2Lt Dan Arnold

STATISTICS FOR MODERN BUSINESS DECISIONS

Second Edition

j	Sometimes used to represent subscripts in a double summation: $$\sum_{j=1}^{m}\sum_{i=1}^{n}X_{ij}$$ $$= (X_{11}+X_{21}+\cdots+X_{n1})$$ $$+(X_{12}+X_{22}+\cdots+X_{n2})$$ $$+(X_{1m}+X_{2m}+\cdots+X_{nm})$$	$\mu_{Y\cdot 12}$	Conditional mean for values of the dependent variable Y for a specified value of the independent variables X_1 and X_2; used in multiple regression analysis, where $\mu_{Y\cdot 12}$ represents the height of the true regression plane
K	Test statistic for Kruskal-Wallis one-factor analysis-of-variance test	N	Number of observations in a population (that is, the population size)
$\log \overline{Y}_X$	Logarithm to base 10 of $\overline{Y}_X$; used in simple regression to find exponential trend curve, $\overline{Y}_X = ab^x$	n	(1) Number of observations in a sample (that is, the sample size) (2) Number of trials in a Bernoulli process
λ (lambda)	Mean rate at which events occur in a Poisson process	$n!$	n factorial, or the product $n \times (n-1) \times (n-2) \times \cdots \times 2 \times 1$
λ_A, λ_S	Mean arrival and service rates used in queuing applications	n_A, n_B	Sample sizes for two-sample tests comparing the parameters of two populations A and B
M	(1) Median of population (2) Monetary amount for calculating utility	n_a, n_b	Number of observations of type a and type b obtained in a sample; applicable to the number-of-runs test
MSA	Mean square (between columns); used to calculate the F statistic in a two-factor analysis of variance when A represents one of the factors about which inferences are to be made	n_j	Size of the jth sample group; used in one-factor analysis of variance with Kruskal-Wallis test
MSB	Mean square (between rows); used to calculate the F statistic in a two-factor analysis of variance when: (1) B represents the blocking variable (2) B represents one of the factors about which inferences are to be made	$O_1, O_2, \ldots$ P	Outcomes in a decision structure (1) Proportion of sample observations having a particular characteristic (2) Proportion of successes from a Bernoulli process
$MSCOL$	Mean square (between columns); used to calculate the F statistic for a Latin-square design in a three-factor analysis of variance	$P[A]$ $P[A\,\vert\,B]$	Probability of event A Conditional probability of event A given event B
MSE	Error mean square; used to calculate the F statistic: (1) (within columns) for a one-factor analysis of variance (2) (residual) for a two-factor or a three-factor analysis of variance	$P[A\ and\ B]$	Probability of the intersection of events A and B; event occurs only when both A and B occur (also called the joint probability of A and B)
$MSROW$	Mean square (between rows); used to calculate the F statistic for a Latin-square design in a three-factor analysis of variance	$P[A\ or\ B]$	Probability of the union of A and B; occurs when either A or B occurs, or when both A and B occur
MST	Mean square; used to calculate the F statistic: (1) (between columns) for the treatments in a one-factor analysis of variance (2) (between letters) in a three-factor analysis of variance using a Latin-square design	$P[X = x]$ $P[X \leqslant x]$	Probability that the random variable X assumes one of several particular values Cumulative probability that X assumes any value less than or equal to a particular value x
m	(1) Sample median (2) Number of variables used in multiple regression and correlation analysis	P^* P_A, P_B	Critical value for P; used in one-sided hypothesis-testing procedure Proportions of observations having a particular characteristic for samples from populations A and B
μ (mu)	Arithmetic mean of a population	P_C	Combined sample proportion; used in two-sample inferences for comparing proportions of two populations
μ_0	Value of the population mean assumed under the null hypothesis		
$\mu_1, \mu_2, \mu_3, \ldots$	Means of populations; used in analysis of variance	P_r^n	Number of permutations of r items taken from a collection of size n when different orders of selection are counted
μ_A, μ_B	Means of populations A and B, which are compared using two samples	p_n, p_0	Prices per unit of an item in year n and in base period 0; used in constructing index numbers
$\mu_{Y\cdot x}$	Conditional mean for values of the dependent variable Y for a specified value of the dependent variable X; used in regression analysis, where $\mu_{Y\cdot x}$ represents the height of the true regression line	π (pi)	(1) Proportion of a population having a particular characteristic (2) Probability of a trial success in a Bernoulli process
		π_0	Value of the population proportion assumed under the null hypothesis
		$\pi_1, \pi_2, \pi_3, \ldots$	Values of population proportions in testing for equality of several population proportions

Statistics
for Modern
Business Decisions
Second Edition

LAWRENCE L. LAPIN

San José State University

 HARCOURT BRACE JOVANOVICH, INC.

New York   San Diego   Chicago   San Francisco   Atlanta

TO INGRID, LISA, AND DANIEL

Cover art by Tadeusz Lapinski

ISBN: 0-15-583775-3

Library of Congress Catalog Card Number: 77-81962

Printed in the United States of America

Illustrations by Vantage Art, Inc.

Preface

In writing this introductory statistics book for students of business and economics, my overriding goal has been to enliven statistics, to make it more interesting and relevant and easier to learn. It is no secret that today's student too often finds statistics boring and irrelevant and more difficult than necessary.

To illustrate that statistics is neither boring nor irrelevant, this book treats it as essentially a decision-making tool and includes many modern concepts and applications. All topics are introduced by carefully chosen examples that illustrate more than technical mathematical concepts. The stage is set, the motivation is provided, and the rationale is given as each new concept is presented. Accordingly, the importance of frequency distributions is highlighted by an application to cryptanalysis. A test of randomness is made something more than just another technique by applying it to the 1970 draft lottery. The fact that sampling is just one source of potential error is emphasized by detailing some of the blunders committed in taking the U.S. Decennial Census. Many of the examples and exercises are clearly related to present-day issues, such as health, conservation, and the environment. Several examples of each major area of business and economics—such as accounting, marketing, finance, production, forecasting, and consumer behavior—serve to richly illustrate the applications of statistics.

A course in high school algebra is the only background required. And although this book should prove more accessible than most, the relevant nature of its presentation has not been achieved at the cost of avoiding reputedly difficult material. Probability, hypothesis testing, and other more difficult topics receive generous explanation, often from several viewpoints. The reader is encouraged to rely more on intuition than on rote memory; less than the customary emphasis is placed on the mechanical and computational aspects of statistics. The computer's role in statistical analysis in managing the more onerous calculations is highlighted throughout the book. Purely mathematical symbology has been minimized; for example, instead of the Boolean cup and bowl notation, the italicized *and* and *or* are used in describing probability concepts.

This second edition features many improvements over the first. The organization has been streamlined, and a smoother topical transition has been achieved through some changes in chapter sequences. About 200 new problems have been added, and many of the original ones have been updated or modified. Most sections within chapters have their own problem sets, permitting the student to easily relate the questions to the concepts just covered. This arrangement also gives the instructor flexibility in picking topics within a chapter. As an added feature, chapters now end with review exercises, allowing the student to gain experience in determining which procedures and concepts to apply. All problems are graded, so that each set begins with easy exercises and increases in difficulty. As a further improvement, much of the statistical jargon and notation has been simplified. All of the second edition's changes should make the book easier to use and to teach from. *Users of the first edition will find a detailed synopsis of the book's changes in the Instructor's Manual.*

The book has been thoroughly class tested in a variety of circumstances and courses in many colleges and universities. The experience of hundreds of instructors has been drawn upon in writing this second edition.

An examination of the table of contents reveals that there is much to choose from in this book. The chapters have been constructed to make it easy for the instructor to design a course to fit individual needs. Classical statistics has not been mixed with statistical decision theory—this book may be used with either emphasis. Many modern texts supplant classical statistics; both the old and the new are available here. Overall, the presentation is familiar except for the inclusion of several topics omitted from most texts. Chapter 14 considers two-sample inferences. Chapters 15 and 16 discuss chi-square applications and analysis of variance. Chapter 17 includes several probability distributions—the hypergeometric, Poisson, exponential, and uniform. These may be conveniently omitted or incorporated in a course without loss of continuity. This second edition includes probability tables for both the binomial and Poisson distributions. Chapter 18 contains some nonparametric statistics most useful for business applications. The Bayesian decision-making procedures of Chapters 19–21 emphasize decision trees; much of the symbology and terminology of decision theory is avoided to allow a simpler and more pragmatic presentation. The three chapters on so-called Bayesian methods have been used primarily to extend statistics to areas where classical procedures have proved inadequate in analyzing decisions under uncertainty.

A glossary of statistical symbols is provided on the endpapers for easy reference. Abbreviated answers to all even-numbered exercises are included in the back of the book. Complete solutions to all exercises are available in the Instructor's Manual, along with more than 100 additional exercises and more than 500 examination questions and their solutions. The Instructor's Manual also provides teaching suggestions and hints on structuring courses. A Study Guide containing over 200 solved problems is also available.

Lawrence L. Lapin

Acknowledgments

I am greatly indebted to the many people who have assisted me in preparing this book. Special thanks go to my colleagues whose comments were invaluable in setting the tone: Robert J. Healey, California State Polytechnic University, Pomona; Richard M. Soland, Ecole Polytechnique, Montreal; and James W. Vigen, California State University, Bakersfield. I am deeply grateful to my students who over many years of debugging the book helped identify the problems a reader might face. There is not enough space to list everyone, but special mention goes to Eileen Player, who assisted in preparing problem material for the Study Guide, and to Wilbur R. Pierce, Jr., who checked all manuscripts for accuracy.

I am also deeply indebted to the following persons, who have used the first edition in their classrooms and have offered helpful suggestions: Moshe Ben-Horim, Montclair State College; F. A. Blackwood, Anne Arundel Community College; Robert O. Boston, Auburn University; Roger L. Burford, Louisiana State University; C. Randall Byers, University of Idaho; Fikert Cuyhun, University of North Dakota; James E. Duffy, John Carroll University; Dennis Geoffroy, University of South Carolina (Sumpter); Herbert Giles, Oklahoma City University; Gary Griepentrog, University of South Carolina; John W. Hagen, California State University (Fresno); James R. Haltiner, University of Virginia; Gaylord Hoyt, Texas A & I University; Gloria J. Hurdle, Colorado College; Henrik Juel, Michigan Technological University; Lester H. Krone, Southern Illinois University; Richard J. Kuzman, University of Virginia; Richard LaBarge, University of New Orleans; Tora M. Larson, East Carolina University; Shu-jan Liang, Loyola University (New Orleans); Donald L. Marx, Louisiana State University; Francis B. May, University of Texas; Frank J. Navratil, John Carroll University; Joe Neely, Hinds Junior College; David E. Nix, Boise State University; T. J. O'Leary, Rochester Institute of Technology; J. Burdeane Orris, Butler University; Leo R. Osterhaus, St. Edwards University; Joseph M. Perry, University of North Florida; Marc J. Schniederjans, St. Louis University; Theresa Shapiro, University of New Orleans; William R. Stewart Jr., University of Maryland; Rao J. Tatikonda, Loyola University (New Orleans); Jack W. Thornton, East Carolina University;

K. E. Wang, California State University (Chico); Peter Wang, Naval Post-graduate School; Jeanne F. Williams, Elon College; H. Williamson, University of Illinois; Julie Zalkind, Duke University.

I am grateful to the Literary Executor of the late Sir Ronald A. Fisher, F.R.S., to Dr. Frank Yates, F.R.S. and to Longman Group Ltd., London, for permission to reprint Tables III and IV from their book *Statistical Tables for Biological, Agricultural and Medical Research* (6th edition, 1974).

L. L. L.

Contents

Five

PROBABILITY, 90

Six

PROBABILITY DISTRIBUTIONS AND EXPECTED VALUE, 145

Seven

THE NORMAL DISTRIBUTION, 193

Eight
STATISTICAL ESTIMATION, 233

Nine
HYPOTHESIS TESTING, 274

Eleven
MULTIPLE REGRESSION AND CORRELATION, 369

Twelve
TIME SERIES ANALYSIS AND FORECASTING, 402

Nineteen
BASIC CONCEPTS OF DECISION THEORY, 646

STATISTICS FOR MODERN BUSINESS DECISIONS

Second Edition

Chapter One
Introduction

The true foundation of theology is to ascertain the character of God. It is by the aid of Statistics that law in the social sphere can be ascertained and codified, and certain aspects of the character of God thereby revealed. The study of statistics is thus a religious service.

Florence Nightingale

Everybody, from some of the remotest people, such as the Bushmen of Africa's Kalahari Desert, to space scientists planning grand tours of the planets use statistics. Surprisingly, the use to which statistics is universally applied is not what most people envision. The word statistics commonly brings to mind masses of numbers, graphs, and tables. These do play a role in statistics, but a limited one. The Kalahari Bushmen cannot count very high, know little mathematics, draw no graphs, and assemble no tables, yet they do use statistics.

1-1   THE MEANING OF STATISTICS

One common thread linking scientist and Bushman is that both *must make decisions in the face of uncertainty*. A successful Bushman locates water in a manner puzzling to some geologists. He sucks through a reed stuck in the sand in what his experience tells him is a likely spot, as if he were drinking a thick milkshake through a straw. Sometimes no water is found, but often enough he does find a "drink hole." His very survival depends on his skill at locating drink holes—on using his experience to cope with uncertainty.

Scientists also depend on experience for determining an optimal space-vehicle configuration—one that can withstand the rigors of a far more hostile environment than that of earth and its atmosphere and survive enough years to fly past Jupiter and eventually to even more distant planets. The communications system must not fail, or the mission itself will be a failure. The system must be super-reliable, so its chances for survival are high. Millions of man-hours of experience can be drawn upon to facilitate design decisions. Even so, there are no guarantees that the chosen design will work as intended. Again, decisions must be made in the face of uncertainty.

Both the Bushman's and the space scientist's mechanisms for making choices utilize limited experience. In this respect they are not substantially different. Also, *both use numerical evidence.* To evaluate communications equipment reliability, components must be tested under stress to determine the number of hours they can function before failing. The scientist's evidence is obviously numerical. But what about the Bushman's? He knows that one set of conditions favors the presence of water more than another. Every wet hole reinforces his learning of factors positive to water, and every dry hole strengthens his awareness of the negative factors. Thus, the Bushman's numerical evidence is the *frequency* of successful drink holes found under various prevailing conditions. Even though presence of water is a qualitative factor, frequencies of occurrence are themselves numerical.

The goal of this book is to describe some of the more useful methods and procedures that can be applied to numerical evidence to facilitate decision-making in the face of uncertainty. So that the reader may achieve a greater appreciation and understanding of how and why these work, certain basic principles will be explained within a theoretical framework.

A concise statement summarizing the subject of this book is the

DEFINITION   *Statistics* is a body of methods and theory applied to numerical evidence in making decisions in the face of uncertainty.

This definition treats statistics as a separate area of academic endeavor, just like physics, history, or botany. As a discipline, statistics has advanced rapidly during the twentieth century to become recognized as a branch of mathematics. Partly due to the relative newness of statistics as a subject of study, the word *statistics* has acquired several meanings.

In its earlier and still most common usage, statistics means a collection of numerical facts or data. In sports, for example, batting averages, rushing yardage and games won or lost are all statistics. Closing prices from the New York Stock Exchange, figures showing sources of income and expenditures for the federal budget, and distances between major cities are also statistics. Your reported income on last year's tax return is a statistic. Examples of this usage are the *vital statistics* for figures on births, deaths, marriages, and divorces, and the titles of publications listing population and economic data, such as the *Statistical Abstract of the United States*. The main distinction between our definition and this usage of the word is its form, plural versus singular. Statistics (singular) *is* a subject of study while statistics (plural) *are* numerical facts.

1-2 THE ROLE OF STATISTICS

Our definition of statistics is particularly appropriate for readers who are primarily interested in applications to business and economics, where there is a high incidence of decisions made under uncertainty. Managerial decisions involving both numerical data and uncertainty are required daily, on matters that range from ordering raw material for products for which demand is uncertain to hiring personnel whose performance cannot be predicted. Statistics is used to answer long-range planning questions, such as when and where to locate facilities to handle future sales of uncertain levels. Statistics can be helpful in formulating strategic policies that affect a firm's survival, such as new product development, pricing, and financing. Economists must choose among alternative policies whose outcomes are determined partly by chance in order to rescue the economy from unemployment and inflation and sustain economic growth. They are called upon by government, business, foundations, and unions to forecast future economic conditions. In doing this they must not only decide what type of data are appropriate, they must also choose from a dazzling array of techniques. Economists rely upon statistical techniques in building, verifying, or implementing economic models.

The social sciences, especially psychology and sociology, also make heavy use of statistics, and so do the physical and life sciences. Geneticists are highly dependent upon statistics. Although this book emphasizes business and economic applications, while other statistics books may be oriented to scientific fields, the statistical elements are identical. The differences are primarily in the choice of examples and the particular techniques emphasized.

1-3 DESCRIPTIVE AND INFERENTIAL STATISTICS

The emphasis upon the decision-making aspects of statistics is a recent one. In its early years, the study of statistics largely consisted of methodology for summarizing or describing numerical data. Any aspects facilitating choice were secondary in importance to the reportorial nature of the subject. This area of study has become known as *descriptive statistics* because it is concerned largely with summary calculations and graphical displays. These methods contrast with the modern approach, where generalizations are made about the whole, called the *population*, by investigating a portion, referred to as the *sample*. Thus, the average income of *all* families in the United States can be estimated from figures obtained from a *few hundred* families. Such a prediction or estimate is an example of an inference. The study of how inferences are made from numerical data is thus called *inferential statistics*.

Our formal definition of statistics applies to both the descriptive and inferential forms. This book emphasizes inferential statistics because of the dynamic role it can play in decision-making. But descriptive statistics remains an important element.

Inferential statistics acknowledges the potential for error that exists in making generalizations from a sample. The seasonal controversy over decisions made by television networks to drop certain programs illustrates some of the principles and problems involved. The information used in these decisions is obtained from a sample of a few hundred viewing families believed to be representative of the viewing public at large. Only those programs indicated by the sample to be most popular are allowed to continue. Although articulate segments of the public complain that their tastes are not represented, the agency that collects the sample data has demonstrated that its audience is selected in accordance with accepted scientific sampling procedures.

The sampling agency knows from probability theory that its errors are likely to be insignificant because it has selected its sample *randomly*. Probability theory measures the chances that an untypical sample will be selected from a population whose characteristics are known. Inferential statistics is based on probability theory, extending its concepts to the measurement of the chance of erroneous generalizations, even when the characteristics of the population are unknown or uncertain.

Because of the important role it plays in statistical inference, we shall discuss probability following descriptive statistics for populations having *known* properties. Then the stage is set for developing statistical inferences about populations whose characteristics are *unknown*.

1-4 DEDUCTIVE AND INDUCTIVE STATISTICS

There is another dichotomy encountered in statistics. Deduction ascribes properties to the specific, starting with the general. For example, probability tells us that if a person is chosen by lottery from a group containing nine men and one woman, then the odds against picking the woman are 9 to 1. We deduce that in about 90 percent of such samples the person will be male. The use of probability to determine the chances of getting a particular kind of sample result is known as *deductive statistics*.

In deductive techniques we know everything in advance about the population and we are concerned with the characteristics of the possible samples that may arise from it. When we reverse directions we are using *inductive statistics*. Induction involves drawing general conclusions from the specific. In statistics this means that inferences about populations are drawn from samples.

The sample is all that is known, and characteristics of the population must be gleaned from the incomplete information available.

Inductive and deductive statistics are completely complementary. We must study how samples are generated before we can turn the tables to generalize from the sample. Deductive statistics is not wholly satisfactory in helping us perform much statistical analysis. The pragmatic aspects of statistics are largely inductive. But we can only understand inductive statistics by first studying deductive statistics.

1-5 STATISTICAL ERROR

Statistics is characterized as partly art and partly science. It is an art because it relies so heavily upon experience and judgment in choosing from the vast panoply of procedures available for analyzing sample information. But it embodies, to various degrees, all elements of the scientific method. The most noteworthy of these is its focus on *error*. Because statistics concerns uncertainty, there is always a chance of making erroneous inferences. Statistical procedures are available for both controlling and measuring the risks of false conclusions. To illustrate this point, we may again consider television viewer sampling.

Those who disagree with the network choices also base their arguments on a sample—the opinions of their own friends and acquaintances. The problem here is that such a sample is biased in favor of persons with similar tastes, education, and social experience. The validity of the sample agency's claims rests upon random selection from the public at large, which allows everyone an equal chance of representation. As we shall see, the agency chooses a sample large enough to keep the chance of error small.

The survey agency cannot be legitimately criticized unless it can be shown that its samples were not random and were therefore biased in favor of specific groups. Even with large samples, bias could be introduced by statistical errors due to improper procedures. Some of the more serious sources of bias will be discussed.

Chapter Two
Describing
Statistical Data

No study is less alluring or more dry and tedious than statistics, unless the mind and imagination are set to work.

William Playfair (1801)

The arrangement and display of statistical data are important elements of descriptive statistics. Raw numbers alone do not indicate any underlying pattern useful for decision making. For example, we might believe that doctors generally have high incomes and that young people usually earn less than older persons. But even if we had access to all tax returns on file with the Internal Revenue Service, without some arranging, sifting, and sorting of the original income data we would not be able to find out if doctors earn more than dentists, if some lawyers do better than most doctors, or if greater experience in a particular occupation leads to the kind of pay increases we expect. Only by organizing the data can we gain information useful for career-planning decisions.

Descriptive statistics is the stage setting for everything else. The basic element of statistics is a single data point, which we call an *observation* because it represents what we actually see. An observation is usually a part of a sample, which itself represents a larger grouping called the population. Sample data can be described in a variety of ways. The most basic summary is found by counting the number of observations falling into various categories. The resulting frequency pattern describes essential features not otherwise apparent and can be helpful in selecting procedures to use in further statistical investigations.

2-1 THE POPULATION AND THE SAMPLE

An observation may be a physical measurement (weight or height), an answer to a question (yes or no), or a classification (defective or nondefective). Observations relevant to a particular decision constitute a population. Stated more formally, we have the following

> **DEFINITION**   A statistical ***population*** is the collection of all possible observations of a specified characteristic of interest.

Note that a statistical population exists whether all, some, or none of the possible observations are actually made. It may be real (such as the height of 30-year-old males in Schenectady in June 1977) or hypothetical (such as the longevity of laboratory rats fed a special diet that is not yet widely used). Because it consists of all possible observations, a population is often referred to synonymously as a *universe*.

Populations and Samples

In contrast to the statistical population, which consists of all possible observations, the *sample* contains only some of the observations. Whether a collection of observations is a population or just a sample depends upon the purpose of the analysis. For example, a medical association may wish to compare physicians' fees to the costs of other kinds of hospital services in order to absolve doctors from total blame for the skyrocketing hospitalization costs experienced in recent years. Here, one population (physicians' fees per hospital stay of all persons treated) would be compared to another population (the costs per patient for ancillary medical and housekeeping services). Depending upon the objectives of the medical association, the populations would comprise fees and costs for the entire nation, for a state, or for a county.

If the population of ancillary costs covered all hospitalized patients released during a particular calendar year, then the charges for all patients released on *a single day* would be a sample. The costs for patients at *a single hospital* during the entire year would also be a sample of the same population.

Again, if the medical association is concerned only with fees and charges for patients discharged on March 1, those data would constitute populations rather than samples. Similarly, if fees at different hospitals were to be compared, then the costs at one hospital would be a separate population.

Elementary Units

A statistical population consists of *observations* of some characteristic of interest associated with the individuals concerned, *not* the individual items or persons themselves. A company may need to know the ages of its employees in order to analyze proposed changes in its retirement program. To find these, the employee records would be searched and the ages determined from dates of birth. Each number determined constitutes an observation of the age characteristic. The entire collection of numbers so obtained is the population; the employees themselves will be referred to as the *elementary units of the population.*

A limitless variety of different populations may be obtained from the same elementary units, depending upon the characteristic of interest. This principle is illustrated in Figure 2-1. Thus an employer could have different populations for political affiliation, sex, marital status, years of education, height, weight, eye color, job classification, and years on present job, where each population is made up of observed characteristics of the same elementary units—the employees.

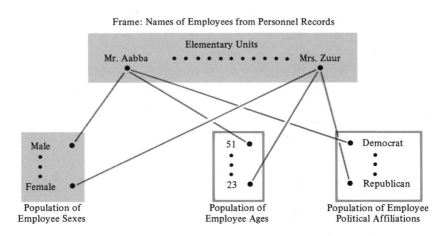

FIGURE 2-1 Illustration of how several different populations may be obtained from the same elementary units.

A population may be *multidimensional*, in which case two or more characteristics are observed for each elementary unit. For example, if we wished to compare the effect of education upon income, observations of both education and income would be required for each employee.

The Frame

How do we define the elementary units of a population? The employer can define his employees as those persons on the payroll, so that the names of all employees may be obtained from pay records. Such a source of elementary units is called a *frame*.

The frame is very important in statistical studies because it helps to define the population. Suppose, for instance, that a sample is taken of voter preference toward candidates in order to predict the outcome of an election. The sample should represent the population of votes to be cast for a specific office. The population of interest is referred to as a *target population*. In selecting the sample of voters, the only frame available to the opinion surveyor is the roll of registered voters. The elementary units listed in this frame may differ from those of the target population, because some people who are registered will not vote. The votes to be cast by registered persons constitute the *working population*, because its frame is the only one currently available. The sample must be drawn from this population.

The potential exists for erroneous sample results, because the candidate preferences may be obtained from some elementary units not part of the target population. In such a case, it may be wise to include in the sample only those persons who are likely to vote. This illustration highlights one difficulty in using a sample to make an inference about a target population. Great care must be exercised in selecting a frame that closely matches that of the target population. The telephone book serves as an inadequate frame for a working population of voter attitudes, because it does not allow certain persons to be presented in the statistical study. Some persons are not listed, because they have recently moved into the community, because they do not own telephones, or for other reasons. A danger exists that a sample chosen from the telephone book will be biased toward a particular opinion not reflective of the target population. In Chapter 4 we will discuss many of the pitfalls associated with sampling.

Qualitative and Quantitative Populations

There are two basic kinds of populations, distinguished by the form of the characteristic of interest. When the characteristic can be expressed numerically, as with height, weight, cost, or income, then the population is *quantitative*. When the characteristic is non-numerical, such as sex, marital status, occupation, or college major, the population is *qualitative*. As we proceed through our presentation of statistics, these two kinds of populations will be discussed separately but in parallel. Different methods will be introduced for describing and summarizing each type. The difference in techniques stems from the fact that arithmetic operations can be performed on numbers, so that, for example, we can calculate the average height for a collection of men, but other procedures must be employed to summarize a qualitative population.

We refer to a particular observation of a qualitative characteristic as an *attribute*. Thus, for the characteristic of marital status, any one of the following attributes might be observed: single, married, divorced, or widowed. An observation of a quantitative characteristic, such as income, will be a particular

TABLE 2-1   Illustration of Possible Observations
for Various Quantitative and Qualitative Populations

Quantitative Population Observations			
Elementary Unit	*Characteristic of Interest*	*Unit of Measurement*	*Possible Variate*
person	age	years	21.3 yrs
microcircuit	defective solder joints	number	5
tire	remaining tread	millimeters	10 mm
account balance	amount	dollars	$5,233.46
employer	female employees	percent	17%
common stock	earnings per share	dollars	$3.49
keypuncher	errors	proportion	.02
light bulb	lifetime	hours	581 hrs
can of food	weight of contents	ounces	15.3 oz

Qualitative Population Observations		
Elementary Unit	*Characteristic of Interest*	*Possible Attributes*
person	sex	male, female
security	type	bond, common stock, preferred stock
building	exterior materials	brick, wood, aluminum
employee	experience	applicable, not applicable
television	quality	defective, nondefective
firm	legal status	corporation, partnership, proprietorship
patient	condition	fair, critical
student	residence	on-campus, off-campus

numerical value or *variate*, such as: $11,928.23, $21,234.15, or $1,095.61. Table 2-1 shows examples of observations from various qualitative and quantitative populations.

EXERCISES

2-1   Consider the data for the number of days employees lost due to illness during August 1978. Give an example of a goal where we may consider these data to be a population; a sample.

2-2   For each of the following problem situations, (1) provide an example of an elementary unit; (2) provide an example of a characteristic of interest; and (3) state whether the population would be qualitative or quantitative.
   (a) An aircraft manufacturer's investment plans will be affected by the fate of a congressional appropriation bill containing funds for a new fighter plane. The company wishes to conduct a survey to facilitate planning.
   (b) A politician plans to study the voter response to pending legislation to determine his platform.
   (c) The Civil Aeronautics Board is seeking operating cost data that will help it establish new rate levels for the New York–Miami airline routes.

2-3   For each of the following situations, discuss whether the suggested frame would be suitable.
   (a) An insurance company is using home theft claims processed in the past

year as its frame to determine the number of thefts from its policy-holders of items valued below $50.

(b) A public health official uses doctors' records of persons diagnosed as suffering from flu as his frame to study the effects of a recent flu epidemic.

(c) A stock exchange official studying the investment attitudes of owners of listed securities uses the active accounts of member brokerage firms as his frame.

2-2 THE FREQUENCY DISTRIBUTION

Finding a Meaningful Pattern for the Data

The ages of a sample of 100 statistics students are shown in Table 2-2. If we wish to describe this sample, how should we proceed? Because the values in Table 2-2 have not been summarized or rearranged in a meaningful manner, we refer to them as *raw data*. We might begin by grouping the ages in a meaningful fashion.

A convenient way to accomplish this is to group them into categories that are two calendar years long, beginning with age 18. Each age will then fall into one of the categories 18.0–under 20.0, 20.0–under 22.0, and so on. We refer to such groupings of values as *class intervals*. Now suppose that we simply count the number of ages falling into each class interval. By summarizing the raw data in this manner, we ought to be able to identify some properties of the sample.

First we list the class intervals in increasing sequence, as in the first column of Table 2-3. Then, going down the list of raw data for each successive age, we place a tally mark beside the corresponding class interval and a check mark beside the number on the original list so that it will not be counted twice. When the tally is complete, we find the total number of observations falling into each class interval by counting the marks. The final result shows the frequency with which ages occur in each class interval and is therefore called a *sample frequency distribution*. We find that 10 of the 100 statistics students fall

TABLE 2-2   Ages of a Sample of 100 Statistics Students

Age in Years									
20.9	33.4	18.7	24.2	22.1	18.9	21.9	20.5	21.9	37.3
57.2	25.3	24.6	29.0	26.3	19.1	48.7	23.5	23.1	28.6
21.3	22.4	22.3	20.0	30.3	31.7	34.3	28.5	36.1	32.6
33.7	19.6	18.7	24.3	27.1	20.7	22.2	19.2	26.5	27.4
22.8	51.3	44.4	22.9	20.6	32.8	27.3	23.5	23.8	22.4
18.1	23.9	20.8	41.5	20.4	21.3	19.3	24.2	22.3	23.1
22.9	21.3	29.7	25.6	33.7	24.2	24.5	21.2	21.5	25.8
21.5	21.5	27.0	19.9	29.2	25.3	26.4	22.7	27.9	22.0
23.3	28.1	24.8	19.6	23.7	26.3	30.1	29.7	24.8	24.7
23.5	22.9	26.0	25.2	23.6	21.0	30.9	21.7	28.3	22.1

TABLE 2-3   Sample Frequency Distribution of Student Ages

Age	Tally	Number of Persons (Class Frequency)
18.0–under 20.0	〜 〜	10
20.0–under 22.0	〜 〜 〜 ///	18
22.0–under 24.0	〜 〜 〜 〜 ///	23
24.0–under 26.0	〜 〜 ////	14
26.0–under 28.0	〜 〜	10
28.0–under 30.0	〜 ///	8
30.0–under 32.0	////	4
32.0–under 34.0	〜	5
34.0–under 36.0	/	1
36.0–under 38.0	//	2
38.0–under 58.0	〜	5
		Total 100

into the class interval 18.0–under 20.0. The number 10 may be referred to as the *class frequency* for the first class interval.

Each class interval has two limits. For the first interval, the *lower class limit* is 18.0 and the *upper class limit* is "under 20.0" (we use the word under to distinguish this limit from 20.0 exactly, which serves as the lower limit of the second class interval). No matter how precisely the raw data are measured, this designation provides no ambiguity in assigning an observation to a particular interval. For example, the age 19.99 years is represented by the first class, while 20.01 years would fall into the second class (20–under 22.0). The *width* of a class interval is found by subtracting its lower limit from the lower limit of the succeeding class interval. For example, the width of the first class interval is $20.0 - 18.0 = 2.0$. All classes but the last one have the same width; as we shall see, beginning or ending class intervals must sometimes be treated differently.

Population Data

The frequency distribution just illustrated applies to sample data. When they are available, the raw data for an entire population could be similarly arranged. In this case, a table of frequencies would constitute a *population frequency distribution*. Ordinarily, only sample results are available, but the present discussion applies to raw data from either a sample or a population.

Graphical Displays

The Histogram
A visual display can be a very useful starting point in describing a frequency distribution. Figure 2-2 graphically portrays the same information that is provided in Table 2-3. In this figure, age is represented on the horizontal axis, which

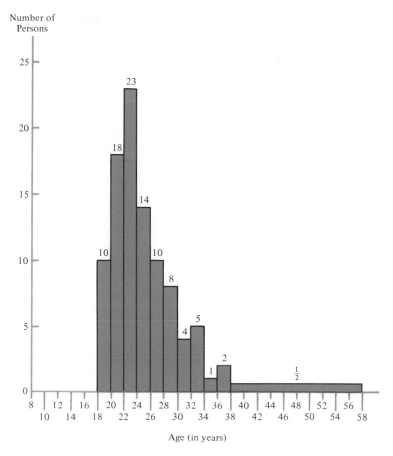

is divided into class intervals two years wide. The classes are represented by bars of varying heights, corresponding to the class frequency—the number of observations falling into each interval. Thus the vertical axis represents frequency. Such a graphical portrayal of a frequency distribution is called a *histogram*.

Since there are 23 ages 22.0 or above to just below 24.0, the corresponding bar is of height 23. Only one person is between 34.0 and 36.0 years old, so the height of that bar is 1. The bars shown for these two class intervals cover the values from 22.0 to just below 24.0 and from 34.0 to just below 36.0, respectively. Neighboring bars touch, emphasizing that age varies continuously on a time scale.

Note that the highest class interval, 38.0 to under 58.0, is 20 years wide— ten times as wide as the standard intervals. With only five ages falling between 38.0 and 58.0, there is, on the average, one-half an observation every two years in this interval. This bar is therefore drawn with height $\frac{1}{2}$. Treating the two-year width as a standard unit, *the area inside any bar* (its height times width in standard units) *equals the number of observations in the corresponding class interval*. Thus, the area inside the first bar is $10 \times 1 = 10$ and the area inside the last one is $\frac{1}{2}$ times the number of standard two-year class intervals, or $\frac{1}{2}(10) = 5$, the number of observations in that category.

The Frequency Polygon

An alternative graphical portrayal of a frequency distribution is the *frequency polygon*, shown in Figure 2-3 for the same population of ages as Figure 2-2 and using the same axes. In Figure 2-3, each class interval is represented by a dot positioned above its midpoint at a height equal to the class frequency. The midpoints are defined by the average of the interval's class limits. Thus, the midpoint of the first interval is $(18.0+20.0)/2 = 19.0$; the second midpoint is 21.0, and so on. The value used for the last interval is $(38.0+58.0)/2 = 48.0$. The dots are connected by line segments to facilitate reading the graph.

Geometrically, a polygon is a closed figure with many sides. To complete the frequency polygon, line segments are drawn from the first and last dots to

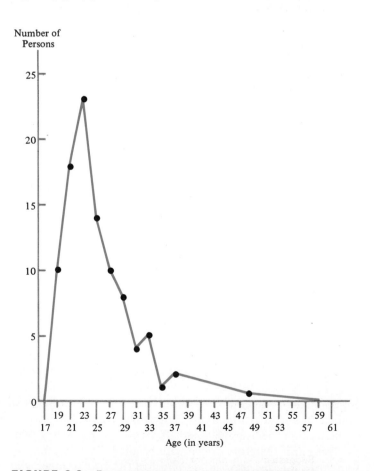

FIGURE 2-3   Frequency polygon for sample of student ages.

the horizontal axis at points one-half the width of a standard class interval below the lowest and above the highest class intervals, in this case touching the axis at 17 and 59. The frequency polygon provides a meaningful frequency only for the observation values corresponding to the midpoints beneath the dots; these are interpreted as the typical values for all observations in the respective class intervals.

The Frequency Curve

When the number of observations is large, the polygon for a sample frequency distribution presents a shape similar to the shape that might be obtained for raw data consisting of the entire population. But since data for the entire population are not ordinarily available, the population frequency distribution is usually portrayed in terms of a *frequency curve* like the one shown in Figure 2-4. The basic shape of a population's frequency curve is usually suggested by the histogram or frequency polygon originally found for sample data. Because populations are usually quite large in relation to the number of observations in a sample, the frequency curve would resemble a frequency polygon or a histo-

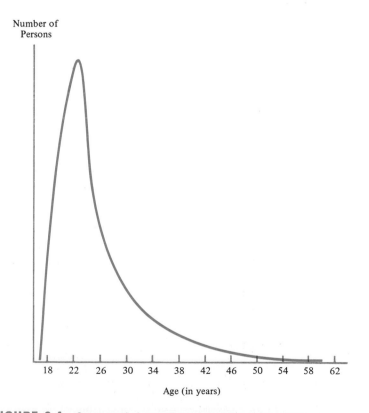

FIGURE 2-4 Suggested shape of smoothed frequency curve for the entire population.

gram with many class intervals of tiny widths. If these intervals were laboriously plotted, the entire collection of population data would present a less jagged graph than that obtainable from sample data alone, and this graph would be almost totally smooth (like the curve in Figure 2-4). Later in this chapter we will discuss some of the shapes commonly encountered for populations.

Descriptive Analysis

We have managed to translate the confusion of the raw data into a pattern based upon frequencies. The frequency distribution tells us two things: It shows how the observations cluster around a central value, and it illustrates the degree of dispersion or difference between observations.

We see that none of the students is younger than 18 and that ages below 28 are most typical. Of these, the most common age is somewhere between 22 and 24, which (from general information obtained from the registrar's office) we know to be higher than usual for the student who enters college right after high school and graduates at about age 22. The students in the sample are generally older; but we can rule out the possibility that they might be graduate students because of the substantial number of younger persons. One guess is that the population could be made up of night students, with the older persons working on their degrees on a part-time basis while holding full-time jobs.

The appropriateness of this conclusion may be substantiated by the incidence of persons over 30, who most likely have financial burdens and cannot afford to be full-time students. Predominantly young, the sample is peppered with persons approaching or exceeding the age of 40. Five of these are relatively so much older that they have been put into a special group—the "over 38s." Their ages (41.5, 44.4, 48.7, 51.3, and 57.2) are spread so thinly along the age scale that it was more convenient to lump these more extreme ages into a single special category.

The foregoing descriptive analysis provides us with an image of this sample that is not immediately available from the raw data. The entire description is based upon frequencies of occurrence—the heart of all statistical analysis. As we shall see in Chapter 5, frequency is the basis for probability theory and as such has a fundamental role in all procedures of statistical inference.

A vivid illustration of how frequency of occurrence can be used to reduce the confusion of raw data is provided by *cryptanalysis*. This also serves to explain frequency distributions for qualitative populations.

The Frequency Distribution of a Qualitative Population

Role of Frequency Distribution in Cryptanalysis
Cryptanalysis is the breaking of codes or ciphers used to keep secret those communications made in the "never-never land" of espionage, foreign intrigue, diplomacy, or matters military. In its simplest form, a *cipher* is a message where

TABLE 2-4   Cipher Message

AOYNS	YIRXJ	AJRRS	OOYIR	YGDYP
MQQCY	CYMOQ	JAPQM	QDPQD	RMGMI
MGXPD	PDQMG	GHVPS	PQJRO	YMQYJ
OKYOA	AJHRJ	IASPD	JIHYM	IDIBA
SGGXM	OOMIB	YKISH	UYOPR	MIQYG
GSPMP	QJOXM	IKCYG	LSPRC	JJPYH
YQCJK	PMIKL	OJRYK	SOYPA	JOBYI
YOMGD	ZDIBM	UJSQL	JLSGM	QDJIP

another alphabet has been substituted for the ordinary one. Consider the example in Table 2-4. To decipher this message, we must find the counterparts to the letters in the original message.

The first step in cryptanalysis is to determine the frequency distribution for the letters in the cipher message, as in Table 2-5. The ciphertext letters are the elementary units from a qualitative population where the possible attributes are the symbols of the alphabet. The frequency distribution for qualitative data provides a count of the number of occurrences for each attribute, so that there is a category for each number that is analogous to the class interval for quantitative data.

The cryptanalyst knows the frequency with which each letter occurs in the ordinary English language. This is provided in Table 2-6, where the letters are shown in lower case to distinguish them from the ciphertext alphabet.

Graphical Portrayal

The frequency distribution of the ordinary English letters is graphed as a histogram in Figure 2-5. When the observations are attributes rather than variates, the bars do not touch each other, reflecting the fact that each category is

TABLE 2-5   Frequency Distribution of Letters in Cipher Message

Letter	Tally	Number of Letters	Letter	Tally	Number of Letters
A	HHH III	8	N	I	1
B	IIII	4	O	HHH HHH HHH	15
C	HHH	5	P	HHH HHH HHH I	16
D	HHH HHH	10	Q	HHH HHH IIII	14
E		0	R	HHH HHH	10
F		0	S	HHH HHH I	11
G	HHH HHH II	12	T		0
H	HHH	5	U	II	2
I	HHH HHH HHH	15	V	I	1
J	HHH HHH HHH II	17	W		0
K	HHH I	6	X	IIII	4
L	IIII	4	Y	HHH HHH HHH HHH I	21
M	HHH HHH HHH III	18	Z	I	1
				Total	200

TABLE 2-6   Frequency Distribution of Letters in 200 Characters of Ordinary English Language Text

Letter	Frequency	Letter	Frequency	Letter	Frequency
a	16	j	1	s	12
b	3	k	1	t	18
c	6	l	7	u	6
d	8	m	6	v	2
e	26	n	14	w	3
f	4	o	16	x	1
g	3	p	4	y	4
h	12	q	$\frac{1}{2}$	z	$\frac{1}{2}$
i	13	r	13	Total	200

SOURCE: David Kahn, *The Codebreakers: The Story of Secret Writing* (New York: Macmillan, 1967), p. 100. Copyright © 1967 by David Kahn.

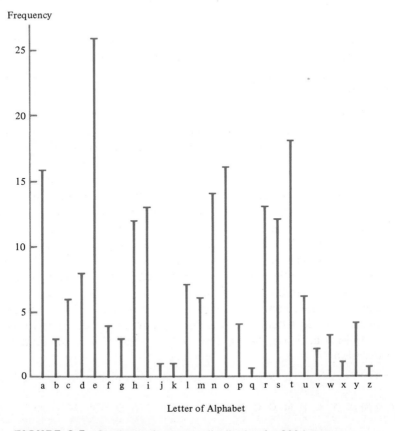

FIGURE 2-5   Qualitative frequency distribution for 200 letters of ordinary English text.

discrete. Sometimes vertical spikes are used instead of bars to emphasize that the observations do not range along a continuous scale.

For samples from qualitative populations, where the characteristic of interest takes the form of various attributes (such as male or female, defective or nondefective, or professional categories such as doctor, lawyer, engineer, or educator), the graphical portrayal of the frequency distribution would be similarly represented.

Sometimes a quantitative frequency distribution is handled in the same way. For example, the number of children in a collection of families would be so represented. Here the possible variates are whole numbers or *integers*, such as 0, 1, 2, 3, or 4. The number of children cannot be fractional, such as 2.67, so they should not be represented on a continuous scale; the possible values are *discrete*. When quantitative observations are discrete, they are graphically portrayed in the same manner as the attributes of a qualitative population.

Frequency Analysis

The letters occurring in ordinary English may be arranged in sequence of decreasing frequency:

English letters	e	t	a	o	n	i	r	s	h	d	l	u	c	m	p	f	y	w	g	b	v	j	k	x	q	z
Frequency	26	18	16	16	14	13	13	12	12	8	7	6	6	6	4	4	4	3	3	3	2	1	1	1	$\frac{1}{4}$	$\frac{1}{4}$
				High										*Medium*										*Low*		

A similar arrangement of the ciphertext letters may be made:

Ciphertext	Y	M	J	P	O	I	Q	G	S	D	R	A	K	C	H	B	L	X	U	N	V	Z	E	F	T	W
Frequency	21	18	17	16	15	15	14	12	11	10	10	8	6	5	5	4	4	2	1	1	1	0	0	0	0	0

There is no reason why we should be so fortunate that this particular message will provide an identical match—letter for letter—strictly on the basis of frequency. But the frequencies can be used to find likely possibilities. For instance, they tell us that the letter e is most frequently used, so e probably corresponds to either the Y, M, J, P, O, or I of the cipher. Similarly, we can identify English text letters likely to correspond to the other letters. Notice the rather dramatic drops in frequency between h and d and again between v and j, which provide clues to considerably narrow our search for a solution.

A more refined analysis is usually the next step in cryptanalysis. It is based upon how frequently each of the higher count ciphertext letters combines with each of the other letters of the alphabet. From experience the cryptanalyst knows that certain two-letter combinations occur more often than others. By a process of elimination, the more common letters can be matched to the ciphertext.

Using the first 50 letters in our message, assuming that we have found Y = e, Q = t, M = a, J = o, D = i, I = n, P = s, and O = r, we obtain the partial translation:

```
A O Y N S Y I R X J A J R R S O O Y I R Y G D Y P
  r e   n       e n       o   o       r r e n   e   i e s

M Q Q C Y C Y M O Q J A P Q M Q D P Q D R M G M I
a t t   e   e a r t o   s t a t i s t i   a   a n
```

In the second row, we have the first eight letters of *statistical*, with the c and l missing. This is strong evidence that R = c and G = l. Substituting these values into the message, we have

```
A  O  Y  N  S  Y  I  R  X  J  A  J  R  R  S  O  O  Y  I  R  Y  G  D  Y  P
   r  e        e  n  c     o        o  c  c        r  r  e  n  c  e  l  i  e  s

M  Q  Q  C  Y  C  Y  M  O  Q  J  A  P  Q  M  Q  D  P  Q  D  R  M  G  M  I
a     t  t     e        e  a  r  t  o        s  t  a  t  i  s ·t  i  c  a  l  a  n
```

A good guess is that S = u and C = h. Filling in the corresponding blanks leads us to further conclude that A = f and N = q.

As further original text letters become known, the remaining letters are increasingly easier to identify, thus filling in the blank spaces below the cipher-text. Finally the cipher is broken; the complete key is

Ciphertext: M U R K Y A B C D E F G H I J L N O P Q S T V W X Z
Original text: a   b c d e f g h i j k l m n o p q r s t u v w x y z

The cipher is constructed by using the word MURKY for the first five original text alphabet letters and listing the remaining cipher letters in alphabetical sequence. The text of the full message reads:

> **Frequency of occurrence lies at the heart of statistical analysis. It allows us to create order from confusion. Meaningfully arranged, numbers can tell us a story and help us choose methods and procedures for generalizing about populations.**

Guidelines for Constructing a Frequency Distribution

The purpose of a frequency distribution is to convert raw data into a meaningful pattern for statistical analysis. In doing this, detail must be sacrificed for insight. Because it lumps individual variates into class intervals, the frequency distribution cannot tell us how the observations within a certain category differ from each other. Only the raw data can provide this information. Thus some less important information is lost in order that more useful information can be gained.

How can the raw data best be condensed into class intervals? This question leads to two others: What range of values should be included in a single category? How many intervals should be used?

Width of Class Intervals

It is desirable that the class intervals be of the same width. This facilitates comparisons between classes and provides simpler calculations of the even more concise summary values to be discussed later in this chapter. As we noted with the distribution of the age data in Table 2-3, it is sometimes better to lump the extreme values in a single category. The need for this becomes quite evident during construction of a frequency distribution for individual annual earnings. Most persons have incomes less than $25,000. A few earn between $25,000 and

$100,000. But the rare, extremely well-to-do have incomes substantially higher. A frequency distribution graph with equal intervals of income width, say, $5,000, would be hard to draw and would not be very readable. The resulting histogram would be somewhat analogous to a few mountain peaks (representing frequency for the lower income levels) sitting to the left of very many successively smaller anthills (representing the number of persons in each progressively rarer, higher income category). This difficulty may be avoided by grouping the higher incomes into a single class.

Thus, higher incomes might be lumped into a category such as "$100,000 or more." Usually such a class interval has no stated upper limit. This is partly due to lack of available data. Another reason is that such an upper limit may dwarf the other intervals to the point that all the categories appear "out of line." Often there is no theoretical upper limit, as might be the case with a frequency distribution for times taken by electronic components to fail. The histogram of a frequency distribution with no upper limit would not usually show a bar for the extreme values, although these should be mentioned with a note.

We cannot really know how wide the class intervals ought to be without knowing how many intervals are to be used.

Number of Class Intervals

There are no rules indicating how many class intervals to use. It is generally recommended that there be between five and 20, but the number is really a matter of personal judgment. The main consideration should be that the interval is not so narrow or so wide that useful information cannot be obtained. Figure 2-6 shows two extreme cases. In diagram (a), the class intervals are so tiny that each has height 1 and the frequency distribution is no better than the raw data themselves. On the other hand, a single class interval like the one in diagram (b) lumps all data into one category, which can only indicate the total amount of dispersion in the observations. We desire something in between these two.

When all intervals are to be the same width, the following rule may be applied to find the required *class interval width.*

$$\text{Class interval width} = \frac{\text{Largest value} - \text{Smallest value}}{\text{Number of class intervals}} \tag{2-1}$$

This is used when the extreme values are not lumped into a special category.

We illustrate this for the 100 observations of fuel consumption in miles per gallon for a fleet of cars listed in Table 2-7. Suppose we desire five class intervals of equal width. We find the required width by taking the difference between the largest and smallest values, $23.9 - 14.1 = 9.8$, and then dividing by 5, getting 1.96 miles per gallon. To ease our task, we can use 2.0 instead of 1.96 for the width and 14.0 instead of 14.1 for the lower limit of our first class interval. The frequency distribution is provided in Table 2-8 and graphed in Figure 2-7(a).

Figure 2-7 also contains histograms for the same gasoline consumption data using 10 class intervals (b) and 20 class intervals (c). Notice that the histogram profiles become progressively "lumpier" as the number of classes

Number of
Observations

Observed Values

(a) A separate class for each observation

Number of
Observations

Observed Values

(b) A single class for all observations

FIGURE 2-6   Illustration of two extreme cases for number
of frequency distribution classes.

TABLE 2-7   Miles per Gallon Achieved
with 100 Medium-Sized Cars (raw data)

19.0	20.8	22.0	22.7	20.0	18.9	16.6	16.8	20.8	14.7
15.1	21.8	21.1	21.5	21.1	15.5	19.3	15.1	20.6	16.8
18.2	20.5	15.3	16.2	16.3	22.8	22.7	21.9	22.5	17.1
19.1	21.6	19.0	18.3	18.6	22.1	17.5	22.9	21.7	18.7
21.9	20.2	14.5	14.1	22.9	20.2	17.3	22.6	19.3	21.7
21.5	22.6	18.7	19.2	22.8	21.6	21.7	20.5	22.7	20.4
18.8	15.1	16.5	20.5	19.1	17.4	19.7	19.2	16.4	21.9
14.3	19.2	19.7	17.1	21.4	21.9	21.7	19.2	23.9	19.6
20.9	18.5	20.2	18.2	20.2	22.4	20.4	21.6	21.3	22.4
20.5	18.1	20.7	21.3	16.9	20.3	23.9	18.8	21.1	21.9

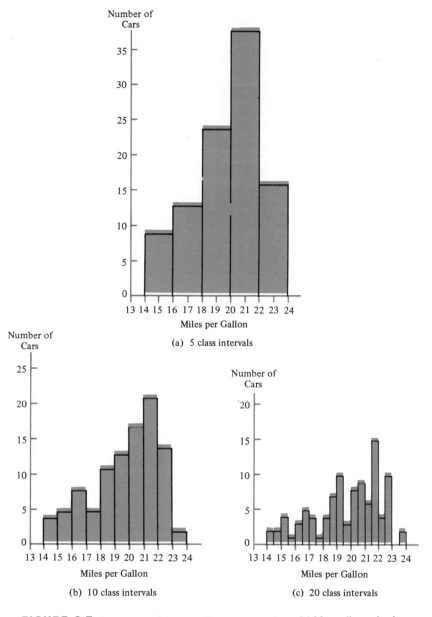

(a) 5 class intervals

(b) 10 class intervals

(c) 20 class intervals

FIGURE 2-7   Histograms for gasoline consumption of 100 medium-sized cars, using three different sets of class intervals.

increases. Both the five-interval and ten-interval graphs provide concise summaries of the data, but a pronounced "sawtooth" effect occurs with 20 intervals. The poorness of the 20-interval summary reflects the large number of intervals in relation to the size of the sample. One way to decide how many class intervals to use would be to try several—plotting a histogram for each and selecting the

TABLE 2-8 Frequency Distribution for Miles per Gallon of 100 Medium-Sized Cars Using 5 Classes

Miles per Gallon	Number of Cars
14.0–under 16.0	9
16.0–under 18.0	13
18.0–under 20.0	24
20.0–under 22.0	38
22.0–under 24.0	16
Total	100

one that provides the most logical explanation of the underlying population pattern. A large number of class intervals will provide more data, but too many will show meaningless oscillations.

EXERCISES

2-4   Using the income data below:

$ 3,145	$15,879	$ 6,914	$ 4,572	$11,374
12,764	9,061	8,245	10,563	8,164
6,395	8,758	17,270	10,755	10,465
7,415	9,637	9,361	11,606	7,836
13,517	7,645	9,757	9,537	23,957
8,020	8,346	12,848	8,438	6,347
21,333	9,280	7,538	7,414	11,707
9,144	7,424	25,639	10,274	4,683
5,089	6,904	9,182	12,193	12,472
8,494	6,032	16,012	9,282	3,331

(a) Construct a frequency distribution having six class intervals of equal width. Round the width to the nearest thousand dollars and use $3,000 as the lower class limit of the first interval.

(b) Draw a histogram showing the distribution from part (a).

2-5   Using the family income data in Exercise 2-4:

(a) Construct a frequency distribution having 12 class intervals of width $2,000, with $3,000 as the lower limit of the first class.

(b) Construct a frequency polygon using the frequency distribution from part (a).

(c) Do you think a better data summary could be gained by using fewer or more class intervals? Discuss the reasons for your choice.

2-6   A brewery has two divisions, one in the East and the other in the West. Separate frequency distributions for the hourly wages of workers in the East and West are provided below.

East		West	
Hourly Wage	Number of Workers	Hourly Wage	Number of Workers
$2.50–under 3.00	150	$2.50–under 3.00	0
3.00–under 3.50	300	3.00–under 3.50	0
3.50–under 4.00	150	3.50–under 4.00	0
4.00–under 4.50	100	4.00–under 4.50	0
4.50–under 5.00	50	4.50–under 5.00	50
5.00–under 5.50	50	5.00–under 5.50	150
5.50–under 6.00	50	5.50–under 6.00	150
6.00–under 6.50	50	6.00–under 6.50	200
6.50–under 7.00	50	6.50–under 7.00	100

(a) Plot frequency polygons for each division separately but on the same graph.

(b) Combine the East and West data into a single all-company frequency distribution.

(c) Plot a frequency polygon for the data obtained in part (b).

(d) Comparing the graphs in part (a) to that in part (c), which presentation do you think provides more meaningful managerial information? Explain.

2-7 Construct a frequency distribution, with a separate category for each alphabetic character, of the first 200 letters of Abraham Lincoln's Gettysburg address:

> Four-score and seven years ago our fathers brought forth on this continent a new nation, conceived in liberty, and dedicated to the proposition that all men are created equal.
>
> Now we are engaged in a great civil war, testing whether that nation, or . . . .

Treat upper and lower case letters the same. Comparing your distribution with that in Table 2-6, do you think that the English used by Lincoln is "ordinary?" Explain.

2-8 Comment on the appropriateness of each of the following class interval widths for a frequency distribution of rates of pay for 100 selected hourly workers in a metropolitan area: $0.05, $0.25, $0.50, $1.00, $2.00.

2-9 The following data have been obtained for the monthly rentals for 45 apartments in a large metropolitan area:

$100	$130	$130	$305	$175
155	150	95	295	210
80	270	135	130	335
230	235	75	90	285
65	345	110	135	185
300	70	250	125	180
150	305	170	95	90
145	90	160	130	80
190	235	75	60	425

(a) Construct a frequency distribution for the above data.

(b) How many classes did you use? Justify your choice.

(c) Did you use equal or unequal class interval widths? Why?

(d) Plot a histogram of your results.

(e) Write a brief summary of your findings.

2-10 Criticize each of the following designations for class intervals of monthly household electricity bills:

(a)	(b)	(c)
$10–15	$11–22	$10–under 15
15–20	21–32	16–under 20
20–25	31–42	21–under 25
etc.	etc.	etc.

2-3 RELATIVE AND CUMULATIVE FREQUENCY DISTRIBUTIONS

Two useful extensions of the basic frequency distribution are the *relative* and the *cumulative* frequency distributions.

A *relative frequency* is the ratio of the number of observations falling into a particular category to the total observations, and may be determined for both quantitative and qualitative data. Relative frequency is a convenient basis for the comparison of similar groups of different size. For example, consider comparing the earnings of workers in sparsely populated Nevada to their counterparts in neighboring California, the most populous state. It would not be very meaningful to state that Nevada has only 6,000 persons achieving a particular level of income, whereas California has 250,000. But if the percentage of such workers is 1 percent in Nevada and only 0.8 percent in California, a realistic comparison between workers in the two states can be made. Analogously, to determine whether the men at a large university have more opportunities to date women on campus than men at a small college have, we must compare the proportion of male students—not the total frequencies.

A *cumulative frequency* is the sum of the frequencies for successively higher classes, and only applies when the observations are numerical. For example, we might find that 8,439 men in a population of 10,000 are less than 6 feet tall; stated differently, 84.39 percent of the population is shorter than 6 feet. Cumulative frequencies can be very useful descriptions of a population, especially when they are expressed relatively as percentages or proportions. We can judge our chances for being accepted by a graduate school, for example, partly according to the percentage of persons obtaining a lower score on the admissions screening examination. (Cumulative frequency is relevent to some probability concepts we will encounter in Chapter 6.)

Relative Frequency Distributions

The relative frequencies for a population are readily obtained for each category. Since a relative frequency is the proportion of all observations falling into a particular category, it is calculated by dividing the number of observations in this category by the total number of observations. Once the frequency distribution itself is obtained, the relative frequency computations are a matter of simple arithmetic. This is illustrated in Table 2-9 for each class interval of data

TABLE 2-9   Calculation of Relative Frequency Distribution of Age of Department Store Accounts Receivable

(1) Age (days)	(2) Number of Accounts (frequency)	(3) Relative Frequency
0–under 30	532	.330
30–under 60	317	.196
60–under 90	285	.176
90–under 120	176	.109
120–under 150	158	.098
150–under 180	147	.091
Totals	1,615	1.000

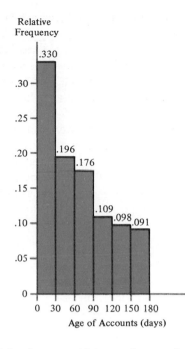

FIGURE 2-8   Relative frequency histogram for age of department store accounts receivable.

on the age of department store accounts receivable (accounts 180 days or older are written off as uncollectible) The relative frequency of accounts less than 30 days old (class interval 0–under 30) is 532/1,615 = .330, which says that 33 percent of all accounts are less than 30 days old. The other relative frequencies are calculated in the same manner, by dividing the class frequency in column (2) by the total number of accounts. The sum of all the relative frequencies must always be 1. Columns (1) and (3) constitute the *relative frequency distribution* for these data. The histogram for this distribution is shown in Figure 2-8. A histogram constructed using relative frequencies will have the same shape as one constructed using original tallies, or absolute frequencies. Only the scale on the vertical axis will change.

Analysis of relative frequencies can sometimes be useful when analysis of absolute frequencies is not. A department store's credit sales will fluctuate considerably over the seasons. If the credit worthiness of the store's customers remains about the same as it has been in the past, then the relative frequency distributions for the ages of accounts receivable obtained during the same calendar month in two successive years should not be noticeably different when growth is steady. This is because the same seasonal pattern will generally persist, even though the total level of sales is higher in the second year. If there is a substantial difference in relative frequencies, it may be due to erratic growth or to a change in the quality of credit customers or in collection procedures. Absolute

TABLE 2-10   Frequency Distributions of Students by Sex

Large University		Small College	
Sex	*Frequency*	*Sex*	*Frequency*
Male	6,000	Male	400
Female	4,000	Female	100
Totals	10,000		500

frequencies cannot isolate the effect of sales growth from the effect of changes in credit procedures.

The relative frequency of men on the two campuses mentioned earlier shows how relative frequency may be used to compare two qualitative populations. Table 2-10 shows the frequency distribution by sex of students in the two schools. The number of men competing for dates in the large university is 6,000; the number in the small college is only 400. The relative frequency distributions are provided in Table 2-11. In terms of relative frequency, there is less competition in the university, where the proportion of men is smaller (.60 in the university versus .80 at the college).

TABLE 2-11   Relative Frequency Distributions of Students by Sex

Large University		Small College	
Sex	*Frequency*	*Sex*	*Frequency*
Male	.60	Male	.80
Female	.40	Female	.20
Totals	1.00		1.00

Cumulative Frequency Distributions

The cumulative frequencies may be determined by adding the frequency for each class interval to the frequencies for preceding intervals. Table 2-12 illustrates this for a sample of 100 annual unit sales figures for television sets sold by retail stores. Here, we find it convenient to express the upper limit of each class interval as "less than" the lower limit of the succeeding interval. The cumulative frequency for sales less than 300 units is found by adding the frequency of sales at or above 100 (but less than 200) to the number of stores having sales at 200 or above (but less than 300), or $0+5 = 5$. The cumulative frequency for a class interval represents the total number of stores having sales levels falling in or below that interval. Columns (1) and (3) of Table 2-12 constitute the *cumulative frequency distribution* for the television sales data.

TABLE 2-12 Calculation of Cumulative Frequencies for Unit Television Set Sales

(1) *Units Sold*	(2) *Number of* *Stores* *(Frequency)*	(3) *Cumulative* *Frequency*
100–less than 200	0	0
200–less than 300	5	$0 + 5 = 5$
300–less than 400	39	$5 + 39 = 44$
400–less than 500	31	$44 + 31 = 75$
500–less than 600	16	$75 + 16 = 91$
600–less than 700	6	$91 + 6 = 97$
700–less than 800	3	$97 + 3 = 100$

The common graphical portrayal for cumulative frequency distributions is shown in Figure 2-9 for the television sales data. The ordinate (vertical height) of a plotted point represents the cumulative frequency for values less than the abscissa (the horizontal scale value). Such a curve is called an *ogive*.

Sometimes it is desirable to calculate cumulative relative frequencies. These are found by adding successive relative frequencies. The largest possible cumulative relative frequency would be 1.0.

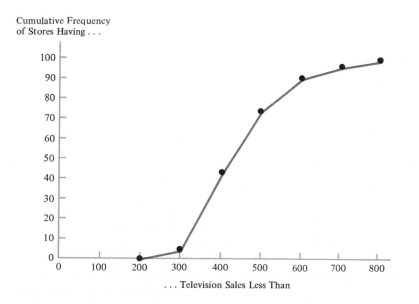

FIGURE 2-9 Ogive for cumulative frequency distribution of television unit sales.

EXERCISES

2-11 The frequency distribution of times between arrivals of injured patients at a hospital emergency room is as follows:

Time (minutes)	Number of Patients
0.0–under 3.0	210
3.0–under 6.0	130
6.0–under 9.0	75
9.0–under 12.0	40
12.0–under 15.0	20
15.0–under 18.0	15
18.0–under 21.0	10

(a) Determine the relative frequency distribution. Then plot the resulting distribution as a histogram.

(b) Determine the cumulative frequency distribution. Then plot this distribution as a "less than" ogive.

2-12 The following is the frequency distribution of consecutive days absent by classified active employees during 1977 in an automobile assembly plant:

Consecutive Days Absent	Number of Employees
0–under 5	3,100
5–under 10	810
10–under 15	510
15–under 20	320
20–under 25	120
25–under 30	30
30–under 60	110

(Employees absent a total of 60 or more consecutive days are reclassified as inactive. Each employee is counted just once, being placed in the category corresponding to his longest absence.)

(a) Determine the relative frequency distribution.

(b) Determine the cumulative *relative* frequency distribution.

(c) Plot a "less than" ogive using the data obtained in part (b).

2-13 The president of an insurance company orders occasional spot checks of the degree of managerial discipline in five regional offices. One factor considered is the relative frequency of tardy and absent employees. On a particular day he ordered an audit of payroll records, which resulted in the following frequency distributions:

Number of Employees by Office

	A	B	C	D	E
Tardy	60	60	10	56	2
Absent	60	30	20	24	15
On job and on time	1,080	510	270	720	233
Total	1,200	600	300	800	250

(a) Determine the relative frequency distributions for each office.

(b) Using office A as a standard, which regions have an excessively high number of tardy employees?

(c) Compared to office A, which regions have an unusually large number of absent employees? Do you think that the managers of these regions are necessarily "softer" than the manager in region A? Explain.

2-14 The cumulative relative frequency distribution for the number of shares owned by each of the 1,000 shareholders in a small nonpublic corporation is provided below.

Number of Shares	Cumulative Proportion of Shareholders
0–under 5,000	0.36
5,000–under 10,000	0.63
10,000–under 15,000	0.81
15,000–under 20,000	0.90
20,000–under 25,000	0.97
25,000–under 30,000	1.00

(a) Determine the relative frequency distribution.
(b) Using your answer to part (a), determine the original frequency distribution.
(c) Using your answer to part (b), determine the cumulative frequency distribution.

2-4 COMMON FORMS OF THE FREQUENCY DISTRIBUTION

Statistical methodology has been developed for analyzing samples taken from populations having various general forms. Thus, by placing populations into various categories, it is possible to increase our analytical powers considerably by using some of the techniques that apply to all populations belonging to the same *distribution family*. All quantitative populations have some form of distribution. Most populations can be classified into a few well-known distributions, although the mathematical equations describing them may be complex. The shape of the sample histogram usually indicates the form of the population distribution.

In Figures 2-10 to 2-14, examples of several of the more common general shapes of frequency curves are sketched alongside representative sample histograms. Figure 2-10 represents the relative frequency distribution of the diameters of a production batch of 1-inch thick steel reinforcing rods. Note that the histogram is fairly symmetrical about the interval 0.995–1.005 inches, with frequency dropping for the next higher and lower intervals. On the left and right the histogram bars become progressively shorter, tapering off at about 0.91 and 1.09 inches, respectively. The smoothed frequency curve beside the histogram is bell-shaped and belongs to a class of populations having the *normal distribution*. We will have more to say about normal curves in Chapter 7. A great many populations have frequency distributions in this category, including many physical measurements.

Figure 2-11 shows the histogram for the television sales data from Table 2-12. Here the data are skewed, because a few stores had quite high sales. Beside the histogram is a frequency curve with the right "tail" longer than the left. This general shape corresponds to a class of skewed distributions where there are few

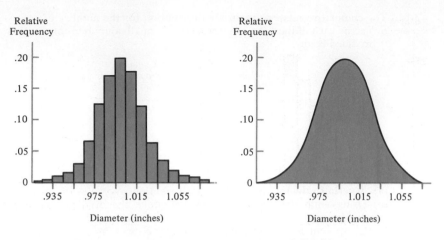

FIGURE 2-10   Sample histogram (left) and population frequency curve (right) for steel rod diameters.

small observations, with proportionately more large observations falling over a wide range of values.

Another type of skewed distribution is provided in Figure 2-12, where the gasoline mileage frequency curve has a longer left tail. In this case, the smaller values are widely spread from 14 through 18 miles per gallon, while the rarer large values fall into a single class, 23.0–under 24.0.

The distribution for the ages of the department store accounts receivable given in Table 2-9 is plotted in Figure 2-13. Here the approximating smoothed

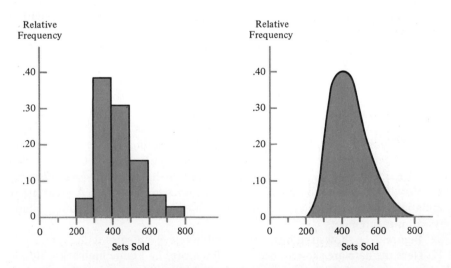

FIGURE 2-11   Sample histogram (left) and population frequency curve (right) for television unit sales.

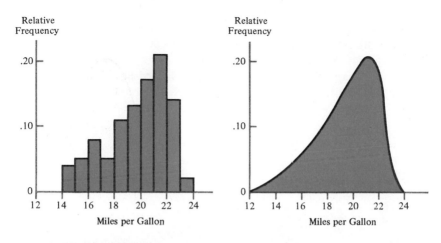

FIGURE 2-12   Sample histogram (left) and population frequency curve (right) for gasoline mileage.

curve has the general shape of a reversed letter J. This type of distribution is sometimes called the *exponential distribution*. Such a frequency curve approximates a great many populations where the observations involve items whose status changes over time. Exponential distributions have been used to characterize equipment lifetimes until failure. They are also common in describing the time between successive arrivals of cars at a toll booth or of emergency patients at a hospital and are therefore very useful in the analysis of waiting-line or queuing situations.

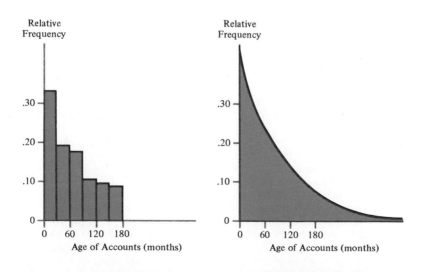

FIGURE 2-13   Sample histogram (left) and population frequency curve (right) for ages of department store accounts receivable.

The left-hand side of Figure 2-14 is the histogram for the lengths of pieces of roofing scrap lumber from a construction job. Any piece shorter than 20 inches (the width between studs) cannot be used. Because the lumber comes from the mill in various lengths, a piece of scrap is likely to be any length between 1 and 20 inches (scrap shorter than 1 inch is not counted here). The histogram is therefore approximated by a rectangle. Because no particular width is favored, such a population is a member of the *uniform distribution* family.

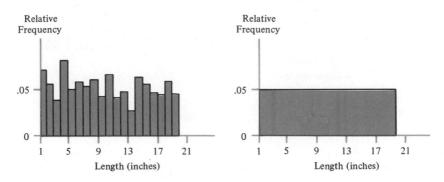

FIGURE 2-14   Sample histogram (left) and population frequency curve (right) for lengths of scrap pieces of lumber.

Later we will encounter other, less common shapes and will discuss how one particular shape—the bimodal—can help to identify nonhomogeneous population influences. By classifying the various shapes of frequency distributions, we obtain better population descriptions and can be selective in choosing statistical techniques for analysis.

EXERCISES

2-15   For each of the following populations for the *ages* of persons, sketch an appropriate shape for the frequency distribution and explain the reasons for your choice.
(a) Science fiction novel readers.
(b) Persons not holding full-time jobs.
(c) Persons having false teeth.
(d) Children in a grammar school.

2-16   For each of the following populations, sketch an appropriate shape for the frequency distribution and explain the reasons for your choice.
(a) Times required by a pharmacist to fill new prescriptions.
(b) Last two digits in numbers assigned to telephones in a metropolitan area.
(c) Number of persons employed by manufacturing firms.
(d) Duration of stay by patients hospitalized with nonchronic diseases.

REVIEW EXERCISES

2-17 The following gasoline mileage data for a taxicab fleet are incomplete:

Miles per Gallon	Number of Cars	Relative Frequency	Cumulative Frequency
6–under 8	—	—	—
8–under 10	23	—	29
10–under 12	—	.34	—
12–under 14	17	.17	—
14–under 16	—	—	92
16–under 18	—	—	—
Totals	100	1.00	

(a) Find the missing values.

(b) Plot the cumulative frequency ogive for this population.

2-18 A sample of students has been selected at a university, and the students' ages have the frequency distribution provided below. Determine the relative and cumulative frequency distributions.

Age (years)	Number of Students
20–under 25	18
25–under 30	23
30–under 35	15
35–under 40	13
40–under 45	7
45–under 50	6
50–under 55	5
55–under 60	5
60–under 65	8
Total	100

2-19 The following data represent the marital status of the heads of households for a sample of welfare recipients:

File No.	Status	File No.	Status	File No.	Status	File No.	Status
00357	M	06315	D	10586	S	16627	M
01112	M	07448	D	10794	S	17051	M
01267	D	07496	S	10813	M	17834	M
01448	S	08523	S	10915	D	18215	D
02536	D	09117	M	17317	W	19006	M
02699	S	09856	W	12225	D	19853	D
03419	M	10013	M	12806	M	20017	W
03212	W	10074	M	13115	W	20556	W
04896	W	10176	M	14083	S	20562	S
05517	M	10324	D	14118	D	21010	M

where S = single, M = married, D = divorced, and W = widowed.

(a) Determine the frequency distribution for this qualitative population.

(b) Construct a histogram for the results obtained in part (a).

2-20 A group of 350 persons has been categorized by sex, marital status, and occupation. The number of persons in each category combination is provided on page 36.

Sex	Marital Status	Occupation	Number of Persons
Male	married	blue collar	75
Male	married	white collar	37
Male	married	professional	12
Male	single	blue collar	55
Male	single	white collar	38
Male	single	professional	3
Female	married	blue collar	13
Female	married	white collar	32
Female	married	professional	2
Female	single	blue collar	12
Female	single	white collar	66
Female	single	professional	5
		Total	350

Construct the frequency distributions for the populations characterized by
(a) sex   (b) marital status   (c) occupation

Chapter Three
Summary
Descriptive Measures

Statisticians commonly limit their inquiries to Averages, and do not revel in more comprehensive views. Their souls seem as dull to the charm of variety as the native of one of our flat English counties, whose retrospect of Switzerland was that, if its mountains could be thrown into its lakes, two nuisances would be got rid of at once.

Sir Francis Galton (1889)

We have seen how the frequency distribution arranges raw data into a meaningful pattern. Now we are ready to investigate further ways to summarize statistical data. Knowledge of the frequency distribution alone is not sufficient for answering many statistical questions. For example, in evaluating a new drug, a pharmaceutical firm must establish whether the drug improves patient recovery. The new drug must somehow be compared to the old one. Sample data can provide recovery times for the two treatments, but a direct comparison of histograms would be cumbersome. Instead, the *average* recovery times for the two drugs would more clearly establish whether the new treatment is better. If the new drug significantly speeds up the average patient's recovery, it should then be used as a replacement.

This chapter considers a variety of summary measures. Each is a number precisely measuring various properties of the observations. For quantitative data, there are two major classes of summary numerical values. One of these measures *central tendency* or *location*, a value around which the observations

37

tend to cluster and which typifies their magnitude. The *arithmetic mean* is one of the more commonly used measures of central tendency. Another broad category of numbers provides measures of *dispersion* or *variability* among the observation values. These measures indicate how the variates differ from each other. Conceptually, the simplest of these is the *range*, which expresses the difference between the largest and smallest observations. For qualitative data, a useful summary measure is the *proportion*, which indicates how frequently a particular attribute is observed.

3-1 STATISTICS, PARAMETERS, AND DECISION MAKING

Summary data measures may correspond either to populations or to samples. A summary measure based upon population data is referred to as a *population parameter* and summarizes a particular property of the entire collection of potential observations. Ordinarily, not all of the population will be observed, and usually only a sample is taken. A summary measure obtained from sample data is referred to as a *statistic*. A statistic is a number conveying a property of just those data actually observed. Corresponding to every population parameter is an analogous sample statistic that can be computed in a similar manner. For instance, the arithmetic mean for a population has a counterpart that is calculated from the sample. Usually the population's mean is not known and may be estimated from an arithmetic mean calculated from sample data.

Population parameters serve a role in decision-making not provided by the frequency distribution alone. For example, a production manager must periodically develop schedules for personnel and equipment based upon some reasonable expectation of performance. Thus, the manager may find that average past productivity levels provide the best indicators of future performance. A frequency distribution for the number of parts produced daily by the assembly department would provide less specific information for a monthly plan than the average daily output. Similarly, a mail order distributor can use sales to readers of a magazine advertisement in evaluating the effectiveness of magazine advertising. A frequency distribution of dollar sales per reader may be less useful for this purpose than the average sales per reader.

When a population is qualitative, the parameter used is the *proportion* of observations having a particular attribute. Thus, a federal agency investigating sex discrimination in employment may be interested in the proportion of females employed in various job categories. If this proportion is judged too low in certain jobs, pressures may be applied to remedy the situation. In quality control, the proportion of defective items often serves as a guideline for accepting or rejecting a production batch or for initiating remedial action.

Populations may be easily compared using parameter values. A young man choosing a career might consider the typical earnings levels achieved by members of the various professions. He may find that half of all doctors in his state earn above $45,000, a *median* income level of this population, while the median income for lawyers is only $25,000. This information may influence him to prefer a medical career to a legal one. A sales manager wishes to spend her last advertising dollars in a medium providing the greatest difference between average sales per 1,000 viewers, listeners, or readers and cost per 1,000. She would thus compare television and radio commercial possibilities to various newspaper, magazine, and billboard advertisements. If, for the same cost per 1,000 readers, an advertisement in magazine A resulted in increased average sales of only $20 per 1,000, while magazine B increased sales on the average by $25 per 1,000, magazine B would be more desirable than A.

When generalizing about a population from a sample, the most common inferences made are those regarding the value of a parameter. The median income of all physicians would be estimated from a limited sample of doctors. The average test score of all persons who will be taking an aptitude test is projected from the scores of the initial few persons taking it. A decision based upon the proportion of defectives in a shipment is made using the results of detailed testing conducted on a sample of items. The procedures of statistical inference are largely concerned with estimating the value of a particular population parameter or with testing to determine whether an assumed value holds.

3-2   THE ARITHMETIC MEAN

The arithmetic mean is the most commonly encountered and best understood of the measures of central tendency. Consider the cash balances (in thousands of dollars) of five manufacturing firms: 101.3, 34.5, 17.6, 83.4, and 52.7. The mean 57.9 is calculated by adding these values and dividing the sum by the number of firms (5):

$$\frac{101.3+34.5+17.6+83.4+52.7}{5} = \frac{289.5}{5} = 57.9$$

If the five cash balances represent only a sample from a population of observations of all medium-sized companies in the nation, then the result of the calculation is a *sample mean* of 57.9 thousand dollars. If, instead, they are the entire set of observations for the population of cash balances at the foundries in Marlborough County, then the above calculation yields a *population mean* equal to 57.9 thousand dollars.

Symbolic Expressions for Calculating the Arithmetic Mean

Since the arithmetic mean is calculated in the same fashion for any group of raw data, it will prove convenient to express it symbolically. Because the value of a particular observation may not yet be known, each observation can also be given a special symbol. The letter X is traditionally used to represent an observed value. To distinguish each observation, we will use the numbers 1, 2, 3, ... as *subscripts*. Thus, X_1 represents the first observation value, X_2 the second, X_3 the third, and so on. The symbol X_1 is referred to as "X sub 1." Another advantage to expressing observation values by symbols is that we may use algebraic expressions to state precisely how each statistical measure is to be calculated, so that the same procedure is indicated for any set of data.

The sample mean is itself represented by the special symbol $\overline{X}$, which we call "X bar." In calculating the sample mean, we must divide the sum of the values by the number of observations made. This is the *sample size*, which is represented by the letter n. We may use the following formula to calculate the *sample mean:*

$$\overline{X} = \frac{X_1 + X_2 + \cdots + X_n}{n} \tag{3-1}$$

This expression applies for any sample result. In our previous illustration, the sample size was $n = 5$ and the observed values were $X_1 = 101.3$, $X_2 = 34.5$, $X_3 = 17.6$, $X_4 = 83.4$, and $X_5 = 52.7$.

A similar calculation applies for the *population mean*, which is traditionally referred to by the Greek letter *mu*, μ. (μ is the equivalent of "m," the first letter in mean. Several other population parameters are also represented by Greek letters.) When all the observation values from the population are available, then μ is found in the same way $\overline{X}$ is. Generally, we do not compute μ directly because the entire population is not usually observed. Ordinarily, the value of μ remains unknown; only $\overline{X}$ is calculated and this value then serves as an estimate of μ.

Sometimes it is convenient to use an even more concise expression than the above formula. Just as the plus sign $+$ means that two quantities are added together, we may represent the sum of several values by a *summation sign*. For this purpose, mathematics employs the upper case Greek *sigma*, $\sum$. We may then express the sample mean by

$$\overline{X} = \frac{X_1 + X_2 + \cdots + X_n}{n} = \frac{\sum_{i=1}^{n} X_i}{n}$$

The term involving the summation sign summarizes the procedure: Take all the X's, add them together, and then divide this result by n. In most statistical applications, where the successive subscripts are the increasing sequence of integral values, 1, 2, ..., n, we may drop the subscripts entirely and use instead the further abbreviated formula:

$$\overline{X} = \frac{\sum X}{n} \tag{3-2}$$

Calculating the Mean from Grouped Data

When the number of observations is very large, calculation of the mean can be a tedious chore, fraught with potential error. If the raw data are to be analyzed by computer, then expression (3-2) indicates the best procedure for finding the sample mean. Otherwise, a shortcut method may sometimes be used.

Generally, the first step in analyzing or describing a collection of raw data is to construct a frequency distribution by arranging the raw data into groups or classes according to size. It is usually possible to obtain a good approximation to the sample mean using only typical values from each group and the corresponding class frequencies. Not only can such a shortcut procedure save time and effort, but it may be the only practicable way to obtain a mean. Sometimes data are published already grouped into classes and the raw data are unavailable.

Representing the class frequencies of successive groups by the letters $f_1, f_2, \ldots$, denoting the corresponding class interval midpoints by the letters $X_1, X_2, \ldots$, and letting n represent the sample size, we may apply the following *shortcut expression for calculating the sample mean from grouped data:*

$$\overline{X} = \frac{f_1 X_1 + f_2 X_2 + \cdots + f_C X_C}{n} = \frac{\sum f X}{n} \tag{3-3}$$

where C is the number of classes.

We illustrate the calculation of the mean in Table 3-1 using the grouped data for the gasoline mileage frequency distribution given in the first two columns.

All values falling within a class interval are represented by the midpoint. The first of these, 15, is found by averaging the limits of the first class interval: $(14.0 + 16.0)/2 = 15$. The remaining class interval midpoints can then be easily found by adding one class interval width (here, 2 miles per gallon) to the preceding class midpoint.

TABLE 3-1   Calculation of the Mean Gasoline Mileage
Using Shortcut with Grouped Data

Gasoline Mileage (miles per gallon)	Number of Cars f	Class Interval Midpoint X	f X
14.0–under 16.0	9	15	135
16.0–under 18.0	13	17	221
18.0–under 20.0	24	19	456
20.0–under 22.0	38	21	798
22.0–under 24.0	16	23	368
Totals	100		1,978

$$\overline{X} = \frac{\sum f X}{n} = \frac{1,978}{100} = 19.78 \text{ miles per gallon}$$

The calculation in expression (3-3) is an example of a *weighted average*. Each class midpoint X_i is weighted by the respective frequency f_i. The sum of the weighted products is then divided by n, which equals the sum of the frequencies or weights. We will encounter weighted averages again in Chapter 6 when we discuss special topics in probability.

The value 19.78 found in Table 3-1 is only an *approximation* of the sample mean and can be expected to differ from the value calculated using expression (3-1). The reason for this is that all gasoline mileages falling within a particular class interval are represented by a single number. Furthermore, grouping the gasoline mileages into different classes would result in different midpoint values and frequencies, and the calculation using expression (3-3) might turn out to be either larger or smaller than 19.78. The raw gasoline mileage data are provided in Table 2-7 (p. 22). The arithmetic mean of these, calculated without grouping the data, is 19.718 miles per gallon. This differs only slightly from the value calculated for $\overline{X}$ using the shortcut method. For practical purposes, the approximation is usually close enough.

Open-Ended Intervals

Special difficulties arise when the data have been grouped so that either the lowest or highest class interval is open-ended, for the midpoint of such an interval is undefined. For example, the frequency distribution of personal earnings may have a class interval of "$100,000 or more." In place of the appropriate fX value for this interval, the total earnings above $100,000 for all persons must be used. If the exact figure is unobtainable, then it must be estimated in some appropriate manner.

EXERCISES

3-1   The following numbers of persons are a firm's monthly hirings during a certain year:

$$14, 6, 12, 19, 2, 35, 5, 4, 3, 7, 5, 8$$

Calculate the arithmetic mean hirings per month.

3-2   A data processing manager has bought remote terminal processing time for running special jobs at two different computer "utilities." He wishes to sign a long-term contract with the firm whose computer causes, on the average, the least delay. The numbers of minutes of delayed processing encountered per week during trial periods with each firm are

CompuQuick	210, 15, 47, 93, 104
Dial-a-Pute	18, 341, 523, 25, 19, 293, 115, 203

Assuming that trial experience is representative of future performance, which firm should get the business? Substantiate your answer with appropriate calculations.

3-3   The sales manager of Kleen Janitorial Supplies allows sales representatives to give special introductory prices to new customers. He wishes to weed out those salespersons who take undue advantage of specials, "milking" them for commissions and bringing in little new continuing business.

Investigating the files for the past 10 months, he has determined for each of the five sales representatives the following sample percentages of specials buyers who placed second orders:

Percentage of Specials Buyers Retained

A	B	C	D	E
36	9	11	33	18
43	16	5	17	17
49	21	6	45	23
18	14	14	29	6
17	33	25	17	31
32	8	12	27	42
24	19	11	61	19
19	17	9	47	13
28	26	28	35	26
36	11	14	14	33

(a) Find the mean percentage of specials buyers retained for each sales-person.

(b) Using your answers to part (a), determine the mean percentage of such customers retained for the sales force as a whole.

(c) Assuming that the sales manager will take remedial action against those salespersons who produce lower than average retention, which salespersons should be singled out for "milking" specials?

3-4 From the frequency distribution given below, calculate the sample mean length of logs arriving at a sawmill:

Length (feet)	Number of Logs f
10.0–under 15.0	107
15.0–under 20.0	253
20.0–under 25.0	1,213
25.0–under 30.0	2,412
30.0–under 35.0	506
35.0–under 40.0	77
40.0–under 45.0	3

3-5 Consider the percentages of specials buyers retained by all salespersons in Exercise 3-3 as a single sample.

(a) Construct a frequency distribution using 6 classes of equal width, starting with 5.0–under 15.0.

(b) Calculate the sample mean using the grouped data of the frequency distribution obtained in part (a).

(c) Calculate the sample mean using ungrouped data. By how much is this above or below your answer to part (b)?

3-3   THE MEDIAN AND THE MODE

The Median

After the mean, the most common measure of central tendency is the *median*. Like the mean, the median provides a numerical value that is typical of quantitative sample observations. The *sample median*, which we denote by the letter m, is the central observation when all the data are arranged in increasing sequence. For the heights 66, 68, 69, 73, and 74 inches, the median is $m = 69$ inches, the central value. If a person 70 inches tall were added to the initial group, then the median would be obtained by averaging the two central values from the following: 66, 68, 69, 70, 73, 74. Thus, the sample median would be $m = (69 + 70)/2 = 69.5$ inches.

In general, the *median is the value above or below which lie an equal number of observations.* We find the median from the raw data by first sequencing the observations from lowest to highest and then selecting the central value if there is an odd number of values or averaging the two central values if there is an even number of observations.

When the data have already been grouped into a frequency distribution, the median will fall somewhere in the first class interval above which fewer than half the observations lie. (Its approximate position in this case can be found by using an interpolation procedure.)

Theoretically, the *population median*, M, can be found in the same fashion from the entire population of observed values. However, just as $\bar{X}$ is used to estimate μ, m is generally calculated from sample observations and then serves as the basis for estimating the value of M.

The Median Contrasted with the Mean

The arithmetic mean and the median are both averages, each in its own sense. The mean is the arithmetic average of variates, and the median is the average of position. When we use the term *average*, we mean the arithmetic mean.

A mean has nice mathematical properties. It can be algebraically manipulated. The combined mean of two populations can be calculated from the individual means. Due to its mathematical properties, many statistical techniques employing the mean have been developed. The median is not as well suited to mathematical operation. For example, the median of a combined population cannot be obtained from the separate component population medians. Because of the mathematical difficulties associated with the median, fewer statistical techniques employ it.

On the other hand, the mean is influenced by extreme values to a much greater degree than the median. Consider the net worth levels of your close friends. Suppose that you meet one of the world's few billionaires and include him in your circle of friends. The mean level of wealth would be so distorted by this person that, according to the mean, your friends would, "on the average," all be multimillionaires—hardly a meaningful summary. But the median would not be significantly influenced by the billionaire. The median is more democratic, each elementary unit having but one "vote" in establishing the central location.

Generally, the median provides a better measure of central tendency than the mean when there are some extremely large or small observations.

The Mode

A third measure that may be used to describe central tendency is the *mode. The mode is the most frequently occurring value in a set of observations.* the simple illustration provided by the collection of five observations: 2, 3, 4, 4, and 7. The mode is 4, because 4 occurs most often.

The interpretation of the statistical mode is analogous to that of the fashion mode. A person dressing in the current style is "in the mode." But a current fashion can be a poor description of what most persons are wearing, because of the variety of styles worn by the general public. In statistics, the mode only tells us which single value occurs most often; it may therefore represent a minority of the observations.

As a basis for decisions, the mode can be insidiously undemocratic. For example, most shoe stores stock only the most popular sizes, so the mode is their deciding parameter. One reason for this is that the turnover on unusual sizes is so low that they are unprofitable. When such sizes are stocked, there is ordinarily little choice of color or style (and what there is will usually be on the conservative side). A significant number of persons have great difficulty buying shoes and may have to resort to mail order purchasing. Not being of modal size, they are forced to be hopelessly out of mode in the sense of fashion as well.

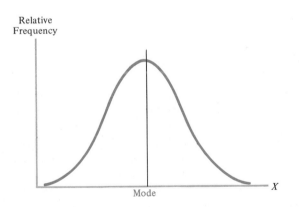

FIGURE 3-1   Illustration of location of mode.

When the data are grouped into classes, the mode is represented by the midpoint of the interval having the greatest class frequency. We refer to this group as the *modal class.* When the frequency distribution is portrayed as a smoothed curve like the one in Figure 3-1, the mode corresponds to the possible observation value lying beneath the highest point on the frequency curve—the location of maximum clustering. The mode can therefore serve as a basis for comparing the typicality of the other measures of central tendency.

Positional Comparison of Measures: Skewed Distributions

When the population has a *symmetrical* frequency curve like the one in Figure 3-2(a), the mean, median, and mode coincide. When the population is not symmetrical, the mean and median will lie to the same side of the mode. The frequency curve in Figure 3-2(b) has a tail tapering off to the right. Such an asymmetrical frequency distribution is *skewed to the right*, so that the population values cluster around a relatively low value, although there are some extremely large observation values. In this case, the mean lies to the right of the mode, reflecting the influence of the larger values in raising the arithmetic average. Although it too is affected by extreme values, the median is not so sensitive as the mean. In a rightward skewed distribution, the median also lies to the right of the mode but somewhere between the mode and the mean.

Because a rightward skewed population will always have a median smaller than its mean, subtracting the median from the mean results in a positive difference. For this reason, such a frequency distribution is said to be *positively*

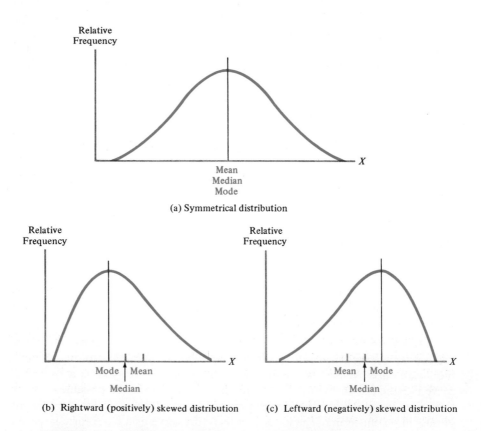

(a) Symmetrical distribution

(b) Rightward (positively) skewed distribution
(c) Leftward (negatively) skewed distribution

FIGURE 3-2 Positional comparison of center measures for symmetrical and skewed frequency distributions.

skewed. This expression also reflects the fact that the tail of the distribution tapers off in a positive direction from the center of the population.

Generally, a characteristic having a lower limit but no theoretical upper boundary will result in positively skewed populations. This would be the case with the annual wages earned by construction workers in the United States. A lower limit would be established by the legal minimum wage. Some blue-collar aristocrats, such as operating engineers (who drive heavy equipment), plumbers, electricians, and steeplejacks, have exceptionally high earnings. In total numbers, however, the high earners are relatively sparse, creating a long, thin, rightward tail in the frequency curve of this population. Many economic data have positively skewed frequency distributions.

Figure 3-2(c) shows a frequency curve *skewed to the left*—the direction toward which its tail points. Because the extremes are relatively small values, the mean lies below the mode. Again, the median will lie somewhere in between the mean and the mode. Subtracting the median from the mean (a smaller value) results in a negative difference. The frequency curve is therefore said to be *negatively skewed.*

Negatively skewed distributions result when the observed values have an upper limit and no significant lower boundary. For example, the ages of viewers watching a famous dance band leader's television program, where the musical taste runs to "old favorites," would be a negatively skewed population. Aimed at a preponderantly middle-aged and elderly audience, with commercials touting denture deodorants, laxatives, and home health care remedies, the show would not be too appealing to the younger set. Some young people might watch it, but not many; a few tots with late bedtimes might appreciate the hoopla and congeniality of the program. These young persons would bring the mean viewing age below what should be considered typical, so that here the *median* age would more truly represent a typical population value.

The median is the most realistic measure of location for data having skewed distributions.

Bimodal Distributions

The mode has been defined as the most frequently occurring population value. But suppose there are two values occurring with equal or nearly equal frequency. Then there are two or more modes. When a population has two modes it is said to be *bimodal.*

The presence of more than one mode has a special significance in statistical analysis: It indicates potential trouble. It is usually dangerous to compare bimodal populations or to draw conclusions about them, because they usually arise when there is some nonhomogeneous factor present in the population. Figure 3-3(a) presents the frequency curve of a population of height measurements for adult patients admitted to a large hospital during the past year. The curve is bimodal, with the two modes at 5'3" and 5'10". In this case, the nonhomogeneous factor is sex, for the two modes result from the fact that an equal

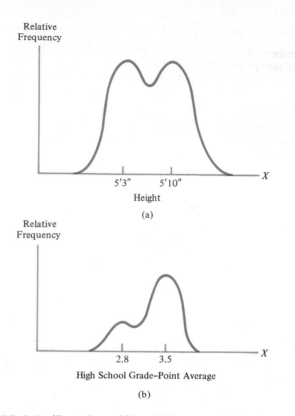

FIGURE 3-3   Illustrations of bimodal frequency distributions.

number of male and female patients are measured. It would be more meaningful to separate the population into male and female populations and analyze the two more homogeneous populations separately.

To illustrate the potential difficulty, suppose we wish to compare patient heights in the year before the new maternity ward opened to those in the current year. The proportion of female patients would be higher in the second year, so the overall mean height would be less. The patients would not have become smaller as a cursory analysis might indicate. If the two populations for each sex were compared separately, the mean heights would not noticeably change over the two-year period.

Figure 3-3(b) shows another population having a double-humped frequency curve. This curve represents the high-school grade-point average of students at a university. Humps in frequency occur at 2.8 and 3.5. Although the mode is 3.5, we would still classify this population as bimodal because there is a nonhomogeneous factor influencing the high-school grades of the students. In this case, the factor is due to a relatively small group of disadvantaged students who are to be given remedial work. Although comparatively ill prepared at present, it is contemplated that their *college* grade-point averages will not substantially differ from those of their fellow students.

EXERCISES

3-6   The numbers of major automobile accidents occurring each month during the past year in a certain city were

$$0, 1, 3, 4, 5, 2, 2, 6, 7, 2, 0, 1$$

Letting these data represent sample data for accidents in cities of similar size, calculate the sample mean, median, and mode.

3-7   The sample frequency distribution for the lifetimes of a particular stereo cartridge is as follows:

Lifetime (hours)	Number of Cartridges
0.0–under 50.0	5
50.0–under 100.0	16
100.0–under 150.0	117
150.0–under 200.0	236
200.0–under 250.0	331
250.0–under 300.0	78
300.0–under 350.0	27
350.0–under 400.0	8

(a) Calculate the sample mean.
(b) Find the sample mode.
(c) Suppose that the sample median has value $m = 205$. Does the mean lie above or below the median? Does this indicate that the distribution is positively or negatively skewed?

3-8   Using the following family installment debt data, determine the sample median.

$2,032	$ 232	$ 493	$5,555
597	4,893	4,432	4,444
203	796	978	329
97	852	1,427	972
3,333	1,712	2,121	438
1,212	1,940	5,067	705
5,769	1,843	4,337	3,976
2,347	3,525	5,213	3,034
2,137	3,414	4,896	5,035
2,049	4,327	2,172	4,222

3-9   The instructor in a statistics course gives four exams of equal weight. From the scores on these, she will determine a single central score value. Suppose that she lets each student decide *in advance of the first test* whether his particular grade will be determined by his mean or by his median test score.

(a) Would you request the mean or the median? Why?
(b) For each of the following hypothetical sets of test scores, indicate whether the mean or the median would provide the greatest central value:

(1)	(2)	(3)	(4)
95	80	80	60
60	50	75	80
75	75	65	90
65	70	60	90

3-10 For each of the following situations, indicate a possible source of non-homogeneity in the data and discuss why the population ought or ought not to be split to better serve the purposes of the statistical study.

(a) Six months ago, a new driver safety program was initiated by a state's highway patrol. For the past year, the governor's office has kept records of the number of weekly accidents. A study is being made to evaluate highway construction standards.

(b) An appliance manufacturer wishes to make a powerful home vacuum cleaner. To be most effective, the cleaner must be heavier than the normal weight for such an appliance. A representative group of employees, including men and women, is used to obtain data on how much weight a person can carry up a flight of stairs without excessive fatigue. These data will be used to set a maximum vacuum cleaner weight.

(c) An automobile manufacturer has obtained data on the total man-hours required to assemble each car made at two identically equipped plants of the same size. Each plant produces cars of makes and models as ordered by dealers in its geographical region. These data will be used to establish production standards for each car model.

3-4 MEASURING VARIABILITY

No one value of central tendency can adequately summarize a set of observations. One value does not indicate how different from each other all the values are. Practically all samples and populations exhibit variability. Nowhere is this more true than in nature. Just as persons come in different shapes and sizes, so all natural phenomena vary in important characteristics. There are wet and dry years. Earthquakes occur with varying intensities. People vary in their talents. The same is true in business. Economic growth is unsteady. Unemployment and product demands fluctuate widely. The time taken to assemble a part will vary from item to item.

Importance of Variability

Measuring variability is just as important as finding central tendency. The role of variability is illustrated in Figure 3-4. Here, we compare the frequency curves of the net earnings for dairies and ranches. These populations, reflecting both good and bad years, were determined in such a way that the median incomes were the same. In each case, the populations are positively skewed; losses occurred for a portion of both dairies and ranches. But the losses incurred by some ranchers were more frequent and were often larger than those of the least profitable dairy. On the other hand, many ranches were more profitable than the best dairies. Ranch earnings exhibit *greater variability* than dairy incomes. Although both forms of agriculture involve cattle and must meet comparable feed requirements, the dairy farmer is blessed with stable milk prices (often due to regulation), while the rancher must sell his beef at the volatile

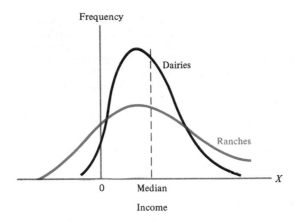

Frequency

Dairies

Ranches

0 Median

Income

X

FIGURE 3-4 Frequency curves for the earnings of dairies and ranches.

market price. The greater variability in income makes ranching a riskier venture than owning a dairy, even though the earnings of both agricultural enterprises have had identical central tendencies (equal medians). Here, statistical variability might help the new agricultural college graduate in choosing between ranching or operating a dairy.

Another illustration of the importance of variability in statistical analysis is provided by a decision to modify a chemical process. Figure 3-5 shows the frequency distributions of processing times required under two methods being

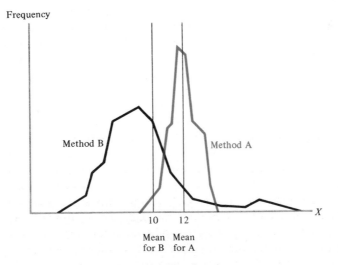

Frequency

Method B

Method A

10 12

Mean Mean
for B for A

X

Completion Time (hours)

FIGURE 3-5 Frequency distributions for the completion times of two chemical processes.

pilot tested. Method A has a mean of 12 hours, whereas method B takes an average of 10 hours. Method B shows substantially greater variability than A. Assuming that both processes cost the same on an hourly basis, B appears to be cheaper. But process A would be easier for planning purposes, because its completion times are less varied. If the final product is perishable or must be made to customer order, so that it cannot be stored in quantity for very long, then method A might turn out to be superior. *In a great many populations, reduction in variability is itself an improvement.*

Variability or dispersion may be measured in two basic ways: in terms of *distances* between particular observation values, or in terms of the *average deviations* of individual observations about the central value.

Distance Measures of Dispersion

Distance measures of dispersion are popular when the only purpose is to describe a collection of data. The most common of these is the *range*, which is obtained by subtracting the smallest observation from the largest. For example, suppose that the five students in a college accounting honors program have the following IQs: 111, 118, 126, 137, 148. The range of these values is $148 - 111 = 37$. The figure 37 represents the total spread in these observations. The range provides a very concise summary of the total variation in a sample or a population. But its major disadvantage as a useful measure is that it ignores all but the two most extreme observations. These two numbers may be very far from typical values, even among the higher and lower observations.

Other distance measures ignore the most extreme observations. These are *interfractile ranges*, which express the differences between two values called fractiles. A *fractile* is a point below which some specified proportion of the value lies. The median is the .50 fractile because half of all observations lie below this value. When expressed as percentages, the analogous measure is called a *percentile*; the median is the 50th percentile. The most commonly used fractiles or percentiles are the *quartiles*. These divide the observations into four groups, each containing a roughly equal number of observations. The .25 fractile, or 25th percentile, is the *first quartile*. This is the value below which 25 percent of the observations lie. The median is the *second quartile*, while the 75th percentile is the *third quartile*.

The most common dispersion measure based upon fractiles is the *interquartile range*. This is the difference between the third and first quartiles and thus *represents the middle 50 percent of the observation values.* Figure 3-6 shows an ogive for family income. The fractile values may be read from this graph. The first quartile is $7,900 and the third quartile is $18,100, so that the interquartile range is $18,100 - $7,900 = $10,200$.

Other interfractile ranges, such as those representing the middle 90 percent or 99 percent, may be used but seldom are.

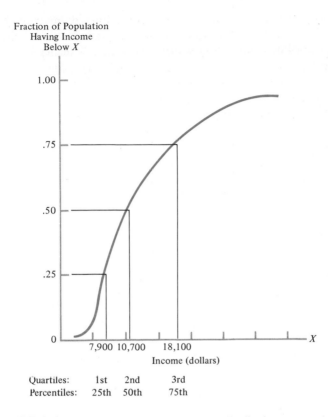

Fraction of Population
Having Income
Below *X*

Quartiles:

Quartiles:	1st	2nd	3rd
Percentiles:	25th	50th	75th

FIGURE 3-6   Cumulative relative frequency distribution
for family income

Measures of Average Deviation

The main disadvantage of the distance measures of dispersion is that they
do not consider every observation. To include all observations, we can calculate
how much each one deviates from the central value and then combine these
deviations through averaging. The most common deviation considered is the
difference between the observed value and the mean:

$$X - \overline{X} \quad \text{for sample data}$$
$$X - \mu \quad \text{for population data}$$

A straightforward averaging of the deviation values will always result in
zero. For example, consider the five values 1, 2, 3, 4, and 5. Their mean is 3.
Subtracting 3 from each number, we obtain deviations -2, -1, 0, 1, and 2.
These add up to zero, so the average deviation is zero. We might avoid this
difficulty by ignoring the minus signs. That is, we could average the *absolute*

values of each deviation (2, 1, 0, 1, and 2) and obtain the *mean deviation* 1.2, which reflects every observation. But because of mathematical difficulties in working with absolute values, two other measures of dispersion are more commonly used.

The Variance and Standard Deviation

The most important measure of variability is found by averaging the *squares* of the individual deviations; the resulting value is the *mean of the squared deviations*. This calculation may be performed on the IQs for the five accounting students previously cited. The mean value is

$$\frac{111+118+126+137+148}{5} = 128$$

The deviations from the mean value are

$$
\begin{aligned}
111-128 &= -17 \\
118-128 &= -10 \\
126-128 &= -2 \\
137-128 &= 9 \\
148-128 &= 20
\end{aligned}
$$

and the mean of the squared deviations is

$$\frac{(-17)^2+(-10)^2+(-2)^2+(9)^2+(20)^2}{5} = \frac{289+100+4+81+400}{5}$$

$$= \frac{874}{5} = 174.8$$

The measure of variability obtained in the above manner is referred to as the *variance*. It may be calculated using data from either the sample or the entire population. When all the population data are available, the above procedure provides the *population variance*, which is represented in abbreviated form by σ^2. (The symbol σ is the lower case Greek *sigma*, and σ^2 is called "sigma squared.") The expression used for calculating the population variance is

$$\sigma^2 = \frac{\sum (X-\mu)^2}{N} \tag{3-4}$$

Here the sum of the squared deviations from the population mean μ is found, and—because every possible observation is made—this sum is divided by the *population size*, denoted by the letter N. In the above illustration the *entire population* consisted of $N = 5$ observations.

In practice, a value for σ^2 cannot be computed because most populations are so large that usually only a sample is taken. For sample data, variability is measured by the *sample variance*, denoted symbolically by s^2. From the following analogous expression *using sample size n in place of N and sample mean* $\overline{X}$ *in place of* μ, we calculate the *sample variance*

$$s^2 = \frac{\sum (X - \overline{X})^2}{n - 1} \tag{3-5}$$

Here the squared deviations from $\overline{X}$ are averaged using only the *n sample observations*. The expression for s^2 has a slightly different form than that for σ^2, with $n - 1$ as the divisor instead of the complete sample size n. For reasons that will be explained in Chapter 8, using $n - 1$ for the divisor makes the resulting s^2 value a better estimate of the usually unknown value for σ^2.

There are two practical difficulties associated with using the variance. One is that the variance is usually a very large number compared to the observations themselves. Thus, if the observations are largely in the thousands, the variance will often be in the millions. Second, the variance is not expressed in the same units as the observations. In the previous example, the variance is 174.8 *squared IQ points*. This is because the deviations, measured in IQ points, have all been squared. The variance of heights, originally measured in feet, will thus be expressed in square feet. The variance for gasoline mileages would be in units of squared miles per gallon.

In spite of these difficulties, the variance has some very nice mathematical properties that make it extremely important in statistical theory. Furthermore, the difficulties may be simply overcome by working with the square root of the variance, called the *standard deviation*. [As an aid, Appendix Table A (page A-1) provides square roots for whole numbers between zero and 1,000.]

The Standard Deviation

Taking the positive square root of the variance in IQ levels, we have

$$\sqrt{174.8} = 13.22$$

which yields the standard deviation in IQ level. The standard deviation is expressed in the same units as the observations themselves; the value 13.22 is a point on the same numerical scale.

The *sample standard deviation* is represented by the letter s without its exponent 2. The following expression may be used to calculate the *sample standard deviation*

$$s = \sqrt{\frac{\sum (X - \overline{X})^2}{n - 1}} \tag{3-6}$$

Note that on both sides of the equation we simply have the square root of the expression for the sample variance. Likewise, for the population parameters,

TABLE 3-2   Calculation of Sample Standard Deviation
for Earnings per Share of Five Common Stocks

Earnings per Share X	Deviation $(X - \bar{X})$	Squared Deviation $(X - \bar{X})^2$
$ 2.34	$2.34 − 3.91 = $ − 1.57	2.4649
4.17	4.17 − 3.91 = 0.26	0.0676
3.56	3.56 − 3.91 = − 0.35	0.1225
9.23	9.23 − 3.91 = 5.32	28.3024
0.25	0.25 − 3.91 = − 3.66	13.3956
$19.55	$ 0.00	44.3530

$$\bar{X} = \sum X/n = \$19.55/5 = \$3.91$$

$$s = \sqrt{\frac{\sum (X - \bar{X})^2}{n - 1}} = \sqrt{\frac{44.3530}{4}} = \$3.33$$

the *population standard deviation* is denoted by σ, and σ is equal to $\sqrt{\sigma^2}$. Both the variance and the standard deviation provide the same information; one can always be obtained from the other. The standard deviation is a practical descriptive measure of dispersion, whereas the variance is generally used in developing statistical theory.

The sample standard deviation is computed in Table 3-2 for the earnings per share of $n = 5$ common stocks. (These five observations are a sample from a very large population.)

Shortcut Calculations of Variance and Standard Deviation

The calculation of the variance and standard deviation can be quite a chore when the number of observations is large. Two short procedures can ease this task. One of these reduces the amount of arithmetic involved. The other technique groups data into classes; s may then be calculated from the frequency distribution, rather than from the original observations, which may be unavailable.

The sample standard deviation may be calculated from individual values with an equation that is mathematically equivalent to expression (3-6) but usually simpler to use. *The shortcut procedure for calculating the sample variance and standard deviation using ungrouped data is*

$$s^2 = \frac{\sum X^2 - n\bar{X}^2}{n - 1} \qquad s = \sqrt{\frac{\sum X^2 - n\bar{X}^2}{n - 1}} \tag{3-7}$$

We illustrate the use of the formula for the standard deviation in Table 3-3 for the earnings per share data given in Table 3-2. This procedure involves only one subtraction in place of the n needed to compute the deviations under the original procedures.

TABLE 3-3   Calculation of Sample Standard Deviation Using
Shortcut Procedure with Ungrouped Common Stock Data

Earnings per Share X	X^2
$ 2.34	5.4756
4.17	17.3889
3.56	12.6736
9.23	85.1929
0.25	.0625
$19.55	120.7935

$$\bar{X} - \sum X/n = \$19.55/5 = \$3.91$$

$$s = \sqrt{\frac{\sum X^2 - n\bar{X}^2}{n-1}} = \sqrt{\frac{120.7935 - 5(3.91)^2}{4}} = \$3.33$$

The shortcut procedure is recommended whenever s is computed by hand or with a calculator.

Just as the mean was calculated from the frequency distribution in Section 3-3, we can use grouped data to calculate the sample variance and standard deviation:

$$s^2 = \frac{\sum f(X - \bar{X})^2}{n-1} \qquad s = \sqrt{\frac{\sum f(X - \bar{X})^2}{n-1}} \qquad (3\text{-}8)$$

However, we would ordinarily use the following *shortcut procedure for calculating the sample variance and standard deviation from grouped data:*

$$s^2 = \frac{\sum fX^2 - n\bar{X}^2}{n-1} \qquad s = \sqrt{\frac{\sum fX^2 - n\bar{X}^2}{n-1}} \qquad (3\text{-}9)$$

These equations are similar to the shortcut expressions for ungrouped data (3-7).

The grouped data computations for the standard deviation are illustrated in Table 3-4, using the gasoline mileages from Table 3-1. The first four columns of Table 3-4 are a reproduction of Table 3-1 for the calculation of $\bar{X}$. Two additional columns, for X^2 and fX^2, are needed to calculate the standard deviation. We find that $s = 2.34$ miles per gallon.

As in calculating the mean from grouped data, only an *approximate* value for the standard deviation may be obtained with this procedure. For most purposes, this is close enough to the true value that would be calculated from either expression (3-6) or (3-7).

Meaning of Standard Deviation

The standard deviation is a parameter that, when combined with statistical techniques, provides a great deal of information. When the population has a special frequency distribution called the normal curve (to be discussed in detail

TABLE 3-4   Calculation of Sample Standard Deviation Using Shortcut Procedure with Grouped Gasoline Mileage Data

(1)	(2)	(3)	(4)	(5)	(6)
		Class			
Gasoline	*Number*	*Interval*			
Mileage	*of Cars*	*Midpoint*			
(miles per gallon)	*f*	*X*	*fX*	*X²*	*fX²*
14.0–under 16.0	9	15	135	225	2,025
16.0–under 18.0	13	17	221	289	3,757
18.0–under 20.0	24	19	456	361	8,664
20.0–under 22.0	38	21	798	441	16,758
22.0–under 24.0	16	23	368	529	8,464
Totals	100		1,978		39,668

$$\bar{X} = \sum fX/n = 1{,}978/100 = 19.78 \text{ miles per gallon}$$

$$s = \sqrt{\frac{\sum fX^2 - n\bar{X}^2}{n-1}} = \sqrt{\frac{39{,}668 - 100(19.78)^2}{99}}$$

$$= \sqrt{5.4865} = 2.34 \text{ miles per gallon}$$

in Chapter 7), we can find the percentage of observations falling within distances of one, two, or three standard deviations from the mean. When the frequency curve of the population has the form of a normal distribution, then about 68 percent of all observations lie within the region $\mu \pm 1\sigma$. For example, suppose a group of men have a mean height of $\mu = 5'9''$ and a standard deviation of $\sigma = 3''$. If these constitute a normal distribution, then 68 percent of all men will be between $\mu - \sigma = 5'6''$ and $\mu + \sigma = 6'0''$ tall. Furthermore, about 95.5 percent of the population will lie within $\mu \pm 2\sigma$, and 99.7 percent will fall within $\mu \pm 3\sigma$.

The normal curve is described mathematically in terms of just two parameters, μ and σ. Thus, for populations characterized by this curve, we can construct a close representation of the entire frequency distribution knowing only these two values, the mean and standard deviation. We will discuss this point more thoroughly in Chapter 7.

A theoretical result referred to as *Chebyshev's Theorem*, after the mathematician who proposed it, indicates that the standard deviation plays a key role in any population.

CHEBYSHEV'S THEOREM   The proportion of observations falling within k standard deviations of the mean is at least $1 - 1/k^2$.

This says that regardless of the characteristics of the population, the following holds:

Standard Deviations k	*Minimum Proportion of Observations Within* $\mu \pm k\sigma$
1	$1 - 1/1^2 = 0$
2	$1 - 1/2^2 = .75$
3	$1 - 1/3^2 = .89$

Since the above principle applies for any population, it is too general to be of much practical use. Usually a more precise determination of how many observations lie within k standard deviations of the mean can be found when the form of a population's frequency distribution is known, as we have shown for the normal curve. The practical significance of Chebyshev's Theorem is that it tells us that a great deal of information is imparted by the population standard deviation.

EXERCISES

3-11 The following are sample gasoline sales figures (thousands of gallons, rounded) for filling stations in a city:

$$35, 47, 57, 16, 12, 73, 102$$

(a) Calculate the sample range.
(b) Calculate the sample variance and the sample standard deviation.

3-12 The following sample data have been obtained for the price–earnings ratios of stocks listed on the New York Stock Exchange:

$$25, 16, 50, 19, 42, 37$$

Calculate the sample variance and sample standard deviation of the above data.

3-13 For each of the following decision situations involving populations, discuss why a central population value may not be wholly adequate by itself.

(a) The population of temperatures actually achieved in each room of a building with standard temperature control settings is being used to determine whether the system ought to be modified.
(b) Balancing an automobile assembly line requires that sufficient personnel and equipment be positioned at each work station so that no one station will be excessively idle. The population of task completion times at each station is used to help determine how this may be done.
(c) In planning for facilities expansion, a hospital administrator requires data on the convalescent time of surgical patients.

3-14 Using the following frequency distribution for the times to failure of a certain kind of fuse, calculate the mean and standard deviation.

Time to Failure (hundreds of hours)	Number of Fuses
0–under 20	500
20–under 40	250
40–under 60	125
60–under 80	61
80–under 100	15
100–under 120	6

3-15 The Educational Testing Service administers the Graduate Management Admissions Test (GMAT). The following cumulative relative frequency distribution applies for a past base period:

Test Score	Cumulative Relative Frequency
200–under 250	.01
250–under 300	.03
300–under 350	.09
350–under 400	.19
400–under 450	.36
450–under 500	.55
500–under 550	.74
550–under 600	.88
600–under 650	.96
650–under 700	.99

(a) On graph paper plot the ogive for the above data.

(b) Assuming that intermediate values may be read to a good approximation from your graph, determine the 0.25, 0.50, and 0.75 fractiles for GMAT scores.

(c) Using your answers to part (b), calculate the interquartile range for GMAT scores.

3-16 The following frequency distribution has been obtained for a sample of $n = 100$ university-student grade-point averages (GPA).

GPA	Number of Students
0–under 1.0	1
1.0–under 2.0	7
2.0–under 3.0	58
3.0–under 4.0	34

Using grouped approximation methods, determine the sample mean and standard deviation.

3-17 In describing the extent of quality control in his company, the president of a rubber company states that the mean weight of a particular tire is 40 pounds, with a standard deviation of 1 pound. He adds that around 68 percent of all tires weigh between 39 and 41 pounds, whereas nearly all tires weigh between 37 and 43 pounds. State the assumptions upon which these statements rest.

3-5   THE PROPORTION

In describing a qualitative population, there is one key measure of interest —the *proportion* of observations falling into a particular category. Like those measures already discussed, the population parameter is a separate entity from the sample statistic. The population parameter is referred to as the *population proportion* and is denoted by the lower-case Greek letter *pi*, π.* The analogous

---

* Statistics has its own special notation, and here π is not the 3.1416 used in geometry to express the ratio of the circumference to the diameter of a circle. Just as μ and σ, the Greek equivalents of *m* and *s*, are the first letters in the words mean and standard deviation, so π, the Greek p, is the first letter in the word proportion.

sample statistic is the *sample proportion*, which is represented by *P*. The following ratio is used to calculate the *sample proportion:*

$$P = \frac{\text{Number of observations in category}}{\text{Sample size}} \qquad (3\text{-}10)$$

A proportion may assume various values between 0 and 1, according to the relative frequency with which the particular attribute occurs. Like the other population parameters, π is ordinarily unknown and may be estimated from the sample results. Statistical procedures for estimating π from *P* are analogous to those used in estimating a population mean from a sample. But there are substantial differences that require parallel statistical development throughout this book.

The proportion is important in many kinds of statistical analysis. For example, it is often used as the basis for taking remedial action. An unusually high proportion of sales returns will be singled out as a managerial problem. A machine producing a large proportion of oversized or undersized items should be adjusted or repaired. The level of impurities in a drug might be expressed as a proportion; if this figure is too high, the drug cannot be used. In many elections for public office in the United States, the winner is the candidate who receives a plurality, that is, the person who gets the highest proportion of votes.

If a sample of $n = 500$ persons contains 200 men and 300 women, then the sample proportion of women is $P = 300/500 = .60$. If a machine has produced a sample of $n = 100$ parts, 5 of which are defective, then the sample proportion of defective parts would be $P = 5/100 = .05$. This same machine might actually produce defective items at a consistently higher rate than experienced in the sample, so that the population proportion of defective parts could be a different value, such as $\pi = .06$. The proportion may also be expressed as a percentage. Thus, 60 percent of the first sample are women, while 5 percent of the items in the second sample are defective.

The proportion is the only measure available for qualitative data. It indicates relatively how many observations fall into a particular category. (When the observations are attributes, such as male or female, central tendency or variability have no meaning.) The type of question answered by *P* or π is *how many* rather than *how much*.

Sometimes we may wish to express the proportion of observations having a collection of attributes. For example, in Table 2-6 (p. 18), we have the frequency distribution of the letters in a representative sample of 200 characters of ordinary English text. We may wish to find the proportion of vowels. We find that "a" occurs 16 times while "e" occurs 26 times, and the frequencies for "i," "o," and "u" are 13, 16, and 6, respectively. Thus, in 200 letters, vowels occur $16 + 26 + 13 + 16 + 6 = 77$ times. The sample proportion of vowels is therefore $P = 77/200 = .385$. These five letters, taken together, occur 38.5 percent of the time in the sample of ordinary English text.

The proportion is not limited to qualitative data. We may also use it to represent the relative frequency of a quantitative category. For example, the median is the .50 fractile. Thus, the proportion of observations falling below the sample median is $P = .50$. Likewise, the sample proportion of items falling below the third quartile is $P = .75$.

EXERCISES

3-18 A government investigator seeks companies exhibiting pronounced discrimination against employees based upon sex. The data on the number of men and women in management positions in five firms within the same industry are provided below:

Firm	A	B	C	D	E
Men	2,342	532	849	1,137	975
Women	156	115	57	145	139

Calculate the proportion of women managers in each firm. Assuming the investigator will more thoroughly study the firm with the lowest proportion of women managers, which firm would be selected?

3-19 Referring to the personal debt data in Exercise 3-8, determine the sample proportion of families whose indebtedness lies below (a) $1,000; (b) $1,500;   (c) $3,000;   (d) $5,000.

3-20 A quality control inspector must reject incoming shipments if the proportion of inspected items found to be defective exceeds .05. For each of the following four shipments: (a) determine the sample proportion of defectives found, and (b) state whether the inspector would accept or reject the shipment.

	(1)	(2)	(3)	(4)
Items inspected	100	500	600	1,000
Items defective	7	25	10	39

3-21 For each of the following situations, discuss whether a mean, a proportion, or both would be an appropriate parameter upon which to base decisions.

(a) A garment manufacturer wishes to ship dresses of the highest quality. Many things can cause a dress to be defective: incorrect sizing, improper seams, creases, missing stitches, and so on.

(b) The Federal Trade Commission requires that the weight of ingredient in packaged goods be indicated on the label. A soap manufacturer wishes to comply. Underweight production batches (populations) are reprocessed rather than shipped. For the sake of efficiency, a large number of packages (elementary units) must be weighed simultaneously, with the weight of the packaging material subtracted to obtain the weight of the ingredients.

(c) A drug maker is testing a new food supplement that he believes will reduce levels of anemia. The supplement is not expected to work on all patients, but when it does, the extent to which it will reduce anemia by increasing the red corpuscle count in the blood will be measurable.

REVIEW EXERCISES

3-22 A statistics instructor needs to analyze the grade-point data for the grades of a random sample of ten statistics students. With 4 points for "A," the possible scores range downward to 0 points for "F." The following data have been obtained from departmental records:

3	2	4	1	0
3	2	2	2	1

(a) Determine the sample range in grade points.
(b) Find the sample mean.
(c) Determine the sample variance for grade points.
(d) Determine the sample standard deviation in grade points.

3-23 The proportions of weed seeds found in boxes of lawn seed mixtures prepared by a grower have the following cumulative relative frequency distribution:

Proportion of Weed Seed	*Cumulative Relative Frequency*
.00–under .01	.05
.01–under .02	.12
.02–under .03	.25
.03–under .04	.37
.04–under .05	.50
.05–under .06	.67
.06–under .07	.75
.07–under .08	.84
.08–under .09	.89
.09–under .10	.90
.10–under .11	.95
.11–under .12	.98
.12–under .13	1.00

For the proportion of weed seed, determine the following:
(a) The .90 fractile. (d) The third quartile.
(b) The 37th percentile. (e) The interquartile range.
(c) The first quartile. (f) The median.

3-24 The mean lifetimes for cartons of 100-watt, long-life lightbulbs have been established to be normally distributed, with mean 1,500 hours and standard deviation 100 hours. Find the upper and lower bounds for the following limits, and indicate the percentage of all cartons where the mean lifetimes fall within these limits:
(a) $\mu \pm 1\sigma$. (b) $\mu \pm 2\sigma$. (c) $\mu \pm 3\sigma$.

3-25 At a particular college, all entering freshmen must take the SATs, a series of aptitude tests. The following percentiles have been determined:

Score	*Percentile*
450	25th
573	50th
615	75th
729	90th
738	95th
752	99th

(a) Find the first, second, and third quartiles.
(b) What is the median score?
(c) Find the interquartile range.

3-26 The following frequency distribution has been obtained for sample data relating to the viable shelf life of a certain brand of bread:

Hours to Deterioration	Number of Loaves
90–under 110	23
110–under 130	37
130–under 150	26
150–under 170	14

Calculate the sample mean and variance using the grouped data.

3-27 The IQ scores achieved by students in a particular school have the cumulative relative frequency distribution provided below:

IQ Score	Cumulative Proportion of Students
70–less than 80	.02
80–less than 90	.12
90–less than 100	.24
100–less than 110	.46
110–less than 120	.65
120–less than 130	.79
130–less than 140	.88
140–less than 150	.97
150–less than 160	1.00

(a) Plot the ogive for the above data.
(b) From your graph, read the following values. (The figures obtained will be only estimates of the actual values.)
    (1) The 50th percentile.
    (2) The .75 fractile.
    (3) The first quartile.
    (4) The median.
    (5) The 90th percentile.
(c) Using your answers from part (b), compute the interquartile range.

3-28 (a) Calculate the sample mean and variance for the following ungrouped examination score sample data:

84	77	67	94	90
81	56	89	77	88
74	76	28	80	58
66	77	89	81	78
77	72	94	93	79
93				

(b) The sample data in (a) have been grouped into the frequency distribution provided below. Calculate the sample mean and variance using the grouped data.

Class Interval	*f*
25–under 35	1
35–under 45	0
45–under 55	0
55–under 65	2
65–under 75	4
75–under 85	11
85–under 95	8
Total	26

(c) The calculation of population parameters using grouped data provides only approximations to their counterparts obtained directly from the ungrouped raw data. Find the amount of error in this approximation procedure for the sample mean by subtracting your answer in part (b) from the value you obtained in (a).

Chapter Four
The Statistical
Sampling Study

By a small sample we may judge the whole piece.

Miguel de Cervantes

Now that we have covered the basic elements of descriptive statistics, we are ready to consider *statistical sampling.* In order to draw conclusions about populations from samples, we call upon inferential statistics, which enables us to determine a population's characteristics by directly observing only a portion, or sample, of the population.

There are many reasons why we resort to a sample rather than a complete enumeration (a *census*) of the population. For one, it is obviously cheaper to observe a part rather than the whole. But there are dangers in using samples, and we should prepare ourselves to cope with them. In this chapter we will investigate various kinds of sampling procedures. Although some are better than others, all may yield samples that are inaccurate and unreliable. We will see how these dangers can be minimized, but some potential for error is the price we must pay for the convenience and savings that samples provide.

4-1 THE NEED FOR SAMPLES

There would be no need for statistical theory if samples were not used to obtain information about the population. Indeed, if the census were employed for this purpose, there would be little need for most of the material contained in this book. Unfortunately, for various reasons, a census may not be practicable and is almost never economical, so that sample information must be relied upon for most applications.

There are six main reasons for sampling in lieu of the census: economy, timeliness, the large size of many populations, inaccessibility of the entire population, destructiveness of the observation, and accuracy.

Economic Advantages of Using a Sample

It should be obvious that the taking of a sample, which involves direct observation of only a portion of the population, would require fewer resources than a census. Consider, for example, a consumer survey attempting to query all the owners of a popular automobile as to their opinions about several proposed colors for next year's model. A questionnaire is to be printed and mailed to all owners. Imagine the clerical chore of simply addressing the envelopes; the cost of the postage alone could easily run into five figures. Consider the bookkeeping problems in tabulating the replies.

Perhaps the greatest difficulty would be to ensure a 100 percent response. A very high proportion of the questionnaires will simply be ignored along with the plethora of other "junk" mail. Most persons can be reached by telephone calls, telegrams, and personal visits. There will invariably be an irascible few who will slam their doors in the face of the company president coming to call, and some who will have to be bribed with a new car to respond. A great many car owners will be very hard to locate, having moved to parts unknown, so that the services of a detective agency may be required to track them down. Some of the owners will never be able to give their replies, having died before the survey is completed. The company would have more trouble completely enumerating its owner population than the FBI has in arresting its ten most wanted men.

As ludicrous as this example is, it does illustrate the very high cost of a census, and it is not an exaggeration. For the type of information desired, the car manufacturer would do well to interview a tiny portion of the car owners. Rare indeed is the circumstance that requires a census of the population, and even rarer is one that justifies its expense.

The Time Factor

A sample may provide an investigator with needed information quickly. Often speed is of paramount importance, as in political polling, where the goal is to determine voter preferences toward candidates for public office from sample evidence. The voting public as a whole is extremely fickle, fluctuating in preference, as polls have indicated, right up to the time of the election. If a poll is to be used to gauge public opinion, it must be very current; the opinions must be obtained, tabulated, and published within a very short period of time. Even if it were physically possible to use a census in such an opinion survey, its results would not be valid because of significant shifts in public opinion over the time required to carry it out.

Frequently a managerial decision based upon a population's characteristics must be made very quickly. A census would not be feasible, so sample evidence must be relied upon. In a highly competitive environment there may not be enough time to wait for a 100 percent response before introducing a new product or changing service patterns.

The Very Large Population

Many populations about which inferences must be made are quite large. Consider, for example, the population of buyers of a particular brand of cereal. If the product is marketed nationally, there may be literally millions of customers No matter how important the information desired by the manufacturer, a census of the population of buyers is likely to be physically impossible. Sample evidence may be the only means available for obtaining information feedback from the buying public.

Some populations appear to be infinite in size. Of course, a truly infinite population of physical objects does not exist. (Scientists have even estimated a finite value for the number of elementary particles in the universe.) Consider the theoretical problems that one would encounter in attempting to census a hypothetical infinite population. No matter what resources were used or how much time was expended, it would be impossible to observe all of the elementary units. At any point in time, the census would be only partially completed—the procedure would be eternal. *Information bearing upon the infinite population can be obtained only from a sample.*

The infinite population is a very convenient one to discuss in theory, because it has many properties that are ideally suited to mathematical techniques. Therefore, it is often desirable to label a whole class of populations "infinite" when they really are not. Most notable are populations whose elementary units result from a continuing process, such as the manufacture of a common consumer product. Since it would be impossible to observe every elementary unit over a reasonable period of time because new ones are continually being created, it would be as difficult to take a census of such a population as it would be to take a census of an infinite population. Hereafter, when we refer to a population as being *infinite,* we mean it is *one for which a census in a reasonable time period is impossible.*

Partly Inaccessible Populations

Some populations contain elementary units that are so difficult to observe that they are in a sense inaccessible. One example is the population of crashed aircraft: Planes that crash and sink in the deep ocean are inaccessible and cannot be directly studied to determine the physical causes of their failure. Similar conditions hold in determining consumer attitudes. Not all of the users of a product can be queried. Some may be incarcerated in prisons or mental hospitals and have limited contact with the outside world. Some individuals may be insulated from harassment by survey takers for more noble reasons; consider the limited accessibility to the President of the United States or the Pope.

Whenever some elementary units are inaccessible, sampling must be used to provide the desired information about the population. The above illustrations demonstrate physical inaccessibility. As a practical matter, an elementary unit's accessibility may be limited for economic reasons alone: Those observations which are deemed too costly to make are, in a real sense, also inaccessible.

Destructive Nature of the Observation

Sometimes the very act of observing the desired characteristic of the elementary unit destroys it for the use intended. Classical examples of this occur in quality control. For instance, in order to test a fuse to determine whether it is defective, it must be destroyed. In order to obtain a census of the quality of a shipment of fuses, all of them must be destroyed. This negates any purpose served by the quality control testing, whose goal is to determine how good the entire shipment is. Clearly, a *sample* of fuses must be used in order to assess the quality of the shipment.

Accuracy and Sampling

A sample may be more accurate than a census. A census, if sloppily conducted, may provide less reliable information than a sample carefully obtained. Indeed, the 1950 U.S. Census provides us with an excellent example.

Example 4-1   Two statisticians noticed a very unusual anomaly in the change of two categories between 1940 and 1950.* They found that an abnormally large number of 14-year-old widows were reported in the 1950 figures: There were 20 times as many as in 1940. Indian divorcees, who had also been extremely rare,

* Ansley J. Coale and Frederick F. Stephan, "The Case of the Indians and Teen-age Widows," *Journal of the American Statistical Association,* LVII (June 1962), 338–437.

had increased by a like magnitude. Unable to justify the changes by any socio-logical trends, they analyzed the data-gathering and processing procedures of the census. After some investigation, it was concluded that the figures could have resulted from the erroneous reversal of the entries on a few of the punched cards used to process the mass of data gathered. In this instance, a census seemed to provide far from reliable or credible results.

Example 4-2 A large utility company had problems of a somewhat different nature with punched cards. The procedure for determining how to allocate the internal costs associated with the keypunching services of the data-processing center had been of a census nature. At the end of each job, no matter what its size, each operator was required to make a detailed entry in a log, specifying how many cards were punched, for whom the job was done, and how much time it took. At the end of each accounting period, the supervisor was required to pre-pare a report for accounting based upon the logs. The data-processing personnel complained about the bother involved in meticulously keeping these records, claiming that it detracted from overall productivity. Furthermore, the accounting people had been receiving complaints from the departments using the key-punching service that they were being inaccurately charged.

A company statistician was called in to analyze the situation and to see if improvements could be made. He found that the root cause of department complaints was attributable to the rather casual manner in which the keypunch operators kept their logs; it proved to be a demanding task, requiring skills that the average operator had not acquired in training. Furthermore, he found that the operators spent about 10 percent of their productive time keeping the records. He proposed to management that a *work sampling* technique be adopted. At random time intervals (three times daily), a bell would be rung; at this time all operators would stop work and fill out a simplified form pertaining only to the current job. Each form contained only the name of the department for which the job was being done. These records provided a basis for allocating keypunching costs to the various departments according to the percentage of forms returned for each department. Over a period of a month, the heavier users of keypunching would have more forms indicating that they requested the service. Since each department used keypunching extensively, the proration of cost from the forms was a much more accurate representation of reality than the previous slipshod procedure. The productivity of the keypunchers increased, and all parties involved were quite satisfied.

EXERCISES

4-1 For each of the following situations, indicate whether a sample or a census would be more appropriate. Explain your choice.
   (a) A manufacturer of automobile spark plugs knows that due to process variations a certain percentage of the plugs will be defective. A thorough test of a spark plug ruins it, yet the production output must be tested in order to determine whether remedial action is necessary.
   (b) NASA must determine the quality of the components of a manned space vehicle.
   (c) A hospital administrator attempting to decide how to improve patient services seeks the attitudes of persons treated.
   (d) A medical researcher wants to determine the possible harmful side effects from a chemical that eases the pain of arthritis.

4-2 For each of the following reasons, give an example of a situation for which a census would be less desirable than a sample. In each case, explain why this is so.

(a) economic   (b) timeliness   (c) size of population
(d) inaccessibility   (e) accuracy   (f) destructive observations

4-2 DESIGNING AND CONDUCTING A SAMPLING STUDY

Much of this book is concerned with how to collect samples in such a way that meaningful conclusions may be drawn about the entire population. Figure 4-1 shows the major stages of a sampling study. The first of these is *planning*, an area that requires careful attention so that the sampling results can achieve the best impact. The second stage is *data collection*, where the plans are followed; here, a major goal is to ensure that observations are free from bias. The last phase is *data analysis and conclusions*, an area to which a major portion of this book will be devoted.

The Importance of Planning

Planning a statistical study is the most important step. Inadequate planning can lead to needless expense when actual data collection begins. Poor planning may result in the eventual invalidation of the entire study. The outcome of the study may even prove strongly counterproductive. Several examples of extreme cases of poor planning will be given in this chapter.

Planning begins with the identification of a population that will achieve the study's goals. This is followed by selection of an observation procedure that might include the design of a questionnaire or the choice of an observation-measuring instrument—a broad category that includes mechanical devices (to record physical data, such as dimensions and weight), various tests (for intelligence, aptitude, personality, or knowledge), sources of data (for example, family income could be obtained from tax records, from employers, or by directly questioning a family member), and survey techniques (written reply, telephone response, or personal interview).

Of equal importance in planning is the choice of the sample type itself. Alternative kinds of samples range from the most "scientific" random samples, like that used in the major public opinion polls, downward to the convenience sample that campus straw votes represent, where practically no heed is paid to how representative the sample might be. The random sample is the most important one, because statistical theory applies to it alone. As we will see, there are a variety of ways to select a sample.

In order to draw proper and valid conclusions from sample data, it is very important that planning include a presampling choice of the statistical procedure to be used later in analyzing the results. Picking an analytical technique *after* sifting through the results may lead to the most insidious kind of

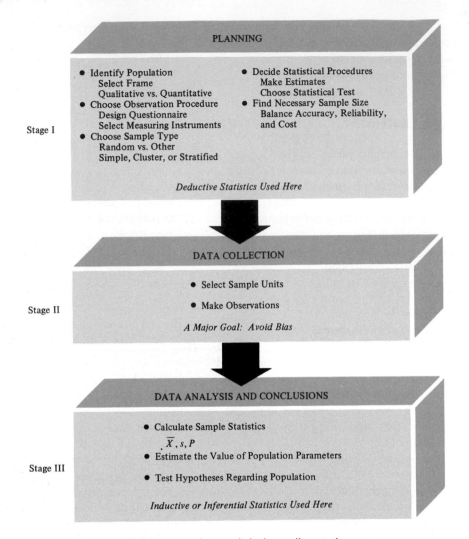

FIGURE 4-1   Major stages in a statistical sampling study.

bias: innocent or intentional selection of a tool that strongly supports the desired conclusion.

A very important planning consideration in any sampling study is how many observations to make. In general, the larger its size, the more closely a random sample is expected to represent its population. But where do we draw the line? Isn't a sample ten times as large ten times as good? The first question will be answered in Chapter 8. To the second, the answer is *no*. As we shall see, selection of sample size is largely an economic matter, for scarce resources (funds available for gathering data) must be traded off against the accuracy and reliability of the result. A point of diminishing returns is soon reached where an extra dollar buys very little in increased sample quality.

Choosing a statistical procedure and selecting an appropriate sample size each involve a heavy dose of deductive statistics, since both of these planning aspects require us to look at how samples are generated from "textbook" populations whose characteristics are fully known.

Data Collection

The second phase of the statistical sampling study—obtaining the raw data—is the one that usually requires the greatest amounts of time and effort. Adequate controls must be provided to prevent observations from becoming biased.

Potential problem areas associated with collecting and managing the data are described in detail in subsequent sections of this chapter. Such problems include observational biases that result when the sample units are measured, queried, or investigated. A poorly asked question and an improperly operated device both lead to incorrect responses. Another source of bias arises because some parts of the population are inaccessible or difficult to observe. Further difficulties may appear after the data are collected: The inevitable ambiguities and contradictions must be dealt with and the results processed so that statistical analyses can be made.

Data Analysis and Conclusions

This last stage of a statistical sampling study is extremely important. Here is where many of the descriptive tools we discussed earlier are used to communicate the results. Our emphasis, however, is placed on drawing conclusions from the necessarily incomplete information available from any sample. This is when statistical inferences are made. The lion's share of statistical theory is directly related to or in support of making generalizations or *inferences* about populations from samples. Inferences generally fall into three broad categories: estimation, hypothesis testing, and association. The choice of which of these to use and the selection from a variety of techniques will depend upon the goals of the study and the resources available.

4-3   BIAS AND ERROR IN SAMPLING

Since a sample is a collection of observations representing a portion of the population, the manner in which the observed units are chosen significantly affects the adequacy of the sample. There may be other factors influencing the representativeness of a sample due to the manner in which the observations are obtained. Here we will indicate some of the pitfalls commonly encountered in sampling and show how many of them may be avoided. Avoidance of certain difficulties is extremely important to achieving the statistician's primary goal: selecting a sample at the lowest cost that will provide the best possible representation consistent with the objective of the study being made.

A sample is expected to mirror the population from which it comes. However, there are no guarantees that any sample will be precisely representative of the population, as chance may dictate that a disproportionate number of untypical observations will be made. In practice, it is rarely known when a sample is unrepresentative and should be discarded, because some population characteristics are unknown (or else no sample would be needed in the first place). Steps must be taken during the planning of the study to minimize the chance that the sample will be untypical.

Sampling Error

What are some of the things that can make a sample unrepresentative of its population? One of the most frequently mentioned is *sampling error*, for which we have the following

> **DEFINITION** *Sampling error* comprises the differences between the sample and the population that are due solely to the particular elementary units that happen to have been selected.

To illustrate sampling error, suppose that a sample of 100 American men are chosen and measured and that they are all taller than seven feet. An obvious conclusion would be that most American males are taller than seven feet. Of course, this is absurd, for most persons do not know a man that tall nor would they even be sure that one existed if some of the most noted basketball players were not that tall. And yet it is possible for the statistician to be unfortunate enough to obtain such a highly unrepresentative sample. However, this is highly unlikely; nature has distributed the rare seven-footers widely among the population.

More dangerous is the sampling error that is not so obvious and for which nature offers little protection. It is not difficult to envision a sample in which the average height is overstated not by a foot, but rather by an inch or two. It is the insidious, unobvious error that is our major concern.

There are two basic causes for sampling error. One is chance; bad luck may result in untypical choices. Since unusual elementary units exist, there is always a possibility that an abnormally large number of them will be chosen. The main protection against this type of error is to use a large enough sample. Another cause of sampling error, sampling bias, is not as easy to remedy.

Sampling Bias

The size of the sample has little to do with the effects of *sampling bias*. In the present context, we provide the

DEFINITION   *Sampling bias* is a tendency to favor the selection of elementary units having particular characteristics.

The bias may be present due to an intentional predilection, but usually it results from a poor sampling plan. A classical example of bias occurred in a poll conducted by the now defunct *Literary Digest* in 1936, when Democrat Franklin D. Roosevelt was running against Republican Alfred M. Landon for the presidency. The poll was a sample of voter preferences, and several million responses were obtained. Its conclusion that Landon would win by a record margin was the exact opposite of what actually happened: Roosevelt received one of the most lopsided victories in American history. The poll's erroneous results have since been attributed to sampling bias. The *Digest* had selected its sample from magazine subscription rolls and telephone directories. Both sources, in the time of the Great Depression, contained a disproportionate number of prosperous persons who favored the laissez-faire Republican platform. The disgruntled majority, strongly in favor of Roosevelt, largely did without telephones and magazines and hence did not receive adequate representation in the sample.

The avoidance of bias in sampling is a major concern of statisticians. Pains must be taken in designing a means of selecting the elementary units so that the more obvious forms of bias will be avoided. In practice, it is very difficult to eliminate all forms of bias. Most notable is the *bias of nonresponse*, which results when—for whatever reason—some elementary units have no chance of appearing in the sample. The cost considerations involved in making sample observations almost guarantee that this particular form of bias will be present to some degree in any sample.

An excellent example is provided by consumer surveys involving food products. It is relatively cheap to obtain opinions about a company's product from persons who remain at home during the day. However, in many areas a large proportion of adult residents are employed in offices or elsewhere and are at home only in the evenings and on weekends. If the surveyors do their sampling during normal working hours, these persons—who also make food-buying decisions—will not be represented. A company wishing to determine whether to expand its line of convenience foods may obtain survey results indicating that such products are not particularly desirable. But, being pressured for time, working persons are often enthusiastic users of such items. A sample that neglected their opinions could well lead to an erroneous marketing decision.

Nonsampling Error

The other main cause of unrepresentative samples is *nonsampling error*. This type of error may occur whether a census or a sample is being used. As with sampling error, it may be either willfully produced by participants in the statistical study or an innocent byproduct of the sampling plans and procedures.

DEFINITION   A *nonsampling error* is an error that is due solely to the manner in which the observation is made.

The simplest example of nonsampling error is inaccurate physical measurement. This may be due to either malfunctioning instruments or poor procedures. Consider the observation of human weights. If persons are asked to state their own weights, no two answers will be of equal reliability. They will have weighed themselves on different scales in various states of poor calibration. An individual's weight fluctuates diurnally by several pounds, so that the time of weighing will affect the answer. The scale reading will also vary with the person's state of undress. Responses will not be of comparable validity unless all persons are weighed under the same circumstances.

Biased observations due to inaccurate measurement can be very innocent but devastating. For example, a French astronomer once proposed a new theory based upon spectroscopic measurements of light emitted by a particular star. When his colleagues discovered that the measuring instrument had been contaminated by cigarette smoke they rejected his findings.

In surveys of personnel characteristics, unintended errors may crop up because of (1) the manner in which the response is elicited, (2) the idiosyncrasies of the persons queried, (3) the purpose of the study, or (4) the personal biases of the interviewer or question writer.

No two interviewers are alike, and the same person may provide different answers to different interviewers. The manner in which a question is formulated can also result in inaccurate responses. Individuals tend to provide false answers to particular questions. A good example of this concerns a person's age. Some people will lie about their age. Asking an age in years can be dangerous, as people ordinarily use their chronological age at their previous birthday, even if it is more than 11 months past. Both problems can be alleviated by asking the date of birth, since the liar would have to do some quick arithmetic to fake the date, and a date of birth is much more accurate than a person's age at his or her last birthday.

The answer to a question could be untrue because the respondee wishes to impress the interviewer. This is especially prevalent with regard to knowledge of current events and to intellectual accomplishments. Numerous examples exist of persons "knowing" about fictitious famous names or stating that they have read books that don't exist. This type of error is the most difficult to prevent, for it involves outright deceit on the part of the respondee. It is important to acknowledge, however, that certain psychological factors induce incorrect responses, and great care must be taken to design the study in such a way as to minimize their effect.

Knowledge of the purpose for which the study is being conducted may tend to create incorrect responses. A classical example of this is the answer to the question: What is your income? If a government agency is asking, then a different figure may be provided than would be given on an application for a home mortgage. A teacher's union seeking to justify a wage increase may get a different response from a member than would his brother-in-law. The union would not likely be given (nor would it really want) the full income (incorporating amounts derived from moonlighting and summer employment), whereas the brother-in-law would probably get a more favorable picture, not only being informed about the income derived from these sources but also hearing about successful investments. One way to protect against such bias is to camouflage the study's goals, perhaps even to employ an independent opinion survey firm in order to keep secret the identity of the course of the investigation. Another remedy is to make the questions very specific, allowing very little room for personal interpretation. For example: Where are you employed?, followed by: What is your salary? Then: Do you have any extra jobs? A sequence of such questions may lead to a more accurate answer to the basic question.

Finally, it should be noted that the personal prejudices of either the study designer or the data collector may tend to *induce bias*. It is not good practice for a person to design a questionnaire relating to a subject about which he or she has strong feelings. Questions may be slanted in such a way that a particular response will be obtained even though it is inaccurate. An example of this is a preference survey sponsored by the makers of brand A, prefaced by the question: Of all the following factors making brand A a superior quality product, which do you think is most important? This could then be followed by a question asking for a preference ranking of a list of products, including brand A (most blatantly, brand A may be the first name on the list). The preliminary question starts the responder thinking about the good features of brand A, creating an atmosphere that will make the later comparison unfair. Another instance of induced error may occur in an experiment for which a technical specialist selects the elementary units to be treated with a new product. For example, when doctors favoring a new drug decide which patients are going to receive it, they may select (consciously or not) those they feel have the best chance of benefiting from its administration. An agronomist may choose certain key plots upon which to apply a new fertilizer, knowing full well that they will provide more favorable yields than others. To protect against induced bias, an individual trained in statistics should have a measure of control over the design and implementation of the entire statistical study. At the very least, someone who is aware of the pitfalls should serve in an auditing capacity.

EXERCISES

4-3 A corporation president has delegated the responsibility for determining employees' attitudes toward a training program run by the personnel department. What dangers are there in asking the personnel manager to dispose of this matter? Suggest a procedure that would overcome these difficulties.

4-4 Those persons who filled out the "long" form for the 1970 U.S. Census were asked to answer questions about their employment. For example, one question asked: How many hours did you work last week? Succeeding questions on the matter all related to the same week, requesting information on type of employer, duties, and so on. The public was asked to provide the data as of April 1, 1970, which fell on the Wednesday right after Easter, so that most of the nation's educators had been on a holiday for the entire week in question. Comment on the possible errors that may result from this set of questions. How might the questionnaire have been improved in order to avoid them?

4-5   A drugstore has recently experienced a significant drop in sales due to the presence in the city of some new discount stores. A questionnaire, filled out by customers who visited the store during one week, asked for comparisons with respect to prices, convenience, and level of service. What do you think of the manner in which the information was obtained? What procedure would you recommend?

4-6   A questionnaire prepared for a study on consumer buying habits contains the question: What is the value of your present automobile(s)? What errors may result from this question? Suggest a better way to obtain the desired response.

4-7   Many personality profiles require that an individual provide answers to multiple-choice questions. The answers are then compiled, and various trait ratings are found. Comment on some of the pitfalls of this procedure. Suggest how some of them may be alleviated.

4-8   The testing of a new drug therapy sometimes involves two patient groups. The patients in one group receive the medication being investigated. The others may receive no medication at all and are often given an innocuous substance, called a *placebo* (often just a sugar pill), that has an appearance identical to the drug being tested. Why is the placebo used?

4-9   A well-known television rating agency provides the networks and advertisers with estimates of the audience size for all nationally televised programs. These estimates are based upon detailed logs maintained by persons in the households surveyed, indicating which stations were watched during each period of the day. The agency has a difficult time recruiting households for its sample, as considerable bother and inconvenience is involved in keeping the logs. It has been estimated by independent observers that an average of 50 families must be approached before one agrees to join the sample. Comment upon the pitfalls that might be encountered when the sample results are taken as representative of the nation's television viewing habits. Can you suggest any ways to minimize these pitfalls? Do you think that the sample observations obtained are in danger of being untypical? Explain.

4-4   SELECTING THE SAMPLE

In the preceding section, we encountered the most common problems associated with statistical studies. The desirability of a sampling procedure depends on both its vulnerability to error and its cost. However, economy and reliability are competing ends, because to reduce error often requires an increased expenditure of resources.

Of the two types of statistical error, only sampling error can be controlled by exercising care in determining the method for choosing the sample. Sampling error may be due to either bias or chance, as we have established. The chance component exists no matter how careful the selection procedures are, and the only way to minimize chance sampling errors is to select a sufficiently large sample. Sampling bias, on the other hand, may be minimized by judicious choice of procedure.

Types of Samples

There are three primary kinds of samples: the convenience sample, the judgment sample, and the random sample. They differ in the manner in which their elementary units are chosen. Each sample will be described in turn, and its desirable and undesirable features will be discussed.

The Convenience Sample

A convenience sample results when the more convenient elementary units are chosen from a population for observation. Dependence on a convenience sample is epitomized by the tendency people have to draw conclusions about the nature of things by relying upon their personal experience as a source of observations. This often results in considerable consternation when more reliable information refutes their inferences.

Convenience samples are the cheapest to obtain. Their major drawback is the extent to which they may be permeated with sampling bias, which tends to make them highly unreliable. An important decision made on the basis of a convenience sample is in great danger of being wrong. The letters received by a member of Congress constitute a convenience sample of constituent attitudes. The legislator need do nothing to receive mail. But the opinions voiced there will rarely be indicative of the attitudes of the entire constituency. Persons with special interests to protect are far more likely to write than the typical voter.

The bias of nonresponse, when present, usually results in a convenience sample. This type of bias can be expected when the telephone—a very convenient device—is used to obtain responses, for the incidence of nonresponse may be relatively high. Many calls will be unanswered, there are unlisted numbers, and some persons have no telephone.

In spite of the obvious disadvantages of convenience samples, they are sometimes suitable, depending upon the purpose of the study. If only approximate information is needed about a population, then a convenience sample may be adequate. Funds for the study may be so limited that only a convenience sample can be afforded. But in such cases the obvious drawbacks must be acknowledged. A convenience sample may lead to only a very insignificant source of bias. For example, when there is no basis for believing that non-responders would provide responses that would, on the whole, be different from those readily available, then there may be little danger in using a telephone survey; but one can never be sure.

The Judgment Sample

A judgment sample is one that is obtained according to the discretion of someone familiar with the relevant characteristics of the population. Judgmental selection of the elementary units is made when the population is very heterogeneous, when the sample is to be very small, or when special skill is required to ensure a representative collection of observations.

Example 4-3   The Consumer Price Index of the U.S. Department of Labor is partly a judgment sample. Those items to be included in establishing the index are chosen on the basis of judgment in order to measure a dollar's purchasing power. Thus, only items or commodities that are used by most people are included; for example, television sets are included, but tape recorders are not. Over time, certain items become obsolete and must be replaced by others; for instance, refrigerators have supplanted iceboxes. Judgment must be employed in deciding what will be replaced, what will be substituted, and when the index will be spliced.* Even within a particular category, there may be several specification categories, and judgment must be exercised by field workers to see that, for example, an item has a particular level of quality or has been changed in terms of quantity. This was the case with the nickel candy bar for 50 years. To maintain price, the quantity of candy in a bar had been declining steadily over the years— each change being tantamount to a price increase—until there was so little candy left that the price was finally raised instead. Certain foods are seasonal, and substitute items must be included in each periodic index determination. Judgment is also used in establishing weights for each item; toothpaste should only be weighted in proportion to its position in a typical family's total expenditure— the typical expenditure is itself a matter of judgment. Finally, judgment is employed in selecting cities to be represented in the surveys; these, too, must be assigned weights.

The judgment sample is obviously prone to bias. Its adequacy is limited by the discernibility of the individual who selects the sample. All of the dangers mentioned in Section 4-3 in connection with induced bias apply to the judgment sample. Clearly, there are instances in which this type of sample is preferred. Indeed, the Consumer Price Index would be unworkable were it not partly based upon judgment samples.

The Random Sample

Perhaps the most important sample type is the random sample. *A random sample is one that allows for the equal probability that each elementary unit will be chosen.* For this reason, it is sometimes referred to as a *probability sample.*

In its simplest form, a random sample is selected in the manner of a raffle. For example, a random sample of ten symphony conductors out of a population of 100 could be obtained by lottery. The name of each symphony conductor would be written on a slip of paper and placed into a capsule. All 100 capsules would then be placed in a box and thoroughly mixed. An impartial party would select the sample by drawing ten capsules from the box.

In actual practice, the physical lottery is cumbersome. There may also be some question as to its randomness. Consider the 1970 draft lottery fiasco. There, the objective was to determine priorities of selection by date of birth. A physical method much like the raffle was used. The results appeared, however, to have a pattern; December birthdays had disproportionately low numbers, while January birthdays had predominantly high numbers. Investigation showed that the undesirable results were due to the fact that the capsules had not been mixed at all; since the December capsules were the last to be placed into the

---

* Rothwell, Doris P. *The Consumer Price Index Pricing and Calculation Procedures* (Washington: U.S. Bureau of Labor Statistics: March 17, 1964).

hopper, many December dates were drawn first. Because low dates implied almost certain draft eligibility, considerable controversy was created, and lawsuits were filed to invalidate the entire lottery.

Sample Selection Using Random Numbers

A more acceptable way to obtain a random sample is to use random numbers. *Random numbers* are digits generated by a process that allows for the equal probability that each possible number will be the next. For example, in a list of five-digit random numbers, each value between 00000 and 99999 has the same chance of appearing at each location. Appendix Table B is a list of five-digit random numbers. These numbers give the appearance of having been selected from a lottery. Indeed, in a special manner, they have been. They were generated by an electromechanical process at the Rand Corporation. These particular numbers have passed many tests and have been certified as pure by the scientific community. Had the Selective Service used such a table of random numbers to select its birthdays, it would have been guilt-free in the eyes of all save those receiving the low numbers.

There are no guarantees that a list of random numbers will not exhibit a pattern of some sort. For example, 8 may follow 7 more frequently than any other value. However, in a long list, a pattern of any sort is highly unlikely (8 should follow 7 about 10 percent of the time).

In order to use random numbers to select our ten conductors, first it will be necessary to assign a number to each member of the population. In this case, we can use two digits; the assigned numbers will therefore run from 00 to 99. It will make no difference how these numbers are assigned, but care must be taken to ensure that the person making the assignments does not know which page of the random number table will be used. In Table 4-1, the 100 conductors have been arranged in alphabetical order and assigned the numbers 00 through 99 in sequence.

The ten conductors will be chosen by reading down the first column of the random numbers table until ten different values are obtained. Note that we only require two-digit numbers, but the table has five-digit entries. This is no problem, for we may use only the first two digits of each entry and ignore the extra digits. If a value is obtained more than once before all ten conductors have been chosen, then that number will be skipped and the next one on the list used instead. The values obtained by starting at the top of the first column of Appendix Table B (page A-11) and reading down the column are listed below, along with the corresponding conductors, who now comprise our sample:

12651	Cantelli	74146	Sanderling
81769	Serafin	90759	Svetlanov
36737	Kletzki	55683	Newman
82861	Silvestri	79686	Schmidt-Isserstedt
21325	Frühbeck de Burgos	70333	Rodzinski

It does not matter how the random number table is read (from left to right, right to left, top to bottom, bottom to top, or diagonally), but it is

TABLE 4-1   Symphony Conductors

00. Abbado	25. Golschmann	50. Mehta	75. Santini
01. André	26. Hannikainen	51. Mitropoulos	76. Sargent
02. Anosov	27. Hollingsworth	52. Monteux	77. Scherchen
03. Ansermet	28. Horenstein	53. Morel	78. Schippers
04. Argenta	29. Horvat	54. Mravinsky	79. Schmidt-Isserstedt
05. Barbirolli	30. Jacquillat	55. Newman	80. Sejna
06. Beecham	31. Jorda	56. Ormandy	81. Serafin
07. Bernstein	32. Karajan	57. Paray	82. Silvestri
08. Black	33. Kempe	58. Patanè	83. Skrowaczewski
09. Bloomfield	34. Kertesz	59. Pedrotti	84. Slatkin
10. Bonynge	35. Klemperer	60. Perlea	85. Smetáček
11. Boult	36. Kletzki	61. Prêtre	86. Solti
12. Cantelli	37. Klima	62. Previn	87. Stein
13. Cluytens	38. Kondrashin	63. Previtali	88. Steinberg
14. Dorati	39. Kostelanetz	64. Prohaska	89. Stokowski
15. Dragon	40. Koussevitzky	65. Rekai	90. Svetlanov
16. Erede	41. Krips	66. Reiner	91. Swarowsky
17. Ferencsik	42. Kubelik	67. Reinhardt	92. Szell
18. Fiedler	43. Lane	68. Rignold	93. Toscanini
19. Fistoulari	44. Leinsdorf	69. Ristenpart	94. Van Otterloo
20. Fricsay	45. Maag	70. Rodzinski	95. Van Remoortel
21. Frühbeck de Burgos	46. Maazel	71. Rosenthal	96. Vogel
22. Furtwängler	47. Mackerras	72. Rozhdestvensky	97. Von Matacic
23. Gamba	48. Markevitch	73. Rowicki	98. Walter
24. Giulini	49. Martin	74. Sanderling	99. Watanabee

important not to read the same number location more than once and not to look ahead before deciding in which direction to proceed. If the numbers are larger than required, the leading or trailing digits may be ignored. If a number on the list has no counterpart in the population (which may happen when the population is smaller than the possible number of random numbers), it may be skipped.

Unlike judgment and convenience samples, random samples are free from sampling bias. No particular elementary units are favored. This still does not guarantee that a random sample will be extremely representative of the population from which it came. The chance effect may cause it not to be. But it will be possible to assess the reliability of a sample in terms of probability. This can be done only with random samples. When sampling bias is present, an objective basis for measuring its effect does not exist. Therefore, *only the random sample has a theoretical basis for quantitative evaluation of its quality.* As we shall see in later chapters, probability is used for such evaluations.

Types of Random Samples

The preceding example is just one type of random sampling scheme. At times it may be desirable to modify the selection procedure without altering the essential features of the random sample. We will refer to the type of sample just discussed as a *simple random sample*, for which we provide the following

DEFINITION   A *simple random sample* is obtained by choosing units in such a way that each unit in the population has an equal chance of being selected.

The Systematic Random Sample

A simple random sample is free of sampling bias. However, using a random number table to choose the elementary units can be a cumbersome procedure. If the sample is to be collected by a person untrained in statistics, then there is the danger that instructions will be misinterpreted and the selections made improperly. To simplify the data collection, instead of using a list of random numbers, the elementary units may be chosen by selecting every 10th or 100th unit, for example, after the first unit has been chosen randomly. Such a procedure is called a *systematic random sample*, for which we have the following

DEFINITION   A *systematic random sample* is obtained by selecting one unit on a random basis and then choosing additional units at even-spaced intervals until the desired number of units have been obtained.

Example 4-4   A telephone company is conducting a billing study in order to justify a new rate structure to the state's public utility commission. Data are to be collected by taking a random sample of individual telephone bills from cities and metropolitan areas classified according to population. Billing data are not available at a single location but are spread throughout the state in several regional accounting offices, where they are stored by telephone number. Time and cost constraints require that the sample information be obtained by the field offices and then forwarded to company headquarters for processing. A company statistical analyst has designed a procedure for each regional office to employ in collecting the samples.

One city has 10,000 telephones sharing the 825 prefix. The telephone numbers run from 825-0000 through 825-9999. A sample size of 200 is required. Dividing the number of telephones by 200, the interval width of 50 is obtained.* Thus the bill for every 50th telephone number will be incorporated into the sample. The analyst chooses a number lying between 0 and 49 at random. Suppose she chooses 37. Her instructions to the regional accounting offices specify that the billing figures for every 50th telephone number, starting with 825-0037, be forwarded to her office. It will then be a simple manual task for a clerk to pull every 50th telephone bill from the files, and the analyst will receive the figures for 825-0037, 825-0087, 825-0137, 825-0187, and so on.

A systematic random sample may be susceptible to sampling bias: Some extraordinary property may be attributable to the elementary units assigned particular numbers, and the initial random number chosen may tend to favor this property. For instance, it is well known that businesses prefer telephone numbers that have an easily recalled pattern (for example, 825-4455). Had the analyst in Example 4-4 chosen the random number 05, then half the sample would have consisted of telephone numbers ending with 55, and it is likely that

---

* Allowances may have to be made for numbers not currently in service. Here we may assume they are all active.

a disproportionate number of businesses would have been represented. If businesses tend to have unusually large telephone bills, then such a listing would provide an obvious source of bias. This bias cannot be remedied by choosing an innocuous starting value such as 09, because, for the same reason, the sample may include too few businesses. The sampling bias can be very subtle in systematic random sampling, but this is the price that must be paid for simplifying the data collection procedures.

The Stratified Sample

In certain instances it is desirable to ensure that various subgroups of a population be represented in the sample in accordance with their respective prevalence in the population. In statistical parlance, these subgroups are referred to as *strata*. Ideally, the population itself should be split into separate entities when it is significantly heterogeneous. In practice, however, this may complicate the statistical analysis. Next best is to force the sample to reflect the population's lack of homogeneity as closely as possible, by guaranteeing that the sample have the same proportions of each subgroup that exist in the population itself. This is accomplished by taking a stratified sample, for which we provide the

DEFINITION   A *stratified sample* is obtained by independently selecting a separate simple random sample from each population stratum.

Whether or not stratification of the population is desirable will depend upon the purpose of the study, but it is usually carried out because certain nonhomogeneities are present in the population. There are also other reasons why a stratified sample may be desirable. It may be more convenient, for example, to collect samples separately from regional centers, as in the preceding example. Or there may be some prevailing reason to divide the population—for instance, to compare strata.

Example 4-5   Voter preference polls have been taken prior to each presidential election in order to infer who would win the election if it were to be held at the time of the poll. Because of the expense involved, the pollsters, working under contract to news agencies, draw a random sample of voters from the entire United States. Sampling is not conducted independently within each state.

The choice of who shall be President is determined by the electoral college. The membership of the college has historically voted as a block by state, with all votes going to the candidate receiving the plurality of that state's votes. American history shows that sometimes the man who receives the most votes from the public can still lose the election in the electoral college. The reason for this disparity is that the winner need only achieve small margins in several large states, even though he loses by large amounts in the rest. Thus he wins a majority of electoral votes while he loses the national plurality. This has happened twice since the Civil War: in 1876, Rutherford B. Hayes won over Samuel J. Tilden, who received the most popular votes, and in 1888, Benjamin Harrison beat the largest popular vote getter, Grover Cleveland. The situation is further distorted by the fact that electoral votes are rationed to each state in accordance to its representation in *both* houses of Congress. Thus Alaska, with about one hundredth the voting population of California, has about one fourteenth as many votes, making each Alaskan voter about seven times as powerful as a Californian.

A sampling scheme that attempts to predict the outcome of an election must treat each state as a separate stratum to adequately cope with the distortion of the electoral college. The sample results must be separately compiled for each state, and the winner of each determined. The results must then be combined in the same proportion as the electoral votes in order to present a distortion-free prediction.

The Cluster Sample

Yet another form of random sampling is used prevalently in consumer surveying, where it is more economical to interview several persons in the same neighborhood. For example, contrast the bother and expense of collecting a thousand responses in a city of 100,000 by simple random sampling with the relative ease of completely canvassing a few selected neighborhoods. In the former case, the chosen elementary units are scattered throughout the city; in the latter, the elementary units live next door to each other. Random sampling would therefore require considerable travel between interviews, while the door-to-door neighborhood canvass would minimize travel time. Because the interviewer will ordinarily be paid by the hour, the simple random sample would be far more expensive.

Neighborhood groupings of people are referred to as *clusters*. Populations may be divided into clusters according to criteria such as geographical proximity, yielding groups that are easy to observe in their entirety. Most often, the clusters that are to be observed are chosen randomly, and hence we make the

DEFINITION   A *cluster sample* is obtained by selecting clusters from the population on the basis of simple random sampling. The sample comprises a census of each random cluster selected.

The only justification for cluster sampling is economic. It is fraught with many dangers of sampling bias. For instance, in neighborhood surveys, similar responses may be obtained from the entire cluster, as people of similar age, family size, income, and ethnic and educational backgrounds tend to live in the same vicinity. There is thus a high risk that persons with certain backgrounds or preferences will not be represented in the sample because the clusters in which they predominate were not chosen; conversely, other groups may be unduly represented.

At this point, it might be helpful to emphasize the similarities and differences between cluster and stratified samples. Both separate the population into groups, but the basis for distinction is usually the homogeneity within strata versus the accessibility of clusters. In stratified samples, all groups are represented, whereas the cluster sample comprises only a fraction of the groups. In a stratified procedure, a sample is taken from within each stratum, while in cluster sampling, a census is conducted within each group. The goal of stratified sampling is to eliminate certain forms of bias; the goal of cluster sampling is to do the job cheaply, which enhances the effects of bias.

Systematic, stratified, and cluster sampling are approximations to simple random sampling. To the extent that the statistical theory applicable to simple random sampling is applied to samples obtained via these other procedures, there will be erroneous conclusions. Throughout much of the remainder of this book, techniques will be developed primarily for analyzing simple random samples. The more complex sampling schemes require more complicated methodology.

EXERCISES

4-10 What types of samples do the following represent?
(a) Telephone callers on a radio "talk" show.
(b) The 30 stocks constituting the Dow-Jones Industrial Average.
(c) The record of a gambler's individual wins and losses from a day of placing one-dollar bets on black in roulette.
(d) The oranges purchased by a homemaker from the produce section of a market.

4-11 In the following situations, would you recommend the use of judgment, convenience, or random sampling, or some combination of these? Explain the reasons for your answer.
(a) A salesman for a large paper manufacturer is preparing a kit of product samples to carry on his next road trip to printing concerns.
(b) A teacher asks her students for suggestions as to how to improve curriculum. She plans to use their suggestions as a basis for a questionnaire concerning curriculum preferences.
(c) A city government wants to compare the wages of its clerical workers to persons holding comparable jobs in private industry.
(d) A utility company plans to purchase a fleet of standard-sized cars from one of four different manufacturers. The criterion for selection will be economy of operation.
(e) A newspaper editor selects letters from the day's mail to print on the editorial page. (Answer from the editor's point of view.)

4-12 An oil company wishes to obtain a random sample of its customers in order to estimate the relative proportion of purchases made from other oil companies. An accountant on the operations staff has recommended that a random sample of credit card customers be selected. An independent survey firm would be retained to obtain detailed records of the following month's purchases, by brand and quantity, for each sample unit. Evaluate this procedure.

4-13 A medical research foundation wishes to obtain a random sample of expectant mothers in order to investigate postnatal developments in their newborn babies. Various metropolitan areas are to be represented. Suggest a procedure that might be used to select the sample in a particular city.

4-14 A certain U.S. Senator is reputed to follow the majority opinion of her constituents on important pending legislation. Over the years, she has accumulated a panel of 20 persons whom her secretary contacts before a major Senate vote. Panel members are replaced only when they die or change their state of residence. Usually the Senator's votes coincide with the majority of this panel. Comment on this policy.

4-15 A random sample is desired for each of the following situations. Indicate whether a cluster, stratified, or combined sampling procedure should be used. Explain the reasons for your choice in each case.

(a) A large retail food chain wishes to determine its customers' attitudes toward trading stamps. Because there is a limited budget for taking the survey, the sample replies are to be obtained by interviewing customers on the store premises.

(b) An agronomist wants to take a sample to compare the effectiveness of two fertilizers. He wishes to test them on a variety of crops and under a range of climate and soil conditions.

(c) An airline is taking a random sample of its first-class and tourist-class passengers in order to obtain a quality assessment of its in-flight meals. The ratings must be taken just after the meals.

4-5 DECIDING STATISTICAL PROCEDURES

A complete discussion of statistical procedures will take up several of the later chapters in this book. All of these procedures make generalizations about a population when only sample data are available. We have called this process inductive or inferential statistics. There are several types of inference, and the procedures to be used depend upon the goals of the study and should be determined during the planning stage. There are many ways to do this.

The simplest procedure estimates a population's parameter, such as its mean, standard deviation, or proportion. The most complicated procedures test some hypothesis regarding the population's characteristics. Ordinarily, several testing schemes may be employed. In all such tests, the proper decision to be made is indicated directly from the sample results. Many tests actually compare two or more populations and require a separate sample from each.

Two-sample statistical testing procedures are used in a variety of business applications. In marketing research they can determine which of two proposed product designs or packaging schemes is more acceptable to the buying public. A drug manufacturer can use samples to determine the more effective chemical formulation. Personnel training often involves choosing between alternative techniques. Thus, a two-sample test might be useful in determining whether on-the-job training is more or less effective than formal classroom instruction.

Although our focus is on business applications, the two-sample statistical procedures are similar to the ones used in education, medicine, and psychology. Often in these fields the status quo must be compared to a proposed improvement. In education, for example, a new teaching method for reading might be evaluated in terms of comprehension test scores. The population of scores achieved by students under the current plan would be compared to the similar test results of another group of readers constituting the elementary units in the population of test scores by children exposed to the new program. Because the new program may or may not be adopted, the associated population does not yet exist. Nevertheless, a sample of children using the new program represents this potentially large group, which makes it a target population. The actual comparison would be made between separate samples from both populations.

The readers in the sample from the current program are referred to as the *control group*, because they are not subjected to anything new. Those children in the second sample constitute the *experimental group*, since these students are using a new procedure on a trial basis primarily to evaluate its merit. Control and experimental groups are encountered in many testing situations, such as in evaluating a new drug or medical procedure, in selecting a more effective fertilizer, or in checking new safety devices.

The simplest procedure for conducting a two-sample test is to select the two groups *independently*, so that the readers in our control and experimental groups would be chosen using separate lists of random numbers. (But both samples would ordinarily be derived from a common frame of applicable students, because the experimental group represents only a target population.) One drawback to independent sampling is that any differences found in the groups' reading comprehension scores could be attributed to causes other than the particular reading programs, such as previous level of reading readiness or home background. The danger that some outside influence may camouflage the actual differences between the two reading programs could be minimized through a stratified sampling scheme, where two separate groups are selected for various categories of student background, or by using large enough groups so that each would provide a representative cross section.

A common method for choosing the control and experimental groups is to pair each elementary unit with one that closely matches it in terms of potential extraneous influences. One member of each pair would be assigned to the experimental group and the other member to the control group. This is called *matched-pairs sampling*. The procedure is epitomized by studies of identical twins, who are genetically the same and who normally share nearly the same environment as well. In our survey, one twin would be assigned to a class having the existing reading program and the other would participate in the new program. Any reading-score differences between sample groups could thereby be confidently isolated to differences in the reading programs and not to other causes. But in practice, twins are rare and are not usually used in such tests. Yet unrelated individuals could still be paired. For example, a new drug for heart patients could be tested with pairs matched in terms of age, sex, weight, marital status, smoking habits, medical histories, and so on, thus producing "near twins." Identical twins who were reared apart have been extensively studied in an attempt to isolate the effects of heredity and environment upon intelligence.

Example 4-6   The experiences of one state during the ecology renaissance of the early 1970s illustrates the pitfalls of inadequate planning when conducting a statistical study. A new law was about to go on the books requiring that all soft drink and beer containers be returnable. This, it was hoped, would eliminate the unsightly refuse problem caused by pop-top cans. The old-fashioned bottle was to be used exclusively. To guarantee that the empty bottles would be returned, a deposit was required by the seller, just as it had been throughout the United States 20 years before.

To assess the effectiveness of the beverage container law, a study was made to determine how it affected accumulations of roadside litter. A random sample of 30 one-mile stretches of highway was chosen, cleared of all beer and soda cans, and then left to the vagaries of normal public neglect and mistreatment for three months before the new law became effective. The 30 miles of highway served as the control group, representing state residents' littering habits when beverage containers were not dictated by law. At the end of three months, the litter was cleared and the cans were counted. For the initial three months under the new law, the same 30 miles—now the experimental group—were again left to accumulate beverage containers (which would only be bottles this time). The accumulations of the two groups were then compared.

This study shows how the same elementary units can sometimes serve in both the control and the experimental groups. In this case, each one-mile segment after the law became effective was matched with itself in a preceding time period. This way traffic conditions and local idiosyncrasies were alike and could not be partly responsible for any differences found between the two groups. However, using the same units in both groups is valid only if no bias is induced upon the second set of observations by the first set. Here is where this study fell apart. When the beverage litter was measured the second time around, precious little of it was found. But all other kinds of litter were practically absent, too. Furthermore, adjacent stretches of highway were abnormally clean. At first blush, environmental officials were ecstatic at the apparent widespread impact of their new law. But they became embarrassed when it was determined that the same pattern prevailed only near the test tracts and not throughout the state.

Who absconded with the litter and why? Perhaps environmentalists—well aware that the new law would be temporary unless it proved effective—got wind of the study and tried to help it along by cleaning up the test stretches. Maybe when the state had cleaned the one-mile parcels, local residents were shamed into picking up some of their own mess.

Upon the advice of a statistician, officials discarded the second set of results and matched the original 30 one-mile stretches of highway with 30 similar ones untainted by having been cleaned. Just one pass was made through the new areas, and only returnable bottles were counted (the old cans did not have to be).

REVIEW EXERCISES

4-16 Starting in the fifth column of the random number table on page A-11, select a simple random sample of ten symphony conductors from those listed in Table 4-1 (page 82). Use only the first two digits of each random number from the table. List the names selected.

4-17 List the names for a systematic random sample of ten symphony conductors. Choose your conductors from those in Table 4-1, assuming that the starting random number provides Sir John Barbirolli for the first name.

4-18 Suppose that each successive ten names in Table 4-1 provides a stratum. Select a stratified random sample containing one conductor from each group. Assume that the following random numbers apply in the respective strata:

$$6, 5, 5, 2, 1, 9, 8, 7, 7, 0$$

(Redesignate the names in each stratum, starting with 0 and ending with 9; maintain the original alphabetical sequence.) List the names selected.

4-19 Treat each successive five names in Table 4-1 as a cluster. A random cluster sample of two clusters from the 20 is to be selected. After assigning a number of 1 through 20 to each cluster, use the random numbers 18 and 4 to find the sample. (Designate the successive clusters as 0, 1, 2, and so on.) List the names obtained.

Chapter Five
Probability

*Let us imagine . . . a person just brought forth into this world. . . .
The Sun would, probably, be the first object that would engage
his attention; but after losing it the first night, he would be
entirely ignorant whether he should ever see it again. . . . But let
him see a second appearance or one return of the Sun, and an
expectation would be raised in him of a second return, and he
might know that there was an odds of 3 to 1 for some probability
of this. This odds would increase, as before represented, with the
number of returns. . . . But no finite number of returns would be
sufficient to produce absolute or physical certainty.*

The Reverend Thomas Bayes (1763)

Probability plays a special role in all our lives, because we use it to measure uncertainty. We are continually faced with decisions leading to uncertain outcomes, and we rely on probability to help us make our choice. Think of the planned outdoor activities, such as picnics or boating, you cancelled because the chance of bad weather seemed too high. Remember those nights before examinations when you decided not to study some topics because they were not likely to be on the test? In business, probability is a pivotal factor in most significant decisions. A department store buyer will order heavily in a new style that is believed likely to sell well. A company will launch a new product when the chance of its success seems high enough to outweigh the possibility of losses due to failure. A new college graduate is hired when the probability of satisfactory performance is judged sufficiently high.

A probability is a numerical value that measures the uncertainty that a particular event will occur. The probability of an event ordinarily represents the *proportion of times under identical circumstances that the event can be expected to occur.* Such a long-run frequency of occurrence is referred to as *objective probability.* In tossing a fair coin, the probability is 1/2 for getting a head. This can be verified by tossing the coin many times—heads will appear about half the time. However, a probability value is often subjective, set solely on the basis of personal judgment. *Subjective probabilities* are used for events having no meaningful long-run frequency of occurrence. For example, an oil wildcatter may express his uncertainty about the presence of oil beneath a possible drilling site in terms of a probability value such as 1/2. One attempt will be made at drilling on that site; since no two sites are identical, there are no other situations like the present one for which the frequency of oil strikes can be determined.

More than 300 years ago, several famous mathematicians initially studied probability scientifically in connection with gambling problems. The theory of probability has since evolved into one of the most elegant and useful branches of mathematics. Today devices ordinarily associated with gambling, such as dice and playing cards, are still useful in illustrating how to find probabilities.

5-1   FUNDAMENTAL CONCEPTS

The Event

Uncertain outcomes are called *events*. In the case of tomorrow's weather, the occurrence of precipitation would be one possible event. Even more specific events may be considered; for example, precipitation could be in the form of rain, hail, or snow. Or events may be quite detailed: 1.2 inches of rain may fall.

A preliminary step in finding an event's probability is to identify all possible outcomes of the uncertain situation. In cataloging possible outcomes or events, it is convenient to discuss them in groupings or *sets*. A complete listing of events is called the *sample space.* Exactly one and only one event on this master list will occur.

The sample space for tossing a coin contains just two events, head and tail, which may be conveniently expressed in set notation as

Sample space = {head, tail}

Head and tail are the *elements* of the sample space. One, and only one, of these events must occur. We rule out such possibilities as the coin landing on its edge or being lost by specifying that they are not legitimate outcomes. That is, the toss is incomplete in such instances and must be repeated until either a head or a tail occurs.

As another illustration, consider the characteristics of a card drawn from a shuffled deck of 52 ordinary playing cards. Here we have

Sample space = {ace of spades, deuce of spades, . . . , king of diamonds}

It is convenient to represent the sample space pictorially as shown in Figure 5-1. Each point in the figure represents an element of the sample space, in this case the drawing of a particular card.

For many situations it is possible to construct more than one sample space. For instance, if we were interested only in the suit of the selected card, we might have used the set

{spade, heart, club, diamond}

For our example, it is convenient to keep the sample space for drawing a card in the more detailed form, making it possible to describe any type of outcome in terms of the more detailed elements—the individual cards. For this reason, we refer to the elements of the sample space shown in Figure 5-1 as *elementary events*. Elementary events are the simplest and most basic outcomes considered.

To extend these concepts, consider the outcomes when three different coins—a penny, a nickel, and a dime—are tossed so that each will show either a head or a tail. The sample space is shown in Figure 5-2. Here the events are ordered triples such as (H,T,H), which represents the outcome "head for the penny, tail for the nickel, head for the dime." Even though three coins are tossed, we may view the tossing of all three as one situation, for which the outcome

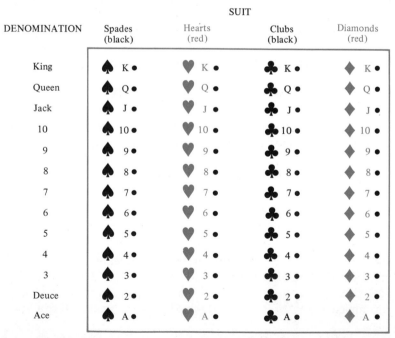

FIGURE 5-1 Sample space describing the card selected randomly from a fully shuffled deck of 52 ordinary playing cards.

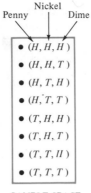

SAMPLE SPACE

FIGURE 5-2 Sample space for the tossing of three coins.

(H,T,H) is a single elementary event. The events (H,T,H) and (T,H,H) differ from (H,T,H), for in each case a different coin has the tail side showing. In describing the sample space for three tosses of the *same coin*, the elementary events would be represented in precisely the same manner—as eight ordered triples. In that case, however, the situation would have three *stages*, so that (H,T,H) would represent the event "head for the first toss, tail for the second toss, head for the third toss." (H,T,H) would be different from the event (T,H,H), because in each the tail appears on a different toss.

We may be interested in more complex outcomes than elementary events. For example, consider the sample space for the outcome from tossing a six-sided die:

$$\text{Sample space} = \{1, 2, 3, 4, 5, 6\}$$

where the elements represent the number of dots on the showing face. The outcome "an even-valued face" is a *composite event*, occurring whenever any one of the elementary events 2, 4, or 6 results. In keeping with our set representation, we denote the possible ways this event may occur by

$$\text{Even-valued face} = \{2, 4, 6\}$$

Such a partial listing is an *event set*. Note that an event set is a *subset* of the sample space: All its elements also belong to the sample space. An event set for an elementary event, such as the king of spades, will contain a single element:

$$\text{King of spades} = \{\text{king of spades}\}$$

For most uncertain situations many composite events are possible. Figure 5-3 shows a few event sets that can be associated with drawing one card from a deck of 52 ordinary playing cards. Each is pictured as a grouping of the applicable elementary events.

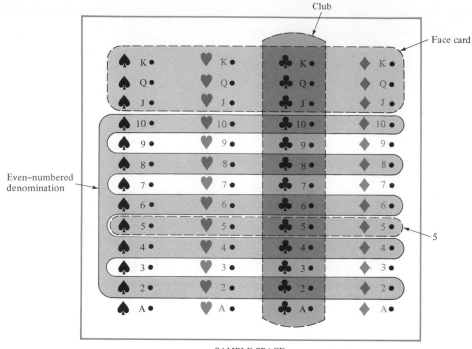

SAMPLE SPACE

FIGURE 5-3   Composite events for drawing a card from a fully shuffled deck of 52 ordinary playing cards.

Basic Definitions of Probability

Classically, the probability of an event is the relative frequency with which it occurs when the identical circumstances are repeated a large number of times. It is thus the ratio of the number of times the event occurs to the number of times the circumstances are faced. The notation used to express the probability of an event is illustrated by the

BASIC DEFINITION

$$P[\text{event}] = \frac{\text{Number of times the event occurs}}{\text{Number of times the situation is repeated}} \tag{5-1}$$

Expression (5-1) indicates that a probability is an empirically derived value obtainable only after repeated experimentation. In practice, actual experimentation is unnecessary for a great many types of events. The probability of some events, such as getting a head in a coin toss, may be obtained by reasoning alone. Knowing that a coin has two sides, assuming that it is evenly balanced, and presuming that it is tossed fairly, we may reasonably expect a head to occur in about half of any number of tosses. Thus we deduce that

$$P[\text{head}] = \frac{1}{2}$$

In a similar manner, we may reason that the probability of drawing the ace of spades from a shuffled deck of cards is 1/52, as there is no reason to suspect that certain of the 52 cards would be favored. Each card should appear with the same frequency in repeated shufflings. Each possible card is equally likely to turn up.

When all elementary events are equally likely, we may determine the probability of an event in the following manner:

PROBABILITY WHEN ELEMENTARY EVENTS ARE EQUALLY LIKELY   When the sample space consists of elementary events reasoned to be equally likely, then

$$P[\text{event}] = \frac{\text{Number of elementary events in its event set}}{\text{Total number of equally likely elementary events}} \qquad (5\text{-}2)$$

Thus, since there is a single way to achieve a head (that is, since its event set is of size $= 1$, because head is an elementary event), expression (5-2) tells us that $P[\text{head}] = 1/2$, where the 2 represents the size of the sample space for one coin toss. The same procedure applies for composite events. For example, since the event "even-valued face" resulting from a die toss occurs whenever any one of the 3 elementary events 2, 4, or 6 is the outcome, and since there are exactly 6 possible elementary events, or showing faces:

$$P[\text{even-valued face}] = \frac{3}{6} = \frac{1}{2}$$

We may use this definition to find the probabilities of the composite events shown in Figure 5-3 for drawing a card from a fully shuffled deck of 52 playing cards:

$$P[\text{club}] = \frac{13}{52} = \frac{1}{4}$$

$$P[\text{face-card}] = \frac{12}{52} = \frac{3}{13}$$

$$P[5] = \frac{4}{52} = \frac{1}{13}$$

$$P\genfrac{[}{]}{0pt}{}{\text{even-numbered}}{\text{denomination}} = \frac{20}{52} = \frac{5}{13}$$

In each case, all cards (elementary events) are equally likely, and since there are 52 of them, the denominator in each case is 52 (the size of the sample space). The numerators are the sizes of the respective event sets (found by counting the number of elementary events—possible cards—in each set). The probabilities are therefore readily obtained by counting the number of elements in the respective sets and computing the ratios.

If the elementary events are not all equally likely, the basic definition of probability must be used. The probabilities must be estimated by repeating the uncertain situation many times. For example, if a die is shaved until it is asymmetrical, it becomes more likely to roll some sides than others. Logical reasoning cannot tell us what the probabilities ought to be for the faces of a shaved die. Only after many tosses can they be estimated from the results actually obtained.

Subjective Probability

Not all events have probabilities that can be obtained in the above fashion. For example, the event "the next U.S. President will be a Democrat" cannot be based on past frequencies alone, since conditions differ from election to election. It makes no sense to divide the number of times a Democrat has won in the past by the number of elections held. Rather, a subjective probability value must be used. Such a number is subjective because people might disagree on the proper value. Chapter 21 describes various procedures for determining subjective probabilities.

Certain and Impossible Events

From our basic definition of probability, it may be noted that a probability will always be between 0 and 1, inclusively. This is because the numerator in the probability fraction can never be negative nor can it be larger than the denominator. Two important observations follow from the definition. First, an event that is certain to occur will have the same value in both the numerator and the denominator, for the same events will result every time (that is, with frequency 1). Thus,

$$P[\text{certain event}] = 1$$

The event "the next President of the United States will be at least 35 years old" is a certain event and has a probability of 1, because the Constitution specifies a minimum age of 35. The event "food prices will rise, fall, or remain unchanged" likewise is certain and has a probability of 1.

At the other extreme, an impossible event's frequency ratio will always have a 0 in the numerator, for such an event will never occur. Thus,

$$P[\text{impossible event}] = 0$$

For example, the U.S. auto industry has limited capacity to produce cars and cannot make 50 million of them in any one year. This outcome for next year is impossible and we can state that

$$P[\text{50 million cars made}] = 0$$

Alternative Expressions of Probability

Probabilities are not always expressed as ratios. They may be expressed as percentages, as odds, or as chances. These other forms are not inconsistent with our definition, because they may all be translated into the basic fraction or ratio form. For example, the probability of a head may be expressed in the following forms:

50 percent probability of a head. (Divide the percent by 100 to get the fraction 1/2.)

50–50 chance of a head. (This means an even chance, a probability of $50/(50+50) = 1/2$.)

1 to 1 odds that a head will occur. [To express odds as a fraction, add the two numbers (in this case, $1+1 = 2$) and place the result in the denominator; then place the first number in the numerator. For 1 to 1 odds, the result is 1/2. As another example, the odds for getting a queen are 4 to 48 or 1 to 12, so that $P[\text{queen}] = 4/(4+48) = 1/(1+12) = 1/13$.]

EXERCISES

5-1 A smoker has eight pipes, two of which are meerschaums. One of his meerschaums has a curved stem. He has a total of four curved-stem pipes. He asks his son to bring him the curved-stem meerschaum. The boy, not knowing rose briar from ivory nor calabash from hookah, selects a curved-stem pipe at random. What is the probability that the father will get the pipe he wants?

5-2 A coin is tossed exactly three times in succession. Here, the sample space has the same form as Figure 5-2. List the elements of the event set for each of the following events and then determine each event's probability:
(a) Exactly two heads appear in the three tosses.
(b) The same side does not appear twice in succession.
(c) The toss sequence ends with a head.
(d) An odd number of tails is obtained.

5-3 A pair of six-sided dice, one red and one green, are tossed. The sides of each die cube exhibit the values 1 through 6:
(a) List the elementary events in the sample space.
(b) List the possible sums of the two showing face values.
(c) For each of your answers to (b), show which elementary events correspond to each possible sum value. Then determine the probability for each sum.

5-4 From your answers to Exercise 5-3, list the elementary events and then determine the probabilities for each of the following composite events:
(a) The sum value lies between 5 and 7, inclusively.
(b) The sum value lies between 8 and 12, inclusively.
(c) The sum value lies outside the range 4 through 9.
(d) The red and green dice have the same value.
(e) The red die has a value greater than the green die.
(f) The red die has a value greater than the green die, and the sum value is greater than or equal to 9.

5-5   Determine the probabilities of the following events:
  (a) That a man chosen randomly from a group of ten men is a doctor, if the group contains two doctors.
  (b) Winning a raffle with a single ticket out of 10,000.
  (c) Getting both heads on one toss each of a dime and a penny. (First determine the sample space.)
  (d) Getting a number greater than 2 for the value of the showing face from the toss of a six-sided die.

5-2   EVENTS AND THEIR RELATIONSHIPS

To ease our task in computing probabilities, it is often helpful to look at relationships between events. Several types of relationships are important. We first consider how events may be combined.

Events Having Components

Some outcomes may be explained by the occurrence of more than one event. For example, getting at least two heads when tossing three coins is equivalent to obtaining exactly two heads or exactly three heads. Dealing yourself the ace of spades may be stated more precisely as getting a card that is both an ace and a spade. The basic event combinations important to probability are expressed in the logical connective sense of "or" and "and."

Union of Events
An outcome that occurs whenever any one of several more specific events happens is called the *union* of those events. This is expressed as

$$A \; or \; B$$

which represents the outcome when either event *A* occurs singly, event *B* occurs singly, or both *A* and *B* occur together. The importance of this relationship is that probability computations can often be simplified by first looking at *A* and *B* separately. Figure 5-4 illustrates how the union of the events "king," "queen," and "jack" provides the event "face card."

Intersection of Events
An outcome that arises only when both *A* and *B* occur is referred to as the *intersection* of events *A* and *B*. We express this as

$$A \; and \; B$$

We sometimes refer to *A and B* as a *joint event*. Figure 5-5 illustrates this concept for three coin tosses. There the event "all heads" is portrayed as the intersection of the events "dime is a head" and "all coins show same side."

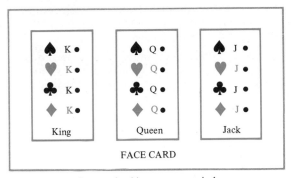

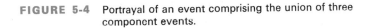

Face card = king *or* queen *or* jack

FIGURE 5-4 Portrayal of an event comprising the union of three component events.

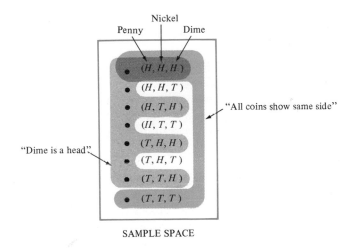

SAMPLE SPACE

FIGURE 5-5 Portrayal of the intersection of two events.

Relationships Between Events

Another type of event relationship involves properties exhibited by two or more events, whether or not they are combined. In developing laws of probability it is important to know if two events can occur jointly. We may also need to know if a collection of events is complete. Sometimes it is helpful to determine whether the occurrence of one event will make another more or less likely or if its effect is neutral.

Mutually Exclusive Events

Several events are *mutually exclusive* if the occurrence of any one event automatically rules out the occurrence of the others. Another way of saying this is that the joint occurrence of the events is itself an impossible event. The following examples illustrate this.

> Example 5-1   Meat-T Pet Food Company is considering its advertising budget for a new brand of dog food. The event of primary interest is the dollar sales figure for next year's operation. The number of possible events, or sales figures, varies from a minimum of zero to a maximum limited only by Meat-T's plant capacity. Since only one of these sales figures will appear in the company's accounts at the end of next year, only one event can occur, and thus the events are mutually exclusive.

> Example 5-2   Consider the events bankruptcy and profit that may result from the current year's operation of a firm. These events are *not* mutually exclusive, since it is possible for a business to make a profit and yet also be forced into bankruptcy by the claims of impatient creditors.

Collectively Exhaustive Events

A collection of events is *collectively exhaustive* if at least one of those events is bound to occur. For example, consider the following events describing the characteristics of a randomly chosen playing card:

$$\text{red suit, black suit, spade}$$

It is certain that one of these events will occur, since together they comprise all possibilities. They are not mutually exclusive, because spades are also black cards. A collectively exhaustive grouping of events may be redundant.

Independent Events

Two events are *independent* when the probability of one is not affected by the occurrence of the other. As an example, consider the outcomes of two successive coin tosses. Assuming that both tosses are fair, we can conclude that getting a head on the second toss is independent of getting a head on the first, because the probability of a head is $\frac{1}{2}$ regardless of whether a head or tail is obtained first. But we cannot conclude that a randomly chosen person's education and income are independent events, since we know that education influences income levels. The probability of a high income is greater for a college graduate than for a high-school dropout.

EXERCISES

5-6   The design engineer for a satellite power system has ordered a mockup test on the ground. The system will run for six months and will use a total of ten power cells. By the end of six months, anywhere between zero and ten cells will have expired, but the exact number is uncertain. List the elementary events in the sample space. Then find the respective event set for the following composite events for the number of dead cells:
(a) Not less than 3 nor more than 7.
(b) Greater than 7.

(c) At the most 4.

(d) Less than 5 or greater than 8.

(e) Less than or equal to 6.

5-7 A six-sided die is tossed. For the following events describing the values of the showing face, list the elementary events.

(a) At least 5 (b) At most 4 (c) 2 or greater (d) 5 or less.

5-8 For the following situations, indicate whether or not the listed events are collectively exhaustive. If they are not, explain why.

(a) A box contains nine objects: three are red, three are blue, and three are white. Two objects are drawn from the box. Some possible color combinations for the pair are: both red, both blue, red and white, both white, and blue and white.

(b) A new job applicant is: (1) either male (*M*) or female (*F*); (2) either a college graduate (*G*) or not (not *G*); and (3) either under 30 (*U*) or 30 or over (*O*). The following events describing the attributes of the applicant are of interest:

M, not G, and O	*F, G, and O*	*F, G, and U*
M, G, and U	*F, not G, and U*	*M, G, and O*
M, not G, and U		

(c) A record disc will be inspected to determine its quality in terms of (1) high (*H*) or low (*L*) electric charge; (2) whether it is scratched (*S*) or not scratched (not *S*); and (3) whether it is warped (*W*) or flat (*F*). The joint events are

H, S, and W	*H, not S, and F*	*L, not S, and W*
H, S, and F	*L, S, and W*	*L, not S, and F*
H, not S, and W	*L, S, and F*	

5-9 For each of the following situations, indicate whether the events are mutually exclusive. If they are not, state why.

(a) Toss of a six-sided die: even-valued result, 1-face, 2-face, 5-face.

(b) Thermometers are inspected and rejected if any of the following is found: poor calibration, inability to withstand extreme temperatures without breaking, not within specified size tolerances.

(c) A manager will reject a job applicant for any of the following reasons: lack of relevant experience, slovenly appearance, too young, too old.

5-3 THE ADDITION LAW

Several laws can ease our task of determining probabilities of complex events. They are used when it is convenient to find values for a complicated probability problem by breaking it into pieces that can be analyzed separately and then combined. The *addition law* serves this purpose for the combination form *A or B*. This law reflects the fact that, due to the logical nature of *or*, the number of ways in which an event may occur is the net sum of the ways in which its component events may occur.

ADDITION LAW

$$P[A \ or \ B] = P[A] + P[B] - P[A \ and \ B] \tag{5-3}$$

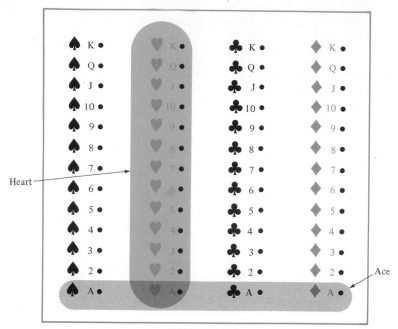

FIGURE 5-6   The union of events "heart" and "ace" is the entire colored and grey area.

As an illustration, consider the event "ace *or* heart" describing the properties of a randomly chosen playing card. The addition law tells us that

$$P[\text{ace } or \text{ heart}] = P[\text{ace}] + P[\text{heart}] - P[\text{ace } and \text{ heart (ace of hearts)}]$$

$$= \frac{4}{52} + \frac{13}{52} - \frac{1}{52} = \frac{16}{52}$$

Figure 5-6 shows that there are 16 elementary events in the sample space that are either ace or heart. Note that the event sets for ace and heart intersect at the ace of hearts. The sizes of the two sets are 4 and 13, respectively, and the ace of hearts is included in both. Therefore, the probability of ace of hearts must be subtracted from the sum of these probabilities in order to provide a result consistent with the basic probability definition. Since 16 cards in the deck are either ace or heart, or both, the correct probability must be 16/52.

The Addition Law for Mutually Exclusive Events

If A and B are mutually exclusive events, their joint occurrence is impossible and $P[A \text{ and } B] = 0$. Therefore, for mutually exclusive events we can state the following

SIMPLIFIED ADDITION LAW

$$P[A \text{ or } B] = P[A] + P[B] \qquad (5\text{-}4)$$

This simplified law applies only when A and B are mutually exclusive events.

As an illustration, suppose that the number of customers arriving at a barbershop during the first 10 minutes it is open can be any value between zero and four, with the following probabilities:

Number of Persons	Probability
0	.1
1	.2
2	.3
3	.3
4	.1

The simplified addition law gives us the probability that exactly two or exactly three persons arrive

$$P[\text{two or three}] = P[\text{two}] + P[\text{three}]$$

$$= .3 + .3 = .6$$

since the two events are mutually exclusive.

The addition law applies for any number of components. For example, the probability that at least one person arrives may be expressed as

$$P[\text{at least one}] = P[\text{one or two or three or four}]$$

$$= P[\text{one}] + P[\text{two}] + P[\text{three}] + P[\text{four}]$$

$$= .2 + .3 + .3 + .1 = .9$$

Events that Are Mutually Exclusive and Collectively Exhaustive

Many uncertain situations involve outcomes that are not only mutually exclusive but also collectively exhaustive. We may use the following addition-law property *whenever the component events are both mutually exclusive and collectively exhaustive.*

$$P[A \text{ or } B \text{ or } C] = P[A] + P[B] + P[C] = 1 \qquad (5\text{-}5)$$

Although the above expression involves three events, in some situations more or fewer event components may be involved. The probabilities of these components sum to one because the two properties make the complex outcome *A or B or C* certain.

Returning to the barbershop example, we see that the five values representing the number of persons exhibit the properties of mutual exclusiveness and are also collectively exhaustive, since one of them is bound to occur (and five or more persons arriving is impossible for this particular barbershop). Thus,

$$P[\text{zero } or \text{ one } or \text{ two } or \text{ three } or \text{ four}]$$

$$= P[\text{zero}] + P[\text{one}] + P[\text{two}] + P[\text{three}] + P[\text{four}]$$

$$= .1 + .2 + .3 + .3 + .1 = 1$$

Viewed another way, we have

$$P[\text{zero } or \text{ at least one}] = P[\text{zero}] + P[\text{at least one}]$$

$$= .1 + .9 = 1$$

The outcomes "zero" and "at least one" have a very special relationship: they are opposites. This feature can be very useful in finding probabilities.

Application to Complementary Events

The addition law can be very useful in dealing with *complementary events* (opposites). An event and its complement are collectively exhaustive, because either one or the other must occur. For example, a person chosen at random must be either male or female (which may be expressed as not male). Since these events are obviously mutually exclusive, for any event A, the addition law provides

$$P[A \text{ } or \text{ not } A] = P[A] + P[\text{not } A] = 1$$

From this it follows that

$$P[A] = 1 - P[\text{not } A] \tag{5-6}$$

This principle can be useful when the event "not A" has a probability value that is easier to find than that of A itself.

Suppose that we wanted a faster way to compute the probability that at least one person would arrive at the barbershop. "At least one" means "some," and *the opposite of some is none.* The complementary event is therefore "zero" customers, and thus

$$P[\text{at least one}] = 1 - P[\text{zero}]$$

$$= 1 - .1 = .9$$

EXERCISES

5-10 A yo-yo manufacturer has determined that his sales, rounded to the nearest hundred thousand, will be 1, 2, 3, or 4. The event set is therefore {1, 2, 3, 4}.

(a) List the elements of the sets for the following events: (1) odd-numbered level of sales, (2) sales of at least 3, (3) sales greater than 1 but less than 4, (4) sales below 4, and (5) sales of 3.

(b) List the elementary events in the event set for the complements of the outcomes in part (a).

5-11 A card is selected from a fully shuffled deck of 52 ordinary playing cards.

(a) Determine the following probabilities, treating the ace as the lowest denomination (one), the king and jack as odd denominations, and the queen as an even denomination:

(1) ace	(4) even	(7) odd *and* below 7
(2) below 7	(5) spade	(8) even *and* spade
(3) odd	(6) ace *and* spade	(9) even *and* below 7

(b) Using the values obtained above, apply the addition law to find the following probabilities:

(1) odd *or* below 7	(3) even *or* below 7
(2) ace *or* spade	(4) even *or* spade

5-12 An antique car parts supplier has determined the following probabilities for the number of annual orders for Locomobile fuel pumps:

Number of Orders	Probability
0	.3
1	.2
2	.1
3	.1
4	.1
5	.1
6	.1
7 or more	0
Total	1.0

Find the probability that there will be:

(a) Less than 4 orders.

(b) Between 2 and 6 orders, inclusively.

(c) At least 1 order.

(d) Between 2 and 4 orders, inclusively.

(e) At the most 2 orders.

5-13 Events *A, B, C* are mutually exclusive and collectively exhaustive, each having a probability of 1/3. Find:

(a) $P[A \text{ or } B]$	(d) $P[A \text{ or } B \text{ or } C]$
(b) $P[\text{not } C]$	(e) $P[\text{not } (A \text{ or } B \text{ or } C)]$
(c) $P[\text{not } (A \text{ or } B)]$	

5-14 The antique car parts supplier in Exercise 5-12 has provided the following probabilities for the annual number of orders for Pierce-Arrow, Duesenberg, and Silver Ghost carburetors:

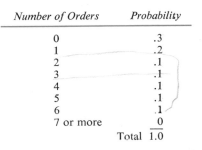

Number of Orders	*Probabilities for* Pierce-Arrow	Duesenberg	Silver Ghost
0	.5	.4	.3
1	.3	.2	.2
2	.2	.1	.2
3	.1	.1	.1
4	.1	.1	.1
5	.1	0	.1
6 or more	0	0	0
	1.3	.9	1.0

For each type of car, determine whether the probability values have been assigned properly in accordance with the addition law for mutually exclusive and collectively exhaustive events. If not, state why.

5-4 CONDITIONAL PROBABILITY AND THE JOINT PROBABILITY TABLE

Conditional Probability

Some uncertain situations can result in the joint occurrence of two or more events. This may happen because several stages are involved, as in tossing a coin more than once, or it may be due to the simultaneous occurrence of several events, such as selecting a person at random who will be either male or female, married or single, and over or under 21 years old. In these cases, new questions arise about the relationship between separate events of a situation. In particular, do the conditions imposed by the occurrence of some events affect the probabilities of the other events? Thus, we may ask whether the probability of getting a head on the eleventh toss ought to be any different when the previous ten tosses had all been heads than if they had all been tails. Or we may question whether the probability that a female under 21 is married should be any different from the probability that an older woman is married. We refer to probability values obtained under the stipulation that some events have occurred or will occur as *conditional probabilities.*

Conditional probability may be illustrated for the outcome of drawing a card from a fully shuffled deck. Suppose another person draws the card without letting you see it, but in a brief glimpse you see that it must be a face card. The deck has only 12 face cards. What is the probability that the card is a king? Although the deck contains 4 kings, our answer is not 4/52, since our surreptitiously gained information indicates that some of the 52 cards are impossible. The sample space has been restricted to the 12 face cards, and the only remaining uncertainty is which of these 12 cards has been removed. In a sense, there is a new "sample space" having the 12 face cards as elementary events. Using basic concepts, we determine that the probability of a king is 4/12 = 1/3. Thus, we may state that the conditional probability of a king *given* face card is

$$P[\text{king} \mid \text{face card}] = \frac{4}{12} = \frac{1}{3}$$

where the vertical bar stands for "given."

Joint Probability Table and Marginal Probabilities

To further illustrate how probabilities may be obtained when there are several simultaneous events, let us consider the following situation.

TABLE 5-1   Number of Credit Applicants by Category

	On Present Job 2 Years or Less (L)	*On Present Job More than 2 Years (M)*	*Total*
Owns Home (O)	20	40	60
Rents Home (R)	80	60	140
Total	100	100	200

The credit applicants of a department store are classified in terms of home ownership and job tenure. Suppose that one application is chosen by lottery from 200, which are grouped into four categories in Table 5-1. The letters O, R, L, and M will be used to simplify the following discussion. Using the probability definition for equally likely events, we can determine the following probability values:

$$P[O \text{ and } L] = \frac{20}{200} = .10 \qquad P[R \text{ and } L] = \frac{80}{200} = .40$$

$$P[O \text{ and } M] = \frac{40}{200} = .20 \qquad P[R \text{ and } M] = \frac{60}{200} = .30$$

The marginal totals may be used to determine the probabilities that the applicant has the respective attributes. For instance, the probability that the applicant owns a home is $P[O] = 60/200 = .30$. In a like manner, we can find $P[R]$, $P[L]$, and $P[M]$. Since only the numbers in the margins of Table 5-1 are needed to compute these probabilities, they are sometimes called *marginal probabilities*.

Construction of the *joint probability table* shown in Table 5-2 may be helpful. The joint events represented by each cell in a joint probability table are mutually exclusive. Thus, the marginal probabilities may also be found by applying the addition law for mutually exclusive events. For example, the event

TABLE 5-2   Joint Probability Table for a Randomly Selected Applicant

	On Present Job 2 Years or Less (L)	*On Present Job More than 2 Years (M)*	*Marginal Probability*
Owns Home (O)	.10	.20	.30
Rents Home (R)	.40	.30	.70
Marginal Probability	.50	.50	1.00

O has two mutually exclusive components: *O and L*, *O and M*. Hence, using the appropriate values from Table 5-2, we determine the probability that the applicant is a homeowner by

$$P[O] = P[(O \text{ } and \text{ } L) \text{ } or \text{ } (O \text{ } and \text{ } M)]$$
$$= P[O \text{ } and \text{ } L] + P[O \text{ } and \text{ } M]$$
$$= .10 + .20 = .30$$

The probability values in the cells of the row (or column) corresponding to the event with the desired characteristic are added to obtain the other marginal probabilities using the addition law:

$$P[R] = P[R \text{ } and \text{ } L] + P[R \text{ } and \text{ } M] = .40 + .30 = .70$$
$$P[L] = P[O \text{ } and \text{ } L] + P[R \text{ } and \text{ } L] = .10 + .40 = .50$$
$$P[M] = P[O \text{ } and \text{ } M] + P[R \text{ } and \text{ } M] = .20 + .30 = .50$$

Computing Conditional Probability from Joint Probability

We are able to compute conditional probabilities by using the joint probability of two events, when it is known, and the probability for the given event. The following expression always applies for any two possible events *A* and *B*:

PROPERTY OF CONDITIONAL PROBABILITY

$$P[A \mid B] = \frac{P[A \text{ } and \text{ } B]}{P[B]} \qquad (5\text{-}7)$$

Applying this property to the credit applicant illustration, we may compute the conditional probability that the applicant owns a home given job tenure of more than two years:

$$P[O \mid M] = \frac{P[O \text{ } and \text{ } M]}{P[M]} = \frac{.20}{.50} = .40$$

Note that the same result could have been obtained from the data in Table 5-1 by calculating the proportion of applicants on their present job more than 2 years who are also homeowners:

$$\frac{40}{40 + 60} = \frac{40}{100} = .40$$

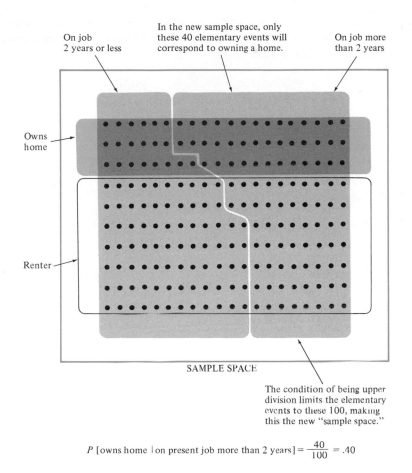

$$P \text{ [owns home | on present job more than 2 years]} = \frac{40}{100} = .40$$

FIGURE 5-7   Portrayal of the concept of conditional probability.

Thus, we see *the conditional probability of A given B is the proportion of times that A occurs out of all the times B occurs.* This explains why we divide the joint probability by the probability of the given event to obtain $P[A \mid B]$.

Figure 5-7 shows how the same result could be obtained directly from a diagram of the sample space by noting that the condition of being on the job more than 2 years limits the outcomes to a new, smaller sample space of size 100. The probability of obtaining a homeowner is now obtained by observing that 40 events out of 100 provide this outcome.

As a further illustration of conditional probability, we may use the preceding property to recompute the probability of getting a king given a face card:

$$P[\text{king} \mid \text{face}] = \frac{P[\text{king } and \text{ face}]}{P[\text{face}]} = \frac{4/52}{12/52} = \frac{4}{12} = \frac{1}{3}$$

Note that in both illustrations the conditional probabilities differ from the corresponding probabilities when there are no stipulations, which we call *unconditional probabilities*. That is,

$$P[\text{king} \mid \text{face}] = \frac{1}{3} \neq \frac{1}{13} = P[\text{king}]$$

$$P[O \mid M] = .40 \neq .30 = P[O]$$

The unconditional and conditional probabilities are not always different. Their comparative values are used in establishing whether there is statistical independence, which will be discussed in Section 5-6.

Expression (5-7) can be used to obtain the conditional probability only when the joint probability of A and B is known. When $P[A \text{ and } B]$ is not known, then the conditional probability must be found by applying the basic concepts of probability, considering outcomes involving B only.

The principle underlying conditional probability is extensively used in our daily decision making. For example, when the sky is heavily overcast, enhancing the chance of rain, you carry an umbrella. Conditional probability is also relied upon in making business decisions. Insurance companies, for example, use it to determine their rates.

Example 5-3   Life insurance companies charge a sizable premium for covering the lives of steeplejacks, miners, divers, and other members of occupational groups who are subject to greater hazards than most people. The mortality tables upon which insurance rates are based indicate that such persons have a shorter life expectancy than the population as a whole; in essence, their probability of dying in any year is higher. Information about an insurance applicant's occupation affects this probability: The likelihood of the event "untimely death" is affected by the occurrence of the event "applicant is a steeplejack."

EXERCISES

5-15   An employment agency specializing in clerical and secretarial help classifies candidates in terms of primary skills and years of experience. The skills are bookkeeping, switchboard, and stenography (we will assume that no candidate is proficient in more than one of these). Experience categories are less than one year, one to three years, and more than three years. There are 100 persons currently on file, and their skills and experience are summarized in the following table.

	Skill			
Experience	*Bookkeeping*	*Switchboard*	*Stenography*	*Total*
Less than One Year	15	5	30	50
One to Three Years	5	10	5	20
More than Three Years	5	15	10	30
Total	25	30	45	100

One person's file is chosen at random. Find the following:
(a) The missing numbers in the table.
(b) $P[\text{stenographer } or \text{ bookkeeper}]$ $45 + 25 = 70/100 = 7/10$
(c) $P[\text{stenographer} \mid \text{more than three years experience}]$ $\frac{10}{30} = \frac{1}{3}$
(d) $P[\text{bookkeeper } or \text{ less than one year experience}]$

5-16 You have drawn a card from a fully shuffled deck of 52 ordinary playing cards. Find:
(a) $P[\text{ace} \mid \text{red}]$ (c) $P[\text{diamond} \mid \text{red}]$
(b) $P[\text{ace of diamonds} \mid \text{red}]$ (d) $P[\text{face card} \mid \text{red}]$

5-17 For events X, Y, and Z, the following probability values hold:
$$P[X \text{ and } Y] = 1/3 \qquad P[X \text{ and } Z] = 1/6$$
$$P[X] = 1/2 \qquad P[Z] = 4/9$$
Answer the following:
(a) Find $P[Y \mid X]$.
(b) Find $P[Z \mid X]$.
(c) Find $P[Y]$, if Y and Z are mutually exclusive and collectively exhaustive.

5-18 A and B are mutually exclusive and collectively exhaustive. If $P[A] = 0.3$, find the following:
(a) $P[B]$ (b) $P[A \text{ and } B]$ (c) $P[A \mid B]$ (d) $P[A \text{ or } B]$

5-19 A new family with two children of different ages has moved into the neighborhood. Suppose that it is equally likely that either child will be a boy or girl. Hence, the following situations are equally likely:

Youngest	Oldest	
boy	boy	(B, B)
boy	girl	(B, G)
girl	boy	(G, B)
girl	girl	(G, G)

$\frac{4}{52} + \frac{1}{24}$

(a) Find P [at least one girl].
(b) If you know there is at least one girl, what is the conditional probability that the family has exactly one boy?
(c) Given that at least one child is a girl, what is the conditional probability that there are two girls?

5-5 MULTIPLICATION LAW

We have seen how the addition law can be used to find the probability of the union of two events. We now introduce the *multiplication law*, which is used to find the probability of the joint occurrence or intersection of two or more events. The multiplication law is especially necessary when the component events have probability values that can be readily found but the joint probability cannot be directly obtained through the basic probability definitions. For instance, the necessary information may not be summarized conveniently in a joint probability table, as it was in the credit applicant illustration in the previous section.

MULTIPLICATION LAW

$$P[A \text{ and } B] = P[A] \times P[B \mid A]$$

and

$$P[A \text{ and } B] = P[B] \times P[A \mid B]$$

(5-8)

This law follows immediately from the basic property of conditional probability. (Each expression is obtained by multiplying both sides of the applicable conditional probability ratio by the given event's probability and canceling terms.)

We may continue with the credit applicant illustration to show how the multiplication law can be applied. Recall that $P[M] = .50$ and also that $P[O|M] = .40$. Applying the multiplication law:

$$P[O \text{ and } M] = P[M] \times P[O|M] = .50(.40) = .20$$

This is the same joint probability value found earlier.

When the joint probabilities are already known, the multiplication law is not needed. But there are situations where only conditional and marginal probabilities are available, and the joint probabilities may be obtained only by using the multiplication law.

Example 5-4   A highway commissioner has found that half of all fatal automobile accidents in his state may be blamed on drunken drivers. Only 4 in 1,000 reported accidents have proved fatal, and 10 percent of all accidents in the state are attributable to drunken drivers. The commissioner wishes to summarize this information in a joint probability table relating to future accidents.

Assuming that the present pattern prevails, the probability that a reported accident happens to be fatal is

$$P[F] = 4/1,000 = .004$$

while the probability that a drunken driver causes the accident (fatal or not) is

$$P[D] = .10$$

and the conditional probability that a drunken driver causes the accident given that it is fatal is

$$P[D|F] = .50$$

The joint probabilities for cause and kind of accident events are provided in Table 5-3. Only the numbers shown in black are directly provided by the data given above. The colored probability values were obtained in the following manner.

TABLE 5-3   Joint Probability Table for Cause and Kind of Automobile Accident

	Fatal (F)	Nonfatal (not F)	Marginal Probability
Drunken Driver (D)	.002	.098	.100
Other Cause (O)	.002	.898	.900
Marginal Probability	.004	.996	1.000

The multiplication law provides the joint probability that a fatal accident is caused by a drunken driver:

$$P[D \text{ and } F] = P[F] \times P[D \mid F]$$
$$= .004(.50) = .002$$

The marginal probabilities for the causes and the types of accidents must sum, respectively, to 1. It therefore follows that

$$P[O] = 1 - P[D] = 1 - .100 = .900$$
$$P[\text{not } F] = 1 - P[F] = 1 - .004 = .996$$

The remaining joint probabilities can be found by utilizing the fact that the joint probabilities in each row and column must sum to the respective marginal probability values. Thus, subtracting the known joint probability value from the marginal probability, we find the unknown joint probability values:

$$P[D \text{ and not } F] = P[D] - P[D \text{ and } F] = .100 - .002 = .098$$
$$P[O \text{ and } F] = P[F] - P[D \text{ and } F] = .004 - .002 = .002$$
$$P[O \text{ and not } F] = P[O] - P[O \text{ and } F] = .900 - .002 = .898$$

Joint Probabilities for More than Two Events

When we wish to find the joint probability of more than two events, the multiplication law may be extended:

$$P[A \text{ and } B \text{ and } C] = P[A] \times P[B \mid A] \times P[C \mid A \text{ and } B] \qquad (5\text{-}9)$$

Suppose that we have a box containing five marbles, each of a different color: yellow, red, green, orange, and purple. Three marbles are selected from the box at random, one at a time, so that all marbles remaining in the box have an equal chance of being selected at each drawing. Once drawn, a marble is not replaced. The following events are designated:

$$A = \text{first marble is yellow}$$

$$B = \text{second marble is green}$$

$$C = \text{third marble is orange}$$

It is easy to establish that $P[A] = 1/5$. If a yellow marble is selected, then only four remain, and one of these is green. Thus, the conditional probability that the second marble will be green given that the first is yellow is $P[B \mid A] = 1/4$. Likewise, should the yellow and green marbles be selected, then the third marble is equally likely to be one of the three colors red, orange, or purple, so that $P[C \mid A \text{ and } B] = 1/3$. The joint probability for A, B, and C may be determined by applying expression (5-9):

$$P[A \text{ and } B \text{ and } C] = \frac{1}{5} \times \frac{1}{4} \times \frac{1}{3} = \frac{1}{60}$$

For a large number of component events, the same approach applies.

Matching-Birthdays Problem

The following example nicely illustrates how the multiplication law may be applied to a large number of events.

> **Example 5-5**   The problem is to determine the approximate probability that there is at least one matching birthday (day and month) among a group of persons. For simplicity, it will be assumed that each day in the year is equally likely to be a person's birth anniversary; February 29 will be combined with March 1. (This assumption is not strictly true; some months are more popular, so that our result will only be approximate.)
>
> It will be simplest to find the probability of the complementary event—no matches—by using the multiplication law. Envision each member of a group of size n being asked in succession to state his or her birthday. We conveniently define our events as follows:
>
> A_i = the ith person queried does not share a birthday with the previous $i-1$ persons.
>
> Then $P[\text{no match}] = P[A_1 \text{ and } A_2 \text{ and} \ldots \text{and } A_{n-1} \text{ and } A_n]$, which is the probability of the event that no person shares a birthday with the preceding persons. Since there is no previous person for the first to match with, the event A_1 is certain, so that:
>
> $$P[A_1] = 1 = \frac{365}{365}$$
>
> Also, we obtain
>
> $$P[A_2 \mid A_1] = \frac{364}{365}$$
>
> because there are 364 days in which the second person may not match birthdays with the first. Continuing in this same manner, we finally obtain
>
> $$P[A_n \mid A_1 \text{ and } A_2 \text{ and} \ldots \text{and } A_{n-1}] = \frac{365 - n + 1}{365}$$
>
> since the nth person cannot have a birthday on the previously cited $n-1$ dates, leaving only $365 - (n-1)$ days allowable for his or her birthday. Therefore, we may apply the multiplication law to obtain:
>
> $$P[\text{no matches}] = \frac{365}{365} \times \frac{364}{365} \times \frac{363}{365} \times \cdots \times \frac{365 - n + 1}{365}$$
>
> The probability of at least one match may be found from this:
>
> $$P[\text{at least one match}] = 1 - P[\text{no matches}]$$

One interesting issue is finding the size of the group for which the probability exceeds 1/2 that there is at least one match. Knowing this number, you can amaze your less knowledgeable friends and perhaps win a few bets. The "magical" group size turns out to be 23.

Why such a low group size? If it were physically possible to list all the ways (triples, sextuples, septuples, and so forth) in which 23 birthdays can match (there are several million, and for each of them a tremendous number of date possibilities), an intuitive appreciation as to why could be attained. Table

TABLE 5-4   Probabilities of at Least One Matching Birthday

Group Size	P[no matches]	P[at least one match]
3	.992	.008
7	.943	.057
10	.883	.117
15	.748	.252
23	.493	.507
40	.109	.891
50	.030	.970
60	.006	.994

5-4 shows the matching probabilities for several group sizes. Note that for groups above 60 there is almost certain to be at least one match.

EXERCISES

5-20 A perfectly balanced coin is tossed fairly twice in succession. Let H_1 and T_1 denote the possible outcomes of the first toss and H_2 and T_2 the possible results from the second toss.
(a) What is the value of $P[H_2 \mid T_1]$?
(b) What is the value of $P[H_2 \mid H_1]$?
(c) Use the multiplication law to find the probability of (1) H_1 *and* H_2, and (2) T_1 *and* T_2.

5-21 Given the following probability values:

$$P[A_2 \mid A_1] = .3 \qquad P[A_1] = .6 \qquad P[A_2] = .4$$
$$P[A_3 \mid A_2] = .4 \qquad P[A_3 \mid A_1 \text{ and } A_2] = .3$$

use the multiplication law to find:

(a) $P[A_1 \text{ and } A_2]$
(b) $P[A_2 \text{ and } A_3]$
(c) $P[A_1 \text{ and } A_2 \text{ and } A_3]$

5-22 A professor grading a statistics examination has promised to give an equal number of A's, B's, C's, and D's. If three students are chosen randomly:
(a) What is the probability that all three will receive different grades?
(b) What is the probability that at least two of the three students will receive the same grade?

5-23 A fruit inspector accepts or rejects shipments of bananas after performing tests on a few sample bunches. He rejects 15 percent of all shipments inspected. Thus far, he has rejected 95 percent of all bad shipments inspected, and 10 percent of all shipments have ultimately proved bad.
(a) Using the above experience as a basis, find the values for the probabilities regarding the outcome of any particular shipment handled by this particular inspector: P[reject], P[bad], P[reject | bad].
(b) Find P[reject *and* bad], using the multiplication law with the appropriate values found in part (a).
(c) Construct a joint probability table showing the joint probabilities and the marginal probabilities for the inspector's actions (accept or reject) and the quality (good or bad) of the banana shipment.

5-6 STATISTICAL INDEPENDENCE, SAMPLING, AND PROBABILITY TREES

In the credit applicant situation illustrated in Section 5-4, there is a difference between the prevalence of long-term and short-term jobholders who own homes. Only 20 percent of the short-term jobholders own their homes, whereas the figure is 40 percent for the others (see Table 5-1, p. 107). Since home ownership is more common among those with more than 2 years on the present job, we may infer that the corresponding events are *dependent*. Likewise, we can say that there is a dependency between home ownership and job tenure for the applicants.

On the other hand, we ordinarily think of the outcomes from tossing two coins as being *independent*. Unless the coins are unfairly tossed, getting a head on the first toss should not influence the outcome of the second. It is very important to determine whether or not events are independent, for in such cases procedures for finding probabilities may often be streamlined. We make the following

> **DEFINITION**   Two events A and B are *statistically independent* if the chance of one is unaffected by the occurrence of the other; that is, if
>
> $$P[A \mid B] = P[A]$$
>
> Whenever the above equality holds, so must the following:*
>
> $$P[B \mid A] = P[B]$$

In our credit applicant illustration, the event "applicant owns his own home" (O) is not independent of (and therefore is dependent upon) the event "applicant has been on his present job more than 2 years" (M). This is indicated by the fact that

$$P[O \mid M] = .40$$

does not equal

$$P[O] = .30$$

so that the requirement of statistical independence is violated.

As another example, a card is drawn from a fully shuffled deck of 52 ordinary playing cards. The events "jack" and "face card" are dependent, since

$$P[\text{jack} \mid \text{face}] = \frac{P[\text{jack } and \text{ face}]}{P[\text{face}]}$$

$$= \frac{4/52}{12/52} = \frac{1}{3}$$

---

* Several events may be *collectively* independent. If they are, every possible conditional probability for all combinations of events must equal the corresponding unconditional probability.

and this differs from

$$P[\text{jack}] = \frac{4}{52} = \frac{1}{13}$$

That "jack" and "face" are dependent is evident from the fact that knowing a card is a face card increases the probability that the card will be a jack. Knowing the occurrence of one event changes the probability that the other event will occur from what the probability would have been without the knowledge of the first event.

Simplification of the Multiplication Law

When events are independent, the joint probabilities may be determined from the multiplication law without using conditional probabilities. *The "unconditional" probabilities thus have the same values as the conditional probabilities.*

MULTIPLICATION LAW APPLIED TO INDEPENDENT EVENTS

$$P[A \text{ and } B] = P[A] \times P[B] \qquad (5\text{-}10)$$

Returning to the playing card illustration, *suit* (heart, club, spade, or diamond) and *denomination* (ace, deuce, three, and so on) are statistically independent. This is because the probability of obtaining an ace is the same (1/13), regardless of whether or not its suit is known—in all cases, exactly one-thirteenth of the cards can be an ace. Thus, the probability that a card is ace *and* heart (the ace of hearts) is the product of the respective *unconditional* probabilities for the component events:

$$P[\text{ace } and \text{ heart}] = P[\text{ace}] \times P[\text{heart}]$$

$$= \frac{1}{13} \times \frac{1}{4} = \frac{1}{52}$$

This concept extends to any number of independent events. For example, suppose that just as many men as women read a particular magazine, that married readers are just as predominant among males as females, and that proportionately there are just as many Democrats in each sex and marital status combination. For a randomly selected reader, his or her sex, marital status, and political affiliation characteristics yield combinations of three independent events. Thus, to compute the probability of selecting a married man who is a Democrat, we may use the multiplication law for independent events:

$$P[\text{man } and \text{ married } and \text{ Democrat}]$$
$$= P[\text{man}] \times P[\text{married}] \times P[\text{Democrat}]$$

Independence and Random Sampling

The selection of a random sample may be viewed as an uncertain situation with several stages. At each stage, some elementary units are removed from a population in such a way that with each successive selection all remaining units have an equal chance of being chosen.

An illustration from manufacturing quality control will be useful. Suppose that 5 percent of all items made by a machine prove to be defective. Let's assume that the incidence of defectives is sufficiently erratic that the attributes of successive items are independent events. In deciding whether or not to readjust the machine, common practice would be to periodically take a sample of items to determine if the number of defectives happens to be excessive. Suppose that three successive items are chosen for this purpose. The multiplication law for independent events could be used to determine the probability that the sample contains all defectives, all good items, or both defective and good items. In order that all possible outcomes can be considered, it is sometimes helpful in such a situation to list all elementary events and find the probabilities for each one.

Probability Tree Diagram

In order to list all elementary events it is sometimes convenient to explain the sampling process in terms of a *probability tree diagram*. Consider the tree diagram provided in Figure 5-8 for the machine being sampled above. Here,

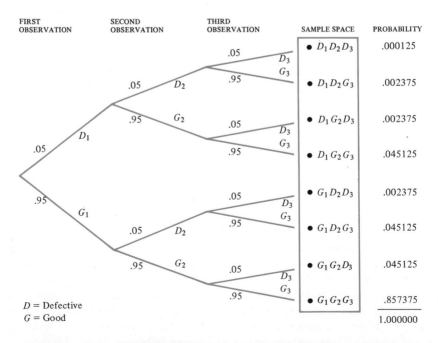

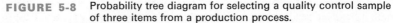

FIGURE 5-8   Probability tree diagram for selecting a quality control sample of three items from a production process.

each successive sample observation outcome is represented by a branch, and the probability of an outcome is indicated alongside its branch. Here we use .05 as the probability of a defective item and .95 for the probability of a good item. Since there are two complementary events possible for each item observed, there are two separate branches for each item—one for defective and one for good. There is a different branching point or *fork* for each observation. Two forks are thus required for the second item—a different one for each possible attribute of the first observation. The probabilities for the events in any one fork must always sum to 1.

Because four distinct outcomes are possible for the quality of the earlier items, four forks are needed for the third observation. To distinguish the outcomes for each item, we use the subscripts 1, 2, and 3. For instance, D_1 means that the first item will be defective; G_2 means that the second will be good. Altogether there are eight paths through the tree, each representing different sample outcomes. Each path leads to a different elementary event, so that the eight end positions provide the sample space for the final sample results.

The probabilities for each elementary event may be found in the manner used earlier, by multiplying together the probability values for the branches on the path leading to that particular event. For instance, the multiplication law may be applied to find the probability that all three items are defective:

$$P[D_1 \text{ and } D_2 \text{ and } D_3] = P[D_1] \times P[D_2] \times P[D_3]$$

$$= (.05)(.05)(.05)$$

$$= .000125$$

Since the events D_1, D_2, and D_3 are independent, we use unconditional probabilities, and in all cases, the probability of obtaining a defective item happens to be the same for every observation to be made. The other outcome probabilities in Figure 5-8 were found in the same way.

Sampling With and Without Replacement

Let us slightly modify our example. Suppose that a population of 100 items, of which 5 percent are defective, is made on the same machine. A three-item sample is *randomly* selected and set aside, and the quality of each item is determined.

The probability tree diagram of this experiment is provided in Figure 5-9. The results of each selection are *not independent*, because with each selection the composition of the remaining items changes. The proportion of defective items remaining increases or decreases, depending upon the quality of the prior selection. Thus, if the first item proves to be defective, so that D_1 occurs, then there are only four defectives left out of 99 remaining items, and the probability that the second item is defective D_2 is 4/99. But if G_1 is the first event, then D_2 has a probability of 5/99, because any one of five remaining defective items could be chosen. These values are *conditional probabilities*, because D_2 has a different

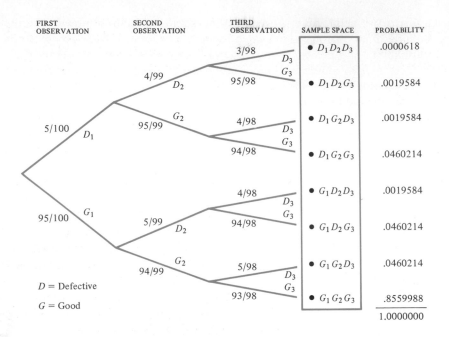

FIGURE 5-9   Probability tree diagram for selecting a quality control sample of three items without replacement from a population of size 100.

chance of occurring in each case. Returning to our original multiplication law, we find the probability of getting all defectives in this revised sampling situation:

$$P[D_1 \text{ and } D_2 \text{ and } D_3] = P[D_1] \times P[D_2 \,|\, D_1] \times P[D_3 \,|\, D_1 \text{ and } D_2]$$

$$= \left(\frac{5}{100}\right)\left(\frac{4}{99}\right)\left(\frac{3}{98}\right)$$

$$= .0000618$$

Note that this result differs from the one obtained when successive observations are independent.

When the population units are set aside after each selection, the sampling is done *without replacement*. If, instead, each inspected item were replaced in the group and again allowed the same chance of being chosen as any of the other items, then the outcomes would have identical probabilities for each observation, as in Figure 5-9. Such a procedure is called *sampling with replacement*. Although intuitively wasteful, sampling with replacement makes for simpler probability calculations. More will be said about this in later chapters.

Independence and the Law of Large Numbers

Another example may prove useful to illustrate a very important property of uncertain situations repeated at several stages, each having outcomes independent of the others.

   Suppose a fair coin is tossed 20 times, and a head appears every time. The probability of this happening is less than one millionth.* Does this mean that in a long series of future tosses 20 extra tail outcomes must occur in order to balance the long-run frequency of occurrence ratio and coincide with "heads" having a probability of 1/2? Also, does this increase the probability of a tail next time?

   The answer to both questions is "no." First, there are no guarantees that any particular sequence of results will exhibit heads even close to one-half of the time. This presents no contradiction here, for there is a nonzero probability that any number of heads—say, 10,000—will occur in sequence. All that can be stated is that it is not very likely there will be many more (or fewer) heads than half the number of tosses. A law of probability, the *law of large numbers*, in essence states that the probability that the result will deviate significantly from that indicated by the theoretical long-run frequency of occurrence becomes small as the number of repetitions (tosses) increases. Thus, if the coin tosses were continued several thousand more times, the effect of the 20 "extra" heads on the resulting frequency would not be very noticeable.

   If the coin-tossing process is fair (that is, if there are no biases in the tossing process in favor of either heads or tails), then it may be inferred that the probability of a head should be 1/2. Also, if the process is fair, then a head would be no more likely to follow a previous head than would a tail; the events of succeeding and preceding tosses are independent. Hence,

$$P[\text{head} \mid \text{head previously}] = P[\text{head}] = 1/2$$

and

$$P[\text{tail}] = 1 - P[\text{head}] = 1/2$$

The probability of a tail should not increase or decrease if the fact is accepted that fairness is present. After obtaining 20 heads in a row, human nature may lead to the inference that the tossing mechanism is indeed unfair. The seemingly aberrant result does not, however, constitute proof of unfairness.

EXERCISES

5-24   A box contains 100 marbles, 60 red and 40 green. There are 30 striped and 70 solid. There are 10 green-striped marbles. One marble is chosen at random from the box.
   (a) Construct a joint probability table summarizing the events describing the properties (color, solid or striped) of the selected marble; include the marginal probabilities.
   (b) Find $P[\text{marble is solid} \mid \text{marble is green}]$.
   (c) Is the event "marble is solid" independent of the event "marble is green"? Why?

---

* This provides rather strong empirical evidence that the coin may indeed be unfair. But—although a rare outcome—this is a possible result even with a fair coin.

5-25 The following probabilities have been obtained for the results of a random experiment: $P[R \text{ and } S] = .10$; $P[R \text{ and } T] = .3$; $P[S \text{ and } T] = .2$; $P[R] = .50$; $P[S] = .4$; and $P[T] = .50$. Specify which of the following pairs of events are statistically independent: R, S; R, T; S, T. State the reasons for your answers.

5-26 Ten percent of the ball bearings in a lot of 50 are known to be overweight. Three bearings are randomly selected, one at a time, and weighed. Each in turn is returned to the lot and allowed the same chance of being selected as the unweighed items. Construct a probability tree diagram for this situation. Find the following probabilities describing the final results of the sampling procedure:
(a) No overweight items are selected.
(b) All the items are found to be overweight.
(c) Exactly one overweight ball bearing is found.

5-27 Repeat Exercise 5-26 if the successively weighed items are not replaced.

5-7 COMMON PITFALLS IN DETERMINING PROBABILITIES

There are several pitfalls encountered in determining probabilities. Most common are the erroneous application of probability laws and using a procedure unworkable for the situation.

Common Errors in Applying the Laws of Probability

Some of the most prevalent errors committed in the determination of probability values are due to the improper use of the laws of probability. A few of the common mistakes are listed here:

(1) Using the addition law to find the probability of the union of several events when they are *not* mutually exclusive, without correcting for the double counting of possible occurrences.

Example 5-6 Suppose that casualty insurance underwriters have established that the probabilities of a city experiencing one of the following natural disasters in the next decade are

tornado	.5
flood	.3
earthquake	.4

We cannot say that the probability of suffering one of these acts is $.5 + .3 + .4 = 1.2$. Clearly, two or more of these disasters may occur over a ten-year period, and some may occur more than once.

(2) Using the addition law when the multiplication law should be used, and conversely. Remember that *or* signifies addition and that *and* signifies multiplication.

For example, the probability of drawing a red face card is the same as that for the event "red *and* face." Recall that:

$$P[\text{red}] = \frac{26}{52} \quad \text{and} \quad P[\text{face}] = \frac{12}{52}$$

If we add these values in trying to find the joint probability:

$$\frac{26}{52} + \frac{12}{52} = \frac{38}{52}$$

we obtain a meaningless result. Since red and face are independent events,

$$P[\text{red } and \text{ face}] = \frac{26}{52} \times \frac{12}{52}$$

$$= \frac{6}{52}$$

(3) Using the multiplication law for independent component events when the events are dependent.

For example, a common commission of this error occurs when replacement is mistakenly assumed in calculating the probability of obtaining a particular sample result. As we have seen, removal of an item from a group changes the group's composition and hence the probabilities that future selections will be of a certain type.

(4) Improperly identifying the complement of an event. For example, *the complement of none is some* (which may be expressed as "one or more," or as "at least one").

The following example, which actually happened, dramatically illustrates how ludicrous results may be obtained through the incorrect application of probability laws.*

Example 5-7 An elderly woman was mugged in the suburb of a large city. A couple was convicted of the crime; the evidence upon which the prosecution rested its case was largely circumstantial. Probability was used to demonstrate that an extremely low probability of one twelve-millionth existed that any specific couple could have committed the crime. The probability value was determined by using the multiplication law for independent events. The events—the characteristics ascribed by witnesses to the couple who actually did the deed—are listed below, along with the assumed probabilities:

Characteristic Event	Assumed Probability
Drives yellow car	1/10
Interracial couple	1/1000
Blonde girl	1/4
Girl wears hair in ponytail	1/10
Man bearded	1/10
Man black	1/3

* For a detailed discussion, see "Trial by Mathematics," *Time*, April 26, 1968, p. 41.

Multiplying the above values, the probability was obtained that any specific couple, chosen at random from the city's population, had all six characteristics:

$$\frac{1}{10} \times \frac{1}{1000} \times \frac{1}{4} \times \frac{1}{10} \times \frac{1}{10} \times \frac{1}{3} = \frac{1}{12,000,000}$$

Since the defendants had all six characteristics and the jury was mystified by the overwhelming strength of the probability argument, they were convicted.

The Supreme Court of the state heard the appeal of one of the defendants. The defense attorneys, after obtaining some good advice on probability theory, attacked the prosecution's analysis on two points: (1) the rather dubiously assumed event probability values, and (2) the invalid assumption of independence implicit in using the multiplication law in the above manner (for example, the proportion of black men having beards may have been greater than the proportion of the population as a whole having beards; also, "interracial couple" and "black man" are definitely not independent events). The judge accepted the arguments of the defense and noted that the trial evidence, even allowing for its incorrect assumptions, was misleading on another score—namely, a high probability that the defendants were the only such couple should really have been determined in order to demonstrate a strong case. Using the prosecution's original figures and its assumptions of independence, it can be demonstrated that the probability is large that at least one other couple in the area had the same characteristics.

Using Inappropriate Procedures

The basic laws of probability should be used only when it is appropriate to do so. For instance, the multiplication law tells us that $P[A \text{ and } B] = P[A] \times P[B \mid A]$ can be used to find the joint probability for *A and B*. But a joint probability can often be found more simply by using a basic definition. For example, to find the probability that a randomly selected card is both a king and a heart, we can immediately observe that $P[\text{king } and \text{ heart}] = 1/52$ since there is one such card among the equally likely 52. It would be extra work to separately get $P[\text{king}] = 1/13$ and $P[\text{heart} \mid \text{king}] = 1/4$ and then find the answer by multiplying: $1/13 \times 1/4 = 1/52$.

And what if either $P[A]$ or $P[B \mid A]$ is unknown? Then the multiplication law cannot be used at all to find $P[A \text{ and } B]$, which must be determined some other way.

Another problem arises with the identity $P[A \mid B] = P[A \text{ and } B]/P[B]$. *This relationship is not the only prescription for computing the conditional probability.* Unless values for both $P[A \text{ and } B]$ and $P[B]$ are known, it's of no use. In such cases, $P[A \mid B]$ can usually be found by using a basic definition of probability under the assumption that *B* must occur. For example, suppose we know only that in a group of persons there are 30 doctors, and that 10 of the doctors are married. Then for a randomly chosen person it follows that $P[\text{married} \mid \text{doctor}] = 10/30 = 1/3$ (only the 30 doctors are considered). We can't first find the values for $P[\text{married } and \text{ doctor}]$ and $P[\text{doctor}]$, because nobody told us how many people are involved altogether.

The most insidious trap in using the above identity to find $P[A|B]$ is illustrated by the following report from a frustrated student: "I don't know $P[A \text{ and } B]$, although $P[B]$ is given. So, I'll get the joint probability from the multiplication law by $P[B] \times P[A|B]$. But I can't do this, since I must divide $P[A \text{ and } B]$ by $P[B]$ to get $P[A|B]$. I therefore need my answer to get the value needed to compute my answer. This is impossible."

To paraphrase Lincoln: Some procedures work all the time and all procedures work some of the time, but all procedures don't work all the time. How you find the answer is dictated by the given data. If the problem is rich in information, you may have a choice of method, and the art is finding the easiest one to apply. When there is a scarcity of given information, there may be only one way to get the answer.

5-8 COUNTING TECHNIQUES

There are uncertain situations whose sample spaces are so large that we cannot list all their elementary events. One can envision situations for which the space contained in all the world's books would not be enough for a complete listing of the possibilities. For example, there are about 400 trillion trillion ways to sequence the 26 letters of the alphabet. Assuming 500,000 entries per book, 100 books per person, 6 billion persons, we have space for only 300,000 trillion entries. Fortunately, probabilities for such events may still be calculated by the use of the techniques to be developed in this section. These enable us to count possibilities by large multiples and to develop rules for employing logical principles to determine what a count should be by taking shortcuts and thereby giving us the capability to deal with astronomical quantities.

Underlying Principle of Multiplication

The most difficult sample spaces to physically enumerate arise when the outcomes are multifaceted. Each elementary event can be categorized in a number of different ways. As we have seen, this might arise when there are several stages, such as successive coin tosses. Or there might be only one stage having several dimensions, like selecting an object that may belong to several categories. For example, a particular order received by an automobile assembly plant can be a complex outcome involving many requested options. The number of possible combinations is so staggering that it is an extreme rarity for two independently ordered cars coming from the same plant to be just alike. In either case, it will be convenient to treat the situation in several stages. Thus, we may envision the car order as one involving first a specification of color, then size of engine, followed by body style (sedan, convertible, or whatever), and so on.

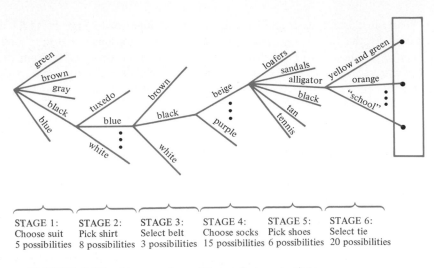

STAGE 1:	STAGE 2:	STAGE 3:	STAGE 4:	STAGE 5:	STAGE 6:
Choose suit	Pick shirt	Select belt	Choose socks	Pick shoes	Select tie
5 possibilities	8 possibilities	3 possibilities	15 possibilities	6 possibilities	20 possibilities

FIGURE 5-10   Diagram of possible wardrobe selections.

When the number of possibilities in a particular stage will be the same no matter what the outcomes of the preceding stages are, our problem is quite simple. We count only the number of possibilities in each stage and then multiply these together.

Example 5-8   Consider the number of possible ways a man could choose to dress himself when selecting items from his wardrobe. Suppose that he has 5 suits, 8 shirts, 3 belts, 15 pairs of socks, 6 pairs of shoes, and 20 ties. Figure 5-10 shows how we may break this situation into stages. The total number of possible choices would then be

$$5 \times 8 \times 3 \times 15 \times 6 \times 20 = 216,000$$

Note that it is impracticable to list all of the possibilities. This would be unnecessary here, anyway. However, if our man is particular about the potential for clashing combinations (if he never wears his white belt with his black suit or his socks with his sandals), then we would have no choice but to laboriously list all possibilities, taking shortcuts whenever possible.

Example 5-9   A deck of 52 ordinary playing cards is thoroughly shuffled and the five top cards are removed. The probability that these cards may be placed in a denominational sequence to form a straight is to be determined. It does not matter in what sequence the cards appear when drawn.

Here, our sample space comprises all possible five-card results. As these are equally likely, we may find the probability of a straight by dividing the number of results involving straights by the size of the sample space. To find the number of five-card straights,* one may begin by listing the possibilities:

* Poker players will recognize that this list would normally include straight flushes (wherein all cards belong to the same suit); these may be eliminated here, thereby reducing the number of possibilities.

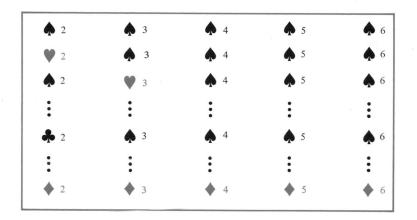

This list, as will be shown, has 1,024 entries. Lists of equal length would have to be constructed for straights beginning with 3, with 4, and so on, up to one beginning with 10 (ace being a high card only). Nine such lists would be required. The total number of five-card straights possible is therefore 9,216. More than 200 pages of this book would be required to show a complete listing.

How did we obtain 9,216? First, we observe that there are nine denominations for the lowest card. All of these denominational groupings are of materially the same form, each containing the same number of possible five-card arrangements. Therefore, if straights beginning with the deuce are investigated first, then the results obtained will be applicable to straights of any denomination. What may be observed from the above list? Note that each possible outcome differs from the others only in the choice of suits for the cards of the five denominations. For the deuce, any one of four suits (hearts, diamonds, clubs, or spades) would be acceptable, and likewise for the 3, 4, 5, and 6. The following list summarizes the possible suit arrangements:

deuce of	3 of	4 of	5 of	6 of
hearts	hearts	hearts	hearts	hearts
diamonds	diamonds	diamonds	diamonds	diamonds
clubs	clubs	clubs	clubs	clubs
or spades	or spades	or spades	or spades	or spades

The total number of suit assignments is found by the following multiplication:

$$\begin{bmatrix} \text{number of} \\ \text{deuce suits} \end{bmatrix} \times \begin{bmatrix} \text{number of} \\ \text{3 suits} \end{bmatrix} \times \begin{bmatrix} \text{number of} \\ \text{4 suits} \end{bmatrix} \times \begin{bmatrix} \text{number of} \\ \text{5 suits} \end{bmatrix} \times \begin{bmatrix} \text{number of} \\ \text{6 suits} \end{bmatrix}$$

which equals

$$4 \times 4 \times 4 \times 4 \times 4 = 4^5 \quad \text{or} \quad 1,024$$

Duplicating the above argument for the eight other denominational categories of straights, we arrive at:

$$\underbrace{9}_{\substack{\text{total number} \\ \text{of possible} \\ \text{denominational} \\ \text{categories}}} \times \underbrace{4^5}_{\substack{\text{total number} \\ \text{of suit} \\ \text{arrangements} \\ \text{for each}}} = \underbrace{9,216}_{\substack{\text{total number} \\ \text{of five-card} \\ \text{straights}}}$$

The number of equally likely situations for the denominator must now be determined before the five-card straight probability can be calculated; this will be done later in this chapter.

The principle used in the foregoing examples is a general one. It may also be applied to certain types of situations of a different nature.

The multiplication principle is applicable even when the same physical object is used over and over again. For example, it tells us that the number of possible outcomes from a sequence of five tosses of the same coin is

$$2 \times 2 \times 2 \times 2 \times 2 = 2^5 = 32$$

Observe that an identical number of outcomes are possible when five different coins are each tossed once.

Number of Ways of Sequencing Objects; The Factorial and Permutations

A large class of situations involves the enumeration of sequences in which objects may occur. The following example illustrates how this may be accomplished.

Example 5-10   ABC Typewriter Company wants to determine the sequence in which to place descriptions of new products in a sales brochure. There are five products to appear (A, B, C, D, and E). How many different sequence versions are possible for the brochure?

The question may be answered by considering each page in succession. Page one may contain any one of the 5 products, thus there are 5 choices; choose one of them. This will then leave 4 products available for page two—4 choices; again, one of these is to be selected. For the first two pages there have been 20 possible choices, partially listed below (you may verify to your satisfaction that there are 20 by completing the list).

Possible Choices of A, B, C, D, and E

Page One	Page Two	Choices for Page Three
A	B	C, D, E
A	C	B, D, E
A	D	B, C, E
A	E	B, C, D
B	A	C, D, E
⋮	⋮	⋮

Suppose that product A is chosen for page one, product B for page two. This leaves products C, D, and E to be assigned to pages three through five. The following 6 choices are possible:

Page Three	Page Four	Page Five
C	D	E
C	E	D
D	C	E
D	E	C
E	C	D
E	D	C

A similar list of equal length may be prepared for any of the other 19 assignments to the first two pages; all such lists would contain 6 entries. For the brochure there are thus 20×6 or 120 different product-to-page sequences possible. This figure could also have been obtained from the following multiplication:

$$5 \quad \times \quad 4 \quad \times \quad 3 \quad \times \quad 2 \quad \times \quad 1$$

| number of choices for first page | number of choices for second page | number of choices for third page | number of choices for fourth page | number of choices for fifth page |

The Factorial

A multiplication of the type used in the foregoing example is called a *factorial* product, or simply a factorial, and is denoted by an exclamation point placed after the highest number. Thus, 5 factorial is

$$5! = 5 \times 4 \times 3 \times 2 \times 1 = 120$$

In general, for any positive whole number n, n factorial ($n!$) may be determined by the following multiplication:

$$n! = n \times (n-1) \times (n-2) \times \cdots \times 2 \times 1 \qquad (5\text{-}11)$$

We define

$$1! = 1$$

$$0! = 1$$

The fact that 0! is 1 is usually a perplexing notion. If you think of 0! as representing the number of different sequences of assigning no (0) products to pages in a brochure with no (0) pages, you may observe that there is only one way of doing this (i.e., there is only one way to sequence nothing).

Factorial values literally become astronomically large for modest values of n. For instance,

$$10! = 3,628,800$$

$$20! = \text{approximately 2.4 billion billion}$$

$$100! = \text{approximately 9 followed by 157 zeros}$$

The Number of Permutations

It is sometimes useful to determine the number of ways in which one may select a number of objects from a given group, considering the order of selection.

Suppose we have n objects from which r are to be removed. The number of ways in which it is possible to select the r objects may be determined from the following product:

$$n \quad \times \quad (n-1) \quad \times \quad (n-2) \quad \times \cdots \times \; (n-r+1)$$

number of	number of	number of	number of
choices for	choices for	choices for	choices for
first object	second object	third object	rth object

Note that when $r-1$ objects have been removed, $n-r+1$ [i.e., $n-(r-1)$] objects remain, leaving this many choices for selection of the rth object. In Example 5-10, $r = 5$ new product descriptions were selected one at a time from $n = 5$ for inclusion in the brochure. There, each possibility differed only as to *sequence*, so that $n = r$. But when r is smaller than n (say we took four new product descriptions for the brochure), each possible group of selections would also differ with respect to *which particular objects were chosen*. Each such possibility is called a *permutation*. A permutation can involve a particular arrangement of fewer objects than the total or a particular sequence of the entire collection. If we multiply the product displayed earlier by $(n-r)!/(n-r)!$, we see that it can be expressed more simply:

$$\frac{n(n-1)\cdots(n-r+1)(n-r)!}{(n-r)!} = \frac{n!}{(n-r)!}$$

This enables us to make the following statement:

NUMBER OF PERMUTATIONS   The number of possible permutations of r objects from a collection of size n, denoted by P_r^n, is

$$P_r^n = \frac{n!}{(n-r)!} \tag{5-12}$$

For the number of permutations of $r = 3$ items out of $n = 5$ in our brochure example,

$$P_3^5 = \frac{5!}{(5-3)!} = \frac{5!}{2!} = 5 \times 4 \times 3 = 60$$

When all objects in the collection are taken,

$$P_n^n = \frac{n!}{(n-n)!} = \frac{n!}{0!} = n!$$

so that in this case the number of permutations is the same as the number of ways to sequence n objects.

The Number of Combinations of Objects

The number of permutations P_r^n considers not only which r objects are selected but also their sequence or arrangement. Sometimes we don't care how the r objects are arranged—we merely wish to determine the number of possible *combinations* of objects.

> **Example 5-11**   Due to a budgetary constraint, ABC Typewriter Company must restrict the number of pages in its sales brochure to three; thus only three of the five products may appear. The three products must be chosen from the five by ABC management. How many combinations of 3 objects out of 5 are there? Each combination may be listed, observing that there are 10:
>
> | | | | | |
> |---|---|---|---|---|
> | ABC | ABE | ACD | BCD | BDE |
> | ABD | ACE | ADE | BCE | CDE |

Again there is an alternative approach to determining the answer. Imagine choosing the items one at a time. We have 5 choices for the first product. This leaves 4 choices for the second. Only 3 products remain for our final choice. Then the following multiplication describes the number of choices:

$$5 \times 4 \times 3$$

But the result of the above product is 60, not 10. The same situations have been accounted for several times each. For instance, the combination ABC has been accounted for in all of the following sequences:

$$ABC \quad BAC \quad CAB \quad ACB \quad BCA \quad CBA$$

These differ only in the order in which the items appear, as the same 3 products are involved in all cases. However, the order in which an item is chosen is not now of interest, only whether it is selected. The redundant accounting may be corrected by dividing the earlier product by the number of sequences in which the 3 items ultimately chosen could have been selected: $3!$, or $3 \times 2 \times 1 = 6$:

$$\frac{5 \times 4 \times 3}{3!} = 10$$

The fraction in the above example may be transformed into a version that will later prove useful in analyzing other situations. Multiplying the numerator and denominator by $2!$ (thereby leaving the ratio's value unchanged) yields

$$\frac{(5 \times 4 \times 3) \times 2!}{3! \times 2!}$$

which may be rewritten as

$$\frac{5 \times 4 \times 3 \times 2 \times 1}{3! \times 2!} = \frac{5!}{3! \times 2!}$$

Another representation is

$$\frac{5!}{3! \times (5-3)!}$$

From this final representation, an easily generalized form for the number of combinations may be inferred:

NUMBER OF COMBINATIONS   The number of combinations of r objects taken from n objects, denoted by C_r^n, may be determined from:

$$C_r^n = \frac{n!}{r!(n-r)!} \tag{5-13}$$

Note that this expression is similar to expression (5-12) for the number of permutations. However, permutations are distinguished by order, while combinations are not. Since there are $r!$ ways to order (or sequence) r objects, the number of combinations is the number of permutations divided by $r!$, so that:

$$C_r^n = \frac{P_r^n}{r!} \tag{5-14}$$

The number of combinations of size $n-r$ may also be determined from expression (5-13) by the following line of reasoning. Whenever there are $n-r$ selected objects, there are r unselected objects; hence, the number of combinations of unselected objects must be the same as the number of combinations of selected objects. In the magazine problem in Example 5-11, there must be ten combinations of 2 (or $5-3$), because for each combination of size 3 listed, there is one combination of size 2 not on the list.

As the expression for the number of combinations is composed of factorials, the numbers may be quite large. Table 5-5 provides some examples of combination sizes.

TABLE 5-5   Number of Combinations of r Objects Taken From n

n	r	$C_r^n = \dfrac{n!}{r!\,(n-r)!}$
6	3	20
8	5	56
12	7	792
20	5	15,504
100	50	$\approx 100{,}000$ trillion trillion

A Final Solution for the Poker Hand

All the tools necessary to finish answering the problem in Example 5-9 have now been developed. The probability of a five-card straight can be found by dividing the number of ways that a five-card straight can occur (which we found to be 9×4^5) by the number of equally likely events. Any combination of five cards is equally likely (since each of the 52 cards in the deck has an equal chance of being on the top of a completely shuffled deck). Therefore, the number of equally likely events is the same as the number of combinations of $r = 5$ cards taken from $n = 52$ cards:

$$C_5^{52} = \frac{52!}{5!(52-5)!}$$

In evaluating this type of fraction, do not try to calculate the denominator and numerator separately, because the numbers become far too large to handle easily and the amount of work required is unwarranted. Instead, follow this procedure.

First, express the fraction in the following manner:

$$\frac{52!}{5!47!}$$

Now, 52! may be factored as

$$52! = 52 \times 51 \times 50 \times 49 \times 48 \times 47!$$

so that

$$\frac{52!}{5!47!} = \frac{52 \times 51 \times 50 \times 49 \times 48 \times 47!}{5!47!}$$

The 47! terms may then be canceled, which gives us

$$\frac{52 \times 51 \times 50 \times 49 \times 48}{5!}$$

Factoring 5!, we obtain

$$\frac{52 \times 51 \times 50 \times 49 \times 48}{5 \times 4 \times 3 \times 2 \times 1}$$

Further cancellation yields:

$$\frac{52 \times 51 \times \overset{\overset{5}{\cancel{10}}}{\cancel{50}} \times 49 \times \overset{\overset{4}{\cancel{12}}}{\cancel{48}}}{\cancel{5} \times \cancel{4} \times \cancel{3} \times \cancel{2} \times 1} = 52 \times 51 \times 5 \times 49 \times 4 = 2{,}598{,}960$$

The resulting figure is the number of possible five-card combinations. Dividing our earlier result for the number of straight combinations by this number, we obtain:

$$P[\text{five-card straight}] = \frac{9 \times 4^5}{\dfrac{52!}{5!(52-5)!}}$$

$$= \frac{9{,}216}{2{,}598{,}960}$$

$$= .00355$$

$$\approx \frac{1}{282}$$

After a large number of attempts at drawing five cards from a deck, you would, on the average, expect to encounter a straight only once in 282 tries. That is, the odds against drawing a five-card straight are about 281 to 1.

EXERCISES

5-28 Calculate the following:

(a) $6!$ (b) $\dfrac{14!}{3!\,11!}$ (c) $8!$ (d) $\dfrac{7!}{4!\,3!} \times \dfrac{11!}{7!\,2!}$

(e) $\dfrac{37!}{4!\,(37-4)!}$

(*Hint* for (e): Express the numerator as a product of numbers and 33 factorial; then cancel.)

5-29 The following famous nursery rhyme contains a counting problem.

> *As I was going to St. Ives,*
> *I met a man with seven wives.*
> *Every wife had seven sacks,*
> *Every sack had seven cats,*
> *Every cat had seven kits,*
> *Kits, cats, sacks, and wives,*
> *How many were going to St. Ives?*

Find (1) the number of cats and (2) the number of kits encountered on the journey.

5-30 A cafeteria has 3 types of salad (carrot, tossed, and bean); 4 entrees (ham, chop suey, meat loaf, and tacos); 3 vegetables (corn, peas, and stewed tomatoes); 6 drinks (cola, iced tea, hot tea, coffee, lemonade, and orange juice); and 4 desserts (ice cream, apple cobbler, apple sauce, and yogurt). For two dollars, you may have 1 salad, 2 different entrees, 2 different vegetables, 1 drink, and 2 different desserts.
(a) How many ways are there to obtain 2 different entrees? (*Hint:* Ignore order of selection.)
(b) How many ways are there to obtain 2 different vegetables?
(c) How many ways are there to obtain 2 different desserts?
(d) How many combinations of two-dollar dinners are allowable when the full quota of items is selected and when there are no duplications? (*Hint:* Do not attempt to diagram the outcomes.)

5-31 A traveling salesman must visit ten cities in one trip. In how many sequences may he make his stops?

5-32 If the top 13 cards are drawn from a deck of 52 ordinary playing cards that has been fully shuffled, they are the equivalent of a bridge hand. How many possible hands are there when the order in which they are obtained does not matter? How many hands are possible when the order does matter? (Answers in terms of factorials are sufficient.)

5-33 Determine the number of possible occurrences for each of the following situations:
(a) A coin is tossed ten times.
(b) Six dice are tossed simultaneously.
(c) One die is tossed six times.
(d) Six objects are selected from ten distinguishable items (order of selection is not considered).

5-34 Seating assignments are being made for the guests at an awards banquet. There are 20 guests (ten couples) to be seated along a table with ten chairs on each side. A name card is to appear at every place setting.

(a) In how many different ways is it possible to place the name cards?

(b) If no man is to sit aside or across from another man, how many arrangements are possible?

(c) If each couple is to sit side by side, how many arrangements are possible when (1) the sexes are alternated, and (2) members of the same sex may sit beside each other?

REVIEW EXERCISES

5-35 There are ten applicants for the position of personnel director. Some characteristics of the candidates are provided in the table below.

Name	Age	College Graduate	Marital Status	Previous Experience
Mr. Braun	28	No	Single	Yes
Mrs. Charles	37	No	Married	Yes
Mr. Feeley	42	No	Single	No
Mr. Gordon	53	Yes	Single	Yes
Ms. Kish	28	Yes	Married	No
Mr. Lambert	35	No	Married	Yes
Mr. Minsky	45	Yes	Married	No
Miss Olivera	33	Yes	Single	Yes
Mr. Snyder	39	No	Single	Yes
Mr. Wasserman	35	No	Married	Yes

The file of one applicant is chosen at random. For each of the following events, indicate the elementary events of its event set and its probability.

(a) College graduate.

(b) Older than 35.

(c) Same age as another applicant.

(d) No previous experience.

(e) Married.

5-36 Suppose that a card is selected from a fully shuffled deck of 52 ordinary playing cards. (For the sample space, refer to Figure 5-1 on page 92.)

(a) List the cards (K-H, 7-D, and so on) that are the elements in the following event sets: (1) heart; (2) ace; (3) below 4; (4) 8 through 10.

(b) Using your answers to part (a), list the elements in the following event sets: (1) heart *and* ace; (2) 8 through 10 *or* ace; (3) 8 through 10 *and* below 4; (4) below 4 *and* ace; (5) below 4 *or* ace.

5-37 Pinochle is a card game played with a special deck consisting of 48 cards. All the cards are above 8 in denomination, and the deck includes aces. A pinochle deck may be compiled from two regular decks by setting aside the denominations 2 through 8. Suppose that this is done with one regular "Bee" deck and one standard "Bicycle" deck.

(a) Draw a sketch of the sample space for one card taken from the shuffled deck. Use a dot to represent each card in the pinochle deck, and make your sketch similar to the one on page 92. (*Hint:* Use two columns for each suit.)

(b) On your sketch, encircle the group of elementary events in the following event sets and write each set's identity beside the corresponding area: king, club, face card, and nine. Then determine the probabilities of these events.

5-38   A General Motors plant manager once remarked, "I've never seen two cars exactly alike come off our assembly line." This is because the number of possible options is so large and the likelihood that two persons will order exactly the same car is so very small.

As an example, consider the abbreviated illustration below, where various options for a hypothetical model car are considered.

Option	Number of Possibilities
Body type (four-door, two-door)	4
Exterior color	8
Interior color	6
Engine size	4
Transmission	3
Suspension	2
Power accessory combinations	4
Sound system combinations	10
Air conditioning	2
Tire type/size	10
Cosmetic combinations	20
Window types	3
Automatic auxiliary features	6

How many possible different cars might be made?

5-39   A box contains four marbles, each of a different color: red (R), yellow (Y), white (W), and blue (B). Three marbles are selected randomly from the box, one at a time, and set aside.
   (a) Construct a three-stage probability tree diagram for this situation. Each fork must contain a branch for every color possible. (Remember, there is one less marble possible at each successive stage.) Label each branch with the corresponding color letter (subscripted with a 1, 2, or 3, depending upon whether it is the first, second, or third marble drawn) and the probability value for that branch.
   (b) Determine the joint probability corresponding to each end position.
   (c) Applying the addition law to the values obtained in (b), find the probability for each of the following composite events: (1) The red marble is selected before the yellow marble; (2) the blue marble is not selected; (3) both the white and the yellow marbles are chosen; (4) the red marble is selected on the first draw and the white marble on the last draw.

5-40   The events listed below pertain to a card selected from a fully shuffled deck of 52 ordinary playing cards. Determine in each case the appropriate relationship (mutually exclusive, collectively exhaustive, both, neither).
   (a) Heart, diamond, 10.   (b) 10, queen, ace.
   (c) Face, nonface.   (d) Face, red, club, spade.

5-41   The following joint probability table represents the particular characteristics of a randomly selected retired military person.

Rank	College Education Yes	College Education No	Marginal Probability
Officer	.21	.13	———
Enlisted	.06	.60	———
Marginal Probability	———	———	1.00

(a) Find the missing marginal probability values.

(b) Find the joint probability that the selected retiree was both an officer and college educated.

(c) Find the conditional probability that the selected person was an officer, given that he or she graduated from college.

(d) Determine the percentage of college-educated persons who were officers.

5-42 An experiment is conducted using three boxes, each containing a mixture of ten red (R) and white (W) marbles. The three boxes have the following compositions:

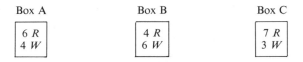

Box A   6 R / 4 W   Box B   4 R / 6 W   Box C   7 R / 3 W

Two marbles are selected randomly. The first is selected from Box A. If it is red, the second marble is to be picked from Box B, but if the first marble is white, the second marble will be taken from Box C. Using R_1 and W_1 to represent the color of the first marble and R_2 and W_2 to represent the color of the second:

(a) Find the following probabilities:

$$P[R_1] \qquad P[W_1]$$
$$P[R_2 \mid R_1] \qquad P[R_2 \mid W_1]$$
$$P[W_2 \mid R_1] \qquad P[W_2 \mid W_1]$$

(b) From your answers to part (a), use the multiplication law to determine the following joint probabilities:

$$P[R_1 \text{ and } R_2]$$
$$P[R_1 \text{ and } W_2]$$
$$P[W_1 \text{ and } R_2]$$
$$P[W_1 \text{ and } W_2]$$

(c) Determine the probabilities that:

(1) One red and one white marble will be chosen.

(2) Either two red or two white marbles will be chosen.

5-43 Have you ever wondered why a royal flush beats four of a kind in straight five-card poker? Recall that a royal flush is an A, K, Q, J, 10 straight of cards in the same suit, while four of a kind consists of four cards of the same denomination plus any fifth card.

Determine the number of five-card hands possible (ignoring the order in which a hand is filled) for obtaining a royal flush and for obtaining four of a kind. Since the rarer hand wins, which one is the best?

5-44 A train detection device for an automated rail network is 99.9 percent reliable. That is, 99.9 percent of the time when there is a stalled train between stations the device detects it, and it indicates that no train is present 99.9 percent of the time when there is not one. The probability that any particular departing train will stall before reaching the next station is .005.

(a) Find the probability that a hazardous situation will arise and a stalled train will go undetected.

(b) How many such situations does the law of large numbers imply that we can expect in one million station departures?

5-45 A horse race is to be run. There are nine qualified entries. Does this mean that after buying a "win" ticket on a randomly chosen horse in the race that you then have a probability of 1/9 of winning? Briefly explain your answer.

5-46   Given the probability data below:

$$P[A] = 1/3 \qquad P[B] = 1/2 \qquad P[C] = 1/4$$
$$P[A \text{ and } B] = 1/8 \qquad P[B \mid C] = 1/3 \qquad P[C \mid A] = 1/5$$
$$P[A \mid B \text{ and } C] = 1/2 \qquad P[A \text{ or } B \text{ or } C] = 17/20$$

(a) Determine the following probabilities:

    (1) $P[A \text{ and } C]$
    (2) $P[B \text{ and } C]$
    (3) $P[A \text{ and } B \text{ and } C]$
    (4) $P[A \mid B]$
    (5) $P[A \mid C]$
    (6) $P[C \mid B]$
    (7) $P[B \text{ and } C \mid A]$
    (8) $P[A \text{ or } B]$
    (9) $P[A \text{ or } C]$
    (10) $P[B \text{ or } C]$

(b) Answer the following:

    (1) Are the events in any letter pair mutually exclusive?
    (2) Do *A*, *B*, and *C* form a collectively exhaustive collection of events?
    (3) Which event pairs are *not* statistically independent?

5-47   A quality control inspector accepts only 5 percent of all bad items and rejects only 1 percent of all good items. Overall production quality of items is such that only 90 percent are good.

(a) Using the above percentage as probabilities for the next item inspected, find:

$$P[\text{accept} \mid \text{bad}]$$
$$P[\text{reject} \mid \text{good}]$$
$$P[\text{good}]$$

(b) Determine the values missing in the following joint probability table:

	Inspector Action		Marginal Probability
Quality	Accept	Reject	
Good			
Bad			
Marginal Probability			

(c) What is the probability that the inspector will accept or reject the next item incorrectly?

5-48   Four strangers wish to compare birth *months*. Assume that all 12 months are equally likely to contain each person's birthday. Then find the probability that there is at least one matching birth month.

5-9   OPTIONAL TOPIC: REVISING PROBABILITIES USING BAYES' THEOREM

In this section, we will introduce a procedure whereby probabilities can be revised when new information is obtained. The notion of revising probabilities is a familiar one, for all of us—even those with no previous experience in calculating probabilities—have lived in an environment ruled by the whims of chance and have made informal probability judgments. We have also intuitively revised these probabilities upon observing certain facts, and have changed our actions accordingly. For example, think how many times you have left home in the morning with no raincoat, only to look up and notice a menacing cloud cover, which sent you back for some protection in case it rained. On first charging outdoors, you behaved in a manner consistent with your judgment that the probability of rain was small. But the presence of clouds caused you to revise this probability significantly upward.

Our concern for revising probabilities arises from a need to make better use of experimental information. We begin here by establishing a fundamental principle that follows immediately from the laws of probability developed earlier in this chapter. This is referred to as *Bayes' Theorem*, after the Reverend Thomas Bayes, who proposed in the eighteenth century that probabilities be revised in accordance with empirical findings.

Such empirical findings may result from very elaborate experiments. In science, for example, many years of effort and much expensive equipment are devoted to such activities as studying physical laws by observing solar eclipses. Empirical findings may also arise from a very minor effort, such as asking a person questions in order to become better acquainted. No matter what their scope, they have one feature in common: *Experimental results provide information.* This information may serve to realign uncertainty. Data obtained by observing a solar eclipse can lend support to hypotheses concerning the effect of the sun's gravity on stellar light rays. They can lead to finer choices for further experiments. A person's responses to your questions may help you decide whether or not you might become friends. You may be led to realize that an ugly person is really beautiful or that a physically attractive person is vain and selfish.

Most information is not conclusive. Any empirical test can camouflage the truth. For instance, some potentially good students will do badly on college entrance examinations and some poor students will score highly. A good example of how such information may be unreliable is illustrated by the oil wildcatter's seismic test. Not completely reliable, a seismic survey can deny the presence of oil in a field already producing it and can confirm the presence of oil under a site already proved dry. Still, such imperfect findings can be valuable. An unfavorable test result can increase the chance of rejecting a poor prospect—college applicant or drilling lease—or a favorable result can enhance the likelihood of selecting a good one.

The information obtained will affect the probabilities of those events which determine the consequences of each act. We can revise the probabilities of these events upward or downward, depending upon the evidence obtained. Thus, the geologist increases the probability that oil will be found if a favorable seismic survey analysis is obtained and decreases the probability if the survey results are unfavorable.

Bayes' Theorem

Consider a situation where two uncertain events E and not E are possible. Suppose that $P[E]$ and $P[\text{not } E]$ have been obtained. These probabilities are referred to as *prior probabilities*, because they represent the chances of the events *before* the results from the empirical investigation are obtained. The investigation itself may have several possible outcomes, each statistically dependent upon E. For any particular result, which we may designate by the letter R, the conditional probabilities $P[R|E]$, $P[R|\text{not } E]$ are often available. The result itself serves to revise the probabilities for E and not E upward or downward. The resulting values are called *posterior probabilities*, since they apply *after* the informational result has been learned.

The posterior probability values are actually conditional probabilities of the form $P[E|R]$, $P[\text{not } E|R]$ that may be found according to

BAYES' THEOREM   The posterior probability of event E for a particular result R of an empirical investigation may be found from:

$$P[E|R] = \frac{P[E]P[R|E]}{P[E]P[R|E] + P[\text{not } E]P[R|\text{not } E]} \tag{5-15}$$

The principle underlying Bayes' Theorem may be best explained in terms of the following example.

Example 5-12   A box contains four fair dice and one crooked die with a leaded weight that makes the six-face appear on two-thirds of all tosses. You are asked to select one die at random and toss it. If the crooked die is indistinguishable from the fair dice and the result of your toss is a six-face, what is the probability that you tossed the crooked die?

The events in question are

$$C = \text{crooked die}$$
$$\text{not } C = \text{fair die}$$

The empirical investigation here is the toss itself, so we use:

$$R = \text{six-face}$$

Since 1 out of 5 dice is crooked, the prior probabilities for the type of die tossed are

$$P[C] = 1/5$$
$$P[\text{not } C] = 4/5$$

Because of the weights inside, we are told that when the crooked die is tossed

$$P[R|C] = 2/3$$

If the fair die is tossed, we know that one of the equally likely sides has a six-face, and

$$P[R|\text{not } C] = 1/6$$

Applying expression (5-15), the posterior probability that the die you tossed is crooked is

$$P[C \mid R] = \frac{P[C]P[R \mid C]}{P[C]P[R \mid C] + P[\text{not } C]P[R \mid \text{not } C]}$$

$$= \frac{(1/5)(2/3)}{(1/5)(2/3) + (4/5)(1/6)}$$

$$- \frac{2/15}{4/15} - \frac{1}{2}$$

Here, we see that the probability of tossing a crooked die must be revised upward from the prior value of 1/5, which applies when there is no information, to 1/2 after we know that the toss resulted in a six-face.

Posterior Probability as a Conditional Probability

Although it has a special interpretation, a posterior probability is merely a conditional probability when some relevant result is given, and it can be found in the same manner:

$$\begin{matrix} \text{Posterior} \\ \text{probability} \\ \text{of event} \end{matrix} = P[\text{event} \mid \text{result}] = \frac{P[\text{event } and \text{ result}]}{P[\text{result}]}$$

A straightforward procedure for calculating an event's posterior probability is first to find the joint probability that the event will occur with the given result and then divide by the probability of that result. This is exactly what expression (5-15) accomplishes. The numerator is the joint probability found by using the multiplication law. The denominator is the probability of obtaining the particular empirical result and is basically the sum of all those joint probabilities for potential outcomes where that result might occur. In practice, expression (5-15) can be cumbersome to use. The data may be given in such a way that the posterior probabilities can be found more directly.

For example, if a statistics class contains just as many men as women, then the prior probability that an examination paper chosen at random will belong to a man (M) would be 1/2. Now suppose that the exams have been graded and 20 percent of the papers received a mark of "C or better" (C) *and* were written by men; a total of 60 percent of the exams were scored "C or better." If a randomly selected test sheet was graded "C," we have sufficient information to calculate the posterior probability that it was written by a man:

$$P[M \mid C] = \frac{P[M \text{ and } C]}{P[C]} = \frac{.20}{.60} = \frac{1}{3}$$

Here, the information regarding the paper's grade causes us to revise downward the probability that it belongs to a man.

Typically, the probability values needed to make a simple calculation such as this are not immediately available. When we use evidence or empirical results to revise probabilities, our knowledge of the various events involved is usually structured so that some preliminary work is necessary to obtain the needed probability value. To accomplish this, it may help to construct a joint probability table first.

Obtaining Posterior Probabilities from the Joint Probability Table

Example 5-13 A noted lawyer specializing in defending corporate clients in personal injury suits thinks that getting a sympathetic jury is half the battle. In large measure, he can winnow a jury panel down to a largely sympathetic group by peremptory challenges. Since a potential juror's leaning in a particular case remains largely concealed during the selection interview, superficial characteristics must be relied upon in accepting or rejecting jury candidates. The lawyer has found that mature and stable persons, those who "made it on their own," are the most likely to be sympathetic to the defendant, while young people tend to have a "social worker attitude" that makes them likely to favor the plaintiff. From post-trial talks with jurors over the years, the lawyer has managed to identify their attitudes toward his clients. He has found that 65 percent of the sympathetic jurors have been older persons. A special bar study in his county has shown that only 30 percent of jury panel members are sympathetic to the defendant in a personal injury suit.

In a negligence suit resulting from an elevator accident, all but one juror has been chosen and both lawyers have no more challenges left. Of the available jurors, six are younger (Y) and four are older (O). Depending upon alphabetical sequence, one of these ten will be the last juror. Thus,

$$P[O] = .4 \quad \text{and} \quad P[Y] = .6$$

Table 5-6 is a joint probability table for characteristics of this last juror. The probability values obtained directly from the data provided above are shown in black. The colored numbers were obtained from these data by first noting that:

$$P[U] = 1 - P[S] = .70$$

The fact that we have been told the following conditional probability:

$$P[O \mid S] = .65$$

enables us to find the joint probability of obtaining an older, more sympathetic juror:

$$P[O \text{ and } S] = P[S]P[O \mid S] = .30(.65) = .195$$

TABLE 5-6 Joint Probability Table Used to Illustrate Posterior Probability Calculation

	Older (O)	Younger (Y)	
Sympathetic (S)	.195	.105	.300
Unsympathetic (U)	.205	.495	.700
	.400	.600	1.000

The remaining values follow from this one and from the fact that the joint probabilities must sum to the respective marginal values.

The prior probability that a sympathetic juror will be obtained is only .30 (which is also the marginal probability for this event). Suppose that an older juror is chosen. The posterior probability that he will also be sympathetic is

$$P[S|O] = \frac{P[O \text{ and } S]}{P[O]} = \frac{.195}{.40} = .488$$

The above example shows how we can calculate posterior probabilities by relying upon basic concepts, instead of using the complicated expression of Bayes' Theorem. Nevertheless, as Table 5-6 shows, essentially the same steps are required in either case.

OPTIONAL EXERCISES

5-49 A local television weather reporter makes a daily forecast indicating the probability that it will rain the next day. On one particular evening, she announces an 80 percent chance of rain (E). The manager of the city golf courses has established a policy that the greens will be watered only if the probability of rain is less than 90 percent. Using the local TV forecast as his prior probability, the manager also relies upon his father-in-law's rheumatism: Historically, the father-in-law gets a "rain pain" (R) on 90 percent of all days followed by rain, but he also gets a pain on 20 percent of the days not followed by rain. The following probabilities therefore apply:

$$P[E] = .80 \qquad P[R|E] = .90 \qquad P[R|\text{not } E] = .20$$

(a) Assuming that the golf course manager's father-in-law is currently receiving pain signals, find the posterior probability that it will rain tomorrow. Should the manager water the greens?

(b) If the manager's father-in-law feels just fine, what is the posterior probability of rain tomorrow?

5-50 A marketing researcher wishes to determine from a given response to a question whether a randomly chosen person will choose BriDent when next purchasing toothpaste. The question will reveal whether the selected person recalls the name BriDent, an event we will designate R. From previous testing, it has been established that 99 percent of those persons buying BriDent had previously recalled the name. It has also been found that only 10 percent of the nonbuyers of BriDent recalled this particular brand name. Since BriDent now has 30 percent of the toothpaste market, the researcher chooses .30 as the prior probability that the person will buy BriDent. Denoting this event by B, we have the following probabilities:

$$P[B] = .30 \qquad P[R|B] = .99 \qquad P[R|\text{not } B] = .10$$

(a) Suppose that the chosen person replies that he remembers BriDent. What is the posterior probability that he will make BriDent his next purchase?

(b) Suppose that he does not remember BriDent. Find the posterior probability that he will pick BriDent when next buying toothpaste.

5-51 An artist has finished a portrait. She believes that the client will have either a warm (W) or cold (C) response, with prior probabilities $P[W] = .90$ and

$P[C] = .10$. In the past, from trying her ideas out on her husband, who either likes (L) or dislikes (D) a piece of work, she has found $P[L\,|\,W] = .80$ and $P[D\,|\,C] = .90$.

(a) Calculate the missing values in the following table:

Prior Probabilities	Conditional Probabilities	Joint Probabilities	Posterior Probabilities
$P[W] = .90$	$P[L\,|\,W] = .80$	$P[L \text{ and } W] = .72$	$P[W\,|\,L] = ?$
$P[C] = .10$	$P[L\,|\,C] = ?$	$P[L \text{ and } C] = ?$	$P[C\,|\,L] = ?$
		$P[L] = ?$	
$P[W] = .90$	$P[D\,|\,W] = ?$	$P[W \text{ and } D] = ?$	$P[W\,|\,D] = ?$
$P[C] = .10$	$P[D\,|\,C] = .90$	$P[C \text{ and } D] = .09$	$P[C\,|\,D] = ?$
		$P[D] = ?$	

(b) What is the posterior probability that the client will respond warmly if the artist's husband likes her portrait?

5-52   An oil wildcatter has assigned a .50 probability to striking oil on his property. He orders a seismic survey that has proved only 80 percent reliable in the past: Given oil it predicts favorably 80 percent of the time; given no oil, it augurs unfavorable with a frequency of .8.

(a) Given a favorable seismic result, what is the probability of oil?

(b) Given an unfavorable seismic result, what is the probability of oil?

5-53   Your friend places two coins, identical in all respects except that one is two-headed, into a box. Without looking, you select one coin from the box and lay it on the table. A head side shows.

(a) What is the prior probability that the coin has two heads?

(b) What is the posterior probability that the coin has two heads?

5-54   A life insurance company gives an aptitude test to sales applicants in order to predict their success at selling. Like most aptitude tests, this one is imperfect. Some high scorers will be poor at selling, lacking the necessary motivation. A few low scorers will turn out to be excellent. Sacrificing justice for efficiency, the company has established a score of 80 as the minimum for hiring. This score was determined after a year of testing new hires, who were divided into two categories—satisfactory and unsatisfactory. The results of the test are summarized below:

	Proportion of Applicants Who		
Performance	Scored Below 80	Scored 80 or Above	Total
Satisfactory	.10	.40	.50
Unsatisfactory	.30	.20	.50
Total	.40	.60	1.00

Since the persons tested represent a typical cross section of applicants, the above figures have been judged acceptable as probabilities for future candidates.

(a) What is the prior probability that a candidate will be satisfactory?

(b) What is the posterior probability that a candidate will perform unsatisfactorily if hired after scoring 80 or above?

(c) What is the posterior probability that a candidate *would have been satisfactory* (if hired) after scoring below 80?

Chapter Six
Probability Distributions and Expected Value

The Curve described by a simple molecule of air or vapor is regulated in a manner just as certain as the planetary orbits; the only difference between them is that which comes from our ignorance.

Marquis de Laplace (1820)

We are now ready to apply probability concepts. Probability is a useful tool for evaluating decisions involving uncertainty. Another important application involves statistical inference, where generalizations are made from samples.

We will not use inferential statistics in this chapter. Rather we focus on *deductive statistics*, where we determine probabilities for getting particular sample results when the population values are known. For example, we will look at a population of Graduate Management Admissions Test scores and see the possible sample outcomes, which will be uncertain events. This approach may seem a bit odd, for it is the reverse of what we usually encounter; known test scores observed in a sample taken from a population having unknown characteristics. But by studying how random samples are generated and what to expect when working with *known* populations, we lay the essential groundwork for evaluating *unknown* populations.

The average test score—or sample mean—is an important value for establishing admissions policies. When its value is uncertain (the case *before* the sample is taken), it must be treated as a variable. Because the sample mean is determined by chance, it is referred to as a *random variable*. The values of a random variable will be treated as uncertain events occurring with a set of probabilities that we call a *probability distribution*. As we shall see, the applicable probabilities may be found from the population frequency distribution.

It is convenient to summarize the information in a probability distribution in terms of one or two key values. Like populations, probability distributions exhibit measures of central tendency and variability. Calculated in a similar manner, an "average" figure for a random variable may be obtained. Such a number is referred to as an *expected value*. The expected value concept may be used as a decision-making tool for comparing probability distributions. Its major role in sampling is that it enables us to analyze the kinds of results that might be obtained from a sampling study. For example, the height of a man randomly chosen from a population having a mean height of 5'10" would be expected to be 5'10". As we will see, the expected value principle can be beneficial in trying to estimate an unknown population mean solely from sample results.

6-1 DISCRETE PROBABILITY DISTRIBUTIONS

The Random Variable Concept

Let us consider a manager's decision problem of selecting among alternative projects for inclusion in next year's budget. One such project may be to expand the capacity of the plant by purchasing new equipment. Various measures, such as cost or profit, may be used to compare the attractiveness of this purchase with competing projects. One common gauge is the investment's *rate of return.**

The actual rate of return achieved will depend upon the particular levels and timing of cash receipts and expenditures attributable to the new equipment. Except for the initial outlay, all of these lie in the future and are therefore subject to uncertainties.

There are many possible rate-of-return outcomes from investing in the equipment. Each outcome consists of many groupings of potential cash flows, several of which may yield the same rate of return. A rate-of-return figure may be calculated for each, using the principles of compound interest. Since it may assume any one of a number of possible values, we may view the rate of return as a *variable*.

We refer to a variable whose value is determined by chance as a *random variable*. Thus, the rate of return to be achieved from the proposed equipment is a random variable. In general, we can make the following

---

* Rate of return is similar to compound interest on savings. A rate of return of 6 percent on an investment means that the same profit could be achieved by placing equivalent funds, depositing all proceeds, in a savings account paying 6 percent simple interest.

DEFINITION A *random variable* is a numerical quantity whose value is determined by the outcome of an uncertain situation.

Before the outcome is known, we must treat the quantity as a variable. The random variable assumes actual numerical value only *after* the uncertainty is resolved.

A situation may have many different kinds of random variables. In the foregoing example, we could have used net cost or net profit over the life of the equipment, instead of rate of return, as the random variable. The values would be calculated in a different manner but from the same data. The elementary events of the sample space would remain unchanged.

Example 6-1 Roulette, the internationally popular casino game, vividly illustrates the relationship between elementary events and random variables. The procedure is for the player to commit himself to a particular bet. A wheel having 38 slots is then spun and a ball is set in motion. The outcome is determined by the slot into which the ball drops. The sample space is therefore one of the 38 slots; 36 of these are numbered from 1 to 36 (half of these are red, the other black) and two green slots are numbered 0 and 00.

There are several ways of placing a roulette bet. For instance, a player may place a dollar on a particular number (say, 7). If the ball drops into the 7-slot, the player receives a $35 payoff;* otherwise he forfeits his bet. Another way to play is to bet on the red field or the black field. If the player bets a dollar on the red field and the ball drops into a red slot, the player receives a dollar; the bet is lost if a black or a green number appears. In either type of gamble, the sample space for the outcome of the spin of a roulette wheel comprises 38 equally likely elementary events.

The random variable of prime interest is the player's winnings. The random variable of the player betting on the 7 has two values: +$35 (if 7 comes up), and −$1 (if the ball drops into any of the other slots). The less venturesome red-player's random variable also has two values: +$1 (if the ball lands in a red slot), and −$1 (if the ball drops into a black or a green slot). For roulette play we have two distinctly different random variables, *depending upon the type of gamble made*.

Figure 6-1 shows how each of the random variables in Example 6-1 is defined in terms of the same sample space. The values of the respective random variables are determined on each play by which elementary event occurs. The arrows show how each elementary event is matched to a particular point on a numerical scale, depending on the choice of random variable. A mathematical interpretation of a random variable therefore is that it is a function that matches or maps the elementary events onto their corresponding points on a numerical scale.

A random variable must assume numerical values. For example, the outcomes of a coin toss—head and tail—are non-numerical. We can associate a random variable with coin tossing only by assigning numbers to these outcomes,

---

* Since there are 38 equally likely slots, the probability of getting 7 is 1/38. To be a fair gamble, the payoff should be 37 to 1, but the house does not pay on 0 or 00, giving it an edge and a built-in source of long-run profits.

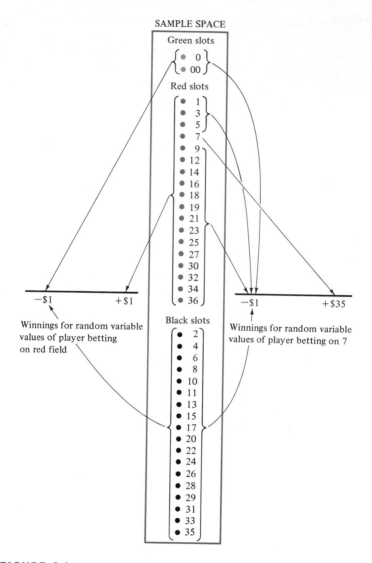

SAMPLE SPACE

Green slots

- 0
- 00

Red slots

- 1
- 3
- 5
- 7
- 9
- 12
- 14
- 16
- 18
- 19
- 21
- 23
- 25
- 27
- 30
- 32
- 34
- 36

−$1   +$1

Winnings for random variable
values of player betting
on red field

−$1   +$35

Winnings for random variable
values of player betting on 7

Black slots

- 2
- 4
- 6
- 8
- 10
- 11
- 13
- 15
- 17
- 20
- 22
- 24
- 26
- 28
- 29
- 31
- 33
- 35

FIGURE 6-1   Portrayal of two different random variables for two types
of roulette gambles.

as would be the case in a wager where a head results in winnings of $1 and tail
in a loss of $1. In this case, the winnings rather than the side showing would be
the random variable, with possible values of $1 and −$1. As we will see in
Section 6-2, an expected value for the random variable can be obtained by an
averaging procedure. Thus, we can determine an average level of winnings from
the coin toss. But there is no way to average the head and the tail, which are
non-numerical.

The Probability Distribution of a Random Variable

The notion of a random variable is fundamental to the application of probability concepts to decision making. It is also necessary to establish a body of statistical theory that can help us interpret sample evidence. In both cases, we need techniques for finding the probabilities for possible random variable values. The relation between a random variable's values and their probabilities is summarized by the *probability distribution.*

Each possible random variable value corresponds to a particular composite event in the underlying sample space. Thus, we may use the procedures introduced in Chapter 5 to obtain the probabilities for each possible value. For example, again consider the random variable of Example 6-1: winnings from a gamble at the roulette table. For the single-number bettor, winnings equal to $35 occur whenever the event "the ball drops into the slot of the number played" occurs. Likewise, winnings equal to −$1 (that is, losing $1) occur when the complementary event "some other slot receives the ball" occurs. There are 37 out of 38 equally likely possibilities that the second event will occur. Thus, the probabilities of our random variable values are equal to the probabilities of the corresponding events. In this instance, denoting the single-number player's winnings by W:

$$P[W = \$35] = 1/38$$

$$P[W = -\$1] = 37/38$$

The probability values assigned to each value correspond to events that are *mutually exclusive.* This is because we specify that each outcome corresponds to exactly one random variable value. In the case of roulette, each slot of the wheel corresponds to a win or to a loss, but not to both. The associated events are also *collectively exhaustive*, meaning that some value for the random variable will always be achieved. In roulette, this corresponds to the fact that the wager must be either lost or won.

Expressing the Probability Distribution

We are now ready to define the probability distribution.

DEFINITION   The *probability distribution* of a random variable X provides a probability for each possible value. These probabilities must sum to 1, and they are denoted by

$$P[X = x]$$

where x represents any one of the possible values that the random variable may assume.

It is advantageous to use a letter as a symbol to denote the random variable. (This is strictly a convenience, as it is in algebra, to keep expressions

TABLE 6-1   Probability Distribution of Rates of Return

Possible Rate of Return x	$P[X = x]$
10%	.05
11	.10
12	.15
13	.17
14	.12
15	.08
16	.09
17	.06
18	.05
19	.05
20	.04
21	.04
Total	1.00

uncluttered.) Symbols will make it easier for us to deal with random variables whose probability values can be determined by mathematical formulas.

Many probability distributions can be expressed in terms of a table like Table 6-1 for the rate of return to be achieved from operating a new piece of equipment. Here we represent the rate of return by the letter X (but any letter would suffice). Note that the probabilities sum to 1, because the events $X = 10$ percent, $X = 11$ percent, ... are mutually exclusive and collectively exhaustive.

Not all probability distributions will be expressed by a table. Sometimes they will be described by an algebraic formula. This is one reason why we use the lower case x to represent the possible values. As the following example demonstrates, there may simply be too many possibilities to conveniently list them all in a table.

Example 6-2 A raffle is to be conducted with 10,000 tickets, numbered consecutively from 1 to 10,000. One ticket is to be selected from a barrel after a thorough mixing. As each ticket is equally likely, the probability that a particular one will be selected is 1/10,000. We define a random variable for the raffle: the number of the selected ticket, to be denoted by Y. This enables us to shorten the statement "The number of the selected ticket will be 7,777" to read

$$Y = 7,777$$

Thus, we can express the probability of this event as

$$P[Y = 7,777] = \frac{1}{10,000}$$

As there are 10,000 outcomes, all having the same probability, we seek a better way to express the probability distribution than by means of a table. We may use a statement of the form

$$P[Y = y] = \frac{1}{10,000} \quad \text{for values of } y = 1, 2, \ldots, 10,000$$

which is equivalent to duplicating the previous probability expression 10,000 times, once for each ticket number. The lower case y is a "dummy" variable, representing one particular ticket number.

It is important to keep in mind that the capital letter Y represents the number of the ticket that *will be* selected and so has no determined value until the raffle is completed. The lower case letter y is a surrogate or stand-in for each ticket number and is a device to avoid 10,000 repetitive statements. We will find that this shorthand representation can be of great value.

Discrete and Continuous Random Variables

Special difficulties arise when random variables do not assume a discrete number of possible values.

Example 6-3   For use in large motors, precision 1 inch-diameter ball bearings must be machined to within a tolerance of .01 of an inch. Each ball bearing is assumed to be so nearly perfectly round that no measuring device commercially available is capable of perceiving otherwise. One million of these ball bearings are used annually.

Each ball bearing sold has been inspected at uniform temperature by measurement, using a pair of "go–no go" gauges (stands with holes through which a bearing being tested is dropped). The diameter of one hole is set for 1.01 inches; the other for .99 inch. Each ball bearing must be small enough to go through the hole in the large gauge, but not so small that it falls through the hole in the small gauge. All oversized and undersized bearings are set aside for salvage.

How many of the million bearings produced annually are precisely 1 inch in diameter? To determine this, a more accurate measuring system must be established. Suppose that a pair of gauges could determine if bearings were within a hundred-thousandth (.00001) of an inch of being exactly 1 inch in diameter. Only about 1,000 ball bearings would pass this test (assuming nearly equal frequency for all values between .99 and 1.01 inches). Those bearings passing this second stage of testing could be measured again, this time with special gauge blocks accurate to within a millionth of an inch. About 100 of these would pass the test. Additional tests using optical equipment could filter out the majority of these bearings, leaving a handful to be measured even more accurately in a fourth stage. But how many would pass the fourth test? Would greater precision of measurement eliminate all of the ball bearings?

We cannot be certain whether one or more of the ball bearings would be precisely 1 inch in diameter, as the standard inch is presently defined and within our capability to measure it. But we can conclude that such ball bearings would be extremely rare.

Consider the random selection of one of these ball bearings. As our random variable, we take the diameter of the ball bearing. We can conclude that the probability that this will be exactly 1 inch is so tiny as to be zero for all practical purposes.

The random variable illustrated in the foregoing example can assume any value on a continuous scale. Such a random variable is therefore given the

DEFINITION   A *continuous random variable* is one that may assume any numerical value on a continuous scale.

Since there are an infinite number of numerical values possible for a continuous random variable, the probability that a particular single value will be attained is zero.

In contrast to the continuous random variable, another class of random variables, called *discrete random variables*, may assume a finite or countable number of numerical values. Examples 6-1 and 6-2 involved discrete random variables.

The dichotomy of discrete versus continuous random variables is important in probability theory because of the type of mathematics required to describe the probability distributions of each. Much of the mathematics needed to handle continuous random variables requires calculus, so that the extensive development of many properties of these variables is beyond the scope of this book. However, continuous random variables share many properties with the discrete class, so that the more significant results attributable to both may be explored using discrete examples.

EXERCISES

6-1   Describe a circumstance that would create a random variable from each of the following:
(a) Tomorrow's weather.
(b) The sex of an unborn child.
(c) The winner of the World Series.

6-2   A gambling game involves a coin toss. The *price* to play is $1 (this is not returned). If the coin lands head-side up, the bettor receives a payment of $2. If a tail occurs, there is no payoff. Letting W represent the net winnings (payoff − cost) from one play of the gamble, determine the probability distribution of W.

6-3   From the following probability distributions for the receipts and expenses of a charity carnival, determine the probability distribution for the net proceeds (receipts − expenses). Levels for receipts are independent of expenditures.

Receipts	Probability	Expenses	Probability
$30,000	1/3	$30,000	1/3
40,000	1/3	40,000	1/3
50,000	1/3	50,000	1/3
	1		1

6-4   "Craps" is a favorite gambling game in which a pair of six-sided dice are tossed. Like roulette, there are many different ways to place a bet. One of these involves "playing the field," where the bettor indicates that he wishes to make a bet with a complicated payoff, depending on which faces of the dice show. If a "field" number, defined by a sum value of 2 through 4 or 9 through 12, occurs, the player wins. Should the roll of dice yield any other total, he loses. A field gamble is further complicated by varying payoffs: 1 to 1 for all field numbers but 2 or 12; 2 to 1 on a 2; and 3 to 1 on a 12. If a bettor wins, he keeps his original bet and is also paid his winnings. If he loses, he forfeits the amount of his wager.

(a) For a bet of $1, find the probability distribution of W, the gambler's net winnings from one field bet in craps. (You may wish to refer to your solution to Exercise 5-3 to obtain the probabilities for the possible dice sums.)

(b) Solve (a) for a bet of $2.

6-2 EXPECTED VALUE AND VARIANCE

Expected Value of a Random Variable

The probability distribution of a random variable is similar to the frequency distribution of a quantitative population because it tells us what the long-run frequency of occurrence will be for each possible outcome when the random situation is repeated. In Chapter 3 we saw that the population mean is a desirable summary, either for comparing populations or for making decisions about the population. Similarly, it is useful to find the average of the random variable values to be achieved from repeated circumstances. Because the outcomes are in the future, the average result is called an *expected value*.

An average, as we saw in Chapter 3, may be calculated in a number of different ways. The computation that we will use here for the expected value is analogous to the computation for finding the mean of grouped data.

> **DEFINITION** The **expected value** of a discrete random variable X, denoted by $E(X)$, is the weighted average of that variable's possible values, where the respective probabilities are used as weights. The expected value may be determined from
>
> $$E(X) = \sum xP[X = x] \qquad (6\text{-}1)$$

To illustrate how we may calculate the expected value for a random variable, let X represent the number of dots on the face showing after a six-sided die is tossed. The probability distribution of X is provided in the first two columns of Table 6-2. Multiplying each possible result by its corresponding

TABLE 6-2 Expected Value Calculation for Die Toss Outcome

(1) Possible Value x	(2) $P[X = x]$	(3) Weighted Value $(1) \times (2) = xP[X = x]$
1	1/6	1/6
2	1/6	2/6
3	1/6	3/6
4	1/6	4/6
5	1/6	5/6
6	1/6	6/6
	6/6 = 1	$E(X) = 21/6 = 3.5$

probability produces a weighted value. Summing these results gives the expected value $E(X) = 3.5$. On the average, the number of dots obtained for the showing faces in a large number of die tosses will be 3.5. Because it is the average value achieved by the random variable X, we sometimes refer to $E(X)$ as the *mean of X*.

Meaning of Expected Value

The expected value has many uses. In a gambling game, it tells us what our long-run average losses per play will be. Sophisticated gamblers know that slot machines pay poorly in relation to the actual odds and that the average loss per play will be less in roulette or dice games. A mathematician, Edward Thorp, caused quite a stir in the early 1960s when he demonstrated that various betting strategies in playing the card game of blackjack will result in positive expected winnings.*

The meaning of the expected value may be explicitly illustrated in terms of long-run frequency. Once again, consider the roulette gambler betting $1 on number 7. We may calculate his expected winnings $E(W)$ as follows:

Possible Winnings w	$P[W = w]$	$wP[W = w]$
+ $35	1/38	+ $35/38
− $1	37/38	− $37/38
		$E(W) = -\$2/38 = -\$.053$

The expected winnings from a single gamble is therefore a loss of 5.3 cents. This means that if the gambler keeps making $1 bets indefinitely, he will lose an average of 5.3 cents on each. Of course, on an individual gamble, he will either win $35 or lose $1. But—again, on the average—he will win $35 in only 1 out of 38 gambles, while he will lose $1 in 37 out of 38.

In both situations just illustrated the expected values of the random variables are not in themselves possible outcomes. Getting 3.5 dots in a single die toss is impossible, and the roulette player will always be dealing in whole dollars. The expected value is an *average result* and may or may not be equal to a possible outcome.

Some Properties of Expected Value

One variable may sometimes be converted into another by means of a mathematical expression, such as $d = \frac{1}{2}gt^2$ for the distance d an object falls by t seconds after its release, or $a = \pi r^2$ for the area of a circle of radius r. In these

---

* See Edward Thorp, *Beat the Dealer*, Second Edition (New York: Random House, 1966). Unlike other gambling games, blackjack allows bets to be placed when the odds are in a player's favor. This is because the card deck may not be reshuffled after each stage of play. By significantly raising his bets at these times, a player will make a profit on the average.

cases, we say that *d* is a *function* of *t* and *a* is a *function* of *r*, or, in symbols, $d = f(t)$ and $a = f(r)$. The function concept is a useful one, because, in working with random variables, it is sometimes necessary to compute the expected value of a function of the original variable.

Several important properties of expected values permit us to take computational shortcuts in evaluating functions of random variables.

1. The expected value of a constant c is equal to the constant:

$$E(c) = c$$

This can be justified immediately by a short example. Suppose a random variable has a single value *c*, as would be the case if *c* represents the age (to the nearest day) of a person randomly chosen from a group of people all born on the same date. No matter who is selected, *c* will be the age obtained. Hence, *c* is also the expected age.

2. The expected value of the product of a constant c and a random variable X is equal to the constant times the expected value of the random variable:

$$E(cX) = cE(X)$$

To see why this is so, consider a random variable *X* whose possible values are expressed in feet. Clearly, if the expected value in inches were desired instead, it could be obtained by multiplying the expected value in feet by 12 [that is, $c \times E(X)$, with $c - 12$], since 1 foot is equal to 12 inches. The result obtained would be the same as if the original measurements had been converted to inches and used to find the expected value. [This would be denoted by $E(cX)$, again with $c - 12$, for each value of *X* would have to be multiplied by 12 before averaging to obtain the expected value.]

3. The expected value of the sum of a constant c and a random variable X is the sum of the constant and the expected value of the random variable:

$$E(c+X) = c+E(X)$$

This property is also easily justified by a simple example. Suppose that bushels of fruit are weighed, one at a time, using the same basket. Then the average weight of bushel baskets of fruit will be the same as the average weight of the bushels without the basket plus the weight of the basket.

These three properties may be combined and summarized as

PROPERTY 6-1　Let *a* and *b* be constants that remain unchanged for all possible values of *X*. Then,

$$E(a+bX) = a+bE(X) \tag{6-2}$$

The Variance of a Random Variable

Just as the expected value of a random variable is analogous to the weighted mean, the variability of random variables may be measured in much the same way as the variability in a population or a sample. The measure we will consider is the variance. Like the mean, the variance of a random variable represents the same thing that it does for the population: the average of the squared deviations from the mean or expected value. The variance is itself an expected value of a function—the squared deviation—so that we make the following

> **DEFINITION**   The *variance* of a random variable X, denoted by $\sigma^2(X)$, is the expected value of the squared deviations from the expected value of the variable, and may be determined from the following expression:

$$\sigma^2(X) = E([X - E(X)]^2) = \sum [x - E(X)]^2 P[X = x] \qquad (6\text{-}3)$$

For computational ease, the following equivalent expression may be used to calculate the *variance of a random variable:*

$$\sigma^2(X) = \sum x^2 P[X = x] - E(X)^2 \qquad (6\text{-}4)$$

Example 6-4   A six-sided symmetrical die is rolled. We denote the number of dots on the showing face by the random variable X. The probability distribution of X is provided by the numbers in columns (1) and (2) of Table 6-3. Column (3) lists the values of x^2. Column (4) contains the weighted products of columns (2) and (3), their sum being

$$\sum x^2 P[X = x] = 15.167$$

The expected number of dots showing was previously found to be $E(X) = 3.5$. Thus, from expression (6-4):

$$\sigma^2(X) = 15.167 - (3.5)^2 = 2.917$$

TABLE 6-3   Calculation of Expected Value for Square of Dots on Die

(1) *Possible Values of X* x	(2) P[X = x]	(3) x²	(4) x²P[X = x]
1	1/6	1	1/6
2	1/6	4	4/6
3	1/6	9	9/6
4	1/6	16	16/6
5	1/6	25	25/6
6	1/6	36	36/6
	6/6 = 1		91/6 = 15.167

Two useful properties of the variance are important.

1. *The variance of the product of a constant and a random variable is equal to the constant squared times the variance of the random variable:*

$$\sigma^2(cX) = c^2\sigma^2(X)$$

To verify that this is true, consider X in units of feet. To express the random variable in inches, we multiply X by 12, to obtain the new random variable $12X$ (here, $c = 12$). As the units in which variance is expressed are the square of the units expressing the random variable [for example, if X is in feet, then $\sigma^2(X)$ is in square feet], then the units expressing $\sigma^2(cX)$ must be c^2 times those for $\sigma^2(X)$ itself. That is, as there are 12^2 square inches in a square foot, then $\sigma^2(12X) = 12^2\sigma^2(X)$.

2. *The variance of the sum of a random variable and a constant equals the variance of the random variable since the added constant has no effect on the variance.*

This may be justified by considering a random variable representing the measured heights of people. Suppose that these people are measured while standing on a block one-inch thick. Since the variance expresses dispersion in the heights, the thickness of the block should not matter.

These two properties together establish

PROPERTY 6-2   Let a and b be two constants. Then,

$$\sigma^2(a+bX) = b^2\sigma^2(X) \tag{6-5}$$

The *standard deviation* of a random variable X, which we will abbreviate here as $\sigma(X)$, will have the same meaning as that of the population. By taking the square root of the variance, we calculate the *standard deviation of a random variable:*

$$\sigma(X) = \sqrt{\sigma^2(X)} \tag{6-6}$$

Expected Value and Sampling

The sampling experiment of randomly selecting an elementary unit from a population is of special interest. Here, the random variable would be the observed value of the chosen unit. Because the long-run average result of repeated sampling experiments should be about the same as the mean of the population, the expected value of the sample observation should equal the mean of the population. A parallel result should hold for the variance, so that we can have the following

RELATION   The value of an elementary unit chosen randomly from a quantitative population is a random variable. Its expected value equals the population mean and its variance equals the population variance.

TABLE 6-4   Frequency Distribution of Number of Children in 1,000 Families in a Town

(1) Number of Children X	(2) Number of Families f	(3) fX	(4) X^2	(5) fX^2
0	63	0	0	0
1	185	185	1	185
2	223	446	4	892
3	207	621	9	1,863
4	153	612	16	2,448
5	87	435	25	2,175
6	53	318	36	1,908
7	21	147	49	1,029
8	5	40	64	320
9	1	9	81	81
10	2	20	100	200
Totals	1,000	2,833		11,101

Example 6-5   The number of children in the 1,000 families residing in a particular town has the frequency distribution presented in Table 6-4. Using the grouped approximation procedures discussed in Chapter 3, the mean number of children μ and the variance σ^2 may be calculated:

$$\mu = \frac{\sum fX}{N} = \frac{2,833}{1,000} = 2.833$$

$$\sigma^2 = \frac{\sum fX^2 - N\mu^2}{N} = \frac{11,101 - 1,000(2.833)^2}{1,000} = 3.075$$

(We use N rather than $n-1$ as the divisor because the data pertain to the entire *population*.)

TABLE 6-5   Probability Distribution for Number of Children in Randomly Selected Family

(1) Possible Number of Children x	(2) $P[X = x]$	(3) $xP[X = x]$	(4) x^2	(5) $x^2 P[X = x]$
0	.063	.000	0	.000
1	.185	.185	1	.185
2	.223	.446	4	.892
3	.207	.621	9	1.863
4	.153	.612	16	2.448
5	.087	.435	25	2.175
6	.053	.318	36	1.908
7	.021	.147	49	1.029
8	.005	.040	64	.320
9	.001	.009	81	.081
10	.002	.020	100	.200
Totals	1.000	2.833		11.101

$$E(X) = \sum xP[X = x] = 2.833$$
$$\sigma^2(X) = \sum x^2 P[X = x] - E(X)^2 = 11.101 - (2.833)^2 = 3.075$$

One family is to be chosen at random. The probability distribution for the selected family's number of children may be obtained from the population frequency distribution in Table 6-4. For example, to find the probability that $X = 2$, we divide the number of two-child families by 1,000: $P[X = 2] = 223/1,000 = .223$. The probability distribution is provided in Table 6-5, where $E(X)$ and $\sigma^2(X)$ are calculated. Note how similar these calculations are to those used earlier to find the population parameters. We use the probabilities in the same manner as class frequencies, and they have corresponding values. We find that $E(X) = 2.833$ and $\sigma^2(X) = 3.075$; these are the same values as the corresponding population parameters, so that $E(X) = \mu$ and $\sigma^2(X) = \sigma^2$.

EXERCISES

6-5 A coin is tossed three times. Let X represent the number of heads obtained. Then determine the probability distribution for X and calculate $E(X)$.

6-6 Determine the probability distribution of the winnings W of the roulette bettor in Example 6-1 when he places a $1 bet on the red field. Calculate $E(W)$. Describe the meaning of your answer.

6-7 The following is the probability distribution for the number of requests a medical laboratory receives daily for blood-typing tests. Find the expected daily number of blood-typing requests.

Number of Requests	Probability
0	.1
1	.2
2	.3
3	.2
4	.1
5	.1

6-8 A scientist studying sleep behavior is interested in the number of rapid-eye-movement (rem) phases achieved by her subjects during eight hours of sleep. The following probability distribution applies for any person not yet studied:

Number of rem Phases	Probability
0	.1
1	.2
2	.3
3	.3
4	.1

Find the expected value and variance for the number of rem phases.

6-9 A laboratory uses a particular breed of rabbit for experiments. In investigating the impact of diet upon litter size, the following probability distributions apply:

Standard Diet		Special Diet	
Litter Size	Probability	Litter Size	Probability
5	.1	5	0.0
6	.2	6	.1
7	.2	7	.2
8	.3	8	.3
9	.1	9	.3
10	.1	10	.1

(a) Find the expected litter sizes using each diet.
(b) Assuming the diet will be chosen that is expected to produce the greatest number of offspring per year, which diet will be used if the expected number of litters per year is 4 with the standard diet and 3.5 with the special diet? (*Hint:* Assume that the number of litters per year is unaffected by the sizes of the individual litters.)

6-10 An investor wishes to buy a stock to be held for one year in anticipation of capital gain. He has narrowed his choice down to High-Volatility Engineering and Stability Power. Both stocks currently sell for $100 per share and yield $5 dividends. The probability distributions for next year's price has been judgmentally assessed for each stock. These are given below, where S_1 = selling price of High-Volatility Engineering and S_2 = selling price of Stability Power

High-Volatility Engineering		Stability Power	
s	$P[S_1 = s]$	s	$P[S_2 = s]$
$ 25	.05	$ 95	.10
50	.07	100	.25
75	.10	105	.50
100	.05	110	.15
125	.10		1.00
150	.15		
175	.12		
200	.10		
225	.12		
250	.14		
	1.00		

(a) Determine the expected prices for a share of each stock.
(b) Should the investor select the stock with the highest expected value? Discuss.

6-3   THE BINOMIAL DISTRIBUTION

In Chapter 2, we saw that populations could be classified as members of basic family groupings, according to the nature of the frequency distribution. The same thing has been done with many random variables encountered in statistics. As the first case, we describe a widely used probability distribution that treats sample outcomes from qualitative populations. In Chapter 7, the normal distribution will be described. In subsequent chapters, additional probability distributions will be introduced in conjunction with various statistical applications.

Many statistical applications involve situations that have only two complementary non-numerical outcomes. Consider these three examples: (1) When deciding to place a magazine advertisement, an advertiser must ultimately consider whether or not the reader will be influenced enough to buy her product. (2) A politician retains a polling agency to find out whether or not he is preferred by a majority of the voters. (3) A medical research team wishes to determine if their new drug does or does not provide patients with some degree of relief. In each of these cases, the relevant answers to be sought are, respectively, the number of persons who will buy, the number of voters favoring the candidate, and how many patients will respond favorably to treatment. Because a great many persons may be involved in all of the foregoing situations, any evidence used to find the answers to questions such as these is usually provided by a sample.

A person selected for the sample will provide one of two opposite responses: purchase the product or not, prefer the candidate or not, or respond to treatment or not. In sampling from such qualitative populations, the only numerical result ordinarily of interest is how many times or in what proportion a particular attribute occurs.

The *number of* persons providing the desired response (such as the number of voters who prefer a candidate) is the key issue in each of our illustrations. Knowing the probability distribution of this random variable should facilitate deciding what course of action to take. For example, the medical researchers would be less apt to promote their drug if only a small number of the sample patients responded favorably to treatment, for the probability of such an outcome would be small if the drug were truly effective.

We may expect each situation to have a different probability distribution. There is no reason (except coincidence) why the probability that 50 voters will prefer the candidate should be the same as the probability that 50 patients will respond favorably to the drug. Yet, there are similarities between these two cases that prove advantageous in finding their respective probability distributions: They have characteristics in common that place them in the same family. Members of this family have a probability distribution referred to as a *binomial distribution*. The binomial distribution is epitomized by coin tossing and can be explained in terms of the following example.

Example 6-6   An evenly balanced coin is fairly tossed five times. This may be viewed as five-stages having the probability tree diagram shown in Figure 6-2, where the sample space is also listed. Our initial problem is to find the probability of obtaining exactly two heads. As each of the 32 outcomes is equally likely, the basic definition of probability allows us to find the answer in the following manner. Count the number of elementary events involving two heads and then divide this result by the total number of equally likely elementary events. The sample space contains 32 elementary events and Figure 6-2 shows that 10 of these are two-head outcomes. Thus, we can determine that

$$P[\text{exactly two heads}] = 10/32$$

As we saw in Chapter 5, it is impracticable to list all possible outcomes unless there are only a few of them. For instance, if 10 tosses were to be considered, then the analogous list would contain 1,024 (2^{10}) entries. For even longer toss sequences, it would be necessary to use the shortcuts and probability laws already developed to ease computation. Before discussing a procedure to simplify finding such probabilities, it will be helpful to relate coin tossing to a similar class of situations.

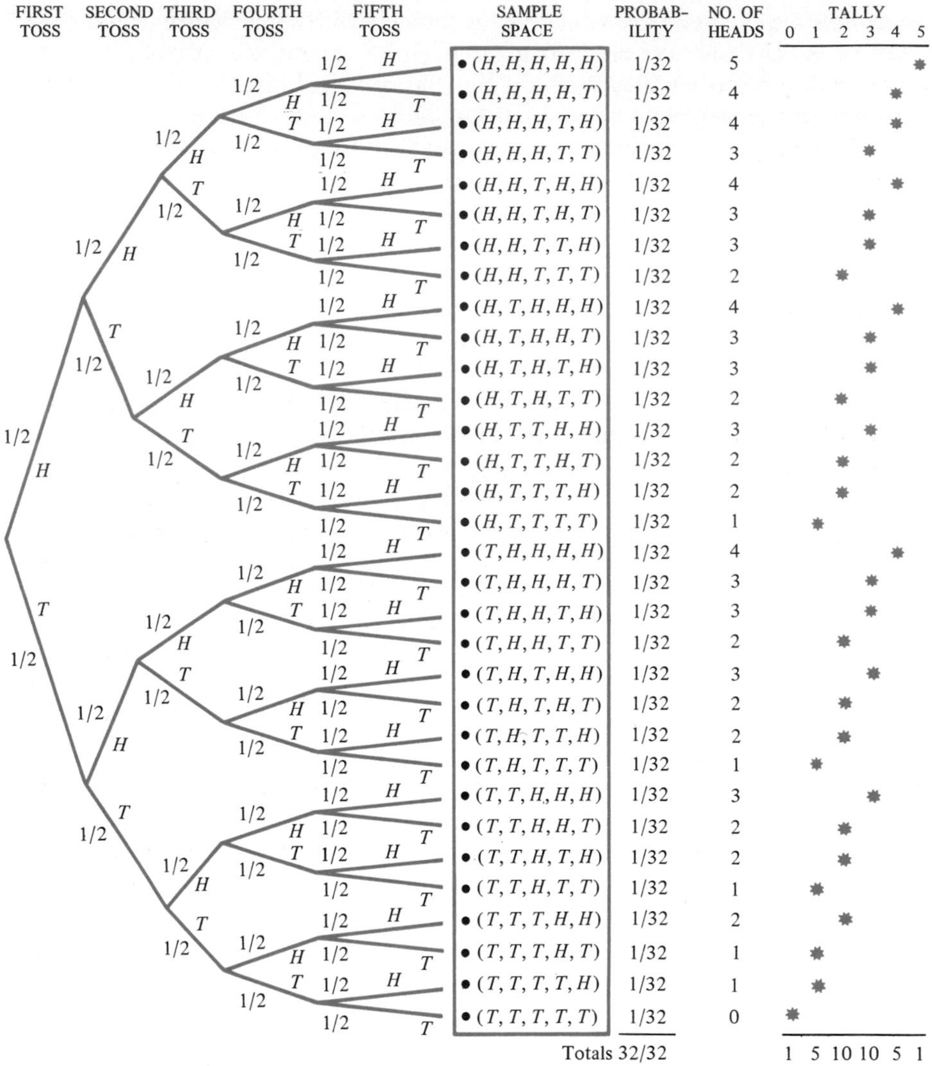
FIRST TOSS
SECOND TOSS
THIRD TOSS
FOURTH TOSS
FIFTH TOSS
SAMPLE SPACE
PROBAB-ILITY
NO. OF HEADS
TALLY 0 1 2 3 4 5
• (H, H, H, H, H) 1/32 5
• (H, H, H, H, T) 1/32 4
• (H, H, H, T, H) 1/32 4
• (H, H, H, T, T) 1/32 3
• (H, H, T, H, H) 1/32 4
• (H, H, T, H, T) 1/32 3
• (H, H, T, T, H) 1/32 3
• (H, H, T, T, T) 1/32 2
• (H, T, H, H, H) 1/32 4
• (H, T, H, H, T) 1/32 3
• (H, T, H, T, H) 1/32 3
• (H, T, H, T, T) 1/32 2
• (H, T, T, H, H) 1/32 3
• (H, T, T, H, T) 1/32 2
• (H, T, T, T, H) 1/32 2
• (H, T, T, T, T) 1/32 1
• (T, H, H, H, H) 1/32 4
• (T, H, H, H, T) 1/32 3
• (T, H, H, T, H) 1/32 3
• (T, H, H, T, T) 1/32 2
• (T, H, T, H, H) 1/32 3
• (T, H, T, H, T) 1/32 2
• (T, H, T, T, H) 1/32 2
• (T, H, T, T, T) 1/32 1
• (T, T, H, H, H) 1/32 3
• (T, T, H, H, T) 1/32 2
• (T, T, H, T, H) 1/32 2
• (T, T, H, T, T) 1/32 1
• (T, T, T, H, H) 1/32 2
• (T, T, T, H, T) 1/32 1
• (T, T, T, T, H) 1/32 1
• (T, T, T, T, T) 1/32 0
Totals 32/32
1 5 10 10 5 1

FIGURE 6-2 Probability tree diagram for five tosses of a fair coin.

The Bernoulli Process

A sequence of coin tosses is one example of a *Bernoulli process*.* A great many situations fall into the same category. All involve a series of situations (such as tosses of a coin), which are referred to as *trials*. With each trial, *there are only two possible complementary outcomes*, like head or tail. Usually one out-

* After Jacob Bernoulli (eighteenth century), who proved a version of the law of large numbers.

come is referred to as a *success* and the other as a *failure*. A success is the outcome of interest, and we seek probabilities for the number of successes that will occur. In the preceding illustration, getting a head would be a success. In some other context, a tail might be considered a success.

Other examples include: the single childbirths in a maternity hospital, where each birth is a trial resulting in a boy or girl; the canning of a vegetable, where each trial is a full can that is slightly overweight or underweight (cans of precisely the correct weight are so improbable that we may ignore them); and the keypunching of numerical data, where each card completed is a trial that will either contain errors or be correct. In all cases, only two opposite trial outcomes are considered.

What further distinguishes these situations as Bernoulli processes is that *the success probability remains constant* from trial to trial. Thus, the probability of getting a head is the same, regardless of which toss is considered—and this must be the case for delivering a boy for any successive birth in the maternity hospital, picking up an overweight can of vegetables, and getting a correctly punched card each time. (The last condition would not hold if a keypuncher tires over time, so that the probability could be larger that an earlier card would be correct than that a later card would be.)

A final characteristic of a Bernoulli process is that *successive trial outcomes must be independent events*. Like a fairly tossed coin, the probability of getting a success (head) must be independent of what occurred in previous trials (tosses). The births in a *single family* might violate this requirement if the parents use certain recent techniques to obtain a second child whose sex is the opposite of their first child. Or a keypuncher's errors may occur in batches, due to fatigue, so that once an error is made it is more likely to be followed by another.

The results of sampling to determine response to advertising, voter preference, or favorable response to drug treatment may all be classified as Bernoulli processes. In order not to violate the requirements of independence and constant probability of success, we must sample with replacement (see Chapter 5, p. 119). This type of sampling allows each person the same chance of being selected each time, and perhaps of being chosen more than once.* The probability of a trial success would in each case be the proportion of persons in the respective population who would provide the desired response.

The Binomial Formula

When the trial outcomes are the results of a Bernoulli process, the number of successes is a random variable having a binomial distribution. The following expression may then be used to find the probability values. It is referred to as

---

* When sampling without replacement, a different probability distribution, the *hypergeometric*, should be used. In practice, when the population is large, the conditions of a Bernoulli process are very nearly met and the binomial distribution is acceptable.

the *binomial formula:*

$$P[R=r] = \frac{n!}{r!(n-r)!}\, \pi^r(1-\pi)^{n-r} \tag{6-7}$$

where R = number of successes achieved

n = number of trials

π = trial success probability

$r = 0, 1, \ldots, n$

Expression (6-7) can be used to determine the probability found earlier for getting $R = 2$ heads in $n = 5$ tosses of a fair coin. In this case, $\pi = P[H] = 1/2$ and $1 - \pi = P[T] = 1/2$, so that

$$P[R=2] = \frac{5!}{2!(5-2)!}\left(\frac{1}{2}\right)^2\left(1-\frac{1}{2}\right)^{5-2} = \frac{5!}{2!\,3!}\left(\frac{1}{2}\right)^2\left(\frac{1}{2}\right)^3$$

$$= 10\left(\frac{1}{2}\right)^5 = \frac{10}{32}$$

The factorial terms in the above product provide the number of outcomes involving exactly 2 heads, which is equal to 10 and represents the number of combinations of 2 particular tosses that may result in heads out of a total of 5 tosses made. The product involving 1/2 represents the probability of getting any one of the 10 two-head sequences that are represented by the end positions of the probability tree diagram in Figure 6-2. Each of these positions is reached by traversing a particular path of 2 head and $5 - 2 = 3$ tail branches. The probability of doing this may be obtained by applying the multiplication law. Since a two-head result can happen in any one of 10 equally likely ways, the addition law of probability indicates that we add 10 of the identical product terms together, or, more simply, multiply by 10.

The entire binomial distribution that corresponds to the number of heads R resulting from $n = 5$ fair tosses of an evenly balanced coin is given in Table 6-6, where the probability values are found by applying the binomial formula for all possible r values. Note that the numerators in the final fractions equal the total number of elementary events found in Figure 6-2 for the indicated number of heads. Those totals represent the number of paths through the tree, and hence the number of combinations corresponding to the sequences involving exactly r heads.

Because the probabilities obtained depend upon the value of r used, the right-hand side of expression (6-7) is a mathematical function in r. Because it provides nonzero probabilities only at specific points between 0 and n, to use a physical analogy, it concentrates its "mass" on these. (Referring to Table 6-6,

TABLE 6-6 Binomial Distribution for the Number of Heads Obtained in Five Coin Tosses

Possible Number of Heads r	$P[R = r]$
0	$\dfrac{5!}{0!\,5!}\left(\dfrac{1}{2}\right)^0\left(\dfrac{1}{2}\right)^5 = \dfrac{1}{32} = .03125$
1	$\dfrac{5!}{1!\,4!}\left(\dfrac{1}{2}\right)^1\left(\dfrac{1}{2}\right)^4 = \dfrac{5}{32} = .15625$
2	$\dfrac{5!}{2!\,3!}\left(\dfrac{1}{2}\right)^2\left(\dfrac{1}{2}\right)^3 = \dfrac{10}{32} = .31250$
3	$\dfrac{5!}{3!\,2!}\left(\dfrac{1}{2}\right)^3\left(\dfrac{1}{2}\right)^2 = \dfrac{10}{32} = .31250$
4	$\dfrac{5!}{4!\,1!}\left(\dfrac{1}{2}\right)^4\left(\dfrac{1}{2}\right)^1 = \dfrac{5}{32} = .15625$
5	$\dfrac{5!}{5!\,0!}\left(\dfrac{1}{2}\right)^5\left(\dfrac{1}{2}\right)^0 = \dfrac{1}{32} = .03125$
	$\overline{1.00000}$

no "mass" is concentrated on any point between 1 and 2, for example, as the probability is zero for any such impossible value of r.) Thus, a function such as expression (6-7) is occasionally referred to as a *probability mass function*.

The designation of which attribute is the "success" is completely arbitrary, but care must be taken to ensure that the appropriate value of π is used. An interesting feature of the binomial formula is that it may also be used to obtain the probability that some number of failures will occur. For instance, the probability of obtaining exactly three tails in five tosses of the coin has the same value as the probability of obtaining two heads, because whenever there are two heads there must be three tails. In general, *when there are r successes, there must be* $n - r$ *failures*.

As we have already noted, different Bernoulli processes will have different probability values. But the number of successes from each process are random variables belonging to the binomial distribution family. Note that the probabilities for all possible values of R depend upon the value of π. Different sizes for n will result in a larger or smaller number of possible values for R and will also affect each probability value. *For purposes of calculating probabilities, one Bernoulli process differs from another only by the values of π and the sizes of n.*

Example 6-7 The administrator of a large airport is interested in the number of aircraft departure delays that are attributable to inadequate control facilities. A random sample of 10 aircraft takeoffs are to be thoroughly investigated. (In Chapter 8, we will discuss the criteria for deciding how large a sample ought to be taken.) If the true proportion of such delays in all departures is .40, what is the probability that 4 of the sample departures are delayed because of control inadequacies?

The sample investigations may be considered as trials in a Bernoulli process. Letting a control-caused delay be a success, the trial success probability is equal to the proportion of such outcomes, so that $\pi = .40$. To obtain the probability of $R = 4$ control-caused delays (successes) using the binomial formula [expression (6-7)] with $\pi = .40$, $n = 10$, and $r = 4$, we have

$$P[R = 4] = \frac{10!}{4!(10-4)!}(.4)^4(1-.4)^{10-4}$$

$$= 210(.4)^4(.6)^6$$

$$= 210(.0256)(.046656)$$

$$= .2508$$

The Proportion of Successes

Ordinarily, the number of successes is a less useful random variable than the *proportion of successes*. The proportion of control-caused aircraft delays would be more meaningful to the administrator in Example 6-7 than the number of delays. The administrator could use this proportion to determine the total number of delays that would be encountered for all prognosticated levels of traffic.

The ratio of the number of successes to the number of trials, denoted by P, is the *proportion of successes*:

$$P = \frac{R}{n}$$

The probabilities of various possible values for P may also be calculated from the binomial formula. From the equality above, we note that $R = nP$. Therefore, when $R = r$, $nP = r$ or $P = r/n$. This allows us to restate the binomial distribution as

$$P\left[P = \frac{r}{n}\right] = \frac{n!}{r!(n-r)!}\pi^r(1-\pi)^{n-r} \tag{6-8}$$

TABLE 6-7   Binomial Distribution for the Proportion of Aircraft Delays ($\pi = .4$)

r	$\dfrac{r}{n} = \dfrac{r}{10}$	$P\left[P = \dfrac{r}{n}\right]$
0	0.0	.0060
1	.1	.0404
2	.2	.1209
3	.3	.2150
4	.4	.2508
5	.5	.2007
6	.6	.1114
7	.7	.0425
8	.8	.0106
9	.9	.0016
10	1.0	.0001
		1.0000

(It is easy to confuse the P inside the brackets with the outside P, our symbol for probability. Remember, $P = r/n$ is an event pertaining to the value of the proportion, while $P[P = r/n]$ is the probability of that event.) The probability distribution of the proportion of control-caused aircraft delays is shown in Table 6-7. Each probability value is calculated from expression (6-8), using $n = 10$ and $\pi = .4$.

The Binomial Distribution Family

To illustrate the concept of a family of binomial distributions, we construct Table 6-8, showing the binomial probability distributions for different trial success probabilities π. Each entry is obtained from expression (6-8).

In each case, a sequence of $n = 5$ trials applies. The same possible outcomes exist, but as shown in Table 6-8, the probabilities for the values of P differ due to the different values of π. When $\pi = .9$, a higher proportion of successes is more likely than when $\pi = .1$. Figure 6-3 shows graphs of these binomial probability distributions, constructed for the values in Table 6-8.

When $\pi = .1$, the probability distribution is quite positively skewed, with the probabilities of small values of P being greatest. As π becomes larger, the skew becomes less pronounced. When $\pi = .5$, the distribution is symmetrical, so that the probability of a particular P value result is equal to the probability of $1 - P$. When π is larger than .5, the distributions become negatively skewed: Low values of P have the smaller probabilities and the intensity of the skew increases with π. Note that the probabilities for $\pi = .1$ are identical, but in *reverse* sequence, to those for $\pi = .9$. This will hold for every complementary pair of π values, such as .3 and .7 or .01 and .99.

The graphs in Figure 6-4 illustrate another interesting feature of the binomial distribution. Here, we fix π at .3 and vary n. Starting with $n = 5$, the number of trials is increased first to 20 and then to 100. With n trials, there are $n + 1$ possible values of P (corresponding to 0, 1, 2, ..., or n successes). For larger n values, we cannot show all of the possibilities as spikes on the graphs, for some of the probabilities are extremely tiny. (For example, when $\pi = .3$

TABLE 6-8   Binomial Probability Distributions When $n = 5$

$$P\left[P = \frac{r}{5}\right]$$

$\dfrac{r}{5}$	$\pi = .1$	$\pi = .3$	$\pi = .5$	$\pi = .7$	$\pi = .9$
.0	.59049	.16807	.03125	.00243	.00001
.2	.32805	.36015	.15625	.02835	.00045
.4	.07290	.30870	.31250	.13230	.00810
.6	.00810	.13230	.31250	.30870	.07290
.8	.00045	.02835	.15625	.36015	.32805
1.0	.00001	.00243	.03125	.16807	.59049

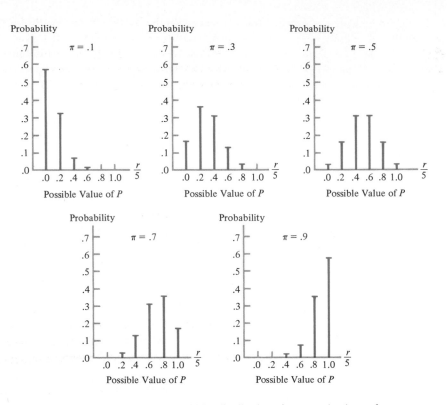

FIGURE 6-3   Binomial probability distributions for several values of π, with $n = 5$.

and $n = 20$, the probability of all successes, or $P[P = 1]$, is less than 40 trillionths.)

Note that the number of spikes increases with n and that the spikes become more closely bunched as n increases. A very significant feature is the tendency for the spikes to assume the "bell shape." In Chapter 7, we will make use of this property to approximate the binomial distribution by the normal distribution. This fundamental property holds for any value of π except 0 and 1 as n becomes large. If $\pi = 0$ or $\pi = 1$, there is only one possible value for P. When $\pi = 0$, no trial can be a success, so P must always equal zero regardless of the size of n. Likewise, when $\pi = 1$, all trials must be successes, so $P = 1$ always.

The Cumulative Probability Distribution

Just as it is sometimes convenient to deal with cumulative frequencies, which are readily determined from the population frequency distribution, we may use *cumulative probabilities* for random variables. These are very simply

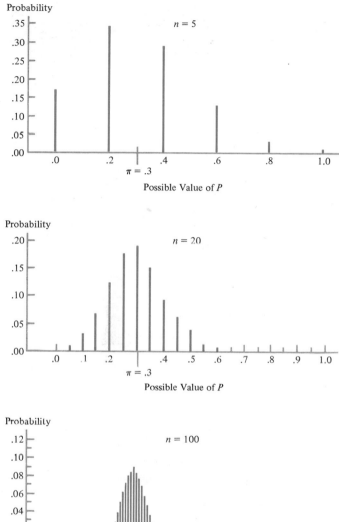

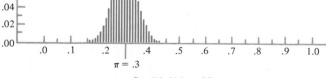

FIGURE 6-4   Binomial distributions for different levels of *n*, with $\pi = .3$.

TABLE 6-9   Cumulative Probability Distribution
             for the Proportion of Aircraft Delays ($\pi = .4$)

(1)	(2)	(3)	(4)
r	$\dfrac{r}{n} = \dfrac{r}{10}$	$P\left[P = \dfrac{r}{n}\right]$	$P\left[P \leqslant \dfrac{r}{n}\right]$
0	0.0	.0060	.0060
1	.1	.0404	.0464
2	.2	.1209	.1673
3	.3	.2150	.3823
4	.4	.2508	.6331
5	.5	.2007	.8338
6	.6	.1114	.9452
7	.7	.0425	.9877
8	.8	.0106	.9983
9	.9	.0016	.9999
10	1.0	.0001	1.0000
		1.0000	

obtained from the probability distribution in Table 6-7 by creating an additional
column (4) for $P[P \leqslant r/n]$, as shown in Table 6-9. The values in this column are
obtained by adding all the preceding entries in the values of $P[P = r/n]$. Thus,

$$P[P \leqslant 0] = P[P = 0] = .0060$$

and

$$P[P \leqslant .1] = P[P = 0] + P[P = .1]$$

$$= .0060 + .0404$$

$$= .0464$$

and

$$P[P \leqslant .2] = P[P = 0] + P[P = .1] + P[P = .2]$$

$$= .0060 + .0404 + .1209$$

$$= .1673$$

Table 6-9 is thus constructed cumulatively from the individual probability values,
so that the values in columns (2) and (4) constitute the *cumulative probability
distribution* of the random variable P.

The probability mass function for the proportion P is graphed in Figure
6-5. The cumulative probability distribution function for P is also shown. The
cumulative probability value corresponding to any particular proportion value
is obtained from the *highest point* on the "stairway" directly above. For instance,
the cumulative probability for values .5 or less is .8338, and not .6331, which
belongs to the lower "step." Note that the size of each step is the same as the
height of the respective spike of the mass function. Thus, the underlying probability distribution may be obtained from the cumulative probability distribu-

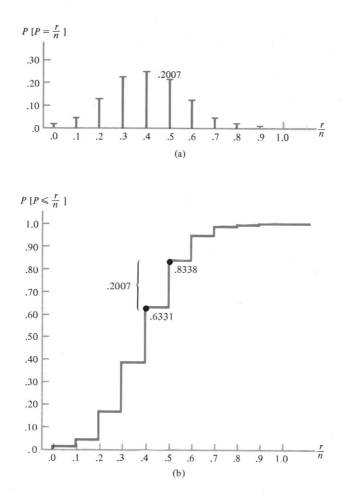

FIGURE 6-5   (a) Binomial probability mass function and (b) cumulative probability distribution function for the proportion of successes from a Bernoulli process with $n = 10$ and $\pi = .4$.

tion by finding these step sizes. For example, to find the probability that $P = .5$ we find the difference

$$P[P = .5] = P[P \leqslant .5] - P[P \leqslant .4]$$
$$= .8338 - .6331 = .2007$$

Using Binomial Probability Tables

Because calculating binomial probabilities involves working with large factorial values and with small numbers raised to large powers, it is convenient to have them computed once and for all. Appendix Table C provides cumulative binomial probability values computed for various sizes of n, with a separate tabulation for each of several π's. Although binomial probability tables may be obtained for individual terms as well, cumulative values are easier to apply in most cases.

It is possible to use this table to compute probabilities for the number or proportion of successes in the variety of situations described below. For purposes of illustration, assume that we are interested in finding probabilities regarding the proportion of $n = 100$ patients who will respond favorably (success) to treatment with a drug that has proved successful 30 percent of the time, so that $\pi = .30$. We will use the portion of Appendix Table C that begins on page A-12.

1. Obtaining a result less than or equal to a particular value. The probability that 40 percent or fewer patients will respond favorably is a cumulative probability value that may be read directly from the table when $r = 40$ successes:

$$P[P \leqslant .40] = P[P \leqslant 40/100] = .9875$$

2. Obtaining a result exactly equal to a single value. Recall that cumulative probabilities represent the sum of individual probability values and are portrayed graphically as a stairway (see Figure 6-5). A single value probability may be obtained by determining the size of the step between two neighboring cumulative probabilities by finding the difference:

$$P\left[P = \frac{r}{n}\right] = P\left[P \leqslant \frac{r}{n}\right] - P\left[P \leqslant \frac{r-1}{n}\right] \qquad (6\text{-}9)$$

For example, the probability that exactly $r = 32$ percent of the patients will respond favorably would be

$$P\left[P = \frac{32}{100}\right] = P\left[P \leqslant \frac{32}{100}\right] - P\left[P \leqslant \frac{31}{100}\right]$$

$$= .7107 - .6331$$

$$= .0776$$

3. Obtaining a result strictly less than some value. In this case, we need only observe that

$$P\left[P < \frac{r}{n}\right] = P\left[P \leqslant \frac{r-1}{n}\right] \qquad (6\text{-}10)$$

For example, the probability that fewer than $r = 30$ percent successes are achieved is the same as the probability that exactly $r - 1 = 29$ percent or less successes are obtained, or

$$P\left[P < \frac{30}{100}\right] = P\left[P \leqslant \frac{29}{100}\right] = .4623$$

4. Obtaining a result greater than or equal to some value. Here, we use the fact that

$$P\left[P \geqslant \frac{r}{n}\right] = 1 - P\left[P < \frac{r}{n}\right] = 1 - P\left[P \leqslant \frac{r-1}{n}\right] \tag{6-11}$$

In finding the probability that at least $r = 20$ percent of the patients will respond favorably, we look up the cumulative probability that $r-1 = 19$ or less will respond and subtract this value from 1, or

$$P\left[P \geqslant \frac{20}{100}\right] = 1 - P\left[P \leqslant \frac{19}{100}\right]$$
$$= 1 - .0089 = .9911$$

Note that the situation is similar when the result must be *strictly greater than* some value. In such a case, we find the cumulative probability for r itself and subtract this from 1. For example, the probability that more than $r = 20$ patients will respond to treatment is 1 minus its complementary probability that 20 or fewer patients respond, or

$$P\left[P > \frac{20}{100}\right] = 1 - P\left[P \leqslant \frac{20}{100}\right]$$
$$= 1 - .0165 = .9835$$

5. Obtaining a result that lies between two values. Suppose we want to find the probability that the proportion of successes will lie somewhere between .25 and .35, inclusively. That is, we want to determine

$$P\left[\frac{25}{100} \leqslant P \leqslant \frac{35}{100}\right]$$

In this case, we obtain the difference between two cumulative probabilities:

$$P\left[P \leqslant \frac{35}{100}\right] - P\left[P \leqslant \frac{24}{100}\right] = .8839 - .1136 = .7703$$

The first term on the left represents all outcomes with 35 or fewer successes, but we do not want to include those outcomes with successes numbering 24 and fewer. By subtracting the second cumulative probability from the first, we account only for those outcomes that are between 25 and 35 percent successful.

6. Finding probabilities when the trial success probability exceeds .5. For brevity, our binomial table stops at $\pi = .5$. Suppose we wish to find probabilities for the number or proportion of successes when the trial success probability is larger (say, .7). To do this, we can still use Appendix Table C by letting R represent the number of failures and π the trial failure probability.

Consider a keypuncher who correctly punches cards 99 percent of the time. Suppose we want to find the probability that at least 95 percent of $n = 100$ cards have been punched correctly. Here, a success represents a correct card and $\pi = .99$. We observe that at least 95 percent correct is the same as 5 percent or less incorrect (failures). For the moment, we use $\pi = 1 - .99 = .01$ as the trial failure probability, and using the portion of Table C on page A-21, we find

$$P\left[P \leqslant \frac{5}{100}\right] = .9995$$

This makes use of the fact that for every success event there is a corresponding failure event with the same probability.

Mean and Variance of Binomial Distribution

The expected value of P may be determined from probabilities obtained from the binomial formula for a particular n and π. Intuitively, however, we would expect the proportion of successes, on the average, to be the same as the trial success probability. For instance, the proportion of heads resulting from a sequence of coin tosses should be $1/2$, on the average, the same as the probability of obtaining a head from a single toss. We therefore have the *expected value of P:*

$$E(P) = \pi \tag{6-12}$$

The variance of P may be calculated from the probability distribution in the manner of expression (6-4), but such calculations can be quite tedious. The following expression, applicable to the binomial distribution, provides the same answer more directly for the *variance of P:*

$$\sigma^2(P) = \frac{\pi(1 - \pi)}{n} \tag{6-13}$$

The expressions just given for $E(P)$ and $\sigma^2(P)$ follow mathematically from the properties of the binomial distribution. Aside from their computational simplicity, an added advantage is that there is no need to compute the probabilities for the possible values of P first. Thus, knowing π and n allows us to quickly find $E(P)$ and $\sigma^2(P)$, making our later task of approximating the binomial distribution a simple one.

Note that since $\sigma^2(P)$ depends upon both the value of π and the number of trials n, if π is held fixed, $\sigma^2(P)$ will decrease as the number of trials increases

Example 6-8   An inspector removes cans of soup from production at randomly chosen times. The proportion of all cans overweight is .05. Thus, the probability that any particular can is overweight will be $\pi = .05$. Letting P represent the proportion of cans the inspector will find overweight, or $E(P) = \pi = .05$, and n represent the number of cans he selects, Table 6-10 shows the values obtained for $\sigma^2(P)$. Since $\sigma^2(P)$ measures dispersion in P, the greater the number of cans selected n, the closer, on the average, the proportion of overweight cans will be to the expected value $E(P)$.

TABLE 6-10 Variance of Proportion P of Overweight Cans Selected
When $\pi = .05$

Number of Cans n	$\sigma^2(P) = \dfrac{.05(.95)}{n}$
2	.02375
5	.0095
10	.00475
100	.000475

Suppose that $n = 10$ cans are selected from production runs of different canned food products and that each run has a different probability π for getting an overweight can. $\sigma^2(P)$ will differ with the type of food, as shown in Table 6-11. Note that $\sigma^2(P)$ is largest when $\pi = .5$. This will always be true, regardless of the size of n.

TABLE 6-11 Variance of P When $n = 10$

Probability of Overweight Can π	$\sigma^2(P) = \dfrac{\pi(1-\pi)}{10}$
.05	.00475
.25	.01875
.50	.025
.75	.01875
.95	.00475

By taking the square root of the variance, we may use the following to calculate the *standard deviation of P:*

$$\sigma(P) = \sqrt{\frac{\pi(1-\pi)}{n}} \tag{6-14}$$

As we will see in Chapter 7, the standard deviation of P is used in many statistical applications.

Now recall that the binomial distribution can be applied to either the proportion of successes P or to the number of successes R. The expected value and variance of R will not be the same as they are for P, but since $R = nP$, the properties of expected value and variance may be used to find $E(R)$ and $\sigma^2(R)$ directly from the shortcut expressions (6-12) and (6-13).

The expected value of R is determined by applying Property 6-1 (page 155), with $a = 0$ and $b = n$, so that $E(nP) = nE(P)$. Thus,

$$E(R) = E(nP) = n\pi \tag{6-15}$$

The variance of R is similarly obtained from Property 6-2 (page 157),

$$\sigma^2(R) = \sigma^2(nP) = n^2\sigma^2(P) = n^2\left(\frac{\pi(1-\pi)}{n}\right)$$

Canceling n terms simplifies the above to

$$\sigma^2(R) = n\pi(1-\pi) \tag{6-16}$$

The standard deviation of R follows directly:

$$\sigma(R) = \sqrt{n\pi(1-\pi)} \tag{6-17}$$

EXERCISES

6-11 Can each of the following situations be classified as a Bernoulli process? If not, state why.
(a) Childbirths in a hospital, the relevant events being the sex of each newborn child.
(b) The outcomes of successive rolls of a die, considering only the events odd or even.
(c) A crooked gambler has rigged his roulette wheel so that whenever the player loses, a mechanism is released that gives the player better odds; likewise, when a player wins, his chance of winning on the next spin is somewhat smaller than before. Consider the outcomes of successive spins.
(d) The measuring mechanism that determines how much dye to squirt into paint being mixed to customer order occasionally violates the required tolerances. The mechanism is very reliable when it is new, but with use it continually wears, becoming less accurate with time. Consider the outcomes (within or not within tolerance) for successive mixings.
(e) A machine produces items that are sometimes too heavy or too wide to be used. The events of interest express the quality of each successive item in terms of both weight and width.

6-12 An evenly balanced coin is fairly tossed seven times.
(a) Determine the probabilities of obtaining: (1) exactly two heads; (2) exactly four heads; (3) no tails; (4) exactly three tails.
(b) What do you notice about your answers to (2) and (4)? Why is this so?

6-13 n parts are randomly chosen from a production process that yields 5 percent defectives.

(a) What is the expected proportion of defectives?

(b) How many defectives are expected when $n = 5$? When $n = 10$? When $n = 100$?

6-14 A political polling agency has contacted a random sample of $n = 50$ persons. The actual proportion of all persons favoring a new law is $\pi = .30$. Assuming that the binomial distribution applies, use Appendix Table C to find the probabilities for the following outcomes relating to the number of favorable responses R:

(a) $R \leqslant 11$ 0.1390 (b) $R = 15$ $.1224$ (c) $R < 18$

(d) $R \geqslant 20$ 0.0478 (e) $R > 25$ (f) $17 \leqslant R \leqslant 23$.

6-15 A fair coin is tossed 20 times in succession. Using Appendix Table C, determine the probability that the proportion of heads obtained is:

(a) Less than or equal to .4.   (d) Greater than or equal to .6.

(b) Equal to .5.   (e) Greater than .65.

(c) Less than .75.   (f) Between .4 and .7, inclusively.

6-16 Using the probability distribution for P provided in Table 6-8 with $\pi = .1$, calculate $E(P)$. Use the definition of expected value, expression (6-1), with r/n in place of x and P in place of X. Your answer should equal π, which here is .1.

6-17 From the probability values in Table 6-8, construct the cumulative probability distribution of P when $n = 5$ and $\pi = .7$.

6-18 A form of malnutrition occurs in 10 percent of all persons. Determine the probabilities of the following malnutrition outcomes for five randomly chosen persons.

(a) All have it.

(b) None have it.

(c) At least one has it.

(d) At least 40 percent have it.

(e) Between 40 and 80 percent, inclusively, have it.

6-19 The chief engineer in a chemical plant has established a testing procedure using five sample vials drawn from the final stage of a chemical process at random times over a 4-hour period. If one or more vials (20 percent or more) have impurities, all the settling tanks are cleaned. Find the probability that the tanks must be cleaned when the process is so clean that the probability of a dirty vial is:

(a) $\pi = .01$ (b) $\pi = .05$ (c) $\pi = .20$ (d) $\pi = .50$

(*Hint:* Use the fact that $P[\text{at least one dirty vial}] = 1 - P[\text{no dirty vials}]$.)

6-20 A production process produces defective parts at the rate of .05. If a random sample of five items are chosen, what is the probability that at least 80 percent of the sample will be defective?

6-21 A lot of 100 items in which 5 percent are defective is sampled *without replacement*. Five items are chosen.

(a) Does the binomial distribution apply here? Explain your answer.

(b) What is the probability that not one of the five sample items is defective?

6-22 A lopsided coin provides a 60 percent chance of a head on each toss. If the coin is tossed 18 times, find the probability that the number of heads obtained is:

(a) Less than or equal to 8.

(b) Equal to 9.

(c) Less than 15.

(d) Greater than or equal to 12.

(e) Greater than 13.

(f) Between 8 and 14, inclusively.

6-4 CONTINUOUS PROBABILITY DISTRIBUTIONS

To begin our discussion of continuous probability distributions, let us consider an uncertain situation involving the selection of a sample from a population.

The frequency distribution obtained from grouping the years of company service of each of the 22,000 employees of the Wheeling Wire Works is given in Figure 6-6. The height of each bar of this histogram represents the relative frequency for durations of employment in the interval covered by the bar. The random variable of interest, which we will denote by the letter X, is the length of service of one person chosen randomly from the population. The time an employee has spent working for the company may be measured on a continuous scale, so that this time may be expressed to any desired fraction of the year. This makes X in our example a *continuous random variable*.

The probability that X lies within a particular class interval will be the same as the relative frequency of persons employed that long.

Recall that the bars of the histogram for a relative frequency distribution have areas proportional to the relative frequency of the variate values in the corresponding interval. Since the relative frequencies must sum to 1, we may consider the total area under the histogram as being equal to 1. There, each class interval is one 5-year unit wide. Thus, the probability that X lies inside a

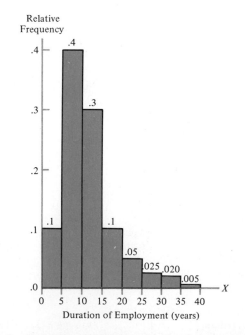

FIGURE 6-6   Frequency distribution of years of employment.

particular class interval equals the area of the bar covering that interval. Therefore, the probability that our employee served between 10 and 15 years must be
.3—the area under the bar or rectangle of the histogram that covers these values,
or width × height = 1 × .3 = .3.

But what if we want to consider an event that is more specific? For
example, we may wish to find the probability that our selected person was
employed between 10.95 and 11.05 years—a range of values lying wholly
within a single class interval. In this case, the frequency distribution does not
provide sufficiently detailed information for us to find the probability directly.

Smoothed Curve Approximation

Our problems arise from the fact that the histogram artificially forces us to
treat population variates in discrete lumps. Each value is arbitrarily placed into
one of a very few class intervals. To accurately consider intervals of any width,
we may construct a smoothed, continuous approximation to the histogram
like the one in Figure 6-7, where the curve is superimposed on the histogram

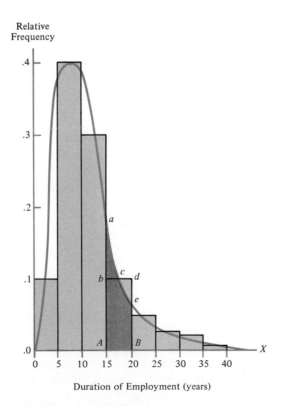

FIGURE 6-7   Frequency distribution from Figure 6-6 approximated
by a continuous curve.

from Figure 6-6. This may then be used to generate any probability values desired.

If the smoothed curve is drawn properly, the area under portions of the curve will correspond closely to the area of the histogram bars for that part of the horizontal axis, and the total area under the curve can also be taken as unity. Thus, in Figure 6-7, the shaded area under the portion of the curve covering the points between *A* and *B* is nearly the same as the corresponding area under the bar covering the values from *A* to *B*. Here, the curve has been drawn so that the wedge-shaped area described by the points *a*, *b*, *c* is nearly the same as the area described by *c*, *d*, *e*. The sum of the areas for portions that are cut off the histogram by the curve should equal the sum of those areas the curve adds by smoothing the corners.

The relative frequency of the population values lying between *A* and *B* in Figure 6-7 may be approximated by the area under the portion of the curve covering these values. We may therefore conclude that *the probability that a continuous random variable assumes some value in an interval is represented by the area under the portion of the continuous curve covering the interval.*

Probability Density Function

As we saw in Chapter 2, population frequency distribution graphs can be categorized according to their general shapes. We can construct smoothed curve approximations for any of these distributions. The process of selecting the curve is in essence one of choosing the appropriate shape. Fortunately, a great deal is known about curves having shapes that fit the more common types of frequency distributions.

Curves of a particular shape can be defined by an equation or function. Thus, we can place population frequency distributions into various groups, according to which mathematical function yields a curve of the shape that best matches that of the population histogram. If we know the function defining the curve, then it is possible to mathematically compute the area over an interval to obtain the required probability.

A unique set of probabilities is obtained from a particular curve. Consider, for example, the two curves in Figure 6-8 for two random variables, *X* and *Y*, whose values range over the same scale. The areas covering the values between points *A* and *B* are different for the two curves because the curve shapes are different. Thus,

$$P[A \leqslant X \leqslant B] \neq P[A \leqslant Y \leqslant B]$$

so that *X* and *Y* have different probability distributions. Note that the thickness or density of the two curves is distributed differently. For this reason, the mathematical expression describing such a curve is sometimes called a *probability density function*. In general, we denote this function by $f(x)$, where the

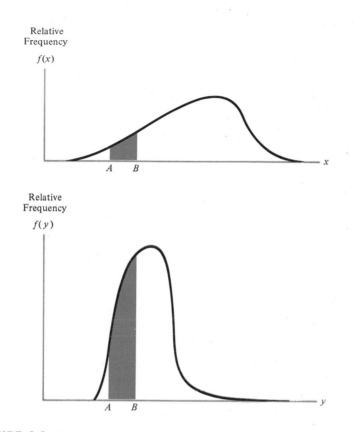

FIGURE 6-8 Two probability density function curves.

lower case x represents the possible values of the random variable X. (Since density is measured on the same scale, we will continue to use "relative frequency" to designate the vertical axis.) The probability density function therefore describes the probability distribution of a continuous random variable, so that a random variable may be categorized by the form of its function. The probability density function is the continuous counterpart to the discrete random variable's probability mass function. But the latter expresses a probability directly, while *it is the area under the density function that yields probability values.*

There is zero area under the portion of the curve that covers a single point. since there is no width. This reflects the fact that for a continuous random variable X, $P[X = x] = 0$, which was established in Example 6-3 (page 151).

Cumulative Probability Distribution

In Section 6-3, we defined the cumulative distribution for the discrete random variable. Analogously, we can make the following

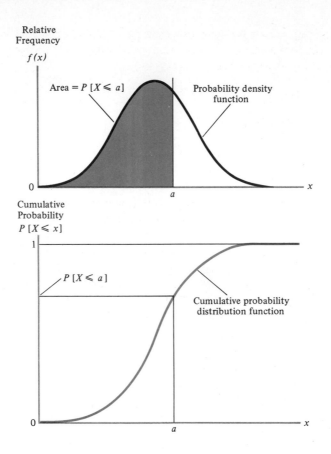

FIGURE 6-9   Graphical expressions of the probability distribution of a continuous random variable.

DEFINITION   The *cumulative probability distribution* of a continuous random variable X is the set of all values expressing $P[X \leq x]$, where x is a particular number. For a given x, the cumulative probability is the total area under the density function covering points to the left of x.

The cumulative probability distribution means precisely the same thing for discrete and continuous random variables. In the former, the cumulative probability graph resembles a stairway (see Figure 6-5) instead of a smoothed curve. In either case, it may be expressed algebraically, as a graph, or as a table of values. The graphical expressions of the probability distribution of a continuous random variable are presented in Figure 6-9.

A property of the cumulative probability distribution of a continuous random variable is that

$$P[X \leq x] = P[X < x]$$

because $P[X = x] = 0$, as we have already seen. (This is also true in the case of the discrete random variable, except when x lies directly beneath a stepping point on the cumulative probability stairway.)

The Expected Value and Variance

As with discrete random variables, we may view the expected value of a continuous random variable as the long-run average result from many repetitions. The variance is also analogous. Both may be calculated from the probability density function, but to do so requires mathematics beyond the scope of this book. For the common distributions we will encounter, the values have already been determined.

Many random variables may have the same basic density function and differ only by the values of the parameters specifying the particular function. They are then said to belong to the same *distribution family*. In Chapter 7, we will discuss one of these families—the normal distribution. Other continuous probability distributions will be introduced in later chapters.

6-5 THE SAMPLING DISTRIBUTION

We are now ready to set the stage for a smooth transition from probability theory to statistical planning and analysis. To do this, we will concern ourselves largely with deductive statistics. Thus, for the time being, it will be assumed that many details regarding the population under investigation are known, and we will study the kinds of *possible* results that may be obtained for samples taken from these populations. It is important to emphasize that the deductive viewpoint is not usually encountered in a real sampling situation. In actual applications, the sample results are known and the population details are unknown. After all, the reason we take a sample is to draw conclusions about a population. The purpose served by reversing our vantage point is that, knowing how sample results are generated and knowing what values are likely to occur, we are better able to answer the more difficult inductive questions encountered in generalizing about an unknown population from a known sample.

One important type of inference to be made from a sample is the estimation of a population parameter such as the mean μ or proportion π. Usually, we would employ the corresponding sample statistics $\overline{X}$ and P in making the estimate.

In the planning stage of a sampling study, before the data are collected, we can speak of $\overline{X}$ and P only in terms of probability. Their values are yet to be determined and will depend upon which particular elementary units happen to be randomly selected from the population. Thus, before the sample results are obtained, $\overline{X}$ and P are random variables. To determine the amount of chance sampling error and to qualify the accuracy of the resulting estimate, we must determine the probability distribution of the statistic used.

We emphasize that at one stage $\overline{X}$ and P are viewed as random variables and at a later phase as statistics whose value can be calculated from observed data. The probability distributions for $\overline{X}$ and P are of key importance. They are called *sampling distributions*, a special term distinguishing probabilities regarding $\overline{X}$ and P from those for other random variables not connected with sampling situations. The sampling distribution of $\overline{X}$ or P is determined in the same way as the probability distribution for any other random variable.

Sampling Distribution of Sample Mean and Proportion

To illustrate how we might find sampling distributions for $\overline{X}$ and P, consider the population of Graduate Management Admission Test (GMAT) scores achieved by four hypothetical Slippery Rock University seniors who have applied to Harvard that is given in Table 6-12. To stretch our point a bit, suppose that the Harvard Business School will admit exactly two applicants from Slippery Rock and that on the basis of total credentials all four of these candidates are viewed equally well. The admissions committee will therefore draw straws, so that the scores of the lucky two will be a random sample from the population of four.

TABLE 6-12   Hypothetical Population of GMAT Scores

Name	GMAT Score
Chen	600
Jones	500
O'Hara	700
Sandor	600

$$\mu = \frac{600+500+700+600}{4} = 600$$

$$\sigma = \sqrt{\frac{(600-600)^2+(500-600)^2+(700-600)^2+(600-600)^2}{4}}$$

$$= \sqrt{5,000} = 70.71$$

Table 6-13 shows the six sample results that are possible and the corresponding values of the sample mean and the proportion of GMAT scores greater than 600. From this information, we can determine the probabilities that the chosen sample will yield possible values for each statistic by finding the number of ways that each value can possibly occur. For example, there are two potential samples where the mean GMAT score is 600, so the probability of this result is $2/6 = 1/3$. The sampling distributions for $\overline{X}$ and P are shown in Table 6-14.

TABLE 6-13   Possible Sample Results for Randomly Selecting Two GMAT Scores Without Replacement

Applicants Selected	GMAT Scores	Sample Mean ($\bar{x}$)	Sample Proportion (p)
Chen, Jones	600, 500	550	0
Chen, O'Hara	600, 700	650	1/2
Chen, Sandor	600, 600	600	0
Jones, O'Hara	500, 700	600	1/2
Jones, Sandor	500, 600	550	0
O'Hara, Sandor	700, 600	650	1/2

TABLE 6-14   Sampling Distribution of $\bar{X}$ and P for GMAT Scores Selected Without Replacement

$\bar{x}$	$P[\bar{X} = \bar{x}]$	$\bar{x}P[\bar{X} = \bar{x}]$	p	$P[P = p]$	$pP[P = p]$
550	1/3	550/3	0	1/2	0
600	1/3	600/3	1/2	1/2	1/4
650	1/3	650/3		1	$E(P) = 1/4$
	1	$E(\bar{X}) = 600$			

Using the procedures outlined earlier in this chapter, we can calculate the expected value, variance, and standard deviation of $\bar{X}$ and P. As the remainder of this chapter will show, these values can be found directly from the population parameters μ, σ, and π when these parameters are known.

The basic concepts underlying the sampling distribution of $\bar{X}$ are shown in Figure 6-10. This distribution may be viewed as roughly analogous to the results that would be obtained if many different samples were taken and the sample mean $\bar{X}$ were calculated each time.

Expected Value of the Sample Mean

The mean of the population of the four GMAT scores in our present illustration is $\mu = 600$, while the population proportion of scores greater than 600 is $\pi = 1/4$. Unlike this example, the full set of data needed to calculate population parameters is ordinarily unavailable, so the values of μ and π are normally estimated from the partial sample results instead. Usually the sample mean $\bar{X}$ and the sample proportion P are calculated and used for this purpose. We will consider how well these estimates perform in Chapter 8. In laying the necessary groundwork, we will now examine two properties of the sampling distribution: its mean, or expected value, and its standard deviation.

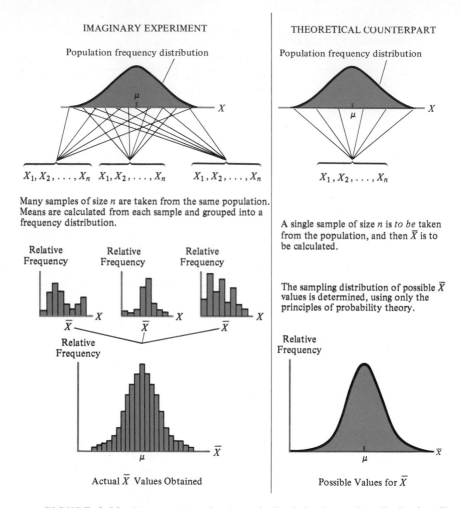

IMAGINARY EXPERIMENT

Population frequency distribution

THEORETICAL COUNTERPART

Population frequency distribution

Many samples of size n are taken from the same population. Means are calculated from each sample and grouped into a frequency distribution.

A single sample of size n is *to be* taken from the population, and then $\overline{X}$ is to be calculated.

The sampling distribution of possible $\overline{X}$ values is determined, using only the principles of probability theory.

Actual $\overline{X}$ Values Obtained

Possible Values for $\overline{X}$

FIGURE 6-10   Interpretation of a theoretically derived sampling distribution. The procedure outlined at the left is never necessary but shows the concepts underlying the theory. The histogram at bottom left is an experimental representation of the sampling distribution at bottom right.

The expected value of $\overline{X}$ is calculated in Table 6-14. Note that $E(\overline{X}) = 600$, which is equal to the population mean μ. In general, this will be true for any random sampling situation, so we have the following relation for the *expected value of* $\overline{X}$:

$$E(\overline{X}) = \mu \tag{6-18}$$

This conclusion is quite plausible. In effect, expression (6-18) says that the long-run average value of sample means is the same as the mean of the population from which the sample observations are taken.

The rationale for this is simple. If $\overline{X}$ is calculated over and over again from different samples taken from the same population, then the successive sample means will tend to cluster about the mean of the population. If a sample of 100 men is taken from a population where the mean height is $\mu = 5'10''$, then the sample mean $\overline{X}$ is expected to be $5'10''$ as well. This does not imply that $\overline{X}$ cannot turn out to be $5'9\frac{1}{2}''$ or $5'10\frac{1}{2}''$, but *on the average* $\overline{X}$ will equal $5'10''$.

The above relationship can be formally justified by looking at the individual sample observations themselves as random variables, each with its own probability distribution. Successive observations may be represented symbolically by X_1 for the first, X_2 for the second, and so forth. The sample mean is the sum of these observations divided by the sample size n. Multiplying the sample mean by the sample size, we obtain:

$$n\overline{X} = X_1 + X_2 + \cdots + X_n \qquad (6\text{-}19)$$

The expected value of $n\overline{X}$ is therefore the same as the expected value of the sum of the individual random variables. It can be shown that the expected value of the sum will always be equal to the sum of the individual expected values:

$$E(n\overline{X}) = E(X_1 + X_2 + \cdots + X_n) = E(X_1) + E(X_2) + \cdots + E(X_n) \quad (6\text{-}20)$$

Since any single sample observation has an expected value equal to the population mean, the right-hand side of expression (6-20) is equal to $n\mu$. Therefore $E(\overline{X}) = \mu$, since $E(n\overline{X}) = nE(\overline{X})$ and the n's cancel.

Standard Deviation of Sample Mean

The standard deviation of the sample mean may be found in a similar manner. In determining it, however, we again encounter the distinction mentioned in Chapter 5 (page 119) between sampling with and without replacement: *Sample outcomes are statistically independent when sampling with replacement and statistically dependent when sampling without replacement.* As we will see, whether or not sample outcomes are independent will affect the value of the standard deviation for $\overline{X}$.

Table 6-15 shows the possible sample results for randomly selecting two of the four Slippery Rock GMAT scores when sampling with replacement. Here there are $4 \times 4 = 16$ equally likely outcomes (because different orders of selection are now counted) and the same name can be selected both times. Although this may seem peculiar, we should keep in mind that sampling is usually not done with replacement.

The sampling distributions of P and $\overline{X}$ are summarized in Table 6-16.

The expected value and the standard deviation for $\overline{X}$ are calculated in Table 6-17. Note that, as earlier, $E(\overline{X}) = 600$. The standard deviation of $\overline{X}$ is $\sigma(\overline{X}) = 50$. In many statistical applications, the standard deviation of a statistic is referred to as its *standard error*. Because we use it so often, the standard error of $\overline{X}$ is represented by the special symbol $\sigma_{\overline{X}}$. Here, $\sigma_{\overline{X}} = 50$.

TABLE 6-15 Possible Sample Results for Randomly Selecting
Two GMAT Scores With Replacement

Applicants Selected	GMAT Scores	Sample Mean ($\bar{x}$)	Sample Proportion (p)
Chen, Chen	600, 600	600	0
Chen, Jones	600, 500	550	0
Chen, O'Hara	600, 700	650	1/2
Chen, Sandor	600, 600	600	0
Jones, Chen	500, 600	550	0
Jones, Jones	500, 500	500	0
Jones, O'Hara	500, 700	600	1/2
Jones, Sandor	500, 600	550	0
O'Hara, Chen	700, 600	650	1/2
O'Hara, Jones	700, 500	600	1/2
O'Hara, O'Hara	700, 700	700	1
O'Hara, Sandor	700, 600	650	1/2
Sandor, Chen	600, 600	600	0
Sandor, Jones	600, 500	550	0
Sandor, O'Hara	600, 700	650	1/2
Sandor, Sandor	600, 600	600	0

TABLE 6-16 Sampling Distributions of $\bar{X}$ and P
for GMAT Scores Selected With Replacement

$\bar{x}$	$P[\bar{X} = \bar{x}]$	p	$P[P = p]$
500	1/16	0	9/16
550	4/16	1/2	6/16
600	6/16	1	1/16
650	4/16		1
700	1/16		
	1		

TABLE 6-17 Calculation of Mean and Standard Deviation for $\bar{X}$
for GMAT Scores Selected With Replacement

$\bar{x}$	$P[\bar{X} = \bar{x}]$	$\bar{x}P[\bar{X} = \bar{x}]$	$\bar{x}^2$	$\bar{x}^2 P[\bar{X} = \bar{x}]$
500	1/16	500/16	250,000	250,000/16
550	4/16	2,200/16	302,500	1,210,000/16
600	6/16	3,600/16	360,000	2,160,000/16
650	4/16	2,600/16	422,500	1,690,000/16
700	1/16	700/16	490,000	490,000/16
		$E(\bar{X}) = 600$		362,500

$$\sigma^2(\bar{X}) = 362,500 - (600)^2 = 2,500$$

$$\sigma_{\bar{x}} = \sigma(\bar{X}) = \sqrt{2,500} = 50$$

We have found that $E(\overline{X}) = \mu$. It is interesting to see if $\sigma_{\overline{X}}$ similarly relates to the population standard deviation. We may use the following expression to calculate the *standard error of $\overline{X}$ when sampling with replacement:*

$$\sigma_{\overline{X}} = \frac{\sigma}{\sqrt{n}} \tag{6-21}$$

This says that the standard error of $\overline{X}$ relates directly to the population standard deviation σ and is inversely proportional to the square root of the sample size. Thus, both population variability and sample size influence the variability in possible values of $\overline{X}$. In Table 6-12, we found that the population of GMAT scores had a standard deviation of $\sigma = 70.71$. In this illustration, $n = 2$, so that

$$\sigma_{\overline{X}} = \frac{70.71}{\sqrt{2}} = \frac{70.71}{1.414} = 50$$

which is the same value for $\sigma_{\overline{X}}$ found in Table 6-17.

To explain why this relation holds, we first note that variability is additive, so that *in sampling with replacement*

$$\sigma^2(n\overline{X}) = \sigma^2(X_1 \mid X_2 \mid \cdots \mid X_n) = \sigma^2(X_1) + \sigma^2(X_2) + \cdots + \sigma^2(X_n) \tag{6-22}$$

This says that the variance of the two selected test scores combined is equal to the sum of the individual score variances, or twice the variance of a single score. There is no canceling effect. Looked at another way, the range also measures variability. Each of the selected GMAT scores may range from 500 (Jones) to 700 (O'Hara), and the sum of any two scores can range from 1,000 (Jones, Jones) to 1,400 (O'Hara, O'Hara)—an interval twice as wide. Here we see that the variability of the sum of *two* variables is *twice* as large as the variability of one variable alone.

Expression 6-22 applies for random variables where the outcomes for any one variable have probabilities that are not influenced by the particular results for the other variables. For example, in the popular casino game of "craps," two dice are tossed and the sum of both dice determines the gambler's reward. The variance of the sum of the showing faces is the sum of the individual variances (found on page 156 to be 2.917), or $2(2.917) = 5.834$. In the parlor game Yahtzee, five dice are tossed, so the variance of their sum would be 5 times 2.917. In both cases, this is because the individual die outcomes are independent events. The respective numerical results are therefore referred to as *independent random variables.* Likewise, whenever random sampling is done with replacement, the results are referred to as an *independent random sample.*

Since $\sigma^2(n\overline{X}) = n^2\sigma^2(\overline{X})$ by Property 6-2 (page 157), it follows that the variance of $\overline{X}$ is the sum of the individual observation variances divided by n^2.

Because each of the n observations has the same variance σ^2 as the population, the following is true:

$$\sigma^2(\overline{X}) = \frac{n\sigma^2}{n^2} \tag{6-23}$$

Canceling the n's and noting that $\sigma_{\overline{X}}^2 = \sigma^2(\overline{X})$, we obtain

$$\sigma_{\overline{X}}^2 = \frac{\sigma^2}{n} \tag{6-24}$$

Taking the square roots of expression (6-24) gives us expression (6-21).

Influence of Sampling Without Replacement

When sampling without replacement, the sample outcomes are not independent. Independence between observations means the same thing as independence between events. For example, suppose that the heights of all adult American males comprise the population of interest. Then, if the first man randomly selected to be in the sample happens to be over seven feet tall, independence requires that this fact will not influence the probability distribution for the second man's height, and so forth for all men selected. However, if the selection is made without replacement, choosing a seven-footer first will have an influence on the second man's height probability. In such cases, the determination of $\sigma_{\overline{X}}$ may become more involved than we have indicated here.

The difficulty arises because, without replacement, variability will no longer be additive and the variance of the sum will be smaller than $n^2\sigma^2$, so that $\sigma_{\overline{X}}$ will be less than $\sigma/\sqrt{n}$ due to a canceling effect. This is because the early selection of an extremely small or large value from a population will reduce the variability of the remaining selections, while the early choice of a middling value will make later observations more varied than they normally would be.*

No practical difficulty exists unless the population is small. For instance, if our population contains 1,000 men, exactly one of whom is over seven feet tall, then independence is violated when sampling without replacement. For a very large population, the degree of dependence will be so slight that it can be ignored. For the United States as a whole, the removal of one seven-footer from the sample would not appreciably change the remaining proportion of persons who are this tall. But in a small population, this could seriously affect the sampling outcome.

In Chapter 7, we will investigate the practical significance of this fact upon sampling without replacement. Independence or dependence between random variables is a very important area of statistics; it will be investigated in later chapters.

---

* These same principles also apply between sample observations representing two distinct populations and between dependent random variables. The difference between the variance of the sum and the sum of the variances may be summarized in terms of the *covariance*, which is half this difference and may be positive or negative.

Mean and Standard Error of *P*

For simple random samples, it is true that the expected value of the sample proportion is the same as the population proportion, or $E(P) = \pi$, which says that the long-run average value of *P* is equal to π. For the GMAT scores in our illustration, the proportion greater than 600 is $\pi = 1/4$, which is equal to $E(P)$ calculated in Table 6-14.

When sampling with replacement, the sampling distribution of *P* is the binomial for the population proportion π (which also represents the trial success probability) and the sample size *n*, which represents the number of trials. As we saw earlier, the standard deviation for *P* may be calculated from π and *n* alone. Again, we will sometimes refer to this as the standard error of *P*, which we denote by σ_P. We may use the following expression to calculate the *standard error of P when sampling with replacement:*

$$\sigma_P = \sqrt{\frac{\pi(1-\pi)}{n}} \qquad (6\text{-}25)$$

When the random sample is a dependent one due to sampling without replacement, expression (6-25) overstates the value for σ_P. As with the standard error for $\overline{X}$, we will further investigate this in Chapter 7.*

EXERCISES

6-23 A sample of size 2 is to be randomly selected *without replacement* from five persons having the following monthly incomes:

Identity	Income
Mr. A	$1,000
Mrs. D	1,200
Mr. J	1,200
Ms. P	1,000
Miss R	900

  (a) Find the sampling distribution of the sample mean.
  (b) Find the sampling distribution of the sample proportion of females.

6-24 Suppose instead that the sample in Exercise 6-23 was chosen *with replacement.*
  (a) Find the sampling distribution of the sample mean.
  (b) Calculate the expected value, variance, and standard deviation of the sample mean.

REVIEW EXERCISES

6-25 You are offered the following proposition. A coin is tossed twice. For each tail you must forfeit one dollar, and for each head you will receive two

---

* The sampling distribution of *P* then becomes the hypergeometric distribution, which is similar to and often approximated by the binomial.

dollars. Determine the probability distribution for your net winnings W. (*Hint:* It will help if you determine which outcomes [for example, (H, T)] apply to each possible amount.)

6-26 During the early 1950s, the card game of canasta was popular throughout the world. In canasta, points are assigned to cards in the following manner: red $3 = 100$ points; joker $= 50$ points; ace or deuce $= 20$ points; 8 through king $= 10$ points; 4 through 7 and black $3 = 5$ points. A canasta deck is composed of two ordinary decks of playing cards, each containing 52 cards and 2 jokers. Determine the probability distribution for the point value of the first card dealt from a shuffled canasta deck.

6-27 Calculate the mean, variance, and standard deviation for your net winnings W in Exercise 6-25, using your probability distribution from that exercise.

6-28 Calculate the mean, variance, and standard deviation for the points of the first card dealt from the canasta deck in Exercise 6-26, using your probability distribution from that exercise.

6-29 Suppose that the proportion of adult U.S. citizens who approve of the way the President does his job is $\pi = .50$. A random sample of $n = 5$ persons is chosen. Using the binomial formula, determine the probability that:
(a) exactly 5 approve   (b) none approve   (c) exactly 3 approve.

6-30 Find the standard deviation for the proportion of successes P found in n Bernoulli trials for the following situations:
(a) $n = 100, \pi = .8$ (b) $n = 25, \pi = .5$ (c) $n = 100, \pi = .10$.

6-31 Forty percent of the voters in a city are black. A jury of 12 persons has been impaneled for a trial. Assuming that every registered voter has an equal chance of being chosen, use Appendix Table C to find the following probabilities for the representation of blacks on the jury:
(a) At least 5 black jurors.
(b) No black jurors.
(c) All black jurors.
(d) At most 10 black jurors.

6-32 The ages of the straight-A students in a certain statistics class are:

Mr. C	24
Miss H	19
Mr. J	21
Mr. M	20
Mrs. T	23

(a) A random sample of two persons is taken *without replacement*. Determine the sampling distribution of the mean age $\bar{X}$, and then determine the value of the standard error of $\bar{X}$.
(b) Calculate the standard deviation of the age *population* of straight-A students. Using this value, determine the standard error of $\bar{X}$ if the random sample of two persons in (a) had been taken *with replacement*.

Chapter Seven
The Normal Distribution

I know of scarcely anything so apt to impress the imagination as the wonderful form of cosmic order expressed by the "Law of Frequency of Error." The Law would have been personified by the Greeks and deified, if they had known of it. It reigns with serenity and in complete self-effacement amidst the wildest confusion. The huger the mob and the greater the apparent anarchy, the more perfect is its sway. It is the supreme law of Unreason. Whenever a large sample of chaotic elements are taken in hand and marshaled in the order of their magnitude, an unsuspected and most beautiful form of regularity proves to have been latent all along. The tops of the marshaled row form a flowing curve of invariable proportions; and each element, as it is sorted into place, finds, as it were, a pre-ordained niche accurately adapted to fit it. If the measurement at any two specified Grades in the row are known, those that will be found at every other Grade, except towards the extreme ends, can be predicted in the way already explained and with much precision.

Sir Francis Galton

The normal distribution is perhaps the most important distribution encountered in statistical applications. One very good reason for this is that so many physical measurements and natural phenomena have actual observed frequency distributions that closely resemble the normal distribution. These include not only distributions for the physical measurements of height and weight of both persons and things, but also other human characteristics, such as IQ. Relative frequencies of these and many more populations closely resemble the normal curve in Figure 7-1 when their histograms are represented graphically by a smoothed curve. But there is a more fundamental reason why the normal distribution is so important to statistics. A theoretical property of the sample mean allows us to use the normal distribution to find probabilities for various sample results. Thus, the normal curve has a basic role to play in situations where inferences are made regarding the value of the population mean when only the sample mean can be calculated directly.

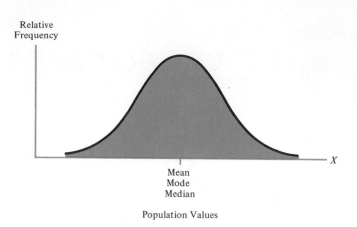

Relative
Frequency

Mean
Mode
Median

Population Values

FIGURE 7-1 Frequency curve for the normal distribution.

7-1 CHARACTERISTICS OF THE NORMAL DISTRIBUTION

Several interesting features are apparent from Figure 7-1. Note that the curve is shaped very much like a bell with a single peak, making it *unimodal*. It is *symmetrical* about its center. A normally distributed population's mean lies at the center of its frequency curve. Because of symmetry, the *median* and the *mode* of the distribution also occur at the curve's center, so that the mean, median, and mode all have the same value. Although it is impracticable to show this on the graph, the tails extend indefinitely in both directions, never quite touching the horizontal axis.

We say that a population having a frequency distribution approximated by the shape of the normal curve is *normally distributed*. If the random variable X is the value of an elementary unit chosen randomly from a normally distributed population, then we also say that X is normally distributed. Furthermore, the normal curve represents the probability density function for X.* The normal curve depends upon only two parameters: the mean μ and the standard deviation σ. No matter what the values of μ and σ, the total area under the normal curve is always 1.

The mean, as we have seen, is a measure of central tendency or location. When normal curves for populations having different means are graphed on the same axis, they will therefore be located at different positions along the horizontal axis. Figure 7-2 illustrates this for three different populations with means of 30, 80, and 120.

---

* The function denoting the height of the curve is

$$f(x) = \frac{1}{\sqrt{2\pi\sigma^2}} e^{-[(x-\mu)^2/2\sigma^2]}$$

where π is the ratio of the circumference to the diameter of a circle (3.1416), and e is the base of natural logarithms (2.7183).

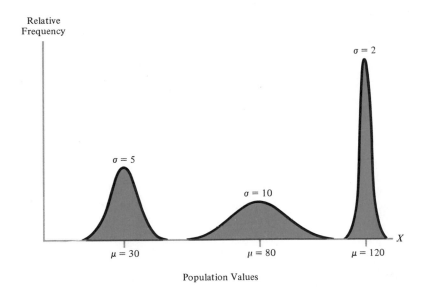

FIGURE 7-2   Three different normal distributions graphed on a common axis.

Figure 7-2 also illustrates that the shape of a normal curve is determined by the population's standard deviation. Distributions with small standard deviations have narrow, peaked "bells," and those with large σ's have flatter curves with less pronounced peaks. The three populations shown in Figure 7-2 have standard deviations of 5, 10, and 2, respectively. A very large class of populations belong to the normal family, and each member differs only by its mean and its standard deviation.

The probability that a normally distributed random variable assumes values within a particular interval equals the area of the portion of the curve covering that interval. The areas can be found by referring to a table, but before we describe how to use this table, note the very useful property of any normal distribution that is illustrated in Figure 7-3. *The area under the normal curve covering an interval symmetrical about the mean depends only upon the distance, measured in standard deviations, that separates the end points from the mean.* For instance, about 68 percent of the population has values lying within one standard deviation in either direction of the mean; that is, the area under the curve over the interval $\mu - \sigma$, $\mu + \sigma$ is .68. This is true no matter what the values of μ and σ happen to be. It is also true that about 95.5 percent of the population has values lying within two standard deviations of the mean, and approximately 99.7 percent fall within three standard deviations.

Example 7-1   The commander of an Army division has wagered with his brother-in-law, who commands a Marine division, that his Army troops are taller. To verify this, the Army commander orders his aide to compile the heights of his soldiers from their medical records. The aide calculates the mean height to be 70 inches and finds that the standard deviation is 2 inches. He also

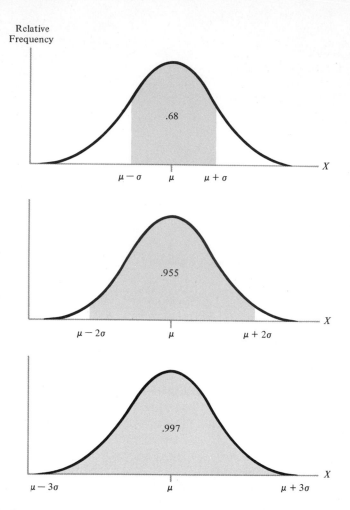

FIGURE 7-3   Relationship between the area under the normal curve and the distance from the mean, expressed in standard deviation units.

constructs a histogram, which exhibits an almost perfect bell shape. Thus, the aide believes that the heights of the Army soldiers may be described in terms of the normal distribution.

The Marine commander arrives at similar conclusions. The mean height of his men is 69.5 inches, with a standard deviation of 2.5 inches. The two populations are compared in Table 7-1. Figure 7-4 shows the frequency curves for these two populations.

The Army commander claims that he wins the bet, as the mean height of his men is .5 inch greater than the mean Marine height. The Marine commander objects, noting that his division contains a greater percentage of very tall men. (Note that the upper tail of the Marines' frequency curve lies above the Army division's curve.) The Army commander agrees, but retorts that there is also a higher percentage of shorter Marines. (Observe the lower tails of the two frequency curves.)

TABLE 7-1 A Summary of Normally Distributed Heights from Two Populations

	Height (inches)	
	Army	Marine
Mean (μ)	70	69.5
Standard deviation (σ)	2	2.5
68 percent lie between $\mu - \sigma$, $\mu + \sigma$	68, 72	67, 72
95.5 percent lie between $\mu - 2\sigma$, $\mu + 2\sigma$	66, 74	64.5, 74.5
99.7 percent lie between $\mu - 3\sigma$, $\mu + 3\sigma$	64, 76	62.5, 77

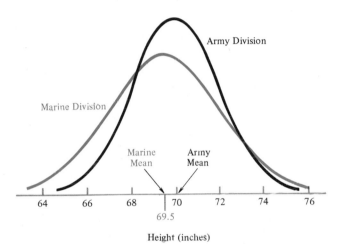

FIGURE 7-4 Normal curves for the heights of the Marine and Army divisions.

This example illustrates a difficulty in comparing populations by using a measure of location, such as the mean. The fact that some Marines are taller than the tallest soldiers is due to the difference in population variabilities. The Marine division is a more disperse group with a larger standard deviation (2.5 inches compared to 2.0 inches for the Army division).

7-2 FINDING AREAS UNDER THE NORMAL CURVE

In order to obtain probability values for normally distributed random variables, we must first find the appropriate area lying under the normal curve. This can be accomplished by using Appendix Table D (page A-23).

We will illustrate how to find the desired areas for the time taken by a particular typesetter to compose 500 lines of standard type. We will assume that the population of times is normally distributed, with a mean of $\mu = 150$ minutes and a standard deviation of $\sigma = 30$ minutes. The time for any given 500 lines, such as the next ones to be composed, represents a randomly chosen time from this population.

The probability that between 150 and 175 minutes will be required is represented by the colored area under the normal curve in Figure 7-5. As we have seen, the area beneath the normal curve between the mean and a certain point depends only upon the number of standard deviations separating the two points. We see that 175 minutes is equivalent to a distance above the mean of .83 standard deviation. This figure is determined by observing that 175 minutes minus the mean of 150 minutes is equal to 25 minutes. Since the standard deviation is 30 minutes, 25 minutes is only a fraction, $25/30 = .83$, of the standard deviation.

Appendix Table D has been constructed for a special curve, called the *standard normal curve,* which provides the area between the mean and a point above it, at a specified distance measured in standard deviations. Because the distance will vary with the situation, it is convenient to represent it by the letter z. Sometimes the value of z is referred to as a *normal deviate*. The distance z that separates a possible normal random variable value x from its mean, expressed in terms of standard deviations, is given by the following expression for the *normal deviate:*

$$z = \frac{x - \mu}{\sigma} \qquad (7\text{-}1)$$

A negative value will be obtained for z when x is smaller than μ.

The first column of Table D lists values of z to the first decimal place. The second decimal place value is located at the head of one of the remaining 10

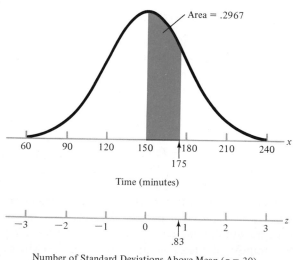

Number of Standard Deviations Above Mean ($\sigma = 30$)

FIGURE 7-5 Determining the area under a normal curve.

columns. The area under the curve between the mean and z standard deviations is found at the intersection of the correct row and column. For example, when $z = .83$, we find the area of .2967 by reading the entry in the .8 row and the .03 column. The area under the normal curve for a completion time between 150 and 175 minutes is thus .2967, which represents the probability that the next 500 lines of print will take this long to set.

Using Normal Curve Table

Appendix Table D provides areas only between the mean and some point above it. But this table may be employed to find areas encountered in other common probability situations, such as those in Figure 7-6. Each of these is described below.

(a) *Area between mean and some point lying below it.* To find the probability that the completion time lies between 125 and 150 minutes, first we calculate the normal deviate from expression (7-1):

$$z = \frac{125-150}{30} = -.83$$

Here, z is negative because 125 is a point lying below the mean. Since the normal curve is symmetrical about the mean, this area must be the same as it would be for a positive value of z of the same magnitude (in this case .2967, as before). It is therefore unnecessary to tabulate areas for negative values of z. The area between the mean and a point lying below it will equal the area between the mean and a point equally distant above it.

(b) *Area to the left of a value above the mean.* To find the probability that the type can be set in 185 minutes or less, we have to find the entire colored area below 185. Here, we must consider the lower half of the normal curve separately. Since the entire normal curve area is 1, the area under the half to the left of 150 must be .5. The area between 150 and 185 is found from Table D, with $z = (185-150)/30 = 1.17$, to be .3790. The entire colored portion is the sum of the two areas, or $.5000 + .3790 = .8790$.

(c) *Area in upper tail.* We find the probability that the number of minutes required exceeds 195 by first finding the area between the mean and 195. The normal deviate is $z = (195-150)/30 = 1.50$, for which Table D yields the area .4332. Since the area in the upper half of the normal curve is .5, our desired area is found by subtracting the unwanted portion, or $.5000 - .4332 = .0668$.

Because the total area under the normal curve is 1, we may use the value of the upper tail area to calculate the area to the left of 195. This may be found by subtracting the upper tail area of .0668 from 1, giving $1.0000 - .0668 = .9332$ as the area to the left of 195 (or the probability that the time will be less than 195 minutes). Similarly, when the area to the left of a point is known, the area to its right can be found by subtracting this value from 1. For example, in (b) above,

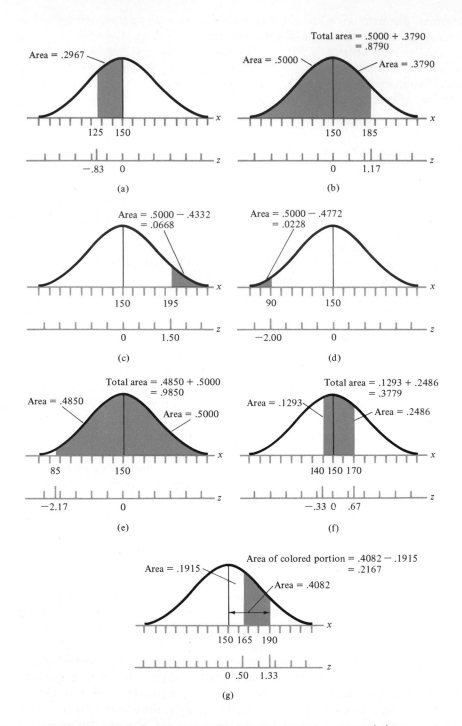

FIGURE 7-6 Various areas under the normal curve. *x* = completion time in minutes; *z* = standard deviations.

we found the area to the left of 185 to be .8790. Thus, the area in the upper tail to the right of 185 must be $1 - .8790 = .1210$.

(d) *Area in lower tail.* We find the probability that 90 minutes or less will be taken to set the type by two steps similar to those in (c) above. First the area between 90 and 150 is found. Using $z = (90 - 150)/30 = -2.00$, we obtain .4772 from Table D. This value is subtracted from .5, yielding $.5000 - .4772 = .0228$.

(e) *Area to the right of a value below the mean.* To find the probability that the completion time will be equal to or greater than 85 minutes, the area between 85 and the mean is added to the area to the right of the mean, which is .5. Here, we calculate $z = (85 - 150)/30 = -2.17$, so that, from Table D, the area is .4850. Adding this to .5, the combined area is $.5000 + .4850 = .9850$.

From this value, the area in the lower tail below 85 may be found by subtracting .9850 from 1: $1 - .9850 = .0150$. Likewise, we may find the area to the right of 90 by subtracting the lower-tail area found in (d) above from 1, or: $1 - .0228 = .9772$.

(f) *Area under portion overlapping the mean.* In order to find the probability that the time taken will be between 140 and 170 minutes, we need only add the portion of the colored area that lies below the mean to the one above it. The respective normal deviate values are calculated to be $z = (140 - 150)/30 = -.33$ and $z = (170 - 150)/30 = .67$. From Table D, the lower area is .1293 and the upper area is .2486, so that the combined area is $.1293 + .2486 = .3779$.

Suppose that we wish to find the probability that between 120 and 180 minutes will be taken. The normal deviates are $z = (120 - 150)/30 = -1$ and $z = (180 - 150)/30 = 1$. From Table D, .3413 is the same area for both sides, so that the combined area is $.3413 + .3413 = .6826$. Because z expresses the number of standard deviation units from the mean, we see that .6826 is a more precise value for the area between $\mu \pm \sigma$ than the value used in Figure 7-3.

(g) *Area between two values lying above or below the mean.* To find the probability that the composition time lies between 165 and 190 minutes, first we have to determine the areas between the mean and each of these two values. The respective normal deviates are therefore $z = (165 - 150)/30 = .50$ and $z = (190 - 150)/30 = 1.33$. From Table D, we see that the area between the mean and 190 is .4082, while the area between the mean and 165 is only .1915. Thus, the colored area is found by subtracting the smaller area from the larger one: $.4082 - .1915 = .2167$.

A similar procedure could be applied for an area lying below the mean. It is also possible to find the value for a complementary situation—that the time will be either below 165 minutes or greater than 190 minutes—by subtracting the colored area from 1, or: $1 - .2167 = .7833$.

Inequalities and Normal Curve Areas

The normal curve represents values lying on a continuous scale, such as height, weight, and time. There is zero probability that a specific value, such as 129.40 minutes, will occur (there is zero area under the normal curve covering a single point). Thus, in finding probabilities, it does not matter whether we use "strict" inequalities, such as the composition time is "less than" ($<$) 129.40

minutes, or an ordinary inequality, such as the time is "less than or equal to" ($\leqslant$) 129.40 minutes. Using $z = (129.40 - 150)/30 = -.69$, the area is the same in either case: $.5000 - .2549 = .2451$.

Cumulative Probabilities and Percentiles

Cases (b) and (d) in our discussion of normal curve areas show how all the values for a normal cumulative probability distribution may be determined. We have seen that the probability of a time of 185 minutes or less is .8790, while the probability of 90 minutes or less is .0228. For values above the mean, when z is positive, we obtain the cumulative probabilities from Table D by simply adding .5 to the tabulated areas. For values below the mean, when z is negative, we subtract the area given by the table from .5 to obtain the cumulative probability.

It is frequently necessary to find a normally distributed population's percentile values. Recall from Chapter 3 that a percentile is the population value below which a certain percentage of the population lies. There, we saw that a percentile or fractile value could be obtained directly from the cumulative relative frequency distribution.

To find a population percentile, we must read Table D in *reverse*, since the specified percentage represents an area under the normal curve. For instance, in our example, the 90th percentile is a particular number of minutes, and the area under the normal curve to the left of this value will be .90. Thus, the area between the mean and the number of minutes to be found will be $.90 - .50 = .40$.

Searching through the body of the table, we select the area that lies closest to this figure. The closest value is .3997. Since .3997 is in the $z = 1.2$ row and the .08 column, the corresponding normal deviate is $z = 1.28$. This means that the desired time is 1.28 standard deviations, or $30 \times 1.28 = 38.4$ minutes, above the mean Adding this to the mean, we find that the 90th percentile is $150 + 38.4 = 188.4$ minutes.

In general, the procedure for finding a percentile is begun by reading Table D in reverse to find z. The corresponding population value x may then be calculated from the following expression, which provides the *percentile for a normal population:*

$$x = \mu + z\sigma \tag{7-2}$$

Note that below the 50th percentile the lower-tail area is used to find z, which in these cases will be negative.

Example 7-2   Human engineers (whose specialty is the problem of integrating human factors into the design of man–machine systems) are designing the cockpit of a new jet aircraft and want to arrange the positions of certain controls so that 95 percent of all pilots can reach them while seated. This will involve finding the maximum reach radius exceeded by 95 percent (but not by 5 percent) of all pilots. Thus, the engineers must find the reach that corresponds to the fifth percentile.

The maximum reach radii of airline pilots are assumed to be approximately normally distributed, with a mean of $\mu = 48$ inches and a standard deviation of

$\sigma = 2$ inches. The engineers seek the point below which the area under the normal curve is equal to .05. This means that Table D must be searched to find the area closest to $.50 - .05 = .45$. It just so happens that two areas are equally close, .4495 and .4505, corresponding to normal deviates of 1.64 and 1.65. The desired figure lies somewhere in between 1.64 and 1.65. For simplicity, the engineers choose 1.64, as they ordinarily wish to err on the side of a larger rather than a smaller tail area.* Since the fifth percentile is below the 50th, they are dealing with a lower-tail area and their normal deviate is negative, so that $z = -1.64$. (The fifth percentile lies *below* the mean and is smaller, so that a distance of 1.64 standard deviations must be *subtracted* from the mean.) From expression (7-2), the fifth percentile is therefore

$$x = 48 - 1.64(2) = 44.72 \text{ inches}$$

Standard Normal Random Variable

The area under any normal curve may be found by using the standard normal curve. This curve provides the probability distribution for the *standard normal random variable Z*. Here, our notation of using capital letters for random variables means that the lower case z represents a point on the scale of possible values for Z. Because z expresses distance in standard deviations above or below the mean, the center of the standard normal curve lies at $z = 0$, so that the expected value of Z is zero. Likewise, the standard deviation of Z is equal to 1.

In the type-composition time illustration, we in essence transformed the original random variable X, the time to complete 500 lines, into the standard normal random variable Z whenever we used Table D to find areas. Such a transformation may be accomplished physically by a procedure consisting of two parts: shifting the center of the curve and then stretching or contracting it. To shift the original curve so that its center lies above the point $x = 0$, subtract μ from each point on the x axis. Then the repositioned curve may be stretched or squeezed so that the scale on the horizontal axis matches the scale for the standard normal distribution. This may be accomplished by dividing all values of the random variable by its standard deviation. The resultant transformed curve will have the same shape as the standard normal curve illustrated in Figure 7-7. The net effect will always be the same, no matter what the values of μ and σ are. The horizontal scale may be either expanded or contracted.

Fortunately, a physical transformation of the original random variable X into the standard normal random variable is unnecessary. Instead, we may algebraically manipulate X itself according to the following expression for the *transformation of X into the standard normal variable:*

$$Z = \frac{X - \mu}{\sigma} \tag{7-3}$$

---

* An interpolation procedure would be more accurate, but to keep our discussions less complicated, throughout this text we will always choose the nearest table value and break ties arbitrarily.

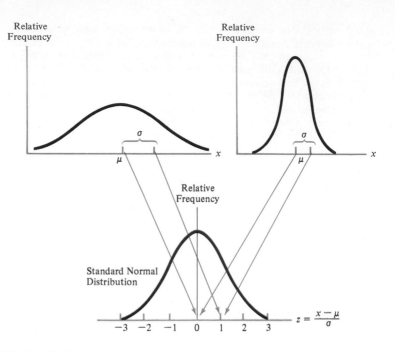

FIGURE 7-7 Illustration of the linear transformation of normal random variables into the standard normal distribution.

Example 7-3 IQ tests are designed so that the scores achieved by a cross section of persons is normally distributed for all practical purposes. One of the most popular is the Stanford-Binet test, which has a mean of $\mu = 100$ points and a standard deviation of $\sigma = 16$. Letting X represent the IQ score achieved by a randomly chosen person, it is possible to determine various probabilities for the value achieved.

For example, we may find the probability that this person's IQ is at most 140:

$$P[X \leqslant 140] = P\left[\frac{X-\mu}{\sigma} \leqslant \frac{140-100}{16}\right]$$

Here we subtract $\mu = 100$ from both sides of the original inequality and then divide by $\sigma = 16$. This change transforms X into the standard normal random variable Z and 140 into the normal deviate value 2.50, so that our original problem is equivalent to evaluating $P[Z \leqslant 2.50]$.

From Appendix Table D, we know that the area between $z = 0$ and $z = 2.50$ is .4938. Thus,

$$P[X \leqslant 140] = P[Z \leqslant 2.50] = .5000 + .4938 = .9938$$

We see that there is a better than 99 percent chance that this person's IQ falls below 140 on the Stanford-Binet scale.

Different IQ tests have standard deviations other than the Stanford-Binet, although the means are generally the same: 100 points. Now suppose we ask the same question for another test with a standard deviation of $\sigma = 10$ points. In this case

$$P[X \leqslant 140] = P\left[\frac{X-\mu}{\sigma} \leqslant \frac{140-100}{10}\right] = P[Z \leqslant 4.0]$$

From Table D, the area between $z = 0$ and $z = 4.0$ is .49997. Thus,

$$P[X \leqslant 140] = .50000 + .49997 = .99997$$

Notice that IQs above 140 are considerably rarer with this test than with the Stanford-Binet.

The fact that different types of IQ tests are scaled differently makes it hard to compare IQ scores. For this reason, various intelligence-test results are often transformed into *standard scores*—normal deviate values which can be calculated from expression (7-1). In this example, 140 points on the Stanford-Binet provides a standard score of 2.50, while 140 points on the other test corresponds to a standard score of 4.0, indicating that a person scoring 140 points on the second test would exhibit a much higher level of intelligence. (To obtain a standard score equal to 4.0 on the Stanford-Binet test, a person would have to be 4 standard deviations above the mean, so that his IQ would be $100 + 4(16) = 164$ on that scale.)

Areas for Large z

Suppose that σ was even smaller than the 10 used in the above example. z would then be so large in absolute value that Table D would not provide the area. Our table has to stop somewhere, for the tails of the normal curve extend indefinitely. In general, whenever z exceeds 3.09, the area between the mean and z is so very close to .5 that for practical purposes .5 would be used in such cases. The upper- and lower-tail areas would be so close to zero that they would be *negligible*. For example, the area below $z = 5$ would be approximately 1, as would the area above $z = -5$, while the areas above $z = 5$ and below $z = -5$ would each be approximately zero.

Concluding Remarks

Recall that the tails of the normal curve never touch the horizontal axis. This implies that there is a probability—although perhaps an infinitesimal one—that the random variable can exceed any value. Consider the distribution of heights of men, for instance. The normal curve quite literally assigns a probability to the event that a man will be born who will grow to be more than one mile tall. Most people would accept that this is impossible, but according to the normal curve the probability of this event is not zero—although it is quite remote. Worse yet, the normal curve says that there are probabilities of men being negatively tall. Absurd as these implications seem, they are merely by-products of employing a convenient mathematical expression to describe a particular curve that happens to fit some empirical frequency distributions very nicely, and they should not detract from the utility of the normal distribution. From the table of areas under the normal curve, only about .13 percent of the area lies beyond a distance of 3σ above the mean. Areas in the tails of the theoretical normal distribution are quite tiny for greater distances. (At 4σ, the tail area is only .003 percent). Any discrepancy between reality and the theoretical normal curve occurring beyond four standard deviations can thus be safely ignored. (A mile-tall man would be more than 40,000 standard deviations from the mean.)

EXERCISES

7-1 The measurement errors for the height of a weather satellite above a ground station are normally distributed, with a mean of zero and a standard deviation of 1 mile. These errors will be negative if the measured altitude is too low and positive if the altitude is too high. Find the probability that for the next orbit the error will be

(a) between zero and $+1.55$ miles.   (e) -1.25 miles or less.
(b) between -2.45 and zero miles.   (f) greater than -1.25 miles.
(c) $+.75$ miles or less.   (g) between $+.10$ and $+.60$ miles.
(d) greater than $+.75$ miles.   (h) between $+1$ and $+2$ miles.

7-2 The lifetime of a particular model of a stereo cartridge is normally distributed, with a mean of $\mu = 1,000$ hours and a standard deviation of $\sigma = 100$ hours. Find the probability that one of these cartridges will last:

(a) between 1,000 and 1,150 hours.   (e) 870 hours or less.
(b) between 950 and 1,000 hours.   (f) longer than 780 hours.
(c) 930 hours or less.   (g) between 700 and 1,200 hours.
(d) more than 1,250 hours.   (h) between 750 and 850 hours.

7-3 The time required by a bank teller to cash a check has been observed to be normally distributed, with a mean of $\mu = 30$ seconds and a standard deviation of $\sigma = 10$ seconds. Find the following percentiles: (a) 10th; (b) 25th;   (c) 50th;   (d) 75th;   (e) 90th.

7-4 The heights of the male students at a particular university were found to be normally distributed, with a mean of $\mu = 5'10''$ and a standard deviation of $\sigma = 2.5''$. Find the height below which the following percentages of men lie: (a) 1;   (b) 5;   (c) 30;   (d) 60;   (e) 95;   (f) 99.

7-5 An architect is designing the interior doors in a men's gymnasium. He wants to make them high enough so that 95 percent of the men using the doors will have at least a 1-foot clearance. Assuming that the heights will be normally distributed, with a mean of 70 inches and a standard deviation of 3 inches, how high must the architect make the doors?

7-6 The quality control manager shuts down an automatic lathe for corrective maintenance whenever a sample of parts it produces has an average diameter either greater than 2.01 inches or smaller than 1.99 inches. The lathe is designed to produce parts with a mean diameter of 2.00 inches, and the sample averages have a standard deviation of .005 inches. Using the normal distribution:

(a) What is the probability that the quality control manager will stop the process when the lathe is operating as designed, with $\mu = 2.00$ inches?
(b) Suppose a part within the lathe wears out and it begins to produce parts that on the average are too wide, with $\mu = 2.02$ inches. What is the probability that the lathe will continue to operate?
(c) Suppose that an adjustment error causes the lathe to produce parts that on the average are too narrow, so that $\mu = 1.99$ inches. What is the probability that the lathe will be stopped?

7-3 SAMPLING DISTRIBUTION OF THE SAMPLE MEAN FOR A NORMAL POPULATION

The normal curve describes the frequency distribution of a great many populations. Notable among these are measurements of persons and things. Some important questions can be answered by applying the normal curve. For instance, a new testing procedure may be analyzed by a counseling center seeking a replacement for their present test. A sample of persons can be given the new test in order to estimate the mean score to be achieved by all those who may ultimately take the test. Because scores obtained with the current test closely fit the normal distribution, there is reason to believe that the normal curve will apply to the new one as well.

We will show how the probability distribution for the sample mean can be determined. It has been established mathematically that under certain circumstances, *when the population frequencies are described by the normal curve, the sampling distribution of X itself is also normally distributed.*

Mean and Standard Deviation of $\overline{X}$

In order to find probabilities for the value of $\overline{X}$, we must determine which particular normal curve applies. Recall that the shape of each normal curve is determined by its mean (expected value) and standard deviation.

Suppose that a random sample of size n is selected from a population with a mean of μ and a standard deviation of σ. In Chapter 6, we showed that the following applies for the *expected value of the sample mean*:

$$E(\overline{X}) = \mu \tag{7-4}$$

This fact is true regardless of the shape of the underlying population distribution.

The standard deviation of $\overline{X}$ depends partly upon the variability of the population, but it also depends partly upon the sample size n. A large sample should be more accurate than a small one; thus, when n is large, $\overline{X}$ values will tend to cluster more tightly about μ than they would if n were small. Both the standard deviation of the population and the size of the sample therefore affect the standard deviation of the sample mean, with large values of n making the standard deviation of the sample mean smaller.

We have referred to the standard deviation of $\overline{X}$ as the *standard error of $\overline{X}$*. One reason for this is that the variability in possible sample mean values provides an indication of the accuracy of estimates to be made. It allows us to quantify chance-caused sampling errors. We may use the following expression to calculate the *standard error (deviation) of $\overline{X}$:*

$$\sigma_{\overline{X}} = \frac{\sigma}{\sqrt{n}} \tag{7-5}$$

This result is true for *any* population whenever the sample observations are independent.

Knowing the values of μ and $\sigma_{\overline{X}}$, we can determine the appropriate normal curve to apply in finding the probability values for $\overline{X}$. The shape of this normal curve is determined by its standard deviation $\sigma_{\overline{X}}$, and its center lies at μ.

Finding Probabilities for $\bar{X}$

We may summarize the foregoing discussions by stating

PROPERTY 7-1   If $\bar{X}$ is the mean of a random sample taken from a normally distributed population having a mean of μ and a standard deviation of σ, then the sampling distribution for $\bar{X}$ is also normal, its mean is also μ, and its standard deviation is $\sigma_{\bar{x}} = \sigma/\sqrt{n}$. This is true no matter what the size of the sample happens to be.*

As an illustration, suppose that $n = 100$ people are chosen as a random sample from a normally distributed population of IQ test scores having an unknown mean of μ and a standard deviation of $\sigma = 10$ points. The sample mean $\bar{X}$ is normally distributed with the same mean and has the standard deviation:

$$\sigma_X = \frac{10}{\sqrt{100}} = \frac{10}{10} = 1$$

The probability may be found that the sample mean differs from the unknown population mean by a level of precision of no more than one point in either direction. We find that:

$$P[-1 \leqslant \bar{X} - \mu \leqslant +1] = P\left[\frac{-1}{1} \leqslant \frac{\bar{X} - \mu}{\sigma_X} \leqslant \frac{+1}{1}\right]$$
$$= P[-1 \leqslant Z \leqslant +1] = .6826$$

Here, $\bar{X}$ was transformed in the usual manner into the *standard normal random variable:*

$$Z = \frac{\bar{X} - \mu}{\sigma_X} \qquad (7\text{-}6)$$

For areas under the normal curve, we find from Table D that the area between the mean and $z = 1$ is .3413. This gave us $2(.2413) = .6826$ for the above probability.

When the population mean is known, we can transform $\bar{X}$ into the standard normal random variable to find a desired probability. For example, suppose that the population mean IQ is $\mu = 100$. Consider the following cases.

(1) The probability that $\bar{X}$ is less than or equal to 101.5 is

$$P[\bar{X} \leqslant 101.5] = P\left[\frac{\bar{X} - \mu}{\sigma_X} \leqslant \frac{101.5 - 100}{1}\right]$$
$$= P[Z \leqslant 1.5]$$
$$= .5000 + .4332 = .9332$$

---

* As we will see in Chapter 8, when σ is *also* of unknown value and n is small, it is necessary to use the Student t statistic instead of $\bar{X}$. This statistic has a different sampling distribution.

(2) The probability that $\bar{X}$ lies between 97 and 102 is

$$P[97 \leqslant \bar{X} \leqslant 102] = P\left[\frac{97-100}{1} \leqslant \frac{\bar{X}-\mu}{\sigma_{\bar{X}}} \leqslant \frac{102-100}{1}\right]$$
$$= P[-3 \leqslant Z \leqslant 2]$$
$$= .49865 + .4772 = .97585$$

(3) The probability that $\bar{X}$ is greater than 102.5 is

$$P[\bar{X} > 102.5] = P\left[\frac{\bar{X}-\mu}{\sigma_{\bar{X}}} > \frac{102.5-100}{1}\right]$$
$$= P[Z > 2.5]$$
$$= .5000 - .4938 = .0062$$

Role Played by the Standard Error of $\bar{X}$

$\sigma_{\bar{X}}$, the standard error of $\bar{X}$, equals the population standard deviation σ divided by the square root of the sample size n. Thus, $\sigma_{\bar{X}}$ will be smaller than σ whenever n exceeds 1. This simply reflects the fact that values for $\bar{X}$ are more alike than individual population values are. The normal curve for the population will therefore be flatter than the one we use to calculate probabilities for $\bar{X}$.

Since the standard error of the sample mean is inversely proportional to the square root of the sample size, the larger the sample is, the smaller $\sigma_{\bar{X}}$ will be. As $\sigma_{\bar{X}}$ becomes smaller, the possible values of $\bar{X}$ cluster more tightly about μ. This is reflected in the shape of the normal curve, which is more peaked when $\sigma_{\bar{X}}$ is small.

As an illustration, the normal curves for the possible values for the sample mean to be calculated from the IQ tests are shown in Figure 7-8 for two different sample sizes: $n = 100$ and $n = 400$. Although only one value of n will actually be used, we can compare the normal curves in order to see which sample size would be more accurate. The curve for the larger sample size is much denser near μ. This means that when $n = 400$, it is more likely that $\bar{X}$ will turn out to be close to μ. The shaded portions represent the probability that $\bar{X}$ will lie within one point of μ. For $n = 100$, we calculated this probability to be .6826. When $n = 400$, the standard error of $\bar{X}$ is

$$\sigma_{\bar{X}} = \frac{10}{\sqrt{400}} = .5$$

The analogous probability is then

$$P[-1 \leqslant \bar{X}-\mu \leqslant +1] = P\left[\frac{-1}{.5} \leqslant \frac{\bar{X}-\mu}{\sigma_{\bar{X}}} \leqslant \frac{+1}{.5}\right]$$
$$= P[-2 \leqslant Z \leqslant +2]$$
$$= 2(.4772) = .9544$$

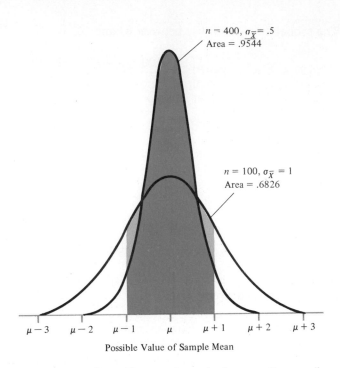

FIGURE 7-8   The effect of increased sample size upon the sampling distribution of $\overline{X}$.

We see that the area covering plus or minus one point from μ is larger for $n = 400$. This fact indicates that a larger sample size provides a more reliable estimate of μ for the same level of precision—plus or minus one point. As the larger sample size is reflected by a smaller value of σ_X, we can conclude that the smaller the value of σ_X, the more accurate the sample result will be.

The standard error of $\overline{X}$ is also affected by the population standard deviation σ. Thus, the size of σ_X depends upon how highly disperse the population values are. This means that the standard error of $\overline{X}$ is a single gauge of sample accuracy that incorporates the effects of both the size of the sample and the variability of the population itself.

We illustrate the effect of population dispersion on sample accuracy by comparing two samples, taken from different populations.

Example 7-4   The mean gasoline mileages of compact and intermediate cars of the same manufacturer are to be estimated by a consumer testing service. It will be assumed that the two car sizes represent different normally distributed populations, with standard deviations of 2 miles per gallon (mpg) for the compacts and 4 mpg for the intermediates. The mileages of intermediate cars are thus a more disperse population.

The standard errors of the sample mean for each type of car are calculated below, assuming that a separate random sample of size $n = 100$ is taken from each population.

$$\text{For compacts:} \qquad \sigma_{\bar{X}} = \frac{2}{\sqrt{100}} = .2$$

$$\text{For intermediates:} \quad \sigma_{\bar{X}} = \frac{4}{\sqrt{100}} = .4$$

Figure 7-9 illustrates the normal curves obtained for the respective sampling distributions of $\bar{X}$. The two curves are drawn on separate graphs to emphasize the fact that different populations are involved, with the compacts having the smaller standard deviation. The colored areas provide the probabilities that each sample mean will lie within $\pm .5$ mpg of the respective unknown population means. These are

$$P[-.5 \leqslant \bar{X} - \mu \leqslant +.5] = P\left[\frac{-.5}{.2} \leqslant \frac{\bar{X} - \mu}{\sigma_{\bar{X}}} \leqslant \frac{+.5}{.2}\right]$$

$$= P[-2.5 \leqslant Z \leqslant +2.5]$$

$$= 2(.4938) = .9876 \quad \text{for compacts}$$

and

$$P[-.5 \leqslant \bar{X} - \mu \leqslant +.5] = P\left[\frac{-.5}{.4} \leqslant \frac{\bar{X} - \mu}{\sigma_{\bar{X}}} \leqslant \frac{+.5}{.4}\right]$$

$$= P[-1.25 \leqslant Z \leqslant +1.25]$$

$$= 2(.3944) = .7888 \quad \text{for intermediates}$$

A more reliable result is obtained for the compacts, whose normal curve for possible sample means provides a tighter clustering of $\bar{X}$ about μ. This is because the standard error of the sample mean is smaller for the compact cars.

Distinguishing s and $\sigma_{\bar{X}}$

The reader is cautioned against confusing $\sigma_{\bar{X}}$ with s. Both are standard deviations, but they represent entirely different phenomena—another reason

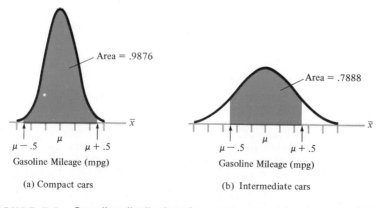

(a) Compact cars   (b) Intermediate cars

FIGURE 7-9 Sampling distributions for sample means taken from populations having different standard deviations.

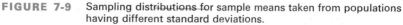

why we usually call $\sigma_{\bar{X}}$ the standard error of $\bar{X}$. Recall that s is the standard deviation of a particular sample result and is actually calculated from the observed sample values at the final stage of sampling; s measures the variability among the observations actually made.

In contrast, $\sigma_{\bar{X}}$ measures the variability of the *possible* $\bar{X}$ values that *might be* obtained and is mainly used in the planning stage. Even though only one numerical value will be achieved for $\bar{X}$, depending upon the sample results, we have demonstrated the need to know the pattern of variation among the possible values that $\bar{X}$ might assume. It is this variation that is summarized by the standard error of the sample mean.

EXERCISES

7-7   A random sample of size n is selected from a normally distributed population. Find $\sigma_{\bar{X}}$ when $\sigma = 10$ for the following values of n: (a) 4; (b) 9; (c) 25; (d) 100; (e) 400; (f) 2,500; (g) 10,000.

7-8   Random samples of size 100 are selected from five normally distributed populations with the following standard deviations σ: (a) .1; (b) 1.0; (c) 5.0; (d) 20; (e) 100. Calculate the value of $\sigma_{\bar{X}}$ for each sample.

7-9   The times taken to install bumpers on cars passing through a particular assembly line are normally distributed with mean time $\mu = 1.50$ minutes and standard deviation $\sigma = .25$ minute. A sample of $n = 25$ cars is obtained and the mean bumper installation time $\bar{X}$ will be calculated.
(a) Find the value of $\sigma_{\bar{X}}$.
Determine the probability that $\bar{X}$ will:
(b) Lie between 1.40 and 1.50 minutes.
(c) Exceed 1.35 minutes.
(d) Fall at or below 1.45 minutes.
(e) Lie between 1.52 and 1.58 minutes.
(f) Fall above 1.65 minutes.

7-10   The city public health department closes down a certain beach when the concentration of *E. coli* bacteria, present in raw sewage, becomes too high. Assume that on a particular day the contamination-level index is normally distributed, with a mean of $\mu = 160$ and a standard deviation of $\sigma = 20$ for each liter of water. A sample of $n = 25$ liters is taken, and the mean index value $\bar{X}$ is found.
(a) Calculate $\sigma_{\bar{X}}$.
Determine the probability that $\bar{X}$ will
(b) Lie between 150 and 160.
(c) Exceed 148.
(d) Fall at or below 153.
(e) Lie between 165 and 170.
(f) Fall above 162.

7-11   The adjusted daily receipts of a pancake house franchise chain are normally distributed with mean $\mu = \$500$ and standard deviation $\sigma = \$100$. A random sample of $n = 25$ days' receipts are chosen for a thorough audit.
(a) What is the probability that $\bar{X}$ will differ from $500 by more than $20 in either direction?
(b) What is the probability that $\bar{X}$ will lie below $420?
(c) Suppose that average daily receipts have grown to an undetermined

level. Assuming that the population standard deviation remains at $\sigma = \$100$, what is the probability that $\overline{X} \geqslant \$600$ when (1) $\mu = \$550$? (2) $\mu = \$600$? (3) $\mu = \$650$? (4) $\mu = \$700$?

7-4 SAMPLING DISTRIBUTION OF $\overline{X}$ WHEN POPULATION IS NOT NORMAL

Even when a sample is selected from a population whose frequency distribution is not normal, for large sample sizes the sampling distribution of the mean will still be approximately normal. Before discussing this result, called the *central limit theorem*, we will consider how the sample size affects the sampling distribution of $\overline{X}$. In doing this, we will use the two facts established in Section 7-3, which hold regardless of the population characteristics: (1) The expected value of $\overline{X}$ is always equal to the population mean μ; and (2) for independent observations, the standard error of $\overline{X}$ is equal to the population standard deviation divided by the square root of the sample size, or $\sigma_{\overline{X}} = \sigma/\sqrt{n}$.

Effect of the Sample Size n upon the Sampling Distribution of $\overline{X}$

Figure 7-10 illustrates the sampling distributions of $\overline{X}$ for samples of various sizes. Here, $\overline{X}$ represents the mean number of bedrooms in a sample of randomly selected homes in a certain city. The same frequency distribution in Table 7-2 was used to generate all the cases shown. Note that as the sample size increases, the number of possible values of $\overline{X}$ grows and the sampling distributions become more symmetrical about μ. Although the number of possible $\overline{X}$ values increases with n, the total variability declines, as evidenced by the tendency of the values farther from μ to decrease in probability while the number of spikes of significant height near μ grows. This tendency is reflected in the standard error of $\overline{X}$, which becomes smaller as n becomes larger. Even more interesting is the pattern presented by the spikes themselves, resembling the bell

TABLE 7-2   Relative Frequency Distribution for the Number of Bedrooms in Residential Units

Number of Bedrooms X	Relative Frequency f	fX
1	.2	.2
2	.3	.6
3	.2	.6
4	.2	.8
5	.1	.5
	1.0	$\mu = 2.7$

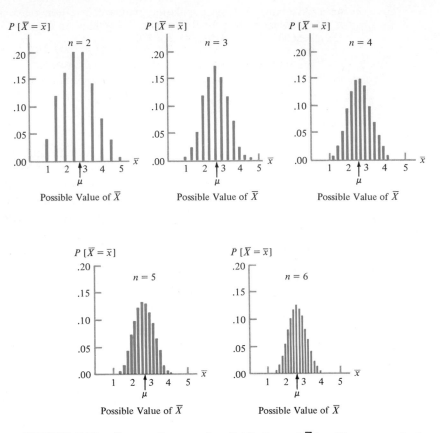

FIGURE 7-10   Comparative sampling distributions of $\overline{X}$ for different sample sizes.

shape that we ordinarily associate with the normal distribution. This tendency is more pronounced with the larger n values.

This illustrates a crucial point of statistical theory, which is substantiated by the central limit theorem to be discussed next. The tendency of the sampling distribution of $\overline{X}$ to assume the bell shape indicates how we can obtain the sampling distribution of $\overline{X}$ even when the population is not normally distributed.

The Central Limit Theorem

The foregoing illustration suggests that the normal distribution may be used as a basis for approximating the sampling distribution of $\overline{X}$. Fortunately, it has been established mathematically that this is indeed the case. It is this fact that has made the normal distribution of such fundamental importance in statistics.

We now state the

CENTRAL LIMIT THEOREM   As the sample size n becomes large, when each of the observations is independently selected from a population having a mean of μ and a standard deviation of σ, the sampling distribution of $\overline{X}$ tends toward a normal distribution with a mean of μ and a standard deviation of $\sigma_{\overline{x}}$.

Note that the central limit theorem is applicable regardless of the shape of the population frequency distribution. It is valid for populations having the skewed, bimodal, uniform, or exponential frequency distributions discussed in Chapter 2. It may be used whether the observation random variable is discrete or continuous. Figure 7-11 shows the sampling distributions of $\overline{X}$ obtained mathematically for samples taken from populations having frequency distributions of various shapes. Note that in every case, as the sample size increases, the sampling distribution of $\overline{X}$ becomes more bell shaped. This occurs more quickly for unimodal, symmetrical populations, which yield bell shapes for small samples; for larger sample sizes, all have shapes of the same form.

The utility of the central limit theorem lies in the fact that it enables us to make an inference about a population without knowing anything more about its frequency distribution than we can glean from a sample, although we must still presume a specific value for σ.

Example 7-5   Much scientific research on human health and psychology is rooted in initial studies of rat physiology and behavior. Over the years, stable populations of these rodents have been established in laboratories around the world. There has been much criticism of the use of such animals in any kind of testing, as various laboratories have their own genetic strains that have been cultured for hundreds of generations in sterile, isolated environments. Thus, two laboratories may obtain entirely different results from identical experiments on their respective races of rats, while a third kind of reaction might be expected when "ill-behaved" wild rats are used.

One researcher has been attempting to break the prevailing rat-research syndrome by duplicating certain medical experiments using only first- and second-generation wild rats captured in the cities. One of his studies involved estimating the mean longevity of rats fed a synthetic food diet. The original laboratory experiment indicated that the population of lifetimes was positively skewed, with a mean of $\mu = 24$ months and a standard deviation of $\sigma = 6$ months. Assuming that the lifetimes of these wild rats have the same distribution, what is the probability that a sample of size $n = 100$ will have a mean lifetime of 25 months or more?

Even though the population is skewed, the central limit theorem indicates that the sampling distribution is normal, with a mean μ of 24 months and a standard deviation of

$$\sigma_{\overline{X}} = \frac{\sigma}{\sqrt{n}} = \frac{6}{\sqrt{100}} = .6$$

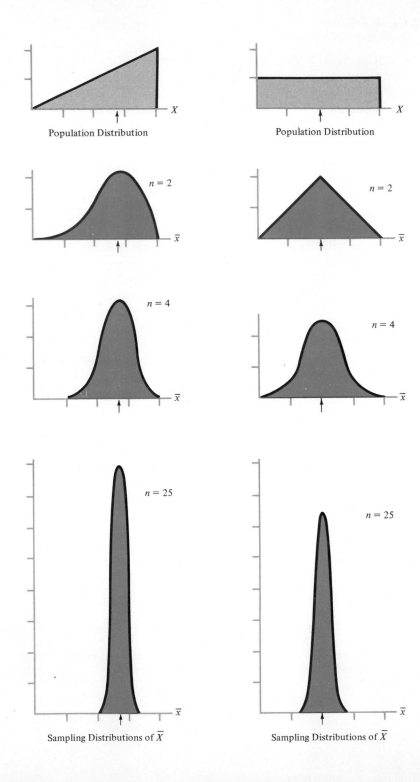

Population Distribution   Population Distribution

$n = 2$ $n = 2$

$n = 4$ $n = 4$

$n = 25$ $n = 25$

Sampling Distributions of $\overline{X}$ Sampling Distributions of $\overline{X}$

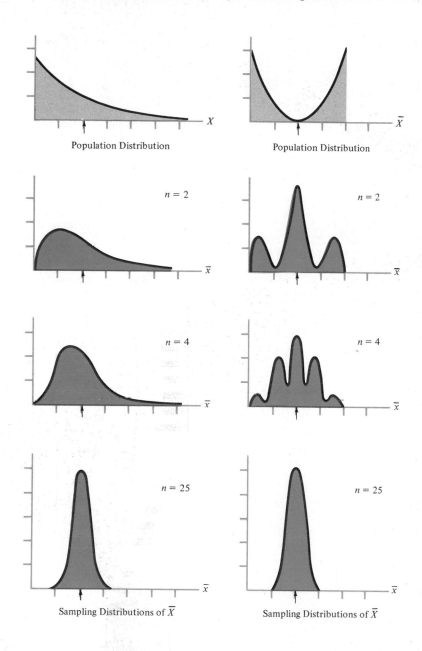

FIGURE 7-11 Illustration of the central limit theorem, showing the tendency toward normality in the sampling distribution of X as n increases, for various populations.

The probability that $\bar{X}$ will be at least 25 months may be calculated by:

$$P[\bar{X} \geqslant 25] = P\left[\frac{\bar{X} - \mu}{\sigma_{\bar{X}}} \geqslant \frac{25 - 24}{.6}\right]$$

$$= P[Z \geqslant 1.67]$$

$$= .5000 - .4525 = .0475$$

Thus, if the same mean and standard deviation apply for the wild rats, then $\bar{X}$ would exceed 25 months in only about 5 percent of these experiments. Such an outcome ought to be relatively rare.

Suppose that $\sigma = 6$ months is indeed the case for wild rats as well. Also, assume that the experimenter actually obtains a mean longevity of $\bar{X} = 30.53$ months with his hardy wild animals! This would make the actual sample mean for wild rats $30.53 - 24 = 6.53$ months greater than the mean for laboratory rats, or more than 10 standard deviations ($10\sigma_{\bar{X}}$) beyond $\mu = 24$. In other words, this outcome is so rare that the upper-tail area under the normal curve will be quite tiny—far too small to even be reflected in our table of areas. The obvious conclusion is that wild rats live substantially longer than laboratory strains fed the same diet, and the actual value of μ is considerably larger than 24 months.

Applicability of the Central Limit Theorem

The central limit theorem is perhaps the most important result of statistical theory. It allows us to develop procedures for making inferences about the means of populations *even when little more than the sample results are known.* The central limit theorem applies universally, whether the population is discrete or continuous.* Thus, the normal curve plays a fundamental role in a great portion of statistical theory. In Chapter 8, we will make use of this result in estimating population means. In Chapter 9, the theorem will be applied in describing procedures for making decisions based upon the sample mean, which may tend to confirm or deny an assumption regarding the true value of the population mean. In the next section of this chapter, we will see that the central limit theorem applies to samples taken from small as well as from large populations. Section 7-6 will then show that the same result allows us to use the normal curve to approximate the binomial distribution.

EXERCISES

7-12 A sample of size $n = 49$ is taken from a population having a mean of $\mu = 100$ and a standard deviation of $\sigma = 14$. Find the probability that $\bar{X}$ will lie between 96 and 104.

7-13 An economist serving as a consultant to a large teamsters' local wishes to obtain an estimate of the mean annual earnings μ of the membership. He will use the mean $\bar{X}$ of a sample of $n = 100$ drivers as an estimate. Assuming that the standard deviation of the membership's annual earnings is $\sigma = \$1,500$, answer the following:

(a) Find the probability that the estimate will lie within \$200 of the actual population mean.

---

* One restriction is that the population must have a finite variance. This is a theoretical limitation of no practical significance to populations ordinarily encountered.

(b) Let n be increased to 400. Find the probability that the estimate will lie within \$200 of the actual population mean. What is the percentage increase in probability over the probability found in (a)?

(c) Determine the probability that the estimate lies within \$100 of the true population mean when $n = 100$. What is the percentage reduction in this result over the probability found in (a)?

7-14 A bus transporation company wishes to estimate the mean mileage that can be obtained on a new type of radial tire. Due to operating methods, a tire may be used on several buses during its useful life. A separate mileage log must therefore be kept on each tire in the sample. Since this procedure is costly, only $n = 100$ tires are to be used. In a previous study on another tire type, a standard deviation of $\sigma - 2{,}000$ miles was determined. It is assumed that the same figure will apply with the new tires.

(a) What is the probability that the sample mean will be within 500 miles of the population mean?

(b) The maintenance superintendent has stated that the new tires may have greater mileage variability than the tires now used. Assuming that the standard deviation is changed to $\sigma = 4{,}000$ miles, find the probability that the sample mean differs from the population mean by no more than 500 miles.

(c) Comparing your answers to parts (a) and (b), what can you conclude about the effect of increased population variability upon the reliability of the sample mean as an estimator?

(d) Suppose that a sample of size $n = 200$ tires is used instead. If a standard deviation of $\sigma = 2{,}000$ miles is determined, find the probability that the sample mean differs from the population mean by no more than 500 miles.

(e) Comparing your answers to parts (a) and (d), what may you conclude about the effect of increased sample size upon the reliability of the sample mean as an estimator?

7-15 In order to determine the optimal number of toll booths to open during various times of the week, the operations manager of a port authority has ordered an extensive study. One unanticipated finding is that the mean time to collect a toll decreases as the traffic becomes heavier. For example, on late Friday afternoon, the collection times were found to have a mean of $\mu = 10$ seconds, with a standard deviation of $\sigma = 2$ seconds. On slower Wednesday mornings, the mean was $\mu = 12$ seconds and the standard deviation was $\sigma = 3$ seconds. A consistency check is now to be made to determine whether the season of the year affects efficiency. Random samples of $n = 25$ cars are taken on Wednesday mornings and Friday afternoons. Assuming that the above results are true population parameters, answer the following:

(a) What is the probability that the Wednesday sample mean will differ by more than 1 second from the assumed mean?

(b) What is the same probability for Friday?

(c) Why do the probabilities found in (a) and (b) differ?

7-5   SAMPLING DISTRIBUTION OF $\overline{X}$ WHEN POPULATION IS SMALL

We have established that for independent sample observations, the standard error for $\overline{X}$ may be obtained from the expression $\sigma_{\overline{X}} = \sigma/\sqrt{n}$. Observations will always be independent when sampling is done with replacement. But, ordinarily, sampling is done *without replacement*. When populations are large in comparison to the sample size, the probability distributions for successive observations are changed imperceptibly by the removal of earlier items. In these cases, we can generally draw the same conclusions that we would if the population were infinite, and thus we can assume independence between observations.

But when the population is small in comparison to the sample size, we must reflect this fact in computing $\sigma_{\bar{X}}$. *The standard error of $\bar{X}$ for small populations is*

$$\sigma_{\bar{X}} = \frac{\sigma}{\sqrt{n}} \sqrt{\frac{N-n}{N-1}} \tag{7-7}$$

where σ = population standard deviation, N = population size, and n = sample size.

Finite Population Correction Factor

The term $\sqrt{(N-n)/(N-1)}$ is referred to as the *finite population correction factor*. When n is small in relation to N, then the factor is very near to 1, so that the standard error obtained from a sample without replacement is close in value to one obtained with replacement. Note that the numerator in the expression will never be greater than the denominator, so that $\sigma_{\bar{X}}$ will be smaller when a sample is taken without replacement. *In practice, the finite population correction is usually ignored whenever n is less than 10 percent of N.*

For samples from small populations, the normal distribution approximately describes the sampling distribution of $\bar{X}$, even though the observations are not independent.

> **Example 7-6** A survey is to be taken of incomes in two cities. City A has a population of $N = 10,000$; city B has a population of $N = 2,500$. It will be assumed that the same standard deviation of $\sigma = \$1,500$ is common to both populations. A sample of size $n = 1,000$ is taken from each.
>
> The following calculations, using expression (7-7), provide the standard error of $\bar{X}$ for city A:
>
> $$\sigma_{\bar{X}} = \frac{\$1,500}{\sqrt{1,000}} \sqrt{\frac{10,000-1,000}{10,000-1}} = \$45.00$$
>
> and, analogously, for city B:
>
> $$\sigma_{\bar{X}} = \frac{\$1,500}{\sqrt{1,000}} \sqrt{\frac{2,500-1,000}{2,500-1}} = \$36.75$$

Note that the standard error of $\bar{X}$ for city B is smaller than that for city A. This is to be expected, since B is a smaller city. But the standard error for city A is only about 23 percent greater, although its population is four times as large.

The probability that $\overline{X}$ *exceeds* the mean by 100 or more may be calculated for each city. For A:

$$P[\overline{X}-\mu \geqslant 100] = P\left[\frac{\overline{X}-\mu}{\sigma_{\overline{X}}} \geqslant \frac{100}{45.00}\right]$$

$$= P[Z \geqslant 2.22]$$

$$= .5000 - .4868 = .0132$$

and for B,

$$P[\overline{X}-\mu \geqslant 100] = P\left[\frac{\overline{X}-\mu}{\sigma_{\overline{X}}} \geqslant \frac{100}{36.75}\right]$$

$$= P[Z \geqslant 2.72]$$

$$= .5000 - .4967 = .0033$$

In either case, the probability of obtaining a sample mean that exceeds the respective mean by \$100 or more is relatively small. Notice, though, that the same sample size provides about the same protection against obtaining extremely large sample values in *both* cities, regardless of the size of either.

In general, we can make the following conclusion:

The probability that the sample mean is unusually small or large is about the same for both small and large populations having the same standard deviation, as long as the sample size is relatively small in relation to the population size.

When n is small in relation to N, the finite population correction factor gets close to 1. Thus, a sample of $n = 1,000$ would yield almost the same finite population factor for a population of $N = 100,000$ as it would for one of $N = 1,000,000$ (.9949 vs. .9995). Thus, if the standard deviations of the two populations are identical, there would be an imperceptible difference in the respective values of $\sigma_{\overline{X}}$ and the probabilities of possible sample results would be nearly identical. In this instance, a sample of size $n = 1,000$ will be almost as reliable in a large population as in one that is one-tenth its size. This is why we concluded in Example 4-5 (page 84) that a sample of Alaskan voters in a presidential election poll would have to be about the same size as a sample of Californian voters for the sample results to be equally reliable.

EXERCISES

7-16 Suppose that a finite population has a standard deviation of $\sigma = 10$. Calculate $\sigma_{\overline{X}}$, the standard error of $\overline{X}$, for each of the following value pairs for the population and sample size:
(a) $N = 1,000$; $n = 500$
(b) $N = 1,000$; $n = 50$
(c) $N = 10,000$; $n = 5,000$
(d) $N = 10,000$; $n = 1,000$
(e) $N = 10,000$; $n = 500$

7-17 A customs official wishes to estimate the mean weight for each of three batches of copper ingots obtained from different smelters. $N = 500$ ingots have arrived from Chile, $N = 1,000$ from Bolivia, and $N = 700$ from Arizona. Samples of $n = 100$ ingots from each batch are weighed. It will be assumed that each smelter produces batches of ingots having a mean weight of $\mu = 100$ pounds, with a standard deviation of $\sigma = 5$ pounds.

(a) Find the probability that each batch yields a sample whose mean lies between 99 and 101 pounds.

(b) Find the analogous probability values when the sample means are obtained from batches 10 times as large (using the same sample size). Do your answers differ significantly between smelters? Explain.

7-18 Suppose that the customs official in Exercise 7-17 establishes a rule to enable him to decide when an entire batch of ingots should be individually weighed. Since weighing is a time-consuming procedure, he wants to do this only when there is strong sample evidence that the ingots are underweight.

Assume that an acceptable batch of $N = 1,000$ ingots has a mean weight of $\mu = 100$ pounds, but that the official does not know this value. He takes a sample of $n = 200$ and calculates $\bar{X}$. Suppose that the batch standard deviation is $\sigma = 5$ pounds. Three decision rules are to be considered:

1. Accept batch (do not weigh all 1,000 ingots) if $\bar{X} \geqslant 100$ pounds.
2. Accept batch if $\bar{X} \geqslant 99.5$ pounds.
3. Accept batch if $\bar{X} \geqslant 99.0$ pounds.

Find the probability under each of the above decision rules that the customs official will accept the batch without weighing all the ingots. If he prefers the rule that maximizes the probability of not weighing all 1,000 ingots, which rule should he choose?

7-6 SAMPLING DISTRIBUTION OF P AND THE NORMAL APPROXIMATION

In Chapter 6, we established that the proportion of successes obtained from a Bernoulli process is a random variable having the binomial distribution. A random sample selected from a population of two complementary attributes may be construed to be a Bernoulli process whenever the population is infinite or whenever the sampling is done with replacement. In other words, the binomial distribution is applicable whenever the sample observations are taken independently.

Advantages of Approximating the Binomial Distribution

The calculation of probabilities from the binomial formula can be quite a chore. In many cases, the task may seem insurmountable. Consider, for example, calculating the probability that $R = 324$ convictions are obtained in the next $n = 2,032$ criminal cases brought to trial in a state, when the average rate of convictions is $\pi = .537$. This would involve evaluating

$$\frac{2,032!}{324!\,(2,032 - 324)!} (.537)^{324} (1 - .537)^{2,032 - 324}$$

The computations would require working with both extremely large and miniscule numbers, making the use of logarithms or other approximations almost mandatory.

Of course, with a high-speed digital computer, the task might be manageable. Binomial probabilities can be calculated and tabulated. But a new problem then arises: For what values of π and n should tables be constructed? Obviously, not all π values can be accommodated, for they are infinite in number (all possible values between 0 and 1). Also, the probability table for a particular π would be quite long for even a moderately large n. Since no table can be constructed that will be satisfactory for all envisionable contingencies, and because one applicable to a moderate number of situations would require a great deal of space, tables are no panacea.*

Normal Distribution as an Approximation

If a satisfactory approximation to the binomial distribution can be used, then the difficulties just discussed can be avoided. Recall that a graph of the binomial distribution tends to be bell shaped as n becomes large (see Figure 6-4, page 169). This suggests that for large sample sizes, the binomial approaches the shape of the normal curve. Indeed, it may be established that the central limit theorem also applies to the proportion of successes P.† This fact proves quite advantageous, because normal curve areas are conveniently tabulated.

In Chapter 6, we established expressions for the mean and the standard deviation of P. The mean of P is

$$E(P) = \pi \qquad (7\text{-}8)$$

Retaining the terminology in the preceding section, the standard deviation of the possible values for the statistic P, calculated from the following expression, is the *standard error of P:*

$$\sigma_P = \sqrt{\frac{\pi(1-\pi)}{n}} \qquad (7\text{-}9)$$

Assuming that P has a sampling distribution shaped like a normal curve, P may be transformed into the standard normal random variable by the following:

$$Z = \frac{P - \pi}{\sigma_P} \qquad (7\text{-}10)$$

---

* Of course, if a high-speed digital computer could be queried whenever the need arose, there would be no need for tables. With the growing accessibility to time-sharing terminals that connect the user directly to a large computer, it may eventually be most convenient to use such a procedure and thus avoid the approximations described in this section.

† Letting each sample success represent a "score" of $X = 1$ and each failure a "score" of $X = 0$, the sample mean "score" $\bar{X}$ is the number of successes divided by n, or $\bar{X} = R/n$. This equals P, the sample proportion of successes.

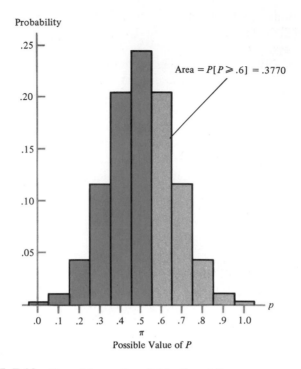

Probability

Area $= P[P \geqslant .6] = .3770$

π

Possible Value of P

FIGURE 7-12   Binomial sampling distribution of P.

The suitability of the approximation may be illustrated by considering the two distributions when $n = 10$ and $\pi = .5$. The actual sampling distribution is plotted in Figure 7-12. The probability values were obtained from Appendix Table C (page A-14). In order to compare this discrete distribution to the continuous normal distribution, the probabilities are presented as bars rather than spikes. The height of each bar represents the probability that P assumes the value at the midpoint of the bar's base. Since the base of each bar may be considered to be of unit width (letting each unit represent a .10 increment on the scale of p), the area of a bar also represents the probability of the P value at the midpoint. The area .3770 of all the bars at or above the point $P = .6$ therefore represents the probability that the value of P obtained will be greater than or equal to .6. This is represented by the gray area in Figure 7-12.

We can obtain the normal approximation to the sampling distribution of P. Here, the mean and the standard error are

$$E(P) = \pi = .5$$

$$\sigma_P = \sqrt{\frac{.5(1-.5)}{10}} = .158$$

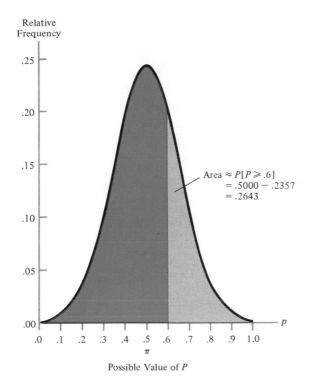

FIGURE 7-13   Normal approximation to the sampling distribution of P, when $n = 10$, $\pi = .5$

The corresponding normal curve is graphed in Figure 7-13. Treating P as an approximately normal random variable, we may find the probability that P lies above .6 as follows:

$$P[P \geqslant .6] = P\left[\frac{P - \pi}{\sigma_P} \geqslant \frac{.6 - .5}{.158}\right]$$

$$= P[Z \geqslant .63]$$

$$= .5000 - .2357 = .2643$$

This probability value is represented by the gray area under the approximating normal curve shown in Figure 7-13.

Note that the area under the normal curve above .6 only approximates the true probability indicated by the gray area under the bars in Figure 7-12. The true probability is .3770, while the normal curve provides a probability of .2643. The discrepancy between the binomial probabilities and those found with the normal curve will be negligible for larger sample sizes. We may better assess the nature of the approximation in Figure 7-14, where the graph for the binomial

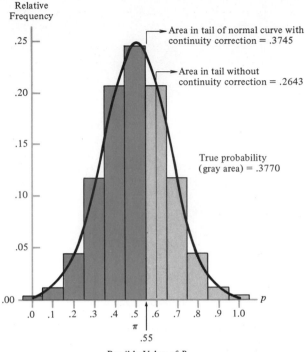

FIGURE 7-14   Comparison of binomial sampling distribution of *P* to its normal approximation

distribution for *P* is superimposed on the normal curve. Here, a continuity correction has been applied to obtain a better approximation.*

Table 7-3 gives the commonly accepted guidelines for using the normal approximation. These guidelines have been constructed according to the popular

---

* From this graph, we can see that a value could have been obtained from the normal curve area above .55 rather than .60:

$$P[P \geqslant .55] = P\left[\frac{P-\pi}{\sigma_P} \geqslant \frac{.55-.50}{.158}\right]$$

$$= P[Z \geqslant .32]$$

$$= .5000 - .1255 = .3745$$

The value .3745 is much closer to the true binomial probability of .3770. Using .55 instead of .60 applies a continuity correction of amount $.5/n = .5/10 = .05$. The need for a continuity correction arises from the fact that the *discrete* binomial distribution is being approximated by a *continuous* normal distribution. Thus, we may improve our normal curve approximation by subtracting $.5/n$ from the lower limit for *P* and adding $.5/n$ to the upper limit. Throughout the remainder of this book, the continuity correction will be ignored, making discussions conceptually simpler. For most sample sizes *n* where the normal approximation will be made, *n* is large enough so that $.5/n$ is relatively tiny and the continuity correction only slightly improves the approximation.

TABLE 7-3 Commonly Accepted Guidelines for Using Normal Approximation to the Binomial

Whenever π Equals	*Use the Normal Approximation Only if n Is No Smaller Than*
.5	10
.40 or .60	13
.30 or .70	17
.20 or .80	25
.10 or .90	50
.05 or .95	100
.01 or .99	500
.005 or .995	1,000
.001 or .999	5,000

rule that the normal approximation to the binomial is adequate whenever both of the following hold:

$$n\pi \geqslant 5$$
$$n(1-\pi) \geqslant 5$$

(7-11)

Some statisticians insist upon even larger sample sizes than those listed in Table 7-3 before the approximation is acceptable. Note that in some cases a very large sample size ought to be used. This is because the skew of the binomial distribution is so pronounced for large or small π that the bell shape is assumed by the binomial distribution only for very large n.

An Example

We may illustrate the usefulness of the normal approximation to the binomial by means of the following example.

Example 7-7 The president of a savings and loan association wants to entice his depositors to move more of their funds from other financial institutions to his firm. He feels that this might be accomplished by offering more services than savings banks traditionally perform. He therefore wants to gauge the potential attraction of safe deposit boxes by estimating the proportion of his firm's customers who now hold them elsewhere. If 50 percent of his current depositors are *assumed* to have safe deposit boxes elsewhere, what is the probability that 40 percent or fewer in a sample of size $n = 100$ customers will hold safe deposit boxes?

We assume that the sample proportion of boxholders has a binomial sampling distribution (because the population is large). Here, $\pi = .50$ and we wish to evaluate the probability that $P \leqslant .40$. Referring to Table 7-3, we see that $n = 100$ is sufficiently large for making the normal approximation. We therefore calculate:

$$\sigma_P = \sqrt{\frac{.50(1-.50)}{100}} = .05$$

Thus,

$$P[P \leqslant .40] = P\left[\frac{P-\pi}{\sigma_P} \leqslant \frac{.40-.50}{.05}\right]$$
$$= P[Z \leqslant -2.00]$$
$$= .5000 - .4772 = .0228$$

So the probability is quite small that 40 percent or fewer of the sample would hold boxes. If a sample result of $P = .40$ were actually obtained, this would be a rare outcome when the actual proportion of users is assumed to be $\pi = .50$. Such sample evidence would strongly indicate that the unknown value of π is smaller than .50.

For $n = 100$, we are fortunate to have the actual cumulative binomial probability values in Appendix Table C. For $\pi = .50$ and $n = 100$, we find that

$$P[P \leqslant .40] = P\left[\frac{R}{n} \leqslant \frac{40}{100}\right] = .0284$$

In this case, the normal approximation provides a value quite close to the actual one.

For a sample of $n = 5$, we could not have used the normal approximation, because Table 7-3 indicates that n would be too small for $\pi = .50$. This desired probability would therefore have to be obtained directly from the binomial distribution.

Distribution of *P* for Samples Taken from a Small Population Without Replacement

As in the case of the sample mean, sampling without replacement requires a different sampling distribution for P. This distribution is called the *hypergeometric distribution*, and it has the same mean as the binomial:

$$E(P) = \pi$$

As with $\bar{X}$, the variability in values of P is smaller when there is no replacement. This is reflected in σ_P. *For small populations, the standard error of P is*

$$\sigma_P = \sqrt{\frac{\pi(1-\pi)}{n}} \sqrt{\frac{N-n}{N-1}} \qquad (7\text{-}12)$$

Expression (7-12) is the standard deviation of the binomial distribution multiplied by the same finite population correction factor that is used with $\bar{X}$.

The normal approximation may be used here in the same manner as it is in sampling with replacement, except that for sampling without replacement the standard error of P is obtained from expression (7-12). Again, we usually ignore the finite population correction when n is less than 10 percent of N.

Example 7-8 A small professional society has $N = 5,000$ members. The president has mailed $n = 500$ questionnaires to a random sample of members asking whether they wish to affiliate with a larger group. Assuming that the proportion of the *entire* membership favoring consolidation is $\pi = .7$, find the probability that the sample proportion P differs from this by no more than .05.

Here we observe that $E(P) = \pi = .7$, and we calculate the standard error from expression (7-12):

$$\sigma_P = \sqrt{\frac{.7(1-.7)}{500}} \sqrt{\frac{5,000-500}{5,000-1}} = .0194$$

The desired probability is then found:

$$P[-.05 \leqslant P - \pi \leqslant .05] = P\left[\frac{-.05}{.0194} \leqslant \frac{P-\pi}{\sigma_P} \leqslant \frac{.05}{.0194}\right]$$

$$= P[-2.58 \leqslant Z \leqslant 2.58]$$

$$= 2(.4951) = .9902$$

An Application of the Normal Approximation to Acceptance Sampling

We may illustrate the usefulness of the normal approximation to the binomial by an example involving *acceptance sampling*. A manufacturer dependent upon an outside supplier for raw materials or components for his own production will want to accept only shipments of some set minimum quality. Because of the expense involved, the decision to accept or reject an incoming shipment is based on a sample of the items received. The procedure for accomplishing this is an acceptance sampling plan. This approach is common in quality control.

Consider a certain automobile assembly plant that obtains its headlamps from a supplier in batches of $N = 500$. The supplier has designed its production operation in such a way that, for various reasons, about 5 percent of its output is defective. The assembly plant quality control manager inspects a sample of size $n = 100$ (without replacement) from each shipment. If 7 or fewer (that is, 7 percent or fewer) items in the sample are found to be defective, he will accept the shipment; otherwise, the batch will be rejected and returned to the supplier.

The number 7 is referred to as the *acceptance number*. It forms the basis for a *decision rule*, which specifies the action to be taken regarding a particular batch. We may determine what the implications are to both the consumer and the producer by using such a rule to calculate various probabilities.

Suppose that a batch of headlamps is received that contains $\pi = .10$ defectives. If the quality control manager knew the π value, he would reject the shipment. But since only a sample will be taken, he may end up accepting this poor batch. What is the probability that the manager will accept the shipment?

The shipment will be accepted if the sample proportion defective P is $\leqslant .07$. Employing the normal approximation, we first find the standard error of P, using expression (7-12):

$$\sigma_P = \sqrt{\frac{.10(1-.10)}{100}}\sqrt{\frac{500-100}{500-1}} = .027$$

The probability of accepting the bad batch is therefore

$$P[P \leqslant .07] = P\left[\frac{P-\pi}{\sigma_P} \leqslant \frac{.07-.10}{.027}\right]$$

$$= P[Z \leqslant -1.11]$$

$$= .5000 - .3665 = .1335$$

Thus, there is a .1335 probability that this poor batch of headlamps will be accepted. Since accepting a bad lot is an incorrect decision that will hurt some users of a product, such a probability value is sometimes referred to as the *consumer's risk*.

The supplier can also be hurt by another kind of erroneous decision. Suppose that an acceptable lot having $\pi = .05$ defectives is shipped. If, by chance, more than 7 defectives are selected, the good shipment will be rejected. To find the probability that this will occur, we again use the normal approximation. The standard error of P is

$$\sigma_P = \sqrt{\frac{.05(1-.05)}{100}}\sqrt{\frac{500-100}{500-1}} = .0195$$

The probability of rejecting the good batch is therefore

$$P[P>.07] = P\left[\frac{P-\pi}{\sigma_P} > \frac{.07-.05}{.0195}\right]$$

$$= P[Z>1.03]$$

$$= .5000 - .3485 = .1515$$

Such a probability that an acceptable shipment will be erroneously rejected is referred to as the *producer's risk*.

The producer's risk and consumer's risk are illustrations of the more general Type I and Type II errors of hypothesis testing to be discussed in Chapter 9. There, we will describe how a decision rule may be constructed to balance both risks and to keep the probabilities of erroneous decisions at desired levels.

EXERCISES

7-19 Find the probability that the proportion P of successes in $n = 100$ trials of a Bernoulli process with trial success probability $\pi = .5$ lies between each of the following pairs of values:
(a) .40, .60   (b) .35, .65   (c) .50, .65   (d) .50, .90.

7-20 Find the probabilities that the proportion P of successes obtained from a Bernoulli process with trial success probability $\pi = .5$ will lie between .4 and .6 when the number n of trials is (a) 64,   (b) 100,   (c) 400.
(d) What relationship do you notice between the probability values obtained and the trial size n? How do you explain this relationship?

7-21 A cannery accepts a shipment of tomatoes whenever P, the proportion that is ripe in a sample of $n = 100$ is $\geqslant .90$. Assuming that shipments are sufficiently large that the sampling process may be represented (with only minor error) as a Bernoulli process, answer the following:
(a) What is the probability of accepting a poor shipment in which the proportion of ripe tomatoes is $\pi = .8$?
(b) What is the probability of rejecting a good shipment in which the proportion of ripe tomatoes is $\pi = .95$?

(c) How do you account for the fact that these probabilities indicate that some shipments of poor quality will be accepted while some shipments of good quality will be rejected?

7-22 Random samples of voter preferences are obtained for the candidates to the U.S. Senate. One is taken from a precinct having $N = 500$ registered voters; the other, from a precinct having $N = 1,000$. In each case, the sample size is $n = 100$. There are just two candidates, a Republican and a Democrat, and, for (a) and (b) below, each voter in the sample favors one of the candidates.

(a) Assuming that the proportion of Republicans in both precincts is $\pi = .40$ and that the voters will adhere strictly to party lines, find the probability for each sample that the majority of the voters polled will favor the Republican candidate.

(b) Same as (a), but with samples of size $n = 49$.

(c) Suppose that some of the voters are "undecided" when polled. Can any sample that includes undecideds be truly reflective of the votes made by the precinct population on election day? Explain.

REVIEW EXERCISES

7-23 As closely as possible, find the following percentiles for a normal distribution of women's heights with a mean of $\mu = 66$ inches and a standard deviation of $\sigma = 1.5$ inches:

(a) 50th   (b) 15th   (c) 95th   (d) 75th   (e) 33rd

7-24 The owners of a large ranch have established that the gestation period of their cows may be represented by the normal distribution with a mean of $\mu = 281$ days and a standard deviation of $\sigma = 5$ days. Assuming that the length of pregnancies for the next 100 births is a random sample from this population, find the probabilities that the mean gestation period will

(a) Exceed 282 days.   (c) Be less than 282.5 days.

(b) Lie between 280 and 282 days.   (d) Be less than 280.5 days.

7-25 The weights of "one-ounce" gold ingots cast by a rare-metals refinery are normally distributed with a mean of $\mu = 28$ grams and a standard deviation of $\sigma = 1$ gram. A shipment of 25 ingots is to be made. Find:

(a) The probability that the mean ingot weighs less than 27.5 grams.

(b) The probability that the entire shipment weighs more than 705 grams.

7-26 The annual incomes of surgeons constitute a highly positively skewed population. Nevertheless, it is still possible—according to the central limit theorem—to find the sampling distribution of the mean of a random sample of these incomes by using the normal distribution. Suppose that the population has an unknown mean of μ and a standard deviation of $\sigma = \$10,000$. An estimate of μ will be made using the value of the sample mean $\bar{X}$. It is desired that this estimate fall within $\pm \$1,000$ of the true mean.

(a) If $n = 100$ incomes, find the probability that the estimate meets the desired accuracy.

(b) If $n = 625$ incomes are used in the sample instead, find the probability that the estimate meets the desired accuracy.

7-27 The IQ scores achieved by the first-grade students in a certain state are normally distributed, with a mean of $\mu = 105$ and a standard deviation of $\sigma = 10$ points. A random sample of n scores is to be selected. Find the standard error of the sample mean and the probability that this mean IQ will exceed 106 points, when: (a) $n = 100$ (b) $n = 25$ (c) $n = 900$

7-28   A parapsychologist is testing the extrasensory perception of a purported clairvoyant. She has a deck of cards, half of which are red and half of which are black. She selects the top card and asks her subject (who is in another room) to identify its color. The procedure is repeated 100 times. Each successive card is replaced in the deck, and the deck is shuffled before the next card is drawn. A subject with no powers of ESP should give the correct color 50 percent of the time, so that $\pi = .5$. Under this assumption, what is the probability that a correct response will be obtained for 65 or more of the 100 cards? (Use the normal approximation.)

7-29   For each of the following sampling situations, indicate (by yes or no) whether the sampling distribution of the sample proportion may be approximated by the normal curve. In each case, assume that the population is quite large in relation to the sample size.
(a) $\pi = .50\ n = 9$ (b) $\pi = .10\ n = 36$ (c) $\pi = .83\ n = 100$
(d) $\pi = .45\ n = 20$ (e) $\pi = .01\ n = 1,000$

7-30   A marketing researcher believes that the proportion of persons favoring a new product is $\pi = .4$. Suppose that a sample of $n = 100$ persons is selected at random.
(a) If the assumed parameter value holds, what is the probability that 50 percent or more of the persons queried will favor the product?
(b) Suppose that the actual parameter value is only $\pi = .37$. What is the probability that 50 percent or more will favor the product?

7-31   A student marks an examination consisting of 36 true-or-false questions by tossing a coin. For each question, he answers true for a head and false for a tail. Assuming that half of the correct answers should be marked true, find the probability he will pass the test by marking at least 75 percent of the answers correctly. (Use the normal approximation.)

7-32   If the population of members of the U.S. Army has a mean of 70 inches and a standard deviation of 3 inches, determine the probabilities that the mean height for a random sample of 100 soldiers will be
(a) Between 70 and 70.5 inches.   (d) Less than 68 inches.
(b) Less than 69.5 inches.   (e) Between 69.4 and 70.8 inches.
(c) Greater than 72 inches.

7-33   A random sample of 100 soldiers is chosen without replacement from a regiment of 900 men. If the mean regiment height is 71 inches, with a standard deviation of 2.5 inches, determine the probabilities that the sample mean height will be
(a) Between 71 and 71.4 inches.   (c) Greater than 71.6 inches.
(b) Less than 70.5 inches.   (d) Between 70.7 and 71.5 inches.

7-34   A company has a policy of measuring the quantities in all bulk products purchased. For instance, on the average, 1,000-foot rolls of transparent tape ought to be close to the specified length. In evaluating 10,000 roll shipments, the purchasing manager has specified the following quality control policy. A random sample of 100 rolls of tape is to be selected, and the mean length determined. If this mean is greater than or equal to 990 feet, the entire shipment is to be accepted; otherwise, the shipment is to be rejected and returned to the manufacturer.
(a) Suppose that a shipment has a mean roll length of only 980 feet, with a standard deviation of 50 feet. Find the consumer's risk or probability of accepting these inferior-quality tapes.
(b) Suppose that a shipment has mean roll length of 1,005 feet, with a standard deviation of 60 feet. Find the producer's risk or probability of rejecting these good-quality tapes.

Chapter Eight
Statistical Estimation

The more numerous the number of observations and the less they vary among themselves, the more their results approach the truth.

Marquis de Laplace (1820)

Many kinds of estimates can be made from sample data. In this chapter we shall be concerned with these estimates and with the procedures for making them. Problems of estimation are crucial in practically every statistical application. This is especially true in business decision making, where often only sample results are available for establishing vital information. For example, samples are used to estimate a product's share of the market—a useful number for many important marketing decisions. Also, statistical estimates provide management with the average times requires to complete various production operations, allowing for intelligent planning and better day-to-day control. Similarly, sample data yield median earnings of subscribers to various magazines, a demographic feature useful to merchandisers in choosing where to place advertisements.

8-1 ESTIMATORS AND ESTIMATES

The use of samples to estimate a population parameter is one of the more prevalent forms of statistical inference. A sample statistic used for this purpose is referred to as an *estimator*. An important segment of statistical theory is concerned with finding statistics that are appropriate to use as estimators. For instance, the sample mean is a particularly good estimator for the population mean. We shall see why this is so.

The Estimation Process

Parameter estimation requires a great deal of planning. The first step is to choose an estimator. Having done that, a major concern is to select appropriate procedures so that sampling error can be controlled. The choice of sampling method—judgment or convenience sampling, or some version of random sampling—will affect this. As we have seen, only random samples are free from sampling bias, so our discussion will center on these. We have also seen that sampling error may be controlled by using a sufficiently large sample, as small samples tend to be less reliable. A practical consideration will be to balance the level of reliability, which is influenced by sampling error, against the costs of obtaining the sample.

Due to chance, the sample statistic actually obtained may not be very close in value to the population parameter, but the only way to be certain of the parameter's value would be to take a census of the population. Therefore, statisticians must develop a methodology that will enable them to assess the reliability of their results. This is tricky business when there is only a theoretical basis for knowing what values are reasonable.

Estimates fall into two categories: point estimates and interval estimates. For example, a commonly quoted figure for the mean height of adult American males is $5'9\frac{1}{2}''$. Such a single value is called a *point estimate*. The major difficulty with a number like $5'9\frac{1}{2}''$ is that it gives us the false impression that it is the true mean value, right down to the smallest fraction of an inch. This is not so. Rather, such a number is the mean of a relatively small sample of heights, and, as we have seen, one sample mean can vary considerably from another—even when both samples are selected from the same population. Reflecting this chance variation, the *interval estimate* specifies a range of values, such as $5'9''$–$5'10''$, within which the population parameter is believed to lie. An interval estimate acknowledges the potential for sampling error by indicating that the parameter lies between two numbers.

Whether a point or an interval estimate is to be made depends upon the objective of the statistical study. Interval estimates would be unsuitable to a manufacturer as the basis for placing orders for raw materials, for the supplier cannot accept an order for "something between 2,000 and 3,000 units." Likewise, knowing only that the wattage of a stereo amplifier lies between 50 and 80 makes it difficult to compare that model to other brands. But the superiority of an interval estimate is evident in many kinds of planning or reporting. For example, knowing that next year's sales might lie between 10,000 and 11,000 units, a company president is able to draw up a realistic budget when the estimate indicates the presence of uncertainty as to the sales level. He can visualize the best and worst cases, and thereby obtain a reasonable basis for evaluating the risks involved.

We are presently concerned only with estimates based upon samples taken from already existing populations or from identifiable target populations. This excludes an entire class of predictions that may be based upon other kinds of information. The most notable of these would be economic forecasts based upon time-series data. For example, every year the news media provide a plethora of forecast levels of the gross national product. Although sampling may be involved in this type of estimate, the major role is played by other factors, such as judgment, current trends, contemplated changes in government policies, and the state of international affairs. Some procedures useful in making such predictions will be discussed in Chapter 10. Another category of excluded predictions concern parameters of some future population. For example, the median annual family income for the United States in 1984 cannot be estimated from the usual sample, because the elementary units cannot be presently defined and the variate values themselves lie in the future. Although the population may be imagined, it cannot be directly observed until 1984.

EXERCISES

8-1 For each of the following situations, indicate whether or not a sample may be selected from some population to make a current estimate. Explain your answers.

   (a) An estimate is to be made of the mean annual lifetime earnings of recent college graduates.

   (b) The taste preferences of the potential buyers of a new product that is not currently on the regular market are to be determined.

   (c) The response of heart patients to a new drug, untried on humans, is to be measured.

   (d) The Federal Power Commission wishes to estimate the kilowatt-hour usage by customers at the end of the coming decade.

8-2 For each of the following parameters, indicate whether you would use a point estimate or an interval estimate and explain your choice.

   (a) The mean age of product buyers, to be used in comparing alternative advertising plans.

   (b) The proportion of an evening's television viewing population watching a particular program, to be presented to advertisers as evidence of the program's drawing power.

   (c) The mean pH value (a measure of acidity) of intermediary ingredients in a chemical process, so that a formula may be developed indicating the amount of neutralizing agent to apply.

   (d) The median income of doctors, to be published in a government report.

8-2 POINT ESTIMATES

Often several alternative statistics can be used as estimators. For instance, to estimate the population mean, we could use any one of three sample statistics: the mean, the median, or the mode. We can guess that the sample mean may be the most suitable estimator, but how can we substantiate our choice?

The most desirable feature of an estimator is that it has a value close to the unknown value of the population parameter. We will need to develop criteria for comparing alternatives in terms of their ability to match this parameter value. The criteria themselves must necessarily be of a theoretical nature, because ordinarily we will have no experimental basis for comparing alternative estimators. Not knowing the population mean, for example, it is not possible to choose between the sample mean or median by their values alone.

Under certain circumstances, the sample mean, median, and mode will each have a value lying close to the population mean. The basic questions are therefore: Which statistic will be the most reliable estimator? And which will require the least expenditure of resources in terms of sample size? An ancillary question, also quite important, is: Do we have an easily applied theoretical procedure for determining the probability that the value obtained for the estimator statistic will lie sufficiently close to the parameter?

Criteria for Statistics Used as Estimators

Three criteria have been developed for comparing statistics in terms of their worth in estimating a parameter. One of these determines whether there is a tendency, on the average, for the statistic to assume values close to the parameter in question. Another considers the reliability of the estimator. A final consideration is whether this reliability improves as the sample size increases. Each of these criteria is defined and discussed below.

Unbiased Estimators

DEFINITION An *unbiased estimator* is a statistic that has an expected value equal to the population parameter being estimated.

The notion of bias, as used here, differs from that previously discussed in that it has nothing to do with the tendency to favor selection of certain population elementary units for the sample. An estimator can be biased even when sampling bias is absent. This is a theoretical type of bias—a statistic that does not, on the average, tend to yield values equal to the parameter is said to be biased. The sample mean $\overline{X}$ is an unbiased estimator of the population mean μ, since we have established that

$$E(\overline{X}) = \mu$$

We may now indicate why we chose to define the sample variance s^2 in the way we did in Chapter 3 (page 55):

$$s^2 = \frac{\sum (X - \overline{X})^2}{n - 1} \tag{8-1}$$

The $n-1$ divisor is used instead of n. However, it may be proven that s^2 (as defined with the $n-1$ divisor) is an unbiased estimator of σ^2, since

$$E(s^2) = \sigma^2$$

An intuitive reason why $n-1$ is used as the divisor is that we obtain a somewhat larger value for the sample variance than the one we obtain by dividing by n. The need for the larger estimator provided by s^2 reflects the fact that ordinarily a sample has less diversity than its population, for the part is rarely more disperse than the whole. (s^2 may turn out to be larger than σ^2, if a disproportionately large number of extreme values are selected for the sample. However, on the average, s^2 values will tend to equal σ^2.)

Efficient Estimators

DEFINITION   One statistic is a more *efficient estimator* than another if its standard error is smaller for the same sample size.

To demonstrate this relationship, we compare the mean and the median of a sample taken from a large, symmetrical population. The sample median is an unbiased estimator of μ when the population is normally distributed. For a large sample size the sample median m has a standard error of

$$\sigma_m = 1.2533 \frac{\sigma}{\sqrt{n}}$$

and we have shown that the standard error of $\overline{X}$ is

$$\sigma_{\overline{X}} = \frac{\sigma}{\sqrt{n}}$$

The standard error of the sample median is 1.2533 times as great as that of the sample mean. This implies that the sample mean is more efficient than the sample median as an estimator of μ. Medians of samples taken from normally distributed populations tend to be more unlike each other than means of the same samples. It follows that the sample mean will make a more reliable estimator of μ.

Consistent Estimators

DEFINITION A statistic is a ***consistent estimator*** of a parameter if the probability that the value of the statistic is very near that of the parameter becomes closer and closer to unity with increasing sample size.

The sample mean is a consistent estimator of the population mean. This is evident because $\sigma_{\bar{X}}$, which expresses the variability in the possible values of $\bar{X}$, becomes smaller as $\sqrt{n}$ grows larger. We also know that the potential values of $\bar{X}$ cluster around μ, so that less variability in these values implies a greater probability that the value actually obtained will be close to μ. As we have seen, $\sigma_{\bar{X}}$ is inversely proportional to $\sqrt{n}$, so that when n becomes quite large, $\sigma_{\bar{X}}$ gets very small; in the limiting case, n is so large ($n = N$) that $\sigma_{\bar{X}}$ becomes zero. This implies that $\bar{X}$ can then assume only one possible value, μ, with a probability of 1. In general, *a statistic whose standard error becomes smaller as n gets larger will be consistent.*

When an estimator is consistent, it then becomes more reliable with larger samples. Consistency alone does not guarantee reliable sample results; this is achieved only by increasing the sample size. But for a larger sample to be more reliable, consistency is a necessary condition. The net effect is that the use of such an estimator allows the statistician to buy more reliability by paying the price to obtain a larger sample. This is not to say that the benefit of increased reliability is worth the price. As with any resource utilization, there is a point of diminishing returns at which the added reliability is not worth the increased cost of a larger sample.

Choosing the Estimator

We may apply the criteria for evaluating the characteristics of the many types of statistics to the comparison of estimators. If we wish to estimate μ, we will achieve better results by using $\bar{X}$ as our estimator than we will by using m. (We would never consider using m to estimate μ, except when the population is believed to be symmetrical.) Both statistics are consistent and unbiased. However, since $\bar{X}$ is more efficient than m, it will be a more reliable estimator of μ for a given expenditure of resources on sampling.

The criteria do not always clearly indicate which statistic is the best one. Each candidate estimator must be analyzed as a separate case, in light of the criteria, since there is no general rule to follow when the best choice is not immediately apparent. Usually, we can say that the better of two estimators that are both unbiased and consistent is the one that is more efficient. But if the better statistic is cumbersome or theoretically difficult to handle, then the second choice will generally be used. (The sample mode is difficult to work with and we will not use it as an estimator.)

Commonly Used Estimators

For the Population Mean

As we have seen, $\bar{X}$ is the most desirable estimator of μ. It is unbiased, consistent, and more efficient than other candidate estimators such as the sample median. It also has a readily obtainable *normal* sampling distribution when the sample is sufficiently large. Knowing the sampling distribution, as we will see in the remainder of this chapter, enables us to choose a sample large enough to achieve a desired level of reliability in our estimate. It also allows us to qualify the estimate actually obtained when the sample results have been collected and tabulated.

Example 8-1   A publisher needs to determine the number of words in one of his books. Rather than having someone count all the words, which would take several hours of painfully boring work, an estimate of the mean number of words per page μ is obtained by counting the number of words on each of 30 randomly chosen pages. The sample mean number of words per page $\bar{X}$ is then calculated. Since there are 600 pages in the book, the estimated number of words is obtained by multiplying $\bar{X}$ by 600. The sample results are shown in Table 8-1.

TABLE 8-1   Sample Results of Words Per Page

Number of Words X	X^2	Number of Words X	X^2
383	146,689	175	30,625
325	105,625	278	77,284
411	168,921	351	123,201
416	173,056	423	178,929
395	156,025	327	106,929
372	138,384	381	145,161
293	85,849	317	100,489
361	130,321	362	131,044
216	46,656	338	114,244
431	185,761	411	168,921
406	164,836	371	137,641
394	155,236	393	154,449
402	161,604	388	150,544
376	141,376	295	87,025
268	71,824	421	177,241
		Totals 10,680	3,915,890

$$\bar{X} = \sum X/n \qquad\qquad s = \sqrt{(\sum X^2 - n\bar{X}^2)/(n-1)}$$
$$= 10{,}680/30 \qquad\qquad\quad = \sqrt{[3{,}915{,}890 - 30(356)^2]/29}$$
$$= 356 \text{ words} \qquad\qquad\quad = \sqrt{3{,}924.48}$$
$$\qquad\qquad\qquad\qquad\qquad = 62.65 \text{ words}$$

The sample mean obtained is

$$\bar{X} = 356 \text{ words}$$

Thus, the point estimate of μ is 356 words. This results in an estimate of

$$356 \times 600 = 213,600$$

words in the entire book.

For the Population Standard Deviation

The sample variance s^2 is an unbiased and consistent estimator of the population variance σ^2. We may take the square root of s^2 to estimate the standard deviation, since σ is the square root of σ^2.

For the previous example, the standard deviation of the number of words per page was calculated in Table 8-1 to be $s = 62.65$ words. This may be used as an estimate of σ, the standard deviation of words per page for the entire book.

For the Population Proportion

The proportion π of elementary units in the population having a particular attribute may be estimated by the corresponding sample proportion P. As we have seen, $E(P) = \pi$, so that P is an unbiased estimator of π. It is also consistent, since the standard error of P

$$\sigma_P = \sqrt{\frac{\pi(1-\pi)}{n}}$$

decreases with increasing n. Thus, the variability in possible P values decreases, so that the probability that the value obtained for P will be very close to π increases as the sample size increases. In the limiting case, when n is the same size as the population, $P = \pi$ with certainty.

> **Example 8-2** A consumer information service was asked to measure the tendency of the average shopper to purchase whatever she or he picks up, whether it is needed or not. A random sample of shoppers was selected for an experiment. Each was asked to prepare a detailed shopping list before embarking on the week's food forage. Then, at the store, each sample shopper was "tailed" and a record kept of each item touched (except for packaged meats and produce). At the end of the shopping, the items on the shopper's original list were compared to those purchased. The number of items bought but not on the list was added to the number of items touched but not bought. This sum represented the total number of impulse items—that is, items not included in the original shopping plans.
>
> The procedure was repeated for several weeks, with separate records kept on each shopper. The proportion P of impulse items bought was then found for every shopper in the sample experiment. One woman accrued a total of 132 impulse items; of these, she purchased 48. Her value of P was therefore determined to be
>
> $$P = \frac{48}{132} = .364$$

which may be taken as a point estimate of the actual proportion of impulse items she would buy under similar circumstances.

The *P*'s for all the shoppers were determined in this manner. Their mean was then used to estimate the proportion of impulse purchases for the shopping population as a whole. The average proportion of such purchases was estimated to be .55. The consumer service therefore advised its clients to keep their hands on their carts and rely on their initial grocery-buying decisions.

EXERCISES

8-3 A survey is taken of the owners of stores in a franchise chain to determine population characteristics of the previous year's earnings by franchisees. A random sample of $n = 10$ stores has been taken, resulting in the following figures (in thousands of dollars, rounded): 15, 5, 2, 7, 25, 19, 11, 9, 13, 42.
   (a) Find a point estimate of the mean earnings for the franchise holders as a group.
   (b) Find a point estimate of the standard deviation of earnings for the population.
   (c) Estimate the proportion of earnings more than $10,000.
   (d) Estimate the proportion of earnings less than $5,000.

8-4 Tossing a die twice in succession may be viewed as analogous to taking a random sample of size $n = 2$ with replacement from a population having 6 observable values (corresponding to the number of dots showing on each side of the die).
   (a) Calculate the range of this population.
   (b) We define the *sample range* to be the difference between the highest and the lowest values obtained from the two tosses. The sampling distribution of the sample range is provided in the table below. Calculate the expected value of the sample range.
   (c) Comparing your answers to (a) and (b), do you conclude that the sample range is an unbiased estimator of the population range? Explain.

Possible Sample Range	Elementary Events	Probability
0	(1, 1) (2, 2) (3, 3) (4, 4) (5, 5) (6, 6)	6/36
1	(1, 2) (2, 1) (2, 3) (3, 2) (3, 4) (4, 3) (4, 5) (5, 4) (5, 6) (6, 5)	10/36
2	(1, 3) (3, 1) (2, 4) (4, 2) (3, 5) (5, 3) (4, 6) (6, 4)	8/36
3	(1, 4) (4, 1) (2, 5) (5, 2) (3, 6) (6, 3)	6/36
4	(1, 5) (5, 1) (2, 6) (6, 2)	4/36
5	(1, 6) (6, 1)	2/36
		36/36

8-3 INTERVAL ESTIMATES OF THE MEAN USING A LARGE SAMPLE

The interval estimate is the preferred form for reporting the results of sampling studies because it serves several purposes: (1) It provides an estimated range of values for the unknown parameter; (2) it acknowledges the presence of uncertainty as to the parameter's actual value; and (3) it may very simply show the degree of precision achieved by the results obtained. Thus, the interval estimate has a distinct advantage over the point estimate. Indeed, it is not uncommon to mistake the point estimate for a precise expression of the parameter value itself. Whenever the evidence is obtained by a sample, perfect results are most improbable.

An interval estimate, being a range of possible values, tacitly illustrates the presence of uncertainty. It is ordinarily accompanied by a statement indicating the degree of uncertainty, expressed as a likelihood that the parameter being estimated actually does lie within the stated interval.

In this section, we will discuss the suitability of an interval estimate and show how it is constructed.

Confidence Interval Estimate of the Mean When σ Is Known

To illustrate how the interval estimate is obtained, we will begin with the problem of estimating a population mean when the standard deviation of the population is known.

Form of the Interval Estimate
We wish to establish an interval containing μ that will be in the form

$$a \leqslant \mu \leqslant b \tag{8-2}$$

We will use the sample mean, our estimator, to accomplish this. Ordinarily, the interval endpoints a and b are chosen in such a way that the interval is centered at the value of $\bar{X}$ actually obtained. Also, we wish to attach to the interval a measure of likelihood, such as .95 or .99, that will vary with the situation and that we will denote by C. Since we know that the sampling distribution of $\bar{X}$ is normal, for any value of C a particular normal deviate value z may be found so that

$$C = P[\mu - z\sigma_{\bar{X}} \leqslant \bar{X} \leqslant \mu + z\sigma_{\bar{X}}] \tag{8-3}$$

The inequality in expression (8-3) may be transformed into the order in expression (8-2) by rearranging the terms inside the brackets so that we obtain

$$C = P[\bar{X} - z\sigma_{\bar{X}} \leqslant \mu \leqslant \bar{X} + z\sigma_{\bar{X}}] \tag{8-4}$$

Although this places μ inside inequalities, μ is constant (and of unknown value) and cannot change. The lower and upper limits for μ are subject to chance variation, since they involve the random variable $\bar{X}$.

The event inside the brackets in expression (8-4) indicates the form of an interval estimate obtained using the actual observed sample mean $\bar{X}$. Using

$\sigma/\sqrt{n}$ in place of $\sigma_{\bar{X}}$, we may use the following expression to calculate the *interval estimate for the population mean:*

$$\bar{X} - z\frac{\sigma}{\sqrt{n}} \leqslant \mu \leqslant \bar{X} + z\frac{\sigma}{\sqrt{n}} \qquad (8\text{-}5)$$

This interval is centered at $\bar{X}$, and the endpoints are partly determined by the value chosen for C, which in turn establishes z (the value of the normal deviate). This interval is sometimes expressed more compactly as $\mu = \bar{X} \pm z\sigma/\sqrt{n}$.

Meaning of an Interval Estimate

Keep in mind that the interval in expression (8-5) may not actually contain μ. This is because the endpoints depend upon the observed value for $\bar{X}$, which may be quite different from the value of μ due to sampling error. *Before* sample results are obtained, there is a probability C that μ will lie within $\bar{X} \pm z\sigma_{\bar{X}}$. But the interval in expression (8-5) is determined by a known value $\bar{X}$ calculated *after* taking the sample, so that we cannot attach a probability measure to it. Once we have a particular value for the sample mean, the interval estimated from it is certain to either contain or not contain μ. But we cannot know which will be true. Figure 8-1 shows the conceptual implications of the interval estimate when $C = .90$.

Confidence Level

Because we cannot attach a probability value to the truthfulness of our interval estimate, we employ instead a related term, the *confidence level*, to which we assign the following

DEFINITION   The ***confidence level***, denoted by C, is the proportion of interval estimates—obtained from many repeated samples (of the same size) taken from the same population—that will contain the actual value of the parameter being estimated. Although a single sample is ordinarily taken, the confidence level is usually expressed as a percentage.

Because in practice just one sample is obtained, so that only a single value of $\bar{X}$ is available, just one interval is constructed from expression (8-5). This is referred to as a *confidence interval*. The level of confidence determines the value of z to be used. The larger the value of C, and hence z, the wider the resulting confidence interval. The value of z required for the construction of an interval corresponding to the desired confidence level may be found by reading in reverse the table of normal curve areas. It will be simpler instead to use Appendix Table E, which directly provides the values of z for common confidence levels.

We will now illustrate how a confidence interval estimate may be obtained. Suppose that a sample of $n = 100$ families is selected from the population of a large city and that the sample mean income is $\bar{X} = \$15,549.63$. We have *prior*

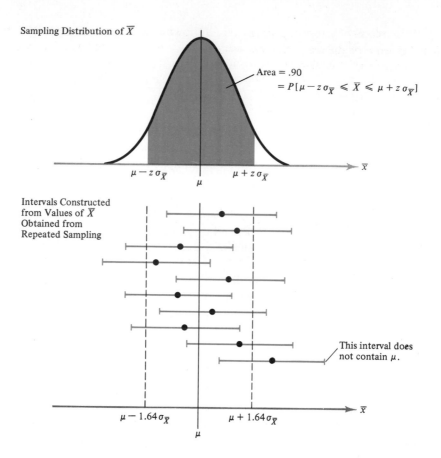

Sampling Distribution of $\overline{X}$

Area = .90
= $P[\mu - z\sigma_{\overline{X}} \leqslant \overline{X} \leqslant \mu + z\sigma_{\overline{X}}]$

Intervals Constructed
from Values of $\overline{X}$
Obtained from
Repeated Sampling

This interval does
not contain μ.

FIGURE 8-1   Illustration of the interval estimate concept. Intervals have been
obtained for ten values of $\overline{X}$ calculated for different samples taken
from the same population. Note that nine of the intervals contain μ.
If many repeated samples were to be taken from a population, the
percentage of intervals obtained that contained μ would be approx-
imately the same as the .90 probability that $\overline{X}$ lies within $\mu \pm 1.64\sigma_{\overline{X}}$.

knowledge that the standard deviation for the population of family incomes is
$\sigma = \$5,000$. We wish to determine a 99-percent confidence interval estimate of
the true population mean μ.

From Appendix Table E, we determine that the normal deviate when
$C = .99$ is $z = 2.57$. Substituting the appropriate values into expression (8-5), we
have as our 99-percent confidence interval estimate

$$\$15,549.63 - 2.57\frac{\$5,000}{\sqrt{100}} \leqslant \mu \leqslant \$15,549.63 + 2.57\frac{\$5,000}{\sqrt{100}}$$

or

$$\$14,264.63 \leqslant \mu \leqslant \$16,834.63$$

We *cannot* say that the stated interval contains μ with a .99 probability. (It either does or does not, but we don't know which case applies.) The proper interpretation of this 99-percent confidence interval is: *If we were to repeat the above procedure often, each time selecting a different sample from the same population, then, on the average, 99 out of every 100 similar intervals obtained would contain μ.*

Confidence Interval Estimate of the Mean When σ Is Unknown

The endpoints of a confidence interval estimate of μ just described depend upon the population standard deviation σ, which is usually unknown and, like μ, must ordinarily be estimated from the sample data. As we saw in Section 8-2, we may use the actual sample standard deviation s as the estimator of σ. For *large samples*, we may therefore use the following *confidence interval estimate of μ when σ is unknown:*

$$\bar{X} - z\frac{s}{\sqrt{n}} \leqslant \mu \leqslant \bar{X} + z\frac{s}{\sqrt{n}} \qquad (8\text{-}6)$$

In effect, the sampling error in using s to estimate σ is ignored. Large values of s will tend to stretch the interval beyond the desired width, and small values of s will have the opposite effect. In practice, ignoring the variability in s is not serious, since, on the average, about as many intervals obtained from repeated samples will contain μ as would be the case if σ were known.

Example 8-3   A bank operating a credit card system wishes to find the time of the month for mailing customer bills that will provide the shortest average time to receipt of cash payment. Currently the bills are mailed at the end of the month, and the average time to receipt is about 10 days. Three samples of customers are randomly selected, one group to be billed on the 5th of the month, another on the 15th, and the final group on the 25th. In order to avoid any bias due to the transition in billing cycle, figures from the fourth month under the new dates constitute the samples. A total of $n = 500$ customers are selected for each sample group. Since the payment of bills is a continuous process, the populations may be treated as infinite. The following results are obtained:

5th of Month	15th of Month	25th of Month
$\bar{X} = 18.30$ days	$\bar{X} = 17.41$ days	$\bar{X} = 5.42$ days
$s = 6.2$	$s = 5.8$	$s = 2.3$

A confidence interval is to be constructed for each group. The desired level of confidence is 99 percent. Thus $z = 2.57$. For the 5th of the month, the confidence interval is calculated, using expression (8-6):

$$18.30 - \frac{2.57(6.2)}{\sqrt{500}} \leqslant \mu \leqslant 18.30 + \frac{2.57(6.2)}{\sqrt{500}}$$

or

$$\mu = 18.30 \pm .71$$

so that

$$17.59 \leqslant \mu \leqslant 19.01 \text{ days} \quad \text{(for 5th)}$$

Analogously, the following confidence intervals are obtained for the other groups:

$$\mu = 17.41 \pm .67 \quad \text{or} \quad 16.74 \leqslant \mu \leqslant 18.08 \text{ days} \quad \text{(for 15th)}$$
$$\mu = 5.42 \pm .26 \quad \text{or} \quad 5.16 \leqslant \mu \leqslant 5.68 \text{ days} \quad \text{(for 25th)}$$

Note that there is so little difference between the results for the 5th and 15th that the confidence intervals overlap. Of the three times of the month, the 25th appears to be the superior billing time. By switching its billing cycle so that bills are mailed on the 25th instead of the month's end, the bank *might* (remember, we do not *know* μ) be able to reduce the collection time average from its present 10 days to some value between 5.16 and 5.68 days, thereby allowing the firm to have longer use of the funds received.

Expression (8-6) applies only when the population itself is large. When the mean of a small population is to be estimated by a sample selected without replacement, then the standard error of $\overline{X}$ includes the finite population correction factor, so that the *confidence interval estimate of μ for small populations is*

$$\overline{X} - z \frac{s}{\sqrt{n}} \sqrt{\frac{N-n}{N-1}} \leqslant \mu \leqslant \overline{X} + z \frac{s}{\sqrt{n}} \sqrt{\frac{N-n}{N-1}} \tag{8-7}$$

Features Desired in a Confidence Interval

Two features are desirable in a confidence interval estimate. One is the level of confidence itself, which expresses the degree of *credibility* that may be attached to the results. The other is the *precision* of the estimate, which is gauged by the width of the interval itself. But credibility and precision are competing ends in themselves. For a fixed sample size, a reduction in the interval width, which causes greater precision, can be achieved only at the expense of reducing z, which is tantamount to using a lower confidence level. Conversely, greater confidence can be obtained only at the expense of precision. Thus, a confidence interval may be very precise but not at all credible, or vice versa. For example, if z were .5 in Example 8-3, then the confidence interval for mailing on the 25th would become

$$\mu = 5.42 \pm .5(2.3)/\sqrt{500} = 5.42 \pm .05$$

or

$$5.37 \leqslant \mu \leqslant 5.47 \text{ days}$$

which is more precise than before, but the confidence level would be only 38 percent. Likewise, increasing the confidence level to 99.8 percent so that $z = 3.08$ would yield the less precise interval estimate

$$\mu = 5.42 \pm 3.08(2.3)/\sqrt{500} = 5.42 \pm .32$$

or

$$5.10 \leqslant \mu \leqslant 5.74 \text{ days}$$

The only way to increase both confidence and precision is to collect a larger sample to begin with. For example, suppose that $n = 1,000$ customers had been used for the billings on the 25th and the same sample results were obtained. With $C = .998$, the confidence interval would be

$$\mu = 5.42 \pm 3.08(2.3)/\sqrt{1,000} = 5.42 \pm .22$$

or

$$5.20 \leqslant \mu \leqslant 5.64 \text{ days}$$

a *more precise* interval with a *greater confidence level* than the one originally obtained.

EXERCISES

8-5 The board of directors of a corporation is evaluating the performance of its corporation president in order to decide whether or not to retain him in the future. One director proposes that each director rate the president—on a scale from 1 to 5—as to the quality of his performance in five areas: (1) sales growth, (2) personnel relations, (3) operating efficiencies achieved, (4) attainment of profit potential, and (5) successful new product development. The ratings will be summarized in terms of frequency distributions, with the mean rating calculated for each category and submitted to the directors at the next meeting, when a vote on retention will take place. The board agrees to the procedure.

The chairman is concerned with the average ratings. He is worried about their precision and wonders what level of confidence should be attached to the results. A trustee who happens to be an expert in statistics diplomatically informs the chairman that these considerations are irrelevant. Explain the basis for the expert's stand.

8-6 Construct a 95-percent confidence interval for the means of large populations, given the following sample results:
(a) With $n = 100$, $\bar{X} = 100.53$ minutes, and $s = 25.3$ minutes.
(b) With $n = 200$, $\bar{X} = 69.2$ inches, and $s = 1.08$ inches.
(c) With $n = 350$, $\bar{X} = \$12.00$, and $s = \$7.00$.

8-7 Repeat Exercise 8-6, assuming in each case that a relatively small population of size $N = 1,000$ was used.

8-8 A personnel director wishes to estimate the mean scores for a proposed aptitude test that may be used in screening applicants for clerical positions. Using a sample of $n = 100$ applicants, she found $\bar{X} = 75.6$ and $s = 14.7$. Assuming that the population is large, construct a 95-percent confidence interval estimate for the true mean.

8-9 A hotel manager desires to improve the level of room service by increasing personnel. To justify the increase, he must estimate the mean waiting time experienced by guests before being served. From a random sample of $n = 100$ orders, the sample mean waiting time was established at 30.3 minutes, with a standard deviation of 8.2 minutes. Construct a 99-percent confidence interval that the manager might use to estimate the actual mean waiting time.

8-10 A tire manufacturer has obtained the following sample results for the tread life of $n = 50$ radial tires tested:

$$\bar{X} = 52,346 \text{ miles}$$
$$s = 2,911 \text{ miles}$$

(a) Construct a 99-percent confidence interval estimate of the mean tread life for all such tires manufactured.

(b) What is the interpretation of the interval you found in part (a)?

(c) Suppose that an estimate having a precision of ± 500 miles is desired. Find the corresponding confidence level.

8-11 In attempting to analyze the causes of the astronomical rise in the cost of medical care over the past decade, a government agency needs to estimate the mean fee for various operations. Suppose that a random sample of 250 splenectomies yields the following results:

$$\bar{X} = \$374.00$$
$$s = \$ 56.25$$

(a) Construct a 99-percent confidence interval estimate of the current mean splenectomy fee.

(b) Suppose that ten years ago, a similar study based upon 150 operations yielded the following results at a 95-percent level of confidence

$$\$130.00 \leqslant \mu \leqslant \$150.00$$

Find the values of $\bar{X}$ and s used to construct this confidence interval.

(c) Using the value of $\bar{X}$ obtained in (b) and the one given in (a) as point estimates of the mean fees in two years, estimate the percentage increase in splenectomy fees over the ten-year period.

8-4 INTERVAL ESTIMATES OF μ WHEN SMALL SAMPLE SIZES ARE USED

We have shown how to construct confidence intervals when the population standard deviation is unknown. We did this by using s (computed from the sample) in place of σ. For the desired level of confidence we used a corresponding normal deviate z. Doing this presumes that $(\bar{X} - \mu)/(s/\sqrt{n})$ is normally distributed. In fact, *the normal distribution is only approximately correct* and is suitable only for large samples. For small sample sizes another distribution applies, and we cannot use values of z in constructing confidence intervals.

The Student *t* Distribution

Shortly after the turn of the century, the statistician W. S. Gosset first studied this problem. Because his employer, a brewery, forbade him to publish, he chose the nom de plume "Student." Gosset derived a probability distribution, now referred to as the Student t distribution, for a random variable t. The sampling distribution of $(\overline{X}-\mu)/(s/\sqrt{n})$ is the t distribution. Whenever the population being sampled is normally distributed,

$$t = \frac{(\overline{X}-\mu)}{s/\sqrt{n}} \tag{8-8}$$

In practice, however, the t distribution may be used for samples taken from any population not highly skewed.

The Student t distribution, like the normal distribution, has a relative frequency curve that is bell-shaped and symmetrical, as shown in Figure 8-2. The single parameter that determines the shape of its curve is called the *number of degrees of freedom*. When t represents $(\overline{X}-\mu)/(s/\sqrt{n})$, the number of degrees of freedom is $n-1$ (because for a fixed value of $\overline{X}$, there are only $n-1$ "free choices" for the values of the n observations used in calculating $\overline{X}$ and s).

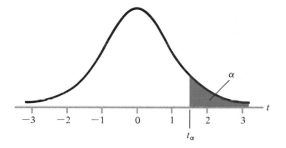

FIGURE 8-2   The Student t distribution.

To find the probability that t exceeds some value, it is necessary to use the table of areas under the Student t distribution in Appendix Table F on page A-25 There is a separate distribution, and hence a separate set of values, for each number of degrees of freedom; these are shown in separate rows in the table. The values in the body of the table are the points t_α corresponding to the respective upper-tail area α (column) and degrees of freedom (row). The reason for this strange layout (compared to the normal curve table) is that we will be concerned with finding the point that corresponds to a given upper-tail area. In order to find t_α so that

$$P[t \geqslant t_\alpha] = \alpha$$

we read down the column headed by the probability value α, stop at the row corresponding to the number of degrees of freedom, and read the desired t_α value.* (As with the normal curve, there is no need to have separate table entries for the left-hand portion of the t curve.)

---

* The reader is cautioned that many other books place the value of the sum of both the lower- and the upper-tail areas at the heads of the columns.

For example, suppose that we wish to find $t_{.01}$ (the value for which the probability is .01 that t is greater than or equal to that value) and that the number of degrees of freedom is 20. From Appendix Table F, we obtain $t_{.01} = 2.528$. Thus

$$P[t \geqslant 2.528] = .01$$

A common guideline is that the Student t distribution need only be used when the sample size is less than 30. For larger samples, the normal distribution is ordinarily used. In actual fact, $(\overline{X} - \mu)/(s/\sqrt{n})$ has the t distribution for samples from normal populations, regardless of the magnitude of n. But for large values of n, the curves for the t distribution and the standard normal curve are very nearly the same. The choice of $n = 30$ as the demarcation point is quite arbitrary, but it is traditional. [As a practical matter, R. A. Fisher, whose table is universally copied (and is used in this book), jumps from 30 to 40 degrees of freedom, so that values in between are unavailable.]

Figure 8-3 shows the curves for the standard normal and t distributions when the number of degrees of freedom is 4. Note that the normal curve lies below the t curve for values lying in the tails. This reflects the fact that the t distribution assigns higher probabilities to extreme-valued outcomes than the normal distribution does, owing to the extra element of uncertainty arising from not knowing σ.

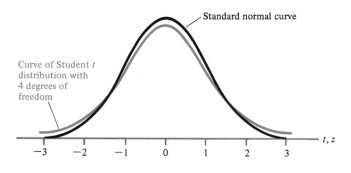

FIGURE 8-3   Comparison of the relative frequency curves of the standard normal distribution and the Student t distribution.

Importance of the t Distribution

The availability of the Student t distribution for making interval estimates has proved advantageous in many applications of statistics where there are often severe limitations upon the size of the samples obtained. The reasons may be economic, since the cost of experimentation with large samples could become prohibitive. Sometimes a large sample cannot be collected quickly enough to provide the answers required. This is the case when observations must be obtained sequentially from a manufacturing process having a low rate of output —large commercial jet aircraft production, for example. Or perhaps the sample observations must be made of rare phenomena, such as nuclear reactor accidents. Experiments in medicine, education, and psychology, where people are observed, are often limited to small samples.

Constructing the Confidence Interval

We may now use t_α—as we used z with large samples—to construct *the confidence interval for estimating the population mean:*

$$\overline{X} - t_\alpha \frac{s}{\sqrt{n}} \leq \mu \leq \overline{X} + t_\alpha \frac{s}{\sqrt{n}} \qquad (8\text{-}9)$$

We use the particular value of t_α that provides the same probability that $\overline{X}$ lies within $\mu \pm t_\alpha s/\sqrt{n}$ as the desired level of confidence C. It may be obtained from Appendix Table F for an upper-tail area of $\alpha = (1 - C)/2$.

To show how this works, let us find a 90-percent confidence interval for sample results obtained from a survey. Since $C = .90$, we have $\alpha = (1 - .90)/2 = .05$. Substituting this value into expression (8-9) gives us

$$\overline{X} - t_{.05} \frac{s}{\sqrt{n}} \leq \mu \leq \overline{X} + t_{.05} \frac{s}{\sqrt{n}}$$

To carry this further, suppose that $n = 25$ and the results obtained gave $\overline{X} = 10.0$ and $s = 5.0$. Then the degrees of freedom would be $n - 1 = 24$, and for an $\alpha = .05$ area under the Student t distribution, $t_{.05} = 1.711$. The 90-percent interval is constructed by substituting these values into expression (8-9),

$$10 - \frac{1.711(5.0)}{\sqrt{25}} \leq \mu \leq 10 + \frac{1.711(5.0)}{\sqrt{25}}$$

so that

$$\mu = 10.0 \pm 1.7$$

or

$$8.3 \leq \mu \leq 11.7$$

Example 8-4   The production manager of an appliance manufacturing company wishes to develop data for a study to determine the quantities of various types of production equipment that should be purchased. An essential element of the study is maintenance costs. The production manager is concerned that too little attention has been paid to the cost of labor lost due to breakdowns. For instance, one assembly production line depends upon parts fabricated by a stamping machine. Occasionally this machine breaks down, taking several hours to repair, and when the buffer stocks of stampings are exhausted, the line must be stopped and many of the workers dismissed for the day. The union contract requires that they receive a full day's wages regardless of the hours actually worked.

TABLE 8-2 Labor Hours Lost Due to
Stamping Machine Breakdowns

Labor Hours Lost X	X^2
205	42,025
1,123	1,261,129
528	278,784
359	128,881
1,421	2,019,241
723	522,729
57	3,249
172	29,584
25	625
Totals 4,613	4,286,247

$\bar{X} = \sum X/n = 4,613/9 = 512.56$ hours

$s = \sqrt{(\sum X^2 - n\bar{X}^2)/(n-1)} = \sqrt{(4,286,247 - 9(512.56)^2)/8}$

$= 490.1$ hours

A larger buffer stock, the size of which currently fluctuates widely throughout the day, would alleviate this problem, but since so many different items may be made in the immediate future, a tremendous investment in work-in-progress inventory would be required to handle all contingencies. An alternative course of action would be to acquire another stamping machine for back-up. In the one year in which the plant has been in operation, the stamping machine has failed 9 times. Table 8-2 shows the direct labor hours lost for each breakdown. An estimate of the mean number of labor hours lost per breakdown is to be obtained. This estimate may then be multiplied by the expected number of breakdowns per year to obtain an estimate of the hours that will be lost annually in the future.

The production manager desires a 95 percent confidence interval to estimate μ, the mean labor hours lost. The number of degrees of freedom is $9 - 1 = 8$. Here $\alpha = (1 - .95)/2 = .025$, so that we obtain $t_{.025} = 2.306$. From expression (8-12), the confidence interval is obtained:

$$512.56 - 2.306(490.1)/\sqrt{9} \leqslant \mu \leqslant 512.56 + 2.306(490.1)/\sqrt{9}$$

so that

$$\mu = 512.56 \pm 376.72$$

and

$$135.84 \leqslant \mu \leqslant 889.28 \text{ hours}$$

Notice that the confidence interval is quite wide, which is to be expected with such a large sample standard deviation and when such a small sample must be employed.

EXERCISES

8-12 Determine the value t_α corresponding to each upper-tail area of the Student t distribution specified below:

	(a)	(b)	(c)	(d)	(e)
α:	.05	.01	.025	.01	.005
Degrees of Freedom:	10	13	21	120	30

8-13 Construct 95-percent confidence intervals for estimates of the means of populations yielding the following sample results:
(a) $n = 6$, $\bar{X} = \$8.00$, $s = \$2.50$.
(b) $n = 15$, $\bar{X} = 15.03$ minutes, $s = .52$ minute.
(c) $n = 25$, $\bar{X} = 27.30$ pounds, $s = 2.56$ pounds.

8-14 Construct 99-percent confidence intervals for (a), (b), and (c) in Exercise 8-13.

8-15 A medical researcher has a contract with a state prison that provides volunteers to test new drugs. He recently tested a drug to be marketed for the treatment of an exotic virus. Each patient was given injections of the live virus until he was infected and was then treated with the drug. Because of the obvious dangers, only 15 volunteers could be obtained. One of the parameters of interest is the mean recovery time. The following recovery times (in days) were obtained:

7	12	17	18	13
9	5	11	6	8
32	9	12	8	18

(a) In preparing the case for presentation to the Food and Drug Administration, a 95-percent confidence interval estimate of the mean recovery time had to be obtained. Find the values of $\bar{X}$ and s, and then calculate the confidence interval used.
(b) What do you think of the appropriateness of ascribing the above result to the population as a whole?

8-16 An electronics firm currently trains its chassis assemblers on the job. It has been proposed that new employees be given one week's training. In order to test the quality of the training program, the output rate of ten trainees is to be compared to that of ten new hires receiving on-the-job training. Each person from the trainee group is matched with one from the other group, according to scores received on an aptitude test. After training, each person is given several chassis to wire, and the time to complete the task is recorded. For each of the $n = 10$ pairs of assemblers, the time of the trainee is subtracted from that of the matching assembler not in the training program. The following results for the differences are obtained:

$$\bar{X} = 3 \text{ minutes}$$

$$s = 2 \text{ minutes}$$

(a) Calculate a 95-percent confidence interval estimate of the mean time difference.
(b) If there is really no difference between the two training methods, then assuming that the population standard deviation is $\sigma = 2$, find the probability that the sample mean would be 3 or more.

8-17 A large casualty insurance company is revising its rate schedules. A staff actuary wishes to estimate the average size of claims resulting from fire damage in apartment complexes having between 10 and 20 units. The current year's claim-settlement experience will be used as a sample. There were 19 claim settlements for buildings in this category. The average claim size was $73,249, with a standard deviation of $37,246. Construct a 90-percent confidence interval estimate of the mean claim size.

8-18 To compare the IQ scores of professional persons, a sociologist administered the Stanford-Binet test to random samples of 16 doctors and 25 lawyers. The following results were obtained:

Doctors	Lawyers
$\bar{X} = 121.4$	$\bar{X} = 128.6$
$s = 12.0$	$s = 15.0$

(a) Construct a 95-percent confidence interval for the mean IQ of doctors.
(b) Construct a 95-percent confidence interval for the mean IQ of lawyers.
(c) Do the sample data indicate that lawyers have higher IQs than doctors? Explain your answer.

8-5 INTERVAL ESTIMATES OF THE POPULATION PROPORTION

The population proportion π may be estimated by an interval, in much the same way as μ. Just as we used $\overline{X}$ to estimate μ, the sample proportion P may be used as the estimator of π. To do this, we take advantage of the normal approximation to the binomial sampling distribution of P (which, as we saw in Chapter 7, is allowable only for certain sample sizes).

We will use P to estimate π by an interval in the form

$$P - z\sigma_P \leqslant \pi \leqslant P + z\sigma_P \qquad (8\text{-}10)$$

Again, we are faced with the difficulty arising from not knowing σ_P (which depends upon π, the value being estimated). This, too, must be determined from the sample results. For this purpose, we may use P in place of π in

$$\sigma_P = \sqrt{\frac{\pi(1-\pi)}{n}}$$

obtaining the point estimate

$$\sqrt{\frac{P(1-P)}{n}}$$

Substituting this into expression (8-10), we obtain the form of our *confidence interval for estimating the population proportion:*

$$P - z\sqrt{\frac{P(1-P)}{n}} \leqslant \pi \leqslant P + z\sqrt{\frac{P(1-P)}{n}} \qquad (8\text{-}11)$$

Expression (8-11) applies for large populations or when sampling with replacement.

Example 8-5   A marketing research firm was retained by a food processor to determine what proportion of food buyers favored the quality of its canned corn over the similar product of one of its major competitors. A panel of $n = 100$ persons was randomly selected. Each panelist was given three cans of brand X and three cans of brand Y with the labels removed. The panelists were asked to use only this corn over a period of two months. Each can was numbered in the sequence in which it was to be used and were assigned so that brand X and brand Y would be alternated. Half of the group started with brand X; the other half with brand Y.

The testers were not told how many brands were involved. They were asked to rate each can of corn on a scale of 1 to 5 for each of four factors: tenderness, sweetness, consistency, and color. The scores were aggregated when all the data had been collected. This was done by brand, so that a comparison could be made—the brand receiving the highest score by a tester would be preferred. The test results are as follows

Number preferring brand X:	59
Number preferring brand Y:	37
Number of ties:	4
Total	100

A 99-percent confidence interval is desired in estimating π, the proportion of the buying population that favors brand X. Thus, $C = .99$, so that the normal deviate obtained from Appendix Table E is $z = 2.57$. The sample proportion of buyers preferring brand X is

$$P = 59/100 = .59$$

We may use expression (8-11) to determine the 99-percent confidence interval

$$.59 - 2.57 \sqrt{\frac{.59(1-.59)}{100}} \leqslant \pi \leqslant .59 + 2.57 \sqrt{\frac{.59(1-.59)}{100}}$$

so that

$$\pi = .59 \pm .13$$

or

$$.46 \leqslant \pi \leqslant .72$$

Should the sample be taken from a small population without replacement, the finite population correction factor is incorporated. In such cases, we use a slightly different *confidence interval for the population proportion for small populations:*

$$P - z \sqrt{\frac{P(1-P)}{n}} \sqrt{\frac{N-n}{N-1}} \leqslant \pi \leqslant P + z \sqrt{\frac{P(1-P)}{n}} \sqrt{\frac{N-n}{N-1}} \qquad (8\text{-}12)$$

EXERCISES

8-19 Find the 99-percent confidence intervals for π, the proportion of undersize boards passing out of a sawmill's planing machine under the following assumptions:
(a) The number of boards measured is $n = 500$, and $P = .25$.
(b) $n = 1,000$ and $P = .1$.
(c) $n = 300$ and $P = .5$.

8-20 A poll has been taken to estimate the President's current popularity. Each person in a random sample of $n = 1,000$ voters was asked to agree with one of the following statements:
(1) The President is doing a good job.
(2) The President is doing poorly.
(3) It is not possible to say.
A proportion of .59 chose statement (1). Assuming that the actual number of voters is very large, construct a 95-percent confidence interval for the population proportion of voters who will choose statement (1).

8-21 Find the 95-percent confidence interval for the proportion of defective items in shipments of parts, when:
(a) $N = 10,000$, $n = 1,000$, and $P = .2$.
(b) $N = 5,000$, $n = 2,000$, and $P = .4$.
(c) $N = 8,000$, $n = 500$, and $P = .01$.

8-22 The highway-patrol director in a certain state has ordered a crackdown on drunken drivers. To see if his safety campaign is working, the director has ordered a sampling study to estimate the proportion of all fatal traffic accidents caused by drinking. In a random sample of $n = 100$ accidents, 42 percent were attributable to alcohol. Assuming that the accident population is large, construct a 95-percent confidence interval for the population proportion.

8-23 A printer has negotiated a contract with a telephone company to print directories. Because a disgruntled customer—stuck with a misspelled name or listed with the number of a mortuary—must suffer for a whole year (and will complain bitterly), the telephone company is anxious to avoid errors. Its contract therefore states that the printer must forfeit $100 for every page containing errors caused by the printing operation.

Counting the errors in a completed directory is an onerous chore. The majority are found by customers' complaints and most of these turn out not to be the printer's fault. Thus, a sample will be taken to determine what penalty to charge the printer. The printer has agreed to these terms. It is so difficult to find errors that many persons must independently search for them. A company accountant selects a sample of 50 pages from a 600-page directory and has 20 people in succession review each page for errors. An estimate will be made of the proportion π of pages containing errors.

(a) Construct a .998 confidence interval estimate of π, if $P = .37$.
(b) The contract spells out that the estimate of π must be a point estimate. What are the losses to the printer if the estimate is too large by .02?
(c) Calculate the probability that the estimator P would be .37 or over if the actual error rate is only $\pi = .35$.

8-6 DETERMINING THE REQUIRED SAMPLE SIZE

A statistic that is consistent becomes more reliable when a larger sample is used. Therefore, the reliability of an estimate made from such a statistic may be controlled by choosing a sample of appropriate size. But what makes a sample size appropriate? That depends upon (1) the disadvantages of erroneous estimates, and (2) the costs of obtaining the sample. As we have indicated, larger samples are more reliable, but they are also more costly. The costs of obtaining the sample must therefore be balanced against any potential damage from error, as reliability and economy are competing ends.

Error and Reliability

The risks of error are dependent upon two things: the chances of making them and the penalties they cause. In a sense, implicit costs are incurred when an estimate is erroneous if it leads to consequences that may be damaging. For example, consider an estimate of a politician's popularity, as expressed by the proportion of voters that prefer him. If the campaign manager estimates a proportion of preference for his candidate that is different from the actual one, then campaign planning may turn out to be far from optimal. In extreme cases, a hopeless campaign might be prolonged to the extent of committing political suicide (for a poor finish could preclude the politician from seeking office in the future), or a very attractive candidate might become too discouraged to continue the battle.

In many statistical applications, it is very difficult to place a monetary value on the results of an incorrect estimate. Also, the seriousness of an error will vary. Being off by half an inch in estimating the mean height of a group of persons would not be as serious as a six-month error in the estimate of expected lifespan, for longevity statistics strongly influence a nation's health planning. Nevertheless, all errors do have some implicit cost. Fortunately, when estimating from samples, the likelihood of major errors is smaller than the likelihood of minor errors. A more reliable sample will yield even smaller chances of major error. In selecting the sample size, the decision-maker must decide what risks are acceptable by considering the chances of making the errors and their implicit costs. Ideally, the sample size chosen should be one that achieves the most desirable balance between the chances of making errors, their costs, and the costs of sampling.

Example 8-6 Lake Airlines, a small regional carrier, derives a substantial amount of business as a feeder to the larger airlines. Passengers purchasing a ticket for a cross-country trip are issued a single ticket for the entire journey at the point of embarkation. When Lake sells these tickets, it is entitled to keep only its portion of the revenue and must forfeit shares to the other airlines involved. The reverse occurs for passengers originating with other airlines who use Lake for a single leg. In these cases, Lake must collect its share of the ticket revenue from the other airline. At the end of each month, the airlines balance their accounts based upon a detailed enumeration of the interairline tickets expired. This has proved to be a very costly and time-consuming process.

A consulting statistician has suggested that the airlines balance their accounts by means of random samples of collected tickets, arguing that only a small portion of the tickets must be analyzed, and so that clerical costs could be considerably reduced. There would be a certain amount of risk, however, for the samples obtained could provide erroneous figures.

Sample Size n	Cost of Collecting Sample	Sampling Error Costs	Total Cost of Sampling
100	$ 100	$40,222	$40,322
1,000	1,000	13,059	14,059
5,000	5,000	5,666	10,666
5,200	5,200	5,454	10,654
6,000	6,000	5,202	11,202
10,000	10,000	4,028	14,028

Using a sample has drawbacks. Because of chance sampling error, Lake's claims against other airlines will be understated in some months and overstated in others. Viewing the long-run average or expected revenue losses as the cost of sampling error, the statistician has computed (by a procedure too detailed to discuss here) the cost for various sample sizes. Assuming that each sample ticket processed costs Lake $1, the costs of sampling have also been calculated. The results are provided in the table on page 257. The sample size yielding the minimum cost to Lake is about $n = 5,200$.

Figure 8-4 illustrates the concepts involved in finding the optimal sample size, which minimizes the total cost of sampling. The costs of collecting the sample data increase with n. But larger samples are more reliable, so that the risks of loss from chance sampling error decline. The total cost of sampling— the sum of collection costs and error costs—will achieve a minimum value for some optimal n. This is the sample size that should be used.

Because of the difficulties associated with finding the costs of sampling error, the procedure illustrated is not usually used to determine the required sample size in traditional applications. Instead, we may focus upon a single number that separates insignificant errors from decidedly undesirable ones. This is called the *tolerable-error level*. In determining this level, we acknowledge that all error is undesirable, but that some error must be accepted as the price for using a sample instead of a census. There are no guarantees that the tolerable error will not be exceeded. However, *large errors may be controlled by keeping the chances of their occurrence small.* Furthermore, as we have seen, reducing the chance of error increases reliability. Thus, we may speak of reliability in terms of the probability that the estimate will differ from the parameter's true value by no more than the tolerable error.

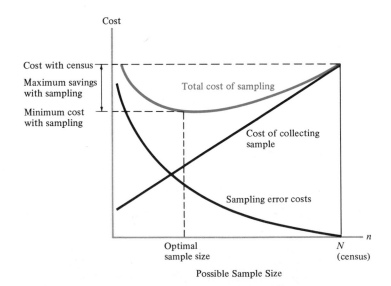

FIGURE 8-4   Relationship among costs in sampling.

Estimating μ by $\overline{X}$

In order to develop a procedure for relating reliability to sample size, we will denote the tolerable error, which is the maximum amount by which the estimate ought to be above or below the parameter, by the letter e, a number in the same units as the parameter being estimated. As applied in traditional statistics, we define reliability in terms of e.

DEFINITION   The *reliability* associated with using $\overline{X}$ to estimate μ is the probability that $\overline{X}$ differs from μ by no more than the tolerable error level e:

$$\text{Reliability} = P[\mu - e \leqslant \overline{X} \leqslant \mu + e] \qquad (8\text{-}13)$$

When the sample is sufficiently large, we have seen that $\overline{X}$ tends to be normally distributed. Estimation reliability may therefore be described in terms of the normal curve. Figure 8-5 illustrates this when the reliability is equal to .95. Here, the colored area provides the probability that $\overline{X}$ will lie within a distance of amount e from μ, either above or below.

For a fixed e, only one normal curve has a shape that provides the desired area. Stated differently, since the shape of a normal curve is specified by its standard deviation, there is only one value of $\sigma_{\overline{X}}$ for which the desired area holds. This may be demonstrated with another case, shown in Figure 8-6. Here the reliability has been established at .80 for the same estimating situation. Note that this curve is flatter than the one in Figure 8-5 for the higher level of reliability. This indicates more variability, so that the curve in Figure 8-6 must have a larger $\sigma_{\overline{X}}$ value.

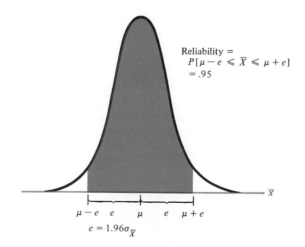

FIGURE 8-5   Relationship among reliability, tolerable error, and the sampling distribution of $\overline{X}$, when reliability (colored area) = .95.

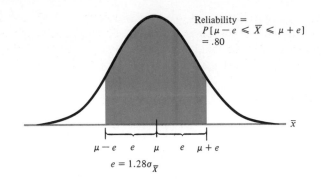

FIGURE 8-6   Relationship among reliability, tolerable error, and the sampling distribution of $\overline{X}$, when reliability (colored area) = .80.

These two examples demonstrate that there is a relation between reliability and the standard deviation of $\overline{X}$. For a specified reliability and tolerable error e, there is a unique corresponding normal curve. Since the shape of this curve is dictated by $\sigma_{\overline{X}}$, the level of reliability itself is determined by the value of $\sigma_{\overline{X}}$. The desired level is ordinarily set in advance of sampling, so that a value for $\sigma_{\overline{X}}$ must be established in order to meet this goal. We must therefore determine the relationship between the desired reliability and the necessary value of the standard deviation of $\overline{X}$.

By rearranging the terms in expression (8-13) and dividing by $\sigma_{\overline{X}}$, we may express the reliability probability as

$$\text{Reliability} = P\left[\frac{-e}{\sigma_{\overline{X}}} \leqslant \frac{\overline{X}-\mu}{\sigma_{\overline{X}}} \leqslant \frac{e}{\sigma_{\overline{X}}}\right] \tag{8-14}$$

Recall that $(\overline{X}-\mu)/\sigma_{\overline{X}}$ is equal to the standard normal random variable, so that we may equivalently state that

$$\text{Reliability} = P\left[\frac{-e}{\sigma_{\overline{X}}} \leqslant Z \leqslant \frac{e}{\sigma_{\overline{X}}}\right] \tag{8-15}$$

Because the normal curve is symmetrical, half of the above probability lies between zero and $e/\sigma_{\overline{X}}$; thus, we may find the appropriate normal deviate for any reliability level. For .95, for example, the area between the mean and $z = 1.96$ is $.95/2 = .4750$. In this case, $\sigma_{\overline{X}}$ must be equal to that unique value permitting the following relationship to hold:

$$1.96 = \frac{e}{\sigma_{\overline{X}}}$$

Likewise, for a reliability of .80, the corresponding normal deviate would be $z = 1.28$, and the following must hold:

$$1.28 = \frac{e}{\sigma_{\overline{X}}}$$

Since each level of reliability corresponds to a unique area under the normal curve, choosing the reliability is tantamount to selecting a value for the normal deviate z. In a sense, a value for z can express the desired reliability level, so that we may summarize the relationship between reliability, tolerable error, and σ_X by means of

$$z = \frac{e}{\sigma_X} \tag{8-16}$$

Keeping e fixed, since the value for z is established by the specified reliability, only $\sigma_{\bar{X}}$ can be adjusted to make the above hold. But if we are sampling from a population, its standard deviation σ is fixed, so that σ_X may be changed only by adjusting the size of the sample. This is so because, as we have seen, σ_X depends upon n (and also upon N, in the case of a small population), so that the reliability of an estimate also depends upon the sample size, and vice versa.

Determining Required Sample Size
in Estimating μ by $\overline{X}$

Independent Sample Observations

Sample observations will be independent either when they are obtained with replacement or when the population is large. In such cases, the standard deviation of $\overline{X}$ is found from

$$\sigma_X = \frac{\sigma}{\sqrt{n}}$$

Since the relationship among reliability, tolerable-error level, and sample size is summarized by expression (8-16), we may substitute the above for σ_X, obtaining

$$z = \frac{e}{\sigma/\sqrt{n}} = \frac{e\sqrt{n}}{\sigma}$$

Squaring both sides of the above expression, then dividing both sides by e^2, and finally multiplying both sides by σ^2, we obtain *the required sample size for sampling with replacement or when the population is large:*

$$n = \frac{z^2\sigma^2}{e^2} \tag{8-17}$$

The above expression tells how large n must be in order to obtain the desired reliability probability that $\overline{X}$ does not differ from μ by more than the tolerable error. This reliability probability fixes a value for z. Appendix Table E provides the values of z for commonly used levels of reliability. The level of the tolerable error e establishes an arbitrary frame of reference for gauging reliability. Both z and e are under the statistician's control. The other factor, the population variance σ^2, remains fixed and is not subject to choice. The effect of each of these three factors is described below.

Three Influences on Sample Size

1. *The required sample size is directly proportional to the population variance.*

Thus, a population that is quite disperse will require a larger sample size than one that exhibits little variability. This tells us that for a constant level of reliability and the same tolerable error, a larger sample size will be necessary to obtain an estimate of the mean for a highly variable population.

Example 8-7 The problem of estimating the mean distance traveled by college professors during the previous summer vacation may be compared to the problem of estimating the mean number of miles that Cadillacs can travel on a tank of gasoline. The mileage of the professors will be quite varied: Some opted to spelunk in Tasmania, while others traveled no further than the local golf course. We can also expect some variability in total gasoline mileage, depending upon the routes traveled, the amount of traffic, who is driving, the brand of gasoline used, and so on. The assumed standard deviation of $\sigma = 500$ miles for the population of distances traveled by professors is 50 times the value of $\sigma = 10$ miles we shall assume for the driving distance of Cadillacs without refueling.

If we desire estimates that differ from the true means by 5 miles or less with a reliability of .99, then, in either case

$$e = 5 \text{ miles}$$
$$z = 2.57$$

From expression (8-17), the sample sizes would be

$$n = \frac{(2.57)^2(500)^2}{5^2} = 66{,}049 \text{ (for professors)}$$

$$n = \frac{(2.57)^2(10)^2}{5^2} = 26.42, \text{ or } 27 \text{ (for Cadillacs)}$$

Note that we must always use the next largest whole number for the sample size. We see that about 2,500 (which is the square of 50) times as many professors as Cadillacs would be needed in the sample in order to provide the same reliability for a tolerable error of 5 miles.

This does not imply that estimating the mean length of professorial odysseys would actually require such a large sample. It is unreasonable to assume that the tolerable error should be as small as the one that might be required by General Motors for its Cadillacs.

2. *The required sample size is inversely proportional to the square of the tolerable error.*

This tells us that decreasing or increasing the tolerable error by a factor results in increasing or decreasing the required sample size by that factor squared. Thus, if we reduce e by half, then we need four times as large a sample

—holding reliability constant. Likewise, if we increase e ten times, the sample size will be one-hundredth as large. Therefore, if we let $e = 50$, ten times the tolerable error used for professors in Example 8-7, then the sample size will be one hundredth as large as before:

$$n = \frac{(2.57)^2(500)^2}{50^2} = 660.49, \text{ or } 661$$

The cost of sampling, as reflected by the sample size, is highly sensitive to the magnitude of the tolerable error. As used in statistics, the tolerable error has roughly the same effect on cost as it does on precision machining. It is an order of magnitude more costly to have machine tolerances of one ten-thousandth of an inch versus one thousandth of an inch.

3. *The required sample size is directly proportional to the square of the reliability-level normal deviate z.*

Thus, doubling z will cause n to be four times as large. We cannot say that doubling z will ordinarily raise reliability by a factor of 2, however, as z does not have a linear relationship to normal curve areas. For example, decreasing z from 2.57 to 1.28 (a reduction in z by about half, so that n would be about one-fourth as large) lowers the reliability from .99 to .80—not quite a 20-percent drop.

The choices of e and z are interrelated, since the reliability usually depends upon the selected tolerable error. Since the tolerable error serves merely as a convenient cutoff point between serious and insignificant errors, its choice may be inseparable from the selection of the reliability level.

Should the sample size be fixed at some level—due to a budgetary limitation or some other practical constraint, like the availability of volunteers to test the effects of a new drug—then the tolerable error can be adjusted upward or downward only by a compensating increase or decrease in the level of reliability. Expression (8-17) shows that by raising or lowering e, z must be correspondingly changed when n and σ are fixed.

Sampling Without Replacement from a Small Population

When the sample is to be taken from a small population of size N, the expression for the standard error of $\overline{X}$ is

$$\sigma_{\overline{X}} = \frac{\sigma}{\sqrt{n}} \sqrt{\frac{N-n}{N-1}}$$

Substituting the terms on the right-hand side into expression (8-16) for $\sigma_{\overline{X}}$ and solving for n, we obtain *the required sample size when sampling without replacement from small populations:*

$$n = \frac{Nz^2\sigma^2}{(N-1)e^2 + z^2\sigma^2} \tag{8-18}$$

Example 8-8   An urban housing research team wishes to estimate the mean monthly rent paid by minority families with one or more children. A sample is to be selected from the residents of a medium-sized city, where $N = 5,000$ such families live. The tolerable error has been set at $e = \$1.00$. Previous studies indicate that the standard deviation should be about $\sigma = \$20.00$. A sample size n must be determined so that the probability that the sample mean differs from the population mean by no more than the tolerable error is .95.

The required normal deviate is found from Appendix Table E to be $z = 1.96$. Substituting these values into expression (8-18), we obtain

$$n = \frac{5,000(1.96)^2(20)^2}{4,999(1)^2 + (1.96)^2(20)^2} = 1,175.5, \text{ or } 1,176$$

Determining Required Sample Size for Estimating π by P

The type of analysis that we applied to the sample mean may also be applied to find the number of observations required to estimate a population proportion from its sample counterpart. The roles of tolerable error and reliability, as they affect n, are completely analogous. Tolerable error e represents the maximum allowable deviation between π and its estimator P, and e is expressed as a *decimal fraction*. Reliability is the probability that P differs from π by no more than e.

Using the normal approximation, the variability in the sampling distribution of P is summarized by σ_P. Analogous to using $\overline{X}$ to estimate μ, we have the requirement that σ_P be of appropriate size so that

$$z = \frac{e}{\sigma_P} \tag{8-19}$$

Since σ_P depends upon n (and upon the population size N as well, when sampling without replacement from a small population), the desired size for σ_P is obtained through the correct choice of n.

Independent Sample Observations

When the sample is obtained from a continuous process, or when N is large, so that the sample outcomes are independent, we have established the standard deviation of P to be

$$\sigma_P = \sqrt{\frac{\pi(1-\pi)}{n}}$$

Note that σ_P, and hence the sampling distribution of P, depends upon π. But it is π that we are trying to estimate. Thus, we cannot know σ_P until π is known. In practice, we must pick a value for π that seems reasonable and use it to establish σ_P. When the sample values are actually obtained, the point estimate made of π may turn out to be smaller or larger than the value used to select σ_P.

Unlike estimating with $\overline{X}$, we cannot, therefore, be sure that our standard deviation of P, and hence n itself, is of an appropriate size to ensure satisfying the prescribed level of reliability (although when using $\overline{X}$, the choice of n depends upon σ, which is not ordinarily known either).

Substituting the expression for σ_P into expression (8-19) and solving the resulting expressions for n, we obtain *the required sample size when sampling with replacement or from a large population:*

$$n = \frac{z^2 \pi (1 - \pi)}{e^2} \qquad (8\text{-}20)$$

Note that this depends upon π, which must be *guessed* before we take the sample to estimate it. We do not use the actual value for π in expression (8-20), because it remains unknown.

Expression (8-20) shows that n is inversely proportional to the square of the tolerable error e and directly proportional to the square of the reliability factor z—just as it is with $\overline{X}$. In place of the population variance, we have the product $\pi(1-\pi)$. Thus, n depends upon π. When the product $\pi(1-\pi)$ is large, then the resulting n must also be large. This term is largest when $\pi = .5$:

$$\pi(1 - \pi) = .5(1 - .5) = .25$$

It can also be quite small, as when $\pi = .001$,

$$\pi(1 - \pi) = .001(.999) = .000999$$

(As indicated in Table 7-3 on page 227, the normal approximation holds for $\pi = .001$ only when $n \geqslant 5,000$.)

> **Example 8-9**   A gas company has noticed that there is a continual discrepancy between the cubic feet of gas leaving its storage tanks and the actual consumption reported by company meter readers. Some of the discrepancy may be caused by inaccurate meters and minor leaks, but much is believed to be due to the lackadaisical behavior of the meter readers. Therefore, the proportion of misread meters is to be estimated for each reader. A sample of homes from each meter reader's route is selected for audit. A company supervisor, whose presence is unknown, will follow each reader on a portion of his route and reread the meters. Later, the figures will be compared. Initially, it will be assumed that 10 percent of the readings are in error in order to choose the sample size (not all readers will have the same error rate, however). The true proportion of erroneous readings is to be estimated within a tolerable error of .02 with a reliability probability of .90.
>
> We have $e = .02$, $z = 1.64$, and a *guess* of .10 for π. Substituting these values into expression (8-20), we obtain the desired sample size for each route:
>
> $$n = \frac{(1.64)^2(.10)(1 - .10)}{(.02)^2} = 605.16, \text{ or } 606$$

Interpreting Sample Results

As noted, whether or not the sample results actually achieved provide the desired risk protection depends upon how good the original guess of π is.

Suppose that the sample results for one meter reader's route indicate that he misread 105 of his 623 meters. For him,

$$P = \frac{105}{623} = .17$$

We must use this value as an estimator of π.

Substituting .17 in place of π in expression (8-20), we see that the sample size that gives the desired reliability should have been approximately

$$n = \frac{(1.64)^2(.17)(1-.17)}{(.02)^2} = 948.8, \text{ or } 949$$

which is larger than the sample size obtained when we assumed $\pi = .10$. The present sample is too small to adequately protect against the risks of an erroneous estimate. (Note that we still do not know the precise value of π and that we never will, but .17 is a better estimate than the value of .10 used initially.)

On the other hand, it is possible to use a sample size larger than the one actually required. For example, another meter reader may have misread only 32 of his meters, so that

$$P = \frac{32}{623} = .051$$

Substituting this value into expression (8-20) in place of π, we obtain

$$n = \frac{(1.64)^2(.051)(1-.051)}{(.02)^2} = 325.4, \text{ or } 326$$

so that, in this case, more observations than necessary would have been obtained.

Samples Taken Without Replacement from a Small Population

The procedure for determining n must be slightly modified when the sample is taken without replacement from a finite population of size N. Recall that the standard error of P must then be found from

$$\sigma_P = \sqrt{\frac{\pi(1-\pi)}{n}} \sqrt{\frac{N-n}{N-1}}$$

Substituting this into expression (8-19) and solving the resulting equation for n, using the level of reliability, population size, and tolerable error, and our initial guess at the value of π, we obtain the following expression for *the required sample size when sampling without replacement from small populations:*

$$n = \frac{Nz^2\pi(1-\pi)}{(N-1)e^2 + z^2\pi(1-\pi)} \tag{8-21}$$

Work-Sampling Applications

One very important concern of production management is work measurement. Because of the great expense involved in collecting the required data, statistical tools have been developed to make the task more efficient.

A generation ago, procedures for obtaining measurements involved stopwatch methods that required continuous monitoring. Sometimes there was one watcher for each worker, so that the cost of gathering the data was high. The development of a statistical technique called *work sampling* relieved management of the burden of the stopwatch, at the same time removing the worker from its purported tyranny.

One goal of such measurements is to establish work standards. These are ordinarily expressed in terms of the time desired to complete a particular task, such as drilling a hole, installing a car bumper, or wiring a circuit board. Standards are established over a period of time by measuring a typical cross section of workers under normal production circumstances. The mean time to completion is estimated for each worker. A frequency distribution of these means is then compiled to set the standard.*

The classical procedure for getting the mean time to assemble a bumper on a car required that the worker be watched continuously and the installation times duly recorded. If a sample of 20 completion times were required, each of about 10 minutes duration, about 200 minutes—or half a day—would be spent by the timer watching just this one worker. If 10 workers in the automobile assembly plant install bumpers, and a sample is to be obtained for each, the timer must therefore spend about 5 days measuring this one operation. But there are hundreds of operations involved in assembling cars, so that a great many timers would be required just to set standards and evaluate performance. The very presence of a timer may bias the observations. It is widely acknowledged that performance is affected if the employee is aware of being measured.†

Work sampling is an alternative to continuous work measurement that can achieve a manyfold increase in the efficiency of the observer. The advantage of work sampling is that the same information obtainable from continuous observation may be achieved instead by many more shorter observations or "glimpses" taken randomly at scattered moments for an extended duration. Suppose that for a week the observer simply walks by the bumper installation station, making a note of what the worker is doing at that moment. It would be possible to do this many times, placing a check mark on a tally sheet for the particular task being performed at that instant. When the tallies have been accumulated at the end of the week, they would form the basis for estimating the proportion of time a worker spends at each task. The underlying principle of work sampling is that *the amount of time spent in a particular state of activity is proportional to the number of observations made of that state.*

---

* For a detailed discussion of setting work standards, see Elwood S. Buffa, *Modern Production Management*, New York: John Wiley & Sons, 1977.

† The famous Hawthorne studies highlight this point. Discussions are contained in many textbooks on management.

Let us suppose that 1,000 observations have been made of an automobile bumper assembler; 858 times he was busy installing, and the rest he was idle. Let us take this figure to calculate $P = 858/1,000 = .858$, which is a point estimate of the actual proportion of time π that the employee was busy installing bumpers. Assuming that all observations were made during the 35 hours in which the installer was officially on station and that he installed 222 bumpers, we may estimate the mean time taken for an installation.

The total time actually spent installing is estimated to be

$$35(.858) = 30.03 \text{ hours}$$

By dividing the time duration by the number of cars completed, the mean installation time μ may be estimated as follows:

$$30.03/222 = .1353 \text{ hour per bumper}$$

$$= 8.1 \text{ minutes per bumper}$$

This is the same type of result that would have been obtained through many hours of continuous observation of the single worker. But the 1,000 work-sampling observations represent only minutes of the observer's time. On each pass through the plant he may collect tally marks for dozens of workers, each of whom performs a variety of tasks. Tallies would be obtained at all hours of the day and for every day of the week. No worker need feel uncomfortable over being watched, and the observer need carry no stopwatch.

The above results are only estimates. The same would be true of stopwatch timing. But work sampling is free of the many sources of potential bias of stopwatch studies. Thus the results may be more reliable as well as cheaper.

Number of Observations Required

To find the number of work-sampling observations required to estimate the mean time the worker takes to install bumpers, a very "rough" estimate would first have to be made of π. Suppose that we use $\pi = .80$. If a 5-percent tolerable error is desired with a 95-percent reliability, then $e = .05$ and $z = 1.96$. Substituting these values into expression (8-20), we have

$$n = \frac{(1.96)^2(.8)(1-.8)}{(.05)^2} = 245.86, \text{ or } 246$$

We may compare this value to the number of stopwatch observations necessary to estimate μ, the mean bumper installation time. Suppose that we know this worker's standard deviation to be $\sigma = 2$ minutes per bumper. With a true value of μ near 8 minutes, a 5-percent tolerable error would correspond to $8(.05) = .4$ minute. Using $e = .4$ and $z = 1.96$, then from expression (8-17) the required sample size would be

$$n = \frac{(1.96)^2(2)^2}{(.4)^2} = 96.04, \text{ or } 97$$

The number of continuous stopwatch observations would be 97 as compared to 246 for work sampling. But recall that the latter would take a few seconds each, whereas the former require several minutes each.

Work sampling has been used in many applications where traditional methods have proven impracticable. Perhaps the greatest advantage occurs when several tasks are performed, with small amounts of time spent on each. For example, consider timing a waitress as she performs dozens of short tasks in seemingly random sequence. A timer would have quite a job timing her as she pours coffee, clears a table, handles the cash register, makes a sundae, makes toast, wipes a table, and so forth. Yet a suitable estimate could be made by work-sampling methods of the amount of time spent per customer on each of these tasks.

Reliability vs. Confidence and Tolerable Error vs. Precision

It may prove helpful at this point to clarify the key concepts that have been introduced in this chapter. An obvious question is: What is the difference between reliability and confidence? Another might be: How do we distinguish between tolerable error and precision? In both cases, are we not really dealing with two terms that are synonymous?

In one sense, confidence and reliability mean the same thing. But the distinction between these concepts is that they apply in *different stages* of a sampling study. The notion of reliability is mainly a concern in the *planning stage*, where an appropriate sample size is found to satisfy the statistical analyst's goals. Greater reliability may only be achieved either by increasing the sample size, and hence the data-collection costs, or by reducing the tolerable-error level. In selecting a reliability level, the statistician seeks to find a satisfactory balance between risks of error and cost. The concept of confidence applies in the last phase of a sampling study—the *data analysis and conclusions stage*. At this final point in an investigation, the statistician is concerned with communicating his results, so that his overriding concern is with *credibility*. Although often of the same value, the reliability need not be equal to the reported confidence level. Indeed, there are instances where the sample size *n* is not under the statistician's control, so that reliability considerations do not even enter into his planning.

We have already encountered the notion of precision in constructing confidence intervals. As the limits of the interval estimate become narrower, we can say that the resulting estimate becomes more precise. Like confidence, precision applies in the final stage of a sampling study. At this point in time, all sample data have been collected and precision can be improved only by a compensating reduction in confidence, or vice versa. The tolerable-error level, on the other hand, is merely a convenient point of demarcation that separates serious errors from those that may be acceptable. It is used only in the planning stage and, with reliability, serves primarily to guide the statistician in selecting an appropriate sample size. Only when the reliability coincidentally equals the confidence level, and the planning guess as to σ or π is on target, will tolerable error be of equal magnitude to reported precision.

EXERCISES

8-24 The mean time required by automobile assemblers to hang a car door is to be estimated. Assuming a standard deviation of 10 seconds, determine the required sample size under the following given conditions.

    (a) The desired reliability of being in error by no more than 1 second (in either direction) is .99.

    (b) The desired reliability is .95 for a tolerable error of 1 second.

    (c) A reliability of .99 is desired, with a tolerable error of 2 seconds. How does the sample size obtained compare with your answer to (a)?

    (d) Same as (a), but suppose that $\sigma = 20$ seconds instead. By how much does the sample size increase or decrease?

8-25 The cost of obtaining the sample in Exercise 8-24 is $1.50 per observation.

    (a) For a tolerable error of 1 second, find the reliability that can be achieved by an expenditure of $300.

    (b) For a reliability of .95, find the tolerable error that must correspond to an expenditure of $300.

8-26 A quality control manager has a flexible sampling policy. Because different parts have different quality requirements, there is a separate policy for each type of part. For example, a pressure seal used on some assemblies must be able to withstand a maximum load of 5,000 pounds per square inch (psi) before bursting. If the mean maximum load of a sample of seals taken from a shipment is less than 5,000 psi, then the entire shipment must be rejected.

    The sampling policy for this item requires a sample to be large enough that the probability that the sample mean differs from the population mean by 10 psi or more (in either direction) is no greater than .05. Historically, it has been established that the standard deviation for bursting pressures of this seal is 100 psi.

    (a) Find the required sample size for a shipment of $N = 10,000$ seals. Then do the same for a shipment of $N = 5,000$ seals. How much larger is the sample size for the larger lot? Why shouldn't it be twice as large?

    (b) If the true mean maximum bursting pressure for the seals in a shipment is actually $\mu = 5,025$ psi, then use your sample size for $N = 10,000$ in (a) to determine the probability that the shipment will be rejected.

8-27 The purchasing officer for a government hospital that orders supplies from many vendors has the following policy: The quality of each shipment is to be estimated by means of a sample that will always include 10 percent of the items, regardless of the size of the shipment. Do you think this is a good policy? Discuss your answer.

8-28 The engineer responsible for the design of a communications satellite wishes to determine how many extra batteries to include in the power supply so that its useful life will be likely to exceed minimum specifications. A random sample of a particular type of battery is selected for testing. The engineer wishes to find the sample size that will provide an estimate of the true proportion π of batteries whose performance will be satisfactory—to an accuracy of $e = .05$ with a .95 reliability. We may assume that the population of batteries is very large.

    (a) Find the necessary sample size, with an initial guess that $\pi = .5$

[which, from expression (8-20), would yield the largest possible sample size needed to satisfy the requirements].

(b) Suppose that after testing the number of batteries found in (a), only 250 prove satisfactory. What is the point estimate of π? If this were the true value of π, how many more batteries were tested unnecessarily?

8-29 A waiter has been observed at 200 random times while on his station. The following tabulation provides the frequency distribution of the tasks he was performing at each observation:

Cleaning tables	10
Taking orders	35
Walking	57
Placing orders	8
Preparing food	20
Picking up orders	15
Delivering orders	10
Calculating bills	10
Preparing or delivering drinks	35

If during the time period over which he was observed he worked a total of 25 hours, exclusive of idle time, and served a total of 1,000 customers, estimate the mean time (in minutes) spent on each of the above tasks per customer.

REVIEW EXERCISES

8-30 An estimate is to be made of the mean number of square feet of scrap and wasted wood per log in the manufacture of one-half-inch exterior plywood. For this purpose, a random sample of 100 logs of various sizes from several mills was chosen. Each log's volume was carefully measured and the theoretical number of square feet of plywood was computed. This value was compared to the actual quantity achieved at the end of production, and the wood loss was calculated. When the study data were assembled, the sample mean and the standard deviation were computed as $\bar{X} = 1,246$ sq ft and $s = 114.6$ sq ft, respectively. Construct a 95-percent confidence interval estimate for the mean wood loss.

8-31 The following salaries were determined for a sample of ten university presidents:

$35,000	$67,500	$51,500	$53,000	$38,000
$42,000	$29,500	$31,500	$46,000	$37,500

(a) Find the value of an efficient, unbiased, and consistent estimator of the mean for the salaries of all university presidents.

(b) Find the value of an unbiased and consistent estimator of the variance for the salaries of all university presidents.

(c) Find the value of an unbiased estimator of the proportion of all university presidents' salaries above $40,000.

8-32 The respective proportions of viewers watching each of the earliest prime-time television programs of one network on four successive nights are to be estimated within a tolerance of $\pm.01$ in such a manner that there is a 95-percent chance that this precision will be achieved (or reliability $= .95$). In doing this, the sample proportion P will be used. Determine the

required sample sizes when the assumed population proportion for:
(a) Tuesday is .3   (b) Wednesday is .6
(c) Thursday is .5   (d) Friday is .1

8-33   A psychologist has designed a new aptitude test to be used by life insurance companies to screen applicants for beginning actuarial positions. In order to estimate the mean score achieved by all future applicants who will eventually take the test, the psychologist has administered it to nine persons. The sample mean and the standard deviation have been calculated as $\bar{X} = 83.7$ and $s = 12.9$ points, respectively. Determine the confidence interval estimates for the mean for each of the following levels of confidence:
(a) 99 percent   (c) 90 percent
(b) 95 percent   (d) 99.5 percent

8-34   The following IQ scores have been obtained for a random sample of persons taken from a large population:

70	110	110
110	100	80
120	110	90

Construct a 95-percent confidence interval estimate of the population mean IQ.

8-35   A random sample of $n = 100$ widths for two-by-fours was selected from a shipment of $N = 500$ boards, The results show that $\bar{X} = 3.5$ inches and $s = .1$ inches. Construct a 95-percent confidence interval estimate of the boards in the entire shipment.

8-36   A pharmaceutical house wants to estimate the mean number of milligrams of drug its machinery inserts into each capsule in four different sizes of pills. In each case, a standard deviation of 1 milligram is assumed to hold and a reliability of 95 percent is desired. However, the amount of error tolerated varies with the pill size. Find the required sample size for:
(a) tiny pills, .05 milligram error   (b) small pills, .1 milligram error
(c) medium pills, .2 milligram error   (d) large pills, .5 milligram error

8-37   The proportion of children born with defects is to be estimated, with a tolerable error of .1 and a reliability of .99. A very conservative guess is that 20 percent of all children born have defects.
(a) Find the necessary sample size.
(b) Suppose that 13 defective children were found, using the sample size in (a), construct a 95-percent confidence interval estimate for the population proportion of children with defects.

8-38   Example 4-2 (page 70) shows how work sampling was used to allocate the expense of keypunching. Suppose that two departments in a company have data keypunched. Three alternatives are possible for determining the charges assigned to the respective departments: (1) Detailed record-keeping (census) at a cost of $200 per day. (2) Stopwatch sampling to estimate the mean daily keypunching time per operator for Department A; then estimating the total daily time for Department A by multiplying this sample mean by the number of operators. (Department B's usage can then be estimated from employee time clock records.) (3) Work sampling to estimate the proportion of all keypunching time for Department A, which when applied to total daily keypunching time yields an estimate equivalent to that in (2).
(a) Suppose that the daily operator keypunching time for Department A, determined by stopwatch sampling, has a standard deviation of $\sigma = .5$ hour. A .95 reliability probability is desired, with a tolerable error of $e = .08$ hour. Find the required sample size n.

(b) Suppose that the proportion of time spent on Department A, determined by a work-sampling study, is presumed to be $\pi = .50$ (a guess). A .95 reliability probability is desired, with a tolerable error of $e = .02$. Determine the required number of observations n.

(c) Suppose that each stopwatch observation costs $1.00, but that each work-sampling observation costs only $.05. Determine the daily costs for each method. Which one is least expensive?

Chapter Nine
Hypothesis Testing

In Chapter 8 we discussed how sample information may be used to estimate a population parameter. In this chapter we introduce another basic type of inference where a sample may be used in deciding between two complementary courses of action. Many important decisions made in the face of uncertainty involve a choice from just two alternatives. For example, the expansion of a company's product line involves a series of decisions as to whether to abandon a new product or enter the next stage of development. At each stage, sample information may be used to help in the decision-making process. A very common example of decisions based directly upon sample outcomes occurs in acceptance sampling, first discussed in Chapter 7. Here a sample is used to determine whether a batch of supplied items appears to be of acceptable quality. Another major use of sample information is in deciding whether to adopt a new procedure. For example, before going to the expense of initiating a training program for its sales department, a company can use the results from a sample of specially trained salespersons to help it decide whether the program would be beneficial.

The statistical methods used in making the type of decisions illustrated above are based upon two complementary assumptions concerning the true nature of a population. For example, a product will be liked by either 50 percent or more of its potential buyers or by fewer than 50 percent. A shipment of parts will have 10 percent or fewer items defective, or it will have a greater percentage defective. A new program will either raise average sales by at least $1,000, or it won't. These assumptions are traditionally referred to as hypotheses. The observation of the sample is viewed as a test. Thus the procedures for making decisions like those illustrated above fall into an area of statistical inference called *hypothesis testing*. Because of their involvement in the decision-making process, hypothesis-testing procedures provide more dynamic forms of statistical inference than the more passive estimating techniques previously encountered.

9-1   BASIC CONCEPTS OF HYPOTHESIS TESTING

We will develop the many concepts tying hypothesis testing together by means of an extensive example involving a decision as to whether to market a new product.

Vita Synthetics, a pharmaceutical manufacturer, has just developed a dietary supplement believed capable of significantly reducing heart disease resulting from a lifetime of poor eating habits.* The product introduces a chemical into the patient's bloodstream that dissolves entrenched arterial deposits of cholesterol. One of the major causes of coronary ailments is a hardening of the arteries caused by the accumulation of cholesterol. By reducing its deleterious effects, the firm's president believes Vita's product would effectively remove cholesterol from the rolls of major killers.

Before the product can be marketed, it must be extensively tested in order to assess its effectiveness in reducing the blood cholesterol levels in human beings; the only evidence obtained to date has been from some limited testing with rhesus monkeys. The Food and Drug Administration will not allow the product to be sold without strong evidence that it will work on humans. For the test, a sample of 100 middle-aged men with no previous history of heart disease is selected. Each man has his cholesterol level measured prior to the experiment, and then each will be given a standard daily dosage of the supplement; any other changes in life style will be discouraged. At the end of the period, each man's cholesterol level is again to be measured.

Past experience with new drugs has shown that widespread acceptance occurs only when the drugs provide substantial relief. The president of Vita Synthetics has determined that the present supplement will be good enough to market only if it can reduce average cholesterol levels by more than 20 percent over a three-month time span.

* This situation is completely hypothetical, and any resemblance to an actual product is coincidental.

Factors Influencing the Decision

On the basis of the experimental results, the company has to decide between the two courses of action: (1) to market the supplement or (2) to postpone marketing and continue developmental research. There are some risks involved due to the uncertainty that will remain with respect to the supplement's true effectiveness even after the evidence has been collected. This residual uncertainty arises from the fact that a sample, whose results may by chance deviate from the population, must be used in the test. The decision really depends upon the answers to several questions, among which are the following.

1. What costs potentially ensue from incorrect decisions? *A decision is incorrect if the action taken is contrary to what would have been done were there no uncertainty.* In this example an incorrect decision would result in (a) marketing an ineffective supplement or (b) not marketing an effective supplement. It is important to understand that incorrect decisions of this type should never occur but for the uncertainties arising from sampling. The costs resulting from incorrect decisions may be expressed in terms of their financial impact on the firm, their social damage, or both.

2. What levels of risk are acceptable? Answering this question essentially requires the manager to look at the possible costs and assess his preferences with respect to various probabilities of incurring such costs. It will be shown that the decision-maker has some, although limited, freedom with which to balance or reduce the risks associated with incorrect decisions. The necessarily subjective evaluations must be his.

3. When does the sample evidence favor a particular assumption or hypothesis regarding the population? A rule must be developed for the decision-maker, so that he may be able to decide whether the sample evidence confirms one of the assumptions, that the dietary supplement either is or is not effective. His decision should be consistent with his attitudes toward the risks involved.

Testing the Value of a Population Mean

Formulating the Hypotheses

So that we may make some generalizations that will be useful in analyzing other testing situations, certain statistical concepts must be introduced. It is common to refer to the possible assumed states of the effectiveness of the supplement in terms of hypotheses. Since management is considering only two possible states, ineffective versus effective, the hypotheses are:

Supplement is ineffective

Supplement is effective

We let μ represent the mean percentage reduction in cholesterol levels experienced by the population of middle-aged men who would take the supplement (if it were made available). It must be emphasized that this is a *target population* that does not exist until (and will not exist unless) the supplement is widely available. However, it is still possible to draw a sample from the "imaginary" population, as the men in the sample will be treated in the same way. The first hypothesis is customarily referred to as the *null hypothesis* (here, "null" represents no change from the natural variation in cholesterol level). In terms of the population parameter μ, we will use the following expression for the *null hypothesis:*

$$H_0: \quad \mu \leqslant 20 \text{ percent}$$

since it has been decided that the supplement ought to be classified as ineffective when the mean percentage reduction in cholesterol levels does not exceed 20 percent. The second hypothesis is called the *alternative hypothesis*. We analogously express the *alternative hypothesis:*

$$H_1: \quad \mu > 20 \text{ percent}$$

corresponding to the mean percentage reduction for an effective supplement. The symbols H_0 and H_1 represent the null and alternative hypotheses, respectively. The hypotheses will always be formulated so that H_0 and H_1 are opposites—when one is true the other is false.

For another special notation in hypothesis testing we add the subscript zero to the symbol for the population parameter. In the present example we have

$$\mu_0 = 20 \text{ percent}$$

which is the pivotal value of the population mean. Generally, the null hypothesis holds for all levels of μ equal to μ_0 or falling on one side of this value and the alternative hypothesis applies otherwise. Unfortunately, we do not know which side applies since the true value of μ remains unknown.

Making the Decision

The decision to be made is the selection of the most appropriate course of action consistent with the sample evidence and the decision-maker's evaluations of risk. The actions may be expressed in terms of the hypotheses. The action "don't market the supplement" corresponds to a belief that the null hypothesis is true (i.e., that the supplement is ineffective); thus it may also be expressed in an equivalent form, "accept the null hypothesis." Analogously, the action "market the supplement" may be expressed as "reject the null hypothesis" or as "accept the alternative hypothesis."

The sample evidence must be expressed in a manner that will meaningfully support one of the hypotheses. The president of Vita Synthetics should want to market his product if it provides a large mean reduction in the cholesterol levels of the sample patients, as this would seem to deny H_0 (that the supplement is truly ineffective). Likewise, it seems that he ought not to market it if the supplement has not been very effective during the sample test, when the evidence would tend to confirm H_0. The sample information may be conveniently summarized in terms of the sample mean $\overline{X}$ of the percentage reduction in cholesterol levels experienced by the test patients. We refer to $\overline{X}$ as the *test statistic*. Our decision-maker will accept H_0 for small values of $\overline{X}$ and reject H_0 for large ones. The question is, where should he draw the line?

Selecting the point of demarcation for $\overline{X}$ is where the president decides what action he will eventually take. For now, we suppose that the value $\overline{X} = 22$ is chosen. The test statistic is then used to formulate a decision rule. A *decision rule* translates sample evidence into the basis for making a choice of action. The value 22 is commonly referred to as the *critical value* or *acceptance number*. Once the critical value is established, we have a decision rule. In this instance, we may express this as:

DECISION RULE

Accept H_0 (don't market the supplement) if $\overline{X} \leqslant 22$

Reject H_0 (market the supplement)   if $\overline{X} > 22$

The decision rule identifies two regions for the possible value of $\overline{X}$. These can be illustrated as follows:

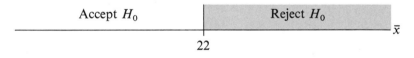

Having established the decision rule, the ultimate action to be taken by the company will be determined by the observed sample results after the test is conducted, the percentage reductions in cholesterol level are observed, and the value of $\overline{X}$ is calculated. This value of $\overline{X}$ will fall within either the acceptance or the rejection region, and H_0 will be accepted or rejected accordingly. When H_0 is rejected, the results are said to be *statistically significant*. Here, we use the word "significant" in a special sense. All hypothesis-testing results are important, but only when the null hypothesis is rejected is the test statistically significant.

The structure of the company's decision is shown in Table 9-1. Two courses of action are considered: market or don't market the supplement. There are also two population states: either the supplement is effective or it is not. For each combination of an action and a supplement quality, the outcome represents either a correct or an incorrect decision. Two possible outcomes are (1) to accept a true null hypothesis and don't market an ineffective supplement, and (2) to reject a false null hypothesis and market an effective supplement. Both of these would be correct decisions. Because of chance sampling error, however, the decision rule may also result in two other, undesirable outcomes,

TABLE 9-1   Hypothesis-Testing Decision Outcome Table

	Possible States of the Population Considered	
Alternative Course of Action	*Null Hypothesis True* $\mu \leqslant 20\ (\mu_0)$ (ineffective supplement)	*Null Hypothesis False* (*Alternative True*) $\mu > 20\ (\mu_0)$ (effective supplement)
Accept Null Hypothesis *resulting* $\overline{X} \leqslant 22$ (don't market)	*Correct Decision* Probability $1-\alpha$ (don't market ineffective supplement)	*Incorrect Decision* Probability β *Type II error* (don't market effective supplement)
Reject Null Hypothesis (*Accept Alternative*) *resulting* $X > 22$ (market)	*Incorrect Decision* Probability α Significance level α *Type I error* (market ineffective supplement)	*Correct Decision* Probability $1-\beta$ (market effective supplement)

where in each case an incorrect decision or an error is made. The incorrect decisions are referred to as Type I and Type II errors. The *Type I error is to reject H_0 when it is true* (market an ineffective supplement), and the *Type II error is to accept H_0 when it is false* (don't market an effective supplement).

To help to evaluate the decision rule, we will find the probability of committing each error. It is conventional to denote the probabilities of these errors as α (alpha) and β (beta), where

$$\alpha = P[\text{Type I error}] = P[\text{reject } H_0 \mid H_0 \text{ true}]$$

$$\beta = P[\text{Type II error}] = P[\text{accept } H_0 \mid H_0 \text{ false}]$$

The value α is sometimes called the *significance level* of the test.

Finding the Error Probabilities

How good was the choice of 22 as the critical value? Recall that the decision-maker should be aware of the risks of incorrect decisions in making his decision and hence in establishing the decision rule. His attitude toward the risks depends upon both the costs resulting from incorrect decisions and the respective probabilities that these incorrect decisions will occur. The classical approach to hypothesis testing focuses on the error probabilities, providing for their adjustment so that acceptable weight is given to the costs. The error probabilities are found by analyzing the sampling distributions of the test statistic when each of the hypotheses is true.

Consider first the case when the null hypothesis is true. Recall that this says that the population mean is no greater than 20 percent, $H_0\colon \mu \leqslant 20$. The null hypothesis holds for any value of μ 20 or below, such as 0, 9.7, or 17.5.

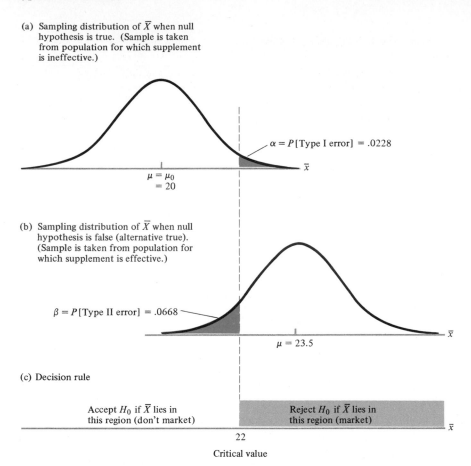

(a) Sampling distribution of $\bar{X}$ when null hypothesis is true. (Sample is taken from population for which supplement is ineffective.)

$\alpha = P[\text{Type I error}] = .0228$

$\mu = \mu_0 = 20$

$\bar{x}$

(b) Sampling distribution of $\bar{X}$ when null hypothesis is false (alternative true). (Sample is taken from population for which supplement is effective.)

$\beta = P[\text{Type II error}] = .0668$

$\mu = 23.5$

$\bar{x}$

(c) Decision rule

Accept H_0 if $\bar{X}$ lies in this region (don't market)

Reject H_0 if $\bar{X}$ lies in this region (market)

$\bar{x}$

22

Critical value

FIGURE 9-1 Sampling distributions of $\bar{X}$ for hypothesis-testing example.

Since we can't consider every possibility, we focus on the extreme case, when the pivotal value μ_0 applies, and set the population mean at $\mu = 20$. The normal curve in the top portion of Figure 9-1 represents the sampling distribution of $\bar{X}$ when the null hypothesis is true and $\mu = \mu_0$ exactly.

Although we don't know the actual value, for purposes of illustration we assume that the population standard deviation for reductions in cholesterol levels is $\sigma = 10$ percent. The corresponding standard error of $\bar{X}$ is

$$\sigma_{\bar{X}} = \sigma/\sqrt{n} = 10/\sqrt{100} = 1$$

The probability of making an incorrect decision of Type I (shown as the colored area to the right of 22 on the top curve) may be calculated:

$$\alpha = P[\bar{X} > 22 \mid H_0 \text{ true } (\mu = \mu_0 = 20)]$$

$$= P\left[\frac{\bar{X} - \mu}{\sigma_{\bar{X}}} > \frac{22 - 20}{1}\right] = P[Z > 2]$$

$$= .5 - .4772 = .0228$$

When the null hypothesis is false (so that the alternative is true), a different sampling distribution for $\overline{X}$ must be used, as is shown in Figure 9-1(b). This is because *the sample is selected from a different population* (namely, that for which the diet supplement is effective) and hence has a different value for μ. As defined, the diet supplement will be effective for any mean percentage reduction in cholesterol level greater than 20 percent. For example, suppose that $\mu = 23.5$ percent and the same standard deviation applies as before. The corresponding probability of a Type II error (shown as the colored area to the left of 22 on the bottom curve) is thus determined to be

$$\beta = P[\overline{X} \leqslant 22 \,|\, H_0 \text{ false } (\mu = 23.5)]$$
$$= P\left[\frac{\overline{X}-\mu}{\sigma_{\overline{X}}} \leqslant \frac{22-23.5}{1}\right] = P[Z \leqslant -1.5]$$
$$= .5 - .4332 = .0668$$

The above calculation may be repeated for any other value for μ greater than 20 percent. For instance, with $\mu = 24.5$, the corresponding value for β would be .0062.

Interpreting the Sample Results

Once a suitable decision rule has been formulated, all that remains is to wait for the sample results. Suppose that the sample mean reduction in cholesterol levels is found to be $\overline{X} = 34.3$ percent. Since this number is greater than the critical value 22, the evidence indicates that the supplement is effective; H_0 *would be rejected and the decision to market would be made.* Another way of stating this is to say that the results would be statistically significant.

Even with $\overline{X}$ so large, there is still no guarantee that the supplement will actually be effective, since the sample could be a poor representation of the population from which it came. The only way to be certain would be to market the supplement and monitor its progress in all heart patients. However, the probability of obtaining a value for $\overline{X}$ this large or greater is infinitesimal if H_0 is true and the supplement is actually ineffective. The normal deviate would be $z = (34.3 - 20)/1 = 14.3$.

EXERCISES

9-1   The following hypotheses are being tested, with $\mu_0 = 150$.

$$H_0: \quad \mu \leqslant \mu_0$$
$$H_1: \quad \mu > \mu_0$$

Suppose that the population standard deviation is $\sigma = 30$ and that a sample of size $n = 100$ is used. Find the Type I error probability α when $\mu = 150$ and the Type II error probability β when $\mu = 160$ assuming that the following decision rule applies:

Accept H_0 if $\overline{X} \leqslant 154$
Reject H_0 if $\overline{X} > 154$

9-2   For each of the following situations, indicate the Type I and Type II errors and the correct decisions.
(a) H_0:   New system is no better than the old one.

(1) Adopt new system when new one is better.
(2) Retain old system when new one is better.
(3) Retain old system when new one is not better.
(4) Adopt new system when new one is not better.
(b) H_0: New product is satisfactory.
   (1) Introduce new product when unsatisfactory.
   (2) Do not introduce new product when unsatisfactory.
   (3) Do not introduce new product when satisfactory.
   (4) Introduce new product when satisfactory.
(c) H_0: Batch of transistors is of good quality.
   (1) Reject good quality batch.
   (2) Accept good quality batch.
   (3) Reject poor quality batch.
   (4) Accept poor quality batch.

9-3 Indicate whether the following statements are true or false. If false, explain why.
(a) The Type II error is the same as accepting the alternative hypothesis when it is false.
(b) Either a Type I or Type II error must occur.
(c) The significance level is the probability of rejecting the null hypothesis when it is true.

9-4 A company introduces a new product into the market.
(a) What null and alternative hypotheses are being tested if the Type I error is to incorrectly conclude that the product will succeed?
(b) What hypotheses are being tested if the Type II error is to incorrectly conclude that the product will succeed?

9-5 For each of the following hypothesis-testing situations, state the Type I and Type II errors in nonstatistical terms (for example, approving a poor drug or disapproving a good drug).
(a) The null hypothesis is that a new manufacturing process is no improvement over the existing one. If sample evidence indicates that it is better, the new process will be adopted.
(b) A union is negotiating with management for a four-day week with nine-hour working days, all at slightly higher pay than at present. The union has argued that due to greater efficiency and higher morale its members' output will actually increase. Choosing as its null hypothesis that productivity will not increase, management will sign the contract if there is adequate evidence that the union claims are true. Otherwise, some hard negotiating sessions are in store.
(c) The objective of a statistical study is to determine whether a stronger consumer protection law is favored by more voters than the present one is. Taking as its null hypothesis that the new law does not meet greater voter approval, a consumer action group will lobby for the new law if there is significant evidence to the contrary.

9-2 FORMULATING HYPOTHESES AND CHOOSING A DECISION RULE

Considerations in Choosing the Decision Rule

The decision rule tells us how to translate a sample result into action. The test statistic $\overline{X}$ served the purpose in the preceding example of the dietary supplement, being compared to a critical value. Because of sampling error, the test statistic may be unusually large or small, thus leading to an erroneous decision. As we have seen, the probabilities of such errors result from the choice of a decision rule. In Chapter 8, we saw that the chances of sampling error may be reduced if a larger sample is used. Thus, the sample size n will also affect the attained probabilities of error; n must be chosen so that the ensuing error probabilities will be of magnitudes consistent with the decision-maker's attitudes toward the risks involved. It is therefore necessary to consider both the sample size and the critical value in selecting an appropriate decision rule.

Effect of Changing the Critical Value

Recall that a decision rule establishes a point of demarcation, called the critical value, which tells us when to accept or reject the null hypothesis, depending upon where the test statistic falls. We will denote the critical value for the test statistic $\overline{X}$ by the symbol $\overline{X}^*$. In the example of the dietary supplement, we established a critical value of $\overline{X}^* = 22$. We will now consider two other decision rules: one with $\overline{X}^* = 22.5$, and another with $\overline{X}^* = 21.5$. With these different rules, how will α and β be changed?

The two situations are portrayed in Figure 9-2. It may be helpful to compare them to the results for the original decision rule in Figure 9-1. In raising the critical value from $\overline{X}^* = 22$ to $\overline{X}^* = 22.5$ [Figure 9-2(a)], we "stack the deck" in favor of accepting and thereby reduce the chance of rejecting H_0 when it is true. The new Type I error probability is smaller, $\alpha = .0062$ compared to the previous figure of .0228. Thus, the new decision rule with $\overline{X}^* = 22.5$ decreases the chance of marketing an ineffective supplement. The price paid in reducing α is to increase the chance that an untypical sample outcome will result in accepting H_0 when it is false. For by increasing $\overline{X}^*$, we also raise the Type II error probability from $\beta = .0668$ to $\beta = .1587$, so that the chance of not marketing an effective supplement is more than doubled. The opposite effect is achieved by reducing the critical value from $\overline{X}^* = 22$ to $\overline{X}^* = 21.5$ [Figure 9-2(b)]; in this case α increases while β decreases.

These illustrations demonstrate that in general the *chance of one error can be reduced only at the expense of increasing the probability of the other.* The decision rule must be chosen so that an acceptable balance is achieved between the chances of the two errors.

Effect of Increasing the Sample Size

The only way to decrease both types of error probabilities is to increase the sample size. This will make the sampling distribution curves like those in Figures 9-1 and 9-2 become more peaked and have shorter tails, as their standard deviations will decrease with larger values of n. The net effect will be smaller error probabilities. For example, if the sample size were increased (so that $n = 150$), then the standard error of $\overline{X}$ in the diet supplement study would be

$$\sigma_{\overline{X}} = \sigma/\sqrt{n} = 10/\sqrt{150} = .816$$

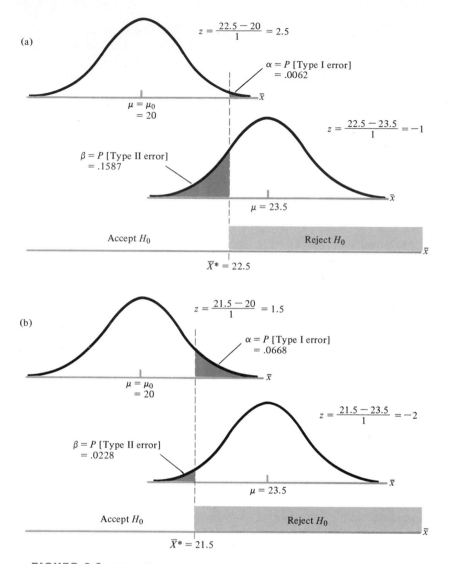

$$z = \frac{22.5 - 20}{1} = 2.5$$

(a)

$$\alpha = P \text{ [Type I error]} = .0062$$

$$\mu = \mu_0 = 20$$

$$z = \frac{22.5 - 23.5}{1} = -1$$

$$\beta = P \text{ [Type II error]} = .1587$$

$$\mu = 23.5$$

Accept H_0 Reject H_0

$$\bar{X}^* = 22.5$$

$$z = \frac{21.5 - 20}{1} = 1.5$$

(b)

$$\alpha = P \text{ [Type I error]} = .0668$$

$$\mu = \mu_0 = 20$$

$$z = \frac{21.5 - 23.5}{1} = -2$$

$$\beta = P \text{ [Type II error]} = .0228$$

$$\mu = 23.5$$

Accept H_0 Reject H_0

$$\bar{X}^* = 21.5$$

FIGURE 9-2   The effect of changing critical value upon error probabilities.

and the error probabilities, using a critical value of $\bar{X}^* = 22$, would be determined as follows:

When Null Hypothesis is True	*When Null Hypothesis is False*
$\alpha = P[X > 22 \mid H_0 \text{ true } (\mu = \mu_0 = 20)]$	$\beta = P[\bar{X} \leqslant 22 \mid H_0 \text{ false } (\mu = 23.5)]$
$= P\left[\dfrac{\bar{X} - \mu}{\sigma_{\bar{X}}} > \dfrac{22 - 20}{.816}\right]$	$= P\left[\dfrac{X - \mu}{\sigma_{\bar{X}}} \leqslant \dfrac{22 - 23.5}{.816}\right]$
$= P[Z > 2.45]$	$= P[Z \leqslant -1.84]$
$= .5000 - .4929 = .0071$	$= .5000 - .4671 = .0329$

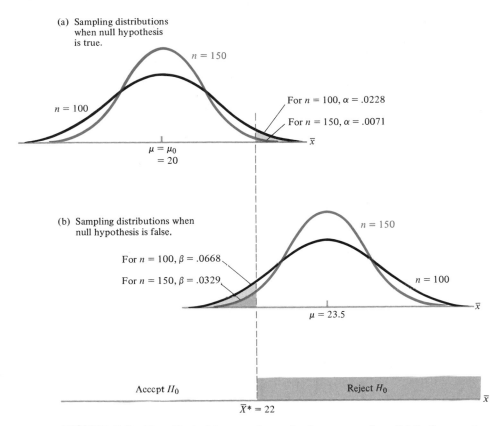

FIGURE 9-3   The effect of increased sample size on sampling distributions and error probabilities.

Figure 9-3 compares these error probabilities to those when the sample size is smaller.

Increasing the sample size reduces the chances that both kinds of incorrect decisions will be made when the same decision rule is applied. This will always be true. There is usually a practical limit as to how large the sample may be, for the cost of sampling may become prohibitive. In the testing of a drug, constraints may be enforced by government regulations limiting the allowable sample size. Usually, cost is the main consideration. Such a study would have limited funding, and increasing the sample size might not be practicable.

Determining Acceptable Error Probabilities

The basic question we will consider here is: Under what circumstances would the decision-maker find another decision rule better? The answer is that the better decision rule is the one that yields the more acceptable levels of risk, which can only be determined after considering the *costs* of incorrect decisions versus the *costs* of taking the sample.

Marketing an ineffective supplement could have deleterious effects upon the long-run success of the pharmaceutical firm. The fact that the supplement did not work well would soon become known, probably generating considerable ill will, which could affect the credibility of the company's claims for its entire product line. In any case, the costs of setting up production and promotion would probably never be recovered. Having "burned his fingers" once, the company president might be reluctant to reenter the diet supplement market for some time, thereby reducing the likelihood of an early solution to the cholesterol problem. Also, the public, becoming somewhat skeptical about all new pharmaceutical developments, would need even stronger evidence that new products will work.

On the other hand, failure to market an effective supplement could result in considerable opportunity losses for the firm. This could lead to a failure to achieve the enviable position of being first in the field, thereby missing the potential dramatic effect upon the firm's profitability and attractiveness as an investment. (For example, the stock of the first firm to successfully market birth-control pills broke existing records for market value appreciation.) There would also be the social cost of the thousands of premature deaths that could have been prevented but for the lack of an available anticholesterol supplement.

Balancing the Risks

The choice of α and β must be made by the decision-maker and must be based upon *subjective evaluations* as to how the risks of incorrect decisions should be balanced. Both kinds of errors are undesirable. A decision rule must be chosen that will provide a lower probability of the more serious error. Only the decision-maker can judge whether losing opportunities to reap rewards from a beneficial drug is more or less serious than placing an ineffective one on the market. Only he can establish the degree to which one error is more abhorrent than the other. He should therefore be wary of setting α and β at arbitrary or traditional levels.

Formulating Hypotheses

The null and alternative hypotheses are opposites, so that when one is true the other is false. This allows us to consider just two actions and two outcomes for each hypothesis, depending upon whether H_0 is true or false. One area of potential confusion is deciding which hypothesis to label H_0. In earlier statistical applications, the null hypothesis corresponded to the assumption that no change occurs, which accounts for the adjective "null." For example, in testing a drug, the usual hypothesis would be that it yields little or no improvement over nature. The H_0 used in the dietary supplement illustration corresponds to this designation. In modern applications, other considerations determine which is the null hypothesis, and H_0 may represent a change rather than no change. For instance, there would have been no material difference in our discussions in Section 9-1 if the H_0 and H_1 designations had been reversed so that the null hypothesis was $\mu \geqslant 20$ instead of $\mu \leqslant 20$. Of course, the other labels would also be different, so that the Type I and Type II errors would also be reversed and so would α and β.

Another often-used guideline is that the null hypothesis ought to be the one that the decision-maker wishes to disprove. *A common practice is to designate as H_0 that hypothesis for which rejecting when true is the more serious error,* so that the Type I error would be worse than the Type II error. As we saw in the dietary supplement illustration, the decision rule was chosen so that this happened to be the case.

Sometimes a hypothesis can be *two-sided.* For example, a manufacturer may wish to test the output of a production process. As his null hypothesis, he may assume that the mean weight μ of his items is the desired output, so he uses $H_0: \mu = \mu_0$. Because, on the average, the items produced may be over- or underweight, the alternative hypothesis would take the form $H_1: \mu \neq \mu_0$; that is, H_0 is violated either when $\mu < \mu_0$ or when $\mu > \mu_0$. Tests with two-sided hypotheses will be discussed in Section 9-4. So far the hypotheses discussed in this chapter have been *one-sided,* as the alternative parameter values lie either all above or all below the H_0 values.

EXERCISES

9-6   The following hypotheses are being tested, with $\mu_0 = 150$.

$$H_0: \quad \mu \leqslant \mu_0$$
$$H_1: \quad \mu > \mu_0$$

Suppose that the population standard deviation is $\sigma = 30$. In each case, find the Type I error probability α when $\mu = 150$ and the Type II error probability β when $\mu = 160$.
(a) $n = 50$, $\bar{X}^* - 155$
(b) $n - 100$, $\bar{X}^* = 156$
(c) $n = 200$, $\bar{X}^* = 154.5$

9-7   A marketing research study is being conducted to determine the demographics of a certain radio station's listeners. The null hypothesis is that the mean family income is less than or equal to $\mu_0 = \$20,000$. The station will be included in a special advertising campaign if the mean income is at a higher level. A random sample of $n = 100$ family incomes is to be collected and the sample mean computed. A decision rule involving $\bar{X}^* = \$21,000$ has been chosen. Assume that the standard deviation in family income is $\sigma = \$6,000$.
(a) Find the value of α when $\mu = \mu_0$ and β when $\mu = \$22,000$.
(b) Will α increase or decrease if the decision rule is changed to a critical value of $\bar{X}^* = \$21,500$? What will be the new value for α? What will be the new value for β? Did β increase or decrease?

9-3   LARGE-SAMPLE TESTS USING THE MEAN

With the basic concepts of hypothesis testing firmly in hand, we are ready to describe the usual procedure for such investigations. Ordinarily, the sampling study begins with the formulation of hypotheses. After some introspection on the part of the decision-maker, a Type I error probability α (significance level) is determined. Having established an appropriate sample size n, everything that follows is largely mechanical: The sample data are collected and a critical value corresponding to the desired value of α is found. Comparing the computed value of the test statistic to this critical value, the decision rule indicates the appropriate action to take.

To illustrate how to find a decision rule to meet prescribed requirements, we next consider an important application of hypothesis testing to quality control.

An Acceptance Sampling Application

Quality control frequently requires decisions about the disposition of batches or lots of items procured from a supplier or produced internally. A manufacturer wishes to protect his finished product by keeping materials supplied from outside at an acceptable level of quality, buying only lots he considers to be "good." Because a sample is used to decide whether a lot is good or bad, hypothesis-testing procedures may be used to determine a choice of action. These also apply when a manufacturer must choose between marketing his own production lot through regular channels or as inferior quality "seconds."

Typically there are two actions involved. Accepting the lot is the same as accepting a hypothesis that is good, while rejecting it is equivalent to rejecting the hypothesis that the lot is good. A good lot may be one having a high mean μ, as would be the case for lifetimes experienced in a shipment of batteries, or one having a low mean, the case for the drying times of a batch of interior house paint.

In Chapter 7 we discussed the two kinds of errors: rejecting a good shipment and accepting a bad shipment. We referred to the probability of the first error as the producer's risk (because a producer desires most to avoid this error), whereas the chance of the second error (which the user wants most to avoid) is the consumer's risk. In acceptance sampling we ordinarily designate as H_0 the hypothesis that the lot is good. This makes the Type I error probability α correspond to the producer's risk, whereas the Type II probability β is the consumer's risk.

To illustrate how a decision rule is obtained in acceptance sampling, we consider a quality control manager's problem of deciding whether or not to fill an office furniture-maker's order with a current batch of springs produced in his company's plant. A sample of $n = 100$ springs will be selected and subjected to a fatigue test. Springs meeting user specifications must withstand a mean stretching force μ of 50 pounds or more before permanent distortion is induced. Thus the following hypotheses are formulated:

$$H_0: \quad \mu \geqslant \mu_0 \, (= 50 \text{ lbs}) \quad \text{(springs are good)}$$
$$H_1: \quad \mu < \mu_0 \qquad\qquad\quad \text{(springs are bad)}$$

The spring manufacturer wishes to be protected against rejecting the null hypothesis when it is true at significance level $\alpha = .05$. The quality control manager must first determine a test statistic to use. Because the hypotheses involve μ, it will be appropriate to use the sample mean $\overline{X}$ of the observed stretching forces. This will be compared to a critical value $\overline{X}*$.

The null hypothesis will be rejected only when the sample results substantially deny it. Thus the lot will be rejected only if the sample mean stretching force $\overline{X}$ lies far enough *below* the 50-pound specification to warrant such action. Thus, $\overline{X}*$ will lie below μ_0. The quality control manager will reject the lot if the observed value for $\overline{X}$ is smaller than $\overline{X}*$ and accept it otherwise.

This situation is shown in Figure 9-4, where the rejection region starts at $\overline{X}*$ and extends below it. The normal curve represents the sampling distribution for the possible values of the sample mean when the springs are actually good. The colored area in the lower tail represents the probability of rejecting the shipment. The value for $\overline{X}*$ must be established so that this area is equal to $\alpha = .05$.

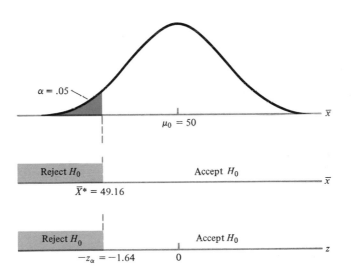

FIGURE 9-4 Sampling distribution of $\overline{X}$, with decision rule and Type I error probability.

Although here H_0 allows μ to be any force $\geqslant 50$ pounds, in setting α, we focus on the smallest of these—placing μ at 50. (In testing with any null hypothesis, we set μ_0 at the value found by ignoring the "$<$" or "$>$" portions, so that the value for α always reflects the extreme case.)

Thus, we use the normal curve with a mean of $\mu_0 = 50$ to represent the sampling distribution of $\overline{X}$. The standard deviation for this curve is $\sigma_{\overline{X}} = \sigma/\sqrt{n}$. Even though we do not know the population standard deviation, we may still use the normal curve because the sample size is large. The quality control manager estimates the value of σ from the sample data by the sample standard deviation $s = 5.1$. Thus $\sigma_{\bar{X}}$ is estimated by

$$\frac{s}{\sqrt{n}} = \frac{5.1}{\sqrt{100}} = .51$$

In employing the normal curve, any value for $\bar{X}$ corresponds to a particular normal deviate by the relation

$$z = \frac{\bar{X} - \mu_0}{\sigma_{\bar{X}}}$$

The test statistic's critical value $\bar{X}^*$ corresponds to a very important normal deviate value corresponding to a normal-curve tail area equal to α. We denote this *critical normal deviate* by the symbol z_α. For simplicity z_α will always be a *positive quantity*. When $\alpha = .05$, we find z_α (which we can also denote as $z_{.05}$) from Appendix Table E to have a value of $z_{.05} = 1.64$. This indicates that $\bar{X}^*$ should be a value lying 1.64 standard deviations below the mean. Thus,

$$\bar{X}^* = \mu - 1.64\sigma_{\bar{X}}$$

Using $s/\sqrt{n} = .51$ as the estimate for $\sigma_{\bar{X}}$, the manager's critical value is

$$\bar{X}^* = 50 - 1.64(.51) = 49.16 \text{ lbs}$$

This may be expressed in terms of the following decision rule:

Accept H_0 (accept the batch for shipment) if $\bar{X} \geqslant 49.16$ lbs

Reject H_0 (reject the batch for shipment) if $\bar{X} < 49.16$ lbs

Suppose that the pressure test is applied to the sample springs and a mean of $\bar{X} = 48.5$ pounds is obtained. In this case, $\bar{X}$ is less than the critical value of 49.16 pounds. Thus, the null hypothesis that the lot is good would be *rejected*, and this particular batch of springs would not be shipped to the office furniture maker. We would say that the test results are statistically significant at level $\alpha = .05$.

As an alternative to the above decision rule, the same choice can be made using normal deviate values. The observed sample mean can be transformed into a particular point on the standard-deviation scale, using $s/\sqrt{n} = .51$ as the estimate of $\sigma_{\bar{X}}$:

$$z = \frac{\bar{X} - \mu_0}{\sigma_{\bar{X}}} = \frac{48.5 - 50}{.51} = -2.94$$

The value $z = -2.94$ gauges how *rare* it would be under the null hypothesis to obtain a sample mean as small or smaller than the $\bar{X}$ value actually observed.

Assuming that 50 pounds is the true population mean distortion stretching force and that the population standard deviation is 5.1, then the area under the normal curve between $\mu_0 = 50$ and $\overline{X} = 48.5$ is found from Appendix Table D to be .4984, so that the probability of getting a result at least as small is $.5 - .4984 = .0016$. Since this probability is smaller than the desired Type I error probability of $\alpha = .05$, the sample result is rare enough under the null hypothesis to justify rejecting it. (Remember that the actual value of σ is not known but has been estimated by $s = 5.1$. Unless 5.1 happens to be the true value, .0016 is only an *approximate* probability.)

The testing approach outlined here can be shortened by comparing the computed value for z to the critical normal deviate z_α, so that H_0 is accepted if $z \geqslant -z_\alpha$ and rejected if $z < -z_\alpha$. Since $z = -2.94$ is smaller than $-z_{.05} = -1.64$, H_0 must be rejected.

In this illustration, the decision rule was actually formulated after the sample data were collected. Such a procedure is correct because once μ_0 is determined, the sample size is prescribed, and the desired significance level is decided, everything that follows is automatic. But it would be improper to change μ_0, n, or α *after evaluating* the sample results. As a practical matter, the decision rule can be established either before or after the data are collected. One advantage of establishing a rule before sampling is that it is then possible to see what Type II error probabilities β result from the initial rule and to make any modifications that may be necessary to provide a better balance between α and β. But, again, the decision rule should never be altered after analyzing the data. Unless σ is known in advance or can be accurately guessed, the decision rule can be found only after the sample statistics have been computed.

Summary of Procedure

It is convenient to categorize hypothesis-testing situations in terms of what portion of the test statistic's sampling distribution corresponds to α. In the preceding illustration, α represents the lower-tail area under the normal curve for $\overline{X}$; this situation is therefore a *lower-tailed test*. In the dietary-supplement example earlier, the hypotheses were designated so that an *upper-tailed test* resulted. It will be convenient if we make the following

DEFINITION   The direction of the inequalities in the hypotheses determines the type of test.

Upper-tailed test:

$$H_0: \quad \mu \leq \mu_0 \qquad\qquad H_1: \quad \mu > \mu_0$$

Lower-tailed test:

$$H_0: \quad \mu \geqslant \mu_0 \qquad\qquad H_1: \quad \mu < \mu_0$$

Upper- and lower-tailed tests are summarized in Figure 9-5.

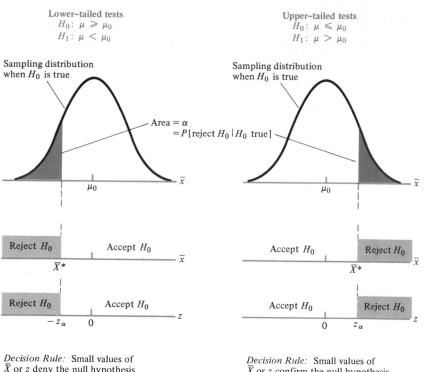

Decision Rule: Small values of $\overline{X}$ or z deny the null hypothesis that μ is large, while large values confirm it.

Decision Rule: Small values of $\overline{X}$ or z confirm the null hypothesis that μ is small, while large values refute it.

FIGURE 9-5   Upper-tailed and lower-tailed testing situations.

Hypothesis Testing Steps

The general approach to one-sided hypothesis-testing situations may be summarized by the following.

1. Specify the null hypothesis and establish the significance level α.
2. Determine the value of the critical normal deviate z_α from Appendix Table E.
3. Establish the *critical value*.

For an upper-tailed test:

$$\overline{X}^* = \mu_0 + z_\alpha \frac{s}{\sqrt{n}} \tag{9-1}$$

For a lower-tailed test:

$$\overline{X}^* = \mu_0 - z_\alpha \frac{s}{\sqrt{n}} \tag{9-2}$$

If the population size N is small, the last term in expressions (9-1) and (9-2) would be multiplied by $\sqrt{(N-n)/(N-1)}$.

Note: If the decision rule is constructed before the sample data are collected, then s would not be available. In those cases, we would use an assumed value for σ in place of s in the above expressions.

4. Formulate the decision rule.

Upper-Tailed Test	*Lower-Tailed Test*
Accept H_0 if $\overline{X} \leqslant \overline{X}^*$ $(z \leqslant z_\alpha)$	*Accept H_0 if $\overline{X} \geqslant \overline{X}^*$ $(z \geqslant -z_\alpha)$*
Reject H_0 if $\overline{X} > \overline{X}^*$ $(z > z_\alpha)$	*Reject H_0 if $\overline{X} < \overline{X}^*$ $(z < -z_\alpha)$*

5. Apply the decision rule to the sample data obtained and accept or reject the null hypothesis. As an alternative procedure, instead of getting $\overline{X}^*$, compute

$$z = \frac{\overline{X} - \mu_0}{s/\sqrt{n}}$$

Illustrations of the Procedure

We continue with our first example, where the marketing of a dietary supplement is being considered. Suppose that Vita Synthetics orders a sample of size $n = 100$ and wishes to find a critical value $\overline{X}^*$ for the test statistic $\overline{X}$ when $\mu_0 = 20$ percent, using a smaller significance level than before, $\alpha = .01$. Since large values of $\overline{X}$ will refute H_0, this is an *upper-tailed test*, and the critical normal deviate z_α corresponds to that point where the upper-tailed area under the normal curve is equal to $\alpha = .01$. Thus, from Appendix Table E we find $z_\alpha = z_{.01} = 2.33$.

Suppose that a sample standard deviation of $s = 11.3$ percent is obtained. Substituting the appropriate values into expression (9-1), we find the critical value

$$\overline{X}^* = 20 + 2.33 \frac{11.3}{\sqrt{100}} = 22.63 \text{ percent}$$

(This is larger than the value $\overline{X}^* = 22$ used before, when the assumed value for the population standard deviation was 10 percent and α had been set at the level of .0228 achieved at the outset.)

Suppose that the sample mean percentage reduction in cholesterol levels turned out to be $\overline{X} = 23.4$ percent. Since this quantity exceeds 22.63, H_0 must be *rejected* and the supplement should be marketed because the evidence indicates that it is effective.

Viewed another way, when $\overline{X} = 23.4$ and $s = 11.3$, expression (9-3) provides the normal deviate

$$z = \frac{23.4 - 20}{11.3/\sqrt{100}} = 3.01$$

Because $z = 3.01$ exceeds $z_{.01} = 2.33$, this indicates that if H_0 were true, the sample outcome would be rarer than the most extreme permitted Type I error. Again we see that H_0 must be rejected.

Example 9-1   Over the past 100 years, there has been a pronounced trend in the United States for successive generations to grow taller than their parents. This tendency has been attributed to improved health care and nutrition. One researcher believes that this trend has reversed, due to the degraded environment, diminished exercise by children, and diets dominated by packaged convenience foods that lack sound nutritional value. To test her theory, the researcher has collected a random sample of heights for $n = 100$ 20-year-old men. As her null hypothesis, she assumes that the past trend is unchanged, so that the mean height of young men is assumed to be at least as high now as it was 20 years before, when it has been established at $\mu_0 = 70$ inches. Thus,

$$H_0: \quad \mu \geqslant 70 \text{ inches} \quad \text{(growth trend continues)}$$
$$H_1: \quad \mu < 70 \text{ inches} \quad \text{(growth trend is reversed)}$$

The researcher chooses $\alpha = .05$ as the significance level. From Appendix Table E, $z_{.05} = 1.64$. As her sample results, she obtains $\bar{X} = 69.75$ inches, with $s = 2.71$ inches. The test is *lower-tailed* (that is, small values of $\bar{X}$ in the lower tail of the normal curve refute H_0). The researcher's critical value for the sample mean is

$$\bar{X}^* = 70 - (1.64)\frac{2.71}{\sqrt{100}} = 69.56 \text{ inches}$$

and her decision rule is:

Accept H_0 (conclude growth trend continues)   if $\bar{X} \geqslant 69.56$
Reject H_0 (conclude growth trend is reversed) if $\bar{X} < 69.56$

In terms of normal deviates, the equivalent decision rule is

Accept H_0 if $z \geqslant -1.64$
Reject H_0 if $z < -1.64$

The normal deviate for the actual sample results is

$$z = \frac{69.75 - 70}{2.71/\sqrt{100}} = -.92$$

Since $\bar{X} = 69.75$ inches is larger than the critical value of 69.56 inches, and $z = -.92$ exceeds -1.64, either decision rule leads to the same conclusion—that the null hypothesis must be *accepted*. This indicates that the test results are not significant at the 5-percent level. The researcher cannot conclude that the present generation is shorter in height than the preceding one. The sample data do not support her theory.

Type II Error Considerations

Example 9-1 raises an important issue in hypothesis testing. In accepting the null hypothesis that the present trend in successively taller generations is continuing, the researcher has used a rule that protects her with a probability of .05 from committing the Type I error of wrongly concluding that the growth trend is over when it is not. *But she may still have made an incorrect decision:* She may have committed the Type II error of accepting the null hypothesis when it is not true. In other words, maybe the growth trend has ended and the true mean height for the present generation is actually some smaller value such as $\mu = 69.5$ inches. If this figure happens to be the true mean, then the probability of incorrectly accepting H_0 would be substantial. The traditional procedure outlined in this chapter always guarantees the desired level for α. But there is the ever-present danger of ignoring the Type II error probability β. As a practical matter, we obtain a smaller β by using a larger sample size. A more detailed discussion of this point will appear in Section 9-7.

EXERCISES

9-8   In testing the hypotheses for a large population,

$$H_0: \quad \mu \leqslant \mu_0 \quad \text{and} \quad H_1: \quad \mu > \mu_0$$

where $\mu_0 = 100$, the desired Type I error probability is $\alpha = .10$. A sample size of $n = 100$ is to be used. Assume that $s = 25$.
(a) Is the test lower-tailed, or upper-tailed?
(b) Find the value of the critical normal deviate z_α.
(c) Using the sample mean $\bar{X}$ as the test statistic, find the critical value $\bar{X}^*$ and formulate the decision rule.
(d) If the sample mean obtained is 102.6, would the decision rule obtained in part (c) lead to accepting or rejecting H_0?

9-9   In testing the hypotheses

$$H_0: \quad \mu \geqslant \mu_0 \quad \text{and} \quad H_1: \quad \mu < \mu_0$$

with $\mu_0 = 30$, the desired Type I error probability is $\alpha = .05$. A sample size of $n - 100$ is to be used. Assume that $s = 10$ and that the population is large.
(a) Is the test upper-tailed or lower-tailed?
(b) Using the sample mean $\bar{X}$ as the test statistic, find the critical value $\bar{X}^*$ and formulate the decision rule.
(c) If the sample mean obtained is 33, should H_0 be accepted or rejected?
(d) Suppose that the population is small with $N - 500$. Determine $\bar{X}^*$ and the decision rule that would apply. In this instance, should H_0 be accepted or rejected?

9-10   For each of the following testing situations, state whether the test is upper- or lower-tailed and find the value of the critical normal deviate z_α. Then, for each sample result obtained, calculate the normal deviate value z and indicate whether the null hypothesis should be accepted or rejected. Finally, for each outcome, determine the approximate probability of obtaining a value of the test statistic as rare as or rarer than the one obtained by finding the tail area under the normal curve corresponding to the computed z. (Assume that the respective populations are large.)
(a) $H_0: \mu \leqslant 105$; $H_1: \mu > 105$; $\alpha = .05$; $n = 100$; $\bar{X} = 108$; and $s = 15$.
(b) $H_0: \mu \geqslant 5$; $H_1: \mu < 5$; $\alpha = .01$; $n = 100$; $\bar{X} = 4.8$; and $s = 2$.
(c) $H_0: \mu \geqslant .8$; $H_1: \mu < .8$; $\alpha = .10$; $n = 36$; $\bar{X} = .6$; and $s = .6$.
(d) $H_0: \mu \leqslant 10$; $H_1: \mu > 10$; $\alpha = .001$; $n = 900$; $\bar{X} = 10.5$; and $s = 6$.

9-11   A psychologist believes that age has an influence on a person's IQ. A random sample of 100 middle-aged persons who had been tested at age 16 were tested again. Subtracting their earlier scores from the new scores, a mean difference of $\bar{X} = 5$ points and a standard deviation of $s = 8$ points were determined. Using $\alpha = .01$ as her significance level, the psychologist wishes to test the null hypothesis $H_0: \mu \leqslant 0$ that no improvement in IQ occurs with age.

(a) Is this test upper- or lower-tailed? Find the critical normal deviate.

(b) Calculate the normal deviate for the test results. Does this value indicate that H_0 must be accepted or rejected?

9-12 A random sample of 100 rolls of paper has been selected from a large shipment by the superintendent of a printing plant. Their lengths have been measured, and the results show that the average length is $\bar{X} = 531$ feet, with a standard deviation of $s = 52$ feet. The null hypothesis that $\mu \geqslant 525$ is to be tested against the alternative that $\mu < 525$.

(a) Assuming that $\alpha = .01$, determine the critical normal deviate. Use this to find the critical value $\bar{X}^*$.

(b) Should the null hypothesis be rejected or accepted? Why?

9-13 A random sample of $n = 100$ department store charge accounts has an average balance of $\bar{X} = \$49.00$ with a standard deviation of $s = \$20.00$. Does this information enable us to reject the hypothesis $\mu \geqslant \$50$ if we test it against the alternative that $\mu < \$50$ at a significance level of $\alpha = .005$?

9-14 In testing the null hypothesis that $\mu \leqslant 80$ for a modified aptitude test, you may presume that the population standard deviation is $\sigma = 16$. You cannot decide whether to use a sample of $n = 64$ or $n = 100$, but you will use the smallest n and corresponding decision rule that provides a β probability of at most .10 for accepting H_0 when μ is actually 85. In all cases, use $\alpha = .05$.

(a) Find the critical value $\bar{X}^*$ and the decision rule when $n = 64$.

(b) Find the critical value $\bar{X}^*$ and the decision rule when $n = 100$.

(c) Calculate the value of β at $\mu = 85$ when $n = 64$ and when $n = 100$. Which sample size should be used?

9-15 A subsystem will be incorporated into a communications satellite if its mean time between failures (MTBF) obtained from a sample of units subjected to environmental testing is greater than or equal to $\bar{X}^* = 500$ hours. This action is equivalent to accepting the null hypothesis that the actual MTBF is $\mu_0 = 550$ hours or more. Assuming that the standard deviation of failure times for the units is $\sigma = 200$ hours and that N is large:

(a) Find the significance level α of the above test, assuming that $n = 100$.

(b) Determine the critical value and formulate the decision rule if it is required that $\alpha = .05$. Use a sample size of $n = 100$.

9-4 TWO-SIDED HYPOTHESIS TESTS USING THE MEAN

In the preceding section we encountered two basic situations where the null hypothesis gets rejected whenever $\bar{X}$ falls far enough to one side or the other of μ_0. Such a procedure is called a *one-sided test*, and may be either upper-tailed or lower-tailed. A different situation is the *two-sided test*, where both extremes in the sample mean, large or small values for $\bar{X}$, will lead to rejecting the null hypothesis.

An important application of hypothesis testing occurs in monitoring quality in production operations. Since quality control is an important branch of applied statistics in which two-sided tests are frequently used, we can illustrate two-sided procedures for testing the mean with the following detailed example.

Illustration of the Testing Procedure

A food company advertises that there are 105 chunks of beef in every 15-ounce can of its chili. It has spent a great deal of money creating the image that it offers a high-quality product, following a policy of including generous portions of expensive ingredients in its canned foods. The company wants to be assured that its policies are being met in chili production. Therefore, periodic checks of the quality of production are made; these consist of taking random samples of 15-ounce chili cans and measuring the quantity of beef in each sample.

Management cannot, of course, ensure that 105 chunks of beef will go into every can, unless each can is carefully filled individually with precisely the desired amount of beef. This is not practicable, because the chili is cooked in large kettles and the ingredients are added as the recipe requires. Each kettle contains several hundred pounds of chili, and the actual number of chunks of beef distributed to each can will vary. Management can control only the mean number of chunks per can. How close the mean actually approaches the desired goal will depend upon the precision used in mixing all of the ingredients during preparation.

Management's goal is therefore to see that the mean number of beef chunks is very close to the advertised 105. If current production has a lower mean, some remedial action must be taken in the kitchen. On the other hand, since beef is by far the most expensive chili ingredient, a mean higher than the desired 105 will also require remedial action. Management wishes to avoid extreme values in the mean beef quantity, both high and low.

Assuming that the standard deviation will be constant under either hypothesis, the following hypotheses regarding the mean number of beef chunks per can are formulated, with $\mu_0 = 105$:

$$H_0: \quad \mu = \mu_0 \quad \text{(no remedial action is required)}$$

$$H_1: \quad \mu \neq \mu_0 \quad \text{(remedial action is required)}$$

The alternative hypothesis states that the mean quantity of beef is *different* from μ_0; the direction of difference is unimportant. This is an example of a *two-sided alternative*.

The decision rule will have the form:

Accept H_0 (do not take action) if $\overline{X}_1^* \leqslant \overline{X} \leqslant \overline{X}_2^*$

Reject H_0 (take action)   if $\overline{X} < \overline{X}_1^*$ or if $\overline{X} > \overline{X}_2^*$

Note that there are two critical values for the test statistic. This is because there are two bases for rejection: insufficient beef and excessive beef.

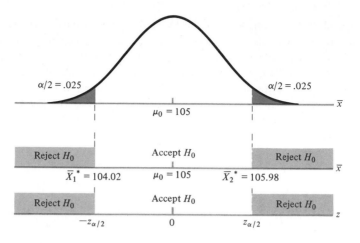

FIGURE 9-6 Sampling distribution of $\overline{X}$, when the null hypothesis is true.

The decision rule is chosen to be symmetrical about μ_0. Figure 9-6 shows the sampling distribution when the null hypothesis is true, as well as the critical values of the decision rule. The sum of the areas in both tails represents the probability of rejection.

In two-sided tests there are two Type I error situations; in this example, a Type I error is to take unnecessary remedial action for either overfilling or underfilling. The significance level α is usually evenly divided between these two errors. There are also two Type II error situations; here, a Type II error results from not taking remedial action either when there is overfilling or when there is underfilling.

Finding Critical Values for the Two-Sided Test

Suppose that a sample of size $n = 100$ is taken and that the sample standard deviation is $s = 5$ chunks per can. The test statistic will be the sample mean chunks found per can $\overline{X}$. Management wants to find a decision rule that will lead to rejecting a true null hypothesis (Type I error) with a probability of .05. The significance level is therefore $\alpha = .05$.

The following provide *the critical values for a two-sided test of the mean:*

$$\overline{X}_1^* = \mu_0 - z_{\alpha/2}\frac{s}{\sqrt{n}}$$

$$\overline{X}_2^* = \mu_0 + z_{\alpha/2}\frac{s}{\sqrt{n}}$$

(9-4)

The critical normal deviate $z_{\alpha/2}$ is a *positive quantity* representing the upper-tail area under the normal curve that corresponds to half of the Type I error probability. Since $z_{\alpha/2}$ expresses distance in standard deviation units, the lower critical value $\bar{X}_1^*$ is found by subtracting $z_{\alpha/2}$ times $s/\sqrt{n}$ (the estimate for $\sigma_{\bar{X}}$) from μ_0; the upper critical value $\bar{X}_2^*$ is found by adding $z_{\alpha/2}$ times $s/\sqrt{n}$ to μ_0. As with one-sided tests, we may construct the decision rule in advance of sampling, provided that σ is known, by using σ in place of s in expression (9-4).

This procedure applies when the population is large. When the sample is taken from a small population, the last term in both equations in expression (9-4) must be multiplied by the finite population correction factor

$$\sqrt{(N-n)/(N-1)}.$$

Returning to our example, Appendix Table E provides the critical normal deviate $z_{\alpha/2} = z_{.025} = 1.96$. Since the population of chili cans is large, we ignore the effect of the population size N in using expression (9-4) to find the critical values for $\bar{X}$:

$$\bar{X}_1^* = 105 - 1.96 \frac{5}{\sqrt{100}} = 104.02$$

$$\bar{X}_2^* = 105 + 1.96 \frac{5}{\sqrt{100}} = 105.98$$

The decision rule may be expressed in terms of these values:

Accept H_0 (do not take action) if $104.02 \leqslant \bar{X} \leqslant 105.98$

Reject H_0 (take action)   if $\bar{X} < 104.02$ *or if* $\bar{X} > 105.98$

Suppose that the sample mean achieved is $\bar{X} = 106.3$. Since this does not lie between the critical values $\bar{X}_1^* = 104.02$ and $\bar{X}_2^* = 105.98$, *management must reject H_0 and take remedial action*. If a different result had been obtained, such as $\bar{X} = 104.5$, then H_0 would have been accepted, as in that case $\bar{X}$ would fall between 104.02 and 105.98.

As with the tests discussed previously, the computation of $\bar{X}_1^*$ and $\bar{X}_2^*$ can be by-passed, and the normal deviate z for the results obtained can be calculated instead. Should z fall within the limits $-z_{\alpha/2}$ to $z_{\alpha/2}$, H_0 would be accepted; otherwise H_0 would be rejected.

With our example, the normal deviate is

$$z = \frac{\bar{X} - \mu_0}{s/\sqrt{n}} = \frac{106.3 - 105}{5/\sqrt{100}} = 2.6$$

This value is greater than $z_{\alpha/2} = 1.96$ so, as before, H_0 must be rejected.

**Explanation of Hypothesis Testing
in Terms of Confidence Intervals**

Two-sided hypothesis-testing procedures may be described in terms of the confidence-interval estimate. The *acceptance region* of this type of test has the form

$$\overline{X}_1^* \leqslant \overline{X} \leqslant \overline{X}_2^*$$

which can be expressed equivalently as

$$\mu_0 - z_{\alpha/2} \frac{s}{\sqrt{n}} \leqslant \overline{X} \leqslant \mu_0 + z_{\alpha/2} \frac{s}{\sqrt{n}}$$

Each two-tailed decision rule must be established so that there is a probability $1 - \alpha$ of accepting H_0 when the null hypothesis that $\mu = \mu_0$ is true. Thus, when $\alpha = .05$, so that $1 - \alpha = .95$, then 95 percent of all samples taken from a population where μ_0 is indeed the true mean will result in accepting this null hypothesis.

Rearranging the above inequality, and replacing the symbol μ_0 with μ, an equivalent expression provides the *confidence interval:*

$$\overline{X} - z_{\alpha/2} \frac{s}{\sqrt{n}} \leqslant \mu \leqslant \overline{X} + z_{\alpha/2} \frac{s}{\sqrt{n}} \tag{9-5}$$

We note that when $\mu = \mu_0$, 95 percent of all samples yield values for $\overline{X}$ and s that provide intervals, calculated from expression (9-5), that contain the value μ_0. But 5 percent of the samples do not contain μ_0. Thus, when $\alpha = .05$, expression (9-5) provides a 95-percent confidence-interval estimate of μ. Finding whether or not H_0 falls into the acceptance region produces the same result as finding whether or not μ_0 falls into the above confidence interval.

We may then approach the two-sided hypothesis-testing procedure by first constructing a confidence interval. *If μ_0 is a value lying inside the confidence interval constructed from the sample results, H_0 must be accepted. But if these limits fall completely above or below μ_0, H_0 must be rejected.* Only 5 percent of these intervals can ever be so far off that they will not bracket μ_0 when it is the true mean; that is, only 5 percent of the time this procedure is employed will the Type I error be committed of rejecting H_0 when it is true.

In the chili illustration, $\overline{X} = 106.3$ beef chunks, $s = 5$, and $n = 100$. Using these data to construct a 95-percent confidence interval, we have

$$106.3 - 1.96 \frac{5}{\sqrt{100}} \leqslant \mu \leqslant 106.3 + 1.96 \frac{5}{\sqrt{100}}$$

or

$$105.32 \leqslant \mu \leqslant 107.28 \text{ beef chunks}$$

Since this interval does not contain the value $\mu_0 = 105$, H_0 must be *rejected*. This is the same conclusion we reached earlier.

EXERCISES

9-16 In testing the hypotheses $H_0: \mu = \mu_0 (= 0)$ and $H_1: \mu \neq \mu_0$, answer the following, assuming that $\sigma = 10$ and that a sample of size $n = 100$ is taken from a large population.

   (a) Assuming that $\alpha = .05$ and that a symmetrical two-tailed test is made, find $z_{\alpha/2}$ and the critical values $\bar{X}_1^*$ and $\bar{X}_2^*$, and then formulate the decision rule.

   (b) Using the decision obtained in (a), calculate the probability of accepting the null hypothesis when $\mu = 1.0$.

   (c) Suppose that the sample results show $\bar{X} = 1.2$ and $s = 9.5$. Calculate the resulting normal deviate. Should H_0 be accepted or rejected?

9-17 For each of the following two-sided testing situations, construct a 95-percent confidence interval for μ and use it to indicate whether H_0 must be accepted or rejected.

   (a) $\mu_0 = 10$; $\bar{X} = 10.1$; $s = .3$; $n = 100$; and N is large.

   (b) $\mu_0 = .72$; $\bar{X} = .705$; $s = .13$; $n = 169$; and $N = 800$.

   (c) $\mu_0 = 0$; $\bar{X} = -.7$; $s = 2.5$; $n = 625$; and N is large.

9-18 A researcher believes that marijuana has a latent effect upon the duration of dreams, but he does not know whether dreaming is increased or decreased. The night's sleep of 36 volunteers is monitored 24 hours after each has experienced a marijuana high. Previous research indicates that, under ordinary conditions, the population mean dream duration is 1.5 hours. Taking that figure as his null hypothesis, he tests this at the .01 significance level against the two-sided alternative. With $\bar{X} = 1.8$ hours and $s = .6$ hours, what conclusion should the researcher make?

9-19 The output of a chemical process is checked periodically in order to determine the level of impurities in the final product. Too many impurities will cause the product to be reclassified; too few are an indication that an expensive catalytic ingredient is being consumed in undesirably large quantities. The process has been designed so that the total amount of impurities desired is $\mu = .05$ gram per liter, with a standard deviation of $\sigma = .02$ gram.

   A sample of 1-liter vials is taken at random times throughout each four-hour period and the level of impurities is measured. The process should be stopped if there are either too many impurities (the tanks are then purged) or too few impurities (the control valves are then readjusted). Criteria are to be established so that the chief engineer can determine when the process should be stopped.

   (a) Formulate the hypotheses for the situation.

   (b) Suppose the chief engineer desires a Type I error probability of $\alpha = .01$ for stopping the process when the mean level of impurities is $\mu_0 = .05$ gram per liter. Find the critical value $\bar{X}^*$ when $n = 100$ liters are used in the sample. Then formulate the decision rule.

   (c) Using the above decision rule, find the probability of erroneously stopping the process when the mean level of impurities shifts to (1) $\mu = .043$; (2) $\mu = .045$; (3) $\mu = .052$; (4) $\mu = .055$. What do you notice about your answers to (2) and (4)? Explain this.

9-5 TESTS OF THE MEAN USING SMALL SAMPLES

Often a statistical decision must be made using data from a small sample. In tests involving people, sample data are frequently skimpy and sample sizes smaller than 30 are quite common. Ordinarily, the population standard deviation σ is not known and must be estimated by its sample counterpart s. As we saw in Chapter 8, the normal curve does not perform satisfactorily as the sampling distribution for $\overline{X}$ under these circumstances. In its place, we therefore employ the Student t distribution.

The Student t statistic is found in the same manner as the normal deviate z—by subtracting the population mean from the observed value of the sample mean—except that we divide this difference by the *estimated* standard error for $\overline{X}$, $s/\sqrt{n}$, instead of the actual value of $\sigma_{\overline{X}}$, $\sigma/\sqrt{n}$, which remains unknown because the value of the population standard deviation is unavailable. (If the value of σ is established in advance of sampling, we may use the procedures outlined in Sections 9-3 and 9-4, and the Student t distribution will not apply.) Under the null hypothesis, μ is equal to an assumed value, μ_0, so that the following expression is used to compute the *Student t test statistic:*

$$t = \frac{\overline{X} - \mu_0}{s/\sqrt{n}} \tag{9-6}$$

Procedure Using *t* Statistic

1. Calculate t from expression (9-6).
2. From Appendix Table F, determine t_α for the desired significance level α. This will always be a positive quantity. For a two-sided test, find $t_{\alpha/2}$ corresponding to an upper-tail area of $\alpha/2$. The number of degrees of freedom is $n-1$.
3. Apply the decision rule:
   (a) For an upper-tailed test:

   $$\text{Accept } H_0 \text{ if } t \leqslant t_\alpha$$
   $$\text{Reject } H_0 \text{ if } t > t_\alpha$$

   (b) For a lower-tailed test:

   $$\text{Accept } H_0 \text{ if } t \geqslant -t_\alpha$$
   $$\text{Reject } H_0 \text{ if } t < -t_\alpha$$

   (c) For a two-sided test:

   $$\text{Accept } H_0 \text{ if } -t_{\alpha/2} \leqslant t \leqslant t_{\alpha/2}$$
   $$\text{Reject } H_0 \text{ if } t < -t_{\alpha/2} \text{ or if } t > t_{\alpha/2}$$

The application of this procedure is illustrated below for a typical statistical problem encountered by a firm deciding whether or not to make a change in its product line. A pivotal factor in such decisions is how the change will affect demand.

Example 9-2   Jumbo Franchises is test marketing a new low-cost dessert for possible replacement of apple turnovers in the standard menu of its 500 hamburger stands. Five typical stands in a large metropolitan area have temporarily incorporated the dessert into their menu, *eliminating* apple turnovers. Jumbo will decide to make the change if the daily demand in the five stands for the new dessert exceeds their historical mean of 1,000 daily requests for apple turnovers. The test is to run for 21 days (seasonal effects and day-of-week fluctuations are ignored), so that $n = 21$.

The hypotheses selected by the Jumbo management, with $\mu_0 = 1,000$, are

$$H_0: \quad \mu \leqslant \mu_0 \quad \text{(new dessert not better)}$$
$$H_1: \quad \mu > \mu_0 \quad \text{(new dessert better)}$$

A one-sided alternative is chosen, since Jumbo management is only concerned with what to do when the new dessert is better; here we have an upper-tailed test. Since rejection of the null hypothesis when it is true would lead to eliminating apple turnovers when they are the best sellers, Jumbo sets the significance level at .01 ($\alpha = .01$).

The following results are obtained from the Jumbo study:

$$\bar{X} = 1,020$$
$$s = 30$$

Applying step 1 of the t-statistic procedure, from expression (9-6) the value of t is determined:

$$t = \frac{1,020 - 1,000}{30/\sqrt{21}} = 3.05$$

We next apply step 2. Jumbo's critical value for an $\alpha = .01$ tail area under the t distribution having $n - 1 = 21 - 1 = 20$ degrees of freedom is found from Table F to be

$$t_\alpha = t_{.01} = 2.528$$

which is positive because the test is upper-tailed.

Applying step 3, Jumbo's decision rule may be expressed as

> *Accept H_0* (don't replace turnovers) if $t \leqslant 2.528$
> *Reject H_0* (replace turnovers)   if $t > 2.528$

Because the resulting value, $t = 3.05$, calculated for Jumbo exceeds the critical value $t_{.01} = 2.528$, step 3 indicates that H_0 must be *rejected*, and the test is significant at level .01. Apple turnovers will be replaced (there is less than a .01 chance that doing so will be incorrect).

An Assumption of the *t* Test

The Student t distribution is based upon the assumption that the underlying population frequency distribution is represented by the normal curve.

As a practical matter, this requirement poses no difficulties, as long as the population frequency distribution is unimodal and fairly symmetrical. Thus, the t test is fairly insensitive to this requirement. Statisticians would say that the t test is, to some degree, *robust* with respect to the non-normality of the population.

To avoid potential difficulties that may arise when the normality assumption does not hold, certain nonparametric tests may be employed. (These will be discussed in Chapter 18.)

EXERCISES

9-20 For each of the following hypothesis-testing situations, calculate the value of the test statistic t. Indicate whether the test is lower-tailed, upper-tailed, or two-sided. Then determine the critical value and formulate the decision rule for each. Indicate whether each H_0 should be accepted or rejected.

(a) $\bar{X} = 13$; $s = 2$; $n = 9$; and $\alpha = .01$.
$H_0: \mu \geqslant 15$ and $H_1: \mu < 15$

(b) $\bar{X} = 170$; $s = 30$; $n = 25$; and $\alpha = .05$.
$H_0: \mu \leqslant 160$ and $H_1: \mu > 160$

(c) $\bar{X} = 102$; $s = 24$; $n = 16$; and $\alpha = .10$.
$H_0: \mu = 100$ and $H_1: \mu \neq 100$

(d) $\bar{X} = -2.8$; $s = 2.0$; $n = 25$; and $\alpha = .01$.
$H_0: \mu = 0$ and $H_1: \mu \neq 0$

9-21 A structural engineer is testing the strength of a newly designed steel beam required in cantilever construction. As his null hypothesis, he assumes that the mean strength will be at most as great as the 100,000 pounds per square inch (psi) for traditional beams. A sample of $n = 9$ new beams has been tested; the results show $\bar{X} = 105,000$ psi, with $s = 10,000$ psi. At the $\alpha = .05$ significance level, should the engineer accept or reject his null hypothesis?

9-22 A random sample of $n = 20$ rolls of wire have been selected, and their lengths have been measured. The results show that the average length is $\bar{X} = 2,031$ m with a standard deviation of $s = 47$ m. The null hypothesis that $\mu \geqslant 2,000$ m is to be tested against the alternative that $\mu < 2,000$ m.

(a) Assuming that $\alpha = .01$, determine the critical value of the test statistic t.

(b) Should the null hypothesis be rejected or accepted? Why?

9-23 Refer to Exercise 9-19. Suppose that a sample of $n = 25$ vials yields an average impurity level of .056 gram with a standard deviation of .03 gram.

(a) Assuming an $\alpha = .01$ significance level, specify the decision rule to be used.

(b) Should the process be stopped, and if so, what type of remedial action is required?

9-24 A statistics professor believes his 25 students are a representative random sample of all beginning statistics students he has taught at the university. At the end of the term, he gives all of his students a standardized test. Over the years, they have established a mean score of 75 points on this test.

The professor wishes to assess the impact of spending twice as much time as before on probability theory, taking some time away from that devoted to all other "core" statistical material. Should he find that this results in a score improvement on his standardized test, he will adopt the new policy in the future. As his null hypothesis, he assumes that there will be no score improvement, so that H_0: $\mu \leqslant 75$ points. The professor assigns an $\alpha = .01$ probability of making the Type I error of adopting the new policy (rejecting H_0) when it does not actually improve test scores.

The sample results show $\bar{X} = 86$ points, with $s = 10$ points. Should the new policy be adopted?

9-25   A cannery inspector desires that the mean weight of ingredients in 16-ounce cans be precisely that figure. If the mean weight falls above or below this figure, some remedial action must be taken. In deciding whether or not to order corrections, he has established an $\alpha = .05$ significance level for a sampling test, so that the Type I error (taking unnecessary action) is avoided 5 percent of the time.

Each hour, a sample of $n = 25$ cans is taken, each can is opened and the contents are weighed.

(a) What is the decision rule for the value of the t statistic?

(b) Suppose that $\bar{X} = 15.9$ ounces and $s = .4$ ounce. Should the inspector take remedial action?

(c) Suppose that $\bar{X} = 16.2$ ounces and $s = .3$ ounce. Should he order corrections?

9-6   HYPOTHESIS TESTS USING THE PROPORTION

The procedures described earlier for testing with the mean can be adapted to tests involving the proportion. The latter situations are encountered when a decision must be made regarding a qualitative population. In such cases, the unknown parameter of interest is the population proportion π. For example, the effectiveness of a new flu vaccine can be determined by the proportion π of treated persons who don't catch the disease when exposed to it. Similarly, the proportion π of users of an existing vaccine who will prefer a new vaccine might serve in deciding whether the latter should be marketed. If π is too small, it may be unprofitable to introduce the new vaccine.

We designate the pivotal value for the population proportion by the symbol π_0. The sample proportion P serves as the test statistic. A critical value P^* for the latter establishes the point of demarcation between accepting or rejecting the null hypothesis. In establishing a value for P^*, we ordinarily use the normal approximation to the underlying binomial sampling distribution for P. For any desired significance level α the corresponding critical normal deviate z_α can be found from Appendix Table E.

We use the following expression to find the *critical value for an upper-tailed test:*

$$P^* = \pi_0 + z_\alpha \sqrt{\frac{\pi_0(1-\pi_0)}{n}} \qquad (9\text{-}7)$$

which arises with the hypotheses $H_0: \pi \leqslant \pi_0$ and $H_1: \pi > \pi_0$. The expression below yields the *critical value for a lower-tailed test:*

$$P^* = \pi_0 - z_\alpha \sqrt{\frac{\pi_0(1-\pi_0)}{n}} \qquad (9\text{-}8)$$

applicable when $H_0: \pi \geqslant \pi_0$ and $H_1: \pi < \pi_0$. (Two-sided tests are usually not made with the proportion.)

When only the critical normal deviate z_α is used in testing, the test statistic is provided by the *normal deviate:*

$$z = \frac{P - \pi_0}{\sqrt{\pi_0(1-\pi_0)/n}} \qquad (9\text{-}9)$$

Example 9-3 Have you ever wondered why most people are right-handed? Right-handers outnumber lefties by 19 to 1, regardless of culture, race, or nationality. One researcher has proposed the following theory to partially justify this phenomenon:

1. Handedness would be strictly a "coin-flipping" proposition, except for environmental influences biasing the development of the right hand.
2. Mothers' hearts tend to be on their left sides.
3. Babies feel secure when they sense heart-beat rhythms and are happier when placed close to their mothers' hearts. Unconsciously accommodating this behavior, babies are held predominantly on the mothers' left side *supported by her left arm.*
4. This leaves only the mother's right arm free for fondling the baby. As the mother's right hand must therefore be used for most hand-to-hand contact, it is easier for her to have contact with the baby's *right hand* because it matches her free hand. Therefore, the baby begins its life using its right hand more than its left.
5. In effect, heart placement helps to determine handedness. If the human heart were on the right side instead, the above theory indicates that more babies than otherwise would end up being left-handed.

To test her theory, the researcher collected a random sample of $n = 100$ new mothers. The bias toward right-handedness was eliminated for their babies. Each mother was asked to wear a tiny amplifier that makes the heart beat loudest on the mother's right side, in effect repositioning the apparent heart location. If the above theory applies, this should favor the motor development of the babies' left hands. Each sample mother was told to wear the device when holding her baby. (The purpose of the study device and the experiment were not known to the mothers to avoid biasing their behavior.) At the end of the experiment, the babies were tested to determine their dominant hand.

As her null hypothesis, the researcher assumed that the proportion π of babies who become left-handed when reared under these experimental conditions will be no more than for the general population:

$$H_0: \quad \pi \leqslant \pi_0 \ (=.05) \ \text{(theory untrue)}$$

The alternative is that experimental conditions will yield a higher proportion of left-handed babies:

$$H_1: \quad \pi > \pi_0 \ \text{(theory true)}$$

Since large values of the sample proportion P of left-handed babies will refute the null hypothesis, this is an *upper-tailed test.* Using an $\alpha = .001$ significance level for the probability of incorrectly rejecting the null hypothesis when it is true, from Appendix Table E we find that $z_\alpha = z_{.001} = 3.08$.

The critical value for the sample proportion is

$$P^* = .05 + 3.08 \sqrt{\frac{.05(1-.05)}{100}} = .117$$

The decision rule is

$$\text{Accept } H_0 \text{ (discard theory) if } P \leqslant .117$$
$$\text{Reject } H_0 \text{ (publish theory) if } P > .117$$

At the end of the experiment, the researcher found that 15 babies were left-handed, so that $P = 15/100 = .15$. Since this is greater than $P^* = .117$, she must *reject* H_0 that the proportion of left-handed babies reared with a left-hand bias is no larger than for the general population. She will therefore publish her findings and promulgate her theory.

To see just how rare this result would be were H_0 true, the normal deviate may be calculated from expression (9-9):

$$z = \frac{.15 - .05}{\sqrt{.05(1-.05)/100}} = 4.59$$

Such a result is quite inconsistent with the null hypothesis rejected above.

Calculating the Error Probabilities

Error probabilities for tests involving the proportion may be found in much the same way as for tests involving means. For this purpose we ordinarily use the normal approximation to the underlying binomial distribution for P. Recall that the standard error for P is expressed as

$$\sigma_P = \sqrt{\frac{\pi(1-\pi)}{n}}$$

As an illustration, consider Example 9-3 and suppose that the null hypothesis is true and $\pi = \pi_0 = .05$. With $n = 100$, the corresponding value for the standard error of P is

$$\sigma_P = \sqrt{\frac{.05(.95)}{100}} = .02179$$

Using the decision rule obtained in the example, the Type I error probability for rejecting the null hypothesis when it is true (and incorrectly concluding that the left-hand theory is true) would be:

$$\alpha = P[P > .117 \mid H_0 \text{ true } (\pi = \pi_0 = .05)]$$
$$= P\left[\frac{P - \pi}{\sigma_P} > \frac{.117 - .05}{.02179}\right]$$
$$= P[Z > 3.08] = .001$$

Of course, the value $\alpha = .001$ was prescribed at the outset in establishing P^* at .117.

Consider now the Type II error probability β. Let's compute this for $\pi = .20$. (Remember that a Type II error can occur if π is any value more extreme than π_0. We choose .20 because it is a convenient value.) We have

$$\sigma_P = \sqrt{\frac{.20(.80)}{100}} = .04$$

which is different than before. *The value of σ_P is different for each possible level for the population proportion.* We have

$$\beta = P[P \leqslant .117 \mid H_0 \text{ false } (\pi = .20)]$$

$$= P\left[\frac{P-\pi}{\sigma_P} \leqslant \frac{.117-.20}{.04}\right]$$

$$= P[Z \leqslant -2.08] = .0188$$

Suppose that the sample result had not yet been obtained. Then using the decision rule found in Example 9-3 there would be almost a 2 percent chance of incorrectly discarding the theory of left-handedness if in fact a substantial proportion (.20) of all babies favor their left after a prolonged simulated switch of their mother's heart placement.

EXERCISES

9-26   The following hypotheses are being tested with $\pi_0 = .10$:

$$H_0: \quad \pi \leqslant \pi_0$$
$$H_1: \quad \pi > \pi_0$$

Suppose that a sample of size $n = 100$ is used. Find the Type I error probability α when $\pi = .10$ and the Type II error probability β when $\pi = .20$ assuming that the following decision rule applies.

Accept H_0 *if* $P \leqslant .16$

Reject H_0 *if* $P > .16$

9-27   Refer to Exercise 9-26. Find the error probabilities when the sample size and critical value are:
(a) $n = 50$, $P^* = .15$ (b) $n = 50$, $P^* = .18$ (c) $n = 200$, $P^* = .18$

9-28   In testing the hypotheses for a large population

$$H_0: \quad \pi \leqslant \pi_0 \ (=.5) \qquad \text{and} \qquad H_1: \quad \pi > \pi_0$$

the desired Type I error probability is $\alpha = .10$. A sample size of $n = 100$ is to be used.
(a) Is the test lower-tailed or upper-tailed?
(b) Find the value of the critical normal deviate z_α.
(c) Using the sample proportion P as the test statistic, find the critical value P^* and formulate the decision rule.
(d) If the sample proportion obtained is .55, would the decision rule obtained in part (c) lead to accepting or rejecting H_0?

9-29 A quality control manager in an electronics assembly plant takes random samples of size $n = 100$ from the items in shipments received from outside suppliers. His decision rule is: If the proportion P of defective items is less than or equal to .07, then accept the shipment; otherwise, reject it. Find the value of α assuming that $\pi_0 = .05$ and the value of β when $\pi = .10$.

9-30 A purchasing department checks samples from each shipment of supplies and returns poor-quality shipments. Policy states that when sampling is used for assessing the quality of a shipment, the probability of erroneously disqualifying a "good" shipment actually having 5 percent or fewer defective should be $\alpha = .05$.

(a) Express the null and alternative hypotheses in terms of the proportion defective π. Is the test lower- or upper-tailed?

(b) Suppose a sample of $n = 100$ items is selected for testing. If the critical value is $P^* = .07$, what is the value for the Type I error probability? (You may assume that N is large.)

(c) Determine the critical value P^* necessary to satisfy the desired α when the sample size is $n = 100$.

9-31 A congressman wishes to test the null hypothesis that at least 50 percent of the voters recognize his name. From a random sample of $n = 25$ persons, only 10 could identify him as a U.S. Representative. Using an $\alpha = .05$ significance level:

(a) Is this test upper- or lower-tailed? Find the critical normal deviate.

(b) Calculate the normal deviate for the test results. Does this value indicate that the null hypothesis must be accepted or rejected?

9-32 A marketing research survey involves a random sample of $n = 100$ cereal buyers from a population where the proportion of the market held by CornChox is to be tested. The food processor will engage in a promotion campaign if CornChox's proportion of buyers is less than or equal to .30, so that the null hypothesis is $\pi \leqslant \pi_0 (= .30)$. But no special promotion is required if $\pi > .30$, the alternative hypothesis. Unfortunately, only the sample result can be known, and a decision rule has been established with a critical value of $P^* = .35$.

(a) What are the values of α (when $\pi = .30$) and β (when $\pi = .40$)?

(b) Will α increase or decrease if the decision rule is changed to a critical value of $P^* = .36$? What will the new value of α be? What will be the new value for β? Did β increase or decrease?

9-33 A personnel manager claims that at least 40 percent of all engineers employed by aerospace firms switch jobs within three years after being hired. The alternative hypothesis is that the rate of job changing is below 40 percent. A significance level of .01 is used.

(a) Find the critical value of the test statistic P, when a sample of 100 engineers is used.

(b) What is the probability that the claim will be accepted when only 30 percent of the engineers actually switch jobs within three years?

(c) Under the assumption of (a), should the claim be accepted or rejected if the sample results show that 25 engineers changed jobs?

9-7 SELECTING THE TEST

Some Important Questions

We have now covered the basic concepts of hypothesis testing as it is applied to means and proportions. It is now time to consider some fundamental questions.

1. *What other test statistics might we use?* Many test statistics other than $\overline{X}$ and P are applicable to hypothesis-testing situations. In the preceding section, we presented one of these based upon the Student t distribution. Usually, the nature of the test determines the type of test statistic to be used. In later chapters, a host of test statistics will be introduced that may be used to compare two or more population parameters, to determine whether or not two population characteristics are independent, and to determine whether or not a sample is random. Even in a single application, such as finding if a new drug results in shorter recovery times, several test statistics might apply; in addition to testing with $\overline{X}$, a number of so-called nonparametric tests (to be described in Chapter 18) may be used.

2. *How can we determine which particular test statistic will work best?* Either $\overline{X}$ or P might be used to obtain the estimate of a population mean in some applications. In certain testing situations, it is also true that a decision can be made using either the sample mean or the sample proportion as the test statistic. Often, we may choose from several alternative procedures. Perhaps the most important factor in making this choice is the relative efficiency of each test.

3. *How might we evaluate a particular decision rule in terms of the protection it provides against both kinds of incorrect decisions: the Type I and Type II errors?* Both types of decision errors should be avoided. But we have seen that when the choice is based upon sample data, some probability for each—α and β—must be tolerated. Ordinarily, only α, the probability of the more serious Type I error, is explicitly considered in selecting a decision rule. But the statistician may revise his initial rule upon finding it woefully inadequate in protecting against the Type II error.

4. *What assumptions underlie the proposed testing procedure, and how do they affect its applicability?* Later in this book, tests will be discussed that are based upon certain key assumptions. In Section 9-5, for example, the t test was described; this test assumes that the population itself is normally distributed. Just how critical are such assumptions? At one extreme, they may so severely limit a test's applicability that it may be totally inappropriate for many decision-making situations. On the other hand, an assumption may prove to be relatively unimportant. A test that works pretty much as it is intended to even when a basic requirement is not exactly met is said to be *robust* with respect to a violation of that assumption.

The Operating Characteristic Curve

With an alternative hypothesis such as $\mu > \mu_0$ (or $\mu < \mu_0$), there is no single Type II error probability value for β. Recall that β is the probability of accepting H_0 when H_0 is false (and H_1 is true). If we use the alternative hypothesis $H_1: \mu > 20$ in the dietary-supplement illustration, we can compute β only for a particular value of μ greater than 20, such as 21, 22, or 24 percent. Figure 9-7 illustrates the values of β obtained for these values of μ using the initial decision rule with $\overline{X}* = 22$, a sample size of $n = 100$, and an assumed standard deviation of $\sigma = 10$ percent.

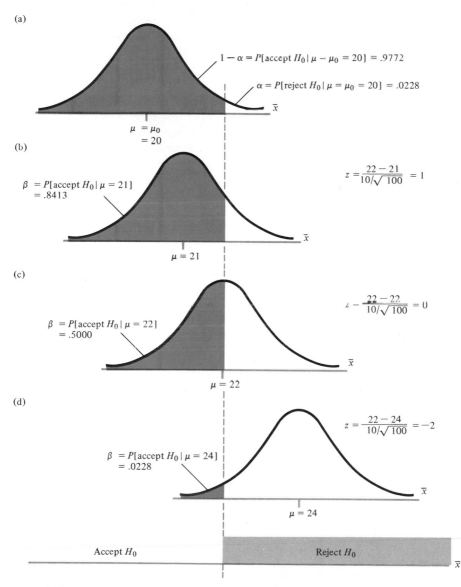

(a)

$1 - \alpha = P[\text{accept } H_0 \,|\, \mu - \mu_0 = 20] = .9772$

$\alpha = P[\text{reject } H_0 \,|\, \mu = \mu_0 = 20] = .0228$

$\mu = \mu_0 = 20$

(b)

$\beta = P[\text{accept } H_0 \,|\, \mu = 21]$
$= .8413$

$z = \dfrac{22 - 21}{10/\sqrt{100}} = 1$

$\mu = 21$

(c)

$\beta = P[\text{accept } H_0 \,|\, \mu = 22]$
$= .5000$

$z = \dfrac{22 - 22}{10/\sqrt{100}} = 0$

$\mu = 22$

(d)

$\beta = P[\text{accept } H_0 \,|\, \mu = 24]$
$= .0228$

$z = \dfrac{22 - 24}{10/\sqrt{100}} = -2$

$\mu = 24$

Accept H_0 Reject H_0

FIGURE 9-7 Probabilities of accepting H_0 for various values of μ. (a) Sampling distribution of $\overline{X}$ when the null hypothesis is true (worst case). (b), (c), (d) Sampling distributions of $\overline{X}$ for various possibilities when the null hypothesis is false.

To evaluate the choice of critical value and sample size, a decision-maker may assess the effects of the entire range of possible values of μ by obtaining the corresponding β's. In Figure 9-8 the probabilities of accepting H_0 for all possible values of μ are plotted on a single graph. From this curve we may obtain the value of β at any level of μ. Such a graph is called an *operating characteristic curve*, which we conveniently shorten to OC curve. An OC curve provides a convenient presentation for evaluating all the risks associated with accepting the null hypothesis (not marketing the supplement). Notice that the OC curve in Figure 9-8 is shaped like an inverted S; this same basic shape applies to all upper-tailed tests. (For a lower-tailed test the OC curve will instead be shaped like a right-side-up S.)

Note that for values of μ close to μ_0, the probability of accepting H_0 is near to $1 - \alpha$. Indeed, when $\mu = \mu_0$, the Type I error and the probability of accepting are complementary, so that the curve at $\mu = \mu_0$ is of height $1 - \alpha$. As μ becomes farther from μ_0, β decreases. In our example, this means that it will be an increasingly rare event to get a value for $\overline{X}$ smaller than $\overline{X}^*$ for larger μ values, as the anticholesterol diet supplement would be even more effective as μ becomes large.

Some statisticians prefer to use the probability of rejecting as the vertical axis of the curve, so that the height of the curve corresponds to $1 - \beta$. Figure 9-9

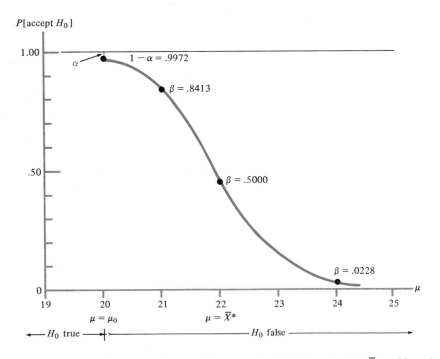

FIGURE 9-8 Operating characteristic curve for decision rule with $\overline{X}^* = 22$ and $n = 100$.

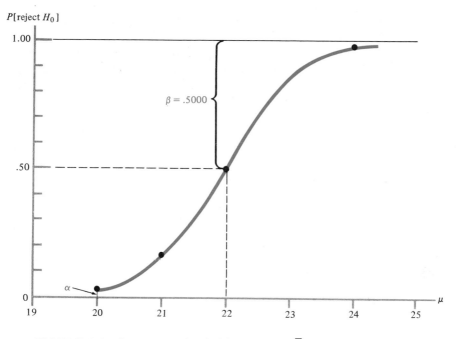

$P[\text{reject } H_0]$

$\beta = .5000$

α

FIGURE 9-9   Power curve for decision rule with $\bar{X}^* = 22$ and $n = 100$.

shows how such a graph looks for the Vita Synthetics decision. This *power curve* provides the same information as the OC curve. By subtracting the heights of points on the power curve from 1, the heights for the corresponding β values on the OC curve may be obtained, and vice versa. It does not really matter which type of curve is used.

Using the OC Curve

Recall that a decision rule is usually found for a fixed sample size n by first setting α and then determining the corresponding critical value. By studying the OC curve, the decision-maker may find that the β values are higher than desired. In Section 9-2 it was established that there are two ways to lower an error probability. One is to revise the critical value, which may be a remedy if the two kinds of risks, α and β, are not suitably balanced by the decision rule. The president of Vita Synthetics could reduce the levels for β (that is, the chances of not marketing supplements of varying degrees of effectiveness) by lowering $\bar{X}^*$, thereby shifting the OC curve leftward. But recall that this can be done only at the expense of increasing the probability α of rejecting a true H_0 (in other words, marketing an ineffective supplement). A decision-maker who finds any reduction in α intolerable can lower the β values only by raising the sample size n. This is a second remedy. In such a case more resources must be devoted to collecting additional sample observations. The resulting test would thereby become more discriminating, and the new OC curve would be steeper in shape.

Efficiency and Power

A very important question considered in advanced applications of hypothesis-testing theory concerns the choice of the test statistic. In many decision situations, there may be a number of statistical tests that can be performed. For instance, in the dietary-supplement example, instead of finding the actual levels of cholesterol reduction in treated patients, the statistician could simply determine how many of the patients achieve a major reduction in their cholesterol levels. Vita Synthetics could then use the proportion P of patients achieving a major reduction, with π_0 representing a desired level for the proportion of all treated persons who might achieve such a reduction. Instead, the choice was the more detailed measure $\overline{X}$, the mean percentage reduction in cholesterol levels. Generally, $\overline{X}$ provides more information than P, so $\overline{X}$ would be a more efficient test statistic than P. That is, for the same sample size and Type I error probability α, the decision rule obtained for $\overline{X}$ should provide smaller Type II error probabilities β (and hence higher probabilities of rejecting H_0 when it is false). The $\overline{X}$ test in this case is said to be more *powerful* than the P test.

9-8 LIMITATIONS OF HYPOTHESIS-TESTING PROCEDURES

In this chapter we presented the *classical* statistical decision analysis. Its applicability to the rather large class of decision problems faced by the modern manager is limited in several ways. Paramount among these is the dependence upon samples for obtaining supportive or contradictory evidence. Many significant decisions must be made without first taking a sample, because a sample is too costly or simply unobtainable. For example, in deciding whether to drill for oil, the wildcatter does not collect direct sample evidence by drilling holes at random as the basis for rejecting or accepting the null hypothesis that there is oil. The only way such evidence may be obtained is to sink the shaft, and this can be done only after the decision has already been made to drill. What evidence is obtained must be of an indirect nature, such as results of geological surveys, seismic tests, and nearby drilling experience. Another limitation of hypothesis testing is its restricted applicability to decisions involving two alternatives when so many decisions involve choosing among a multitude of alternatives.

Even when classical hypothesis testing is applicable, there are improvements that may be made. One is to expand the process so that more information may be utilized. For instance, the fact that certain values of the population decision parameter may be more likely than others can be put to use by the decision-maker so as to reduce the effective likelihoods of incorrect decisions. Methods for doing this will be described in Chapter 20. A further limitation of the classical approach is that it does not in any way facilitate the resolution of the problem faced by a decision-maker in assessing the risks associated with the incorrect decisions; this subject is covered further in Chapter 21. The cost of collecting the sample is not explicitly considered in the classical treatment. Chapter 20 shows how we can relate the costs of selecting the sample to those of the ensuing risks, so that an optimal course of action can be achieved.

REVIEW EXERCISES

9-34 For each of the following situations, find the Type I error probability α that corresponds to the stated decision rule. In all cases, use a sample size of $n = 100$ and assume that the population is large.
(a) *Accept H_0 if $P \leqslant .15$*   *Reject H_0 if $P > .15$*
  when $\pi_0 = .1$.
(b) *Accept H_0 if $\bar{X} \geqslant 12$*   *Reject H_0 if $\bar{X} < 12$*
  when $\mu_0 = 14$ and $\sigma = 18$.
(c) *Accept H_0 if $\bar{X} \leqslant 100$*   *Reject H_0 if $\bar{X} > 100$*
  when $\mu_0 = 97$ and $\sigma = 20$.
(d) *Accept H_0 if $P \geqslant .42$*   *Reject H_0 if $P < .42$*
  when $\pi_0 = .5$.

9-35 Each of the following hypothesis-testing situations contains a sample size of $n = 100$ taken from a large population, and an $\alpha = .05$ significance level is desired. In each case, (1) give the value of μ_0; (2) indicate whether the test is lower-tailed, upper-tailed, or two-sided; (3) find the critical value(s) for $\bar{X}$; (4) calculate the normal deviate for the sample results; and (5) state whether H_0 should be accepted or rejected.
(a) $H_0: \mu \geqslant 25$; $H_1: \mu < 25$; $\bar{X} - 23.0$; and $s = 4.7$.
(b) $H_0: \mu \leqslant 14.7$; $H_1: \mu > 14.7$; $\bar{X} = 15.3$; and $s = 1.5$.
(c) $H_0: \mu = 168$; $H_1: \mu \neq 168$; $\bar{X} = 169$; and $s - .92$.

9-36 In the manufacture of a certain brand of paper, the desired thickness is .06 millimeter. If the mean thickness of the individual sheets is above or below this value, then the machinery must be adjusted. Because the amount of production time lost during adjustment is considerable, unnecessary adjustments should occur no more than 5 percent of the time. Historically, it has been established that the standard deviation in sheet thickness is $\sigma = .003$ millimeter. Each day a random sample of 100 sheets of paper is selected, and based upon the sample mean thickness, a decision of whether or not to adjust the equipment is made.
(a) State H_0 and H_1 in equation form. Is the test lower-tailed, upper-tailed, or two-sided?
(b) Does adjusting the machine correspond to accepting or rejecting H_0?
(c) Does not adjusting the machine correspond to accepting or rejecting H_0?
(d) Calculate the critical value(s) for the test statistic $\bar{X}$ and then formulate the decision rule.
(e) Calculate the Type II error probability, using the decision rule from part (d) and assuming that (1) the mean thickness is actually .061 millimeter, and (2) the mean thickness is actually .0597 millimeter.

9-37 A presidential candidate plans to campaign in only those primaries where he is preferred by at least 20 percent of the voters in his party. A random sample of 100 voter preferences is to be obtained from each state. In each case, the null hypothesis will be that the state meets the above criterion.
(a) Identify the appropriate parameter for the test. Formulate the null and alternative hypotheses in terms of specific values for this parameter.

(b) What test statistic should be used? Is the test upper- or lower-tailed?

(c) If an $\alpha = .05$ Type I error probability is desired, find the critical value for the test statistic and then formulate the decision rule.

(d) Based upon your answers to (c), indicate whether the null hypothesis should be accepted or rejected in each of the following states. Also indicate whether or not the candidate will enter the campaign in each of these states.

State	Number in Sample Preferring Candidate
New Hampshire	12
Florida	23
Wisconsin	15
Massachusetts	10

9-38 To assess the time required to cure a disease using an experimental drug, the drug is administered to a sample of $n = 25$ persons. The medical team is basing its decision whether or not to continue its research upon whether or not the drug is deemed effective. An $\alpha = .01$ Type I error probability is desired for not continuing the research when the drug indeed yields a mean advantage in cure time of at least two days over present treatment time.

(a) State H_0 and H_1 in equation form. Is the test lower-tailed, upper-tailed, or two-sided?

(b) What test statistic should be used here? Determine the critical value for this test statistic and express the decision rule.

(c) Suppose that the sample results for the cure-time advantage are $\bar{X} = 1.5$ and $s = .5$ day. Should the null hypothesis be accepted or rejected? Does this mean that the drug experiment must be continued or terminated?

9-39 A shoe manufacturer must decide whether or not to tighten down on the sizing department's work. Due to ordinary variability, a shoe does not fall precisely into a size, like $8\frac{1}{2}$ EEE. Finished shoes must be individually measured and then classified to the nearest appropriate size. In order to determine whether or not to take corrective action, the plant manager orders a sample size of 100 randomly selected shoes to be meticulously resized and the proportion that were originally correctly sized determined. As his null hypothesis, he assumes that the true proportion of all shoes incorrectly sized will be $\leqslant .05$, the desirable level. He must construct a decision rule that will reject this hypothesis when it is true with a probability of .05.

(a) Is this test lower- or upper-tailed? Determine the critical value P^* and express the decision rule.

(b) Calculate the probability of making the Type II error, assuming that the true proportion of missized shoes is .10.

9-40 A company psychologist wishes to give his standard screening examination to some recent job applicants in order to decide whether or not job seekers score more highly than applicants did ten years ago. If they do, he will use a new examination in the future. The test is to be administered to a random sample of $n = 25$ persons. In analyzing the results, the psychologist desires only a 1-percent chance of incorrectly changing procedures when the actual mean screening examination score is $\leqslant 86$, the historical mean figure ten years ago. Assuming that the mean score achieved by the sample group is 88, with a standard deviation of 10 points, should the present screening examination be kept or changed?

Chapter Ten
Regression and Correlation Analysis

Induction, analogy, hypotheses founded upon facts and rectified continually by new observations, a happy tact given by nature and strengthened by numerous comparisons of its indications with experience, such are the principal means for arriving at truth.

Marquis de Laplace (1820)

In many important business decisions it is necessary to predict the values of unknown variables. A personnel manager is concerned with predicting the success of a job applicant, which may be expressed in terms of his or her productivity. A production manager for a chemical company may wish to predict the levels of impurities in a final product. Many economists make predictions of gross national product (GNP). In each case, knowledge of one factor may be used to better predict another factor. The personnel manager may use screening examination scores as the basis for predicting future on-the-job performance. The production manager may use process temperatures or concentrations of ingredient chemicals to forecast impurities. The economist may use current interest rates, unemployment levels, and government spending in making GNP prognostications.

In this chapter we will discuss the techniques that fit into a broad category called *regression and correlation analysis*. Regression and correlation analysis comprises a body of statistical methodology that investigates the relation between variables. In Chapter 8, we initially investigated one form of statistical inference by using the sample mean to estimate the value of the population mean. In Chapter 9, a second kind of inference was described—one that uses a sample mean to test a hypothesis about a population mean. In this chapter, a third kind of statistical inference is to be introduced. Here, we will be concerned with measuring the *association* between two or more variables.

Regression analysis tells us how one variable is related to another. It provides an equation wherein the known value of one variable may be used to estimate the unknown value of the other. For instance, it can be used by a cost accountant to estimate the total cost (an unknown variable) of machining the number of parts (a known variable) scheduled to be produced in the following month. The information obtained can then be used to establish a budget by which managerial performance can be gauged. Similarly, a foreman in charge of an assembly line can use regression analysis to predict the unknown number of man-hours necessary to complete a job of known size. As another example, the future sales potential at a site being considered for a fried chicken franchise outlet can be estimated by measuring the traffic density along its access road and then substituting this value into a mathematical equation. By including other relevant factors, such as distance to closest competitor or the number of apartment units within walking distance, a finer estimate of sales potential might be obtained. When several variables are used to make a prediction, the technique used is called *multiple regression*; it will be discussed in Chapter 11.

Correlation analysis tells us the degree to which two variables are related. It is useful in expressing the efficiency achieved by using one variable to estimate the value of another. Correlation analysis can also identify which factors of a multiple-characteristic population are highly related, either directly or by a common connection to another variable.

Regression analysis takes its name from studies made by Sir Francis Galton around the turn of this century. Galton compared the heights of persons to the heights of their parents. His major conclusion was that the offspring of unusually tall persons tend to be shorter than their parents, while children of unusually short parents tend to be taller. In a sense, the successive generations of offspring from tall persons "regress" downward toward the mean height of the population, while the reverse is true of the offspring from short families.* Since one variable (the height of the parent) was used to predict another (the height of the child), the original term "regression" came to be applied to more general analyses involving the prediction of one variable by another. Aside from the context of prediction, the term "regression" as used in this chapter has little relationship to Galton's original notion of regressing toward the mean.

---

* But the distribution of heights for the total population continues to have the same variability from generation to generation. This is because the more prevalent parents of near-average height produce more tall offspring than do the relatively rare tall parents.

10-1 REGRESSION ANALYSIS

The primary goal of regression analysis is to obtain predictions of one variable using the known values of another. These predictions are made by means of an equation such as $Y = a + bX$, which provides the estimate of an unknown variable Y when the value of another variable X is known. Such an expression is referred to as a *regression equation*. Knowing the regression equation, a prediction of Y may be readily obtained from a given X. Unlike the results from ordinary mathematical equations (such as $A = b \times h$ for the area of a rectangle, or interest $= i \times P \times t$, where i is the rate of interest, P is the principal, and t is the time), we cannot be certain about the value of Y obtained from the regression equation. This is due to inherent statistical variability. Thus, predictions made from the regression equation are subject to error and are only *estimates* of the true values.

TABLE 10-1   Sample Observations of Rail Distance and Transportation Times for 10 Shipments by a Parts Supplier

Customer	Rail Distance to Destination (miles) X	Transportation Time (days) Y
1. Muller Auto Supply	210	5
2. Taylor Ford	290	7
3. Auto Supply House	350	6
4. Parts N'Spares	480	11
5. Jones & Sons	490	8
6. A. Hausman	730	11
7. Des Moines Parts	780	12
8. Pete's Parts	850	8
9. Smith Dodge	920	15
10. Gulf Distributors	1,010	12

Regression analysis begins with a set of data involving pairs of observed values, one number for each variable. Table 10-1 shows the observations of transportation time and distance for a sample of 10 rail shipments made by an automobile parts supplier. These data will be used to arrive at predictions of transit times for future shipments. From these the regression equation will be determined. Because using a sample gives rise to sampling error, the regression equation obtained may not be truly representative of the actual relationship between the variables. In order to reduce the chances of large sampling error, a sample size considerably greater than 10 ought to be used. We have taken such a small number here merely for ease in showing calculations.

The Scatter Diagram

A first step in regression analysis is to plot the value pairs as points on a graph as in Figure 10-1. The horizontal axis corresponds to values of the variable distance, denoted by the letter X. The vertical scale represents values of the variable time, for which we use the designation Y. A point is found for each shipment. For example, the shipment to Jones & Sons, located at a distance of $X = 490$ miles from the plant, took $Y = 8$ days to arrive. This is represented by the point ($X = 490$, $Y = 8$) on the graph. The points obtained in Figure 10-1 are spread in an irregular pattern. For this reason, such a plot is referred to as a *scatter diagram*.

The parts supplier wishes to use the known rail distance to the customer as the basis for predicting an order's unknown transportation time. It is customary

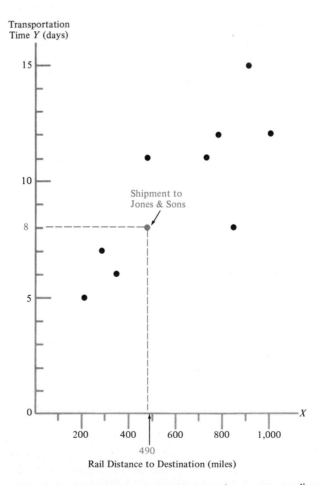

FIGURE 10-1 Scatter diagram for shipments by a parts supplier (values from Table 10-1).

to refer to the variable whose value is known as the *independent variable*, the possible values of which are represented by the X axis of the scatter diagram. The variable whose value is being predicted is called the *dependent variable*. The values on the Y axis represent the possible magnitudes of the dependent variable. Thus, rail distance X is the independent variable, because it is determined by the shipment's destination only, while the transportation time Y is the dependent variable, because it is in part predictable from rail distance.

These designations follow from simple algebra, where the X axis represents the independent variable and the Y axis provides values for the dependent variable by means of a function or an equation. Thus, Y is a function of X. The dependence of Y upon X does not necessarily mean that Y is *caused* by X. The type of relationship found by regression analysis is a statistical one. (We can find a statistical relationship expressing family houschold expenditures as a dependent variable that is a function of an independent variable, family disposable income. But having money to spend does not mean that appliances will be purchased.

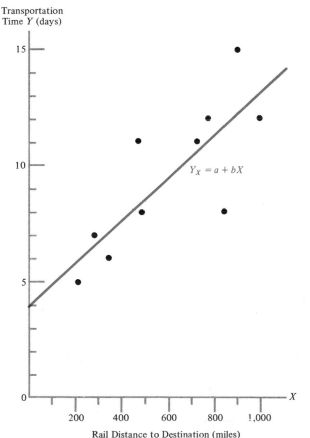

FIGURE 10-2   Fitting a regression line to a parts supplier's data.

A purchase is a voluntary decision that is merely allowed to occur because money has been made available; a purchase need not be made just because there is sufficient income.)

The Data and the Regression Equation

The next step in regression analysis is to find a suitable function to use for the regression equation, which will provide the predicted value of Y for a given value of X. The clue to finding an appropriate regression equation is the general pattern presented by the points on the scatter diagram. A cursory examination of the transportation data in our example indicates that a straight line, like the one shown in Figure 10-2, might be a meaningful summary of the information provided by the sample. This line seems to "fit" the rough scatter pattern of the data points.

Regression Line

A linear relationship between the variables X and Y is conceptually the simplest. The general equation for a straight line is $Y = a + bX$. The constant a is the value of Y obtained when $X = 0$, so that $Y = a + b(0) = a$. This is the value for Y at which the line intersects the Y axis, so that a may be referred to as the Y *intercept*. The constant b is the *slope* of the line. It represents the change in Y due to a one-unit increase in the value of X. Figure 10-3 shows the line for the equation $Y = 3 + 2X$. Here, the Y intercept is $a = 3$ and the slope is $b = 2$. Y increases by two units for every one-unit change in X. To review how to find the value of Y for X, suppose we wish to find the Y corresponding to $X = 5$. Substituting 5 for X in the above expression, we obtain $Y = 3 + 2(5) = 13$. The same value may be read directly from Figure 10-3 by following the vertical black line from $X = 5$ to the line relating Y to X. The vertical distance represents the value of Y. Any point on the line, for example ($X = 5$, $Y = 13$), can be described by the horizontal distance from the Y axis (5) and the vertical distance from the X axis (13).

The line used to describe the relationship between Y and X is generally obtained from sample data and is called the *estimated regression line*. It expresses the average relationship between the variables X and Y. The estimated regression line provides an estimate of the mean level of the dependent variable Y, when the value of X is specified. We use the symbol $\bar{Y}_X$ ("Y-bar sub X") to represent the values obtained from the linear *estimated regression equation:*

$$\bar{Y}_X = a + bX \tag{10-1}$$

With $\bar{Y}_X$, we distinguish estimates of the dependent variable from the observed data points, which, for simplicity, are denoted by the symbol Y. When expression (10-1) is applied to a specific X, the resulting $\bar{Y}_X$ is a *predicted* value for the dependent variable. As we will see, the values a and b in this expression are found from sample data. They are referred to as *estimated regression coefficients*.

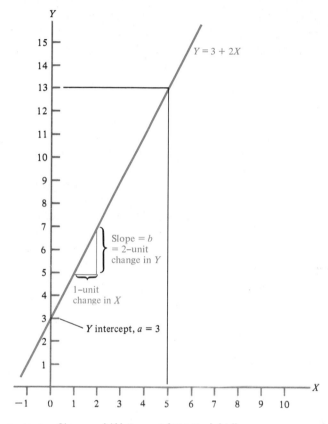

FIGURE 10-3   Slope and Y intercept for a straight line.

Regression Curves

It must be emphasized that a straight line is not always an appropriate function relating Y to X. The scatter diagrams in Figure 10-4 show cases where various types of nonlinear functions more closely fit the data. Note that all the functions are curves. Such relationships between X and Y are called *curvilinear*.

Figure 10-4(a) shows the relationship between crop yield Y and quantity X of fertilizer applied. The curve fits data obtained from test plots to which various amounts of fertilizer have been applied. As the amount of fertilizer increases to a certain point, it proves beneficial in increasing the harvest. But beyond this point, the benefits become negative, because additional fertilizer burns plant roots and causes the crop yield to decline. The greatest increases in Y occur for small values of X, with Y increasing at a decreasing rate. The peak value of Y may be referred to as the "point of negative returns," after which Y decreases at an increasing rate. This curve expressing Y as a function of X has the shape of an inverted U. One regression equation that could be used here is the form $Y = a + bX - X^2$.

This is contrasted to the U-shaped curve in Figure 10-4(b), where incremental or marginal cost Y of production is plotted against volume X. The

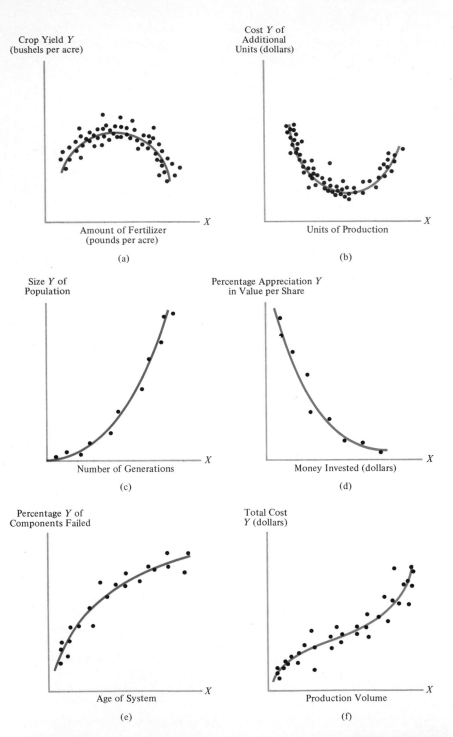

FIGURE 10-4 Examples of curvilinear relationships found for scatter diagrams.

regression equation has the form $Y = a + bX + X^2$. Data points have been obtained for the various levels of activity experienced in a plant. For low levels of plant activity, factors of production are not employed efficiently and unit costs are high. As volume increases, the cost of each additional unit declines as inputs become more efficiently employed. Increases in efficiency become less pronounced, until a point is reached where extra production can be handled, but less efficiency than before, and marginal costs begin to rise.

In Figure 10-4(c), the size Y of a population of *Drosophila* (fruit flies) is shown as a function of the number of generations X since the colony was established. The data points represent observations made after successive hatchings. There are no natural checks upon the population growth, since the flies are reared in an artificial environment. The curve obtained is an exponential or geometric growth curve, so that Y is related to X by an expression like $Y = a^X$ or $Y = X^c$. Plots of the world's human population growth during the past several centuries have the same basic shape. With exponential growth, Y increases at an increasing rate for larger values of X.

This is in contrast to the negative exponential curve in Figure 10-4(d), where the percentage appreciation Y in the value of each share of a mutual fund is plotted against the total money invested by the fund. The points represent several successful mutual funds at various stages of growth. The appropriate regression equation would be in the form $Y = ae^{-bX}$. Negative exponential curves correspond to values of Y that decrease at a decreasing rate as X becomes large. A rationale for such a result is that a small mutual fund can be very selective in choosing its portfolio, so that it has the opportunity to buy small-company stocks that may appreciate greatly. But as the fund grows larger, it cannot buy as heavily into the rather limited number of small, growing companies and must invest more money in the stocks of larger, less promising firms.

Figure 10-4(e) shows a logarithmic curve relating the percentage Y of original components of a particular kind that have failed to the age X of the system. The points were obtained from the histories of several systems. Some components survive almost indefinitely, although most of the original ones fail early. Here, the values for Y increase at a decreasing rate as X becomes large. We may express Y in terms of X by the equation $Y = a + b \log(1 + X)$.

In Figure 10-4(f), the total costs Y of production experienced by a plant over a particular time period are plotted against the associated levels of activity X. These points are fitted by a curve that shows total cost increasing at a decreasing rate as greater volumes of production are achieved. Beyond a point of diminishing returns for X, the larger volume reduces incremental efficiency and the curve shows the values of Y increasing at an increasing rate.

Throughout the remainder of this chapter, only linear relationships will be considered. The procedure for determining which particular line best fits the data is called *linear regression analysis*. One reason for our emphasis on linear equations is that they are easier to explain. The methods of analysis are also simpler and may be directly extended to curvilinear relationships. Straight lines are useful for describing a great many phenomena, so they are among the most common regression relationships.

Some Characteristics of the Regression Line

Some important general properties of the regression line and its fit to the data are illustrated in Figure 10-5. We will first consider the manner in which *Y* is related to *X*. There are two basic kinds of regression lines. If the values of the dependent variable *Y* increase for larger values of the independent variable *X*, then *Y* is *directly related* to *X*, as is shown in Figure 10-5(a). Here, the slope of the line is positive, so that *b* is greater than zero; this is because *Y* will increase as *X* becomes larger. Figure 10-2 shows that transportation time and rail distance are directly related variables. Other examples of directly related variables are age and salary (during employment years), weight and daily caloric intake, and the number of passengers and the quantity of luggage on commercial aircraft flights. In Figure 10-5(b), the slope of the regression line is negative, with the value of *b* less than zero. Here, *Y* becomes smaller for larger values of *X*, so the variables *X* and *Y* are *inversely related*. Examples of inverse relationships include remaining tire tread and miles driven, crop damage by insects and the quantity of insecticide applied, and the typical economic demand curve where demand decreases as price increases.

The degree to which two variables are related is reflected by the amount of scatter of the data points about the regression line. In Figure 10-5(c), the data points all lie on the regression line. This unusual "perfect fit" indicates that *X* and *Y* are *perfectly correlated*. In Figure 10-5(d), the data points are widely scattered about the regression line, so that we may say that the data indicate that *X* and *Y* are weakly correlated. Contrast this scatter diagram with the one in Figure 10-5(a), where the points cluster more closely about the line. Predictions of *Y* tend to be more accurate when there is less scatter, for then the sample results are less varied in relation to the regression line. As we saw in Chapter 8, small sample variability indicates a smaller standard error in the estimate; the sampling error is less pronounced, and more reliable estimates are obtained. When there is less scatter, the degree of correlation is higher. This suggests that correlation analysis can be used to qualify the accuracy of estimates made from the regression line. When *X* and *Y* are *uncorrelated*, as in Figure 10-5(e), the regression line is horizontal, indicating that values of *Y* have sizes independent of the value of *X*. This means that *X* is a worthless predictor of *Y*, so that the poorest predictions of *Y* are obtained by regression when *Y* is uncorrelated with *X*.

Fitting the Data by a Straight Line

How do we determine which particular regression line to use? One simple procedure would be to use our judgment, positioning a straight edge until it appears to summarize the linear pattern of the scatter diagram and then drawing the line. The equation of this regression line can then be found by reading its *Y* intercept and slope directly from the graph. Although this procedure may be adequate for some applications, estimates for *Y* obtained in this way are often crude. A major drawback to using freehand methods in fitting a line is that two persons will usually draw different lines for the same data. Freehand fitting can

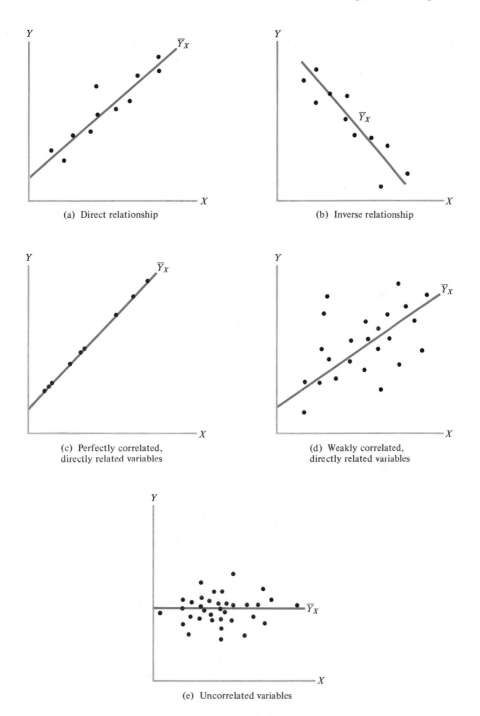

FIGURE 10-5 Properties of the regression line and possible relationships between variables.

therefore create unnecessary controversy regarding the conclusions of the data analysis. Another serious objection is that statistical methodology cannot then be employed to qualify (by confidence limits, for instance) the errors of estimation.

These difficulties may be overcome by using a statistical method to fit the line to the data. The most common technique is the *method of least squares*, which will be discussed in Section 10-2. This procedure, from many different points of view, provides the best possible fit to a set of data and thereby the best possible predictions.

EXERCISES

10-1   On a sheet of graph paper, construct the following regression lines and indicate whether X and Y are directly or inversely related:
(a) $\bar{Y}_X = -5 + 2X$ (b) $\bar{Y}_X = 5 + 3X$ (c) $\bar{Y}_X = 20 - 2X$

10-2   Plot a scatter diagram for the following data on a piece of graph paper. Then, using a ruler, draw a line through the data points that appears to summarize the underlying relationship between X and Y. From your graph, determine the values for a and b, and then write the equation corresponding to your regression line.

Number of Pages X	Hours of Typing Time Y	Number of Pages X	Hours of Typing Time Y
10	20	100	50
20	10	40	40
20	30	60	40
30	30	110	30
50	20	120	50

10-3   Plot a scatter diagram for each of the following sets of data. Sketch the shape of the regression curve that best seems to fit each relationship.

(a)		(b)		(c)	
Number of Men X	Output per Man-Hour Y	Number of Units X	Total Cost Y	Minutes Between Rest Periods X	Pounds Lifted per Minute Y
5	10	600	$11,000	5.5	350
8	4	50	3,100	9.6	230
1	3	470	10,200	2.4	540
1	2	910	15,700	4.4	390
1	7	160	6,300	.5	910
8	8	950	19,500	7.9	220
7	10	690	13,900	2.0	680
10	2	90	1,800	3.3	590
2	5	310	8,800	13.1	90
3	8	1,000	25,700	4(2	520

10-4   Consider the two variables, family savings and income. For each of the following studies, indicate which of these two variables would be independent and which would be dependent.
(a) A bank wishes to predict the increase in its time deposits due to a 10-percent increase in the salaries of state employees—whose incomes are known.

(b) A mutual fund wishes to use its customers' purchases of stock (a form of savings) to predict their incomes. This information will be used by its salespersons to identify leads for increased business.

(c) An economist wishes to forecast increases in savings due to inflationary wage settlements.

10-2 METHOD OF LEAST SQUARES

Introduction

Least squares regression is a technique for fitting a regression equation to the observed data. The least squares criterion has a great many desirable properties that make it the most commonly used tool in regression analysis. Although much of this chapter is restricted to linear relationships between two variables, the procedures we will describe here can be extended to a variety of situations where a curvilinear fit is desired. We will begin by describing how the method of least squares is applied to our previous parts supplier data, which are again plotted in Figure 10-6. The least squares criterion requires that a line be chosen to fit our data so that the *sum of the squares of the vertical deviations separating the points from the line will be a minimum*. The deviations are represented by the lengths of vertical line segments that connect the points to the estimated regression line in the scatter diagram.

Rationale for Least Squares

To explain how this procedure may be interpreted, we investigate the shipment to Jones & Sons, which is located at a distance of $X = 490$ miles from the supplier's plant. Our data (page 319) show that $Y = 8$ days were required for the shipment to arrive. This transportation time is also represented on the graph by the vertical distance along the thin line from the X axis at $X = 490$ to the corresponding data point. The predicted or estimated transportation time for the *next* shipment to Jones & Sons may be obtained by finding the vertical distance all the way up to the regression line. This is the height of the thin line plus the length of the vertical segment, a total of $\bar{Y}_X = \bar{Y}_{490} = 8.4$ days. The difference between the observed transportation time, $Y = 8$ days, and the predicted value for Y is the difference $Y - \bar{Y}_X = Y - \bar{Y}_{490} = 8 - 8.4 = -.4$ days. .4 is the length of the colored vertical line segment connecting the point to the regression line. Because the observed value of Y lies below the predicted value, a negative deviation is obtained; if the observed Y lay above the line, the deviation would be positive. The vertical deviation represents the amount of *error associated with using the regression line to predict* a future shipment's transportation time. We want to find values for a and b that will minimize the sum of the squares of these vertical deviations (or prediction errors):

$$\sum (Y - \bar{Y}_X)^2 \tag{10-2}$$

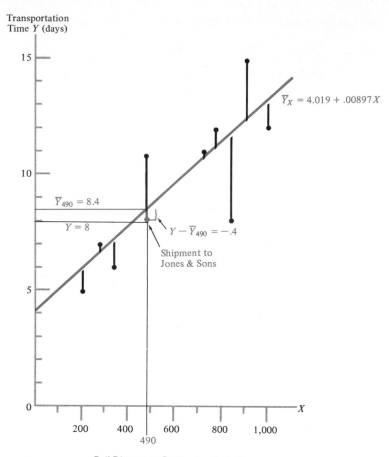

FIGURE 10-6 Fitting a regression line to a parts supplier's data using method of least squares.

One reason for minimizing the sum of the squared vertical deviations is that some of the differences $Y - \bar{Y}_X$ are negative while others are positive. For any set of data, a great many lines can be drawn for which the sum of the unsquared deviations would be zero, but most of these lines would poorly fit the data.

Finding the Regression Equation

Substituting $a + bX$ for $\bar{Y}_X$ into expression (10-2), the sum to be minimized becomes

$$\sum (Y - a - bX)^2$$

which is a function having two unknowns, a and b. Mathematically, it may be shown that the required values must simultaneously satisfy the following expressions, referred to as the *normal equations**:

$$\sum Y = na + b \sum X \tag{10-3}$$

$$\sum XY = a \sum X + b \sum X^2 \tag{10-4}$$

Solving the above algebraically, we obtain the following expression for b:

$$b = \frac{n \sum XY - \sum X \sum Y}{n \sum X^2 - (\sum X)^2} \tag{10-5}$$

The equation for a may then be obtained from expression (10-3) by solving for a:

$$a = \frac{1}{n} \left(\sum Y - b \sum X \right) \tag{10-6}$$

The above expressions may be further simplified using the mean values $\overline{X} = (\sum X)/n$, $\overline{Y} = (\sum Y)/n$ in order to compute the *estimated regression coefficients:*

$$b = \frac{\sum XY - n\overline{X}\,\overline{Y}}{\sum X^2 - n\overline{X}^2} \tag{10-7}$$

$$a = \overline{Y} - b\overline{X} \tag{10-8}$$

Note that b must be calculated before a is.

The advantage of calculating a and b from expressions (10-7) and (10-8) is that every step involves computations with values of moderate size. Although this may increase the danger of rounding errors, such errors ordinarily prove to be negligible.

Illustration of the Method

We are now ready to find the regression equation for the parts supplier's regression line obtained from the $n = 10$ observations. In order to evaluate the expressions for a and b, we must perform a set of intermediate calculations (shown in Table 10-2). To find b, we must calculate $\overline{X}$, $\overline{Y}$, $\sum XY$, and $\sum X^2$. Columns of values for X, Y, XY, and X^2 are used for this purpose. An extra column for the squares of the dependent variable observations, Y^2, is computed for use in later discussions of the regression line. Using the intermediate values obtained, we can first find the value for b using expression (10-7):

$$b = \frac{\sum XY - n\overline{X}\,\overline{Y}}{\sum X^2 - n\overline{X}^2} = \frac{64{,}490 - 10(611.0)(9.5)}{4{,}451{,}500 - 10(611.0)^2} = \frac{6{,}445}{718{,}290} = .00897$$

---

* The word "normal" as used here has nothing to do with the normal curve. Rather, *normal equations* receive their name from a mathematical property of linear algebra.

TABLE 10-2 Intermediate Calculations for Obtaining
the Parts Supplier's Estimated Regression Line

(1) Shipment Destination	(2) Rail Distance X	(3) Transportation Time Y	(4) XY	(5) X^2	(6) Y^2
1. Muller Auto Supply	210	5	1,050	44,100	25
2. Taylor Ford	290	7	2,030	84,100	49
3. Auto Supply House	350	6	2,100	122,500	36
4. Parts N'Spares	480	11	5,280	230,400	121
5. Jones & Sons	490	8	3,920	240,100	64
6. A. Hausman	730	11	8,030	532,900	121
7. Des Moines Parts	780	12	9,360	608,400	144
8. Pete's Parts	850	8	6,800	722,500	64
9. Smith Dodge	920	15	13,800	846,400	225
10. Gulf Distributors	1,010	12	12,120	1,020,100	144
Totals	6,110	95	64,490	4,451,500	993

$$\bar{X} = \frac{\Sigma X}{n} = \frac{6,110}{10} = 611.0 \qquad \bar{Y} = \frac{\Sigma Y}{n} = \frac{95}{10} = 9.5$$

$$\Sigma XY = 64,490 \qquad \Sigma X^2 = 4,451,500 \qquad \Sigma Y^2 = 993$$

Substituting $b = .00897$ into expression (10-8), we obtain

$$a = 9.500 - .00897(611.0)$$

$$= 9.500 - 5.481 = 4.019$$

Thus we have determined the following equation for the estimated regression line graphed in Figure 10-6:

$$\bar{Y}_X = 4.019 + .00897X$$

We may now use the above regression equation to predict the transportation time $\bar{Y}_X$ for a shipment of known rail distance X from the parts supplier's plant. For instance, when $X = 490$, we have

$$\bar{Y}_{490} = 4.019 + .00897(490)$$

$$= 8.414$$

Thus the prediction for the transportation to a customer 490 miles away is $\bar{Y}_{490} = 8.4$ days (rounded). This is the same value previously read from the graph of the regression line in Figure 10-6.

A Check for Computational Accuracy
The least squares regression line has two important features. One is that it goes through the point $(\bar{X}, \bar{Y})$ corresponding to the mean of the observations

of X and Y. The other is that the sum of the deviations of the Y's from the regression line is zero. That is,

$$\sum (Y - \bar{Y}_X) = 0 \qquad (10\text{-}9)$$

Thus, the positive and negative deviations about the regression line cancel, so that the least squares line goes through the center of the data scatter. This can be a useful check to determine if any miscalculations were made in finding a and b. In Table 10-3, the deviations are calculated for the parts supplier's data. (The sum of the deviations is slightly greater than zero, .002, due to rounding errors.)

TABLE 10-3   Computation of Deviations About Parts Supplier's Regression Line as a Check for Consistency

X	Y	$\bar{Y}_X = a + bX$ $= 4.019 + .00897X$	$Y - \bar{Y}_X$
210	5	5.903	−.903
290	7	6.620	.380
350	6	7.159	−1.159
480	11	8.325	2.675
490	8	8.414	−.414
730	11	10.567	.433
780	12	11.016	.984
850	8	11.644	−3.644
920	15	12.271	2.729
1,010	12	13.079	−1.079
			$\sum (Y - \bar{Y}_X) = 0.002$

Meaning and Use of the Regression Line

Once the regression equation has been obtained, predictions or estimates of the dependent variable may be made. For purposes of planning, the parts supplier now has a basis for determining his order-filling priorities so that there will be a reasonable chance that shipments will be received by customers at the required times. His estimated regression equation is $\bar{Y}_X = 4.019 + .00897X$. The value $a = 4.019$ represents an estimate of the Y intercept. An interpretation of this value is that about four days of "overhead" are built into all rail shipments. This roughly corresponds to the time a shipment spends in delivery to and from the railhead, being loaded and unloaded, and waiting between various stages of the shipping process. The slope $b = .00897$ reflects the impact of distance alone upon the total transportation time. For each additional mile, an estimated .00897 day is added to the total time. Stated another way, each additional 100 miles of distance adds roughly .9 day to the transportation time. Note that b is positive, indicating that transportation time varies directly with distance—the greater the distance, then the longer, on the average, it will take for a shipment to be delivered.

Knowing that Jones & Sons is 490 miles distant, the $\overline{Y}_{490} = 8.4$ days may be used as a point estimate of the transportation time required for the shipment. But the proper interpretation of 8.4 days is that *on the average* all future shipments to Jones & Sons will require about this much time in transit. It is an average because the conditions existing for successive shipments to this customer will vary due to a host of factors, such as freight train schedules, total freight to be handled, loading and unloading conditions, and routing of the box car. The times will vary from shipment to shipment. In general, the dependent variable Y will vary for a given X. Furthermore, the same regression equation will be used for other customers at a 490-mile distance; shipments to these others may travel on other roads having different characteristics. This leads us to the next important consideration of regression analysis.

Measuring Variability of Results

The fundamental expression of variability available from the sample data is a measure of the spread or scatter about the estimated regression line. As we have noted, estimates made from the regression line will be more precise when the data are less scattered. Hence, we may investigate the degree of scatter to determine an expression for the error involved in making estimates through regression. This suggests employing a measure that fits naturally into the scheme of least squares regression. Recall that we obtained the Y intercept a and the slope b of the regression line by minimizing the squared deviations about the regression line, $\sum (Y - \overline{Y}_X)^2$. As we saw in selecting the fundamental measure of a population's variability, the variance is the average of the squared deviations from the mean. This suggests that we can similarly select as our measure of variability the mean of the squared deviations about the regression line for a sample of size n:

$$\frac{\sum (Y - \overline{Y}_X)^2}{n}$$

Standard Error of the Estimate

The square root of the mean squared deviations is referred to as the *standard error of the estimate* about the regression line. This suggests that we may use it to estimate the true variability in Y. For convenience we will modify the above expression before taking its square root, using

$$s_{Y \cdot X} = \sqrt{\frac{\sum (Y - \overline{Y}_X)^2}{n-2}} \qquad (10\text{-}10)$$

as our standard error of the estimate. Here, we use the letter s in accordance with our convention to indicate that the calculations have been made from sample data. The subscript $Y \cdot X$ indicates that the deviations are about the regression line, which provides values of Y for given levels of X. We divide the sum of the squared deviations by $n-2$, which will make $s_{Y.X}^2$ an unbiased estimator of the true variance of the Y values about the regression line. We subtract 2 from n because 2 degrees of freedom are lost since the values of a and b making up the expression for $\overline{Y}_X$ have been calculated from the same data.

The standard error of the estimate resembles the *sample standard deviation* calculated for the individual Y's, which we designate as s_Y:

$$s_Y = \sqrt{\frac{\sum (Y-\overline{Y})^2}{n-1}} \tag{10-11}$$

Here, X does not appear in the subscript because s_Y makes no reference to the values for X. The sample standard deviation is the square root of the mean of the squared deviations about the center $\overline{Y}$ of the sample: $(Y-\overline{Y})^2$. Thus, s_Y represents the *total variability* in Y. Ordinarily, the deviations about $\overline{Y}$ are larger than their counterparts about the estimated regression line, so that s_Y will be larger than $s_{Y.X}$. Figure 10-7 illustrates this concept. Note that s_Y and $s_{Y.X}$ summarize the dispersions of separate sample frequency distributions.

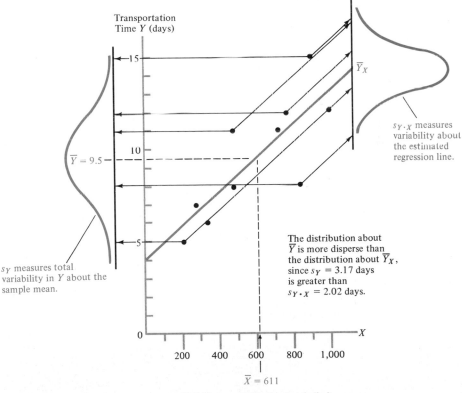

FIGURE 10-7 Illustration of the difference between total variability and variability about the estimated regression line.

Although expression (10-10) serves to define $s_{Y \cdot X}$, in practice it is cumbersome to use in calculating the standard error, because the $\overline{Y}_X$ values must first be calculated from the estimated regression equation. The following mathematically equivalent expression is often used instead for *the standard error of the estimate:*

$$s_{Y \cdot X} = \sqrt{\frac{\sum Y^2 - a\sum Y - b\sum XY}{n-2}} \qquad (10\text{-}12)$$

This is simpler to use than expressions appearing in some other textbooks because it allows us to take advantage of the calculations of a and b that we already made when determining the regression equation. We will use expression (10-12) to calculate $s_{Y \cdot X}$ for our parts supplier illustration. Using the values obtained previously for a and b and taking the intermediate calculations from Table 10-2, we have

$$s_{Y \cdot X} = \sqrt{\frac{993 - 4.019(95) - .00897(64,490)}{10-2}}$$

$$= 2.02 \text{ days}$$

Variability and Knowledge of X

The standard error of the estimate directly expresses the degree of scatter in the data. In the extreme case, when there is no scatter, all the Y observations fall on the regression line, as shown in Figure 10-5(c), and the vertical deviations are all zero, making $s_{Y \cdot X} = 0$. This presents strong evidence that the true variability of the Y's about the regression line is zero, so that the regression line provides perfect predictions. But when the degree of scatter is high, making $s_{Y \cdot X}$ large, the values of the dependent variable are quite disperse, so that for a given X, the predictions of Y made from the regression line are subject to considerable sampling error.

When knowledge of X is ignored, so that a regression line is not available, we have seen that the total variability in Y is summarized by the sample standard deviation s_Y, which may be more conveniently calculated from

$$s_Y = \sqrt{\frac{\sum Y^2 - n\overline{Y}^2}{n-1}} \qquad (10\text{-}13)$$

Using the parts supplier's data from Table 10-2, we find

$$s_Y = \sqrt{\frac{993 - 10(9.5)^2}{10-1}} = 3.17 \text{ days}$$

This value of s_Y is larger than the value found earlier for $s_{Y \cdot X}$, reflecting the fact that the variability about the regression line is smaller than the total variation in Y. This is indicated in Figure 10-7, where the underlying frequency curve for deviations about the estimated regression line is more compact than the one that might be constructed for the Y's without a knowledge of X. Thus, a prediction interval calculated using s_Y would be wider. A general conclusion is that predictions will tend to be more reliable and accurate when X is used as a predictor than when it is not.

EXERCISES

10-5   A statistician for the Civil Aeronautics Board has selected a random sample of ten freight invoices in order to determine an equation that relates destination distance to freight charges for a standard-sized crate. He obtains the following results:

Distance (in hundreds of miles)	Charge (to nearest dollar)
14	68
23	105
9	40
17	79
10	81
22	95
5	31
12	72
6	45
16	93

(a) Plot a scatter diagram for the above data.
(b) Using the method of least squares, determine the equation for the estimated regression line.
(c) Check your calculations by computing $\sum(Y-\bar{Y}_x)$. Allowing for rounding errors, this should equal zero. If it does not, find your error. Then plot the regression line on the scatter diagram.

10-6   For each of the following sets of data, determine the estimated regression equation $\bar{Y}_x = a + bX$.
(a) $\bar{X} = 10$; $\bar{Y} = 20$; $\sum XY - 3{,}000$; $\sum X^2 = 2{,}000$; $n = 10$.
(b) $\bar{X} = 10$; $\bar{Y} = 20$; $\sum XY = 1{,}000$; $\sum X^2 = 2{,}000$; $n = 10$.
(c) $\bar{X} = 50$; $\bar{Y} = 10$; $\sum XY = 30{,}000$; $\sum X^2 = 135{,}000$; $n = 50$.

10-7   A personnel manager wishes to evaluate various employee aptitude tests in order to find one that will predict productivity. A sample of $n = 100$ electronics assembly workers has been selected. Each person is administered a test currently being evaluated, and his or her aptitude score X is determined. The production foreman has previously evaluated the performance of each worker by means of a productivity index Y. The following intermediate calculations have been obtained:

$$\sum X = 5{,}000 \qquad \sum Y = 600 \qquad \sum XY = 50{,}000$$
$$\sum X^2 = 350{,}000 \qquad \sum Y^2 = 8{,}600$$

Suppose the test is adopted. Determine the regression equation $\bar{Y}_x = a + bX$ and plot it on graph paper.

10-8   A government economist wishes to establish the relationship between annual family income X and savings Y. A sample of $n = 100$ families has been randomly chosen from various income levels between \$5,000 and \$20,000. A thorough investigation of these families has been made, and the following intermediate calculations have been obtained (X and Y are measured in thousands of dollars):

$$\sum X = \$1{,}239 \qquad \sum Y = \$79$$

$$\sum XY = 1{,}613 \qquad \sum X^2 = 17{,}322 \qquad \sum Y^2 = 293$$

(a) Determine the equation for the estimated regression line.
(b) State the meaning of the slope b and Y intercept a.
(c) Calculate $s_{Y \cdot X}$ and s_Y. Does a comparison between these indicate that the regression line may be a useful tool for predicting family savings? Why or why not?

10-9   A stereo-cartridge manufacturer has conducted a regression analysis to estimate the average cartridge lifetime (in hours) at various record tracking forces X (in grams). The following regression equation has been obtained for a sample of $n = 100$ cartridges that were played until worn out at various tracking forces: $\bar{Y}_X = 1{,}300 - 200X$. The standard error of the estimate for cartridge lifetimes about this line is $s_{Y \cdot X} = 100$ hours.

(a) Plot the regression line on graph paper.
(b) State the meaning of the slope of the regression line.
(c) Calculate $\bar{Y}_X$ when $X = 1$, $X = 2$, and $X = 3$ grams.

10-3 ASSUMPTIONS AND PROPERTIES OF LINEAR REGRESSION ANALYSIS

The introduction to regression in the preceding section is largely a mechanical process of fitting a line to the data. In this section, we will provide the assumptions of a theoretical model for regression analysis. Our purpose is to lay the groundwork for measuring the error associated with using the regression line in making estimates.

Assumptions of Linear Regression Analysis

Suppose that in our parts supplier illustration we consider each possible transportation time Y for *all* shipments, past and future, to customers at a specified distance X from the plant. For this fixed X, the values of Y represent a population, and they will fluctuate and cluster about a central value. Similarly, for any other rail distance X, there will be an analogous population of Y values. Since the means of these populations depend upon the respective values for X, we may represent them symbolically by $\mu_{Y \cdot X}$, where, as before, the subscript $Y \cdot X$ signifies that the values of Y are for a given value of X.

Figure 10-8 portrays several populations for Y, showing how they fit into the context of linear regression. This graph is three dimensional, with an extra axis perpendicular to the XY plane. This vertical axis represents the relative frequency for Y at a specified level X. The curves are drawn with their centers at a distance $\mu_{Y \cdot X}$ from the X axis. Thus, we may refer to $\mu_{Y \cdot X}$ as the *conditional mean* of Y given X. There will be a different frequency curve for each X. Here,

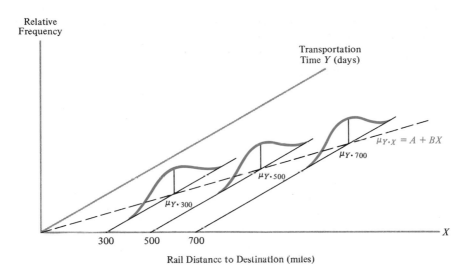

FIGURE 10-8   Populations for *Y* at various levels given for *X*.

we show these curves for all shipments to destinations of $X = 300$, $X = 500$, and $X = 700$ miles. The respective conditional means are denoted by $\mu_{Y \cdot 300}$, $\mu_{Y \cdot 500}$, and $\mu_{Y \cdot 700}$.

The Assumptions

Linear regression analysis makes four theoretical assumptions about the populations for *Y*:

1. All populations have the same standard deviation, denoted by $\sigma_{Y \cdot X}$, no matter what the value of *X* is.
2. The means $\mu_{Y \cdot X}$ all lie on the same straight line, having the equation

$$\mu_{Y \cdot X} = A + BX \qquad (10\text{-}14)$$

which is the expression for the *true regression line*.
3. Successive sample observations are independent.
4. The value of *X* is known in advance.

Sometimes an additional assumption is that the population for *Y* be normally distributed. But many regression analysis results do not require such a strong and sometimes unrealistic condition.

Estimating the True Regression Equation

We have seen how the method of least squares may be used to derive the estimated regression equation $\bar{Y}_X = a + bX$. We will now investigate how this equation is related to the true regression equation $\mu_{Y \cdot X} = A + BX$. The values

A and *B*, which we will call the *true regression coefficients*, are generally unknown. The reason for our choice of the notation $\bar{Y}_X$ is now apparent: $\bar{Y}_X$ will be used to estimate $\mu_{Y \cdot X}$, in the same way we used $\bar{X}$ to estimate μ in Chapter 8. The two regression equations differ only in the values for the *Y* intercept and slope. We may consider *a*, which is calculated from the sample data by expression (10-8), to be a point estimate of *A*. Likewise, from expression (10-7), we consider *b* the estimate of *B*.

The values calculated for *a* and *b* depend upon the sample observations obtained. The equation $\bar{Y}_X = 4.019 + .00897X$ relating transportation time to distance resulted from the particular times of the ten shipments chosen for the sample. Had different shipments been chosen, the regression equation obtained from them would most likely differ—perhaps considerably so—from the one we found.

When *a* and *b* are calculated by the method of least squares, they are *unbiased estimators* of the true coefficients *A* and *B*. This means that if the experiment of collecting samples is repeated a large number of times, and the regression line is found by the least squares method each time, then the average value of the *Y* intercepts *a* would tend to be close to the true *Y* intercept *A*. Likewise, on the average, the values of *b* would be close to their target, *B*. Unbiasedness was one of several properties mentioned in Chapter 8 as desirable to any estimator. One reason for the universal choice of the least squares criterion for fitting a regression line to the data is that this method exhibits so many of these desirable features. It has been established that of all unbiased estimators for linear regression coefficients, the least squares criterion provides the estimators of smallest variance, making the method of least squares the *most efficient* of all conceivable estimators. Being the most efficient, *a* and *b* minimize chance sampling error, so that estimates made from the regression line $\bar{Y}_X = a + bX$ are the most reliable ones for a fixed sample size. The values for *a* and *b* obtained by the least squares method are also *consistent* estimators of *A* and *B*.* Recall from Chapter 8 that a consistent estimator becomes progressively closer to the target parameter with increasing sample size. This can be attributed to the sampling distributions of *a* and *b*, whose variances decrease with *n*.

10-4   STATISTICAL INFERENCES USING THE REGRESSION LINE

A variety of inferences may be made using the estimated regression line. These fall into two broad categories: (1) predictions of the dependent variable, and (2) inferences regarding the regression coefficients *A* and *B*. Since predictions are made more often, we will discuss them first.

---

* When the *Y*'s are normally distributed, the least squares estimators fall into a broad class referred to as maximum likelihood estimators (MLE). In addition to being consistent, the MLE are most efficient and are normally distributed.

Prediction Intervals in Regression Analysis

The major goal of regression analysis is to predict Y from the regression line at given levels of X. This may be done in two ways. One involves predicting the value of the conditional mean $\mu_{Y \cdot X}$. However, sometimes it is useful to make a second kind of prediction—one for an individual Y value rather than for a mean.

For example, the parts supplier might want to predict the mean transportation time that will be achieved by all shipments over a distance of 500 miles. In this case, $X = 500$, and the best point estimate for $\mu_{Y \cdot X}$ will be the fitted Y value from the regression line, which we denote by $\overline{Y}_X$. Here, $\overline{Y}_X = \overline{Y}_{500}$, and

$$\overline{Y}_{500} = a + b(500)$$

$$= 4.019 + .00897(500)$$

$$= 8.50 \text{ days}$$

This same value may be used to estimate the transportation time for a particular shipment over the same distance. To distinguish a mean value from an *individual value*, both of which can only be estimated from the sample, we use the special symbol Y_I.

Either kind of estimate will involve sampling error, which can be acknowledged and expressed in terms of confidence intervals. Because of the special nature of regression analysis, the numbers obtained are usually referred to as *prediction intervals*.

Prediction Interval for Conditional Mean

A prediction interval is found in a manner similar to the way the confidence intervals we encountered in Chapter 8 were derived. There, we used

$$\mu = \overline{X} \pm z \frac{s}{\sqrt{n}} \qquad \text{for large samples}$$

and

$$\mu = \overline{X} \pm t_\alpha \frac{s}{\sqrt{n}} \qquad \text{for small samples}$$

where $s/\sqrt{n}$ served as the estimator of $\sigma_{\overline{X}} = \sigma/\sqrt{n}$, the standard error of $\overline{X}$.

In regression analysis, Y (not X) is the variable being estimated, and in the present notational context, intervals of analogous form are required to estimate a conditional mean for Y:

$$\mu_{Y \cdot X} = \overline{Y}_X \pm (z \text{ or } t_\alpha) \text{ (estimated } \sigma_{\overline{Y}_X})$$

The standard error for $\overline{Y}_X$, which we denote by $\sigma_{\overline{Y}_X}$, represents the amount of variability in possible $\overline{Y}_X$ values at the particular level for X for which a prediction is desired. In the context of transportation time a somewhat different line $\overline{Y}_X = a + bX$ (such as $\overline{Y}_X = 3.5 + .011X$ or $\overline{Y}_X = 4.2 + .009X$) might have fitted the least squares procedure if some other random sample of ten shipments had been selected. Thus, for some other sample $\overline{Y}_{500}$, the point estimate of transportation time when $X = 500$, might have computed to a different value than 8.50 days. For every level of X, the potential set of $\overline{Y}_X$ values would have a distribution with a standard deviation of $\sigma_{\overline{Y}_X}$.

There are two components of the variability in $\overline{Y}_X$:

$$\sigma^2_{\overline{Y}_X} = \begin{array}{c} \text{Variability in the} \\ \text{mean of } Y\text{'s} \end{array} + \begin{array}{c} \text{Variability caused by the} \\ \text{distance of } X \text{ from } \overline{X} \end{array}$$

The first source is analogous to the variability in the sample mean, which as we saw in Chapter 8, depends upon the potential standard deviation and the sample size. The second source of variation is associated with the distance that X lies from $\overline{X}$. Figure 10-9 shows why this is so. Here, several estimated regression lines have been plotted, each representing different samples of shipments taken from the same population. (Although each sample involves the same X's and thus the same level for $\overline{X}$, each involves slightly different values for a, b, and $\overline{Y}$.) Note that these lines tend to diverge and that their separations become greater as the distance between X and $\overline{X}$ increases. Therefore, the values of $\overline{Y}_X$ become more varied the farther they are from $\overline{X}$.

Small Sample Predictions
With small samples (generally, when $n < 30$), the following expression is used to calculate the *prediction interval for the conditional mean:**

$$\mu_{Y \cdot X} = \overline{Y}_X \pm t_\alpha s_{Y \cdot X} \sqrt{\frac{1}{n} + \frac{(X - \overline{X})^2}{\sum X^2 - n\overline{X}^2}} \qquad (10\text{-}15)$$

Here, t_α is the value of t found from Appendix Table F for which the upper-tailed area under the t curve is α—an amount equal to half of 1 minus the confidence level. The degrees of freedom are $n - 2$ (rather than $n - 1$ used in earlier chapters) because $s_{Y \cdot X}$ depends upon the two values a and b calculated from the sample results.

Representing $\mu_{Y \cdot X}$ when $X = 500$ as $\mu_{Y \cdot 500}$, we may construct the 95-percent prediction interval for the conditional mean transportation time using

---

* Mathematically, it can be shown that the variance in $\overline{Y}_X$ may be found from

$$\sigma^2_{\overline{Y}_X} = \sigma^2_{Y \cdot X}\left(\frac{1}{n} + \frac{(X - \overline{X})^2}{\sum X^2 - n\overline{X}^2}\right)$$

The estimated standard error for $\overline{Y}_X$ follows, using $s_{Y \cdot X}$ in place of $\sigma_{Y \cdot X}$.

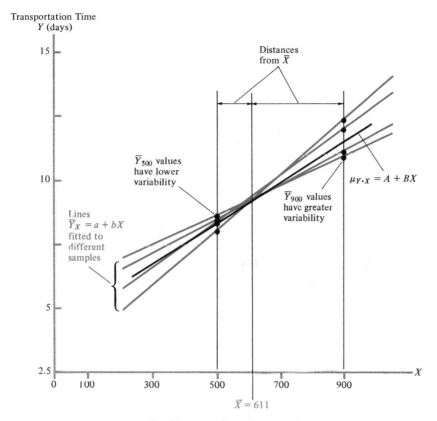

Transportation Time
Y (days)

Distances
from $\bar{X}$

$\bar{Y}_{500}$ values
have lower
variability

$\mu_{Y \cdot X} = A + BX$

$\bar{Y}_{900}$ values
have greater
variability

Lines
$\bar{Y}_X = a + bX$
fitted to
different
samples

$\bar{X} = 611$

Rail Distance to Destination (miles)

FIGURE 10-9   Illustration of how variability in $\bar{Y}_X$ increases for larger distances separating X from $\bar{X}$.

$10-2 = 8$ degrees of freedom. Since $\alpha = (1-.95)/2 = .025$, we find that $t_{.025} = 2.306$, and therefore

$$\mu_{Y \cdot 500} = \bar{Y}_{500} \pm t_{.025} s_{Y \cdot X} \sqrt{\frac{1}{n} + \frac{(500-\bar{X})^2}{\sum X^2 - n\bar{X}^2}}$$

$$= 8.50 \pm 2.306(2.02) \sqrt{\frac{1}{10} + \frac{(500-611)^2}{4,451,500 - 10(611)^2}}$$

$$= 8.50 \pm 1.59$$

or

$$6.91 \leqslant \mu_{Y \cdot 500} \leqslant 10.09 \text{ days}$$

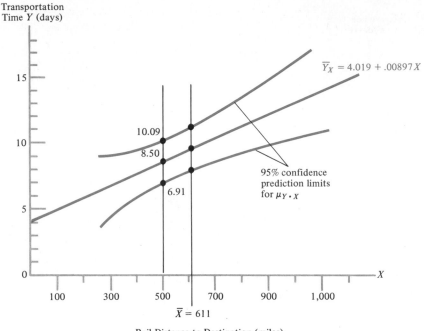

FIGURE 10-10   Confidence limits for predictions of mean transportation time.

We would therefore conclude that the transportation time for destinations 500 miles from the plant is *on the average* somewhere between 6.91 and 10.09 days. Our confidence that this statement is correct rests upon the procedure used, which provides similar intervals containing the true mean about 95 percent of the time.

We may calculate 95-percent confidence intervals for the other values of X, thus obtaining prediction limits for $\mu_{Y \cdot X}$ over the entire range of X. In Figure 10-10, this has been done for the parts supplier's data. Note that the width of the confidence band is dependent upon the distance of the X values from the mean. As we already noted, this is because the slope error is magnified—σ_{Y_X} increases as the distance separating X from $\overline{X}$ increases. Since one term is zero for $X = \overline{X}$, the narrowest portion of the band occurs here. Thus, we may conclude that estimates of $\mu_{Y \cdot X}$ made from the regression line are most precise for X values near their mean, with precision decreasing for values farther from $\overline{X}$.

Large Sample Predictions

When n is large (30 or more), the normal curve applies, in which case the normal deviate z replaces t_α in expression (10-15). Further simplification is ordinarily made for large samples, for then the fraction involving X values becomes very small. Thus, we may use an abbreviated but approximate expression for the *prediction interval for the conditional mean using large samples:*

$$\mu_{Y \cdot X} = \overline{Y}_X \pm z \frac{s_{Y \cdot X}}{\sqrt{n}} \tag{10-16}$$

Note that expression (10-16) resembles the one we used to construct a confidence interval for the population mean. Here, $\overline{Y}_X$ is analogous to the sample mean, while $s_{Y \cdot X}$ replaces s.

Prediction Interval for Individual Value of *Y* Given *X*

Predicting an individual value of Y given X is similar to predicting the mean. If our parts supplier wished to predict the transportation time of the next shipment over a distance of $X = 500$ miles, then the same point estimate, $\overline{Y}_{500} = 8.50$ days would be made from the regression equation. The following expression provides *the prediction interval for an individual value of Y when using small samples:*

$$Y_I = \overline{Y}_X \pm t_\alpha s_{Y \cdot X} \sqrt{\frac{1}{n} + \frac{(X - \overline{X})^2}{\sum X^2 - n\overline{X}^2} + 1} \tag{10-17}$$

Expression (10-17) is the same as expression (10-15) for $\mu_{Y \cdot X}$, except that an extra 1 has been added to the sum under the square root sign. This reflects the fact that when $\overline{Y}_X$ is used to estimate Y_I, a third source of variability is present—the dispersion of individual Y values about the regression line. (Even if the true regression line were known, the Y's at a particular level for X would have a variance of $\sigma^2_{Y \cdot X}.$*)

We may now construct a 95-percent confidence interval for Y_I, using the parts supplier's data when $X = 500$. Substituting the appropriate values into expression (10-17), we predict Y_I:

$$Y_I = \overline{Y}_{500} \pm t_{.025} s_{Y \cdot X} \sqrt{\frac{1}{n} + \frac{(500 - \overline{X})^2}{\sum X^2 - n\overline{X}^2} + 1}$$

$$= 8.50 \pm 2.306(2.02) \sqrt{\frac{1}{10} + \frac{(500 - 611)^2}{4,451,500 - 10(611)^2} + 1}$$

$$= 8.50 \pm 4.92$$

---

* So that we must add $\sigma^2_{Y \cdot X}$ to $\sigma^2_{\overline{Y}_X}$:

$$\sigma^2_{\overline{Y}_X} = \sigma^2_{Y \cdot X}\left(\frac{1}{n} + \frac{(X - \overline{X})^2}{\sum X^2 - n\overline{X}^2}\right) + \sigma^2_{Y \cdot X} = \sigma^2_{Y \cdot X}\left(\frac{1}{n} + \frac{(X - \overline{X})^2}{\sum X^2 - n\overline{X}^2} + 1\right)$$

Using $s_{Y \cdot X}$ in place of $\sigma_{Y \cdot X}$ we obtain the estimated standard error for the estimator of Y_I.

or
$$3.58 \leqslant Y_I \leqslant 13.42 \text{ days}$$

Note that this interval is considerably wider than the interval obtained previously for $\mu_{Y \cdot 500}$. This is to be expected, because Y_I is the estimate for the transportation time of *a particular shipment*, not a mean, and the greater width is attributable to the added variability that would be present even if the true regression line were available in making the prediction.

For *large samples*, the normal curve may be assumed, so that an appropriate normal deviate value z replaces t_α. Ordinarily, we can use the following abbreviated equation for computing *the prediction interval of an individual value of Y when using large samples:*

$$Y_I = \overline{Y}_X \pm zs_{Y \cdot X} \tag{10-18}$$

Dangers of Extrapolation

In establishing a regression equation, a set of observations is used that covers a limited range of values for the independent variable X. Caution must be exercised when making predictions of the dependent variable Y whenever X falls outside this range. Such predictions are called *extrapolations*.

In the parts supplier illustration, the regression line was computed for ten shipments whose distances ranged from 210 to 1,010 miles. Suppose we wished to use our results to predict the transportation time for a shipment to a customer separated from the plant by 2,000 miles, a distance considerably greater than the largest used in calculating the regression line. How reliable would such an extrapolation be? This depends upon whether our assumption of a linear relationship between time and distance is valid for shipments over great distances. There is simply no way to know this without including some longer shipments in the sample. As noted earlier in this chapter, the selection of a straight line was motivated by the general appearance of the data's scatter. Perhaps with a few additional points for distances between 1,000 and 2,000 miles, a curvilinear relationship might provide a better fit. There may be a good logical basis for assuming that a line will prevail—but then we might expect its slope to be flatter or steeper because of the influence from additional data points. On the other hand, there are reasonably sound arguments that longer distances ought to involve less time-consuming recomposition of trains (adding and removing box cars), so that the additional time per extra mile (i.e., the slope of the regression curve) decreases for longer trips. This might be the case for 2,000-mile shipments to the Pacific Coast from a midwestern plant. Railroads in the western United States generally cover greater distances than eastern ones do, and because of the lower industrial concentrations toward the west, they may require less switching of box cars at intermediate stops. There would also be greater distances covered between stops. Thus we might reasonably expect that a higher proportion of the total transportation time would actually be spent rolling instead of sitting, and that the rolling would be at higher speeds. Because longer shipments would invariably go to the Pacific Coast, we might therefore justify a curvilinear relationship between time and distance.

Regression analysis is limited only to the range of actual observations. These observations—and not qualitative reasoning—are used to quantify the relationship between X and Y. Qualitative reasoning is useful initially in selecting the form of the regression equation (linear versus curvilinear) and later in interpreting the results, but it cannot be used in place of actual observation. We are not ruling out extrapolation here but are merely indicating its potential pitfalls. If there are no data available beyond the range of required predictions, then extrapolation may be the only suitable alternative. Keep in mind that *extrapolation assigns values using a relationship that has been measured for circumstances differing from those for the prediction.*

Circumstances may differ for reasons other than extrapolation. Should the underlying populations change over time—as would be the case for changes in railroad operations or technology—then the regression line would not represent the shipments in subsequent years. Often, a regression analysis is short-lived in its applicability because underlying relationships can change over time.

Inferences Concerning Slope of Regression Line*

Second in importance to prediction intervals are inferences concerning the slope B of the true regression line. This is especially true in statistical applications where the underlying relationship between X and Y is more important than predicting Y for a particular level of X. For example, much economic theory relies upon regression analysis to substantiate hypothetical models requiring supply and demand curves; the *coefficients* of these demand and supply equations —rather than a predicted quantity for a given price—are the main interest. Similarly, a metallurgist might use regression analysis to develop a mathematical relationship between alloy concentrations and strength properties; he might be more concerned with how much extra shearing force is needed to break a metal for each unit increase in one alloy material than in predicting a particular force (that is, he might wish to estimate B rather than $\mu_{Y \cdot X}$).

Confidence Interval Estimate of B

An unbiased estimate of slope B of the true regression line may be obtained from its sample counterpart b. The following equation† is used to construct a

---

* Much of the material in this section relies on background material in Chapter 9 and may be skipped with no loss of continuity.

† Here we use the principle that
$$B = b \pm t_\alpha(\text{estimated } \sigma_b)$$
It can be established that
$$\sigma_b = \frac{\sigma_{Y \cdot X}}{\sqrt{\sum X^2 - n\bar{X}^2}}$$
Using $s_{Y \cdot X}$ in place of $\sigma_{Y \cdot X}$, we obtain an estimate of the standard error for b.

confidence interval estimate for B:

$$B = b \pm t_\alpha \frac{s_{Y \cdot X}}{\sqrt{\sum X^2 - n\overline{X}^2}} \tag{10-19}$$

where t_α is found from Appendix Table F for $n-2$ degrees of freedom.

We may use our parts supplier illustration to apply this procedure. Suppose that a 95-percent confidence interval is desired of the true regression coefficient B. Using $\alpha = (1-.95)/2 = .025$ and $10-2 = 8$ degrees of freedom, we have, from Table F, $t_\alpha = t_{.025} = 2.306$. Using the intermediate calculations from Table 10-2 and the values previously determined for b and $s_{Y \cdot X}$, we have as our 95-percent confidence interval:

$$B = .00897 \pm 2.306 \frac{2.02}{\sqrt{4,451,500 - 10(611)^2}}$$

$$= .00897 \pm .00550$$

$$.00347 \leqslant B \leqslant .01447$$

This means that we are 95 percent confident that the true value of B, the mean number of days required for transporting a shipment each additional mile, lies between .00347 and .01447. Repeating this procedure with 100 different samples, then, about 95 percent of the time we will construct such an interval containing the true value of B.

This interval estimate of B is not very precise and would probably be of little use to the parts supplier. As with the confidence interval for the population mean discussed in Chapter 8, precision can be increased by using a larger sample. It is advisable that a sample considerably larger than the one used in this illustration be taken.

In practice, when n is large, the Student t distribution closely fits the normal distribution. In these cases, the normal deviate z may replace t_α in expression (10-19) to˙determine the confidence interval for B.

Testing Hypotheses about B

We may extend tests of hypotheses to inferences about B. Ordinarily, the fact of greatest importance in testing for the value of B is whether it equals zero. Figure 10-11 illustrates a regression line having zero slope. Note that no matter what the value of X, $\mu_{Y \cdot X}$ remains at A parallel to the X axis. Thus, if $B = 0$, then, since the population distributions for Y have the same mean and variance, we may usually conclude that the Y distributions are identical for all values of X. This means that there is no statistical relationship between X and Y; we will bring up this point again later in context with our discussion of correlation. Thus, if $B = 0$, regression analysis will be of no value in making predictions of Y.

In making the two-sided test, our hypotheses are

$$H_0: \quad B = 0$$

$$H_1: \quad B \neq 0$$

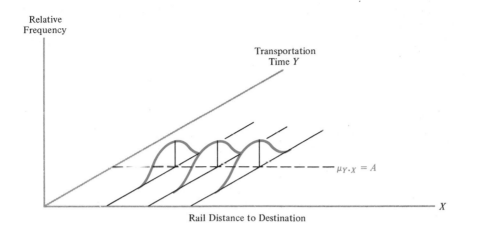

FIGURE 10-11 Illustration of a true regression line having zero slope, so that X and Y are uncorrelated.

If we choose .05 (1 minus the previous confidence level) as our significance level, then we only need to find out if our confidence interval contains the point $B = 0$. If it does not, we may reject the null hypothesis. Because the lower limit of the 95-percent confidence interval calculated previously is .00347, a number greater than $B = 0$, we may reject the null hypothesis at a .05 significance level, concluding that rail distance does affect transportation time.

It may be appropriate instead to employ a one-sided upper-tailed test with $H_1: B > 0$. This would be better if Y varies directly with X, as seems natural in the case of transportation time and distance. The first step is to calculate the t statistic:

$$t = \frac{b}{\frac{s_{Y \cdot X}}{\sqrt{\sum X^2 - n\bar{X}^2}}} \tag{10-20}$$

The value obtained is then compared to the critical value t_α, found from Table F, that corresponds to the prescribed significance level α. If t is smaller than t_α, the null hypothesis is accepted. The reverse is true for a lower-tailed test, where the alternative is that $B < 0$ (the case when Y bears an inverse relationship to X.)

We may illustrate the one-sided test with the parts supplier's results. For example, if we use $\alpha = .005$, then from Table F and using $10 - 2 = 8$ degrees of freedom, we obtain the critical value $t_{.005} = 3.355$. Applying expression (10-20), we have

$$t = \frac{.00897}{\frac{2.02}{\sqrt{4,451,500 - 10(611)^2}}} = 3.769$$

Since $t = 3.769$ exceeds the critical value $t_{.005} = 3.355$, the null hypothesis is *rejected* at a significance level of $\alpha = .005$, which indicates that the slope of the true regression line is greater than zero.

EXERCISES

10-10 The estimated regression line providing the yield (bushels) per acre of corn when X pounds of nitrate fertilizer is applied $\hat{Y}_X = 50 + .1X$. This result was obtained from a sample of $n = 100$ acres for which $s_{Y \cdot X} = 5$ bushels. Calculate 95-percent prediction intervals for $\mu_{Y \cdot X}$ and Y_I when $X = 150$ pounds.

10-11 The relationship between the total weight Y (in pounds) of luggage stored in an aircraft's baggage compartment and the number of passengers X on the flight manifest is $\hat{Y}_X = 250 + 27X$. This will be used by superintendents at airports to determine how much additional freight can safely be stored on a flight, after taking into consideration the fuel load and the weight of the passengers themselves. The data were obtained from a sample of $n = 25$ flights. Other results are: $s_{Y \cdot X} = 100$ pounds, $s_Y = 300$ pounds, $\sum X^2 = 64{,}000$, and $\bar{X} = 50$. Construct a 95-percent confidence interval estimate for both $\mu_{Y \cdot X}$ and Y_I when: (a) $X = 50$;   (b) $X = 75$; (c) $X = 100$.

10-12 From a sample of 400 families, a city planner has found the number of square feet in each home X and the size of each family Y. He has established the following estimated regression line in order to predict the family size for given square-footage levels: $\hat{Y}_X = .5 + .002X$. The values $s_Y = .30$ and $s_{Y \cdot X} = .10$ have been obtained. When the home has 1,000 square feet, construct 95-percent prediction intervals for (a) the mean family size, and (b) the number of persons in a particular family.

10-13 The credit manager of a department store has determined the following regression equation for a customer credit-rating index X and the proportion of customers Y who eventually incur bad debts: $\hat{Y}_X = .09 - .002X$. The index values range from zero to 40. A sample of $n = 25$ is taken, and other calculations show that $\sum X^2 = 23{,}000$, $s_{Y \cdot X} = .02$, and $\bar{X} = 30$.

   (a) Determine the 90-percent confidence prediction interval for the mean proportion of customers with ratings of $X = 20$ who will incur bad debts.

   (b) The proper interpretation for Y_I is in this case the *probability* that a particular individual will incur a bad debt. Determine the 90-percent confidence interval for Y_I when $X = 20$.

10-14 Referring to the information provided in Exercise 10-11:

   (a) Construct a 99-percent confidence interval estimate of the slope B of the true regression line.

   (b) In testing H_0 that $B = 0$ against the two-sided alternative that $B \neq 0$, should the null hypothesis be accepted or rejected at the .01 significance level?

   (c) In testing H_0 that $B \leq 0$ against the one-sided alternative that $B > 0$, should the null hypothesis be accepted or rejected at the .01 significance level?

10-15 Referring to the information provided in Exercise 10-13:

   (a) Construct a 95-percent confidence interval estimate of slope B of the true regression line.

   (b) In testing H_0 that $B = 0$ against the two-sided alternative that $B \neq 0$, should the null hypothesis be accepted or rejected at the .05 significance level?

(c) In testing H_0 that $B \geqslant 0$ against the one-sided alternative that $B < 0$, should the null hypothesis be accepted or rejected at the .05 significance level?

10-5   CORRELATION ANALYSIS

The goal of correlation analysis is to measure the *degree* to which two variables are related. Regression analysis provides an equation by which one variable's value may be estimated from another's. Correlation analysis shows how closely two variables can move together by means of a single number calculated from the same data.

Correlation analysis is very useful as an auxiliary tool in regression analysis, because it can be used to describe how well the regression line explains the variation in the values of the dependent variable. It is used instead of regression when the only question is how strongly two variables are related. One such application is in isolating statistically related characteristics of a population in order to explain their differences. For example, a pharmacologist may be interested in identifying those chemicals that can be formulated into a drug to alleviate various symptoms of a particular disease, such as anemia, pain, and poor appetite. A highly positive correlation between dosages X of a specific chemical and appetite Y (as measured by the quantity of food consumed) may make the chemical a good candidate for inclusion in the final drug.

The central focus of correlation analysis is to find a suitable index indicating how strongly X and Y are related. It is convenient to initially treat correlation as an adjunct to regression analysis, so this index will first be explained by using the regression line. Later, a parallel explanation will be given that does not require prior knowledge of the estimated regression line.

Measuring Degree of Association

As we saw in Section 10-1, the degree to which X and Y are related may be explained in terms of the magnitude of data scatter about the regression line. One extreme case occurs when scatter is so great that the regression line has a zero slope and is parallel to the X axis, as shown in Figure 10-12(a). Here, values of Y have no relationship to the value of X. We say that the degree of correlation is zero, since knowledge of X cannot add to the accuracy of predictions of Y. Figure 10-12(b) illustrates the opposite extreme. Here, a perfect fit between Y and X observations is achieved because all the data points happen to lie on the same line. Since there is no scatter about the regression line, the data indicate that Y will change by some predetermined amount for each increment in X, showing the strongest possible relationship between X and Y. We can say that the degree of correlation is perfect, so that knowledge of X allows perfect predictions of Y.

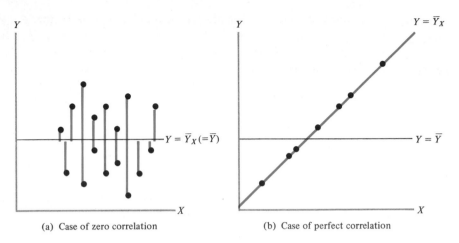

(a) Case of zero correlation   (b) Case of perfect correlation

FIGURE 10-12   Two extreme cases illustrating degrees of correlation.

We will now develop two indices to summarize the strength of association. The more important is the *coefficient of determination*, which expresses the relative reduction in the variation of Y that can be attributed to a knowledge of X and its relationship to Y by way of the regression line. From this, another useful index, the *correlation coefficient*, may then be obtained.

Sample Coefficient of Determination

In Section 10-2, the scatter of data about the estimated regression line was summarized by the standard error of the estimate $s_{Y \cdot X}$. Its square, $s_{Y \cdot X}^2$, is the *mean* of the squared vertical deviations of the data points around the regression line. It is now convenient to summarize the scatter with the *sum* of the squared deviations about $\bar{Y}_X$:

$$\sum (Y - \bar{Y}_X)^2$$

This may be compared to the scatter of the sample observations about their mean, represented by

$$\sum (Y - \bar{Y})^2$$

which is the sum of the squared vertical deviations around the horizontal line $Y = \bar{Y}$. (The above sums of squares are easily recognizable as the numerators of $s_{Y \cdot X}^2$ and s_Y^2, respectively.)

These sums of squares will be used to construct the indices measuring strength of association. When we compared $s_{Y \cdot X}$ to s_Y previously, we saw that their relative sizes reflect the predictive power of knowing X. Using the corresponding sums of squares, we may construct the *sample coefficient of determination* to express how strongly X is associated with Y:

$$r^2 = 1 - \frac{\sum (Y - \bar{Y}_X)^2}{\sum (Y - \bar{Y})^2} \tag{10-21}$$

When X and Y have a zero correlation, as they do in Figure 10-12(a), the regression line has a zero slope and $\bar{Y}_X = \bar{Y}$, in which case the deviations about $\bar{Y}_X$ are the same as those about $\bar{Y}$. This makes the numerator the same as the denominator in expression (10-21), so that the fraction must be equal to 1; thus, $r^2 = 1 - 1 = 0$. If X and Y are perfectly correlated, as in Figure 10-12(b), then $\sum (Y - \bar{Y}_X)^2 = 0$, so that $r^2 = 1 - 0 = 1$. The value obtained for r^2 must lie somewhere between 0 and 1.

Population Coefficient of Determination

Recall that data observations are taken from a sample and may present a distorted image of the true association between X and Y. The sample coefficient of determination may indicate either a stronger or a weaker relationship than actually exists. The true measure of association is obtained from the *population coefficient of determination*, defined by

$$\rho^2 = \frac{\sigma_Y^2 - \sigma_{Y \cdot X}^2}{\sigma_Y^2} = 1 - \frac{\sigma_{Y \cdot X}^2}{\sigma_Y^2} \tag{10-22}$$

The symbol ρ is the Greek letter *rho*. There, $\sigma_{Y \cdot X}^2$ is the variance of the various population distributions for Y and σ_Y^2 is the variance of the combined population of Y's. The former expresses the variation in Y about the true regression line $\mu_{Y \cdot X} = A + BX$, while the latter indicates the variability of Y about its true mean without regard to X. The difference between the variances, $\sigma_Y^2 - \sigma_{Y \cdot X}^2$, in the numerator of the first expression for ρ^2 represents the net reduction in the variance in Y that is due to knowing X and the true regression line. Dividing this difference by σ_Y^2 gives us ρ^2. This may be interpreted as the proportional reduction in the variance of Y due to regression.

The expressions for ρ^2 and r^2 are similar. Each is 1 minus the ratio of variability about a regression line to the variability about a mean value for Y. ρ^2 is defined in terms of true parameter values, while r^2 is based upon sample values that are estimators of their population counterparts. Thus, we may consider the sample coefficient of determination r^2 as a point estimator of its population counterpart ρ^2.*

---

* Some texts define the sample coefficient of determination as

$$r_a^2 = 1 - \frac{s_{Y \cdot X}^2}{s_Y^2}$$

which can be obtained directly from expression (10-22), using the unbiased point estimators $s_{Y \cdot X}^2$ and s_Y^2 for the variances $\sigma_{Y \cdot X}^2$ and σ_Y^2. r_a^2 is referred to as the *adjusted coefficient of determination* and is related to r^2 by

$$r_a^2 = 1 - (1 - r^2)\left(\frac{n-1}{n-2}\right)$$

For large values of n, r^2 is nearly identical to r_a^2. We do not use r_a^2 because of difficulties with the divisors $(n-2)$ and $(n-1)$ used to calculate $s_{Y \cdot X}^2$ and s_Y^2. An expression equivalent to (10-21) is

$$r^2 = 1 - \frac{s_{Y \cdot X}^2}{s_Y^2}\left(\frac{n-2}{n-1}\right)$$

Calculating the Coefficient of Determination

In actual practice, calculating r^2 from expression (10-21) can be quite cumbersome. Instead, we may use the estimated regression coefficients and the intermediate values obtained in finding these coefficients to calculate r^2 from the following mathematically equivalent expression for the *sample coefficient of determination:*

$$r^2 = \frac{a\sum Y + b\sum XY - n\bar{Y}^2}{\sum Y^2 - n\bar{Y}^2} \tag{10-23}$$

This equation uses values previously obtained from regression analysis.

In the parts supplier illustration, we may calculate r^2 from expression (10-23), using $a = 4.019$, $b = .00897$, and the intermediate calculations from Table 10-2:

$$r^2 = \frac{4.019(95) + .00897(64,490) - 10(9.5)^2}{993 - 10(9.5)^2}$$

$$= \frac{57.78}{90.50} = .64$$

Interpretation of Coefficient of Determination

How should we interpret our finding that $r^2 = .64$? Our initial motivation in comparing variation about $\bar{Y}_X$ to variation about $\bar{Y}$ was to show how knowledge of X can reduce errors in predicting Y. We next establish that r^2 can be deduced from an explanation of variations in Y.

Figure 10-13 shows the regression line calculated from the parts supplier's sample of transportation times. Suppose that a point estimate is required of the next order's transportation time. If we don't bother to use the regression equation—in effect ignoring distance X—then our best estimate of the required time is $\bar{Y} = 9.5$ days. If the rail distance of the order is $X = 920$ miles, $\bar{Y}$ would not provide a very good estimate. We represent the resulting event by the *total deviation* of the estimate from the observed transportation time, $Y = 15$, for that distance: $Y - \bar{Y} = 15 - 9.5 = 5.5$. If we use the regression line calculated from the data, then our best estimate would be instead $\bar{Y}_X = \bar{Y}_{920} = 12.3$ (rounded), which lowers the error so that the actual deviation from the estimate would be: $Y - \bar{Y}_X = 15 - 12.3 = 2.7$. By using the regression line, our error has been reduced by an amount $\bar{Y}_X - \bar{Y} = 12.3 - 9.5 = 2.8$. Thus, part of the total error may be attributed to using the regression line, so that $\bar{Y}_X - \bar{Y} = 2.8$ is the *explained deviation*. The remaining portion of the error is due to unidentifiable causes, so that $Y - \bar{Y}_X = 2.7$ is an *unexplained deviation*. The total deviation of the observed Y may then be expressed as

$$(Y - \bar{Y}) = (\bar{Y}_X - \bar{Y}) + (Y - \bar{Y}_X) \tag{10-24}$$

which we can state in words:

Total deviation = Explained deviation + Unexplained deviation

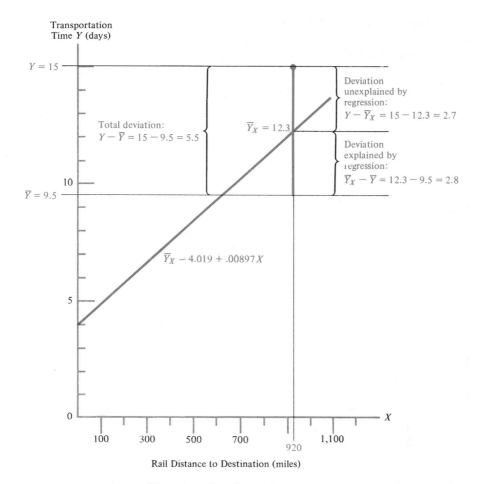

Rail Distance to Destination (miles)

FIGURE 10-13 Illustration of total, explained, and unexplained variation in *Y*.

The above relationship suggests that the *total variation* in *Y* has two components, one of which may be explained:

Total variation = Explained variation + Unexplained variation

The total variation expresses the amount of vertical scatter of the data points about their mean $\bar{Y}$. This may be measured by $\sum (Y-\bar{Y})^2$. Likewise we use $\sum (Y-\bar{Y}_X)^2$ to express the unexplained variation, the magnitude of scatter about the estimated regression line. The explained variation may therefore be expressed as the difference:

$$\text{Explained variation} = \sum (Y-\bar{Y})^2 - \sum (Y-\bar{Y}_X)^2$$

If we determine the ratio of the explained to the total variation, we obtain:

$$\frac{\text{Explained variation}}{\text{Total variation}} = \frac{\sum (Y-\bar{Y})^2 - \sum (Y-\bar{Y}_x)^2}{\sum (Y-\bar{Y})^2} = 1 - \frac{\sum (Y-\bar{Y}_x)^2}{\sum (Y-\bar{Y})^2}$$

The right-hand side of the above equation is the sample coefficient of determination, which is also expression (10-21), so that we have

$$r^2 = \frac{\text{Explained variation}}{\text{Total variation}} = 1 - \frac{\sum (Y-\bar{Y}_x)^2}{\sum (Y-\bar{Y})^2} \qquad (10\text{-}25)$$

This provides us with the following interpretation of r^2: *The sample coefficient of determination is the proportion of the total variation in Y explained by the regression line.* In our illustration, we calculated $r^2 = .64$. This signifies that 64 percent of the total variation, or scatter, of transportation times Y about their mean can be explained by the relationship between this variable and rail distance X, as estimated by the regression line for X and Y.

Because the unexplained variation can never exceed the total variation, their ratio is at most 1, so again we see that the greatest possible value of r^2 is 1. Likewise, when the explained variation is zero, so that the knowledge of the regression line cannot reduce the errors of prediction, the value for r^2 must be zero. This corresponds to the case previously discussed where the regression line is horizontal and has both slope and correlation of zero.

Correlation Coefficient

Although the rationale for using the coefficient of determination to express the degree of relationship between X and Y is well justified, statisticians sometimes use another value calculated from the sample data. This is called the *sample correlation coefficient*, which is the square root of the coefficient of determination, calculated from

$$r = \sqrt{r^2} \qquad (10\text{-}26)$$

The *population correlation coefficient* ρ is defined analogously,

$$\rho = \sqrt{\rho^2} \qquad (10\text{-}27)$$

We may consider r to be a point estimator of ρ.

The square root of any number may be positive or negative. This fact may make the correlation coefficient a more useful expression of the strength of association. The sign of r, positive or negative, can be used to signify the *direction* of the relationship between X and Y. Thus if Y varies *directly* with X, then r is *positive*. And when Y bears an *inverse* relationship to X, r is *negative*.

For the parts supplier data, the sample correlation coefficient is

$$r = \sqrt{r^2} = \sqrt{.64} = .80$$

We choose a positive sign for r because, since transportation time increases as rail distance increases, X and Y are directly related.

Figure 10-14 shows the values of the correlation coefficient r calculated for various sets of data. The values of $r = \sqrt{r^2}$ may range from -1 to 1. Negative values for r are obtained for the data sets in diagrams (b) and (d), where Y varies inversely with X. The slope of the estimated regression lines fitted to each set of these data will be negative, because Y decreases with increasing X. In diagrams (a) and (c), the correlation coefficients are positive, because in both cases the data indicate a direct relationship between X and Y, and the slope of the estimated regression lines will be positive. Thus *the sign for the correlation coefficient must be the same as for the slope of the regression line.*

Just like the coefficient of determination, the value of the correlation coefficient approaches zero as the degree of scatter becomes greater. Diagrams (a) and (c) in Figure 10-14 illustrate this point: In (a), the data are perfectly correlated, so that $r = 1$; in (c), considerable scatter indicates a smaller degree of correlation, so that $r = .95$. Likewise, for the perfectly correlated data in diagram (b), $r = -1$, while the less correlated, more scattered data in (d) yield $r = -.57$. As with r^2, $r = 0$ signifies a zero correlation. Diagrams (e) and (f) represent two instances where $r = 0$.

In (e), there is no apparent relationship between X and Y. Diagram (f) also shows $r = 0$, indicating no statistical relationship between X and Y; yet the data there appear to have a well-pronounced curvilinear relationship. Thus, the conclusion of no relationship is fallacious in this case, indicating that our *correlation coefficient must be restricted to instances where the underlying relationship between X and Y is believed to be linear.* Different procedures are required for calculating the strength of association for data having a curvilinear relationship.

Comparison of r and r^2

As we have already seen, the sample coefficient of determination r^2 shows the proportion of the total variation in Y that is explained by the regression line. As an adjunct to regression analysis, r^2 is a more useful measure of association. Since r is a decimal fraction, it will always be larger (in absolute value) than r^2. Thus, $r = .70$ may give us the false impression that the variation in Y can be explained to a great extent through regression. The reduction in total variation amounts to only $r^2 = (.70)^2 = .49$, which is less than $1/2$. Statisticians employing regression analysis usually prefer to use the coefficient of determination r^2 to explain the strength of association between X and Y.

When regression analysis is not used, however, the correlation coefficient r may be more meaningful. In such a case, r would be calculated from a different expression (which is to be explained next) that automatically provides the proper sign indicating whether a direct or an inverse relationship exists.

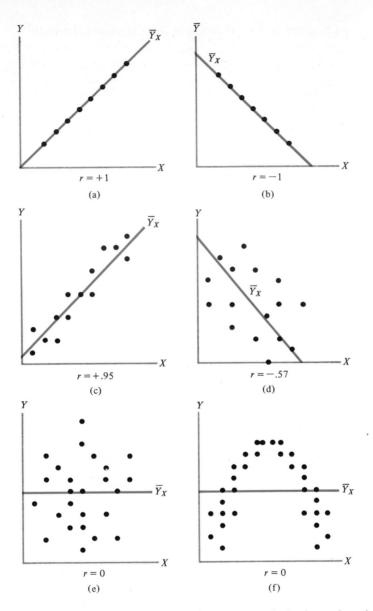

FIGURE 10-14 Scatter diagrams for sample results having various degrees of correlation.

Correlation Explained Without Regression

The value of the correlation coefficient may be computed without performing regression analysis first. In many statistical applications, only the correlation coefficient is desired. For example, in determining if a chemical's concentration X improves patient recovery time Y, a medical researcher may only be interested in finding out whether or not raising the drug's dosage reduces symptoms. That is, he would be concerned with the *degree* to which X and Y are related, which could be determined from the correlation coefficient. The researcher may not be at all interested in *predicting* the number of days it will take a patient given a 50 cc dosage to recover, which is what he would learn from a regression line.

We may directly calculate from the following expression* for *the sample correlation coefficient*:

$$r = \frac{\sum XY - n\bar{X}\bar{Y}}{\sqrt{(\sum X^2 - n\bar{X}^2)(\sum Y^2 - n\bar{Y}^2)}} \qquad (10\text{-}28)$$

For example, we may use the intermediate calculations found earlier for rail distance X and transportation time Y:

$$n = 10 \qquad\qquad \bar{X} = 611 \qquad\qquad \bar{Y} = 9.5$$

$$\sum XY = 64{,}490 \qquad \sum X^2 = 4{,}451{,}500 \qquad \sum Y^2 = 993$$

Substituting these values into expression (10-28), the sample correlation co-efficient is

$$r = \frac{64{,}490 - 10(611)(9.5)}{\sqrt{[(4{,}451{,}500 - 10(611)^2][993 - 10(9.5)^2]}} = .80$$

which is the same value that we found earlier by using expression (10-23) to obtain r^2 and then taking the positive square root.

To explain the foregoing procedure for calculating r, we can express the sample correlation coefficient in an equivalent form. The numerator may be rewritten equivalently as $\sum (X - \bar{X})(Y - \bar{Y})$; also, the two terms in the denominator are the same as the sample variances of the X and Y values without the $n - 1$ divisors. Thus,

$$r = \frac{\sum (X - \bar{X})(Y - \bar{Y})}{\sqrt{[(n-1)s_X^2][(n-1)s_Y^2]}} = \frac{\sum (X - \bar{X})(Y - \bar{Y})}{(n-1)s_X s_Y}$$

Here, we use s_X^2 to represent the sample variance of the X's in order to distinguish it from s_Y^2, which summarizes the total variability in the sample Y's. The above expression may then be further transformed into the following equivalent expression for r:

$$r = \frac{\sum \left(\dfrac{X - \bar{X}}{s_X}\right)\left(\dfrac{Y - \bar{Y}}{s_Y}\right)}{n - 1} \qquad (10\text{-}29)$$

* This equation may be obtained from expression (10-23) for r^2. First substitute $\bar{Y} - b\bar{X}$ for a. Then the right-hand side of expression (10-7) on page 331 may be substituted for b. After canceling and collecting terms in the equation that results, taking the square root of both sides provides the above expression for r.

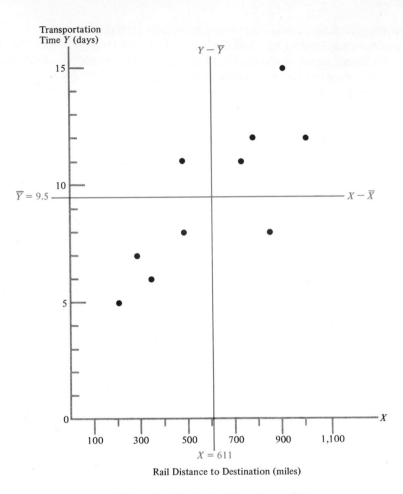

FIGURE 10-15 Illustration for explanation of correlation without using regression line.

This relationship suggests that the sample correlation coefficient may be explained in terms of the deviations $X - \bar{X}$ and $Y - \bar{Y}$.

Figure 10-15 shows how these deviations can be plotted on the original scatter diagram by shifting the horizontal axis upward and the vertical axis to the right. The new axes are relabeled $X - \bar{X}$ and $Y - \bar{Y}$, with their origin at the points where $X = \bar{X}$ and $Y = \bar{Y}$. This graph shows how transportation time and distance move together in terms of the deviation products, the sum of which is denoted by

$$\sum (X - \bar{X})(Y - \bar{Y})$$

If Y increases with X, then most of the deviations will fall in the northeast and southwest quadrants. Thus, the sum of the deviation products will be positive, reflecting a direct relationship between X and Y. But if the points are predominantly in the northwest and southeast quadrants, indicating that Y decreases for increasing X, this sum will be negative. If the points are scattered nearly evenly throughout all four quadrants, indicating poor responses of Y to X, the sum of the deviation products will be close to zero. Thus, we may conclude that the deviation-product sum will carry the same sign as the correlation coefficient and will have a value of zero when X and Y demonstrate no statistical relationship.

By itself, the deviation-product sum cannot serve as a suitable index of correlation, because it is affected by the units employed. To compensate for this, each deviation may be standardized by dividing by the respective sample standard deviation and obtaining $(X-\bar{X})/s_X$ and $(Y-\bar{Y})/s_Y$. Then the sum of the products would be the same value no matter what units were used for X (e.g., furlongs, kilometers, yards, or light years) and Y (e.g., fortnights, seconds, weeks, or years). Expression (10-29) shows that the resultant standardized deviation-product sum actually underlies the r computation. To account for the influence of the sample size (for instance, the standardized deviation-product sum would be about 10 times as large if the sample size were 10 times as large), this is divided by $n-1$. The resulting index for r is therefore an average of standardized deviation products.

Correlation and Causality

The correlation coefficient measures only the strength of *association* between two variables. This is a statistical relationship, and a large positive or

TABLE 10-4   Calculation of Correlation Coefficient for the Sperm Whale Catch and Common Stock Price Index.

Year	Number of Sperm Whales Caught (thousands) X	Standard and Poor's Common Stock Price Index Y	X^2	Y^2	XY
1964	29	81	841	6,561	2,349
1965	25	88	625	7,744	2,200
1966	27	85	729	7,225	2,295
1967	26	92	676	8,464	2,392
1968	24	99	576	9,801	2,376
Totals	131	445	3,447	39,795	11,612

$$\sum X = 131 \qquad \bar{X} = 26.2 \qquad \sum Y = 445 \qquad \bar{Y} = 89$$
$$\sum X^2 = 3,447 \qquad \sum Y^2 = 39,795 \qquad \sum XY = 11,612$$

$$r = \frac{\sum XY - n\bar{X}\bar{Y}}{\sqrt{(\sum X^2 - n\bar{X}^2)(\sum Y^2 - n\bar{Y}^2)}} = \frac{11,612 - 5(26.2)(89)}{\sqrt{[3,447 - 5(26.2)^2][39,795 - 5(89)^2]}} = -.89$$

SOURCES: *Yearbook of Fishery Statistics,* Food and Agriculture Organization, United Nations, and *Economic Report of the President, February* 1970.

negative value for r does not indicate whether a high value of one variable may cause the other to be large. Examples of nonsense or *spurious* correlations abound. We may illustrate such a correlation by finding the value for r that measures the association between the number of sperm whales X caught from 1964 to 1968 and Standard and Poor's Price Index for 500 stocks Y. The intermediate calculations are provided in Table 10-4. We find $r = -.89$, indicating a highly negative correlation between X and Y. How do we interpret this result? Clearly, there is no apparent logical connection between whaling and the New York Stock Exchange prices for common stocks. The values of X and Y have simply moved in opposite directions by approximately the same relative amounts for the five years considered. Statistically, large values of X have occurred with small values of Y, and vice versa. Obviously, r does not measure *causation* here, for we cannot say that the increasing stock prices have caused a declining catch of sperm whales, nor the reverse.

Statistical Inferences About ρ^*

The population correlation coefficient ρ is the square root of the population coefficient of determination. The latter is defined by 1 minus the ratio of the variance of Y about the true regression line to the variance of Y about its mean. In order to make probability statements regarding ρ, *both* X and Y must be treated as random variables. Correlation theory requires this to be so before we can qualify inferences about ρ. When using r as the estimator, one additional restrictive—and often unrealistic—assumption is ordinarily made to avoid mathematical difficulties in finding the sampling distribution of r. This is that X and Y have a particular joint probability distribution called the bivariate normal distribution. Discussion of this distribution is beyond the scope of this book. For this reason, we will not describe the sampling distribution of r, and we therefore cannot discuss how to construct confidence interval estimates of ρ.

The far more common inference desired is a test to decide whether $\rho = 0$; that is, whether there is any statistical relationship at all between X and Y. For this purpose, we may substitute the test regarding the slope of the regression line described in Section 10-4. Recall that a slope of zero for the regression line indicates a zero correlation. Thus, a test of whether $B = 0$ may be used to reject or to accept the null hypothesis $\rho = 0$. *A test rejecting the null hypothesis that $B = 0$ will also reject the assumption that $\rho = 0$.*

EXERCISES

10-16 Determine the value of the sample correlation coefficient for each of the following situations:
(a) $\bar{Y}_X = 10 + 2X$; $r^2 = .974$ (c) $\bar{Y}_X = 1.1 + 5.5X$; $r^2 = .950$
(b) $\bar{Y}_X = .3 - .1X$; $r^2 = .640$ (d) $\bar{Y}_X = 20 - 2X$; $r^2 = .810$

---

* This section relies on background material in Chapter 9 and may be skipped with no loss of continuity.

10-17 For each of the following situations, indicate whether a correlation analysis, a regression analysis, or both would be appropriate. In each case, give the reasons for your choice.

(a) In order to choose advertising media, an agency account executive is investigating the relationship between a woman's age and her annual expenditures on a client firm's cosmetics.

(b) A trucker needs to establish a decision rule that will enable him to determine when to inspect or to replace his tires, based upon the number of miles driven.

(c) A government agency wishes to identify which field offices of various sizes (in numbers of employees) are out of alignment with the prevailing pattern of working days lost due to sick leave.

(d) A research firm conducts attitude surveys in two stages. The first stage identifies coincident factors, such as age and income. The second stage is more detailed, involving separate study to predict values of one variable using the known values of other variables associated with it in the initial stage.

10-18 The following data represent disposable personal income and personal consumption expenditures (in billions of dollars) for the United States during the five-year period from 1964 through 1968. (Source: *Economic Report of the President, February 1970.*)

Year	Disposable Personal Income X	Personal Consumption Expenditures Y
1964	438	401
1965	473	433
1966	512	466
1967	547	492
1968	590	537

(a) Use the method of least squares to find the estimated linear regression equation that provides consumption expenditure predictions for specified levels of disposable income.

(b) Is the Y intercept negative or positive? Why do you think this is so?

(c) State verbally the meaning of the slope of the regression line.

(d) Using your intermediate calculations from (a) and the values found for the estimated regression coefficients, calculate the coefficient of determination using expression (10-23).

10-19 In helping to evaluate the effectiveness of a retraining program, a personnel manager is studying the following results obtained for a sample of $n = 10$ employees. The data provide productivity indices before and after retraining.

Employees	Score Before X	Score After Y
Grace Brown	90	83
Patrick Gray	75	72
Lisa White	80	84
Homer Black	65	76
John Green	85	77
Linda Jones	90	82
Carl Smith	95	95
Freddy Tyler	75	68
Lisa Adams	70	78
Karen Johnson	60	55

(a) Use the method of least squares to determine the equation for the estimated regression line.

(b) Calculate the sample coefficient of determination using expression (10-23).

(c) What percentage of the total variation in Y is explained by the estimated regression line?

10-20 Referring to the information contained in Exercise 10-18 and to your answers to that exercise:

(a) What percentage of the total variation in Y is explained by the regression line?

(b) What is the value of the correlation coefficient?

(c) Calculate the correlation coefficient another way, using expression (10-28).

10-21 A statistics instructor wants to know if there is a correlation between his students' homework point totals and their average examination scores. A random sample of five of his students has produced the following results:

Homework Point Total X	Average Examination Score Y
140	90
80	80
90	60
150	80
110	70

Calculate the correlation coefficient for the above data.

10-6 COMMON PITFALLS AND LIMITATIONS OF REGRESSION AND CORRELATION ANALYSIS

There are several limitations and pitfalls associated with linear regression and correlation analysis that should be given special mention. These may be categorized as being due to (1) violations of the theoretical assumptions, (2) improper use of the regression equation and correlation coefficient, and (3) misinterpretation of these coefficients. Regression and correlation are powerful tools, but ludicrous conclusions may be drawn if they are not used properly.

Relevancy of Past Data

Care must be taken in using past data to determine a future relationship. Regression analysis is often used in forecasting with time series, which we shall discuss in Chapter 12. There the independent variable is time, with the dependent variable Y being forecast. The source of data is history, so that often a time span of many years is encompassed by the observed Y values. A very serious danger is that the conditional distributions for Y may have changed character over time. The regression equation accounts for a shift in the conditional means of *Y*, but it assumes that the variance is constant. Thus if there is reason to believe that the values of *Y* are becoming more or less volatile over time, a critical assumption of regression analysis is violated. In addition to difficulties with the variance, the observations over the years are usually statistically *dependent*, violating another assumption of regression theory. The net effect of such violations is that probabilistic interpretations of inferences are invalid and cannot be used.

Because relationships are apt to change over time, special care should be taken when past data are used to predict a future value of the dependent variable. The hazards are most pronounced in forecasting with time series, but similar difficulties may arise whenever the data are collected over a long time period. This would be the case in attempting to express the cost of a production run by means of a regression line relating it to quantity produced. A very useful result of such an analysis is identification of fixed and variable cost components, so that the *Y* intercept is the estimated fixed cost per production run, while the slope of the regression line provides an estimate of variable costs per unit. Since production runs may be infrequent, obtaining sufficient data points for predictions precise enough to be useful may require historical experience from several years. But during this period, a great many changes—in labor and material costs, in efficiency (due to technological improvements), or in facilities—can cause unknown changes in the relationship between cost and production volume.

The regression assumptions presume that the same conditions prevail at all levels of production, which is probably not the case. For example, low production volumes may predominate in early time periods, with higher volumes in later years. The slope of the regression line obtained may be unduly steep, exaggerating the true cost–volume relationship if prices have been increasing over the duration. If there is inflation, labor rates and per-unit material prices will rise with time, so that all basic historical accounting data ought to be recalculated at present wage and price levels prior to regression analysis, if that is at all possible.

Cause-and-Effect Relationships

Earlier in this chapter we noted that regression and correlation analysis only provides a statistical relationship between two variables. It cannot tell us whether the values of *X* cause the values of *Y*. There may be a cause-and-effect relationship, but not necessarily. Possibly there is not even a logical reason for a relationship. (Although for any practical problem there is ordinarily some reasonable connection.) We have illustrated this by the spurious correlation found for the sperm whale catch and stock prices. Often the relationship between two variables may be explained by their interactions with a common factor. Thus we might find that a straight line provides a very close fit to the scatter diagram that relates the number of major oil slicks polluting our coasts to the number of electrical power failures. Clearly, one set of events is not caused by the other, but both may be explained by a common linkage: the demand for energy.

10-7   CURVILINEAR REGRESSION ANALYSIS

As we have seen in the earlier sections of this chapter, the assumption of a linear relationship between two variables is the simplest, but it does not always provide the best explanation. We have shown several examples where the relationship between X and Y is curvilinear.

The method of least squares may be applied to curvilinear relationships. The simplest of these finds a regression equation of the form

$$\bar{Y}_X = a + bX + cX^2 \qquad (10\text{-}30)$$

which is the equation for a parabola. It differs from a linear equation by the term containing X^2. Sometimes a curve may be used that involves higher powers of X, such as X^3 or X^4. An additional regression coefficient is required for each higher power of X. The regression equations so obtained are referred to mathematically as polynomials. It is unusual in applications of regression analysis to go beyond a polynomial involving X^3.

As with linear regression, the values for a, b, and c may be determined from a simultaneous solution of normal equations:

$$\sum Y = na + b \sum X + c \sum X^2$$

$$\sum XY = a \sum X + b \sum X^2 + c \sum X^3 \qquad (10\text{-}31)$$

$$\sum X^2 Y = a \sum X^2 + b \sum X^3 + c \sum X^4$$

For curves involving X^3 terms, one more normal equation is required. In general, if the highest power of X is X^n, then $n+1$ unknown regression coefficients must be found by simultaneously solving $n+1$ normal equations.

A detailed discussion of curvilinear regression analysis is given in Chapter 12 as one tool for time series analysis.

REVIEW EXERCISES

10-22 For each of the following results, calculate (1) the sample coefficient of determination, and (2) the sample correlation coefficient.
(a) $\bar{Y}_X = 10 + .5X$; $\sum Y = 200$; $\sum XY = 5{,}000$; $\sum Y^2 = 5{,}250$; $n = 10$.
(b) $\bar{Y}_X = 15 - .5X$; $\sum Y = 500$; $\sum XY = 8{,}000$; $\sum Y^2 = 4{,}500$; $n = 100$.

10-23 A security analyst wants to be convinced that the efficiency of capital utilization, expressed by the annual turnover of inventory, actually does have an effect upon a manufacturer's earnings. A sample of five firms is chosen, and the following results are obtained:

Company	Inventory Turnover X	Earnings as a Percent of Sales Y
A	3	10
B	4	8
C	5	12
D	6	15
E	7	13

Calculate the correlation coefficient for the above data.

10-24 A linear least squares relationship is used to determine how the grade-point average Y (GPA is measured on a scale where 4.0 is "straight A") of a particular student in a certain university relates to his or her average weekly study time X (in hours per week). A random sample of 100 students was selected, and the following intermediate calculations were obtained:

$$\sum X = 3,000 \qquad \sum Y = 260 \qquad \sum XY = 8,050$$

$$\sum X^2 = 92,500 \qquad \sum Y^2 = 775$$

(a) Find the estimated regression equation.

(b) State in words the meaning of the slope of your estimated regression line.

10-25 An economist has established that personal income X may be used to predict personal savings Y by the relationship $\bar{Y}_x = 24.0 + .06X$ (billions of dollars). For each of the following levels of personal income, calculate the predicted value for personal savings:

(a) $X = \$300$ billion (b) $X = \$500$ billion (c) $X = \$700$ billion

10-26 A California rancher has kept records over the past $n = 10$ years of the amount of rainfall X (in inches) in his county and of the number of alfalfa bales Y he has had to buy to supplement grazing grass for his herd until the excess cattle could be sold. The following estimated regression line has been obtained: $\bar{Y}_x = 20,000 - 500X$. The rancher has calculated $s_Y = 1,000$ bales, $s_{Y \cdot X} = 500$ bales, and $\sum X^2 = 2,500$. The mean rainfall for the time period considered has been $\bar{X} = 15$ inches. In order to arrange banking financing, the rancher wishes to predict how much alfalfa he must buy for the remainder of the current year. Since the dry season has arrived, he knows how much rain has fallen. Construct 95-percent prediction intervals for the required number of bales if this year's rainfall is

(a) 15 inches (b) 20 inches (c) 10 inches.

10-27 An agronomist believes that over a limited range of fertilizer-application levels X (in gallons per acre), a prediction of crop yield Y (in bushels per acre) may be obtained using linear least squares regression. Using a sample of $n = 25$ plots, she has established that $\bar{Y}_x = 50 + .05X$, with $s_Y = 8$ bushels per acre, $s_{Y \cdot X} = 2$ bushels per acre, $\bar{X} = 210$ gallons, and $\sum X^2 = 1,105,000$.

(a) Construct a 95-percent prediction interval for the conditional mean bushels per acre $\mu_{Y \cdot X}$ for an application of 200 gallons of fertilizer per acre.

(b) Construct a 95-percent prediction interval for the yield of a particular one-acre plot where 200 gallons of fertilizer will be applied.

10-28 Suppose that the estimated regression line providing total ingredient cost for chemical batches of size X (in thousands of liters) is $\bar{Y}_X = \$30,000 + \$5,000X$. This result was obtained from a sample of $n = 100$ production runs, for which $s_{Y \cdot X} = \$400$.

(a) Construct the 95-percent prediction interval for the conditional mean batch cost $\mu_{Y \cdot X}$ when $X = 10,000$ liters.

(b) Construct the 99-percent prediction interval for the total cost of the next 10,000-liter batch.

Chapter Eleven
Multiple Regression and Correlation

Measurement does not necessarily mean progress. Failing the possibility of measuring that which you desire, the lust for measurement may, for example, merely result in your measuring something else—and perhaps forgetting the difference—or in ignoring some things because they cannot be measured.

George Udny Yule

The techniques discussed in Chapter 10 for the analysis of the relationship between two variables are referred to as *simple* regression and correlation analysis. There we learned how to find a regression equation to make predictions of a dependent variable when the value of a single independent variable is known. We noted that such predictions may be too imprecise for practical application due to a substantial amount of the variation in Y being unexplainable by X. In this chapter these techniques are expanded to *multiple regression and correlation analysis*, which includes *several* independent predictor variables. The total variation in Y may then be explained by two or more variables, which in many situations will allow for more precise predictions than are possible through simple regression.

The essential advantage in using two or more independent variables is that it allows greater use of available information. For example, a regression line expressing a new store's sales in terms of the population of the city it serves should yield a poorer sales forecast than an equation that also considers median income, number of nearby competitors, and the local unemployment rate. A plant manager ought to more precisely predict the cost for processing a new order if he considers, in addition to the size of that order, the total volume of orders, his current manpower level, or the production capacity of available equipment. A marketing manager ought to more finely gauge the sales response to a magazine advertisement by considering in addition to its circulation, the demographical features of its readers, such as median age, median income, or proportion of urban readers.

11-1 LINEAR MULTIPLE REGRESSION INVOLVING THREE VARIABLES

Linear multiple regression analysis extends the simple linear regression analysis of Chapter 10 by considering two or more independent variables. In the case of two independent variables, denoted as X_1 and X_2, we use *the estimated multiple regression equation:*

$$Y_C = a + b_1 X_1 + b_2 X_2 \qquad (11\text{-}1)$$

Here we use Y_C, with the subscript C for "computed," to denote values for Y calculated from the estimated regression equation. This is analogous to $\bar{Y}_X$ used before, but in dealing with several independent variables it is too cumbersome to place X_1 and X_2 in subscripts. With two independent variables and one dependent variable, a total of three variables must be considered. The sample data will consist of three values for each sample unit observed, so that a scatter pattern portraying these observations will be three dimensional.

Regression in Three Dimensions

We can explain how such data can be portrayed in three dimensions using the analogy with the walls and floor of a room. Letting a corner of the room represent the situation when all three variables have value zero, we may represent the data points by marbles suspended in space at various distances from the floor and the two walls. A marble's height above the floor can represent the value of Y for that observation. Its distance from the wall on the left may then represent the observed value for X_1, while the distance to the other wall on the right expresses the value found for X_2. A pictorial representation of one three-dimensional scatter is shown in Figure 11-1 for a hypothetical set of data.

The regression equation (11-1) corresponds to a plane.* This plane must be

---

* Although Y is related to X_1 and X_2 by a plane instead of a line, we still say that the relationship is linear. The three-dimensional extension of a two-dimensional line is a plane. Although a line can also exist in three dimensions, it is defined as the intersection of two planes. Thus a three-dimensional line is like a point in two dimensions, which can be defined by the intersection of two lines.

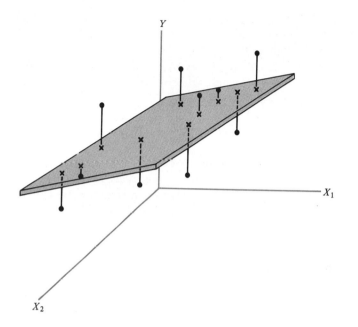

FIGURE 11-1   Regression plane for multiple regression, using three variables.

slanted in such a way that it provides the best fit to the sample data. We refer to the three-dimensional surface so obtained as the *regression plane*. The choice of this plane is analogous to determining how to position a pane of glass through the suspended marbles so that it has an inclination approximating that presented by the pattern of scatter. Of course, we want the same regression plane to be obtained by everyone, so we will adapt the method of least squares to three dimensions for this purpose.

The constants a_1, b_1, and b_2 in the equation of the regression plane, $Y_C = a + b_1 X_1 + b_2 X_2$, are called the estimated regression coefficients. As with $\overline{Y}_X = a + bX$, a is the value of Y where the regression plane cuts the Y axis, so that we still refer to a as the Y intercept. The interpretation of b_1 and b_2 is somewhat different than in simple regression. The constant b_1 expresses the net change in Y for a one-unit increase in X_1, holding X_2 fixed at a constant value. We may view b_1 as the slope of the edges obtained by slicing the regression plane with cuts made parallel to the X_1 axis at a distance X_2 from the origin. Likewise, b_2 is the net change in X_2, holding X_1 fixed. Because b_1 or b_2 alone only partially show the total movement in Y in response to increases in the respective independent variables, they are referred to as *estimated partial regression coefficients*.

For example, suppose that student college grade point average (GPA) Y (on a scale of 4) is related to high school GPA, denoted by X_1, and Scholastic Aptitude Test (SAT) score X_2 (in hundreds of points) by the equation $Y_C = -1.8 + .8X_1 + .3X_2$. Here $a = -1.8$, so that the regression plane cuts the Y axis at $Y = -1.8$. The regression coefficient $b_1 = .8$ signifies that a student's college

GPA can be predicted to be .8 point higher for each additional point in his high school GPA, regardless of how well he has done in the SAT. The constant $b_2 = .3$ indicates that each additional 100 points on the SAT is estimated to add .3 point to a student's college GPA, no matter what his high school GPA. Thus, a "straight A" high school student (GPA = 4.0) scoring 750 on the SAT would have a predicted college GPA of

$$Y_C = -1.8 + .8(4.0) + .3(7.5) = 3.65$$

which is an "A minus" average. Because of individual differences in background, motivation, study load, high school grading levels, and so forth, for the sample of students used to obtain the above regression equation, we cannot assume that this particular student will necessarily achieve a 3.65 GPA. As noted in Chapter 10, we must account for variability in Y, both inherent and due to sampling error.

11-2   MULTIPLE REGRESSION USING LEAST SQUARES

Mathematically, the method of least squares involves inclining the regression plane in such a way that the sum of the squared vertical deviations from its surface to the data points is minimized. The dots in Figure 11-1 represent the observed data points. Their vertical deviations from the plane are shown as line segments. The crosses indicate the points on the regression plane having the same values for X_1 and X_2 as the corresponding data points. The height of a cross above the X_1X_2 plane (i.e., the floor) represents the value of Y_C computed from expression (11-1). The difference between the observed and computed heights, $Y - Y_C$, will be positive for dots lying above the regression plane and negative for those lying below, so that the method of least squares minimizes.

$$\sum (Y - Y_C)^2 \tag{11-2}$$

As with simple regression, the coefficients of the estimated regression plane may be determined by solving a set of three equations in three unknowns. As before, these are referred to as the *normal equations:*

$$\sum Y = na + b_1 \sum X_1 + b_2 \sum X_2$$
$$\sum X_1 Y = a \sum X_1 + b_1 \sum X_1^2 + b_2 \sum X_1 X_2 \tag{11-3}$$
$$\sum X_2 Y = a \sum X_2 + b_1 \sum X_1 X_2 + b_2 \sum X_2^2$$

These may be obtained from the equation for a plane, $Y = a + b_1 X_1 + b_2 X_2$. The first normal equation is found by summing up each term of the regression equation and using the fact that $\sum a = na$. The second normal equation can likewise be obtained by first multiplying every term in the regression equation by X_1 and then summing the resulting products. The third equation can similarly be found by multiplying through by X_2 and then summing.*

We do not here introduce separate expressions for the regression coefficients, since the resulting equations would be extremely involved and cumbersome to use. Thus we find a_1, b_1, and b_2 by first calculating the required sums from the data for the various combinations of Y, X_1, and X_2. These are then substituted into the normal equations, which are solved simultaneously. To show how this works, we introduce the following illustration.

A Supermarket Illustration

In order to illustrate how to find the estimated multiple regression equation, we consider the problem of predicting profit Y (in thousands of dollars) for supermarkets in a large metropolitan area. As independent variables we use the total sales (in tens of thousands of dollars) X_1 of foods and X_2 of non-foods. For simplicity of calculation we use only the 10 hypothetical observations shown in Table 11-1.

TABLE 11-1   Profit and Sales of Food and Non-Food Items
for Ten Hypothetical Supermarkets

Supermarket Number	Profit (thousands of dollars) Y	Sales of Foods (tens of thousands of dollars) X_1	Sales of Non-Foods (tens of thousands of dollars) X_2
1	20	305	35
2	15	130	98
3	17	189	83
4	9	175	76
5	16	101	93
6	27	269	77
7	35	421	44
8	7	195	57
9	22	282	31
10	23	203	92

One reason for splitting total sales into food and non-food categories is that stores will differ significantly from each other in their offerings of non-food items. Virtually all will handle tobacco and cleaning agents. But some will have liquor departments, offer lines of convenience hardware and small appliances, or handle clothing articles. Separate sales figures for the two categories are easily obtainable, because the food items (in this particular locale) are not

* This procedure is a mnemonic aid. Calculus was used to actually derive equations (11-3).

subject to sales tax, whereas the non-food items are. The non-food items typically have higher markups and move more slowly off the shelf. Thus, treating food and non-food sales separately ought to provide a better prediction of a store's profit than total sales.

The intermediate calculations necessary to find the regression equation are shown in Table 11-2. The first eight columns contain the individual variable values and the squared and product terms. Column (9) contains the values for Y^2, which are not needed to obtain the regression coefficients and will be used later. Substituting the appropriate column totals into expressions (11-3), we obtain the following normal equations:

$$191 = 10a + 2{,}270b_1 + 686b_2$$

$$48{,}690 = 2{,}270a + 594{,}832b_1 + 139{,}565b_2$$

$$12{,}579 = 686a + 139{,}565b_1 + 52{,}682b_2$$

Solving these equations simultaneously for the unknowns a, b_1, b_2, we obtain the solutions:

$$a = -23.074$$

$$b_1 = .1148$$

$$b_2 = .2349$$

The simultaneous solution of three normal equations by hand can be quite a chore. This task, as we will see later in this chapter, can be enormously simplified by using a computer.

TABLE 11-2 Intermediate Calculations for Obtaining Regression Coefficients

(1) Y	(2) X_1	(3) X_2	(4) X_1Y	(5) X_2Y	(6) X_1X_2	(7) X_1^2	(8) X_2^2	(9) Y^2
20	305	35	6,100	700	10,675	93,025	1,225	400
15	130	98	1,950	1,470	12,740	16,900	9,604	225
17	189	83	3,213	1,411	15,687	35,721	6,889	289
9	175	76	1,575	684	13,300	30,625	5,776	81
16	101	93	1,616	1,488	9,393	10,201	8,649	256
27	269	77	7,263	2,079	20,713	72,361	5,929	729
35	421	44	14,735	1,540	18,524	177,241	1,936	1,225
7	195	57	1,365	399	11,115	38,025	3,249	49
22	282	31	6,204	682	8,742	79,524	961	484
23	203	92	4,669	2,116	18,676	41,209	8,464	529
191	2,270	686	48,690	12,569	139,565	594,832	52,682	4,267

$$\Sigma Y = 191 \qquad \Sigma X_1 = 2{,}270 \qquad \Sigma X_2 = 686$$

$$\bar{Y} = 19.1 \qquad \bar{X}_1 = 227.0 \qquad \bar{X}_2 = 68.6$$

$$\Sigma X_1 Y = 48{,}690 \qquad \Sigma X_2 Y = 12{,}569 \qquad \Sigma X_1 X_2 = 139{,}565$$

$$\Sigma X_1^2 = 594{,}832 \qquad \Sigma X_2^2 = 52{,}682 \qquad \Sigma Y^2 = 4{,}267$$

The above values for a, b_1, and b_2 provide the estimated multiple regression equation

$$Y_C = -23.074 + .1148X_1 + .2349X_2$$

This equation may then be used to forecast the profit of a particular store. Suppose that a new store is built that will have estimated sales of $2,500,000 for foods and $750,000 for non-foods, so that $X_1 = 250$ and $X_2 = 75$. The estimated store profit for these sales levels would be

$$Y_C = -23.074 + .1148(250) + .2349(75) = 23.244 \text{ or } \$23,244$$

Interpreting the Results

We may interpret the value $b_1 = .1148$ as follows: For each ten thousand dollar increase in food sales there will be an estimated .1148 thousand or 114.8 dollar increase in profits, holding the sales of non-food items at any fixed level. Likewise, each 10,000 additional dollars from the sale of non-food items results in an estimated profit increase of $b_2 = .2349$ thousand or $234.90 for any fixed amount of food sales. Thus the marginal contribution of non-foods to profits is, dollar for dollar, slightly more than twice that of the foods. The result $a = -23.074$ signifies that $23,074 of "fixed" costs, on the average, must be absorbed before a store can show a profit. These correspond to those expenses, such as rent, which continue whether or not the store is open. The $23,074 figure may vary considerably from the actual fixed costs of any particular store, because of sampling error and due to different store characteristics. It also depends upon (1) the linear model being appropriate and (2) the validity of extrapolation down to zero sales for both types of items.

Advantages of Multiple Regression

Two interesting questions may be posed regarding the use of multiple rather than simple regression analysis. First, is the simultaneous analysis of two independent variables through multiple regression any improvement over that obtained through two separate simple regressions? Second, how can we show that the accuracy of predictions is improved by the use of multiple regression analysis? We will begin to answer these questions by continuing with our supermarket illustration.

Three two-dimensional diagrams of the supermarket data are shown in Figure 11-2. In Figure 11-2(a), profit is plotted against sales of food items. Food sales X_1 by itself might be a fairly reliable predictor of profit Y, since there is a high value of .76 for the sample correlation coefficient. Denoting this particular sample correlation coefficient by the double-subscripted symbol r_{Y1}, where $Y1$ indicates that the strength of association between the variables Y and X_1 is being measured, we have $r_{Y1} = .76$. A similar figure may be obtained for any pair of the three variables. Thus, analysis relating profit Y to the sales X_2 of non-food

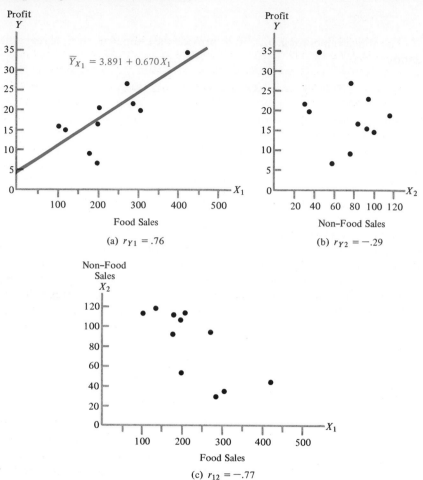

FIGURE 11-2 Scatter diagrams for variable pairs using supermarket data.

items provides another sample correlation coefficient, $r_{Y2} = -.29$. A cursory examination of this second relationship, shown in Figure 11-2(b), seems to indicate that non-food sales have little effect upon profits. Does this indicate that non-food sales would be a poor predictor of a store's income? Two-variable analysis seems to contradict our previous finding that profit will increase by an estimated \$234.90 for each additional \$10,000 in non-food sales. How might we explain this?

Limitations of Simple Regression and Correlation Analysis

A comparison of food sales X_1 to non-food sales X_2, as represented by the scatter diagram in Figure 11-2(c), shows a pronounced negative correlation between these two variables. We distinguish the sample correlation coefficient in this case from the others by using the subscript 12: here, $r_{12} = -.77$. Supermarkets having higher than average food sales tend to have lower than average non-food sales, while the reverse is true for stores with below average food sales.

The low-food-volume operators have managed to survive and achieve profits in face of competition from stores more successful at selling food by specializing heavily in non-food items. The two stores having annual food sales below $1.5 million have extraordinarily large profits, which are not very well explained by food sales alone. Their data points lie considerably above the regression line in Figure 11-2(a). The impact of non-food sales is camouflaged by the interaction of food and non-food sales.

This illustrates a general inadequacy in using simple regression to separately determine how a dependent variable relates to several independent variables. The same is true of correlation. Separate simple correlations of Y versus X_1 and Y against X_2 seem to indicate that food item sales would be a far better predictor of profit than non-food sales. A two-variable analysis indicates that X_2 has a negligible correlation with Y of $r_{Y2} = -.29$. But it would be a blunder to discard X_2 because it shows such a small correlation with Y. This is because X_2 is highly negatively correlated with X_1, $r_{12} = -.77$, so that its influence on Y can be explained only by considering how Y relates to both X_1 and X_2 through multiple regression. The interactions between the predictor variables themselves must first be determined before a variable can be discarded. We shall present techniques of multiple regression and correlation analysis used to provide this information.

Standard Error of the Estimate

We have seen that the errors in making predictions from the regression line are smaller when the scatter of the data is less pronounced. The degree of such variation in Y can be expressed by the standard error of the estimate for values of Y. The same is true in multiple regression. The standard error of the estimate for values of Y about the regression plane is defined by

$$S_{Y \cdot 12} = \sqrt{\frac{\sum (Y_C - Y)^2}{n - 3}} \qquad (11\text{-}4)$$

We use a different subscript notation, $Y \cdot 12$, to show that two independent variables X_1 and X_2 are being used to predict Y. As in simple regression, the standard error of the estimate is found by taking the square root of the mean squared deviations of observed Y values from the estimated regression plane. The divisor $n - 3$ is chosen because three degrees of freedom are lost in estimating the regression coefficients. This makes $S_{Y \cdot 12}^2$ an unbiased estimator of the variance of Y about the true regression plane. In practice, it is simpler to use the following expression to calculate *the standard error of the estimate:*

$$S_{Y \cdot 12} = \sqrt{\frac{\sum Y^2 - a \sum Y - b_1 \sum X_1 Y - b_2 \sum X_2 Y}{n - 3}} \qquad (11\text{-}5)$$

which does not require the calculation of Y_C for every data point.

Using the data in Table 11-2 and the regression constants found previously, we calculate the standard error of the estimate for the supermarket data:

$$S_{Y \cdot 12} = \sqrt{\frac{4{,}267 - (-23.074)(191) - .1148(48{,}690) - .2349(12{,}569)}{10 - 3}}$$

$$= 4.343 \text{ thousand dollars.}$$

This value may be compared to the corresponding standard error found in a simple regression for profit Y and food sales X_1. Using X_1 as the only independent variable, and then applying the procedures of Chapter 10 to the supermarket data, we find the regression line

$$\overline{Y}_{X_1} = 3.891 + .0670 X_1$$

The scatter of data about this regression *line* is summarized by the standard error of the estimate

$$s_{Y \cdot X_1} = 5.719 \text{ thousand dollars}$$

Comparing this with the standard error of the estimate about the regression *plane*, $S_{Y \cdot 12} = 4.343$, we see that multiple regression provides a better interpretation of the data. As we noted earlier, the standard error expresses the amount of variation in Y that is left unexplained by regression analysis. Since $S_{Y \cdot 12}$ is smaller than $s_{Y \cdot X_1}$, our regression plane (incorporating both food and non-food sales as *two* independent variables) explains more of the variation in Y than the regression line does (where food sales serves as the *single* independent variable and there is more unexplained variation). This indicates that inclusion of non-food sales data in the analysis will indeed provide better predictions of store profit. Before we see how such predictions can be made from multiple regression results, we must clarify some theoretical points.

Assumptions of Multiple Regression

The assumptions of linear multiple regression are similar to those of simple regression. The least squares method provides a plane that is an estimate of

$$\mu_{Y \cdot 12} = A + B_1 X_1 + B_2 X_2 \qquad (11\text{-}6)$$

where $\mu_{Y \cdot 12}$ denotes the conditional mean of Y, given X_1 and X_2. The true regression coefficients are A, B_1, and B_2. Their values remain unknown and are estimated by a, b_1, and b_2, respectively. For each combination of X_1 and X_2 there is a corresponding point on the true regression plane. The height of this point is $\mu_{Y \cdot 12}$, the mean of the corresponding populations for Y. As with simple regression, each such distribution is assumed to have the same variance $\sigma_{Y \cdot 12}^2$.

It is possible to extend the theoretical developments of simple regression to multiple regression in order to make inferences of A, B_1, and B_2. For instance, a confidence interval can be obtained for B_1 using estimator b_1, just as we did for B with b. Prediction intervals for $\mu_{Y \cdot 12}$ and individual values for Y can also be constructed using the estimated regression plane.

Prediction Intervals in Multiple Regression

Prediction Interval to Estimate Mean Value of Y

The procedures for constructing prediction intervals to qualify estimates made from the regression plane are similar to those in simple regression. The following equation* provides *the prediction interval estimate for $\mu_{Y \cdot 12}$:*

$$\mu_{Y \cdot 12} = Y_C \pm t_\alpha \frac{S_{Y \cdot 12}}{\sqrt{n}} \qquad (11\text{-}7)$$

where Y_C is the value for Y computed from the regression plane at the given levels for X_1 and X_2, and t_α is the critical value of the t statistic for an upper-tailed area α (half of 1 minus the confidence level) when the degrees of freedom are $n-3$.

We may illustrate this with the supermarket data. Suppose that $\mu_{Y \cdot 12}$ is to be estimated by a 95 percent confidence interval, so that $\alpha = .025$. This is done for all stores having food sales of \$2,000,000 and non-food sales of \$500,000. Thus (in ten-thousand dollar units), $X_1 = 200$ and $X_2 = 50$, and the corresponding height of the regression plane is

$$Y_C = -23.074 + .1148(200) + .2349(50) = 11.631 \text{ (thousand dollars)}$$

From Appendix Table F, the critical value for $n-3 = 7$ degrees of freedom is $t_\alpha = t_{.025} = 2.365$. Substituting these values and $S_{Y \cdot 12} = 4.343$ into expression (11-7), we obtain the prediction interval:

$$\mu_{Y \cdot 12} = 11.631 \pm \frac{2.365(4.343)}{\sqrt{10}}$$

$$= 11.631 \pm 3.248$$

$$8.383 \leqslant \mu_{Y \cdot 12} \leqslant 14.879 \text{ (thousand dollars)}$$

Thus we are 95 percent confident that the true mean profit for all such stores lies between \$8,383 and \$14,879. This interval is probably too wide for practical planning purposes, largely due to the small sample size used.

---

* This equation is an approximation of a more complicated one, sometimes used in other textbooks, which provides nearly the same values for most sample sizes n.

As with all sampling situations, a larger sample would provide an even more precise estimate of mean store profit. *When the sample size is large (30 or more), the normal distribution can be used,* so that t_α is replaced in expression (11-7) by the normal deviate z for an upper-tailed normal curve area α.

Prediction Interval to Estimate Individual Y

An individual value of Y is denoted here by Y_I. The following expression provides *the prediction interval estimate for Y_I:*

$$Y_I = Y_C \pm t_\alpha S_{Y \cdot 12} \sqrt{\frac{n+1}{n}} \tag{11-8}$$

We illustrate this for the college GPA example (page 371) by finding the 95-percent confidence interval for the college GPA, Y, of a student whose high school GPA is $X_1 = 2.75$ and whose SAT score is 480, so that $X_2 = 4.80$. The college GPA may be computed from the regression equation:

$$Y_C = -1.8 + .8X_1 + .3X_2$$
$$= -1.8 + .8(2.75) + .3(4.80)$$
$$= 1.84$$

We will use $n = 20$ and $S_{Y \cdot 12} = .2$. From Table F, using $20 - 3 = 17$ degrees of freedom, the critical value is $t_\alpha = t_{.025} = 2.110$. The student's college GPA is predicted with 95 percent confidence by

$$Y_I = 1.84 \pm 2.110(.2) \sqrt{\frac{20+1}{20}}$$
$$= 1.84 \pm .43$$

$$1.41 \leqslant Y_I \leqslant 2.27$$

When n is large, expression (11-8) is modified by replacing t_α by the appropriate normal deviate z.

Inferences Regarding Regression Coefficients

There are important questions in regression analysis concerning the true partial regression coefficients B_1 and B_2. Although we can estimate B_1 and B_2 from sample data by b_1 and b_2, sampling error may exist. Because two or more coefficients are dealt with in a multiple regression, special procedures must be used when making inferences about them. These are considered in Chapter 16, where we discuss the analysis of variance. As an optional topic to that chapter we apply hypothesis testing concepts to multiple regression coefficients.

EXERCISES

11-1   An economist wishes to predict the incomes of restaurants over two years old. This prediction will be made from a regression equation using total floor space and number of employees. For a sample of $n = 5$ restaurants, the following data have been obtained:

Income (thousands of dollars) Y	Floor Space (thousands of square feet) X_1	Number of Employees X_2
20	10	15
15	5	8
10	10	12
5	3	7
10	2	10

(a) Calculate the estimated regression equation for the given data.

(b) State the meaning of the partial regression coefficients b_1 and b_2.

11-2   Suppose that a college admissions director has used high school GPA X_1 and IQ score X_2 to predict college GPA Y. Using the regression equation

$$Y_C = .5 + .8X_1 + .003X_2$$

predict the college GPA for each of the four students whose scores are as shown:

	(a)	(b)	(c)	(d)
High School GPA	2.9	3.0	2.7	3.5
IQ Score	123	118	105	136

11-3   The editor of a statistics journal wishes to use the intermediate sample data calculations provided below to determine a regression equation that predicts the total typing hours Y for article drafts. As independent variables, she uses number of words in the draft X_1 (expressed in tens of thousands) and an index X_2 for level of difficulty on a scale from 1 (least difficult) to 5 (most difficult).

$$n = 25 \qquad \sum Y = 200 \qquad \sum X_1 = 100 \qquad \sum X_2 = 75$$

$$\sum X_1 Y = 1,000 \qquad \sum X_2 Y = 800 \qquad \sum X_1^2 = 600$$

$$\sum X_2^2 = 325 \qquad \sum Y^2 = 3,800 \qquad \sum X_1 X_2 = 200$$

(a) Determine the equation for the regression plane $Y_C = a + b_1 X_1 + b_2 X_2$.

(b) Explain the meaning of values obtained for b_1 and b_2.

11-4   A record manufacturer uses special machines to press a recording's grooves onto blank disks from a die. Each die lasts for about 1,000 pressings. Because of the time constraints inherent in the record business, it is sometimes necessary to use several pressing machines simultaneously. Since each machine requires an expensive die disk and many production runs are completed before the useful lifetime of each die disk has been achieved, this raises production costs. For $n = 100$ production runs, the total manufacturing cost Y (in thousands of dollars) has been determined for the number of pressings made X_1 (in thousands) and the number of die disks required X_2. The following results have been calculated:

$$Y_C = 1.082 + 1.2X_1 + .553X_2$$

$$\bar{Y} = 32.0 \qquad \bar{X}_1 = 23.0 \qquad \bar{X}_2 = 6.0$$

$$\sum Y^2 = 104{,}000 \qquad \sum X_1 Y = 75{,}000 \qquad \sum X_2 Y = 15{,}000$$

(a) Calculate the estimated cost Y_C for each of the following production runs:

Run	Number of Pressings (thousands)	Number of Die Disks
(1)	15	5
(2)	20	3
(3)	15	4
(4)	100	10

(b) Calculate the standard error of the estimate for values of Y about the regression plane.
(c) For each production-run situation in (a), construct the 95-percent confidence interval for the *mean* production costs.
(d) Same as (c), but construct intervals for costs estimates for *individual* production runs.

11-5   Referring to the information contained in Exercise 11-3 and to your answers to that exercise:
(a) Determine the equation for the estimated regression line $\bar{Y}_{X_1} = a + bX_1$, using only a single independent variable X_1.
(b) Calculate $s_{Y \cdot X_1}$, using X_1 instead of X in expression (10-12) on page 336, and $S_{Y \cdot 12}$, using expression (11-5). Do you think the inclusion of the level of difficulty variable X_2 will result in better predictions than those obtained using X_1 alone? Why?
(c) Suppose that a particular article containing 50,000 words is rated at a difficulty level of 3. Determine the prediction interval for the typing hours required at a 95-percent confidence level. Do the same for the mean typing time of all articles of the same length and difficulty.

11-3   REGRESSION WITH MANY VARIABLES: COMPUTER APPLICATIONS

Multiple regression may use more than two independent variables. For example, in predicting supermarket profit we might use the *size* of the store as well as food sales and non-food sales. Inclusion of this third independent variable, denoted by X_3, would provide the regression equation

$$Y_C = a + b_1 X_1 + b_2 X_2 + b_3 X_3 \tag{11-9}$$

In solving for the regression coefficients, additional product sums involving X_3 must be computed and four normal equations must be solved simultaneously.

Ordinarily, the necessary calculations are made with a digital computer rather than by hand, so a detailed discussion of the computations will not be provided in this book.

As in multiple regression with X_1 and X_2, by including X_3 we may compute the standard error of the estimate about the regression *hyperplane*. (Including Y, there will now be four variables, so the regression surface cannot be graphed in only three dimensions. Expression (11-9) yields a four-dimensional plane, which mathematicians call a "hyperplane.") The standard error, denoted by the symbol $S_{Y \cdot 123}$, is calculated in the same way we calculate $S_{Y \cdot 12}$, but with the extra term $b_3 \sum X_3$ in the numerator; the denominator will be $n - 4 = 10 - 4 = 6$. The number of degrees of freedom will also be $n - 4$, and we may calculate the prediction intervals as we did before with this reduced value.

When more predictor variables are desired, we can expand the regression analysis by including X_4, X_5, and so on. When there are m total variables (one dependent and $m - 1$ independent), the number of degrees of freedom will be $n - m$, which is used as the denominator for computing the standard error and in finding t_α for the construction of prediction intervals.

To illustrate multiple regression with three independent variables, a computer application will be discussed next.

Using the Computer in Multiple Regression Analysis

By hand, the computations necessary to perform a regression analysis are at best tedious, even with the assistance of a hand-operated calculator. Although hand calculation may be feasible when the number of observations and the number of independent variables are small, such tedium can be alleviated by using a digital computer. The computer not only saves time and energy but also prevents the inevitable cascade of errors that occurs whenever one error, such as mispunching a calculator button, is committed. Also, a computer generally provides greater levels of accuracy because of its superior capability in handling a large number of significant figures.

It is not necessary for the user to prepare his or her own computer program to perform regression and correlation analysis. Library programs already written for this purpose are widely available. These "canned" programs vary considerably in their format and in the type of output data they provide, but they generally include a determination of the regression coefficients (a, b_1, b_2, and so on), standard errors, and correlation coefficients. Such programs can be quite elaborate. They may include lower-dimensional regression equations for various variable combinations, values for the t statistic (used in constructing confidence intervals for regression coefficients and in obtaining prediction intervals), and coefficients of partial determination (discussed in Section 11-5). The most complex programs provide inference-making computations too sophisticated to include here.

Here we will describe how to use one particular program: the Multiple Linear Regression Routine of the International Timesharing Corporation.

Although this program is of the time-sharing type, similar programs are available that operate in a batch-processing mode. In those cases, the input data and operating parameters must be punched onto cards rather than fed directly through a teletype terminal.

To illustrate the use of the computer, we will expand our supermarket illustration to include a third independent variable—the size of the store in thousands of square feet. To do this, we will augment our previous sample data by including the ten observations for X_3 provided in Table 11-3.

TABLE 11-3   Sample Observations of Supermarket Profits, Using Food Sales, Non-Food Sales, and Size of Store as Independent Variables

Supermarket Number	Food Sales (tens of thousands of dollars) X_1	Non-Food Sales (tens of thousands of dollars) X_2	Store Size (thousands of square feet) X_3	Profit (thousands of dollars) Y
1	305	35	35	20
2	130	98	22	15
3	189	83	27	17
4	175	76	16	9
5	101	93	28	16
6	269	77	46	27
7	421	44	56	35
8	195	57	12	7
9	282	31	40	22
10	203	92	32	23

Based on the data in Table 11-3, Figure 11-3 shows the log of terminal communications, how the data are entered, and the output of the regression analysis. The computer results indicate that profit predictions may be made from the estimated regression equation

$$Y_C = -10.170 + .027X_1 + .097X_2 + .525X_3$$

We may interpret the values for the partial regression coefficients. The value $b_1 = .027$ indicates that a store's profit will increase by an estimated .027 thousand = 27 dollars for each additional $10,000 in food sales, holding other variables fixed. This is smaller than the value for b_1 found in the previous three-variable regression, but b_1 has a different meaning here. Instead of a single additional variable, two variables, both non-food sales and store size, are accounted for and are being held constant. Likewise, $b_2 = .097$ indicates that, holding store size and food sales constant, store profits will increase by an estimated $97 for each $10,000 in non-food sales. The independent variable X_3, store size, has a partial regression coefficient of value $b_3 = .525$, indicating that a supermarket can increase its profits by an estimated $525 for each thousand square feet in additional floor space.

I T S STATISTICAL PACKAGE

WANT TO SEE STAT INDEX? NO
WANT ADVANCED USER STATUS(YES OR NO)? NO
TYPE THE CODE OF THE ROUTINE YOU WISH TO USE MU
TYPE NO. OF VARIABLES AND OBSERVATIONS 4.,10
DATA ORDERED BY OBSERVATION OR BY VARIABLE(OBS OR VAR)? OBS
ENTER DATA FILE NAME OR 'TERMINAL' -- TERMINAL
INPUT DATA IN FORM XX.X,XX.X,XX.X,...XX.X (RET)
305,35,35,20
130,98,22,15
189,83,27,17
175,76,16,9
101,93,28,16
269,77,46,27
421,44,56,35
195,57,12,7
282,31,40,22
203,92,32,23
LISTING(YES OR NO)? YES
VARIABLE

OBS.	1 X_1	2 X_2	3 X_3	4 Y
1	305.0000	35.0000	35.0000	20.0000
2	130.0000	98.0000	22.0000	15.0000
3	189.0000	83.0000	27.0000	17.0000
4	175.0000	76.0000	16.0000	9.0000
5	101.0000	93.0000	28.0000	16.0000
6	269.0000	77.0000	46.0000	27.0000
7	421.0000	44.0000	56.0000	35.0000
8	195.0000	57.0000	12.0000	7.0000
9	282.0000	31.0000	40.0000	22.0000
10	203.0000	92.0000	32.0000	23.0000

DO YOU WISH TRANSFORMATIONS OF DATA? NO
DO YOU WISH TO SAVE THIS DATA ON A DISK FILE? NO
ENTER NUMBER OF INDEPENDENT VARIABLES IN THE FORM XX ⌈RET⌉ 3
ENTER COLUMN NUMBERS OF THE INDEPENDENT VARIABLES IN
THE FORM XX,XX,... ETC. ⌈RET⌉ 1,2,3
ENTER COLUMN NUMBER OF DEPENDENT VARIABLE IN THE FORM XX 4

VARIABLE NO.	MEAN	STANDARD DEVIATION	CORRELATION X VS Y	REGRESSION COEFFICIENT	STD. ERROR OF REG.COEF.	COMPUTED T VALUE
1 $\bar{X}_1$	227.000	94.011 s_{X_1}	.760 r_{Y1}	.027 b_1	.012	2.246
2 $\bar{X}_2$	68.600	24.994 s_{X_2}	-.286 r_{Y2}	.097 b_2	.030	3.219
3 $\bar{X}_3$	31.400	12.442 s_{X_3}	.979 r_{Y3}	.525 b_3	.059	8.869
DEPENDENT						
4 $\bar{Y}$	19.100	8.293 s_Y				

INTERCEPT   -10.170243 a
MULTIPLE CORRELATION COEFFICIENT $R_{Y \cdot 123}$ .992399
STANDARD ERROR OF ESTIMATE   1.249868 $S_{Y \cdot 123}$

WANT TABLE OF RESIDUALS(YES OR NO)? YES
DO YOU WANT TO OUTPUT RESIDUALS TO A FILE(YES OR NO)? NO

                           TABLE OF RESIDUALS

OBSERVATION	Y OBSERVED	Y ESTIMATED	RESIDUAL	RES. PCNT. OF EST.
1	20.000	19.837	-.163	-.822
2	15.000	14.399	-.601	-4.176
3	17.000	17.162	.1621	.941
4	9.000	10.332	1.332	12.894
5	16.000	16.277	.277	1.704
6	Y 27.000	Y_c 28.711	Y_c-Y 1.711	5.960
7	35.000	34.865	-.135	-.387
8	7.000	6.930	-.070	-1.006
9	22.000	21.450	-.550	-2.563
10	23.000	21.037	-1.963	-9.332

WANT ANOTHER MULTIPLE LINEAR REGRESSION(YES OR NO)? NO

FIGURE 11-3   Computer run for multiple regression, using sample
              supermarket data.

The substantial changes in the values a, b_1, and b_2 from the earlier multiple regression indicate that including store size X_3 as one of the independent variables should lead to better profit predictions. This improvement can be seen by comparing the standard error of the estimate of $S_{Y.123} = 1.250$ thousand dollars (shown in the computer printout) to the earlier one of 4.343 thousand dollars. Including the additional variable X_3 for store size considerably reduces the standard error of the estimate for Y. This indicates that profit can be predicted with greater precision when store size is included as well as food and non-food sales.

EXERCISES

11-6 For the family data given in the table below:
   (a) Determine the coefficients for the estimated regression line $\bar{Y}_{X_1} = a + bX_1$ and calculate $s_{Y.X_1}$.

Family	Total Spending Y	Income X_1	Size X_2	Additional Savings X_3
A	8,000	10,000	3	1,000
B	7,000	10,000	2	1,500
C	7,000	9,000	2	700
D	12,000	16,000	4	1,800
E	6,000	7,000	6	200
F	7,000	9,000	4	500
G	8,000	8,000	6	0
H	7,000	8,000	5	100
I	10,000	12,000	6	200
J	8,000	11,000	2	1,000

   (b) Determine the coefficients for the estimated regression plane $Y_C = a + b_1 X_1 + b_2 X_2$ and calculate $S_{Y.12}$.
   (c) Does a comparison of the values $S_{Y.12}$ and $s_{Y.X_1}$ suggest that including family size has been worthwhile in predicting total spending? Explain.

11-7 *Computer exercise:* Using the data in the table in Exercise 11-6:
   (a) Determine the coefficients for the estimated regression hyperplane

$$Y_C = a + b_1 X_1 + b_2 X_2 + b_3 X_3$$

   (b) Determine the value for $S_{Y.123}$.
   (c) Compare the values of $S_{Y.123}$ and $S_{Y.12}$ (from Exercise 11-6). Does your comparison suggest that including the additional savings variable has proved worthwhile in predicting total spending? Explain your answers.

11-4 DUMMY VARIABLE TECHNIQUES

It is sometimes necessary to determine how a dependent variable is related to quantitative independent random variables when there are nonhomogeneous factors influencing their interaction. Often such factors are qualitative in nature.

For example, in printing a book, the cost of typesetting can be expressed by an equation involving the size of the book and the number of figures and tables. But this cost is also affected by the kind of book. A technical book using many special symbols and characters (like this one) requires a considerable amount of hand work and is, page for page, more expensive to set than a literary anthology. "Kind of book" can be viewed as a qualitative variable that influences composition cost. Although regression analysis requires all variables to be quantitative, qualitative variables may be incorporated into the framework of multiple regression through the introduction of dummy variables.

There are two major kinds of statistical studies where dummy variables may be used. Those made with sample data collected at a single point in time are sometimes referred to as *cross-sectional studies*. Studies made using observations collected over an extended time period use *time series data*. In business and economics, time series data are very important because observations of a dependent variable, such as consumption of electricity or gross national product, can only be obtained periodically. Often, time itself becomes the independent variable. Unavoidable historical heterogeneous influences, such as war or recession, may be treated as qualitative variables, and their effects must be somehow identified. Another important use for qualitative variables in time series is to identify seasonal influences and relate them to the dependent variable.

Using a Dummy Variable

We illustrate the dummy variable technique in Figure 11-4 for data relating composition costs to total number of words for a hypothetical sample of textbooks. The books have been printed during one year by a firm under contract to various publishers. The data points for technical books are shown as crosses, while the dots represent nontechnical texts. As we have noted, the technical books tend to be more costly, so that the crosses cluster higher than the dots. Two parallel lines have been constructed for the scatter diagram. The top one, fitting the data for the technical books, represents an upward shift in composition costs due to extensive hand typesetting.

These lines have been obtained by means of a linear least squares *multiple* regression with two independent variables, word length X_1 and type of book X_2. X_2 is a dummy variable that takes on only two values, 1 or 0, depending upon whether or not a book is technical. We may envision X_2 as a "switching" variable that is "on" when an observation is made of a technical book and "off" for an ordinary text. The estimated multiple regression equation is of the form

$$Y_C = a + b_1 X_1 + b_2 X_2$$

where $X_2 = 0$ for nontechnical books and $X_2 = 1$ for technical books. This is the equation for a plane in three-dimensional space. However, we have restricted X_1 in such a way that only two parallel slices through the plane at $X_2 = 0$ and

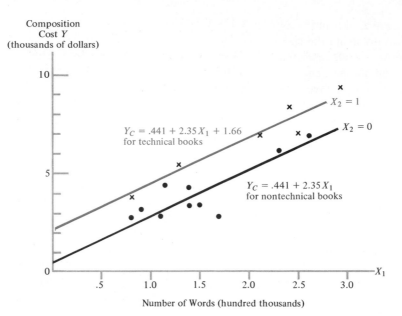

FIGURE 11-4   Results from multiple regression with dummy variable, showing projected lines.

$X_2 = 1$ are possible. These are projected onto the $X_1 Y$ plane as the two estimated regression lines in Figure 11-4, the equations for which are

$$Y_C = a + b_1 X_1 + b_2 \quad \text{for technical books}$$
$$Y_C = a + b_1 X_1 \qquad \text{for nontechnical books}$$

The value of a is the Y intercept for nontechnical books. The value for b_1 is the incremental or variable cost per additional word for either type of book. The amount b_2 represents the additional estimated cost—here assumed to be fixed in nature—associated with setting the type for a technical book. Thus the Y intercept for technical books is a total fixed cost estimated to be $a + b_2$.*

Table 11-4 shows the data for this example. Solving the corresponding normal equations, the following regression constants are obtained:

$$b_1 = 2.35$$
$$b_2 = 1.66$$
$$a = .441$$

and the estimated regression equation is

$$Y_C = .441 + 2.35 X_1 + 1.66 X_2$$

---

* A more general model would allow for different variable costs for technical books, which might be more realistic and would allow lines of different slope for the two types of texts.

TABLE 11-4 Intermediate Calculations for Multiple Regression
with Dummy Variable in Textbook Illustration

(Cost Y in thousands of dollars; length X_1 in hundreds of thousands of words)

Cost Y	Length X_1	X_2	$X_1 Y$	$X_2 Y$	$X_1 X_2$	X_1^2	X_2^2	Y^2
4.2	1.4	0	5.88	0	0	1.96	0	17.64
2.8	1.1	0	3.08	0	0	1.21	0	7.84
3.3	1.4	0	4.62	0	0	1.96	0	10.89
3.9	.8	1(T)	3.12	3.9	.8	.64	1	15.21
6.7	2.6	0	17.42	0	0	6.76	0	44.89
7.0	2.5	1(T)	17.50	7.0	2.5	6.25	1	49.00
9.3	2.9	1(T)	26.97	9.3	2.9	8.41	1	86.49
2.7	.8	0	2.15	0	0	.64	0	7.29
6.9	2.1	1(T)	14.49	6.9	2.1	4.41	1	47.61
2.8	1.2	0	3.36	0	0	1.44	0	7.84
5.4	1.3	1(T)	7.02	5.4	1.3	1.69	1	29.16
6.1	2.3	0	14.03	0	0	5.29	0	37.21
8.3	2.4	1(T)	19.92	8.3	2.4	5.76	1	68.89
3.3	1.5	0	4.95	0	0	2.25	0	10.89
3.1	.9	0	2.79	0	0	.81	0	9.61
75.8	25.2	6	147.30	40.8	12.0	49.48	6	450.46

$$\Sigma Y = 75.8 \qquad \Sigma X_1 = 25.2 \qquad \Sigma X_2 = 6$$
$$\bar{Y} = 5.053 \qquad \bar{X}_1 = 1.680 \qquad \bar{X}_2 = .400$$
$$\Sigma X_1 Y = 147.3 \qquad \Sigma X_2 Y = 40.8 \qquad \Sigma X_1 X_2 = 12.0$$
$$\Sigma X_1^2 = 49.48 \qquad \Sigma X_2^2 = 6 \qquad \Sigma Y^2 = 450.46$$

For the two values of X_2, the multiple regression equation provides

$$Y_C = .441 + 2.35 X_1 \qquad \text{for nontechnical books}$$

and

$$Y_C = .441 + 2.35 X_1 + 1.66$$

or

$$Y_C = 2.101 + 2.35 X_1 \qquad \text{for technical books}$$

We may interpret these lines as follows. The value $a = .441$ represents an estimated setup or fixed cost of \$441 applicable, on the average, to every book set in type. The partial regression coefficient value $b_1 = 2.35$, which is also the slope of each of the lines for the two kinds of books, is the estimated average variable cost of \$2,350 for each additional 100,000 words in length, or 2.35 cents per additional word. This applies to both technical and nontechnical books. The other partial regression coefficient, $b_2 = 1.66$, applies only to technical texts and indicates the estimated additional average fixed cost of handsetting special characters, \$1,660 per book, so that these books involve an average fixed cost estimated to be \$441 + \$1,660 = \$2,101 each.

The importance of treating kind of book as a separate variable is that this allows us to properly identify the relationship between composition cost and

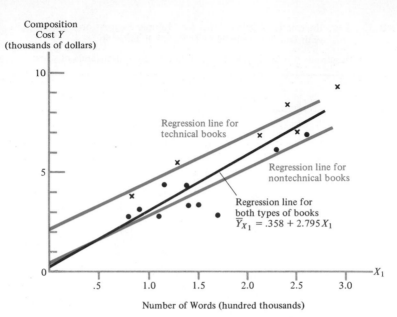

FIGURE 11-5   Graphical comparison of linear least squares regression and multiple regression with dummy variable.

book length. Using the dummy variable X_2, we can treat the two kinds of books separately and yet still glean the common information that both types yield in relating book length to cost. We certainly should not ignore the kind of book in determining the relationship between these primary variables. Doing so can lead to very erroneous conclusions, as is shown in Figure 11-5, where a simple linear regression line relates Y to X_1. This line does not fit the data nearly as well as the two lines obtained from multiple regression, and the amount of scatter about this single line is substantially greater than that achieved for the parallel lines obtained from our dummy variable multiple regression.

But why can't we do just as well by making two separate linear regression analyses, splitting the observations into separate samples for technical and non-technical books? If the sample sizes are large, this would be more desirable than multiple regression with dummy variables, because then we could have lines of different slopes reflecting the possibility that technical books may also have higher (or lower) variable costs. However, in this illustration the number of technical books observed was small, so that there may be considerable error in doing a separate regression analysis for each type of book.

Using a Dummy Variable with Time Series

We have noted situations where regression analysis using dummy variables with time series data may be advantageous. One of these involves isolation of the effect of nonhomogeneous influences, such as war and peace or recession and economic expansion, upon the relationship between two or more variables. Such variables are characterized by the uncontrollability of the sampling experiment, so that observations can be collected only as they occur over time. The statistician or economist cannot make a large number of "peacetime-only" observations in order to determine a relationship between personal consumption expenditures and disposable personal income, for the data are available only with peacetime and war years intermingled. Separate analyses would be less reliable, because of the scarcity of observations, than a multiple regression analysis treating war as a dummy variable. The procedure for the latter is completely analogous to the one illustrated for the printing of textbooks. The wartime observations would be separated from peacetime ones by means of a dummy switching variable. This involves fitting a regression plane to the three-dimensional data array, with values for personal consumption expenditure and disposable personal income variables, and with the dummy variable taking the value 0 for peacetime and 1 for wartime years.

Figure 11-6 shows the two projected regression lines obtained from the regression plane using disposable personal income and war to predict personal

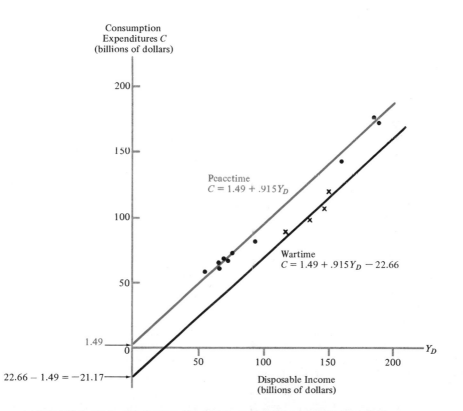

FIGURE 11-6   Illustration of multiple regression with dummy variable: consumption function during wartime and peacetime.

consumption expenditures for the United States, using data from 1935–1949. Because of World War II's dramatic disruptions to personal lives and the economy, there was a significantly different pattern of consumer spending during the 1942–1945 period. This was due to a host of factors, such as rationing and the appropriation of production facilities for military materiel.

The equation for the regression plane is

$$C = 1.49 + .915Y_D - 22.66W$$

where C represents personal consumption expenditures, Y_D is the traditional economists' designation for disposable income (taken here to be an independent variable), and W is a dummy variable ($W = 0$ for peacetime and $W = 1$ for wartime). When $W = 0$, the regression plane becomes the line

$$C = 1.49 + .915Y_D \quad \text{(in peacetime)}$$

which may be interpreted as an estimate of the *aggregate consumption function.* The slope of this line, .915, is the personal consumption expenditure for each dollar increase in disposable income. For the economy as a whole, 91.5 cents from each extra dollar of personal income is estimated to be spent on consumption. In the terminology of economics, .915 is the *marginal propensity to consume.* When $W = 1$, then with $b_2 = -22.66$ the regression line (the consumption function) shifts downward by an amount of 22.66 billion dollars, reflecting a general drop in personal expenditures due to the shortage of many goods formerly purchased by individuals. Notice that this shifted regression line has the same slope, reflecting the fact that the marginal propensity to consume is the same as before.*

If the time series data were expanded to include the 1950s and 1960s, the effect of two other wars, in Korea and Vietnam, would be much less pronounced. These smaller wars were not very disruptive to consumer spending habits, since there were no major shortages or rationing. For this reason, a better fit to the time series could be obtained by treating these later war years like peacetime. (So that perhaps the dummy variable, wartime *rationing*, would then be a better designation.)

EXERCISES

11-8   Six women and four men have taken a test that measures their manual dexterity and patience in using their hands with tiny objects. Each has then gone through a week of intensive training as electronics assemblers, followed by a month at actual assembly, during which their productivity was measured by a relative index having values ranging from 0 to 10 (with 10 for the most productive worker). The results obtained are provided in Table 11-5.

---

* As we have noted, this may not be realistic, but it is a necessary consequence of the linear multiple regression model.

TABLE 11-5

Subject	Productivity Index Y	Test Score X_1	Sex
a	5.2	5.8	F
b	6.0	8.5	M
c	6.5	8.2	F
d	2.0	3.5	F
e	2.7	6.5	M
f	10.0	9.5	F
g	6.4	9.8	M
h	6.6	9.2	M
i	3.5	4.0	F
j	4.0	5.5	F

(a) Plot the data on a scatter diagram, using dots for women and crosses for men.

(b) Using a dummy variable having value $X_2 = 1$ for women and $X_2 = 0$ for men, determine the coefficients for the equation $Y_C = a + b_1 X_1 + b_2 X_2$ of the estimated regression plane. Draw the lines corresponding to $X_2 = 0$ and $X_2 = 1$ on your scatter diagram.

(c) State in words the meaning of the partial regression coefficients.

(d) Determine the estimated regression line obtained when the sex of the subjects is ignored, and plot it on your scatter diagram.

11-9 The data in Table 11-6 provide personal savings and personal income (in billions of dollars) for the time period 1935–1949.

(a) Plot the data as a scatter diagram showing peacetime years with dots and wartime years with crosses.

TABLE 11-6

Year	Personal Savings Y	Personal Income X_1	War Year
1935	2	60	
1936	4	69	
1937	4	74	
1938	1	68	
1939	3	73	
1940	4	78	
1941	11	96	
1942	28	123	yes
1943	33	151	yes
1944	37	165	yes
1945	30	171	yes
1946	15	179	
1947	7	191	
1948	13	210	
1949	9	207	

SOURCE: *Economic Report of the President, February 1970.*

(b) Using as values for the dummy variable $X_2 = 0$ for peacetime and $X_2 = 1$ for wartime, determine the estimated regression equation $Y_C = a + b_1 X_1 + b_2 X_2$.

(c) Plot the two lines obtained from this equation corresponding to wartime and peacetime on your scatter diagram.

11-10   Referring to the information contained in Exercise 11-8 and your answers to that exercise, answer the following.

(a) Compute the average test scores separately for the men and the women. Then compute the average productivity index for men and for women.

(b) Based upon these averages, what conclusion can you draw with respect to the average test score results for the sample men as compared to those for the women? Can the same conclusion be drawn for the productivity index?

(c) How do you reconcile your conclusion in part (b) with the interpretation of the partial regression coefficient b_2?

11-5   MULTIPLE CORRELATION

Sample Coefficient of Multiple Determination

The concept of correlation may be extended to multiple variables. As with the simple linear relationships discussed earlier in this chapter, we will begin by describing the *sample coefficient of multiple determination* as an index of association. When the multiple regression involves only two independent variables, X_1 and X_2, this is denoted symbolically by $R_{Y.12}^2$ and represents the ratio of variation in Y explained by the regression plane to the total variation:

$$R_{Y.12}^2 = \frac{\text{Explained variation}}{\text{Total variation}} = 1 - \frac{\sum(Y-Y_C)^2}{\sum(Y-\bar{Y})^2} \qquad (11\text{-}10)$$

The *sample multiple correlation coefficient* is defined to be the square root of the coefficient of multiple determination, $R_{Y.12} = \sqrt{R_{Y.12}^2}$. The sign of $R_{Y.12}$ is always considered positive.

A shorter, equivalent version of expression (11-10) is used* to calculate the *sample coefficient of multiple determination:*

$$R_{Y.12}^2 = 1 - \frac{s_{Y.12}^2}{s_Y^2}\left(\frac{n-m}{n-1}\right) \qquad (11\text{-}11)$$

As before, m represents the number of variables used, and here $m = 3$.

To illustrate this computation we again use the results found earlier for

---

* $R_{Y.12}^2$ is said to be unadjusted for degrees of freedom. The adjusted coefficient of multiple determination may be derived from

$$R_{aY.12}^2 = 1 - \frac{S_{Y.12}^2}{s_Y^2}$$

For large n, $R_{aY.12}^2$ is nearly the same as $R_{Y.12}^2$.

the multiple regression for store profit Y when food sales X_1 and non-food sales X_2 are the only independent variables. The standard deviation in sample profit is

$$s_Y = \sqrt{\frac{\sum Y^2 - n\bar{Y}^2}{n-1}} = \sqrt{\frac{4{,}267 - 10(19.1)^2}{9}} = 8.293 \text{ thousand dollars}$$

From before we have $S_{Y \cdot 12} = 4.343$. Substituting these values into expression (11-11), we have

$$R^2_{Y \cdot 12} = 1 - \frac{(4.343)^2}{(8.293)^2}\left(\frac{10-3}{10-1}\right) = .787$$

The interpretation of $R^2_{Y \cdot 12} = .787$ is that an estimated 78.7 percent of the total variation in Y may be explained by knowledge of the regression plane and the values for X_1 and X_2. Only $100 - 78.7 = 21.3$ percent of the variation in Y is estimated due to other causes, such as chance, plus other factors not explicitly considered—for example, store size, location, and advertising.

When the supermarket data were expanded to include an additional independent variable for store size, X_3, the estimated regression equation was recalculated to be $Y_C = -10.170 + .027X_1 + .097X_2 + .525X_3$. As noted earlier, the standard error of the estimate for Y about this higher-dimensional regression hyperplane was significantly smaller than when store size was ignored. This indicates that, in this case, more of the total variation in Y may be explained by raising the number of regression variables. To see by how much the total variation in Y explained by regression has risen, we obtain the coefficient of multiple determination when X_3 is included in the analysis. The computer printout in Figure 11-3 provides the value $R_{Y \cdot 123} = .9924$. Squaring this, we have

$$R^2_{Y \cdot 123} = \frac{\text{Explained Variation}}{\text{Total Variation}} = (.9924)^2 = .985$$

Thus the total variation in Y explainable by regression increases from 78.7 percent to 98.5 percent when store size X_3 is included as an additional independent variable. This further illustrates that expanding regression analysis to include more variables may increase the reliability of predictions.

We now consider a set of indices helpful in determining whether or not it is worthwhile to include additional variables in the regression analysis.

Partial Correlation

Let's begin by comparing the results of a simple regression analysis relating store profit Y to food sales X_1 alone. As we have seen, the equation for the estimated regression line is

$$\bar{Y}_{X_1} = 3.891 + .0670X_1$$

and the simple coefficient of determination is $r_{Y1}^2 = (.760)^2 = .578$. Suppose we now incorporate non-food sales X_2 as a second independent variable. We have seen that better predictions for Y will result from doing this. To quantify the improvement achieved with a higher-dimensional regression analysis, we can calculate the proportional reduction in previously unexplained variation. This provides a further index of asosciation, $r_{Y2 \cdot 1}^2$, called the *coefficient of partial determination*, that measures the correlation between Y and X_2 while the other independent variable X_1 is still considered but held constant. The subscript $Y2 \cdot 1$ indicates this. The coefficient is calculated from

$$r_{Y2 \cdot 1}^2 = \frac{\text{Reduction in unexplained variation}}{\text{Previously unexplained variation}} = \frac{R_{Y \cdot 12}^2 - r_{Y1}^2}{1 - r_{Y1}^2} \qquad (11\text{-}12)$$

Substituting the values found earlier into expression (11-12) gives us

$$r_{Y2 \cdot 1}^2 = \frac{.787 - .578}{1 - .578} = .495$$

The difference, $R_{Y \cdot 12}^2 - r_{Y1}^2$, represents the reduction in unexplained variation (which is also the increase in explained variation). The value $r_{Y2 \cdot 1}^2 = .495$ tells us that 49.5 percent of the variation in store profit Y that was left unexplained by a simple regression with food sales X_1 alone can be explained by the regression obtained from including non-food sales X_2.

In multiple regression analysis, the coefficient of partial determination or its square root, the *partial correlation coefficient*, provides an index of the correlation between two variables *after* the effects of all the other variables have been considered. Thus, the value .495 expresses the net association between store profit Y and non-food sales X_2 while food sales X_1 are held constant but are still accounted for.

The value $r_{Y2 \cdot 1}^2 = .495$ may be compared to the *simple* coefficient of determination between Y and X_2, $r_{Y2}^2 = (-.286)^2 = .082$. The former provides a truer impact of including X_2 in the multiple regression analysis than would be indicated by a simple correlation analysis using only X_2. When evaluating the potential merits of a predictor variable, the coefficients of partial determination (or the partial correlation coefficients) are sometimes employed in, determining which independent variables to include (a superior method to using the simple counterpart coefficient). We can illustrate how the coefficient of partial determination may be used to do this.

In discussing a third independent variable X_3 (size of store), a multiple regression was run on the computer. The coefficient of partial determination may be found from

$$r_{Y3 \cdot 12}^2 = \frac{\text{Reduction in unexplained variation}}{\text{Previously unexplained variation}} = \frac{R_{Y \cdot 123}^2 - R_{Y \cdot 12}^2}{1 - R_{Y \cdot 12}^2} \qquad (11\text{-}13)$$

Substituting the coefficients of multiple determination obtained from the previous two multiple regressions using the supermarket data, we have

$$r_{Y3 \cdot 12}^2 = \frac{.985 - .787}{1 - .787} = .930$$

Thus, $r_{Y3 \cdot 12}^2 = .930$ tells us that there is a 93.0 percent reduction in previously unexplained variation by including X_3. This additional variable has been quite effective in increasing the sharpness of the multiple regression analysis.

Table 11-7 shows how the amount of variation in Y explainable by regression has increased through successive inclusions of additional variables. Note how the variation in Y is reduced from $s_Y = 8.293$ that was obtained when no regression was performed. Variation is expressed by the successive standard errors of the estimates of Y about the respective regression surfaces (line, plane, and hyperplane) shown in column (3). Paralleling the declining standard errors are increases in the proportion of variation explained by regression, shown in column (4). Column (5) shows the proportional reduction in previously unexplained variation in Y resulting from the additional variable.

The total explainable variations in Y will not always be increased by including additional variables. It is not always obvious that an additional factor will sharpen rather than cloud the predictive powers of regression analysis. Good common sense must be exercised in selecting variables for which there is a meaningful nonstatistical explanation of their influence on the dependent variable. Sales is one factor used to calculate profit, so that it has a logical connection. Likewise, a larger store requires a greater investment in facilities and

TABLE 11-7 Summary of How Successively Higher-Dimensional Regression Equations Have Increased the Explained Variation in Y When Additional Variables are Included in Supermarket Illustration

(1) Independent Variables Included	(2) Additional Variable	(3) Standard Error of Estimate (thousands of dollars)	(4) Proportion of Variation Explained	(5) Proportional Reduction in Previously Unexplained Variation
none	—	$s_Y = 8.293$	0.000	—
X_1	X_1	$s_{Y \cdot X1} = 5.719$	$r_{Y1}^2 = .578$[a]	$\dfrac{.578 - 0}{1 - 0} = .578 = r_{Y1}^2$
X_1, X_2	X_2	$s_{Y \cdot 12} = 4.343$	$R_{Y \cdot 12}^2 = .787$	$\dfrac{.787 - .578}{1 - .578} = .495 = r_{Y2 \cdot 1}^2$
X_1, X_2, X_3	X_3	$s_{Y \cdot 123} = 1.250$	$R_{Y \cdot 123}^2 = .985$	$\dfrac{.985 - .787}{1 - .787} = .930 = r_{Y3 \cdot 12}^2$

[a] This value is the simple coefficient of determination calculated for the regression line $\bar{Y}_{X_1} = 3.891 + .0670 X_1$.

may be operated more efficiently than a smaller one, so that store size can be reasoned to have a direct relation to profits.

EXERCISES

11-11 The following intermediate calculations have been made by an economist using sample data relating annual family spending Y to income X_1, family size X_2, and annual savings X_3. A sample of size $n = 100$ was used, and all monetary figures are in thousands of dollars.

$$\bar{Y} = 10 \qquad \bar{X}_1 = 12 \qquad \bar{X}_2 = 5 \qquad \bar{X}_3 = 1$$

$$\sum Y^2 = 11{,}400 \qquad \sum X_1 Y = 13{,}000 \qquad \sum X_2 Y = 6{,}000 \qquad \sum X_3 Y = 500$$

Plane A: $Y_C = 1.7 + .4X_1 + .7X_2$ (using only X_1 and X_2)

Plane B: $Y_C = 4.3 + .3X_1 + .6X_2 - .9X_3$ (using X_1, X_2, and X_3)

(a) Calculate $S_{Y.12}$ and $R^2_{Y.12}$. What percentage of the variation in Y may be explained by the regression plane A?

(b) Suppose that $S_{Y.123} = .722$ and $R^2_{Y.123} = .964$. What percentage of the variation in Y may be explained by the regression hyperplane B?

(c) Has the standard error of the estimate for Y been reduced by the inclusion of X_3 in the regression analysis?

(d) Determine the proportions of unexplained variation in Y by using the regression equations for planes A and B. What proportional change in previously unexplained variation is achieved by adding X_3 to the analysis? Does this increase or reduce the unexplained variation?

11-12 Suppose that the economist in Exercise 11-11 has determined for *another sample* that the simple coefficient of determination between Y and X_1 is .50 and that between Y and X_2 it is .60. He has also found the coefficient of multiple determination to be .75, considering only X_1 and X_2.

(a) Calculate the coefficients of partial determination $r^2_{Y1.2}$ and $r^2_{Y2.1}$.

(b) State the meaning of the values you obtained in (a).

(c) Compare the values in (a) to their respective simple coefficients of determination. Why may the corresponding values differ?

11-13 A wholesale distributor of business forms has developed three predictors of sales Y (in thousands of dollars) achieved by its representatives in the field. For each salesperson, X_1 represents the score on a sales aptitude test, X_2 the score on a motivation test, and X_3 the total years of sales experience. The following intermediate calculations have been obtained for sample data representing $n = 30$ salespersons.

$$\bar{Y} = 50 \qquad \bar{X}_1 = 10 \qquad \bar{X}_2 = 5 \qquad \bar{X}_3 = 5$$

$$\sum Y^2 = 80{,}600 \qquad \sum X_1 Y = 16{,}000 \qquad \sum X_2 Y = 8{,}500 \qquad \sum X_3 Y = 8{,}100$$

Plane A: $Y_C = 10 + 3X_1 + 2X_2$ (excluding X_3)

Plane B: $Y_C = 5 + 2X_1 + 1X_2 + 4X_3$ (including X_3)

(a) Calculate $S_{Y.12}$ and $R^2_{Y.12}$. What percentage of the variation in Y may be explained by the regression plane A?

(b) $R^2_{Y.123} = .964$. What percentage of the variation in Y may be explained by the regression hyperplane B?

    (c) Calculate the partial coefficient of determination for adding X_3 to the analysis. What is the percentage reduction in previously unexplained variation from adding X_3 to the analysis?

    (d) Do you believe that years of sales experience ought to be included in predictions of sales performance? Why?

1-6 THE ROLE OF THE COMPUTER IN MULTIVARIATE ANALYSIS

The digital computer can play a significant role in multivariate analysis. Unlike many statistical applications where it serves only to save hand calculations, the computer can facilitate analysis itself when several variables are involved. We discuss two applications of computers that considerably increase analytical capacity. One of these extends multiple regression and correlation; the other may be used as a substitute for the methods in this chapter.

Stepwise Multiple Regression

Modern data centers have computer programs in their libraries that can be used to handle a variety of statistical problems. One group of such programs is used to perform *stepwise multiple regression,* which includes additional predictor variables one at a time, in successive stages, each raising the dimensions of the analysis by one. A great many independent variables can be handled on the computer using this procedure. One such program selects the most promising independent variable—the one that provides the greatest reduction in the unexplained variation in Y—at each stage. In doing this, the computer performs simple regression separately for each independent variable, printing the results for the best one. The next step of the program performs separate multiple regressions, each combining one of the remaining independent variables with those selected in the previous stages. Again, the one that reduces unexplained variation the most is chosen to be included in all future stages. The process continues in successively higher dimensions either until every variable has been included in a multiple regression involving them all, or until no further reduction in the unexplained variation is possible. Such a program efficiently saves all previous calculations necessary for the higher-dimensional analysis.

The output from such a program can be rich—providing at each step the various multiple and partial coefficients of determination. In addition, it may provide simple correlations for all variable pairs.

Many assumptions concerning the linearity of the data are automatically made by such computer programs. As with any other application, in multivariate analysis the computer does not eliminate the need for good judgment. It is best used in intermediate stages of the analysis. Computer printouts must be thoroughly evaluated to determine if there is a meaningful explanation of why some variables are excluded and others are included. A variable may be rejected because it does not reduce the unexplained variance that is actually due to a strong curvilinear relation between the variable and Y.

The use of a digital computer may be extended to consider curvilinear multiple regression. This involves even longer computations than the linear case considered in this chapter. The most complex of multivariate techniques are well suited to the digital computer.

Automatic Interaction Detector

Some analysts feel that the assumptions of regression analysis are so overpowering that its usefulness is severely limited in practical applications. As the number of variables considered grows, so does the propensity for these assumptions to be violated. One technique especially amenable to the digital computer avoids most of the restrictions of regression and correlation analysis. Automatic Interaction Detector (AID) is a computer program developed at the University of Michigan* that has been used to predict a dependent variable such as annual earnings Y by considering a host of independent demographic variables. The procedure is very useful for surveys commonly encountered in marketing research.

The program separates the population into homogeneous groups, by successively subdividing the sample observations. At various stages the data are split according to the values of a particular independent variable, such as education level. This splitting reduces the total unexplained variation in the income level by the greatest possible amount. For example, high school graduates may earn substantially more than those who have not completed their education. If wage earners are separated into two groups based upon education level, the unexplained variation in Y in either group may be considerably less than the total before the split. Each group is thereafter treated separately, being further split, perhaps on the basis of different independent variables that provide the maximum further reduction in unexplained variation. Thus, the high school graduates may be further split according to additional levels of education, while the incomes of nongraduates, which may differ most because of their racial background, would be split in accordance with this qualitative variable.

Figure 11-7 demonstrates how a sample might be successively split into groups. The independent variable and its value chosen for a split is that which can explain the most variation in Y. Splitting is continued either until a group contains too few observations or until no further reduction in the unexplained variation of Y is possible. The 10 groups at the terminal positions of the tree represents the final subdivision of the sample. Predictions of an individual's annual earnings may be made by first identifying which of these 10 groupings he or she belongs to. The estimate of Y is taken to be the sample mean, $\bar{Y}$, of

* For a detailed description see John A. Sonquist and James N. Morgan, *The Detection of Interaction Effects*, Survey Research Center, University of Michigan, 1964.

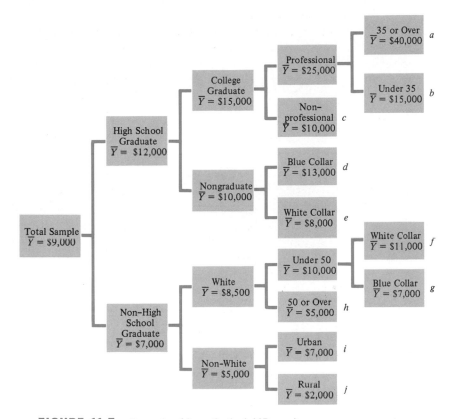

FIGURE 11-7   Example of hypothetical AID results.

that group. For example, a person in group *e* would be a high school graduate who did not finish college and is a white collar worker. The mean earnings of sample individuals falling into this category is $\bar{Y} = \$8,000$; this is the "best" estimate of the annual earnings for any member of the population having the same characteristics.

The main advantages of a computer program like AID are that (1) absolutely no assumptions need to be made about the distribution of Y about some regression surface and (2) there is no concern as to whether the linear model is really appropriate. Each sample grouping may be considered as randomly chosen from the corresponding population. Thus, statistical inferences may be made about the respective population means using the techniques of Chapters 8 and 9.

Chapter Twelve
Time Series Analysis and Forecasting

Some people hate the very name of statistics, but I find them full of beauty and interest. Whenever they are not brutalized, but delicately handled by the higher methods, and are warily interpreted, their power in dealing with complicated phenomena is extraordinary. They are the only tools by which an opening can be cut through the formidable thicket of difficulties that bars the path of those who pursue the Science of man.

Sir Francis Galton (1889)

Every successful business and organization must plan for the future. Quite a dazzling array of statistical tools are available to facilitate this task. In this chapter we focus upon statistical methodology that can transform past experience into forecasts of future events. Thus, a government economist can forecast annual personal income five years into the future by projecting from the trend indicated by the levels of personal income in previous years, and use this information to predict future tax revenue. An electric company can decide that the demand for power will grow at a rate similar to that which has prevailed during the previous decade in order to project its generating capacity requirements five, ten, or twenty years into the future. A department store buyer can use past experience to decide when to make purchases and in what quantities. In each case, values of the variable being predicted are available for several past periods of time. Such data are called *time series*. Statistical procedures that use such values are called *time series analysis*.

2-1   THE TIME SERIES AND ITS COMPONENTS

Time series are best described in terms of a graph like the one shown in Figure 12-1, in which the gross national product (GNP) of the United States is plotted against time for the period 1929 to 1975. The graph shows that the GNP has grown over the years, but that this growth has been erratic, being faster in some years than others. Wide swings are evident, the GNP declining during the

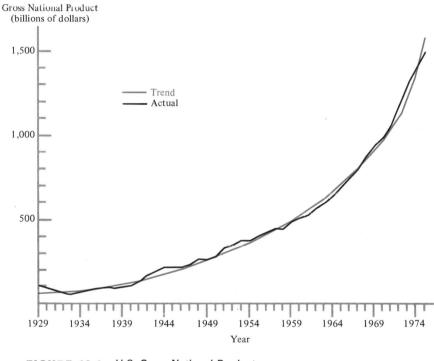

FIGURE 12-1   U.S. Gross National Product
(SOURCE: *Economic Report of the President,* 1970, 1976).

Great Depression of the 1930s and then rising rapidly with the advent of World War II. One goal of time series analysis is to identify the swings and fluctuations of a time series and sort them into various categories. This is done through arithmetic manipulation of the numerical values obtained.

Several models may be used to characterize time series. The classical model

used by economists provides the clearest explanation of the following four time series components of variation and how they relate to each other:

1. Secular trend (T_t)
2. Cyclical movement (C_t)
3. Seasonal fluctuation (S_t)
4. Irregular variation (I_t)

With calendar time as the independent variable, these components are related to a dependent variable by mathematical equations. The dependent variable is denoted by the symbol Y_t, where the subscript refers to a period of time. Examples of Y_t are annual sales, number of passenger-miles flown by domestic airlines, and acre-feet of water supplied to a city.

Secular trend is defined as the long-range general movement in Y_t over an extended period of time. Thus, the world's human population has experienced a long upward trend since men and women first appeared on this planet. Airline passenger-miles flown has experienced a similar upward trend over a much shorter duration. Some variables have experienced a downward trend, declining over time. Paralleling the rise in air traffic has been a general pronounced reduction in the number of railroad passengers in the United States in the past thirty years. In this chapter we will develop methods for isolating trend from other variational components in a time series. This is done by means of a *trend curve*, such as that shown for GNP in Figure 12-1. Here, trend is conveniently summarized by a smooth curve about which the actual time series winds in an erratic fashion. This curve expresses the general long-term movement in GNP over time. The short-term, less regular movement may be explained in terms of the other time series components.

Cyclical movement in time series data is characterized by wide swings—usually of a year or more in duration—upward or downward from the secular trend. These are temporary in nature. Such movement is ordinarily typified by alternating periods of economic expansion and contraction or recession. Cyclical movement often accompanies external distortions to an economy brought about by anomalous events such as a war. The cyclical component of time series variation is the most difficult to analyze, since the cycles vary in length and intensity. Each is caused by a host of factors, which may differ in their effect from one cycle to the next, and there is usually some controversy over which causes are most significant.

Seasonal fluctuation is a generally recurring upward and downward pattern of movement in Y_t, usually on an annual basis. A classic example of seasonal fluctuation is the household consumption of fossil fuels, such as oils, coal, or natural gas. Because of heating requirements in the winter, consumption is higher in December through March than in any other period throughout the year. Less obvious seasonal influences are felt in the demand for practically all goods and services. Department store sales fluctuate widely throughout the year, peaking in the weeks prior to Christmas and falling considerably in January and February.

Irregular variations are among the most perplexing ones encountered in time series. These are characterized by events that are completely unpredictable and sometimes are referred to as random factors. Such causes of variation are distinguished, by their irregularity, from the trend, cyclical and seasonal, components, which are collectively referred to as *systematic influences*. The list of important random factors includes wars, strikes, election results, and presidential assassinations. Unpredictable events can precipitate, accentuate, or terminate a time series' cyclical movement. Because of the problems of separating long-term cyclical movement from random causes, short-term random factors are ordinarily the only ones included in the irregular category. All time series variations that cannot be explained by secular trend, cyclical movement, or seasonal fluctuation are identified as irregular.

12-2   THE CLASSICAL TIME SERIES MODEL

The classical time series model, originally used by economists, combines the four components by an equation of the form

$$Y_t = T_t \times C_t \times S_t \times I_t \tag{12-1}$$

This says that there are factors associated with each component that can be multiplied together to provide the value of the dependent variable. Another version of the classical time series model assumes that the components are additive. There is no substantial difference between the two models, so we will focus on the *multiplicative model*, which provides more convenient explanations.*

We may explain this model by means of a hypothetical time series, the sales Y_t of stereo speakers. We will construct this time series starting with the trend component T_t, shown in Figure 12-2 as a straight line relating sales to time period. Each successive quarter raises the level of sales by .2 million. Thus, with initial sales of 1 million units, by the summer of 1976, 10 periods later, these have grown to $1 + .2(10) = 3$ million units. In the absence of all other influences, this graph provides the time series

$$Y_t = T_t \qquad \text{(ignoring other components)}$$

Now consider the influence of cyclical movement upon the series that produces sales temporarily above the trend in good years, or below it in lean years. For convenience, we express the cyclical effect as a proportion of trend, shown in Figure 12-3(a). This curve, called a sine wave, yields regular oscillatory movement in C_t over time. Each cycle has an eight-quarter duration, with a

---

* By taking the log of both sides of the multiplicative model in expression (12-1), we obtain $\log(Y_t) = \log(T_t) + \log(C_t) + \log(S_t) + \log(I_t)$. The series $\log(Y_t)$ may be treated as an additive model with components $\log(T_t)$ for trend, $\log(C_t)$ for cyclical movement, etc.

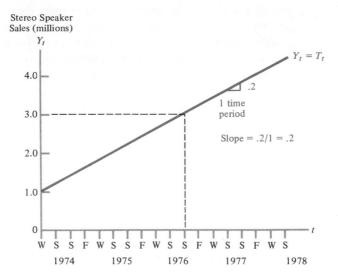

FIGURE 12-2   Trend line for hypothetical sales of stereo speakers.

peak or trough every other summer. Although C_t may be expressed as a proportion of trend, it is convenient to express it in terms of a percentage. The average value of C_t throughout an entire cycle is taken as 100 percent. In the summer of 1976, the value of C_t is 150 percent, indicating that sales are 50 percent above the trend during that quarter.

The trend for the summer of 1976 is $T_t = 3.0$, so that by including cyclical movement we have:

$$Y_t = T_t \times C_t \qquad \text{(ignoring seasonal and irregular components)}$$

$$= 3.0 \times \frac{150}{100} = 4.5 \text{ (million speakers)}$$

The time series for speaker sales with this added component is graphed in Figure 12-3(b), where the curve for C_t has been superimposed upon the trend line.

The seasonal fluctuations in stereo speaker sales may be handled in the same manner as cyclical movement. We may view these as short-term swings about the longer term sales level indicated by the combined trend and cyclical components. Sales will lie above this level during the busy season and below it during slack times. Thus we can view S_t as a proportion of long-term sales level established by T_t and C_t, again conveniently expressed as a percentage.

The values of S_t, referred to as *seasonal indexes*, are shown in Figure 12-4. The values are 80 percent for the winter quarter, 110 percent for the spring quarter, 60 percent for the summer quarter, and 150 percent for the fall. These sum to 400 percent, the number of quarterly periods in a year times 100 percent, so that they average 100 percent for a complete year. For the summer of 1976,

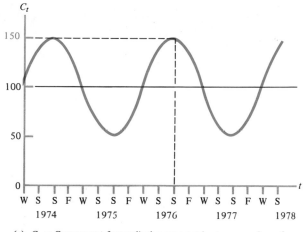

(a) C_t = Component for cyclical movement in stereo speaker sales
(percentage of trend)

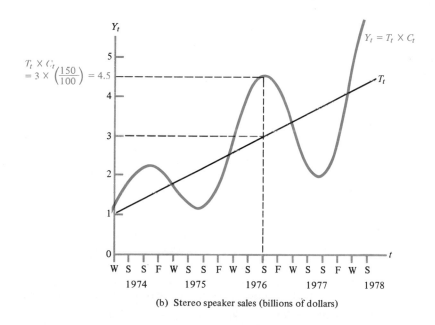

(b) Stereo speaker sales (billions of dollars)

FIGURE 12-3   Cyclical movement component for stereo speaker hypothetical
sales and time series showing only trend and cyclical components.

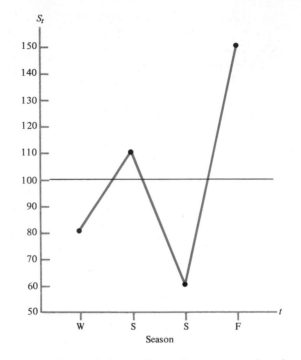

FIGURE 12-4 Seasonal fluctuations of stereo speaker hypothetical sales. S_t = Seasonal index of fluctuation about the long-term sales level expressed as a percentage of $T_t \times C_t$.

an "off" season, we must adjust downward the 4.5 million sales figure found previously. Since the seasonal index for summer is $S_t = 60$ percent, indicating that sales are only 60 percent of "normal" in this period, the sales figure obtained for the summer of 1976 by including seasonal fluctuation is:

$$Y_t = T_t \times C_t \times S_t \qquad \text{(ignoring irregular component)}$$

$$= 3.0 \times \left(\frac{150}{100}\right) \times \left(\frac{60}{100}\right) = 2.7 \text{ (million speakers)}$$

The time series obtained by superimposing the seasonal fluctuations upon longer term sales is shown in Figure 12-5.

The irregular component of variation in speaker sales remains to be considered. As with C_t and S_t, we represent this by a percentage I_t. Viewing all irregular movement as short term in nature, we may consider I_t as the factor coming last, raising or lowering sales from the level established by the regular pattern of the systematic factors already considered. The values used to construct the graph for I_t shown in Figure 12-6 have been obtained from a random number table representing values selected from a normal population, so that the long-run average value of I_t is 100 percent. A standard deviation of 2 percent is assumed.

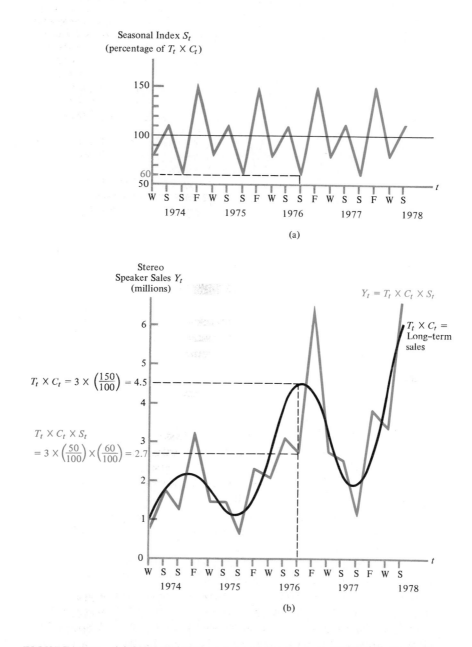

FIGURE 12-5   (a) Seasonal index component for stereo speaker hypothetical sales and (b) time series showing only trend, cyclical, and seasonal components.

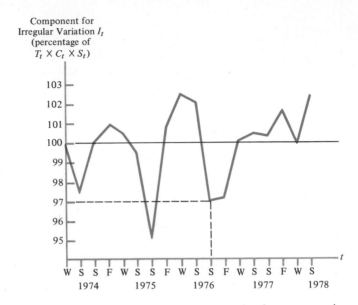

Component for
Irregular Variation I_t
(percentage of
$T_t \times C_t \times S_t$)

FIGURE 12-6   Component of irregular fluctuation for stereo speaker
hypothetical sales.

For the summer of 1976, the value obtained for I_t is 97 percent. This indicates that some unpredictable circumstances, such as several good musical summer television "replacements," have perhaps caused people to be less than ordinarily interested in stereo speakers, reducing sales to a level of only 97 percent of what would be "normal" according to the systematic time series components. Thus, we further adjust stereo speaker sales considering all time series elements:

$$Y_t = T_t \times C_t \times S_t \times I_t$$

$$= 3.0 \times \left(\frac{150}{100}\right) \times \left(\frac{60}{100}\right) \times \left(\frac{97}{100}\right)$$

$$= 2.619 \text{ (million speakers)}$$

The irregular variations may be superimposed upon the curve previously obtained using all the other components, providing a complete hypothetical time series for stereo speaker sales. The variational influence of each component is summarized in Figure 12-7, where the final time series is obtained.

We have illustrated how a hypothetical time series may be synthesized from the assumed characteristics of the four components. In actual applications, we may not know any of these features, and usually we must start with the raw time series data, reversing the procedures by shifting the data to sort out and identify the components. This chapter will discuss some of the procedures used for doing this.

The classical time series model has limitations. The multiplicative relationship among trend, cyclical, seasonal, and irregular components has been

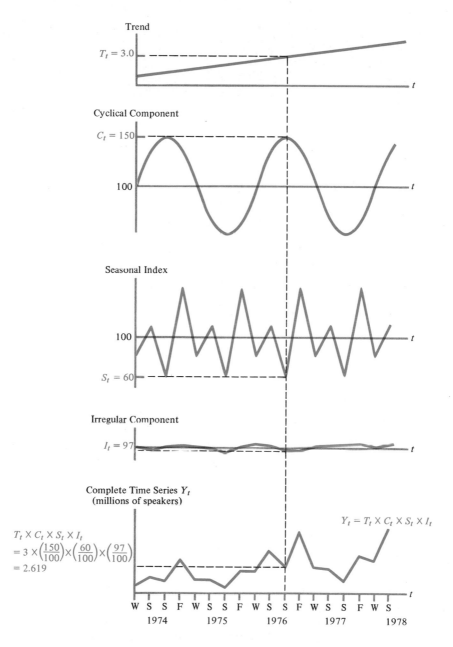

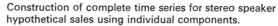

FIGURE 12-7   Construction of complete time series for stereo speaker hypothetical sales using individual components.

criticized as being oversimplified and unrealistic. A large number of possible relationships other than multiplicative could exist among T_t, C_t, S_t, and I_t, and some of these may be more appropriate. Other models use more factors; for example, Y_t is sometimes assumed to also depend upon Y_{t-1}, the value from the preceding time period. As we shall see, several different techniques are available for isolating the components themselves, so that for a specific time series the classical model yields no unique solution. In spite of these difficulties, the model is easy to understand and to explain and can provide a basis for useful time series analysis.

More sophisticated time series models have been developed. The field of *econometrics*, which employs specialized statistical tools to explain and predict economic activity, embodies techniques for analyzing time series data. An especially powerful tool uses variables from several different times series to predict values of other variables of interest. To do this, variables called leading indicators, which have historically moved upward or downward ahead of the time series being analyzed, are identified and combined mathematically. The general level of economic activity in a future time period may be predicted by a relationship between such leading indicators as business inventories, housing starts, and new durable goods orders.

Other models explain time series movement in terms of its past behavior only, without isolating seasonal and cyclical components. One technique for doing this is *exponential smoothing*, which involves the averaging of past data, giving greater weight to current values. Another approach, called spectral analysis, describes a time series mathematically in terms of periodic functions such as sine and cosine.

The mathematics necessary to describe these more advanced techniques is beyond the scope of this book. The remainder of this chapter is restricted largely to procedures developed around the classical model.

EXERCISES

12-1 Higbee Mills has projected that sales for 19X2 will grow by $100,000 per quarter. Assuming that sales during the fall quarter of 19X1 are $1,000,000, determine the trend sales levels for the winter, spring, summer, and fall quarters of 19X2.

12-2 Bixbee Mills had sales of $1,000,000 in the fall of 19X1. The trend indicates that sales are growing at a compound rate of 9 percent per quarter. Determine the trend levels for the winter, spring, summer, and fall quarters of 19X2.

12-3 The Variety Galore Store wishes to forecast its sales for the next calendar year. The following components have been determined by its accountant:

Quarter t	Trend T_t	Cyclical Component C_t	Seasonal Index S_t
Winter	$100,000	90	80
Spring	110,000	110	70
Summer	121,000	100	100
Fall	133,100	90	150

Determine the forecasts of sales Y_t for each quarter.

12-4   The sales data for Humpty Dumpty Toys, Inc. have been analyzed, and the trend, cyclical, seasonal, and irregular components have been determined for the preceding four quarters' operations. Find the missing values in the table below, assuming that the time series components are multiplicative.

Quarter *t*	Trend T_t	Cyclical Component (*percentage*) C_t	Seasonal Index (*percentage*) S_t	Irregular Component (*percentage*) I_t	Sales Y_t
Winter	$1,000,000	107	50	101	
Spring	1,100,000	105	70		$820,000
Summer	1,200,000	105		98	987,840
Fall	1,300,000		200	97	2,622,880

2-3   ANALYSIS OF SECULAR TREND

The trend component of a time series is perhaps the most valuable one in making forecasts using time series data. Trend analysis focuses upon finding an appropriate trend line that summarizes the movement of the series over an extended period of time. As we have seen, a trend line often takes the form of a curve. In this section several approaches for determining trend are investigated. All of these involve treating the historical data points like a scatter diagram, which we first encountered in conjunction with regression analysis in Chapter 10. The objective of trend analysis is similar to that of regression: to find a trend curve that summarizes the historical scatter of the dependent variable Y_t over time. Either of two general approaches may be taken in fitting the data. In this chapter we will discuss modification of regression techniques to isolate the trend element. Another approach is to obtain a trend curve through judgment alone, so that a curve is sketched through the data by hand. This may be adequate and as valid as finding the trend by using statistical procedures, but little can be said about a freehand procedure. As in regression analysis, two persons can be expected to arrive at different trend curves unless they use the same statistical procedure.

The regression techniques discussed in Chapter 10 are severely limited when applied to time series data. Most of the assumptions, such as independence, normality, and constant variance, are usually not relevant to time series data. Thus it is impossible to attach a measure of statistical confidence to a prediction made from a trend line. This should be evident because a forecast must deal with the future, using the past only as a guide. There are no assurances that future influences on the time series will operate like those in the past. Furthermore, a prediction using a trend curve is a projection beyond the range of observations (there are no future data points), so that forecasting with the time series is subject to the major difficulty of extrapolation usually avoided in regression analysis.

Describing Trend

In the hypothetical time series for stereo speaker demand discussed in the last section, secular trend was represented by a straight line. A straight-line trend assumes that Y_t changes at a constant rate. An increasing series will thus have a positively sloping trend line, while a declining one will be represented by a line with a negative slope.

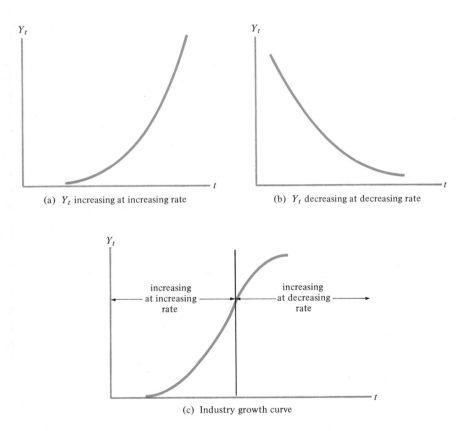

(a) Y_t increasing at increasing rate

(b) Y_t decreasing at decreasing rate

(c) Industry growth curve

FIGURE 12-8   Shapes of commonly encountered trend curves.

Most time series do not involve long-term behavior that changes constantly over time. In business or economic situations a variable will usually increase or decline at a rate that itself changes from period to period. Some basic shapes for nonlinear trend curves frequently encountered are provided in Figure 12-8. For example, consider the movement in GNP levels over a prolonged period. The GNP for the United States has increased by more in the recent past than it did following World War II, so that the trend is represented best by a curve with increasing and positive slope as in diagram (a). In absolute terms, the American GNP has been increasing in recent times at an increasing rate.*

Diagram (b) shows the trend for a time series that decreases at a decreasing rate. The level of activity for a declining industry may sometimes be represented by such a curve. The decline is initially dramatic but becomes more gradual with time. An example of such a trend is the number of railroad passengers carried in the United States each year during the 1950s and 1960s.

The long-range growth of a firm or an industry may sometimes be explained in terms of a trend having the shape in Figure 12-8(c). Here, output increases at an increasing rate when innovative products are brought onto the market to satisfy emerging needs. As the industry matures, rapid growth is replaced by a period of gradual increases; product sales still increase, but at a decreasing rate. Ultimately, sales peak and a period of stagnation begins. Such S-shaped curves are therefore called *growth curves*. Two growth curves frequently encountered in statistics are the logistic and the Gompertz.

The particular shape to portray the trend of a specific time series is selected partly by studying the scatter of the data on a graph. The choice should be a basic shape that not only seems to closely fit the historical data but also coincides with good judgment about how it should be related to future data. There are no rules to tell us which shape must be used. Judgment and experience play the dominant role, so that fitting a trend curve to make forecasts is as much an art as a science.

Determining Linear Trend Using Least Squares

Time series covering a small number of years can usually be fitted by a straight line. The usual procedure is to adapt the method of least squares. This involves finding the *regression equation:*

$$\overline{Y}_X = a + bX \tag{12-2}$$

$\overline{Y}_X$ represents computed value for the dependent variable of the time series, in keeping with our previous regression notation. The letter X represents the time period, which serves as the independent variable. We use X instead of t because the task of computing the regression coefficients may be considerably simplified by expressing time relative to some base period. For example, suppose that the time series comprises observations for the years 1974, 1975, 1976, and 1977. Rather than using the four-digit year numbers for X, we can instead let $X = 0$ represent 1974, $X = 1$ stand for 1975, which is one time period later than 1974, and so forth. Thus, the successive values used for X in these four years would be 0, 1, 2, and 3. The values of $\overline{Y}_X$ are used to obtain the corresponding trend values T_t.

---

* The *percentage* rate of *growth* in real GNP has been more or less constant at about 3 percent, even though the absolute rate of increase in GNP has been rising. Percentage growth rate is expressed relative to the current position and works like compound interest paid by a bank. The original savings account balance will increase at an increasing rate, so that the shape in diagram (a) applies over time, even though the percentage rate of interest or growth remains constant.

The regression coefficients a and b are obtained by the method of least squares by solving the normal equations:

$$\sum Y = na + b \sum X$$
$$\sum XY = a \sum X + b \sum XY \tag{12-3}$$

The summations are carried out for successive periods of time. The letters X and Y represent the time periods observed and their associated value for the dependent variable. It may be simpler to obtain a and b from the following equations for the *estimated regression coefficients:*

$$b = \frac{\sum XY - n\bar{X}\bar{Y}}{\sum X^2 - n\bar{X}^2} \tag{12-4}$$

$$a = \bar{Y} - b\bar{X} \tag{12-5}$$

Illustration of Procedure

We illustrate this procedure for the total level of civilian employment in the United States from 1966 through 1975. The time series data are provided in the first two columns of Table 12-1. The results are $b = 1.47$ and $a = 72.95$, so that the trend equation is $\bar{Y}_X = 72.95 + 1.47X$, with $X = 0$ at 1966.

TABLE 12-1 Computations for Fitting Least Squares Line to Employment Data

Year	Year in Transformed Units X	Total Civilian Employment (in millions) Y	XY	X^2
1966	0	72.9	0	0
1967	1	74.4	74.4	1
1968	2	75.9	151.8	4
1969	3	77.9	233.7	9
1970	4	78.6	314.4	16
1971	5	79.1	395.5	25
1972	6	81.7	490.2	36
1973	7	84.4	590.8	49
1974	8	85.9	687.2	64
1975	9	84.8	763.2	81
	45	795.6	3,701.2	285

$$\sum X = 45 \qquad \sum Y = 795.6 \qquad \sum XY = 3{,}701.2 \qquad \sum X^2 = 285$$
$$n = 10 \qquad \bar{X} = 4.5 \qquad \bar{Y} = 79.56$$

$$b = \frac{\sum XY - n\bar{X}\bar{Y}}{\sum X^2 - n\bar{X}^2} = \frac{3{,}701.2 - 10(4.5)(79.56)}{285 - 10(4.5)^2} = 1.47$$

$$a = \bar{Y} - b\bar{X} = 79.56 - 1.47(4.5) = 72.95$$

$$\bar{Y}_x = 72.95 + 1.47X \qquad (X = 0 \text{ at } 1966)$$

SOURCE OF DATA: *Economic Report of the President, 1976.*

This equation indicates that the trend value for 1966 is an employment level of 72.95 million and that Y_t increases by 1.47 million per year. Because we have transformed the calendar years, it is important to indicate the base year: $X = 0$ for 1966. The trend line and time series obtained are plotted in Figure 12-9.

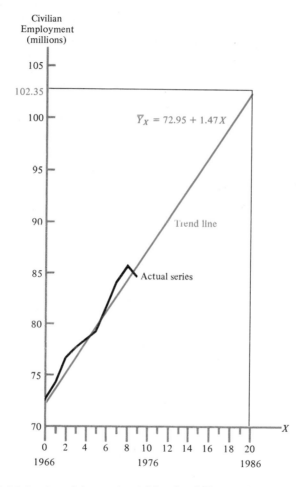

FIGURE 12-9   Actual data and trend line for civilian employment in the United States.

Projecting Trend Line

The trend line may be used to project the level of employment for 1986. We must use $X = 20$, because this year is $X = 1986 - 1966 = 20$ periods beyond the base year. From the trend equation, we project employment for 1986 as:

$$\bar{Y}_X = 72.95 + 1.47(20)$$

$$= 102.35 \text{ (million)}$$

The projected trend line is shown in Figure 12-9 as the dashed portion of the line extending beyond the time periods actually observed. It is emphasized that the estimate of 102.35 is an *extrapolation*; its validity depends upon the assumption that the ensuing 10 years will exhibit growth similar to that existing in the past. The assumption of linearity is perhaps a poor one to use here, for the labor force grows in the same manner as the population, which for the United States has been nonlinear. Had more past years been used, a curve with slope increasing over time would have provided a closer fit to the actual time series data. Even then, good judgment would be an essential element. Ordinarily many more than 10 years are required to determine a basic pattern for trend.

Modifying Trend for Periods Shorter than One Year

Trend values are usually obtained from annual data, to avoid distortions brought about by seasonal and irregular fluctuations. When time series analysis is extended to consider the seasonal and cyclical components, it may be necessary to modify a trend equation to obtain monthly or quarterly values. Consider, for example, the trend line for civilian employment:

$$\overline{Y}_X = 72.95 + 1.47X$$

with X in years and $X = 0$ at the *middle* of 1966. Suppose we wish to obtain monthly trend values. The new values of X will represent the number of months from the base and will be centered at the middle of each month. Thus, we want to have $X = 0$ for January 15, 1966, which is 5.5 months prior to the middle of 1966 (July 1, 1966). Each successive month will increase $\overline{Y}_X$ by one-twelfth the annual increment: $b/12 = 1.47/12 = .1225$. The slope of the new line will be .1225. The intercept a will be reduced by an amount $5.5(.1225) = .67$ (rounded), so that the new Y intercept is $72.95 - .67 = 72.28$. The equation of the modified trend line is

$$\overline{Y}_X = 72.28 + .1225X$$

with X in months and $X = 0$ at January 15, 1966.

The same general approach would apply in getting quarterly trend equations. The slope would be one-fourth as large, and the point $X = 0$ would be shifted to the middle of the winter quarter, February 15, which is 1.5 quarters from the middle of the year. When trend is itself fitted directly to deseasonalized quarterly or monthly data, the trend equation need not be modified.

Nonlinear Trend: Exponential Trend Curve

For many time series a straight line provides a poor fit to the data. A straight line assumes that Y_t increases (or decreases) by a constant amount each year. This assumption is not valid for most time series, where Y_t may change at either an increasing or decreasing rate. Figure 12-10 shows the time series for

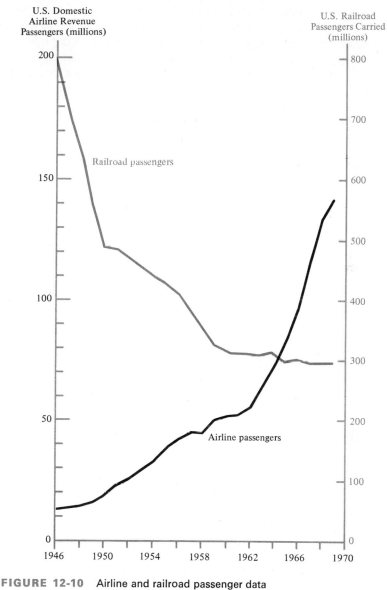

U.S. Domestic
Airline Revenue
Passengers (millions)

U.S. Railroad
Passengers Carried
(millions)

Railroad passengers

Airline passengers

FIGURE 12-10   Airline and railroad passenger data
(SOURCE: *Moody's Transportation Manual,* 1970).

domestic airline fare-paying passengers from 1946 to 1969. Here the number of
passengers has increased at an increasing rate over time. This is contrasted with
the number of railroad passengers carried, also shown, where the trend is
decreasing but at a seemingly decreasing rate.

Part of the rail passenger drop may be explained by a preference for airplane travel and part by wider use of the automobile. Few passenger trains run

over long distances in the United States, and these have been declining so very fast that the government now runs rail passenger service. The leveling-off at around 300 million passengers may be attributed to the growing significance of commuters who now comprise a high proportion of rail passengers.

Either of these time series may be fitted by a J-shaped or exponential curve. For the airline passenger data, the equation would be of the form:

$$\overline{Y}_X = ab^X \qquad (12\text{-}6)$$

where b is a constant (always positive) raised to the power of the number of time periods beyond the base year, and a is a constant multiple. The railroad passenger series has a negative exponential shape, so that the appropriate equation is

$$\overline{Y}_X = ab^{-X} \qquad (12\text{-}7)$$

where the minus sign before the X is used because $\overline{Y}_X$ decreases for increasing X.

The chief advantage of using an exponential curve for fitting a trend is evident when taking the logarithm of both sides of expression (12-6). When an exponential trend curve is converted in this manner, we have the equation for *the logarithmic trend line*:

$$\log \overline{Y}_X = \log a + X \log b \qquad (12\text{-}8)$$

This equation has the form of a straight line using $\log \overline{Y}_X$ for the values on the vertical scale, with intercept of $\log a$ and slope $\log b$.

Figure 12-11(a) shows the graph of the exponential trend curve $\overline{Y}_X = 5(7)^X$, so that $a = 5$ and $b = 7$. Substituting these values into expression (12-8), we have

$$\log \overline{Y}_X = \log 5 + X \log 7$$

$$= .6990 + .8451X$$

The logarithm values are obtained from Appendix Table G. The logarithmic trend line in diagram (b) is drawn with $\log \overline{Y}_X$ as the dependent variable, so that the vertical axis is expressed in log Y units. Both the exponential trend curve and the corresponding logarithmic trend line provide the same information, and values of $\overline{Y}_X$ may be obtained from the value for $\log \overline{Y}_X$, and vice versa.

This suggests the possibility of fitting historical time series data to an exponential trend curve, using the method of least squares to first find the logarithmic trend line. This may be accomplished by taking the logarithm of the observed time series values Y, determining the regression coefficients $\log a$ and $\log b$. For this purpose we modify the earlier equations for a and b, obtaining the *logarithmic regression coefficients*:

$$\log b = \frac{\sum X \log Y - \overline{X} \sum \log Y}{\sum X^2 - n\overline{X}^2}$$

$$\qquad (12\text{-}9)$$

$$\log a = \frac{\sum \log Y}{n} - \overline{X} \log b$$

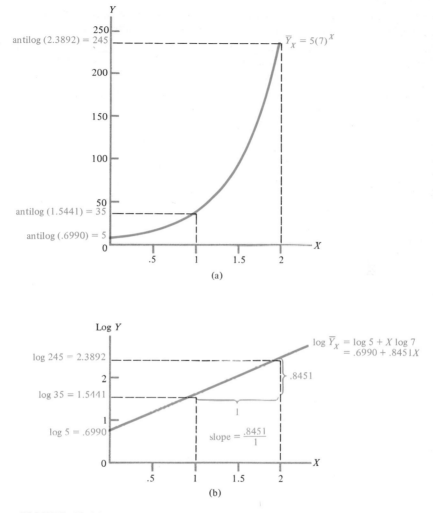

FIGURE 12-11   Graphs of exponential curve and corresponding logarithmic trend line.

These expressions replace a, b, and Y values by log a, log b, and log Y. To avoid possible confusion of symbols, we use the fact that $n\bar{Y} = \sum Y$ and replace $n\bar{Y}$ with $\sum$ log Y.

Illustration of Procedure

The procedure is illustrated by the calculations in Table 12-2 using the airline passenger data. Substituting the appropriate values into expression (12-9), the slope of the logarithmic trend line is

$$\log b = \frac{497.7083 - 11.5(38.7612)}{4,324 - 24(11.5)^2} = .0452$$

$$\log a = (38.7612)/24 - 11.5(.0452) = 1.0953$$

TABLE 12-2 Computations for Fitting Exponential Trend Curve to Data for Number of U.S. Domestic Airline Passengers

Year	Years Beyond Base Period X	Number of Passengers (in millions) Y	log Y	X log Y	X^2
1946	0	12.2	1.0864	0	0
1947	1	12.9	1.1106	1.1106	1
1948	2	13.2	1.1206	2.2412	4
1949	3	15.1	1.1790	3.5370	9
1950	4	17.4	1.2405	4.9620	16
1951	5	22.7	1.3560	6.7800	25
1952	6	25.0	1.3979	8.3874	36
1953	7	28.7	1.4579	10.2053	49
1954	8	32.5	1.5119	12.0952	64
1955	9	38.0	1.5798	14.2182	81
1956	10	41.7	1.6201	16.2010	100
1957	11	44.8	1.6513	18.1643	121
1958	12	44.4	1.6474	19.7688	144
1959	13	50.5	1.7033	22.1429	169
1960	14	51.6	1.7126	23.9764	196
1961	15	52.0	1.7160	25.7400	225
1962	16	55.3	1.7427	27.8832	256
1963	17	63.2	1.8007	30.6119	289
1964	18	72.1	1.8579	33.4422	324
1965	19	83.6	1.9222	36.5218	361
1966	20	97.8	1.9903	39.8060	400
1967	21	118.7	2.0745	43.5645	441
1968	22	134.4	2.1284	46.8248	484
1969	23	142.3	2.1532	49.5236	529
	276	1,270.1	38.7612	497.7083	4,324

$$n = 24 \qquad \sum X = 276 \qquad \sum \log Y = 38.7612$$

$$\bar{X} = 11.5 \qquad \sum X \log Y = 497.7083 \qquad \sum X^2 = 4,324$$

SOURCE OF DATA: *Moody's Transportation Manual*, 1970.

The logarithmic trend line has the equation

$$\log \bar{Y}_X = 1.0953 + .0452X \qquad (12\text{-}10)$$

The values for a and b may be found by taking the antilogs of the above coefficients:

$$a = \text{antilog } (1.0953) = 12.45$$

$$b = \text{antilog } (.0452) = 1.11$$

The equation for the exponential trend curve is then found by substituting these values for a and b into expression (12-8):

$$\bar{Y}_X = 12.45(1.11)^X \qquad (X = 0 \text{ at } 1946)$$

In computing trend values, the above equation form would not ordinarily be used. Instead, the log $\bar{Y}_X$ values would be calculated from the fitted logarithmic trend line of expression (12-10). The $\bar{Y}_X$ values can be easily obtained from the antilogs of these. For example, to find the $\bar{Y}_X$ for 1969, we have $X = 1969 - 1946 = 23$. Thus,

$$\log \bar{Y}_{23} = 1.0953 + .0452(23) = 2.1349$$

$$\bar{Y}_{23} = \text{antilog } (2.1349) = 136.4 \text{ million passengers}$$

The value is fairly close to the actual figure of 142.3 million passengers carried in 1969.

The trend curve and the original time series are shown in Figure 12-12. This graph has an *arithmetic* vertical scale. The time series behavior in the early years is hardly noticeable, while the points in later years rise by progressively larger amounts. So as not to exaggerate the importance of the later data, exponential trend curves are sometimes graphed with a compressed vertical scale called the *semilogarithmic*. The ruling on such a scale is made so that equal

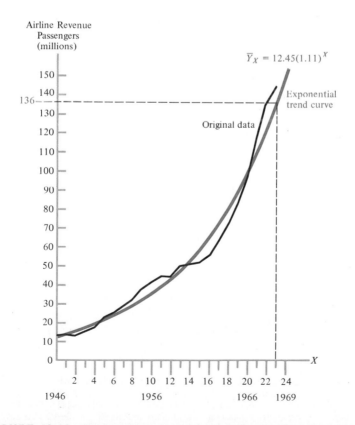

FIGURE 12-12   Exponential trend and original data for airline passengers.

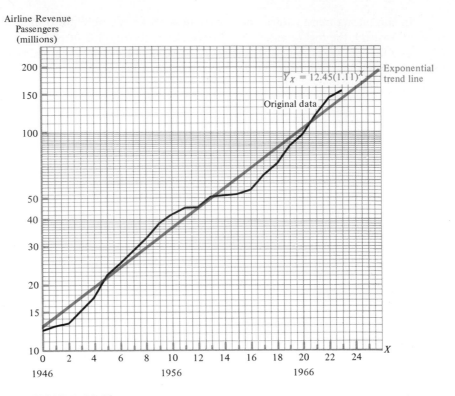

FIGURE 12-13 Exponential trend and original data for airline passenger data plotted on semilogarithmic graph paper.

vertical distances correspond to values of Y that have increased by the same percentage. This is accomplished by spacing the scale marks at distances that correspond to the logarithm of their heights.

Figure 12-13 shows the airline passenger time series and trend plotted with a semilogarithmic vertical scale. The exponential trend curve plots as a straight line, indicating that the number of passengers grew at a constant percentage rate during the period shown. The value $b = 1.11$ indicates that this rate was .11, or 11 percent, per year.*

Parabolic Trend

Another commonly used procedure is to fit data having a nonlinear trend by a *parabola*. The following is the *expression for the parabolic trend curve:*

$$\overline{Y}_X = a + bX + cX^2 \tag{12-11}$$

---

* Recall that the expression for determining the amount A to which a principal amount P will grow at an interest rate i per year is: $A = P(1+i)^n$, where n is the number of time periods. The trend starts in 1946 at 12.45 and $\overline{Y}_X = 12.45(1.11)^X = 12.45(1+.11)^X$. The .11 represents the percentage rate of growth in passengers and is analogous to i, while 12.45 is similar to P, and X, like n, is the number of years beyond 1946.

As noted in Chapter 10, the method of least squares may be extended to find the values for the constants a, b, and c appearing above. These determine the shape of the parabola that best fits the data. The constant values are determined by solving a set of simultaneous normal equations involving terms $\sum X^2 Y$, $\sum X^2$, $\sum X^3$, and $\sum X^4$. When dealing with time series data, the values of X typically increase by one unit for successive time periods, so that we may simplify the computations considerably by transforming the independent variable, with the time center of the data represented by the number 0. Denoting the centered values by x, calculated by subtracting $\overline{X}$ from each value X, the normal equations may be rewritten, replacing X by x. This considerably simplifies the computations, since $\sum x$ and $\sum x^3$ are equal to zero. We thus use the following to determine the *parabolic regression coefficients:*

$$\sum Y = na + c \sum x^2$$
$$\sum x^2 Y = a \sum x^2 + c \sum x^4$$
$$b = \frac{\sum xY}{\sum x^2}$$

(12-12)

We illustrate how a parabolic trend curve may be obtained using the U.S. cotton consumption data in Table 12-3 for the 23 years 1947–1969. The center of the data occurs in 1958, where $x = 0$. The values of x are negative for years before 1958. From the intermediate values in Table 12-3, we obtain the value for b:

$$b = \frac{-19.10}{1,012} = -.01887$$

The values for a and c are found by substituting the appropriate totals into the first two normal equations:

$$205.08 = 23a + 1,012c$$

$$9,110.68 = 1,012a + 79,748c$$

Since 23, the coefficient of a in the first equation, divides evenly into its counterpart in the second to yield an even 44, we may make these terms the same by multiplying all terms in the first equation by 44, getting

$$9,023.52 = 1,012a + 44,528c$$

$$9,110.68 = 1,012a + 79,948c$$

Subtracting the first equation from the second, the a terms cancel and we obtain

$$87.16 = 35,420c$$

TABLE 12-3 Parabolic Trend Calculations for U.S. Cotton Consumption

Year	Years Beyond Base X	Years from Center of Data $x = X - \bar{X}$	Cotton Consumption (millions of bales) Y	xY	x^2	x^2Y	x^4
1947	0	−11	9.55	−105.05	121	1,155.55	14,641
1948	1	−10	9.10	−91.00	100	910.00	10,000
1949	2	−9	7.87	−70.83	81	637.47	6,561
1950	3	−8	9.65	−77.20	64	617.60	4,096
1951	4	−7	10.04	−70.28	49	491.96	2,401
1952	5	−6	9.19	−55.14	36	330.84	1,296
1953	6	−5	9.32	−46.60	25	233.00	625
1954	7	−4	8.53	−34.12	16	136.48	256
1955	8	−3	9.07	−27.21	9	81.63	81
1956	9	−2	8.97	−17.94	4	35.88	16
1957	10	−1	8.36	−8.36	1	8.36	1
1958	11	0	8.13	0	0	0	0
1959	12	1	8.98	8.98	1	8.98	1
1960	13	2	8.71	17.42	4	34.84	16
1961	14	3	8.53	25.59	9	76.77	81
1962	15	4	8.72	34.88	16	139.52	256
1963	16	5	8.39	41.95	25	209.75	625
1964	17	6	8.94	53.64	36	321.84	1,296
1965	18	7	9.30	65.10	49	455.70	2,401
1966	19	8	9.65	77.20	64	617.60	4,096
1967	20	9	9.22	82.98	81	746.82	6,561
1968	21	10	8.57	85.70	100	857.00	10,000
1969	22	11	8.29	91.19	121	1,003.09	14,641
	253	0	205.08	−19.10	1,012	9,110.68	79,948

$$\bar{X} = \frac{253}{23} = 11 \qquad \sum Y = 205.08 \qquad \sum xY = -19.10$$

$$\sum x^2 = 1,012 \qquad \sum x^2Y = 9,110.68 \qquad \sum x^4 = 79,948$$

SOURCE OF DATA: *Moody's Industrial Manual*, 1970.

so that

$$c = \frac{87.16}{35,420} = .00246$$

The value for a may be determined by rearranging the original first equation and substituting .00246 for c:

$$a = \frac{1}{23}[205.08 - 1,012(.00246)] = 8.808$$

The parabolic trend curve for the cotton consumption data is thus expressed by the equation:

$$\bar{Y}_X = 8.808 - .01887x + .00246x^2$$

where $x = 0$ at 1958 (middle of year). We may convert the above equation back into the units X by substituting $X - \overline{X} = X - 11$ for x:

$$\overline{Y}_X = 8.808 - .01887(X - 11) + .00246(X - 11)^2$$

which reduces to

$$\overline{Y}_X = 9.310 - .07297X + .00246X^2$$

where $X = 0$ at 1947.

    The foregoing calculations were based upon an *odd* number of years. The procedure is identical when the number of years is even, except that the values of x are then fractional. For example, if 1970 were included with the data, then the center would fall on December 31, 1958, and the values for x would be -11.5, $-10.5, \ldots$.

    The parabolic trend curve is plotted in Figure 12-14 along with the original time series. Note that the parabola is mildly U-shaped. This reflects the fact that although U.S. cotton consumption suffered a decline in the years following

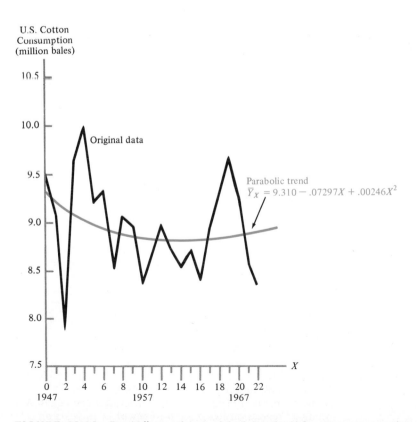

FIGURE 12-14   Parabolic trend and original data for U.S. cotton consumption.

World War II, as new synthetic fiber substitutes were brought onto the market, it has resumed growth at a gradual rate since the late 1950s.

Parabolic trend curves will usually serve as well as exponential curves. Like the exponential, a parabola can be used for some nonlinear declining series as well as for increasing ones. Exponential curves would be inappropriate, however, where a decline is followed by growth, as in U.S. cotton consumption, and the trend is U-shaped. In these cases the parabola is usually suitable.

A parabola may be fitted to the railroad passenger series in Figure 12-10 where there has been a decline at a decreasing rate. However, in extrapolating the trend into the future, the parabola will eventually turn upward, indicating a rapid growth in the number of railroad passengers that is a mirror image of the preceding decline. This seems to be quite opposite to the prognostications of the U.S. railroads, who gladly surrendered their passenger service in 1971 to a government corporation, Amtrak, which immediately terminated more than half the U.S. passenger trains. Indeed, arguments are strong for further decline in the number of rail passengers, so that a parabolic trend—although nicely fitting past data—may be decidedly inferior to a decreasing exponential one that cannot turn upward.

EXERCISES

12-5 A certain large retailing corporation has experienced the following annual sales:

Year	Sales	Year	Sales
1967	$18 million	1973	$ 82 million
1968	28	1974	89
1969	26	1975	108
1970	43	1976	121
1971	55	1977	155
1972	54		

(a) Plot the above time series data on ordinary graph paper.
(b) Would a straight line provide a suitable summary of the trend in sales? Explain.

12-6 The electricity usage (in million kilowatt-hours) in a region served by a certain utility company from 1968 through 1977 is provided below:

Year	Consumption	Year	Consumption
1968	205	1973	241
1969	206	1974	267
1970	223	1975	268
1971	234	1976	277
1972	231	1977	290

(a) Plot the above time series data on a graph.
(b) Using the method of least squares, determine the equation for the estimated regression line $\bar{Y}_X = a + bX$ with X in years and $X = 0$ in 1968. Draw this line on your graph.

(c) Using your answer to part (b), estimate the electricity consumption for 1986.

12-7 Using the data provided in Exercise 12-5, answer the following:

(a) Representing sales by Y, use least squares regression of log Y on X, where X is in years and $X = 0$ for 1967, to find the logarithmic trend line, log $\bar{Y}_X = \log a + X \log b$.

(b) Determine the exponential trend equation $\bar{Y}_X = ab^X$.

(c) What is the annual percentage growth in sales indicated by the trend equation found in part (b)?

(d) Using the trend equation from part (a), what is the projected sales level for 1982?

12-8 Using the data provided in Exercise 12-5, answer the following:

(a) Representing sales by Y, use least squares regression of Y on x, where x is in years and $x = 0$ for 1972, to find the parabolic trend equation, $\bar{Y}_X = a + bx + cx^2$.

(b) What is the projected trend in sales for 1982?

12-9 For each of the following trend equations, make the required modifications.

(a) $\bar{Y}_X = 1{,}000{,}000 + 120{,}000X$, with X in years and $X = 0$ for July 1, 1970. This expresses the number of employees in a utility industry. Find (1) $\bar{Y}_X$ for monthly employment with X in months and base January 15, 1970; (2) $\bar{Y}_X$ for quarterly employment with X in quarters and base winter 1970 (February 15, 1970).

(b) $\bar{Y}_X = 10{,}000 + 600X$ with X in years and $X = 0$ for July 1, 1971. This expresses the number of welfare recipients in a particular county. Find (1) $\bar{Y}_X$ for the number of welfare recipients in months X with base January 15, 1969, and (2) $\bar{Y}_X$ for the number of welfare recipients in quarters X with base February 15, 1969.

(c) $\bar{Y}_X = 10 - .01x + .002x^2$, with x in years, when $x = 0$ in 1960. Find $\bar{Y}_X$ when $X = 0$ in 1951, assuming $\bar{X} - 9$.

12-4 ANALYSIS OF SEASONAL FLUCTUATION

Short-range planning in business and in government will ordinarily consider seasonal patterns. A successful organization must manage its resources to function efficiently when operating at peak level. When lower level activity resumes, the same facilities and personnel must be retained and readied for a new peak. Few organizations are free from seasonal cycles, which we ordinarily associate with a calendar year. We may generalize the notion of a season to incorporate more or less regular patterns or cycles that recur over successive time periods of a year or less in duration. We may thus have "seasonal" fluctuation on a monthly, weekly, or even daily basis. Payroll departments operate on cycles of a month or less. Restaurants operate on a daily cycle punctuated by busy periods at mealtimes and also on a weekly cycle, with a different business pattern on weekdays than on weekends. Of primary interest in time series analysis, however, will be seasonal cycles one year long.

In this section we discuss a procedure for isolating seasonal fluctuations in time series data. Identifying seasonal patterns is a necessary first step in short-range planning. The management of a firm whose business drops in May is not alarmed if it is only the beginning of an annual seasonal trough. Likewise, government economists recognize that in certain months the Consumer Price Index will rise or fall due solely to the influence of seasonal factors such as changing varieties of produce on the market. In order to monitor performance, of a business or of an economy, it has proven useful to "deseasonalize" time series data in order to determine whether a current drop or rise is greater than usual. A technique for doing this is described at the end of this section.

Ratio-to-Moving-Average Method

In presenting the classical time series model, we showed how the seasonal fluctuation may be considered as short-term oscillations about the longer range time series pattern established by the trend and cyclical elements. In constructing the hypothetical time series for stereo speaker sales, the seasonal fluctuations were superimposed onto the pattern established by the trend line and cyclical movement. This was accomplished by multiplying the long-term level of sales by a predetermined seasonal index, which takes on a specific value for each quarter of the year.

Various techniques exist for isolating seasonal fluctuations. We discuss only the ratio-to-moving-average method, which is somewhat more complex than the others but is most widely used. This approach reverses the sequence used in constructing the hypothetical stereo speaker time series. Starting with the actual time series, the trend and cyclical elements are isolated together in what is referred to as a "smoothed" time series analogous to that in Figure 12-3(b) (p. 407). The isolation of the long-term elements is accomplished by means of *four-quarter moving averages*.

To obtain the moving averages, the procedure begins with four-quarter moving totals. The values for four successive quarters, beginning with the first of the series, are added together to obtain the initial four-quarter total. Then the first quarter is dropped from this figure and the fifth added to provide the second total. This procedure continues until the last quarter has been included. An adjustment is then made so that the data will be centered to correspond to the same time position as the original data. This is accomplished by adding together each successive pair of four-quarter totals. These final sums are then converted into four-quarter moving averages.

Each average represents an entire year, so that the seasonal fluctuations are averaged out of the time series. As the random or irregular variations tend to occur throughout the year, raising or lowering the time series level from what it would otherwise have been, these tend to be eliminated by the averaging process taken over an entire year. The four-quarter moving average is intended to eliminate both the seasonal and short-term irregular elements, so that all that remains are the cycle and trend. This is the goal, although a perfect separation may not be achieved. If seasonal fluctuations are not stable and their timing fluctuates somewhat from year to year, then not all the seasonal movement may be removed. Likewise, portions of a cyclical variation may seem like seasonal fluctuations when a longer term upturn or downward swing of the time series coincides with the busy or slack season. Thus, the smoothing process may average out part of the cyclical element as well.

The element of oscillation of the original series about the smoothed one is next determined for each period, as a percentage of the dependent variable value in the smoothed series. These percentages are then analyzed separately by season for all the years, and a typical value is found to be used as the seasonal index for that quarter.

In the context of the classical time series model, the ratio-to-moving-average method is summarized by the expression

$$\frac{Y_t}{\text{Moving average}} = \frac{T_t \times C_t \times S_t \times I_t}{T_t \times C_t} = S_t \times I_t \qquad (12\text{-}13)$$

The moving average provides trend and cycle, so that $T_t \times C_t$ is obtained for each time period. Dividing Y_t by the moving average is thus equivalent to canceling the $T_t \times C_t$ terms from the multiplicative model, and only the seasonal and irregular components, expressed by $S_t \times I_t$, remain.

Illustration of Procedure

To illustrate this procedure, data for average weekly freight car loading are provided in Table 12-4. The original data are listed in column (2). These numbers may be viewed as corresponding to the middle of their respective quarters: February 15, May 15, August 15, and November 15. In column (3), the moving totals for four successive quarters are obtained. For 1968 the quarterly figures are 508.0, 565.7, 549.7, and 543.7 thousands of carloads. The total of these is 2,167.1, which represents an entire year's carloading figures. (But since the original data are weekly averages, this is not an annual total.) The number 2,167.1 corresponds to the midyear, or July 1, 1968, the date that separates the summer quarter from the spring. Each four-quarter moving total corresponds to a date dividing two quarters. Thus the entries in column (3) are positioned in the table to fall between the quarters. In order to arrive at a value for each quarter, these numbers must be adjusted.

To illustrate this procedure, consider the first two entries in column (3). The value 2,167.1 is a total of weekly carloading averages for the six months prior to and succeeding July 1, 1968. The next number, 2,166.4, represents the weekly carloadings for the year centered at October 1, 1968. The sum of these is 4,333.5, which represents two overlapping years of carloadings and encompasses five quarters. This number is placed in the row for the summer quarter 1968, corresponding to the date August 15, 1968, halfway between July 1 and October 1. Since three quarters have been counted twice, a total of eight quarterly figures are represented by the value 4,333.5. Similar entries in column (4) are obtained for the remaining quarters. The four-quarter moving average for August 15, 1968, is obtained by dividing the sum 4,333.5 by 8, obtaining 541.7. This is entered in column (5) where four-quarter moving averages have been similarly obtained for the remaining quarters.

TABLE 12-4 Ratio-to-Moving-Average and Deseasonalizing Calculations for Average Weekly Carloadings

(1) Quarter	(2) Average Weekly Carloadings (thousands)	(3) Four-Quarter Moving Total	(4) Sum of Two Successive Four-Quarter Totals	(5) Four-Quarter Moving Average [(4)÷8]	(6) Original Data as Percentage of Moving Average [(2)÷(5)]×100	(7) Seasonal Index	(8) Deseasonalized Data [(2)÷(7)]×100
1968							
Winter	508.0					96.11	528.7
Spring	565.7	2,167.1				103.66	545.7
Summer	549.7	2,166.4	4,333.5	541.7	101.48	100.25	548.3
Fall	543.7	2,162.4	4,328.8	541.1	100.48	99.98	543.8
1969							
Winter	507.3	2,158.0	4,320.4	540.1	93.93	96.11	527.8
Spring	561.7	2,171.3	4,329.3	541.2	103.79	103.66	541.9
Summer	545.3	2,162.7	4,334.0	541.8	100.65	100.25	543.9
Fall	557.0	2,151.3	4,314.0	539.3	103.28	99.98	557.1
1970							
Winter	498.7	2,129.7	4,281.0	535.1	93.20	96.11	518.9
Spring	550.3	2,086.0	4,215.7	527.0	104.42	103.66	530.9
Summer	523.7	2,073.0	4,159.0	519.9	100.73	100.25	522.4
Fall	513.3	2,048.7	4,121.7	515.2	99.63	99.98	513.4
1971							
Winter	485.7	2,002.0	4,050.7	506.3	95.93	96.11	505.4
Spring	526.0	1,946.0	3,948.0	493.5	106.59	103.66	507.4
Summer	477.0	1,928.3	3,874.3	484.3	98.49	100.25	475.8
Fall	457.3	1,916.0	3,844.3	480.5	95.17	99.98	457.4

1972							
Winter	468.0	1,939.3	481.9	3,855.3	97.12	96.11	486.9
Spring	513.7	1,993.3	491.6	3,932.6	104.50	103.66	495.6
Summer	500.3	2,028.0	502.7	4,021.3	99.52	100.25	499.1
Fall	511.3	2,047.6	509.5	4,075.6	100.35	99.98	511.4
1973							
Winter	502.7	2,077.3	515.6	4,124.9	97.50	96.11	523.0
Spring	533.3	2,100.3	522.2	4,177.6	102.13	103.66	514.5
Summer	530.0	2,109.3	526.2	4,209.6	100.72	100.25	528.7
Fall	534.3	2,108.3	527.2	4,217.6	101.35	99.98	534.4
1974							
Winter	511.7	2,085.3	524.2	4,193.6	97.62	96.11	532.4
Spring	532.3	2,030.7	514.5	4,116.0	103.46	103.66	513.5
Summer	507.0					100.25	505.7
Fall	479.7					99.98	479.8

SOURCE OF DATA: *Moody's Transportation Manual*, 1975.

The four-quarter moving averages are graphed in Figure 12-15 along with the original time series data. Note that two quarters are "lost" at the beginning and end of the series. Assuming that the series curve provided by the moving averages, shown as a dashed line, represents only trend and cyclical elements, the fluctuations of the original data about this curve illustrate the seasonal and irregular components. Expression (12-13) indicates that the combination of these, $S_t \times I_t$, may be obtained by dividing the original data by the corresponding four-quarter moving average. For the summer of 1968, the actual carloading value is 549.7 thousand per week. Dividing by the corresponding moving

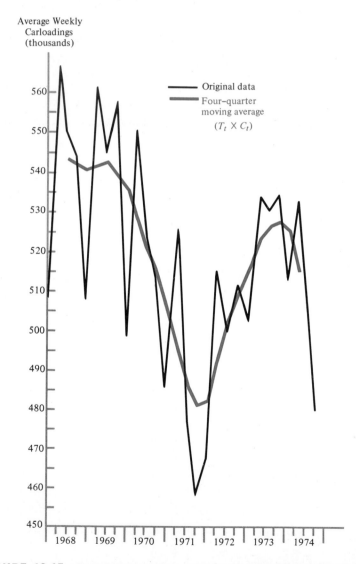

FIGURE 12-15   Four-quarter moving average and original data for average weekly carloadings.

average of 541.7 and multiplying by 100, we obtain the *percentage of moving average*:

$$\frac{549.7}{541.7} \times 100 = 101.48$$

In column (6) of Table 12-4 the percentages of moving averages are provided for the remaining quarters. These are plotted in Figure 12-16. Note the repetitive nature of the oscillations, which are more or less regular from one time period to the next. However, the pattern is not precisely the same for all years, due to the presence of the irregular variation. The remaining step in the ratio-to-moving-average method is to completely isolate a seasonal index by removing the irregular component.

The classical model assumes that short-term random influences will either raise or decrease the Y_t value from the level at which it would otherwise have been for a particular quarter. Viewing the summer quarters in several different years, the irregular fluctuations will have a positive effect in some years and a negative influence in others. Throughout the duration of the time series we may assume that the average effect of random factors will be zero. The percentage of moving average values represent only the time series component product $S_t \times I_t$; therefore, assuming S_t constant for the same quarter from one year to the next, the variation in these numbers must be due to the irregular component I_t. We may then isolate S_t by averaging the $S_t \times I_t$ values for the same season.

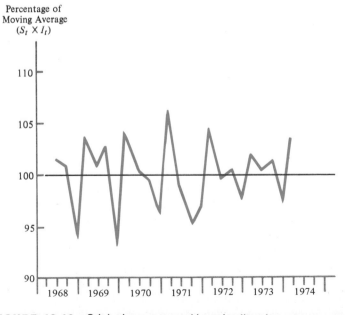

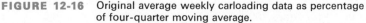

FIGURE 12-16   Original average weekly carloading data as percentage of four-quarter moving average.

The procedure for "averaging out" the I_t eliminates the more extreme $S_t \times I_t$ values, finding a central value for each quarter. This is illustrated in Table 12-5, where the percentage of moving average values for the several years are collected together by quarters. Thus the values from column (6) of Table 12-4 are placed into four separate groups, one for each season. Note that for winter the values range from a low of 93.20 for 1970 to a high of 97.62 for 1974. To represent the true seasonal factor, the median will be used. For winter, this value is 96.53. For the remaining groups, the successive medians are 104.11, 100.69, and 100.42. From these medians, a seasonal index can be obtained for each quarter. Their sum is 401.75. A further adjustment is necessary so that the resulting seasonal indexes sum to 400, which is accomplished by multiplying each median times 400/401.75. For instance, for the winter quarter, we obtain the seasonal index 96.53(400/401.75) = 96.11.

TABLE 12-5   Calculation of Seasonal Indexes from Percentages of Moving Average for Carloading Data of Table 12-4

Year	Winter	Spring	Summer	Fall
1968			101.48	100.48
1969	93.93	103.79	100.65	103.28
1970	93.20	104.42	100.73	99.63
1971	95.93	106.59	98.49	95.17
1972	97.12	104.50	99.52	100.35
1973	97.50	102.13	100.72	101.35
1974	97.62	103.46		
Median	96.53	104.11	100.69	100.42

Total of medians = 401.75

Seasonal index = $\dfrac{400}{401.75} \times$ median

= | 96.11 | 103.66 | 100.25 | 99.98 |

Monthly Data

A quarter may be too long a period to be useful. Many businesses will use a 12-month seasonal cycle. The general procedures that we illustrated for quarterly data also apply to monthly figures. First, 12-month moving totals are obtained. These are then centered by finding the sum of two successive 12-month moving totals. The 12-month moving average is found by dividing the centered totals by 24, the number of monthly figures included. As with quarters, the percentage of moving average is then found by dividing the original monthly data by the respective moving averages. Seasonal indexes are obtained by grouping together all the percentages for the same month in each year, so that 12 groups are obtained. The median of each monthly group is then found. The sum of the medians is determined. The final step is to adjust these so that their sum is 1,200, 12 months in a year times 100 percent.

Deseasonalized Data

The ratio-to-moving-average method isolates the seasonal indexes. These may be used to deseasonalize the original time series data. Removing the seasonal effect provides a series that may prove useful in analyzing longer term movement in the series. The resulting series is sometimes used instead of the smoothed data to identify cyclical activity. Deseasonalized data may be used, for instance, to compare successive time periods to aid in determining whether a turning point in the current cycle has been reached. For example, inflation may be expressed in terms of the Consumer Price Index (CPI), computed by the U.S. Bureau of Labor Statistics, which measures the percentage change in current prices beyond a base period. (See Chapter 13 for a detailed discussion of the CPI.) Government economists establish current monetary and fiscal policies upon the level of the CPI, after removing the seasonal influence. Thus, a slower increase in the deseasonalized CPI may indicate that the peak in an inflationary period has been reached. Monthly deseasonalized CPI values may also be converted on an annual basis. Thus, an increase of .5 percent over the previous month's value would be multiplied by 12 to provide an annual rate of inflation of 6 percent.

Removal of seasonal fluctuations is accomplished by dividing the original time series data points by the corresponding seasonal indexes. In terms of the classical model this is expressed symbolically by

$$\text{Deseasonalized value} = \frac{Y_t}{\text{Seasonal index}}$$

$$= \frac{T_t \times C_t \times S_t \times I_t}{S_t} = T_t \times C_t \times I_t \qquad (12\text{-}14)$$

Dividing Y_t by the seasonal index removes the S_t component from the series, leaving only the trend, cyclical, and irregular components, $T_t \times C_t \times I_t$. The deseasonalized carloading data are shown in column (8) of Table 12-4. In column (7) the seasonal indexes are entered, the values corresponding to the respective quarter in each year. The original data values in column (2) are then divided by the seasonal index in column (7) and multiplied by 100. The resulting values are deseasonalized and shown in column (8). For instance, for the winter of 1968, the actual average number of weekly carloadings is 508.0 thousand. The seasonal index is 96.11. Thus, for this time period we have

$$\text{Deseasonalized value} = \frac{508.0}{96.11} \times 100 = 528.7 \text{ (thousand)}$$

The deseasonalized weekly carloading data are plotted in Figure 12-17. Eliminating seasonal movement makes it simpler to identify the longer term oscillations that we have identified as cyclical. In the next section of this chapter, a procedure is discussed for isolating the cyclical component.

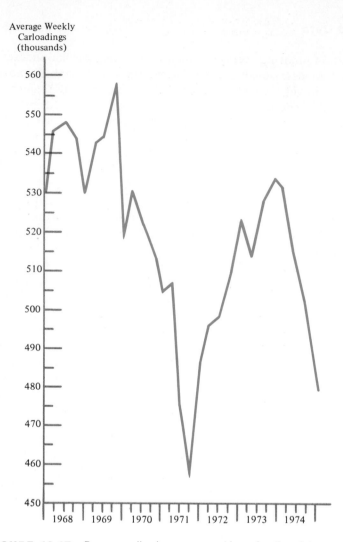

FIGURE 12-17   Deseasonalized average weekly carloading data.

Forecasting with Seasonal Indexes

Seasonal indexes are useful in making short-term forecasts. These are accomplished by first determining a trend over the annual period. Seasonal adjustments are then made for each of the shorter periods within the year. For example, suppose that a department store wishes to forecast monthly sales for the next calendar year. The following trend equation has been determined:

$$\overline{Y}_X = 1,025,000 + 50,000X$$

TABLE 12-6 Calculations of Monthly Forecast
for Department Store Sales

(1)	(2)	(3)	(4)	(5)
			Monthly Sales	Monthly Sales
		Seasonal	Trend Levels	Forecast
Month	X	Index	$\bar{Y}_X$	$[(3) \times (4)] \div 100$
January	0	56.7	$1,025,000	$ 581,175
February	1	64.5	1,075,000	693,375
March	2	62.1	1,125,000	698,625
April	3	99.9	1,175,000	1,173,825
May	4	83.6	1,225,000	1,024,100
June	5	67.4	1,275,000	859,350
July	6	58.2	1,325,000	771,150
August	7	100.1	1,375,000	1,376,375
September	8	110.6	1,425,000	1,576,050
October	9	137.7	1,475,000	2.031,075
November	10	167.3	1,525,000	2,551,325
December	11	191.9	1,575,000	3,022,425
		1,200.0		

with X in months and $X = 0$ at January 15 of next year. The calculations of monthly sales forecast are provided in Table 12-6. The 12 monthly seasonal indexes are provided in column (3). The monthly sales trend levels are calculated in column (4) for the above trend line equation. For January, the trend value of $1,025,000 is multiplied by 56.7 percent to obtain the forecast sales of $581,175. The sales forecasts for all 12 months are shown in column (5).

EXERCISES

12-10 The following percentages of moving average values have been obtained for a dairy's ice cream sales. Determine the seasonal index for each quarter.

		Quarter		
Year	Winter	Spring	Summer	Fall
1969			156	111
1970	49	92	137	109
1971	53	93	148	108
1972	52	91	162	104
1973	51	89	153	110
1974	51	90	151	112
1975	48	88		

12-11 A certain men's clothing chain has experienced the following quarterly sales data (in millions of dollars) for the 5 years 1973–1977.

	1973	1974	1975	1976	1977
Winter	3.9	7.8	12.9	13.9	13.5
Spring	6.1	10.6	15.2	14.4	18.2
Summer	4.3	6.9	10.3	10.2	14.2
Fall	10.8	13.5	18.7	17.3	20.7

(a) Plot the above time series data on a graph.

(b) Determine the four-quarter moving averages.

(c) Calculate the percentage of moving average values and use them to determine the seasonal indexes.

(d) Deseasonalize the original sales data and plot them on your graph.

12-12 In arranging for short-term credit with its bank, the Make-Wave Corporation must project its cash needs on a monthly basis. To help in doing this, seasonal indexes must be developed from the following historical data on cash requirements (in hundreds of thousands of dollars).

(a) Using 12-month moving averages, determine the seasonal index number for each month by means of the ratio-to-moving-average method.

(b) Make-Wave's cash needs for the coming year are forecast to be on the average equal to $1,000,000 per month. Using the seasonal indexes calculated in (a), estimate the cash requirements for each month.

	1973	1974	1975	1976	1977
January	2.7	2.9	3.5	2.5	4.2
February	5.4	6.4	7.3	8.1	9.6
March	9.3	10.1	11.3	7.9	12.4
April	2.4	4.1	3.8	5.2	6.2
May	6.1	7.8	8.1	9.2	8.7
June	7.3	7.4	6.9	8.1	8.3
July	6.5	5.5	6.5	7.6	6.6
August	9.7	9.6	8.9	9.3	9.8
September	13.4	13.5	14.3	15.8	16.3
October	10.6	10.7	11.5	12.6	13.4
November	5.1	4.8	6.5	7.2	6.9
December	3.4	2.8	3.9	4.1	6.1

12-13 Suppose that the following seasonal indexes have been obtained by Make-Wave Corporation:

Month	Index	Month	Index
January	40	July	90
February	100	August	120
March	140	September	180
April	60	October	140
May	110	November	80
June	90	December	50
		Total	1,200

(a) Use these indexes to deseasonalize the data provided in Exercise 12-12.

(b) Plot the original data for 1976 and 1977 on a graph. Then plot the deseasonalized data for both years on the same graph.

(c) Is the rise in 1977 cash requirements from August to September abnormally large? Explain.

12-5   CYCLICAL MOVEMENT AND IRREGULAR FLUCTUATION

Cyclical movement in time series data is the most troublesome of the systematic components to analyze. Unlike seasonal fluctuation, which is repetitious and more or less regular from one year to the next, the longer term oscillations we call cycles are erratic. Seasonal influences are predictable and occur periodically. It is virtually certain, for example, that a department store will achieve greater sales in the fall quarter than in any other period within a particular year. With cyclical variation, the peak may occur at any point within a calendar year, and the cycle's duration may vary from one to several years in length. Cyclical activity ordinarily varies in both intensity and distance from peak to successive peak. This makes the task of forecasting a cycle a formidable, and perhaps impossible, one.

Identification of past cycles in time series data is itself difficult. One problem is that true separation of trend and cyclical movement is ordinarily impossible with the statistical tools available. As we have seen, the trend curve obtained is largely a matter of judgment. There is no reason why, for instance, least squares regression must be used in fitting the data except that it may be less controversial. Again, it is a matter of individual choice as to how many time periods will be included and which particular regression procedure—for example, exponential versus parabolic—will be used. A different trend line will result from each of the various techniques. In any case, the resulting trend line cannot be relied upon to completely separate the trend from cyclical and irregular components.

Isolating Cyclical Movement: Residual Method

In the preceding section we indicated a procedure whereby seasonal fluctuation can be isolated from the other time series components. Similar techniques may be used to isolate the cyclical components from the others. In illustrating how this is done, we will continue with the time series data for weekly carloadings. When the original data are deseasonalized, the resulting time series may be represented symbolically by expression (12-14), which is rewritten here:

$$\frac{Y_t}{\text{Seasonal index}} = \frac{T_t \times C_t \times I_t \times S_t}{S_t} = T_t \times C_t \times I_t$$

The above product indicates that only the trend, cyclical, and irregular components remain. The deseasonalized carloading data are shown in column (8) of Table 12-4.

As the first step in isolating cyclical movement, we will remove trend from the deseasonalized data so that all that remain are the cyclical-irregular components. To find the trend component, the procedures of Section 12-2 will be employed to find a regression equation with time, in quarters, as the independent variable and weekly carloadings as the dependent variable. We will represent the carloading trend thus obtained by the symbol $\overline{Y}_X$. According to the multiplicative model, the deseasonalized values may be divided by the respective $\overline{Y}_X$ terms to isolate the cyclical-irregular components. Symbolically, this is achieved by

$$\frac{\dfrac{Y_t}{\text{Seasonal index}}}{\overline{Y}_X} = \frac{T_t \times C_t \times I_t}{T_t} = C_t \times I_t \qquad (12\text{-}15)$$

The product $T_t \times S_t$ is thereby eliminated from the series. That product represents the *predictable* time series components, as these are what would be expected in the absence of the less predictable cyclical-irregular components, summarized by the remaining $C_t \times I_t$ product.

After the cyclical-irregulars have been separated by canceling predictables out of the original data, the cyclical component must next be isolated from the irregulars. The procedure we have outlined involves, first, the isolation of three components by deseasonalization, then the reduction of these to two by canceling out the trend, and finally, separation of the cyclical component. At each stage, the residual components that remain are further separated. The procedure is therefore referred to as the *residual method*.

The procedure for isolating the cyclical movement in average weekly carloadings from 1968 through 1974 is illustrated in Table 12-7. The deseasonalized quarterly data obtained in Section 12-4 are provided in column (2). A logarithmic trend line, $\log \overline{Y}_X = 2.73012 - .00128X$, has been fitted to these using the procedures of Section 12-3. The values for $\log \overline{Y}_X$ have been obtained for each quarter, using $X = 0$ for the winter of 1968 and incrementing X by 1 for each successive quarter. The trend values $\overline{Y}_X$ in column (3) have been found by taking the antilogs of the logarithmic trend values. For example, when $X = 0$, $\log \overline{Y}_X = 2.73012$, and antilog $(2.73012) = 537.2$, which is the trend value for the winter of 1968.

The cyclical-irregular component, expressed as a percentage of trend, is obtained by dividing each deseasonalized carloading figure by the corresponding trend value. These are shown in column (4) and represent $C_t \times I_t$. For the winter of 1968, we obtain the first entry in column (4), $(528.7/537.2) \times 100 = 98.42$. The final step is removal of the irregular variation I_t.

The irregular variation, assumed to be largely of a short-term nature, may be eliminated with a moving average in a manner similar to the one used in finding seasonal indexes. The procedure for doing this with the cyclical-irregular component is simpler. Various methods may be used; the one considered here is a three-quarter weighted moving average. Recall that a four-quarter moving average was used in obtaining the seasonal indexes because the original data had

TABLE 12-7 Calculations for Isolating Cyclical Time Series Component for Carloading Data

(1)	(2)	(3)	(4)	(5)	(6)
Year and Quarter	Deseasonalized Weekly Carloading Data	Trend $\bar{Y}_X$	Cyclical-Irregular Component as Percent of Trend $[(2) \div (3)] \times 100$	Weighted Three-Quarter Moving Total	Cyclical Component $(5) \div 4$
1968					
Winter	528.7	537.2	98.42		
Spring	545.7	535.6	101.89	404.88	101.22
Summer	548.3	534.0	102.68	409.37	102.34
Fall	543.8	532.5	102.12	406.34	101.59
1969					
Winter	527.8	530.9	99.42	403.34	100.84
Spring	541.9	529.3	102.38	407.23	101.81
Summer	543.9	527.8	103.05	414.35	103.59
Fall	557.1	526.2	105.87	413.68	103.42
1970					
Winter	518.9	524.7	98.89	405.14	101.29
Spring	530.9	523.1	101.49	402.02	100.51
Summer	522.4	521.6	100.15	400.52	100.13
Fall	513.4	520.0	98.73	395.08	98.77
1971					
Winter	505.4	518.5	97.47	391.81	97.95
Spring	507.4	517.0	98.14	386.05	96.51
Summer	475.8	515.5	92.30	371.75	92.94
Fall	457.4	513.9	89.01	365.34	91.34
1972					
Winter	486.9	512.4	95.02	376.06	94.02
Spring	495.6	510.9	97.01	387.02	96.76
Summer	499.1	509.4	97.98	393.66	98.42
Fall	511.4	507.9	100.69	402.64	100.66
1973					
Winter	523.0	506.4	103.28	409.15	102.29
Spring	514.5	504.9	101.90	412.08	103.02
Summer	528.7	503.5	105.00	418.35	104.59
Fall	534.4	502.0	106.45	424.27	106.07
1974					
Winter	532.4	500.5	106.37	422.10	105.53
Spring	513.5	499.0	102.91	413.82	103.46
Summer	505.7	497.6	101.63	402.88	100.72
Fall	479.8	496.1	96.71		

to be averaged over an entire year to completely eliminate the one-year (i.e., four-quarter) seasonal cycle. Using four quarters required an additional step to center the moving total at the middle of each quarter, so that in effect two overlapping four-quarter moving totals were averaged. Thus, a total of five quarters were included in each moving average. Since we now wish only to eliminate irregular variation, fewer quarters can be used, and with three quarters there is no need for centering adjustments.

The moving average tends to smooth the time series. It is common to choose weights for each quarter so that information is not lost by excessive smoothing. Here we will use the values 1, 2, 1 as weights. This means that the

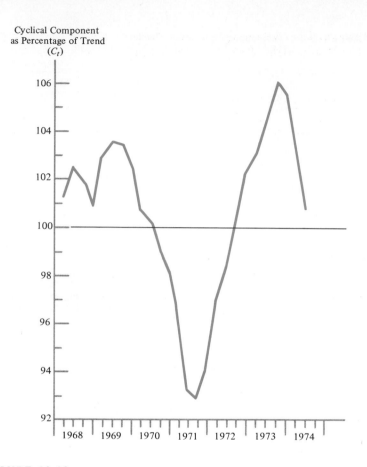

Cyclical Component
as Percentage of Trend
(C_t)

FIGURE 12-18 Cyclical component of average weekly carloading time series as a percentage of trend.

current quarter has twice the weight of the preceding and succeeding quarters. Other weights may be used. The four-quarter centered moving averages discussed in Section 12-4 are really weighted five-quarter moving averages, with weights 1, 2, 2, 2, 1.

The first weighted moving average is calculated for the spring of 1968 by obtaining a three-quarter weighted total. Two times the cyclical-irregular factor for this quarter, 2(101.89), is added to the corresponding values for the previous and following periods, 98.42 and 102.68: 1(98.42)+2(101.89)+1(102.68) = 404.88. The number 404.88 is entered in column (5). The cyclical component is obtained by dividing the total by the sum of the weights, 1+2+1 = 4: 404.88/4 = 101.22. This value is placed in column (6), where the other cyclical factors have been similarly calculated.

The cyclical variation for the carloading data is summarized in Figure 12-18. During the seven-year period covered, there appears to be one full peak-to-peak cycle. This cycle begins in the summer of 1969 and ends in the fall of 1973. The deep trough reflects the recession of 1970–1972.

Isolating the Irregular Fluctuations

To complete our discussion of time series analysis, we identify specific values for the irregular component. Because irregular fluctuations reflect no systematic influence, they are not ordinarily computed and are of little practical use in traditional forecasting methods. But the I_t values will be helpful in completing our presentation.

The multiplicative model tells us that

$$\text{Irregular value} = I_t = \frac{Y_t}{T_t \times C_t \times S_t}$$

The three components in the denominator have been identified for each quarter of the carloading data. For example, we have for Winter 1974,

$$Y_t = 511.7 \quad \text{(from Table 12-4)}$$

$$T_t = \overline{Y}_X = 500.5 \quad \text{(from Table 12-7)}$$

$$C_t = 105.53 \quad \text{(from Table 12-7)}$$

$$S_t = 96.11 \quad \text{(from Table 12-5)}$$

Thus, for that quarter we have

$$I_t = \frac{511.7}{500.5 \times \left(\frac{105.53}{100}\right) \times \left(\frac{96.11}{100}\right)} \times 100 = 100.80$$

Table 12-8 shows the irregular components computed for the entire set of carloading data.

A Complete Synthesis of the Time Series

Now that all four components have been identified, we can reconstruct the original carloading time series using the multiplicative model for the components. The results are provided in Table 12-8. This table merely summarizes the results obtained in the chapter. We would not ordinarily use all four time series components in forecasting future values. For that purpose we would use trend and seasonal values only, because the cyclical and irregular variations cannot ordinarily be predicted.

TABLE 12-8 A Complete Synthesis of the Original
Carloading Times Series from its Components

Quarter	Original Data Y_t	Time Series Components				Product $Y_t = T_t \times C_t \times S_t \times I_t$
		Trend T_t	Cyclical C_t	Seasonal S_t	Irregular I_t	
1968						
Winter	508.0					
Spring	565.7	535.6	101.22	103.66	100.66	565.7
Summer	549.7	534.0	102.34	100.25	100.34	549.7
Fall	543.7	532.5	101.57	99.98	100.55	543.7
1969						
Winter	507.3	530.9	100.84	96.11	98.59	507.3
Spring	561.7	529.3	101.81	103.66	100.55	561.7
Summer	545.3	527.8	103.59	100.25	99.49	545.3
Fall	557.0	526.2	103.42	99.98	102.37	557.0
1970						
Winter	498.7	524.7	101.29	96.11	97.63	498.7
Spring	550.3	523.1	100.51	103.66	100.97	550.3
Summer	523.7	521.6	100.13	100.25	100.02	523.7
Fall	513.3	520.0	98.77	99.98	99.96	513.3
1971						
Winter	485.7	518.5	97.95	96.11	99.51	485.7
Spring	526.0	517.0	96.51	103.66	101.70	526.0
Summer	477.0	515.5	92.94	100.25	99.31	477.0
Fall	457.3	513.9	91.34	99.98	97.44	457.3
1972						
Winter	468.0	512.4	94.02	96.11	101.08	468.0
Spring	513.7	510.9	96.76	103.66	100.25	513.7
Summer	500.3	509.4	98.42	100.25	99.54	500.3
Fall	511.3	507.9	100.66	99.98	100.03	511.3
1973						
Winter	502.7	506.4	102.29	96.11	100.97	502.7
Spring	533.3	504.9	103.02	103.66	98.91	533.3
Summer	530.0	503.5	104.59	100.25	100.39	530.0
Fall	534.3	502.0	106.07	99.98	100.36	534.3
1974						
Winter	511.7	500.5	105.53	96.11	100.80	511.7
Spring	532.3	499.0	103.46	103.66	99.47	532.3
Summer	507.0	497.6	100.72	100.25		
Fall	479.7					

EXERCISES

12-14 The Piñon Nut Company sells exotic seeds and nuts. A company statistician has developed a price index for the raw products it purchases. The deseasonalized values for this index are provided below:

	1970	*1971*	*1972*	*1973*	*1974*	*1975*	*1976*
Winter	101.1	98.0	105.7	110.3	105.2	108.4	121.1
Spring	98.4	96.9	110.2	108.9	106.4	110.3	119.7
Summer	96.2	98.5	114.0	107.6	103.9	119.4	119.4
Fall	97.8	99.7	111.3	107.3	106.2	118.0	117.5

The quarterly trend is determined from the equation $\bar{Y}_X = 100 + .7X$ with $X = 0$ for winter 1970.
(a) Determine the cyclical component for the price index.
(b) Graph your results.

REVIEW EXERCISES

12-15 Consider the following sales data for bottles (thousands) of Malabug, a mosquito repellant made by Albers, Crumbly, and Itch.

	1973	1974	1975	1976	1977
Winter	21	35	39	78	54
Spring	42	54	82	146	114
Summer	60	91	117	136	160
Fall	12	14	38	30	29
Total	135	194	276	390	357

(a) Determine the trend line regression equation using annual sales.
(b) What is the trend level of sales for 1977?

12-16 Use the Malabug sales data in Exercise 12-15.
(a) Find the seasonal index values for each quarter.
(b) Plot the original time-series data and the four-quarter moving average on a graph.

12-17 Suppose that the following trend line applies for sales of Malabug at individual quarters, $\bar{Y}_X = 35 + 3X$ ($X = 0$ at February 15, 1973), and that the seasonal indexes are

Winter	60
Spring	120
Summer	180
Fall	40

(a) Calculate the quarterly trend values and deseasonalize the data given in Exercise 12-15.
(b) Determine for each quarter the cyclical-irregular component as a percentage of trend.
(c) Identify the cyclical component for each quarter.

12-18 Find the equation for the semilogarithmic trend line for the Malabug quarterly sales data given in Exercise 12-15. What sales level is forecast for Winter 1980?

12-19 A complete time-series analysis of the unit sales of Bri-Dent toothpaste has resulted in the following conclusions:
(1) Quarterly trend (in millions) may be determined from

$$\bar{Y}_X = 10 + .5X \qquad (X = 0 \text{ at February 15, 1973})$$

(2) The cyclical component percentages for 1977 are

Winter	105.7
Spring	103.2
Summer	101.4
Fall	98.6

(3) The seasonal indexes are:

Winter	105
Spring	110
Summer	85
Fall	100

(4) The irregular time-series component percentage values for 1977 are

Winter	98
Spring	101
Summer	100
Fall	102

Find the original sales data for the quarters of 1977.

Chapter Thirteen
Index
Numbers

The whole art of statistical inference lies in the reconciliation of random mathematics with biased samples. Every new problem has some fresh kind of bias and might contain some new pitfall.

W. S. Gossett (1933)

13-1 PRICE INDEXES

Inflation is a decrease in the purchasing power of money, evident to consumers as a pervasive increase in the prices of goods and services over a period of time. Many factors may contribute to inflation, but whatever the root causes at any particular time, the first step in prescribing possible remedies is to measure the amount of inflation. This is most commonly accomplished by measuring changes in price levels.

How do we measure changes in price? We only have to shop for groceries to notice that it is natural for prices to fluctuate. Some items, such as watermelon, are seasonal and sell at "outrageous" prices before they reach their peak supply and then sell for a small fraction of their previous high. Other items have no seasonal basis to explain their price fluctuations. To obtain a meaningful measure of inflation, the prices of all goods and services must somehow be represented.

449

A numerical value that summarizes price levels is called a *price index*. For such an index, the seasonal rise in the price of a commodity like strawberries should not have any significant influence. But increases in strawberry prices from one May to the next should. Likewise, only goods that are important to a great many people ought to be considered. Van Gogh paintings have increased steadily in price over the past 50 years, but such a price rise affects a minuscule percentage of persons and may be ignored.

Measuring price changes in the United States is an official task of the Department of Labor. Its Bureau of Labor Statistics periodically publishes the well-known Consumer Price Index or CPI.

It was the question of price changes that led to the development of the first price index more than 200 years ago by G. R. Carli, an Italian who compared the change in the prices of grain, wine, and oil from the years 1500 to 1750.* Carli's original index was a crude one compared to today's CPI, which is quite elaborate and complicated.

Price indexes have other uses besides being barometers of inflation. Economic models deal with *real* wages and *real* income, so that wages and income are adjusted to account for changing price levels by means of index numbers. Actual economic growth is ordinarily expressed in terms of change in real national product, which is found by using a price index to adjust annual GNP values computed at current price levels to values comparable to those of a prior period.

13-2 AGGREGATE PRICE INDEXES

Simple Price Relatives Index

The simplest price index measures the change over time in the price of a single item. The retail prices per pound of frying chicken sold at a particular store from 1967 through 1977 provided in Table 13-1 illustrate this index. The *base period*, the point in time to which all later prices are compared, is 1967. This is expressed by the equation 1967 = 100, which means that the index expresses all prices relative to that of 1967. Index numbers are ordinarily expressed in percentages. In 1967 the price of chicken was $0.47 per pound. The *price relative* for 1968, when chicken cost $0.45 per pound, is the ratio of the two prices, .45/.47 = .96, which indicates that in 1968 the price of chicken was 96 percent as high as in 1967. The price index for 1968 is thus 96. In a similar manner, the 1969 price of $0.41 is divided by the 1967 price, .41/.47 = .87, so that for 1969 the index is 87, the percentage of the price that prevailed in 1967; this is a 100 − 87 = 13 percent price reduction. Index values so obtained are called *percentage price relatives*.

* Bruce D. Mudgett, *Index Numbers*. New York: John Wiley & Sons, 1951, p. 6.

TABLE 13-1   Percentage Price Relatives Index
for Frying Chicken

Year	Price per Pound	Price Relative to 1967	Index
1967	$0.47	1.00	100
1968	0.45	.96	96
1969	0.41	.87	87
1970	0.39	.83	83
1971	0.37	.79	79
1972	0.38	.81	81
1973	0.40	.85	85
1974	0.42	.89	89
1975	0.51	1.09	109
1976	0.57	1.21	121
1977	0.63	1.34	134

Expressed symbolically in terms of the base period price p_0 and the price p_n in a given period, we have the *percentage price relatives index:*

$$I = \frac{p_n}{p_0} \times 100 \tag{13-1}$$

It is sometimes convenient to use the calendar years as subscripts, so that for 1975 the price index would be expressed as

$$I = \frac{p_{75}}{p_{67}} \times 100 = \frac{.51}{.47} \times 100 = 109$$

Price relatives for a single item are limited in usefulness. Price changes in a single commodity such as chicken do not indicate the general movement in prices. Of greater importance in economic planning and in comparing conditions from year to year would be a composite price index that covers many different items. The rise in the price of chicken will not significantly affect the life styles of most persons. But a rise in food prices may, especially for those whose incomes are fixed. Thus an index that considers several food items can help us measure the change in the standard of living of a large number of people.

Aggregate Price Indexes

In Table 13-2 the prices for selected meats, poultry, and fish sold at the same retail outlet are provided for the years 1975, 1976, and 1977. A price index for several items may be determined in a manner similar to that used previously for frying chicken. This would involve the calculation of an *aggregate* of the prices for each year, by summing together the prices for the four items. Such an

TABLE 13-2 Prices per Pound for Selected Food Items

Year	Rib Roast	Pork Chops	Canned Tuna	Frying Chicken
1975	$1.20	$0.90	$1.12	$0.51
1976	1.35	0.92	0.99	0.57
1977	1.47	1.08	1.08	0.63

aggregate may be either unweighted or weighted. Extending the previous notation, we determine the *unweighted aggregate price index:*

$$I = \frac{\sum p_n}{\sum p_0} \times 100 \qquad (13\text{-}2)$$

Using 1975 = 100, we obtain the price aggregate:

$$\sum p_{75} = \$1.20 + 0.90 + 1.12 + 0.51 = \$3.73$$

For 1976, the price aggregate is

$$\sum p_{76} = \$1.35 + 0.92 + 0.99 + 0.57 = \$3.83$$

so that the percent relative price index is

$$I = \frac{\sum p_{76}}{\sum p_{75}} \times 100 = \frac{\$3.83}{\$3.73} \times 100 = 103 \text{ (rounded)}$$

Thus the aggregate price of these foods has increased by 3 percent from 1975 to 1976.

Simple unweighted price aggregates are subject to certain difficulties. One problem is that the price index obtained is affected by a factor other than price, the *units* upon which the prices are based. In computing the above index numbers, each food item was expressed in the same units of 1 pound. Except for canned tuna, the foods listed are sold by the pound. If instead we had used $6\frac{1}{2}$ ounces, the weight of a standard can of tuna, as the unit of measurement, we would have obtained (rounded to the nearest cent) $0.46 for 1975, $0.40 for 1976, and $0.44 for 1977. Thus the price index for 1976 would have been 106 instead of 103.

One way to eliminate potential distortion caused by choice of units is to weight items in such a way that any units may be used. As a bonus, a weight may be given to each item in relation to its importance, thereby yielding a more meaningful measure of price change. For most households, the prices of rib roast and other beef products are much more significant than the price of canned tuna, since beef is more of a staple item and should weigh more heavily in the index.

The weights traditionally used in price indexes are quantities denoted by the letter q. The product $p \times q$ represents total value and is unaffected by the units chosen, because p is price per unit and q is the number of units. A meaningful price index is one that uses quantities in proportion to the importance or usage of the item. Thus, in establishing an index intended to measure a family's purchasing power, the quantities of each item purchased by a typical family would be used. When the $p \times q$ terms are summed for several items, the resulting value is referred to as a *weighted price aggregate*, which is denoted by $\sum pq$.

Various indexes may be computed from weighted price aggregates. The differences among those presented in this book are due to the choice of quantities used. We first consider the *Laspeyres index:*

$$I = \frac{\sum p_n q_0}{\sum p_0 q_0} \times 100 \tag{13-3}$$

The numerator $\sum p_n q_0$ represents the value of all the items purchased in time period n. The Laspeyres index uses quantity weights q_0 from the base period, so that only the prices are allowed to change. The denominator $\sum p_0 q_0$ provides the value of the same quantities of these commodities when they are purchased in the base period.

Table 13-3 shows the weekly quantities (in pounds) of selected food items assumed to be purchased by a typical family in 1975, the base period. The Laspeyres index for 1976 is calculated from expression (13-3) using the quantities for 1975 and prices for 1975 and 1976:

$$I = \frac{\sum p_{76} q_{75}}{\sum p_{75} q_{75}} \times 100 = \frac{\$11.86}{\$10.96} \times 100 = 108$$

Thus the prices for the selected items in 1976 are 8 percent higher than in the 1975 base period, which has index value 100.

TABLE 13-3 Price and Quantity Data for Food Items Used in Calculating Laspeyres Index, 1975=100

Item	Price per Pound 1975 p_{75}	Price per Pound 1976 p_{76}	Quantity (pounds) 1975 q_{75}	Value of Items 1975 $p_{75} q_{75}$	Value of Items 1976 $p_{76} q_{75}$
Rib roast	$1.20	$1.35	5	$6.00	$6.75
Pork chops	0.90	0.92	2	1.80	1.84
Canned tuna	1.12	0.99	1	1.12	0.99
Frying chicken	0.51	0.57	4	2.04	2.28
				$10.96	$11.86

$$\text{Laspeyres index} = \frac{\sum p_{76} q_{75}}{\sum p_{75} q_{75}} \times 100 = \frac{\$11.86}{\$10.96} \times 100 = 108$$

Another commonly used weighted aggregate price index is the *Paasche index:*

$$I = \frac{\sum p_n q_n}{\sum p_0 q_n} \times 100 \tag{13-4}$$

The Paasche index is similar to the Laspeyres, but the quantities q_n from the current period are used in calculating the price aggregate. If the quantities of the various items consumed by a typical family change over time, the two indexes will provide different percentage changes.

For example, in 1976 the market for canned tuna was seriously disturbed by concern over the porpoises killed in tuna nets. This possibly caused a drop in the level of consumption of tuna from the previous year. For the sake of illustration, suppose that the typical family in 1976 consumed only $\frac{1}{2}$ pound of tuna per week, raising its consumption of chicken to $4\frac{1}{2}$ pounds, while the quantities of rib roast and pork chops remained constant at 5 and 2 pounds. The weighted price aggregates are, for 1975,

$$\sum p_{75} q_{76} = \$1.20(5) + \$0.90(2) + \$1.12(\tfrac{1}{2}) + \$0.51(4\tfrac{1}{2}) = \$10.655$$

and for 1976,

$$\sum p_{76} q_{76} = \$1.35(5) + \$0.92(2) + \$0.99(\tfrac{1}{2}) + \$0.57(4\tfrac{1}{2}) = \$11.65$$

The Paasche index is calculated from expression (13-4):

$$I = \frac{\sum p_{76} q_{76}}{\sum p_{75} q_{76}} \times 100 = \frac{\$11.65}{\$10.655} \times 100 = 109$$

According to this index, the prices in 1976 were 9 percent, not 8 percent, higher than in 1975.

Ordinarily the discrepancies between the Laspeyres and Paasche indexes can be expected to grow as the time differential between the base period and current period becomes greater. There are two basic causes for widening disagreement. The primary one is the changing tastes of consumers. Newer items used in the index will, over time, tend to supplant the older ones in importance. We need only list some of the meat products heavily purchased 50 years ago to illustrate this point. Kidneys, tripe, heart, brains, and tongue are today hard to find in the ordinary supermarket, and are now largely used in processed meats, such as frankfurters. The Laspeyres index would use the earliest quantities for all items, giving high weight to some items hardly consumed at all and little weight to newer but more popular ones.

A second explanation for the discrepancy between the Paasche and Laspeyres indexes is that in a period of inflation there may be a downward shift in quantities consumed of higher priced items. Persons of fixed income will buy less steak and eat more hamburger as prices rise. If wages rise as fast or faster than prices, the reverse may be true.

The Paasche index may thus be more realistic than the Laspeyres, because changes in taste and earnings—as reflected in revised quantity weights—are considered as well as price. For reasons indicated below, the Paasche index is more difficult to work with than the Laspeyres, so that a generalized version of the latter is usually preferred. To overcome the difficulties of shifting consumer emphasis of various items, the base period may be revised from time to time to bring an index up to date. The Consumer Price Index, for example, is revised about every 10 years, to a new base period.

Generally, the use of base-period quantities to weight prices, as with the Laspeyres index, is preferred to the current quantities of the Paasche index. One reason for this is that it is expensive to collect data to find quantity weights, so that to do so every year would require a greater expenditure of resources than to use a single set of quantities for all years. Another difficulty in using current weights is that the base period's weighted aggregate must be recomputed for each new period considered. As we shall see, this is an important consideration in shifting the base period of an index. When different quantity weights have been used for each period, the change of base can be accomplished only be re-computing the index for all periods. The data required to make these calcula-tions may not be available, and the various shortcut procedures depend upon the use of the same weights in all time periods. A final advantage of using the same quantity weights in all years is that the percentage change in prices between two periods, neither of which need be a base, can then be determined from the index numbers obtained for each of the years.

It is convenient to consider a price index similar to the Laspeyres that uses arbitrarily chosen quantity weights q_a. This is the *fixed-weight aggregate price index*:

$$I = \frac{\sum p_n q_a}{\sum p_0 q_a} \times 100 \qquad (13\text{-}5)$$

Expression (13-5) provides the Laspeyres price index [expression (13-3)] when $q_a = q_0$. The major advantages of this more general index are that, along with the Laspeyres, it is free from period-to-period changes in the quantity weights and that, unlike the Laspeyres, its weights are not tied to a single base period.

EXERCISES

13-1   A random sample of 100 households has been selected in order to establish a price index for housing utilities. The following average annual figures have been obtained.

	Prices (dollars per unit)				Quantities			
	1974	1975	1976	1977	1974	1975	1976	1977
Electricity	1.97	2.05	2.09	2.10	62	64	68	70
Gas	7.90	8.25	8.60	8.80	8.7	9.0	9.5	10.1
Water	.29	.30	.31	.32	296	297	298	300
Telephone	2.40	2.45	2.50	2.50	55	56	58	60

The units are: thousand kilowatt hours for electricity, hundred therms for gas, hundred cubic feet for water, and hundred message unit equivalents for the telephone.

Calculate unweighted aggregate price indexes for 1975–1977 with the data on page 455, using 1974 = 100.

13-2 Using the 1974 quantities as weights, calculate the Laspeyres price indexes for 1975–1977, using the data in Exercise 13-1, with 1974 = 100. What is the percentage increase in 1977 prices over those of 1974?

13-3 Using the quantities for the current year as weights, calculate the Paasche indexes for 1975–1977, using the data in Exercise 13-1, with 1974 = 100. What is the percentage increase in 1977 prices over those of 1974?

13-4 Use the following quantity weights q_a: 65, 10, 300, 50 for electricity, gas, water, and telephone. Answer the following, using the data from Exercise 13-1.

(a) For a 1976 base, calculate the fixed-weight aggregate price index for 1977. What is the percentage increase in 1977 prices over the preceding year's?

(b) Use a 1977 base to calculate the fixed-weight aggregate price index for 1976. Determine the percentage increase in 1977 prices using these index numbers. Is your answer the same as in (a)? Explain.

13-3 PRICE RELATIVES INDEXES

The simplest index encountered at the outset of this chapter was the percentage price relative for a single commodity. This is provided by the ratio of the current price p_n to the base price p_0 times 100:

$$\text{Percentage price relative} = \frac{p_n}{p_0} \times 100 \qquad (13\text{-}6)$$

The indexes presented so far for two or more quantities involved price aggregates. Price indexes may also be constructed by taking averages of price relatives. As with price aggregates, these may be either weighted or unweighted. The simplest index computed from p_n/p_0 ratios for N items is the *unweighted price relatives index*:

$$I = \frac{\sum \dfrac{p_n}{p_0} \times 100}{N} \qquad (13\text{-}7)$$

Table 13-4 illustrates how this index is computed for the four food items previously considered. For 1976 the unweighted price relatives index is 103.7. Note that this is smaller than two of the aggregate price indexes previously obtained for the same data: 108 for the Laspeyres and 109 for the Paasche.

Aside from its simplicity, the unweighted price relatives index has one positive feature. It is independent of the units in which prices are expressed. The

TABLE 13-4   Calculation of Unweighted Price
Relatives Index for Selected Items

	Price per Pound		
	1975	*1976*	*Percentage*
			Price Relative
Item	p_{75}	p_{76}	$(p_{76}/p_{75}) \times 100$
Rib roast	$1.20	$1.35	112.5
Pork chops	0.90	0.92	102.2
Canned tuna	1.12	0.99	88.4
Frying chicken	0.51	0.57	111.8
			414.9

$$I = \frac{\sum (p_{76}/p_{75} \times 100)}{4} = \frac{414.9}{4} = 103.7$$

same value would be obtained whether tuna were priced in units of $6\frac{1}{2}$ ounces or by the pound. But, like the unweighted price aggregate index, all items are treated as equally important. As we have seen, this can make such an index less meaningful as a measure of how households are affected by general price increases.

The importance of the individual items is handled in the aggregate price indexes by using quantity weights. For price relatives, the analogous measure for the importance of each commodity is its total value. For a consumer index, this would correspond to the total amount paid for each item. The following expresses the *weighted price relatives index:*

$$I = \frac{\sum \left(\frac{p_n}{p_0} \times 100\right) v}{\sum v} \tag{13-8}$$

where $v =$ value of the item, which is here equal to price $\times$ quantity. Various combinations of price and quantities may be used. Only three are mentioned here.

When $v = p_0 q_0$, then the index

$$I = \frac{\sum \left(\frac{p_n}{p_0} \times 100\right) p_0 q_0}{\sum p_0 q_0} \tag{13-9}$$

is obtained. This is algebraically equivalent to the Laspeyres index [expression (13-3)], because the p_0 terms in the numerator cancel, so that the numerator is 100 times the price aggregate for period n when base period weights q_0 are used.

The weighted price relatives index computation when $v = p_0 q_0$ is provided in Table 13-5. The index number obtained, 108, is exactly the same as the value obtained in Table 13-3 for the Laspeyres index.

TABLE 13-5   Calculation of Weighted Price Relatives
Index for Selected Items

(1)	(2)		(3)	(4)	(5)	(6)
	Price per Pound		*Percentage Price Relative*	*Quantity (pounds)*		*Weighted Price Relative*
	1975	*1976*	$\dfrac{p_{76}}{p_{75}} \times 100$	*1975*	*Value*	$(3) \times (5)$
Items	p_{75}	p_{76}		q_{75}	$v = p_{75}q_{75}$	
Rib roast	$1.20	$1.35	112.5	5	$6.00	$675.00
Pork chops	0.90	0.92	102.2	2	1.80	183.96
Canned tuna	1.12	0.99	88.4	1	1.12	99.01
Frying chicken	0.51	0.57	111.8	4	2.04	228.07
					$10.96	$1,186.04

$$I = \frac{\sum \left(\dfrac{p_{76}}{p_{75}} \times 100\right) p_{75}q_{75}}{\sum p_{75}q_{75}} = \frac{\$1,186.04}{\$10.96} = 108$$

When $v = p_0 q_n$, then the following index is obtained:

$$I = \frac{\sum \left(\dfrac{p_n}{p_0} \times 100\right) p_0 q_n}{\sum p_0 q_n} \qquad (13\text{-}10)$$

This index is equivalent to the Paasche index of expression (13-4).

When $v = p_0 q_a$, then the index is

$$I = \frac{\sum \left(\dfrac{p_n}{p_0} \times 100\right) p_0 q_a}{\sum p_0 q_a} \qquad (13\text{-}11)$$

which is identical in value to the fixed-weight aggregate price index [expression (13-5)].

Other values of v could be used, but they would not be as meaningful. We see that the three weighted price relatives indexes are equivalent to the weighted price aggregate indexes discussed, so that numerical values calculated from the two sets will be equal. Whether to use price relatives instead of aggregates is a matter of the availability of data, and in some cases price relatives are simplest to acquire. The Bureau of Labor Statistics uses price relatives in computing the Consumer Price Index because of the tremendous substitution of items involved.

EXERCISE

13-5   From the price data of Exercise 13-1 (page 455), calculate the percentage price relatives for each utility item for the years 1975–1977, using 1974 = 100. Then, assuming value weights of $150, $90, $100, and $150 for electricity, gas, water, and telephone, determine the weighted price relatives indexes.

13-4 THE CONSUMER PRICE INDEX

The Consumer Price Index measures changes in prices that affect the cost of living for a large fraction of the U.S. population.* This is achieved by means of a "market basket" of goods and services that consists of about 400 items. These comprise most major expenses incurred by a typical city wage earner, including food, clothing, medical treatment, entertainment, rent, and transportation. Table 13-6 shows the major goods and service categories comprising

TABLE 13-6 Groups of Goods and Services Priced for the Consumer Price Index, Their December 1963 Relative Importance, and the Number of Items Priced

Major Groups	*Relative Importance*			*Number of Items Priced*	
All Items	100.00			398	
Food	22.43			105	
Food at home		17.89			96	
Cereals and bakery products			2.45		9
Meats, poultry, and fish			5.63		29
Dairy products			2.80		7
Fruits and vegetables			3.02		29
Other food at home			3.99		22
Food away from home		4.54			9
Housing	33.2			81	
Shelter		20.15			18
Rent			5.50		1
Hotels and motels			.38		1
Home ownership			14.27		16
Fuel and utilities		5.26			10
Household furnishings and operation		7.82			53
Apparel and Upkeep	10.63			77	
Men's and boys' apparel			2.86		19
Women's and girls' apparel			4.08		35
Footwear			1.51		11
Other apparel			2.18		12
Transportation	13.88			34	
Private		12.64			29
Public		1.24			5
Health and Recreation	19.45			101	
Medical care		5.70			38
Personal care		2.75			12
Reading and recreation		5.94			34
Other goods and services		5.06			17
Miscellaneous	.38				

SOURCE: U.S. Bureau of Labor Statistics.

* A nontechnical discussion of the CPI is contained in U.S. Department of Labor, *The Consumer Price Index: A Short Description*, 1967.

the CPI and the number of items in each. Also shown is the relative importance as a percentage of the total market basket, given to the items in each major grouping.

The CPI has been published continuously since 1913, although major modifications have been made in the method of computation, data collection, contents of the market basket, and base period. Since World War II there have been three base periods: 1947–1949, 1957–1959, and the single year, 1967, or about one change every 10 years. The CPI closely resembles the Laspeyres index, which, as we have noted, uses fixed quantities for weights. Because of the shifting importance of items, it is advantageous to revise the weights periodically. The weight revisions for the CPI do not necessarily occur at the same time as the shift of base, which is one reason why the CPI is not a Laspeyres index.

The CPI is based upon sample data, so sampling error is present. Furthermore, only a few key items are included, because it would be prohibitively expensive to collect data on all products and services provided in the U.S. Even for the limited 400 items, it would be impossible to monitor every transaction in order to obtain exact prices. Instead, average prices are used as estimates. These are obtained for all of the larger metropolitan areas and for a select group of smaller ones. Separate price indexes are computed for each city and then averaged by means of population weights, so that price levels in the larger cities have greater importance.

The data-collecting procedures are far too elaborate for detailed discussion in this book.* A few key features are important. The price data are obtained from a few randomly selected stores in each area. The store types are chosen to be representative of the merchandise classes from a recent Census of Retail Trade. The selection is made by *quota sampling*, where a specified number or quota of stores from each category is sought.

A very significant problem encountered in obtaining pricing data is that of product quality changes. When a product's quality declines while its price is fixed, it amounts to the same thing as a price increase. The nickel candy bar, now gone, is a good example. For over 50 years the price of many brands of candy bars was held at 5 cents, even though inflation had been recurrent. The amount of candy per bar was gradually reduced in order to cover the rising costs of manufacture. The Bureau of Labor Statistics has published detailed quality specifications on the items included in the price index in order to measure the real changes in price.

The CPI is a hybrid of two indexes discussed previously. In the early periods following a switch of base periods, it is the same as the Laspeyres index. But because the value (or quantity) weights used in recent times have been switched several periods after the base period was revised, the computations for a fixed-weight index must be used. The reason for this complicated scheme is that CPI base periods have been changed whenever the current index level was judged too high for further meaningful comparisons. The value data necessary

---

* For a comprehensive discussion, see Doris P. Rothwell, *The Consumer Price Index Pricing and Calculation Procedures* (Preliminary). Washington, D.C.: U.S. Bureau of Labor Statistics, March 17, 1964.

for revising weights are obtained from special studies that may occur in a different year than the base period. For example, in the late 1960s, the CPI base period was 1957–1959 = 100. A change in weights was made in December 1963 in accordance with the 1960–1961 Consumer Expenditure Survey.

Table 13-7 shows the consumer price index values over 1940–1975 when 1967 = 100.

TABLE 13-7   Consumer Price Index Values (1967 = 100)

1940	42.0	1950	72.1	1960	88.7	1970	116.3
1941	44.1	1951	77.8	1961	89.6	1971	121.3
1942	48.8	1952	79.5	1962	90.6	1972	125.3
1943	51.8	1953	80.1	1963	91.7	1973	133.1
1944	52.7	1954	80.5	1964	92.9	1974	147.7
1945	53.9	1955	80.2	1965	94.5	1975	161.2
1946	58.5	1956	81.4	1966	97.2		
1947	66.9	1957	84.3	1967	100.0		
1948	72.1	1958	86.6	1968	104.2		
1949	71.4	1959	87.3	1969	109.8		

13-5   DEFLATING TIME SERIES USING INDEX NUMBERS

A major use of a price index such as the CPI is to measure the "real" values in economic time series data expressed in monetary amounts. For example, the United States gross national product is calculated in current dollars, so that price changes over time are reflected in the original data. GNP is the basic measure of economic growth, so that to determine how much the physical goods and services have grown over time, increases in value due to price should not be included. It is possible for the quantity of goods and services to actually fall during a recession, while inflation causes the GNP to rise due solely to price increases. Real economic growth may be determined by using a price index to *deflate* GNP values.

Table 13-8 provides the values for GNP and its price deflator index during 1963–1975. Note that the index values have been continually increasing. The GNP has also been rising during this period of inflation. To isolate the changes in real GNP, the effect of rising prices may be found by transforming the actual values obtained for current dollars into their equivalent in the 1972 base dollars. This is achieved by dividing the original GNP data by the respective deflator index numbers. Thus in 1963 the GNP was 594.7 billion dollars, and the index was 71.59. Since prices were lower in 1963 than for the average base period, *real* GNP should have been higher and is found by dividing 594.7 by 71.59 percent:

$$\text{Real 1963 GNP} = \frac{594.7}{71.59} \times 100 = 830.7 \text{ billion dollars}$$

The original data show that in 1974, a recession year, the GNP grew from 1,306.4 to 1,406.8 billion dollars. But prices grew faster. The high levels of unemployment in 1974 actually caused a drop in real GNP, from 1,233.4 billion 1972

TABLE 13-8   Actual U.S. Gross National Product,
Price Deflator Index, and Real GNP

Year	(1) *Price Deflator Index* *(1972 = 100)*	(2) *U.S. GNP in Current Dollars* *(billions)*	(3) *Real GNP* *(billions)* *(2) ÷ (1) × 100*
1963	71.59	$594.7	$830.7
1964	72.71	635.8	874.4
1965	74.32	688.1	925.9
1966	76.76	753.0	981.0
1967	79.02	796.3	1,007.7
1968	82.57	868.5	1,051.8
1969	86.72	935.5	1,078.8
1970	91.36	982.4	1,075.3
1971	96.02	1,063.4	1,107.5
1972	100.00	1,171.1	1,171.1
1973	105.92	1,306.4	1,233.4
1974	116.20	1,406.8	1,210.7
1975	126.35	1,499.0	1,186.4

SOURCE: *Economic Report of the President, 1976.*

dollars to 1,210.7 billion 1972 dollars, found by dividing the actual GNP by the deflator index value of 116.20.

Economic models are often expressed in terms of real or price-adjusted values. Thus, we may use price indexes to find real wages, real income, or real production. To determine whether a typical worker's salary has risen enough to provide an increased standard of living, a price index can be used to compare take-home wages to prices. Thus if wages grow by 5 percent while prices grow by 6 percent, there has been a change in real wages (and hence, living standard) of $105/106 - 1 = -.01$ or a 1 percent decline. If the worker's union has enough clout, his standard of living may rise even during a period of inflation. Thus a 10 percent wage increase when there is a 6 percent CPI rise results in a $110/106 - 1 = .038$ or 3.8 percent increase in real wages.

EXERCISE

13-6   The average gross weekly earnings by persons employed in manufacturing, as reported in the 1976 *Economic Report of the President*, are provided below:

Year	Earnings		Year	Earnings
1963	$99.63		1970	$133.73
1964	102.97		1971	142.44
1965	107.53		1972	154.69
1966	112.34		1973	166.06
1967	114.90		1974	176.40
1968	122.51		1975	189.51
1969	129.51			

Using the CPI values in column (1) of Table 13-7, deflate the above time series to obtain "real" gross earnings with a base 1967 = 100.

3-6   QUANTITY INDEXES

Up to this point we have dealt only with price index numbers. The other major type of index number is the quantity index, which measures changes in physical volume over time. One of the most important is the Index of Production published monthly by the U.S. Federal Reserve Board. This index provides a summary of the total amount of goods produced in a given period relative to production during a base period. The index is composed of products in three broad categories or market groupings—consumer goods, equipment, and materials—with separate indexes published for major items. Index numbers are also reported in terms of major industry groupings—durable, nondurable, mining, and utilities. This index is an important barometer of economic conditions and is used by government agencies and businesses in short-range planning.

Quantity indexes are constructed in the same manner as price indexes. Because it is quantity that is being measured, the q values are changed each period. Prices are used as weights, so that the more expensive products are weighted more heavily. As with price indexes, the weights ordinarily remain constant from one reporting period to the next, so that the p values are usually not changed. Thus, algebraic expressions for computing quantity indexes can be obtained from those developed in the preceding sections for price changes by reversing the roles of p and q. For instance, the Laspeyres procedure may be adapted to measure change in quantities, providing the equation

$$I = \frac{\sum q_n p_0}{\sum q_0 p_0} \times 100 \tag{13-12}$$

The numerator and denominator are weighted quantity aggregates. As with price indexes, these are both total values of items. Since prices are held constant at the base period level, an increase in quantities from one period to the next will increase total value (there are then more items), and the quantity index will therefore rise.

3-7   SHIFTING AND SPLICING INDEX NUMBER SERIES

We shall conclude with a discussion of two technical points concerning time series of index numbers: (1) how the base period of the index may be *shifted* and (2) the related issue of how two indexes covering different periods of time may be combined into a single series by *splicing*.

Shifting the Base

An index such as the Consumer Price Index is considered by most persons to be a measure of the dollar's purchasing power. When discussing inflation, journalists often translate the CPI with statements like "in January 1971 a dollar is worth only 73 cents in 1959 purchasing power." For persons experiencing the rapid inflation of 1970–1971, 1959 seemed like such a long time ago that comparisons with prices during this base period became hard to relate to. The U.S. Bureau of Labor Statistics in 1971 shifted the base period of the CPI forward to 1967, thereby making inflationary comparisons more meaningful and easier. At the time of writing, further inflation is causing similar problems, and a newer base period is expected.

What are the implications of a shifted base, and how is such a shift accomplished? Table 13-9 shows a price index for sporting goods with a base period of 1965. The index numbers in column (1) were calculated using the Laspeyres method, expression (13-3). The base period of this index is shifted to 1975 in column (2). The numbers must be transformed so that the index number for the new base year is equal to 100. This is accomplished by dividing each value in the original series by 140, the original index number for 1975, and then multiplying by 100. The index numbers for years preceding 1975 are thus projected backward from the new base. The index for 1965 is thus $(100/140) \times 100 = 71.4$, and for 1970 it is $(112/140) \times 100 = 80.0$.

The values in column (2) may be viewed as the purchasing power of 1975 dollars. Thus a 1975 dollar buys the same quantity of sporting goods that could have been purchased in 1970 for 80 cents. The original and shifted series provide the same year-to-year percentage price increases. For instance, in 1966, prices increased by 4 percent over 1965, as the index number in column (1) is 104 for 1961 and 100 for 1965. In column (2) the 1965 index is 71.4 and the 1966 index is

TABLE 13-9   Original and Shifted Price Indexes
for Sporting Goods

Year	(1) *Original* *Price Index* *(1965 = 100)*	(2) *Price Index* *with Shifted Base* *(1975 = 100)*
1965	100	71.4
1966	104	74.3
1967	106	75.7
1968	107	76.4
1969	110	78.6
1970	112	80.0
1971	115	82.1
1972	117	83.6
1973	125	89.3
1974	131	93.6
1975	140	100.0
1976	147	105.0

74.3; thus, using the new base, 1966 prices are still $74.3/71.4 = 1.04$ or 104 percent of those for 1965.

Symbolically, ignoring the 100 factor, the shift in index number for 1975 is achieved by dividing $\sum p_{70}q_{65}/\sum p_{65}q_{65}$ by $\sum p_{75}q_{65}/\sum p_{65}q_{65}$, so that the sums involving $p_{65}q_{65}$ cancel, and the resulting index is

$$\frac{\sum p_{70}q_{65}}{\sum p_{75}q_{65}} \times 100 = 80.0$$

The quantity weights q_{65} in the above expression are still those used in 1965. The new 1975 base index shows prices relative to 1965 and is therefore no longer a Laspeyres index. As noted in Section 13-2, changing tastes and new products may make the weights given to the items in 1965 obsolete. Shifting the base period does not by itself bring an index up to date. One way to avoid this difficulty would be to revise the 1975 weights. In this case, the above shifting procedure would no longer apply, and the weighted aggregates would have to be recalculated for every year. In practice, revision of quantity weights would not be carried backward. Real problems, for example, would be created by using 1975 weights for sporting equipment not yet invented in 1965. Instead, the index for 1975 and future years would be computed using 1975 weights. The original series and the new series would then be spliced.

Splicing Index Time Series

Splicing of two sets of price index numbers covering different periods of time is usually required when there is a major change in quantity weights. It may also be necessary due to a new method of calculation or the inclusion of new commodities in the index. Such a change is usually accompanied by a

TABLE 13-10   Splicing Two Index Number Series

Year	(1) Old Price Index (1965 = 100)	(2) Revised Price Index (1970 = 100)	(3) Spliced Price Index (1970 = 100)
1965	100.0		87.6
1966	102.3		89.6
1967	105.3		92.2
1968	107.6		94.2
1969	111.9		98.0
1970	114.2	100.0	100.0
1971		102.5	102.5
1972		106.4	106.4
1973		108.3	108.3
1974		111.7	111.7
1975		117.8	117.8
1976		121.6	121.6

change in base period as well. In Table 13-10, old and revised price index numbers with 1965 = 100 are combined into a new series with 1970 = 100.

The procedure for projecting the earlier index number backward from 1970 is identical to shifting the base from 1965 to 1970, the same method previously discussed. For 1970 there is a value for the old and new series. The two series must overlap before they can be spliced to provide a continuous new series. The value of 114.2 for 1970 has been calculated with the weights used in the old series. The value of 100.0 for 1970 is used to obtain the weights for the new series. For all years after 1970, the new weights are used in calculating the index numbers.

Chapter Fourteen

Inferences Using
Two Samples

The great tragedy of science —the slaying of

a beautiful hypothesis by an ugly fact.

Thomas Huxley

A very important area of statistical inference involves using data from two samples, each representing a different population. A comparison of the two sample means may lead to the conclusion that one population tends to have larger values than the other. Two-sample inferences are important in a great many experiments where the impact of a change is being assessed. For example, a drug manufacturer may compare the effectiveness of a new treatment to that of an existing procedure. Thus, an experimental chemotherapy agent for leukemia and an existing drug may be compared in terms of their respective remission rates. Two separate samples—one for each drug—would ordinarily be required, because this controls treatment conditions by limiting the explanation of potential findings to differences in drugs rather than to other factors that could influence recovery.

Generalizations from two samples may take the form of an estimate or a test. Estimates may be made of the differences in the respective population means, proportions, or variances. Two-sample hypothesis testing procedures conclude either that one population has greater values than the other or that the differences between the two are not significant. Two-sample procedures follow the same dichotomies we identified in Chapter 9: one-sided versus two-sided tests; using the proportion versus the mean; and small versus large samples. In addition to these, the existence of two populations may involve a further choice: whether to use independent or matched-pairs samples. Matching the sample observations usually results in a considerable reduction in the number of observations that might otherwise be required.

14-1 CONFIDENCE INTERVALS FOR THE DIFFERENCE IN MEANS USING LARGE SAMPLES

The simplest two-sample inference involves estimating the difference between two population parameters. We begin by constructing a confidence interval estimate of the difference between the two population means.

For convenience, we will designate the populations by the letters A and B. Following this notation, *the population means are*

$$\mu_A = \text{Mean of population } A$$

$$\mu_B = \text{Mean of population } B$$

Which population corresponds to a particular letter is arbitrary. Usually, A designates the population presumed to have the larger mean. *The difference in population means is*

$$D = \mu_A - \mu_B \qquad (14\text{-}1)$$

This value may be estimated from the sample results. There are two ways of doing this, depending upon whether the observations are made independently or by matching pairs.

Independent Samples

The simplest case to consider is when the sample observations are selected independently. Sample means from the respective populations are designated as $\overline{X}_A$ and $\overline{X}_B$. *The difference between sample means is*

$$d = \overline{X}_A - \overline{X}_B \qquad (14\text{-}2)$$

This statistic is an unbiased estimator of D, the difference in population means. The samples used in calculating expression (14-2) may differ in size, and the number of observations taken for the respective samples are represented by the symbols n_A and n_B.

As we have seen, the sampling distributions of $\overline{X}_A$ and $\overline{X}_B$ may each be approximated by the normal curve for sufficiently large samples. Because the samples are chosen independently, it may be established that d *will also be approximately normally distributed, with a mean of* $D = \mu_A - \mu_B$ *and a standard deviation* of*

$$\sigma_d = \sqrt{\frac{\sigma_A^2}{n_A} + \frac{\sigma_B^2}{n_B}} \qquad (14\text{-}3)$$

where σ_A^2 and σ_B^2 are the respective population variances. Ordinarily, when μ_A and μ_B are unknown, σ_A^2 and σ_B^2 will also be unknown. The respective sample variances s_A^2 and s_B^2 may be used as estimators of these parameters. For *large samples* (in general, 30 or more observations for each), we thereby obtain

$$s_d = \sqrt{\frac{s_A^2}{n_A} + \frac{s_B^2}{n_B}} \qquad (14\text{-}4)$$

as an estimate of σ_d.

We are now ready to construct the confidence interval estimate for the difference in population means. We select a normal deviate z corresponding to the desired confidence level, so that we estimate the difference in population means by the interval

$$D = d \pm z s_d \qquad (14\text{-}5)$$

Since D and d are differences in means, a more convenient expression of *the confidence interval for the difference in population means when using independent samples is*

$$\mu_A - \mu_B = \overline{X}_A - \overline{X}_B \pm z \sqrt{\frac{s_A^2}{n_A} + \frac{s_B^2}{n_B}} \qquad (14\text{-}6)$$

Example 14-1   A statistics professor wishes to compare a new textbook to her old one. She teaches two sections of the same course. The professor continues to use the old book in section B, while she uses the new book in section A. Both sections of the course contain 30 students, and the respective classes are conducted in nearly identical fashion. Since the quality of the new book is being evaluated, we may refer to those students in section A as the experimental group and to those in section B as the control group. The students have been randomly assigned to section A or B, and each may be viewed as a sample of all students taking statistics in the professor's classes.

The effectiveness of each textbook can be measured in terms of the combined examination scores achieved by the students on common tests given throughout the term. Population A represents the potential scores of all students at the university who might use the new textbook in a course taught by this particular

---

* Here, we use the fact that $\overline{X}_A$ and $\overline{X}_B$ are independent random variables, so that the variance of their sum or difference equals the sum of the individual variances:

$$\sigma_d^2 = \sigma^2(\overline{X}_A - \overline{X}_B) = \sigma^2(\overline{X}_A) + \sigma^2(\overline{X}_B) = \frac{\sigma_A^2}{n_A} + \frac{\sigma_B^2}{n_B}$$

professor; population B represents the potential scores these same students would receive using the old textbook. Both sets of scores are target populations, because not all students will have the same statistics professor, use the same books, or take identical examinations.

The sample results are provided in Table 14-1. These data will be used to

TABLE 14-1   Sample Results for Students in Two Classes Using New and Old Textbooks

	Students Using New Book (A)			Students Using Old Book (B)	
Student Initials	Combined Exam Score X_A	X_A^2	Student Initials	Combined Exam Score X_B	X_B^2
C.A.	95	9,025	C.A.	85	7,225
L.A.	87	7,569	J.A.	74	5,476
A.B.	84	7,056	O.A.	59	3,481
I.B.	79	6,241	P.A.	71	5,041
P.B.	78	6,084	W.A.	48	2,304
B.C.	93	8,649	D.B.	78	6,084
M.C.	72	5,184	D.C.	94	8,836
D.D.	92	8,464	M.C.	75	5,625
E.E.	89	7,921	B.E.	92	8,464
S.F.	68	4,624	F.E.	85	7,225
T.G.	73	5,329	J.F.	76	5,776
V.G.	53	2,809	S.G.	69	4,761
G.I.	81	6,561	G.H.	82	6,724
F.L.	90	8,100	F.J.	76	5,776
M.L.	77	5,929	J.K.	85	7,225
N.L.	86	7,396	S.L.	70	4,900
G.M.	83	6,889	K.M.	69	4,761
H.M.	91	8,281	M.M.	71	5,041
T.M.	68	4,624	D.N.	80	6,400
N.N.	81	6,561	A.O.	91	8,281
Q.P.	75	5,625	L.P.	77	5,929
P.R.	76	5,776	A.S.	90	8,100
P.S.	64	4,096	B.S.	88	7,744
S.S.	63	3,969	T.S.	60	3,600
W.S.	61	3,721	W.S.	47	2,209
M.T.	83	6,889	L.T.	74	5,476
S.T.	72	5,184	N.T.	63	3,969
W.T.	69	4,761	T.T.	63	3,969
T.W.	59	3,481	L.V.	71	5,041
W.W.	53	2,809	P.W.	60	3,600
	2,295	179,607		2,223	169,043

estimate the difference in mean population scores, $D = \mu_A - \mu_B$. For this study, $n_A = n_B = 30$. (It is not necessary for the two samples to be of the same size, even though they happen to be in our example.) The following statistics are obtained:

$$\bar{X}_A = 2,295/30 = 76.5 \qquad\qquad \bar{X}_B = 2,223/30 = 74.1$$

$$s_A^2 = \frac{179,607 - 30(76.5)^2}{30 - 1} = 139.29 \qquad s_B^2 = \frac{169,043 - 30(74.1)^2}{30 - 1} = 148.92$$

The professor wants to construct a 95-percent confidence interval estimate for $\mu_A - \mu_B$. The required normal deviate is $z = 1.96$, and from expression (14-6) we have

$$\mu_A - \mu_B = 76.5 - 74.1 \pm 1.96 \sqrt{\frac{139.29}{30} + \frac{148.92}{30}}$$

$$= 2.4 \pm 6.08$$

or

$$-3.68 \leqslant \mu_A - \mu_B \leqslant 8.48$$

Thus, the mean difference in scores is estimated to lie between -3.68 and 8.48. The limit -3.68 indicates that the *disadvantage* in mean scores using book A might be 3.68 points (so that book B might be better), while 8.48 tells us that the *advantage* in mean scores using book A might be as great as 8.48 points.

The interpretation of the above interval is that were this experiment to be repeated several times, then this procedure would yield interval estimates containing the true $\mu_A - \mu_B$ difference about 95 percent of the time. Note that this estimate is not very precise and does not clearly indicate much difference between the effectiveness of the two books. Next, we will investigate another procedure that we might have used on this sample.

Matched-Pairs Sampling

A *matched-pairs sample* is obtained by making each population A observation in such a way that the selected elementary unit is matched with a "twin" from population B. For example, in evaluating a new drug, each patient in the control group would have an experimental partner of the same sex, with a similar occupation, family environment, and medical history, and close in age, weight, height, build, and other physiological characteristics. In job-placement testing, partners might be matched by aptitudes and intelligence, experience, socio-economic level, and productivity. In every case, matching would be accomplished in terms of those factors that might influence the characteristic being measured.

The individual differences for each pair can be used as the basis for estimating population differences. Matched-pairs sampling thus attempts to explain the differences in individual pairs in terms of differences due to the factor studied, while minimizing the variability in observations that may result from extraneous influences. The net effect is to reduce the impact of sampling error and thus to obtain greater sampling efficiency.

To illustrate how matched pairs may be obtained, we will expand the sampling study in Example 14-1. Suppose that the professor in our example decides to match students in the two classes. Her matching criteria should be selected so that each student pair is closely alike in aptitude for statistics and in achievement in related areas. Since the students *should be matched before actual sample observations are made*—a safeguard that minimizes bias in selecting actual pairs—she cannot use the two classes' performances on statistics tests for this purpose.

The professor may use quantitative SAT scores as a matching criterion for statistical aptitude. These could easily be obtained from the registrar's office for the enrolled students. As a measure of achievement, she might use the students' grades in the prerequisite mathematics course—data also obtainable from student records. Suppose that the professor uses these indicators to match her students. Table 14-2 shows one matching assignment, using mathematics grades as the main ranking device and SAT scores to obtain a finer sorting of students with identical mathematics grades. In terms of these criteria, two "A" students having respective SAT scores of 706 and 713 constitute the first pair; similarly, two "C" students scoring 455 and 454 are the nineteenth pair.

The observations may be designated by the symbols

X_{A_i} = Sample value for population A partner in ith matched pair

X_{B_i} = Sample value for population B partner in ith matched pair

TABLE 14-2   Matching of Students in Terms of Mathematics Grades and Quantitative SAT Scores

	Students Using New Book (A)			Students Using Old Book (B)		
Pair	Student Initials	Mathematics Grade	Quantitative SAT	Student Initials	Mathematics Grade	Quantitative SAT
1	A.B.	A	706	A.O.	A	713
2	B.C.	A	702	A.S.	A	698
3	C.A.	A	674	B.E.	A	685
4	D.D.	A	660	B.S.	A	659
5	E.E.	A	622	C.A.	A	610
6	F.L.	B	685	D.C.	A	507
7	G.M.	B	683	D.N.	B	671
8	G.I.	B	623	D.B.	B	654
9	H.M.	B	583	F.J.	B	612
10	I.B.	B	582	F.E.	B	596
11	L.A.	B	581	G.H.	B	575
12	N.L.	B	525	J.K.	B	533
13	M.T.	B	489	J.F.	B	477
14	M.L.	B	425	J.A.	B	454
15	M.C.	C	523	K.M.	B	426
16	N.N.	C	512	L.P.	C	544
17	Q.P.	C	510	L.T.	C	523
18	P.R.	C	468	L.V.	C	481
19	P.B.	C	455	M.C.	C	454
20	P.S.	C	421	M.M.	C	409
21	S.F.	C	411	N.T.	C	408
22	S.S.	C	394	O.A.	C	402
23	S.T.	C	359	P.A.	C	383
24	T.M.	C	342	P.W.	C	336
25	T.G.	C	326	S.L.	C	326
26	T.W.	C	308	S.G.	C	315
27	W.S.	C	295	T.S.	D	435
28	W.T.	D	421	T.T.	D	386
29	V.G.	D	351	W.A.	D	321
30	W.W.	D	288	W.S.	D	317

For each sample couple, we may find *the matched-pair difference:*

$$d_i = X_{A_i} - X_{B_i} \qquad (14\text{-}7)$$

(d_i should not be confused with the unsubscripted d used earlier, which expresses the difference between the means of two independent samples rather than individual pairs.)

In the usual manner, we find *the mean of the matched-pair differences:*

$$\bar{d} = \frac{\sum d_i}{n} \qquad (14\text{-}8)$$

where n is the *number of pairs* observed in the sampling study. Analogously, we determine *the standard deviation of the matched-pair differences:*

$$s_{d\text{-paired}} = \sqrt{\frac{\sum d_i^2 - n\bar{d}^2}{n-1}} \qquad (14\text{-}9)$$

Here $\bar{d}$ represents the mean of n separate matched-pair differences and has an expected value of $D = \mu_A - \mu_B$. This is the same fact noted for the d discussed previously for differences in means of entire independent samples. Both d and $\bar{d}$ may be used to draw inferences about the difference between the means of populations A and B. However, each matched-pair difference d_i can be treated like a single observation, so that $\bar{d}$ has the same properties described in earlier chapters for $\bar{X}$. Thus, the central limit theorem indicates that for a sufficiently large sample (usually 30 or more), $\bar{d}$ *is approximately normally distributed, with a mean of D and a standard deviation estimated from*

$$\frac{s_{d\text{-paired}}}{\sqrt{n}}$$

This makes it possible to select a normal deviate z corresponding to a desired confidence level, so that we may estimate $D = \mu_A - \mu_B$ by *the confidence interval for the difference in population means when matched pairs are used:*

$$\mu_A - \mu_B = \bar{d} \pm z \frac{s_{d\text{-paired}}}{\sqrt{n}} \qquad (14\text{-}10)$$

Returning to the statistics professor's estimation problem of the difference in population mean scores using the new and old books, the values for the matched-pair differences appear in Table 14-3. For $n = 30$ pairs, the professor obtained the following results:

$$\bar{d} = 2.4 \qquad s_{d\text{-paired}} = 5.01$$

TABLE 14-3 Calculation of Matched-Pair Differences for Student Scores Using New and Old Books

| | *Student Pair* | | *Combined Exam Scores* | | | |
| | Group A | Group B | Group A | Group B | Difference | |
i	Student	Student	X_{A_i}	X_{B_i}	d_i	d_i^2
1	A.B.	A.O.	84	91	−7	49
2	B.C.	A.S.	93	90	3	9
3	C.A.	B.E.	95	92	3	9
4	D.D.	B.S.	92	88	4	16
5	E.E.	C.A.	89	85	4	16
6	F.L.	D.C.	90	94	−4	16
7	G.M.	D.N.	83	80	3	9
8	G.I.	D.B.	81	78	3	9
9	H.M.	F.J.	91	76	15	225
10	I.B.	F.E.	79	85	−6	36
11	L.A.	G.H.	87	82	5	25
12	N.L.	J.K.	86	85	1	1
13	M.T.	J.F.	83	76	7	49
14	M.L.	J.A.	77	74	3	9
15	M.C.	K.M.	72	69	3	9
16	N.N.	L.P.	81	77	4	16
17	Q.P.	L.T.	75	74	1	1
18	P.R.	L.V.	76	71	5	25
19	P.B.	M.C.	78	75	3	9
20	P.S.	M.M.	64	71	−7	49
21	S.F.	N.T.	68	63	5	25
22	S.S.	O.A.	63	59	4	16
23	S.T.	P.A.	72	71	1	1
24	T.M.	P.W.	68	60	8	64
25	T.G.	S.L.	73	70	3	9
26	T.W.	S.G.	59	69	−10	100
27	W.S.	T.S.	61	60	1	1
28	W.T.	T.T.	69	63	6	36
29	V.G.	W.A.	53	48	5	25
30	W.W.	W.S.	53	47	6	36
			2,295	2,223	72	900

$$\bar{d} = \frac{\sum d_i}{n} = \frac{72}{30} = 2.4$$

$$s_{d\text{-paired}} = \sqrt{\frac{\sum d_i^2 - n\bar{d}^2}{n-1}} = \sqrt{\frac{900 - 30(2.4)^2}{29}}$$

$$= \sqrt{25.0759} = 5.01$$

(Note that 2.4 is the same point estimate for $\mu_A - \mu_B$ that we found earlier using the same data as independent samples.) A 95-percent confidence interval estimate for $\mu_A - \mu_B$ is constructed, using expression (14-10) and the normal deviate value $z = 1.96$:

$$\mu_A - \mu_B = 2.4 \pm 1.96 \left(\frac{5.01}{\sqrt{30}} \right)$$

$$= 2.4 \pm 1.79$$

or

$$.61 \leqslant \mu_A - \mu_B \leqslant 4.19$$

This confidence interval is more precise than the previous one using the student test data as independent samples. A comparison of these two procedures follows.

Matched Pairs Compared to Independent Samples

Which procedure—independent sampling or matched pairs—is best? As a first step in answering this question, we might compare the sample sizes necessary to provide identical levels of estimation reliability for the same tolerable error.

Generally, the comparative advantage of matched-pairs sampling depends upon how closely the matching scheme used correlates population *A* values with population *B* values. A good matching criterion should eliminate most extraneous sources of variation, so this correlation would ordinarily be quite high.

A sample-size comparison is easiest to make when there are just as many observations from *A* as from *B*, so that $n_A = n_B$. We may also presume that population variabilities are similar, so that σ_A and σ_B are approximately equal. Under these conditions, it is possible to mathematically prove that *matched-pairs sampling requires a smaller sample size than independent sampling, and this reduction in required sample size is proportional to the population correlation coefficient*. Thus, if *A* and *B* have a correlation coefficient of .9, then a 90-percent savings in sample size is possible by using matched pairs. That is, 10 times as many observations are needed for independent samples to yield the same precision and reliability as with matched pairs. If the correlation coefficient were .99, then independent sampling would require 100 times as many observations as matched-pairs sampling.

Returning to our original question, we might wonder why independent samples are used at all. In part, independent sampling is prevalent both because pair matching is often difficult and because each observation takes a great deal of time. Sometimes it is impossible to advantageously match elementary units. Successful matching generally requires a large amount of available data on every unit. Not only must these data be studied just to establish relevant matching criteria—perhaps using multiple regression and correlation techniques—but they must then be carefully applied when the sample units are paired. Once the matched-pairs machinery has been set in motion, further sampling costs are comparable, observation by observation, to those of independent sampling. For a study involving continued monitorship over a long period of time, matched-pairs samples have a distinct cost advantage. This makes them preferred in medical studies, where the fixed cost of establishing the sample pairs is small in comparison to total expenses.

EXERCISES

14-1   The business school dean at State U. wants to compare the GMAT scores of his graduates to those of non-business students. Two independent random samples produced the following data:

Business	Non-Business
$n_A = 100$	$n_B = 150$
$\bar{X}_A = 620.1$	$\bar{X}_B = 576.4$
$s_A^2 = 1,874$	$s_B^2 = 2,057$

Construct a 95-percent confidence interval for the difference in population means.

14-2   A government meteorologist wishes to find the difference in mean annual tornado intensity (verified annual number of occurrences per 10,000 square miles) for two Midwestern states. Assuming that past tornado events over a ten-year period in the two states represent independent random samples of long-run weather patterns, he has plotted all reported tornadoes on a map and obtained the following intensity data:

State A	State B
$n_A = 96$	$n_B = 114$
$\bar{X}_A = .53$	$\bar{X}_B = .34$
$s_A^2 = 1.2$	$s_B^2 = 1.5$

Construct a 99-percent confidence interval for the difference in mean annual tornado intensity.

14-3   A Federal Aviation Agency statistician must determine how two airlines differ in their ability to meet flight schedules. From routes common to both airlines, he has randomly selected 100 actual arrival times for each. Each observation has been matched not only by route but by date and by time of day. From these data, the number of minutes late in every matched pair was determined for each airline (negative values were used for early arrivals). The sample mean and the standard deviation for the differences (the late time for airline A minus the late time for airline B) were determined as

$$\bar{d} = 2 \text{ minutes}$$

$$s_{d\text{-paired}} = 3 \text{ minutes}$$

Construct a 95-percent confidence interval estimate for the difference in mean amount of late time for the two airlines.

14-4   A city manager wants to know what gasoline savings would be made by converting the tires on all city cars. New tires were ordered for 200 cars; half of these cars used steel radial tires and the rest were equipped with the standard cord variety. Cars in the two groups were matched by make, model, age, use (police, building inspection, or whatever), and general condition. A month-long test revealed that the mean increase in gasoline mileage when radial tires were used was 2 miles per gallon. The standard deviation in gasoline savings for the paired cars was also 2 miles per gallon. Construct a 95-percent confidence interval estimate for the savings advantage in mean gasoline mileage that radial tires would create if they were adopted for all city cars.

4-2 HYPOTHESIS TESTS FOR COMPARING TWO MEANS USING LARGE SAMPLES

Rather than estimate the difference between two population means, it may be desirable to apply hypothesis-testing procedures to determine whether or not population *A* values are significantly larger or smaller than population *B* values. These methods would permit choices to be made. Thus, an experimental compensation program may be adopted because the statistical test concludes that workers paid under it attain higher mean productivity than those paid through the existing program. A new drug may be rejected by a hospital staff because it does not have a mean relief level that significantly exceeds the present one. The owner of a taxicab fleet may find sample results indicating that a new tire supplier should be awarded a contract because his tires wear longer than the current brand. In each of these cases, sample data are required for both the control group and the experimental group.

In two-sample tests, the null hypothesis may take any one of the following forms:

$$H_0: \ \mu_A \geqslant \mu_B \quad \text{or} \quad H_0: \ D \geqslant 0 \qquad \text{(lower-tailed test)}$$
$$H_0: \ \mu_A \leqslant \mu_B \quad \text{or} \quad H_0: \ D \leqslant 0 \qquad \text{(upper-tailed test)}$$
$$H_0: \ \mu_A = \mu_B \quad \text{or} \quad H_0: \ D = 0 \qquad \text{(two-sided test)}$$

The equivalent expressions on the right are found by subtracting μ_B on both sides of the original inequalities and using the fact that $D = \mu_A - \mu_B$. As in estimating the difference between two means, two-sample hypothesis tests may be applied to independent samples as well as to matched pairs.

Independent Samples

When samples are selected independently, the appropriate test statistic is $d = \bar{X}_A - \bar{X}_B$. As we have seen, for sufficiently large samples *d* is approximately normally distributed, with a mean of *D* and a standard deviation of σ_d. We must choose a critical value for *d*, which we will denote as d^*, that provides a decision rule corresponding to the desired significance level. When population *A* values are presumed larger, so that $\mu_A \geqslant \mu_B$ and the null hypothesis is $H_0: D \geqslant 0$, extremely negative values for *d* will refute H_0. The Type I error probability α is then represented by a lower-tailed area under the normal curve for *d*. Therefore, we have the following *decision rule for a lower-tailed test:*

Accept H_0 if $d \geqslant d^*$

Reject H_0 if $d < d^*$

For an upper-tailed test the reverse rule applies.

In finding d^*, we use the fact that under H_0 the normal curve for d must be centered at $D = 0$. The critical normal deviate for the test is z_α, and d^* is therefore located z_α standard deviations away from this mean. Estimating σ_d by s_d, we have

$$d^* = z_\alpha s_d \quad \text{or} \quad d^* = -z_\alpha s_d \tag{14-11}$$

depending on whether the test is upper- or lower-tailed. Substituting the terms in expression (14-4) for s_d, we have *the critical value for the difference in sample means:*

$$d^* = z_\alpha \sqrt{\frac{s_A^2}{n_A} + \frac{s_B^2}{n_B}} \quad \text{for an upper-tailed test}$$

$$\tag{14-12}$$

$$d^* = -z_\alpha \sqrt{\frac{s_A^2}{n_A} + \frac{s_B^2}{n_B}} \quad \text{for a lower-tailed test}$$

If the values of the population variances are known in advance of sampling, then σ_A^2 and σ_B^2 can be used in place of s_A^2 and s_B^2 in expression (14-12).

Example 14-2   In evaluating the effectiveness of a new automobile engine in controlling exhaust emissions, the U.S. Environmental Protection Agency might conduct a sampling study like the one we will describe here. The experimental group (A) consisted of $n_A = 50$ prototype rotary engines of a type proposed to replace conventional engines. The control group (B) contained $n_B = 100$ piston engines equipped with catalytic converters. (Note that different sample sizes were used for the two groups.)

The EPA wishes to use the null hypothesis that the mean sulfur-dioxide emissions level in parts per million (ppm) from all rotary engines is at least as great as that from the current engines, $H_0: \mu_A \geqslant \mu_B$. Since rejection of this hypothesis will result in permitting a manufacturer to install the rotary engine in all its cars, the EPA has established an $\alpha = .01$ significance level for the test; that is, there is a one-percent chance of making the incorrect decision and concluding that rotary engines are cleaner than piston engines when the opposite is true.

The sample results for sulfur dioxide emissions were

Rotary Engine	*Piston Engine*
$\bar{X}_A = 25$ ppm	$\bar{X}_B = 30$ ppm
$s_A^2 = 90$	$s_B^2 = 100$

From Appendix Table E we have $z_{.01} = 2.33$. Since the test is lower-tailed, expression (14-12) provides

$$d^* = -2.33 \sqrt{\frac{90}{50} + \frac{100}{100}} = -3.90$$

The decision rule for applying $d = \bar{X}_A - \bar{X}_B$ is therefore

Accept H_0 (refuse rotary engine) if $d \geqslant -3.90$

Reject H_0 (permit rotary engine) if $d < -3.90$

Since the actual difference in sample means is

$$d = \bar{X}_A - \bar{X}_B = 25 - 30 = -5$$

which is a value smaller than $d^* = -3.90$, the EPA must *reject* H_0 and allow the manufacturer to substitute the rotary engine.

The calculation of d^* may be bypassed, using the fact that $z = d/s_d$, so that we may calculate *the normal deviate for the sample results:*

$$z = \frac{\bar{X}_A - \bar{X}_B}{\sqrt{\dfrac{s_A^2}{n_A} + \dfrac{s_B^2}{n_B}}} \qquad (14\text{-}13)$$

We may then compare this value to z_α. In the preceding example,

$$z = \frac{25 - 30}{\sqrt{\dfrac{90}{50} + \dfrac{100}{100}}} = -2.99$$

which is smaller than $-z_{.01} = -2.33$, and again we see that H_0 must be rejected.

Two-Sided Tests

When population A values are presumed smaller and $\mu_A \leqslant \mu_B$, so that $H_0: D \leqslant 0$, the test is upper-tailed. The procedure is analogous to the one in Example 14-2, except that large positive values for d or z result in rejecting H_0. For a two-sided test, where it is assumed that $\mu_A = \mu_B$ and that the null hypothesis is $H_0: D = 0$, the critical normal deviate is $z_{\alpha/2}$ (corresponding to an upper-tail area equal to one-half the desired significance level) and the critical values d_1^* and d_2^* are found, so that our rule is

> *Accept H_0 if $d_1^* \leqslant d \leqslant d_2^*$*
>
> *Reject H_0 if $d < d_1^*$ or if $d > d_2^*$*

The following expressions provide *the critical values for the difference in sample means:*

$$d_1^* = -z_{\alpha/2}\sqrt{\frac{s_A^2}{n_A} + \frac{s_B^2}{n_B}}$$

$$\qquad (14\text{-}14)$$

$$d_2^* = z_{\alpha/2}\sqrt{\frac{s_A^2}{n_A} + \frac{s_B^2}{n_B}}$$

Using the value for z calculated from expression (14-13) instead, H_0 would be accepted if z fell within $\pm z_{\alpha/2}$ and would be rejected outside these limits.

Often the two-sided test is conducted in conjunction with a confidence interval estimate of $D = \mu_A - \mu_B$. In Example 14-1, we found the 95-percent confidence interval for the difference in population mean statistics scores for students using a new book A and students using an old book B to be

$$-3.68 \leqslant \mu_A - \mu_B \leqslant 8.48$$

Since this interval contains the value 0, the null hypothesis for those data, $H_0: \mu_A = \mu_B$ (or $D = \mu_A - \mu_B = 0$), must be *accepted* at the $\alpha = 1 - .95 = .05$ significance level.

Matched-Pairs Sampling

When matched pairs are used, we find the pair differences $d_i = X_{A_i} - X_{B_i}$ and then calculate their mean $\bar{d}$ and standard deviation $s_{d\text{-paired}}$. Using $\bar{d}$ as the test statistic, for sufficiently large samples, we may presume that the normal curve applies. We may therefore represent critical values by $\bar{d}*$ for a one-sided test or by $\bar{d}_1^*$ and $\bar{d}_2^*$ for a two-sided test. The hypothesis-testing decision rules may be summarized as follows:

Upper-Tailed Tests	*Lower-Tailed Tests*
$H_0: \mu_A \leqslant \mu_B$ or $D \leqslant 0$	$H_0: \mu_A \geqslant \mu_B$ or $D \geqslant 0$
Accept H_0 if $\bar{d} \leqslant \bar{d}*$ $(z \leqslant z_\alpha)$	*Accept H_0 if $\bar{d} \geqslant \bar{d}*$ $(z \geqslant -z_\alpha)$*
Reject H_0 if $\bar{d} > \bar{d}*$ $(z > z_\alpha)$	*Reject H_0 if $\bar{d} < \bar{d}*$ $(z < -z_\alpha)$*

Two-Sided Tests

$$H_0: \quad \mu_A = \mu_B \quad \text{or} \quad D = 0$$

Accept H_0 if $\bar{d}_1^* \leqslant \bar{d} \leqslant \bar{d}_2^*$ $(-z_{\alpha/2} \leqslant z \leqslant z_{\alpha/2})$
Reject H_0 if $\bar{d} < \bar{d}_1^*$ or if $\bar{d} > \bar{d}_2^*$ (if $z < -z_{\alpha/2}$ or if $z > z_{\alpha/2}$)

The critical values are:

$$\bar{d}* = z_\alpha \frac{s_{d\text{-paired}}}{\sqrt{n}} \qquad \text{for an upper-tailed test}$$

$$\bar{d}* = -z_\alpha \frac{s_{d\text{-paired}}}{\sqrt{n}} \qquad \text{for a lower-tailed test}$$

(14-15)

With two-sided tests:

$$\bar{d}_1^* = -z_{\alpha/2} \frac{s_{d\text{-paired}}}{\sqrt{n}}$$

$$\bar{d}_2^* = z_{\alpha/2} \frac{s_{d\text{-paired}}}{\sqrt{n}}$$

(14-16)

while the computed normal deviate z may be found using

$$z = \frac{\bar{d}}{s_{d\text{-paired}}/\sqrt{n}} \qquad (14\text{-}17)$$

Example 14-3 Perhaps the most controversial application of statistics has been in cigarette-smoking studies. One researcher interested in the tendency among middle-aged American men toward angina pectoris conducted an elaborate matched-pairs sampling investigation to determine if the onset of this disease is accelerated by heavy smoking. Random samples of male smokers and non-smokers were chosen from medical records. To speed her investigation, the researcher decided not to follow each patient until detection of the disease, but instead to study only those men already suffering from angina.

Each smoker was matched to a nonsmoker, first by age and then in accordance with life style, occupation, medical history, and general physical characteristics. The actual matching was determined from carefully prepared dossiers, where all references to the status of the circulatory system and the heart were deleted by an independent physician. (It is very important that any data directly relevant to the variable being observed not influence the matching, thereby eliminating an obvious source of bias.)

As her null hypothesis, the researcher assumed that the mean age at which angina was first detected was the same for smokers and nonsmokers:

$$H_0: \quad \mu_A = \mu_B$$

A total of $n = 100$ pairs were obtained by matching, and the sample ages X_{A_i} for smokers and X_{B_i} for nonsmokers when angina was first detected were determined. The individual matched-pair differences d_i were then computed and the following statistics were obtained:

$$\bar{d} = -1.3 \text{ years}$$
$$s_{d\text{-paired}} = 2.4 \text{ years}$$

Using an $\alpha = .05$ significance level, the critical normal deviate for this two-sided test was $z_{\alpha/2} = z_{.025} = 1.96$. The critical values for $\bar{d}$ were computed to be

$$\bar{d}_1^* = -1.96\left(\frac{2.4}{\sqrt{100}}\right) = -.47$$

$$\bar{d}_2^* = 1.96\left(\frac{2.4}{\sqrt{100}}\right) = .47$$

The applicable decision rule was therefore

Accept H_0 (conclude smoking does not matter) if $-.47 \leqslant \bar{d} \leqslant .47$

Reject H_0 (conclude smoking affects angina)   if $\bar{d} < -.47$ or if $\bar{d} > .47$

Since $\bar{d} = -1.3$ years is smaller than $-.47$, the null hypothesis that smokers and nonsmokers contract angina at the same mean age had to be *rejected*, and the researcher had to conclude that smoking hastens the occurrence of angina.

Solved another way, we may calculate the normal deviate by using expression (14-17) to obtain

$$z = \frac{-1.3}{2.4/\sqrt{100}} = -5.42$$

which is less than $-z_{.025} = -1.96$, and again we see that H_0 had to be rejected.

The value $\bar{d} = -1.3$ in the above example serves as a point estimate for the difference $D = \mu_A - \mu_B$, indicating that for the sample results obtained, angina occurs on the average 1.3 years sooner among smokers than among non-smokers. A 95-percent confidence interval estimate of the difference in population mean ages could be obtained directly from the above results:

$$\mu_A - \mu_B = -1.3 \pm .47$$

or

$$-1.77 \leqslant \mu_A - \mu_B \leqslant -.83 \text{ years}$$

The above confidence interval might have been used as the basis for testing the original hypothesis. We can see how this works by continuing with the earlier example of the statistics professor comparing two textbooks.

We will apply the confidence-interval results for the matched pairs the professor obtained in a two-sided test where her null hypothesis was that the new statistics book yields mean scores no different from those obtained with the old book; that is, $H_0: \mu_A = \mu_B$. For the data in Section 14-1, we found the 95-percent confidence interval

$$.61 \leqslant \mu_A - \mu_B \leqslant 4.19$$

which does not contain the value 0. Thus, in this example, H_0 must be rejected at the $\alpha = .05$ significance level.

Efficiency of Matched-Pairs Testing

Note that the above result contradicts our earlier conclusion from the independent sample data, for in this particular application, matched-pairs sampling proved to be a more discriminating procedure. (*Never use both methods on the same data*; we did it here only to compare the techniques.)

The earlier arguments for and against matched-pairs sampling can be applied to hypothesis-testing situations as well. A matched-pairs test is much more efficient or powerful than a test from independent sampling. With matched pairs, a much smaller sample size can generally be used to provide similar protection against Type I and Type II errors. However, matched-pairs sampling is more costly and is applicable only in those situations where suitable matching criteria and supporting data are available.

EXERCISES

14-5   A physician must compare two treatments for venereal disease. Because new bacteria strains have evolved that are resistant to antibiotics, a formerly obsolete chemical cure has been revived. The doctor wishes to test the null hypothesis that patient recovery time using penicillin to treat gonorrhea is less than or equal to the duration of sulfa-drug treatment. If this hypothesis is rejected, he will use sulfa drugs on future patients;

if the sample results are not significant, he will continue to administer penicillin. A random sample of $n_A = 100$ patients were selected from those treated with penicillin, and another group of $n_B = 50$ patients were given sulfa. The following results were obtained:

Penicillin	Sulfa
$\bar{X}_A = 10$ days	$\bar{X}_B = 9$ days
$s_A^2 = 10$	$s_B^2 = 3$

(a) Is this test lower-tailed or upper-tailed?

(b) If an $\alpha = .01$ significance level is desired, find the doctor's critical value for the difference in sample means. Which treatment should he use in the future?

(c) Calculate the normal deviate for the sample results. What is the smallest significance level at which this value indicates the null hypothesis could have been rejected?

14-6 To combat aphid infestation, a farmer must decide whether he should spray his fruit trees with pesticide or inundate them with ladybugs. He sprays a sample of 250 trees and uses ladybugs on another sample of 250 trees. His null hypothesis is that spraying produces a yield as high as that obtained using the natural predators. His sample results for spraying provide a mean of 10 bushels of good fruit per tree, with a standard deviation of 3 bushels. With ladybugs, the mean is 10.5 bushels of good fruit per tree with a standard deviation of 1 bushel. Using as his test statistic the mean yield from spraying minus the mean yield from ladybugs, should the farmer accept or reject the null hypothesis at the .05 significance level?

14-7 A soft drink bottler wanted to determine whether or not noncaloric drinks help people who have weight problems. Although these drinks reduce caloric intake, they do not reduce overall appetite levels like sugared drinks do. The company dietician matched 36 pairs of obese persons in terms of weight, sex, diet, life style, eating habits, and prior fattiness problems. The experimental group (A) was asked to use only diet soft drinks and to substitute artificial sweeteners. Both groups were to continue with their regular diets, but the control group (B) was asked to avoid noncaloric beverages of any kind. At the end of six months, the weight change was determined for each person. As her null hypothesis, the dietician assumes that the mean weight reduction will be the same for both groups. The mean of the matched-pairs differences has been found to be a one-pound reduction in favor of noncaloric drinks. The standard deviation was 2 pounds. If an $\alpha = .01$ significance level is desired for this two-sided test:

(a) Find the critical values for the mean matched-pair difference.

(b) What conclusion should the dietician reach?

(c) Calculate the normal deviate for the test results. What is the lowest significance level at which she may reject her null hypothesis?

14-8 Referring to the confidence interval found in Exercise 14-2 for the differences in mean annual tornado intensity in two states, should the meteorologist accept or reject the null hypothesis that the mean intensity is the same in both states if he uses an $\alpha = .01$ significance level?

14-9 Refer to the confidence interval found in Exercise 14-3 for the difference in the mean number of minutes late for two airlines. At the $\alpha = .05$ significance level, should the FAA accept or reject the null hypothesis that the mean minutes late is the same for both airlines?

14-10   Refer to the confidence interval found in Exercise 14-4 for the savings in mean gasoline mileage using radial tires. At the $\alpha = .05$ significance level, should the city manager accept or reject the null hypothesis that mean gasoline consumption is the same for radial as for standard tires?

14-3   INFERENCES FOR TWO MEANS USING SMALL SAMPLES

Thus far, we have considered inferences about two populations made from large samples. In such cases, the normal curve provides the sampling distributions for d and $\bar{d}$. But if small sample sizes must be used, the normal approximation proves inadequate in testing situations when the population variance is unknown. In these cases, the Student t distribution must be used instead.

Estimating the Difference in Means: Independent Samples

When independent samples are used, confidence intervals may be constructed for the difference in population means, $D = \mu_A - \mu_B$, in nearly the same manner we presented earlier. Again, we use $d = \bar{X}_A - \bar{X}_B$ to estimate D. In place of the normal deviate z, we use t_α (obtained from Appendix Table F). In addition, the standard error for d must be calculated somewhat differently.

When small samples are used (as a practical rule, whenever *both* n_A and n_B are less than 30), applicability of the Student t distribution requires that *both populations have the same variance*, so we must assume that $\sigma_A^2 = \sigma_B^2 = \sigma^2$. The standard error for d may therefore be expressed in a slightly different form than before:

$$\sigma_d = \sqrt{\frac{\sigma^2}{n_A} + \frac{\sigma^2}{n_B}} = \sigma \sqrt{\frac{1}{n_A} + \frac{1}{n_B}} \tag{14-18}$$

Under this requirement, s_A^2 and s_B^2 serve as unbiased estimators of σ^2. An even better estimate of. σ^2 may be obtained by pooling the sample results. Thus, σ_d may be estimated by taking the square root of a weighted average of the sample variances. The following expression (the first term of which has its denominator reduced by 2 in order to yield an unbiased estimator) is used to estimate σ_d:

$$s_{d\text{-small}} = \sqrt{\frac{(n_A - 1)s_A^2 + (n_B - 1)s_B^2}{n_A + n_B - 2}} \sqrt{\frac{1}{n_A} + \frac{1}{n_B}} \tag{14-19}$$

Using independent samples, the confidence interval estimate for the difference in population means is

$$\mu_A - \mu_B = \bar{X}_A - \bar{X}_B \pm t_\alpha s_{d\text{-small}} \tag{14-20}$$

In finding t_α from Appendix Table F for a confidence level of C, we choose $\alpha = (1-C)/2$. The number of degrees of freedom is equal to $n_A + n_B - 2$. In effect, the combined sample size $n_A + n_B$ must be reduced by 2, because one degree of freedom is lost in calculating each of the two sample variances.

Example 14-4   An astronomer wishes to compare the resolution (magnification accuracy) of two large telescopes. One telescope, located in the Southern Hemisphere, is refractive and uses a thick transparent lens to focus light from distant galaxies. Of purported equal power is a reflective telescope in the Northern Hemisphere that focuses starlight by means of polished mirrors. Although different galaxies may be viewed from each hemisphere, the density of galaxies in space is considered the same in either case.

The astronomer has taken $n_A = 16$ pictures with the refractive telescope at randomly chosen coordinates in the South; a counterpart random sample of $n_B = 26$ frames has been exposed by the reflective telescope in the North. Camera and film type were the same at both sites, and all exposures were made for exactly one hour on clear nights. The detectable galaxies in each frame were counted, and the following sample means and variances for the respective counts were obtained:

$$\bar{X}_A = 29.5 \qquad \bar{X}_B = 21.4$$
$$s_A^2 = 96.3 \qquad s_B^2 = 112.4$$

The standard error for the differences in sample means, $d = \bar{X}_A - \bar{X}_B$, is

$$s_{d\text{-small}} = \sqrt{\frac{(16-1)96.3 + (26-1)112.4}{16+26-2}} \sqrt{\frac{1}{16} + \frac{1}{26}} = 3.277$$

Using these data, a 95-percent confidence interval was constructed for the difference in population mean galaxy counts. For $16 + 26 - 2 = 40$ degrees of freedom and using $\alpha = (1 - .95)/2 = .025$, $t_{.025} = 2.021$. Thus,

$$\mu_A - \mu_B = 29.5 - 21.4 \pm 2.021(3.277)$$
$$= 8.1 \pm 6.62$$

or

$$1.48 \leqslant \mu_A - \mu_B \leqslant 14.72$$

The advantage in resolution of the refractive telescope (A) over the reflective one (B) is therefore estimated to fall somewhere between 1.48 and 14.72 galaxies.

Estimating the Difference in Means: Matched Pairs

In matched-pairs sampling, we estimate $D = \mu_A - \mu_B$ by $\bar{d}$, the mean of the individual matched-pair differences. Using small samples (generally, when the number of pairs is $n < 30$), the only difference is that the normal deviate z is replaced by t_α. The standard error of $\bar{d}$ remains the same, and it is estimated from the standard deviation of individual paired differences $s_{d\text{-paired}}$. *Using matched-pairs samples, the confidence interval estimate for the difference in population means is*

$$\mu_A - \mu_B = \bar{d} \pm t_\alpha \frac{s_{d\text{-paired}}}{\sqrt{n}} \tag{14-21}$$

We choose a value t_α that corresponds to the confidence level, using $n-1$ degrees of freedom.

> **Example 14-5**   A systems analyst for the Marlborough County Data Center has proposed adopting the dynamic-core allocation system used in neighboring Kent County. Since both counties have identical computers and otherwise identical software (program systems), a special test is to be administered to estimate the savings in mean "throughput" time for processing regular job batches under the proposed system. Designating Marlborough's present system A and the new system B, a random sample of $n = 25$ batches has been run twice, once in each county. Thus, the two processing times for one batch constitute the observations of a matched pair. For the ith batch, d_i represents the throughput time on the Marlborough computer run minus the analogous figure from the Kent operation. The following results were obtained:
>
> $$\bar{d} = 25 \text{ minutes}$$
>
> $$s_{d\text{-paired}} = 20 \text{ minutes}$$
>
> A 95-percent confidence interval estimate of the savings in mean batch throughput time from using dynamic-core allocation can then be constructed. For $25-1 = 24$ degrees of freedom with $\alpha = (1-.95)/2 = .025$, $t_{.025} = 2.064$, so that the estimated mean time advantage for using dynamic-core allocation is
>
> $$\mu_A - \mu_B = 25 \pm 2.064 \frac{20}{\sqrt{25}}$$
>
> $$= 25 \pm 8.3$$
>
> or
>
> $$16.7 \leqslant \mu_A - \mu_B \leqslant 33.3 \text{ minutes per batch}$$
>
> The above interval indicates that Marlborough's present computer software can be improved by using dynamic-core allocation, which will reduce mean batch processing time between 16.7 and 33.3 minutes.

Hypothesis Tests for Comparing Two Means: Independent Samples

When small independent samples are used in testing hypotheses regarding μ_A and μ_B, the value

$$t = \frac{\bar{d} - D}{s_{d\text{-small}}} \tag{14-22}$$

is the test statistic. Under the various null hypotheses typically encountered, a value of zero is always assumed for $D = \mu_A - \mu_B$. Thus, using the expression for $s_{d\text{-small}}$ given earlier, we may calculate *the t statistic for independent samples:*

$$t = \frac{\bar{X}_A - \bar{X}_B}{\sqrt{\dfrac{(n_A - 1)s_A^2 + (n_B - 1)s_B^2}{n_A + n_B - 2}} \sqrt{\dfrac{1}{n_A} + \dfrac{1}{n_B}}} \tag{14-23}$$

The critical value corresponding to the desired significance level α may be found from Appendix Table F for $n_A + n_B - 2$ degrees of freedom. For lower-tailed tests, with the null hypothesis $H_0: \mu_A \geqslant \mu_B$, H_0 must be rejected when $t < -t_\alpha$. With $H_0: \mu_A \leqslant \mu_B$, the test is upper-tailed and H_0 must be rejected when $t > t_\alpha$. With $H_0: \mu_A = \mu_B$, the critical value is $t_{\alpha/2}$. Here, H_0 must be accepted when t lies within $\pm t_{\alpha/2}$; otherwise it must be rejected.

Example 14-6 Drinking coffee affects many people's sleep. One investigator compared the effects of coffee on habitual drinkers with the effects on occasional drinkers. Independent random samples of $n_A = 10$ light and $n_B = 15$ heavy coffee drinkers were obtained. One night's sleep was monitored for each subject, and before retiring, every person was given a cup of coffee. As her null hypothesis, the researcher assumes that the light coffee drinkers will go to sleep at least as fast as the heavy coffee drinkers. In terms of mean time to onset of sleep, $H_0: \mu_A \leqslant \mu_B$. The following test data were obtained:

Light Coffee Drinkers	Heavy Coffee Drinkers
$\bar{X}_A = 45$ minutes	$\bar{X}_B = 36$ minutes
$s_A^2 = 706$	$s_B^2 = 654$

This is an upper-tailed test. The number of degrees of freedom is $10 + 15 - 2 = 23$. For an $\alpha = .05$ significance level, $t_{.05} = 1.714$. Substituting the above results into expression (14-31), the following value is obtained for the test statistic:

$$t = \frac{45 - 36}{\sqrt{\frac{9(706) + 14(654)}{23}}\sqrt{\frac{1}{10} + \frac{1}{15}}} = .85$$

Since .85 is smaller than $t_{.05} = 1.714$, H_0 must be *accepted*. The results are not statistically significant, and the sample data do not refute the null hypothesis that light drinkers will go to sleep at least as quickly as heavy drinkers after one cup of coffee.

Hypothesis Tests for Comparing Two Means: Matched Pairs

Matched-pairs tests with small samples involve the test statistic

$$t = \frac{\bar{d} - D}{s_{d\text{-paired}}/\sqrt{n}} \tag{14-24}$$

where $\bar{d}$ and $s_{d\text{-paired}}$ are the mean and standard deviation of the sample matched-pair differences. Under the typical null hypothesis, $D = \mu_A - \mu_B$ is zero and we may therefore simplify expression (14-24) in calculating *the t statistic for matched pairs:*

$$t = \frac{\bar{d}}{s_{d\text{-paired}}/\sqrt{n}} \tag{14-25}$$

The critical value t_α for the desired significance level α is found from Appendix Table F by using $n-1$ degrees of freedom. For a two-sided test, we use $t_{\alpha/2}$ as the critical value.

To illustrate this procedure, suppose that the systems analyst in Example 14-5 desired to test the null hypothesis that the Kent County dynamic-core allocation system (B) was as slow or slower than Marlborough's present one (A). In this case, the analyst would use $\mu_A \leqslant \mu_B$ for H_0, indicating that the new system's mean processing time is at least as great as the present system's. Here, a one-sided, upper-tailed test would apply.

Suppose that an $\alpha = .05$ significance level is desired. For 24 degrees of freedom, the critical value for the test statistic is $t_{.05} = 1.711$. The test statistic calculated from the earlier data is

$$t = \frac{25}{20/\sqrt{25}} = 6.25$$

which we see is larger than the critical value, and H_0 must therefore be *rejected*. The analyst would conclude that Kent County's data processing system is faster than Marlborough's present system.

EXERCISES

14-11   Estimate the difference in mean gasoline mileage in two car models by a 95-percent confidence interval if the following results apply for independent samples.

Car A	Car B
$n_A = 10$	$n_B = 10$
$\bar{X}_A = 14$ mpg	$\bar{X}_B = 12.5$ mpg
$s_A^2 = 2$	$s_B^2 = 2.5$

14-12   Suppose that the drivers of the two cars in Exercise 14-11 were matched according to their driving skills. The mean and the standard deviation for the differences in gasoline mileage found by subtracting car B's mpg from car A's are

$$\bar{d} = 1.5 \text{ mpg}$$
$$s_{d\text{-paired}} = 1.2 \text{ mpg}$$

Construct a 95-percent confidence interval for the difference in mean gasoline mileage.

14-13   A city manager wanted to estimate the advantage in the mean lifetime of a new type of tire compared to an existing tire. A taxicab company cooperated in a test where 10 cars were equipped with two of each type of tire. A record was kept of each car's total mileage until both tires of the same type had to be replaced. For each car, the replacement mileage for the present tire (B) was subtracted from the corresponding figure for the new tire (A). The mean difference in mileage was 2,000 miles, with a standard deviation of 2,000 miles.

(a) Construct a 95-percent confidence interval estimate for the difference in mean tire lifetimes.

(b) Should the null hypothesis that the mean lifetimes are identical be accepted or rejected at the 5-percent significance level?

14-14 Suppose that a test similar to the one in Exercise 14-13 was performed on another group of cars. Here, 15 cars were fully equipped with the new tire (A) and 10 cars were equipped with the old tire (B). No attempt was made to match the cars. The sets of four tires were replaced when driving each car became hazardous. The mileage results showed

$$\bar{X}_A = 35{,}000 \text{ miles} \qquad \bar{X}_B = 33{,}000 \text{ miles}$$
$$s_A^2 = 6{,}500{,}000 \qquad s_B^2 = 7{,}000{,}000$$

(a) Construct a 95-percent confidence interval estimate for the difference in mean tire lifetimes.

(b) Should the null hypothesis that the mean tire lifetimes are identical be accepted or rejected at the 5-percent significance level?

14-15 One aspect of horticulture is to find and nurture genetic strains of plants with favorable characteristics. In trees grown for timber, it is desirable to select fast-growing seeds. Two parent strains of a certain species are being compared in test plots. The following data have been obtained for the third-year growth of seedlings:

Strain A	Strain B
$n_A = 14$	$n_B = 28$
$\bar{X}_A = 2.4$ feet	$\bar{X}_B = 2.6$ feet
$s_A^2 = .25$	$s_B^2 = .35$

Should the null hypothesis that seedling growth for strain A is at least as great as seedling growth for strain B be accepted or rejected at the 5-percent significance level?

14-16 A real estate property manager wishes to compare net monthly incomes under two different leasing agreements. Plan A has tenants sign for a lower rent but requires them to pay for all small repairs themselves. Under plan B, the tenant pays more rent but is not responsible for repairs. As the null hypothesis the manager assumes that plan B yields at least as great a mean income as plan A. The following data have been obtained for independent random samples of 15 leases each:

Plan A	Plan B
$\bar{X}_A = \$132.45$	$\bar{X}_B = \$128.06$
$s_A^2 = 123$	$s_B^2 = 95$

Can the manager reject the null hypothesis using a 5-percent significance level?

14-17 Suppose that the astronomer in Example 14-4 wishes to compare the near-range resolution of the Southern Hemisphere refractive telescope (A) with the resolution of the Northern Hemisphere reflective telescope (B). Since Jupiter can be seen from both sites simultaneously, shots of this planet from both telescopes were made at the same time on 15 different nights throughout the year. The photographs were then analyzed to determine the number of Jovian moons that could be detected in each. The mean difference in moon counts was found to be .3 moon, with a standard deviation of .7 moon. Must the null hypothesis that the reflective telescope provides at least as high a moon count be accepted or rejected at the 5-percent significance level?

14-18 A company's telephone salespeople are all currently salaried. To improve incentives, management will convert the compensation either to a commission-only basis or to a salary-plus-commission plan. The null hypothesis is that the mean sales per solicitor will be the same under either plan. To test the schemes, random samples of 25 salespeople from each of two different offices were matched into pairs according to past sales records. After a trial six months, the sales of the salary-plus-commission partner were subtracted from the corresponding figure for the commission-only person. A mean difference of $100 was obtained with a standard deviation of $25. At the 5-percent significance level, which compensation plan, if any, is the better one?

14-4 HYPOTHESIS TESTS FOR COMPARING PROPORTIONS

Qualitative populations may be compared in terms of their respective proportions. We can extend the hypothesis-testing concepts of the preceding section to using sample proportions as the basis for comparison. Such testing may be useful, for example, to a politician who must determine whether or not the popularity of new legislation differs between two groups of constituents. Similarly, a television network might compare the proportions of potential audiences preferring its two comedies over a third, all shown on different nights, in deciding whether or not to reschedule programs.

As before, we employ the designations π_A and π_B to represent the two population proportions. *The difference between population proportions is*

$$D = \pi_A - \pi_B \tag{14-26}$$

The respective sample proportions, designated P_A and P_B, may be used to estimate D by *the difference in sample proportions:*

$$d = P_A - P_B \tag{14-27}$$

Using d as the test statistic, a decision rule may be constructed to test one of the following null hypotheses:

$$H_0: \ \pi_A \geqslant \pi_B \quad \text{or} \quad H_0: \ D \geqslant 0 \qquad \text{(lower-tailed test)}$$

$$H_0: \ \pi_A \leqslant \pi_B \quad \text{or} \quad H_0: \ D \leqslant 0 \qquad \text{(upper-tailed test)}$$

$$H_0: \ \pi_A = \pi_B \quad \text{or} \quad H_0: \ D = 0 \qquad \text{(two-sided test)}$$

Ordinarily, the sampling distributions of P_A and P_B can be approximated by the normal curve when sample sizes are large enough. Because the samples are selected independently, it follows that d can be assumed to be normally distributed, with a mean of $D = \pi_A - \pi_B$ and a standard deviation of*

$$\sigma_d = \sqrt{\frac{\pi_A(1-\pi_A)}{n_A} + \frac{\pi_B(1-\pi_B)}{n_B}} \qquad (14\text{-}28)$$

Under any of the above null hypotheses, we may assume that $\pi_A = \pi_B$, so that $D = 0$ and the sample results may be treated as if they came from the same population. As an estimator of either π_A or π_B, the sample results may be pooled to compute *the combined sample proportion:*

$$P_C = \frac{n_A P_A + n_B P_B}{n_A + n_B} \qquad (14\text{-}29)$$

The standard deviation for d is then estimated by

$$s_d = \sqrt{P_C(1-P_C)\left(\frac{1}{n_A} + \frac{1}{n_B}\right)} \qquad (14\text{-}30)$$

Again, we use the symbol d^* to represent the critical value for d. This must be chosen so that a decision rule is obtained that corresponds to the desired significance level. As in our earlier two-sample tests, the critical normal deviate z_α indicates how many standard deviations d^* lies above or below the mean $D = 0$. Thus, $d^* = \pm z_\alpha s_d$, and we may express *the critical value for the difference in sample proportions:*

$$d^* = z_\alpha \sqrt{P_C(1-P_C)\left(\frac{1}{n_A} + \frac{1}{n_B}\right)} \qquad \text{for an upper-tailed test}$$

$$(14\text{-}31)$$

$$d^* = -z_\alpha \sqrt{P_C(1-P_C)\left(\frac{1}{n_A} + \frac{1}{n_B}\right)} \qquad \text{for a lower-tailed test}$$

The possible forms of the decision rule are analogous to those forms discussed in connection with the difference in independent sample means.

An alternative approach is to compute *the normal deviate value for the sample results:*

$$z = \frac{P_A - P_B}{\sqrt{P_C(1-P_C)\left(\frac{1}{n_A} + \frac{1}{n_B}\right)}} \qquad (14\text{-}32)$$

---

* As with the difference in independent sample means, it follows that the variance of $d = P_A - P_B$ is the sum of the respective variances for the individual sample proportions.

which may be compared to z_α to determine whether H_0 must be accepted or rejected.

Two-Sided Tests

For a two-sided test using $z_{\alpha/2}$ as the critical normal deviate, we use the following expressions to calculate *the critical values for the difference in sample proportions:*

$$d_1^* = -z_{\alpha/2}\sqrt{P_C(1-P_C)\left(\frac{1}{n_A}+\frac{1}{n_B}\right)}$$

(14-33)

$$d_2^* = z_{\alpha/2}\sqrt{P_C(1-P_C)\left(\frac{1}{n_A}+\frac{1}{n_B}\right)}$$

Example 14-7   A television programming director has decided to replace his network's Monday night comedy show "Grundy's Mondays" with one of two candidate comedy series: "The Sky is Falling" or "Mr. McGregor's Garden." Although either of the new programs should have a wider appeal than the present one, the director wants to pick the new comedy that best suits the whims of the present Monday-night audience. To determine this, special pilots of "Sky" and "McGregor" were shown on nonsuccessive weeks in the "Grundy" time slot. Two independent random samples of regular "Grundy" viewers who also watched both comedy pilots were then selected, and the sample proportion favoring each of the new shows was then determined. As his null hypothesis, the program director assumed that the respective population proportions of viewers preferring each of the program pilots over "Grundy's Mondays" are the same. Therefore, using A to designate "Sky" and B for "McGregor", H_0: $\pi_A = \pi_B$. In this problem, a two-sided test applies.

With $n_A = 150$ and $n_B = 100$, the respective sample proportions favoring the new programs were

$$P_A = .80 \text{ and } P_B = .70$$

These results provide a difference in proportions of

$$d = P_A - P_B = .80 - .70 = .10$$

The combined sample proportion favoring a change in programs is found by substituting the above values into expression (14-29):

$$P_C = \frac{150(.80) + 100(.70)}{150 + 100} = .76$$

Even though these results indicate that "Grundy" is not well liked by its current audience, the program director will use the limited sample results to choose a replacement only if one new show is significantly preferred over the other. Otherwise, further investigations will be required to pick a new show. The director therefore desires an $\alpha = .10$ significance level for this test, so that there is just a 10-percent chance of picking the new show that was not most preferred by "Grundy" addicts. Substituting $P_C = .76$ and $z_{.05} = 1.64$ for $z_{\alpha/2}$ in expression (14-33), the critical values for the difference in sample proportions are

$$d_1^* = -1.64\sqrt{.76(1-.76)\left(\frac{1}{150}+\frac{1}{100}\right)} = -.09$$

$$d_1^* = .09$$

and the decision rule for $d = P_A - P_B$ is

> *Accept H_0* (investigate further) if $-.09 \leqslant d \leqslant .09$
>
> *Reject H_0* (use "McGregor") if $d < -.09$
>
> *or* (use "Sky") if $d > .09$

Since $d = .10$ is greater than .09, H_0 must be *rejected* and the program director should replace "Grundy" with "The Sky is Falling."

A shorter procedure would be to find the normal deviate for the sample results by using expression (14-32):

$$z = \frac{.80 - .70}{\sqrt{.76(1 - .76)\left(\frac{1}{150} + \frac{1}{100}\right)}} = 1.81$$

Since 1.81 exceeds $z_{.05} = 1.64$, we see again that H_0 must be rejected.

EXERCISES

14-19 Suppose that the television network programming director in Example 14-7 signed a contract for "Mr. McGregor's Garden" (*B*) but that he would be willing to use "The Sky is Falling" (*A*) instead if significantly more viewers favored it. For the same numerical results obtained in that example:

(a) What null hypothesis is being tested? Is the test two-sided, lower-tailed, or upper-tailed?

(b) At the $\alpha = .025$ significance level, determine the critical value(s) for the director's decision. Which program do the data indicate should be used?

(c) Using the normal deviate z for the sample results, what is the smallest significance level at which the null hypothesis can be rejected?

14-20 A political polling firm has been retained by a congressional candidate. In order to organize his strategy in the final weeks of the campaign, he needs to know whether he is stronger in the suburbs (*A*) or in the cities (*B*). Independent random samples of 100 voters in each category have been polled, and these data indicate the candidate is preferred by 48 percent in the suburbs and 53 percent in the cities. As his null hypothesis, he has assumed that he is equally strong in both areas. At the $\alpha = .05$ significance level, what conclusion should he make from the sample results?

14-21 An aerospace statistician is evaluating a prototype aircraft radar system to see if it can detect a plane passing through the edges of the radar horizon better than the existing system can. Two independent samples of 100 test flights have been made using both systems, and the respective proportions detected have been computed. A 5-percent chance is desired as protection against incorrectly concluding that the new system (*A*) has a detection probability (a population proportion of flights detected at the horizon) higher than the old system (*B*) does. The test results yield $P_A = .80$ and $P_B = .70$.

(a) Formulate the null hypothesis. Is the test two-sided, lower-tailed, or upper-tailed?

(b) Based upon the sample results, can the statistician conclude that the new system is better?

14-5   FURTHER REMARKS

In this chapter, we have considered two-sample inferences regarding population means and proportions. In testing means, either independent or matched-pairs samples may be employed, and each procedure has its advantages as well as its drawbacks. Generally, matched-pairs sampling makes more efficient use of sample information, but it is more elaborate and costly.

Again, we have encountered the basic dichotomy between large and small samples. With large samples, we make use of the fact that when the population standard deviations are known, the central limit theorem indicates that the respective estimators and test statistics are approximately normally distributed. Ordinarily, however, σ_A^2 and σ_B^2 are unknown and may be estimated by s_A^2 and s_B^2. In all such cases, the Student t distribution applies instead of the normal distribution. But for large samples, the normal curve is nearly identical to the Student t distribution, so that we use it anyway.

A requirement of the Student t distribution is that the parent population be normally distributed. As we saw in Chapter 9, this usually presents no problem unless the population is highly skewed. In independent, two-sample tests that have small n's, there is the additional requirement that both population variances be equal. If there is reason to believe that σ_A^2 is much different than σ_B^2, the t statistic should not be used on small, independent samples.

Further statistical procedures can be employed in making inferences regarding σ_A^2 and σ_B^2. Up to this point, we have largely skirted the issue of making inferences concerning variances. When the necessary sampling distributions have been described in their more traditional applications we will discuss these procedures. Chapters 15 and 16 will primarily focus upon testing for independence and comparing three or more population parameters.

REVIEW EXERCISES

14-22   A statistician who is also a baseball fan is interested in how major league batting averages differ between home and away games. He has selected 25 batters at random and has kept detailed records of their performances. As his null hypothesis, the statistician assumes that the mean batting average of hitters away from home is at least as large as the mean average they attain playing on their home field. After compiling his data and separately computing the batting averages, the statistician found the mean difference in a player's batting average to be .028 in favor of the home games. The standard deviation in the differences was computed to be .056.

(a) At the $\alpha = .05$ significance level, what conclusion should the statistician make?

(b) Construct a 95-percent confidence interval for the advantage in mean batting average attained by playing at home.

14-23 Consider the sample data shown below for the weights and ages of athletic and nonathletic men, all approximately 6 feet tall and all of medium build.

Athletic Men (A)		Nonathletic Men (B)	
Weight	Age	Weight	Age
151	22	152	21
148	24	153	26
156	31	149	33
155	37	162	35
157	41	165	39
161	42	168	44
158	49	157	47
168	51	178	49
149	55	161	57
174	61	186	59

(a) Calculate the sample means and variances for the weights of the two groups.

(b) Treating the weights as independent random samples, should the null hypothesis that the population mean weight for athletic men will be at least as large as that for nonathletic men be accepted or rejected at the $\alpha = .10$ significance level?

14-24 Referring to Exercise 14-23, assume that the data represent observation pairs matched by age.

(a) Compute the weight differences for each pair, subtracting the non-athlete's weight from the athlete's. Then find the mean and the standard deviation of these matched-pair differences.

(b) Treating the weights as matched-pairs samples, should the null hypothesis that the population mean weight for athletic men is at least as large as that for nonathletic men be accepted or rejected at the $\alpha = .10$ significance level?

14-25 A company tested two cereals to determine the taste preferences of potential buyers. Two different panels of persons were selected; the individuals on one were asked to taste brand *A*, while the others were asked to taste brand *B*. Each person was then asked if he or she would buy the product tasted. The following results were obtained:

	Cereal A	Cereal B
Number who would buy:	75	80
Number who would not buy or who were undecided:	50	60
	125	140

Consider the null hypothesis that there is no difference in the proportion of potential buyers who would desire to buy either product. At the 5-percent significance level, should H_0 be accepted or rejected?

14-26 An agronomist compared the corn-crop yields per acre on which a nitrate-based fertilizer was used with corn yields from plots on which a sulfate-based fertilizer was used. A sample of 100 acres using nitrates (*A*) yielded an average of 56.2 bushels per acre, with a variance of 156.25. The sample of 150 acres fertilized with sulfates (*B*) yielded an average of 52.6 bushels per acre, with a variance of 190.44. For each of the null hypotheses (a), (b), and (c): (1) Express H_0, using the appropriate symbols; (2) construct the decision rule for the difference in sample means for an $\alpha = .05$ significance level; and (3) find the value of the test statistic and indicate whether H_0 must be accepted or rejected.

(a) There is no difference in resulting crop yields between the two fertilizers.

(b) The nitrates provide at least the yield of the sulfates.

(c) The sulfates provide at least the yield of the nitrates.

14-27 A car rental company wishes to determine which of two types of gasoline will provide the most miles per gallon. Two independent random samples of 15 cars were selected. Each car was driven 2,000 miles by employees on normal business, but a different type of gasoline was used in each sample. The results were

Type A	Type B
$\bar{X}_A = 15.0$ mpg	$\bar{X}_B = 14.8$ mpg
$s_A^2 = 1.44$	$s_B^2 = .81$

(a) Construct a 95-percent confidence interval estimate for the difference in mean gasoline mileages.

(b) Should the null hypothesis that there is no difference between the gasolines be accepted or rejected at the $\alpha = .05$ significance level?

14-28 Suppose that the plots used to test the nitrate- and sulfate-based fertilizers in Exercise 14-26 were selected so that the two types of fertilizers were placed on neighboring one-acre plots and that the yield of each sulfate-fertilized acre (B) was subtracted from the yield of its neighboring nitrate-fertilized acre (A). From a total of 100 pairs, the mean matched-pairs difference was 1.3 bushels, with a standard deviation of 3.2 bushels. Should the null hypothesis that there is no difference in yields due to choice of fertilizer be accepted or rejected at the $\alpha = .05$ significance level?

14-29 Suppose that the company in Exercise 14-27 matched the cars using gasoline A with those using gasoline B, that the cars in each pair were nearly identical in many respects (make, age, engine size, accessories, and so on), and that both groups of cars were driven over the same route by the same professional driver. The results showed that the mean difference in gasoline mileage between the cars using gasoline A and the cars using gasoline B was .2 mile per gallon, with a standard deviation of .1.

(a) Construct a 95-percent confidence interval estimate for the difference in mean gasoline mileages.

(b) Should the null hypothesis that there is no difference in the gasolines be accepted or rejected at the $\alpha = .05$ significance level?

Chapter Fifteen
Chi-Square Applications

*The frequent observation that things of a sort
are disposed together in any place would lead
us to conclude, upon discovering there any
object of a particular sort, that there are laid
up with it many others of the same sort.*

The Reverend Thomas Bayes (1763)

Thus far, we have described procedures using the normal and Student t distributions, but many important statistical applications go beyond these distributions. In this chapter, we investigate the *chi-square distribution*, which will considerably expand our basic repertoire.

In Section 15-1, we apply the chi-square distribution to sample data *in testing whether or not two variables are independent.* As we have seen in applications of probability, statistical independence is an important concept, because it allows us to considerably simplify the multiplication law. Even more important, independence between sample observations permits us to streamline procedures considerably. Perhaps it is most important to know if variables are independent when alternative methods and treatments are evaluated.

When population variables are qualitative characteristics (such as marital status, political affiliation, sex, state of health, type of treatment, or kind of response), then the presence or absence of independence between variables can be used to draw important conclusions. For example, if a pharmaceutical manufacturer knows that preventive measures (vaccinated, unvaccinated) and resistance (diseased, not diseased) are dependent, then it may be concluded that a vaccine is effective. A marketing researcher who learns that highest education level (elementary, high shcool, college) and brand preference (candidates A, B, C) are dependent might use this information to help choose advertising media. If severity of automobile accidents (property damage, injury, fatalities) is found to be dependent upon where they occur (city streets, rural roads, highways), a public safety director may decide to revise traffic law-enforcement procedures.

The second area of statistical inference we investigate in this chapter is *comparing several population proportions*. This application is closely related to testing for independence. A procedure comparing two populations was described in Chapter 14, but when three or more populations are involved, the testing procedure makes use of the chi-square distribution.

Although these two applications of the chi-square distribution are the most common in business decision making, others exist. Inferences regarding the population variance are discussed as an optional topic later in this chapter. Chapter 17 considers a chi-square procedure called the goodness-of-fit test.

15-1 INDEPENDENCE AND THE CHI-SQUARE DISTRIBUTION

The first new application of statistical inference we will investigate is testing to determine if two qualitative population variables are independent. In doing this, we will describe a special test statistic whose sampling distribution is the chi-square.

Independence Between Qualitative Variables

To describe what we mean by independence between two qualitative variables or population characteristics, we will briefly consider a basic concept of probability. Recall that two events A and B are statistically independent if the occurrence of either event does not affect the probability of the other. More formally, this states that A and B are independent if

$$P[A \mid B] = P[A]$$

or, in other words, if the conditional and unconditional probabilities are equal. Thus, we see that drawing an ace from a fully shuffled deck of 52 ordinary playing cards is statistically independent of drawing a club because

$$P[\text{ace} \mid \text{club}] = 1/13 = 4/52 = P[\text{ace}]$$

Viewed another way, the proportion of aces in the club suit (1/13) is the same as the proportion of aces in the entire deck (4/52).

We can extend this concept of statistical independence to populations and samples. Consider a population whose elementary units may be classified in terms of two qualitative variables, *A* and *B*. Variable *A* might represent a person's sex, so that it would have two possible attributes—male and female; likewise, variable *B* might be political party, so that its attributes would be Democrat, Republican, and so on. Let us assume that men occur in the same proportion throughout the entire population as they do among Democrats. Under that assumption, we could then conclude that for the attributes of a randomly selected person,

$$P[\text{male} \mid \text{Democrat}] = P[\text{male}]$$

so that the *events* male and Democrat are statistically independent. If this is the case, then the multiplication law of probability for independent events tells us that

$$P[\text{male } and \text{ Democrat}] = P[\text{male}] \times P[\text{Democrat}]$$

If a similar fact holds for all attribute combinations, the population variables will exhibit a very important property:

DEFINITION   Two qualitative population variables *A* and *B* are *independent* if the proportion of the total population having any particular attribute of *A* is the same as it is in the part of the population having a particular attribute of *B*, no matter which attributes are considered. This implies that the frequency of units having any particular attribute pair may be found by multiplying the respective frequencies for the individual attributes and dividing by the total number of observations.

Example 15-1   A symphony orchestra has 100 members. Of these, 70 are men and 30 are women. Each member is categorized by the type of instrument he or she plays: woodwind, brass, string, or percussion. The table below shows the frequencies of the members in terms of two characteristics: sex and instrument. Here, the two characteristics are independent. The ratio of male woodwind players to the total number of woodwind players is $21/30 = .7$. The same value is obtained for male brass, string, or percussion player ratios, respectively: 14/20, 21/30, and 14/20 all equal .7, the proportion of men in the orchestra. Likewise, the ratio of female woodwind players to the total woodwinds is .3, which is the same as the ratio for any other instrument played by females and is also the proportion of females in the orchestra.

	Instrument Category				
Sex	(1) *Woodwind*	(2) *Brass*	(3) *String*	(4) *Percussion*	Total
(1) *Male*	21	14	21	14	70
(2) *Female*	9	6	9	6	30
Total	30	20	30	20	100

Since sex and instrument are independent, the frequency of male string players is equal to the product of the frequency for the respective attributes divided by the total number of players in the orchestra:

$$\frac{70 \times 30}{100} = 21$$

Likewise, the frequency of female string players is found by multiplying the number of females by the number of string players and dividing by 100:

$$\frac{30 \times 30}{100} = 9$$

Testing for Independence

In situations where the population frequencies are unknown, the presence or absence of independence between two variables must also be unknown. A sample may be used to test for independence, but to do this, we must extend the principles of hypothesis testing used previously. It will be helpful if we proceed by developing the following illustration.

Superior Oil Company markets its products through two distinctly different kinds of service station outlets. One is a company-owned chain, selling gasoline and other products under the Superior label. The other is a chain of franchised dealerships—independently owned and managed—advertised with Superior but also identified as Sentinel stations. The reason for the double identity is twofold.

(1) By creating two types of stations, the company believes that it appeals to two segments of the market: both those preferring to buy from a big operator and those who like to deal with a local dealer (thereby receiving more individual attention and service).

(2) The company-owned stations are major operations, located in high-volume traffic areas where the capital investment must be huge. A company-owned station in these locations is believed to be most effective and profitable.

Another advantage is that, when traveling on major highways, a customer who trades at a Sentinel station will stop at conveniently located company-owned stations. Likewise, an urban customer of Superior's company-owned stations will be more likely to trade at a Sentinel station when traveling on side roads or in rural areas.

Superior's new chairman is concerned about the value of operating in this fashion. He wonders whether the extra promotional costs are really justified and even if there are actually two separate market segments. He has requested that his chief statistician conduct a survey to determine if there is any significant difference between the Sentinel customers and those trading at company-owned stations.

The statistician has mailed a questionnaire to a random sample of 200

TABLE 15-1   Contingency Table for Actual Sample Results from a Superior Oil Customer Survey

	Customer Preference		
Reason	(1) *Sentinel Station*	(2) *Company Station*	*Total*
(1) *Location*	32	8	40
(2) *Quality of service*	12	2	14
(3) *Cleanliness*	13	3	16
(4) *Personal attention*	56	35	91
(5) *Mechanical service*	11	13	24
(6) *Staff appearance*	6	9	15
Total	130	70	200

credit card customers. The replies received have been partially tabulated in Table 15-1. Each subject has been categorized as preferring Sentinel or company stations. The primary reason given for each person's preference is placed in one of six categories: location, quality of service, cleanliness, personal attention, mechanical service, and staff appearance.

The Contingency Table

In Table 15-1, the customer preference variable is represented by a column for each station type and the second variable by a row for each primary reason given for preferring a particular type of station. (Customers were asked to state their primary reason only.) The cell formed by the intersection of a row and column represents a possible classification for a customer's responses. The value within each cell is the tally for those subjects classified as having that cell's corresponding attributes. These cell numbers are referred to as *actual frequencies.* Such an arrangement of data is called a *contingency table,* because it accounts for all combinations of the factors being investigated—in other words, for all contingencies.

Using the statistician's data, we wish to find out whether or not the customer's primary stated reason for choosing where to trade actually matters in the final selection of the particular type of station. The null hypothesis is that the type of station preferred is not related to the stated reason. Stated another way, *the null hypothesis is that the two variables are independent.* The first step in accepting or rejecting H_0 is to determine the kind of results that might be expected if the variables were truly independent.

Expected Frequencies

The sample results that would be obtained on the average if the null hypothesis of independence were true serve as a basis for comparison. We refer to these hypothetical data as the *expected sample results.* To see how they deviate from the actual results, another contingency table must be constructed. The differences between the actual and the expected results can then be summarized by comparing the two contingency tables.

Table 15-2 is the contingency table for the expected results of this study. The total numbers of observations for each reason and type of station are the same. Because they are calculated in a manner consistent with the null hypothesis of independence, the cell entries are referred to as *expected frequencies.* Since these quantities, which appear in color in Table 15-2, are *expected* rather than actual values, it is not necessary for the cell entries to be whole numbers. (Generally, two places of accuracy after the decimal point provide adequate precision.)

TABLE 15-2   Contingency Table for Expected Sample
Results Under the Null Hypothesis of Independence
for Superior Oil Variables

	Customer Preference		
Reason	(1) *Sentinel Station*	(2) *Company Station*	Total
(1) *Location*	26.00	14.00	40
(2) *Quality of service*	9.10	4.90	14
(3) *Cleanliness*	10.40	5.60	16
(4) *Personal attention*	59.15	31.85	91
(5) *Mechanical service*	15.60	8.40	24
(6) *Staff appearance*	9.75	5.25	15
Total	130	70	200

To facilitate our comparison, we will represent the actual and expected frequencies symbolically. We use the letter f for frequency, with the subscripts a for actual and e for expected. For convenience, we use the letter i to represent any particular row, where here i may equal any number between 1 and 6; likewise, the letter j represents the column, here equal to 1 or 2. Thus, for row i and column j, $f_a(i, j)$ denotes the actual frequency and $f_e(i, j)$ the expected frequency.

The actual frequency f_a values for the Superior Oil study results were provided initially in Table 15-1. The expected frequency $f_e(1, 1) = 26.00$ for the cell in row (1) and column (1) of Table 15-2 was found by multiplying the row (1) and the column (1) totals and dividing by the sample size:

$$26.00 = \frac{40 \times 130}{200}$$

In general, the following procedure is used to calculate *the expected frequency of the cell in the ith row and jth column:*

$$f_e(i, j) = \frac{r_i c_j}{n} \qquad (15\text{-}1)$$

where r_i is the marginal total of row i, c_j is the marginal total of column j, and n is the sample size. All of the expected frequencies in Table 15-2 were calculated in this manner. For example, the expected number of subjects who gave cleanliness as their reason and prefer company stations is 5.60 and appears in the cell of row (3) and column (2). Here, $r_3 = 16$ and $c_2 = 70$, so that

$$f_e(3, 2) = \frac{16 \times 70}{200} = 5.60$$

In both the actual and the expected contingency tables, r_i and c_j mean the same thing and both have the property that

$$\sum r_i = \sum c_j = n$$

The Chi-Square Statistic

The actual and expected frequencies must be compared so that the null hypothesis of independence can be accepted or rejected. A decision rule must be established that provides a desirable balance between the probabilities of making the Type I error of rejecting independence when it indeed exists and of making the Type II error of accepting independence when it does not exist. In practice, when the sample size is fixed in advance—as in our gas station illustration—we are free to control only the Type I error probability α.

We need a test statistic that does two things: It must measure the amount of deviation between the actual and expected results, and it must have a sampling distribution that enables us to determine the Type I error probability α.

Such a statistic may be computed from the cell entries in the actual and expected contingency tables. It is based upon the individual differences between actual and expected frequencies in each cell. The following expression is used to calculate the *chi-square statistic:*

$$\chi^2 = \sum \frac{(f_a - f_e)^2}{f_e} \qquad (15\text{-}2)$$

where the symbol χ is the Greek lower case *chi* (pronounced kie) and χ^2 is read as "chi square." The summation is taken over all cells in the contingency table. Table 15-3 shows the χ^2 calculations for the Superior Oil study results. Here, we find that $\chi^2 = 16.929$.

TABLE 15-3   Chi-Square Calculations for
Superior Oil Results

(Row, Column)	Actual Frequency f_a	Expected Frequency f_e	$f_a - f_e$	$(f_a - f_e)^2$	$\dfrac{(f_a - f_e)^2}{f_e}$
(1, 1)	32	26.00	6.00	36.0000	1.385
(1, 2)	8	14.00	−6.00	36.0000	2.571
(2, 1)	12	9.10	−2.90	8.4100	.924
(2, 2)	2	4.90	2.90	8.4100	1.716
(3, 1)	13	10.40	2.60	6.7600	.650
(3, 2)	3	5.60	−2.60	6.7600	1.207
(4, 1)	56	59.15	−3.15	9.9225	.168
(4, 2)	35	31.85	3.15	9.9225	.312
(5, 1)	11	15.60	−4.60	21.1600	1.356
(5, 2)	13	8.40	4.60	21.1600	2.519
(6, 1)	6	9.75	−3.75	14.0625	1.442
(6, 2)	9	5.25	3.75	14.0625	2.679
	200	200.00	0.00		$\chi^2 = 16.929$

The possible values of χ^2 range upwards from zero. If the deviation between f_a and f_e is large for a particular cell, then so is the squared deviation $(f_a - f_e)^2$. In calculating χ^2, each squared deviation is divided by f_e, to ensure that any differences are not exaggerated simply because a large number of observations are obtained. Large $(f_a - f_e)^2/f_e$ ratios occur when actual and expected results differ considerably, making χ^2 large. Therefore, the more the sample results deviate from what would be expected if the two observed variables were independent, the larger the value of χ^2 will be, and vice versa.

Before we can draw any conclusions about the customer preference and reason variables, we must determine whether or not the value for χ^2 obtained from the sample is consistent with H_0 that these variables are independent. Even if they were independent, sampling error makes it highly unlikely that the f_e and f_a values will match perfectly. Thus, the computed value for χ^2 will usually be greater than zero. The sampling distribution for χ^2 will tell us how big this statistic must be before we can reject the assumption of independence.

The Chi-Square Distribution

The chi-square distribution is a theoretical probability distribution that, under the proper conditions, may be used as the sampling distribution of χ^2. It is described by a single parameter, the number of degrees of freedom, which means much the same as it did in our previous discussion of the Student t distribution. (The procedure for determining the number of degrees of freedom will be given a little later.)

Figure 15-1 shows curves for the chi-square distributions when the degrees of freedom are 2, 4, 10, and 20. Note that these curves are positively skewed but that as the degrees of freedom increase, the degree of skew declines. As the

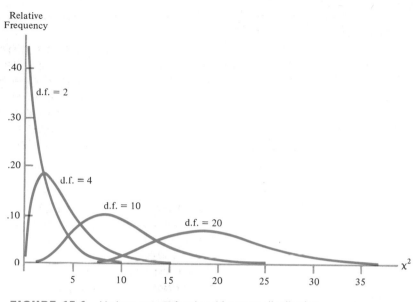

FIGURE 15-1   Various curves for the chi-square distribution.

number of degrees of freedom becomes large, the chi-square approaches the normal distribution.

Appendix Table II provides upper-tailed areas for the chi-square distribution. Denoting the value of the χ^2 statistic for which the upper-tailed area is α by χ_α^2, we have

$$\alpha = P[\chi^2 \geqslant \chi_\alpha^2]$$

As with the Student t distribution, there is a separate distribution for each number of degrees of freedom, and a row corresponding to each of these numbers appears in the table of upper-tail areas. The tail areas are given at the head of each column, and the entries in the body of the table are the corresponding values of χ_α^2. The curve for the chi-square distribution with 5 degrees of freedom is shown in Figure 15-2. To find the upper 5-percent value of χ^2, denoted by $\chi_{.05}^2$, we read the entry in the 5 degrees of freedom row and in the column for area .05, obtaining $\chi_{.05}^2 = 11.070$. Thus, we have

$$.05 = P[\chi^2 \geqslant 11.070]$$

We can also use Appendix Table H to find areas above points lying in the lower portion. For example, for an upper-tail area of .90, we obtain the value $\chi_{.90}^2 = 1.610$ at 5 degrees of freedom (see Figure 15-2).

Degrees of Freedom for the Contingency Table
Recall that row and column totals were used to estimate the expected frequencies in Table 15-2 for the Superior Oil study. The cell entries in that con-

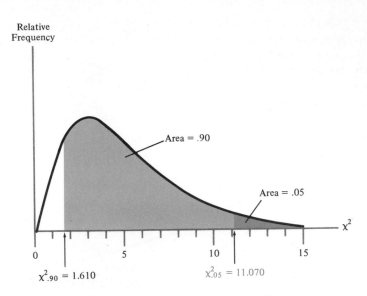

FIGURE 15-2 Chi-square curve for 5 degrees of freedom.

tingency table were found by multiplying the respective marginal totals for the row and column and then dividing by the sample size. Because the six row totals must sum to n, the values of any five rows automatically fix the value of the sixth. Knowing r_1, r_2, r_3, r_4, r_5, and n, the value for r_6 follows directly. We can say that five of the row totals are "free," while the sixth is "fixed." Likewise, only one of two column totals is free. Although there are $6 \times 2 = 12$ cells, we are free to specify only $5 \times 1 = 5$ of these cells, where the free rows and columns intersect. Our number of degrees of freedom is therefore 5. In general, we establish the following rule:

The number of degrees of freedom for a contingency table is determined by

$$(\text{Number of rows} - 1) \times (\text{Number of columns} - 1)$$

The Decision Rule

Suppose that our researcher wants to protect himself at the $\alpha = .05$ significance level against making the Type I error of concluding that the selected station type and stated reason for that choice are dependent when these variables are in fact independent. From the table of chi-square areas, we have already found that $\chi^2_{.05} = 11.070$ using 5 degrees of freedom. The appropriate decision rule would then be

Accept H_0 (conclude that the variables are independent) if $\chi^2 \leqslant 11.070$

Reject H_0 (conclude that the variables are dependent)   if $\chi^2 > 11.070$

Ordinarily the decision rule will be established once the design (number of categories in the rows and columns) and the significance level are determined, *before* gathering any data on the problem.

The interpretation of $\chi^2_{.05} = 11.070$ is that due to chance sampling error, this number will be exceeded on the average by only 5 percent of all χ^2 values calculated from repeated samples, each taken from a population where the null hypothesis is true. Thus, if the two variables are independent, about 5 percent of the sample results will disagree so much that independence will be rejected. Each of these samples will have a computed value, such as 13.5 or 14.2, that exceeds 11.070.

The above decision rule illustrates a convenient feature of this procedure: *All chi-square tests that compare frequencies are upper-tailed.* Stated another way, large χ^2 values tend to refute H_0, while small values confirm the null hypothesis. Since our statistician's computed value of $\chi^2 = 16.929$ is larger than $\chi^2_{.05}$, *the null hypothesis that the type of station preferred is independent of the primary stated reason must be rejected* at the .05 significance level. The statistician must assume that the type of station preferred by a customer is influenced by his primary reason for selecting where he trades.

The Type II Error

Had a smaller significance level such as $\alpha = .001$ been desired, then the researcher would have obtained $\chi^2_{.001} = 20.517$ from Appendix Table H for 5 degrees of freedom. Since this value is larger than the computed value of 16.929, the null hypothesis of independent variables would have been accepted. In such a case, there may be considerable chance of committing the Type II error of accepting H_0 when the variables are not independent. (In our illustration, this would mean concluding that reason for choice does not influence type preference when it does.) There are many ways in which such errors may occur, and finding β probabilities is a task too difficult to consider here. Only by making the sample size large can the chance of a Type II error be kept within reasonable boundaries.

Limitation on Using the Chi-Square Distribution

The true sampling distribution of χ^2 calculated from expression (15-2) is only approximated by the chi-square distribution. The nature of this approximation is somewhat analogous to substituting the normal distribution in place of the binomial distribution in certain instances. Ordinarily, the approximation is adequate if the sample size is sufficiently large. In practice, the sample will be large enough when the *expected* frequencies for each cell value round to 5 or more. Should some of these be smaller than 5, this requirement may be met by combining two rows or columns before calculating χ^2. A corresponding reduction in the degrees of freedom would then have to be made to account for the lower number of cells.

EXERCISES

15-1 Find the value of the chi-square statistic that holds for each upper-tail area α and each number of degrees of freedom stated on page 508 (top).

	(a)	(b)	(c)	(d)	(e)
α	.05	.01	.99	.10	.80
Degrees of freedom	10	20	18	6	29

15-2 A marketing researcher is testing to determine if a person's sex is independent of his or her preference for fruits. For each of the following situations where the sample results have been summarized, find the degrees of freedom and the critical value. Then indicate whether the null hypothesis of independence should be accepted or rejected.

(a) Bananas, apples, and pears are considered. $\chi^2 = 7.85$ and $\alpha = .05$.

(b) Pineapples, guavas, papayas, and passionfruit are considered. $\chi^2 = 15.23$ and $\alpha = .01$.

(c) Boysenberries, blueberries, huckleberries, blackberries, and strawberries are considered. $\chi^2 = 7.801$ and $\alpha = .10$.

(d) Plums, apricots, peaches, cherries, persimmons, and nectarines are considered. $\chi^2 = 10.99$ and $\alpha = .05$.

15-3 Various random samples have been selected and the chi-square statistics have been computed for each of the following independence-testing situations. For the stated significance level, determine the applicable number of degrees of freedom and the corresponding critical value in each situation. Then indicate whether or not the null hypothesis of independence should be accepted for each of the actual chi-square statistics obtained.

(a) Sex (male, female) versus marital status (single, married), with $\alpha = .05$ and $\chi^2 = 3.62$.

(b) College major (liberal arts, science, social science, professional) versus type of employment (manufacturing, service, government), with $\alpha = .01$ and $\chi^2 = 23.885$.

(c) Number of siblings (0, 1, 2, 3 or more) versus desired family size (0, 1, 2, 3 or more), with $\alpha = .10$ and $\chi^2 = 14.753$.

(d) Political affiliation (Republican, Democrat, other) versus sexual attitude (repressive, permissive), with $\alpha = .01$ and $\chi^2 = 8.063$.

15-4 A contingency table of actual sample frequencies is given below:

	Marital Status		
Preference	(1) *Single*	(2) *Married*	Total
(1) *Brand A*	20	10	30
(2) *Brand B*	20	50	70
Total	40	60	100

(a) Complete the contingency table for the expected frequencies under the null hypothesis of independence between marital status and brand preference.

(b) Calculate the chi-square statistic.

(c) Find the number of degrees of freedom and the critical value for the test at the $\alpha = .01$ significance level.

(d) Should the null hypothesis that marital status and brand preference are independent be accepted or rejected?

15-5 An advertiser wishes to determine whether there are any significant differences in regular series program preferences between male and female television viewers. A random sample of persons have been interviewed.

Each person has been asked to indicate which one of five program types he or she prefers. The results are provided below:

	Viewer's Sex		
Preferred Program Type	(1) Male	(2) Female	Total
(1) Western	32	18	50
(2) Situation comedy	17	13	30
(3) Drama	27	33	60
(4) Comedy	13	7	20
(5) Variety	24	16	40
Total	113	87	200

The null hypothesis is that a viewer's sex and preference are independent.
(a) Determine the contingency table of the expected results.
(b) Calculate the χ^2 statistic.
(c) How many degrees of freedom are associated with this test statistic?
(d) Assume that the advertiser wishes to protect himself against the Type I error of incorrectly concluding that sex is dependent upon preference at a significance level of $\alpha = .01$. Determine the critical value for the test statistic. Should the hypothesis of independence be accepted?
(e) Would your conclusion in (d) change if an $\alpha = .05$ significance level were chosen instead? Explain.

15-6 Repeat Exercise 15-5, but suppose that the following data were obtained instead:

	Viewer's Sex		
Preferred Program Type	(1) Male	(2) Female	Total
(1) Western	37	13	50
(2) Situation comedy	21	23	44
(3) Drama	26	32	58
(4) Comedy	19	15	34
(5) Variety	22	18	40
Total	125	101	226

15-2 TESTING FOR EQUALITY OF SEVERAL PROPORTIONS

An important statistical question involves a comparison of several population parameters. In Chapter 14, we described the inferences for two populations and the tests comparing *two* population means or proportions. There, we considered the problem of deciding which of two television programs was preferred by using the proportions of two independent samples taken from different populations. But what if more than two programs were to be compared? It would still be possible to make pair comparisons as we did in Chapter 14, but sometimes it is better to test the population proportions simultaneously to see if they really differ. With more than two populations, we must take a different approach. For comparing several proportions, the procedures used earlier in testing for independence may be applied.

Illustration of Procedure

We will illustrate the procedure for testing several proportions with a situation commonly encountered in the advertising field.

An advertising agency wishes to determine whether there are any differences in terms of recall among three kinds of magazine advertisements. One ad is humorous, the second is quite technical, while the third provides a pictorial comparison with competing brands. A national magazine with three regional editions is chosen for the test, and a different quarter-page advertisement is placed in each of its editions. A random sample of persons is chosen from a list of subscribers in each region, and one month after the ads have appeared, each person in the sample is visited. All are shown five ads of similar format, four of which are fakes, and are asked if they remember any of the five ads. Those selecting the correct ad are included in the tally of rememberers, while those unable to select the correct ad are classified as nonrememberers. Following the identification test, a brief quiz is administered to determine whether or not the magazine was read (thus avoiding prestige bias by persons falsely claiming to have read the ad), and nonreaders are eliminated from the sample.

Null Hypothesis
The null hypothesis is that there are no differences in the mnemonic properties of the three kinds of advertisements. This may be expressed in terms of the proportions of the readers of the three magazine editions who remembered the advertisements. Thus, letting π_1 represent the proportion remembering the first ad, π_2 the second, and π_3 the third, we may express the null hypothesis

$$H_0: \quad \pi_1 = \pi_2 = \pi_3$$

The alternative hypothesis suitable for this test is that at least two proportions differ.

Test Statistic
The results obtained are provided in Table 15-4. Recall that in testing for independence, the expected cell frequencies are determined by assuming equal ratios or proportions. In testing for independence, we are therefore testing for

equality of proportions. The same procedures may also be used here. From the sample results, we obtain the frequencies shown in Table 15-5. Applying expression (15-1), the contingency table for the results to be expected under the null hypothesis can then be determined (Table 15-6).

The χ^2 test statistic may be calculated in the same manner as in testing for independence. The calculations are provided in Table 15-7. The number of degrees of freedom is

$$(\text{No. of rows} - 1) \times (\text{No. of columns} - 1) = (2 - 1) \times (3 - 1) = 2$$

TABLE 15-4   Results of Mnemonic Advertising Samples

	Type of Advertisement		
	(1) *Humorous*	(2) *Technical*	(3) *Comparative*
Number of rememberers	25	10	7
Number of nonrememberers	73	93	108
Number of readers	98	103	115
Proportion of rememberers	$P_1 = .255$	$P_2 = .097$	$P_3 = .061$

TABLE 15-5   Contingency Table for Actual Observed Frequencies

	Type of Advertisement			
	(1) *Humorous*	(2) *Technical*	(3) *Comparative*	Total
(1) *Rememberers*	25	10	7	42
(2) *Nonrememberers*	73	93	108	274
Total	98	103	115	316

TABLE 15-6   Contingency Table for Expected Frequencies

	Type of Advertisement			
	(1) *Humorous*	(2) *Technical*	(3) *Comparative*	Total
(1) *Rememberers*	13.025	13.690	15.285	42
(2) *Nonrememberers*	84.975	89.310	99.715	274
Total	98	103	115	316

TABLE 15-7 χ^2 Calculations for Mnemonic Advertisement Study

(Row, Column)	Actual Frequency f_a	Expected Frequency f_e	$f_a - f_e$	$(f_a - f_e)^2$	$\dfrac{(f_a - f_e)^2}{f_e}$
(1, 1)	25	13.025	11.975	143.4006	11.010
(1, 2)	10	13.690	−3.690	13.6161	.995
(1, 3)	7	15.285	−8.285	68.6412	4.491
(2, 1)	73	84.975	−11.975	143.4006	1.688
(2, 2)	93	89.310	3.690	13.6161	.152
(2, 3)	108	99.715	8.285	68.6412	.688
	316	316.000	0.000		$\chi^2 = 19.024$

Testing the Hypothesis

The chosen level of significance is $\alpha = .01$. Appendix Table H shows us that this corresponds to a critical value of $\chi^2_{.01} = 9.210$. This is smaller than the calculated value of the test statistic, $\chi^2 = 19.024$, so that *the null hypothesis of equal proportions must be rejected* at the .01 significance level. The agency must conclude that the three ads are not equally easy to remember. (The results are also significant at the .001 level, since $\chi^2_{.001} = 13.815$.)

EXERCISES

15-7   In planning campaign strategy concerning a particular issue, a congressional candidate wishes to determine if there are any differences in the proportion of voters who favor the issue among her rural, suburban, and urban constituents. She has collected sample data of opinions and has obtained the following results:

	Rural	Suburban	Urban
In favor	65	63	52
Not in favor	35	37	48

(a) Construct a contingency table for the expected frequencies.
(b) Calculate the chi-square statistic.
(c) Find the number of degrees of freedom and the critical value associated with this test at the $\alpha = .01$ significance level.
(d) Must the null hypothesis that the proportion in favor is the same among constituent types be accepted or rejected?

15-8   A pastry chef wishes to determine whether the proportion of unsatisfactory bear claws is affected by oven temperature. He has baked batches of them at 350°, 400°, and 425°, and has obtained the following results:

	Temperature		
	350°	400°	425°
Number satisfactory	132	128	111
Number unsatisfactory	14	17	35

If the chef wishes to test the null hypothesis of identical proportions at an $\alpha = .05$ significance level, what conclusion should he reach?

15-9 The quality control manager of an electronics assembly plant wants to know if the day of the week influences the number of faulty cable harness assemblies. He suspects that on Mondays and Fridays the error rate is significantly higher than on other days. If he finds that the day of the week does make a difference, he will conduct a more detailed study to determine which days are worse and will recommend that cables be assembled only on certain days. He has collected a random sample of assemblies produced on different days of the week and has obtained the following results:

	Day of the Week				
	Monday	*Tuesday*	*Wednesday*	*Thursday*	*Friday*
Number of faulty assemblies	32	12	15	18	27
Number of correct assemblies	95	87	91	79	73

If the manager wishes to test the null hypothesis of identical proportions of faulty assemblies at an $\alpha = .05$ significance level, what conclusion should he reach?

15-10 The quality control manager in an appliance factory wishes to determine if the proportion of defective toasters is affected by the speed of the assembly line. He has taken three samples of size 100 from the line when it was run at three different speeds. The proportions of defectives obtained are: for 100 parts per hour, .05; for 150 parts per hour, .07; and for 200 parts per hour, .10.

Will he conclude that the proportions differ if he wishes to protect himself at level $\alpha = .01$ against wrongly deciding so? What is the lowest significance level at which the results will lead him to conclude that the proportions of defectives changes with line speed?

5-3 OTHER CHI-SQUARE APPLICATIONS

Testing for independence and comparing several population proportions are the most common uses of the chi-square distribution in business decision making. But this versatile distribution has wider application.

The following optional section tells us how the chi-square distribution can be used in making inferences about the population variance. Until now we have not estimated the population variance σ^2 by means of *confidence intervals*, nor have we tested *hypotheses about* σ^2. Although important, inferences concerning σ^2 have a lower priority than those for μ and π, where we use $\overline{X}$ and P as estimators and test statistics. We will use s^2 in the same fashion. We have waited until now to do this because of the role the chi-square distribution plays in the sampling distribution for s^2.

Chapter 17 considers a fourth chi-square application. There the *goodness-of-fit test* is described. That procedure is useful in determining whether a variety of technical assumptions hold with respect to the characteristics of the population sampled. The goodness-of-fit procedure also allows us to decide whether a particular probability distribution actually applies.

REVIEW EXERCISES

15-11 In developing nations, birth control is not yet widespread. A government population planning official in an Asian country must determine if traditional contraceptive procedures will work with the rural poor. Using a sample of 250 women, each practicing one of four methods of contraception for two years, he has obtained the following results:

	Contraceptive Method				
	(1) IUD	(2) Pill	(3) Mechanical	(4) Other	Total
(1) *Pregnant*	20	10	30	30	90
(2) *Not pregnant*	40	50	50	20	160
Total	60	60	80	50	250

Should the population planner conclude that any of the four contraceptive procedures will work? (Use $\alpha = .01$.)

15-12 A marketing student wishes to test the null hypothesis that people's sexual attitudes are independent of the kinds of cars they own. A random sample of 100 persons was selected, and each was interviewed and placed into a "dominant" sexual-attitude category. The following results were obtained:

Dominant Sexual Attitude	Previously Purchased Car			
	(1) Foreign	(2) Small	(3) Large	Total
(1) *Repressed*	3	6	11	20
(2) *Ho-hum*	13	25	12	50
(3) *Swinger*	14	9	7	30
Total	30	40	30	100

At the $\alpha = .05$ significance level, what conclusion should the student make?

15-13 A sales manager is determining a marketing strategy. To do this, he must determine whether his product's appeal is generally broad, or whether it varies from region to region. A sampling study provided him with the following regional data:

	East	Central	South	West
Number preferring	21	29	23	16
Number not preferring	39	41	27	24

Should the manager conclude that the product is equally preferred in all regions? (Use $\alpha = .01$.)

15-14 Suppose that the manager in Exercise 15-13 wishes to test the null hypothesis that the product is equally strong in the East and in the West. Using an $\alpha = .05$ significance level, what should he conclude?

15-15 A market researcher for a soap manufacturer wishes to determine whether the amount of time people spend watching daytime television influences their choice of type of laundry bleach. He took a random sample of 260 persons and determined their viewing habits and which bleach they used most. The results are:

Television Viewing Time	Bleach Types		
	Liquid Chlorine	Dry Chlorine	Oxygen
Light	53	5	38
Moderate	29	10	35
Heavy	45	8	37

Should he conclude that television viewing time and type of bleach used are independent? Test at the $\alpha = .05$ level of significance.

15-16 Suppose that the market researcher in the previous problem has decided that the amount of television viewing time affects the choice of bleach type. He now wishes to decide whether preference for "soap operas" or game shows affects the choice of bleach. Another sample is collected. The following results are obtained.

Program Preference	Bleach Types		
	Liquid Chlorine	Dry Chlorine	Oxygen
Soap opera	58	5	55
Game show	48	13	47
Other	16	12	27

Are preference of daytime programming and type of bleach used independent? Test at the $\alpha = .05$ level of significance.

15-4
OPTIONAL TOPIC: INFERENCES REGARDING THE POPULATION VARIANCE

An important area of statistics is concerned with making inferences about the population variance σ^2. As we have seen, knowledge of population variability is an important element of statistical analysis. For instance, a training director may choose a particular teaching method because it provides low dispersion in trainee productivity levels, thus making the instructor's job less demanding than a high-variability procedure would. Likewise, a bank policy might favor a single waiting line that feeds into several teller windows rather than separate lines, because it has been estimated that the single line will minimize variability in customer waiting times—even though the mean time spent in line is the same in either case. For a car rental company, tires with a low variability in wear may be preferred to more durable tires with greater variability in useful lifetime, simply because it is cheaper to replace an entire set of tires periodically for each car.

Like the population mean, σ^2 *is ordinarily unknown and its value must be estimated using sample data.* Until now, we have been using the sample variance

$$s^2 = \frac{\sum X^2 - n\bar{X}^2}{n-1}$$

in making point estimates of σ^2. These estimates were made as an adjunct to inferences regarding μ, where confidence intervals and hypothesis-testing decision rules have been constructed using s^2 in place of σ^2.

Although less common than inferences for μ, inferences for σ^2 may be similarly made. To this end, s^2 may be used as an unbiased and consistent estimator of the population variance, playing the analogous role with σ^2 that $\bar{X}$ does with μ. Thus, s^2 serves as the basis either for constructing confidence interval estimates or for testing hypotheses about σ^2.

Probabilities for the s^2 Variable

In the *planning stage* of a sampling study, s^2 must be treated as a random variable, since its value is yet to be determined and is subject to chance variation. In discussing how to apply probability analysis to s^2, it will be helpful to briefly review our earlier treatment of $\bar{X}$.

Recall that when σ^2 is unknown, the Student t distribution is used to make inferences about the population mean. This is because the random variable $t = (\bar{X} - \mu)/(s/\sqrt{n})$ is so distributed that probability statements with respect to $\bar{X}$ must be made in terms of the Student t distribution. For instance,

$$\alpha = P\left[\frac{\bar{X} - \mu}{s/\sqrt{n}} \geq t_\alpha\right]$$

The chi-square distribution assigns a role to s^2 that is similar to the role the Student t assigns to $\bar{X}$. *Before the sample data are collected, s^2 must be viewed as a random variable* (just as $\bar{X}$ is). Multiplying s^2 by $n-1$ and dividing by σ^2 converts it into *the chi-square random variable:*

$$\chi^2 = \frac{(n-1)s^2}{\sigma^2} \tag{15-3}$$

which has the chi-square distribution.* Thus, it is possible to find probabilities for this variable:

$$\alpha = P\left[\frac{(n-1)s^2}{\sigma^2} \geq \chi_\alpha^2\right] \tag{15-4}$$

when the number of degrees of freedom is $n-1$.

To illustrate this, suppose that a sample of $n = 25$ heights has been randomly selected from a population of men where the population standard deviation is $\sigma = 3$ inches. We are interested in finding the value for s^2 that only 5 percent of such samples is expected to exceed. From Appendix Table H, we have $\chi_{.05}^2 = 36.415$ for $25-1 = 24$ degrees of freedom. Thus, using the fact that $\sigma^2 = 3^2 = 9$,

$$.05 = P\left[\frac{24s^2}{9} \geq 36.415\right]$$

Multiplying both sides of this inequality by 9 and dividing by 24, we have

$$.05 = P\left[s^2 \geq \frac{9(36.415)}{24}\right] = P[s^2 \geq 13.66]$$

We see that there is a probability of .05 that the sample variance will exceed 13.66. Stated differently, there is only a 5-percent chance that the variability in the sample will be so extreme that the sample standard deviation s will exceed $\sqrt{13.66} = 3.7$ inches.

To find the probability that s^2 falls within a range of numbers, two limits are required for the chi-square variable. These may be chosen so that χ^2 is just as likely to fall below its *lower limit*, denoted by χ_L^2, as it is to fall above its *upper limit* χ_U^2. For example, if these limits are to be chosen for a .90 probability:

$$.90 = P\left[\chi_L^2 \leq \frac{(n-1)s^2}{\sigma^2} \leq \chi_U^2\right]$$

In this case, the χ^2 values are found from Appendix Table H for $n-1 = 25 - 1 = 24$ degrees of freedom. The upper-tail areas are .95 for the lower limit and .05 for the upper limit, and the area under that portion of the chi-square curve between the limits is .90:

$$\chi_L^2 = \chi_{.95}^2 = 13.848$$
$$\chi_U^2 = \chi_{.05}^2 = 36.415$$

Two separate tabled values are required to find the limits χ_L^2 and χ_U^2, because the chi-square distribution is *positively skewed*. This is in contrast to

---

* Like the Student t distribution, the chi-square distribution requires that the *population* be normally distributed.

our earlier applications involving the normal and Student t curves, both of which are symmetrical.

Again, using $\sigma = 3$ inches, we have

$$.90 = P\left[13.848 \leqslant \frac{24s^2}{9} \leqslant 36.415 \right]$$

so that

$$.90 = P\left[\frac{9(13.848)}{24} \leqslant s^2 \leqslant \frac{9(36.415)}{24} \right] = P[5.19 \leqslant s^2 \leqslant 13.66]$$

Thus, there is a 90-percent chance that a sample of $n = 25$ observations from a population where $\sigma = 3$ inches will provide a sample variance lying between 5.19 and 13.66 (in other words, that s will lie between $\sqrt{5.19} = 2.3$ and $\sqrt{13.66} = 3.7$ inches).

Confidence Interval Estimate of σ^2

The foregoing probability analysis presumes that the value of the population variance is known. This is not usually the case in a sampling situation. *After the sample data are collected*, s^2 can be calculated and can serve as the basis for making inferences about the unknown σ^2. Treating σ^2 as the unknown quantity and s^2 as the known, we may transform the probability interval for s^2,

$$\chi_L^2 \leqslant \frac{(n-1)s^2}{\sigma^2} \leqslant \chi_U^2 \tag{15-5}$$

into the form for making an interval estimate of σ^2. Separate algebraic manipulations of the two inequality portions of expression (15-5) provide the following procedure for constructing a *confidence interval estimate for σ^2*:

$$\frac{(n-1)s^2}{\chi_U^2} \leqslant \sigma^2 \leqslant \frac{(n-1)s^2}{\chi_L^2} \tag{15-6}$$

Here, χ_L^2 and χ_U^2 must be chosen from Appendix Table H, using $n-1$ degrees of freedom, to correspond to the confidence level desired.

> **Example 15-2**   A sociologist estimated the variability of IQ, as measured on the Stanford-Binet scale, for the inmates at a certain state prison. For a sample of $n = 30$ prisoners, he obtained a standard deviation of $s = 10.2$ points, considerably below the corresponding figure of 16 points for all test takers.
>
> The sample variance is $s^2 = (10.2)^2 = 104.04$. Using this result, we may construct a 90-percent confidence interval estimate for the variance in IQ of the prison population. For $30-1 = 29$ degrees of freedom. Table G provides the following lower and upper limits for the chi-square variable:
>
> $$\chi_L^2 = \chi_{.95}^2 = 17.708$$
> $$\chi_U^2 = \chi_{.05}^2 = 42.557$$

Substituting these and the sample results into expression (15-6), we obtain the following interval estimate for σ^2:

$$\frac{(30-1)104.04}{42.557} \leqslant \sigma^2 \leqslant \frac{(30-1)104.04}{17.708}$$

or

$$70.8969 \leqslant \sigma^2 \leqslant 170.3840$$

To estimate the population standard deviation of these results, we may take the square root of each term and obtain the following 90-percent confidence interval for σ:

$$\sqrt{70.8969} \leqslant \sigma \leqslant \sqrt{170.3840}$$

or

$$8.42 \leqslant \sigma \leqslant 13.05$$

Since this interval lies well below 16, the sociologist might safely conclude that the prisoners have a lower variability in IQ than the population as a whole. Later in this section, we will see how such comparisons may be made using hypothesis-testing concepts.

In explaining why inmates have less variability in IQ, the sociologist concludes: You can't be very dull and still be a serious criminal; besides, retarded persons who commit crimes are incarcerated in other kinds of institutions. On the other hand, the smartest people have, by and large, avoided a life of crime. In effect, the tails of the normal curve for IQ are underrepresented in prisons, which explains the lower variability in measured intelligence.

Testing Hypothesis Regarding σ^2

Hypothesis tests regarding σ^2 may be conducted in a manner similar to the tests described in earlier chapters. The null hypothesis regarding σ^2 may be either one- or two-sided. Decision rules may be constructed in terms of the chi-square variable, which serves as the test statistic. Using the hypothesized value of the population variance, denoted by σ_0^2, the appropriate *test statistic is*

$$\chi^2 = \frac{(n-1)s^2}{\sigma_0^2} \tag{15-7}$$

The significance level α establishes the critical values for this statistic.

One-Sided Tests
For one-sided tests, the decision rule is based upon either χ_α^2, which must correspond to the upper tail of the chi-square curve, or $\chi_{1-\alpha}^2$ for the lower tail of that curve. This is because for a lower-tailed test the critical value for χ^2 must be that point *below* which the area is α. The cases may be summarized as follows:

Lower-Tailed Test	*Upper-Tailed Test*
$H_0: \;\; \sigma^2 \geqslant \sigma_0^2$	$H_0: \;\; \sigma^2 \leqslant \sigma_0^2$
Accept H_0 if $\chi^2 \geqslant \chi_{1-\alpha}^2$	*Accept H_0 if* $\chi^2 \leqslant \chi_\alpha^2$
Reject H_0 if $\chi^2 < \chi_{1-\alpha}^2$	*Reject H_0 if* $\chi^2 > \chi_\alpha^2$

Example 15-3 That predictability and variability are related can be illustrated by the attitudes of people who wait in lines. A lengthy waiting time is more acceptable if the variability is smaller, even though the average wait may be the same. When the variability is smaller, the inconvenience of waiting becomes more predictable. This accounts for the fact that many businesses and government offices dealing with the public have instituted a "single-line" policy as a replacement for the earlier, chaotic procedure of having independent lines form at various service areas (like windows at a post office). Although the mean waiting time is not greatly affected by the single-line policy, the variability in waiting time is.

A particular postmaster has determined that the current procedure of separate lines yields a standard deviation in waiting times on late December mornings of $\sigma_0 = 10$ minutes per customer. He has decided to implement the single-line policy on a trial basis to see if a reduction in waiting-time variability occurs.

A sample of 30 customers were monitored, and their waiting times were determined. The sample standard deviation was $s = 5$ minutes per customer. As his null hypothesis, the postmaster assumes that the variance in waiting times will be at least as great under the experimental procedure

$$H_0: \quad \sigma^2 \geqslant \sigma_0^2 \quad (10^2 = 100)$$

This test is lower-tailed. At an $\alpha = .01$ significance level, we find for $30 - 1 = 29$ degrees of freedom that the critical value for the chi-square statistic is

$$\chi^2_{1-\alpha} = \chi^2_{.99} = 14.256$$

The postmaster's decision rule is

Accept H_0 (and retain the old procedure) if $\chi^2 \geqslant 14.256$
Reject H_0 (and adopt the new procedure) if $\chi^2 < 14.256$

From expression (15-7), the test statistic has the value

$$\chi^2 = \frac{(30-1)(5)^2}{(10)^2} = 7.25$$

Since 7.25 is smaller than $\chi^2_{.99} = 14.256$, H_0 must be *rejected* and the postmaster should adopt the new single-line system.

Two-Sided Tests

When the null hypothesis takes the form $H_0: \sigma^2 = \sigma_0^2$, a two-sided test applies. Large or small values for the sample variance tend to refute H_0. Thus, either a large or a small calculation for χ^2 will result in rejecting H_0. As with the two-sided tests we discussed in earlier chapters, a convenient procedure for making a decision is to construct a confidence interval corresponding to the significance level. If σ_0^2 falls outside this interval, H_0 must be rejected; if the interval contains σ_0^2, H_0 must be accepted.

To illustrate this procedure, we again consider the variance in prisoner IQs in Example 15-2. There, we obtained the 90-percent confidence interval

$$70.8969 \leqslant \sigma^2 \leqslant 170.3840$$

Suppose that the sociologist in our example wished to test the null hypothesis that the variability in prisoner IQs is the same as the IQ variability in the general population as a whole, where the Stanford-Binet test has a standard deviation of 16. To do this, he would use

$$H_0: \quad \sigma^2 = \sigma_0^2 \quad (16^2 = 256)$$

Since $\sigma_0^2 = 256$ lies above the upper limit of the 90-percent confidence interval, H_0 must be *rejected* at the $\alpha = .10$ significance level. The sociologist must conclude that prisoner IQs have a lower variability than IQs in the general population. In fact, H_0 could be rejected at the lower significance level $\alpha = .02$. (As an exercise, you may verify this by constructing a 98-percent confidence level.)

Normal Approximation for Large Sample Sizes

The chi-square distributions in Appendix Table H are not given above 30 degrees of freedom. *For values of n larger than 30, we may approximate the chi-square distribution by the normal curve.* It may be shown that χ^2 has a mean equal to the degrees of freedom and a variance equal to twice that amount. Thus, we may compute the applicable normal deviate from

$$z = \frac{\chi^2 - (n-1)}{\sqrt{2(n-1)}} \tag{15-8}$$

Expression (15-8) is useful for testing hypotheses about σ^2. In order to construct a confidence interval, however, it is more convenient to express the critical values of χ^2 in terms of the tabled value of z by the equivalent expressions

$$\chi_L^2 = \chi_{1-\alpha}^2 = n - 1 - z\sqrt{2(n-1)}$$

and $\tag{15-9}$

$$\chi_U^2 = \chi_\alpha^2 = n - 1 + z\sqrt{2(n-1)}$$

Example 15-4 A medical researcher ordered a sampling study to see how effectively a particular tranquilizer induces sleep. The drug was administered to a sample of $n = 100$ patients. The sample standard deviation in times required until onset of sleep was computed as $s = 7.3$ minutes. Based upon this result, the researcher may construct a 95-percent confidence interval for the variance in time to sleep. Using $z = 1.96$ (so that the area under the normal curve between $\pm z$ is .95 and the area in each of the two tails is $\alpha = .025$) the following limits for the chi-square variable can be found from expression (15-9):

$$\chi_L^2 = \chi_{.975}^2 = 99 - 1.96\sqrt{2(99)}$$
$$= 99 - 27.58 = 71.42$$
$$\chi_U^2 = \chi_{.025}^2 = 99 + 27.58 = 126.58$$

Substituting these values into expression (15-6), with $s = 7.3$ and $n = 100$:

$$\frac{99(7.3)^2}{126.58} \leqslant \sigma^2 \leqslant \frac{99(7.3)^2}{71.42}$$

or

$$41.68 \leqslant \sigma^2 \leqslant 73.87$$

Taking the square root of each term reveals a 95-percent confidence that the population standard deviation will fall between 6.46 and 8.59 minutes.

Suppose that our researcher wanted to test the null hypothesis that the variability in the new sleeping drug is the same as the variability in the old one, where previous records show that the standard deviation is 8 minutes. Thus, he would have

$$H_0: \quad \sigma^2 = \sigma_0^2 \quad (8^2 = 64)$$

Since this value falls inside the 95-percent confidence interval for σ^2, the researcher must *accept* H_0 at the $\alpha = .05$ significance level and conclude that the two drugs are identical in variability of time necessary to induce sleep.

OPTIONAL EXERCISES

15-17 For each of the following situations, construct a 90-percent confidence interval estimate for the population variance:
(a) $s^2 = 20.3$ (b) $s^2 = 101.6$ (c) $s^2 = .53$ (d) $s^2 = 7.78$
  $n = 25$ $n = 12$ $n = 15$ $n = 20$

15-18 For each of the following hypothesis-testing situations: (1) indicate whether the test is lower-tailed or upper-tailed; (2) find the critical value for the chi-square statistic for the indicated significance level; and (3) calculate χ^2, and state whether H_0 must be accepted or rejected.
(a) $H_0: \sigma^2 \geqslant 16$; $n = 25$; $\alpha = .05$; $s^2 = 19$.
(b) $H_0: \sigma^2 \leqslant 100$; $n = 10$; $\alpha = .01$; $s^2 = 105$.
(c) $H_0: \sigma^2 \geqslant .64$; $n = 19$; $\alpha = .10$; $s^2 = .59$.
(d) $H_0: \sigma^2 \leqslant 6.1$; $n = 17$; $\alpha = .05$; $s^2 = 10.1$.

15-19 A sociologist has administered the Stanford-Binet test to 30 randomly chosen persons in a particular city in order to draw conclusions regarding the IQ scores of professionals. The sample standard deviation obtained was $s = 12.7$.
(a) Assuming that the population standard deviation for the IQs of nonprofessional persons is 14, should the null hypothesis that professionals have at least as great a variability in IQ be accepted or rejected at the $\alpha = .05$ significance level?
(b) Suppose that the population standard deviation for attorneys is 10.3. Should the null hypothesis that professional people as a whole have a variability in IQ that is no larger be accepted or rejected at the $\alpha = .05$ significance level?
(c) Construct a 90-percent confidence interval estimate for the variance in professional IQ scores. Does your answer indicate that the variability in IQ for this group is different from the variability for the general population, where the standard deviation is 16? (Use $\alpha = .10$.)

15-20 Suppose that the researcher in Example 15-4 used another drug on $n = 200$ patients, where the standard deviation in time to sleep was $s = 8.2$ minutes.
(a) Construct a 95-percent confidence interval for the population variance for the time to sleep.

(b) Suppose the researcher wished to test the null hypothesis that this drug will have the same variability as the one presently used, where the standard deviation is 8 minutes. What conclusion should he reach at the $\alpha = .05$ significance level?

15-21 A consumer agency has tested a random sample of $n = 100$ sets of radial tires. The sample standard deviation in tire-set lifetimes was determined to be $s = 2,000$ miles.

(a) Construct a 99-percent confidence interval estimate for the population variance in lifetimes of radial tires.

(b) Should the agency conclude that radial tires have a different lifetime variability than nonradial tires, which have a population standard deviation of 2,500 miles? (Use $\alpha = .01$.)

Chapter Sixteen
Analysis
of Variance

*In order to recognize the best of the treatments
in use in the healing of a malady, it is sufficient
to test each of them on an equal number of
patients, making all the conditions exactly
similar.*

Marquis de Laplace (1820)

This chapter describes procedures for analyzing several quantitative populations. The central focus is a statistical application called *analysis of variance*, which is actually a method for comparing the means of more than two populations.

This kind of analysis is very useful in many areas of decision making. A manufacturer can use it in determining the most effective packaging for a product. It can indicate to a production manager whether various ingredient combinations really make a difference in the quality of the final product. In agriculture, analysis of variance may be helpful in determining if crop yields differ according to the kinds of fertilizers or pesticides used.

The basic questions considered in this chapter have been posed earlier in Chapter 14, where we compared two population means using two samples—control and experimental groups. When more than two samples are involved, however, a radically different approach is required.

Since analysis of variance deals with means, it may appear to be misnamed, but as we will see, *this procedure achieves its goal by comparing sample variances*. In doing this, a new probability distribution—the *F distribution*—must be used.

16-1 ANALYSIS OF VARIANCE AND THE *F* DISTRIBUTION

Analysis of variance uses sample data to compare several *treatments* in order to determine if they achieve different results. Here, we use the word "treatment" in a broad sense that includes not only medical therapy but other factors a researcher might investigate. Thus, an agronomist may consider several concentrations of fertilizer as "treatments" for crops. Similarly, alternative package design in a marketing research program may represent a different "treatment" in the final stage of a product's development. Sample data can be obtained by applying the respective treatments to different samples. These sample data may then be analyzed to determine if the treatments differ.

Testing for Equality of Means

As an illustration, consider the data in Table 16-1 obtained for three different fertilizer schemes being evaluated by a lawn-sod farmer. Here, the total dosages are the same, but the fertilizer application sizes and frequencies have been varied. The sample observations represent the number of square yards of marketable sod obtained from random plots of 100 square yards, all seeded with

TABLE 16-1 Sample Fertilizer Treatment Yields (square yards) for Three Fertilizing Schemes

		Fertilizer Treatment		
Sample Observation Number		*(1)* *Quarter Dosage* *Once Weekly*	*(2)* *Half Dosage* *Every Two Weeks*	*(3)* *Full Dosage* *Every Four Weeks*
1		77	83	80
2		79	91	82
3		87	94	86
4		85	88	85
5		78	85	80
	Totals	406	441	413
	Means	$\bar{X}_1 = 81.2$	$\bar{X}_2 = 88.2$	$\bar{X}_3 = 82.6$

$$\bar{\bar{X}} = \frac{406 + 441 + 413}{5(3)} = 84$$

the same variety of grass mix. In each case, a random sample of five plots was subjected to one of the three treatments.

The analysis of variance procedure used to determine whether fertilizing affects sod yields involves two variables, and we may note some similarities between this situation and regression analysis. The method of fertilizing is a qualitative variable, which is sometimes referred to as a *factor*. Each treatment is a *factor level*. The factor is analogous to the independent variable in regression analysis. The sod yield is the *response variable*, which must be quantitative, and since the response achieved may depend upon the particular treatment used, this variable plays a role similar to the dependent variable used in regression analysis. Although analysis of variance is primarily concerned with *qualitative factors*, it can also be used with quantitative factors. In such cases, the factors are fixed at a few key levels and constitute *quantitative categories* rather than continuous variates.

The sod farmer must compare the alternative fertilizer schemes to see if they provide different mean yields of marketable sod. In effect, he wishes to test the null hypothesis that the population mean yield per 100 square yards of seeded surface is the same under each treatment. Using subscripts 1, 2, and 3 for the respective treatment, we may express the *null hypothesis*

$$H_0: \quad \mu_1 = \mu_2 = \mu_3$$

The corresponding alternative hypothesis is that the means are not equal; that is, that at least one pair of the μ's differ.

The procedures described in this chapter actually test a somewhat stronger null hypothesis—that the treatment populations are identical, or in other words, that they have the same frequency distribution form. In particular, this assumption means that each treatment population has the same common value for its variance.

The concepts underlying this procedure are illustrated in Figure 16-1. When the sample data are combined, they appear to be observations from a single, highly disperse population, as shown in (a). But when each treatment is viewed separately, these same sod yields appear to belong to three separate populations with smaller variances, as indicated in (b). Under the null hypothesis, however, the treatment populations have identical means and the same variance, so that an identical frequency curve like the one in (c) applies for each method of fertilizing.

As with earlier hypothesis-testing procedures, we must convert the sample data into a test statistic and see whether or not the value achieved refutes H_0. Before we do this, it is necessary to establish some notation and concepts.

Summarizing the Data

Each sample plot yield in Table 16-1 may be represented by a symbol X_{ij}, where i refers to the row or observation number and j refers to the column. In each column, the values are the sample observations made from the corresponding treatment populations. For example, $X_{32} = 94$ square yards—the sod yield

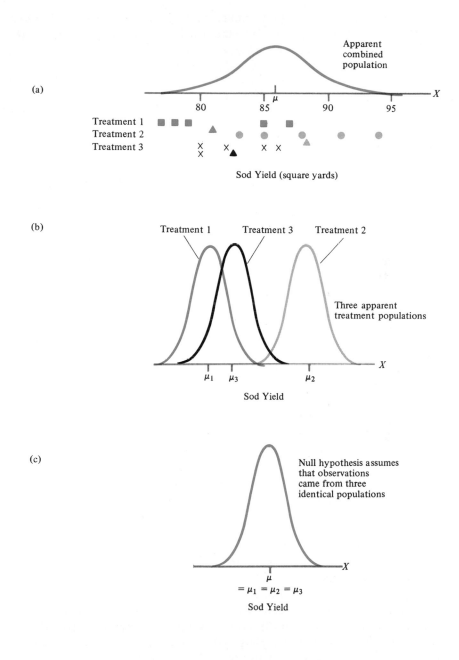

FIGURE 16-1   Concepts underlying analysis of variance.

for the third test plot in the second sample, where treatment (2), half the fertilizer dosage every two weeks, was used. In the usual manner, we can calculate the *sample mean for the jth treatment column:*

$$\overline{X}_j = \frac{\sum_i X_{ij}}{r} \qquad (16\text{-}1)$$

where all the observations in the jth column are summed and divided by the number of observations made under that treatment, r = the number of rows. In our example, $j = 1$, 2, or 3, depending upon which treatment is being considered. For the first treatment, the sample mean is found by summing the values in column (1) and dividing by $r = 5$:

$$\overline{X}_1 = \frac{77 + 79 + 87 + 85 + 78}{5} = 81.2 \text{ square yards}$$

The other sample means can be similarly calculated as $\overline{X}_2 = 88.2$ and $\overline{X}_3 = 82.6$ square yards.

To facilitate testing the null hypothesis, we require that the data from the three samples be pooled in calculating the *grand mean:*

$$\overline{\overline{X}} = \frac{\sum_j \sum_i X_{ij}}{rc} \qquad (16\text{-}2)$$

Here, we denote the grand mean by $\overline{\overline{X}}$ ("X double bar"). The double summation indicates that first we obtain the column totals and then we sum these figures for all treatments. The resultant total is divided by the combined sample size. We denote the number of treatments or columns by the letter c; in this illustration, there are $c = 3$ treatments. The combined sample size is therefore $rc = 5(3) = 15$. The grand mean for this illustration was computed in Table 16-1 to be $\overline{\overline{X}} = 84$ square yards.

Using Variability to Identify Differences

As with any testing problem, a test statistic is desired that will (1) highlight the differences between the observed sample results and what would be expected under the null hypothesis, and (2) have a convenient sampling distribution to measure the effect of chance sampling error. As we have seen, the amount of sampling error may be easily estimated from the variability of the sample results. We may also use the variability of the results to express differences. For instance, if several values are unalike, then we have seen that their dispersion—expressed by a range, variance, or standard deviation—will be greater than it will if the values are nearly the same. When many values are involved, their collective differences can be summarized by one of these measures of variability.

Since we are dealing with several populations, it is convenient to use the sample data to measure three sources of variability: (1) *treatments variation*, which measures how the sample results differ under the various treatments; (2) *error*, which collectively summarizes how the observations vary within their respective samples; and (3) *total variation* of the sample observations without regard to the populations to which they belong.

Treatments Sum of Squares

To summarize the variability between sample results, we use the following for the *treatments sum of squares:*

$$SST = r \sum (\bar{X}_j - \bar{\bar{X}})^2 \qquad (16\text{-}3)$$

In calculating SST, we sum squared deviations of the sample treatment means from the grand mean and then multiply by the number of observations r made under each treatment. For the results from our sod-fertilizing experiment we find

$$SST = 5[(81.2 - 84)^2 + (88.2 - 84)^2 + (82.6 - 84)^2]$$
$$= 5(7.84 + 17.64 + 1.96) = 137.2$$

We multiply by $r = 5$, the number of observations per treatment (or the number of rows), so that with $c = 3$ treatments or columns, all of the $rc = 15$ observations are represented.

The treatments sum of squares expresses the variation between columns, which is often referred to as *explained variation*. This is because SST is obtained from differences in the sample means. Thus, SST summarizes those differences in sample results that might be due to inherent differences in the treatment populations rather than to chance alone.

Error Sum of Squares

We summarize the variability within samples by summing the squared deviations of the individual observations about their respective sample means. This variability is referred to as the *error sum of squares:*

$$SSE = \sum \sum (X_{ij} - \bar{X}_j)^2 \qquad (16\text{-}4)$$

Table 16-2 shows the calculation of the error sum of squares for the results of the sod-fertilizing experiment. There, we obtain $SSE = 190.80$. In performing this calculation, it is convenient to maintain the same column arrangement we used initially, first totaling the squared deviations for each treatment and then summing these to obtain SSE. As with SST, SSE accounts for each individual sample observation made.

The error sum of squares expresses variation within the columns. This is sometimes called *unexplained variation*, because the error sum of squares measures differences between sample values that are due to chance (or residual)

TABLE 16-2 Calculation of the Error Sum of Squares for the Sod-Fertilizing Experiment

i	$(X_{i1} - \bar{X}_1)^2$	$(X_{i2} - \bar{X}_2)^2$	$(X_{i3} - \bar{X}_3)^2$
1	$(77 - 81.2)^2 = 17.64$	$(83 - 88.2)^2 = 27.04$	$(80 - 82.6)^2 = 6.76$
2	$(79 - 81.2)^2 = 4.84$	$(91 - 88.2)^2 = 7.84$	$(82 - 82.6)^2 = .36$
3	$(87 - 81.2)^2 = 33.64$	$(94 - 88.2)^2 = 33.64$	$(86 - 82.6)^2 = 11.56$
4	$(85 - 81.2)^2 = 14.44$	$(88 - 88.2)^2 = .04$	$(85 - 82.6)^2 = 5.76$
5	$(78 - 81.2)^2 = 10.24$	$(85 - 88.2)^2 = 10.24$	$(80 - 82.6)^2 = 6.76$
	$\overline{80.80}$	$\overline{78.80}$	$\overline{31.20}$

$$SSE = \sum \sum (X_{ij} - \bar{X}_j)^2 = 80.80 + 78.80 + 31.20 = 190.80$$

variation, for which no identifiable cause can be found. This is in contrast to *SST*, which explains the variation between samples in terms of differences in treatment populations.

Total Sum of Squares

If we initially ignore the groupings of the sample observations, then we can determine the sum of squares for a single combined sample. The result obtained is called the *total sum of squares:*

$$\text{Total } SS = \sum \sum (X_{ij} - \bar{\bar{X}})^2 \tag{16-5}$$

We may calculate the total sum of squares for our 15 observations:

$$\text{Total } SS = (77 - 84)^2 + (79 - 84)^2 + \cdots + (80 - 84)^2 = 328$$

Note that if we add the treatments and error sums of squares, we obtain the same result:

$$SST + SSE = 137.20 + 190.80 = 328$$

In general, it can be mathematically shown that

$$\text{Total } SS = SST + SSE \tag{16-6}$$

for any set of sample results.

Computational Difficulties

When sample sizes are large, sum of squares calculations can be quite burdensome. In such cases, computations may be considerably simplified by using shortcut expressions for *SST* and *SSE*. Since the more straightforward procedures presented here work just as well for small samples, short-cut expressions have not been included in this book. Instead, *it is recommended that large problems be run on a computer.* Canned programs that perform analysis of variance for a variety of situations are widely available from most large computer centers and time-sharing facilities.

The Test Statistic

Expression (16-6) shows that the two components of total variation are explained (*SST*) and unexplained (*SSE*) variations. Our task is to determine whether the explained variation is significant enough to warrant rejecting the null hypothesis that the treatment populations have identical means.

Comparing Variations

As our test statistic, we must use a summary measure to express how much the sample results deviate from what is expected when the null hypothesis is true. This may be achieved by comparing the explained and the unexplained variations. Regardless of whether or not H_0 is true, we should expect some error or unexplained variation within each sample, as this is natural in any random sampling experiment. But according to H_0—that population means are identical for all methods of fertilization—the amount of explained treatments variation between samples should be small. That is, the respective sample means should be about the same. If, in fact, the population means are equal, then the explained and unexplained variation components should be of comparable size. To compare them, we will use their ratio.

Mean Squares

To find this ratio, we cannot immediately divide the sums of squares. Recall that *SSE* is the sum of $r \times c$ squared differences (for the 15 observations in our example), while only c squares (representing the 3 samples in our example) are used to calculate *SST*. Each sum of squares must be converted into an average before *SSE* and *SST* are comparable. We then have sample variances, which we will call *mean squares* to avoid confusion with population variances. Mean squares may be viewed as estimators of the population variances, which, under the assumption that the samples are taken from identical populations, are equal to a common value of σ^2. These estimators are unbiased when the proper divisors are chosen. First, we define the *treatments mean square:*

$$MST = \frac{SST}{c-1} \tag{16-7}$$

In a similar manner, we define the *error mean square:*

$$MSE = \frac{SSE}{(r-1)c} \tag{16-8}$$

Returning to our sod-fertilizing illustration, we have

$$MST = \frac{137.2}{3-1} = 68.6 \quad \text{and} \quad MSE = \frac{190.8}{(5-1)3} = 15.9$$

Note that the treatments mean square is more than four times as large as the error mean square. Under the null hypothesis of identical population means, they should be nearly the same. Such a large difference seems unlikely, but it may be "explained" by differences between populations. We have yet to determine just how unlikely this large discrepancy would be if the populations were in fact identical.

The ANOVA Table

It is helpful to summarize the computations for analysis of variance in the format of Table 16-3. Called an ANOVA table (an acronym for "ANalysis Of VAriance"), this table conveniently arranges the intermediate calculations. As we will see later in this chapter, the ANOVA table is important in organizing the computations for more complicated experiments, because it provides the degrees of freedom, the sum of squares, and the mean square for each source of variation. The degrees of freedom are the divisors we use to calculate the mean squares. The test statistic, which will be discussed next, is the value in the column labeled *F*.

The F Statistic

We now have two sample variances, *MST* and *MSE*. In keeping with our earlier discussions, we may refer to the treatments mean square as the variance explained by treatments and to the error mean square as the unexplained variance. In calculating the ratio of these variances, we obtain our *test statistic:*

$$F = \frac{\text{Variance explained by treatments}}{\text{Variance left unexplained}} = \frac{MST}{MSE} \tag{16-9}$$

For our example, we calculate

$$F = \frac{68.6}{15.9} = 4.31$$

Under the null hypothesis, we would expect values for *F* to be close to 1, because *MST* and *MSE* would then both be unbiased estimators of the common population variance σ^2. Since they would have the same expected value, the sample should yield like values for *MST* and *MSE*, and the ratio of these values should

TABLE 16-3   ANOVA Table for Sod-Fertilizing Experiment

Variation	Degrees of Freedom	Sum of Squares	Mean Square	F
Explained by Treatments (between columns)	$c-1 = 2$	$SST = 137.2$	$MST = 137.2/2$ $= 68.6$	MST/MSE $= 68.6/15.9$ $= 4.31$
Error or Unexplained (within columns)	$(r-1)c = 12$	$SSE = 190.8$	$MSE = 190.8/12$ $= 15.9$	
Total	$rc-1 = 14$	$SS = 328$		

be near 1. In order to formulate a decision rule, we must establish the sampling distribution of this test statistic. From this, we can find a critical value that will tell us whether the calculated value of F is large enough to cause rejection of the null hypothesis. The probability distribution we use to do this is called the F distribution. Before describing this distribution, we must clarify what is meant by degrees of freedom.

Degrees of Freedom

We may view the divisor $c-1$ in the calculation for MST as the number of degrees of freedom associated with using MST to estimate σ^2. Here, finding the sum of squares involves calculating $\overline{X}$, which may be expressed in terms of the $\overline{X}_j$'s. For a fixed $\overline{X}$, all but one of the c $\overline{X}_j$'s are free to vary.

Analogously, the $(r-1)c$ divisor in the calculation for MSE is the number of degrees of freedom associated with using MSE to estimate σ^2. This is due to the fact that in finding the sum of squares, each term includes an $\overline{X}_j$ calculated from the X_{ij} values. For a given value of $\overline{X}_j$, only $r-1$ of the X_{ij}'s are free to assume any value. For c treatments, the number of free variables is therefore only $(r-1)c$.

Thus, a pair of degrees of freedom are associated with the F statistic. This pair sums to the total number of observations minus one. In our sod-fertilizing example, $r = 5$ and $c = 3$, so that the following degrees of freedom apply:

$$\text{For the numerator:} \quad c-1 = 3-1 = 2$$

$$\text{For the denominator:} \quad (r-1)c = (5-1)3 = 12$$

and $2+12 = 14$, a value 1 less than the total number of observations.

The F Distribution

Under the proper conditions, we may employ the F distribution to obtain probabilities for possible values of F. Like those for the chi-square and t distributions, the F distribution is characterized by degrees of freedom. Because the F statistic is defined as a ratio, the F distribution has two kinds of degrees of freedom. As we have seen, we associate one of these with the numerator and one with the denominator.

Figure 16-2 shows curves for the F distribution when the degrees of freedom for the numerator and denominator, respectively, are: 6 and 6; 20 and 6; and 30 and 30. Note that the F distribution curve is positively skewed, with possible values ranging from zero to infinity. There is a different distribution and curve for each pair of degrees of freedom.

Since the F distribution is continuous, probabilities for the values of F are provided by the areas under the curves. The critical values for upper-tail areas under the F distribution are provided in Appendix Table I. The table is constructed in the same manner as the tables for the t and chi-square distributions. Due to space limitations, only two upper-tail areas are considered.

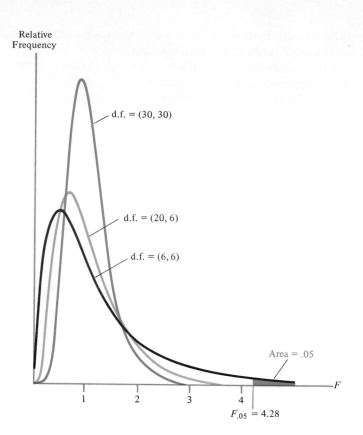

FIGURE 16-2 Various *F* distribution curves.

In Appendix Table I, the rows correspond to the number of degrees of freedom in the denominator and the columns correspond to the number of degrees of freedom in the numerator. The entries in the body of the table are critical values, designated as F_α, where $\alpha = .01$ or $.05$. To find $F_{.01}$ and $F_{.05}$ when the numerator and the denominator degrees of freedom are 6 and 6, we read the entries from column 6 and row 6. The boldface type is the value for $F_{.01}$ and the lightface type is the value for $F_{.05}$, so the values are $F_{.01} = 8.47$ and $F_{.05} = 4.28$. Thus

$$P[F \geqslant 8.47] = .01$$

$$P[F \geqslant 4.28] = .05$$

The second probability is represented by the colored area under the curve for this distribution, beginning at $F_{.05} = 4.28$. Because the tails of the *F* curve are so long and narrow, the graph in Figure 16-2 does not show the area above $F_{.01}$. These values signify that in repeated experiments, values of *F* exceeding 4.28

will be obtained on an average of 5 percent of the time and values exceeding 8.47 will be obtained about 1 percent of the time.

Testing the Hypothesis

Large values for the F statistic tend to refute the null hypothesis of equal population means. For a significance level established at $\alpha = .01$ or $\alpha = .05$, Appendix Table I provides the critical value F_α for the following decision rule:

$$Accept \ H_0 \ if \ F \leqslant F_\alpha$$

$$Reject \ H_0 \ if \ F > F_\alpha$$

Suppose that an $\alpha = .05$ Type I error probability is desired for incorrectly concluding that the population means for the various sod-fertilizing treatments are not identical. Using 2 as the degrees of freedom for the numerator and 12 for the denominator, Table I provides $F_{.05} = 3.88$. Since the calculated value $F = 4.31$ exceeds this critical value, the null hypothesis must be *rejected* and we must conclude that the methods of fertilizing differ.

(If the decision maker required greater protection against the Type I error and used the smaller significance level of $\alpha = .01$, the opposite conclusion would be reached, since $F_{.01} = 6.93$, which is larger than the calculated value for F.)

Additional Comments

What should the sod farmer do after rejecting the null hypothesis of identical population means? Obviously, he should pick the fertilizer treatment that will maximize mean sod yield. But his results are only sample data, which are subject to sampling error. He could arrive at a decision by comparing individual treatments. (A procedure for doing this will be described in Section 16-2.)

The analysis of variance procedure we have described thus far has considered just one type of treatment—sod fertilization. This one factor explained enough of the variation in sod yield to justify our conclusion that the fertilizer treatments have different effects. But there may be other explanations for differences in sample yields: for example, varying soil conditions or watering schedules. In Section 16-3, procedures for analyzing two factors will be discussed, and later we will see how as many as three factors may be incorporated into the analysis. As more factors are included, the testing procedures become more discriminating and efficient.

The theoretical conditions under which the F distribution applies to our problem are (1) the populations for each sample must be *normally distributed* with identical mean and variance (standard deviation), and (2) all sample observations are *independent*. The requirement of normality is shared with the

Student t distribution. As we noted in our discussion of the t distribution, as long as the populations are not highly skewed, departures from normality are not considered serious. In Chapter 18, an alternative procedure that does not require the assumption of normality—the Kruskal-Wallis test—will be discussed.

Because we have already established the sample sizes, we are free only to set the value of the Type I error probability α for falsely rejecting the null hypothesis of identical fertilizer treatment means. As we saw in Chapter 9, no matter what the sample size, a critical value may be obtained that always guards against erroneous rejection of the null hypothesis. But when H_0 is accepted after comparing F to the critical value, there may be a very large chance of committing the Type II error and accepting a false hypothesis. To protect against erroneous acceptance, much larger samples should generally be used than those in our sod-fertilizing experiment.

EXERCISES

16-1   For each pair of degrees of freedom and each significance level provided below, indicate the critical value F_α for the F statistic above which the stated tail area holds.

	(a)	(b)	(c)	(d)
α	.01	.05	.05	.01
Numerator d.f.	10	12	5	10
Denominator d.f.	10	8	26	5

16-2   A chemical engineer is investigating different pressure settings to determine whether pressure affects particular synthetics in terms of quantity produced. Once for every chemical, three sample batches, each of size 5, are run at low, medium, and high pressures. For each synthetic, H_0 is that the mean output is identical under all pressure settings. In the following cases, find the appropriate critical value and then indicate whether H_0 should be accepted or rejected.
(a) For synthetic X, $F = 5.32$ and $\alpha = .01$.
(b) For synthetic Y, $F = 4.97$ and $\alpha = .05$.
(c) For synthetic Z, $F = 6.43$ and $\alpha = .05$.

16-3   A statistics instructor teaches three small experimental sections of the same course. In each of these, he uses a different book. The instructor wishes to test the null hypothesis that the mean scores achieved on a standard examination by all students using a particular textbook at his university will be identical. He has administered this test to his students, and the 9 scores obtained from each class constitute a random sample from the respective population of university-wide scores. In applying the F test, find the respective degrees of freedom. Then, in each of the situations below, find whether the null hypothesis should be accepted or rejected at the stated significance level.
(a) $F = 4.86$ and $\alpha = .01$.   (c) $F = 5.91$ and $\alpha = .01$.
(b) $F = 4.59$ and $\alpha = .05$.   (d) $F = 3.19$ and $\alpha = .05$.

16-4   Quicker Oats is contemplating changing the shape of its box from the quaint cylinder presently in use. In an experiment, different random samples were selected from five stores of similar size in the same region, and for several days, one of three candidate boxes was substituted for the cylinder. Total boxes sold have been determined as follows:

	Box Shape		
Sample Store	(1) Pyramid	(2) Rectangle	(3) Cube
1	110	57	92
2	85	65	81
3	69	73	66
4	97	49	71
5	78	77	70

(a) Calculate the individual sample means and the grand mean.
(b) Determine the treatments and error sums of squares. Use these values to find the total sum of squares.
(c) Construct the appropriate ANOVA table.
(d) At the $\alpha = .05$ significance level, should the null hypothesis that the mean sales are identical regardless of box shape be accepted or rejected?

16-5 In assessing the impact of the level of impurities in a particular ingredient upon the solubility of her company's aspirin tablets, a statistician wishes to test the null hypothesis that the mean dissolving time is the same regardless of the impurity level. In test batches, the following dissolving times measured in seconds were obtained:

	Level of Impurities		
Observation	(1) 1 percent	(2) 5 percent	(3) 10 percent
1	2.01	1.95	2.30
2	1.82	2.21	2.29
3	1.74	2.14	2.17
4	1.90	1.93	2.06
5	2.03	2.07	2.58

(a) Construct the applicable ANOVA table.
(b) At the $\alpha = .05$ significance level, what should the statistician conclude?

16-6 A detergent manufacturer advertises that its product will remove all stains except oil-based paint in any kind of water. A consumer information service reporting on detergent quality is testing this claim. Wash loads were run in five randomly chosen homes in each of three areas— areas with hard, soft, or moderately soft water. Each wash load contained an assortment of rags and cloth scraps stained with food products, grease, and dirt over a 100-square-inch area. After washing, the number of square inches still stained was determined, and the following results were obtained:

	Level of Water Hardness		
Observation	(1) Hard	(2) Moderate	(3) Soft
1	5	4	4
2	3	7	0
3	2	8	1
4	10	3	3
5	6	2	2

(a) Using an $\alpha = .01$ level of significance, will the consumer service conclude that the type of water affects the effectiveness of the detergent?

(b) Are there any factors besides water type that might "explain" some of the sources of variation?

16-2 ESTIMATING TREATMENT MEANS AND DIFFERENCES

Once the null hypothesis of equal treatment population means has been rejected, what do we do next? Continuing with the sod farmer's experiment, we have concluded that the sod yields differ according to the fertilizing treatment applied. But what should the farmer do? He might simply select the procedure with the greatest mean yield. But in doing so, he must acknowledge that chance sampling error still clouds the results. In this section, we will extend the analysis of variance results by describing further procedures that can help us translate them into action.

There are two basic aspects to this extended analysis. First, we will individually estimate the means of the treatment populations. Then, we will compare treatments by estimating the differences between pairs of population means. In both cases, the confidence interval estimation techniques encountered earlier in this book may be applied.

Confidence Intervals for Treatment Population Means

Recall that for a single sample, a confidence interval may be constructed for the population mean according to

$$\mu = \overline{X} \pm t_\alpha \frac{s}{\sqrt{n}}$$

where α is selected so that the chosen confidence level equals $1 - 2\alpha$ (and t_α is the critical value for which the upper-tail area under the Student t curve is α), s is the sample standard deviation, and n is the sample size. When several samples have been taken from different populations, only slight modifications are necessary to obtain a similar expression for each of the respective population means $\mu_1, \mu_2, \ldots$

Remember that the treatment populations were presumed to have identical variances σ^2. Thus, a better estimator for σ^2 can be achieved by pooling the sample results, using the unexplained variance MSE in place of a single sample variance s^2. In estimating μ_j, the population mean for the jth treatment, we may use sample treatment mean $\overline{X}_j$ as the estimator. In place of n, we use the number of observations r made under that treatment. Finally, the number of degrees of freedom used in finding t_α is $(r-1)c$, the same figure we used in computing MSE.

Thus, we obtain the following expression for computing the *confidence interval estimate of μ_j*:

$$\mu_j = \overline{X}_j \pm t_\alpha \sqrt{\frac{MSE}{r}} \qquad (16\text{-}10)$$

Returning to the fertilizing experiment results in the previous section, we may construct a 95-percent confidence interval estimate for the mean sod yield for treatment (1). For $(r-1)c = (5-1)3 = 12$ degrees of freedom, Appendix Table F provides $t_{.025} = 2.179$. With $\overline{X}_1 = 81.2$ and $MSE = 15.9$, we obtain the following estimated mean yield of marketable sod per 100 square yards:

$$\mu_1 = \overline{X}_1 \pm t_{.025} \sqrt{\frac{MSE}{5}}$$

$$= 81.2 \pm 2.179 \sqrt{\frac{15.9}{5}}$$

$$= 81.2 \pm 3.9$$

or

$$77.3 \leqslant \mu_1 \leqslant 85.1 \text{ square yards}$$

Similarly, the confidence intervals for the other treatments are

$$84.3 \leqslant \mu_2 \leqslant 92.1 \text{ square yards}$$

$$78.7 \leqslant \mu_3 \leqslant 86.5 \text{ square yards}$$

Comparing Treatment Means Using Differences

In Chapter 14, we investigated various procedures for using two sample means to estimate the difference in population means. In the case of independent samples, we used a confidence interval of the form

$$\mu_A - \mu_B = \overline{X}_A - \overline{X}_B \pm t_\alpha s_{d\text{-small}}$$

where $s_{d\text{-small}}$ represents an estimate of the standard error of the difference $d = \overline{X}_A - \overline{X}_B$ that is found by pooling the sample standard deviations. Although here we use number subscripts, the procedure may be extended to any treatment pair. In place of $s_{d\text{-small}}$, we may use $\sqrt{2MSE/r}$, again reflecting the fact that the common population variance is estimated by MSE. The presence of the 2 indicates that the variability is additive for two samples. Thus, we have the following *confidence interval estimate for the difference $\mu_2 - \mu_1$*:

$$\mu_2 - \mu_1 = \overline{X}_2 - \overline{X}_1 \pm t_\alpha \sqrt{\frac{2MSE}{r}} \qquad (16\text{-}11)$$

where t_α is chosen to correspond to the confidence level and the degrees of freedom are $(r-1)c$ as before. Applying this expression to our fertilizing experiment results, the 95-percent confidence interval for the difference in mean sod yields between treatments (2) and (1) is

$$\mu_2 - \mu_1 = 88.2 - 81.2 \pm 2.179 \sqrt{\frac{2(15.9)}{5}}$$

$$= 7 \pm 5.5$$

or

$$1.5 \leqslant \mu_2 - \mu_1 \leqslant 12.5 \text{ square yards}$$

Thus, we estimate that the advantage in mean sod yield of using treatment (2) over treatment (1) is somewhere between 1.5 and 12.5 square yards.

We may use the above confidence interval to test the null hypothesis that the treatment means are equal. The fact that the interval does not overlap zero indicates that $H_0: \mu_1 = \mu_2$ can be *rejected*, and we can only conclude that μ_1 and μ_2 differ at the $1-.95 = .05$ significance level. Thus, we can recommend that the sod farmer choose treatment (2) over treatment (1), with only a .05 probability that this action could be incorrect if the treatments actually yield identical results.

Other 95-percent confidence intervals may be similarly constructed for the remaining pairs:

$$\mu_3 - \mu_1 = 1.4 \pm 5.5 \quad \text{or} \quad -4.1 \leqslant \mu_3 - \mu_1 \leqslant 6.9 \quad \text{square yards}$$

$$\mu_3 - \mu_2 = -5.6 \pm 5.5 \text{ or } -11.1 \leqslant \mu_3 - \mu_2 \leqslant -.1 \text{ square yards}$$

The first confidence interval contains zero, indicating that $H_0: \mu_3 = \mu_1$ must be accepted at the 5-percent significance level. However, the null hypothesis that $\mu_3 = \mu_2$ must be rejected.

Multiple Comparisons

The preceding methods simply extend earlier concepts to the analysis of variance. But their interpretation may be somewhat misleading. The confidence and significance levels obtained apply only to the *single* estimate or test and *not to the entire series* of estimates or tests. It would be incorrect to tie the three confidence intervals together in a single statement, such as: "Treatment (2) yields greatest mean sod yield, while treatments (1) and (3) are similar to each other but are both inferior to (2)." This is because *as a set* these three confidence intervals correspond to less than a 95-percent confidence level. Stated another way, there is greater than a .05 chance that there will be at least one erroneous rejection of an individual null hypothesis that a pair of treatments has the same mean. The separate inferences are interdependent.

This problem can be alleviated by constructing somewhat wider confidence intervals, a procedure referred to as *multiple comparisons*. Because of their relative complexity, a discussion of these methods is beyond the scope of this book.*

EXERCISES

16-7   The following ANOVA table and mean calculations apply to the results of a study seeking to determine if a person's attitude toward his present job influences the number of years he has remained in that position. The treatments were three job attitudes: (1) dislike, (2) apathetic, and (3) enjoy. A sample of 4 persons was used for each treatment.

Variation	Degrees of Freedom	Sum of Squares	Mean Square	F
Treatments	2	104	52	8.7
Error	9	54	6	
Total	11	158		

$\bar{X}_1 = 2$ years $\bar{X}_2 = 4$ years $\bar{X}_3 = 9$ years $\bar{X} = 5$ years

(a) Construct 95-percent confidence intervals for the treatment population means.

(b) Construct 95 percent confidence intervals for the differences $\mu_2 - \mu_1$, $\mu_3 - \mu_2$, and $\mu_3 - \mu_1$.

(c) Referring to your answers to (b), do the population means for attitudes (3) and (1) appear significantly different at the 5-percent level?

16-8   Referring to the data in Exercise 16-4 (page 536) and to your answers to that exercise:

(a) Construct a 95-percent confidence interval estimate for the mean sales of the pyramid-shaped box.

(b) Construct a 95-percent confidence interval for the difference found by subtracting the mean sales of the rectangular box from the mean sales of the pyramid box. Do the two styles have different mean sales at the $\alpha = .05$ significance level?

16-9   Referring to Exercise 16-5 (page 537) and to your answers to that exercise, determine whether the 1-percent and 10-percent impurity levels provide significantly different mean dissolving times. (Use $\alpha = .05$.)

16-3   TWO-FACTOR ANALYSIS OF VARIANCE

In analyzing the sod-yield data in Table 16-1, we saw that the test results were significant enough (but barely so) to warrant rejecting H_0 of identical

---

* A complete description of three multiple comparison procedures, due to J. W. Tukey, Henry Scheffé, and Bonferroni, respectively, are described in John Neter and William Wasserman, *Applied Linear Statistical Models* (Homewood, Ill.: Richard D. Irwin, 1974), Chapter 14.

treatment means at the 5-percent level. For $\alpha = .01$, however, H_0 would have to be accepted, because we found too much unexplained variation in sod yields to justify rejecting H_0 at this lower level. Is it possible to lower the level of unexplained variation by explaining a portion of it in terms of another factor? Perhaps some of the differences in yield could be explained in terms of varying soil qualities, the slopes of plots, or different watering methods, for example.

Suppose that every sample observation consisted of three neighboring plots in each of five separate parcels owned by the farmer and that every treatment was randomly assigned to one plot in each parcel. We could then treat the parcel as a second factor in the analysis. Although the sod farmer is interested in finding out how yields are affected by fertilizer treatments—and not by the parcels themselves (which are permanent features of the farm)—consideration of parcels as a second factor may still help to explain some of the differences achieved in sod yields. In this section, we will describe a procedure for doing this, called *two-factor analysis of variance*.

There are two basic forms of two-factor analysis of variance. We will illustrate the first form by expanding our analysis of the sod-fertilizing experiment, where inferences will be made with respect to the original factor only. Later in this section, we will investigate situations where inferences are made regarding both factors.

The Randomized Block Design

Each parcel of land is referred to as a *block*. Table 16-4 arranges the original sod-yield data by block and treatment. This experiment has a *randomized block design*, since treatments have been randomly assigned to units within each block.

TABLE 16-4 Two-Factor Layout for Sod-Fertilizing Experiment Using Parcels as Blocks and with Sod Yield (square yards) as the Response Variable

| | Fertilizer Treatment | | | Mean Yield (square yards) |
| | (1) Quarter Dosage Once Weekly | (2) Half Dosage Every Two Weeks | (3) Full Dosage Every Four Weeks | |
Blocks				
(1) *Parcel A*	77	83	80	$\bar{X}_1. = 80$
(2) *Parcel B*	79	91	82	$\bar{X}_2. = 84$
(3) *Parcel C*	87	94	86	$\bar{X}_3. = 89$
(4) *Parcel D*	85	88	85	$\bar{X}_4. = 86$
(5) *Parcel E*	78	85	80	$\bar{X}_5. = 81$
Mean Yield (square yards)	$\bar{X}_{.1} = 81.2$	$\bar{X}_{.2} = 88.2$	$\bar{X}_{.3} = 82.6$	$\bar{X} = 84$

Although our illustration represents a block as a contiguous, presumably rectangular area (like a "city block"), the term actually refers to a second factor in the analysis that is used primarily to reduce the unexplained variation by having homogeneous sample units in each block. Here, the blocking factor is of no inherent interest, and its primary use is to reduce the unexplained variation in the response variable. This same design can also be used to evaluate several training programs in terms of productivity; but if the trainees in a variety of plants are to be tested, the experimental results will be more discriminating if the plants are blocked according to size and region (either of which can influence productivity), with an equal representation of each block in the various training programs.

The sod farmer is still faced with his earlier question: Are mean sod yields affected by fertilizer treatments? His null hypothesis is the same as before:

$$H_0: \quad \mu_1 = \mu_2 = \mu_3$$

Extending the procedure outlined in Section 16-1, which we now refer to as *one-factor analysis of variance*, we have another source of variation that may be explained by differences between blocks. In addition to treatments and error variation, *blocks variation* is a third component of total variation. We may measure each of these three component variations by computing a sum of squares and a mean square. But before we do this, we must expand upon our earlier notation.

Sample Mean Calculations

As before, each observation is denoted by X_{ij}, but here i refers to the ith block and j to the treatment. In addition to the column means used for treatments, we now find row means for each block. To help distinguish between these, the row means are designated by symbols of the form $\overline{X}_{i\cdot}$ and the column means are represented as $\overline{X}_{\cdot j}$'s. The subscripted dots signify that more than one factor is being considered. The following calculation provides the *sample mean for the ith block*:

$$\overline{X}_{i\cdot} = \frac{\sum\limits_j X_{ij}}{c} \tag{16-12}$$

where all the observations in the ith row are summed and divided by the number of entries in that row, which is the number of columns c. In our example, $i = 1, 2, 3, 4,$ or 5, depending upon which block we are considering. For block (4), representing plots in parcel D, the sample mean is found by summing the values in row (4) and then dividing by $c = 3$:

$$\overline{X}_{4\cdot} = \frac{85 + 88 + 85}{3} = \frac{258}{3} = 86$$

The sample means for the remaining rows are provided in the margins of Table 16-4.

Likewise, we may calculate the *sample mean for the jth treatment:*

$$\overline{X}_{\cdot j} = \frac{\sum\limits_{i} X_{ij}}{r} \qquad (16\text{-}13)$$

These values are also provided in Table 16-4.

As before, the mean of all observations in the combined sample—which may be computed by averaging either the row or the column means—serves as the *grand mean:*

$$\overline{\overline{X}} = \frac{\sum \overline{X}_{i\cdot}}{r} = \frac{\sum \overline{X}_{\cdot j}}{c} \qquad (16\text{-}14)$$

The Two-Factor ANOVA Table

The two-factor ANOVA table for our sod-fertilizing experiment is provided in Table 16-5, which is similar to Table 16-3 but contains an additional row for the blocks variation. For blocks, the number of degrees of freedom is $r-1$, the number of rows minus one. Also, note that the number of degrees of freedom for the error row is $(r-1)(c-1)$, accounting for the fact that one degree of freedom each is lost from the rows and columns.

Here, the treatments sum of squares *SST* expresses variation between the column means; it is found as before, by summing the squared deviations of the column means from the grand mean and then multiplying by the number of rows. Analogously, the variation between the row means is expressed by summing their squared deviations from the grand mean and then multiplying by the number of columns to obtain the *blocks sum of squares:*

$$SSB = c \sum (\overline{X}_{i\cdot} - \overline{\overline{X}})^2 \qquad (16\text{-}15)$$

TABLE 16-5 Two-Factor ANOVA Table for Sod-Fertilizing Experiment Using Randomized Block Design

Variation	Degrees of Freedom	Sum of Squares	Mean Square	F
Explained by Treatments (between columns)	$c-1 = 2$	$SST = 137.2$	$MST = 137.2/2$ $= 68.6$	MST/MSE $= 68.3/3.6$ $= 19.06$
Explained by Blocks (between rows)	$r-1 = 4$	$SSB = 162$	$MSB = 162/4$ $= 40.5$	*
Error or Unexplained (residual)	$(r-1)(c-1) = 8$	$SSE = 28.8$	$MSE = 28.8/8$ $= 3.6$	
Total	$rc-1 = 14$	$SS = 328$		

* In the randomized block design, *F* is not ordinarily calculated for blocks.

In our example,

$$SSB = 3[(80-84)^2 + (84-84)^2 + (89-84)^2 + (86-84)^2 + (81-84)^2]$$
$$= 3(16+0+25+4+9) = 162$$

A New Source of Explained Variation

Together, *SST* and *SSB* account for the explained variation in sod yields. *SST* explains this variation in terms of differences in fertilizer treatments; *SSB*, in terms of differences between parcels of land. Left unexplained by either fertilizing or parcels is the residual variation in sod yield, which is expressed by the error sum of squares *SSE*. It may be shown mathematically that the total sum of squares is the sum of the three components:

$$\text{Total } SS = SST + SSB + SSE \tag{16-16}$$

By calculating the total sum of squares and then subtracting *SSB* and *SST*, we may determine the *error sum of squares:*

$$SSE = \text{Total } SS - SST - SSB \tag{16-17}$$

Earlier, the total sum of squares for sod yields was found to be 328. Thus, for that experiment,

$$SSE = 328 - 137.2 - 162 = 28.8$$

Note that *SSE* is smaller than it was in our earlier one-factor analysis of variance, because much of the formerly unexplained variation in sod yields can now be attributed to differences in parcels or blocks.

The mean square for each component of variation is computed by dividing the respective sum of squares by the applicable number of degrees of freedom. We may calculate the *blocks mean square:*

$$MSB = \frac{SSB}{r-1} \tag{16-18}$$

For our example,

$$MSB = \frac{162}{5-1} = 40.5$$

The value of the treatments mean square remains at $MST = 68.6$, unchanged from our earlier one-factor analysis of variance. Dividing *SSE* by a smaller number of degrees of freedom than before, we calculate the *error mean square for two-factor analysis of variance:*

$$MSE = \frac{SSE}{(r-1)(c-1)} \tag{16-19}$$

For the sod-fertilizing experiment,

$$MSE = \frac{28.8}{(5-1)(3-1)} = 3.6$$

Recall that each mean square is really a sample variance and serves as an estimator of the common variance of the treatment populations.

Testing the Null Hypothesis

We are now ready to test the null hypothesis. First we calculate the appropriate *F statistic:*

$$F = \frac{\text{Variance explained by treatment factor}}{\text{Variance left unexplained}} \qquad (16\text{-}20)$$

This is accomplished by dividing the respective mean squares. The *F* statistic for the fertilizer treatments is

$$F = \frac{MST}{MSE} = \frac{68.6}{3.6} = 19.06$$

To see if these results are significant, we must find the critical value for 2 numerator and 8 denominator degrees of freedom in Appendix Table I. We see that the calculated value for *F* is greater than both $F_{.05} = 4.46$ and $F_{.01} = 8.65$, indicating that we must *reject* the null hypothesis that population fertilizer treatment means are identical at the 1-percent significance level.

Although it is possible to calculate a value of *F* for blocks using *MSB*, this variable is of secondary interest and is used primarily to allow finer discrimination between treatments. Later in this section, we will investigate two-factor experiments where inferences may be made regarding both factors.

Increased Efficiency of Two-Factor Analysis

Our example illustrates how two-factor analysis of variance can be more efficient than one-factor analysis. We obtained a much larger value of *F* for treatments than before, allowing us to reject H_0 (equal fertilizing population means) at a smaller significance level than we could in the one-factor analysis. This is because including parcels as a second factor considerably reduced the previously unexplained variation in sod yield.

Making Inferences About Both Factors

Another kind of two-factor analysis of variance is performed when inferences using both factors are made. To illustrate this, consider the data in Table 16-6, where factor *A* (acidity level) and factor *B* (chlorine concentration) are

TABLE 16-6 Two-Factor Layout and Sample Results for Relating Monthly Drop in Swimming Pool Alkalinity (ppm) to Acidity Levels and Chlorine Concentrations

Factor B *(Chlorine Concentration)*	Factor A *(Acidity Level)*				*Sample Mean*
	(1) *pH 7.2*	(2) *pH 7.4*	(3) *pH 7.6*	(4) *pH 7.8*	
(1) *Low*	23	18	9	7	$\bar{X}_1. = 14.25$
(2) *Medium*	10	12	8	4	$\bar{X}_2. = 8.50$
(3) *High*	9	9	7	4	$\bar{X}_3. = 7.25$
Sample Mean	$\bar{X}._1 = 14$	$\bar{X}._2 = 13$	$\bar{X}._3 = 8$	$\bar{X}._4 = 5$	$\bar{\bar{X}} = 10$

Total $SS = \sum\sum (X_{ij} - \bar{\bar{X}})^2$:

$$
\begin{array}{llll}
(23-10)^2 = 169 & (18-10)^2 = 64 & (9-10)^2 = 1 & (7-10)^2 = 9 \\
(10-10)^2 = 0 & (12-10)^2 = 4 & (8-10)^2 = 4 & (4-10)^2 = 36 \\
(9-10)^2 = \underline{1} & (9-10)^2 = \underline{1} & (7-10)^2 = \underline{9} & (4-10)^2 = \underline{36} \\
170 & 69 & 14 & 81
\end{array}
$$

Total $SS = 170 + 69 + 14 + 81 = 334$

$$
\begin{aligned}
SSA &= r \sum (\bar{X}._j - \bar{\bar{X}})^2 \text{ (between-columns variation)} \\
&= 3[(14-10)^2 + (13-10)^2 + (8-10)^2 + (5-10)^2] \\
&= 3(16+9+4+25) = 162
\end{aligned}
$$

$$
\begin{aligned}
SSB &= c \sum (\bar{X}_i. - \bar{\bar{X}})^2 \text{ (between-rows variation)} \\
&= 4[(14.25-10)^2 + (8.50-10)^2 + (7.25-10)^2] \\
&= 4(18.0625 + 2.25 + 7.5625) = 111.5
\end{aligned}
$$

$$
SSE = \text{Total } SS - SSA - SSB = 334 - 162 - 111.5 = 60.5
$$

used to explain the monthly drop in alkalinity (in parts per million or ppm) for a random sample of swimming pools. Pool acidity and chlorine are set at various levels to satisfy sanitation requirements, but for each combination of these factor levels, the drop in alkalinity must be periodically offset by adding soda ash.

Here, we wish to make inferences regarding the underlying populations for the alkalinity-drop response variable at various levels for both factors. In this example, the sample units (swimming pools) have been randomly assigned with equal probability to each factor combination. Such a two-factor study has a *completely randomized design*, as opposed to the randomized block design described earlier, where the unit assignments to blocks are fixed by their nature because of location, characteristics, or some other fixed factor. In a completely randomized design involving two factors, there is a separate treatment for each combination of levels for the two factors, represented by the cells in Table 16-6.

The particular design used here allows us to *test the two null hypotheses* described below.

1. The response (alkalinity-drop) means for factor A populations (acidity levels) are identical.
2. The response (alkalinity-drop) means for factor B populations (chlorine concentrations) are identical.

A separate test may be performed on each hypothesis using the same data. Again, this shows that a two-factor analysis can be more efficient than separate one-factor analyses. (As we indicate in Section 16-4, the two-factor analysis sometimes answers questions that cannot even be considered in one-factor analyses.)

Since there is a separate treatment for each cell, it is necessary to modify our previous notation somewhat. For this purpose, we use *SSA* and *SSB* to denote the factor *A* and factor *B* sums of squares. These are calculated in Table 16-6 in the same manner as their counterparts in the randomized block design, where *SSA* is based upon the deviations of *column means* and *SSB* is based upon the deviations of *row means*. The total and the error sums of squares are also calculated in Table 16-6 in the same way as before.

The ANOVA table for this experiment is provided in Table 16-7. The respective mean squares, *MSA*, *MSB*, and *MSE*, are found by dividing the corresponding sum of squares by the applicable number of degrees of freedom. We find the values of the *F* statistic:

$$\textit{For factor A (acidity level): } F = \frac{MSA}{MSE} = 5.36$$

and

$$\textit{For factor B (chlorine concentration): } F = \frac{MSB}{MSE} = 5.53$$

In the case of factor *A*, the degrees of freedom are 3 for the numerator and 6 for the denominator. Appendix Table H provides $F_{.05} = 4.76$. Since this value is smaller than the calculated *F*, we must *reject* the null hypothesis that the acidity level population means are identical at the $\alpha = .05$ significance level. Similarly, for 2 and 6 degrees of freedom for factor *B*, we have $F_{.05} = 5.14$, and the second

TABLE 16-7   Two-Factor ANOVA Table for Completely Randomized Design for Experiment for Effects of Acidity and Chlorine Levels on Drop in Swimming Pool Alkalinity

Variation	Degrees of Freedom	Sum of Squares	Mean Square	F
Explained by Factor A—Acidity Level (*between columns*)	$c-1 = 3$	$SSA = 162$	$MSA = 162/3$ $= 54$	MSA/MSE $= 54/10.08$ $= 5.36$
Explained by Factor B—Chlorine Concentration (*between rows*)	$r-1 = 2$	$SSB = 111.5$	$MSB = 111.5/2$ $= 55.75$	MSB/MSE $= 55.75/10.08$ $= 5.53$
Error or Unexplained (*residual*)	$(r-1)(c-1) = 6$	$SSE = 60.5$	$MSE = 60.5/6$ $= 10.08$	
Total	$rc-1 = 11$	$SS = 334$		

null hypothesis of identical population means for chlorine concentration must also be *rejected* at the $\alpha = .05$ significance level.

An Important Assumption
In the above example, we make the important assumption that the factor effects are *additive*, so that the population treatment mean is raised or lowered from some "background" level by a different constant amount for each level of every treatment. But this may not be true, for there may be an *interaction* between the two factors that cannot be explained by either one alone. For example, the mean alkalinity drop in swimming pools may be more severe if the acidity level is high when the chlorine concentration is decreased than would be indicated by combining the separate effects. By not accounting for such interactions, the testing procedure outlined above may be less discriminating.

EXERCISES

16-10 A randomized block design is being used to test the null hypothesis that mean responses are identical under five treatments, with four levels used for the blocking factor. The following data are obtained:

$$SST = \ \ 84$$
$$SSB = 132$$
$$\text{Total } SS = 288$$

(a) Construct the ANOVA table.
(b) Should the null hypothesis of identical population means be accepted or rejected at the $\alpha = .01$ significance level?

16-11 Suppose that the sample data in Exercise 16-4 (page 536) represent three observations from stores in each of five regions. Treating "region" as the blocking variable and referring to your answers to that exercise:
(a) Determine the sample means for each row. Then compute the blocks sum of squares.
(b) Construct the ANOVA table for this experiment.
(c) Comparing the value of *SSE* to that obtained in Exercise 16-4, what can you conclude regarding the effect upon unexplained variation of adding the blocking variable?
(d) At the $\alpha = .01$ significance level, should the null hypothesis of identical mean sales for each box shape be accepted or rejected?

16-12 An economist wishes to assess the effects of factor *A* (education) with five levels and factor *B* (occupation) with four levels upon a person's annual earnings. The following data have been obtained in each category for 20 randomly chosen persons:

$$SSA = \ \ \ 800{,}000$$
$$SSB = \ \ \ 900{,}000$$
$$\text{Total } SS = 2{,}000{,}000$$

(a) Construct a one-factor ANOVA table, using education as the only treatment. At the $\alpha = .05$ significance level, can you conclude that the treatment means differ?
(b) Construct a one-factor ANOVA table, using occupation as the only treatment. At the $\alpha = .05$ significance level, can you conclude that the treatment means differ?

(c) Construct a two-factor ANOVA table, using both education and occupation. What can you conclude about the respective null hypotheses for identical mean incomes for education levels and occupation? (Use $\alpha = .01$.)

(d) Do you notice any discrepancy between the one-factor and two-factor results? Explain.

16-13 A computer programming instructor conducted an experiment to determine the effects upon student achievement of the computer languages he taught and of the types of computers he used. Over a period of four terms, he taught 16 classes, and each class was given a standard achievement test. The mean scores achieved by the respective classes are provided below:

	Language			
Types of Computer	(1) BASIC With No FORTRAN	(2) BASIC With Some FORTRAN	(3) FORTRAN With No BASIC	(4) FORTRAN With Some BASIC
(1) Batch/No Time Share	64	74	68	69
(2) Batch/Some Time Share	86	83	85	84
(3) Time Share/ No Batch	88	90	84	87
(4) Time Share/ Some Batch	84	92	69	89

(a) Compute the row, column, and grand means.

(b) Construct the two-factor ANOVA table.

(c) At the $\alpha = .01$ significance level, can the instructor conclude that *languages* make a difference in achievement?

(d) At the $\alpha = .01$ significance level, can the instructor conclude that *computer types* make a difference in achievement?

16-4 LATIN SQUARES AND OTHER ANOVA DESIGNS

So far in this chapter, we have considered basic analysis of variance procedures involving one and two factors. But analysis of variance is a very broad topic, and we have barely scratched the surface. In this section, we will touch upon the breadth and depth of this topic, and we will conclude by discussing a very useful procedure for analyzing three factors.

Important ANOVA Considerations

Analysis of variance situations may be classified in a number of ways. Some of the important ones are discussed in the following paragraphs.

Factorial Design

Thus far, we have encountered examples where all combinations of the factors have been covered. In our sod-fertilizing experiment, we investigated three levels for the fertilizing factor and five levels for the parcel blocking factor. Each level for both factors was represented in the sample data. Such experiments are called *complete factorial designs.* But sometimes only a fraction of the combinations can be studied, either because of expense or because some are infeasible (as would be the case in our example if some parcels had soil that could not absorb heavy applications of fertilizer). Such experiments are said to have a *fractional factorial design.* At times, it may be useful to omit certain factor combinations but to still incorporate all factorial levels in the experiment. This is called an *incomplete factorial design.* A useful experiment in this category is one conducted with a *Latin square design*, the procedure we will describe later in this section for analyzing three factors.

Factor Levels Considered

In our illustrations thus far, we have established in advance the levels for the factors we have investigated. For instance, the three fertilizing policies were established before the data were collected. That study involved a *fixed-effects experiment.* This is in contrast to a *random-effects experiment* where the factor levels are not established in advance and are subject to chance, as would be the case when the levels constitute a sample from a larger population. For example, suppose that a medical society is studying doctors' incomes, using "specialty" and "region where educated" as factors. Data might be compiled from one medical school in each region, so that the school selected is just a sample and the levels of the education factor are themselves samples. Because of the added complexity, a detailed discussion of random-effects experiments is beyond the scope of this book.

Interactions

As we saw in Section 16-2, analysis of variance can be extended to answer other important questions. There, we saw how pairs of treatments may be compared. Often of considerable importance are the interactions between one or more factor levels that exist when together they have an added influence that they do not have individually. Techniques for analyzing interactions are so complex that we have limited the experiments in this book to applications where interactions can be ignored.

Sample Size and Replication

Statisticians use the word *replication* to indicate that an experiment is repeated. The number of repetitions is the number of replications. When a single sample is used, this number is the sample size. Larger sample sizes have the advantage of reducing sampling error. In hypothesis-testing situations, the chance of the Type II error of accepting a false null hypothesis becomes smaller as the level of n is raised. When two or more samples are used, we compare population parameters or estimate their differences. In either case, the usual advantages to large sample sizes are accrued, but of course, larger samples are more expensive.

In our analysis of variance illustrations, replication occurred only in the one-factor application where five plots were used for each fertilizer treatment. Our two-factor experiments involved a single observation for each factor combination, and the designs for these experiments did not involve replication. More complicated designs (not described in this book) incorporate replication when multiple observations are made for each cell. Doing so can be useful. To investigate interaction effects, such a replication scheme is required.

Randomization

We classified our two-factor analysis of the sod-fertilizing treatments as a randomized block design. There, the sample units within each parcel were assigned to treatments randomly. The advantage of doing this is that slight differences between plots within parcels were allowed no systematic influence—as might be the case, for instance, if the plot receiving the best irrigation was always heavily fertilized. Often an important element in sampling studies, such an assignment of sample units to treatments is referred to as *randomization*. For example, in evaluating the effectiveness of training programs, it is important to account for the differences among instructors. This can be accomplished by randomly assigning a particular training program to each instructor. Such a randomization is less discriminating than treating "instructors" as a separate blocking variable, but the latter would force each instructor to train once under each treatment program, which would be both time consuming and burdensome.

The Latin Square Design

Until this point, we have discussed only one- and two-factor designs. We will now consider a *three-factor analysis* involving one treatment factor of interest and two blocking variables.

A psychologist conducting an experiment to evaluate the effects on achievement-test performance of three different training methods may choose a design that incorporates other factors that might explain performance variability, such as a trainee's aptitude and age. Thus, the psychologist might block the sample subjects in terms of three levels of aptitude and three levels of age. A total of nine blocks would be necessary—one for each aptitude and age-level combination. In a complete design, three treatments must be considered for each case, so that a minimum of 27 subjects would be required. In the case of four treatments and two blocking variables, each also having four levels, a minimum of $4^3 = 64$ subjects would be required for a complete design. For a moderate number of levels, a very large number of sample units may be required, and such experiments can be very expensive.

One way of reducing the number of sample units is to use an incomplete design where not all combinations of treatments and blocks are represented. An efficient procedure for doing this is the *Latin square design*. Here, the number of treatments is limited to just the number of levels used for the blocks. In the case of the training-method evaluation, this can be done with just 9 instead of 27 subjects. Table 16-8 shows the data obtained in this experiment for a sample of 9 persons. The letters in the cells pertain to the particular program applied. These same letters form the *Latin square:*

$$
\begin{array}{ccc}
A & B & C \\
B & C & A \\
C & A & B
\end{array}
$$

This arrangement of Latin letters is designed so that each letter appears exactly once in each column and in each row. Other Latin squares for 4 and 5 letters are

$$
\begin{array}{cccc}
A & B & C & D \\
B & A & D & C \\
C & D & A & B \\
D & C & B & A
\end{array}
\qquad
\begin{array}{ccccc}
A & B & C & D & E \\
B & A & E & C & D \\
C & D & A & E & B \\
D & E & B & A & C \\
E & C & D & B & A
\end{array}
$$

Since a letter represents a particular treatment, and a different level of the blocking variables corresponds to each column and row, *the Latin square design forces each treatment to be applied exactly once under each level of both blocking variables.*

The sample means in Table 16-8 have been calculated in the usual manner for the rows and columns. The treatment sample means are found by summing

TABLE 16-8   Layout and Sample Data for Latin Square Design Using Achievement Test Scores to Evaluate Training Programs

Row Blocking Factor (Aptitude)	*Column Blocking Factor (Age)*			*Sample Mean for Row*
	(1) *Young*	(2) *Middle*	(3) *Old*	
(1) *Low*	A 82	B 87	C 80	$\bar{X}_1. = 83$
(2) *Medium*	B 92	C 82	A 81	$\bar{X}_2. = 85$
(3) *High*	C 90	A 83	B 88	$\bar{X}_3. = 87$
Sample Mean for Column	$\bar{X}._1 = 88$	$\bar{X}._2 = 84$	$\bar{X}._3 = 83$	$\bar{\bar{X}} = 85$
Treatment: Training Program Sample Mean	A $\bar{X}_A = 82$	B $\bar{X}_B = 89$	C $\bar{X}_C = 84$	

the cell responses having the corresponding letter and then dividing by the number of cells having that letter. The respective means are denoted as $\bar{X}_A$, $\bar{X}_B$, and $\bar{X}_C$, and their values are given in Table 16-8. For training program A, the sample mean calculation is

$$\bar{X}_A = \frac{82+81+83}{3} = 82$$

In the usual way, we calculate the *sums of squares for the row and column blocking factors:*

$$SSROW = r\sum(\bar{X}_{i.} - \bar{\bar{X}})^2 \qquad (16\text{-}21)$$
$$= 3[(83-85)^2 + (85-85)^2 + (87-85)^2]$$
$$= 3(4+0+4) = 24$$

$$SSCOL = r\sum(\bar{X}_{.j} - \bar{\bar{X}})^2 \qquad (16\text{-}22)$$
$$= 3[(88-85)^2 + (84-85)^2 + (83-85)^2]$$
$$= 3(9+1+4) = 42$$

In Latin square designs, the number of rows and columns are the same, so that $c = r (=3$, here). The number of treatments must also be equal to the number of rows. We have the *treatments sum of squares:*

$$SST = r[(\bar{X}_A - \bar{\bar{X}})^2 + (\bar{X}_B - \bar{\bar{X}})^2 + (\bar{X}_C - \bar{\bar{X}})^2] \qquad (16\text{-}23)$$
$$= 3[(82-85)^2 + (89-85)^2 + (84-85)^2]$$
$$= 3(9+16+1) = 78$$

The total sum of squares is found as before, by squaring the deviations of the column responses about the grand mean and then summing these totals:

(1)	(2)	(3)
$(82-85)^2 = 9$	$(87-85)^2 = 4$	$(80-85)^2 = 25$
$(92-85)^2 = 49$	$(82-85)^2 = 9$	$(81-85)^2 = 16$
$(90-85)^2 = 25$	$(83-85)^2 = 4$	$(88-85)^2 = 9$
$\overline{83}$	$\overline{17}$	$\overline{50}$

Total $SS = 83+17+50 = 150$

The following difference provides the *error sum of squares:*

$$SSE = \text{Total } SS - SST - SSROW - SSCOL \qquad (16\text{-}24)$$
$$= 150-78-24-42 = 6$$

The ANOVA table is provided in Table 16-9. The degrees of freedom are $r-1=2$ for all factors and $(r-1)(r-2)=2$ for the error. The mean squares are calculated in the usual fashion.

The test statistic is

$$F = \frac{MST}{MSE} = 13.0$$

From Appendix Table I, for 2 degrees of freedom in the numerator and 2 in the denominator, we see that $F_{.01} = 99.00$ and $F_{.05} = 19.00$. Since both critical values are larger than the calculated value for F, the null hypothesis of identical treatment population means must be *accepted*, and we must conclude that the training programs do not differ.

TABLE 16-9   Latin Square Design ANOVA Table

Variation	Degrees of Freedom	Sum of Squares	Mean Square	F
Explained by Treatments (between programs)	$r-1=2$	$SST = 78$	$MST = 78/2$ $= 39$	MST/MSE $= 39/3.0$ $= 13.0$
Explained by Column Blocks (between ages)	$r-1=2$	$SSCOL = 42$	$MSCOL = 42/2$ $= 21.0$	*
Explained by Row Blocks (between aptitudes)	$r-1=2$	$SSROW = 24$	$MSROW = 24/2$ $= 12$	*
Error or Unexplained (residual)	$(r-1)(r-2)=2$	$SSE = 6$	$MSE = 6/2$ $= 3.0$	
Total	$r^2-1=8$	$SS = 150$		

* F is not ordinarily calculated for blocking variables.

The primary advantage of the Latin square design is that it reduces the number of sample units needed in testing with three factors. But our illustration also points out an important disadvantage to this design: The Latin square design has a small number of degrees of freedom, making it very hard to reject the null hypothesis of identical population means unless SST is very large in relation to SSE. This type of test becomes more discriminating, however, if several observations are made for each cell or if the number of treatments is increased. Another drawback to the Latin square design is that it is limited to situations where exactly the same number of levels are used for both the blocking variables and the treatments.

EXERCISES

16-14 Indicate whether or not each of the following arrangements forms a Latin square:

(a)

A	B
B	A

(b)

A	B	C	D
B	C	D	A
C	D	A	B

(c)

A	B	C
B	C	A
C	A	C

(d)

E	A	D	C	B
A	C	B	D	E
D	E	C	B	A
B	D	A	E	C
C	B	E	A	D

(e)

D	C	B	A
C	D	A	B
B	A	C	D
A	B	D	C

16-15 The following sums of squares were obtained, using a four-by-four Latin square design:

$$SST = 97$$
$$SSCOL = 53$$
$$SSROW = 48$$
$$\text{Total } SS = 236$$

Construct the ANOVA table. What can you conclude regarding the treatment means? (Use $\alpha = .05$.)

16-16 A Latin square design can be used to make inferences regarding three separate factors. Suppose that the following sums of squares were obtained for a five-by-five design:

$$SST = 157 \quad \text{(factor } X\text{)}$$
$$SSCOL = 77 \quad \text{(factor } Y\text{)}$$
$$SSROW = 143 \quad \text{(factor } Z\text{)}$$
$$\text{Total } SS = 452$$

(a) Construct the ANOVA table, calculating the appropriate F statistics for each factor.
(b) For which factors are the population means significantly different? (In each case, use $\alpha = .01$.)

16-17 The sample data below represent scores achieved on a classical music appreciation test. The "treatment" of interest is the age of the subject:

$$A = \text{preteen}$$
$$B = \text{teen-ager to 25}$$
$$C = \text{over 25}$$

Two blocking variables, "family background" and "intelligence," were used:

	Intelligence		
Family Background	(1) Low	(2) Medium	(3) High
(1) Blue Collar	A 78	B 88	C 68
(2) White Collar	B 90	C 82	A 74
(3) Professional	C 87	A 79	B 92

(a) Construct the ANOVA table for the Latin square design.
(b) At the $\alpha = .05$ significance level, can you conclude that mean music appreciation scores differ for the various age levels?

REVIEW EXERCISES

16-18 A researcher conducting a study on human behavior offered a contest to the students in four psychology classes. Points were given for the number of nonsense syllables memorized during a class period. Rewards varied between classes. Using a random sample of five students from each class, the following numbers of correct syllables were obtained:

	Number of Points in Reward			
Student	(1) $\frac{1}{2}$	(2) 1	(3) $1\frac{1}{2}$	(4) 2
1	18	32	46	52
2	34	48	58	73
3	27	25	37	46
4	31	26	48	63
5	20	39	61	56

(a) Determine the sample means, calculate the sums of squares, and construct the ANOVA table for this experiment.
(b) Should the researcher conclude that motivation to perform meaningless tasks is affected by the level of reward? (Use $\alpha = .01$.)
(c) Construct 95-percent confidence interval estimates for $\mu_4 - \mu_1$. Do rewards of $\frac{1}{2}$ and 2 points provide significantly different motivation at the 5-percent level?

16-19 Consider the following results for a two-factor experiment where six levels were used for factor A and five levels were used for factor B:

$$SSA = 78$$
$$SSB = 65$$
$$\text{Total } SS = 183$$

(a) Construct the ANOVA table for this experiment.
(b) At the $\alpha = .01$ significance level, what can you conclude regarding the null hypotheses of equal population means for the levels of the respective factors?

16-20 A job-performance evaluator is concerned with how workers' performance ratings are affected by their skill levels. Three levels are considered:

Unskilled (A)
Semiskilled (B)
Skilled (C)

Using a sample of three workers from each level, with productivity and attitude serving as blocking variables, the following data were obtained:

	Attitude		
Productivity	(1) *Poor*	(2) *Fair*	(3) *Good*
(1) *Low*	A 50	B 79	C 105
(2) *Medium*	B 74	C 106	A 63
(3) *High*	C 98	A 61	B 93

(a) Calculate the sample means and the sums of squares.
(b) Construct the ANOVA table for the Latin square design.
(c) At the $\alpha = .01$ significance level, what can you conclude regarding the effect of skill level on the mean performance ratings?

16-21 A school psychometrist arranged for a special study to evaluate the effects of testing environment on the performance of high-school students taking the SAT. Group *A* students were allowed to take the test in their home-rooms in the presence of their regular teachers. Group *B* students also took the test in their homerooms, but they were proctored by strangers. Group *C* students were examined in distant cities with their regular teachers serving as proctors. Group *D* students took the test in a distant city, under the supervision of strangers. The students in the experiment were carefully blocked in terms of motivation and academic performance. The following data were obtained:

	Motivation			
Academic *Performance*	(1) *Poor*	(2) *Fair*	(3) *Good*	(4) *Excellent*
(1) *Poor*	A 342	B 313	C 325	D 324
(2) *Fair*	B 368	A 406	D 349	C 401
(3) *Good*	C 377	D 348	A 512	B 493
(4) *Excellent*	D 455	C 482	B 575	A 634

(a) Calculate the sample means and the sums of squares.
(b) Construct the ANOVA table.
(c) Do the data suggest that test surroundings affect SAT performance? (Use $\alpha = .01$.)

16-22 Referring to Exercise 16-21 and to your answers to that exercise:
(a) Construct a one-factor ANOVA table, using "test surroundings" as the treatment and ignoring blocking factors. Can you reject the null hypothesis of identical population means at the $\alpha = .05$ significance level?
(b) Using only the "academic performance" blocking variable, construct a two-factor ANOVA table for a randomized block design, again with "test surroundings" as the treatment. Can you reject the null hypothesis of identical population means? (Use $\alpha = .05$.)

(c) What does a comparison of your one-, two-, and three-factor ANOVA tables suggest regarding the discrimination of testing when "academic performance" and "motivation" are used as the blocking variables?

16-5
OPTIONAL TOPIC:
ANALYSIS OF VARIANCE
FOR MULTIPLE REGRESSION RESULTS

Regression analysis and analysis of variance are closely related topics. Regression analysis is concerned with finding an estimated regression equation that can be used to predict the mean values of a dependent variable for given levels of independent variables. With three independent variables, the estimated regression equation is expressed as

$$Y_C = a + b_1 X_1 + b_2 X_2 + b_3 X_3$$

Analysis of variance presumes that a particular relationship—usually a linear one—exists between the mean response and given levels of factor variables, and it is concerned with finding whether the relationship differs for various levels of these variables. This is done by using an F ratio to compare explained to unexplained variation.

Regression analysis also involves a comparison of the variation in the dependent variable Y that is explained by the regression plane to the total variation. In regression analysis, this ratio provides the coefficient of multiple determination, which measures the strength of association between the variables. By considering the total variation in regression as the sum of two components,

$$\text{Total variation} = \begin{array}{c} \text{Variation} \\ \text{explained by} \\ \text{regression} \end{array} + \begin{array}{c} \text{Variation} \\ \text{left} \\ \text{unexplained} \end{array} \qquad (16\text{-}25)$$

we may extend analysis of variance procedures to testing various hypotheses about the underlying regression coefficients B_1, B_2, and B_3 of the true regression line.

In keeping with our present terminology, the variation explained by regression may be presented by the *regression sum of squares*, which we denote as *SSR*. The ratio of explained to total variation provides the coefficient of multiple determination:

$$R^2_{Y \cdot 123} = \frac{\text{Explained variation}}{\text{Total variation}} = \frac{SSR}{\text{Total } SS} \qquad (16\text{-}26)$$

The *error sum of squares*, which here summarizes variation left unexplained, is the difference between total and explained variation

$$SSE = \text{Total } SS - SSR$$

$$\begin{array}{ccc} \text{Unexplained} \\ \text{variation} \end{array} = \begin{array}{c} \text{Total} \\ \text{variation} \end{array} - \begin{array}{c} \text{Explained} \\ \text{variation} \end{array} \qquad (16\text{-}27)$$

The respective sums of squares may be computed using the following equations:

$$SSR = a\sum Y + b_1 \sum X_1 Y + b_2 \sum X_2 Y + b_3 \sum X_3 Y - n\bar{Y}^2$$

$$SSE = \sum Y^2 - a\sum Y - b_1 \sum X_1 Y - b_2 \sum X_2 Y - b_3 \sum X_3 Y \quad (16\text{-}28)$$

$$\text{Total } SS = \sum Y^2 - n\bar{Y}^2$$

The above values may be used to test the null hypothesis that the multiple regression coefficients for X_1, X_2, and X_3 are all zero:

$$H_0: \quad B_1 = B_2 = B_3 = 0$$

This test is accomplished by computing the mean squares. The *regression mean square* is

$$MSR = \frac{SSR}{m-1} \qquad (16\text{-}29)$$

where m is the total number of variables in the regression analysis. (Here, $m = 4$ and represents the number of degrees of freedom for MSR.) The *error mean square* is

$$MSE = \frac{SSE}{n-m} \qquad (16\text{-}30)$$

where $n - m$ is the number of degrees of freedom and represents the difference between the number of observations and the number of variables in the multiple regression. The test statistic is

$$F = \frac{\text{Variance explained by regression}}{\text{Variance left unexplained}} = \frac{MSR}{MSE} \qquad (16\text{-}31)$$

Ordinarily, a computer is used to perform multiple regression analysis, and these computations are performed at the same time. As an example, consider our supermarket example in Chapter 11, where we obtained the following estimated regression equation using the computer printout in Figure 11-3 (page 385):

$$Y_C = -10.170 + .027X_1 + .097X_2 + .525X_3$$

The ANOVA table for these results is provided in Table 16-10. There, $F = 130.2$.

TABLE 16-10   ANOVA Table for Multiple Regression using Supermarket Data of Chapter 11

Variation	Degrees of Freedom	Sum of Squares	Mean Square	F
Explained by Regression	$m-1 = 3$	$SSR = 609.527$	$MSR = SSR/3$ $= 203.18$	$\dfrac{203.18}{1.56} = 130.2$
Unexplained	$n-m = 6$	$SSE = \quad 9.373$	$MSE = SSE/6$ $= 1.56$	
Total	$n-1 = 9$	$SS = 618.900$		

From Appendix Table I, using 3 numerator and 6 denominator degrees of freedom, we find $F_{.01} = 9.78$. Since the calculated F is considerably larger than this critical value, the null hypothesis that all multiple regression coefficients are equal to zero must be *rejected*.

Chapter Seventeen
Further Probability Distributions and the Goodness-of-Fit Test

All events, even those which . . . do not seem to follow the great laws of nature, are a result of it just as necessarily as the revolutions of the sun.

Marquis de Laplace (1820)

There are several probability distributions of special importance in business decision making. Five of these have already been considered. This chapter describes four more, two discrete and two continuous.

Of the two discrete probability distributions to be described, the first is the hypergeometric. The hypergeometric distribution provides the same information as the binomial but is appropriate for a common situation where the binomial should not be used: when sampling is done without replacement from a small qualitative population. The other is the Poisson distribution, which is also similar to the binomial. Instead of the number of successes obtained in a fixed sample, the Poisson distribution provides probabilities for the number of events that will occur over a specified time interval or in some given space. The number of possible events is not fixed but rather is unlimited. The Poisson has been used to ascribe probabilities for such things as the number of customers arriving at a store during some specified period of time or for the number of errors made by a typist on any given page.

Two continuous distributions, the uniform and the exponential, are also discussed. These may be used in the same manner as the normal to obtain probabilities for the size of items randomly chosen from quantitative populations having frequency distributions shaped like a rectangle or a reversed J, respectively. The uniform distribution assumes that all possible values are equally likely, a common circumstance for many physical or random phenomena. The exponential distribution, closely related to the Poisson, provides probabilities for such things as the time between customer arrivals or the number of words between a typist's errors.

These distributions have been included in this book not only because of their tremendous importance to sampling applications but also because they play important roles in some quantitative methods used in analyzing decisions such as setting policies for inventory control, designing facilities, and managing existing operations. The Poisson, exponential, and uniform distributions are crucial in many models of waiting lines or queues. The uniform distributions also is fundamental to Monte Carlo simulation techniques.

Many quantitative techniques assume that a particular probability distribution applies. Such assumptions may not coincide with reality. Statistical procedures are available for verifying them, using sample data. This chapter concludes with a hypothesis-testing procedure for determining whether or not a sample comes from a population having a frequency distribution of a particular shape or if a sample result is consistent with some process having certain theoretical properties. This is referred to as a goodness-of-fit test, because it measures how well sample data fit the results expected when the assumed probability distribution applies.

17-1   THE HYPERGEOMETRIC DISTRIBUTION

As we have seen, the binomial distribution may be used to find the probabilities for the number of successes from a Bernoulli process. The requirements thereby imposed severely limit the applicability of the binomial distribution to samples from small populations, where the units must be chosen *with replacement*. Ordinarily a sample is chosen from a population *without replacement*. When items are selected from a shipment of parts in order to determine the quality of the shipment, those items inspected are usually set aside and not allowed to be redundantly reevaluated. As we noted in Chapter 4, there are instances where the sampling process itself destroys the item, so that under these circumstances it would be impracticable to sample with replacement. The hypergeometric distribution allows us to find the probabilities for the number of defective parts or, in general, for the number of successes in samples taken without replacement from small populations.

Finding Probabilities When Sampling Without Replacement

To illustrate the basic principles underlying the hypergeometric distribution, we will first look at a simple example.

Example 17-1   A box contains 6 black and 4 white marbles. Four marbles are selected randomly, one at a time, from the box. Once selected, a marble is set aside. We want to find the probability distribution of the number of black marbles obtained, a random variable which we denote by R.

Figure 17-1 shows the probability tree diagram for this random experiment, in terms of four stages. At each stage the color composition of the marbles remaining in the box is provided. The branches on the path leading to the end position (B, W, W, W) are shown as black lines. Initially there are 6 black and 4 white marbles. The probability that the first selection is black is therefore 6/10. If the first marble is black, 5 black and 4 white marbles remain for the second selection. The conditional probability that the second marble is white given that the first is black is thus 4/9. Continuing along this path we see that, the conditional probabilities of white as the third selection, followed by white again on

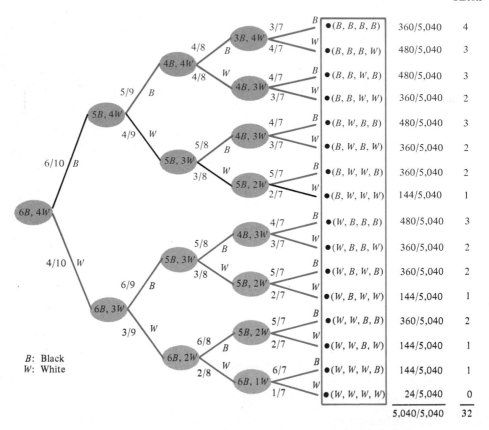

FIGURE 17-1   Probability tree diagram for sampling without replacement from box containing 6 black and 4 white marbles.

the fourth selection, are, respectively, 3/8 and 2/7. Applying the general form of the multiplication law, we obtain

$$P[B, W, W, W] = P[B]P[W \mid B]P[W \mid B, W]P[W \mid B, W, W]$$

$$= \left(\frac{6}{10}\right)\left(\frac{4}{9}\right)\left(\frac{3}{8}\right)\left(\frac{2}{7}\right) = \frac{144}{5,040}$$

Note that there are altogether four end positions of the tree diagram yielding exactly 1 black marble (which can be the first, second, third, or fourth marble selected), all of them having equal probabilities. The probability of exactly 1 black marble may be obtained by summing these, applying the addition law for mutually exclusive events. Alternatively, denoting by R the number of black marbles obtained, we may multiply the preceding result by 4 to get

$$P[R = 1] = 4\left(\frac{144}{5,040}\right) = \frac{576}{5,040}$$

Expressing the Hypergeometric Distribution

It is usually more convenient to use a combinatorial approach to find the desired probabilities. It will be helpful if we first note that the ultimate outcome from the random experiment will be the same if we choose all four marbles simultaneously. The number of outcomes (accounting for which particular marbles are selected; only the color and sequence of selection are represented in Figure 17-1) is the same as the number of combinations of 4 marbles out of 10: C_4^{10}. The number of outcomes yielding exactly 1 black is the number of ways to obtain 1 black out of 6, C_1^6, times the number of ways to select the 3 white out of 4, C_3^4. Thus we may also express the above probability as

$$P[R = 1] = \frac{C_1^6 C_3^4}{C_4^{10}}$$

We can verify that this ratio is identical in value to our previous result by expressing it in factorials:

$$P[R = 1] = \frac{\left(\dfrac{6!}{1!5!}\right)\left(\dfrac{4!}{3!1!}\right)}{\dfrac{10!}{4!6!}}$$

which, by rearranging and canceling terms, equals

$$\frac{6 \times 4 \times 4! \times 6!}{10!} = \frac{6 \times 4 \times 4!}{10 \times 9 \times 8 \times 7}$$

$$= 4\left(\frac{6}{10}\right)\left(\frac{4}{9}\right)\left(\frac{3}{8}\right)\left(\frac{2}{7}\right) = \frac{576}{5,040}$$

To find the probability for the number of successes, R, in a sample of size n taken *without replacement* from a population of size N, we use the following expression for the *hypergeometric probability distribution:*

$$P[R = r] = \frac{C_r^S C_{n-r}^{N-S}}{C_n^N} \qquad (17\text{-}1)$$

where $r = 0, 1, \ldots, n$ or S (whichever is smaller) and S = number of successes in the population.

In our example, $n = 4$, $N = 10$, and $S = 6$. Thus we may find, using expression (17-1) with $r = 4$, so that $n - r = 4 - 4 = 0$,

$$P[R = 4] = \frac{C_4^6 C_0^4}{C_4^{10}} = \frac{360}{5{,}040}$$

which is the same as $P[B, B, B, B]$ in Figure 17-1. (You may verify that the results obtained by adding together the appropriate end position probabilities from Figure 17-1 will agree with those using expression (17-1), for 0, 2, and 3 black marble outcomes as well.)

Example 17-2 The hypergeometric distribution may be used to determine the probability of being dealt five cards that are all hearts from a deck of fully shuffled ordinary playing cards. Poker players call such a hand a flush. Since there are 13 hearts in the deck, $S = 13$. We have $r = 5, n = 5$, and $N = 52$, so that from expression (17-1)

$$P[\text{heart flush}] = \frac{C_5^{13} C_0^{39}}{C_5^{52}}$$

$$= \frac{\dfrac{13!}{5!8!} \times \dfrac{39!}{0!39!}}{\dfrac{52!}{5!47!}}$$

$$= \left(\frac{13}{52}\right)\left(\frac{12}{51}\right)\left(\frac{11}{50}\right)\left(\frac{10}{49}\right)\left(\frac{9}{48}\right) = \frac{33}{66{,}640} \approx \frac{1}{2{,}019}$$

The probability calculated in Example 17-2 applies for a flush in any specified suit, since each has 13 cards, so that the same constants may be used in the hypergeometric probability expression. To get the probability of a flush regardless of suit (the kind that is used in determining poker odds), we may apply the addition law for mutually exclusive events to the 4 satisfying events (one for each suit—hearts, diamonds, clubs, or spades). Thus,

$$P[\text{flush}] = 4\left(\frac{33}{66{,}640}\right) = \frac{132}{66{,}640}$$

$$= .00198 = \frac{1}{505}$$

The odds against receiving a flush are therefore 504 to 1.*

---

* When the straight and royal flushes are separately categorized, then the above odds increase to 508 to 1. Our calculations did not eliminate flushes that are also straights.

In a similar manner, we may find the probability of getting four of a kind in a five-card hand. Consider first getting four aces. Here we have $r = 4$, $S = 4$, $n = 5$, and $N = 52$, so that from expression (17-1):

$$P[4 \text{ aces}] = \frac{C_4^4 C_1^{48}}{C_5^{52}}$$

$$= \frac{\dfrac{4!}{4!0!} \times \dfrac{48!}{1!47!}}{\dfrac{52!}{5!47!}}$$

$$= 5\left(\frac{4}{52}\right)\left(\frac{3}{51}\right)\left(\frac{2}{50}\right)\left(\frac{1}{49}\right)\left(\frac{48}{48}\right) = \frac{1}{54,145}$$

(One interpretation of the factor 5 in the third line of the above expression is that there are 5 different sequence positions possible for getting the non-ace.) Since there are 13 denominations in a deck of cards, we may multiply the above probability by 13 to get the probability of four of a kind where denomination is not specified. (Multiplying by 13 is really applying the addition law for 13 mutually exclusive, equiprobable events: 4 twos, 4 threes, etc.) We thus obtain

$$P[4 \text{ of a kind}] = \frac{13}{54,145} = .00024 = \frac{1}{4,165}$$

so that the odds against getting four of a kind are 4,164 to 1. This explains why such a hand is superior in poker to a flush (non-straight variety); a flush is more than 8 times as likely.

Hypergeometric Distribution for the Proportion of Successes

As we noted in discussing the binomial distribution, we are usually more interested in the proportion of successes in the sample than in the number of successes. As before, we will denote by π and P the proportion of successes in the population and sample, respectively. Thus, since

$$P = \frac{R}{n} \quad \text{and} \quad \pi = \frac{S}{N}$$

we may modify expression (17-1) to provide the *hypergeometric probability distribution for the proportion*:

$$P\left[P = \frac{r}{n}\right] = \frac{C_r^{\pi N} C_{n-r}^{(1-\pi)N}}{C_n^N} \tag{17-2}$$

with $r = 0, 1, 2, \ldots, n$ or πN (whichever is smaller).

It may be established mathematically that the expected value and variance of P are:

$$E(P) = \pi$$

$$\sigma^2(P) = \pi(1-\pi)\left(\frac{N-n}{N-1}\right) \qquad (17\text{-}3)$$

Note that $E(P)$ is the same as with the binomial distribution, while $\sigma^2(P)$ here differs from its binomial counterpart by the $(N-n)/(N-1)$ term. This factor, as we saw in Chapter 7, plays an important role in analyzing samples taken from finite populations. Note, though, that as N gets very large, the term becomes close to 1. This suggests that for large N, the hypergeometric distribution probabilities should not differ much from those calculated with the binomial formula.

Example 17-3 Diablo Pyrotechnics, Ltd. is investigating a new compound to use in its Fantastic Spiroid rockets. It is supposed to produce a larger and brighter explosive pattern. Unfortunately, the new compound is highly unstable, so that some unknown proportion of the rockets will produce a loud pop instead of the intended dazzling display. The company sales manager wishes to know what the proportion of duds will be so that he can set prices to account for the uncertain results the customer must expect. He has decided to use a sample of rockets from the upcoming test shots in estimating this proportion.

Diablo has produced 100 Fantastic Spiroids for a variety of tests. A sample of 5 is chosen at random. Supposing that 20 percent of the rockets produced will be duds, then the probability that the proportion of duds in the sample will be between 0 and 40 percent may be determined from expression (17-2), using $n = 5$, $\pi = .20$, and $N = 100$:

$$P[0 \leqslant P \leqslant .40] = P[P = 0] + P[P = .2] + P[P = .4]$$

$$= P\left[P = \frac{0}{5}\right] + P\left[P = \frac{1}{5}\right] + P\left[P = \frac{2}{5}\right]$$

$$= \frac{C_0^{20} C_5^{80}}{C_5^{100}} + \frac{C_1^{20} C_4^{80}}{C_5^{100}} + \frac{C_2^{20} C_3^{80}}{C_5^{100}}$$

$$= \left(\frac{80}{100}\right)\left(\frac{79}{99}\right)\left(\frac{78}{98}\right)\left(\frac{77}{97}\right)\left(\frac{76}{96}\right) + 5\left(\frac{20}{100}\right)\left(\frac{80}{99}\right)\left(\frac{79}{98}\right)\left(\frac{78}{97}\right)\left(\frac{77}{96}\right)$$

$$+ \frac{5 \times 4}{2}\left(\frac{20}{100}\right)\left(\frac{19}{99}\right)\left(\frac{80}{98}\right)\left(\frac{79}{97}\right)\left(\frac{78}{96}\right)$$

$$= .3193 + .4201 + .2073 = .9467$$

Comparison to Binomial Distribution

We may compare this result to that obtainable from the binomial distribution (which would be *improper* to use here). Consider the second term in the above probability sum; this is the probability of getting exactly one dud in a sample of size 5. Using the binomial formula,

$$C_1^5(.2)^1(.8)^4 = .4096$$

which is close to the .4201 calculated above. Note that the binomial here understates the true probability; for some other values of r, it will overstate it. If N is quite large, the binomial probabilities will be very close to those of the hypergeometric distribution.

EXERCISES

17-1 A personnel manager randomly selects $n = 3$ different names from a file of $N = 10$ job applicants, $S = 5$ of whom are experienced. Construct a probability tree diagram with a separate stage for each person chosen, with forks containing branches for the events experienced and inexperienced. Enter the appropriate probability values on each branch. Then use the multiplication law to determine the probability for each end position. From your tree, determine the following probabilities:
(a) No selected persons are experienced.
(b) Only one selected person is experienced.
(c) Exactly two persons are experienced.
(d) All persons are experienced.

17-2 A personnel manager selects $n = 5$ names from a file containing $N = 10$ job applicant records. $S = 7$ of the 10 are experienced. Find an expression for the probability that
(a) Exactly three of the selected persons are experienced.
(b) Exactly four of those chosen are experienced.

17-3 A procurement analyst for a corporation buys light bulbs by the gross (i.e., a dozen dozen, or 144). From each batch, $n = 5$ bulbs are selected and tested under excessive voltage (which destroys them for further use) in order to determine whether the entire batch of bulbs contains an excessive number of defectives. The analyst's rule for disposing of a batch is: When the sample contains no defectives, the batch is accepted; otherwise the batch is rejected and returned to the supplier for full credit, with no charges made for the destroyed bulbs.
(a) What is the probability that a "good" batch containing $S = 5$ defective bulbs will be rejected?
(b) What is the probability that a "poor" batch containing $S = 30$ defective bulbs will be accepted?
(c) Do you think that the rule provides protection against rejecting "good" batches and accepting "bad" batches? Explain.

17-4 The producer of the light bulbs in Exercise 17-3 occasionally takes a sample of $n = 50$ bulbs at random from the production line. Will the hypergeometric distribution help him to determine probabilities for the number of defectives to be found? Explain.

17-5 What is the probability of getting three or more kings when drawing five cards from a fully shuffled deck of cards? Using this answer, find the probability of getting three or more cards of the same denomination.

17-2 THE POISSON DISTRIBUTION

Many practical statistical problems involve events occurring over time. One of the most notable is how to design a facility to service customers arriving at unpredictable times. Knowledge of the probability distribution of the number of arrivals may help the designer to achieve an optimal balance between the amount of facility idle time and the time spent by customers waiting in line. For example, a bank may need to determine how many tellers to hire for a new branch office. This will be affected by the pattern of customer arrivals over a period of time. During 5 minutes, the number of newly arrived customers can be expected to vary from 0, 1, 2, or perhaps 20 or more up to the limit of space available in the bank. There will be times when all tellers are busy, so that lines will form. Of course, the bank may decide to have ten tellers when five would be sufficient to handle any day's transactions, because customers do not enjoy waiting and may switch their business to a competing bank if they feel unduly delayed. Many familiar events, such as airplanes landing at an airport with limited capacity, persons arriving at a bank of elevators in a busy office building, or telephone calls arriving at a switchboard, call for similar decisions.

Decisions where idle time is balanced against waiting time fall into the broad class of waiting line or *queuing* problems. In analyzing arrival patterns, we are concerned not with the nature of the event (an arrival) but rather with the number of event occurrences. Questions involving occurrences over time are also common in establishing inventory policies and in setting criteria for the reliability of a system. In some businesses, the distribution of customer orders over a period of time may be critical to finding the best inventory level. Enough stock must be available to fill orders, but too large an inventory could be quite costly. In designing systems to achieve a desired level of reliability, the pattern of failures over time is also an important consideration. For example, the probability distribution of the number of component malfunctions during the life of a communications satellite may be helpful in determining how much redundant capability ought to be provided. Likewise, a hospital would want a heart-lung machine to have a very small probability of malfunctioning during open-heart surgery.

The Poisson Process

There are many different patterns of unpredictable occurrences of events over time. A large class of situations in which events occur randomly can be characterized as a *Poisson process*, named after the eighteenth-century mathematician and physicist Siméon Poisson.

There are two very important probability distributions associated with a Poisson process. One, to be described here, provides probabilities for the *number* of events occurring in a time interval. This is the *discrete* Poisson distribution. Also of great interest is the *continuous* exponential distribution, used for finding the probabilities of *times between* the event occurrences; it is discussed in Section 17-4.

It is interesting and helpful to note some similarities between the Poisson and Bernoulli processes. Recall that the binomial distribution provides probabilities for the number of events of a *particular kind* (successes) occurring in n independent trials of a random experiment. With a Poisson process, there is no fixed number of trials; the events occur randomly over time—which is continuous. There is only one kind of event (instead of two complementary ones—success and failure—as in a Bernoulli process), such as arrival of a customer or an equipment breakdown. Of interest is the number of events occurring during some time period, such as one hour.

The Poisson Distribution

The probabilities for the number of events X that occur in a Poisson process in a period of duration t may be obtained from the following expression for the *Poisson distribution:*

$$P[X = x] = \frac{e^{-\lambda t}(\lambda t)^x}{x!} \tag{17-4}$$

where $x = 0, 1, 2, \dots$. The constant e is the base of natural logarithms and is equal to 2.7183. The factor λt *is the mean number of events occurring during* t. The parameter λ (lambda) *represents the mean rate at which events occur during the process.* That is, on the average, λ events per unit time will occur. Multiplying λ, a rate, by t, a duration of time, results in the mean number of events occurring in a period of length t, λt.* Note that we place no upper limit on the number of possible events that may occur; that is, X may assume any integral value from 0 to infinity.

The Poisson distribution is completely specified by the process rate λ and the duration t. Its mean and variance are identical and are expressed in terms of these parameters as

$$E(X) = \lambda t$$
$$\sigma^2(X) = \lambda t \tag{17-5}$$

Example 17-4   Sammy Lee owns a one-man barber shop. One of his customers informs Sammy that during the lunch-time rush his customers arrive in a pattern that is approximately a Poisson process having a mean rate of 6 persons per hour. If Sammy takes 15 minutes (.25 hour) to cut one man's hair, what is the probability that exactly 2 new customers will arrive before he is finished?

We have $\lambda = 6$ customers per hour and $t = .25$ hour. Therefore,

$$\lambda t = 6(.25) = 1.50 \text{ customers}$$

From expression (17-4) we obtain

$$P[X = 2] = \frac{e^{-1.50}(1.50)^2}{2!}$$

Appendix Table J provides values of the powers of e. We find that $e^{-1.50} = .223130$, so that

$$P[X = 2] = \frac{.223130(1.50)^2}{2!} = .2510$$

---

* In many books, $t = 1$, a standard unit of time, and λ represents the mean number of occurrences over a standard time period. There, $\lambda t = \lambda \times 1 = \lambda$.

If the duration t is increased, then the probability will be different. The probabilities for large numbers of arrivals will become greater. This seems logical, since more time is allowed for events to occur. For example, if $t = .4$ hour, then $\lambda t = 6(.4) = 2.4$, so that

$$P[X = 2] = \frac{e^{-2.4}(2.4)^2}{2!} = \frac{.090718(2.4)^2}{2!} = .2613$$

which is larger than before. Analogously, the probabilities for few arrivals will be reduced when t is increased.

Assumptions of a Poisson Process

As we have indicated, the events of a Poisson process occur randomly over time. Three assumptions are required to distinguish it from other types of occurrence patterns.

1. A Poisson process has *no memory*. That is, the number of events occurring in one interval of time is *independent* of what happened in previous time periods.
2. The process rate λ *must remain constant* for the entire duration considered.
3. It is extremely *rare* for more than one event to occur in a small interval of time; the shorter the duration, the rarer the occurrence of two or more events becomes. And the probability for exactly one event occurring in such an interval is approximately λ times its duration.

If we divide a duration into small time segments, letting each represent a trial with just two possible outcomes, (a) exactly one event occurring or (b) a non-occurrence, then the Poisson probabilities may be roughly represented by the binomial distribution. This is only approximately so, as more than one event may occur in each time segment (so that each "trial" actually has more than two possible outcomes—violating Bernoulli process assumptions). But our third assumption makes the probability of the occurrence of more than one event close to zero. When the time segments are very tiny, the approximation becomes quite close, and expression (17-4) is obtained mathematically from the binomial formula.

Practical Limitations of the Poisson Distribution

A very serious mistake to be avoided when applying the Poisson distribution is to assume that the mean event occurrence rate λ holds over an extended duration when it does not. Many queuing situations, for example, involve random arrivals whose rate changes with the time of day, day of week, season, or other circumstances. The mean rate of vehicle arrivals at a metropolitan toll plaza will be different at 9 AM than at 3 AM; it will be different on Fridays than on Mondays; and it will be greater in the fall than in the summer, when many drivers are on vacation. It is still proper to treat a variety of such situations as a Poisson process, but care must be taken to keep short the durations considered and to apply the appropriate value of λ. Thus a bank may find it best to keep only a third of its teller windows open at 10:30 AM on Tuesday, when λ is small,

TABLE 17-1   Poisson Probabilities When $\lambda t = 1.50$

x	$P[X = x]$
0	.2231
1	.3347
2	.2510
3	.1256
4	.0470
5	.0141
6	.0036
7	.0007
8	.0002
9	.0000

but it will probably be optimal to keep them all open around 5 PM on a Friday that is also the first of the month, when transaction traffic proves heaviest.

In Table 17-1 the probabilities for several possible values of X have been calculated for $\lambda t = 1.50$. Although not shown on the table, the Poisson distribution sets no limit on the number of customers who may arrive. There is a nonzero probability that as many as 20 or even 100 customers may arrive in the 15-minute interval considered in Example 17-4. But the probability of these outcomes is quite tiny. For the same reasons as those we noted with the normal distribution, even absurd outcomes have nonzero probabilities. An implication of expression (17-4) is that since this bizarre event has a nonzero probability, it is possible that 10,000 men would try to crowd into Sammy's barber shop during the 15 minutes. As with the normal distribution, a random variable only approximately has a Poisson distribution. For a large number of situations, the approximation is often empirically well justified. For example, a statistician has shown that the number of U.S. Supreme Court vacancies experienced in a given year very closely fits a Poisson distribution. Some studies have shown that the deaths of Prussian army recruits kicked by horses and the very rare freeze-ups of Lake Zurich are closely approximated by the Poisson process. Of far more practical significance, as we have indicated, a vast number of waiting line, reliability, and inventory situations are adequately characterized by the Poisson process.

Using Poisson Probability Tables

As for the binomial probabilities, hand computation of Poisson probabilities can be an onerous chore. Cumulative values of these are computed for levels of λt ranging from .1 to 20.0 in Appendix Table K. As with the binomial, individual probability terms are not provided, because they may be obtained easily from the respective cumulative values.

The table provides values for $P[X \leqslant x]$. For example, to find the cumulative probability values for the number of cars arriving at a toll booth during an interval $t = 10$ minutes, when the arrival rate is $\lambda = 2$ per minute, we look in Table K on the page where $\lambda t = 2(10) = 20$.

The probability that the number of arriving cars is less than or equal to 15 is

$$P[X \leqslant 15] = .1565$$

whereas the probability that 20 or fewer cars arrive during the 10 minutes is

$$P[X \leqslant 20] = .5591$$

As with the cumulative binomial tables discussed in Chapter 6, it is possible to obtain the individual term, the greater than, the less than, the greater than or equal to, and the interval Poisson probability values by using Table K. For example, to find $P[X = x]$, we must determine the difference

$$P[X = x] = P[X \leqslant x] - P[X \leqslant x-1]$$

Thus, the probability that exactly 15 cars arrive in 10 minutes is

$$P[X = 15] = P[X \leqslant 15] - P[X \leqslant 14] = .1565 - .1049 = .0516$$

In a like manner, we may obtain the probability that the number of cars arriving lies between x_1 and x_2 from the difference

$$P[x_1 \leqslant X \leqslant x_2] = P[X \leqslant x_2] - P[X \leqslant x_1 - 1]$$

Thus, the probability that between 16 and 20 cars arrive is

$$P[16 \leqslant X \leqslant 20] = P[X \leqslant 20] - P[X \leqslant 15] = .5591 - .1565 = .4026$$

To find the greater than or the greater than or equal to probability values, we use the facts that

$$P[X > x] = 1 - P[X \leqslant x]$$

and

$$P[X \geqslant x] = 1 - P[X \leqslant x-1]$$

For our toll booth illustration,

$$P[X > 20] = 1 - P[X \leqslant 20] = 1 - .5591 = .4409$$

and

$$P[X \geqslant 20] = 1 - P[X \leqslant 19] = 1 - .4703 = .5297$$

Likewise, we may determine the probability that the number of arrivals is less than some amount by utilizing the fact that

$$P[X < x] = P[X \leqslant x-1]$$

and thus

$$P[X < 16] = P[X \leqslant 15] = .1565$$

Applications Not Involving Time

Although usually presented with events occurring over time, a Poisson process may be an appropriate characterization of events occurring in space as well. If we consider as events the finding of objects spread randomly over a space, such as misspelled names in a telephone directory, then encountering objects while the space (in this case, pages of the directory) is searched may also be viewed as a Poisson process. This particular application has proven fruitful in quality control and in such esoteric areas as developing search techniques for radar, establishing tactics for ships transiting mine fields, and hunting for submarines. Here λ would represent the mean number of events per unit distance (e.g., inch), area (e.g., square mile), or space (e.g., cubic centimeter). More generally, λ may be the mean number of events of a particular kind per observation made of the phenomena in question. Thus λ may be 3 errors per page or it may be 5 bad debts per 1,000 installment contracts. The "durations" would be analogous: the space searched, the number of pages scanned, the number of contracts written, etc.

Example 17-5 The commodore of a tuna fishing fleet has ordered a search of the Pacific Ocean in the Humboldt Current off the coast of South America for a school of tuna. To widen the area of search, an amphibious aircraft is used. The plane can search for a distance of 600 miles. Flying at an altitude of 5,000 feet, the spotter will notice a large school of fish within a lateral distance of ten miles to either side of the aircraft. Thus the area searched in a day would be $2(10)600 = 12,000$ square miles.

There is no reason for tuna to be at any particular location in the million square mile fishing area, so that the disposition of schools throughout is completely random. Historically, we will assume that it has been established that the mean density of large tuna schools in the Humboldt is 1 per 100,000 square miles.

A storm is forecast to reach the fishing area in 6 days. The boats require at least one day to return to port. What is the probability that at least one school will be located no later than one day before the storm?

Since there is 1 school per 100,000 square miles, $\lambda = .00001$ school per square mile. The value of t (here representing area) is $5 \times 12,000 = 60,000$ square miles (5 days times the area searched in a day). Thus, $\lambda t = .00001 (60,000) = .60$, which represents the mean number of schools to be encountered in 5 days of searching. To find the probability that at least one school is encountered, we may find the complementary probability that none is located and subtract this result from 1. Thus, from expression (17-4),

$$P[X \geqslant 1] = 1 - P[X = 0]$$

$$= 1 - \frac{e^{-.60}(.60)^0}{0!}$$

$$= 1 - e^{-.60}$$

$$= 1 - .549 = .451$$

Suppose that no tuna are found and that after docking for the storm, the search is resumed. We may find how many days must be committed to the search in order to ensure a probability of .95 that at least one school will be found. Since a Poisson process has no memory, we must start all over again, because *for probability-calculating purposes the previous search does not count.* Otherwise the number of schools encountered in the first and second searches would be dependent events, violating the basic Poisson process assumptions. (The size of the remaining search area may not even be reduced, since schools may enter or might already have entered the area previously scanned.) Thus, we want to find t such that

$$.95 = P[X \geqslant 1] = 1 - P[X = 0]$$

$$= 1 - \frac{e^{-\lambda t}(\lambda t)^0}{0!}$$

$$= 1 - e^{-\lambda t}$$

or

$$e^{-\lambda t} = 1 - .95 = .05$$

From Appendix Table J, we see that $e^{-y} = .05$ (rounded) when $y = 3.00$, so that using $\lambda t = 3.00$ we will have the smallest t for the above condition to hold. Thus, dividing 3.00 by the number of schools encountered per square mile, $\lambda = .00001$, we obtain the total search area t required:

$$t_* = \frac{\lambda t}{\lambda} = \frac{3.00}{.00001} = 300,000 \text{ square miles}$$

Dividing this area by the area searched per day, we obtain the days required to yield a .95 probability of finding at least one school of tuna:

$$\frac{300,000 \text{ square miles}}{12,000 \text{ square miles per day}} = 25 \text{ days}$$

These 25 days are *in addition to the 5 days already spent searching.*

EXERCISES

17-6   Between 9 and 10 AM on Saturday, the peak business period, customers arrive at Sammy Lee's barber shop at a mean rate of $\lambda = 5$ per hour. During the Thursday slump, between 2 and 3 PM, customers arrive at Sammy's at the rate of $\lambda = 1$ per hour. In either case, the arrivals may be represented as a Poisson process.

   (a) Does this mean that there will always be more customers arriving during the peak than during the slump? Explain.

   (b) Compare the probability of exactly two customers arriving during Sammy's slump to that of the same number arriving during his peak.

   (c) If the mean rate of arrivals for the week as a whole is three customers per hour, then can Sammy use the Poisson distribution with $\lambda = 3$ to find the probability that next week's arrivals will be between 100 and 150? Explain.

17-7   Suppose that a typesetter makes on the average $\lambda = .5$ error per page. What is the probability he will make no errors in the first $t = 10$ pages? What is the probability that he will make exactly five errors in the first ten pages?

17-8   During the late Friday rush at a bank, an average of $\lambda = 5$ customers per minute arrive. What is the probability that no customers arrive during a specified 1-minute interval?

17-9   A family receives an average of $\lambda = 2$ pieces of regular mail each day that letters are delivered. Assume that the Poisson distribution applies.
   (a) What is the probability that they go the next two consecutive days without getting any mail?
   (b) What is the probability that, given two days without mail, they will go another two days without mail?

17-10   In each of the following situations, use Appendix Table K to find the probabilities that the stated number of events occur in a Poisson process at the rate of $\lambda = 8$/hour when the duration considered is:
   (a) $t = 2$ hours, 10 or fewer events.
   (b) $t = 1.5$ hours, 6 or more events.
   (c) $t = 1$ hour, exactly 3 events.
   (d) $t = .1$ hour, between 1 and 5 events.

17-11   A typist commits errors at the rate of .01 per word. Assuming that a Poisson process applies, use Appendix Table K to find the probabilities that the number of errors committed in a 500-word letter will be:
   (a) exactly 5;   (b) zero;   (c) more than 10;   (d) between 3 and 7.

17-12   A California Central Valley tomato grower wishes to protect his crop against destruction by aphids. Two alternatives are open to him: Spray with a powerful insecticide that may harm the local ecology or wait for the ladybugs to eat the aphids. Each spring, massive flights of ladybugs are wafted by wind currents across the California valleys from their Sierra Nevada hibernating points. Unfortunately, where and when a flight of ladybugs lands is purely a matter of chance. Wherever there are plenty of aphids, they lay eggs that rapidly hatch. If at least one flight of ladybugs lands on part of the grower's crop within five days, they and their larvae will devour all the aphids. Otherwise he will spray, killing all aphids and the unfortunate late-coming aphid-eaters as well, for by that time irreparable crop damage will have been suffered. On any given day 10 percent of the Central Valley is covered by ladybugs. Assume that the arrivals of ladybugs may be considered a Poisson process. (The size of the farm may be ignored.)
   (a) Assuming that the mean arrival rate is $\lambda = .1$ flock per day, what is the probability that no flocks arrive during $t = 5$ days?
   (b) What is the probability that the farmer won't have to spray?

17-13   Two tourists are enjoying the view from San Francisco's Golden Gate Bridge. They have decided to spend a half hour waiting for ships to pass under the bridge. Suppose that ship arrivals at the Golden Gate (leaving or entering San Francisco Bay) are a Poisson process at the mean rate of $\lambda = .2$ per hour. Find the probability that the tourists will see passing beneath them (a) no ships;   (b) 1 ship;   (c) 2 ships.

17-3   THE UNIFORM DISTRIBUTION

The uniform distribution provides probabilities for a random variable that has equal chances of assuming any value on a continuous scale. For example, it provides the probability that a wheel of fortune will stop so that its pointer lies within a particular segment. The uniform distribution has many interesting applications. One of the more notable occurs in conjunction with generating random numbers, which are used for selecting a random sample.

The uniform distribution has the following probability density function:

$$f(x) = \begin{cases} \dfrac{1}{b-a} & \text{if } a \leqslant x \leqslant b \\ 0 & \text{otherwise} \end{cases} \qquad (17\text{-}6)$$

The top portion of Figure 17-2 shows the density functions obtained for two different sets of values for *a* and *b*. Each is a horizontal line segment of constant height $1/(b-a)$ over the interval from *a* to *b*. Outside the interval, $f(x) = 0$. This means that for a uniformly distributed random variable *X*, values below *a* or above *b* are impossible.

Recall from Chapter 6 that the probability that *X* will fall below a point is provided by the area under the density curve to the left of that point. The cumu-

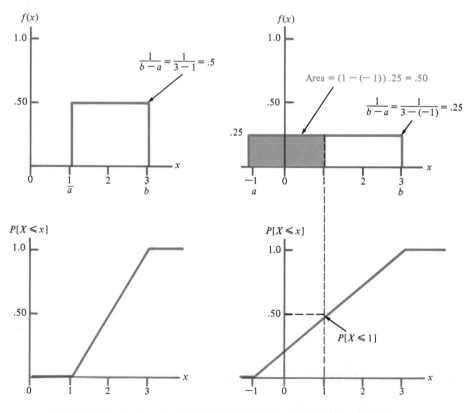

FIGURE 17-2 Top: Uniform density functions. Bottom: Cumulative distribution functions.

lative probability distribution function, $P[X \leqslant x]$, provides these areas. This is determined for values of x between a and b by finding the area of the rectangle of height $1/(b-a)$ and base $x-a$, obtained by multiplying these two values together. To the left of a, the cumulative probabilities must be zero, while the probability that X lies below points beyond b must be 1. The following expression thus provides *cumulative probabilities for the uniform distribution:*

$$P[X \leqslant x] = \begin{cases} 0 & \text{if } x < a \\ \dfrac{x-a}{b-a} & \text{if } a \leqslant x \leqslant b \\ 1 & \text{if } b < x \end{cases} \qquad (17\text{-}7)$$

The cumulative distribution functions for the two cases are shown in the bottom half of Figure 17-2.

Example 17-6   A traveling salesman must change planes at Peoria en route to New Haven. His Peoria-bound plane is scheduled to arrive 20 minutes prior to the New Haven flight departure. If that flight is missed, he must spend 12 hours in Peoria waiting for the next plane. Assuming that his plane's arrival time is uniformly distributed over the interval from being 1 hour early to 1 hour late, what is the probability that he will be stuck in Peoria (that is, that his Peoria-bound plane is more than 20 minutes late)?

Here $a = -60$ minutes while $b = +60$ minutes. Let X be the arrival time in Peoria. From expression (17-7),

$$\begin{aligned} P[\text{stuck in Peoria}] &= P[X > 20] \\ &= 1 - P[X \leqslant 20] \\ &= 1 - \frac{20-(-60)}{60-(-60)} \\ &= 1 - \frac{80}{120} = \frac{40}{120} = \frac{1}{3} \end{aligned}$$

It is easy to obtain an expression for the expected value of a uniformly distributed random variable. This is the center of the interval (a, b):

$$E(X) = \frac{a+b}{2} \qquad (17\text{-}8)$$

To verify this, we need only notice that the expected value of X is the long-run average result obtained from repeating the same random experiment. Since all values between a and b have the same chance of occurring, the average of a and b, $(a+b)/2$, would be the long-run average of the individual outcomes.

The variance of a uniform random variable must be obtained mathematically. It is given by

$$\sigma^2(X) = \frac{(b-a)^2}{12} \qquad (17\text{-}9)$$

Often it is necessary to find the probability that a uniform random variable falls between two values. For instance, suppose that $a = 10$ and $b = 15$. Then we can determine the probability that X lies between 11 and 14. This probability will be equal to the rectangular area between 11 and 14. As with finding areas under the normal curve, we may determine the result by subtracting the smaller probability (area) from the larger one, so that

$$P[11 \leqslant X \leqslant 14] = P[X \leqslant 14] - P[X \leqslant 11]$$
$$= \frac{14-10}{15-10} - \frac{11-10}{15-10} = \frac{3}{5} = .6$$

(Like the normal, and any other continuous distribution, $P[X \leqslant x] = P[X < x]$, so that the distinction between $\leqslant$ and $<$ is unimportant.)

EXERCISES

17-14 A lumber mill cuts logs into planks 10 feet long. After cutting, the trimmed plank ends are apt to be any length smaller than 10 feet. What proportion of the trimmings have lengths between (a) 4 and 6 feet; (b) 3 and 7 feet; (c) 2.5 and 6.4 feet; (d) 5.52 and 8.52 feet?

17-15 A pilot is navigating his airplane by "dead reckoning" over the ocean. He does not know his precise speed and actual heading, since he has no way to gauge the effects of wind. He is flying at night and intends to home on a light ship. The minimum distance at which the plane will pass the light ship is uniformly distributed, from 0 miles to 50 miles. Assuming clear visibility, what is the probability that the pilot will see the light ship when flying at an altitude providing a line-of-sight range of (a) 50 miles; (b) 40 miles; (c) 30 miles; (d) 10 miles?

17-16 A farmer is scheduled to begin reaping his wheat at 6 AM, July 1, the date on which the combines belonging to his cooperative will be available. Harvesting must begin within 4 days after ripening or the crop will be lost. It cannot be reaped before it is ripe. If his wheat is not ready for reaping on the scheduled date or ripens too early, then the farmer must pay for private equipment. Assuming that the crop will ripen at a time uniformly distributed from 6 AM, June 23, through 6 AM, July 3, what is the probability that the farmer will not be forced to rent his combines from outside? (June has 30 days.)

17-4 THE EXPONENTIAL DISTRIBUTION

The Need to Consider Time Between Events

In a previous section we introduced the Poisson process as one situation whose outcomes are events occurring randomly over time (or space). The Poisson distribution provides the probabilities that a particular number of events will occur. Of great importance in business applications is the time duration (or space encountered) *between* the events. To a person waiting in a bank line, the number of persons arriving before him is of little importance if his line moves quickly; his prime concern is the length of his wait. The commodore whose fleet has enough capacity to capture just one school of tuna cares only about how long it will take to locate the first one.

In this section we will present the exponential distribution, which for a Poisson process provides the probabilities for the time (or space traversed) between events or until the first event occurrence. As an illustration, consider cars arriving at a toll collection station. Figure 17-3 illustrates this concept.

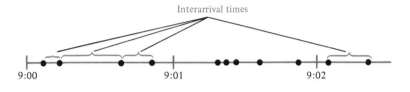

Time of Arrival at Toll Booth

FIGURE 17-3   Times for random arrivals of cars at a toll booth.

Each dot represents a car and is positioned so that its horizontal distance from the origin (at 9:00 AM) indicates when it arrives at the station. Such a graph could be constructed from an aerial photograph taken at 9:00 AM of the two miles of highway leading to the station; assuming that all cars are traveling at the speed limit, we could directly translate each car's distance from the station into its arrival time. Note that the dots in Figure 17-3 are scattered across the page with no apparent pattern, as if placed there randomly. This pattern is typical Poisson process.

Finding Interevent Probabilities

The gaps between the dots in Figure 17-3 represent the interarrival times, or times between successive arrivals of cars. The exponential distribution is concerned with the size of the gaps, measured in time units, separating successive cars. Although the dots are scattered randomly over time, the relative frequency of interarrival times of various sizes is predictable. Suppose that the cars arriving at the toll station were observed for several minutes, and that the time of each car's arrival was noted. Those data would provide a histogram similar to the one in Figure 17-4(a). This approximates the shape of the underlying frequency curve in Figure 17-4(b), the height of which may be determined for any interarrival time t (or generally, for the time or space between any two events in a Poisson process) from

$$f(t) = \lambda e^{-\lambda t} \tag{17-10}$$

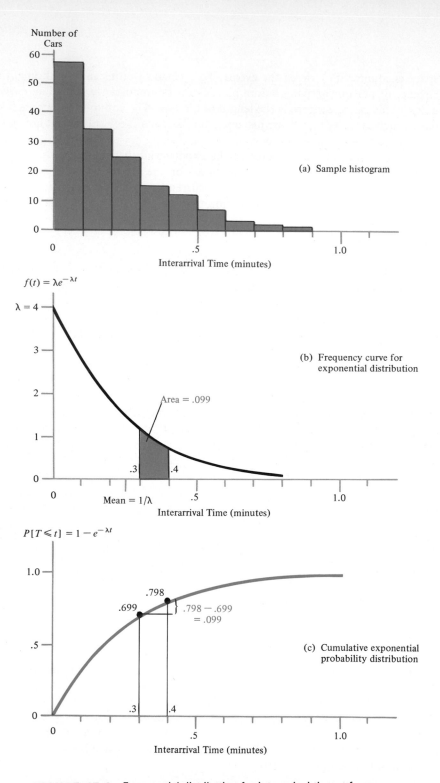

FIGURE 17-4 Exponential distribution for interarrival times of cars at a toll station.

Expression (17-10) is the probability density function for the exponential distribution. The particular distribution applicable to a specific situation depends only on the level of λ. In our toll-station illustration, a mean arrival rate of $\lambda = 4$ cars per minute applies. Note that the frequency curve intersects the vertical axis at height λ. The mean and standard deviation of the exponential distribution are identical and may be expressed in terms of λ as

$$E(T) = 1/\lambda$$
$$\sigma(T) = 1/\lambda$$

(17-11)

where our random variable is T, the uncertain time (or space) between any two successive events. (Unlike the Poisson distribution, the *standard deviation* equals the mean, while the variance equals the mean squared.)

Note that the mean time between arrivals is the reciprocal of the mean rate of arrivals. Thus if $\lambda = 4$ *cars per minute*, then the mean time between arrivals is $1/\lambda = 1/4 = .25$ *minute per car*. Another feature of the exponential distribution is that *shorter durations are more likely than longer ones*. Note that the curve in Figure 17-4(b) decreases in height and the slope becomes less pronounced as t becomes larger. The tail of the exponential curve, like the tails of the normal curve, never touches the horizontal axis, indicating that there is no limit on how large the interarrival time t might conceivably be.

Like those for the normal curve, probabilities for the exponential random variable may be found by determining the area under the frequency curve. The following expression provides the *cumulative probability for the exponential distribution:*

$$P\lfloor T \leqslant t \rfloor = 1 - e^{-\lambda t}$$

(17-12)

where T represents the time (or space) between any two successive events. Figure 17-4(c) shows the cumulative probability graph when $\lambda = 4$. Appendix Table J may be used to find values for $e^{-\lambda t}$.

For example, using $\lambda = 4$ cars per minute, we find the probability that the interarrival time between any two cars is less than or equal to $t = .4$ minute:

$$P[T \leqslant .4] = 1 - e^{-4(.4)} = 1 - e^{-1.6}$$
$$= 1 - .201897$$
$$= .798 \text{ (rounded)}$$

And the probability that this time is $t = .3$ minute or less is

$$P[T \leqslant .3] = 1 - e^{-4(.3)} = 1 - e^{-1.2}$$
$$= 1 - .301194$$
$$= .699 \text{ (rounded)}$$

The probability that an interarrival time between .3 and .4 minute will be achieved is thus

$$P[.3 \leqslant T \leqslant .4] = .798 - .699$$

$$= .099$$

The above value is the area under the exponential frequency curve in Figure 17-4(b) between times of .3 and .4 minute.

Applications of the Exponential Distribution

Because a Poisson process has no memory, expression (17-12) is also valid if T represents the time between any two events—whether near the beginning of the process or near the end. The burning out of light bulbs in a new building, a process often characterized as a Poisson process, illustrates this point. The probability that the time from the 99th burnout to the 100th exceeds 50 hours would be the same as that for the period between the 78th and 79th or for the period of initial connection to the 1st burnout. A very common application of the exponential distribution is to situations in which the process is intermittent. Thus the time taken by a bank teller to service a customer might be an exponential random variable, so that the Poisson process ends when all customers have been processed. The teller is then "idle" (not making a transaction, although there may be other work to do during these occasions). The amount and pattern of idle time is a function of both the arrivals and the service. A new phase of the Poisson process begins with the arrival of the next customer.

One point should be made clear. There is no reason why the teller's service times must be exponentially distributed. Their historical frequency distribution may yield a histogram having a shape very different from that provided in Figure 17-4. In that case, the situation clearly would not fit the assumptions of a Poisson process. Whether the exponential distribution should be used is a matter of how closely it fits the situation. An exponential distribution, for instance, assigns low probabilities to long interevent times and high probabilities to short ones. But maybe both long and short are rare, and a normal distribution more appropriate.

Reliability Applications

One important application of the exponential distribution occurs in establishing specifications for the reliability of equipment that will fail at some future time according to the probability pattern of this distribution. Operating requirements are often established in terms of mean-time-between failures (MTBF), which from expression (17-11) is the inverse of the mean failure rate λ (which represents the mean number of failures per unit time): $1/\lambda$.

The MTBF figure itself may be established by a requirement that the equipment achieve some probability of lasting a minimum time before failing.

Example 17-7   Suppose that certain items must be designed so that 90 percent of them will last more than 100 hours. Here the failure rate λ and MTBF $1/\lambda$ must be determined. The requirements may be expressed as: Choose λ so that

$$.90 = P[T > 100] = 1 - P[T \leqslant 100]$$
$$= 1 - (1 - e^{-\lambda(100)})$$
$$= e^{-\lambda(100)}$$

From Appendix Table J, we see that the closest value is $e^{-y} = .905$ (rounded) when $y = .10$. Thus, setting $\lambda(100) = .10$, we obtain

$$\lambda - \frac{.10}{100} = .001 \text{ failure per hour}$$

and

$$\text{MTBF} = \frac{1}{\lambda} = \frac{1}{.001} = 1,000 \text{ hours}$$

We may find the probability that a particular part built to these specifications will fail between 200 and 600 hours after operation by subtracting the probability that failure occurs by 200 hours from the probability that it occurs on or before 600 hours:

$$P[200 \leqslant T \leqslant 600] = P[T \leqslant 600] - P[T \leqslant 200]$$
$$= (1 - e^{-.001(600)}) - (1 - e^{-.001(200)})$$
$$= e^{-.2} - e^{-.6}$$
$$= .819 - .549 = .270$$

(As with the previously discussed continuous distributions, the distinction between $<$ and $\leqslant$ is unimportant.)

The following example shows a reliability application involving the decision about the quantity of equipment needed to meet certain requirements.

Example 17-8   A hospital is reviewing its contingency plans for coping with power failures. Due to the increased demand for electricity and the inability of power companies to keep pace in generating capacity, electrical blackouts have been occurring at more frequent intervals and for longer durations. But certain hospital functions, such as surgery, require a continuous power supply. The hospital has one emergency generator connected to auxiliary electrical circuits in critical locations. The concern now is what happens if the auxiliary power should fail during a blackout while essential services are being rendered. Funds for a back-up generator are being sought to reduce the chance of this event.

Assuming that the present generator has mean time between failures $(1/\lambda)$ rated as 100 hours, what is the probability that it will fail during the next 10-hour blackout?

Here $\lambda = .01$ failure per hour. From expression (17-12),

$$P[T \leqslant 10] = 1 - e^{-.01(10)} = 1 - e^{-.10}$$
$$= 1 - .904837 = .095 \text{ (rounded)}$$

Thus the probability is .095 that a failure will occur and .905 that it will not. The chance of failure is rather high, considering the stakes involved. Suppose that there are $n = 5$ such blackouts in one year. The probability that the generator works through all of them may be determined using $\pi = .905$ and $r = 5$ in the binomial formula:

$$C_5^5(.905)^5(.095)^0 = .61$$

an unsafe value, to be sure.

Consider how dramatically the probability changes with the purchase of additional back-up generators. We will assume that the generators operate independently and simultaneously. Suppose first that one additional generator is purchased. The probability that both generators fail in a 10-hour period would be $(.095)^2 = .0090$. Thus the probability that at least one works throughout is

$$1 - .0090 = .9910$$

Considering five blackouts, the probability that at least one generator works during all the blackouts may be obtained from the binomial formula with $r = n = 5$ and $\pi = .991$:

$$C_5^5(.991)^5(.009)^0 = .956$$

When three generators are used, the probability that all fail in 10 hours becomes .00086, and the probability of no interruptions throughout five blackouts increases to .9957.

A Queuing Application

A very fruitful application of the exponential distribution has been its use in queuing problems. The following simple example illustrates one such possible application.

Example 17-9   There is a single centralized tool cage at the Miller Machine Works where machinists must obtain special parts needed for their equipment. The cage clerk has just retired and must be replaced. The plant superintendent wants to replace him with an experienced machinist whose direct costs are $10.00 per hour. This runs counter to company policy, which dictates that the position is for a clerk and should be filled with a $5.00-per-hour person. The superintendent insists that the machinist will be better, because with his special knowledge he can provide service twice as quickly. Furthermore, the superintendent has constructed a very convincing argument.

He has assumed that the arrivals at the tool cage are a Poisson process with mean rate λ_A men per hour and that the service time distribution for the clerk is exponential with mean rate λ_S men per hour (that is, counting just those times when someone is being serviced by the cage clerk). By a mathematical deduction, it may be established that the total time W that a machinist must wait at the tool cage—both in line and while being serviced—has an exponential distribution with expected value

$$E(W) = \frac{1}{\lambda_S - \lambda_A}$$

Thus, if $\lambda_S = 10$ per hour and $\lambda_A = 5$ per hour, then

$$E(W) = \frac{1}{10 - 5} = .2 \text{ hour}$$

Since a machinist is unproductive while waiting in line or being serviced, which takes an average of $1/\lambda_S$ hours, his direct costs of $10.00 per hour are lost during these times. Thus the total expected hourly cost of manning the tool cage with a clerk is the cost of machinists' unproductive time plus the cost of the clerk. Since each machinist must be unproductive $E(W)$ hours, on the average, and there are λ_A arriving per hour, the total expected cost per hour is

$$\$\lambda_A[E(W)]10.00+5.00 = \$5(.2)10.00+5.00$$
$$= \$15.00$$

If an experienced machinist mans the cage, then he services at twice the clerk's rate, $\lambda_S = 2(10) = 20$ machinists per hour, so that

$$E(W) = \frac{1}{20-5} = \frac{1}{15} = .067 \text{ hour}$$

Thus using a cost of $10.00 per hour for the man in the tool room, we obtain a total expected cost per hour of

$$\$5(.067)10.00+10.00 = \$13.35$$

By using an experienced machinist, an average of $1.65 per hour can be saved.

EXERCISES

17-17   On Tuesday mornings, customers arrive at the Central Valley National Bank at a rate of $\lambda = 1$ per minute. What is the probability that the time between the next two successive arrivals will be (a) shorter than 1 minute;   (b) longer than 5 minutes;   (c) between 2 and 5 minutes?

17-18   The final settlement claims filed by policyholders of a casualty insurance company involving amounts of $100,000 or more are events from a Poisson process with a mean rate of $\lambda = 1$ per working day. Funds earmarked for large-claims settlement are invested in short-term government bonds at an interest rate of 5 percent, so that the timing of settlements affects company profits. What is the probability that the next large claim must be settled (a) within 5 days;   (b) sometime after 2 days;   (c) in between 2 and 5 days?

17-19   An automobile manufacturer wishes to determine the terminal mileage for the warranty coverage on the power train of its new compact car. A warranty is desired such that no more than 9.5 percent of the cars will have to use it. Assume that the time between power train failures is exponentially distributed for each car. How many miles should warranty coverage last when the power trains fail at a mean rate of once every 100,000 miles driven, so that $\lambda = .00001$ failure per mile?

17-20   The tuna fleet commodore of Example 17-5 has embarked from port and begins an air search for tuna. The airplane searches 20 square miles for every mile traveled. Schools of tuna are randomly distributed over the fishing area at a mean density of one school per 100,000 square miles.
(a) Find λ, the rate at which tuna schools are located per mile flown.
(b) What is the probability that the first school will be located before the search aircraft has flown 5,000 miles?
(c) How many miles must the airplane be capable of traveling in order to guarantee a .90 probability of spotting at least one school of tuna?

17-21   C. A. Gopher & Sons is excavating a site requiring the removal of 100,000 cubic yards of material. Mr. Gopher has the choice of using a scoop loader or a shovel crane. He has leased 10 trucks at $20 per hour. A scoop loader costs $40 per hour, while the cost of a shovel crane is $60 per hour. Once work has been started, the trucks arrive according to a Poisson process with a mean rate of $\lambda_A = 7$ trucks per hour. The truck-filling times are exponentially distributed. A scoop loader can fill trucks at an average rate of $\lambda_S = 10$ per hour. The shovel crane is faster, on the average capable of filling $\lambda_S = 15$ trucks per hour. (For simplicity, we assume the same truck arrival rate, regardless of equipment used.)

Since the number of truck arrivals required to excavate the site is fixed by the amount of dirt, the optimal choice of filling equipment will be one that will minimize the combined hourly costs of truck *unproductive time* plus the cost of the filling equipment. Adapting the procedures used in Example 17-9, determine the optimal equipment choice.

17-22   One of the fundamental principles of designing a system to be reliable is that it have redundant (i.e., duplicate) critical subsystems. Suppose that two power supplies are to be used simultaneously on a communications satellite. Assuming the lifetime of each to be exponentially distributed, operating independently, what is the probability that the satellite will function for 1,000 hours before total power failure when the mean time between failures $(1/\lambda)$ of each power supply is (a) 500 hours;   (b) 1,000 hours;   (c) 5,000 hours.

17-5   TESTING FOR GOODNESS-OF-FIT

In this section we make inferences regarding the type of distribution, using a procedure called the *goodness-of-fit test*. The goodness-of-fit test determines whether or not sample data could have been generated according to a particular probability distribution, such as the Poisson or exponential. It can also indicate whether or not the frequency distribution for the sampled population has a particular shape, such as the normal curve. It achieves this by comparing the sample frequency distribution (histogram) to the assumed theoretical frequency distribution (frequency curve).

Importance of Knowing the Distribution

We have seen that many models used in statistical applications require specification of probability distributions. For example, techniques developed for analyzing waiting lines in order to determine appropriate service facilities (e.g., how many tellers for a bank) often assume that the number of arrivals has a Poisson distribution. Every rule developed in such queuing models depends upon this assumption. (Other queuing models depend upon other specified distributions.) As we have noted, the validity of using the Poisson distribution to characterize a random variable ought to be established by collecting substantiating evidence. Recall that a Poisson process requires the following: (1) no memory (occurrences are independent over time), (2) constant mean occurrence rate, and (3) small likelihood that two or more events will occur at about the same time. The lack of any of these requirements will make the Poisson distribution inappropriate. Only by actual observation of the random process (or one believed to be identical in structure) can it be confirmed that the above conditions are met.

When the Poisson distribution is wrongly used in place of the appropriate arrival distribution, then the entire queuing solution is invalid. Consider, for example, the arrivals of baggage articles at the claim area of an airport. This may be a process with constant mean arrival rate and no memory, but it blatantly violates the requirement for rarity of simultaneous arrivals, as hundreds of pieces of luggage may arrive on a single flight. A facility designed to handle a fast-moving trickle of baggage (which is the case for Poisson arrivals) would be totally incapable of coping with an infrequent deluge of luggage. The difficulty of providing for this particular type of queuing situation was dramatically illustrated in Rome in 1970, just after the introduction of the jumbo Boeing 747 jets; three of the new jets landed within minutes of each other, and it took 3 hours for all passengers to find their luggage.

In sampling studies, knowledge of the population distribution may be very important. As we have seen, certain statistical applications rest upon theoretical foundations that require particular population distributions. For example, the validity of the Student t distribution in making inferences about μ from small samples is limited to populations where the *normal curve* closely represents the underlying distribution. The random number list used in selecting the sample units is presumed to be *uniformly distributed* (that is, the number 21763 is just as likely to be the next number on a five-digit list as is any other value between 00000 and 99999). The *binomial distribution* provides probabilities for a variety of qualitative populations; but a violation of the underlying assumptions (constant π, independent and complementary trial outcomes) may invalidate the use of the binomial formula for this purpose.

There are more practical reasons for wanting to know the population distribution rather than only μ or σ^2. Many standardized tests used to measure aptitude and achievement are designed partly to provide scores that are normally distributed. This permits a common interpretation of resultant scores in terms of standard-deviation units. Recall that *the distance of a person's score above or below the mean, in standard deviation units, can be directly translated into a percentile value if the normal curve applies to the population.* Thus, a personnel analyst or college admissions officer may readily resolve the conflicting scales on the various screening tests if their respective standard deviations are known. This is often done by converting data into *standard scores*, which are the same as normal deviates.

Conducting the Test

In testing for goodness-of-fit, the following hypotheses apply:

H_0: The sample is from a population having a designated distribution (for example, Poisson, normal).

H_1: The sample is from a population having some other distribution.

A decision rule must be developed so that the sample evidence can be translated into action. As in our earlier treatment, we will express the rule in terms of a critical value for some test statistic. If the computed value for this test statistic lies to one side of the critical value, we will accept the null hypothesis; otherwise, we will reject it. Again, this procedure will contain two possible kinds of error: accepting a false null hypothesis and rejecting a true null hypothesis. The following illustration explains the procedure.

The SAT (Scholastic Aptitude Test) has been designed to represent a population of high-school seniors who receive a mean score of 500, with a standard deviation of 100. Furthermore, this population is assumed to be normally distributed. A university president has asserted that her students—all of whom took the SAT before matriculation—are representative of that population. Based upon a random sample of 200 student SAT scores, a statistics professor at the university constructed the histogram in Figure 17-5 and then superimposed the normal curve assumed by the president on the histogram. The professor disagrees with the president, since the histogram is positively skewed, with a lower mean and a greater variability than the purported population frequency distribution indicates.

Not convinced by the graphical evidence, the president asks the statistician for a more conclusive argument. The professor begins by arranging the sample data in the frequency distribution provided in Table 17-2. (Note that the three

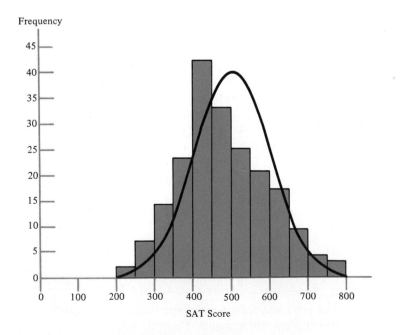

FIGURE 17-5   Sample histogram and assumed normal curve for student SAT scores.

lowest and the three highest class intervals from the histogram have been grouped into two broader categories; the reason for doing this will be explained later in this section.)

TABLE 17-2 Frequency Distribution for SAT Scores of a Sample of University Students

SAT Score	Number of Students f_a
$\leqslant 350$	23
351–400	23
401–450	42
451–500	33
501–550	25
551–600	21
601–650	17
> 650	16
	200

As we have seen with testing problems, we must determine whether the results we obtain are typical for the null hypothesis. To do this we must compare them with the results expected under the following null hypothesis:

H_0: University SAT scores are normally distributed with a mean of $\mu = 500$ and a standard deviation of $\sigma = 100$.

In sampling from any population, there is no reason why the frequency distribution of sample results must precisely resemble that of the population. Because of the presence of sampling error, a perfect match is an extremely unlikely outcome. But a drastically different shape for the frequency distribution is also unlikely. For testing purposes, we will compare the actual sample result to the frequency distribution of the sample results expected under the assumption of the null hypothesis. This is the distribution obtainable "on the average" from a large number of repeated sample selections from the population.

The numbers of occurrences in each class interval obtained under the null hypothesis are referred to as the *expected frequencies*. They are determined by multiplying the proportion of population values lying within each class interval by the sample size used. Here, a normal distribution is hypothesized for the population. Therefore, the expected frequency for SAT scores at or below 350 can be found by multiplying together (1) the area under the normal curve covering scores $\leqslant 350$ and (2) the sample size $n = 200$.

To obtain the area, we determine the normal deviate:

$$z = \frac{x - \mu}{\sigma} = \frac{350 - 500}{100} = -1.5$$

Reading Appendix Table D, this corresponds to a lower-tail area of .5000 − .4332 = .0668. Multiplying by the sample size, we obtain the expected frequency .0668 × 200 = 13.36 students. The remaining expected frequencies can be calculated in a similar manner and appear in Table 17-3.

TABLE 17-3   Expected Frequencies for Student SAT Scores Under the Null Hypothesis

(1) *SAT Score* *x = Upper Class Limit*	(2) *Normal* *Deviate* $z = \dfrac{x-500}{100}$	(3) *Area to* *Left of* *x*	(4) *Area of* *Class* *Interval*	(5) *Expected* *Frequency* f_e *[(4) × 200]*
350	−1.5	.0668	.0668	13.36
400	−1.0	.1587	.0919	18.38
450	− .5	.3085	.1498	29.96
500	0	.5000	.1915	38.30
550	.5	.6915	.1915	38.30
600	1.0	.8413	.1498	29.96
650	1.5	.9332	.0919	18.38
> 650	∞	1.0000	.0668	13.36
			1.0000	200.00

The Test Statistic

As the test statistic, we need a number that summarizes the amount of deviation between the frequencies of SAT scores actually obtained and the expected frequencies. The chi-square statistic serves this purpose.

Since our data are available for ranges or intervals of numerical values, we will treat the frequencies for each interval individually. We use the symbol f_e to denote the expected frequency of sample values in a particular class interval. Similarly, we use f_a to denote the actual observed frequency of values in the same class interval obtained from the sample. To compute the test statistic, we use the following expression for the *chi-square statistic for a goodness-of-fit test:*

$$\chi^2 = \sum \frac{(f_a - f_e)^2}{f_e} \tag{17-13}$$

These computations are made for the SAT scores in Table 17-4 using the actual and expected frequencies found earlier. There we obtain the value $\chi^2 = 21.614$.

The Decision Rule

Suppose that our statistician desires an $\alpha = .01$ significance level. This means that he wants to have only a 1-percent chance of rejecting a true null hypothesis that the university SAT score distribution is the one assumed by the president.

The degrees of freedom in a chi-square test correspond to the number of

TABLE 17-4 Calculation of the χ^2 Test Statistic for SAT Scores

SAT Score	Actual Frequency f_a	Expected Frequency f_e	$f_a - f_e$	$(f_a - f_e)^2$	$\dfrac{(f_a - f_e)^2}{f_e}$
$\leqslant 350$	23	13.36	9.64	92.9296	6.956
351–400	23	18.38	4.62	21.3444	1.161
401–450	42	29.96	12.04	144.9616	4.839
451–500	33	38.30	-5.30	28.0900	.733
501–550	25	38.30	-13.30	176.8900	4.619
551–600	21	29.96	-8.96	80.2816	2.680
601–650	17	18.38	-1.38	1.9044	.104
> 650	16	13.36	2.64	6.9696	.522
	200	200.00	0.00		$\chi^2 = 21.614$

f_e values that we are "free" to set. Because the number of f_e's must sum to the sample size n, all but one f_e are free to vary. Thus, in testing for goodness of fit, *the number of degrees of freedom is equal to the number of categories minus one.* As we will see, this rule must be modified slightly in some cases.

From Appendix Table H, we use $8 - 1 = 7$ degrees of freedom for eight categories and find the critical value $\chi^2_{.01} = 18.475$. The meaning of this number is that if the university SAT score distribution is normal with a mean of 500 and a standard deviation of 100, then there is a 1-percent chance that a sample will be obtained that yields a χ^2 value equal to or greater than 18.475. We may formulate the decision rule as

Accept H_0 (conclude that the university SAT score distribution is normal with $\mu = 500$ and $\sigma = 100$)

$$\text{if } \chi^2 \leqslant \chi^2_\alpha \ (18.475)$$

Reject H_0 (conclude that the SAT score distribution is different)

$$\text{if } \chi^2 > \chi^2_\alpha$$

Since the computed value of the test statistic is $\chi^2 = 21.614$, which exceeds the tabled critical value of $\chi^2_{.01} = 18.475$, the statistician must *reject H_0*. He must conclude that the university students' SAT scores are not normally distributed with the stated mean and standard deviation. The president now has some mighty convincing evidence that she is wrong.

The Type II Error
In testing for goodness of fit, the probability β of accepting a false null hypothesis (the Type II error) is not well defined. This is because there are so many ways in which the null hypothesis can be false. And if the sample does come from some other distribution, this must be specified in order to calculate β. A different β will be obtained if the sample actually comes from an exponential

distribution than if it comes from a uniform distribution. In general, the larger the sample, the better the protection against Type II errors will be.

Testing with Unknown Population Parameters

In the testing procedure just illustrated, the population mean and standard deviation were specified in advance. Most often, not only are we concerned with identifying the family (normal, uniform, exponential, Poisson, etc.) to which the underlying distribution belongs, but also we may need to find the appropriate particular distribution of that family. For example, in addition to not knowing whether a sample comes from a normal distribution, we may also lack knowledge of μ and σ. The unknown population parameters may themselves have to be estimated from the sample data. As an additional feature, the goodness-of-fit test can incorporate these estimations.

To illustrate this, we will continue with our present example. (Again, we caution that only one of these procedures should be used on the same data. We use both methods here only for ease of discussion and so that the two methods may be compared.) In Table 17-5 the sample mean and the sample standard

TABLE 17-5 Calculation of Sample Mean
and Standard Deviation for SAT Score Data

Class Interval	Frequency f	Midpoint X	fX	X^2	fX^2
201–250	2	225	450	50,625	101,250
251–300	7	275	1,925	75,625	529,375
301–350	14	325	4,550	105,625	1,478,750
351–400	23	375	8,625	140,625	3,234,375
401–450	42	425	17,850	180,625	7,586,250
451–500	33	475	15,675	225,625	7,445,625
501–550	25	525	13,125	275,625	6,890,625
551–600	21	575	12,075	330,625	6,943,125
601–650	17	625	10,625	390,625	6,640,625
651–700	9	675	6,075	455,625	4,100,625
701–750	4	725	2,900	525,625	2,102,500
751–800	3	775	2,325	600,625	1,801,875
	200		96,200		48,855,000

$$\bar{X} = \frac{\sum fX}{n} = \frac{96,200}{200} = 481$$

$$s = \sqrt{\frac{\sum fX^2 - n\bar{X}^2}{n-1}} = \sqrt{\frac{48,855,000 - 200(481)^2}{200-1}} = 113.93$$

deviation for the SAT score data are computed to be $\bar{X} = 481$ and $s = 113.93$.

Suppose that our statistician had instead chosen to use these values as estimators of μ and σ. His null hypothesis may be expressed as:

H_0: The sample is from a normally distributed population where $\mu = 481$ and $\sigma = 113.93$.

The alternative hypothesis includes all other possible distributions—even a normal distribution having other values for μ and σ. Remember that μ and σ have been estimated here from the sample observations.

The expected frequency calculations under the statistician's new hypothesis appear in Table 17-6 and the chi-square statistic is computed in Table 17-7. In Chapter 15 we indicated that when calculating χ^2, each expected frequency should round to a value of at least 5. Thus, the first two categories are grouped, since the expected frequency 4.24 for $\leqslant 250$ is smaller than 5. Likewise, the

TABLE 17-6   Expected Frequencies for Student SAT Scores When Parameters Are Estimated from Sample Data

(1) SAT Score $x = $ Upper Class Limit	(2) Normal Deviate $z = \dfrac{x-481}{113.93}$	(3) Area to Left of x	(4) Area of Class Interval	(5) Expected Frequency f_e [(4) × 200]
$\leqslant 250$	-2.03	.0212	.0212	4.24
300	-1.59	.0559	.0347	6.94
350	-1.15	.1251	.0692	13.84
400	$-.71$	.2388	.1137	22.74
450	$-.27$	.3936	.1548	30.96
500	.17	.5675	.1739	34.78
550	.61	.7291	.1616	32.32
600	1.04	.8508	.1217	24.34
650	1.48	.9306	.0798	15.96
700	1.92	.9726	.0420	8.40
750	2.36	.9909	.0183	3.66
> 750		1.0000	.0091	1.82
			1.0000	200.00

TABLE 17-7   Calculation of the χ^2 Test Statistic for SAT Scores When Parameters Are Estimated from Sample Data

SAT Score	Actual Frequency f_a	Expected Frequency f_e	f_a-f_e	$(f_a-f_e)^2$	$\dfrac{(f_a-f_e)^2}{f_e}$
$\leqslant 250$	2 \}9	4.24 \}11.18	-2.18	4.7524	.425
251–300	7	6.94			
301–350	14	13.84	.16	.0256	.002
351–400	23	22.74	.26	.0676	.003
401–450	42	30.96	11.04	121.8816	3.937
451–500	33	34.78	-1.78	3.1684	.091
501–550	25	32.32	-7.32	53.5824	1.658
551–600	21	24.34	-3.34	11.1556	.458
601–650	17	15.96	1.04	1.0816	.068
651–700	9	8.40	.60	.3600	.043
701–750	4 \}7	3.66 \}5.48	1.52	2.3104	.422
> 750	3	1.82			
	200	200.00	0.00		$\chi^2 = \overline{7.107}$

frequency for > 750 is combined with the preceding class interval, yielding the expected frequency 5.48 for the combined category. These combinations reduce the number of final categories in Table 17-7 to ten. (Because the expected frequencies used here are different from those used previously, there are a total of two more final categories in Table 17-7 than there are in Table 17-5.)

Number of Degrees of Freedom

When population parameters are estimated from the sample data, one additional degree of freedom is lost for each parameter. Thus, we have for the *total number of degrees of freedom:*

$$\text{d.f.} = \text{Number of categories} \qquad (17\text{-}14)$$
$$- \text{Number of parameters estimated} - 1$$

In the present illustration we have

$$\text{d.f.} = 10 - 2 - 1 = 7$$

(Although we gained categories from the earlier illustration, ordinarily fewer degrees exist when population parameters are estimated.)

Suppose that the statistician uses the same significance level as before. Because the degrees of freedom are unchanged, we have the same critical value of $\chi^2_{.01} = 18.475$. Since the computed value of $\chi^2 = 7.107$ (from Table 17-7) is smaller than 18.475, H_0 must be *accepted*. This is the reverse of the conclusion we reached using our previous null hypothesis. Although the data significantly refute a normally distributed population with a mean of $\mu = 500$ and a standard deviation of $\sigma = 100$ when these parameters are specified in advance, the results are quite consistent with the null hypothesis of normality when the same parameters are estimated from the sample data. (The latter null hypothesis cannot even be rejected at the 30 percent level, for we can see from Appendix Table H that 7.107 lies between $\chi^2_{.50} = 6.346$ and $\chi^2_{.30} = 8.383$. Thus, at least 30 percent of the time we can expect samples from such a population to be even more untypical than the one we òbtained here.)

Testing for an Assumed Probability Distribution

As we noted at the outset, whether or not a particular probability distribution applies can be crucial when using probability concepts for decision making, such as in queuing investigations. To determine if a particular probability distribution applies, we can use the goodness-of-fit test in the same way as before. The following example applies this procedure.

Example 17-10 A publisher wishes to design a "boiler plate" clause in its contracts with printers composing its books so that notice of pending penalties or incentives may be determined from a sample of galley proofs *before the book is* *completed.* Thus the printer is served notice as to how his profits from the book will be affected by continuation of poor performance or maintenance of good quality. From the publisher's point of view, such notification will serve to encourage greater printer managerial control and result in a more speedily produced end product. Whether or not a sample may be used for this purpose will depend upon the probability distribution of the number of errors per 100 lines of print.

If the number of errors has Poisson distribution, then the occurrences of errors throughout the printing may be considered to be a Poisson process. This implies that it is extremely rare for several errors to be adjacent to each other. Another property of a Poisson process is that the mean rate of error commission would be constant, no matter which part of the book is sampled. Thus a sample taken from the first chapter may be appropriate for inferring the accuracy of the rest of the book.

On the other hand, if the number of errors closely fits some other distribution, such as the normal, then the mean error rate need not be constant throughout the book. Also, the errors may tend to cluster in difficult portions, such as tables or mathematical expressions. Galleys from all parts of the book may be required to make an assessment of its accuracy. Determination of penalty or incentive would have to wait for the composition of the entire book. If this is the case, there would be no need for sampling at all, since the ultimate settlement of accounts, adjusted for penalty or incentive, must take place after a thorough time-consuming phase of proofreading by publisher and author. There is nothing to be gained by haranguing the printer at such a late stage. Except for corrections, his composition work is largely done.

The decision whether or not to implement an early penalty-incentive notification therefore depends upon the probability distribution of the number of errors. From files containing galley proofs of all recently published books having comparable complexity, a random sample is taken of $n = 40$ segments of type 100-lines long.

Table 17-8 shows the sample frequency distribution for the number of errors per 100 lines. The mean number of errors in the sample is $\bar{X} = 3.15$. Thus, the mean error rate per line times the number of lines is

$$\lambda t = 3.15$$

TABLE 17-8   Frequency Distribution of Number of Printer's Errors

Number of Errors per 100 Lines	Total Number of Errors in Category	Observed Frequency f_a
0	0	5
1	9	9
2	10	5
3	21	7
4	16	4
5	10	2
6	18	3
7	14	2
8	8	1
9	0	0
10	20	2
	126	40

$$\bar{X} = 126/40 = 3.15$$

The hypotheses are:

H_0: The population of printer's errors has a Poisson distribution with $\lambda t = 3.15$.

H_1: Population of printer's errors has some other distribution.

The *alternative hypothesis includes all other possible distributions*—possibly even Poisson but with λt at some other value. We emphasize that λt has been estimated from the observations.

The expected frequencies for each error category are calculated in column (4) of Table 17-9 by multiplying the Poisson probabilities in column (3) by $n = 40$. Note that some of the expected frequencies must be grouped so that each category involves an f_e rounding to 5 or more.

TABLE 17-9 Chi-Square Calculations Under Poisson Distribution Null Hypothesis

(1) Number of Errors x	(2) Actual Error Frequencies f_a	(3) Poisson Probabilities	(4) Expected Error Frequencies f_e	(5) $f_a - f_e$	(6) $(f_a - f_e)^2$	(7) $\dfrac{(f_a - f_e)^2}{f_e}$
0	5 ⎫ 14	.0428	1.71 ⎫ 7.11	6.89	47.472	6.68
1	9 ⎭	.1350	5.40 ⎭			
2	5	.2124	8.50	-3.50	12.250	1.44
3	7	.2233	8.93	-1.93	3.725	.42
4	4	.1759	7.04	-3.04	9.242	1.31
5	2 ⎫	.1106	4.42 ⎫			
6	3	.0581	2.32			
7	2	.0261	1.04			
8	1 ⎬ 10	.0106	.42 ⎬ .40	1.60	2.560	.31
9	0	.0036	.14			
10	2	.0011	.04			
11 or more	0 ⎭	.0005	.02 ⎭			
	$\overline{40}$	$\overline{1.0000}$	$\overline{39.98^{a}}$			$\overline{10.16}$

$$f_e = 40P[X = x] = 40\,\frac{e^{-3.15}(3.15)^x}{x!}$$

$$\chi^2 = \sum \frac{(f_a - f_e)^2}{f_e} = 10.16$$

[a] Total would be 40, except for rounding errors.

The number of degrees of freedom is $5 - 1 - 1 = 3$, since only one parameter (the mean λt of the Poisson distribution) is estimated from the sample data. Assuming a desired significance level of $\alpha = .05$, Appendix Table H provides the chi-square critical value of $\chi^2_{.05} = 7.815$. The chi-square value computed in Table 17-9, $\chi^2 = 10.16$, exceeds the critical value. Thus, the null hypothesis that the error distribution is Poisson with $\lambda t = 3.15$ must be *rejected*. The publisher will therefore not write an early incentive-penalty notification clause into its printing contracts.

EXERCISES

17-23 The vice-president for personnel of a large insurance company wishes to establish hiring policies for the company's clerical personnel. A key element of the company's screening procedures is the scores of applicants on a verbal aptitude screening examination. This test is to be used to match capabilities to job requirements. Some applicants may be "over-qualified" for various positions and "underqualified" for others. Personnel planning requires that the percentages of the applicant population having scores at various levels be determined. This will involve specification of the frequency distribution, which can only be inferred from a limited sample taken. It will be significantly simpler to generate plans if the population is normally distributed. Thus the vice-president wishes to conduct a goodness-of-fit test for a normal null hypothesis. The psychologists who designed the test maintain that an ordinary cross section of persons have achieved a mean of 72 and a standard deviation of 10. The observed results by a sample of 100 persons applying for positions at the company is provided below:

Score	Frequency
below 40	8
40–50	7
50–60	18
60–70	25
70–80	32
80–90	3
over 90	7
	100

(a) Using the values provided by the psychologist, construct a table of expected frequencies. (Use .4490 for the area between the mean and $z = 3.2$.)

(b) Calculate the χ^2 statistic. (Remember to group the lower frequencies.)

(c) How many degrees of freedom are associated with this test statistic?

(d) Suppose that the vice-president wishes to protect himself at level .05 against rejecting the normal hypothesis when true. Determine the critical value for the test statistic.

(e) Should the normal hypothesis be accepted or rejected? What is the smallest significance level that you can determine at which the hypothesis can be rejected?

17-24 Suppose that the insurance company vice-president in Exercise 17-23 does not believe that the psychologist's parameters are valid for her applicant population. Instead she wishes to use the sample results to estimate μ and σ. For the 100 test scores, the mean is 64.5 and the standard deviation is 16.8.

(a) Calculate the table of expected frequencies. Then calculate the test statistic. At a significance level of .05, should the null hypothesis be accepted or rejected?

(b) Is the lowest probability at which the data allows rejecting lower or higher than in 17-23(e) above?

17-25 The Seven-High Bottling Company has been using a refillable bottle that has proven to be relatively safe from exploding. To modernize its image, a sleeker Seven-High bottle is being sought. Because of the obvious dangers to the company posed by exploding bottles, tests are being conducted on a new bottle and the special seal devised for it. This will be accomplished on a special testing device in which bottles filled with Seven-High are heated and shaken. For the old bottle, it has been established that the number of bottles tested between explosions on this device is approximately exponentially distributed, with a mean of 3 bottles between explosions. It is hoped that the new bottle will have the same distribution. A sample of 1,000 new bottles is tested. The frequency distributions obtained are provided below. The null hypothesis is that the distribution of the number of new bottles tested between explosions is identical to that for the old bottles. The alternative is that some other distribution applies.

(a) Calculate χ^2.

(b) How many degrees of freedom are associated with this test statistic?

(c) State in a sentence the Type I error; the Type II error.

(d) If a significance level of .05 is desired, determine the critical value of the test statistic. What does this number mean? Formulate the decision rule. Should the null hypothesis be rejected?

(e) If the significance level of .02 is instead considered, then how do your answers to (d) change?

Number of Bottles Between Explosions	Class Interval	Actual Frequency	Expected Frequency
0	0– .999	97	86.75
1	1– 1.999	54	65.25
2	2– 2.999	58	49.50
3	3– 3.999	25	28.00
4	4– 4.999	27	21.00
5	5– 5.999	15	15.80
6	6– 6.999	10	12.70
7	7– 7.999	5	9.30
8	8– 8.999	11	6.20
9	9– 9.999	2 ⎱	3.10 ⎱
10	10–10.999	0 ⎰	3.10 ⎰
11	11–11.999	2 ⎱	3.10 ⎱
12	12–12.999	1 ⎬	3.10 ⎬
13 or more	≥ 13	3 ⎰	3.10 ⎰
		310	310.00

17-26 Before random number tables were widely available, some statisticians used telephone digits. One concern with such numbers is whether they occur with the proper frequency. Assuming that the last four digits in the Manhattan telephone directory are used to generate decimal values between 0 and 1, a random sample of 100 successive numbers was obtained, and the following frequency distribution was determined. (A 0000 suffix is counted as 1.0000.)

Class Interval	Number of Values Obtained
.0001– .1000	13
.1001– .2000	12
.2001– .3000	10
.3001– .4000	9
.4001– .5000	9
.5001– .6000	11
.6001– .7000	9
.7001– .8000	11
.8001– .9000	7
.9001–1.0000	9
	100

Using as your null hypothesis the assumption that the above numbers were obtained from a *uniformly distributed* population, so that all values between 0 and 1 are equally likely to occur:

(a) Construct a table of expected frequencies.

(b) Find the value of the χ^2 statistic.

(c) At the $\alpha = .10$ significance level, what conclusion can you make?

17-27 An automobile manufacturer wishes to determine the frequency distribution of warranty-financed repairs per car for its new minicar, the Colt. The number of such repairs per new automobile on its current line of cars has been established to have a Poisson distribution with parameter λ, the mean rate of repairs per car. The value of λ varies with the line of car. Management believes that Colt will have nearly the same number of repairs distribution as Pony, its next larger car. For Pony, $\lambda = 3$ repairs per year. A random sample of 43 cars is selected for a year's study. Special records are kept on each year. The distribution of repairs per car obtained is provided below.

Number of Repairs	Frequency of Cars
0	1
1	2
2	5
3	9
4	7
5	5
6	3
7	5
8 or more	6
	43

Calculate the table of expected frequencies, using Poisson probabilities with $\lambda t = 3$. Then determine the value of the test statistic. Should the null hypothesis be accepted or rejected at a significance level of .05?

REVIEW EXERCISES

17-28 A random sample of $n = 3$ persons is to be taken from a group of $N = 10$, $S = 4$ of whom are women. Find the probability that the sample contains exactly two women, assuming:

(a) That the sampling is done with replacement.

(b) That the sampling is done without replacement.

17-29 Suppose you deal yourself a poker hand consisting of 5 cards from a standard deck of playing cards. Find the probability that you will get all the aces.

17-30 During noon hour on Fridays, customers arrive at a mean rate of 2 per minute to the tellers' windows of Chase-Haste Bank. The pattern of arrivals is considered to be purely random.

(a) Find the probability that exactly 7 customers arrive between 12:15 and 12:17.

(b) What is the probability that the first customer arrives before 12:01?

17-31 A computer program generates random decimal values in such a way that any value between 0 and 1 is equally likely to be obtained each time. Find the probability that the next number is (a) less than .5;   (b) between .25 and .35;   (c) greater than .99;   (d) greater than or equal to .05.

17-32 A particular production process yields 10 percent defective items.

(a) Assuming that production is a Bernoulli process, find the probability that in the next 100 items made there will be at least 5 defectives.

(b) Assuming that production is a Poisson process, with defectives occurring at the mean rate of 10 per hour, find the probability that at least 5 defectives occur in any specific hour.

17-33 A communications satellite's power cells have an exponential time-to-failure distribution. The mean time between failures is 100 hours.

(a) What is the probability that any particular power cell will fail prior to 500 hours of operation?

(b) Suppose that there are four power cells altogether, that they operate independently, and that the satellite will function as long as there is at least one working cell. What is the probability that the satellite can still communicate at the end of its 500th hour of operation?

17-34 A random number generator yields uniformly distributed random decimals between 0 and 1. Consider the sampling distribution for the mean $\bar{X}$ of 12 such decimals. $\bar{X}$ itself has an expected value (mean) of .5 and a standard deviation of 1/12.

(a) What probability distribution applies for $\bar{X}$?

(b) Find the probability that $\bar{X}$ falls between .4 and .6.

17-35 The actual frequency distribution of rush-hour automobile accidents reported in a certain city for a 100-day period is given in the table below. Assuming that these data represent a random sample from a population where the number of daily accidents has the Poisson distribution at a mean rate of 5 per day, we obtain the expected frequencies in the last column.

Number of Accidents per Day	Actual Frequency (days)	Expected Frequency (days)
$\leqslant 2$	13	13
3	8	14
4	22	18
5	24	18
6	15	15
7	8	10
8	5	6
$\geqslant 9$	5	6
	100	100

Are the sample data consistent with the indicated Poisson distribution? Use $\alpha = .05$.

17-36 The times between reported automobile accidents in a different city during rush hours are provided below for a random sample of 200 accidents. Alongside are the expected frequencies that would apply if the population were exponentially distributed with a mean accident rate of one every 20 minutes.

Time Between Accidents (minutes)	Actual Frequency	Expected Frequency
0–10	62	78.6
10–20	55	47.8
20–30	32	29.0
30–40	21	17.6
40–50	12	10.6
50–60	8	6.4
> 60	10	10.0
	200	200.0

Are the sample data consistent with the indicated exponential distribution? Use $\alpha = .10$.

Chapter Eighteen
Nonparametric Statistics

Out of the mouths of babes and sucklings
hath He perfected praise! In the last few
evenings I have wrestled with a double
humped curve and have overthrown it.

Walter F. R. Weldon (1892)

Most of the hypothesis-testing procedures discussed earlier in this book involve inferences concerning population parameters such as the mean. These tests are therefore referred to as *parametric*, and their test statistics are sometimes called *parametric statistics*. The sampling distributions for the statistics used in these tests usually depend upon assumptions about the *populations* from which the samples are obtained. Particularly stringent are the assumptions of the Student t statistic, used for tests of means when the sample sizes are small, and the F statistic, used in analysis of variance. Both the t and F sampling distributions assume that the sampled populations are normal.

Without complete enumeration, there is no way to tell for certain that the populations are actually normal. Even if the population distribution is known, the normal distribution is a theoretical "nicety" that serves only as a mathematically convenient representation, for we have seen that no real population is truly normal. When a sample must be used, further complications arise due to chance error. Slight deviations from normality may be tolerated in using the t

and *F* tests, but in certain cases a population not meeting the assumption of normality can invalidate the results of the statistical test.

18-1 THE NEED FOR NONPARAMETRIC STATISTICS

In this chapter, we will present statistical tests that make no assumptions about the shape of population distributions. For this reason, they are often referred to as being "distribution free." Many of these same statistics require no assumptions regarding population parameters. Thus, they have come to be more commonly referred to as *nonparametric statistics*. A nonparametric test has been defined as one that makes no hypothesis about the value of a population parameter.* We have already used a nonparametric statistic, the chi-square, in testing for independence. There, we made no assumptions about the distribution of the populations nor did our hypotheses involve suppositions about parameters.†

Advantages of Nonparametric Statistics

Nonparametric statistics have many nice properties; among these is their ease of calculation. They often have sampling distributions that can be easily explained by the simplest laws of probability. But their major advantage is that they are encumbered by few restrictive assumptions. This is particularly important when, for various reasons, samples cannot be large. For instance, nonparametric statistics are vital to behavioral scientists, because large samples are the exception in long-term experiments involving people.

In addition to explicit assumptions regarding the shape of a population, certain parametric tests make assumptions about the population parameters *not being tested*. For example, equal variances are assumed in using the Student *t* statistic to test for differences in population means with independent samples (see Section 14-3). Implicitly, another assumption often made by parametric tests involving means is that the population values are continuous. A great many populations, although they involve variates, have values that are inherently not continuous. A large class of such values cannot be combined arithmetically.

Many practical research problems require subjective ratings on a numerical scale. For example, if a subject rates the taste of brand *A* beets as 5, brand *C* beets as 4, and brand *B* as 3, he is really expressing his order of preference: *A* is better than *C*, which is better than *B*. The numbers have no real meaning in themselves (ratings of 999, 2, and -30, respectively, would express the same thing), so that the mean of such numbers is not very meaningful.

---

* Some tests not strictly adhering to this requirement are nevertheless classified as nonparametric.
† The χ^2 is a hybrid in that it is sometimes employed as a parametric statistic. For example, χ^2 may be used as a test statistic for hypotheses regarding a population's variance.

Numbers that primarily express preference, ranking, hierarchy, and so on, are convenient symbols that convey order, and their numerical values are said to belong to an *ordinal scale*. Distance between values has no inherent meaning. Thus, standard arithmetic operations are not consistent when applied to ordinal numbers. Any statistical test requiring the calculations of means or variances would be largely invalid when applied to samples from populations whose variates are ordinal. *Usually, for such populations only nonparametric tests are valid.*

Another deficiency of parametric tests is their preoccupation with the mean and the variance, much of which stems from the nice mathematical properties of these measures. Except for symmetrical distributions, the median is a more meaningful measure of central tendency than the mean. Various inter-fractile ranges depict dispersion more vividly than the standard deviation. For example, to the unsophisticated (that is, to almost everybody), knowing that the incomes of 90 percent of all doctors in a particular region lie between $20,000 and $150,000 is more meaningful than knowing that $\sigma = \$25,000$. Some non-parametric tests are well suited for testing hypotheses regarding medians,while the popular parametric tests are limited to the less meaningful mean. Further-more, medians are equally valid measures whether the variates are continuous or ordinal.

Disadvantages of Nonparametric Statistics

There are, of course, disadvantages to using nonparametric statistics. Their primary drawback is that they tend to ignore much sample information that is gleaned by their parametric counterparts. This makes them generally less efficient. But it has been argued that although they are less efficient, researchers using nonparametric statistics have more confidence in their methodology than they do if they must adhere to the unsubstantiable assumptions inherent in parametric tests like the Student *t*. One handicap of nonparametric tests is that there are so many from which to choose that researchers must pay more heed to the extra dimension of efficiency in designing a statistical study.

Topics Covered

In this chapter, we will introduce some of the more popular and relatively efficient nonparametric tests. Most of these will be nonparametric counterparts of procedures discussed earlier in this book. We will begin by describing a series of tests that compare two populations. In analyzing independent samples, the Wilcoxon rank-sum test and the Mann-Whitney U test will be introduced. Then the sign test and the Wilcoxon signed-rank test will be described for matched-pairs sampling, followed by a discussion of the number-of-runs test for random-ness. The Spearman rank correlation coefficient will also be discussed. The chap-ter will conclude with an alternative to the F test—the Kruskal-Wallis procedure for one-factor analysis of variance. An optional final section describes the Kolmogorov-Smirnov test for goodness of fit.

18-2 COMPARING TWO POPULATIONS USING INDEPENDENT SAMPLES: THE WILCOXON RANK-SUM TEST

Two methods (independent samples and matched pairs) were proposed in Chapter 14 for making a decision that involves the choice of the population with the greater mean, but these tests are adequate only when the populations are normally distributed, or closely so. Here we introduce another procedure to use with independent samples, the *Wilcoxon rank-sum test*, which is free of the possibly invalid assumptions of normality. This test is named after the statistician Frank Wilcoxon, who first proposed it in 1945.

Description of Test

The Wilcoxon test compares two samples—a control and an experimental group—taken from two populations. All null hypotheses share a common assumption that the samples were selected from identical populations, which is more stringent than assuming that they have identical means. The test is therefore based upon the principle that the two samples may be treated as though they came from a common population. Under the various null hypotheses encountered, the data for the two samples may be combined. The observed values in the pooled sample are then ranked from smallest to largest; the smallest value is assigned a rank of 1, the next smallest value is ranked 2, and so forth. After the rankings are obtained, the samples are separated and the sums of the ranks are calculated for each. The rank sums obtained are used as test statistics.

As an illustration, we will compare type A and type B fertilizers for effectiveness in increasing the yield of corn. In this experiment, ten Corn Belt farmers set aside one-acre plots for testing. Five acres chosen randomly are to use type A and five are to use type B. It is assumed that the two fertilizers are equally effective, so that the hypotheses are

H_0: Types A and B fertilizers are equally effective.

H_1: Types A and B fertilizers differ in effectiveness.

Based upon the yields in the sample plots, H_0 will be either accepted or rejected. In effect, the *null hypothesis states that the population of yields for plots fertilized with type A is identical to the corresponding population using type B*. The alternative hypothesis is that the two populations differ somehow. Since the alternative might be true either if A is better than B or if B is better than A, this particular experiment involves a *two-sided test*.

The yields obtained from the sample plots are provided in Table 18-1, and the pooled sample results are ranked in Table 18-2. If the fertilizers are equally effective, then we would expect type A to be ranked low and high about as many times as type B. A convenient comparison can be made in terms of the sums of the ranks obtained for the respective samples. *For this purpose, the sum of the ranks for sample A is the test statistic.* Using the ranks in Table 18-2 and letting W represent this rank sum, we have

$$W = 1+2+3+4+7 = 17$$

We can calculate the rank sum for sample B similarly, but its value is more easily obtained by subtracting W from the total rank sum, which is 55 here.* Thus, the sample B rank sum is $55 - 17 = 38$. A comparison of the two rank sums shows that type A fertilizer has a value less than half as large as type B, indicating that type A will result in predominantly lower corn yields. Although this seems to contradict the null hypothesis that the two types of fertilizer are equally effective, we still must determine if these results are significant enough to warrant rejecting H_0. To do this, we need only investigate the properties of W obtained for sample A. (Because the sample B rank sum is automatically determined by the value of W, we only need consider the rank sum for sample A.)

The Sampling Distribution of the Rank Sum W

Under the hypothesis of identical effectiveness, any five of the ten ranks for the pooled samples can belong to population A; that is, the first rank is no more likely to belong to sample A than to B. This holds for any rank. In other words, if the fertilizers are equally effective, then the smallest yield is just as likely to have been obtained from a plot where type A has been applied as from a plot where type B has been used, and likewise for the highest yield or for any of the yields in between. Thus, assuming a true null hypothesis, we may view the

TABLE 18-1   Corn Yields Obtained in Test of Two Fertilizers

	Yield (bushels)				
Type A	42.3	38.7	42.8	35.6	47.2
Type B	61.4	45.3	46.4	53.1	50.1

TABLE 18-2   Ranks of Fertilizer Test Yields

Type	A	A	A	A	B	B	A	B	B	B
Yield	35.6	38.7	42.3	42.8	45.3	46.4	47.2	50.1	53.1	61.4
Rank	1	2	3	4	5	6	7	8	9	10

* The sum of N integers, $1, 2, \ldots, N$, is obtained from $N(N+1)/2$. When $N = 10$, the sum is $10(10+1)/2 = 55$.

sample results as only one possible outcome from an uncertain situation having as many equally likely outcomes as there are ways to select five ranks for sample *A* out of a total of ten ranks.

The sampling distribution for *W* could be found by listing all of the rank combinations. Treating these elementary events as equally likely, we could then determine exact probabilities for rank sums such as 16, 17, 18, 19, and so on. For most test situations, however, this would be tedious.

Instead, we can approximate the distribution of *W* by the normal curve, which works well for most sample sizes encountered. For this purpose, the following expression* is used to calculate *the normal deviate for the sample results:*

$$z = \frac{W - \dfrac{n_A(n_A + n_B + 1)}{2}}{\sqrt{\dfrac{n_A n_B(n_A + n_B + 1)}{12}}} \tag{18-1}$$

where n_A and n_B represent the number of sample observations made from populations *A* and *B*, respectively.

Substituting $n_A = n_B = 5$ and $W = 17$ into expression (18-1), the normal deviate for the fertilizer test results is

$$z = \frac{17 - \dfrac{5(5+5+1)}{2}}{\sqrt{\dfrac{5(5)(5+5+1)}{12}}} = \frac{17 - 27.5}{\sqrt{22.9167}} = -2.19$$

Small values of *W*, and hence negative *z*'s, reflect that smaller ranks have been assigned to sample *A*, which would be consistent with a situation where the values of population *A* are smaller than the values of *B*. For large *W*'s and positive *z*'s, the reverse holds. The value $z = -2.19$ strongly indicates that fertilizer *A* generally produces lower yields than *B* does. Before we can determine the appropriate action to take, we must find out whether or not -2.19 significantly refutes the null hypothesis that both fertilizers are equally effective.

The usual decision rules apply for the rank-sum test. For one-sided tests, the critical normal deviate z_α that corresponds to the desired significance level is obtained from Appendix Table E. For two-sided tests, $z_{\alpha/2}$ is used.

Suppose that a significance level of $\alpha = .05$ is desired in the fertilizer experiment. We find $z_{.025} = 1.96$, so the decision rule is

Accept H_0 (conclude fertilizers equally effective) if $-1.96 \leqslant z \leqslant 1.96$

Reject H_0 (conclude *A* most effective) if $z > 1.96$
or (conclude *B* most effective) if $z < -1.96$

---

* Here, we use the fact that $z = [W - E(W)]/\sigma(W)$, where the mean of *W* is half the total rank sum, $E(W) = n_A(n_A + n_B + 1)/2$, and it can be shown that the variance of *W* is $\sigma^2(W) = n_A n_B(n_A + n_B + 1)/12$.

Since the computed value of the normal deviate $z = -2.19$ is smaller than -1.96, H_0 must be *rejected*. The sample results indicate that fertilizer B is more effective at the $\alpha = .05$ significance level.

Application to One-Sided Tests

To show how this procedure may be applied in a one-sided test, consider the following example.

Example 18-1 A toy manufacturer wishes to compare two compensation plans. One would use an incentive wage; the other calls for a straight hourly wage. A sample of 10 men are placed under the incentive plan; we refer to these as group A. This group is to be compared with a sample of 15 men, group B, who are paid by the hour. Management will substitute a wage incentive plan if it demonstrates an improvement in productivity over the regular hourly wage. To be tested at a level of significance $\alpha = .05$ is the null hypothesis that the incentive compensation plan does not result in improved output:

H_0: Population A values are less than or equal to those of population B.

Since a preponderance of high ranks for sample A should refute H_0, this test is *upper-tailed*. The combined sample data were ranked as shown in Table 18-3. (The special handling of tying scores is explained below.) The rank sum for the sample A outputs is

$$W = 5 + 7.5 + 11 + 12 + 17 + 19 + 20 + 23 + 24 + 25 = 163.5$$

Applying expression (18-1) with sample sizes $n_A = 10$ and $n_B = 15$, the normal deviate is

$$z = \frac{163.5 - \dfrac{10(10+15+1)}{2}}{\sqrt{\dfrac{10(15)(10+15+1)}{12}}} = \frac{33.5}{\sqrt{325}} = 1.86$$

Management desires an $\alpha = .05$ significance level. Thus, $z_{.05} = 1.64$. Since the computed value for z is larger than 1.64, management must *reject H_0* that population A outputs are no larger than those for population B and conclude that incentive compensation yields greater productivity than does hourly compensation.

The Problem of Ties

Several ties were encountered in ranking the data in Table 18-3. For instance, two sample A workers shared the output level of 148 and two sample B workers achieved the same output of 147. *As long as ties occur within the same sample group, successive ranks may be assigned arbitrarily to the tying sample observations.* Thus, we ranked the two 147 outputs as 9 and 10 and the two 148 outputs as 11 and 12.

A difficulty arises, however, when ties occur between sample groups, because the choice of ranks affects W. *When ties occur between sample groups, each observation is assigned the average of the ranks for that value.* The ranks of 7 and 8 would have applied to the two outputs of 146 had they been in the same

TABLE 18-3   Sample Data for Experiment Comparing
Two Compensation Plans

Unit Output Under Incentive Compensation X_A	Unit Output Under Hourly Compensation X_B	X_A^2	X_B^2
148	143	21,904	20,449
146	137	21,316	18,769
152	149	23,104	22,201
157	151	24,649	22,801
144	146	20,736	21,316
148	155	21,904	24,025
160	147	25,600	21,609
154	150	23,716	22,500
154	147	23,716	21,609
156	138	24,336	19,044
1,519	145	230,981	21,025
	153		23,409
	155		24,025
	149		22,201
	138		19,044
	2,203		324,027

Sample	B	B	B	B	A	B	A	B	B	B	A	A	B	B
Output	137	138	138	143	144	145	146	146	147	147	148	148	149	149
Rank	1	2	3	4	5	6	7.5	7.5	9	10	11	12	13	14

	B	B	A	B	A	A	B	B	A	A	A
	150	151	152	153	154	154	155	155	156	157	160
	15	16	17	18	19	20	21	22	23	24	25

$n_A = 10$ $n_B = 15$

$\bar{X}_A = \dfrac{1,519}{10} = 151.90$ $\bar{X}_B = \dfrac{2,203}{15} = 146.87$

$s_A^2 = \dfrac{230,981 - 10(151.90)^2}{9}$ $s_B^2 = \dfrac{324,027 - 15(146.87)^2}{14}$

$\quad = 27.21$ $\quad = 33.22$

sample. However, since one worker in *each* sample achieved the same output
level, the values receive equal ranks of $(7+8)/2 = 7.5$.

Comparison of Wilcoxon and Student t Tests

The data from Example 18-1 may be used to compare the Wilcoxon rank-
sum test to the Student t test for independent samples. Substituting the intermediate calculations from Table 18-3 into expression (14-23), we obtain

$$t = \frac{151.90 - 146.87}{\sqrt{\dfrac{9(27.21) + 14(33.22)}{10 + 15 - 2}}\sqrt{\dfrac{1}{10} + \dfrac{1}{15}}}$$

$$= \frac{5.03}{\sqrt{30.8682}\sqrt{.1667}} = 2.218$$

Using $\alpha = .05$ with $n_A + n_B - 2 = 23$ degrees of freedom, Appendix Table F provides $t_{.05} = 1.714$. Since the computed value for t is larger than 1.714, the t test also indicates that H_0 must be *rejected*.

Similar results were obtained using both tests. (Once again, it should be emphasized that a particular test would normally be chosen in advance of sampling and that only one test would ordinarily be used on any given data. Both tests were applied here only to compare the two techniques.) Generally, the t test is more efficient or powerful than the Wilcoxon, so, using the same data, the t test should provide a lower probability α of incorrectly rejecting H_0. However, the Student t test requires that the *populations* be normally distributed, which is often not the case.* Also, the Wilcoxon test can be used for experiments where the observations are measured on an ordinal scale, whereas the t test cannot. *The Wilcoxon rank-sum test can therefore be more widely used.*

EXERCISES

18-1   A taxicab company must decide whether to replace its brand A batteries with brand B. It will do so if testing shows that brand B is more effective. The null hypothesis is that brand A is at least as effective as B. Ten new brand A batteries have been installed in a random sample of cars, and 15 new brand B batteries have been installed in another group of randomly chosen cars. The number of days until the battery requires replacement is to be determined for each car. The results obtained are (in days to replacement):

> *Brand A*   323, 178, 246, 195, 402, 603, 496, 328, 213, 187
> *Brand B*   421, 327, 609, 433, 519, 504, 183, 455, 365, 615,
>   504, 312, 513, 497, 723

(a) Is an upper-tailed or a lower-tailed test appropriate here?
(b) Rank the sample results and calculate W.
(c) Suppose that management wishes to protect itself against incorrectly deciding to change battery brands at a .05 level of significance. Find the critical value for the test statistic. Should the battery brands be changed?

18-2   Suppose that the company in Exercise 18-1 installed 100 brand A batteries and 150 brand B batteries, and that $W = 11,500$. Using the normal approximation, should management reject the null hypothesis that brand A is at least as effective as B at the .05 significance level?

18-3   Suppose that the physician in Exercise 14-5 (page 482) uses the Wilcoxon rank-sum test on a sample of eight patients treated with penicillin and on a group of ten patients to whom sulfa was administered, and that he obtains the following results for the number of days required to cure a virulent strain of venereal disease:

> *(A) Penicillin*   15, 9, 12, 22, 14, 9, 10, 15
> *(B) Sulfa*   7, 8, 10, 6, 7, 7, 4, 13, 11, 5

(a) Rank the sample data and calculate W.
(b) The doctor's null hypothesis is that the treatments are equally effective. Formulate his decision rule, assuming that in the future he

---

* Both procedures require equal population variances.

will use the treatment he finds most effective but that otherwise he will test further. (Use $\alpha = .05$.)

(c) What action should the doctor take?

18-4 A farm cooperative wishes to select the fastest railroad for shipments to Central City, served by both the CW&B and Sun Belt lines. A random sample of less-than-carload shipments via each line were selected for detailed monitoring, and the following results were obtained for hours required to complete shipments:

$$(A) \quad CW\&B \quad 10, 18, 12, 15, 27$$
$$(B) \quad Sun \ Belt \quad 14, 19, 22, 23, 25, 19, 24, 31, 26$$

Shipments are currently made on the Sun Belt line. The null hypothesis is that the Sun Belt is at least as fast as CW&B.

(a) Is an upper- or a lower-tailed test appropriate here?

(b) Rank the sample results and calculate W.

(c) Suppose that protection against erroneously choosing the wrong railroad must be at the $\alpha = .025$ significance level. Should the null hypothesis be accepted or rejected?

18-5 Two security analysts for a mutual fund want to compare their trading strategies. Each takes a random selection of ten stocks and trades them for a year. Analyst A's procedure is a bit revolutionary, so the null hypothesis is that analyst B's method will provide percentage rates of return at least as great as A's. The following results (in percentage rates of return) have been obtained:

A	10	-5	15	23	113	57	-51	203	33	44
B	11	27	9	9	18	-4	-8	53	112	6

(a) Is an upper- or a lower-tailed test appropriate here?

(b) Find the critical value for the $\alpha = .10$ significance level. Formulate the decision rule.

(c) Calculate W.

(d) Should H_0 be accepted or rejected at the $\alpha = .10$ significance level?

18-3 THE MANN-WHITNEY U TEST

The *Mann-Whitney U test* is often used in comparing two populations with independent samples. This procedure is actually equivalent to the Wilcoxon rank-sum test, and the two procedures lead to identical conclusions.

The Mann-Whitney U test proceeds like the Wilcoxon, by ranking the combined sample data and then calculating the sum W of the sample A ranks. The following test statistic is used:

$$U = n_A n_B + \frac{n_A(n_A + 1)}{2} - W \tag{18-2}$$

The normal curve also serves as the approximate sampling distribution for U. The following calculation provides the normal deviate for the sample results:

$$z = \frac{U - \dfrac{n_A n_B}{2}}{\sqrt{\dfrac{n_A n_B(n_A + n_B + 1)}{12}}} \tag{18-3}$$

If expression (18-2) for U is substituted into expression (18-3) and the terms are collected, the same expression for z that is used in the Wilcoxon rank-sum test is obtained but with reversed signs. Since the Wilcoxon procedure is equivalent to the U test and involves fewer steps, its use is recommended.

18-4 COMPARING TWO POPULATIONS USING MATCHED PAIRS: THE SIGN TEST

In this section, we will discuss a nonparametric test for the differences between two populations that involves samples of *matched pairs*. This is the *sign test*, so named because it considers only the direction of difference in each sample pair, which may be expressed by either a plus or a minus sign. Like the Wilcoxon rank-sum test for independent samples, the sign test may be applied to a wider variety of situations than the parametric t test we described in Chapter 14. The sign test evaluates null hypotheses where population A values are (1) at least as great as B's; (2) at most as large as B's; or (3) equal to B's. The test makes no assumptions whatsoever about the shape or the parameters for the population frequency distributions. (The Wilcoxon test involved null hypotheses where the targeted experimental and the control populations were considered identical.)

Description of the Test

The sign test will be described in terms of the following example.

The Blue-Beard Razor Blade Company wishes to compare its prototype "Rapier" blade with a competitor's "Scimitar" brand to determine whether the Rapier is of superior quality. A sampling study is to be conducted, and the Rapier brand will be marketed only if testing shows that Rapier is superior to Scimitar; otherwise, more effort will be devoted to improving Rapier.

A random sample of a representative cross section of 20 men is chosen for the test. Each man will shave one side of his face with the Rapier blade and the other side with the Scimitar for five consecutive days. At the end of the test, each man will rate the two blades in each of five categories: closeness of shave, shaving comfort, durability of sharpness, ease of effort, and residual facial discomfort during the day. The highest rating is 10 points, and the lowest is a point value of zero. The points in each category are added together, so that a blade receiving top ratings in all five categories will be given a score of 50 and a blade rating lowest in all categories will be given a score of zero. Fractional scoring is allowed.

Blade assignment is randomly made by tossing a coin to determine which side of each man's face will be shaved with the Rapier blade. The identities of the blades are not known to the men participating in the experiment. The same blade will be used on the same side of a subject's face throughout the experiment.

The hypotheses are expressed as:

H_0: Rapier is not superior to Scimitar.

H_1: Rapier is superior to Scimitar.

Suppose that the data provided in Table 18-4 were obtained from the experiment. We must determine a test statistic that will enable us to accept or reject the null hypothesis.

TABLE 18-4   Experimental Results of Razor Blade Test

Test Subject Number	Score Received		Difference	Sign
	Rapier	Scimitar		
1	48.0	37.0	+11.0	+
2	33.0	41.0	−8.0	−
3	37.5	23.4	+14.1	+
4	48.0	17.0	+31.0	+
5	42.5	31.5	+11.0	+
6	40.0	40.0	0.0	tie
7	42.0	31.0	+11.0	+
8	36.0	36.0	0.0	tie
9	11.3	5.7	+5.6	+
10	22.0	11.5	+10.5	+
11	36.0	21.0	+15.0	+
12	27.3	6.1	+21.2	+
13	14.2	26.5	−12.3	−
14	32.1	21.3	+10.8	+
15	52.0	44.5	+7.5	+
16	38.0	28.0	+10.0	+
17	17.3	22.6	−5.3	−
18	20.0	20.0	0.0	tie
19	21.0	11.0	+10.0	+
20	46.1	22.3	+23.8	+

The Test Statistic

The null hypothesis allows us to consider the special case where the blades may be of equal quality. If the blades are identical in quality, the scores obtained for Rapier and Scimitar would be due only to the side of face shaved with Rapier. The first subject in Table 18-4 has assigned a higher score to Rapier. This may be due to the blade, but it may also be due to the fact that he is right-handed and shaved the left side of his face with Scimitar, which would be more cumbersome. If this is the case, then the coin flip, not the blade quality, resulted in the difference in ratings. Under the presumption of equal quality, the opposite conclusion would be made if the coin toss resulted in a tail instead of a head. Then, the score for Rapier would be 37.0 and the score for Scimitar would be 48.0.

For each matched pair, the difference in sample values is determined. In our illustration, the differences in Table 18-4 have been obtained by subtracting the Scimitar score from the Rapier score.

We can now determine whether the data support or refute the null hypothesis. For this purpose, we use only the signs of the difference for each pair. The rating scheme used in the experiment resulted in three ties. In these cases, it is assumed that there are truly some differences too subtle to assess, but since they are impossible to identify, the tied outcomes are eliminated from the analysis. This leaves us with $20 - 3 = 17$ pairs with sign differences.

Note the preponderance of positive signs in Table 18-4. Since a larger number of positive signs is evidence that Rapier is favored over Scimitar, the decision may be based upon the number of positive signs. Therefore, an appropriate *test statistic for the sign test is:*

$$R = \text{number of positive signs}$$

In our illustration, $R = 14$. Although this value is larger than the number of minus signs because a majority of the sample rated Rapier blades higher than Scimitar blades, we must still determine whether R is large enough to warrant rejecting H_0. Our first step will be to find the sampling distribution for R.

Sampling Distribution of Test Statistic R

Under the presumption of identical blade quality, each of the signs in Table 18-4 could have been reversed; that is, the probability of a positive sign difference for each matched pair is .5, just as if the results had been determined by the toss of a coin. Thus, we may determine the probability of how untypical our results are under the null hypothesis by using the *binomial distribution*. The probability of obtaining a positive sign difference for any particular pair would be $\pi = .5$, and we have $n = 17$ pairs. The probabilities for the possible number of positive signs R may be found by using Appendix Table C, which gives cumulative probabilities for the binomial distribution. Using $\pi = .5$ and $n = 17$, for example, we find that

$$P[R > 11] = 1 - P[R \leqslant 11] = 1 - .9283 = .0717$$

The Decision Rule

As in all hypothesis-testing situations, a decision rule must be found here that coincides with the significance level desired. This decision rule will determine a *critical value* R^* for the number of positive signs. Since large values of R favor Rapier and tend to refute H_0 that Rapier is not superior to Scimitar, H_0 must be rejected for large values of R. The probability of incorrectly rejecting H_0 for large values of R is represented by upper-tail probabilities of the binomial distribution, making the test in this illustration *upper-tailed*.

To find R^*, we assume that the Blue-Beard Razor Blade Company has established the significance level at $\alpha = .05$. In this case, *we must select R^* so that the probability that the number of positive signs exceeds R^* is no larger than* α. We have already found that 11 is too small to be the critical value, since $P[R > 11] = .0717$, which is greater than .05. The next larger value is 12, for which Appendix Table C provides

$$P[R > 12] = 1 - P[R \leqslant 12] = 1 - .9755 = .0245$$

Since 12 is the smallest value yielding a probability less than .05, we use $R^* = 12$ as the critical value.

The appropriate decision rule is

$$Accept\ H_0\ (\text{do not market Rapier}) \quad \text{if } R \leqslant 12$$

$$Reject\ H_0\ (\text{market Rapier}) \qquad \text{if } R > 12$$

Because the actual number of positive signs $R = 14$ exceeds $R^* = 12$, H_0 that Rapier is not superior to Scimitar must be *rejected* at the $\alpha = .05$ significance level. The Blue-Beard Razor Blade Company should therefore market its new Rapier blade. There is less than a .05 chance that this action will prove incorrect.

The decision rule for a lower-tailed test is the reverse. In such a case, the smallest value for R^* is chosen, so that $P[R < R^*]$ is no larger than α. It is also possible to apply the procedure to two-sided hypothesis tests. This would involve two critical values for R.

The Normal Approximation

When the sample size is large, the probabilities for extreme values of R may be determined by using the normal approximation to the binomial distribution. In Chapter 6, we established that the mean and the standard deviation for the number of successes R (here, a success is a positive sign) were

$$E(R) = n\pi = n(.5) = n/2$$

$$\sigma(R) = \sqrt{n\pi(1-\pi)} = \sqrt{n(.5)(1-.5)} = \sqrt{n/4}$$

so that substituting these parameters into $z = [R - E(R)]/\sigma(R)$ and simplifying the numerator and the denominator gives us the following expression for the *normal deviate for the sample results:*

$$z = \frac{2R - n}{\sqrt{n}} \tag{18-4}$$

The usual decision rules apply, using the critical normal deviates z_α for one-sided tests and $z_{\alpha/2}$ for two-sided tests. The following example illustrates how the normal approximation may be applied.

Example 18-2   An educational researcher conducted an experiment to determine if elementary-school language programs might be improved by a new approach to vocabulary and spelling. Rather than the usual memorization methods, the researcher believes that the same amount of time and effort devoted to additional reading would be more effective. Fourth-grade students from various classes in several schools were divided into two groups. Children in the control group A took the standard language program in their home rooms. Students in the experimental group B went to special classes during language periods, where they read, submitted book reports, and discussed assigned outside reading.

As her null hypothesis, the researcher assumes that the new procedure does not improve language skills, as measured by scores on an achievement test. Thus:

H_0: A scores are at least as great as B scores (new procedure is no improvement).

H_1: A scores are lower than B scores (new procedure is an improvement).

Each child in group B was matched to a group A counterpart in his or her own classroom who had similar skills and aptitudes. Toward the end of the school year, both groups were tested. After subtracting the B child's score from the A child's score, the number of positive sign differences were then determined. Since a small value for R will refute the null hypothesis, this test is *lower-tailed*. Using a significance level of $\alpha = .05$, the critical normal deviate is $z_{.05} = 1.64$ and the decision rule is

Accept H_0 (do not recommend new procedure) if $z \geqslant -1.64$

Reject H_0 (recommend new procedure)   if $z < -1.64$

TABLE 18-5   Sample Data for Experiment
Comparing Two Language-Skill Teaching Procedures

Pair i	Control Group A Score X_{A_i}	Experimental Group B Score X_B	Difference $d_i = X_{A_i} - X_{B_i}$	Sign	d_i^2
1	65	67	-2	$-$	4
2	72	66	$+6$	$+$	36
3	74	77	-3	$-$	9
4	81	90	-9	$-$	81
5	76	72	$+4$	$+$	16
6	95	95	0	tie	0
7	63	68	-5	$-$	25
8	85	95	-10	$-$	100
9	90	98	-8	$-$	64
10	64	60	$+4$	$+$	16
11	78	72	$+6$	$+$	36
12	86	94	-8	$-$	64
13	89	96	-7	$-$	49
14	75	73	$+2$	$+$	4
15	93	96	-3	$-$	9
16	78	90	-12	$-$	144
17	92	92	0	tie	0
18	67	63	$+4$	$+$	16
19	88	95	-7	$-$	49
20	79	88	-9	$-$	81
21	60	75	-15	$-$	225
22	90	95	-5	$-$	25
23	82	78	$+4$	$+$	16
24	73	85	-12	$-$	144
25	86	82	$+4$	$+$	16
			$\overline{-81}$		$\overline{1,229}$

$$\bar{d} = \frac{-81}{25} = -3.24$$

$$s_{d\text{-paired}} = \sqrt{\frac{1,229 - 25(-3.24)^2}{25-1}} = 6.35$$

The data in Table 18-5 were obtained. Here, we see that there were two ties; eliminating these leaves $n = 23$ pairs to consider. The number of positive signs was $R = 8$. Thus, expression (18-4) provides

$$z = \frac{2(8) - 23}{\sqrt{23}} = -1.46$$

Since this value is greater than $-z_{.05} = -1.64$, the researcher must *accept* H_0 that the new procedure is no improvement and must not recommend its adoption.

Comparison of Sign and Student *t* Tests

The sign test may be compared to the analogous parametric procedure described in Chapter 14 for matched-pairs testing. There, the Student *t* test was used with small samples. Substituting the mean of the matched-pairs differences and their estimated standard error (both calculated in Table 18-5) and using $n = 25$ as the sample size, expression (14-25) provides

$$t = \frac{-3.24}{6.35/\sqrt{25}} = -2.551$$

Using $\alpha = .05$, from Appendix Table F for $25 - 1 = 24$ degrees of freedom, the critical value is $-t_{.05} = -1.711$. Since the computed value for *t* is smaller than -1.711, the Student *t* test indicates that H_0 should be *rejected*. This conclusion is opposite to the decision we reached using the sign test for the same data.

As with the Wilcoxon test, this reflects the fact that *when applicable* the *t* test is more powerful and therefore more efficient. Its greater discrimination is due to the fact that the relative sizes of the matched-pairs differences—as well as their signs—are used in calculating *t*. However, the *t* test requires that the *populations* of all potential matched-pairs differences be normally distributed (or nearly so). *When this requirement is not met, the sign test is the valid test to use.*

EXERCISES

18-6   In each of the following situations, the sign test will be used to determine the appropriate action.
(1) Indicate whether the test is lower- or upper-tailed.
(2) Use Appendix Table C to find the critical value R^* for the number of positive sign differences.
(3) Formulate the appropriate decision rule.
(4) Indicate whether H_0 should be accepted or rejected at the stated significance level for the result provided.

(a)	(b)	(c)	(d)
$H_0: A\text{'s} \geqslant B\text{'s}$	$H_0: A\text{'s} \leqslant B\text{'s}$	$H_0: A\text{'s} \geqslant B\text{'s}$	$H_0: A\text{'s} \leqslant B\text{'s}$
$n = 18$	$n = 100$	$n = 50$	$n = 19$
$\alpha = .05$	$\alpha = .01$	$\alpha = .01$	$\alpha = .05$
$R = 4$	$R = 58$	$R = 13$	$R = 13$

18-7 A car rental company must determine whether its cars should burn leaded (A) or unleaded (B) gasoline. Fifteen pairs of cars are selected: one car from each pair uses leaded gasoline; the other, unleaded. The cars in each pair are nearly identical in essential respects. These cars were driven in the same manner over the same routes. The null hypothesis is that unleaded gasoline provides at least as good mileage as leaded gasoline. The following sample results were obtained:

Pair	Miles per Gallon Leaded (A)	Unleaded (B)	Pair	Miles per Gallon Leaded (A)	Unleaded (B)
1	15.3	14.7	9	15.0	13.8
2	18.1	17.9	10	16.2	16.1
3	14.9	15.0	11	15.9	14.2
4	17.3	17.3	12	21.3	20.6
5	13.7	12.3	13	18.4	17.7
6	11.8	9.2	14	19.3	17.4
7	20.3	19.7	15	9.8	7.6
8	15.2	14.7			

(a) Determine the sign difference (leaded minus unleaded mileage) for each pair.

(b) Find the value for the test statistic R, the number of positive signs. Is an upper- or a lower-tailed test required?

(c) Under the assumption that both gasolines provide equally good gasoline mileage, determine the probability that a result would be obtained that is as untypical as the actual one. (Use Appendix Table C.)

(d) Assuming that leaded gas will be used if it provides better mileage, would it be used if the desired significance level is $\alpha = .001$?

18-8 For the gasoline mileages in Exercise 18-7, suppose that the normal approximation is used to test the same null hypothesis at the $\alpha = .05$ significance level when the number of automobile pairs is $n = 100$. Assume that $R = 60$. Which type of gasoline would be used?

18-9 Suppose that the researcher in Example 14-3 (page 476) found the signs of differences in mean age for contracting angina pectoris by subtracting the onset age of the nonsmoker (B) from that of the smoker (A), obtaining $R = 30$ positive signs. As her null hypothesis, the researcher assumes that smoking makes no difference in the speed of the disease. Using an $\alpha = .01$ significance level, what should she conclude regarding the effect of smoking on the age when angina occurs?

18-10 A pharmaceutical firm wishes to determine if a new appetite suppressor supplement reduces weight more effectively than the one now marketed. If so, the new supplement will replace the current one. A random sample of 20 pairs of persons chosen for testing are paired so that all factors reasoned to influence weight buildup are nearly the same for each pair: Women are paired with women, smokers are paired with smokers, physically inactive types are paired, and so forth. One pair member is administered the new supplement, and the other is given the old supplement. The null hypothesis is that the new supplement is at most as effective as the old one. A supplement is said to be more effective if it brings about a greater percentage weight reduction in three months of use. The results are:

	Reduction Percentage			Reduction Percentage	
Pair	New Supplement	Old Supplement	Pair	New Supplement	Old Supplement
1	10	−2	11	15	8
2	5	3	12	13	12
3	7	1	13	14	10
4	8	10	14	13	5
5	4	2	15	7	8
6	15	11	16	11	3
7	12	13	17	−2	−3
8	18	5	18	0	−2
9	3	−2	19	16	9
10	8	12	20	9	8

(a) Determine the sign difference (percentage for new minus that for old) for each pair.

(b) Find the test statistic R, the number of positive signs. Is an upper- or a lower-tailed test required?

(c) Calculate the normal deviate for the sample results.

(d) Making the normal approximation, express the decision rule at the $\alpha = .05$ significance level. What course of action is indicated by the sample results?

18-11 A chemical supplier wishes to determine whether a new preservative will provide a longer shelf life for the bread of its bakery customers. Ten bakeries have used the new preservative in some of their dough and have provided the supplier with two fresh loaves of standard bread, one baked with their regular preservative and the other baked with the new preservative. The following shelf lives have been obtained:

	Shelf Life (days)	
Bakery	Old Preservative	New Preservative
1	5.7	6.3
2	4.2	3.9
3	6.5	6.7
4	3.4	3.6
5	6.1	6.3
6	5.3	5.7
7	4.9	5.2
8	3.7	3.7
9	2.8	3.7
10	4.3	4.5

(a) Use the sign test with binomial probabilities to determine whether to accept or reject the null hypothesis that the new preservative yields shelf lives that are at most as long as the old preservative at an $\alpha = .05$ level of significance.

(b) Repeat this test using the t statistic.

18-5 THE WILCOXON SIGNED-RANK TEST FOR MATCHED PAIRS

Thus far, we have described three nonparametric procedures. The first of these is based upon rank sums and applies to independent samples. The second is equivalent to the first. The third is applicable when the sample data are matched into pairs. The first test is concerned only with the ranking of sample data and not with the relative magnitudes of the differences between sample groups. The third considers the direction but not the size of differences in sample pairs.

A test that considers both the direction and the magnitude of differences in matched sample pairs would exhibit both features of the above procedures. Such a test was proposed by Frank Wilcoxon. In this section, we will describe his *Wilcoxon signed-rank test*, a procedure based upon both rank sums and the signs of paired differences.

Description of the Test

The Wilcoxon signed-rank test is based upon matched-pairs differences. Ignoring signs, the *absolute values* of the differences are ranked from low to high. Once these rankings have been assigned, those ranks corresponding to the original positive matched-pairs differences are summed. This procedure can be summarized in the following steps, which provide *the test statistic V:*

1. Calculate the differences $d_i = X_{A_i} - X_{B_i}$ for all sample pairs.
2. Ignoring signs, rank the absolute values of the d_i's. Do not rank zero differences.
3. Calculate $V =$ sum of ranks for positive d_i's.

The statistic V may be used to test the same hypotheses as the sign test. In every application, H_0 includes the special case where *A and B values are generated by identical populations.* If this is true, then each matched-pairs difference has a 50–50 chance of having a positive or a negative sign. Furthermore, positive or negative differences of the same absolute size should be equally likely. This indicates that under H_0, about half the ranks ought to correspond to positive differences and that the sum of these ranks V should be close to half the total rank-sum value. To determine whether the value of V significantly refutes H_0, we must examine its sampling distribution.

The Sampling Distribution of the Test Statistic V

As with the earlier Wilcoxon test, a detailed probability accounting will provide the exact sampling distribution of V. However, for most sample sizes encountered, we may use the normal curve instead. The following expression* is used to calculate the *normal deviate for the sample results:*

$$z = \frac{V - \frac{n(n+1)}{4}}{\sqrt{\frac{n(n+1)(2n+1)}{24}}} \tag{18-5}$$

---

* Here, we use the fact that $z = [V - E(V)]/\sigma(V)$, where the mean of V is half the total rank sum $n(n+1)/2$ and it can be shown that the variance of V is $\sigma^2(V) = n(n+1)(2n+1)/24$.

The value for n is the number of nonzero differences found in the sample. As in the sign test, we ignore ties with sample pairs, since they provide matched-pairs differences of zero.

The computed z may be compared to the appropriate critical normal deviate to determine the course of action to take. As an illustration, we will reconsider Example 18-2, where an educational researcher conducted an experiment to compare two methods of lanaguage-skill instruction. Table 18-6 shows the data she obtained. Recall that A observations represent the scores achieved by fourth-grade students under a traditional memory-drill method designed to expand vocabulary and improve spelling. Scores for the experimental group B were achieved by fourth-graders taking a special outside reading program in lieu of the regular procedure. The hypothesis to be tested is H_0: A scores are at least as great as B scores (new procedure is no improvement over old procedure).

Ignoring the signs, the ranks for the nonzero matched-pairs differences in Table 18-6 were assigned to the absolute amounts, starting with 1 for the lowest. Assigning absolute values to pairs of opposite signs is handled exactly as we discussed in the Wilcoxon rank-sum test. Thus, the pairs with differences

TABLE 18-6 Sample Data for Experiment
Comparing Two Language-Skill Teaching Procedures
with Assignment of Signed Ranks

Pair i	Experimental Group A Score X_{A_i}	Control Group B Score X_{B_i}	Difference $d_i = X_{A_i} - X_{B_i}$	Sign	Rank of Absolute Values of Matched-Pairs Differences
1	65	67	-2	$-$	1.5
2	72	66	$+6$	$+$	12
3	74	77	-3	$-$	3
4	81	90	-9	$-$	18
5	76	72	$+4$	$+$	5
6	95	95	0	tie	—
7	63	68	-5	$-$	10
8	85	95	-10	$-$	20
9	90	98	-8	$-$	16
10	64	60	$+4$	$+$	6
11	78	72	$+6$	$+$	13
12	86	94	-8	$-$	17
13	89	96	-7	$-$	14
14	75	73	$+2$	$+$	1.5
15	93	96	-3	$-$	4
16	78	90	-12	$-$	21
17	92	92	0	tie	—
18	67	63	$+4$	$+$	7
19	88	95	-7	$-$	15
20	79	88	-9	$-$	19
21	60	75	-15	$-$	23
22	90	95	-5	$-$	11
23	82	78	$+4$	$+$	8
24	73	85	-12	$-$	22
25	86	82	$+4$	$+$	9

-2 and $+2$, which tie for the smallest absolute value, both receive the average of the two lowest ranks $(1+2)/2 = 1.5$. As before, ties between positive or negative differences only are ignored.

The sum of the ranks for the eight positive differences is

$$V = 12+5+6+13+1.5+7+8+9 = 61.5$$

The corresponding normal deviate is found from expression (18-5), using $n = 23$ nonzero pair differences:

$$z = \frac{61.5 - \dfrac{23(24)}{4}}{\sqrt{\dfrac{23(24)(46+1)}{24}}} = \frac{-76.5}{\sqrt{1,081}} = -2.33$$

Since small values of V and resultant negative z's indicate that the B values are preponderantly larger than the A values—the opposite of what the null hypothesis implies—this test is *lower-tailed*. At the $\alpha = .05$ significance level, $z_{.05} = 1.64$. Since the computed value of $z = -2.33$ is smaller than -1.64, the Wilcoxon signed-rank test indicates that the null hypothesis should be *rejected* and that the researcher should conclude that the experimental language program is an improvement over the traditional procedure.

Comparison of the Wilcoxon Signed-Rank and the Sign Tests

The conclusion just reached is contradictory to the one we reached previously. Using these data, the sign test accepted the same null hypothesis at the identical significance level. With the sign test, we obtained $z = -1.46$, which corresponds to a lower-tail normal curve area of $.5 - .4279 = .0721$, the lowest significance level at which H_0 could have been rejected using that test. The Wilcoxon signed-rank test provides $z = -2.33$, corresponding to a lower-tail normal curve area of $.5 - .4901 = .0099$. Thus, the probability of incorrectly rejecting H_0 is much lower with the Wilcoxon than with the sign test. This reflects the fact that the Wilcoxon signed-rank test is more powerful; that is, for the same sample size, it is more discriminating or more efficient than the sign test.

The greater efficiency of the Wilcoxon procedure results from the greater amount of information it derives from the sample data. The test considers the sizes of the differences as well as their signs. Why, then, is the less efficient sign test used at all? One reason for its popularity is that the sign test is simpler to use. Another is that when there are very many ties between differences of opposite signs, the Wilcoxon signed-rank test needs adjustment to be applicable. *A further advantage of the sign test is that its assumptions are less restrictive than the Wilcoxon's.* It does not assume that A and B values have identical population frequency distributions (and, hence, equal variances), as does the Wilcoxon signed-rank test.

EXERCISES

18-12 In each of the following situations, the Wilcoxon signed-rank test will be used to determine the appropriate action:

(a)	(b)	(c)	(d)
H_0: A's $\leqslant B$'s	H_0: A's $\geqslant B$'s	H_0: A's $\leqslant B$'s	H_0: A's $\geqslant B$'s
$n = 18$	$n = 100$	$n = 50$	$n = 19$
$\alpha = .05$	$\alpha = .01$	$\alpha = .01$	$\alpha = .05$
$V = 40$	$V = 2{,}065$	$V = 890$	$V = 44$

(1) Indicate whether the test is lower- or upper-tailed.
(2) Find the appropriate decision rule.
(3) Indicate whether H_0 should be accepted or rejected at the stated significance level for the result provided.

18-13 Consider the data in Table 14-3 (page 476) for the examination scores achieved by two groups of students, one using a new statistics book (A) and the other using an old statistics book (B). There, the professor assumed the null hypothesis that the scores would be identical for the two groups.
(a) Is this test one- or two-sided?
(b) Formulate the professor's decision rule at the $\alpha = .05$ significance level.
(c) Determine the value of the test statistic V. What conclusion does this value indicate the professor should make?

18-14 Using the data in Exercise 18-11 (page 620), compute the test statistic V. Should the null hypothesis that the new preservative yields shelf lives at most as long as the old preservative yields be accepted or rejected at the $\alpha = .05$ significance level?

18-15 Use the sample data provided in Exercise 18-7 (page 619) to apply the Wilcoxon signed-rank test. Assuming that leaded gasoline will be used only if it provides significantly better mileage than unleaded gasoline, determine which gasoline the data indicate will be used. (Use $\alpha = .0010$.)

18-6 TESTING FOR RANDOMNESS: THE NUMBER-OF-RUNS TEST

The Need to Test Randomness

We have seen that in order to use probabilities to qualify inferences about populations based on sample results, the observations must be randomly obtained. The question of whether a sample is random is especially critical in those instances when sample evidence from rare occurrences is collected over time. For example, production delays due to equipment malfunction, the causes or costs of aircraft accidents, or the IQs of identical twins reared apart are data for which evidence can be collected only historically. It is not possible to collect sample evidence through random sampling in a short time. Thus, the samples available are not random in the usual sense, but they may be analyzed as if they were, provided the data appear to be random.

Sample data collected over time are not random if there is some sort of serial dependency, so that the order in which particular attributes or variates of similar size occur is affected by what happened previously. To apply statistical methodology in such circumstances, it must be verified that the order in which the observations are obtained is similar to the order expected from a truly random sample.

The Number-of-Runs Test

A very useful procedure is to separate the sample results into two opposite categories: defective, nondefective; above 80, 80 or below; or fatal, nonfatal. Then the data can be represented chronologically as a string of category designations. For example, suppose that a company has administered a screening aptitude test to 20 new employees over the last two years and wishes to use the test scores as a basis for making judgments regarding future hirings. Letting *a* represent a score above the median and *b* a score below, then the results could be represented by a string of *a*'s and *b*'s, as in

Sequence 1: $a\ b\ b\ a\ a\ a\ b\ b\ a\ b\ b\ b\ b\ a\ a\ a\ b\ b\ a\ a$

The braces indicate *runs* of a particular category: in this sequence, 5 of *a* and 4 of *b*. *A run is a succession of one or more observations in the same category.* The hypothesis-testing procedure uses the number of runs as a basis for determining randomness.

The underlying rationale of using runs to test for randomness is that too few runs or too many runs are unlikely if the sample is truly random over time. For instance, consider the following two-run result:

Sequence 2: $a\ a\ a\ a\ a\ a\ a\ a\ a\ a\ b\ b\ b\ b\ b\ b\ b\ b\ b\ b$

The first 10 employees hired all scored highly, while the later hires received scores below the median. Such a result is indeed peculiar and quite rare from a random process. It might be explained by a change in screening procedure. For instance, the dropping of a personnel agent, who did some screening of his own, after the 10th hire may account for such an outcome. On the other hand, a 20-run result would also be highly unlikely:

Sequence 3: $b\ a\ b\ a\ b\ a\ b\ a\ b\ a\ b\ a\ b\ a\ b\ a\ b\ a\ b\ a$

Such a history could be obtained by a policy of attempting to maintain a balance in employee aptitudes or by some obscure altruistic motives on the part of the personnel manager, such as having a fixed ratio of disadvantaged workers.

The number-of-runs test is based upon the following null hypothesis:

H_0:   The sampling is random. Therefore, each sequence position has the same prior chance of obtaining an *a* as any other.

The alternative is that the sample is not random.

The test statistic is the number of runs for category a, denoted R_a. (We could just as well use the number of runs for category b, or the total number of runs; all provide nearly the same results.) For the screening test results of sequence 1, the number of a runs is $R_a = 5$; likewise, we have $R_a = 1$ for sequence 2 and $R_a = 10$ for sequence 3. To facilitate formulating an appropriate decision rule, we will first describe the sampling distribution for R_a.

The Sampling Distribution for the Number of Runs R_a

Basic concepts of probability may be applied to show that R_a has the *hypergeometric distribution*. Like the binomial, probability values for this distribution are tedious to compute and are usually tabled. It is more convenient to approximate the probabilities by using the normal curve. The following expression* may be used to calculate the *normal deviate for the sample results:*

$$z = \frac{R_a - \dfrac{n_a(n_b+1)}{n_a+n_b}}{\sqrt{\dfrac{n_a(n_b+1)(n_a-1)}{(n_a+n_b)^2}\left(\dfrac{n_b}{n_a+n_b-1}\right)}} \tag{18-6}$$

where n_a and n_b denote the number of a's and b's in the sample. For the three test-score sequences, $n_a = n_b = 10$ and the following normal deviates apply:

$$\text{Sequence 1:} \quad z = \frac{5 - \dfrac{10(10+1)}{10+10}}{\sqrt{\dfrac{10(10+1)(10-1)}{(10+10)^2}\left(\dfrac{10}{10+10-1}\right)}}$$

$$= \frac{5-5.5}{\sqrt{1.3026}} = \frac{5-5.5}{1.14} = -.44$$

$$\text{Sequence 2:} \quad z = \frac{1-5.5}{1.14} = -3.95$$

$$\text{Sequence 3:} \quad z = \frac{10-5.5}{1.14} = 3.95$$

The Decision Rule

Continuing with our screening-test illustration, suppose that we desired an $\alpha = .05$ significance level for the probability of incorrectly concluding that the test scores were randomly generated. *The testing procedure is two-sided,*

---

* Here, we use the relation $z = [R_a - E(R_a)]/\sigma(R_a)$, where the mean of R_a is

$$E(R_a) = n_a(n_b+1)/(n_a+n_b)$$

and

$$\sigma^2(R_a) = \frac{n_a(n_b+1)(n_a-1)}{(n_a+n_b)^2}\left(\frac{n_b}{n_a+n_b-1}\right)$$

since H_0 is refuted by either too few or too many a runs. The critical normal deviate is $z_{.025} = 1.96$, and the appropriate decision rule is

Accept H_0 (conclude scores are random)   if $-1.96 \leqslant z \leqslant 1.96$

Reject H_0 (conclude scores are not random) if $z < -1.96$ *or* if $z > 1.96$

Applying the above rule to sequence 1, the normal deviate $z = -.44$ lies within ± 1.96, so H_0 must be *accepted*. At the 5-percent significance level, we may conclude that the test scores in sequence 1 were randomly generated. Since the normal deviates for sequences 2 and 3 lie outside the acceptance region, we must *reject H_0* for either sequence, concluding that the test scores in each case were not randomly generated.

Testing the 1970 Draft Lottery for Randomness

Example 18-3 In December 1969, the U.S. Selective Service initiated a new procedure for determining the priorities for inducting young men into compulsory military service. Starting with the 19-year-olds born in 1950, a revised policy was implemented which drafted these younger men before the older ones. A 19-year-old man who was not drafted in 1970 would have a lower priority of being drafted in 1971 than the new crop of men born in 1951. As the manpower requirements for draftees in 1970 were much less than the number of available men, a method was devised to determine the induction priorities for 1970 by lottery.

Capsules were to be drawn from a barrel. Those men whose birthdays were drawn first would almost certainly be drafted in 1970. Those born on dates chosen near the end of the lottery would be almost certain of never having to enter military service.

Newspapers devoted wide coverage to the lottery. Some drew an imaginary line at 183 (half the number of days in a leap year), concluding that those whose numbers were 183 or below were "vulnerable," while those having numbers greater than 183 were "safe."

Table 18-7 gives the calendar dates and the corresponding draft-priority numbers obtained from the lottery in December 1969. Note that birthdays early in the year tend to be preponderantly "safe," while those late in the year comprise a majority of "vulnerables." This leads us to question whether the lottery was truly random. To help identify the runs in priority numbers, safe values are marked with a dot on the left and vulnerable values are marked with a dot on the right.

We may use the number-of-runs test to answer this question, because the draft lottery fits all the necessary assumptions. We will make one slight interpretation. The capsules contained *dates*, so that the sequence in which a date was drawn determined the draft priority for that date. It will be simpler if we envision a completely analogous experiment in which capsules containing numbers from 1 through 366 are drawn one at a time, the first capsule corresponding to January 1, the second to January 2, and so forth throughout the year. The number inside each capsule represents the draft priority for that date. All possible sequences of priority numbers are equally likely, so that our underlying assumption regarding the sampling distribution of R_a is met.

TABLE 18-7 Determination of Number of Runs of Low Priority Numbers from 1970 Draft Lottery

| | January Draft-priority number | | February Draft-priority number | | March Draft-priority number | | April Draft-priority number | | May Draft-priority number | | June Draft-priority number |
Birth-day		Birth-day		Birth-day		Birth-day		Birth-day		Birth-day	
1	·305	1	86·	1	108·	1	32·	1	·330	1	·249
2	159·	2	144·	2	29·	2	·271	2	·298	2	·228
3	·251	3	·297	3	·267	3	83·	3	40·	3	·301
4	·215	4	·210	4	·275	4	81·	4	·276	4	2u·
5	101·	5	·214	5	·293	5	·269	5	·364	5	28·
6	·224	6	·347	6	139·	6	·253	6	155·	6	110·
7	·306	7	91·	7	122·	7	147·	7	35·	7	85·
8	·199	8	181·	8	·213	8	·312	8	·321	8	·366
9	·194	9	·338	9	·317	9	·219	9	·197	9	·335
10	·325	10	·216	10	·323	10	·218	10	65·	10	·206
11	·329	11	150·	11	136·	11	14·	11	37·	11	134·
12	·221	12	68·	12	·300	12	·346	12	133·	12	·272
13	·318	13	152·	13	·259	13	124·	13	·295	13	69·
14	·238	14	4·	14	·354	14	·231	14	178·	14	·356
15	17·	15	89·	15	169·	15	·273	15	130·	15	180·
16	121·	16	·212	16	166·	16	148·	16	55·	16	·274
17	·235	17	·189	17	33·	17	·260	17	112·	17	73·
18	140·	18	·292	18	·332	18	90·	18	·278	18	·341
19	58·	19	25·	19	·200	19	·336	19	75·	19	104·
20	.280	20	·302	20	·239	20	·345	20	183·	20	·360
21	·186	21	·363	21	·334	21	62·	21	·250	21	60·
22	·337	22	·290	22	·265	22	·316	22	·326	22	·247
23	118·	23	57·	23	·256	23	·252	23	·319	23	109·
24	59·	24	·236	24	·258	24	2·	24	31·	24	·358
25	52·	25	179·	25	·343	25	·351	25	·361	25	137·
26	92·	26	·365	26	170·	26	·340	26	·357	26	22·
27	·355	27	·205	27	·268	27	74·	27	·296	27	64·
28	77·	28	·299	28	·223	28	·262	28	·308	28	·222
29	·349	29	·285	29	·362	29	·191	29	·226	29	·353
30	164·			30	·217	30	·208	30	103·	30	·209
31	·211			31	30·			31	·313		

| | July Draft-priority number | | August Draft-priority number | | September Draft-priority number | | October Draft-priority number | | November Draft-priority number | | December Draft-priority number |
Birth-day		Birth-day		Birth-day		Birth-day		Birth-day		Birth-day	
1	93·	1	111·	1	·225	1	·359	1	19·	1	129·
2	·350	2	45·	2	161·	2	125·	2	34·	2	·328
3	115·	3	·261	3	49·	3	·244	3	·348	3	157·
4	·279	4	145·	4	·322	4	·202	4	·266	4	165·
5	·188	5	54·	5	82·	5	24·	5	·310	5	56·
6	·327	6	114·	6	6·	6	87·	6	76·	6	10·
7	50·	7	168·	7	8·	7	·234	7	51·	7	12·
8	13·	8	48·	8	·184	8	·283	8	97·	8	105·
9	·277	9	106·	9	·263	9	·342	9	80·	9	43·
10	·284	10	21·	10	71·	10	·220	10	·282	10	41·
11	·248	11	·324	11	158·	11	·237	11	46·	11	39·
12	15·	12	142·	12	·242	12	72·	12	66·	12	·314
13	42·	13	·307	13	175·	13	138·	13	126·	13	163·
14	·331	14	·198	14	1·	14	·294	14	127·	14	26·
15	·322	15	102·	15	113·	15	171·	15	131·	15	·320
16	120·	16	44·	16	·207	16	·254	16	107·	16	96·
17	98·	17	154·	17	·255	17	·288	17	143·	17	·304
18	·190	18	141·	18	·246	18	5·	18	146·	18	128·
19	·227	19	·311	19	177·	19	·241	19	·203	19	·240
20	·187	20	·344	20	63·	20	·192	20	·185	20	135·
21	27·	21	·291	21	·204	21	·243	21	156·	21	70·
22	153·	22	·339	22	160·	22	117·	22	9·	22	53·
23	172·	23	116·	23	119·	23	·201	23	182·	23	162·
24	23·	24	36·	24	·195	24	·196	24	·230	24	95·
25	67·	25	·286	25	149·	25	176·	25	132·	25	84·
26	·303	26	·245	26	18·	26	7·	26	·309	26	173·
27	·289	27	·352	27	·233	27	·264	27	47·	27	78·
28	88·	28	167·	28	·257	28	94·	28	·281	28	123·
29	·270	29	61·	29	151·	29	·229	29	99·	29	16·
30	·287	30	·333	30	·315	30	38·	30	174·	30	3·
31	·193	31	11·			31	79·			31	100·

SOURCE: *U.S. News & World Report*, December 15, 1969, p. 34. Reprinted from *U.S. News & World Report*. Copyright 1969 U.S. News & World Report, Inc.

Suppose we test the null hypothesis that the lottery is random at a significance level of $\alpha = .01$. Our decision rule may be found by determining the critical value $z_{\alpha/2} = 2.57$ from Appendix Table E. We may express our decision rule as

Accept H_0 (conclude lottery was random)   if $-2.57 \leqslant z \leqslant 2.57$

Reject H_0 (conclude lottery was not random) if $z < -2.57$ *or* if $z > 2.57$

From Table 18-7 we observe that there are 86 runs of safe (low-priority) a's and 86 runs of vulnerable (high-priority) b's. Thus, $R_a = 86$. From expression (18-6), we calculate the corresponding normal deviate, using $n_a = n_b = 183$:

$$z = \frac{86 - \dfrac{183(183+1)}{(183+183)}}{\sqrt{\dfrac{183(183+1)(183-1)}{(183+183)^2}\left(\dfrac{183}{183+183-1}\right)}} = -1.253$$

Since z lies between the critical values -2.57 and 2.57, this value falls into the acceptance region and we can conclude that *the draft lottery numbers were randomly selected.*

Referring to the table of areas under the normal curve, $z = -1.253$ corresponds to a lower-tail area of about .105, so that the null hypothesis can only be rejected at a level of significance of twice this amount, or approximately $\alpha = .21$.

Meaningfulness of Results

The draft lottery example was included in this book partly because of the controversy the lottery stirred in 1970. As we indicated in Chapter 4, the U.S. Selective Service was vehemently criticized because the capsules were selected in such a haphazard way. The criticism resulted from the disparity of the numbers in Table 18-7. Investigations of the procedure used showed that the capsules were placed into the barrel by month, starting with January and ending with December. The mixing of the capsules was superficial, so that more December dates than January dates, for example, were on the top. It has been convincingly argued that the lottery was unfair to young men having birthdays late in the year. Several lawsuits were initiated to invalidate the lottery for this reason.

But our number-of-runs test does not provide nearly sufficient evidence to refute the hypothesis of random selection. Our lowest possible significance level leading to rejection is very high—greater than .20. In many scientific applications, for example, a significance level as low as .01 or .001 is usually required before results are worthy of inclusion in the body of the theory. Most persons employing statistics would regard a significance level of about .20 as highly "insignificant" in establishing that the null hypothesis is untrue and would therefore either reserve judgment or accept the null hypothesis.

This example points out a major inadequacy of using hypothesis testing as a basis for drawing conclusions about how well data fit a particular assumption. This inadequacy is fundamental to the entire statistical approach of explaining outcomes in terms of probabilities. Our number-of-runs model is not refined enough to incorporate all information (for example, the manner in which the capsules were supposedly mixed and then selected). It focuses on results only; all other relevant information is ignored. The same statistician who would conclude that the *results* are not significant enough to warrant rejection would, upon hearing a *description of the procedure* for capsule selection, be almost certain to dismiss the same null hypothesis with the full strength of his convictions, *regardless of what results were obtained.*

One important question remains. Why was such a typical run statistic value calculated for the 1970 draft lottery, when it was so convincingly argued that it was far from random? We note that although circumstances were far from ideal, there was *some mixing* of the capsules. Capsules were often withdrawn by plunging the fingers deeply into the barrel, so that even the top capsules were not guaranteed an early withdrawal and the bottom capsules were not immune from an early grasp. Thus, these operating factors contributed some aspects of randomness. As the numbers in Table 18-7 indicate, the number of vulnerable dates for February, May, June, July, September, and October did not deviate by very much from half the number of days in these months.

Undoubtedly embarrassed and goaded by public pressure, the Selective Service revised its procedures for the 1971 draft lottery. Two sets of capsules were used—one containing dates and the other containing priority numbers. Mixing machines were employed, and the drawings consisted of simultaneously selecting a capsule from each barrel and matching the respective date and priority number. The randomness of this procedure was beyond reproach.

Other Tests for Randomness

We have only considered a single test for randomness, based upon the *number* of runs. A similar test not described here is based upon the *lengths* of runs. Number-of-runs tests consider only the *sequence* of numbers. In some situations, it is desirable to test for other features, such as the *frequency* of various values or their *serial correlation* (which measures the tendency of certain numbers to be followed by other numbers).

To illustrate the need to consider all these features, examine the problem of testing how suitable it would be to use computer-generated random numbers (which only appear random and are properly called pseudorandom numbers) to select sample units. A number-of-runs test would accept as random the following sequence of digits:

$$1\ 9\ 9\ 9\ 1\ 1\ 1\ 9\ 9\ 1\ 1\ 1\ 9\ 9\ 9\ 9\ 1\ 1\ 1\ 9\ 9$$

Clearly, such a sequence would be inadequate in selecting a random sample. The number-of-runs test does not detect the frequency with which each digit (in this case, zero through 9) occurs. For a list of true random numbers, each digit is expected to occur 10 percent of the time, so that the uniform distribution represents the underlying population of values. Testing procedures (the goodness-of-fit test) exist to determine whether or not the above sequence came from a population having that distribution. Such a test would therefore result in eliminating the particular computer-generation scheme as unsuitable.

A test for serial correlation could be applied to the following sequence

$$2\ 7\ 6\ 9\ 5\ 3\ 2\ 1\ 0\ 7\ 6\ 9\ 5\ 4\ 3\ 8\ 7\ 6\ 4\ 0$$

to detect unrandomlike patterns—that each occurrence of 7 is followed by a 6, for example. Such quirks are ignored by both number-of-runs and goodness-of-fit tests, either of which would lead to accepting the above sequence as being consistent with its respective null hypothesis.

A detailed discussion of the various tests of randomness and how they may be combined as a series is beyond the scope of this book.*

EXERCISES

18-16 The following four sequences of men and women represent the order in which persons of the respective sexes were admitted to various graduate programs. In each case below, there are 10 men and 10 women.

(1) *M W M W W W M M M W M M M W M W M W W M M W*
(2) *M W M M W M W W W M W M M W M W W W M W M W*
(3) *M M M M W W W W W W M M M M M M W W W W W*
(4) *M W W M W M M M W M W M W M W M W M W W M*

(a) Using an $\alpha = .05$ significance level, formulate the appropriate decision rule for testing the null hypothesis that the sexes of the persons admitted were randomly determined for each successive admission. Let R_a represent the number of runs of women.
(b) Applying your decision rule from (a), indicate whether an H_0 of randomness must be accepted or rejected for each sequence.

18-17 A fair coin tossed 16 times produced a total of 8 heads and 8 tails. There is some doubt as to whether these successive tosses were random events. Using the number of head runs as R_a, apply the normal approximation to determine whether H_0 that the tosses were random should be accepted or rejected for each of the following sequences. (Use $\alpha = .05$.)

(a) *H T T T H T T H T T H H H T H H H*
(b) *H H H T T T T H H H H H H T T T T*
(c) *H T H T H T T H H T H T H T H T*
(d) *H H T T H H T T T H H H T H T T*

18-18 The results of the 1971 draft lottery are provided in Table 18-8.
(a) Determine the number of runs of vulnerable dates (those having priority 183 or less).
(b) Remembering that there are only 365 dates, calculate the normal deviate corresponding to your result.
(c) What is the lowest significance level at which the null hypothesis of random selection can be rejected? (Recall that the runs test is two-sided.)

18-19 Toss a coin 30 times, recording whether a head or a tail occurs for each toss. Then test your results for randomness, using the number-of-runs test with the normal approximation. At a significance level of .10, can you reject the null hypothesis that you are a fair coin tosser?

18-20 The successive terms in the expansions of certain constants, such as $\pi = 3.1416\ldots$, have been proposed as substitutes for random numbers. In testing for one property of the numbers obtained in this fashion, a

* For a comprehensive discussion for testing the randomness of number lists, see J. W. Schmidt and R. E. Taylor, *Simulation and Analysis of Industrial Systems* (Homewood, Ill.: Richard D. Irwin, 1970), Chapter 6.

TABLE 18-8   1971 Draft Lottery Results

	January Draft-priority number		February Draft-priority number		March Draft-priority number		April Draft-priority number		May Draft-priority number		June Draft-priority number
Birthday		Birthday		Birthday		Birthday		Birthday		Birthday	
1	133	1	335	1	14	1	224	1	179	1	65
2	195	2	354	2	77	2	216	2	96	2	304
3	336	3	186	3	207	3	297	3	171	3	135
4	99	4	94	4	117	4	37	4	240	4	42
5	33	5	97	5	299	5	124	5	301	5	233
6	285	6	16	6	296	6	312	6	268	6	153
7	159	7	25	7	141	7	142	7	29	7	169
8	116	8	127	8	79	8	267	8	105	8	7
9	53	9	187	9	278	9	223	9	357	9	352
10	101	10	46	10	150	10	165	10	146	10	76
11	144	11	227	11	317	11	178	11	293	11	355
12	152	12	262	12	24	12	89	12	210	12	51
13	330	13	13	13	241	13	143	13	353	13	342
14	71	14	260	14	12	12	202	14	40	14	363
15	75	15	201	15	157	15	182	15	344	15	276
16	136	16	334	16	258	16	31	16	175	16	229
17	54	17	345	17	220	17	264	17	212	17	289
18	185	18	337	18	319	18	138	18	180	18	214
19	188	19	331	19	189	19	62	19	155	19	163
20	211	20	20	20	170	20	118	20	242	20	43
21	129	21	213	21	246	21	8	21	225	21	113
22	132	22	271	22	269	22	256	22	199	22	307
23	48	23	351	23	281	23	292	23	222	23	44
24	177	24	226	24	203	24	244	22	22	24	236
25	57	25	325	25	298	25	328	25	26	25	327
26	140	26	86	26	121	26	137	26	148	26	308
27	173	27	66	27	254	27	235	27	122	27	55
28	346	28	234	28	95	28	82	28	9	28	215
29	277			29	147	29	111	29	61	29	154
30	112			30	56	30	358	30	209	30	217
31	60			31	38			31	350		

	July Draft-priority number		August Draft-priority number		September Draft-priority number		October Draft-priotity number		November Draft-priority number		December Draft-priority number
Birthday		Birthday		Birthday		Birthday		Birthday		Birthday	
1	104	1	326	1	283	1	306	1	243	1	347
2	322	2	102	2	161	2	191	2	205	2	321
3	30	3	279	3	183	3	134	3	294	3	110
4	59	4	300	4	231	4	266	4	39	4	305
5	287	5	64	5	295	5	166	5	286	5	27
6	164	6	251	6	21	6	78	6	245	6	198
7	365	7	263	7	265	7	131	7	72	7	162
8	106	8	49	8	108	8	45	8	119	8	323
9	1	9	125	9	313	9	302	9	176	9	114
10	158	10	359	10	130	10	160	10	63	10	204
11	174	11	230	11	288	11	84	11	123	11	73
12	257	12	320	12	314	12	70	12	255	12	19
13	349	13	58	13	238	13	92	13	272	13	151
14	156	14	103	14	247	14	115	14	11	14	348
15	273	15	270	15	291	15	310	15	362	15	87
16	284	16	329	16	139	16	34	16	197	16	41
17	341	17	343	17	200	17	290	17	6	17	315
18	90	18	109	18	333	18	340	18	280	18	208
19	316	19	83	19	228	19	74	19	252	19	249
20	120	20	69	20	261	20	196	20	98	20	218
21	356	21	50	21	68	21	5	21	35	21	181
22	282	22	250	22	88	22	36	22	253	22	194
23	172	23	10	23	206	23	339	23	193	23	219
24	360	24	274	24	237	24	149	24	81	24	2
25	3	25	364	25	107	25	17	25	23	25	361
26	47	26	91	26	93	26	184	26	52	26	80
27	85	27	232	27	338	27	318	27	168	27	239
28	190	28	248	28	309	28	28	28	324	28	128
29	4	29	32	29	303	29	259	29	100	29	145
30	15	30	167	30	18	30	332	30	67	30	192
31	221	31	275			31	311			31	126

SOURCE: *U.S. News & World Report*, July 13, 1970, p. 27. Reprinted from *U.S. News & World Report*. Copyright 1969 U.S. News & World Report, Inc.

statistician's resultant data were 45 successive four-digit numbers 5,000 or above (*a*) and 55 numbers below 5,000 (*b*). Testing the null hypothesis of randomness (or, more correctly, the appearance of randomness) at the $\alpha = .05$ significance level, he found $R_a = 26$. What must the statistician conclude regarding the "randomness" of successive terms in the π expansion?

18-21 Before random number tables were constructed, a group of British statisticians used the London telephone directory to select random samples. You are to determine whether your local directory can be used for this purpose.
(a) Select a page from the telephone directory and determine the number of runs of even last digits of the telephone numbers. Using the normal approximation, can you conclude that the sequence of odd and even last digits is not random at a significance level of .01?
(b) Regardless of your results in (a), do you think that telephone numbers would be suitable random numbers? Discuss.

18-7   THE RANK CORRELATION COEFFICIENT

In Chapter 10, the sample correlation coefficient r was introduced as an index measuring the degree of association between two variables X and Y. Nonparametric statistics can be employed to provide alternative measures of correlation. One such statistic is the *Spearman rank correlation coefficient:*

$$r_s = 1 - \frac{6 \sum (X - Y)^2}{n(n^2 - 1)} \tag{18-7}$$

where X and Y are the *ranks* of the two variables measured.

The rank correlation coefficient was derived directly from the conventional correlation coefficient [as calculated in expression (10-28), page 359], except that ranks are used for X and Y instead of the observation values themselves. The fact that the sums of the ranks and their squares and the rank means are automatically known for each sample size n (for example, when $n = 5$, $\sum X = 1 + 2 + 3 + 4 + 5 = 15$ and $\bar{X} = 15/5 = 3$, always) permits us to use the equivalent and simpler calculation in expression (18-7).

To illustrate the rank correlation coefficient, consider the data in Table 18-9. Here, observations have been made of the average number of weekly hours a sample of $n = 10$ university students spent studying and their grade-point averages for the term.

Beginning with 1 for the lowest value, the observations for each variable in Table 18-9 were ranked. *Tying observations were given the average of the successive ranks that would have been assigned had the values been different.* Thus, the two figures of 17 study hours were both equally ranked as $(2 + 3)/2 = 2.5$, and each of the two GPAs of 3.6 received a rank of $(7 + 8)/2 = 7.5$.

The differences in ranks were determined and their squares were calculated. The sum of the squared rank differences is $\sum (X - Y)^2 = 9.00$. The rank

TABLE 18-9   Rank Correlation Calculations for Study Hours and GPA

Variables		Ranks			
Study Hours	GPA	For Study Hours X	For GPA Y	Rank Difference X − Y	(X − Y)²
24	3.6	6	7.5	−1.5	2.25
17	2.0	2.5	1	1.5	2.25
20	2.7	4	4	0.0	0.00
41	3.6	8	7.5	.5	.25
52	3.7	10	9	1.0	1.00
23	3.1	5	5	0.0	0.00
46	3.8	9	10	−1.0	1.00
17	2.5	2.5	3	− .5	.25
15	2.1	1	2	−1.0	1.00
29	3.3	7	6	1.0	1.00
				0.0	9.00

correlation coefficient between average weekly study hours and GPA is

$$r_s = 1 - \frac{6(9.00)}{10(10^2 - 1)} = 1 - \frac{54}{990} = .946$$

This indicates a high correlation between study time and grades.

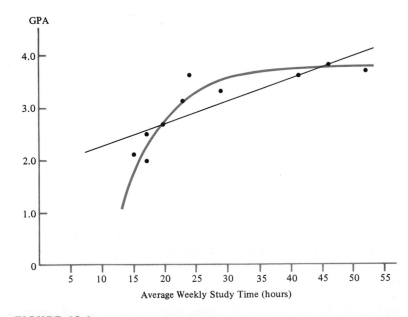

FIGURE 18-1   Illustration of inadequacy of conventional correlation coefficient when data are curvilinear.

Usefulness of Rank Correlation

The rank correlation coefficient is useful in many situations where the conventional correlation coefficient is not suitable. Recall from Chapter 10 that the conventional r is based upon the assumption that the underlying relationship is linear. Consider the study time and GPA data in Table 18-9 when they are plotted in Figure 18-1. The graph shows a pronounced curvilinear relationship between these variables, summarized by the colored curve. Here, GPA increases with study time, but each additional hour of study time produces a progressively smaller improvement in grades. A least squares regression would fit the black line to the sample data, and the conventional correlation coefficient (through the coefficient of determination r^2) would express the proportion of variation in GPA explained by this line. Obviously, the regression line poorly fits the data here, as confirmed by the much lower conventional correlation value of $r = .58$ obtained.

EXERCISES

18-22   The following daily data were obtained for a sample of $n = 10$ smokers who drink coffee:

Packs Smoked	Cups Drunk
.5	3
1.0	4
.5	5
1.5	6
2.0	4
2.5	6
1.0	3
.5	2
1.5	7
2.0	5

Calculate the rank correlation coefficient.

18-23   Referring to Exercise 10-19 on page 363, determine the rank correlation coefficient for the productivity indices.

18-24   Referring to Exercise 10-23 on page 366, calculate the rank correlation coefficient for turnover and earnings.

18-8   ONE-FACTOR ANALYSIS OF VARIANCE: THE KRUSKAL-WALLIS TEST

Alternative to the *F* Test

In Chapter 16, we presented a testing procedure for determining whether differences exist among several means, using the F test to perform analysis of variance. A very serious drawback to the *F* test is that it requires the populations to be normal. As noted in our preceding discussion of nonparametric tests, this assumption may invalidate the testing procedure.

An alternative to the *F* test is the Kruskal-Wallis one-factor analysis of variance, named after W. H. Kruskal and W. A. Wallis, who introduced it in 1952. It is really an extension of the Wilcoxon rank-sum test to the analysis of several samples.

Description of the Test

Underlying Principle

The primary difference from the *F* test is that the Kruskal-Wallis test is based upon a test statistic computed from ranks determined for pooled sample observations. Its null hypothesis is that the rank assigned to a particular observation has an equal chance of being any number between 1 and *n*, regardless of the sample group to which it belongs. We will illustrate this procedure with the following detailed example.

A college computer instructor wishes to determine if there is really any difference in programming aptitudes between students in different majors. The students in his college can be classified into four major groups: science, liberal arts, business, and engineering. He selected a random sample of students in each category and administered a computer programming aptitude test to them. Their scores and score ranks appear in Table 18-10. (Although no ties were found for these data, ranks are only averaged when tying observations occur between two or more sample groups.)

TABLE 18-10   Test Scores and Ranks for Computer Programming by Major

(1) Science		(2) Liberal Arts		(3) Business		(4) Engineering	
Score	Rank	Score	Rank	Score	Rank	Score	Rank
85	12	95	19	67	3	90	15
73	7	54	1	74	8	65	2
96	20	72	6	84	11	92	17
91	16	81	10	68	4	94	18
88	14	69	5	87	13		
				77	9		

$$T_1 = 69 \qquad T_2 = 41 \qquad T_3 = 48 \qquad T_4 = 52$$
$$T_1^2 = 4{,}761 \qquad T_2^2 = 1{,}681 \qquad T_3^2 = 2{,}304 \qquad T_4^2 = 2{,}704$$
$$n_1 = 5 \qquad n_2 = 5 \qquad n_3 = 6 \qquad n_4 = 4$$
$$\frac{T_1^2}{n_1} = 952.2 \qquad \frac{T_2^2}{n_2} = 336.2 \qquad \frac{T_3^2}{n_3} = 384.0 \qquad \frac{T_4^2}{n_4} = 676.0$$

Score:	54	65	67	68	69	72	73	74	77	81	84	85	87	88	90	91	92	94	95	96
Rank:	1	2	3	4	5	6	7	8	9	10	11	12	13	14	15	16	17	18	19	20

At a significance level of $\alpha = .05$, the instructor wishes to test the null hypothesis

H_0:   There are no programming aptitude differences between major groups.

The alternative hypothesis is that college major makes a difference in aptitude.

As with the Wilcoxon tests, the null hypothesis implies that the four sample groups are obtained from the same population. Under the null hypothesis, therefore, each score in Table 18-10 has the same prior probability of receiving any rank of 1 through 20.

Test Statistic

For our test statistic, we choose to compare variabilities of the ranks in each column. As we saw with the F test, the sum of squares may be used for this purpose. For convenience in obtaining a meaningful statistic, the sum of squares is not directly calculated. Instead, the sum of ranks for each category T_j is computed. A sum of the squares of these sums, each term weighted by the reciprocal of the sample size n_j of the jth group, is obtained. The following calculation provides the *Kruskal-Wallis test statistic:*

$$K = \frac{12}{n(n+1)}\left(\sum \frac{T_j^2}{n_j}\right) - 3(n+1) \tag{18-8}$$

where $n - \sum n_j$.

The sampling distribution of K is approximately chi-square with $m-1$ degrees of freedom, where m is the number of categories. Thus, in order to find the critical value, we use Appendix Table H, which provides critical values for specified tail areas.

In our example, $m = 4$, so there are $m-1 = 4-1 - 3$ degrees of freedom. Letting $\alpha = .05$, our critical value found from the chi-square table is $\chi^2_{.05} = 7.815$. Our decision rule is therefore

Accept H_0 (conclude major makes no difference) if $K \leqslant 7.815$

Reject H_0 (conclude major makes a difference)   if $K > 7.815$

Substituting the values from Table 18-10 into expression (18-8), we calculate K, using $n = 20$:

$$K = \frac{12}{20(20+1)}(952.2 + 336.2 + 384.0 + 676.0) - 3(20+1)$$

$$= 4.097$$

Since K is smaller than $\chi^2_{.05}$, *we must accept the null hypothesis that there are no differences.*

EXERCISES

18-25 A chemical engineer wishes to know whether the mean time required to complete a chemical reaction is affected by the proportion of impurities present. Samples of reactions have been conducted with several different proportions of impurities. The reaction times obtained are provided below:

Proportion of Impurities

.001	.01	.05	.10
Reaction Times (minutes)			
103	104	153	207
111	113	127	183
107	117	143	173
105	120	119	
	113	138	
		143	

(a) Rank the sample results.

(b) Calculate the test statistic K.

(c) How many degrees of freedom are associated with this test statistic?

(d) Using a significance level of $\alpha = .05$, can the null hypothesis that the proportion of impurities does not affect the reaction times be rejected?

18-26 Referring to the sod-yield data in Table 16-1 on page 525, apply the Kruskal-Wallis test to the null hypothesis that mean yields are identical under all fertilizer treatments. (Use $\alpha = .05$.) What conclusion should be made?

18-27 An insurance company wishes to determine if there is any difference due to the type of profession in the mean amount of whole life insurance held by its professional policyholders. A random sample of policyholders is selected for a thorough study. The results obtained are:

Insurance Coverage

Physicians	Lawyers	Dentists
$200,000	$ 50,000	$ 80,000
150,000	100,000	45,000
40,000	95,000	155,000
35,000	10,000	325,000
110,000	300,000	
	75,000	

Determine whether the null hypothesis of no difference must be accepted or rejected at a .05 significance level.

REVIEW EXERCISES

18-28 In testing the null hypothesis that drug *A* yields relief from sinus headaches for at least as long as drug *B*, a statistician selects two independent samples of 30 sinus sufferers each and asks a physician to administer drug

A to one group and drug *B* to the other. The number of pills taken over a fixed time period is used to compute each sufferer's mean relief duration score. In ranking the scores of the two groups, he found that $W = 826$. Should H_0 be accepted or rejected at the $\alpha = .05$ significance level?

18-29 Suppose that the statistician grouped the patients in Exercise 18-28 into 30 pairs, matched on the basis of medical history, age, sex, and life style. Also, assume that exactly the same individuals received the respective drugs. (*Note:* We would never use both the Wilcoxon rank-sum test and the sign test for matched pairs on the same data. This is an illustration only of how results may vary between the two tests.) The difference in relief duration for each pair was found by subtracting the mean time of the drug *B* patient from the corresponding figure of his partner. A total of $R = 5$ positive differences resulted, and there were 5 ties. Should H_0 be accepted or rejected at the $\alpha = .05$ significance level?

18-30 Repeat Exercise 18-29, applying the Wilcoxon signed-rank test when the sample data provide $V = 30$.

18-31 Referring to the data in Exercise 16-5 on page 537, apply the Kruskal-Wallis test to determine whether the dissolving time of aspirin tablets differs with the level of impurities. (Use $\alpha = .01$.)

18-32 Referring to the data in Exercise 10-5 on page 337, calculate the rank correlation coefficient.

18-33 A statistics professor asked his students to use their judgment in constructing their own random number lists from scratch. The purpose of the experiment was to demonstrate how faulty this procedure can be. One student obtained the following list. Proceeding down one column at a time, determine the number of runs of small values (0 through 4) and then determine whether the null hypothesis of randomness should be accepted or rejected. (Use $\alpha = .05$.)

4	6	9	9	0
8	1	2	3	6
3	9	8	8	2
7	2	3	2	3
9	4	7	7	4
0	8	1	5	8
2	7	7	1	5
1	6	3	7	3
8	0	4	0	8
5	3	6	5	0

OPTIONAL TOPIC:
18-9 TESTING FOR GOODNESS OF FIT—
THE KOLMOGOROV-SMIRNOV ONE-SAMPLE TEST

An Alternative to the Chi-Square Test

In Chapter 17, the chi-square test was introduced as a procedure for inferring whether a sample is obtained from a population having a particular distribution. As a test for goodness of fit, the chi-square test has some serious limitations. The most significant of these is the requirement for a large sample. Recall that a rule for using the chi-square distribution is that each class interval must have an expected frequency of at least 5. Unless n is quite large, only the most frequent class intervals will retain their data; the less frequent class intervals must be combined before computing χ^2 and, in doing this, information is lost. When a very tiny sample is all that is available, the chi-square test cannot be used at all.

An alternative goodness-of-fit test is the *Kolmogorov-Smirnov one-sample test*, named after A. Kolmogorov and N. V. Smirnov, two Russian mathematicians who provided the theoretical foundations upon which this test rests. The test approaches the problem by comparing the observed cumulative frequency distribution of the sample to that expected from the population specified by the null hypothesis. The test statistic obtained is the maximum deviation between the observed and the expected distributions.

Description of the Test

The Kolmogorov-Smirnov test will be developed from the following example.

In order to simulate a new scheduling policy, Ace Airlines wishes to determine whether the take-off delay times at El Paso are normally distributed. Only one percent of the biweekly El Paso departures have resulted in unpredictable delays. Thus, over a ten-year period, only 11 delays have occurred. The durations are provided in Table 18-11. From studies of other airports, Ace has judged that delays at El Paso should have a mean of 3 hours with a standard deviation of 1 hour. The following null hypothesis is therefore formulated:

H_0: The aircraft take-off delays are normal with $\mu = 3$ hours and $\sigma = 1$ hour

The alternative hypothesis is that some other distribution describes the population.

TABLE 18-11   Durations of Aircraft
Take-off Delays at El Paso

Duration (hours) X	X^2
2.1	4.41
1.9	3.61
3.2	10.24
2.8	7.84
1.0	1.00
5.1	26.01
.9	.81
4.2	17.64
3.9	15.21
3.6	12.96
2.7	7.29
31.4	107.02

The Test Statistic

To find the value of the test statistic, we first establish the cumulative *relative* frequency distribution obtained for our sample results. This is shown in Table 18-12. Since the frequencies are relative, each sample value occurs with a frequency of $1/11 = .0909$. The observations are not grouped in the usual manner. Instead, the durations obtained are listed in column (1) of Table 18-12 in increasing order of size. The cumulative frequencies in column (2) are obtained by adding the relative frequencies. Thus, .1818 is the frequency of durations of 1.0 hour or less (obtained by adding together the .0909 frequencies for .9 and 1.0 hours) and .6363 is the frequency of delays of 3.2 hours or less. We denote the actual frequency of values less than or equal to x by $F_a(x)$.

TABLE 18-12   Actual Observed and Theoretical Expected Cumulative Frequencies for Take-off Delay Durations with Calculations of Test Statistic

(1) Duration of Delays (in hours) from Sample x	(2) Actual Observed Cumulative Frequency of Durations $\leqslant x$ $F_a(x)$	(3) $z = \dfrac{x-\mu}{\sigma}$	(4) Expected Cumulative Frequency of Durations $\leqslant x$ $F_e(x)$	(5) Deviation $F_a(x)-F_e(x)$
.9	.0909	-2.1	.0179	.0730
1.0	.1818	-2.0	.0228	.1590
1.9	.2727	-1.1	.1357	.1370
2.1	.3636	$-.9$	.1841	.1795
2.7	.4545	$-.3$	.3821	.0724
2.8	.5454	$-.2$	.4207	.1247
3.2	.6363	.2	.5793	.0570
3.6	.7272	.6	.7257	.0015
3.9	.8181	.9	.8159	.0022
4.2	.9090	1.2	.8849	.0241
5.1	.9999	2.1	.9821	.0178

$$D = \max |F_a(x) - F_e(x)| = .1795$$

The expected frequencies under the null hypothesis, denoted by $F_e(x)$, must coincide with the normal curve for $\mu = 3$ and $\sigma = 1$. In column (3) of Table 18-12, the normal deviates z are calculated for each value of x. The cumulative frequencies in column (4) are readily obtainable from Appendix Table D. For the negative values of z, the lower-tail areas corresponding to cumulative frequencies may be obtained by subtracting the area in Appendix Table D from .5. Thus, when $x = 1.9$, $z = -1.1$, and Table D provides the area .3643, so that the expected frequency is

$$F_e(1.9) = .5 - .3643 = .1357$$

For positive z values, Table D provides areas between the mean and z standard deviations. These must be added to .5 to provide the cumulative frequencies.

Thus, when $x = 4.2$, $z = 1.2$, so Table D provides the area .3849. The cumulative frequency is therefore $F_e(4.2) = .5 + .3849 = .8849$.

The deviation between the actual and expected frequencies is calculated in column (5) of Table 18-12 for each duration. Large deviations indicate poorness of fit of the actual to the expected values. This type of comparison is illustrated in Figure 18-2, where the two cumulative frequency distributions are plotted on the same graph. The actual frequencies lie above the expected ones for all values of x obtained from the sample. The vertical distance between the two curves indicates the magnitude of the deviations. The largest deviation occurs at $x = 2.1$, where

$$F_a(2.1) - F_e(2.1) = .1795$$

We will use this as our test statistic, denoting it by D. In general, the following expression provides the *Kolmogorov-Smirnov statistic:*

$$D = \max \ |F_a(x) - F_e(x)| \qquad (18\text{-}9)$$

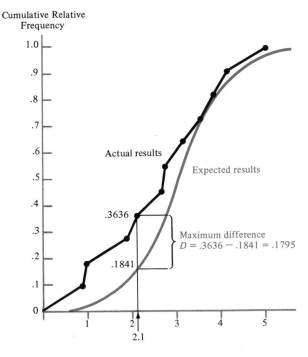

FIGURE 18-2   Actual and expected cumulative frequency distributions of El Paso take-off delays.

Note that we are interested only in absolute values; that is, the sign of the difference is unimportant, so that negative differences are treated like positive ones. Our test statistic, D, is the maximum frequency deviation.

Finding the Decision Rule and the Critical Value
The form of the decision rule is

> *Accept* H_0 (conclude normal distribution applies)   if $D \leqslant D_\alpha$
>
> *Reject* H_0 (conclude some other distribution applies) if $D > D_\alpha$

Large deviations tend to refute the null hypothesis. We will denote the critical value D_α, where α is the significance level or probability of rejecting a true null hypothesis. To find the value of D_α, we must first find the sampling distribution of our test statistic D.

Because the sampling distribution of D is very complex to describe and quite mathematical in nature, we will not describe its properties here. Instead, we will employ Appendix Table L in order to find the critical values of D. This table provides critical values D_α for several significance levels α and *sample sizes n*. (Unlike the chi-square test, these tabulated values depend upon the entire sample size and not upon the number of sample groups.) Thus, we can find D_α such that

$$P[D \geqslant D_\alpha] = \alpha$$

For example, suppose that we wish to see whether the sample results are significant at $\alpha = .05$. We obtained $D = .1795$ in Table 18-12 with a sample size of $n = 11$. From Appendix Table L, we obtain as our critical value the entry in the row for $n = 11$ and the column for $\alpha = .05$, or $D_{.05} = .35242$. Since this value is greater than D, *the null hypothesis is accepted*. In fact, setting α as high as .10 leads to the same conclusion. The sample of take-off delays appears to be quite consistent with the null hypothesis of normality.

Investigating the Type II Error
It is interesting to note that in accepting the null hypothesis, there is a high likelihood of making a Type II error. Suppose that instead we chose a uniform distribution between .5 and 5.5 hours as our null hypothesis. Table 18-13 shows the calculation we would obtain from this distribution. The $F_e(x)$ values are obtained by calculating the proportion of the distance between .5 and 5.5 represented by the corresponding value for x.

Although here $D = .1690$, our sample could reasonably be expected to have come from a uniform distribution. We have no basis for choosing between the normal and the uniform distributions. All we can say is that *there is no significant evidence to reject either*. Using a larger sample size is the only recourse we have for avoiding the Type II error.

TABLE 18-13   Calculation of the Test Statistic for
Uniform Distribution Hypothesis

(1) *Duration of* *Delays (in hours)* *Obtained from* *Sample* *x*	(2) $F_a(x)$	(3) $F_e(x)$	(4) $F_a(x) - F_e(x)$
.9	.0909	.0800	.0109
1.0	.1818	.1000	.0818
1.9	.2727	.2800	−.0073
2.1	.3636	.3200	.0436
2.7	.4545	.4400	.0145
2.8	.5454	.4600	.0854
3.2	.6363	.5400	.0963
3.6	.7272	.6200	.1072
3.9	.8181	.6800	.1381
4.2	.9090	.7400	.1690
5.1	.9999	.9200	−.0799

$$D = \max |F_a(x) - F_e(x)| = .1690$$

Comparison with the Chi-Square Test

Comparisons have been made of the relative efficiencies of the χ^2 and Kolmogorov-Smirnov tests. The latter has been established to be more powerful for small samples; that is, for a fixed sample size, the Kolmogorov-Smirnov test provides a higher probability of rejecting a false null hypothesis.

A major disadvantage of the Kolmogorov-Smirnov test is that it does not allow us to estimate any of the population parameters from the sample data. *The population parameters must be specified in advance of testing.* Thus, in our example, we could not use $\overline{X}$ and s as estimates of μ and σ. (Had this been allowed, then the fit would have been even closer.) The χ^2 test allows us to do this—at the price of a reduced number of degrees of freedom.

OPTIONAL EXERCISES

18-34   A postmaster wishes to establish whether the Friday lunchtime arrivals at a new branch post-office follow a Poisson distribution. From previous tests, he has estimated that the mean arrival rate is 2 customers per minute. A sample of the arrivals in 100 random one-minute time segments has been collected over a two-month period. The results obtained and the expected sample frequencies appear below:

	Actual Observed Results			*Expected Sample Results*	
Number of Arrivals	*Actual Frequency*	*Relative Frequency*		*Number of Arrivals*	*Relative Frequency*
0	8	.08		0	.1353
1	19	.19		1	.2707
2	28	.28		2	.2707
3	24	.24		3	.1804
4	14	.14		4	.0902
5	2	.02		5	.0361
6	3	.03		6	.0120
7	1	.01		7	.0034
8	0	.00		8	.0009
9	1	.01		9	.0002
					.9999

(a) Determine the cumulative relative frequencies for the actual and expected results.

(b) Calculate the maximum deviation D.

(c) What is the lowest significance level at which the null hypothesis of a Poisson distribution with $\lambda = 2$ can be rejected?

(d) Calculate the χ^2 statistic for this test. (Remember that χ^2 is based upon true frequencies instead of relative ones. Also recall that the low frequencies must be grouped.)

(e) What is the lowest significance level at which the null hypothesis may be rejected using the χ^2 test?

(f) In this example, which test do you believe is more discriminating: the χ^2 or the Kolmogorov-Smirnov? Explain.

18-35 Suppose that the postmaster in Exercise 18-34 estimated instead that 2.5 arrivals per minute apply. The following expected relative frequencies should be used:

Number of Arrivals	*Relative Frequency*
0	.0821
1	.2052
2	.2565
3	.2138
4	.1336
5	.0668
6	.0278
7	.0099
8	.0031
9	.0009
10	.0002
	.9999

(a) Determine the cumulative relative frequencies for the actual and the expected results.

(b) Calculate the maximum deviation D.

(c) Can the postmaster reject the null hypothesis that the arrivals are Poisson at a significance level of $\alpha = .10$?

18-36 Referring to the data in Exercise 17-23 (page 599), apply the Kolmogorov-Smirnov test at the $\alpha = .10$ significance level to determine whether or not the sample data are consistent with the indicated normal distribution.

Chapter Nineteen
Basic Concepts of Decision Theory

There is no more miserable human being than one in whom nothing is habitual but indecision.

William James

Modern analysis of decision making under uncertainty has its roots in the area of study called *statistical decision theory*. Although most major developments in this field have occurred during the last fifty years, many contributions were made more than two hundred years ago by the same pioneer mathematicians who formulated the theory of probability. In addition to probability, decision theory contains elements of statistics, economics, and psychology.

The central focus of this book is on the use of statistical procedures in decision making. This chapter considers the structural properties of decisions in general. We make a basic distinction between decision making under certainty, where no elements are left to chance, and decision making under uncertainty, where one or more random factors affect a choice's outcome.

We begin our discussion of decision theory by considering an underlying structural framework. This is followed by a presentation of the main decision-making criterion—the Bayes decision rule—which is based upon expected values.

Our picture of decision theory is enriched through consideration of several other criteria. For various reasons, we shall see that the Bayes decision rule, which chooses the act that has the best expected payoff, is the favored criterion. Decision-theoretical concepts largely expand on this rule, since it is the only one that uses all the information at the disposal of the decision maker. When the proper payoff measure is used, the Bayes decision rule always leads to the most desirable choice. The device making this possible is the utility payoff, which measures a decision-maker's preference; utility theory is a special field within the broader context of decision theory.

This chapter surveys decision theory. In the remaining chapters we will consider special topics. Chapter 20 discusses how experimental information may be systematically incorporated into decision making. Chapter 21 describes utility theory and provides the details for obtaining and using utility values. Much of Chapter 21 is devoted to the practical problems of obtaining and using subjective probabilities.

19-1 CERTAINTY AND UNCERTAINTY IN DECISION MAKING

The least complex applications of decision theory are found in *decision making under certainty*. Perhaps the simplest decision of this sort is selecting what clothes to wear; although the possible combinations of various items of attire may be numerous, we all manage to quickly make our choices with little bother. But not all decisions are this easy—remember your childhood and how hard it was to choose from among an assortment of candy bars. Nor are all decisions under certainty as trivial as choosing the day's apparel.

When the outcomes are only partly determined by the decision-maker's choice, so that the result is affected also by random factors, a decision takes on added complexity. We must somehow cope with the unpredictability resulting from our choices. To set the stage in structuring a decision under uncertainty, consider the choice of whether to carry an umbrella or some other rain protection throughout the day. Here we are faced with two alternatives: carrying an ungainly item that can, in the event of rain, help to defer a cleaning bill or a cough, versus challenging the elements with hands free, hoping not to be caught in the rain. Lack of human skill at accurate weather prediction causes us to be uncertain whether it will rain. Yet faced with the daily needs of life we must make our decision in spite of our uncertainty. This illustrates a common *decision under uncertainty*: a choice of action must be made even though its outcome is unknown and determined by chance.*

---

* This class of decisions has often been divided into categories—decision making under *risk*, where outcome probabilities are known, and under *uncertainty*, where these probabilities are unknown. We make no such distinction and assume that probabilities may always be found somehow—either objectively through long-run frequency, or subjectively.

19-2   STRUCTURING DECISIONS INVOLVING UNCERTAINTY

We will now present a framework within which we may explain how and why particular choices are made. Our decisions in coping with weather illustrate the essential features of all decisions under uncertainty. We choose the umbrella when the chance of rain seems uncomfortably high, whereas we do without it when rain is unlikely. But two people occasionally make different choices. Is there a correct decision? If so, how do we explain that two persons do not always make the same choice? We can begin to answer these questions by identifying several key elements common to all such decisions and then structuring them in a convenient form for analysis.

Elements of Decisions

Every decision problem under certainty exhibits two elements: *acts* and *outcomes*. The decision-maker's choices are the acts. For example, in the choice among three television programs in the 9 PM time slot, each program represents a potential act. The outcomes may be characterized in terms of the enjoyment we might derive from each of the various programs.

If the decision is made under uncertainty, a third element exists. This involves *events*. Continuing with the rain uncertainty illustration, the acts are "carry an umbrella" and "leave the umbrella home." All decisions involve selection of an act. But the outcomes resulting from each act are uncertain, because *an outcome is determined partly by choice and partly by chance*. For the act "carry an umbrella" there are two possible outcomes: (1) unnecessarily carting rain paraphernalia and (2) weathering a shower fully protected. The other act, "leave the umbrella at home," has either of the outcomes: (1) getting unnecessarily wet and (2) remaining dry and unencumbered. Again, whether the first or second happens depends only on the occurrence of rain. The outcome for any particular chosen act is dependent on which *event*, rain or no rain, occurs.

Decision Table

To facilitate analysis, a decision problem may be summarized by a *decision table*, which indicates the relationship between pairs of decision elements. The decision table for the umbrella illustration is provided in Table 19-1. Each row corresponds to an event; each column corresponds to an act. The outcomes appear as entries in the body of the table. Each event–act combination has a specific outcome, reflecting the fact that it is the interplay between act and event that determines the ultimate result.

The acts included in the decision table are only those the decision maker wishes to consider. In the above illustration, staying home is another possible

TABLE 19-1   Decision Table for the Umbrella Decision

	Act	
Event	*Carry Umbrella*	*Leave Umbrella Home*
Rain	Stay dry	Get wet
No Rain	Carry unnecessary burden	Be dry and free

act, which we exclude because it is not contemplated. The acts are mutually exclusive and collectively exhaustive, so that exactly one will be chosen. The events are also mutually exclusive and collectively exhaustive. A more elaborate decision structure might consider events for various amounts or durations of rain. Then each amount or duration event considered would have two outcomes, one for each of the two acts.

Decision Tree Diagram

A decision problem can also be conveniently illustrated with a *decision tree diagram* like that shown in Figure 19-1. This portrayal proves especially convenient for decision problems with choices that must be made at different times over an extended duration. It is similar to the probability tree diagrams used previously. The choice of acts is shown as a fork with a separate branch for each

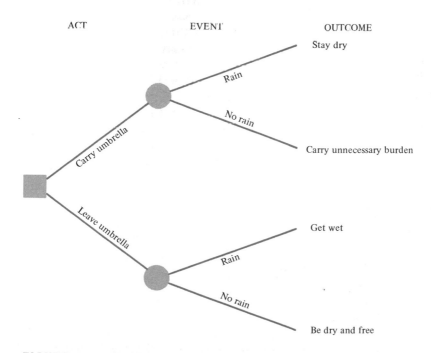

FIGURE 19-1   Decision tree diagrams for the umbrella illustration.

act. The events are also represented by branches in separate forks. Because decision tree diagrams can be quite elaborate, we must distinguish act forks from event forks; to do so we use squares for act-fork nodes and circles for event-fork nodes. A basic guideline for constructing such a diagram is that the flow should be chronological from left to right. The acts are shown on the initial fork, because the decision must be made *before* the actual event is known. The events are thus shown as branches in the second-stage forks. The outcome resulting from an event–act combination is shown as the end position of the corresponding path from the base of the tree.

Ranking the Alternatives and the Payoff Table

In this chapter we shall concern ourselves with how the choice of act should be determined. Everyone who has faced the problem of coping with rain has managed to make an umbrella decision. But we wish to analyze the decision-making process in order that better decisions can be made. In doing this, we focus on two measures: one for *uncertainty* and one for the comparative worth or *payoff* of the outcomes to the decision maker. These two key elements are interwoven into the fabric of decision theory.

For now we will consider examples with outcomes that have obvious associated numerical values as payoffs. These payoffs may be dollars, expressing profits, costs, or assets, or some other numerical value. Every outcome—that is, every event–act combination—will have a payoff value. Since the payoffs actually received after having chosen a particular act are conditional on whichever event happens, they are sometimes referred to as *conditional values*. These values may be conveniently arranged in a *payoff table*, as indicated in Table 19-2 for the gambling decision. This arrangement is also called a *conditional value table*. The decision is to choose one of two acts, gamble or don't gamble. Regardless of the choice made, a coin will be tossed with two possible events: head or tail. The possible outcomes correspond to the four event–act combinations. A wager of $1 will be made if the decision maker gambles. Viewing net winnings as a payoff measure, $1 represents the result if a head occurs when the act to gamble is chosen. Likewise, the payoff is −$1 when a tail results. If the player chooses to not gamble, there is no wager, so the payoff will be the same regardless of the coin toss results: $0 in either case.

TABLE 19-2   Payoff Table for the Decision
Whether or Not to Gamble

Event	Act	
	Gamble	*Don't Gamble*
Head	$1	$0
Tail	−$1	$0

Objectives and Payoff Values

In determining payoffs to be assigned to outcomes we shall assume that the decision maker wishes to select a course of action that will bring him closest to some objective. We shall suppose that each decision outcome may somehow be ranked in terms of how close it brings the decision maker to his goal. If the decision maker selects as a payoff some measure expressing the degree of goal attainment, then the payoff table will provide a meaningful basis for comparison, thus enhancing the decision-maker's ability to make a good choice.

For example, if a business decision-maker's goal is to achieve a high level of profits, then a natural payoff for each outcome would be its profit. But profit is a valid measure for a limited set of objectives. It is by no means the top concern of all business managers. The founder of a successful corporation may have a goal of maintaining personal control, possibly consciously keeping profits low to avoid having the firm look too attractive to another merger-minded entrepreneur.

Viewed in a more general context, decision making may have many different kinds of goals, each requiring a distinct payoff measure. Consider the following illustrations.

When the United States made its World War II decision to develop the atomic bomb, three different technologies could have been pursued. Had the goal been to select the technology that minimized cost, then only the one believed least costly would have been chosen. Instead, the goal was to develop an operational bomb before the Germans did; thus, the overriding objective was a quick attainment of nuclear-weapons capability. The course of action chosen was to develop all three technologies simultaneously: the most expensive alternative, but also the fastest. *Time savings* was the payoff measure used.

In selecting alternative designs for manned spacecraft, NASA has demonstrated the importance of safety. Thus, *systems reliability* is a more valid measure to use for payoff than time or cost would be. The latter were extremely important in the race to the moon, but they served more as constraints on the number of alternative system designs, rather than as measures of goal attainment, especially following the Apollo disaster in 1967.

In designing defensive military systems, the objective is to maximize survivability in the face of a host of enemy threats. A commonly used payoff for ranking alternatives is the *probability of damage* resulting from an attack. Here too, although time and cost are important, they are often secondary considerations.

Decision makers with different goals may select unlike measures for payoffs when they each consider the same set of alternatives. As the following example shows, the best choice for each may be a different course of action.

Example 19-1 Charles Snyder, Herman Brown, and Sylvia Gold want to choose from among three routes from Los Angeles to San Francisco. The routes are: (1) Interstate No. 5, which is a freeway nearly all the way and has a high minimum speed limit; (2) State Highways 118 and 33, which are fairly direct and have no minimum speed limit; and (3) State Highway 1, which winds along the Pacific coast and is slow and long but very beautiful. Mr. Snyder is a salesman who travels to San Francisco regularly; his goal is to reach his destination as quickly as possible. Mr. Brown is an economy "nut"; he wants to reach San Francisco as cheaply as possible. Ms. Gold is on vacation and loves to drive on hilly, winding, scenic roads; she wishes to select the route yielding the greatest driving pleasure.

Table 19-3 provides the payoffs that each person would assign to the three routes. Mr. Snyder uses time savings, in comparison to the slowest route, as his payoff measure. Thus, he chooses Interstate 5, which yields the greatest payoff of 4 hours. Mr. Brown likes to drive at a moderate speed that provides maximum gasoline mileage, while taking as short a route as possible. His payoff measure is gasoline savings (based on the amount of gasoline required on the most expensive route), so that he chooses the back roads, State Highways 118 and 33, where he saves 7 gallons. Ms. Gold has rated the routes in terms of points of interest, type of scenery, and number of hills and curves. This rating serves as her payoff measure, so that for her the best route is scenic State Highway 1, which rates 10.

TABLE 19-3   Payoffs for the Alternative Routes Relevant to the Goals of Three Decision Makers

	Payoff Measure		
	Mr. Snyder	*Mr. Brown*	*Ms. Gold*
Alternative Route	*Time Savings (hours)*	*Fuel Savings (gallons)*	*Enjoyment (subjective rating)*
Interstate 5	4	3	1
Highways 118 & 33	3	7	3
Highway 1	0	0	10

We may conclude that *the selection of a payoff measure should be made so that the payoff will rank outcomes by the degree to which they attain a decision-maker's goals.* It is the goal that dictates which measures are valid. A disturbing feature of many decision problems is that there may be no obvious payoff measure with which to rank outcomes, when their effects are subjective. We will directly confront this problem by means of utility theory in Chapter 21. Utilities are values that correspond to a decision-maker's preferences for the outcomes.

Tippi-Toes: A Case Illustration

As a detailed example of a business decision under uncertainty, we consider a hypothetical toy manufacturer who must choose among four prototype designs for Tippi-Toes, a dancing ballerina doll that does pirouettes and bourrées. Each prototype represents a different technology for the moving parts, all powered by small electric motors using batteries. One is a complete arrangement of gears and levers. The second is similar, using springs instead of levers. Another works on the principle of weights and pulleys. The movement of the fourth design is controlled pneumatically through a system of valves that open and close at the command of a small solid-state computer housed in the head cavity. The dolls are identical in all functional aspects.

Tippi-Toes will be sold through distributors, who will be charged an average price of $10. The choice of movement design will depend solely on comparative contributions to profits. Gears and levers will provide the lowest tooling and setup costs, $100,000, but the highest per unit variable cost, $5. Spring action will have slightly higher fixed cost, $160,000, with somewhat lower variable costs, $4 per unit. A computer-controlled pneumatic movement will involve the highest fixed cost, $500,000, and the lowest per unit variable costs, $2. The weights and pulleys will have a fixed cost of $300,000 and variable costs of $3. All other costs are classified as overhead and are identical for each movement type. The demand for Tippi-Toes is uncertain, but management feels that one of the following events will occur:

> Light demand (25,000 units)
> Moderate demand (100,000 units)
> Heavy demand (150,000 units)

Table 19-4 is constructed with payoffs expressed in terms of total contribution to profit and overhead. Our payoffs represent the contributions for the various event–act combinations. For example, if 25,000 dolls are sold and the gears and levers movement is chosen, the total contribution to profit and overhead is computed as follows:

Revenue − Total variable costs − Fixed costs

$$= \$10(25,000) - \$5(25,000) - \$100,000 = \$25,000$$

The payoff entries in Table 19-4 are calculated in this manner.

In this example, the toy manufacturer has considered only three possible levels of demand. This will simplify our analysis. Demand need not be precisely 25,000 or 100,000 units. The problem could be analyzed for several hundred thousand possible levels of demand, say from 0 to 500,000 dolls. The techniques we will develop can be applied to a more detailed probability distribution. Because of the computational requirements, an approximate probability distribution might consider demand to the nearest 100, 1,000, or 10,000 units.

TABLE 19-4   Payoff Table for the Tippi-Toes Decision

	Act (Choice of Movement)			
Event	*Gears and Levers*	*Spring Action*	*Weights and Pulleys*	*Pneumatic*
Light Demand	$ 25,000	−$ 10,000	−$125,000	−$300,000
Moderate Demand	400,000	440,000	400,000	300,000
Heavy Demand	650,000	740,000	750,000	700,000

A continuous distribution having nice mathematical properties might also be used as an approximation to the discrete demand distribution.

Our example has only four alternatives. In the practical business decision-making environment, the number of possible alternatives can be large. For instance, the decision regarding what mix of toys to sell could easily involve trillions of alternatives. *The decision analysis need only include every alternative that the decision maker wishes to consider.* This includes "doing nothing" when there is no compelling reason for choosing one of the alternatives. The search for attractive alternatives is essential to good decision making. However, decision analysis cannot tell us what should and should not be considered, even though it can be useful in guiding our selection.

Reducing the Number of Alternatives: Inadmissible Acts

Regardless of the process we ultimately select for making a choice, an initial screening may be made to determine if there are any acts that will never be chosen. To illustrate this, consider the payoffs in Table 19-4. An interesting feature is exhibited by the payoffs of two acts: the weights and pulleys, and the pneumatic. No matter which demand event occurs, the weights and pulleys act leads to a greater payoff. For instance, if a light demand occurs, the payoff for weights and pulleys is −$125,000, which is more favorable than the −$300,000 payoff from the pneumatic movement; a similar finding results by comparing these two acts for the other possible demand events. Thus the weights and pulleys movement will always be a superior choice to the pneumatic one. We say that the first act *dominates* the second one. An act dominates another one whenever it achieves a better or equal payoff regardless of which events occur, and when it is strictly better for one or more events.

In general, whenever an act is dominated by another one, it is inadmissible. We see that the pneumatic movement is an *inadmissible act*. The toy-manu-facturer's decision can be simplified by eliminating that movement from further consideration. Removing the pneumatic act leaves us with the modified payoff table in Table 19-5.

A simple way to find whether an act is inadmissible is to see if every entry in its column is less than or equal to the corresponding entry in some other

TABLE 19-5   Modified Payoff Table for the Tippi-Toes Decision

	Act (Choice of Movement)		
Event	*Gears and Levers*	*Spring Action*	*Weights and Pulleys*
Light Demand	$ 25,000	−$ 10,000	−$125,000
Moderate Demand	400,000	440,000	400,000
Heavy Demand	650,000	740,000	750,000

particular column. It is easily verified that this is not true for the entries in Table 19-5, so the remaining movement acts must remain. They may be called *admissible acts*.

EXERCISES

19-1 A young bachelor is deciding whether to spend his Christmas vacation at a ski resort or surfing in Hawaii. He must commit himself to one of these alternatives in the early fall, since reservations have to be made months in advance. He really enjoys skiing more than surfing. Unfortunately he cannot be certain about December snow conditions; should there be poor snow, his ski trip will be ruined. The Hawaii trip would be a sure thing. But if he must go there when the snow is good elsewhere, his trip will be somewhat spoiled by regrets that he did not arrange to ski.
(a) Construct his decision table.
(b) Draw his decision tree diagram.

19-2 Peggy Jones, the founder of a computer-programming services firm, wishes to arrange expansion into the manufacture of peripheral equipment. Funds must be raised to build and operate the necessary facilities. Three alternatives are available: (1) issue additional common stock, (2) sell bonds, and (3) issue nonvoting preferred stock. A common stock issue will provide a strong financial base for future expansion through borrowing, but will considerably reduce the Jones family's percentage of ownership and control from its current 100 percent. New common stock will also cause future earnings to be divided into smaller amounts per share to existing shareholders. Bonds will allow existing shareholders to take all the benefits of new earnings, but will also result in greater risk of forced liquidation if the new venture proves unsuccessful. Preferred stockholders have no claims on the firm's assets but will drastically reduce the rate of earnings participation by existing common stockholders. Table 19-6 summarizes the forecast financial status of the firm if the manufacturing venture is successful.

TABLE 19-6

Possible Payoff Measure	Alternatives for Financing		
	Additional Common Stock	Bonds	Preferred Stock
1. Earnings after taxes and preferred dividends	$5,000,000	$3,500,000	$4,000,000
2. Common shares outstanding	1,000,000	500,000	500,000
3. Earnings per common share	$5.00	$7.00	$8.00
4. Jones' percentage of common ownership	50	100	100
5. Emergency line of credit	$1,000,000	$400,000	$500,000
6. Earnings available for common dividends	$5,000,000	$2,000,000	$4,000,000
7. Maximum possible dividends per share of common stock	$5.00	$4.00	$8.00

For each of the following goals, suggest an appropriate payoff measure. Then use it to identify the best and worst alternative choices for financing, in terms of the degree to which the *single* goal is met. Indicate any ties.

(a) Maintain a high percentage of control by Jones family.

(b) Maximize earnings of Jones family shares.

(c) Maximize availability of short-term credit.

(d) Maximize potential for cash dividends to Jones family.

19-3   An appliance manufacturer wishes to select one of three feasible proto-type designs for a new high-intensity fluorescent lamp. Lamp *A* will cost $100,000 for tooling plus $20 each for labor, parts, and materials. The fixed and variable costs for the other two candidates are $50,000 and $35 for *B* and $200,000 and $10 for *C*. The lamp will sell for $50. There are three possible equally likely levels of unit sales for the lamp, which are independent of the design chosen: E_1, 4,000; E_2, 8,000; and E_3, 12,000. For the design decision, profit will be used as the payoff.

(a) Construct the payoff table.

(b) Construct the decision tree diagram.

19-4   Identify any inadmissible acts in the following payoff table.

			Act		
Event	A_1	A_2	A_3	A_4	A_5
E_1	3	4	4	5	1
E_2	6	2	1	4	2
E_3	1	8	8	7	3

19-3   EXPECTED PAYOFF AND DECISION TREE ANALYSIS

How does one choose an act? When there is no uncertainty, the answer is straightforward: Select the act that yields the highest payoff (although finding this particular optimal act can be a very difficult task when the alternatives are many). But with uncertain events, the act having the greatest payoff for one event may have a lower payoff than a competing act for some other event. Later in the chapter we consider several criteria that may be used. For the present, we use expected value as the basis for decision making.

Maximizing Expected Payoff: Bayes Decision Rule

Suppose that our toy manufacturer accepts the following probabilities for the Tippi-Toes demand:

Light demand	.10
Moderate demand	.70
Heavy demand	.20
	1.00

If we treat the payoff values for each act as separate random variables, where the above probability values apply in each case, we can calculate the expected payoff for each act as shown in Table 19-7. We find that the spring-action movement results in the maximum expected payoff of $455,000. Thus, using maximum expected payoff as a decision-making criterion, our toy manufacturer would select the spring-action movement for the Tippi-Toes doll.

TABLE 19-7   Calculation of Expected Payoffs
for the Tippi-Toes Decision   *ЄPO*

Demand Event	Prob- ability	Gears and Levers		Spring Action		Weights and Pulleys	
		Payoff	Payoff× Probability	Payoff	Payoff× Probability	Payoff	Payoff× Probability
Light	.10	$ 25,000	$ 2,500	−$ 10,000	−$ 1,000	−$125,000	−$ 12,500
Moderate	.70	400,000	280,000	440,000	308,000	400,000	280,000
Heavy	.20	650,000	130,000	740,000	148,000	750,000	150,000
Expected payoff:			$412,500		$455,000		$417,500

The criterion of selecting the maximum expected payoff act is sometimes referred to as the *Bayes decision rule*. This criterion is named after Thomas Bayes, whom we associate with using empirical evidence for revising prior probabilities, because maximization of expected payoff is a suitable rule to use when decision making involves such experimental information.

The criterion of maximum expected payoff makes full use of information about the chances of the various payoffs. But, as we shall see, it is not a perfect device and can lead to a choice that is not truly the most desirable one. However, we shall see also that it is a suitable basis for decision making under uncertainty when the payoff values are themselves selected with great care.

Decision Tree Analysis

So far we have encountered decisions under uncertainty that may be portrayed in terms of a payoff table. But some problems are too complex to be represented in that fashion. Difficulties arise when the same events do not apply for all acts. For example, a contractor might need to choose between seeking a construction job for a dam or one for an airport. Not having sufficient resources to bid on both, the contractor must choose just one. Regardless of the job chosen, there is some probability (which may differ for the two projects) of winning the job bid on. Separate sets of events and probabilities are required for each act.

Often, decisions must be made at two or more points in time, with uncertain events occurring between decisions. Sometimes such problems may be analyzed in terms of a payoff table. But usually the earlier choice of act has bearing on the type, quantity, and probabilities of later events. This makes it cumbersome at best to attempt to force the decision into the limited confines of the rectangular arrangement of a payoff table.

Advantages of Decision Trees

A decision tree diagram, described earlier, may also be used to portray a decision problem. The tree representation allows us to meaningfully arrange the elements of a complex decision without the restrictions of the tabular format. It has further advantages in that it serves as a marvelous management communication tool because the tree makes every course of action and all possible outcomes easy to see.

To emphasize the need for a more general decision structure, consider again the toy manufacturer's decision evaluated earlier with a payoff table. We purposely kept that decision uncomplicated. There is merit in doing so, for some excluded factors may be unimportant. But there are also dangers from oversimplification that can lead to a less than optimal choice.

For instance, we eliminated the computer-controlled pneumatic doll-movement act, because it was dominated by weights and pulleys. But a computer-controlled movement might be adapted to an entire line of mechanical toys, thereby making the movements of all such toys cheaper than otherwise. A decision to do this can be made only at a later point in time, and then only if this particular movement is used. Such attractive alternatives have a value to the decision maker and ought to be reflected in the formulation of the decision structure.

Other factors might also be considered. For instance, the amount of advertising to use could be incorporated into the decision analysis. This would affect the total doll sales, and a decision to use more advertising may possibly make the choice of another doll movement more attractive than the choice made previously.

Our problem also assumed that the respective doll movements were equally attractive to the buyer. This need not be the case. In a society of rapidly expanding technology, the computer-controlled doll may be sold at a premium. Its sales might be increased if it is advertised as the "first doll with a genuine brain." A legitimate act would be to include different promotional appeals for each type of doll movement. Any differences in the sales potentials might be reflected by the event probabilities, which need not be the same for each act.

We recognize that the outcome of a decision about marketing a new product is not determined wholly by the simple interaction of a product-choice act with a consumer-demand event. The initial choice is simply the first in what can be a rather long, complicated chain of decisions to be made where intervening uncertain events must be encountered. For instance, later decisions must be made about the product's distribution, its intended market, its level of advertising, its method of production, its production schedule, and so forth. Each of these decisions will be influenced by uncertainties.

The ultimate outcome of such an involved decision may not be determined for years. During this period, new decisions must be made continually. Decision tree analysis accounts for this and also allows for the continual updating of the informational data base as a finer gauging of future uncertainties becomes possible. We illustrate decision tree analysis with a detailed discussion of a hypothetical situation.

Ponderosa Record Company: A Case Illustration

The president of Ponderosa Record Company, a small independent recording studio, has just signed a contract with a four-person group, the Fluid Mechanics, whom he heard at a recent music festival. The contract covers a single album and may be extended at the company's option for two years. Tapes have been cut, and Ponderosa must decide whether or not to market the recording. If they market the record, the pressing run must be decided. Its size will depend on whether a choice is made to test market the record or to immediately place it on a national market. If test marketing is to be done, then a 5,000-record run will be made and promoted regionally; this may result in a later decision to distribute nationally an additional 45,000 records, for which a second pressing run must be made. If immediate national marketing is chosen, a pressing run of 50,000 records will be made. Regardless of the test marketing results, the president may decide to enter the national market or decide not to.

It is the nature of Ponderosa's business that a record is either a complete success or a failure in its market. A successful recording sells all records pressed, while a failure's sales are practically nil. Success in a regional market does not guarantee success nationally, but it is a fairly reliable predictor.

The Decision Tree Diagram

The structure of the Ponderosa decision problem is provided by the decision tree diagram in Figure 19-2. Decisions are to be made at two different points in time, or stages. The immediate choice requires selecting one of two acts: test market or don't test market. These acts are shown as branches on an initial fork at node *a*. Suppose that test marketing is chosen. Then the result to be achieved in the test marketplace is uncertain. This is reflected by an event fork at ,node *b*, the branches representing favorable and unfavorable outcomes. Regardless of which event occurs, a new decision is required: to market nationally or to abort. These acts occur at a later stage, and their choice is shown as a pair of act forks, one each corresponding to the two different conditions under which this decision may be made: at node *c* when the test marketing is favorable and at node *d* when it is unfavorable. If national marketing is chosen at either node *c* or node *d*, the success or failure of the recording still remains unknown, and the possible events are reflected on the decision tree as branches on the terminal event forks at nodes *f* and *g*.

If the initial choice at decision point *a* is don't test market, a further choice at decision point *e* must be made whether to market nationally or to abort. As before, node *h* reflects the two uncertain events arising from a choice to market nationally. The path leading to *h* contains one "dummy" branch, a diagrammatical convenience to allow event and act forks of similar form to appear at

ACT   EVENT   ACT   EVENT   OUTCOME

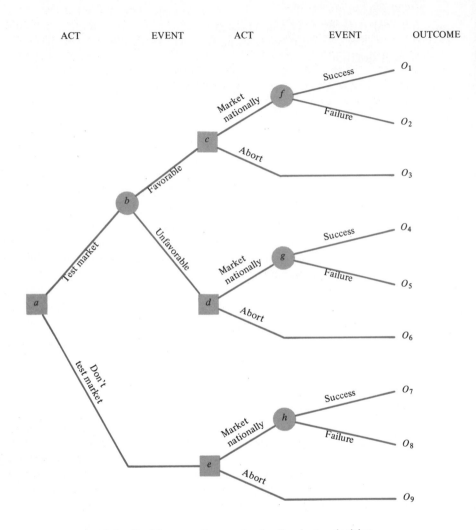

FIGURE 19-2   Decision tree diagram for the Ponderosa decision.

the same stage of the problem. This also allows all paths to terminate at a common stage. Thus, all abort acts are followed by one dummy branch.

Every path leading from the base of the decision tree leads to a terminal position corresponding to an outcome of the decision. Each possible combination of acts and events, or path, has a distinct outcome. For instance, O_1 represents the following sequence of events and acts: test market, favorable, market nationally, success.

A first step in analyzing the decision problem is to obtain a payoff for each outcome.

Determining the Payoffs

The terms of the contract with the Fluid Mechanics call for a $5,000 payment if records are produced. Ponderosa arranges with a record manufacturer to make its pressings. Each pressing run has a $5,000 fixed charge plus $0.75 for each record. The record jackets, handling, and distribution cost an additional $0.25 per record. The total variable cost per record is thus $1.00. Using these figures, we may calculate the immediate cash effect of each act in the decision tree. These will be referred to as *partial cash flows.*

Act		Partial Cash Flow	
Test Market		−$ 5,000	(for fee)
		− 5,000	(fixed cost of pressing)
		− 5,000	(variable costs of 5,000 records at $1.00)
	Total	−$15,000	
Don't Test Market		$0	
Market Nationally		−$ 5,000	(for fee)
(*without test*)		− 5,000	(fixed cost of pressing)
		− 50,000	(variable costs of 50,000 records at $1.00)
	Total	−$60,000	
Abort		$0	

The negative cash flows indicate expenditures. We show each partial cash flow on the respective branches from decision points a and e of the decision tree in Figure 19-3. In a similar manner, we determine the partial cash flows for the acts in the forks at decision points c and d: −$50,000 for marketing nationally ($5,000 fixed pressing charge plus $1.00 each in variable costs for 45,000 records) and $0 for abort.

Ponderosa receives $2 for each record sold through retail outlets. Since the events, favorable and unfavorable, or success and failure, represent sales of all and no records, respectively, the partial cash flows may be obtained by multiplying the number of records sold by $2. The partial cash flows for the events of the fork at node b are therefore +$10,000 (for 5,000 records sold) and $0 (for no sales). Also, the amounts for events at nodes f and g are +$90,000 (for 45,000 records sold) and $0, while for the events from node h we obtain +$100,000 and $0.

The payoff for each outcome may be obtained by adding the partial cash flows on the branches of the path leading to its terminal position. Thus for O_1 we add the partial cash flows: −$15,000, +$10,000, −$50,000, and +$90,000. The payoff is thus +$35,000. The payoffs calculated for each outcome are shown at the respective terminal positions in Figure 19-3.

Assigning Event Probabilities

Our decision maker wishes to choose that act which yields the maximum expected payoff. Before such a choice can be determined, probability values must be assigned to the events in the decision structure. Suppose that Ponderosa's president believes that the chance of favorably test marketing the recording is .50, so that the probability of unfavorable is its complement $(1 - .50)$, or also

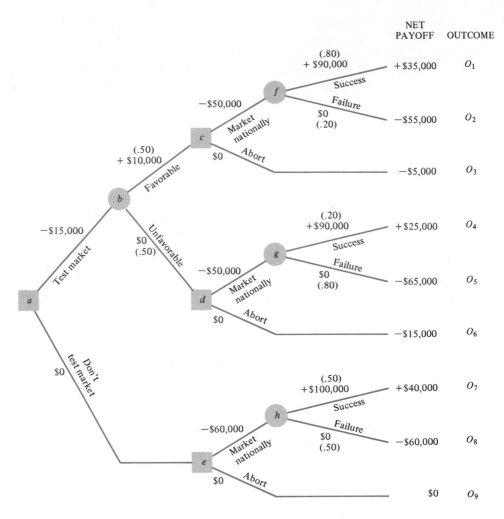

FIGURE 19-3   The Ponderosa decison tree diagram showing partial cash flows and probabilities on branches with net-cash-flow payoffs at end positions.

.50. These values are placed in parentheses along the branches at node *b* in Figure 19-3. In assigning probability values to the success and failure events for national marketing, our decision maker is faced with three distinctly different situations. If there should be no test marketing, the chance of national success is judged to be .50. Favorable test marketing demonstrates that the record appeals to the regional segment of the market, so that the chance of national success in that case is judged to be a much higher .80; this is a *conditional* probability, where the given event is a favorable test. Likewise, unfavorable test marketing would be a likely precursor of things to come nationally, so that the conditional probability of success is then judged to be .20. The following probability values are placed on the branches for the events in the remaining forks of the decision tree diagram: at node f, .80 for success, .20 for failure; at node g, .20 for success, .80 for failure; and at node h, .50 for success, .50 for failure. (It is just coincidental that the probability of national marketing success given unfavorable test marketing equals .20, which is also the probability of national marketing failure after favorable test marketing. Our decision maker could possibly have determined another value, such as .10, to be appropriate as the conditional probability of national success given an unfavorable regional outcome.)

Backward Induction

We are now ready to analyze the decision problem posed in the foregoing example. Our decision maker wishes to select an immediate act at decision point a. The first act we evaluate is test marketing. What is the expected payoff for this act? Referring to Figure 19-3, we see that six outcomes, O_1 through O_6, may result from this choice. How can we translate the corresponding payoffs into an expected value? This is not possible without first specifying the intervening acts at nodes c and d that will be chosen. In general, *it is impossible to evaluate an immediate act without first considering all later decisions that result from this choice*.

Thus, to find the expected payoff for the test marketing act, our decision maker must first decide whether to market nationally or abort if (1) test marketing has proven favorable or (2) test marketing was unfavorable. This illustrates an essential feature of analyzing multistage decisions: *evaluations must be made in reverse of their natural chronological sequence*. Before deciding whether to test market, our decision maker must first decide what to do if the test marketing is favorable or if it is unfavorable. The procedure for making such evaluations is called *backward induction*.

Let us make this point clearer by describing the procedure for our problem. For simplicity, the Ponderosa president's decision tree diagram is redrawn in Figure 19-4 with the partial cash flows left off.

Consider the act fork at decision point c. If Ponderosa's president chooses to market nationally, then he is faced with the event fork at node f. With probability .80, marketing nationally will be a success, in which case a net payoff of $+\$35,000$ is achieved; failure has a .20 probability and leads to a net payoff of $-\$55,000$. The expected payoff may be determined for this event fork as follows:

$$.80(\$35,000)+.20(-\$55,000) = +\$17,000$$

The amount $+\$17,000$ is entered on the decision tree at node f, since this is the expected payoff from the act to market nationally. For convenience we place the expected payoff for a sequence of acts and events above the applicable node.

The act to abort, at decision point c, leads to a certain payoff of $-\$5,000$. Since the expected payoff of the act to market nationally is larger, $+\$17,000$,

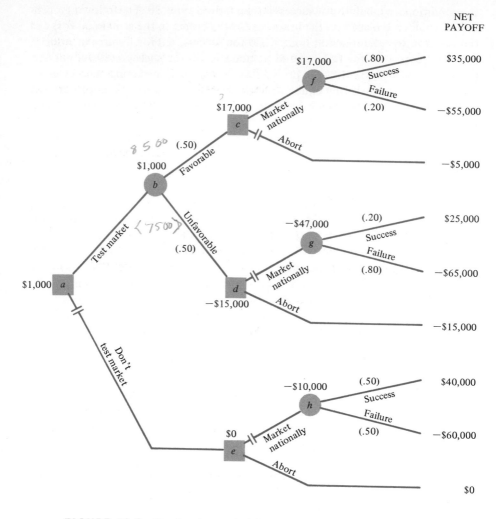

NET
PAYOFF

$17,000   (.80) $35,000

Success

f

Failure

$17,000   Market nationally   (.20)   −$55,000

c

Abort

8 5 6⁰   (.50)

$1,000   Favorable   −$5,000

b

−$47,000   (.20) $25,000

Unfavorable   Success

g

(.50)   Failure

Test market ⟨750⟩   Market nationally   (.80)   −$65,000

d

$1,000   *a*   −$15,000   Abort   −$15,000

Don't test market

−$10,000   (.50) $40,000

Success

h

Failure

$0   Market nationally   (.50)   −$60,000

e

Abort

$0

FIGURE 19-4   The Ponderosa decision tree diagram showing backward induction analysis.

the latter act should be chosen over aborting. We may reflect this future choice by "pruning" from the tree the branch corresponding to abort; this act merits no further consideration, since on reaching decision point *c*, the president would choose instead to market nationally. That is, if the decision maker were to have decided originally to test market and then this turned out to be favorable, he would choose to market nationally. We thus assign +$17,000 as the expected payoff resulting from making the best choice at decision point *c*. We bring back the amount +$17,000 to be entered on the diagram above the node at *c*.

As a rule of thumb in performing backward induction, ultimately all but one act will be eliminated at each decision point (except in the case of ties), so that all but branches leading to the greatest expected payoff will be pruned. Only the *best single payoff* from the later stage is brought backward to the preceding decision point (square). *Branch pruning takes place in act forks only, never in event forks.* Event forks (circles), instead, always involve an expected value calculation, so that an average payoff is always computed from the later stage values.

The available choices when test marketing results are unfavorable may be handled in the same way. First we calculate the expected payoff at node *g* arising from the act to market nationally:

$$.20(+\$25{,}000) + .80(-\$65{,}000) = -\$47{,}000$$

We place this figure on the diagram above node *g*. Since the act to abort leads to a payoff of $-\$15{,}000$, which is larger than $-\$47{,}000$, the branch for the act to market nationally is pruned from the tree. The best choice when the test marketing fails is to abort. We therefore bring back and enter the amount $-\$15{,}000$ on the diagram above the node at decision point *d*.

In a similar fashion, the expected payoff of the event fork at node *h*, when the initial choice is to market nationally, is determined as follows:

$$.50(+\$40{,}000) + .50(-\$60{,}000) = -\$10{,}000$$

At node *e* we do notice that abort is superior to the act to market nationally, so that the branch of the latter is pruned from the tree. Our decision maker must now compare the acts at decision point *a*. We see that the expected payoff from the act to test market is still to be determined. This is the expected payoff for the event fork at node *b*, which has two event branches. The branch corresponding to success leads to a portion of the tree with an expected payoff of $17,000. The other branch leads to a later choice whose expected payoff we have evaluated at $-\$15{,}000$. We may calculate the expected payoff at node *b* using these two amounts:

$$.50(+\$17{,}000) + .50(-\$15{,}000) = +\$1{,}000$$

We enter the amount $+\$1{,}000$ on the diagram above node *b*.

We can now compare the test marketing act at decision point *a* to not testing. We see that test marketing's expected payoff is higher: $+\$1{,}000$ versus $0 for not testing. Thus, our decision maker would choose to test market, leading to an expected payoff of $1,000; this amount is brought back and placed above node *a*. The branch corresponding to don't test market is pruned. Our backward induction is complete.

A decision has been indicated. Our decision maker should choose to test market the Fluid Mechanics record. Then if the test marketing is favorable, he must market nationally; if it is not, he ought to abort the recording. This result is illustrated in Figure 19-4 by the unpruned branches remaining in the decision tree. Because the consequences of immediate acts could not be determined until later decisions were resolved, the decision was analyzed using backward induction.

Additional Remarks

The later-stage choices are not irrevocable, and this analysis does not preclude a later change of the decision-maker's mind. New information may be received before the future decision at *c*, for instance, indicating a need to revise the chance of national success downward. If there is bad publicity about one of the Fluid Mechanics, for example, the expected payoff from national marketing might be smaller than that obtained by aborting. The possible changing conditions do not invalidate the original backward induction analysis. *The choice to test market is the best decision that can be made with the currently available information.* Although test marketing was chosen primarily on the strength of expected payoffs following the initial acts, we assume during our analysis that there is no reason to suspect an adverse personal public reaction to the Fluid Mechanics. If there were grounds for expecting such an event, an additional event fork should have been included in the decision tree.

The decision tree structure is suitable for analyzing decisions extending over a long time period. It indicates the best course of action for the current decision. But as time progresses, some uncertainties may be reduced and new ones might arise. Previously identified future optimal acts may turn out to be obviously poor choices, and brand new candidates may be determined. The relevant portion of the decision tree can be updated and revised prior to each new immediate decision. But each such decision is analyzed in the same general manner, using the best information available at the time a choice has to be made.

Although a decision tree is analyzed by moving backward in time, the analysis is really forward-looking. It indicates the optimal course of action to take when reaching future decision points. The dollar amounts brought backward to each branching-point node represent the best payoff the decision maker can expect to achieve if at a later time he should arrive at that position. Regardless of what events have occurred, the course of action optimal for the future choices is indicated by the original analysis (provided the basic structure and information used has not changed, like the bad publicity possibility indicated above).

EXERCISES

19-5 Consider the following payoff table.

		Act Payoff		
Event	Probability	A_1	A_2	A_3
E_1	.3	$10,000	$20,000	$ 5,000
E_2	.5	5,000	−10,000	10,000
E_3	.2	15,000	10,000	10,000

Compute the expected payoffs for each act. According to the Bayes decision rule, which act should be chosen?

19-6 Recompute the expected payoffs for the Tippi-Toes decision in Table 19-5 assuming that the demand event probabilities are now:

Light demand	.20
Moderate demand	.50
Heavy demand	.30

According to the Bayes decision rule, which act should the toy manufacturer choose?

19-7 For the decision tree diagram in Figure 19-5, perform backward induction analysis to determine the maximum expected payoff strategy. The event probabilities and payoffs are shown on the tree.

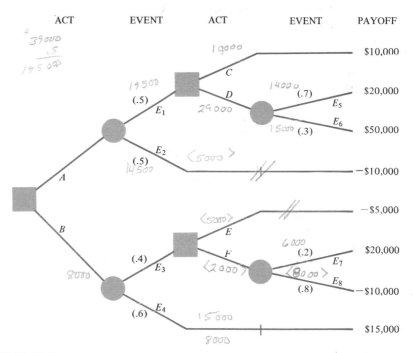

ACT	EVENT	ACT	EVENT	PAYOFF

FIGURE 19-5

19-8 Suppose that the president of Ponderosa Record Company uses the following probability values to analyze his decision.

$P[\text{national marketing success}\,|\,\text{favorable test marketing}] = .9$
$P[\text{national marketing failure}\,|\,\text{unfavorable test marketing}] = .6$
$P[\text{national marketing success}] = .7$
$P[\text{test marketing success}] = .75$

Repeat the decision tree analysis used in the chapter to determine the optimal strategy. Assume that all payoffs remain unchanged.

19-9 The manager of an oil company's data-processing operations personally interviews applicants for jobs as keypunchers. Persons hired with no previous experience are placed in a one-month training program on a

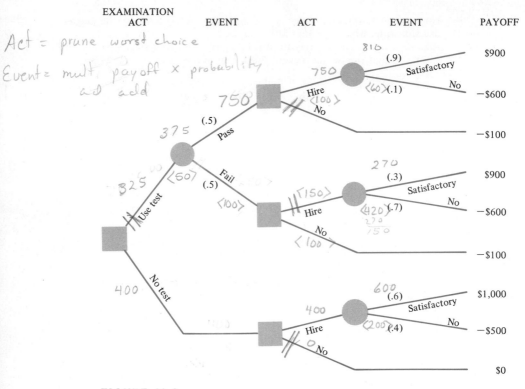

EXAMINATION
ACT   EVENT   ACT   EVENT   PAYOFF

Act = prune worst choice

Event = mult. payoff × probability
*   and add*

FIGURE 19-6

trial basis. Satisfactory employees are retained, while the others are let go. Most of the persons let go in the past have been found lacking in aptitude. The manager is contemplating contracting for the testing services of a personnel agency, which for a $100 fee per applicant will administer a battery of aptitude tests. She has developed the decision tree in Figure 19-6 to help her make her hiring decisions. The event probabilities are indicated on the corresponding branches of the tree. As a payoff measure she has chosen per employee net recoverable training expenses. For trainees retained, all expenses except testing fees are recoverable; they also contribute an additional salary savings of $1,000 over hiring already experienced personnel. For trainees not retained, neither the $500 training costs nor the testing fee are recoverable. Perform backward induction to determine what strategy or course of action will maximize expected payoff.

19-10 The president of Hercules Helicopter Corporation must decide whether to propose to design and perhaps later to build a new all-purpose jungle-copter for the Army. If Hercules submits a proposal, two results are possible: (1) it may win an R & D contract, or (2) it may lose to a competitor. If Hercules wins the contract, the following choice will still have to be made: either (a) invest in personnel and facilities with the hope of winning a follow-on production contract, or (b) not invest. In either case (a) or (b), Hercules may win or lose the follow-on production contract, but additional investment would increase its chances of winning. Diagram the Hercules decision problem.

19-11 Buzzy-B Toys must decide the course of action for a new whistling yo-yo. An initial decision must be made whether or not to market it at all or to first conduct a test marketing program. After test marketing has been done, a decision must be made whether to abandon or nationally distribute the yo-yo.

A national success will increase profits by $500,000, and a failure will reduce them by $100,000, while abandoning the product will not change profits. The test marketing will cost Buzzy-B a further $10,000.

If no test marketing is done, the probability of a national success has been judged to be .45. The assumed probability for a favorable test marketing result is .50. The conditional probability of national success given favorable test marketing is .80 and that for national success given unfavorable test results is .10.

Construct the decision tree diagram and perform backward induction to determine the optimal course of action using net change in profits as the payoff.

9-4 FURTHER CRITERIA FOR MAKING A CHOICE

A primary aim of statistical decision theory is to establish systematic means for choosing an act. This is accomplished largely through the payoff table. Various *decision-making criteria* may be employed in selecting the best act. The payoff measure itself is a key element in selecting rules for decision making, and decision theory considers a variety of these in addition to the Bayes decision rule discussed earlier.

Maximin Payoff

No decision-making theory could be complete without considering various rules that might be used in selecting the most desirable act. We will begin with the simplest criterion: *maximin payoff*. This procedure guarantees that the decision maker can do no worse than achieve the best of the poorest outcomes possible. As an illustration, we will use the payoff table of Table 19-8, which presents the toy-manufacturer's choice of doll movement for the Tippi-Toes doll.

Suppose that our toy manufacturer wishes to make his choice of act so as

TABLE 19-8 Payoff Table for the Tippi-Toes Decision

	Act (Choice of Movement)		
Event	*Gears and Levers*	*Spring Action*	*Weights and Pulleys*
Light Demand	$ 25,000	−$ 10,000	−$125,000
Moderate Demand	400,000	440,000	400,000
Heavy Demand	650,000	740,000	750,000

to ensure a favorable outcome no matter what happens. This may be accomplished by taking a pessimistic viewpoint, determining the worst outcome for each act, regardless of event. For the gears and levers act, the lowest possible payoff is $25,000 when light demand occurs. The lowest payoff for the spring-action movement is a negative amount, −$10,000, also obtained when demand is light. For the weights and pulleys movement it is −$125,000. By choosing the act that yields the largest of these payoffs, our decision maker can guarantee a minimum return that is the best of the worst. In this case, a gears and levers movement for the doll will guarantee the toy manufacturer a payoff of at least $25,000.

The gears and levers act is the act with the maximum of the minimum payoffs. This may be stated more concisely: gears and levers is the *maximin payoff act*. To show how this may be determined in general, we reconstruct the payoff table in Table 19-9.

How suitable is the maximin payoff criterion? This depends on the nature of the decision. Consider the decision problem in Table 19-10. Here we have a situation where the decision maker chooses A_1 over A_2. You may feel that A_2 would be a better choice if the chance of E_2 were high enough. The maximin

TABLE 19-9   Determining Maximin Payoff Act
for the Tippi-Toes Decision

| | Act (Choice of Movement) | | |
| | Gears and Levers | Spring Action | Weights and Pulleys |
Event			
Light Demand	$ 25,000	−$ 10,000	−$125,000
Moderate Demand	400,000	440,000	400,000
Heavy Demand	650,000	740,000	750,000
Column minimums	$ 25,000	−$ 10,000	−$125,000

Maximum of column minimums = $25,000

Maximin payoff act = Gears and levers

TABLE 19-10   Maximin Payoff Determination
for a Hypothetical Decision

| | Act | |
Event	A_1	A_2
E_1	$0	−$1
E_2	1	10,000
Column minimum	$0	−$1

Maximum of column minimums = $0

Maximin payoff act = A_1

TABLE 19-11   Payoff Table for a Hypothetical Decision

	Act	
Event	A_1	A_2
E_1	$1	$10,000
E_2	−1	−10,000

decision maker is giving up an opportunity to gain $10,000 in order to avoid a possible loss of $1. To avoid losing $1, the decision maker is choosing an act that will guarantee at least the maintenance of the status quo. One can envision circumstances, however, where A_1 would be the best choice of act. Suppose that our decision maker has only $1 and must use this to pay a debt to a loan shark or lose his life. In that case the payoffs do not realistically represent the true value assigned them by the decision maker.

Consider the situation whose payoffs are given in Table 19-11. Here the maximin payoff act is A_1. This would be a good choice for a decision maker who could not tolerate a loss of $10,000, no matter how unlikely it was. Few people would risk losing their business by choosing an act leading to the possibility of bankruptcy unless the odds were extremely small. But an individual who could survive a loss of $10,000 would find A_2 superior if the probability of E_2 were substantially lower than E_1.

Our examples illustrate a key deficiency of maximin payoff: It is an extremely conservative decision criterion and can lead to some very bad decisions. Any alternative with slightly larger risks is passed over in favor of a comparatively risk-free alternative, which can be far less attractive. Taken to its ludicrous extreme, a maximin payoff policy would force any firm out of business. No inventories would be stocked, because there is always a possibility of unsold items. No new products would be introduced, because one can never be certain of their success. No credit would be granted, because one can always count on some customers not paying.

Another major deficiency of the maximin criterion exists if the likelihoods of the various events are known. Maximin payoff is mainly suited to decision problems whose probabilities are unknown and cannot be reasonably assessed. As our illustrations indicated, maximin payoff in extreme cases—the person hounded by loan sharks or the business that could go bankrupt—can lead to the best decision. But most of us, when faced with the same decision, would not choose the maximin payoff act because we attach different measures of worth to the outcomes. As we shall see later, utility values may be used to explicitly measure the true relative worth of the various decision outcomes.

Maximum Likelihood Criterion

Another rule that has served as a model for decision-making behavior is the *maximum likelihood criterion*. Here the focus is on the most likely event, to the exclusion of all others. Table 19-12 illustrates this criterion for the toy-manufacturer's decision analyzed previously.

For this decision we see that a moderate demand has the highest probability of .7. The maximum likelihood criterion tells us to ignore the light and heavy demand events completely, in effect to assume that they will not occur. This rule then tells us to choose the best act assuming that a moderate demand will occur. In this example, the *maximum likelihood act* is to use the spring-action doll movement, which for a moderate demand provides the greatest profit of $440,000.

How suitable is the maximum likelihood criterion for decision making? Using it, we don't explicitly consider the range of outcomes for the spring-action set—from a $10,000 loss if a light demand occurs to a $740,000 profit if it is heavy. We also ignore much of the rest of the possible outcomes, including the best (selecting weights and pulleys when demand is heavy, which yields a $750,000 profit) and the worst (selecting weights and pulleys when demand is light, which leads to a $125,000 loss). In a sense, the maximum likelihood criterion would have us "play ostrich," ignoring much that might happen. If this is so, why is it discussed here?

We describe this criterion partly to be complete, but mainly because it seems so prevalent in the decision-making behavior of individuals and businesses. We may use it to explain certain anomalies that would otherwise be hard to rationalize. These quirks are epitomized by the so-called "hog cycle" in the raising and marketing of pigs, which relates to the more or less predictable two-year-long pork price movement from higher to lower levels and back again to high prices. Hog farmers have been blamed for this, since they expand their herds when prices are high, so that one year later the supply of mature hogs is excessive and prices are driven downward; then when prices are low, these same farmers reduce their herds, cutting the supply of marketable hogs, and the next year's prices consequently rise.

Why don't the farmers break this cycle? After all, it doesn't seem rational to be wrong consistently in timing hog production. One explanation is that the hog farmers use the maximum likelihood criterion. In their minds, the most

TABLE 19-12 Determining Maximum Likelihood Act
for the Tippi-Toes Decision

Demand Event	Probability	Act (Choice of Movement)		
		Gears and Levers	Spring Action	Weights and Pulleys
Light	.10	$ 25,000	−$ 10,000	−$125,000
Moderate	.70	400,000	440,000	400,000
Heavy	.20	650,000	740,000	750,000

Most likely event = Moderate demand
Maximum row payoff = $440,000
Maximum likelihood act = Spring action

likely future market price is the current one—and we know that this has proven to be very poor judgment. Given that premise, the maximum likelihood act is to increase herd sizes when current prices are high and to decrease them when prices are low. This peculiarity in human behavior extends to other decisions. The small investor has been accused of buying most heavily just as the stock market peaks and selling most strongly at the bottom. Even sophisticated corporate managers too often accentuate business cycles by investing excessively in plant and inventory just prior to recessions and retrenching prior to recovery. Such decision making is not unlike that of the hog farmers.

Criterion of Insufficient Reason

Another criterion that has been employed is *insufficient reason*. This may be used when a decision maker has no information about the chances of the events. In this case, no event may be regarded as more likely than another, and all events are assigned equal probability values. Since the events are collectively exhaustive and mutually exclusive, the probability of each must be

$$\frac{1}{\text{Number of events}}$$

Using these probabilities, one chooses the act with the maximum expected payoff.

A major criticism of this criterion is that there are few situations where some knowledge of the relative chances of events is not available. When it is available, the Bayes decision rule employing more realistic probabilities would be more valid.

Bayes Decision Rule Preferred

The foregoing three criteria have obvious inadequacies. *None of the three incorporates all information* available to the decision maker. Maximin payoff totally ignores probabilities for the events. Although this has been argued to be a strength when probabilities are not easily determined, there are few circumstances where judgment cannot be used in arriving at acceptable probability values.

The maximum likelihood criterion ignores all events but the most likely one, even if that event happens to be a lot less likely than the union of the rest. (For instance, among 20 events the most likely one may have a probability of .10, with a .90 probability that one of the other 19 events will occur.)

The criterion of insufficient reason essentially asks us to violate our judgments and "willy nilly" assume that all events are equally likely; this must be so even with such listed events as war and peace and boom and depression.

The Bayes decision rule has proven to be the central focus of statistical decision theory when all relevant evidence is used in determining a choice of action. It makes the greatest use of information. It alone allows us to extend decision theory to incorporate sampling or experimental information. Its major deficiency occurs when alternatives involve different magnitudes of risk. To illustrate the point, consider the decision structure in Table 19-13. Acts A_1 and A_2 are equally attractive under the criterion of maximum expected payoff, which is $500,000, the same amount for either act. Yet most decision makers would clearly prefer A_2, because it avoids the rather large risk of a million-dollar loss.

TABLE 19-13   Payoff Table for a Hypothetical Decision

		Act A_1		Act A_2	
Event	Probability	Payoff	Payoff × Probability	Payoff	Payoff × Probability
E_1	.5	− $1,000,000	− $ 500,000	$250,000	$125,000
E_2	.5	2,000,000	1,000,000	750,000	375,000
Expected payoff:			$ 500,000		$500,000

The paradox here may be resolved not by choosing another criterion, but rather by reconsidering the values chosen for the payoffs. The theory of utility presented in Chapter 21 provides a way of setting the payoffs at values that express their true worth to the decision maker.

Bayes Decision Rule and Utility

We have made a strong case for using expected values as the basis for decision making under uncertainty. As we have seen, a criterion based on expected value uses all the available probability data and gives proper weight to every outcome; the other criteria use fewer structural elements from the decision. Expected value also provides us with a gauge for evaluating additional sources of information that can be used in decision making.

But when applied to monetary payoffs, the Bayes decision rule—maximizing expected profit and minimizing expected cost or loss—often leads to a less preferred choice.

Perhaps the best example of this occurs in casualty insurance decisions— where the choices are to buy a policy or to not buy one. Most persons have liability insurance for their cars, and most carry greater coverage than the legal minimum. It is well-known that the policy-owner's annual cost for that insurance exceeds the expected loss from an accident. (This is because insurance companies must charge more than what they expect to pay in claims, just to meet overhead and expenses.) But according to the Bayes decision rule, the best decision is not to insure—it has the greater expected monetary payoff (that is, the expected cost of not insuring is less than the cost of insurance). This contradicts the true preference of most people.

Similar breakdowns of the Bayes decision rule occur whenever a person prefers a less risky alternative to one that involves considerable risk but actually has a greater expected monetary payoff. Since other decision-making criteria have serious defects too, how should we objectively analyze decisions where great risks are involved?

Fortunately, *decision theory copes with attitude toward risk through an adjustment in the payoff values themselves.* This is accomplished by establishing for every outcome a true-worth index called a *utility* value. Thus, a decision may be analyzed using utilities instead of dollars or other standard payoff measures.

In Chapter 21 we will describe the theory of utility and its application in great detail. There is one very important principle established there: *when the Bayes decision rule is applied in a decision having utilities as payoffs, it always indicates the most preferred course of action.* This makes that rule the theoretically perfect criterion for decision making, no matter how complex the decision happens to be.

EXERCISES

19-12   You have decided to participate in a gamble with the following monetary payoffs:

	Act	
Event	*Choose Red*	*Choose Black*
Red Occurs	$1	− $2
Black Occurs	−1	100

(a) What is the maximin payoff act?

(b) Suppose that the probability of red is .99. Calculate the expected payoffs from each act. Which act is best under the Bayes decision rule? What act would you choose?

(c) Suppose the probability of red is .5. Calculate the expected payoffs for the acts. Which act has the maximum expected payoff? What act would you choose?

(d) In view of your answers to the above questions, what do you think of the maximin payoff decision criterion?

19-13   A decision maker must choose among three acts. The payoff table, along with the event probabilities, is provided below.

		Act		
Event	*Probability*	A_1	A_2	A_3
E_1	.3	$10	$15	$20
E_2	.4	15	20	15
E_3	.3	25	15	15

(a) Which is the maximin payoff act?
(b) Which act is the maximum likelihood act?
(c) Calculate the expected payoffs. According to the Bayes decision rule, which act should be chosen?

19-14   A farmer intends to sign a contract to provide a cannery with his entire crop. He must choose one of the following five vegetables: corn, tomatoes, beets, asparagus, and cauliflower. His entire 1,000 acres will be planted with the selected crop. The yield of each vegetable will be affected to various degrees by the weather. The following table indicates the approximate productivities for dry, moderate, and damp weather. It also lists the price per bushel that has been offered.

Weather Type	*Approximate Yield (Bushels per Acre)*				
	Corn	*Tomatoes*	*Beets*	*Aspara-gus*	*Cauli-flower*
Dry	20	10	15	30	40
Moderate	35	20	20	25	40
Damp	40	10	30	20	40
Price/bushel	$1.00	$2.00	$1.50	$1.00	$0.50

(a) Using approximate total cash receipts when the crop is sold as a payoff measure, construct the payoff table for this farmer's decision.
(b) Identify any inadmissible acts, and eliminate them from the payoff table.
(c) What is the maximin payoff act?
(d) Supposing that the following probability values have been assigned for the weather, calculate the expected payoff for each act and identify the act having the maximum expected payoff.

Weather	Probability
Dry	.3
Moderate	.5
Damp	.2

19-5   DECISION MAKING USING STRATEGIES

One important aspect of decision making is using information that might be helpful in making a choice. We may expand the concepts developed so far to accommodate such information. Business has numerous examples of these kinds of decision situations. In establishing an employment policy based on a screening test, an employer must use an applicant's score as the basis for hiring or rejecting that person. Regardless of the score achieved, when hired, a person will ultimately perform satisfactorily or not. In receiving components for possible assembly into a final product, manufacturers generally use the information contained in a random sample before deciding to accept or reject a shipment; the ultimate quality of the entire shipment will be known only after this decision has been made. As a further example, consider the choice between adding a new product to the line or abandoning it. The results of a marketing research study might be used before deciding; the success or failure of the new product will be known only after it has been introduced.

All of the above situations are decisions with two points of uncertainty. The first of these is the kind of information obtained—the screening test score, the number of defective sample items, or the results of the survey. The second uncertainty concerns the ultimate outcome—the new employee's performance, the quality of the shipment, the new product's performance. Between these points in time a decision has to be made. The act chosen may depend on the particular event that occurred before.

It is possible to determine in advance the best acts to select for each informational event. The resulting decision rule is called a *strategy*. The ultimate decision requiring our analysis is the selection of the particular strategy. We will show how this is done by means of an illustration that contains sampling and inspection.

The Cannery Inspector: A Case Illustration

A cannery inspector monitors tests for mercury contamination levels before authorizing shipments of canned tuna. The procedure is to randomly select two crates of canned fish from a shipment and determine the parts per million of mercury. The number of these crates R exceeding government contamination guidelines is then determined. The inspector may then approve (A) or disapprove (D) the shipment. If approved, the shipment is sent to distributors who perform more detailed testing and determine whether the entire shipment's average mercury levels are excessive (E) or tolerable (T). An excessively contaminated shipment is returned to the cannery. If the company inspector originally refuses shipment, the production batch is sent to the rendering department to be converted into pet food. At this time, it is determined whether the entire shipment does indeed contain excessive average levels of mercury contamination.

The decision tree diagram for the inspector's decision is provided in Figure 19-7. Eight strategies, denoted symbolically by S_1 through S_8, are identified in Table 19-14. A strategy must specify which act, approve or disapprove, to choose for each possible test result. Thus, we see that strategy S_1 is

TABLE 19-14   Strategies for the Cannery Inspector's Decision

Test Result Event	Strategy							
	S_1	S_2	S_3	S_4	S_5	S_6	S_7	S_8
$R = 0$	A	A	A	D	A	D	D	D
$R = 1$	A	A	D	A	D	A	D	D
$R = 2$	A	D	A	A	D	D	A	D

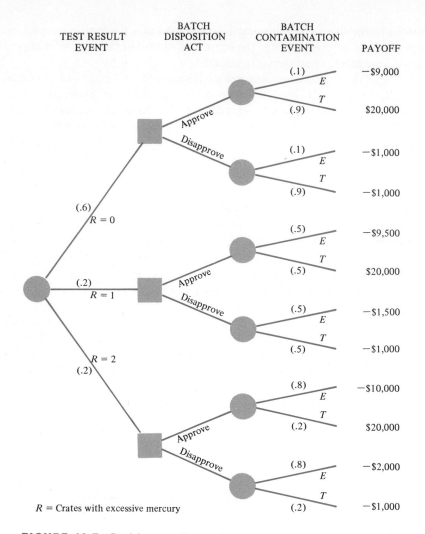

| TEST RESULT EVENT | BATCH DISPOSITION ACT | BATCH CONTAMINATION EVENT | PAYOFF |

FIGURE 19-7   Decision tree diagram for the cannery inspector.

a decision rule specifying that the shipment must be approved no matter what the number of excessively contaminated crates R happens to be. Strategy S_2 specifies approval if $R = 0$ or $R = 1$, but disapproval if $R = 2$. Eight strategies are possible because for each of the 3 events there are 2 choices and thus $2^3 = 8$ distinct decision rules.

A table may be constructed showing the payoff for each strategy–event combination. The payoff table obtained, shown in Table 19-15, is identical in form to those discussed for single-stage decisions, but strategies are used instead of acts. One difference is that there are uncertainties at two stages: (1) the number of excessively contaminated crates in the sample, and (2) whether the

TABLE 19-15 Payoff Table for the Cannery Inspector's
Decision Using Strategies (Payoffs in Thousands of Dollars)

Joint Event	Strategy							
	S_1	S_2	S_3	S_4	S_5	S_6	S_7	S_8
$R = 0$ *and E*	− 9	− 9	− 9	− 1	− 9	− 1	− 1	−1
$R = 0$ *and T*	20	20	20	− 1	20	− 1	− 1	−1
$R = 1$ *and E*	− 9.5	− 9.5	− 1.5	− 9.5	− 1.5	− 9.5	− 1.5	−1.5
$R = 1$ *and T*	20	20	− 1	20	− 1	20	− 1	−1
$R = 2$ *and E*	− 10	− 2	− 10	− 10	− 2	− 2	− 10	−2
$R = 2$ *and T*	20	− 1	20	20	− 1	− 1	20	−1

contamination level of the entire production batch will be found, on the average, excessive or tolerable. The six joint events are of the form $R = 0$ *and E, $R = 2$ and T*. The cell entry payoff values are the same as in the decision tree in Figure 19-7 and correspond to the joint event that occurs for the specified strategy. Thus, if the joint event $R = 2$ *and E* occurs when S_1 is used, the payoff is − 10 thousand dollars, since this particular strategy has the inspector approve shipment whenever $R = 2$. If the inspector is using S_2, the same event will indicate disapproval, and because there is an excessive average batch-mercury-level, the payoff is − 2 thousand dollars.

This strategy-selection decision can be analyzed by applying any of the various criteria we have encountered earlier and treating each strategy in the same way as an act in a simpler decision structure. However, we will continue by maximizing expected payoff.

Extensive and Normal Form Analysis

This particular decision may be analyzed using the Bayes decision rule and maximizing expected payoff through either (1) backward induction on the decision tree or (2) direct computation from the values in the payoff table to find the strategy with the maximum expected payoff. *The two approaches will provide identical results.* When a decision tree is used, the procedure is called an *extensive form analysis.* Analysis performed on the payoff table is referred to as *normal form analysis.*

Figure 19-8 shows the extensive form analysis. The probability value determined for each event is shown on the corresponding branch. Backward induction shows that the best procedure is to approve the shipment when $R = 0$ or $R = 1$ and to reject the shipment when $R = 2$; referring to Table 19-14, we see that this corresponds to strategy S_2.

The results of the normal form analysis are shown in Table 19-16. Strategy S_2 has the maximum expected payoff of 10.95 thousand dollars, which is the same as the result obtained in the extensive form analysis. Indeed, every strategy listed in Table 19-14 can be represented by a unique pruned tree, as shown in

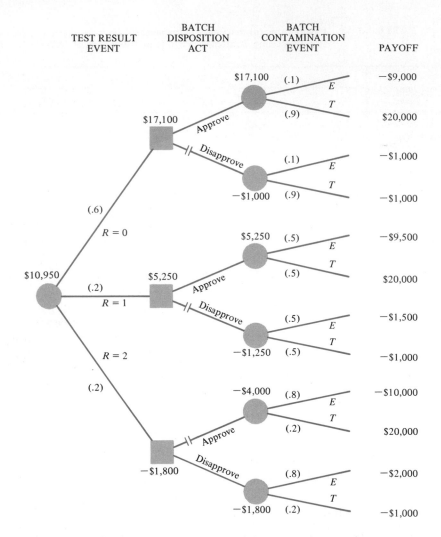

TEST RESULT EVENT	BATCH DISPOSITION ACT	BATCH CONTAMINATION EVENT	PAYOFF

FIGURE 19-8   Extensive form analysis of the cannery inspector's problem, using the decision tree diagram.

Figure 19-9. Fortunately, extensive form analysis requires that we prune the tree just once. In terms of computational efficiency, this makes decision tree analysis superior because fewer computations are required, and it is not even necessary to catalog the various strategies. In backward induction, only the maximum expected payoffs need be brought back to the earlier branching point.

Often extensive form analysis using a decision tree is the only approach possible, because the problem structure cannot be forced into the rectangular format of a payoff table. This is especially true of problems having two or more decision points, such as the Ponderosa Record Company example (see Figure

TABLE 19-16   Expected Payoff Calculation for the Cannery Inspector's
Decision Using Strategies (Payoffs in Thousands of Dollars)

(1) *First-Stage Event Probability*	(2) *Second-Stage Event Probability*	(3) *Joint Probability [(1) × (2)]*	(4) *Payoff for S_2*	(5) *Payoff × Joint Probability [(3) × (4)]*
$P[R = 0] = .6$	$P[E \mid R = 0] = .1$	.06	− 9	− .54
$P[R = 0] = .6$	$P[T \mid R = 0] = .9$	.54	20	10.80
$P[R = 1] = .2$	$P[E \mid R = 1] = .5$	.10	− 9.5	− .95
$P[R = 1] = .2$	$P[T \mid R = 1] = .5$	.10	20	2.00
$P[R = 2] = .2$	$P[E \mid R = 2] = .8$	.16	− 2.0	− .32
$P[R = 2] = .2$	$P[T \mid R = 2] = .2$	.04	− 1.0	− .04
			Expected payoff =	10.95

Strategy:	S_1	S_2	S_3	S_4	S_5	S_6	S_7	S_8
Expected payoff:	10.51	10.95	9.21	−.35	9.65	.09	−1.65	−1.21

19-3 on page 662). Only problems with a symmetrical tree like that in Figure 19-8 can be analyzed either way in terms of expected payoff.

EXERCISES

19-15 Suppose that the following probabilities apply instead for the cannery inspector illustration:

Test Result	*Probability*	*Conditional Probabilities*	
$R = 0$	.4	.2 (E)	.8 (T)
$R = 1$	.3	.6 (E)	.4 (T)
$R = 2$	.3	.9 (E)	.1 (T)

(a) Do a new extensive form analysis (using a corrected decision tree) to determine the strategy that maximizes expected payoff.
(b) Do a new normal form analysis (using corrected joint probabilities) to select the strategy that maximizes expected payoff.

19-16 A cannery manager classifies each truckload of apricots purchased under contract from local orchards as either underripe, ripe, or overripe. Then the manager must decide whether a particular truckload will be used for dried apricots (*D*) or for apricot preserves (*P*). A truckload of apricots used in preserves yields a profit of $6,000 if the fruit has a high sugar content, but only $4,000 if the sugar content is low (because costly extra sugar must be added). Regardless of sugar content, a truckload of dried apricots yields a profit of $5,000. In either case, the actual sugar content can be determined only during final processing.

The probability for an underripe truckload is .3, for a ripe one it is .5, and for an overripe one it is .2. The following probabilities have been established for sugar content for given levels of ripeness:

	Underripe	Ripe	Overripe
Low Sugar	.9	.4	.2
High Sugar	.1	.6	.8
	1.0	1.0	1.0

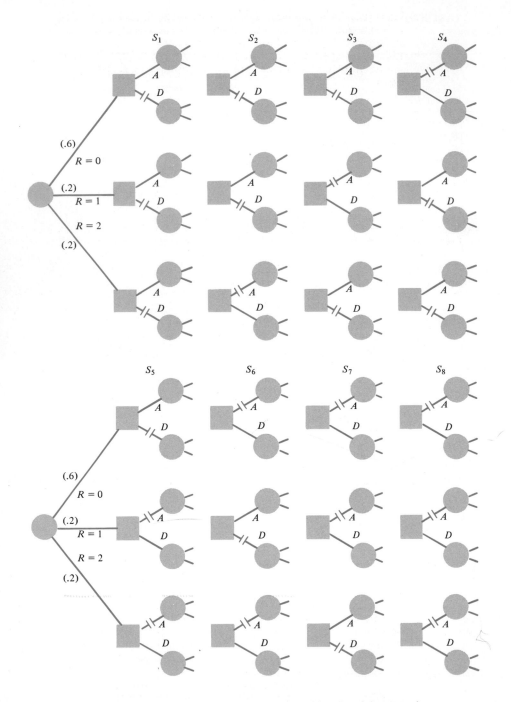

FIGURE 19-9   Pruned tree diagrams illustrating the eight strategies for the cannery inspector.

(a) Construct the manager's decision tree diagram and perform an extensive form analysis to determine the maximum expected payoff strategy for disposing of a truckload of apricots.
(b) List the possible strategies for disposing of a truckload. Perform a normal form analysis to select the strategy yielding greatest expected profit.

19-6 OPPORTUNITY LOSS AND EXPECTED VALUE OF PERFECT INFORMATION

Is it worthwhile to buy information that may help us choose the better act? Information is usually not free. Resources, for example, are required to take a sample or to administer a test. Here we attempt to place a value on such information. In doing this, we introduce the concept of opportunity loss.

Opportunity Loss

Suppose that we view each possible outcome in terms of a measure expressing the difference in payoff between the act chosen and the best that could have been achieved. Such a measure is referred to as an *opportunity loss*, to which we give the following

DEFINITION   The *opportunity loss* for an outcome is the amount of payoff forgone by not selecting the act that has the greatest payoff for the event that actually occurs.

Table 19-17 shows how the opportunity losses are obtained for the payoffs for the toy-manufacturer's doll-movement decision. The opportunity losses are

TABLE 19-17   Determination of Opportunity Losses for the Tippi-Toes Decision

Demand Event	Payoff			Row Maximum
	Gears and Levers	Spring Action	Weights and Pulleys	
Light	$ 25,000	−$ 10,000	−$125,000	$ 25,000
Moderate	400,000	440,000	400,000	440,000
Heavy	650,000	740,000	750,000	750,000

Row maximum − Payoff = Opportunity loss
(thousands of dollars)

Light	25− 25 =	0	25−(−10) = 35	25−(−125) =	150	
Moderate	440−400 =	40	440− 440 = 0	440− 400 =	40	
Heavy	750−650 =	100	750− 740 = 10	750− 750 =	0	

calculated by first determining the best outcomes for each event, the maximum payoff in each row. The payoffs in each row are then subtracted from the row maximums.

The *opportunity loss table* is shown in Table 19-18. All opportunity loss values are non-negative, since they measure how much worse off the decision maker is by choosing an act other than the best for the occurring event. Let us consider the meaning of the values. For example, suppose that the gears and levers movement is chosen and a light demand occurs. The opportunity loss is zero, because, referring to Table 19-17, we see that no better payoff than $25,000 could have been achieved if another act had been chosen. But if gears and levers are used and a heavy demand occurs, the opportunity loss must then be $100,000. This is because that movement does not have the greatest payoff for a heavy demand; the weights and pulleys movement with a payoff of $750,000 does. Since for this event choosing gears and levers has a payoff of only $650,000, the payoff difference, $750,000 − $650,000 = $100,000, represents the additional payoff forgone. It should be emphasized that the $100,000 opportunity loss is not a loss in the accounting sense, for a net positive contribution of $650,000 to profits is obtained. Rather, the opportunity to achieve an additional $100,000 has been missed. We might say that the decision maker would have $100,000 in *regret* by not having chosen weights and pulleys instead of gears and levers, should demand prove to be heavy.

TABLE 19-18   Opportunity Loss Table for the Tippi-Toes Decision

	Act (Choice of Movement)		
Event	*Gears and Levers*	*Spring Action*	*Weights and Pulleys*
Light Demand	$ 0	$35,000	$150,000
Moderate Demand	40,000	0	40,000
Heavy Demand	100,000	10,000	0

Bayes Decision Rule and Opportunity Loss

Since an opportunity loss is a numerical outcome, we can calculate the expected value of the opportunity losses for each act to be considered. Our goal is to select the act with the minimum expected opportunity loss. The expected opportunity loss for each act is calculated in Table 19-19 for the toy-manufacturer's decision. We see that the expected opportunity loss for the gears and levers movement is $48,000. Note that the minimum expected opportunity loss is $5,500 for the spring-action act. This act would be our decision-maker's choice under this criterion. The spring-action movement is the *minimum expected opportunity loss act*.

We saw earlier that the spring-action movement was also the maximum expected payoff act and was thus the best choice according to the Bayes decision

TABLE 19-19   Calculation of Expected Opportunity Losses for the Tippi-Toes Decision   *Easier to do*

Demand Event	Probability	Gears and Levers		Spring Action		Weights and Pulleys	
		Loss	Loss × Probability	Loss	Loss × Probability	Loss	Loss × Probability
Light	.10	$ 0	$ 0	$35,000	$3,500	$150,000	$15,000
Moderate	.70	40,000	28,000	0	0	40,000	28,000
Heavy	.20	100,000	20,000	10,000	2,000	0	0
Expected opportunity loss:			$48,000		$5,500		$43,000

rule. Our new criterion leads to the same choice. It may be established mathematically that this will always be so. Since either criterion will always lead to the same choice, we can say that the *Bayes decision rule is to select the act having the maximum expected payoff or the minimum expected opportunity loss.*

Expected Value of Perfect Information

So far we have pictured our toy manufacturer selecting an act without benefit of any additional information beyond that acquired through experience with other toys. But it is possible to obtain better information about next season's demand through test marketing, from opinion and attitude surveys, or from inside information concerning competitors' plans. How much would the decision maker be willing to pay for additional information?

Expected Payoff with Perfect Information

It will be helpful to consider the payoff that can be expected from improved information about the events. We will take the extreme case, where the decision maker can acquire *perfect information*. Using this information, the decision maker could guarantee selection of the act yielding the greatest payoff for whatever event actually occurs. Because we wish to investigate the worth of such information *before* it is obtained, we will determine the *expected payoff with perfect information.*

To calculate the expected payoff with perfect information, we determine the highest payoff for each event. This is illustrated for the doll-movement decision in Table 19-20. The maximum payoff for each demand level is determined by finding the largest payoff in each row. Thus, for a light demand we find that choosing gears and levers gives the largest payoff, $25,000. If perfect information indicated that light demand was certain to occur, our decision maker would choose that movement. Similarly, $440,000 is the maximum payoff possible for moderate demand, and this amount can be achieved only if the spring-action movement is chosen. Likewise, $750,000 is the maximum possible

TABLE 19-20   Calculation of Expected Payoff with Perfect
Information for the Tippi-Toes Decision   *ε POW PI*

Demand Event	Prob- ability	Act			Maximum Payoff for Event	Maximum Payoff × Probability
		Gears and Levers	Spring Action	Weights and Pulleys		
Light	.10	$ 25,000	−$ 10,000	−$125,000	$ 25,000	$ 2,500
Moderate	.70	400,000	440,000	400,000	440,000	308,000
Heavy	.20	650,000	740,000	750,000	750,000	150,000

Expected payoff with perfect information = $460,500

payoff when a heavy demand occurs, corresponding to a choice of the weights and pulleys movement. The last column of Table 19-20 shows the products of the maximum payoffs and their respective event probabilities. Summing these, we obtain $460,500 as the expected payoff with perfect information. This figure represents the average payoff the toy manufacturer would experience if he were faced with the same situation repeatedly and always selected the act yielding the best payoff for the event indicated by the perfect information. Keep in mind that the $460,500 represents the payoff that will on the average be achieved, viewed from some point in time *before* the information has been made available. *After* the information has been obtained, exactly one of the payoffs, $25,000, $440,000, or $750,000, is bound to occur. When the information is actually obtained, the payoff is a known certainty.

Expressing the Worth of Perfect Information

We may now answer our question regarding the worth of perfect information to the decision maker. As we have seen, the Bayes decision rule leads to the choice of a particular act that maximizes the expected payoff without regard to any additional information. We shall refer to this value as the *expected payoff under uncertainty*. Since this is the best that our decision maker can do with no new information, and the expected payoff with perfect information is the average payoff that can be anticipated with the best possible knowledge, then the worth to him of perfect information is expressed by the difference in these two amounts. We call the resulting number the *expected value of perfect information*, which is conveniently represented by the abbreviation EVPI. We have the following expression for the *expected value of perfect information*:

EVPI = Expected payoff with perfect information
 − Expected payoff under uncertainty (with no information)   (19-1)

For the toy-manufacturer's decision, we obtain the EVPI by subtracting the expected payoff under uncertainty of $455,000 (calculated in Table 19-7 on page 657) from the $460,500 expected payoff with perfect information:

$$\text{EVPI} = \$460,500 - \$455,000 = \$5,500$$

In this case the EVPI represents the greatest amount of money the decision maker would be willing to pay to obtain perfect information about what the doll's demand will be. Stated differently, $5,500 is the increase in the decision-maker's expected payoff that can be attributed to perfect knowledge of demand. Neither the $455,000 nor the $460,500 has any meaning *after* the perfect information is obtained. Thus, the EVPI of $5,500 can be interpreted only *before* the perfect information has become known.

The expected value of perfect information is analogous to the expected claim from a hypothetical insurance policy that provides our decision maker with the difference between the payoff actually achieved and the best payoff that could have been achieved had the event that was to occur been known. Table 19-21 shows the calculation of the expected claim, which is the same

TABLE 19-21   EVPI Calculation Using a Hypothetical Insurance Policy

(1) *Demand* *Event*	(2) *Probability*	(3) *Payoff for* *Optimal Act,* *Spring* *Action*	(4) *Greatest* *Payoff* *for* *Event*	(5) *Hypothetical* *Insurance* *Claim* *[(4)−(3)]*	(6) *Claim ×* *Probability* *[(2)×(5)]*
Light	.10	−$ 10,000	$ 25,000	$35,000	$3,500
Moderate	.70	440,000	440,000	0	0
Heavy	.20	740,000	750,000	10,000	2,000
			EVPI = Expected hypothetical insurance claim =		$5,500

figure, $5,500. Because the EVPI expresses how much worse off the decision maker is, on the average, by being uncertain which act will be best, it is sometimes called the *cost of uncertainty.*

EVPI and Opportunity Loss

Note that the amount $5,500 is the same as the minimum expected opportunity loss calculated in Table 19-19 for the optimal choice of act under uncertainty (without perfect information). Note also that the hypothetical claim entries in column (5) of Table 19-21 are the same values as the individual opportunity losses for the spring-action movement. The expected value of these is $5,500, the EVPI. Thus we see that *the expected value of perfect information is equal to the expected opportunity loss for the optimal act.*

Therefore we may calculate the expected value of perfect information by calculating the expected opportunity losses. The minimum of these is the EVPI. Table 19-22 summarizes the relationships among expected payoff, expected opportunity loss, and expected value of perfect information for the toy-manufacturer's decision. Note that, for any act, the sum of the expected payoff and the expected opportunity loss is equal to the expected payoff with perfect information.

Since in practice perfect information is nonexistent in most real-world

TABLE 19-22   Relationships Among Expected Payoff,
Expected Opportunity Loss, and EVPI
for the Tippi-Toes Decision

	Gears and Levers	Spring Action	Weights and Pulleys
Expected payoff	$412,500	$445,000	$417,500
Expected opportunity loss	48,000	5,500	43,000
Expected payoff with perfect information	$460,500	$460,500	$460,500

Expected value of perfect information (EVPI) = $5,500   ⌐ Optimal act

decision making, why do we care about the EVPI? Our answer is that it helps us to establish a limit on the worth of less-than-perfect information. For example, if a marketing-research study aimed at predicting demand costs $6,000, which exceeds the EVPI by $500, then it should not be ordered—regardless of its quality. The concepts involving decision making with experimental information are investigated further in Chapter 20.

EXERCISES

19-17 Using the payoff table below, construct an opportunity loss table.

Event	Act A_1	Act A_2
E_1	100	90
E_2	−50	20

	A_1	A_2
ε_1	0	10 (100−90)
ε_2	(50)−20 70	0

19-18 Using the opportunity loss table below, determine which act yields the lowest expected opportunity loss.

Event	Probability	Act A_1	Act A_2	Act A_3
E_1	.4	10 4	0 0	20 8
E_2	.5	0 0	30 15	40 20
E_3	.1	50 5	5 5	0 0

9   20   28

19-19 For the payoff table on page 689, answer the following:
(a) What is the maximum expected payoff? To what act does this correspond? E_3 / A_2
(b) What is the expected payoff with perfect information?
(c) Using your answers from (a) and (b), calculate the expected value of perfect information.

(d) What is the minimum expected opportunity loss?

(e) What do you notice about your answers to (c) and (d)?

		Act		
Event	Probability	A_1	A_2	A_3
E_1	1/3	10	20	30
E_2	1/3	40	−10	20
E_3	1/3	20	50	20

19-20 A paper company is planning its capital investment expenditures for new equipment. Two alternative machines are being considered for the manufacture of kraft paper used in cardboard boxes. Machine A costs $100,000 and produces paper at an operating cost of $10 per ton, including materials and labor. Machine B costs $500,000 and makes paper at an operating cost of $5 per ton. The company currently buys kraft paper for $20 per ton from another mill. Total kraft-paper requirements throughout the next five years is the major uncertainty affecting choice of machines. Management has chosen as its payoff measure total five-year savings over purchasing the paper from outside.

(a) How many tons of paper must be used before machine A has been "paid off"? How many for machine B?

(b) What is the number of tons that will yield equal savings from either machine?

(c) Suppose two levels of total production are judged equally likely: 50,000 tons and 100,000 tons. Construct the payoff table. Then determine the maximum expected payoff act.

(d) Construct the opportunity loss table for this decision. Then determine the minimum expected opportunity loss act.

(e) Was the same act chosen in (c) and (d)? Why was this so?

19-21 An oil wildcatter must decide whether to drill on a candidate drilling site. His judgment leads him to the conclusion that there is a 50-50 chance of oil. If he drills and strikes oil, his profit will be $200,000. But if the well turns up dry, his net loss will be $100,000.

(a) Using the Bayes decision rule, should the wildcatter drill or abandon the site?

(b) What is the wildcatter's EVPI?

(c) A seismologist offers to conduct a high-reliability seismic survey. The results could be used in helping the wildcatter make the decision. What is the most the wildcatter would consider paying for such seismic information?

REVIEW EXERCISES

19-22 Use the payoff table below to answer the following questions.

		Act				
Event	Probability	A_1	A_2	A_3	A_4	A_5
E_1	.2	10	20	10	15	20
E_2	.2	−5	10	−5	10	−5
E_3	.6	15	5	10	10	10

(a) Find any inadmissible acts, and list all those acts that dominate them. Cross out the columns in the payoff table that represent any inadmissible acts.

(b) Find the minimum payoff for each admissible act. Which act is the maximin payoff act?

(c) Which act is the maximum likelihood act?

(d) Calculate the expected payoff for each admissible act. According to the Bayes decision rule, which act is best?

(e) Find the EVPI.

19-23 Refer to the payoff table in Exercise 19-22.

(a) Construct the opportunity loss table (include all acts).

(b) Compute the expected opportunity losses for each act. According to the Bayes decision rule, which act is best?

19-24 A product manager for a soap manufacturer wants to determine whether or not to market a new toothpaste. The present value of all future profits for a successful toothpaste is $1,000,000, whereas failure of the brand would result in a net loss of $500,000. Not marketing it would not change profits. The manager has judged that the toothpaste would have a 50–50 chance of success.

(a) Construct the payoff table for this decision.

(b) Which act will maximize expected payoff?

(c) What is the expected payoff under uncertainty?

(d) Compute the decision-maker's EVPI. What is the minimum expected opportunity loss?

19-25 Suppose that the manager in Exercise 19-24 will order a consumer testing program costing $50,000. Consumer testing will be either favorable (40-percent chance) or unfavorable. Given a favorable test result, the chance of product success is judged to be 80 percent. But for an unfavorable test result, the toothpaste's success probability has been judged to be only 30 percent.

(a) Construct a decision tree diagram assuming that testing is used. Then perform backward induction to find the optimal strategy for using the test results.

(b) Identify the basic strategies involving the results of the consumer testing program. Construct a payoff table with these strategies as the choices and the joint market outcomes and test results as the events. Then conduct a normal form analysis to determine which strategy maximizes expected payoff.

19-26 A newsdealer must decide how many copies of a particular magazine to stock in December. He will not stock less than the lowest possible demand nor more than the highest. Each magazine costs him $0.50 and sells for $1.00. At the end of the month, unsold magazines are thrown away. Three levels of monthly demand are equally likely: 10, 11, and 12. If demand exceeds stock, sales will equal stock.

(a) Using December profit as his payoff, construct the newsdealer's payoff table.

(b) According to the maximin criterion, how many copies should he stock?

(c) Which number of copies will provide the greatest expected payoff?

19-27 A government official wishes to decide the best way to control crop damage from the gypsy moth. Three methods for attacking the pest are: (1) Spray with DDT; (2) Use a scent to lure and trap males, so that those that remain must compete for mating with a much larger number of males that have been sterilized in a laboratory and then released; and

(3) Spray with juvenile hormone, which prevents the larvae from developing into adults.

The net improvement in current and future crop losses using DDT is zero, for it is assumed that DDT will never completely eradicate the moth.

The scent-lure program has probability .5 of leaving a low number of native males, with a .5 chance of a high number. Once the scent-lure results are known, a later choice must then be made either to switch back to DDT or to release sterile males. The cost of the scent lures is $5 million and that for sterile males is an additional $5 million. But if this two-phase program is successful, the present and future crop savings will be $30 million. If scent lures leave the remaining native male population small, there is a 90-percent chance of success using sterile males, otherwise there is only a 10-percent chance of success with sterile males. A failure results in zero crop savings.

The juvenile hormone must be synthesized at a cost of $3 million. There is only a .20 probability that the resulting product will work. If it does, the crop savings would be $50 million, as the gypsy moth would become extinct. If not, crop savings would be zero.

Construct a decision tree diagram for the official's decision. Using crop savings minus cost as the payoff measure (relative to using DDT, which has zero payoff), determine the maximum expected payoff course of action.

Chapter Twenty

Bayesian Analysis of Decisions Using Experimental Information

Antecendently to all experience, it would be improbable as infinite to one, that any event, beforehand imagined, should follow the application of any natural object to another. . . . But if the same event has followed without interruption in any one or more experiments, then some degree of uniformity will be observed; reason will be given to expect the same success in further experiments.

Reverend Thomas Bayes (1763)

We usually associate the term "experiment" with a test or investigation. Experiments may be very elaborate, as in science where many years of effort and much expensive equipment are devoted to activities such as studying physical laws by observing solar eclipses. Or they may be very simple, such as asking a person questions in order to become better acquainted. No matter what their scope, all experiments have one feature in common: *they provide information*. This information may serve to realign uncertainty. Information obtained by observing a solar eclipse can support hypotheses regarding the effect of the sun's gravity on stellar light rays. A person's response to your questions can help you decide whether he or she is worth befriending. *An experiment can help us make better decisions under uncertainty*. Scientists can become more certain that the sun's gravity has an effect on light rays, and their observations can lead to finer choices for further experiments. The answers to our questions can convince us that an ugly person is really beautiful or that a physically beautiful person is vain and selfish.

Most experiments, however, are not conclusive. Any test can camouflage the truth. For instance, some potentially good employees will flunk well-designed employment screening tests, while some incompetents will pass them. Another good example is the seismic survey, which provides geological information about deep underground rock structures and is used to explore for oil deposits. Unfortunately, a seismic survey can deny the presence of oil in a field already producing oil and confirm the presence of oil under a site already proven to be dry. Still, such imperfect experiments can be of value. An unfavorable test result can increase the chance of rejecting a poor prospect—job applicant or drilling site—and a favorable one can enhance the likelihood of selecting a good prospect.

In this chapter, we will incorporate experimentation into the framework of our decision-making analysis. The information obtained will affect the probabilities of those events that determine the consequences of each act. We can revise the probabilities of these events upward or downward depending on the evidence obtained. Thus a geologist will increase the subjective probability of oil on obtaining a favorable seismic survey analysis and lower it if the survey is unfavorable.

The seismic survey epitomizes experimental information in decision making. In business situations several other classic sources of such information are commonly employed. A marketing research study serves to realign uncertainty regarding the degree of success a new product will achieve in the marketplace. An aptitude test is often used to help predict a job applicant's future success or failure should he or she be hired—a decision involving considerable uncertainty. A sampling study is frequently employed in quality-control decisions to facilitate decisions relating to how satisfactorily items are produced or the amount of defective items arriving from a supplier.

In this chapter, we first investigate how to revise probabilities in accordance with experimental results. In doing this we will apply the probability concepts associated with Bayes' Theorem discussed in Chapter 5. We meld this probability information with all the decision elements by means of a decision tree diagram. How much information is incorporated into the decision serves as a prelude to a more general analysis of the initial choice to experiment. For example: Would an oil wildcatter use a seismic survey if it cost $50,000?

The remainder of the chapter is concerned with decisions using sample information. We consider for the first time the decision whether or not to sample at all. Another important question answered is: How large should n be?

20-1 REVISING PROBABILITIES: POSTERIOR ANALYSIS

In a typical situation, the decision maker has some kind of judgment about the uncertain events. This may be expressed as a set of *prior probabilities* regarding the occurrence of the respective events. On occasion, such judgment must be quantified in terms of subjective probabilities, since the events in question frequently arise from nonrepeatable circumstances. At other times, the prior probabilities may be objective in nature. In accordance with the information obtained from the experiment, the event uncertainties are realigned to obtain *posterior probabilities*. Figure 20-1 shows the sequence of steps in this procedure, exactly the one originally proposed by Thomas Bayes.

The Oil Wildcatter: A Case Illustration

As an illustration, we will use an oil wildcatter's decision whether to drill for oil at a leased site. He is contemplating hiring a geologist to conduct a detailed seismic survey of the area. For the present we are only concerned with the probability portion of this problem.

As a first step, the wildcatter must *exercise judgment* regarding the likelihood of striking oil. Since no two unproven drilling sites are very much alike,

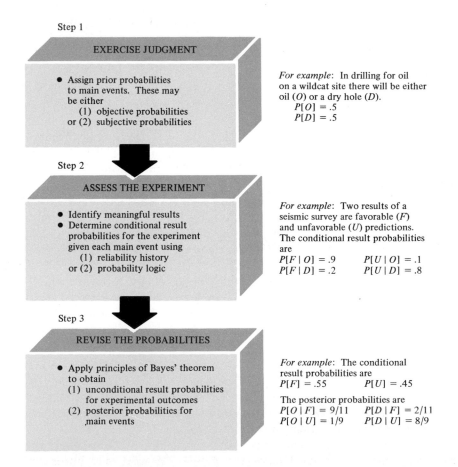

Step 1

EXERCISE JUDGMENT

- Assign prior probabilities to main events. These may be either
    - (1) objective probabilities
    - or (2) subjective probabilities

For example: In drilling for oil on a wildcat site there will be either oil (*O*) or a dry hole (*D*).
$$P[O] = .5$$
$$P[D] = .5$$

Step 2

ASSESS THE EXPERIMENT

- Identify meaningful results
- Determine conditional result probabilities for the experiment given each main event using
    - (1) reliability history
    - or (2) probability logic

For example: Two results of a seismic survey are favorable (*F*) and unfavorable (*U*) predictions. The conditional result probabilities are
$$P[F \mid O] = .9 \qquad P[U \mid O] = .1$$
$$P[F \mid D] = .2 \qquad P[U \mid D] = .8$$

Step 3

REVISE THE PROBABILITIES

- Apply principles of Bayes' theorem to obtain
    - (1) unconditional result probabilities for experimental outcomes
    - (2) posterior probabilities for main events

For example: The conditional result probabilities are
$$P[F] = .55 \qquad P[U] = .45$$

The posterior probabilities are
$$P[O \mid F] = 9/11 \qquad P[D \mid F] = 2/11$$
$$P[O \mid U] = 1/9 \qquad P[D \mid U] = 8/9$$

FIGURE 20-1   Steps in performing the probability portion of the decision analysis when experimental information is used.

there is no historical frequency that can be used for this purpose. The wild-catter must therefore rely on a subjective probability value. Suppose that he believes there is a 50–50 chance of striking oil. Letting O represent oil and D stand for dry hole, the prior probabilities of the basic events are

$$P[O] = .5$$
$$P[D] = .5$$

As the next step, the wildcatter *assesses the experiment*, the seismic survey in this case. He starts by contemplating what results would be meaningful to him. Although the seismic output might be very complex and varied, for simplicity we suppose that the geologist's analysis will lead to only two meaning-ful results: a favorable (F) prediction for oil or an unfavorable one (U). It is necessary to obtain *conditional result probabilities* for the respective seismic outcomes given each possible basic event. Ordinarily, the conditional result probabilities for the experiment may be obtained objectively, either through estimation from historical frequencies or by applying the underlying logic of probability. Thus, we might refer to these values as "logical-historical" prob-abilities to help distinguish them from the several types encountered.

In the present example, the geologist has kept a "batting average" for the procedure. Historical records show that on 90 percent of known producing oil fields his prediction of oil has proven favorable. That is, 90 percent of similar seismic survey data have provided favorable oil predictions when indeed oil exists; in other words, the seismic survey method is 90 percent reliable in arriving at a favorable forecast when oil is actually present. (Of course, such a number should not be biased by the fact that the seismic survey result may have affected the earlier decisions to drill on those sites. A reliability figure is best obtained through a special study where the tester itself is tested; this might be done by taking special seismic measurements on already producing sites.) Through simulated readings on known dry holes, the geologist has also determined that the survey is only 80 percent reliable in making an unfavorable prediction when no oil is present. The appropriate conditional result probabilities are

$$P[F|O] = .90 \quad \text{and} \quad P[U|O] = .10$$
$$P[F|D] = .20 \quad \text{and} \quad P[U|D] = .80$$

The above probabilities are "historical" and in the nature of statistical estimates of the underlying values, since they are based on limited samples of drilling sites. (Note that the conditional probability of a favorable result given oil is greater than that for an unfavorable prediction given dry; there is no reason why a test must be equally discerning in both directions.)

In other situations, conditional result probabilities for an informational experiment may be obtained more directly without using past history. This would be true, for example, in assessing a quality-control sample. The precise probability distribution for the sample result may be determined through logical deduction, based only on probability principles and the type of events that characterize the sampled population. Later, we will see how such "logical" probabilities may be determined using the binomial distribution.

The final step toward incorporating experimental information into the probability portion of decision analysis is to *revise the probabilities*. This revision ordinarily results in two kinds of probability values, each applicable at a different stage of uncertainty. The *posterior probabilities* serve for the main events and the *unconditional result probabilities* for the experimental outcomes themselves. Although the underlying concepts of Bayes' Theorem are used in arriving at these values, a somewhat more streamlined procedure, illustrated in Figure 20-2, proves more convenient when using decision trees to analyze a decision.

Using Probability Trees

We start with the probability tree diagram 20-2(a). This portrays the *actual chronology* of events. Here the first fork represents the events for the site status: oil or dry. The second stage is represented by a fork for the seismic survey results. This particular arrangement represents the sequence in which the events actually arise: first, nature determined (several million years ago) whether this site would cover an oil field; second, our present-day geologist conducts a seismic test. The actual chronology also adheres to the manner in which the probability data are initially obtained. The wildcatter has directly assessed the probabilities for the site status events; and the geologist has indicated the reliabilities for the survey. Thus, the values given earlier for the prior probabilities of oil and dry and the conditional result probabilities are placed on the corresponding branches in diagram (a).

Probability tree diagram 20-2(b) represents the *informational chronology*. This is the sequence in which the decision maker finds out which events occur. First the wildcatter obtains the result for the seismic survey, portrayed by the initial event fork. Then, if he chooses to drill, he ultimately determines whether or not the site covers an oil field. This is the sequence of events as they would appear on a decision tree (which will be discussed later). But this particular chronology does not directly correspond to the inital probability data. Additional work is needed to get the probability values shown on tree diagram 20-2(b).

We start by multiplying together the branch probabilities on each path in tree diagram 20-2(a) to obtain the corresponding joint probability values. The same numbers apply regardless of chronology, so the joint probabilities can be transferred to diagram (b). This must be done with care, since the in-between joint outcomes are not listed in the same order in (b) as in (a) because analogous paths (event sequences) differ between the diagrams. For example, in diagram (a) we obtain the joint probability of oil and an unfavorable seismic result

$$P[O \text{ and } U] = P[O] \times P[U|O] = .5 \times .1 = .05$$

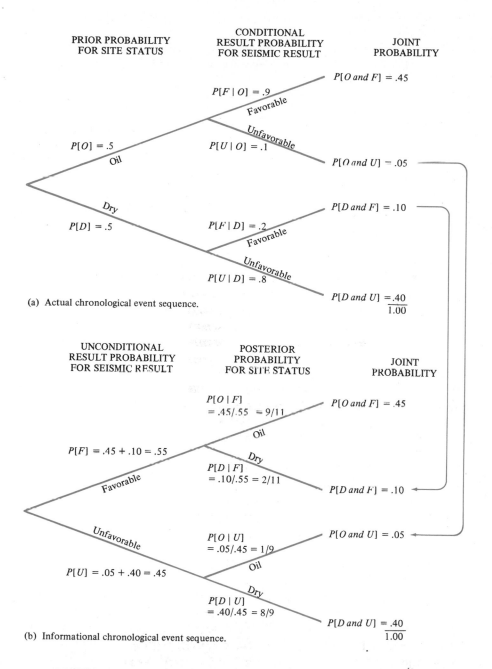

FIGURE 20-2   Probability tree diagrams showing event chronologies for drilling a wildcat well and using a seismic survey.

This is the second joint probability in (a) and corresponds to the third end position in (b).

Next, we work entirely in diagram (b). First, we compute the unconditional result probabilities at the first stage. Here we use the addition law to obtain

$$P[F] = P[O \text{ and } F] + P[D \text{ and } F] = .45 + .10 = .55$$

$$P[U] = P[O \text{ and } U] + P[D \text{ and } U] = .05 + .40 = .45$$

These values are placed on the applicable branches at the first stage. Finally, the posterior probabilities for the second-stage events are computed using the basic property of conditional probability:

$$P[A \mid B] = \frac{P[A \text{ and } B]}{P[B]} \tag{20-1}$$

Thus, we determine the posterior probability for oil given a favorable seismic survey result:

$$P[O \mid F] = \frac{P[O \text{ and } F]}{P[F]} = \frac{.45}{.55} = \frac{9}{11}$$

This value is placed on the second-stage branch for oil preceded by the earlier branch for a favorable result. In a like manner, the other posterior probabilities shown in diagram (b) are each found by dividing the respective end-position joint probability by the probability on the preceding branch.

Revision of probabilities in the manner illustrated above is generally required whenever experimental information is used in decision making. This happens because we ordinarily get our probabilities in the reverse chronology from that needed to analyze the problem.

Posterior Analysis

Figure 20-3 is the decision tree diagram illustrating the wildcatter's choices once the seismic results are known. Here we have assumed that (1) the lease will be sold for $250,000 upon striking oil; (2) the cost of drilling is $100,000; and (3) the seismic survey will cost $25,000. We show the decision to drill or to abandon the lease as following the seismic survey result, since the wildcatter obviously would not decide before finding out the geologist's prediction. The revised probabilities found earlier for the informational chronology are used. Since the posterior probabilities for the site status events apply at the two decision points, using this decision tree as the basis for decision making is called *posterior analysis*.

Note that there is no event fork following the act to abandon the lease, because the oil wildcatter will never find out if there is oil unless he drills for it.

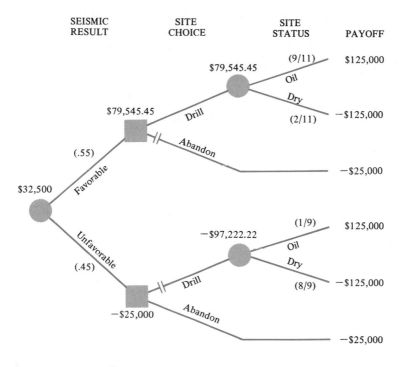

FIGURE 20-3   The wildcatter's decision tree diagram when seismic survey is taken.

(The uncertainty still exists, nevertheless; it would do no harm to have event forks for oil versus dry at those points, but the payoff would be −$25,000 in either case, and an identical conclusion would be reached.)

Performing the backward induction, we see that the wildcatter would prune the abandon branch and drill if a favorable seismic result were obtained and would do the opposite in the case of an unfavorable prediction. Even though drilling will lead to identical payoffs for either seismic result, the posterior probabilities of oil and dry are different for the favorable and unfavorable predictions. The expected payoff from drilling is $79,545.45 for the favorable seismic, but it is a negative value, −$97,222.22, in the case of an unfavorable one. His expected payoff for the optimal strategy is $32,500. This number will be useful, as we shall see later, in determing whether the seismic survey should be used at all.

Obviously Non-Optimal Strategies

In the simpler decision structures, it may be convenient to streamline the decision tree diagram. For the wildcatter's problem, we can conclude that he would prune the same branches regardless of the numbers involved. Since he is paying $25,000 for the seismic survey and this experiment provides fairly reliable predictions, he should choose acts consistent with the information obtained. But the tree in Figure 20-3 allows for three other strategies: drill regardless of result (prune both abandon branches); abandon in either case (prune the two branches for drill); and do the opposite of what is predicted (prune the drill branch if the seismic is favorable and prune the abandon branch if it is unfavorable). The last strategy is ridiculous and would never be considered. The other two are inferior to drilling or to abandoning without benefit of seismic results, since in either case the $25,000 cost could be saved. Such inferior strategies are *obviously non-optimal strategies*.

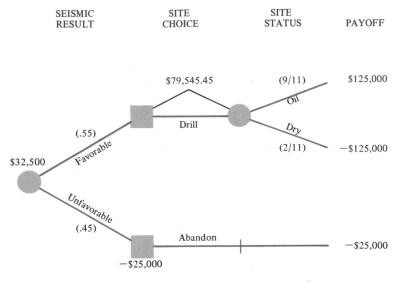

FIGURE 20-4   The simplified wildcatter's decision tree diagram with obviously non-optimal strategies left off.

Figure 20-4 shows how the wildcatter's decision tree diagram could have been drawn by excluding the obviously non-optimal strategies. This representation might help simplify an otherwise complex decision tree. However, for expository convenience, we will always use the complete tree structure presented earlier. When more than two acts or experimental results are involved, it is not easy to determine which strategies are obviously non-optimal.

EXERCISES

20-1   For the probability tree diagram in Figure 20-5 showing the actual chronological sequence of events, determine the missing values for the end position joint probabilities. Then find the missing values for the informational chronology probability tree diagram in Figure 20-6.

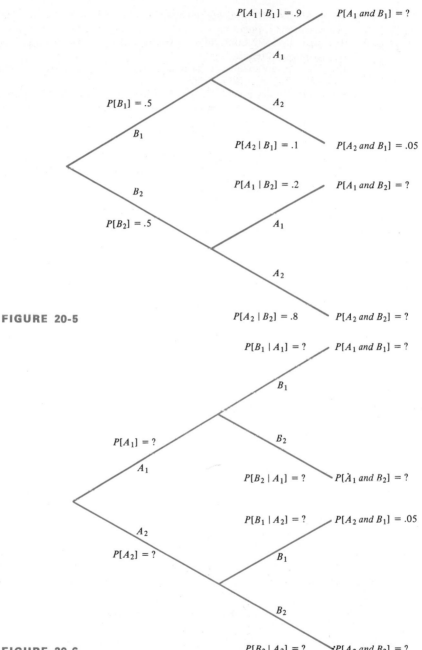

FIGURE 20-5

FIGURE 20-6

20-2   An oil wildcatter has assigned a .40 probability to striking oil on his property. He orders a seismic survey that has proved only 80 percent reliable in the past. Given oil, it predicts favorably 80 percent of the time; given no oil, it augurs unfavorable with a frequency of .8.

Construct probability trees for the actual and informational chronologies, and indicate the appropriate probability values for each branch and end position.

20-3 The structure of a boat-builder's decision is provided in Figure 20-7.
  (a) List all strategies.
  (b) Perform an extensive form analysis using backward induction to determine the optimal strategy.

20-4 Referring to the boat-builder's decision in Figure 20-7, suppose that $50,000 is saved by not conducting test marketing. Answer the following. (Assume that the payoffs in Figure 20-7 include the cost of test marketing.)
  (a) Expand the boat-builder's decision tree diagram to show an initial act fork for the decision whether to test market. Revise the monetary payoffs for those end positions resulting from not test marketing, and assume that without test marketing the prior probability of high sales is .5.

TEST MARKETING RESULT	CHOICE OF HULL MATERIAL	SALES EVENT	PAYOFF

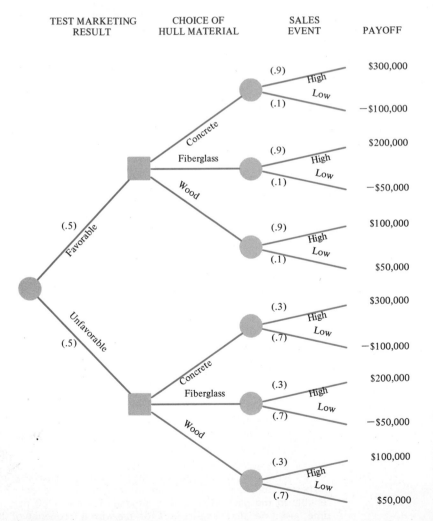

FIGURE 20-7

(b) Perform backward induction analysis to determine whether the builder would choose to test market.

20-5 The following payoff table for marketing choices for a new film has been determined by the management of a motion picture studio.

Box Office Result Events	Distribute as "A" Feature	Sell to TV Network	Distribute as "B" Feature
Success ,3	$ 5,000,000	$1,000,000	$3,000,000
Failure ,7	−2,000,000	1,000,000	−1,000,000

The prior probability of a box office success has been judged to be .3. The studio plans a series of sneak previews. Historically, it has found that favorable previews have been obtained for 70 percent of all successful films previewed, while unfavorable previews have resulted from 80 percent of the box office failures subjected to such experimentation.
(a) Construct the probability tree diagrams for the actual and informational chronologies.
(b) Construct a table showing all possible strategies for management contingent upon the results of the sneak preview.
(c) Construct a tree diagram for the studio's decision, assuming that it will definitely use the sneak preview.
(d) Perform backward induction analysis. What is the optimal course of action? To which strategy in part (b) does this correspond?

20-6 Your friend places two coins, identical in all respects except that one is two-headed, into a box. Without looking, you select one coin from the box and lay it on the table.
(a) What is the prior probability that the two-headed coin gets selected?
(b) You may examine the showing face as a source of predictive information about which coin was selected. Construct the probability tree diagram for the actual chronology of events.
(c) After you have examined the showing face of the coin, you may then turn it over to see what is on the other side. Construct the probability tree diagram for the informational chronology.
(d) If a head shows (before turning the coin over), what is the posterior probability that the two-headed coin was selected?

20-2 DECISION TO EXPERIMENT: PREPOSTERIOR ANALYSIS

We have illustrated the use of experimental information and have described posterior analysis, which indicates what act to select for each experimental outcome. Now we will incorporate the additional choice of whether or not to obtain such information in the first place. Thus the decision is expanded to include an initial stage involving selection of acts concerning experimentation. The procedure that evaluates this expanded decision is sometimes referred to as *preposterior analysis.*

To illustrate how to incorporate the decision to use experimental information, we expand the oil wildcatter's decision. Figure 20-8 shows the decision

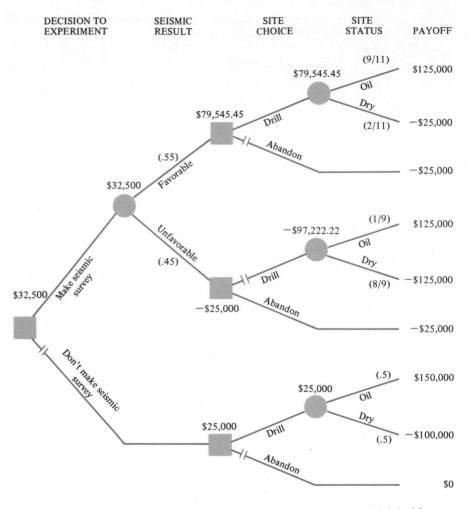

DECISION TO EXPERIMENT	SEISMIC RESULT	SITE CHOICE	SITE STATUS	PAYOFF

FIGURE 20-8 The wildcatter's decision tree diagram with the initial decision regarding seismic.

structure. The added decision about whether or not to make the seismic test is treated as an initial decision point, which is the initial act fork having branches for making and for not making the seismic test. If the seismic survey is used, there follows an event fork relating to the seismic result to be achieved; here the unconditional result probabilities apply. These events are followed by the final decision to drill or to abandon. If the wildcatter drills, the last set of event forks represent the oil and dry events and the posterior probabilities apply. If the initial decision is to not make the seismic survey, then the choice to drill or abandon must be made without any information, which is shown as the act fork at the bottom of the tree. In this case, drilling leads to a final event fork for the site status events. Here the prior probabilities originally obtained apply for oil and dry. The payoffs in this bottom portion of the tree are $25,000 greater than their counterparts directly above, since the cost of the seismic survey is saved.

We now have a two-stage decision problem to analyze. Performing backward induction on the top portion of Figure 20-8, we obtain the result found earlier: Using the seismic survey yields an expected payoff of $32,500. We find that not using the survey leads to a smaller expected payoff of only $25,000. Thus, at the first decision point, the branch for don't make the seismic is pruned. The course of action maximizing expected payoff is: Make the seismic survey; if it is favorable, drill, but if it is unfavorable, abandon.

Role of EVPI

In some situations the foregoing procedure may be considerably shortened. Recall that the expected value of perfect information, or EVPI, indicates the worth of the best possible or ideal information about the events in the main decision. Usually information obtained through experiments is far from perfect in its predictive powers. If such evidence would cost more than it can at best be worth, it should obviously not be obtained. In Table 20-1 the wildcatter's

TABLE 20-1   Calculation of the Wildcatter's EVPI

Event	Probability	Payoff		Row Maximum	Row Maximum × Probability
		Drill	Abandon		
Oil	.5	$150,000	$0	$150,000	$75,000
Dry	.5	−100,000	0	0	0
	1.0				$75,000

Expected payoff with perfect information = $75,000
Expected payoff under uncertainty (drilling) = .5($150,000)+.5(−$100,000) = $25,000
EVPI = $75,000−$25,000 = $50,000

EVPI is calculated to be $50,000. (Here the prior probabilities are used, since the seismic survey does not apply.) Had the cost of the seismic survey been a higher figure, say $60,000, the oil wildcatter would be better off not bothering with it, regardless of how reliable its predictions would be. In effect, the seismic branch would be pruned from the tree, without any need to calculate posterior probabilities or to do any of the preposterior analysis described above. Of course, this shortcut applies only when the cost of the information exceeds the EVPI. Since the wildcatter had to spend only $25,000, which is smaller than the $50,000 EVPI, in this case the complete preposterior analysis was required.

EXERCISES

20-7   The exploration manager for a small oil company must decide whether to drill on a parcel of leased land or to abandon the lease. To aid in making this choice he can first decide whether to pay $30,000 for a seismic survey, which will confirm or deny the presence of the anticlinal structure necessary for oil. He has judged his prior probability of oil to be .30. For oil-producing fields of similar geology, his experience has shown that the chance of a confirming seismic is .9; but for dry holes with about the same features, the probability that a seismic survey will deny oil has been established to be only .7. Drilling costs have been firmly established at $200,000. If oil is struck, his company plans to sell the lease for $500,000.

(a) What is the manager's EVPI for the basic decision, using profit as the payoff measure? Comparing this value to the cost of the seismic survey, can we conclude definitely that no survey would be used?

(b) Construct the manager's decision tree diagram, and determine the appropriate payoffs.

(c) Find the revised probabilities for the informational chronology, and place these values on the corresponding branches of your decision tree diagram.

(d) Perform backward induction analysis to determine the course of action providing maximum expected profit.

20-8   Lucky Jones must decide whether to participate in a card game offered by Inscrutable Smith. For the price of $5, Jones will draw a card from an ordinary deck of playing cards. If the card is a king, then Smith pays Jones $60 (so that Jones wins $55). But if it is not a king, Jones receives nothing for the $5. Smith, eager for action, offers Jones an additional enticement. For $3 Jones can draw a card without looking at it. Smith will then tell Jones whether or not the card is a face card. If Jones wishes to continue, for an additional payment of $5 the game will proceed as before.

(a) Construct a decision tree diagram showing the structure of Jones' decision.

(b) Determine the probabilities for the events and the total profit for end position.

(c) What course of action provides Jones with the greatest expected payoff?

20-9   The decision tree diagram in Figure 20-9 has been determined for a marketing manager deciding how to introduce a new product. She has determined a .40 prior probability for marketing success.

(a) From a consumer survey costing $30,000, she can obtain an 80 percent reliable indication of the product's impact in the marketplace. Thus, the probability of a favorable survey result given market success is .80, while that for an unfavorable result given market failure is .80. Find the posterior probabilities of the market events and the unconditional result probabilities for the survey events.

(b) For a sales program in a test region costing $50,000, the results are judged 95 percent reliable. Find the posterior and unconditional result probabilities.

(c) Using the information given in the statement of the problem and your answers to parts (a) and (b), perform backward induction to find the optimal course of action. (The payoffs in Figure 20-9 include the cost of experimenting.)

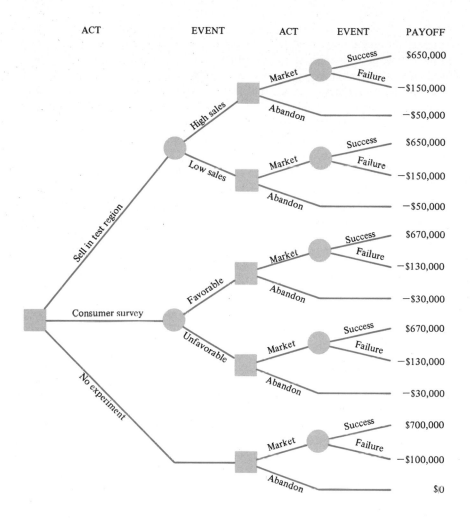

ACT	EVENT	ACT	EVENT	PAYOFF

FIGURE 20-9

DECISION MAKING WITH SAMPLE INFORMATION

Until now we have considered the general problem of decision making with experimental information. We now consider a decision commonly en-countered in business situations in which there are just *two acts* and the experi-ment is taking a *random sample* from a population whose characteristics affect the ultimate payoffs. The decision-maker's choice depends on the particular sample result obtained.

Recall that two types of populations are encountered in these sampling experiments. One is the *qualitative population*, which is comprised of units classified into categories—for example, persons, who might be categorized by occupation (blue-collar, professional, etc.), sex (male, female), or preferences (liking a product, disliking it); or production items, which may be classified in terms of quality (satisfactory, unsatisfactory), weight (below the limit, above it), or color (light, medium, dark). The other type, the *quantitative population*, associates a numerical value to each unit—for example, persons who could be measured in terms of income levels, aptitude test scores, or years of experience; or things that may have a numerical value for weight, volume, quantity of an ingredient, and so forth.

A sample from a qualitative population tells us how many sample units fall into a particular category, and this number reflects the prevalence of that attribute in the population, which in turn affects the payoff associated with the attribute's incidence. For example, in deciding how to dispose of a supplier's shipment, a receiving inspector may find that 12 of the items in a random sample of 100 are defective, which indicates a high probability that the entire shipment is bad, and returning it might maximize expected payoff. The payoffs in such a problem can often be expressed in terms of the proportion π of the population having the key attribute (for example, proportion defective in the entire shipment). As with most decision making using experiments, the value of π itself and the number of defectives that will turn up in the sample are both uncertain. Probabilities for the latter can be determined by using the binomial distribution.

A sample taken from a quantitative population provides a similar basis for action, such as accepting or rejecting a machine setting in a chemical process. Here, the mean quantity of a particular ingredient in each gallon may be the determining factor in establishing the payoff. The population mean μ measures the central quantity of the ingredient in all gallons made under that setting. The true value of μ is uncertain. A second area of uncertainty involves the quantities in the sample itself; here the sample mean $\overline{X}$ may serve as the basis for decision making.

In this section, we consider how to integrate sample information into the basic decision-making structure. As in the preceding section, the procedure will involve prior probabilities for π or μ, which must be revised to coincide with possible sample results to provide posterior probabilities for these population parameters. Backward induction with revised probabilities will provide the optimal decision rule, based on the sample statistic that will be obtained. The analysis may be expanded to consider how sample observations must be made.

We begin our discussion of sampling as a source of experimental information with the case of the qualitative population, where the binomial distribution determines the conditional result probabilities.

Decision Making with Binomial Probabilities

Charles Stereo: An Acceptance Sampling Illustration
Charles Stereo is a chain of retail outlets specializing in sound equipment. Because of its high volume, Charles stocks its inventory of stereo pickup

cartridges by ordering lots of 100 units from various manufacturers. Bertrand Charles, the owner, wishes to decide whether to accept or reject a particular lot from one supplier, DICO. Each cartridge in a rejected lot is thoroughly inspected by Charles, and those actually found to be defective are replaced by the supplier. An accepted lot is parceled out uninspected to the retail stores for sale to customers, who are relied upon to find the defective cartridges, which Charles replaces without charge from its inventory. DICO will not give Charles credit for cartridges already used by retail customers, even if they were originally defective.

One of the Charles employees has suggested that the company sample incoming lots, using the information thereby obtained as a basis for deciding whether a lot should be accepted or rejected. Charles is a bit skeptical about the advantages of sampling, since even after inspection of randomly chosen items he cannot be certain of the value of the lot proportion defective π. The employee volunteers to analyze the decision and chooses as a payoff measure the gross profit from a 100-item lot.

Detailed records have been kept of all DICO cartridges received by Charles. From these the frequencies of lot proportions defective have been found. These frequencies serve as estimates of the prior probabilities for values of π of .10, .20, and .30 as shown below.

Possible Lot Proportion Defective π	Prior Probability
.10	.4
.20	.3
.30	.3
	1.0

To simplify our analysis, we consider values of π only to the nearest whole 10 percent (the same procedures would apply if we considered $\pi = .05$, .07, ..., .35).

Structure of Decision

Consider a sample of size $n = 2$, for example, for the Charles decision problem as shown in Figure 20-10. An immediate choice, represented by the act fork at decision point a, is required to determine whether or not to sample. If the choice is made to inspect the two randomly chosen items, the possible outcomes for the number of defectives are $R = 0$, $R = 1$, or $R = 2$, shown as events on the fork at b. The choices to accept or reject the lot are represented by act branches in the forks at decision points c, d, e, and f. After the acts to accept or reject, the lot proportion defective π is determined. π is found either through 100-percent inspection, in the case of rejection, or by a tally of returned cartridges if the lot is accepted. The various possible values of π are shown as events on forks g through n.

The payoffs for each end position are determined by adjusting a $1,000

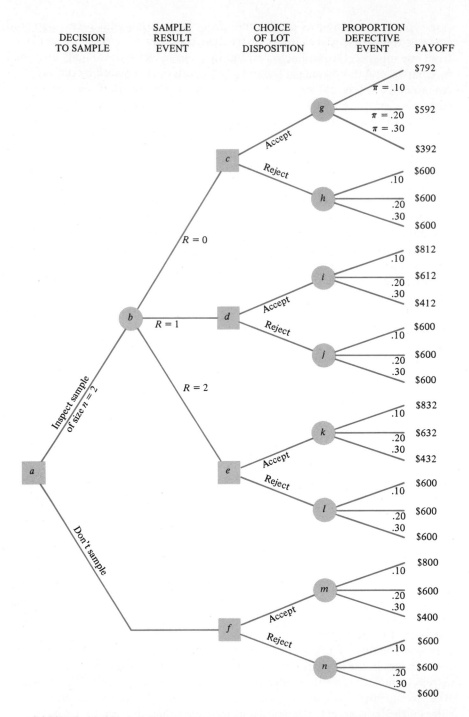

FIGURE 20-10 The decision tree for the Charles Stereo sampling decision.

lot markup downward to account for the costs of inspection and losses from used defective cartridges returned by customers.

The payoff corresponding to the act sequence, don't sample and then accept, is found by subtracting the losses on 100π defective cartridges at \$20 each from \$1,000:

$$\text{Payoff} = \$1,000 - 100\pi(\$20)$$

When $\pi = .10$, the payoff from position m is then $\$1,000 - 100(.10)(\$20) = \$800$. The payoffs for the event fork at branching point m are calculated in the same manner.

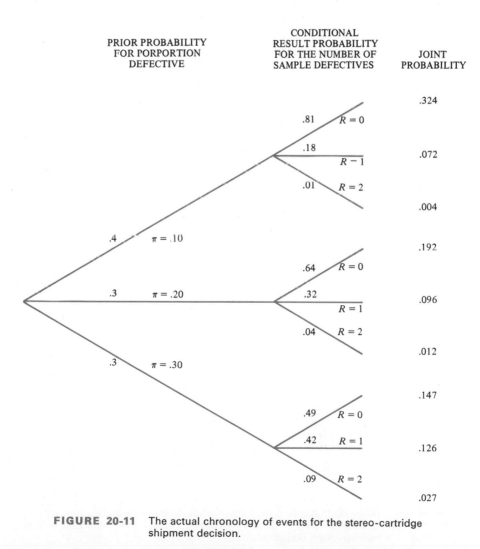

PRIOR PROBABILITY FOR PORPORTION DEFECTIVE	CONDITIONAL RESULT PROBABILITY FOR THE NUMBER OF SAMPLE DEFECTIVES	JOINT PROBABILITY

FIGURE 20-11   The actual chronology of events for the stereo-cartridge shipment decision.

Charles incurs a $4 cost for each cartridge it inspects prior to sale or return for supplier credit. Rejecting a 100-item lot, therefore, results in a $400 loss, so that the payoffs for the act sequence, don't sample and then reject, are all equal to $1,000 − $400 = $600, regardless of the value of π.

When sampling is considered, there is a 2($4) = $8 cost for the two items inspected. If the lot is accepted, there will be a $20 loss on only the defective cartridges not found; the number of these is $100\pi - R$. Thus the payoffs for the act sequence, sample and then accept, are calculated from

$$\text{Payoff} = \$1,000 - \$8 - \$20(100\pi - R)$$

For example, the end position of the event fork at k, for the branch $\pi = .10$ following from event $R = 2$, has payoff

$$\$1,000 - \$8 - \$20(10 - 2) = \$832$$

Determining Event Probabilities

The actual event chronology is provided in Figure 20-11. Here the first stage represents the prior probabilities for the proportion of defective cartridges in the shipment, and the second stage provides the conditional result probabilities for the number of defectives in the sample. The later probabilities are calculated in Table 20-2 by using the binomial distribution.* (When n is large, it may be more convenient to obtain the binomial probabilities from Appendix Table C.)

TABLE 20-2 Binomial Conditional Result Probabilities for the Number of Defectives in the Sample

π	r	$P[R = r] = \dfrac{n!}{r!(n-r)!}\pi^r(1-\pi)^{n-r}$
.10	0	$1(.10)^0(.90)^2 = .81$
.10	1	$2(.10)^1(.90)^1 = .18$
.10	2	$1(.10)^2(.90)^0 = .01$
		$\overline{1.00}$
.20	0	$1(.20)^0(.80)^2 = .64$
.20	1	$2(.20)^1(.80)^1 = .32$
.20	2	$1(.20)^2(.80)^0 = .04$
		$\overline{1.00}$
.30	0	$1(.30)^0(.70)^2 = .49$
.30	1	$2(.30)^1(.70)^1 = .42$
.30	2	$1(.30)^2(.70)^0 = .09$
		$\overline{1.00}$

* Here the population of cartridges is of fixed size. Unless the sampling is done with replacement, there is some error in using binomial probabilities. But when the population is large in relation to n, such errors are negligible.

We may categorize these as being "logical," since they are based entirely on probability concepts rather than on past frequencies.

Figure 20-12 shows the informational chronology for the sampling experiment. In the first stage the unconditional result probabilities for the number of sample defectives are provided. This is in accordance with the sequence in which Charles Stereo finds the outcomes that apply. Next, the posterior probabilities for the population proportion of defective cartridges are given. This informational chronology provides the revised probabilities used in the complete decision tree diagram in Figure 20-13.

Each level of π corresponds to a *different population,* so that a separate set of binomial probabilities is required for each. In calculating those values

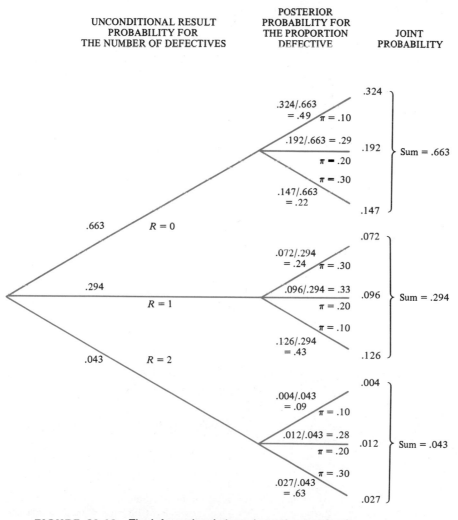

FIGURE 20-12   The informational chronology of events for the stereo-cartridge decision.

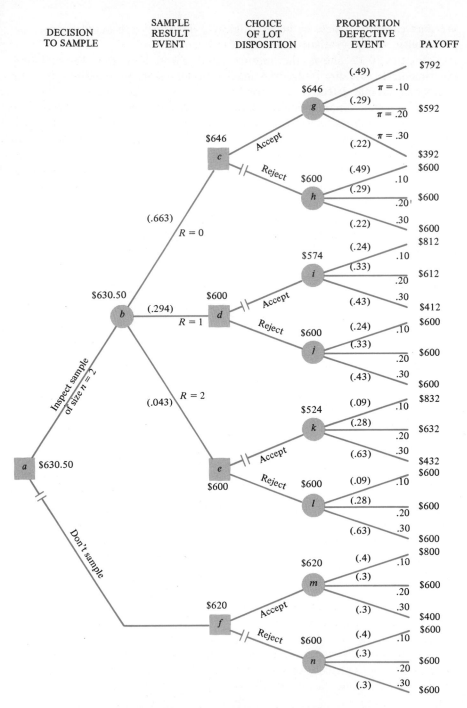

FIGURE 20-13 The Charles Stereo decision tree diagram.

it is important that the level for π not be confused with its prior probability. For example, in calculating the conditional result probabilities for the number of sample defectives when $\pi = .10$, we use .10 as the trial success probability π, not .4; the latter value is the prior probability for the event and applies in a later step of the analysis.

After they have been determined, the binomial probabilities are placed on the corresponding second-stage branches of the actual-chronology probability tree. The joint probabilities are then found by multiplying the probabilities on the respective branches. In doing this, *do not confuse the events with their probabilities.* Remember, $\pi = .10$, $\pi = .20$, and $\pi = .30$ are the *events*, analogous to low, moderate, or high numbers of defectives in the population. (As events, it makes no sense to combine the values for π arithmetically—so since they should not be added together, they certainly do not have to sum to 1!) The prior probabilities .4, .3, and .3 are the multipliers. Thus, the top joint probability in Figure 20-11 is

$$P[\pi = .10 \ and \ R = 0] = .4 \times .81 = .324$$

and the other joint probabilities are calculated in the same way.

Backward Induction Analysis

Let us first consider the results of sampling. The expected payoff of the fork at *g*, following accepting, is $646, which is larger than the $600 at *h*, the expected payoff for rejecting. Thus, if a sample result of $R = 0$ is obtained, accepting is superior because the sample evidence indicates that the lot is likely to be low in defectives. The amount $646 is brought back to node *c*, and the branch for reject is pruned. But if $R = 1$, rejecting would lead to a greater expected payoff of $600 at *j* compared to the $574 payoff from accepting at *i*. The accept branch is therefore pruned, and $600 is brought back to node *d*. Here the sample evidence indicates the lot will likely contain a high proportion of defectives, and therefore 100-percent sampling will prove more profitable than selling uninspected cartridges. Likewise, rejecting provides the greatest expected payoff when $R = 2$ at decision point *e*, so that $600 is brought back to node *e*, and the accept branch is pruned. The overall expected payoff from sampling is $630.50, calculated for the event fork at *b* using the expected payoffs of the optimal acts for the respective sample results. If no sample is taken, the greatest expected payoff of $620 is obtained by accepting the lot, for then the expense of 100-percent inspection is greater, on the average, than the losses from returned items. The branch for rejecting is pruned, and $620 is brought back to node *f*. We see that the expected payoff from sampling is $630.50 versus $620 for not sampling. Sampling is the better choice of act. Thus we prune the branch for the act not to sample, bringing $630.50 back to node *a*.

The Decision Rule

From our decision tree we observe that when the number of defectives is $R = 0$, the chosen act is to accept. But when $R = 1$ or more, rejecting yields a higher expected payoff. This demonstrates the principle that as the number of defective items in the sample becomes large, the evidence favors the higher lot-proportion-defective events. We refer to the largest value of R for which the lot will be accepted as the decision-maker's *acceptance number*, which we denote C. In this example, the acceptance number is $C = 0$. With a sample size of $n = 2$, our decision maker will thus apply the following *decision rule*:

$$\text{Accept the lot if } R \le C$$

$$\text{Reject the lot if } R > C$$

In two-action decision problems involving sampling, everything boils down to selecting such a decision rule. The optimal strategy is therefore equivalent to finding that value for C which maximizes expected payoff.

In Section 20-4 we will consider whether or not a different sample size might provide an even greater expected payoff than the one obtained for $n = 2$.

Decision Rules Based on the Sample Mean

A completely analogous procedure to decision making with binomial probabilities applies when samples are taken from quantitative populations.

A Computer Memory Device Decision

To illustrate decision making with the sample mean, we consider the decision faced by a computer center about the kind of peripheral memory storage device to use in its computer system. The two proposed units are based on laser technology, and both will operate more efficiently than the current memory storage. One of the choices, based on photographic principles, uses special film for storing the data. The other alternative uses holography, a process by which a three-dimensional image is retrieved from a special wafer. A photographic memory unit costs less to lease than a holographic one, but it is slower and thus more costly to operate; their storage capacities and reliabilities are identical.

Table 20-3 shows the annual costs for the proposed memory units and

TABLE 20-3   Annual Costs and Savings
for Memory Storage Units

Type of Unit	Annual Cost		Annual Savings	
	Lease	*Access*	*Lease*	*Access*
Magnetic (current)	$900,000	$180,000	—	—
Photographic	300,000	122,500	$600,000	$ 57,500
Holographic	450,000	60,000	450,000	120,000

the current magnetic one. The lease costs are fixed, while the access costs vary with the number of bits retrieved or stored. Access costs are based on the value of the processing time lost while retrieving and storing data with peripheral memory. They are expressed in dollars per gigabit (billion bits) per day. Based on the given cost data, Table 20-3 also shows the annual savings of the proposed units over the present obsolescent memory unit.

The annual savings achieved under either alternative depends on the daily volume of peripheral memory access. Although the actual number of bits stored or retrieved varies daily, the mean daily access level can be used to establish average annual access savings for each alternative. When this is added to the fixed lease cost, the resulting mean total annual savings serves as the payoff measure for this decision; a single-year figure is appropriate here, since all leases run for just one year and are subject to annual review. This payoff depends on the mean daily gigabits accessed μ, which represents the average volume taken over all days.

The computer facility manager is uncertain about the value of μ, since historical data on the density of peripheral memory traffic are incomplete. Although he believes access volume on any given day might fall anywhere between some negligible level and perhaps 18 gigabits, he will base his analysis on two possible levels for the mean, $\mu = 2$ and $\mu = 3$ gigabits per day; each value is judged to be equally likely.

Figure 20-14 shows the manager's decision structure when no sample information is available. Notice that different payoff values for mean annual

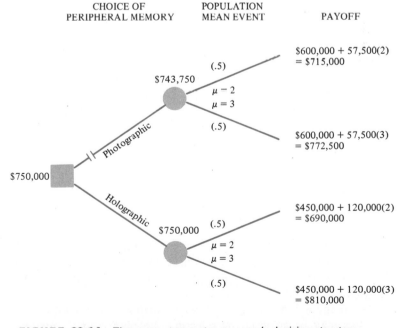

| CHOICE OF PERIPHERAL MEMORY | POPULATION MEAN EVENT | PAYOFF |

$743,750

(.5)
$\mu = 2$
$\mu = 3$
(.5)

$600,000 + 57,500(2)
= $715,000

$600,000 + 57,500(3)
= $772,500

Photographic

$750,000

Holographic

$750,000 (.5)
$\mu = 2$
$\mu = 3$
(.5)

$450,000 + 120,000(2)
= $690,000

$450,000 + 120,000(3)
= $810,000

FIGURE 20-14 The computer center manager's decision structure when no sample is used.

savings are obtained for each type of unit and μ combination. Using prior probabilities of .5 for $\mu = 2$ and .5 for $\mu = 3$, we find that the holographic memory unit provides the greatest expected payoff of $750,000 in mean annual savings.

Decision Making with Sample Information

We now consider the manager's analysis using sample data. He believes that for an extra few hundred dollars per day he can determine the precise level of peripheral memory access on sample days by adding a special accounting program to the software system. Any sampling cost arises from the slower processing that results. Suppose that a sample of $n = 9$ days is to be used for this purpose.

Since the sample data will be used to predict mean daily access level, it is appropriate to summarize the sampling results in terms of the sample mean memory access level, computed from

$$\bar{X} = \frac{X_1 + X_2 + \cdots + X_n}{n}$$

where X_1, X_2, etc. are the observed levels for individual sample days. A large $\bar{X}$ will lend credence to the greater population mean value of $\mu = 3$ gigabits per day, while a small $\bar{X}$ will support $\mu = 2$. But since the sample results are not yet known, the actual value for $\bar{X}$ is uncertain. In Chapter 7, we investigated properties of the sample mean; for large n it is approximately normally distributed (under appropriate conditions, assumed to apply here) with mean μ. For our discussion we will use the *approximate* conditional result probabilities for $\bar{X}$ given in Table 20-4.

TABLE 20-4   Approximate Conditional Result Probabilities for $\bar{X}$

Possible Mean	Conditional Probability Given $\mu = 2$	Conditional Probability Given $\mu = 3$
$\bar{X} = 1$	.35	.05
$\bar{X} = 2$	.35	.25
$\bar{X} = 3$	.25	.35
$\bar{X} = 4$	.05	.35

The manager's decision tree diagram using sample information is provided in Figure 20-15. The revised probabilities used there are obtained from Figure 20-16. The decision tree analysis assumes that each sample observation involves a cost of $100, so that with $n = 9$ the payoffs are each $900 smaller than before.

Backward induction in Figure 20-15 indicates that maximum expected annual savings may be achieved by selecting the photographic memory unit

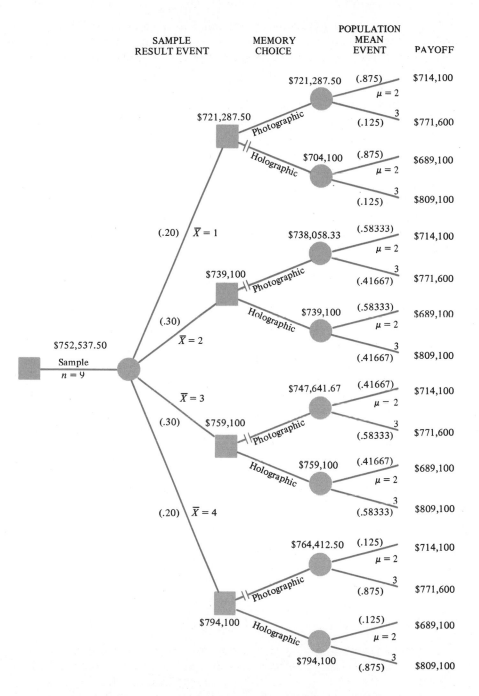

FIGURE 20-15   The computer center manager's decision structure using a sample of size *n* = 9.

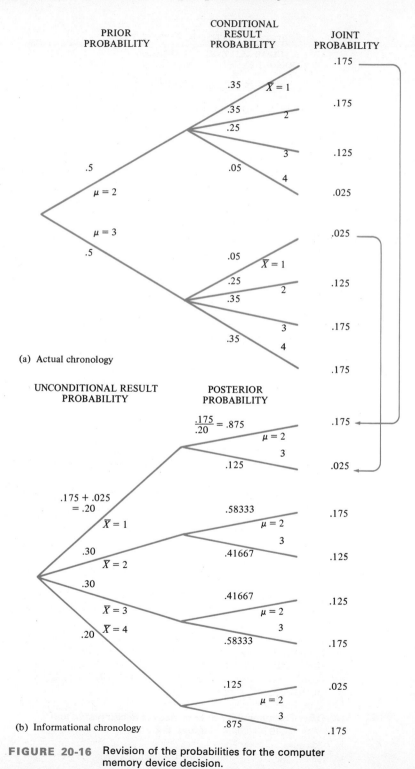

FIGURE 20-16 Revision of the probabilities for the computer memory device decision.

for $\bar{X} = 1$ and the holographic peripheral storage for $\bar{X} = 2$, $\bar{X} = 3$, or $\bar{X} = 4$. We may express this result in terms of the decision rule:

Select photographic unit if $\bar{X} \leq C$

Select holographic unit if $\bar{X} > C$

where $C = 1$ gigabit per day.

Comparing the final expected payoff in Figure 20-14 with the one in Figure 20-15, we see that the computer center manager would be better off taking a sample with $n = 9$ and using the above decision rule (resulting in an expected payoff of $752,537.50) than he would by selecting the holographic memory and not using sample data (where the expected payoff would be only $750,000). We know that sampling is better. But we have yet to determine which sample size would be best. This question is investigated in the next section.

EXERCISES

20-10 The president of Admiral Mills believes that the proportion of children π who will like Crunchy Munchy has the following probability distribution.

Possible Proportion π	Probability
1/4	1/3
1/2	1/3
3/4	1/3
	1

He wishes to revise these probabilities so that a strategy may be devised for later test marketing. Three children have been chosen at random, given Crunchy Munchy, and then asked if they like it.
(a) Construct the actual chronological probability tree diagram for the outcomes of this experiment, using values of π as the events of the branches in the first-stage fork and the number of children found to like Crunchy Munchy as the second-stage branches.
(b) Enter the probabilities given above for the possible π values on the appropriate branches. Then use the binomial formula to find the probabilities of the branches in the remaining forks, entering these on your diagram.
(c) Calculate the joint probabilities for each end position.
(d) Construct the informational chronological probability tree diagram, reversing the event sequences. Thus, the first fork will provide branches for the number of children liking Crunchy Munchy, followed by forks for the values of π. Determine the probabilities for the events represented by each branch.
(e) If all three children like Crunchy Munchy, what are the posterior probabilities for π?

20-11 Let π be the proportion of dogs that will like SuperPooch. Suppose that the following probabilities have been established for π: $P[\pi = .20] = .1$, and $P[\pi = .30] = .9$. A random sample of the responses of $n = 2$ dogs is obtained. Using Appendix Table C, determine the noncumulative values for the conditional result probabilities for the number of dogs that will like SuperPooch, given the respective values for π. Then determine the posterior probabilities for π if:

(a) no dogs are found to like the food.
(b) exactly one dog likes it.
(c) both dogs like it.

20-12 Consider a slight modification of the peripheral memory device decision discussed in the text. Suppose that the following prior probabilities apply instead for the mean memory access level:

$$\mu = 2 \text{ gigabits per day: } .6$$
$$\mu = 3 \text{ gigabits per day: } .4$$

Compute the new probabilities for the actual and informational chronologies in Figure 20-16, assuming that the same conditional result probabilities apply.

20-4 DECIDING ABOUT THE SAMPLE: PREPOSTERIOR ANALYSIS

Our first example of decision making with sample information concerned Charles Stereo. We saw that rather than accepting each lot, it would be better to first take a sample of size $n = 2$ and accept only those lots where no sample defectives are found. But we have not yet investigated the possibility that a different sample size might be even better. Although more observations will result in added cost, the increased sample reliability may provide a net gain in expected payoff. An analysis of various sample sizes determines exactly what kind of information to acquire. In keeping with our previous discussions, we refer to such an evaluation as *preposterior analysis*.

Determining the Optimal Sample Size

How large a sample should be taken? We can investigate the choice of sample size the same way we determined whether or not to sample. By explicitly considering each possible level of n as an act in the decision structure, we can use the principles developed so far to analyze the fully generalized decision. This decision involves not only the choice of whether to use experimental evidence, but also the selection of the evidence to be obtained.

We can accomplish this for our acceptance sampling illustration (Charles Stereo) by augmenting the decision structure as shown in Figure 20-17. Here four possible sample sizes are considered: $n = 1$, $n = 2$, $n = 3$, and $n = 4$. Each of these is a separate choice in an initial act fork. A sample of size n has $n + 1$ possible sample outcomes, as the number of defectives may be $R = 0$, $R = 1, \ldots,$ or $R = n$. Thus, the number of events in the sample outcome forks varies with the size of n, there being $n + 1$ branches for each.

The posterior probabilities for the possible values of π will differ with n

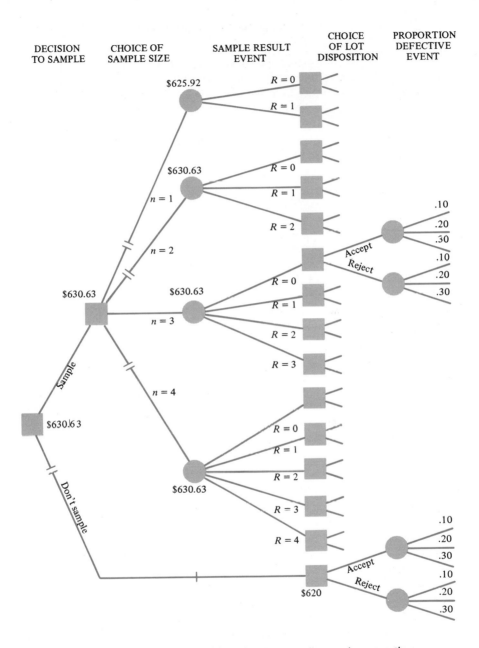

| DECISION
TO SAMPLE | CHOICE OF
SAMPLE SIZE | SAMPLE RESULT
EVENT | CHOICE
OF LOT
DISPOSITION | PROPORTION
DEFECTIVE
EVENT |

$625.92 $R = 0$ $R = 1$

$630.63 $R = 0$ $R = 1$ $n = 1$ $R = 2$

$n = 2$

.10
.20
.30

Accept
Reject

.10
.20
.30

$630.63 $630.63 $R = 0$ $R = 1$ $n = 3$ $R = 2$ $R = 3$

$n = 4$

Sample

$630.63

Don't sample

$630.63 $R = 0$ $R = 1$ $R = 2$ $R = 3$

.10
.20
.30

$R = 4$

Accept
Reject

.10
.20
.30

$620

FIGURE 20-17 The Charles Stereo decision tree diagram incorporating the choice of sample size.

and the sample outcome and must be recalculated for each sample size considered. The end position payoffs for the paths of the decision tree depend on both the losses from returned defective cartridges and the cost of sampling and must also be calculated separately. Once these have been determined, analysis of the decision can proceed in the manner previously used. By backward induction, the sample size yielding the maximum expected payoff can then be determined.

The following expected payoffs have been determined for the other values of n as they were for $n = 2$.

Act	Expected Payoff
$n = 1$	$625.92
$n = 2$	630.50
$n = 3$	630.63 maximum
$n = 4$	630.36

Of the four sample sizes considered, $n = 3$ has the maximum expected payoff of $630.63. The expected payoff rises when the sample size is increased from 2 to 3 and then declines for larger values of n. Thus, $n = 3$ is the *optimal sample size* for Charles Stereo to use in establishing an acceptance plan, and the branches in the decision tree of Figure 20-17 representing the other choices of n are pruned. The expected payoff from the decision to sample is $630.63.

In a more general acceptance sampling problem, a large number of possible values of n may have to be evaluated before the optimal sample size can be determined. This could involve a staggering amount of calculation, leaving little recourse other than to use a digital computer to find the n that yields maximum expected payoff.*

Valuing Sample Information

Recall that the EVPI establishes the worth of perfect information and represents the difference in payoffs expected with perfect information and with no information at all:

EVPI = Expected payoff with perfect information
        − Expected payoff under uncertainty (with no information)

For the computer center manager's decision discussed earlier, we have established that the best course of action when there is no information is to use the holographic memory having

Expected payoff under uncertainty = $750,000

---

* In his book *Analysis of Decisions Under Uncertainty* (New York: McGraw-Hill, 1969), Robert Schlaifer describes a program developed at Harvard University to determine the optimal sample size for binomial or hypergeometric sampling.

If a perfect hypothetical predictor were available for the unknown value of the population daily mean memory access level, the manager would select the photographic memory, for a payoff of $715,000, when $\mu = 2$, and the holographic memory, for a $810,000 payoff, when $\mu = 3$. Thus, we have

Expected payoff with perfect information $= .5(\$715,000) + .5(\$810,000)$

$$= \$762,500$$

Thus, the expected value of perfect information is

$$\text{EVPI} = \$762,500 - \$750,000 = \$12,500$$

The EVPI sets a limit on how much the manager would be willing to pay for any kind of experimental information helpful in predicting the value of μ.

As we have seen, the EVPI can be useful as a rough gauge for deciding whether further information is worthwhile to pursue. If the EVPI is tiny then sample information can hardly be attractive and an immediate decision should be made from prior knowledge alone. Thus, *if the EVPI is very small no preposterior analysis should be performed.*

Expected Value of Sample Information

Another measure similar to the EVPI expresses the worth of the information contained in the sample. The following calculation establishes the *expected value of sample information:*

EVSI = Expected payoff with sample information
    − Expected payoff under uncertainty (with no information)   (20-1)

To illustrate, we continue with the computer memory decision. In Figure 20-15 we obtained the expected payoff of $752,537.50 for using a sample of size $n = 9$ and applying the indicated decision rule for $\bar{X}$. That figure reflects *net* payoffs and includes the $900 cost of sampling. The expected payoff with sample information, like its counterpart for perfect information, does not include the cost of the information and must be based upon *gross* payoffs. Adding back the $900, we have

Expected payoff with sample information $= \$753,437.50$

Thus, for the memory device decision we have

$$\text{EVSI} = \$753,437.50 - \$750,000 = \$3,437.50$$

The above amount establishes how much better off, on the average, the computer center manager would be by having the $n = 9$ sample result rather than no information at all. The EVSI is totally analogous to the EVPI, but applies to less reliable information gleaned from the sample. Like the EVPI, the EVSI establishes an upper limit on what a decision maker should pay to get the sample results.

Expected Net Gain of Sampling

Preposterior analysis often begins with gross payoffs rather than net payoffs, and thus sampling costs must be integrated at a later stage. (One reason for waiting to include the sampling cost is that it is sometimes easier to minimize expected opportunity loss than to maximize expected payoff; it is more convenient in such an approach to include sampling costs at the end.)

In terms of gross annual savings the manager is better off by the EVSI of $3,437.50 if he has the sample results and then applies the optimal decision rule with $C = 1$. Thus, the manager should be willing to pay anything up to $3,437.50 for the sample, but he would not use it if it cost more. *As long as the cost of sampling is less than the EVSI, the decision maker is better off with the sample than without it.*

In order to obtain the peripheral memory access levels for the sample days, a special program must be added to the operating system that will slow down the processing of each job. As a result, the computer must be run longer than otherwise—an added expense. We have assumed that doing this costs an extra $100 per day. The total cost of sampling for $n = 9$ days is therefore $900. Since this figure is smaller than the EVSI, the computer center manager should prefer sampling to deciding without the information sampling provides.

How large should n be? As a practical matter, n can be no larger in this example than the number of days remaining before the peripheral unit must be ordered. However, this question is ordinarily a matter of economics. To help in deciding, we might compute the EVSI for several levels of n, subtracting the sampling cost in each case. Each resulting value represents the *expected net gain of sampling*, or ENGS. Treating n as a variable, we have the following expression for the *expected net gain of sampling:*

$$\text{ENGS}(n) = \text{EVSI}(n) - \text{Cost}(n) \qquad (20\text{-}2)$$

Thus, when $n = 9$, we have

$$\text{ENGS}(9) = \text{EVSI}(9) - \text{Cost}(9)$$
$$= \$3,437.50 - \$900$$
$$= \$2,537.50$$

Comparable figures could be obtained for other n's, and the optimal sample size would be the one having the greatest expected net gain.

Table 20-5 shows the EVSI and ENGS results for the Charles Stereo decision. The optimal sample size of $n = 3$ (identified earlier in Figure 20-17) is the one with the greatest ENGS, $10.63. Note that EVSI increases as n does, reflecting the greater reliability of larger samples. But sampling cost grows by

TABLE 20-5 EVSI and ENGS Values for the Charles Stereo Decision

Sample Size n	(1) Expected Payoff (Net)	(2) Expected Payoff (Gross)	(3) Expected Payoff Under Uncertainty	(4) EVSI(n) [(2)−(3)]	(5) Cost (n)	(6) ENGS(n) [(4)−(5)]
1	$625.92	$629.92	$620	$ 9.92	$ 4	$ 5.92
2	630.50	638.50	620	18.50	8	10.50
3*	630.63	642.63	620	22.63	12	10.63
4	630.36	646.36	620	26.16	16	10.36

* Optimal n.

$4 per observation, and we see that ENGS peaks at $n = 3$ and drops thereafter. Similar results will be found for most sampling situations. Ordinarily our search for the optimal n ends when we find an ENGS that is smaller than the preceding one.

EXERCISES

20-13 The decision tree diagram in Figure 20-18 has been determined for deciding whether or not to accept shipments from a particular supplier.
(a) Perform backward induction. Which choice—no sample, sampling with $n = 1$, or sampling with $n = 2$—should be made?
(b) What is the optimal value for the acceptance number C if $n = 1$ is used? If $n = 2$ is used?

20-14 Suppose that the prior probabilities for the proportion π of CornChox buyers favoring a new package design are $P[\pi = .4] = .5$ and $P[\pi = .6] = .5$. Suppose further that if the new design is used, the present value of future profits will decrease by $10,000 when $\pi = .4$ and increase by $10,000 when $\pi = .6$. Sampling is very expensive, costing $500 per observation.
(a) Which act provides the greatest expected payoff, don't sample or sample with $n = 1$?
(b) Which act provides the greatest expected payoff, $n = 1$ or $n = 2$? What can you conclude about the optimal sample size?

20-15 Suppose that the peripheral memory device example in the text were modified so that the following prior probabilities apply for the population mean memory access level:

$$\mu = 2 \text{ gigabits per day: } .3$$
$$\mu = 3 \text{ gigabits per day: } .7$$

The decision tree diagram in Figure 20-19 now applies.
(a) Perform backward induction.
(b) What is the value for C that maximizes expected payoff? Formulate the optimal decision rule.
(c) For a sample costing $900 calculate the EVSI.
(d) Determine the expected net gain of sampling.

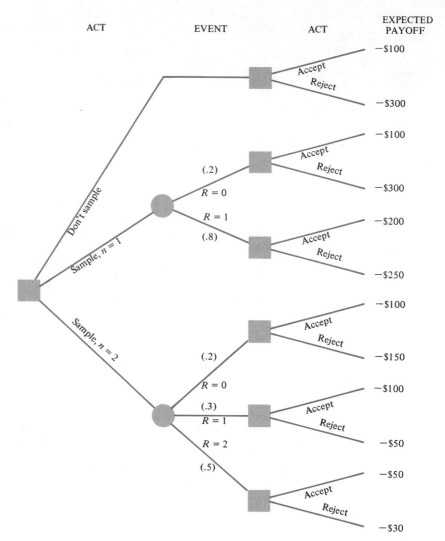

FIGURE 20-18

20-16 A chemical process yields a mean μ grams of active ingredient for every liter of raw material processed. Because of variations in the raw material and in the control settings, the true population mean for any particular batch is unknown until processing is complete. From past history, the plant superintendent has judged that the following prior probabilities apply for μ:

Possible Mean μ	Probability
25 g	.3
30	.4
35	.3

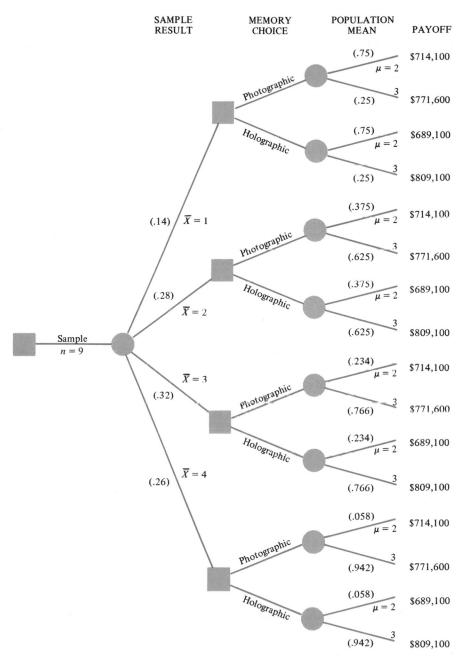

| SAMPLE RESULT | MEMORY CHOICE | POPULATION MEAN | PAYOFF |

FIGURE 20-19

Early in the processing of the current batch, it is planned to select a random sample of $n = 3$ liters, and the amount of active ingredient will be precisely determined. From these readings, the sample mean will be calculated. Suppose that the following approximate conditional result probabilities apply:

	Probabilities for $\bar{X}$		
$\bar{X}$	$\mu = 25$ g	$\mu = 30$ g	$\mu = 35$ g
25 g	.7	.2	.2
30	.2	.6	.3
35	.1	.2	.5

Construct the actual chronological probability tree diagram. Using this, find the tree for the informational chronology and compute the unconditional result probabilities and the posterior probabilities for μ.

20-17 Refer to Exercise 20-16. The plant superintendent must decide whether or not to adjust the control settings in processing a chemical batch. Suppose that the following payoff table applies.

Population Mean μ	Acts	
	Adjust	*Leave Alone*
25 g	$ 500	$-$500
30	0	0
35	$-1,000$	500

(a) Assuming that no sample is used, what course of action maximizes expected payoff?

(b) Find the plant superintendent's EVPI. Would he use a sample to facilitate his decision if it cost $400? If it cost only $200? (Answer yes, no, or maybe.) Explain.

20-18 Refer to Exercises 20-16 and 20-17 and your answers to those exercises.

(a) Construct the plant superintendent's decision tree diagram assuming that he is committed to taking the sample. Use gross payoff figures.

(b) Use backward induction to determine the value for C (for accepting the need for adjustment) that maximizes expected gross payoff. Indicate the optimal decision rule for him to use.

(c) Calculate the EVSI.

(d) Suppose that a sample of $n = 3$ liters costs $50 to take. Calculate the superintendent's expected net gain of sampling.

20-5   DECISION THEORY AND TRADITIONAL STATISTICS

To complete our discussion of decision making with sample information, a few comments should be made about the procedure presented here and the traditional statistical approach. In the two examples, we obtained the following optimal decision rules for the chosen sample sizes:

Accept the shipment if $R \leqslant C (= 0)$

Reject the shipment if $R > C$

and

Select photographic unit if $\bar{X} \leqslant C(=1)$

Select holographic unit if $\bar{X} > C$

This type of result is usually obtained in a statistical testing procedure. However, the process for determing C is totally different.

Hypothesis Testing Concepts Reviewed

In traditional statistics, the basic uncertainty is couched in special terminology. The main events are expressed as *hypotheses*. Each decision has two kinds of hypotheses. One is referred to as the *null hypothesis* (originally used to represent "no change"), and the other as the complementary *alternative hypothesis*. In the language of classical staistics, we might have the following hypotheses for the quality-control inspection problem:

Null hypothesis: Shipment is good ($\pi = .10$)

Alternative hypothesis: Shipment is poor ($\pi > .10$)

and, for the computer memory decision.

Null hypothesis: Photographic unit is best ($\mu = 2$)

Alternative hypothesis: Holographic unit is best ($\mu = 3$)

The decision rules provided earlier may be expressed in terms of the respective pair of hypotheses. They take the following form for the inspection decision:

Accept the null hypothesis if $R \leqslant C$

Reject the null hypothesis if $R > C$

For the computer memory decision:

Accept the null hypothesis if $\bar{X} \leqslant C$

Reject the null hypothesis if $\bar{X} > C$

(Rejecting the null hypothesis is the same as accepting the alternative hypothesis.)

Traditional statistics focuses on the worst outcomes of the decision. These are called errors, and there are two types. The Type I error occurs when the null hypothesis is rejected when it is actually true. The Type II error is to accept the null hypothesis when it is false. In the stereo-cartridge inspection problem, these errors are

Type I error: Reject shipment when it is good

Type II error: Accept shipment when it is poor

In the other example, the Type I error would be to use the holographic memory when the photographic one is better, while the Type II error would be to select the photographic one when the holographic one is superior. (In either case, there are two correct choices, accepting the null hypothesis when it is true and rejecting the null hypothesis when it is false.)

The decision structure for traditional statistical analysis is shown in Table 20-6. The main events themselves are not assigned probabilities. Rather, the controlling factors in establishing the decision rule (value for C) are the probabilities for the two kinds of errors:

$$\alpha = P[\text{Type I error}] = P[\text{rejecting null hypothesis when it is true}]$$

$$\beta = P[\text{Type II error}] = P[\text{accepting null hypothesis when it is false}]$$

These probabilities are usually set in advance of sampling and are actually conditional probabilities (where the status of the null hypothesis, true or false, is the given event). Conventionally, the Greek letters α (alpha) and β (beta) are used to represent the error probabilities. In the stereo-cartridge inspection example, α represents the probability of rejecting a good shipment and is sometimes referred to as the *producer's risk*. Likewise, β is the probability for accepting a poor shipment, which is the *consumer's risk*.

TABLE 20-6   Decision Table for the Traditional Statistical Decision

	Act	
Event	*Accept Null Hypothesis* (*Accept shipment*; *select photographic*)	*Reject Null Hypothesis* (*Reject shipment*; *select holographic*)
Null hypothesis is true (Shipment good; photographic best)	Correct decision	Type I error (Return good shipment; select holographic when photographic is best) α = Target probability
Null hypothesis is false (Shipment poor; holographic best)	Type II error (Accept poor shipment; select photographic when holographic is best) β = Target probability	Correct decision

Both types of errors are undesirable. But obviously, neither can be avoided entirely. Traditional statistics is concerned with selecting the sample size n and the decision rule (value for C) such that an acceptable balance is achieved between α and β. If n is held fixed, one error probability can be reduced only by increasing the probability for the other one. Often, the sample size itself is dictated by economic or other considerations. For this reason, it is often possible to control only one error completely.

Generally, the hypotheses are formulated in such a way that the Type I error is the more serious one. The tolerable probability for this error is specified at a level such as $\alpha = .01$, $\alpha = .05$, or $\alpha = .10$. Then the value is chosen for C that guarantees this α is not exceeded.

Let us see how this would work for our stereo-cartridge inspection problem. Suppose we use $\alpha = .05$. Thus, C must be the smallest value such that

$$P[\text{rejecting null hypothesis when true}] \leqslant \alpha$$

or

$$P[R > C \mid \pi = .10] \leqslant .05$$

For $C = 0$, the probability of incorrectly rejecting a good shipment is (from Table 20-2)

$$P[R > 0] = 1 - P[R = 0] = 1 - .81 = .19$$

which is greater than the targeted Type I error probability of $\alpha = .05$. Trying $C = 1$, we have

$$P[R > 1] = P[R = 2] = .01$$

which is smaller than $\alpha = .05$. The optimal decision rule using the traditional procedure is $C = 1$.

The above value for C differs from the one found previously $(C = 0)$. *The optimal rule using decision-theoretical analysis will often differ from that obtained with the traditional statistical hypothesis test.*

Contrasting the Two Approaches

Why did the two approaches lead to different decision rules? The differences between the procedures are outlined below.

(1) The decision-theoretical procedure considered the payoffs from every possible outcome. Payoffs are not explicitly considered in hypothesis testing, although they may influence the choice of α.

(2) Prior probabilities are used directly in the decision-theoretical approach. As with payoffs, these ought to play some role in establishing α.

(3) Hypothesis testing proceeds directly from the prescribed α to the

decision rule. The decision-theoretical analysis arrives at the optimal decision rule by means of the Bayes decision rule, using appropriate posterior probabilities and the payoffs for each outcome. The resulting decision maximizes expected payoff.

Which procedure is best? Decision theory is plagued by subjective prior probabilities, considered by many to be the weakest link in its analytical chain. Many statisticians deny the existence of subjective probabilities, thereby relegating much of statistical decision theory to the ash heap. A major feature making traditional hypothesis-testing procedures more universally accepted is that there is no explicit need for prior probabilities at all. *But the uncertainties regarding the population parameter still exist*, and traditional statistical procedures must also involve some sort of subjective assessment of these uncertainties when desired error probabilities are being established. In hypothesis testing, everything hinges on the prescribed significance level α (and also upon β, when there is the freedom or the capability to prescribe β). Unless care is taken in finding α, inferior decisions are bound to occur. Decision theory allows for consistent and systematic treatment of chance and payoffs, as well as of attitude toward risk. It does not place so great a burden on the decision maker by requiring him or her to do everything in one fell swoop by choosing a single number, "an α for all seasons."

When the outcomes do not have a natural numerical payoff measure, or when the decision maker is risk seeking or risk averse, then decision theory's strengths rest on a foundation of utility values. As is shown in Chapter 21, obtaining utilities requires a set of assumptions about attitudes, which are obtained by means of an elaborate procedure. Although any difficulties involved in employing utilities can be avoided by traditional statistics, α embodies everything, so that even more care must be exercised in choosing the appropriate target value.

A final, and perhaps the most significant, advantage of decision theory is that *it considers whether or not a sample should even be used*. As we have seen, a greater expected payoff might be achieved by deciding what to do immediately without incurring the expense of a sample. Traditional statistics never satisfactorily copes with this question. Also, the choice of proper sample size is too often an *ad hoc* process in traditional statistics. (All too often a sample size of 30 is used, for example, because the Student t table stops at 30 degrees of freedom.) Decision theory explicitly considers the costs of the various sample sizes.

EXERCISES

20-19 A market researcher wishes to determine whether to accept the null hypothesis regarding the proportion π of Appleton smokers who will switch to a new mentholated version, Mapleton. Her null hypothesis is that $\pi = .1$. She takes a random sample of 100 current Appleton smokers who will be contacted in 6 months to see if they switched. She wishes to protect against the Type I error with probability $\alpha = .005$. Using Appendix Table C, determine the smallest acceptance number C such that the probability that the number of switchers exceeding this is less than or equal to the desired α. Then formulate her decision rule.

20-20 Referring to Problem 20-19, suppose that the following prior probabilities are obtained for π:

π	Probability
.05	1/3
.10	1/3
.15	1/3
	1

The following conditional result probabilities apply for the number of switchers R:

	$\pi = .05$	$\pi = .10$	$\pi = .15$
$R \leqslant 17$	1.0000	.9900	.7633
$R = 18$	0	.0054	.0739
$R \geqslant 19$	0	.0046	.1628

The decision-maker's payoffs, including the cost of sampling, are as follows:

	Accept Null Hypothesis	Reject Null Hypothesis
$\pi = .05$	\$10,000	$-\$2,000$
$\pi = .10$	5,000	0
$\pi = .15$	$-2,000$	4,000

(a) Calculate the posterior probability distribution for π, given each of the above sample result events, and the unconditional result probabilities.

(b) Construct the market researcher's decision tree diagram. Enter the appropriate probabilities found in part (a) onto the branches, and place the payoffs along the respective end positions.

(c) Should the decision maker accept or reject the null hypothesis if $R = 18$? Compare your result with that in Problem 20-19.

▬6 CONCLUDING REMARKS

In this chapter we have shown how to analyze decision making with sampling. Using the procedures described, we can exercise judgment about the population characteristics by assigning prior probabilities to the possible values of the decision parameter π or μ. The benefits and costs of sampling can be systematically evaluated, and in doing this, the payoffs for every outcome can be explicitly accounted for. Thus, it is possible to even consider the question of whether or not to sample in the first place. The decision-theoretical principles permit a more thorough analysis than traditional statistics provides.

The procedures of this chapter have drawbacks. The main difficulties arise from the nature of decision tree analysis itself. Because the possible number of sample results and population parameters can be huge, many problems are too big to conveniently fit on a tree. Some problems would require such a large amount of computational effort that a computer might be needed in evaluating them.

But decision tree analysis involves a more fundamental problem. It is an inherently *discrete* procedure, since each event must be represented by a separate branch. Many problems involve continuous random variables. For example,

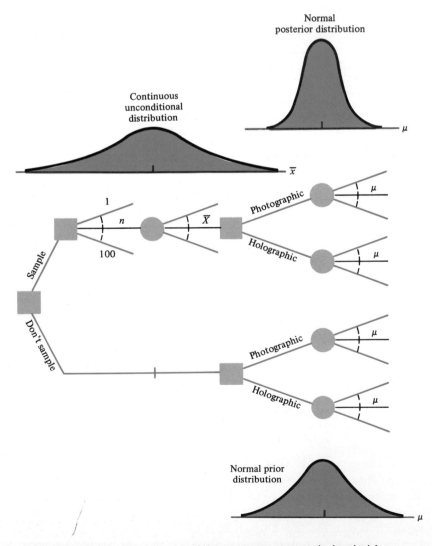

FIGURE 20-20   The structure of the computer memory device decision when a normal prior distribution applies for the population mean.

π and μ may range over a continuous spectrum of possible values. Also, the sample mean $\overline{X}$ is often a continuous variable generally represented by the normal distribution. Figure 20-20 shows a more realistic representation of the decision faced by the computer center manager. The curves reflect the underlying probability distributions, which would ordinarily be continuous. In this chapter we have really approximated the continuous variables by a few representative values. Chapter 21 is partly concerned with how such discrete approximations are made.*

REVIEW EXERCISES

20-21 Solve Exercise 5-50 (page 143) using probability trees for the actual and informational chronologies.

20-22 The makers of Quicker Oats oatmeal have packaged this product in cylindrical containers for 50 years. The usual box had been believed inseparable from the product's image. But with consumer tastes changing, the new marketing vice-president wonders whether younger people regard the round box as old-fashioned and unappealing. The vice-president wishes to analyze the case for a rectangular box that will save significantly on transportation costs due to the elimination of dead space in the packing cartons. It is also believed that the change can actually expand Quicker Oats' market by uplifting the product's image. But previous study has shown that a small segment of the existing market buys the oatmeal primarily for the round box; these customers would be lost by the change. The following payoff table has been established for the present net worth of retaining the old box versus implementing the new one.

National Market Response to New Box Events	Act	
	Retain Old Box	Use New Box
W: Weak	$0	−$2,000,000
M: Moderate	0	0
S: Strong	0	3,000,000

As prior probabilities for new box response events, the marketing chief has judged the following values: $P[W] = .20$, $P[M] = .30$, $P[S] = .50$. A "barometer" city is chosen for six months' test marketing of the new box. Three outcomes are possible: sales decreased (D), unchanged (U), and increased (I). Historical experience with other products has established the following conditional result probabilities:

$$P[D\,|\,W] = .8 \qquad P[D\,|\,M] = .2 \qquad P[D\,|\,S] = 0$$
$$P[U\,|\,W] = .2 \qquad P[U\,|\,M] = .4 \qquad P[U\,|\,S] = .1$$
$$P[I\,|\,W] = 0 \qquad P[I\,|\,M] = .4 \qquad P[I\,|\,S] = .9$$

* As an alternative to making approximations, we could deal directly with the continuous case using the normal loss function. A detailed discussion is contained in Lawrence L. Lapin, *Quantitative Methods for Business Decisions* (New York: Harcourt Brace Jovanovich, 1976), Chapter 15.

(a) Construct the probability tree diagrams for the actual and informational chronologies.

(b) Construct the Quicker Oats decision tree diagram, assuming that test marketing will be used.

(c) Perform backward induction. Then for each test outcome, indicate the maximum expected payoff act. What is the optimal strategy?

20-23 Your friend gives you a choice between two gambles involving the random selection of a coin from a box. The box contains two coins: one has two heads and one is ordinary. If you choose gamble A, he will pay you $2 if the coin is two-headed, but you must pay him $1 if the coin is the ordinary one. If you choose gamble B, he will toss the coin for the price of $1. Seeing the showing side, you may then decide to stop or continue. If you continue, the coin is then examined, and the same money amounts are exchanged as in gamble A.

(a) Construct a decision tree diagram for the choice between the two gambles. Evaluate each end position, using your profit as the payoff measure.

(b) Find the appropriate event branch probabilities.

(c) Perform backward induction to determine which gamble provides the maximum expected payoff.

(d) Formulate the optimal decision rule for gamble B, indicating whether you should stop or continue for each possible coin toss result.

20-24 A presidential campaign manager asks two politicians what they believe to be the true proportion π of voters favoring their party's candidate. The respective replies are .40 and .50. The manager's judgment leads to assigning equal chances that any one of them is correct. A random sample of $n = 100$ registered voters will be chosen, and the number R preferring the candidate will be found. The following results are of interest: $R < 40$, $40 \leqslant R \leqslant 50$, and $R > 50$.

(a) Construct a probability tree diagram for the actual chronology, using the sample results in the second stage. Appendix Table C provides the conditional result probabilities.

(b) Determine the probability tree diagram for the informational chronology.

(c) What is the posterior probability that $\pi = .40$, (1) given $R < 40$? (2) given $40 \leqslant R \leqslant 50$? (3) given $R > 50$?

20-25 A quality control inspector must determine the optimal sample size for deciding whether to accept or reject incoming shipments. The following payoffs apply for various assumed levels of the proportion defective.

Proportion Defective	Prior Probability	Accept	Reject
$\pi = .05$	.3	$100	$-100
$\pi = .10$	.4	0	0
$\pi = .20$	.3	-100	100

The following expected payoffs with sample information (ignoring the cost of sampling) have been obtained:

Sample Size	Expected Payoff
$n = 1$	$ 9.00
$n = 2$	15.70
$n = 3$	20.50
$n = 4$	24.22

(a) Find the expected payoff with sample information when $n = 5$. What acceptance number applies for the number of sample defectives R?

(b) Assuming that each sample observation costs $3, determine ENGS($n$) for $n = 1$ through 5. What is the optimal sample size?

20-26 The marketing manager of Blitz Beer must determine whether or not to sponsor Blitz Day with the Gotham City Hellcats. She is uncertain what the effect of the promotion will be in terms of mean increase in daily sales volume that would result during the 100-day baseball season. The cost of sponsorship is $10,000, and each can of Blitz has a marginal cost of 20 cents and sells for 40 cents. Two levels are judged equally likely for the mean increase in sales for the season: $\mu = 490$ and $\mu = 530$ cans per day.

(a) Construct the manager's payoff table.

(b) If the manager wishes to maximize expected payoff, what action should she take?

(c) Further experimental information may be desired before making a final decision. Calculate the EVPI. Can a sample from the underlying population, assuming it is cheap enough, even be helpful in this decision? Explain.

Chapter Twenty-One
Accounting
for Attitudes
and Judgment

*Suppose that you are allowed to participate
in a far-fetched lottery where the price is $100
if you win and death if you lose. Is there any
probability of winning for which you would
be indifferent between the status quo and
playing?*

In this chapter our goal is to make some of the more relevant results of decision theory workable in practice. The criteria discussed in Chapter 19 all require that the decision structure be given. Of crucial importance are two elements of this structure: the *payoffs* associated with the outcomes and the event *probabilities*. These elements are perhaps the most difficult to obtain. As we have seen, a meaningful payoff measure must be related to the decision-maker's goals. But this is not enough, for even when the payoffs are known, *an individual's attitudes determine their true worth*. The assignment of probability values to events also requires further study. Most decisions of any consequence involve events arising from nonrepeatable random experiments, so that *subjective probabilities* are the only available measures of uncertainty. To be of value in evaluating alternative choices, *the decision-maker's judgment must be exercised to the fullest extent in determining subjective probabilities*. Thus, meaningful analysis of a real decision often requires incorporation of the decision-maker's personal values and judgments into the problem's structure.

The crucial role of attitude and judgment in any decision may be illustrated by the divergent behavior of different persons faced with the same decision. The umbrella situation nicely demonstrates this point. *How can we explain why everyone does not carry an umbrella when we do?* To a certain extent we can say that not all individuals are equally adept at selecting and exercising appropriate decision criteria. This is one possible explanation. With much justification, however, we can conclude that the difference in behavior may also be explained by differing attitudes toward the consequences. Getting wet may be fun to some people, but to others it is viewed as an invitation to pneumonia and possibly the first step into a premature grave. Some persons think it chic to carry rain paraphernalia when it's not raining; others would as soon lug around a ball and chain. Even if we can find two persons with identical attitudes toward the decision consequences, we will find that occasionally they make opposite decisions. Such a difference can be explained if they do not have identical judgments regarding the chance of rain. One person may rely on Weather Service radio broadcasts as a source of information, judging the forecaster's subjective probabilities to be adequate. Another person may instead depend upon his lumbago pains as a fairly reliable measure of the probability of rain.

In this chapter we discuss utility as an alternative expression of payoff that is reflective of a person's attitudes. We begin by discussing the rationale for buying insurance. A brief historical discussion of utility is then presented, and the underlying assumptions of a theory of utility are provided. Finally, a procedure is presented whereby utility values can be determined. The utility function so obtained provides a basis for discussion of some basic attitudes toward risk. The chapter concludes with a discussion of subjective probability, during which a rationale is presented for subjective probabilities and some methodology is provided to facilitate determining these through judgment.

21-1 ATTITUDES, PREFERENCES, AND UTILITY

Chapter 19 presented various procedures and criteria that help decision makers choose in the presence of uncertainty. In all cases, a payoff value for each outcome is required in order to analyze the decision. As we have seen, not all outcomes have an obvious numerical payoff. In this section, we indicate how payoffs may be determined in such cases. Later in this chapter, we develop methods of quantifying such consequences as reduced share of the market, loss of corporate control, and antitrust suits. Even when numerical outcomes can be naturally determined, we have noted that it may be unrealistic to select the act with the maximum expected payoff. In some cases, an extremely risky act fares better under the Bayes decision rule than one obviously preferred. As noted in Chapter 19, this difficulty is not the fault of the Bayes criterion, but rather is caused by payoff values that do not reflect their true worth to the decision maker.

Decision to Buy Insurance

The inadequacy of using such obvious measures as dollar costs or profits for payoffs may be vividly illustrated by evaluating an individual's decision whether or not to buy fire insurance.

> **Example 21-1** Spiro Pyrophobis wishes to decide whether to buy a fire insurance policy for his home. For simplicity there are only two relevant events, fire and no fire. Our decision-maker's payoffs will be expressed in terms of his out-of-pocket costs, which we shall represent by negative numbers. Our question is: Will the Bayes decision rule lead to the choice of act actually preferred?
>
> In answering this question, we will use the hypothetical payoff table provided in Table 21-1. Here we have greatly simplified the decision by considering just one kind of coverage to be supplied by a single company. The acts are to buy or not buy an annual policy with a $100 premium charge. Should there be a fire, we assume his home and all its contents, valued at $40,000, will be completely destroyed; partial damage is impossible. We also assume that the company will reimburse our homeowner fully for all fire losses. In addition, we suppose that the home and its contents are fully owned and, if destroyed, will be replaced at identical cost by our hapless decision maker.

TABLE 21-1   Payoff Table for the Decision
to Buy Fire Insurance

		Act			
		Buy Insurance		*Don't Buy Insurance*	
Event	*Probability*	*Payoff*	*Payoff×* *Probability*	*Payoff*	*Payoff×* *Probability*
Fire	.002	− $100	− $ .20	− $40,000	− $80.00
No fire	.998	− 100	− 99.80	0	0
Expected payoff:			− $100.00		− $80.00

For homes in the category of Mr. Pyrophobis', the insurance company actuaries have established that historically 2 out of every 1,000 such homes burn down each year. The probability of such a fire has therefore been set at 2/1,000 = .002 for Mr. Pyrophobis. Thus, the complementary event, no fire, has probability 1 − .002 = .998. Using these probability values, we calculate the expected payoffs for each act in Table 21-1. The maximum expected payoff is − $80, which corresponds to the act don't buy insurance and is larger than the − $100 payoff from buying fire insurance.

In the example just given, the *Bayes decision rule indicates that it is optimal to buy no insurance.* Yet most persons faced with this decision do choose to buy insurance. Loss of a home, which for many persons comprises the major portion of a lifetime's savings, is a dreadful prospect. The expenditure of an annual premium, although not exactly appealing, buys a feeling of security that seems to outweigh the difference between the expected payoffs. Furthermore, insurance policy premiums are intentionally set at a price higher than the expected cost of potential claims (or equivalently, the policyholder's expected dollar loss); they must be, if the insurance company is to pay wages and achieve profits. Thus the buying of insurance may be looked on as an unfair gamble, where the payout is not in the buyer's favor. An individual can expect to pay more in insurance premiums than he will collect in claims.* Most persons feel blessed at not having to file a claim.

The Bayes decision rule selects the less preferred act. Does this mean that it is an invalid criterion? Rather than answer no immediately, let us consider the payoffs used. The true worth of the outcomes is not reflected by the dollar payoffs. A policyholder is willing to pay more than the expected dollar loss for "peace of mind." We can say that the policyholder derives greater "utility" from having insurance. If dollar losses are valued on a scale of true worth or *utility*, then each additional dollar loss will make our decision maker feel disproportionately worse off. Thus a 10-percent reduction in wealth may be more than twice as bad as a 5-percent reduction. The same would ordinarily be true for gains in dollar wealth; the second increase may not raise the sense of well being as much as the first. In the parlance of economics, *the policyholder's marginal utility for money is decreasing*. Each successive dollar brings a smaller increase in utility; each additional dollar loss reduces utility by a greater amount than before.

Thus, we may question the validity of using dollars as our payoff measure. Instead, we might find it fruitful to use an outcome's worth or utility as the payoff.

Numerical Utility Values

We seek numbers that express the true worth of the payoffs corresponding to decision consequences. We have referred to such numbers as utilities. Much investigation has been made of the true worth of monetary payoffs. The early eighteenth-century mathematician Daniel Bernoulli pioneered in efforts to develop a measure of utility. He proposed that *the true worth of one's wealth is the logarithm of the amount of money*. Thus a graphical relationship between utility and money would have the basic shape of the curve in Figure 21-1. Note that this curve has a slope that, although always positive, decreases as the amount of money increases, reflecting the assumption of decreasing marginal utility for money.

Saint Petersburg Paradox

A gambling game called the Saint Petersburg Paradox led Bernoulli to his conclusion. In the game, a balanced coin is fairly tossed until the first head appears. The gambler's winnings are based upon the number of tosses made

---

* Life insurance, ordinarily a form of savings, is excluded.

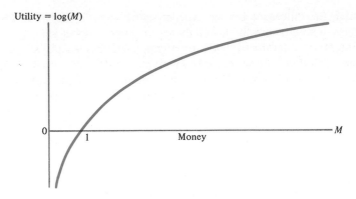

FIGURE 21-1 The utility function for money assumed by Bernoulli.

before the game ends. If a head appears on the first toss, the player wins $2. If not, the "kitty" is doubled to $4—the reward if a head appears on the second toss. If a tail occurs, the kitty is doubled again. The pot keeps doubling at every coin toss. The winnings achieved is $2 raised to the power of the number of tosses until and including the first head. It will be most interesting if you pause to think what amount you would be willing to pay for the privilege of playing this game.

The probability that $n+1$ tosses occur before payment is the probability that there is a run of n tails and that the $(n+1)$st toss is a head: $(1/2)^{n+1}$. The payoff for $n+1$ tosses is 2^{n+1}. We may therefore calculate the player's expected receipts from the sum

$$\$2(1/2)+\$2^2(1/2)^2+\$2^3(1/2)^3+\cdots=\$1+\$1+\$1+\cdots=\$\infty$$

Since the number of 1's in this sum is unlimited, the *expected receipts from a play of this game are infinite*! How much were you willing to pay to play? Whatever amount you chose, it must have been a finite amount, and thus less than the expected receipts. Thus the expected payoff from this gamble is also infinite, no matter what price is paid to play.

Few people are willing to pay more than $10 to play the game. Even at this price, a player would come out ahead in only 1 out of 8 games, on the average. At $500, you would show a profit in an average of only 1 out of 256 gambles. The natural reticence of players to pay very much for this gamble led Bernoulli to his conclusion about the utility for money. In general, we say that a person has *decreasing marginal utility for money* if he prefers not to participate in a gamble where the expected receipts exceed the price to play.

Validity of Logarithmic Values

Other early mathematicians, through different paths of reasoning, arrived at conclusions similar to Bernoulli's: that the marginal utility for money is decreasing. They proposed other utility curves with the same basic shape. A major fault of these early works is that they do not account for individual differences in the assignment of worth. More modern treatment of utility in the abstract sense was advanced by Von Neumann and Morgenstern in their 1947 book *Theory of Games and Economic Behavior*. There they proposed that a utility curve can be tailored for any individual, provided certain assumptions about the individual's preferences hold. These assumptions allow several valid basic utility-curve shapes, including curves similar to Bernoulli's. We shall investigate some of these later in the chapter.

Outcomes Without a Natural Payoff Measure

So far, we have concentrated on examples where the outcomes have a natural numerical payoff measure, such as dollars profit, gasoline gallons saved, or time. But we have noted decisions with outcomes for which there are no such numbers. As decision makers, we ought to be able to assess the relative worths of such outcomes.

For most decisions, it is possible to determine preferences—but we do not propose that this task is always easy. Indeed, value judgments may be the most difficult step in analyzing a decision. Consider the young student choosing one of several top universities, the child selecting a candy bar, the bachelor contemplating losing his freedom by getting married, the tired corporate founder pondering merger and retirement versus retaining control and delegating operating responsibility to his son-in-law, or the innocent person choosing between pleading guilty to manslaughter or facing a trial for murder. If we assume the capability to rank the consequences in order of preference, we can extend the notion of utility so that numerical payoffs can be made for the most intangible outcomes.

EXERCISES

21-1   Suppose that you are offered a gamble by Ms. I. M. Honest, a representative of a foundation studying human behavior. A fair coin is to be tossed. If a head occurs, you will receive $10,000 from Ms. Honest. But if the result is a tail, you must pay her foundation $5,000. If you do *not* have $5,000, a loan will be arranged, which must be repaid over a five-year period at $150 per month but can be deferred until you have graduated from school.
(a) Calculate your expected profit from participating in this gamble.
(b) Would you be willing to accept Ms. Honest's offer? Does your answer indicate that your marginal utility for money is decreasing?

21-2   Mr. Smith has offered you a deal similar to that of Ms. Honest in Problem 21-1. If a head occurs, he will hand you $1.00. But if the result is a tail, you must pay Mr. Smith $0.50.
(a) Calculate your expected profit by participating in this gamble.
(b) Would you be willing to accept Mr. Smith's offer?

21-3   Suppose a homeowner with a house valued at $40,000 was offered tornado insurance for an annual premium charge of $500. Suppose that there are just two mutually exclusive outcomes, complete damage or none from a tornado, and that the probability of damage from a tornado is .0001.

(a) Construct the homeowner's payoff table for a decision whether to buy tornado insurance.

(b) Calculate the decision-maker's expected monetary payoff for each act. Which has the maximum expected payoff?

(c) Suppose the homeowner decides not to buy tornado insurance. Does this contradict decreasing marginal utility for money? Explain.

21-2   UTILITY THEORY

The fundamental proposition of the modern treatment of utility is that it is possible to obtain a numerical expression of one's preferences. For a set of outcomes ranked by preference, we can assign utility values that convey these preferences. The largest utility number is assigned to the most preferred outcome, the next largest to the second most preferred, and so forth. Suppose, for instance, that in contemplating a menu you prefer New York steak to baked halibut. Were you to assign utility values to these entrees in accordance with your preferences, then if the utility of steak is 5, that is, u(steak) = 5, u(halibut) must be some number smaller than 5.

Before describing how specific-utility numbers can be obtained, we shall first discuss some of the assumptions underlying the theory of utility.

Assumptions of Utility Theory

Various assumptions have been made about the determination of utilities.* These have one feature in common: that the values obtained pertain only to a *single individual* who behaves *consistently* in accordance with his or her own tastes.

Preference Ranking

The first assumption of utility theory is that a person can determine for any pair of outcomes O_1 and O_2 whether he or she prefers O_1 to O_2, prefers O_2 to O_1, or regards both equally. This assumption is particularly nice when we consider monetary values, for then we can assume that more money is always better than less. But as we have seen, a preference ranking can be very difficult when qualitative alternatives are considered. Can a person always determine a preference or establish indifference between outcomes? If not, then utilities cannot be found for these outcomes.

---

* Those discussed in this book are simplifications of the original axioms postulated by Von Neumann and Morgenstern.

Transitivity of Preference

The second assumption is that if A is preferred to B and B is preferred to C, then A must be preferred to C. This property has been called *transitivity* and reflects an individual's consistency. Again, when we are dealing with monetary figures for outcomes, we can usually assume transitivity.

Before discussing the assumptions of utility any further, we will introduce gambles between outcomes so that uncertainty may be incorporated into the determination of utility.

Gambles and Expected Utility

We are presently concerned with making choices under uncertainty. Thus the payoffs for decison acts are unknown, and each act may be viewed as a *gamble* with uncertain rewards. To evaluate such decisions, we must extend the concept of utility to gambles.

Recall that the Bayes decision rule involves comparisons between the expected payoffs of acts or strategies, so that the "optimal" choice has the maximum expected payoff. But the major difficulty with this criterion, as we have seen, is that the indicated course of action can be less attractive than some other. For example, the Bayes decision rule tells us not to buy fire insurance under circumstances when most persons would believe insurance most desirable. We wish to overcome this obstacle by using utilities in place of ordinary dollar payoffs. Thus, we require that the expected utility payoffs provide a valid means for comparing actions so that the action having the greatest expected utility is actually preferred to the alternative actions. Thus, buying fire insurance should have greater expected utility than not buying it.

But we can go one step further. Suppose that the most preferred action has the greatest expected utility, the next most preferred the next greatest, and so forth. If this is so, then expected utility would express preference ranking, and *expected utility values would themselves be utilities*. Each would express the worth of a *gamble* between outcomes and would be obtained by averaging the utility values of the outcomes, using their respective probabilities as weights. This may be stated more precisely as a property of utility theory:

> In any gamble between outcome A and outcome B, with probabilities q for A and $1-q$ for B

$$u(\text{gamble}) = qu(A) + (1-q)u(B)$$

(21-1)

Thus the utility of a gamble between two outcomes equals the expected utility of the gamble. When acts having uncertain outcomes are viewed as gambles, an act's utility equals the expected utility of its outcomes. *With utilities as payoffs, the Bayes decision rule would indicate that the act having maximum expected utility is optimal*, so that this criterion would always select the most preferred act or strategy.

Determining Expected Utilities

To see how this works, suppose that our homeowner in the example values the dollar changes in his assets according to the following utility function:

$$u(M) = \sqrt{M + 40,000} - 200$$

where M expresses the change in cash position associated with each outcome.

Table 21-2 shows the utility calculations and the expected utility calculations for the acts buy insurance and don't buy insurance. For instance, when no insurance is bought and there is a fire, there is a loss, so that $M = -\$40,000$, a negative change in cash position. The utility for this outcome is obtained by the calculation

$$u(-\$40,000) = \sqrt{-40,000 + 40,000} - 200$$

$$= \sqrt{0} - 200 = -200$$

TABLE 21-2 Determination of Utilities for Outcomes of the Fire Insurance Decision and Calculation of Expected Utilities

(1) Event	(2) Probability	(3) Cash Change M	(4) Utility $\sqrt{M + 40,000} - 200$	(5) Utility × Probability
		Buy Insurance		
Fire	.002	− $100	−.25	−.0005
No fire	.998	− 100	−.25	−.2495
			Expected utility =	−.2500
		Don't Buy Insurance		
Fire	.002	− $40,000	− 200	−.40
No fire	.998	0	0	0
			Expected utility =	−.40

The utilities for the other outcomes are calculated in a similar manner; $u(0) = 0$, while $u(-\$100) = -.25$.

Each act is a gamble. Buying insurance is a gamble having two identical outcomes in terms of dollar expenditure, −$100, since the same amount applies whether or not there is a fire. Buying no insurance is a gamble with cash outlays of −$40,000 if there is a fire and $0 if there is no fire. The utilities of the respective acts are thus the expected utilities of the corresponding gambles. Therefore, we see from Table 21-2 that the expected utilities are −.25 for buying insurance and −.4 for not buying insurance. Since buying insurance has the higher utility, it must be preferred by the decision maker; stated differently, the act to buy insurance has the maximum expected utility payoff, so the Bayes decision rule indicates that it is the optimal choice.

We see that when we use utilities as payoff values, the "proper" result is obtained with the Bayes decision rule. We may not, however, conclude that with utilities as payoffs this criterion will always lead to a decision to buy insurance. The choice depends on the relation between the chance of fire and the insurance policy's price. Suppose, for example, that the price of a policy is raised to $200, so that the utility of the dollar payoffs for buying insurance is

$$u(-\$200) = \sqrt{-200 + 40{,}000} - 200$$
$$= \sqrt{39{,}800} - 200 = -.50$$

The expected utility for buying insurance is $-.50$, so that if the probability of fire remains the same as before, the act don't buy insurance would have utility $-.4$, which is greater than $-.50$, so that don't buy insurance is the preferred act. This is the opposite of the choice made above. The insurance has become too expensive to be attractive.

Many persons facing the same circumstances would buy insurance even if the premium were raised to $1,000 or more. *Their tastes would be different, and this would be reflected by different utility values for each outcome.* The price of a policy may partly explain why there is a prevalence of coverage against fire while there is a paucity of protection against natural disasters, such as earthquakes, tornados, or floods. One reason why people do not generally buy such insurance policies might be the high premium required by insurance companies for such coverage (if it is offered at all) in relation to the probabilities (which are difficult to obtain actuarily for such rare phenomena).

Assumption of Continuity

The third assumption of utility theory is that of *continuity*. This says there is some gamble having the best and worst outcomes as rewards that the individual regards as equally preferable to some middling or in-between outcome. To illustrate continuity, consider the following example.

Example 21-2 Homer Briant has a small hardware store in a declining neighborhood. He is contemplating a move. Because he is still young and has no special skills, he will not consider leaving the hardware business. A move cannot be guaranteed to be successful since relocating will involve maximum stretching of his lines of credit, and there will be no time for a gradual buildup of business. Moving will therefore bring either an improvement over his present business or disaster. Thus, he will be faced with one of the following outcomes:

Most preferred O_3: increasing sales (if move is a success)
O_2: decreasing sales (if he stays)
Least preferred O_1: imminent bankruptcy (if move is a failure)

Whether a move will be a success depends largely on luck or chance. Our assumption of continuity presumes that there is some probability value q of a successful move that will make Mr. Briant indifferent between staying and moving. Figure 21-2 shows a decision tree diagram for his decision. The fork at node b represents a gamble between O_3 and O_1 resulting from the act to move.

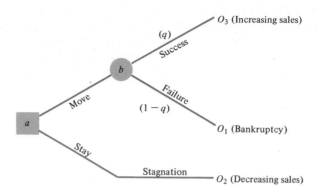

O_3 (Increasing sales)

(q)
Success

b

Failure
$(1 - q)$

Move

a

O_1 (Bankruptcy)

Stay

Stagnation
O_2 (Decreasing sales)

FIGURE 21-2 Mr. Briant's decision tree diagram for possible business relocation.

Continuity may be justified by observing that if the value of q is near 1, so that a move will almost certainly be a success, Mr. Briant would prefer the gamble of moving to staying. But if q is close to 0, making bankruptcy a near certainty, he will prefer to stay in his present location. Thus, there must be a value of q somewhere between 0 and 1 beyond which his preference will pass from O_2 to the gamble; this value of q makes the gamble equally attractive as O_2.

Continuity is a crucial assumption of utility theory, yet it may be hard to accept, especially if the outcomes include the ultimate one, death.

Suppose that you are allowed to participate in a far-fetched lottery where the price is $100 if you win and death if you lose. Is there any probability of winning for which you would be indifferent between the status quo and playing? A natural response is that this is not a very meaningful gamble. All right then, let us recast the situation. Suppose that you are informed by a reliable source that you can drive your car one mile down the road where a man is passing out $100 bills, one to a person. There are no gimmicks and there will be no inconvenience from a mob of people. Would you go? If your answer is yes, then consider your chances of getting killed in an automobile accident on your journey. For the past several years, approximately 50,000 persons have been killed from such accidents in the United States annually. Thus, although quite small, the probability of your rather untimely death occurring while collecting your $100 prize is not zero. Going to get your $100 is a gamble with death as a possibility, and you prefer the gamble to the status quo. Suppose now that we increase the chance of death. To reach the man you must cross a condemned bridge. Would you still go? Probably not, as the chance of death would be significantly higher. Somewhere between these two cases is a probability for safely getting your $100, with a complementary probability of death, for which you would be indifferent between the status quo and the gamble.

Assumption of Substitutability

A fourth assumption of utility allows us to revise a gamble by *substituting* one outcome for another regarded equally well. The premise is that the person will be indifferent between the original and revised gambles. The substitutability assumption may be illustrated by means of the following example.

> **Example 21-3**   A husband and wife cannot agree how to spend Saturday night. In desperation they agree to a gamble where the toss of a coin will determine the kind of entertainment they will select. If a head occurs, they will spend the evening at the opera (her preference), and if a tail, they will go to a basketball game. Suppose that the wife changes her mind and wants instead to go to a dance. The husband dislikes dancing just as much as the opera. He would then be indifferent between tossing for the opera or basketball and a revised gamble between dancing and basketball. This will hold regardless of the odds, providing the chance of going to the basketball game remains the same for the original and revised gambles.

The principle of substitutability also holds if we treat a gamble as an outcome. For any outcome we may substitute an *equivalent gamble*, one regarded equally as well as the outcome the gamble replaces, having as rewards two other outcomes. For example, suppose that the wife instead insists on a movie, where she wants to see a romance story, while he feels that to be compensated for being

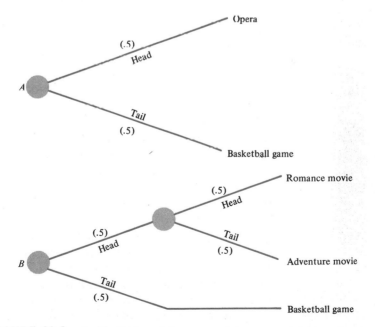

FIGURE 21-3   An illustration of the assumption of substitutability. The gamble at *A* is regarded equally as well as the two-stage gamble at *B*.

dragged to a movie, they should see an adventure film. Suppose that the husband is indifferent between an opera or a coin toss determining which of the two movies will be seen. The second coin toss is an equivalent gamble to the opera outcome. Thus the husband should be indifferent between the single- and two-stage gambles in Figure 21-3.

Assumption of Increasing Preference

The final assumption of utility theory concerns any pair of gambles with identical outcomes. The gamble that has the greater probability for the more desirable outcome must be preferred. Thus, the preference for gambles between the same two outcomes increases with the probability of attaining the better outcome. That this is plausible should be apparent. Suppose you are offered the proposition that when a coin is tossed it pays you $100 if a head occurs and nothing for a tail. The probability of winning $100 is 1/2. It should be obvious that this gamble would be decidedly inferior to one where the outcomes are the same but where the probability of winning is greater than 1/2.

Determining Utility Values

We are now ready to show how utility values may be assigned to outcomes. Figure 21-4 outlines the procedure for doing this. The numbers are obtained by using a series of gambles between a pair of outcomes.

The Reference Lottery

The process begins with a preference ranking of all outcomes to be considered. The most preferred and least preferred outcomes are determined, and then a gamble between these is used to establish the individual's utilities. We call this a *reference lottery*. It has two events: win, corresponding to achieving the best outcome, and lose, for attaining the worst outcome. Such a gamble is purely *hypothetical* and only provides a framework for assessing utility. The events win and lose do not relate to any events in the actual decision structure and are used to divorce the reference lottery from similar but real gambles. *The probability of winning the hypothetical reference lottery is a variable*, changed according to the attitudes of the decision maker and denoted q.

The initial assignment of utility values for the best and worst outcomes is *completely arbitrary*, so that any numbers may be used. It does not matter what values are chosen; different values for these arbitrary utilities will result in different utility scales. This is just like temperature, where two different and quite arbitrary values are used to define the Fahrenheit and Celsius scales. The choices of 32° Fahrenheit and 0° Celsius for the freezing point of water, with 212°F and 100°C for the boiling point, have resulted in quite different values in the two scales for any particular temperature.

(1) All outcomes are ranked. A convenient designation is to let a subscript denote the order of preference:

Decreasing preference
$$O_n \longleftarrow \text{Best}$$
.
.
.
$$O_2$$
$$O_1 \longleftarrow \text{Worst}$$

(2) Utilities for best and worst outcomes are arbitrarily assigned:

$$u(O_n)$$
.   Utilities for intermediate
.   outcomes are to be found.
.
$$u(O_2)$$
$$u(O_1)$$

(3) A reference lottery is formulated. This is a gamble having rewards O_n if won and O_1 if lost. The probability q of winning the reference lottery is treated as a variable, to be changed at the will of the decision maker. The reference lottery is strictly hypothetical.

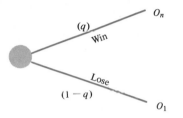

(4) For each intermediate outcome, the decision maker establishes a value of q making him indifferent between the outcome itself and the reference lottery.

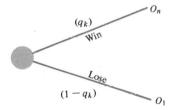

Thus for outcome O_k a win probability q_k is determined that results in a reference lottery regarded equally as well as O_k.

(5) The utility of O_k may be determined. It is equal to the expected utility for the reference lottery with win probability q_k.

$$u(O_k) = q_k u(O_n) + (1 - q_k)u(O_1)$$

FIGURE 21-4   The procedure for establishing utility values for a set of outcomes.

Obtaining Utility Values

Once the extreme utility values are set, the decision maker then may use the reference lottery to obtain utilities for intermediate outcomes. This is accomplished by varying the win probability q until the decision maker establishes a value of q that serves as a *point of indifference* between achieving that outcome for certain or letting the reward be determined by the reference lottery. That particular value of q makes the reference lottery a gamble equivalent to the intermediate outcome so evaluated. As we have seen, the assumption of continuity makes this possible. We may again add meaning to this procedure by considering the similarities with temperature. The decision-maker's subjective evaluation is analogous to designing a thermometer. A thermometer is designed by determining a core diameter such that a substance such as mercury can rise to various levels in its tubular cavity. For each level of heat, there corresponds a height to which the mercury must rise. With the Celsius scale the 100-degree mark corresponds to the mercury's height when the thermometer is inserted into boiling water. Various levels of heat between freezing and boiling points of water correspond to marks at prescribed heights above the thermometer's zero mark, allowing heat to be relatively measured in degrees. In an analogous manner, the values of q established to make the decision maker indifferent between respective intermediate outcomes and the reference lottery serve to relatively measure his or her preferences. The indifference values of q are like the markings on a thermometer, where the different outcome preferences are analogous to different levels of heat. These values of q are established through introspection, and they have nothing to do with the actual chance of winning, just as the design of a thermometer is not related to tomorrow's temperature.

Once an indifference value of q has been established for an outcome, its utility value may be determined. This is accomplished by calculating the expected value of the reference lottery with that value of q. Letting O_1 and O_n represent the least and most preferred outcomes, we may then find the utility of an outcome O_k of intermediate preference from

$$u(O_k) = q_k u(O_n) + (1 - q_k) u O_1) \qquad (21\text{-}2)$$

Here q_k is the value of q making the decision maker *indifferent* between the certain achievement of O_k and taking his chances with the reference lottery. The utility value $u(O_k)$ is analogous to a numerical degree value placed beside a marking on a thermometer.

An Example

To show how this works, we continue with the illustration of Homer Briant contemplating relocation of his small business. He has ranked his preferences for the outcomes of increasing sales (O_3), decreasing sales (O_2), and bankruptcy (O_1). The reference lottery is shown in Figure 21-5. Suppose that the utility values of the extreme outcomes are arbitrarily set at 10 and -5:

$$u(O_3) = 10$$

$$u(O_1) = -5$$

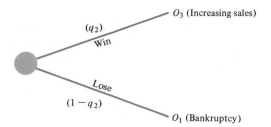

FIGURE 21-5 The reference lottery for Mr. Briant's decision.

Suppose now that Mr. Briant contemplates the reference lottery in terms of 100 marbles in a box, some labeled W for win and the rest labeled L for lose. A marble will be selected at random, and if it has a W, then he will be guaranteed outcome O_3, increasing sales, but if it is marked with an L, he will go bankrupt with certainty, achieving outcome O_1. He is then asked what number of W marbles he would require before he would be indifferent between facing declining sales, outcome O_2, or taking his chances with the lottery. After considerable thought, Mr. Briant replies that 75 W marbles would make him regard O_2 and the reference lottery equally well. Thus he establishes a reference lottery win probability q_2 that makes it an equivalent gamble to outcome O_2:

$$q_2 = 75/100 = .75$$

This probability may be used in expression (21-2) to calculate the utility of declining sales:

$$u(O_2) = q_2 u(O_3) + (1 - q_2) u(O_1)$$
$$= .75(10) + .25(-5)$$
$$= 6.25$$

Attitude Versus Judgment

It must be emphasized that the value $q_2 = .75$ is merely a device used to establish indifference. *The probability selected for winning the lottery has nothing to do with the chance that the most favorable outcome will occur.* In setting $q_2 = .75$, the decision maker is expressing an *attitude* toward one outcome in terms of the rewards of a hypothetical gamble. This value was obtained by looking inward in an attempt to balance his tastes and aspirations between remaining in a declining business or gambling to improve it. He is assumed capable of switching roles from this kind of introspection to that of dispassionate *judgment* when asked later what he believes his actual chance is that moving his business will be a success. To arrive at the probability of success, our decision maker must use his experience and knowledge of such factors as the history of failures by relocated businesses, prevailing economic conditions, and possible competitor reactions.

Suppose that Mr. Briant judges his chance of success after moving to be 1/2. We may now analyze his decision problem by applying the Bayes decision rule with utilities as payoffs. The decision tree diagram is shown in Figure 21-6. The expected utility payoff for the event fork at *b* is 2.5, which is the utility achieved by moving. Since this value is smaller than the 6.25 utility achieved by remaining in his present location, Homer Briant should not move. Thus we prune the branch corresponding to the act to move and bring the 6.25 utility payoff back to node *a*.

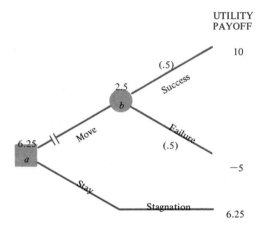

FIGURE 21-6   Mr. Briant's decision tree diagram showing backward induction analysis with utility payoffs.

Utility and the Bayes Decision Rule

This example illustrates why the Bayes decision rule is valid when utility payoffs are used. The basic property [expression (21-1)] states that the utility of a gamble is the expected value of the utilities assigned to its rewards. Since any act with uncertain outcomes may be viewed as a gamble, the act providing the greatest utility, and hence the one that must be preferred, is the one with the maximum expected utility payoff. The Bayes decision rule can therefore be viewed as just an extension of utility theory, the criterion serving only to translate one's preferences into a choice of act. Homer Briant decides to stay put because, of the two acts, this provides the greatest utility—which can only be the case, our theory states, if remaining in the present location is the preferred act. *In arriving at a choice, both the decision-maker's attitudes toward the consequences and his judgment regarding the chances of the events are considered and integrated.* The choice indicated by the Bayes criterion is optimal because it is preferred above all others.

Had some other success probability, say .90, been determined, Mr. Briant would relocate, since doing so would have the highest utility: $.9(10) + .1(-5) = 8.5$. This might be the case, for example, if he learned that his major would-be competitor's business was to be taken over by his incompetent son. Changing the probability of events reflects only the decision-maker's judgment regarding factors influencing their occurrence. Only the *expected* utilities of uncertain *acts* can be affected by revision of event probabilities. Regardless of the chance of relocation's success, the decision-maker's utilities for the ultimate *outcomes* must remain unchanged. Only a change of taste or attitude can justify revision of these. This might be caused by a death in his family or brought about by a change in personal finances.

EXERCISES

21-4   A contractor must determine whether to buy or rent equipment required to do a job up for bid. Because of lead-time requirements in getting the equipment, he must decide before knowing whether the contract is won. If he buys, a contract would result in $120,000 profit, net of equipment resale returns; but should he lose the job, then the equipment will have to be sold at a $40,000 loss. By renting, his profit from the contract, if he wins it, will be only $50,000, but there will be no loss of money if the job is not won. His chances of winning are 50–50. The contractor's utility function is $u(M) = \sqrt{M + 40,000}$.
   (a) Construct the contractor's payoff table using profit as the measure.
   (b) Calculate the expected profit payoff for each act. According to the Bayes decision rule, what act should he select?
   (c) Construct the contractor's payoff table when utilities are used for payoffs.
   (d) Calculate the expected utility payoff for each act. Which act provides the maximum expected utility?
   (e) Which act should the decision maker choose? Explain.

21-5   Another decision maker has as her utility function for monetary gains, $u(M) = \sqrt{M + 10,000}$. The size of a certain monetary gain that would make her indifferent between two more extreme amounts must have utility equal to the gamble's expected utility, u_g.
   (a) Show that she would be indifferent between zero gain and a 50–50 gamble between $30,000 and −$10,000.
   (b) What amount of certain monetary gain would make her indifferent between it and a 50–50 gamble with rewards $80,000 or −$7,500? Use the fact that $M = (u(M))^2 - 10,000$.
   (c) What is the most she would be willing to pay as the annual premium for an insurance policy covering theft of her coin collection, valued at $10,000, if the chance of a theft sometime during the year were .1? If the probability were .01? If the probability were .001?

21-6   Consider the following outcomes that you may achieve; no rights are transferable.
   • 100 new records of your choice
   • A grade of *C* on the next examination covering utility
   • A year's assignment to Timbuktu, Mali
   • Confinement to an airport during a three-day storm
   • A month of free telephone calls to anywhere
   (a) Rank these in decending order of preference, designating them O_5, O_4, O_3, O_2, and O_1.
   (b) Let the utilities be $u(O_5) = 100$ for the best outcome and $u(O_1) = 0$ for the worst. Consider a box containing 1,000 marbles, some labeled

Win, the remainder labeled Lose. If a Win marble is selected at random from the box, you will achieve O_5. If a Lose marble is chosen, you attain O_1. Determine how many marbles of each type would make you indifferent between gambling or achieving O_2. Determine the same for O_3 and O_4.

(c) The corresponding probabilities q_k of winning may be determined by dividing the respective number of Win marbles by 1,000. Use these to calculate $u(O_4)$, $u(O_3)$, and $u(O_2)$.

21-3 THE UTILITY FOR MONEY AND ATTITUDES TOWARD RISK

Applying the Utility Function in Decision Analysis

The reference lottery may be used to construct a utility function for money. For this purpose we select as the best outcome some amount of money no smaller than the greatest possible payoff. The worst outcome is likewise no larger than the lowest payoff. Monetary outcomes offer some special advantages. The amount can be measured on a continuous scale, so that the utility function itself will be continuous. This suggests that it may be determined by finding an appropriate smoothed curve relating money values to their utilities. To do this, only a few key dollar amounts and some knowledge of the curve's general shape need be evaluated. The curve obtained by fitting the points so obtained may then serve as an approximation to the utility function.

Such a curve is shown in Figure 21-7 for the Ponderosa Record Company

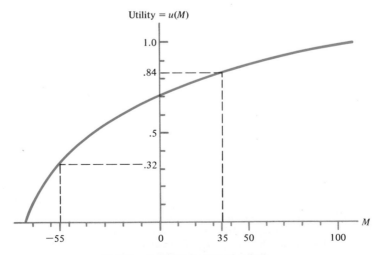

Monetary Payoff (thousands of dollars)

FIGURE 21-7 The utility function for the president of the Ponderosa Record Company.

decision of Chapter 19. This utility curve has been derived according to the procedures just described by applying a reference lottery and using a few key monetary amounts as the outcomes. The reference lottery used is between the amounts +$100,000 (for win) and −$75,000 (for lose), which for ease of evaluation are more extreme than any possible payoff. Arbitrary utility values of $u(+\$100,000) = 1$ and $u(-\$75,000) = 0$ were set for simplicity.

In practice, a utility function is empirically found by personally interviewing the decision maker. It will ordinarily be described graphically rather than by a mathematical equation, with utilities read directly from the curve.

We may use the utility curve in Figure 21-7 to analyze the Ponderosa president's decision problem. The original decision tree diagram is reconstructed in Figure 21-8. The utilities corresponding to each monetary payoff have been obtained from the utility curve. For instance, we find the utilities for the

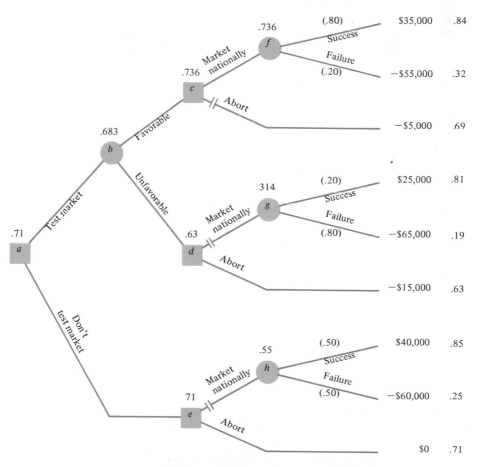

MONETARY
PAYOFF   UTILITY

$35,000	.84
−$55,000	.32
−$5,000	.69
$25,000	.81
−$65,000	.19
−$15,000	.63
$40,000	.85
−$60,000	.25
$0	.71

FIGURE 21-8   The Ponderosa decision tree diagram showing backward induction analysis with utility payoffs.

monetary payoffs \$35,000 and −\$55,000 to be .84 and .32, respectively. The backward induction may be performed using utilities instead of dollars. The analysis proceeds in the same fashion as in Chapter 19.

We begin by determining the expected utility for a terminal event fork of the tree. The expected utility of the event fork at branching point f is calculated:

$$.8(.84) + .2(.32) = .736$$

The value .736 is entered above node f and represents the expected utility of the act to market nationally in the fork at c. The choice of acts at decision point c can now be determined. Aborting leads to an outcome utility of .69, which is lower than the .736 expected utility of marketing nationally, so that the abort branch is pruned, and .736 is brought back to be entered above node c. The rest of the backward induction is conducted using utilities instead of dollars, in the usual manner.

Using utilities, we thus find that the optimal choice is don't test market and abort. The two alternatives that involve marketing the record are too risky to the president of Ponderosa. Recall that a different conclusion was reached in Chapter 19, where expected monetary values were used. But since utility values express the true worth of monetary outcomes, our latest solution is the valid one to use.

Attitudes Toward Risk and the Shape of the Utility Curve

The utility function for money may be used as a basis for describing a person's attitudes toward risk. Three basic attitudes have been characterized. The polar cases are the *risk averse* individual, who takes only favorable gambles, and the *risk seeker*, who will pay a premium for the privilege of participating in a gamble. Between these extremes lies the *risk neutral* individual, who assigns the face value of money as its true worth. The utility functions for each basic attitude are shown in Figure 21-9. Each function has a different shape, corresponding to the decision-maker's fundamental outlook. All three utility functions

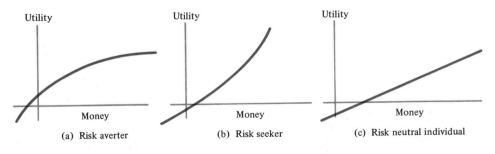

(a) Risk averter   (b) Risk seeker   (c) Risk neutral individual

FIGURE 21-9   A graphical portrayal of utility functions for basic attitudes toward risk.

show that utility increases as monetary gain rises. This reflects the underlying assumption of utility theory that utility increases with preference, which is combined with an additional assumption that more money will always increase one's well being, so that the outcomes having greater payoff are more preferred. (This may not be a strictly true assumption, but except for eccentrics, most persons behave in a manner supporting it.)

The Risk Averter

Throughout most of his or her life, a typical person is risk averse. Such an individual buys plenty of casualty insurance. He or she is typified by a disdain for actions involving high risks—the chance of a large monetary loss. Only a gamble that will yield an expectation of a considerable payoff will be attractive. A risk averse person's utility drops ever more severely as losses become larger, while the utilities for positive amounts do not grow as fast with monetary gains. The risk averter's marginal utility for money diminishes as the rewards get better. His or her utility curve [Figure 21-9(a)] has decreasing positive slope as the level of monetary payoff becomes larger. Such a curve is *concave* when viewed from below.

The Risk Seeker

The risk seeker's behavior is the opposite. Many of us are risk seekers at some stages of our lives. This attitude is epitomized by the "high roller" whose behavior seems reckless. This person is motivated by the possibility of achieving the maximum reward in any gamble. The risk seeker will prefer *some* gambles having a negative expected monetary payoff to the status quo. The greater the maximum reward, the wider is the risk seeker's divergence from the risk averter's behavior. The risk seeker is typically self-insured, believing that the risk is superior to forgoing money spent on premiums. The risk seeker's marginal utility for money is increasing: Each additional dollar brings a disproportionately greater sense of well being; and although the loss of one more dollar still hurts, its impact is felt only slightly more severely for large absolute levels of loss than for small ones. Thus the risk seeker's utility curve, shown in Figure 21-9(b), has increasing slope as the monetary change improves. This curve is *convex* when viewed from below.

Risk Neutrality

Our third characterization of attitude toward risk is that of risk neutrality. A risk neutral individual is one who prizes money at its face value. The utility function for such an individual is thus a straight line, as shown in Figure 21-9(c). His or her utility for a gamble equals the utility of the expected monetary payoff. Such an individual buys no casualty insurance, since the premium charge is greater than the expected loss. Risk neutral behavior is epitomized by individuals with enormous wealth. Decisions of large corporations are often based on the Bayes decision rule applied directly to monetary payoffs, reflecting that increments in dollar assets are valued at their face amount.

Generally, risk neutrality holds true only over a limited range of money values. Many large firms, for example, do not carry casualty insurance. But nearly all giant corporations will insure against extremely large losses; for example, airlines buy hijacking insurance. The same holds true for individuals. Many risk averse persons are risk neutral when the stakes are small. The player in office World Series pools falls into this category; losses are hardly noticeable and winnings allow for indulging in some luxury. (Small gambles may add spice to a person's life—they are a form of entertainment. Thus a person might play poker with more skillful persons, where the expected payoff would be negative, just for the fun of it.) That people are risk neutral for small risks is illustrated by their car insurance purchases. Many generally risk averse people have deductible comprehensive coverage on automobile policies, and when their car gets old, usually only the liability coverage is kept. Again this is reflective of risk neutrality over a limited range of monetary outcomes. This does not contradict the curve shapes in Figures 21-9(a) and (b), for throughout a narrow monetary interval each curve can be approximated by a straight-line segment.

Further Remarks

Many persons will exhibit both risk averse and risk seeking attitudes depending on the range of monetary values considered. Consider an entrepreneur starting his own business. Here the risks are definitely huge—a lifetime's savings, plenty of hard work, burnt career bridges, a heavy burden of debt, and a significant chance of bankruptcy. A person embarking upon the hard road of self-employment may often be viewed as a risk seeker. He is motivated primarily by the rewards, monetary and otherwise, of being his own boss. Let us take his development to the point where his business is becoming established and he is viewed by his peers as a future pillar of the community. His attitude toward risk will have evolved to a point where he may now be characterized as risk averse. He is much more conservative (there is now something to conserve). Hardly any deal would be imaginable where he would be willing to risk everything he owns to further his wealth.

We can conceive that an individual's attitudes will switch back and forth between risk seeking and risk aversion over time. Usually a risk seeker has some definite goal or *aspiration level*, which a specific level of money will allow him to achieve. A young man needing enough money to buy his first motorcycle might be willing to participate in an unfair gamble if winning would provide sufficient cash for a down payment. The young professional may speculate in volatile stocks until he or she earns enough money to make a down payment on a fancy home. For such risk-seeking people, losing is not much worse than the status quo. But once the goal is achieved, the risk seeker's outlook changes, and with sated appetite he becomes a risk averter, until some new goal enters his horizon.

A utility curve for such an individual is shown in Figure 21-10. The horizontal axis is total wealth, as measured in monetary units, rather than changes in current cash position. Here the utility function is convex until an aspiration level is reached. Until that goal is achieved, the person is risk seeking. Upon reaching his goal the individual becomes a conservative risk averter until

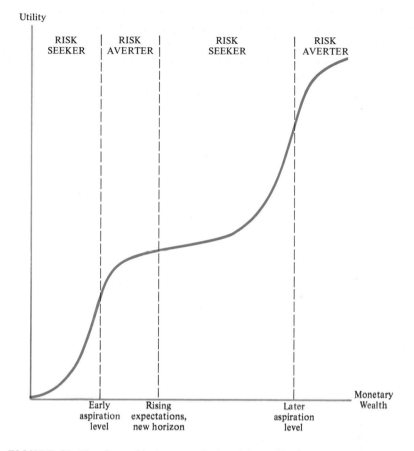

FIGURE 21-10   A graphical portrayal of evolving utility function for an individual over a long time period.

more wealth permits germination of a newer, higher order goal. Then the cycle begins all over again with risk seeking, followed by another spell of risk aversion.

Such a curve portrays behavior over a long period of time and is only an idealization of a long-run utility function. A great many factors can cause an individual's attitudes to change over time, and it may not be possible to obtain meaningful measures of the influence of remote goals. Generally a utility curve's validity is very short-lived and will change with factors such as age, life style, family size, and total wealth. To be successfully employed, the utility function ought to be updated prior to each decision.

EXERCISES

21-7   Suppose that Alvin Black's attitude toward risk is generally averse. For each of the following 50–50 gambling propositions, indicate whether he

(1) would be willing, (2) might desire, or (3) would be unwilling to participate. Explain the reasons for your choices.
(a) $10,000 versus $0.
(b) $10,000 versus −$1,000.
(c) $15,000 versus −$10,000.
(d) $500 versus −$600.
(e) $20,000 versus $10,000.

21-8   Lucille Brown is risk neutral. Would she buy comprehensive coverage on her automobile if she agreed with company actuaries regarding the probability distribution of future claim sizes? Explain.

21-9   Victor White is a risk seeker. Does this necessarily imply that he will never buy casualty insurance? Explain.

21-10   J. P. Tidewasser has just undergone the first traumatic phase of determining his utility function for a range of money values. By his response to a series of gambles, it has been established that he is indifferent between the 50–50 gambles listed below and receiving the certain amounts of money shown on the right.

Rewards of Gamble		Equivalent Amount
+$30,000	−$10,000	$ 0
+ 30,000	0	+ 10,000
0	− 10,000	− 7,000
+ 10,000	− 7,000	1,000

(a) If he sets $u(\$30,000) = 1$ and $u-(\$10,000) = 0$, then determine what his utility should be for $0.
(b) Calculate his utilities for +$10,000 and −$7,000.
(c) Calculate his utility for +$1,000. Do you notice any inconsistencies between this and previous answers?

21-11   Hoopla Hoops is a retail boutique catering to current crazes. The owner must decide whether or not to stock a batch of Water Wheelies. Each item costs $2.00 and sells for $4.00. Unsold items cannot be returned to the supplier, who sells them in batches of 500. The following probability distribution is assumed to apply for the demand to be experienced for Water Wheelies:

Demand	Probability
100	.05
200	.10
300	.15
400	.20
500	.20
600	.15
700	.10
800	.05
	1.00

By demand we mean the potential for sales. No more than what is demanded may be sold; but if demand exceeds on-hand inventory, then not all of it can be fulfilled.
(a) Calculate the expected demand. If you assume that the expected demand were actually to occur, what profit corresponds to this amount? Using the utility curve in Figure 21-11, determine the utility value that corresponds.

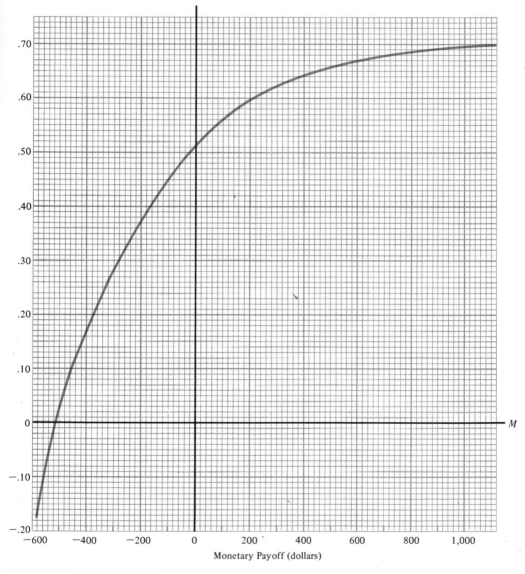

Utility = $u(M)$

Monetary Payoff (dollars)

FIGURE 21-11

(b) Calculate the expected profit from stocking 500 Water Wheelies. Does this differ from the amount found in part (a)? Explain this. Also, determine the utility value for the expected profit.

(c) Calculate the expected utility for stocking 500 Water Wheelies. (First, calculate the profit for each level of possible demand; then find the utility of each; finally, apply the probability weights.) Which act, stocking or not stocking Water Wheelies, provides the greatest expected utility?

        (d) Compare your utility values from (a), (b), and (c). Do these differ? Explain. Which one applies?

21-12 Consider the plight of the decision maker in Exercise 19-9 (p. 667). She must interview dozens of candidates annually for keypunching jobs. Losses of her recoverable training expenses can therefore be significant. Suppose that she has constructed the utility function shown in Figure 21-11. Answer the following:

        (a) Redraw Figure 19-6.

        (b) For each end position's monetary payoff value, determine the decision-maker's approximate utility values from the curve in Figure 21-11.

        (c) Perform backward induction analysis using utilities as payoffs. Which strategy is optimal?

21-4   ASSESSING PROBABILITIES THROUGH JUDGMENT

Although probability concepts have been extensively used in earlier chapters, little discussion has been devoted to subjective probabilities. Applicable to nonrepeatable circumstances, such as introducing a new product or drilling a wildcat oil well, subjective probabilities must be arrived at through *judgment*. This is in contrast to the long-run-frequency basis used to establish objective probabilities, which is valid only when elements of repeatability are present. Because so many business decisions involve one-shot situations that are impossible to repeat exactly, there is a strong need for subjective probabilities when analyzing decision making under uncertainty. This section illustrates procedures for translating judgment into those subjective probability values necessary for implementing Bayesian analysis to help solve real-world decision problems.

Probabilities Obtained from History

Historical experience may be a convenient starting point for assigning probabilities. All that is necessary to calculate the historical frequency of an event is knowledge of how many times it has occurred in the past and the number of opportunities when it could have occurred. This is how fire insurance underwriters get their probabilities for determining expected claim sizes used to establish policy charges. With tens of thousands of buildings involved, *the event frequencies themselves define the probabilities*, because in the traditional sense probability fundamentally expresses long-run frequency of occurrence.

Difficulties do arise in using historical frequencies as probabilities. One is the limited extent of history—not enough data may be available for anything but a rather crude frequency estimate. Unless the number of similar past circumstances is large, statistical estimates of event frequencies may be unreliable. Past history may be suitable for setting fire insurance rates. But past frequency cannot be wholly adequate, indeed is unavailable, for finding probability distributions for a great many variables encountered in business, such as the demand for a new product.

Another serious difficulty arises as conditions change over time. The recent experience of automobile casualty insurance firms serves as an example of how changing conditions can make historical frequencies unsuitable for obtaining probabilities. Car insurers, who have consistently complained about losing money on collision and comprehensive coverage, have found that past experience has proven a poor predictor of the future levels of damage claims. The fault lies not with sampling error, virtually nonexistent because data obtained constitute a census, but rather in changing circumstances. Cars have been becoming steadily less sturdy, so that minor impacts that would hardly dent an older car can cause serious damage to a new one. The costs of repairs have also been rising in a pronounced inflationary spiral. More cars are sharing roads that are not increasing at the same rate, while driving habits are also changing; this affects the accident rate. Losses due to auto theft have been increasing as the result of new social pressures.

Using historical frequencies to estimate probabilities of future auto insurance claims may be compared to tossing a die, some side of which is shaved before each toss. We do not know which side is shaved nor by how much. Under these circumstances we can never obtain a reasonable probability distribution for the respective sides from historical frequencies alone.

Subjective Probabilities

In order to apply basic decision-making models based upon expected payoff or utility, we must employ probabilities. Past history can sometimes provide probability values that fit into the mold of long-run frequencies. But the applicability of such data is limited to events with a rich history, such as insurance claims. Even when they are available, these data can be misleading owing to the forces of change.

In many business decisions, there is ordinarily no recourse but to use subjective probabilities, which are not tied to a long-run frequency of occurrence, because so many decisions are "one shot" in nature and may be characterized by essentially nonrepeatable uncertainties. Good *judgment* may be the only recourse available for transforming such uncertainties into a set of probabilities for the various events involved.

We have seen that decision making under uncertainty is really analogous to gambling. Unlike card games, lotteries, dice, or roulette, most real-life gambles can be analyzed only with the help of subjective probabilities. As noted, these must reflect an amalgam of the decision-maker's judgment and experience.

How do we obtain a subjective probability?

We may consider subjective probabilities as "betting odds." That is, they can be treated just like the probabilities that the decision maker would desire in a lottery situation—of his or her own design—in which the payoffs are identical in every respect to those possible from the actual decision being evaluated. For example, suppose a contractor assigns a subjective probability of .5 to the event of winning a contract that will increase profits by $50,000, while losing will cause a $10,000 loss. The contractor then ought to be indifferent between preparing a bid for this contract and gambling on a coin toss where a head provides a $50,000 win and a tail results in a $10,000 loss. The subjective probability of winning the contract may be transformed directly into an "objective" .5 probability of getting a head from a coin toss. Assuming indifference between the real-life gamble and a hypothetical coin toss, we can substitute the latter into the decision analysis.

One practical benefit of such a hypothetical-for-real substitution is that subjective probabilities may be used in conjunction with the traditional long-run frequency type. In effect, apples and oranges may be mixed, thus providing for wider acceptance of the decision-theoretical analysis. More significantly, a hypothetical gamble or lottery can provide a convenient means of obtaining the subjective probability value itself.

> **Example 21-4** A project engineer has a choice of two technologies for designing a prototype sonar system. He may use Doppler shift or acoustic ranging. If he uses Doppler shift, time becomes a crucial factor. To analyze his decision he must determine the probability of completing his project on time. If he is late, the project will be canceled, and he will be out of a job. But if he is early or on time, his contract will be extended for two more years. Figure 21-12(a) shows the event fork of concern.
>
> Suppose that he considers a hypothetical lottery, shown in Figure 21-12(b), where one marble will be randomly selected from a box containing 100. Some marbles are labeled *E* (for early), the rest are marked *L* (for late). In this hypothetical gamble, selecting an *E* marble will result in an extended contract, but drawing an *L* marble will result in a canceled contract. Our engineer can determine the mix of *L* and *E* marbles. He is asked what mixture will make him *indifferent* between letting his future be decided by trying the Doppler shift design or by selecting a marble from the box.
>
> Suppose that he determines that 70 *E* marbles and 30 *L* marbles would make him indifferent. This means that the probability of selecting an *E* marble is .70.

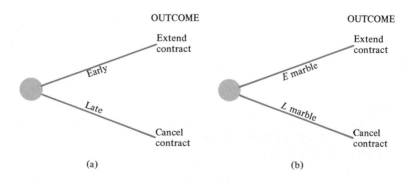

(a)   (b)

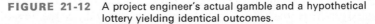

FIGURE 21-12   A project engineer's actual gamble and a hypothetical lottery yielding identical outcomes.

The .70 figure may be viewed as his judgmental assessment that he will be early or on time by using Doppler shift. Thus our decision maker can use .70 for the probability of being early in analyzing his decision, with .70 used for the early event branch of the fork in Figure 21-12(a).

Arriving at subjective probabilities by substituting the real-life gamble for an equally preferred lottery is a useful procedure when the number of possible events is small. But this method can be quite cumbersome when there are more than a handful of events. In business applications, we are often faced with variables, such as product demand, with many possible levels. Such uncertain quantities are best handled with an entire *probability distribution.*

As we have seen, probability distributions may be divided into two categories. Discrete probability distributions apply to variables, such as the demand for cars, that must be a whole number. Continuous probability distributions, on the other hand, represent variables such as time, which may be expressed on a continuous scale and can be measured to any degree of precision desired. When the number of possibilities is great, discrete variables are often treated as approximately continuous. For this reason, we focus on finding continuous probability distributions.

We next consider the case of using judgment to determine the normal distribution, which constitutes perhaps the most common distribution family encountered in business decision making with continuous variables. After the normal curve, we discuss the more general problem of establishing a probability distribution for *any* random variable.

EXERCISES

21-13 For each of the following situations, discuss whether historical frequencies can be used meaningfully to estimate probabilities:
(a) For first-year salary levels of business school graduates.
(b) For the faces obtained by tossing an asymmetrical die.
(c) Of dying during the next year, for persons in various age, health, sex, and occupational categories.

21-14 Using your judgment, assess the probability that you will receive an "A" on your next statistics examination. To help you achieve this, imagine that your instructor will let you obtain your grade by lottery, so that 100 slips of paper—some saying A, the rest not A—will be put into a hat and mixed. You will then draw one of these slips at random. The letter obtained will be the grade you receive. How many A slips must there be to make you indifferent between letting your grade be determined by lottery or by earning it?

21-5 DETERMINING A NORMAL CURVE JUDGMENTALLY

The normal distribution plays an important role in decision making. In large measure, this is due to the fact that probabilities for sample means can usually be characterized by a normal curve (because of the central limit theorem, discussed in Chapter 7). But the normal curve might apply in many applications other than sampling. Physical measurements often occur with a frequency pattern matched by the normal curve. This feature makes it especially important in production applications, where natural fluctuations in size, density, concentrations, etc., cause individual units to vary according to the normal distribution. Test scores used to determine personal aptitudes or achievement are often so characterized. Questions of facility design, as they relate to waiting lines—whether in manufacturing, retailing, or data-processing situations—must consider time needed to service customers, complete jobs, or produce production units; these service times are often normally distributed.

Since the normal distribution is so prevalent in a broad spectrum of decision-making situations, we give it special emphasis in this chapter. As we have seen, any normal distribution is uniquely defined in terms of two parameters, the mean μ and standard deviation σ. Except in the rare circumstances when these parameters are known precisely, it is impossible to measure their values directly without expensive sampling procedures. It may be more convenient to exercise judgment in determining μ and σ. With these two quantities, we can specify the entire normal distribution. (In fact, it may be optimal not to take samples at all—we considered this question in Chapter 20. Often sampling is itself impossible because no population currently exists from which observations can be taken.)

The mean of the subjective normal curve for any quantity X believed to have that distribution may be established by selecting the *midpoint* of all possible values. *The subjective mean μ is that point judged to have a 50–50 chance that any value X will lie at or above it or, instead, below it.* This value is actually the *median* level, since it is just as likely for X to fall below as above the point so identified. Because the normal curve is symmetrical, this central value must also equal the mean.

For example, suppose that an engineer is evaluating a new teleprocessing terminal design to determine if a prototype should be fabricated. Based on the physical characteristics of the unit compared with those of existing equipment of similar scope, the engineer concludes that messages might be printed at a rate of between 30 and 70 lines per second varying with the type of message. Because the unit has never been built, the true rate X for a typical message is uncertain. The engineer assumes that this quantity is normally distributed (because similar data in related applications have been found to fit well to the normal curve).

To establish the mean printing rate, the engineer is asked to establish a level such that it is equally likely for X to fall above or below it. This might be phrased in terms of a coin toss: "Suppose you must find a middle value for X such that it would be difficult for you to choose whether an actual printing rate lies above or below it. That is, if your professional reputation depended on being correct and you had to make a prediction for X, you would be willing to select one side or the other of that value by tossing a coin. Where does your midpoint lie?" After some thought the engineer might reply: "I think it is a coin-tossing proposition that the printing rate experienced in actual testing might fall above or below 50 lines per second." This establishes the desired midpoint and hence the mean of the subjective probability distribution, $\mu = 50$ lines per second.

Relating the judgmental evaluation to coin tossing makes the problem easy for a person not used to dealing with probability. The 50–50 gamble is the easiest to envision. We may extend this concept to finding the standard deviation as well. *The subjective standard deviation σ can be found by establishing a middle range of values centered at μ such that an equal chance is judged for X lying inside or outside that interval.* To see why this works, let's review some properties of the normal curve.

In Chapter 7, we established that the area under the normal curve between any two points is established by the distances separating each point from the mean with distance expressed in standard-deviation units. This standardized distance may be represented by a value for the normal deviate z, where for any particular point x, the corresponding normal deviate may be computed from

$$z = \frac{x - \mu}{\sigma}$$

We seek two possible values for X, equally distant from μ, such that the area between them is .50. This means that the area between μ and the upper limit must be half this, or .25. From the normal curve areas in Appendix Table D, the normal deviate value of $z = .67$ provides the closest area, .2486. We may use $z = .67$ in finding σ.

Figure 21-13 illustrates the underlying principles involved. The area between μ and $\mu + .67\sigma$ is about .25, so that the area in the interval $\mu \pm .67\sigma$ is

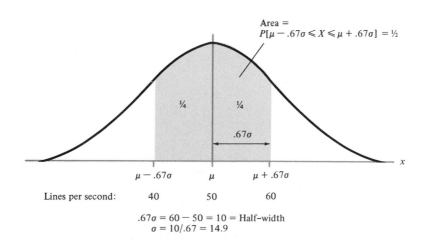

Area =
$P[\mu - .67\sigma \leqslant X \leqslant \mu + .67\sigma] = \frac{1}{2}$

¼   ¼

$.67\sigma$

$\mu - .67\sigma$ μ $\mu + .67\sigma$

Lines per second: 40   50   60

$.67\sigma = 60 - 50 = 10 =$ Half-width
$\sigma = 10/.67 = 14.9$

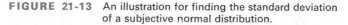

FIGURE 21-13   An illustration for finding the standard deviation of a subjective normal distribution.

about .50. If we know the distance separating the upper limit $\mu+67\sigma$ and mean μ, the *half-width* of the interval, we may then determine the corresponding value for σ by setting $.67\sigma$ equal to that distance:

$$.67\sigma = \text{Upper limit} - \mu$$

Dividing both sides by .67, we obtain the following *expression for the judgmental standard deviation:*

$$\sigma = \frac{\text{Upper limit} - \mu}{.67} = \frac{\text{Half-width}}{.67} \qquad (21\text{-}4)$$

Thus, in finding σ we need only establish the width of the middle range. This quantity is sometimes called the *interquartile range*. This evaluation is tantamount to establishing that half-width such that there is a 50–50 chance that any particular value for X falls within μ plus or minus this amount.

The engineer in our example is next asked to establish the half-width of the central interval. This query might take the form: "We now want to consider a range of values centered at $\mu = 50$ characters per second where you think it is just as likely that the actual printing rate will fall inside or outside of it. To find the interval we must determine an amount such that μ plus or minus that quantity determines the range." The engineer might respond: "I would guess that plus or minus 10 lines per second is suitable for this purpose. This means that there is a coin-flipping chance that the actual printing rate falls somewhere between $50-10 = 40$ and $50+10 = 60$ lines per second." This establishes the half-width of 10 lines per second for the middle range, and the standard deviation may be computed as follows:

$$\sigma = \frac{10}{.67} = 14.9 \text{ lines per second}$$

The subjective probability distribution for the actual printing time of the proposed terminal is now specified. Combining this with economic data, we may then apply decision-theoretical concepts to evaluate various alternatives regarding the manufacturing or marketing of the proposed unit.

EXERCISES

21-15 A bank manager believes that the time taken by a typical teller to write a money order is normally distributed. He has established that (1) it is a 50–50 proposition that this task will take more than 45 seconds; and (2) it is "even money" that the required time for any particular transaction will be from one-half to a full minute.
   (a) Determine the mean and standard deviation of the subjective probability distribution.
   (b) Find the probabilities that a particular money order requires
       (1) between 50 and 70 seconds.
       (2) less than 25 seconds.
       (3) more than one minute.
       (4) between 20 and 50 seconds.

21-16   Establish your own subjective probability distribution for the heights of adult males residing within 50 miles of the campus. Using the normal curve obtained, establish the following probabilities that a randomly chosen man is
(a) less than 6 feet 2 inches.
(b) taller than 5 feet 6 inches.
(c) taller than your father.

21-6   JUDGMENTAL ASSESSMENT OF A GENERAL PROBABILITY DISTRIBUTION

The preceding procedure is a limited one. Although the normal distribution is very common, it is the exception. We now consider how judgment may be exercised to determine probability distributions in general. This procedure applies when there is no reason to believe that a particular curve shape, such as the normal, applies.

Our generalized procedure applies to any variable with a large number of possible values, such as product demand. Millions of levels of demand might be possible for a food product, for example. In analyzing the choice between capital investment alternatives, a food manufacturer would require probabilities for various levels of demand. How might the manufacturer arrive at a probability distribution for demand? It would at best be tedious to attempt to assign an individual probability to each demand level, starting with 0 units and considering each possibility up to 5 or 10 million units. Not a very pleasing prospect. Any numbers so obtained would likely be unrealistic, and individual assessment of a particular demand, say 333,333 units, would involve a probability value too tiny to have much meaning.

A natural and fairly simple procedure for judgmentally obtaining a probability distribution is to use cumulative probabilities. By posing a series of 50–50 gambles, it is quite simple for a decision maker to judgmentally determine a random variable's cumulative probability distribution. Each response provides a point that may be represented on a graph; a smoothed curve may then be drawn through the points. This curve completely specifies the underlying probability distribution. The following illustration shows how this procedure may be carried out.

The president of a food manufacturing concern wishes to obtain the probability distribution for a brand new snack product's demand. This will be used to facilitate analysis of the decision whether or not to introduce it into the market. A statistical analyst on the staff asks a series of questions, obtaining answers that help in formulating later questions. The interview proceeds on the next page.*

---

* This procedure was inspired by that of Howard Raiffa in his book *Decision Analysis: Introductory Lectures on Choices Under Uncertainty* (Reading, Mass.: Addison-Wesley, 1968).

Q. What do you think the largest and smallest possible levels of demand are?

A. Certainly demand will exceed 500,000 units. But I would set an upper limit of 3 million units. I don't think that under the most favorable circumstances we could sell more than this amount.

Q. Okay, we have determined the range of possible demand. Now I want you to tell me what level of demand divides the possibilities into two equally likely ranges. For example, do you think demand will be just as likely to fall above 2,000,000 as below?

A. No. I'd rather pick 1,500,000 units as the 50–50 point.

Q. Very good. Now let's consider the demand levels below 1,500,000. If demand were to fall somewhere between 500,000 and 1,500,000 units, would you bet that it lies above or below 1,000,000?

A. Above. I would say that a demand of 1,250,000 units would be a realistic dividing point.

Q. We will use that amount as our 50–50 point. Let's do the same thing for the upper range of demand.

A. If I were to pick a number, I would choose 2,000,000 units. I feel that demand is just as likely to fall into the 1.5 to 2 million range as into the 2 to 3 million range.

Q. Excellent. We're making good progress. To get a finer fix on the points obtained so far, I now want you to tell me whether you think demand is just as likely to fall between 1.25 and 2 million units as outside that range.

A. Inside. I suppose this means I am being inconsistent.

Q. Yes it does. Let's remedy this. Do you think that we ought to raise the 1,250,000 dividing point or lower the 2 million unit figure?

A. Lower the 2 million figure to 1.9 million.

Q. Let's check to see if this disturbs our other answers. Do you think that 1,500,000 splits demand over the range from 1,250,000 to 1,900,000 into two equally likely regions?

A. Yes, I am satisfied that it does.

Q. Just a few more questions. Suppose demand is above 1,900,000. What level splits this demand range into two equally likely regions?

A. I'd say 2,200,000.

Q. Good. Now supposing demand is between 2,200,000 and 3,000,000, where would you split?

A. I would guess that 2,450,000 units would be the 50–50 point.

Q. How about when demand is below 1,250,000?

A. Try 1,100,000 units.

Q. And when demand is between 500,000 and 1,100,000 units?

A. I think demand is far more likely to be close to the higher figure. I would bet on 950,000 units.

Table 21-3 shows the information obtained through the interview. The initial decision to divide demand at 1,500,000 units makes this level the 50-

TABLE 21-3   A Food Manufacturer's Judgmental Assessment
of Fractiles for Demand of a New Snack Food

Fractile	Amount
0	500,000
.0625	950,000
.125	1,100,000
.25	1,250,000
.50	1,500,000
.75	1,900,000
.875	2,200,000
.9375	2,450,000
1.000	3,000,000

percent point or median. Since .5 has been judged the chance that demand will
be below 1,500,000, we will refer to this as the .5 fractile. This means that the
probability is .5 that the actual demand will be 1,500,000 units *or less*. Our
decision maker has chosen to divide the range from 500,000 to 1,500,000 units
at a demand level of 1,250,000. Believing that the chance of demand falling into
this range is .5, the president has judged the chance that demand will be at or
below 1,250,000 units to be .5(.5) = .25; we refer to 1,250,000 units as the .25
fractile. Again this establishes a .25 probability that demand will be less than or
equal to 1,250,000. Likewise, the median of the range from 1,500,000 to 3,000,000
units is 1,900,000, which thus becomes the .75 fractile, since the probability is
.5 + .5(.5) = .75 that demand will fall somewhere below 1,900,000 units. The
analyst has proceeded by finding the medians of the regions working outward
from previously found 50 percent points. Thus, the .125 fractile, 1,100,000 units,
is the median demand for possible levels below the .25 fractile (1,250,000 units),
which had to be determined first. The median of demands above 1,900,000
units is the .875 fractile, 2,200,000 units. Similarly, the median of the demands
below 1,100,000 is the .0625 fractile, 950,000 units, while the median demand
level beyond 2,200,000 is the .9375 fractile, 2,450,000.

The fractiles and the corresponding demands are plotted as points in
Figure 21-14. The vertical axis represents the cumulative probability of demand.
A curve has been smoothed through these points. This serves as an approximation of the cumulative probability distribution for the snack's first-year demand.
The curve has an S shape, slope first increasing and then decreasing over higher
levels of demand. The slope changes most rapidly for large and small demands,
so that more points in these regions provide greater accuracy. This is why we
have worked outward from the median in assessing the demand fractiles.

This example illustrates how we may obtain a very detailed measurement
of judgment by posing a few 50–50 gambles. As a rule of thumb, the seven
fractile values used above, ranging from .0625 to .9375, are adequate for this
purpose. There is little to be gained by trying for more, since further gambles
might result in a lumpy curve and would probably not alter the basic shape
anyway. Besides, there is no reason to "gild the lily" nor to try the decision-

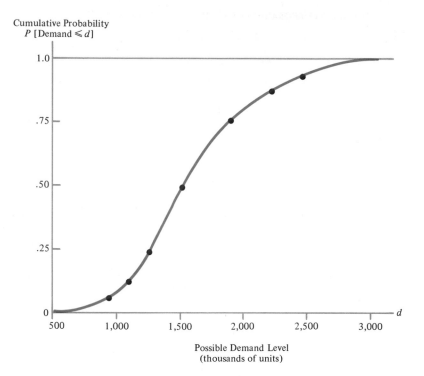

Cumulative Probability
P [Demand ⩽ d]

Possible Demand Level
(thousands of units)

FIGURE 21-14 The cumulative probability distribution function obtained
for a new snack product using judgmental assessments.

maker's patience. A curve obtained by this procedure provides about as good
a reading judgment as is humanly possible.

Common Shapes for Subjective Probability Curves

Ordinarily, subjective probability distributions found in the above manner
will provide S-shaped graphs elongated at either the top or the bottom. Such
graphs represent underlying probability distributions skewed to the left or to
the right, as the corresponding frequency curves in Figure 21-15(a) and (b)
show. Although skewed distributions are the most common ones for business
and economic variables, a symmetrical distribution, shown in (c), is also possible.

Lumpy cumulative probability graphs like the one shown in Figure
21-15(d), where there are two stacked S-shaped curves, are to be avoided. The
corresponding frequency curve has the two-humped shape that typifies a
bimodal distribution. Such distributions reflect some underlying nonhomogeneous influence operating differently for the low value possibilities than for the
higher ones. In statistical applications, the bimodal distribution is epitomized

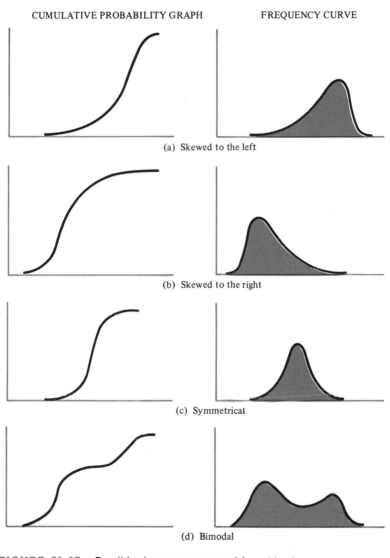

CUMULATIVE PROBABILITY GRAPH   FREQUENCY CURVE

(a) Skewed to the left

(b) Skewed to the right

(c) Symmetrical

(d) Bimodal

FIGURE 21-15   Possible shapes encountered for subjective probability distributions.

by combining heights of men and women. In statistics, it is more meaningful to portray male and female heights separately in terms of two curves.

Similar treatment applies to subjective probability distributions. Should such a result occur, for example, in assessing the next model year's demand for cars, there might be some identifiable factor in the decision-maker's mind that could explain the bimodality. A good example would be the possibility of an oil embargo like that experienced in 1973–74. If such is the case, the assessment should be broken into greater detail: (1) Find a subjective probability for an embargo; (2) determine the subjective probability distribution for automobile demand assuming an embargo occurs; and (3) separately establish a second distribution for demand given that no embargo occurs.

If there is no identifiable explanation, lumpiness in the cumulative probability graph might be due to inconsistencies in expressing judgment. The inconsistencies might be resolved by moving one or more points to the left or right and re-posing the succeeding 50–50 gambles. One easy consistency check is to see if the interquartile range, from the .25 fractile (1,250,000 units in the above example) to the .75 fractile (1,900,000 units) does indeed provide a 50–50 proposition for falling inside or outside of it. Should the decision maker believe the inside to be more likely, then the middle range should be narrowed, either by raising the .50 fractile (to perhaps 1,300,000 units) or by reducing the .75 fractile (to maybe 1,800,000 units). Conversely, if the outside is favored, one of the fractiles should be changed in the opposite direction.

Approximating the Subjective Probability Distribution

The cumulative S curve is difficult to use directly in decision analysis, where expected values must be determined. Expected-value calculations are ordinarily made with a table that lists the possible variable values and their probabilities. To obtain such a table, it is necessary to approximate the cumulative probability curve by a series of steps, as shown in Figure 21-16.

Each possible variable value is represented by an interval. A fairly good approximation is obtained with ten intervals of equal width. The probabilities for each are shown as the step sizes at the upper limit for the respective interval. The probabilities for individual intervals are determined by the difference between successive cumulative probability values. All values in an interval are represented by a typical value. For this purpose, the midpoint is used.

To see how this might be done, suppose that the decision maker now wishes to establish subjective probabilities for intervals of demand from 500,000 to 3,000,000 units, in increments of 250,000. Table 21-4 shows how these have been obtained by reading values from the cumulative probability curve. We may use the probabilities so obtained to determine the approximate expected demand. A representative value is used for this purpose. We have used the interval midpoints in arriving at 1,587,500 units as the expected demand. The same probability values and representative demands can be used to find the expected payoff from introducing the new snack. For each representative level of demand, the total payoff can be determined. The weighted average of these, using the probabilities in Table 21-4, would then yield the expected payoff, which could be used in the total analysis.

The interval probabilities may be used to plot the histogram for demand, as in Figure 21-17. The height of .25 for the bar covering the interval from 1,250,000 to 1,500,000 units represents the probability that demand will fall

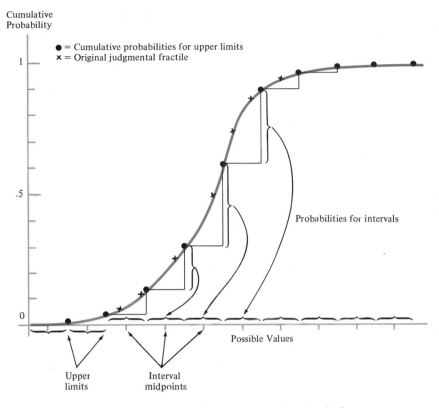

FIGURE 21-16   An illustration of how to approximate a continuous distribution using 10 intervals.

TABLE 21-4   Demand Probabilities for Intervals and Approximation of Expected Demand Calculation

(1) *Demand Interval (thousands)*	(2) *Interval Midpoint (thousands)*	(3) *Probability of Demands at or below Upper Limit (obtained from curve)*	(4) *Probability of Demand Interval*	(5) *Demand× Probability [(2) × (4)]*
500– 750	625	.02	.02	12.50
750–1,000	875	.08	.06	52.50
1,000–1,250	1,125	.25	.17	191.25
1,250–1,500	1,375	.50	.25	343.75
1,500–1,750	1,625	.68	.18	292.50
1,750–2,000	1,875	.80	.12	225.00
2,000–2,250	2,125	.89	.09	191.25
2,250–2,500	2,375	.95	.06	142.50
2,500–2,750	2,625	.98	.03	78.75
2,750–3,000	2,875	1.00	.02	57.50

Approximate expected demand = 1,587.50

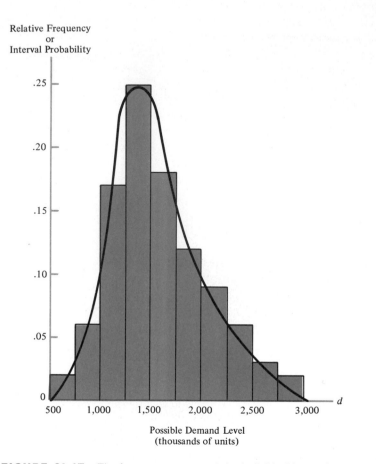

FIGURE 21-17   The frequency curve and the individual interval probabilities obtained for a new snack product demand using judgmental assessments.

somewhere between these amounts. Superimposed onto this histogram is a smoothed curve representing the judgmental frequency curve for demand. Note that the curve is positively skewed.

Concluding Remarks

We have seen that probability values for decision making may sometimes be obtained from past history. But past history is of limited use in business situations, and it may not exist at all for nonrepeatable circumstances. We have emphasized directly assessing a decision-maker's judgment and not many useful traditional statistical techniques. But it should be noted that the latter also rely heavily on judgmental inputs (usually of an indirect nature).

It is not necessary for a decision maker to obtain subjective probabilities personally. Such judgment can be delegated. For example, the chairman of General Motors might rely on various officers within the corporation to determine some or all of the probabilities used in analyzing a decision. After all, this is an area in which expert opinion should be used whenever possible. Although exercising judgment to find subjective probabilities is similar to assessing attitude toward decision outcomes (constructing and then using a utility curve), it is dangerous for any decision maker to delegate that role to others. Attitude is highly personal and expresses unique taste, whereas judgment can be shared. (Collective assessment of attitude is absolutely prohibited by the axioms of utility theory. However, there is no reason why a committee cannot determine the subjective probabilities to be used.)

EXERCISES

21-17   Calculate the cumulative probability function for the random variable, unit sales, whose probability distribution is provided below. Then construct a graph showing the cumulative probabilities as a step function.

Possible Sales Level s	$P[Sales = s]$
0	.1
1	.2
2	.3
3	.2
4	.1
5	.1
	1.0

21-18   Using the cumulative probability distribution function in Figure 21-18, determine the following probabilities:
(a) $P[D > 500]$ (b) $P[D \leqslant 150]$
(c) $P[D \geqslant 300]$ (d) $P[200 \leqslant D \leqslant 800]$

21-19   Using the cumulative distribution probability graph in Figure 21-18, determine the following fractiles:
(a) .10;   (b) .50;   (c) .125;   (d) .75;   (e) .37.

21-20   Envision your income during the first full calendar year after graduation. Establish your own subjective probability distribution for the adjusted gross income figure that you will then report to the IRS. (If applicable, include your spouse's earnings, interest, dividends, etc.) If your graph has an unusual shape, try to eliminate any inconsistencies or to identify the nonhomogeneous factors (pregnancy, unemployment, divorce, etc.) that might explain the shape. Remember, you are the expert about yourself.

21-21   Using the cumulative probability distribution for demand in Figure 21-18, construct the probability distribution of demand, using five intervals in increments of 200. Selecting the midpoints of these intervals as representative values, determine the approximate expected demand.

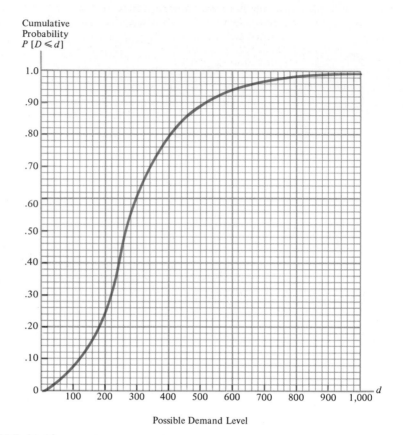

Cumulative
Probability
$P[D \leqslant d]$

Possible Demand Level

FIGURE 21-18

REVIEW EXERCISES

21-22 Actor Nathan Summers likes to wear costumes in front of audiences. He likes most dressing up like a little old lady. He hates to dress up like an animal. Somewhere in between these lies his preference for wearing a cowboy suit. Assigning utility 10 for being a lady and -5 for being an animal, what is his utility for playing a cowboy if he is indifferent between this outcome and a coin toss determining which of the other roles he will play?

21-23 A tornado-damage home insurance policy would cost Hermie Hawks $1,000 per year. Assuming that any actual damage from a tornado to Hermie's house, valued at $100,000, would be total destruction, and assuming that the probability of a tornado hitting his house during the year to be .0025, answer the following.

(a) Assuming that Hermie is risk neutral, what would his Bayes-decision-rule optimal decision be regarding buying tornado insurance? Show your computations.

(b) How much above its expected claim size is the insurance company charging Hermie for its combined overhead and profit on the proposed policy?

(c) Hermie's utility function for any change in his monetary position is, for any amount M,

$$u(M) = 10,000 - (M/1,000)^2$$

In order to maximize his expected utility, what action should Hermie take?

(d) What annual insurance premium charge would make Hermie indifferent between buying or not buying tornado insurance?

21-24 Suppose that the president of Ponderosa Record Company has a utility function for money $u(M) = [(M+65,000)/10,000]^2$.

(a) Redraw Figure 21-8 (page 759), and calculate the utility for each end position.

(b) Perform backward induction analysis using the new utilities you have calculated. Which strategy is optimal?

(c) On a piece of graph paper, plot the utilities calculated in part (a) as a function of monetary payoffs M. Sketch a curve through the points. Of what attitude toward risk is the shape of your curve indicative?

21-25 Suppose that a person faced with the decision structure provided in Figure 19-5 (page 667) has the utility function shown in Figure 21-19. Answer the following:

(a) Redraw the decision tree diagram of Figure 19-5, entering the appropriate probability values on the corresponding branches.

(b) For each end position's monetary payoff value, determine the decision-maker's approximate utility values from the curve in Figure 21-19.

(c) Perform backward induction analysis using utilities as payoffs. Which strategy is optimal?

21-26 An automobile production manager believes that the time taken to install a new car bumper is normally distributed. He has established (1) that it is a 50–50 proposition that this task will take more than 60 seconds and (2) that it is "even money" that the required time for any particular car will be between 45 and 75 seconds.

(a) Determine the mean and standard deviation of the subjective probability distribution.

(b) Find the probabilities that the installation for a particular car will take:
  (1) between 50 and 70 seconds.
  (2) less than 25 seconds.
  (3) more than one minute.
  (4) between 20 and 90 seconds.

21-27 The following fractiles apply to the subjective probability distribution for a new product's demand:

Fractile	Quantity
.0625	10,000
.125	25,000
.250	35,000
.500	40,000
.750	45,000
.875	55,000
.9375	75,000

Establish the probabilities that demand will fall within the following limits:
(a) 10,000 to 40,000
(b) 35,000 to 75,000
(c) 25,000 to 55,000
(d) 25,000 to 45,000

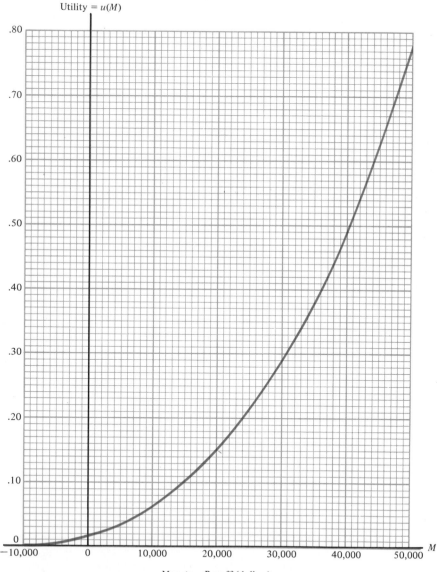

FIGURE 21-19

21-28 The following approximation has been obtained for the subjective probability distribution for a product's demand:

Demand D	Probability
1,000	.08
2,000	.18
3,000	.36
4,000	.18
5,000	.10
6,000	.04
7,000	.03
8,000	.02
9,000	.01

(a) Determine the expected demand.
(b) Suppose that the payoff for each level of demand is determined by the following expression

$$\text{Payoff} = \begin{cases} -\$500 + .3D & \text{if } D \leqslant 5,000 \\ \$1,000 & \text{if } D > 5,000 \end{cases}$$

Calculate the expected payoff.
(c) Suppose that the decision-maker's utility function for money is provided in Figure 21-11. Calculate the expected utility.

Selected References

The Role of Statistics
Careers in Statistics. The American Statistical Association (no date available).
Huff, Darrell. *How to Lie with Statistics.* New York: W.W. Norton, 1954.
Moroney, M.J. *Facts from Figures.* Baltimore: Penguin Books, 1965.
Reichmann, W.J. *Use and Abuse of Statistics.* New York: Oxford University Press, 1962.
Wallis, W.A., and H.V. Roberts. *The Nature of Statistics.* New York: The Free Press, 1965.

Probability
Feller, William. *An Introduction to Probability Theory and Its Applications,* Vol. 1, 3rd ed. New York: John Wiley & Sons, 1968.
Hodges, J.L., Jr., and E.L. Lehmann. *Elements of Finite Probability.* San Francisco: Holden-Day, 1965.
Laplace, Pierre Simon, Marquis de. *A Philosophical Essay on Probabilities.* New York: Dover Publications, 1951.
Lindgren, B.W., and G.W. McElrath. *Introduction to Probability and Statistics,* 3rd ed. New York: Macmillan, 1969.
Mosteller, F., R. Rourke, and G. Thomas, Jr. *Probability and Statistics.* Reading, Mass.: Addison-Wesley, 1961.
Parzen, Emmanuel. *Modern Probability Theory and Its Applications.* New York: John Wiley & Sons, 1960.

Regression and Correlation Analysis
Ezekiel, Mordecai, and Karl A. Fox. *Methods of Correlation and Regression Analysis,* 3rd ed. New York: John Wiley & Sons, 1959.
Johnston, J. *Econometric Methods,* 2nd ed. New York: McGraw-Hill, 1972.
Neter, John, and William Wasserman. *Applied Linear Statistical Models.* Homewood, Ill.: Richard D. Irwin, 1974.
Williams, E.J. *Regression Analysis.* New York: John Wiley & Sons, 1959.
Wonnacott, Ronald J., and Thomas H. Wonnacott. *Econometrics.* New York: John Wiley & Sons, 1970.

Time Series Analysis and Index Numbers
Brown, Robert G. *Smoothing, Forecasting and Prediction of Discrete Time Series.* Englewood Cliffs, N.J.: Prentice-Hall, 1963.
McKinley, David H., Murray G. Lee, and Helene Duffy. *Forecasting Business Conditions.* The American Bankers Association, 1965.
Mudgett, Bruce D. *Index Numbers.* New York: John Wiley & Sons, 1951.
Spencer, Milton H., Colin G. Clark, and Peter W. Hoguet. *Business and Economic Forecasting: An Econometric Approach.* Homewood, Ill.: Richard D. Irwin, 1965.

Analysis of Variance and Design of Experiments
Cochran, William G., and Gertrude M. Cox. *Experimental Designs,* 2nd ed. New York: John Wiley & Sons, 1957.

Cox, D.R. *Planning of Experiments*. New York: John Wiley & Sons, 1958.
Guenther, W.C. *Analysis of Variance*. Englewood Cliffs, N.J.: Prentice-Hall, 1964.
Mendenhall, William. *An Introduction to Linear Models and the Design and Analysis of Experiments*. Belmont, Calif.: Wadsworth, 1968.
Neter, John, and William Wasserman. *Applied Linear Statistical Models*. Homewood, Ill.: Richard D. Irwin, 1974.
Scheffe, Henry. *The Analysis of Variance*. New York: John Wiley & Sons, 1959.

Nonparametric Statistics
Bradley, James V. *Distribution-Free Statistical Tests*. Englewood Cliffs, N.J.: Prentice-Hall, 1968.
Conover, W.J. *Practical Nonparametric Statistics*. New York: John Wiley & Sons, 1971.
Gibbons, J. *Nonparametric Statistical Inference*. New York: McGraw-Hill, 1971.
Hájek, Jaroslav. *Nonparametric Statistics*. San Francisco: Holden-Day, 1969.
Kraft, Charles H., and Constance van Eeden. *A Nonparametric Introduction to Statistics*. New York: Macmillan, 1968.
Noether, Gottfried E. *Introduction to Statistics: A Fresh Approach*. Boston: Houghton Mifflin, 1971.
Siegel, Sydney. *Nonparametric Statistics for the Behavioral Sciences*. New York: McGraw-Hill, 1956.

Decision Theory and Utility
Aitchison, J. *Choice Against Chance*. Reading, Mass.: Addison-Wesley, 1970.
Brown, R.V., A.S. Kahr, and C. Peterson. *Decision Analysis for the Manager*. New York: Holt, Rinehart and Winston, 1974.
Chernoff, H., and L.E. Moses. *Elementary Decision Theory*. New York: John Wiley & Sons, 1959.
Jones, J.M. *Introduction to Decision Theory*. Homewood, Ill.: Richard D. Irwin, 1977.
Luce, R.D., and H. Raiffa. *Games and Decisions*. New York: John Wiley & Sons, 1957.
Miller, D.W., and M.K. Starr. *Executive Decisions and Operations Research*, 2nd ed. Englewood Cliffs, N.J.: Prentice-Hall, 1969.
Morris, W.T. *Management Science: A Bayesian Introduction*. Englewood Cliffs, N.J.: Prentice-Hall, 1968.
Pratt, J.W., H. Raiffa, and R. Schlaifer. *Introduction to Statistical Decision Theory*. New York: McGraw-Hill, 1965.
Raiffa, H. *Decision Analysis: Introductory Lectures on Choices Under Uncertainty*. Reading, Mass.: Addison-Wesley, 1968.
Schlaifer, R. *Analysis of Decisions Under Uncertainty*. New York: McGraw-Hill, 1969.
———. *Introduction to Statistics for Business Decisions*. New York: McGraw-Hill, 1961

Statistical Tables
Beyer, William H. (ed.). *Handbook of Tables for Probability and Statistics*, 2nd ed. Cleveland, Ohio: The Chemical Rubber Co., 1968.
Burington, Richard S., and Donald C. May. *Handbook of Probability and Statistics with Tables*, 2nd ed. New York: McGraw-Hill, 1970.
Fisher, R.A., and F. Yates. *Statistical Tables for Biological, Agricultural and Medical Research*. London: Longman Group, 1963.
National Bureau of Standards. *Tables of the Binomial Distribution*. Washington, D.C.: U.S. Government Printing Office, 1950.
Owen, D.B. *Handbook of Statistical Tables*. Reading, Mass.: Addison-Wesley, 1962.
Pearson, E.S., and H.O. Hartley. *Biometrika Tables for Statisticians*, 3rd ed. Cambridge, England: Cambridge University Press, 1966.
The Rand Corporation. *A Million Random Digits with 100,000 Normal Deviates*. New York: The Free Press, 1955.

Appendix

TABLE A Squares, Square Roots, and Reciprocals

N	$\sqrt{N}$	N^2	$\sqrt{10N}$	$1000/N$	N	$\sqrt{N}$	N^2	$\sqrt{10N}$	$1000/N$
					50	7.07107	2500	22.36068	20.00000
1	1.00000	1	3.16228	1000.00000	51	7.14143	2601	22.58318	19.60784
2	1.41421	4	4.47214	500.00000	52	7.21110	2704	22.80351	19.23077
3	1.73205	9	5.47723	333.33333	53	7.28011	2809	23.02173	18.86792
4	2.00000	16	6.32456	250.00000	54	7.34847	2916	23.23790	18.51852
5	2.23607	25	7.07107	200.00000	55	7.41620	3025	23.45208	18.18182
6	2.44949	36	7.74597	166.66667	56	7.48331	3136	23.66432	17.85714
7	2.64575	49	8.36660	142.85714	57	7.54983	3249	23.87467	17.54386
8	2.82843	64	8.94427	125.00000	58	7.61577	3364	24.08319	17.24138
9	3.00000	81	9.48683	111.11111	59	7.68115	3481	24.28992	16.94915
10	3.16228	100	10.00000	100.00000	60	7.74597	3600	24.49490	16.66667
11	3.31662	121	10.48809	90.90909	61	7.81025	3721	24.69818	16.39344
12	3.46410	144	10.95445	83.33333	62	7.87401	3844	24.89980	16.12903
13	3.60555	169	11.40175	76.92308	63	7.93725	3969	25.09980	15.87302
14	3.74166	196	11.83216	71.42857	64	8.00000	4096	25.29822	15.62500
15	3.87298	225	12.24745	66.66667	65	8.06226	4225	25.49510	15.38462
16	4.00000	256	12.64911	62.50000	66	8.12404	4356	25.69047	15.15152
17	4.12311	289	13.03840	58.82353	67	8.18535	4489	25.88436	14.92537
18	4.24264	324	13.41641	55.55556	68	8.24621	4624	26.07681	14.70588
19	4.35890	361	13.78405	52.63158	69	8.30662	4761	26.26785	14.49275
20	4.47214	400	14.14214	50.00000	70	8.36660	4900	26.45751	14.28571
21	4.58258	441	14.49138	47.61905	71	8.42615	5041	26.64583	14.08451
22	4.69042	484	14.83240	45.45455	72	8.48528	5184	26.83282	13.88889
23	4.79583	529	15.16575	43.47826	73	8.54400	5329	27.01851	13.69863
24	4.89898	576	15.49193	41.66667	74	8.60233	5476	27.20294	13.51351
25	5.00000	625	15.81139	40.00000	75	8.66025	5625	27.38613	13.33333
26	5.09902	676	16.12452	38.46154	76	8.71780	5776	27.56810	13.15789
27	5.19615	729	16.43168	37.03704	77	8.77496	5929	27.74887	12.98701
28	5.29150	784	16.73320	35.71429	78	8.83176	6084	27.92848	12.82051
29	5.38516	841	17.02939	34.48276	79	8.88819	6241	28.10694	12.65823
30	5.47723	900	17.32051	33.33333	80	8.94427	6400	28.28427	12.50000
31	5.56776	961	17.60682	32.25806	81	9.00000	6561	28.46050	12.34568
32	5.65685	1024	17.88854	31.25000	82	9.05539	6724	28.63564	12.19512
33	5.74456	1089	18.16590	30.30303	83	9.11043	6889	28.80972	12.04819
34	5.83095	1156	18.43909	29.41176	84	9.16515	7056	28.98275	11.90476
35	5.91608	1225	18.70829	28.57143	85	9.21954	7225	29.15476	11.76471
36	6.00000	1296	18.97367	27.77778	86	9.27362	7396	29.32576	11.62791
37	6.08276	1369	19.23538	27.02703	87	9.32738	7569	29.49576	11.49425
38	6.16441	1444	19.49359	26.31579	88	9.38083	7744	29.66479	11.36364
39	6.24500	1521	19.74842	25.64103	89	9.43398	7921	29.83287	11.23596
40	6.32456	1600	20.00000	25.00000	90	9.48683	8100	30.00000	11.11111
41	6.40312	1681	20.24846	24.39024	91	9.53939	8281	30.16621	10.98901
42	6.48074	1764	20.49390	23.80952	92	9.59166	8464	30.33150	10.86957
43	6.55744	1849	20.73644	23.25581	93	9.64365	8649	30.49590	10.75269
44	6.63325	1936	20.97618	22.72727	94	9.69536	8836	30.65942	10.63830
45	6.70820	2025	21.21320	22.22222	95	9.74679	9025	30.82207	10.52632
46	6.78233	2116	21.44761	21.73913	96	9.79796	9216	30.98387	10.41667
47	6.85565	2209	21.67948	21.27660	97	9.84886	9409	31.14482	10.30928
48	6.92820	2304	21.90890	20.83333	98	9.89949	9604	31.30495	10.20408
49	7.00000	2401	22.13594	20.40816	99	9.94987	9801	31.46427	10.10101
50	7.07107	2500	22.36068	20.00000	100	10.00000	10000	31.62278	10.00000

TABLE A   (*continued*)

N	$\sqrt{N}$	N^2	$\sqrt{10N}$	$1000/N$	N	$\sqrt{N}$	N^2	$\sqrt{10N}$	$1000/N$
100	10.00000	10000	31.62278	10.00000	150	12.24745	22500	38.72983	6.66667
101	10.04988	10201	31.78050	9.90099	151	12.28821	22801	38.85872	6.62252
102	10.09950	10404	31.93744	9.80392	152	12.32883	23104	38.98718	6.57895
103	10.14889	10609	32.09361	9.70874	153	12.36932	23409	39.11521	6.53595
104	10.19804	10816	32.24903	9.61538	154	12.40967	23716	39.24283	6.49351
105	10.24695	11025	32.40370	9.52381	155	12.44990	24025	39.37004	6.45161
106	10.29563	11236	32.55764	9.43396	156	12.49000	24336	39.49684	6.41026
107	10.34408	11449	32.71085	9.34579	157	12.52996	24649	39.62323	6.36943
108	10.39230	11664	32.86335	9.25926	158	12.56981	24964	39.74921	6.32911
109	10.44031	11881	33.01515	9.17431	159	12.60952	25281	39.87480	6.28931
110	10.48809	12100	33.16625	9.09091	160	12.64911	25600	40.00000	6.25000
111	10.53565	12321	33.31666	9.00901	161	12.68858	25921	40.12481	6.21118
112	10.58301	12544	33.46640	8.92857	162	12.72792	26244	40.24922	6.17284
113	10.63015	12769	33.61547	8.84956	163	12.76715	26569	40.37326	6.13497
114	10.67708	12996	33.76389	8.77193	164	12.80625	26896	40.49691	6.09756
115	10.72381	13225	33.91165	8.69565	165	12.84523	27225	40.62019	6.06061
116	10.77033	13456	34.05877	8.62069	166	12.88410	27556	40.74310	6.02410
117	10.81665	13689	34.20526	8.54701	167	12.92285	27889	40.86563	5.98802
118	10.86278	13924	34.35113	8.47458	168	12.96148	28224	40.98780	5.95238
119	10.90871	14161	34.49638	8.40336	169	13.00000	28561	41.10961	5.91716
120	10.95445	14400	34.64102	8.33333	170	13.03840	28900	41.23106	5.88235
121	11.00000	14641	34.78505	8.26446	171	13.07670	29241	41.35215	5.84795
122	11.04536	14884	34.92850	8.19672	172	13.11488	29584	41.47288	5.81395
123	11.09054	15129	35.07136	8.13008	173	13.15295	29929	41.59327	5.78035
124	11.13553	15376	35.21363	8.06452	174	13.19091	30276	41.71331	5.74713
125	11.18034	15625	35.35534	8.00000	175	13.22876	30625	41.83300	5.71429
126	11.22497	15876	35.49648	7.93651	176	13.26650	30976	41.95235	5.68182
127	11.26943	16129	35.63706	7.87402	177	13.30413	31329	42.07137	5.64972
128	11.31371	16384	35.77709	7.81250	178	13.34166	31684	42.19005	5.61798
129	11.35782	16641	35.91657	7.75194	179	13.37909	32041	42.30839	5.58659
130	11.40175	16900	36.05551	7.69231	180	13.41641	32400	42.42641	5.55556
131	11.44552	17161	36.19392	7.63359	181	13.45362	32761	42.54409	5.52486
132	11.48913	17424	36.33180	7.57576	182	13.49074	33124	42.66146	5.49451
133	11.53256	17689	36.46917	7.51880	183	13.52775	33489	42.77850	5.46448
134	11.57584	17956	36.60601	7.46269	184	13.56466	33856	42.89522	5.43478
135	11.61895	18225	36.74235	7.40741	185	13.60147	34225	43.01163	5.40541
136	11.66190	18496	36.87818	7.35294	186	13.63818	34596	43.12772	5.37634
137	11.70470	18769	37.01351	7.29927	187	13.67479	34969	43.24350	5.34759
138	11.74734	19044	37.14835	7.24638	188	13.71131	35344	43.35897	5.31915
139	11.78983	19321	37.28270	7.19424	189	13.74773	35721	43.47413	5.29101
140	11.83216	19600	37.41657	7.14286	190	13.78405	36100	43.58899	5.26316
141	11.87434	19881	37.54997	7.09220	191	13.82027	36481	43.70355	5.23560
142	11.91638	20164	37.68289	7.04225	192	13.85641	36864	43.81780	5.20833
143	11.95826	20449	37.81534	6.99301	193	13.89244	37249	43.93177	5.18135
144	12.00000	20736	37.94733	6.94444	194	13.92839	37636	44.04543	5.15464
145	12.04159	21025	38.07887	6.89655	195	13.96424	38025	44.15880	5.12821
146	12.08305	21316	38.20995	6.84932	196	14.00000	38416	44.27189	5.10204
147	12.12436	21609	38.34058	6.80272	197	14.03567	38809	44.38468	5.07614
148	12.16553	21904	38.47077	6.75676	198	14.07125	39204	44.49719	5.05051
149	12.20656	22201	38.60052	6.71141	199	14.10674	39601	44.60942	5.02513
150	12.24745	22500	38.72983	6.66667	200	14.14214	40000	44.72136	5.00000

TABLE A (*continued*)

N	$\sqrt{N}$	N^2	$\sqrt{10N}$	1000/N	N	$\sqrt{N}$	N^2	$\sqrt{10N}$	1000/N
200	14.14214	40000	44.72136	5.00000	250	15.81139	62500	50.00000	4.00000
201	14.17745	40401	44.83302	4.97512	251	15.84298	63001	50.09990	3.98406
202	14.21267	40804	44.94441	4.95050	252	15.87451	63504	50.19960	3.96825
203	14.24781	41209	45.05552	4.92611	253	15.90597	64009	50.29911	3.95257
204	14.28286	41616	45.16636	4.90196	254	15.93738	64516	50.39841	3.93701
205	14.31782	42025	45.27693	4.87805	255	15.96872	65025	50.49752	3.92157
206	14.35270	42436	45.38722	4.85437	256	16.00000	65536	50.59644	3.90625
207	14.38749	42849	45.49725	4.83092	257	16.03122	66049	50.69517	3.89105
208	14.42221	43264	45.60702	4.80769	258	16.06238	66564	50.79370	3.87597
209	14.45683	43681	45.71652	4.78469	259	16.09348	67081	50.89204	3.86100
210	14.49138	44100	45.82576	4.76190	260	16.12452	67600	50.99020	3.84615
211	14.52584	44521	45.93474	4.73934	261	16.15549	68121	51.08816	3.83142
212	14.56022	44944	46.04346	4.71698	262	16.18641	68644	51.18594	3.81679
213	14.59452	45369	46.15192	4.69484	263	16.21727	69169	51.28353	3.80228
214	14.62874	45796	46.26013	4.67290	264	16.24808	69696	51.38093	3.78788
215	14.66288	46225	46.36809	4.65116	265	16.27882	70225	51.47815	3.77358
216	14.69694	46656	46.47580	4.62963	266	16.30951	70756	51.57519	3.75940
217	14.73092	47089	46.58326	4.60829	267	16.34013	71289	51.67204	3.74532
218	14.76482	47524	46.69047	4.58716	268	16.37071	71824	51.76872	3.73134
219	14.79865	47961	46.79744	4.56621	269	16.40122	72361	51.86521	3.71747
220	14.83240	48400	46.90416	4.54545	270	16.43168	72900	51.96152	3.70370
221	14.86607	48841	47.01064	4.52489	271	16.46208	73441	52.05766	3.69004
222	14.89966	49284	47.11688	4.50450	272	16.49242	73984	52.15362	3.67647
223	14.93318	49729	47.22288	4.48430	273	16.52271	74529	52.24940	3.66300
224	14.96663	50176	47.32864	4.46429	274	16.55295	75076	52.34501	3.64964
225	15.00000	50625	47.43416	4.44444	275	16.58312	75625	52.44044	3.63636
226	15.03330	51076	47.53946	4.42478	276	16.61325	76176	52.53570	3.62319
227	15.06652	51529	47.64452	4.40529	277	16.64332	76729	52.63079	3.61011
228	15.09967	51984	47.74935	4.38596	278	16.67333	77284	52.72571	3.59712
229	15.13275	52441	47.85394	4.36681	279	16.70329	77841	52.82045	3.58423
230	15.16575	52900	47.95832	4.34783	280	16.73320	78400	52.91503	3.57143
231	15.19868	53361	48.06246	4.32900	281	16.76305	78961	53.00943	3.55872
232	15.23155	53824	48.16638	4.31034	282	16.79286	79524	53.10367	3.54610
233	15.26434	54289	48.27007	4.29185	283	16.82260	80089	53.19774	3.53357
234	15.29706	54756	48.37355	4.27350	284	16.85230	80656	53.29165	3.52113
235	15.32971	55225	48.47680	4.25532	285	16.88194	81225	53.38539	3.50877
236	15.36229	55696	48.57983	4.23729	286	16.91153	81796	53.47897	3.49650
237	15.39480	56169	48.68265	4.21941	287	16.94107	82369	53.57238	3.48432
238	15.42725	56644	48.78524	4.20168	288	16.97056	82944	53.66563	3.47222
239	15.45962	57121	48.88763	4.18410	289	17.00000	83521	53.75872	3.46021
240	15.49193	57600	48.98979	4.16667	290	17.02939	84100	53.85165	3.44828
241	15.52417	58081	49.09175	4.14938	291	17.05872	84681	53.94442	3.43643
242	15.55635	58564	49.19350	4.13223	292	17.08801	85264	54.03702	3.42466
243	15.58846	59049	49.29503	4.11523	293	17.11724	85849	54.12947	3.41297
244	15.62050	59536	49.39636	4.09836	294	17.14643	86436	54.22177	3.40136
245	15.65248	60025	49.49747	4.08163	295	17.17556	87025	54.31390	3.38983
246	15.68439	60516	49.59839	4.06504	296	17.20465	87616	54.40588	3.37838
247	15.71623	61009	49.69909	4.04858	297	17.23369	88209	54.49771	3.36700
248	15.74802	61504	49.79960	4.03226	298	17.26268	88804	54.58938	3.35570
249	15.77973	62001	49.89990	4.01606	299	17.29162	89401	54.68089	3.34448
250	15.81139	62500	50.00000	4.00000	300	17.32051	90000	54.77226	3.33333

TABLE A (*continued*)

N	$\sqrt{N}$	N^2	$\sqrt{10N}$	$1000/N$	N	$\sqrt{N}$	N^2	$\sqrt{10N}$	$1000/N$
300	17.32051	90000	54.77226	3.33333	350	18.70829	122500	59.16080	2.85714
301	17.34935	90601	54.86347	3.32226	351	18.73499	123201	59.24525	2.84900
302	17.37815	91204	54.95453	3.31126	352	18.76166	123904	59.32959	2.84091
303	17.40690	91809	55.04544	3.30033	353	18.78829	124609	59.41380	2.83286
304	17.43560	92416	55.13620	3.28947	354	18.81489	125316	59.49790	2.82486
305	17.46425	93025	55.22681	3.27869	355	18.84144	126025	59.58188	2.81690
306	17.49286	93636	55.31727	3.26797	356	18.86796	126736	59.66574	2.80899
307	17.52142	94249	55.40758	3.25733	357	18.89444	127449	59.74948	2.80112
308	17.54993	94864	55.49775	3.24675	358	18.92089	128164	59.83310	2.79330
309	17.57840	95481	55.58777	3.23625	359	18.94730	128881	59.91661	2.78552
310	17.60682	96100	55.67764	3.22581	360	18.97367	129600	60.00000	2.77778
311	17.63519	96721	55.76737	3.21543	361	19.00000	130321	60.08328	2.77008
312	17.66352	97344	55.85696	3.20513	362	19.02630	131044	60.16644	2.76243
313	17.69181	97969	55.94640	3.19489	363	19.05256	131769	60.24948	2.75482
314	17.72005	98596	56.03570	3.18471	364	19.07878	132496	60.33241	2.74725
315	17.74824	99225	56.12486	3.17460	365	19.10497	133225	60.41523	2.73973
316	17.77639	99856	56.21388	3.16456	366	19.13113	133956	60.49793	2.73224
317	17.80449	100489	56.30275	3.15457	367	19.15724	134689	60.58052	2.72480
318	17.83255	101124	56.39149	3.14465	368	19.18333	135424	60.66300	2.71739
319	17.86057	101761	56.48008	3.13480	369	19.20937	136161	60.74537	2.71003
320	17.88854	102400	56.56854	3.12500	370	19.23538	136900	60.82763	2.70270
321	17.91647	103041	56.65686	3.11526	371	19.26136	137641	60.90977	2.69542
322	17.94436	103684	56.74504	3.10559	372	19.28730	138384	60.99180	2.68817
323	17.97220	104329	56.83309	3.09598	373	19.31321	139129	61.07373	2.68097
324	18.00000	104976	56.92100	3.08642	374	19.33908	139876	61.15554	2.67380
325	18.02776	105625	57.00877	3.07692	375	19.36492	140625	61.23724	2.66667
326	18.05547	106276	57.09641	3.06748	376	19.39072	141376	61.31884	2.65957
327	18.08314	106929	57.18391	3.05810	377	19.41649	142129	61.40033	2.65252
328	18.11077	107584	57.27128	3.04878	378	19.44222	142884	61.48170	2.64550
329	18.13836	108241	57.35852	3.03951	379	19.46792	143641	61.56298	2.63852
330	18.16590	108900	57.44563	3.03030	380	19.49359	144400	61.64414	2.63158
331	18.19341	109561	57.53260	3.02115	381	19.51922	145161	61.72520	2.62467
332	18.22087	110224	57.61944	3.01205	382	19.54482	145924	61.80615	2.61780
333	18.24829	110889	57.70615	3.00300	383	19.57039	146689	61.88699	2.61097
334	18.27567	111556	57.79273	2.99401	384	19.59592	147456	61.96773	2.60417
335	18.30301	112225	57.87918	2.98507	385	19.62142	148225	62.04837	2.59740
336	18.33030	112896	57.96551	2.97619	386	19.64688	148996	62.12890	2.59067
337	18.35756	113569	58.05170	2.96736	387	19.67232	149769	62.20932	2.58398
338	18.38478	114244	58.13777	2.95858	388	19.69772	150544	62.28965	2.57732
339	18.41195	114921	58.22371	2.94985	389	19.72308	151321	62.36986	2.57069
340	18.43909	115600	58.30952	2.94118	390	19.74842	152100	62.44998	2.56410
341	18.46619	116281	58.39521	2.93255	391	19.77372	152881	62.52999	2.55754
342	18.49324	116964	58.48077	2.92398	392	19.79899	153664	62.60990	2.55102
343	18.52026	117649	58.56620	2.91545	393	19.82423	154449	62.68971	2.54453
344	18.54724	118336	58.65151	2.90698	394	19.84943	155236	62.76942	2.53807
345	18.57418	119025	58.73670	2.89855	395	19.87461	156025	62.84903	2.53165
346	18.60108	119716	58.82176	2.89017	396	19.89975	156816	62.92853	2.52525
347	18.62794	120409	58.90671	2.88184	397	19.92486	157609	63.00794	2.51889
348	18.65476	121104	58.99152	2.87356	398	19.94994	158404	63.08724	2.51256
349	18.68154	121801	59.07622	2.86533	399	19.97498	159201	63.16645	2.50627
350	18.70829	122500	59.16080	2.85714	400	20.00000	160000	63.24555	2.50000

TABLE A (continued)

N	$\sqrt{N}$	N^2	$\sqrt{10N}$	1000/N	N	$\sqrt{N}$	N^2	$\sqrt{10N}$	1000/N
400	20.00000	160000	63.24555	2.50000	450	21.21320	202500	67.08204	2.22222
401	20.02498	160801	63.32456	2.49377	451	21.23676	203401	67.15653	2.21729
402	20.04994	161604	63.40347	2.48756	452	21.26029	204304	67.23095	2.21239
403	20.07486	162409	63.48228	2.48139	453	21.28380	205209	67.30527	2.20751
404	20.09975	163216	63.56099	2.47525	454	21.30728	206116	67.37952	2.20264
405	20.12461	164025	63.63961	2.46914	455	21.33073	207025	67.45369	2.19780
406	20.14944	164836	63.71813	2.46305	456	21.35416	207936	67.52777	2.19298
407	20.17424	165649	63.79655	2.45700	457	21.37756	208849	67.60178	2.18818
408	20.19901	166464	63.87488	2.45098	458	21.40093	209764	67.67570	2.18341
409	20.22375	167281	63.95311	2.44499	459	21.42429	210681	67.74954	2.17865
410	20.24846	168100	64.03124	2.43902	460	21.44761	211600	67.82330	2.17391
411	20.27313	168921	64.10928	2.43309	461	21.47091	212521	67.89698	2.16920
412	20.29778	169744	64.18723	2.42718	462	21.49419	213444	67.97058	2.16450
413	20.32240	170569	64.26508	2.42131	463	21.51743	214369	68.04410	2.15983
414	20.34699	171396	64.34283	2.41546	464	21.54066	215296	68.11755	2.15517
415	20.37155	172225	64.42049	2.40964	465	21.56386	216225	68.19091	2.15054
416	20.39608	173056	64.49806	2.40385	466	21.58703	217156	68.26419	2.14592
417	20.42058	173889	64.57554	2.39808	467	21.61018	218089	68.33740	2.14133
418	20.44505	174724	64.65292	2.39234	468	21.63331	219024	68.41053	2.13675
419	20.46949	175561	64.73021	2.38663	469	21.65641	219961	68.48357	2.13220
420	20.49390	176400	64.80741	2.38095	470	21.67948	220900	68.55655	2.12766
421	20.51828	177241	64.88451	2.37530	471	21.70253	221841	68.62944	2.12314
422	20.54264	178084	64.96153	2.36967	472	21.72556	222784	68.70226	2.11864
423	20.56696	178929	65.03845	2.36407	473	21.74856	223729	68.77500	2.11416
424	20.59126	179776	65.11528	2.35849	474	21.77154	224676	68.84766	2.10970
425	20.61553	180625	65.19202	2.35294	475	21.79449	225625	68.92024	2.10526
426	20.63977	181476	65.26868	2.34742	476	21.81742	226576	68.99275	2.10084
427	20.66398	182329	65.34524	2.34192	477	21.84033	227529	69.06519	2.09644
428	20.68816	183184	65.42171	2.33645	478	21.86321	228484	69.13754	2.09205
429	20.71232	184041	65.49809	2.33100	479	21.88607	229441	69.20983	2.08768
430	20.73644	184900	65.57439	2.32558	480	21.90890	230400	69.28203	2.08333
431	20.76054	185761	65.65059	2.32019	481	21.93171	231361	69.35416	2.07900
432	20.78461	186624	65.72671	2.31481	482	21.95450	232324	69.42622	2.07469
433	20.80865	187489	65.80274	2.30947	483	21.97726	233289	69.49820	2.07039
434	20.83267	188356	65.87868	2.30415	484	22.00000	234256	69.57011	2.06612
435	20.85665	189225	65.95453	2.29885	485	22.02272	235225	69.64194	2.06186
436	20.88061	190096	66.03030	2.29358	486	22.04541	236196	69.71370	2.05761
437	20.90454	190969	66.10598	2.28833	487	22.06808	237169	69.78539	2.05339
438	20.92845	191844	66.18157	2.28311	488	22.09072	238144	69.85700	2.04918
439	20.95233	192721	66.25708	2.27790	489	22.11334	239121	69.92853	2.04499
440	20.97618	193600	66.33250	2.27273	490	22.13594	240100	70.00000	2.04082
441	21.00000	194481	66.40783	2.26757	491	22.15852	241081	70.07139	2.03666
442	21.02380	195364	66.48308	2.26244	492	22.18107	242064	70.14271	2.03252
443	21.04757	196249	66.55825	2.25734	493	22.20360	243049	70.21396	2.02840
444	21.07131	197136	66.63332	2.25225	494	22.22611	244036	70.28513	2.02429
445	21.09502	198025	66.70832	2.24719	495	22.24860	245025	70.35624	2.02020
446	21.11871	198916	66.78323	2.24215	496	22.27106	246016	70.42727	2.01613
447	21.14237	199809	66.85806	2.23714	497	22.29350	247009	70.49823	2.01207
448	21.16601	200704	66.93280	2.23214	498	22.31591	248004	70.56912	2.00803
449	21.18962	201601	67.00746	2.22717	499	22.33831	249001	70.63993	2.00401
450	21.21320	202500	67.08204	2.22222	500	22.36068	250000	70.71068	2.00000

TABLE A (*continued*)

N	$\sqrt{N}$	N^2	$\sqrt{10N}$	1000/N	N	$\sqrt{N}$	N^2	$\sqrt{10N}$	1000/N
500	22.36068	250000	70.71068	2.00000	550	23.45208	302500	74.16198	1.81818
501	22.38303	251001	70.78135	1.99601	551	23.47339	303601	74.22937	1.81488
502	22.40536	252004	70.85196	1.99203	552	23.49468	304704	74.29670	1.81159
503	22.42766	253009	70.92249	1.98807	553	23.51595	305809	74.36397	1.80832
504	22.44994	254016	70.99296	1.98413	554	23.53720	306916	74.43118	1.80505
505	22.47221	255025	71.06335	1.98020	555	23.55844	308025	74.49832	1.80180
506	22.49444	256036	71.13368	1.97628	556	23.57965	309136	74.56541	1.79856
507	22.51666	257049	71.20393	1.97239	557	23.60085	310249	74.63243	1.79533
508	22.53886	258064	71.27412	1.96850	558	23.62202	311364	74.69940	1.79211
509	22.56103	259081	71.34424	1.96464	559	23.64318	312481	74.76630	1.78891
510	22.58318	260100	71.41428	1.96078	560	23.66432	313600	74.83315	1.78571
511	22.60531	261121	71.48426	1.95695	561	23.68544	314721	74.89993	1.78253
512	22.62742	262144	71.55418	1.95313	562	23.70654	315844	74.96666	1.77936
513	22.64950	263169	71.62402	1.94932	563	23.72762	316969	75.03333	1.77620
514	22.67157	264196	71.69379	1.94553	564	23.74868	318096	75.09993	1.77305
515	22.69361	265225	71.76350	1.94175	565	23.76973	319225	75.16648	1.76991
516	22.71563	266256	71.83314	1.93798	566	23.79075	320356	75.23297	1.76678
517	22.73763	267289	71.90271	1.93424	567	23.81176	321489	75.29940	1.76367
518	22.75961	268324	71.97222	1.93050	568	23.83275	322624	75.36577	1.76056
519	22.78157	269361	72.04165	1.92678	569	23.85372	323761	75.43209	1.75747
520	22.80351	270400	72.11103	1.92308	570	23.87467	324900	75.49834	1.75439
521	22.82542	271441	72.18033	1.91939	571	23.89561	326041	75.56454	1.75131
522	22.84732	272484	72.24957	1.91571	572	23.91652	327184	75.63068	1.74825
523	22.86919	273529	72.31874	1.91205	573	23.93742	328329	75.69676	1.74520
524	22.89105	274576	72.38784	1.90840	574	23.95830	329476	75.76279	1.74216
525	22.91288	275625	72.45688	1.90476	575	23.97916	330625	75.82875	1.73913
526	22.93469	276676	72.52586	1.90114	576	24.00000	331776	75.89466	1.73611
527	22.95648	277729	72.59477	1.89753	577	24.02082	332929	75.96052	1.73310
528	22.97825	278784	72.66361	1.89394	578	24.04163	334084	76.02631	1.73010
529	23.00000	279841	72.73239	1.89036	579	24.06242	335241	76.09205	1.72712
530	23.02173	280900	72.80110	1.88679	580	24.08319	336400	76.15773	1.72414
531	23.04344	281961	72.86975	1.88324	581	24.10394	337561	76.22336	1.72117
532	23.06513	283024	72.93833	1.87970	582	24.12468	338724	76.28892	1.71821
533	23.08679	284089	73.00685	1.87617	583	24.14539	339889	76.35444	1.71527
534	23.10844	285156	73.07530	1.87266	584	24.16609	341056	76.41989	1.71233
535	23.13007	286225	73.14369	1.86916	585	24.18677	342225	76.48529	1.70940
536	23.15167	287296	73.21202	1.86567	586	24.20744	343396	76.55064	1.70648
537	23.17326	288369	73.28028	1.86220	587	24.22808	344569	76.61593	1.70358
538	23.19483	289444	73.34848	1.85874	588	24.24871	345744	76.68116	1.70068
539	23.21637	290521	73.41662	1.85529	589	24.26932	346921	76.74634	1.69779
540	23.23790	291600	73.48469	1.85185	590	24.28992	348100	76.81146	1.69492
541	23.25941	292681	73.55270	1.84843	591	24.31049	349281	76.87652	1.69205
542	23.28089	293764	73.62065	1.84502	592	24.33105	350464	76.94154	1.68919
543	23.30236	294849	73.68853	1.84162	593	24.35159	351649	77.00649	1.68634
544	23.32381	295936	73.75636	1.83824	594	24.37212	352836	77.07140	1.68350
545	23.34524	297025	73.82412	1.83486	595	24.39262	354025	77.13624	1.68067
546	23.36664	298116	73.89181	1.83150	596	24.41311	355216	77.20104	1.67785
547	23.38803	299209	73.95945	1.82815	597	24.43358	356409	77.26578	1.67504
548	23.40940	300304	74.02702	1.82482	598	24.45404	357604	77.33046	1.67224
549	23.43075	301401	74.09453	1.82149	599	24.47448	358801	77.39509	1.66945
550	23.45208	302500	74.16198	1.81818	600	24.49490	360000	77.45967	1.66667

TABLE A (*continued*)

N	$\sqrt{N}$	N^2	$\sqrt{10N}$	$1000/N$	N	$\sqrt{N}$	N^2	$\sqrt{10N}$	$1000/N$
600	24.49490	360000	77.45967	1.66667	650	25.49510	422500	80.62258	1.53846
601	24.51530	361201	77.52419	1.66389	651	25.51470	423801	80.68457	1.53610
602	24.53569	362404	77.58866	1.66113	652	25.53429	425104	80.74652	1.53374
603	24.55606	363609	77.65307	1.65837	653	25.55386	426409	80.80842	1.53139
604	24.57641	364816	77.71744	1.65563	654	25.57342	427716	80.87027	1.52905
605	24.59675	366025	77.78175	1.65289	655	25.59297	429025	80.93207	1.52672
606	24.61707	367236	77.84600	1.65017	656	25.61250	430336	80.99383	1.52439
607	24.63737	368449	77.91020	1.64745	657	25.63201	431649	81.05554	1.52207
608	24.65766	369664	77.97435	1.64474	658	25.65151	432964	81.11720	1.51976
609	24.67793	370881	78.03845	1.64204	659	25.67100	434281	81.17881	1.51745
610	24.69818	372100	78.10250	1.63934	660	25.69047	435600	81.24038	1.51515
611	24.71841	373321	78.16649	1.63666	661	25.70992	436921	81.30191	1.51286
612	24.73863	374544	78.23043	1.63399	662	25.72936	438244	81.36338	1.51057
613	24.75884	375769	78.29432	1.63132	663	25.74879	439569	81.42481	1.50830
614	24.77902	376996	78.35815	1.62866	664	25.76820	440896	81.48620	1.50602
615	24.79919	378225	78.42194	1.62602	665	25.78759	442225	81.54753	1.50376
616	24.81935	379456	78.48567	1.62338	666	25.80698	443556	81.60882	1.50150
617	24.83948	380689	78.54935	1.62075	667	25.82634	444889	81.67007	1.49925
618	24.85961	381924	78.61298	1.61812	668	25.84570	446224	81.73127	1.49701
619	24.87971	383161	78.67655	1.61551	669	25.86503	447561	81.79242	1.49477
620	24.89980	384400	78.74008	1.61290	670	25.88436	448900	81.85353	1.49254
621	24.91987	385641	78.80355	1.61031	671	25.90367	450241	81.91459	1.49031
622	24.93993	386884	78.86698	1.60772	672	25.92296	451584	81.97561	1.48810
623	24.95997	388129	78.93035	1.60514	673	25.94224	452929	82.03658	1.48588
624	24.97999	389376	78.99367	1.60256	674	25.96151	454276	82.09750	1.48368
625	25.00000	390625	79.05694	1.60000	675	25.98076	455625	82.15838	1.48148
626	25.01999	391876	79.12016	1.59744	676	26.00000	456976	82.21922	1.47929
627	25.03997	393129	79.18333	1.59490	677	26.01922	458329	82.28001	1.47710
628	25.05993	394384	79.24645	1.59236	678	26.03843	459684	82.34076	1.47493
629	25.07987	395641	79.30952	1.58983	679	26.05763	461041	82.40146	1.47275
630	25.09980	396900	79.37254	1.58730	680	26.07681	462400	82.46211	1.47059
631	25.11971	398161	79.43551	1.58479	681	26.09598	463761	82.52272	1.46843
632	25.13961	399424	79.49843	1.58228	682	26.11513	465124	82.58329	1.46628
633	25.15949	400689	79.56130	1.57978	683	26.13427	466489	82.64381	1.46413
634	25.17936	401956	79.62412	1.57729	684	26.15339	467856	82.70429	1.46199
635	25.19921	403225	79.68689	1.57480	685	26.17250	469225	82.76473	1.45985
636	25.21904	404496	79.74961	1.57233	686	26.19160	470596	82.82512	1.45773
637	25.23886	405769	79.81228	1.56986	687	26.21068	471969	82.88546	1.45560
638	25.25866	407044	79.87490	1.56740	688	26.22975	473344	82.94577	1.45349
639	25.27845	408321	79.93748	1.56495	689	26.24881	474721	83.00602	1.45138
640	25.29822	409600	80.00000	1.56250	690	26.26785	476100	83.06624	1.44928
641	25.31798	410881	80.06248	1.56006	691	26.28688	477481	83.12641	1.44718
642	25.33772	412164	80.12490	1.55763	692	26.30589	478864	83.18654	1.44509
643	25.35744	413449	80.18728	1.55521	693	26.32489	480249	83.24662	1.44300
644	25.37716	414736	80.24961	1.55280	694	26.34388	481636	83.30666	1.44092
645	25.39685	416025	80.31189	1.55039	695	26.36285	483025	83.36666	1.43885
646	25.41653	417316	80.37413	1.54799	696	26.38181	484416	83.42661	1.43678
647	25.43619	418609	80.43631	1.54560	697	26.40076	485809	83.48653	1.43472
648	25.45584	419904	80.49845	1.54321	698	26.41969	487204	83.54639	1.43266
649	25.47548	421201	80.56054	1.54083	699	26.43861	488601	83.60622	1.43062
650	25.49510	422500	80.62258	1.53846	700	26.45751	490000	83.66600	1.42857

TABLE A   (*continued*)

N	$\sqrt{N}$	N^2	$\sqrt{10N}$	1000/N	N	$\sqrt{N}$	N^2	$\sqrt{10N}$	1000/N
700	26.45751	490000	83.66600	1.42857	750	27.38613	562500	86.60254	1.33333
701	26.47640	491401	83.72574	1.42653	751	27.40438	564001	86.66026	1.33156
702	26.49528	492804	83.78544	1.42450	752	27.42262	565504	86.71793	1.32979
703	26.51415	494209	83.84510	1.42248	753	27.44085	567009	86.77557	1.32802
704	26.53300	495616	83.90471	1.42045	754	27.45906	568516	86.83317	1.32626
705	26.55184	497025	83.96428	1.41844	755	27.47726	570025	86.89074	1.32450
706	26.57066	498436	84.02381	1.41643	756	27.49545	571536	86.94826	1.32275
707	26.58947	499849	84.08329	1.41443	757	27.51363	573049	87.00575	1.32100
708	26.60827	501264	84.14274	1.41243	758	27.53180	574564	87.06320	1.31926
709	26.62705	502681	84.20214	1.41044	759	27.54995	576081	87.12061	1.31752
710	26.64583	504100	84.26150	1.40845	760	27.56810	577600	87.17798	1.31579
711	26.66458	505521	84.32082	1.40647	761	27.58623	579121	87.23531	1.31406
712	26.68333	506944	84.38009	1.40449	762	27.60435	580644	87.29261	1.31234
713	26.70206	508369	84.43933	1.40252	763	27.62245	582169	87.34987	1.31062
714	26.72078	509796	84.49852	1.40056	764	27.64055	583696	87.40709	1.30890
715	26.73948	511225	84.55767	1.39860	765	27.65863	585225	87.46428	1.30719
716	26.75818	512656	84.61678	1.39665	766	27.67671	586756	87.52143	1.30548
717	26.77686	514089	84.67585	1.39470	767	27.69476	588289	87.57854	1.30378
718	26.79552	515524	84.73488	1.39276	768	27.71281	589824	87.63561	1.30208
719	26.81418	516961	84.79387	1.39082	769	27.73085	591361	87.69265	1.30039
720	26.83282	518400	84.85281	1.38889	770	27.74887	592900	87.74964	1.29870
721	26.85144	519841	84.91172	1.38696	771	27.76689	594441	87.80661	1.29702
722	26.87006	521284	84.97058	1.38504	772	27.78489	595984	87.86353	1.29534
723	26.88866	522729	85.02941	1.38313	773	27.80288	597529	87.92042	1.29366
724	26.90725	524176	85.08819	1.38122	774	27.82086	599076	87.97727	1.29199
725	26.92582	525625	85.14693	1.37931	775	27.83882	600625	88.03408	1.29032
726	26.94439	527076	85.20563	1.37741	776	27.85678	602176	88.09086	1.28866
727	26.96294	528529	85.26429	1.37552	777	27.87472	603729	88.14760	1.28700
728	26.98148	529984	85.32292	1.37363	778	27.89265	605284	88.20431	1.28535
729	27.00000	531441	85.38150	1.37174	779	27.91057	606841	88.26098	1.28370
730	27.01851	532900	85.44004	1.36986	780	27.92848	608400	88.31761	1.28205
731	27.03701	534361	85.49854	1.36799	781	27.94638	609961	88.37420	1.28041
732	27.05550	535824	85.55700	1.36612	782	27.96426	611524	88.43076	1.27877
733	27.07397	537289	85.61542	1.36426	783	27.98214	613089	88.48729	1.27714
734	27.09243	538756	85.67380	1.36240	784	28.00000	614656	88.54377	1.27551
735	27.11088	540225	85.73214	1.36054	785	28.01785	616225	88.60023	1.27389
736	27.12932	541696	85.79044	1.35870	786	28.03569	617796	88.65664	1.27226
737	27.14774	543169	85.84870	1.35685	787	28.05352	619369	88.71302	1.27065
738	27.16616	544644	85.90693	1.35501	788	28.07134	620944	88.76936	1.26904
739	27.18455	546121	85.96511	1.35318	789	28.08914	622521	88.82567	1.26743
740	27.20294	547600	86.02325	1.35135	790	28.10694	624100	88.88194	1.26582
741	27.22132	549081	86.08136	1.34953	791	28.12472	625681	88.93818	1.26422
742	27.23968	550564	86.13942	1.34771	792	28.14249	627264	88.99438	1.26263
743	27.25803	552049	86.19745	1.34590	793	28.16026	628849	89.05055	1.26103
744	27.27636	553536	86.25543	1.34409	794	28.17801	630436	89.10668	1.25945
745	27.29469	555025	86.31338	1.34228	795	28.19574	632025	89.16277	1.25786
746	27.31300	556516	86.37129	1.34048	796	28.21347	633616	89.21883	1.25628
747	27.33130	558000	86.42916	1.33869	797	28.23119	635209	89.27486	1.25471
748	27.34959	559504	86.48699	1.33690	798	28.24889	636804	89.33085	1.25313
749	27.36786	561001	86.54479	1.33511	799	28.26659	638401	89.38680	1.25156
750	27.38613	562500	86.60254	1.33333	800	28.28427	640000	89.44272	1.25000

TABLE A (*continued*)

N	$\sqrt{N}$	N^2	$\sqrt{10N}$	1000/N	N	$\sqrt{N}$	N^2	$\sqrt{10N}$	1000/N
800	28.28427	640000	89.44272	1.25000	850	29.15476	722500	92.19544	1.17647
801	28.30194	641601	89.49860	1.24844	851	29.17190	724201	92.24966	1.17509
802	28.31960	643204	89.55445	1.24688	852	29.18904	725904	92.30385	1.17371
803	28.33725	644809	89.61027	1.24533	853	29.20616	727609	92.35800	1.17233
804	28.35489	646416	89.66605	1.24378	854	29.22328	729316	92.41212	1.17096
805	28.37252	648025	89.72179	1.24224	855	29.24038	731025	92.46621	1.16959
806	28.39014	649636	89.77750	1.24069	856	29.25748	732736	92.52027	1.16822
807	28.40775	651249	89.83318	1.23916	857	29.27456	734449	92.57429	1.16686
808	28.42534	652864	89.88882	1.23762	858	29.29164	736164	92.62829	1.16550
809	28.44293	654481	89.94443	1.23609	859	29.30870	737881	92.68225	1.16414
810	28.46050	656100	90.00000	1.23457	860	29.32576	739600	92.73618	1.16279
811	28.47806	657721	90.05554	1.23305	861	29.34280	741321	92.79009	1.16144
812	28.49561	659344	90.11104	1.23153	862	29.35984	743044	92.84396	1.16009
813	28.51315	660969	90.16651	1.23001	863	29.37686	744769	92.89779	1.15875
814	28.53069	662596	90.22195	1.22850	864	29.39388	746496	92.95160	1.15741
815	28.54820	664225	90.27735	1.22699	865	29.41088	748225	93.00538	1.15607
816	28.56571	665856	90.33272	1.22549	866	29.42788	749956	93.05912	1.15473
817	28.58321	667489	90.38805	1.22399	867	29.44486	751689	93.11283	1.15340
818	28.60070	669124	90.44335	1.22249	868	29.46184	753424	93.16652	1.15207
819	28.61818	670761	90.49862	1.22100	869	29.47881	755161	93.22017	1.15075
820	28.63564	672400	90.55385	1.21951	870	29.49576	756900	93.27379	1.14943
821	28.65310	674041	90.60905	1.21803	871	29.51271	758641	93.32738	1.14811
822	28.67054	675684	90.66422	1.21655	872	29.52965	760384	93.38094	1.14679
823	28.68798	677329	90.71935	1.21507	873	29.54657	762129	93.43447	1.14548
824	28.70540	678976	90.77445	1.21359	874	29.56349	763876	93.48797	1.14416
825	28.72281	680625	90.82951	1.21212	875	29.58040	765625	93.54143	1.14286
826	28.74022	682276	90.88454	1.21065	876	29.59730	767376	93.59487	1.14155
827	28.75761	683929	90.93954	1.20919	877	29.61419	769129	93.64828	1.14025
828	28.77499	685584	90.99451	1.20773	878	29.63106	770884	93.70165	1.13895
829	28.79236	687241	91.04944	1.20627	879	29.64793	772641	93.75500	1.13766
830	28.80972	688900	91.10434	1.20482	880	29.66479	774400	93.80832	1.13636
831	28.82707	690561	91.15920	1.20337	881	29.68164	776161	93.86160	1.13507
832	28.84441	692224	91.21403	1.20192	882	29.69848	777924	93.91486	1.13379
833	28.86174	693889	91.26883	1.20048	883	29.71532	779689	93.96808	1.13250
834	28.87906	695556	91.32360	1.19904	884	29.73214	781456	94.02127	1.13122
835	28.89637	697225	91.37833	1.19760	885	29.74895	783225	94.07444	1.12994
836	28.91366	698896	91.43304	1.19617	886	29.76575	784996	94.12757	1.12867
837	28.93095	700569	91.48770	1.19474	887	29.78255	786769	94.18068	1.12740
838	28.94823	702244	91.54234	1.19332	888	29.79933	788544	94.23375	1.12613
839	28.96550	703921	91.59694	1.19190	889	29.81610	790321	94.28680	1.12486
840	28.98275	705600	91.65151	1.19048	890	29.83287	792100	94.33981	1.12360
841	29.00000	707281	91.70605	1.18906	891	29.84962	793881	94.39280	1.12233
842	29.01724	708964	91.76056	1.18765	892	29.86637	795664	94.44575	1.12108
843	29.03446	710649	91.81503	1.18624	893	29.88311	797449	94.49868	1.11982
844	29.05168	712336	91.86947	1.18483	894	29.89983	799236	94.55157	1.11857
845	29.06888	714025	91.92388	1.18343	895	29.91655	801025	94.60444	1.11732
846	29.08608	715716	91.97826	1.18203	896	29.93326	802816	94.65728	1.11607
847	29.10326	717409	92.03260	1.18064	897	29.94996	804609	94.71008	1.11483
848	29.12044	719104	92.08692	1.17925	898	29.96665	806404	94.76286	1.11359
849	29.13760	720801	92.14120	1.17786	899	29.98333	808201	94.81561	1.11235
850	29.15476	722500	92.19544	1.17647	900	30.00000	810000	94.86833	1.11111

TABLE A (*continued*)

N	$\sqrt{N}$	N^2	$\sqrt{10N}$	1000/N	N	$\sqrt{N}$	N^2	$\sqrt{10N}$	1000/N
900	30.00000	810000	94.86833	1.11111	950	30.82207	902500	97.46794	1.05263
901	30.01666	811801	94.92102	1.10988	951	30.83829	904401	97.51923	1.05152
902	30.03331	813604	94.97368	1.10865	952	30.85450	906304	97.57049	1.05042
903	30.04996	815409	95.02631	1.10742	953	30.87070	908209	97.62172	1.04932
904	30.06659	817216	95.07891	1.10619	954	30.88689	910116	97.67292	1.04822
905	30.08322	819025	95.13149	1.10497	955	30.90307	912025	97.72410	1.04712
906	30.09983	820836	95.18403	1.10375	956	30.91925	913936	97.77525	1.04603
907	30.11644	822649	95.23655	1.10254	957	30.93542	915849	97.82638	1.04493
908	30.13304	824464	95.28903	1.10132	958	30.95158	917764	97.87747	1.04384
909	30.14963	826281	95.34149	1.10011	959	30.96773	919681	97.92855	1.04275
910	30.16621	828100	95.39392	1.09890	960	30.98387	921600	97.97959	1.04167
911	30.18278	829921	95.44632	1.09769	961	31.00000	923521	98.03061	1.04058
912	30.19934	831744	95.49869	1.09649	962	31.01612	925444	98.0816C	1.03950
913	30.21589	833569	95.55103	1.09529	963	31.03224	927369	98.13256	1.03842
914	30.23243	835396	95.60335	1.09409	964	31.04835	929296	98.18350	1.03734
915	30.24897	837225	95.65563	1.09290	965	31.06445	931225	98.23441	1.03627
916	30.26549	839056	95.70789	1.09170	966	31.08054	933156	98.28530	1.03520
917	30.28201	840889	95.76012	1.09051	967	31.09662	935089	98.33616	1.03413
918	30.29851	842724	95.81232	1.08932	968	31.11270	937024	98.38699	1.03306
919	30.31501	844561	95.86449	1.08814	969	31.12876	938961	98.43780	1.03199
920	30.33150	846400	95.91663	1.08696	970	31.14482	940900	98.48858	1.03093
921	30.34798	848241	95.96874	1.08578	971	31.16087	942841	98.53933	1.02987
922	30.36445	850084	96.02083	1.08460	972	31.17691	944784	98.59006	1.02881
923	30.38092	851929	96.07289	1.08342	973	31.19295	946729	98.64076	1.02775
924	30.39737	853776	96.12492	1.08225	974	31.20897	948676	98.69144	1.02669
925	30.41381	855625	96.17692	1.08108	975	31.22499	950625	98.74209	1.02564
926	30.43025	857476	96.22889	1.07991	976	31.24100	952576	98.79271	1.02459
927	30.44667	859329	96.28084	1.07875	977	31.25700	954529	98.84331	1.02354
928	30.46309	861184	96.33276	1.07759	978	31.27299	956484	98.89388	1.02249
929	30.47950	863041	96.38465	1.07643	979	31.28898	958441	98.94443	1.02145
930	30.49590	864900	96.43651	1.07527	980	31.30495	960400	98.99495	1.02041
931	30.51229	866761	96.48834	1.07411	981	31.32092	962361	99.04544	1.01937
932	30.52868	868624	96.54015	1.07296	982	31.33688	964324	99.09591	1.01833
933	30.54505	870489	96.59193	1.07181	983	31.35283	966289	99.14636	1.01729
934	30.56141	872356	96.64368	1.07066	984	31.36877	968256	99.19677	1.01626
935	30.57777	874225	96.69540	1.06952	985	31.38471	970225	99.24717	1.01523
936	30.59412	876096	96.74709	1.06838	986	31.40064	972196	99.29753	1.01420
937	30.61046	877969	96.79876	1.06724	987	31.41656	974169	99.34787	1.01317
938	30.62679	879844	96.85040	1.06610	988	31.43247	976144	99.39819	1.01215
939	30.64311	881721	96.90201	1.06496	989	31.44837	978121	99.44848	1.01112
940	30.65942	883600	96.95360	1.06383	990	31.46427	980100	99.49874	1.01010
941	30.67572	885481	97.00515	1.06270	991	31.48015	982081	99.54898	1.00908
942	30.69202	887364	97.05668	1.06157	992	31.49603	984064	99.59920	1.00806
943	30.70831	889249	97.10819	1.06045	993	31.51190	986049	99.64939	1.00705
944	30.72458	891136	97.15966	1.05932	994	31.52777	988036	99.69955	1.00604
945	30.74085	893025	97.21111	1.05820	995	31.54362	990025	99.74969	1.00503
946	30.75711	894916	97.26253	1.05708	996	31.55947	992016	99.79980	1.00402
947	30.77337	896809	97.31393	1.05597	997	31.57531	994009	99.84989	1.00301
948	30.78961	898704	97.36529	1.05485	998	31.59114	996004	99.89995	1.00200
949	30.80584	900601	97.41663	1.05374	999	31.60696	998001	99.94999	1.00100
950	30.82207	902500	97.46794	1.05263	1000	31.62278	1000000	100.00000	1.00000

TABLE B   Random Numbers

12651	61646	11769	75109	86996	97669	25757	32535	07122	76763
81769	74436	02630	72310	45049	18029	07469	42341	98173	79260
36737	98863	77240	76251	00654	64688	09343	70278	67331	98729
82861	54371	76610	94934	72748	44124	05610	53750	95938	01485
21325	15732	24127	37431	09723	63529	73977	95218	96074	42138
74146	47887	62463	23045	41490	07954	22597	60012	98866	90959
90759	64410	54179	66075	61051	75385	51378	08360	95946	95547
55683	98078	02238	91540	21219	17720	87817	41705	95785	12563
79686	17969	76061	83748	55920	83612	41540	86492	06447	60568
70333	00201	86201	69716	78185	62154	77930	67663	29529	75116
14042	53536	07779	04157	41172	36473	42123	43929	50533	33437
59911	08256	06596	48416	69770	68797	56080	14223	59199	30162
62368	62623	62742	14891	39247	52242	98832	69533	91174	57979
57529	97751	54976	48957	74599	08759	78494	52785	68526	64618
15469	90574	78033	66885	13936	42117	71831	22961	94225	31816
18625	23674	53850	32827	81647	80820	00420	63555	74489	80141
74626	68394	88562	70745	23701	45630	65891	58220	35442	60414
11119	16519	27384	90199	79210	76965	99546	30323	31664	22845
41101	17336	48951	53674	17880	45260	08575	49321	36191	17095
32123	91576	84221	78902	82010	30847	62329	63898	23268	74283
26091	68409	69704	82267	14751	13151	93115	01437	56945	89661
67680	79790	48462	59278	44185	29616	76531	19589	83139	28454
15184	19260	14073	07026	25264	08388	27182	22557	61501	67481
58010	45039	57181	10238	36874	28546	37444	80824	63981	39942
56425	53996	86245	32623	78858	08143	60377	42925	42815	11159
82630	84066	13592	60642	17904	99718	63432	88642	37858	25431
14927	40909	23900	48761	44860	92467	31742	87142	03607	32059
23740	22505	07489	85986	74420	21744	97711	36648	35620	97949
32990	97446	03711	63824	07953	85965	87089	11687	92414	67257
05310	24058	91946	78437	34365	82469	12430	84754	19354	72745
21839	39937	27534	88913	49055	19218	47712	67677	51889	70926
08833	42549	93981	94051	28382	83725	72643	64233	97252	17133
58336	11139	47479	00931	91560	95372	97642	33856	54825	55680
62032	91144	75478	47431	52726	30289	42411	91886	51818	78292
45171	30557	53116	04118	58301	24375	65609	85810	18620	49198
91611	62656	60128	35609	63698	78356	50682	22505	01692	36291
55472	63819	86314	49174	93582	73604	78614	78849	23096	72825
18573	09729	74091	53994	10970	86557	65661	41854	26037	53296
60866	02955	90288	82136	83644	94455	06560	78029	98768	71296
45043	55608	82767	60890	74646	79485	13619	98868	40857	19415
17831	09737	79473	75945	28394	79334	70577	38048	03607	06932
40137	03981	07585	18128	11178	32601	27994	05641	22600	86064
77776	31343	14576	97706	16039	47517	43300	59080	80392	63189
69605	44104	40103	95635	05635	81673	68657	09559	23510	95875
19916	52934	26499	09821	87331	80993	61299	36979	73599	35055
02606	58552	07678	56619	65325	30705	99582	53390	46357	13244
65183	73160	87131	35530	47946	09854	18080	02321	05809	04898
10740	98914	44916	11322	89717	88189	30143	52687	19420	60061
98642	89822	71691	51573	83666	61642	46683	33761	47542	23551
60139	25601	93663	25547	02654	94829	48672	28736	84994	13071

SOURCE: The Rand Corporation, *A Million Random Digits with 100,000 Normal Deviates.* New York: The Free Press, 1955. Reproduced with permission of The Rand Corporation.

TABLE C   Cumulative Values for the Binomial Probability Distribution

$$P[R \leqslant r] = P[P \leqslant r/n]$$

n = 1

π	.01	.05	.10	.20	.30	.40	.50
r							
0	0.9900	0.9500	0.9000	0.8000	0.7000	0.6000	0.5000
1	1.0000	1.0000	1.0000	1.0000	1.0000	1.0000	1.0000

n = 2

π	.01	.05	.10	.20	.30	.40	.50
r							
0	0.9801	0.9025	0.8100	0.6400	0.4900	0.3600	0.2500
1	0.9999	0.9975	0.9900	0.9600	0.9100	0.8400	0.7500
2	1.0000	1.0000	1.0000	1.0000	1.0000	1.0000	1.0000

n = 3

π	.01	.05	.10	.20	.30	.40	.50
r							
0	0.9703	0.8574	0.7290	0.5120	0.3430	0.2160	0.1250
1	0.9997	0.9927	0.9720	0.8960	0.7840	0.6480	0.5000
2	1.0000	0.9999	0.9990	0.9920	0.9730	0.9360	0.8750
3	1.0000	1.0000	1.0000	1.0000	1.0000	1.0000	1.0000

n = 4

π	.01	.05	.10	.20	.30	.40	.50
r							
0	0.9606	0.8145	0.6561	0.4096	0.2401	0.1296	0.0625
1	0.9994	0.9860	0.9477	0.8192	0.6517	0.4752	0.3125
2	1.0000	0.9995	0.9963	0.9728	0.9163	0.8208	0.6875
3	1.0000	1.0000	0.9999	0.9984	0.9919	0.9744	0.9375
4	1.0000	1.0000	1.0000	1.0000	1.0000	1.0000	1.0000

n = 5

π	.01	.05	.10	.20	.30	.40	.50
r							
0	0.9510	0.7738	0.5905	0.3277	0.1681	0.0778	0.0313
1	0.9990	0.9774	0.9185	0.7373	0.5282	0.3370	0.1875
2	1.0000	0.9988	0.9914	0.9421	0.8369	0.6826	0.5000
3	1.0000	1.0000	0.9995	0.9933	0.9692	0.9130	0.8125
4	1.0000	1.0000	1.0000	0.9997	0.9976	0.9898	0.9688
5				1.0000	1.0000	1.0000	1.0000

TABLE C   (*continued*)

n = 6

π	.01	.05	.10	.20	.30	.40	.50
r							
0	0.9415	0.7351	0.5314	0.2621	0.1176	0.0467	0.0156
1	0.9985	0.9672	0.8857	0.6554	0.4202	0.2333	0.1094
2	1.0000	0.9978	0.9841	0.9011	0.7443	0.5443	0.3438
3	1.0000	0.9999	0.9987	0.9830	0.9295	0.8208	0.6563
4	1.0000	1.0000	0.9999	0.9984	0.9891	0.9590	0.8906
5	1.0000	1.0000	1.0000	0.9999	0.9993	0.9959	0.9844
6				1.0000	1.0000	1.0000	1.0000

n = 7

π	.01	.05	.10	.20	.30	.40	.50
r							
0	0.9321	0.6983	0.4783	0.2097	0.0824	0.0280	0.0078
1	0.9980	0.9556	0.8503	0.5767	0.3294	0.1586	0.0625
2	1.0000	0.9962	0.9743	0.8520	0.6471	0.4199	0.2266
3	1.0000	0.9998	0.9973	0.9667	0.8740	0.7102	0.5000
4	1.0000	1.0000	0.9998	0.9953	0.9712	0.9037	0.7734
5	1.0000	1.0000	1.0000	0.9996	0.9962	0.9812	0.9375
6				1.0000	0.9998	0.9984	0.9922
7					1.0000	1.0000	1.0000

n = 8

π	.01	.05	.10	.20	.30	.40	.50
r							
0	0.9227	0.6634	0.4305	0.1678	0.0576	0.0168	0.0039
1	0.9973	0.9428	0.8131	0.5033	0.2553	0.1064	0.0352
2	0.9999	0.9942	0.9619	0.7969	0.5518	0.3154	0.1445
3	1.0000	0.9996	0.9950	0.9437	0.8059	0.5941	0.3633
4	1.0000	1.0000	0.9996	0.9896	0.9420	0.8263	0.6367
5	1.0000	1.0000	1.0000	0.9988	0.9887	0.9502	0.8555
6				0.9999	0.9987	0.9915	0.9648
7				1.0000	0.9999	0.9993	0.9961
8					1.0000	1.0000	1.0000

n = 9

π	.01	.05	.10	.20	.30	.40	.50
r							
0	0.9135	0.6302	0.3874	0.1342	0.0404	0.0101	0.0020
1	0.9966	0.9288	0.7748	0.4362	0.1960	0.0705	0.0195
2	0.9999	0.9916	0.9470	0.7382	0.4628	0.2318	0.0898
3	1.0000	0.9994	0.9917	0.9144	0.7297	0.4826	0.2539
4	1.0000	1.0000	0.9991	0.9804	0.9012	0.7334	0.5000
5	1.0000	1.0000	0.9999	0.9969	0.9747	0.9006	0.7461

TABLE C (*continued*)

$n = 9$

π r	.01	.05	.10	.20	.30	.40	.50
6	1.0000	1.0000	1.0000	0.9997	0.9957	0.9750	0.9102
7				1.0000	0.9996	0.9962	0.9805
8					1.0000	0.9997	0.9980
9						1.0000	1.0000

$n = 10$

π r	.01	.05	.10	.20	.30	.40	.50
0	0.9044	0.5987	0.3487	0.1074	0.0282	0.0060	0.0010
1	0.9957	0.9139	0.7361	0.3758	0.1493	0.0464	0.0107
2	0.9999	0.9885	0.9298	0.6778	0.3828	0.1673	0.0547
3	1.0000	0.9990	0.9872	0.8791	0.6496	0.3823	0.1719
4	1.0000	0.9999	0.9984	0.9672	0.8497	0.6331	0.3770
5	1.0000	1.0000	0.9999	0.9936	0.9526	0.8338	0.6230
6	1.0000	1.0000	1.0000	0.9991	0.9894	0.9452	0.8281
7				0.9999	0.9999	0.9877	0.9453
8				1.0000	1.0000	0.9983	0.9893
9						0.9999	0.9990
10						1.0000	1.0000

$n = 11$

π r	.01	.05	.10	.20	.30	.40	.50
0	0.8953	0.5688	0.3138	0.0859	0.0198	0.0036	0.0005
1	0.9948	0.8981	0.6974	0.3221	0.1130	0.0302	0.0059
2	0.9998	0.9848	0.9104	0.6174	0.3127	0.1189	0.0327
3	1.0000	0.9984	0.9815	0.8369	0.5696	0.2963	0.1133
4	1.0000	0.9999	0.9972	0.9496	0.7897	0.5328	0.2744
5	1.0000	1.0000	0.9997	0.9883	0.9218	0.7535	0.5000
6	1.0000	1.0000	1.0000	0.9980	0.9784	0.9006	0.7256
7				0.9998	0.9957	0.9707	0.8867
8				1.0000	0.9994	0.9941	0.9673
9					1.0000	0.9993	0.9941
10						1.0000	0.9995
11							1.0000

TABLE C   (*continued*)

$n = 12$

π	.01	.05	.10	.20	.30	.40	.50
r							
0	0.8864	0.5404	0.2824	0.0687	0.0138	0.0022	0.0002
1	0.9938	0.8816	0.6590	0.2749	0.0850	0.0196	0.0032
2	0.9998	0.9804	0.8891	0.5583	0.2528	0.0834	0.0193
3	1.0000	0.9978	0.9744	0.7946	0.4925	0.2253	0.0730
4	1.0000	0.9998	0.9957	0.9274	0.7237	0.4382	0.1938
5	1.0000	1.0000	0.9995	0.9806	0.8821	0.6652	0.3872
6	1.0000	1.0000	0.9999	0.9961	0.9614	0.8418	0.6128
7	1.0000	1.0000	1.0000	0.9994	0.9905	0.9427	0.8062
8				0.9999	0.9983	0.9847	0.9270
9				1.0000	0.9998	0.9972	0.9807
10					1.0000	0.9997	0.9968
11						1.0000	0.9998
12							1.0000

$n = 13$

π	.01	.05	.10	.20	.30	.40	.50
r							
0	0.8775	0.5133	0.2542	0.0550	0.0097	0.0013	0.0001
1	0.9928	0.8646	0.6213	0.2336	0.0637	0.0126	0.0017
2	0.9997	0.9755	0.8661	0.5017	0.2025	0.0579	0.0112
3	1.0000	0.9969	0.9658	0.7473	0.4206	0.1686	0.0461
4	1.0000	0.9997	0.9935	0.9009	0.6543	0.3530	0.1334
5	1.0000	1.0000	0.9991	0.9700	0.8346	0.5744	0.2905
6	1.0000	1.0000	0.9999	0.9930	0.9376	0.7712	0.5000
7	1.0000	1.0000	1.0000	0.9988	0.9818	0.9023	0.7095
8				0.9998	0.9960	0.9679	0.8666
9				1.0000	0.9993	0.9922	0.9539
10					0.9999	0.9987	0.9888
11					1.0000	0.9999	0.9983
12						1.0000	0.9999
13							1.0000

TABLE C   (*continued*)

n = 14

π r	.01	.05	.10	.20	.30	.40	.50
0	0.8687	0.4877	0.2288	0.0440	0.0068	0.0008	0.0001
1	0.9916	0.8470	0.5846	0.1979	0.0475	0.0081	0.0009
2	0.9997	0.9699	0.8416	0.4481	0.1608	0.0398	0.0065
3	1.0000	0.9958	0.9559	0.6982	0.3552	0.1243	0.0287
4	1.0000	0.9996	0.9908	0.8702	0.5842	0.2793	0.0898
5	1.0000	1.0000	0.9985	0.9561	0.7805	0.4859	0.2120
6	1.0000	1.0000	0.9998	0.9884	0.9067	0.6925	0.3953
7	1.0000	1.0000	1.0000	0.9976	0.9685	0.8499	0.6047
8				0.9996	0.9917	0.9417	0.7880
9				1.0000	0.9983	0.9825	0.9102
10					0.9998	0.9961	0.9713
11					1.0000	0.9994	0.9935
12						0.9999	0.9991
13						1.0000	0.9999
14							1.0000

n = 15

π r	.01	.05	.10	.20	.30	.40	.50
0	0.8601	0.4633	0.2059	0.0352	0.0047	0.0005	0.0000
1	0.9904	0.8290	0.5490	0.1671	0.0353	0.0052	0.0005
2	0.9996	0.9638	0.8159	0.3980	0.1268	0.0271	0.0037
3	1.0000	0.9945	0.9444	0.6482	0.2969	0.0905	0.0176
4	1.0000	0.9994	0.9873	0.8358	0.5155	0.2173	0.0592
5	1.0000	0.9999	0.9978	0.9389	0.7216	0.4032	0.1509
6	1.0000	1.0000	0.9997	0.9819	0.8689	0.6098	0.3036
7	1.0000	1.0000	1.0000	0.9958	0.9500	0.7869	0.5000
8				0.9992	0.9848	0.9050	0.6964
9				0.9999	0.9963	0.9662	0.8491
10				1.0000	0.9993	0.9907	0.9408
11					0.9999	0.9981	0.9824
12					1.0000	0.9997	0.9963
13						1.0000	0.9995
14							1.0000

TABLE C (*continued*)

$n = 16$

π r	.01	.05	.10	.20	.30	.40	.50
0	0.8515	0.4401	0.1853	0.0281	0.0033	0.0003	0.0000
1	0.9891	0.8108	0.5147	0.1407	0.0261	0.0033	0.0003
2	0.9995	0.9571	0.7892	0.3518	0.0994	0.0183	0.0021
3	1.0000	0.9930	0.9316	0.5981	0.2459	0.0651	0.0106
4	1.0000	0.9991	0.9830	0.7982	0.4499	0.1666	0.0384
5	1.0000	0.9999	0.9967	0.9183	0.6598	0.3288	0.1051
6	1.0000	1.0000	0.9995	0.9733	0.8247	0.5272	0.2272
7	1.0000	1.0000	0.9999	0.9930	0.9256	0.7161	0.4018
8	1.0000	1.0000	1.0000	0.9985	0.9743	0.8577	0.5982
9				0.9998	0.9929	0.9417	0.7728
10				1.0000	0.9984	0.9809	0.8949
11					0.9997	0.9951	0.9616
12					1.0000	0.9991	0.9894
13						0.9999	0.9979
14						1.0000	0.9997
15							1.0000

$n = 17$

π r	.01	.05	.10	.20	.30	.40	.50
0	0.8429	0.4181	0.1668	0.0225	0.0023	0.0002	0.0000
1	0.9877	0.7922	0.4818	0.1182	0.0193	0.0021	0.0001
2	0.9994	0.9497	0.7618	0.3096	0.0774	0.0123	0.0012
3	1.0000	0.9912	0.9174	0.5489	0.2019	0.0464	0.0064
4	1.0000	0.9988	0.9779	0.7582	0.3887	0.1260	0.0245
5	1.0000	0.9999	0.9953	0.8943	0.5968	0.2639	0.0717
6	1.0000	1.0000	0.9992	0.9623	0.7752	0.4478	0.1662
7	1.0000	1.0000	0.9999	0.9891	0.8954	0.6405	0.3145
8	1.0000	1.0000	1.0000	0.9974	0.9597	0.8011	0.5000
9				0.9995	0.9873	0.9081	0.6855
10				0.9999	0.9968	0.9652	0.8338
11				1.0000	0.9993	0.9894	0.9283
12					0.9999	0.9975	0.9755
13					1.0000	0.9995	0.9936
14						0.9999	0.9988
15						1.0000	0.9999
16							1.0000

TABLE C   (*continued*)

$n = 18$

π	.01	.05	.10	.20	.30	.40	.50
r							
0	0.8345	0.3972	0.1501	0.0180	0.0016	0.0001	0.0000
1	0.9862	0.7735	0.4503	0.0991	0.0142	0.0013	0.0001
2	0.9993	0.9419	0.7338	0.2713	0.0600	0.0082	0.0007
3	1.0000	0.9891	0.9018	0.5010	0.1646	0.0328	0.0038
4	1.0000	0.9985	0.9718	0.7164	0.3327	0.0942	0.0154
5	1.0000	0.9998	0.9936	0.8671	0.5344	0.2088	0.0481
6	1.0000	1.0000	0.9988	0.9487	0.7217	0.3743	0.1189
7	1.0000	1.0000	0.9998	0.9837	0.8593	0.5634	0.2403
8	1.0000	1.0000	1.0000	0.9957	0.9404	0.7368	0.4073
9				0.9991	0.9790	0.8653	0.5927
10				0.9998	0.9939	0.9424	0.7597
11				1.0000	0.9986	0.9797	0.8811
12					0.9997	0.9942	0.9519
13					1.0000	0.9987	0.9846
14						0.9998	0.9962
15						1.0000	0.9993
16							0.9999
17							1.0000

$n = 19$

π	.01	.05	.10	.20	.30	.40	.50
r							
0	0.8262	0.3774	0.1351	0.0144	0.0011	0.0001	0.0000
1	0.9847	0.7547	0.4203	0.0829	0.0104	0.0008	0.0000
2	0.9991	0.9335	0.7054	0.2369	0.0462	0.0055	0.0004
3	1.0000	0.9868	0.8850	0.4551	0.1332	0.0230	0.0022
4	1.0000	0.9980	0.9648	0.6733	0.2822	0.0696	0.0096
5	1.0000	0.9998	0.9914	0.8369	0.4739	0.1629	0.0318
6	1.0000	1.0000	0.9983	0.9324	0.6655	0.3081	0.0835
7	1.0000	1.0000	0.9997	0.9767	0.8180	0.4878	0.1796
8	1.0000	1.0000	1.0000	0.9933	0.9161	0.6675	0.3238
9				0.9984	0.9674	0.8139	0.5000
10				0.9997	0.9895	0.9115	0.6762

TABLE C   (*continued*)

n = 19

π	.01	.05	.10	.20	.30	.40	.50
r							
11				0.9999	0.9972	0.9648	0.8204
12				1.0000	0.9994	0.9884	0.9165
13					0.9999	0.9969	0.9682
14					1.0000	0.9994	0.9904
15						0.9999	0.9978
16						1.0000	0.9996
17							1.0000

n = 20

π	.01	.05	.10	.20	.30	.40	.50
r							
0	0.8179	0.3585	0.1216	0.0115	0.0008	0.0000	0.0000
1	0.9831	0.7358	0.3917	0.0692	0.0076	0.0005	0.0000
2	0.9990	0.9245	0.6769	0.2061	0.0355	0.0036	0.0002
3	1.0000	0.9841	0.8670	0.4114	0.1071	0.0160	0.0013
4	1.0000	0.9974	0.9568	0.6296	0.2375	0.0510	0.0059
5	1.0000	0.9997	0.9887	0.8042	0.4164	0.1256	0.0207
6	1.0000	1.0000	0.9976	0.9133	0.6080	0.2500	0.0577
7	1.0000	1.0000	0.9996	0.9679	0.7723	0.4159	0.1316
8	1.0000	1.0000	0.9999	0.9900	0.8867	0.5956	0.2517
9	1.0000	1.0000	1.0000	0.9974	0.9520	0.7553	0.4119
10				0.9994	0.9829	0.8725	0.5881
11				0.9999	0.9949	0.9435	0.7483
12				1.0000	0.9987	0.9790	0.8684
13					0.9997	0.9935	0.9423
14					1.0000	0.9984	0.9793
15						0.9997	0.9941
16						1.0000	0.9987
17							0.9998
18							1.0000

TABLE C (*continued*)

n = 50

π r	.01	.05	.10	.20	.30	.40	.50
0	0.6050	0.0769	0.0052	0.0000	0.0000	0.0000	0.0000
1	0.9106	0.2794	0.0338	0.0002	0.0000	0.0000	0.0000
2	0.9862	0.5405	0.1117	0.0013	0.0000	0.0000	0.0000
3	0.9984	0.7604	0.2503	0.0057	0.0000	0.0000	0.0000
4	0.9999	0.8964	0.4312	0.0185	0.0002	0.0000	0.0000
5	1.0000	0.9622	0.6161	0.0480	0.0007	0.0000	0.0000
6	1.0000	0.9882	0.7702	0.1034	0.0025	0.0000	0.0000
7	1.0000	0.9968	0.8779	0.1904	0.0073	0.0001	0.0000
8	1.0000	0.9992	0.9421	0.3073	0.0183	0.0002	0.0000
9	1.0000	0.9998	0.9755	0.4437	0.0402	0.0008	0.0000
10	1.0000	1.0000	0.9906	0.5836	0.0789	0.0022	0.0000
11	1.0000	1.0000	0.9968	0.7107	0.1390	0.0057	0.0000
12	1.0000	1.0000	0.9990	0.8139	0.2229	0.0133	0.0002
13	1.0000	1.0000	0.9997	0.8894	0.3279	0.0280	0.0005
14	1.0000	1.0000	0.9999	0.9393	0.4468	0.0540	0.0013
15	1.0000	1.0000	1.0000	0.9692	0.5692	0.0955	0.0033
16				0.9856	0.6839	0.1561	0.0077
17				0.9937	0.7822	0.2369	0.0164
18				0.9975	0.8594	0.3356	0.0325
19				0.9991	0.9152	0.4465	0.0595
20				0.9997	0.9522	0.5610	0.1013
21				0.9999	0.9749	0.6701	0.1611
22				1.0000	0.9877	0.7660	0.2399
23					0.9944	0.8438	0.3359
24					0.9976	0.9022	0.4439
25					0.9991	0.9427	0.5561
26					0.9997	0.9686	0.6641
27					0.9999	0.9840	0.7601
28					1.0000	0.9924	0.8389
29						0.9966	0.8987
30						0.9986	0.9405
31						0.9995	0.9675
32						0.9998	0.9836
33						0.9999	0.9923
34						1.0000	0.9967
35							0.9987
36							0.9995
37							0.9998
38							1.0000

TABLE C (*continued*)

$n = 100$

π	.01	.05	.10	.20	.30	.40	.50
r							
0	0.3660	0.0059	0.0000	0.0000	0.0000	0.0000	0.0000
1	0.7358	0.0371	0.0003	0.0000	0.0000	0.0000	0.0000
2	0.9206	0.1183	0.0019	0.0000	0.0000	0.0000	0.0000
3	0.9816	0.2578	0.0078	0.0000	0.0000	0.0000	0.0000
4	0.9966	0.4360	0.0237	0.0000	0.0000	0.0000	0.0000
5	0.9995	0.6160	0.0576	0.0000	0.0000	0.0000	0.0000
6	0.9999	0.7660	0.1172	0.0001	0.0000	0.0000	0.0000
7	1.0000	0.8720	0.2061	0.0003	0.0000	0.0000	0.0000
8	1.0000	0.9369	0.3209	0.0009	0.0000	0.0000	0.0000
9	1.0000	0.9718	0.4513	0.0023	0.0000	0.0000	0.0000
10	1.0000	0.9885	0.5832	0.0057	0.0000	0.0000	0.0000
11	1.0000	0.9957	0.7030	0.0126	0.0000	0.0000	0.0000
12	1.0000	0.9985	0.8018	0.0253	0.0000	0.0000	0.0000
13	1.0000	0.9995	0.8761	0.0469	0.0001	0.0000	0.0000
14	1.0000	0.9999	0.9274	0.0804	0.0002	0.0000	0.0000
15	1.0000	1.0000	0.9601	0.1285	0.0004	0.0000	0.0000
16	1.0000	1.0000	0.9794	0.1923	0.0010	0.0000	0.0000
17	1.0000	1.0000	0.9900	0.2712	0.0022	0.0000	0.0000
18	1.0000	1.0000	0.9954	0.3621	0.0045	0.0000	0.0000
19	1.0000	1.0000	0.9980	0.4602	0.0089	0.0000	0.0000
20	1.0000	1.0000	0.9992	0.5595	0.0165	0.0000	0.0000
21	1.0000	1.0000	0.9997	0.6540	0.0288	0.0000	0.0000
22	1.0000	1.0000	0.9999	0.7389	0.0479	0.0001	0.0000
23	1.0000	1.0000	1.0000	0.8109	0.0755	0.0003	0.0000
24				0.8686	0.1136	0.0006	0.0000
25				0.9125	0.1631	0.0012	0.0000
26				0.9442	0.2244	0.0024	0.0000
27				0.9658	0.2964	0.0046	0.0000
28				0.9800	0.3768	0.0084	0.0000
29				0.9888	0.4623	0.0148	0.0000
30				0.9939	0.5491	0.0248	0.0000
31				0.9969	0.6331	0.0398	0.0001
32				0.9984	0.7107	0.0615	0.0002
33				0.9993	0.7793	0.0913	0.0004
34				0.9997	0.8371	0.1303	0.0009
35				0.9999	0.8839	0.1795	0.0018

TABLE C   *(continued)*

$n = 100$

π r	.01	.05	.10	.20	.30	.40	.50
36				0.9999	0.9201	0.2386	0.0033
37				1.0000	0.9470	0.3068	0.0060
38					0.9660	0.3822	0.0105
39					0.9790	0.4621	0.0176
40					0.9875	0.5433	0.0284
41					0.9928	0.6225	0.0443
42					0.9960	0.6967	0.0666
43					0.9979	0.7635	0.0967
44					0.9989	0.8211	0.1356
45					0.9995	0.8689	0.1841
46					0.9997	0.9070	0.2421
47					0.9999	0.9362	0.3086
48					0.9999	0.9577	0.3822
49					1.0000	0.9729	0.4602
50						0.9832	0.5398
51						0.9900	0.6178
52						0.9942	0.6914
53						0.9968	0.7579
54						0.9983	0.8159
55						0.9991	0.8644
56						0.9996	0.9033
57						0.9998	0.9334
58						0.9999	0.9557
59						1.0000	0.9716
60							0.9824
61							0.9895
62							0.9940
63							0.9967
64							0.9982
65							0.9991
66							0.9996
67							0.9998
68							0.9999
69							1.0000

TABLE D Areas Under the Standard Normal Curve

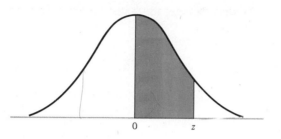

0   z

The following table provides the area between the mean and normal deviate value *z*.

Normal Deviate z	.00	.01	.02	.03	.04	.05	.06	.07	.08	.09
0.0	.0000	.0040	.0080	.0120	.0160	.0199	.0239	.0279	.0319	.0359
0.1	.0398	.0438	.0478	.0517	.0557	.0596	.0636	.0675	.0714	.0753
0.2	.0793	.0832	.0871	.0910	.0948	.0987	.1026	.1064	.1103	.1141
0.3	.1179	.1217	.1255	.1293	.1331	.1368	.1406	.1443	.1480	.1517
0.4	.1554	.1591	.1628	.1664	.1700	.1736	.1772	.1808	.1844	.1879
0.5	.1915	.1950	.1985	.2019	.2054	.2088	.2123	.2157	.2190	.2224
0.6	.2257	.2291	.2324	.2357	.2389	.2422	.2454	.2486	.2518	.2549
0.7	.2580	.2612	.2642	.2673	.2704	.2734	.2764	.2794	.2823	.2852
0.8	.2881	.2910	.2939	.2967	.2995	.3023	.3051	.3078	.3106	.3133
0.9	.3159	.3186	.3212	.3238	.3264	.3289	.3315	.3340	.3365	.3389
1.0	.3413	.3438	.3461	.3485	.3508	.3531	.3554	.3577	.3599	.3621
1.1	.3643	.3665	.3686	.3708	.3729	.3749	.3770	.3790	.3810	.3830
1.2	.3849	.3869	.3888	.3907	.3925	.3944	.3962	.3980	.3997	.4015
1.3	.4032	.4049	.4066	.4082	.4099	.4115	.4131	.4147	.4162	.4177
1.4	.4192	.4207	.4222	.4236	.4251	.4265	.4279	.4292	.4306	.4319
1.5	.4332	.4345	.4357	.4370	.4382	.4394	.4406	.4418	.4429	.4441
1.6	.4452	.4463	.4474	.4484	.4495	.4505	.4515	.4525	.4535	.4545
1.7	.4554	.4564	.4573	.4582	.4591	.4599	.4608	.4616	.4625	.4633
1.8	.4641	.4649	.4656	.4664	.4671	.4678	.4686	.4693	.4699	.4706
1.9	.4713	.4719	.4726	.4732	.4738	.4744	.4750	.4756	.4761	.4767
2.0	.4772	.4778	.4783	.4788	.4793	.4798	.4803	.4808	.4812	.4817
2.1	.4821	.4826	.4830	.4834	.4838	.4842	.4846	.4850	.4854	.4857
2.2	.4861	.4864	.4868	.4871	.4875	.4878	.4881	.4884	.4887	.4890
2.3	.4893	.4896	.4898	.4901	.4904	.4906	.4909	.4911	.4913	.4916
2.4	.4918	.4920	.4922	.4925	.4927	.4929	.4931	.4932	.4934	.4936
2.5	.4938	.4940	.4941	.4943	.4945	.4946	.4948	.4949	.4951	.4952
2.6	.4953	.4955	.4956	.4957	.4959	.4960	.4961	.4962	.4963	.4964
2.7	.4965	.4966	.4967	.4968	.4969	.4970	.4971	.4972	.4973	.4974
2.8	.4974	.4975	.4976	.4977	.4977	.4978	.4979	.4979	.4980	.4981
2.9	.4981	.4982	.4982	.4983	.4984	.4984	.4985	.4985	.4986	.4986
3.0	.49865	.4987	.4987	.4988	.4988	.4989	.4989	.4989	.4990	.4990
4.0	.49997									

© 1970 by Harcourt Brace Jovanovich, Inc., and reproduced with their permission from *Statistical Analysis for Decision Making* by Morris Hamburg.

TABLE E   Normal Deviate Values

Normal Deviates for Statistical Estimation

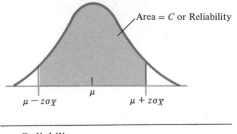

Reliability or Confidence Level C	Normal Deviate z
.80	1.28
.90	1.64
.95	1.96
.98	2.33
.99	2.57
.998	3.08
.999	3.27

Critical Normal Deviates for Hypothesis Testing

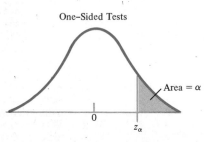

One–Sided Tests

Significance Level α	Normal Deviate z_α	Significance Level α	Normal Deviate $z_{\alpha/2}$
.10	1.28	.10	1.64
.05	1.64	.05	1.96
.025	1.96	.025	2.24
.01	2.33	.01	2.57
.005	2.57	.005	2.81
.001	3.08	.001	3.27

TABLE F　Student t Distribution

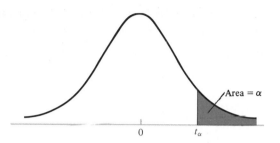

Area $= \alpha$

0　　t_α

The following table provides the values of t_α that correspond to a given upper-tail area α and a specified number of degrees of freedom.

Degrees of Freedom	Upper-Tail Area α									
	.4	.25	.1	.05	.025	.01	.005	.0025	.001	.0005
1	0.325	1.000	3.078	6.314	12.706	31.821	63.657	127.32	318.31	636.62
2	.289	0.816	1.886	2.920	4.303	6.965	9.925	14.089	22.327	31.598
3	.277	.765	1.638	2.353	3.182	4.541	5.841	7.453	10.214	12.924
4	.271	.741	1.533	2.132	2.776	3.747	4.604	5.598	7.173	8.610
5	0.267	0.727	1.476	2.015	2.571	3.365	4.032	4.773	5.893	6.869
6	.265	.718	1.440	1.943	2.447	3.143	3.707	4.317	5.208	5.959
7	.263	.711	1.415	1.895	2.365	2.998	3.499	4.029	4.785	5.408
8	.262	.706	1.397	1.860	2.306	2.896	3.355	3.833	4.501	5.041
9	.261	.703	1.383	1.833	2.262	2.821	3.250	3.690	4.297	4.781
10	0.260	0.700	1.372	1.812	2.228	2.764	3.169	3.581	4.144	4.587
11	.260	.697	1.363	1.796	2.201	2.718	3.106	3.497	4.025	4.437
12	.259	.695	1.356	1.782	2.179	2.681	3.055	3.428	3.930	4.318
13	.259	.694	1.350	1.771	2.160	2.650	3.012	3.372	3.852	4.221
14	.258	.692	1.345	1.761	2.145	2.624	2.977	3.326	3.787	4.140
15	0.258	0.691	1.341	1.753	2.131	2.602	2.947	3.286	3.733	4.073
16	.258	.690	1.337	1.746	2.120	2.583	2.921	3.252	3.686	4.015
17	2.57	.689	1.333	1.740	2.110	2.567	2.898	3.222	3.646	3.965
18	.257	.688	1.330	1.734	2.101	2.552	2.878	3.197	3.610	3.922
19	.257	.688	1.328	1.729	2.093	2.539	2.861	3.174	3.579	3.883
20	0.257	0.687	1.325	1.725	2.086	2.528	2.845	3.153	3.552	3.850
21	.257	.686	1.323	1.721	2.080	2.518	2.831	3.135	3.527	3.819
22	.256	.686	1.321	1.717	2.074	2.508	2.819	3.119	3.505	3.792
23	.256	.685	1.319	1.714	2.069	2.500	2.807	3.104	3.485	3.767
24	.256	.685	1.318	1.711	2.064	2.492	2.797	3.091	3.467	3.745
25	0.256	0.684	1.316	1.708	2.060	2.485	2.787	3.078	3.450	3.725
26	.256	.684	1.315	1.706	2.056	2.479	2.779	3.067	3.435	3.707
27	.256	.684	1.314	1.703	2.052	2.473	2.771	3.057	3.421	3.690
28	.256	.683	1.313	1.701	2.048	2.467	2.763	3.047	3.408	3.674
29	.256	.683	1.311	1.699	2.045	2.462	2.756	3.038	3.396	3.659
30	0.256	0.683	1.310	1.697	2.042	2.457	2.750	3.030	3.385	3.646
40	.255	.681	1.303	1.684	2.021	2.423	2.704	2.971	3.307	3.551
60	.254	.679	1.296	1.671	2.000	2.390	2.660	2.915	3.232	3.460
120	.254	.677	1.289	1.658	1.980	2.358	2.617	2.860	3.160	3.373
∞	.253	.674	1.282	1.645	1.960	2.326	2.576	2.807	3.090	3.291

SOURCE: E.S. Pearson and H.O. Hartley, *Biometrika Tables for Statisticians*, Vol. I. London: Cambridge University Press, 1966. Partly derived from Table III of Fisher and Yates, *Statistical Tables for Biological, Agricultural and Medical Research*, published by Longman Group Ltd., London (previously published by Oliver & Boyd, Edinburgh, 1963). Reproduced with permission of the authors and publishers.

TABLE G   Four-Place Common Logarithms

N	0	1	2	3	4	5	6	7	8	9	1	2	3	4	5	6	7	8	9
														Proportional Parts					
10	0000	0043	0086	0128	0170	0212	0253	0294	0334	0374	4	8	12	17	21	25	29	33	37
11	0414	0453	0492	0531	0569	0607	0645	0682	0719	0755	4	8	11	15	19	23	26	30	34
12	0792	0828	0864	0899	0934	0969	1004	1038	1072	1106	3	7	10	14	17	21	24	28	31
13	1139	1173	1206	1239	1271	1303	1335	1367	1399	1430	3	6	10	13	16	19	23	26	29
14	1461	1492	1523	1553	1584	1614	1644	1673	1703	1732	3	6	9	12	15	18	21	24	27
15	1761	1790	1818	1847	1875	1903	1931	1959	1987	2014	3	6	8	11	14	17	20	22	25
16	2041	2068	2095	2122	2148	2175	2201	2227	2253	2279	3	5	8	11	13	16	18	21	24
17	2304	2330	2355	2380	2405	2430	2455	2480	2504	2529	2	5	7	10	12	15	17	20	22
18	2553	2577	2601	2625	2648	2672	2695	2718	2742	2765	2	5	7	9	12	14	16	19	21
19	2788	2810	2833	2856	2878	2900	2923	2945	2967	2989	2	4	7	9	11	13	16	18	20
20	3010	3032	3054	3075	3096	3118	3139	3160	3181	3201	2	4	6	8	11	13	15	17	19
21	3222	3243	3263	3284	3304	3324	3345	3365	3385	3404	2	4	6	8	10	12	14	16	18
22	3424	3444	3464	3483	3502	3522	3541	3560	3579	3598	2	4	6	8	10	12	14	15	17
23	3617	3636	3655	3674	3692	3711	3729	3747	3766	3784	2	4	6	7	9	11	13	15	17
24	3802	3820	3838	3856	3874	3892	3909	3927	3945	3962	2	4	5	7	9	11	12	14	16
25	3979	3997	4014	4031	4048	4065	4082	4099	4116	4133	2	3	5	7	9	10	12	14	15
26	4150	4166	4183	4200	4216	4232	4249	4265	4281	4298	2	3	5	7	8	10	11	13	15
27	4314	4330	4346	4362	4378	4393	4409	4425	4440	4456	2	3	5	6	8	9	11	13	14
28	4472	4487	4502	4518	4533	4548	4564	4579	4594	4609	2	3	5	6	8	9	11	12	14
29	4624	4639	4654	4669	4683	4698	4713	4728	4742	4757	1	3	4	6	7	9	10	12	13
30	4771	4786	4800	4814	4829	4843	4857	4871	4886	4900	1	3	4	6	7	9	10	11	13
31	4914	4928	4942	4955	4969	4983	4997	5011	5024	5038	1	3	4	6	7	8	10	11	12
32	5051	5065	5079	5092	5105	5119	5132	5145	5159	5172	1	3	4	5	7	8	9	11	12
33	5185	5198	5211	5224	5237	5250	5263	5276	5289	5302	1	3	4	5	6	8	9	10	12
34	5315	5328	5340	5353	5366	5378	5391	5403	5416	5428	1	3	4	5	6	8	9	10	11
35	5441	5453	5465	5478	5490	5502	5514	5527	5539	5551	1	2	4	5	6	7	9	10	11
36	5563	5575	5587	5599	5611	5623	5635	5647	5658	5670	1	2	4	5	6	7	8	10	11
37	5682	5694	5705	5717	5729	5740	5752	5763	5775	5786	1	2	3	5	6	7	8	9	10
38	5798	5809	5821	5832	5843	5855	5866	5877	5888	5899	1	2	3	5	6	7	8	9	10
39	5911	5922	5933	5944	5955	5966	5977	5988	5999	6010	1	2	3	4	5	7	8	9	10
40	6021	6031	6042	6053	6064	6075	6085	6096	6107	6117	1	2	3	4	5	6	8	9	10
41	6128	6138	6149	6160	6170	6180	6191	6201	6212	6222	1	2	3	4	5	6	7	8	9
42	6232	6243	6253	6263	6274	6284	6294	6304	6314	6325	1	2	3	4	5	6	7	8	9
43	6335	6345	6355	6365	6375	6385	6395	6405	6415	6425	1	2	3	4	5	6	7	8	9
4	6435	6444	6454	6464	6474	6484	6493	6503	6513	6522	1	2	3	4	5	6	7	8	9
45	6532	6542	6551	6561	6571	6580	6590	6599	6609	6618	1	2	3	4	5	6	7	8	9
46	6628	6637	6646	6656	6665	6675	6684	6693	6702	6712	1	2	3	4	5	6	7	7	8
47	6721	6730	6739	6749	6758	6767	6776	6785	6794	6803	1	2	3	4	5	5	6	7	8
48	6812	6821	6830	6839	6848	6857	6866	6875	6884	6893	1	2	3	4	4	5	6	7	8
49	6902	6911	6920	6928	6937	6946	6955	6964	6972	6981	1	2	3	4	4	5	6	7	8
50	6990	6998	7007	7016	7024	7033	7042	7050	7059	7067	1	2	3	3	4	5	6	7	8
51	7076	7084	7093	7101	7110	7118	7126	7135	7143	7152	1	2	3	3	4	5	6	7	8
52	7160	7168	7177	7185	7193	7202	7210	7218	7226	7235	1	2	2	3	4	5	6	7	7
53	7243	7251	7259	7267	7275	7284	7292	7300	7308	7316	1	2	2	3	4	5	6	6	7
54	7324	7332	7340	7348	7356	7364	7372	7380	7388	7396	1	2	2	3	4	5	6	6	7
N	0	1	2	3	4	5	6	7	8	9	1	2	3	4	5	6	7	8	9

TABLE G *(continued)*

N	0	1	2	3	4	5	6	7	8	9	Proportional Parts 1	2	3	4	5	6	7	8	9
55	7404	7412	7419	7427	7435	7443	7451	7459	7466	7474	1	2	2	3	4	5	5	6	7
56	7482	7490	7497	7505	7513	7520	7528	7536	7543	7551	1	2	2	3	4	5	5	6	7
57	7559	7566	7574	7582	7589	7597	7604	7612	7619	7627	1	2	2	3	4	5	5	6	7
58	7634	7642	7649	7657	7664	7672	7679	7686	7694	7701	1	1	2	3	4	4	5	6	7
59	7709	7716	7723	7731	7738	7745	7752	7760	7767	7774	1	1	2	3	4	4	5	6	7
60	7782	7789	7796	7803	7810	7818	7825	7832	7839	7846	1	1	2	3	4	4	5	6	6
61	7853	7860	7868	7875	7882	7889	7896	7903	7910	7917	1	1	2	3	4	4	5	6	6
62	7924	7931	7938	7945	7952	7959	7966	7973	7980	7987	1	1	2	3	3	4	5	6	6
63	7993	8000	8007	8014	8021	8028	8035	8041	8048	8055	1	1	2	3	3	4	5	5	6
64	8062	8069	8075	8082	8089	8096	8102	8109	8116	8122	1	1	2	3	3	4	5	5	6
65	8129	8136	8142	8149	8156	8162	8169	8176	8182	8189	1	1	2	3	3	4	5	5	6
66	8195	8202	8209	8215	8222	8228	8235	8241	8248	8254	1	1	2	3	3	4	5	5	6
67	8261	8267	8274	8280	8287	8293	8299	8306	8312	8319	1	1	2	3	3	4	5	5	6
68	8325	8331	8338	8344	8351	8357	8363	8370	8376	8382	1	1	2	3	3	4	4	5	6
69	8388	8395	8401	8407	8414	8420	8426	8432	8439	8445	1	1	2	2	3	4	4	5	6
70	8451	8457	8463	8470	8476	8482	8488	8494	8500	8506	1	1	2	2	3	4	4	5	6
71	8513	8519	8525	8531	8537	8543	8549	8555	8561	8567	1	1	2	2	3	4	4	5	5
72	8573	8579	8585	8591	8597	8603	8609	8615	8621	8627	1	1	2	2	3	4	4	5	5
73	8633	8639	8645	8651	8657	8663	8669	8675	8681	8686	1	1	2	2	3	4	4	5	5
74	8692	8698	8704	8710	8716	8722	8727	8733	8739	8745	1	1	2	2	3	4	4	5	5
75	8751	8756	8762	8768	8774	8779	8785	8791	8797	8802	1	1	2	2	3	3	4	5	5
76	8808	8814	8820	8825	8831	8837	8842	8848	8854	8859	1	1	2	2	3	3	4	5	5
77	8865	8871	8876	8882	8887	8893	8899	8904	8910	8915	1	1	2	2	3	3	4	4	5
78	8921	8927	8932	8938	8943	8949	8954	8960	8965	8971	1	1	2	2	3	3	4	4	5
79	8976	8982	8987	8993	8998	9004	9009	9015	9020	9025	1	1	2	2	3	3	4	4	5
80	9031	9036	9042	9047	9053	9058	9063	9069	9074	9079	1	1	2	2	3	3	4	4	5
81	9085	9090	9096	9101	9106	9112	9117	9122	9128	9133	1	1	2	2	3	3	4	4	5
82	9138	9143	9149	9154	9159	9165	9170	9175	9180	9186	1	1	2	2	3	3	4	4	5
83	9191	9196	9201	9206	9212	9217	9222	9227	9232	9238	1	1	2	2	3	3	4	4	5
84	9243	9248	9253	9258	9263	9269	9274	9279	9284	9289	1	1	2	2	3	3	4	4	5
85	9294	9299	9304	9309	9315	9320	9325	9330	9335	9340	1	1	2	2	3	3	4	4	5
86	9345	9350	9355	9360	9365	9370	9375	9380	9385	9390	1	1	2	2	3	3	4	4	5
87	9395	9400	9405	9410	9415	9420	9425	9430	9435	9440	0	1	1	2	2	3	3	4	4
88	9445	9450	9455	9460	9465	9469	9474	9479	9484	9489	0	1	1	2	2	3	3	4	4
89	9494	9499	9504	9509	9513	9518	9523	9528	9533	9538	0	1	1	2	2	3	3	4	4
90	9542	9547	9552	9557	9562	9566	9571	9576	9581	9586	0	1	1	2	2	3	3	4	4
91	9590	9595	9600	9605	9609	9614	9619	9624	9628	9633	0	1	1	2	2	3	3	4	4
92	9638	9643	9647	9652	9657	9661	9666	9671	9675	9680	0	1	1	2	2	3	3	4	4
93	9685	9689	9694	9699	9703	9708	9713	9717	9722	9727	0	1	1	2	2	3	3	4	4
94	9731	9736	9741	9745	9750	9754	9759	9763	9768	9773	0	1	1	2	2	3	3	4	4
95	9777	9782	9786	9791	9795	9800	9805	9809	9814	9818	0	1	1	2	2	3	3	4	4
96	9823	9827	9832	9836	9841	9845	9850	9854	9859	9863	0	1	1	2	2	3	3	4	4
97	9868	9872	9877	9881	9886	9890	9894	9899	9903	9908	0	1	1	2	2	3	3	4	4
98	9912	9917	9921	9926	9930	9934	9939	9943	9948	9952	0	1	1	2	2	3	3	4	4
99	9956	9961	9965	9969	9974	9978	9983	9987	9991	9996	0	1	1	2	2	3	3	3	4
N	0	1	2	3	4	5	6	7	8	9	1	2	3	4	5	6	7	8	9

TABLE H   Chi-Square Distribution

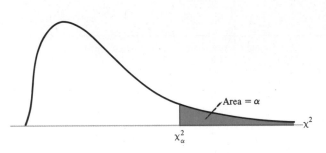

The following table provides the values of χ_α^2 that correspond to a given upper-tail area α and a specified number of degrees of freedom.

Degrees of Freedom	Upper-Tail Area α						
	.99	.98	.95	.90	.80	.70	.50
1	$.0^3157$	$.0^3628$	.00393	.0158	.0642	.148	.455
2	.0201	.0404	.103	.211	.446	.713	1.386
3	.115	.185	.352	.584	1.005	1.424	2.366
4	.297	.429	.711	1.064	1.649	2.195	3.357
5	.554	.752	1.145	1.610	2.343	3.000	4.351
6	.872	1.134	1.635	2.204	3.070	3.828	5.348
7	1.239	1.564	2.167	2.833	3.822	4.671	6.346
8	1.646	2.032	2.733	3.490	4.594	5.527	7.344
9	2.088	2.532	3.325	4.168	5.380	6.393	8.343
10	2.558	3.059	3.940	4.865	6.179	7.267	9.342
11	3.053	3.609	4.575	5.578	6.989	8.148	10.341
12	3.571	4.178	5.226	6.304	7.807	9.034	11.340
13	4.107	4.765	5.892	7.042	8.634	9.926	12.340
14	4.660	5.368	6.571	7.790	9.467	10.821	13.339
15	5.229	5.985	7.261	8.547	10.307	11.721	14.339
16	5.812	6.614	7.962	9.312	11.152	12.624	15.338
17	6.408	7.255	8.672	10.085	12.002	13.531	16.338
18	7.015	7.906	9.390	10.865	12.857	14.440	17.338
19	7.633	8.567	10.117	11.651	13.716	15.352	18.338
20	8.260	9.237	10.851	12.443	14.578	16.266	19.337
21	8.897	9.915	11.591	13.240	15.445	17.182	20.337
22	9.542	10.600	12.338	14.041	16.314	18.101	21.337
23	10.196	11.293	13.091	14.848	17.187	19.021	22.337
24	10.856	11.992	13.848	15.659	18.062	19.943	23.337
25	11.524	12.697	14.611	16.473	18.940	20.867	24.337
26	12.198	13.409	15.379	17.292	19.820	21.792	25.336
27	12.879	14.125	16.151	18.114	20.703	22.719	26.336
28	13.565	14.847	16.928	18.939	21.588	23.647	27.336
29	14.256	15.574	17.708	19.768	22.475	24.577	28.336
30	14.953	16.306	18.493	20.599	23.364	25.508	29.336

TABLE H   (*continued*)

Degrees of Freedom	Upper-Tail Area α						
	.30	.20	.10	.05	.02	.01	.001
1	1.074	1.642	2.706	3.841	5.412	6.635	10.827
2	2.408	3.219	4.605	5.991	7.824	9.210	13.815
3	3.665	4.642	6.251	7.815	9.837	11.345	16.268
4	4.878	5.989	7.779	9.488	11.668	13.277	18.465
5	6.064	7.289	9.236	11.070	13.388	15.086	20.517
6	7.231	8.558	10.645	12.592	15.033	16.812	22.457
7	8.383	9.803	12.017	14.067	16.622	18.475	24.322
8	9.524	11.030	13.362	15.507	18.168	20.090	26.125
9	10.656	12.242	14.684	16.919	19.679	21.666	27.877
10	11.781	13.442	15.987	18.307	21.161	23.209	29.588
11	12.899	14.631	17.275	19.675	22.618	24.725	31.264
12	14.011	15.812	18.549	21.026	24.054	26.217	32.909
13	15.119	16.985	19.812	22.362	25.472	27.688	34.528
14	16.222	18.151	21.064	23.685	26.873	29.141	36.123
15	17.322	19.311	22.307	24.996	28.259	30.578	37.697
16	18.418	20.465	23.542	26.296	29.633	32.000	39.252
17	19.511	21.615	24.769	27.587	30.995	33.409	40.790
18	20.601	22.760	25.989	28.869	32.346	34.805	42.312
19	21.689	23.900	27.204	30.144	33.687	36.191	43.820
20	22.775	25.038	28.412	31.410	35.020	37.566	45.315
21	23.858	26.171	29.615	32.671	36.343	38.932	46.797
22	24.939	27.301	30.813	33.924	37.659	40.289	48.268
23	26.018	28.429	32.007	35.172	38.968	41.638	49.728
24	27.096	29.553	33.196	36.415	40.270	42.980	51.179
25	28.172	30.675	34.382	37.652	41.566	44.314	52.620
26	29.246	31.795	35.563	38.885	42.856	45.642	54.052
27	30.319	32.912	36.741	40.113	44.140	46.963	55.476
28	31.391	34.027	37.916	41.337	45.419	48.278	56.893
29	32.461	35.139	39.087	42.557	46.693	49.588	58.302
30	33.530	36.250	40.256	43.773	47.962	50.892	59.703

SOURCE: From Table IV of Fisher and Yates, *Statistical Tables for Biological, Agricultural and Medical Research*, published by Longman Group Ltd., London (previously published by Oliver & Boyd, Edinburgh, 1963). Reproduced with permission of the authors and publishers.

TABLE I   *F* Distribution

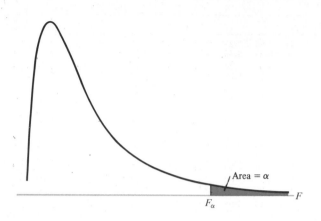

The following table provides the values of F_α that correspond to a given upper-tail area α and a specified degrees of freedom pair. The values of $F_{.05}$ are in lightface type, while those for $F_{.01}$ are given in boldface type. The number of degrees of freedom for the *numerator* mean square is indicated at the head of each *column*, while the number of degrees of freedom for the *denominator* mean square determines which *row* is applicable.

Degrees of Freedom in Denominator	Degrees of Freedom in Numerator											
	1	2	3	4	5	6	7	8	9	10	11	12
1	161	200	216	225	230	234	237	239	241	242	243	244
	4,052	**4,999**	**5,403**	**5,625**	**5,764**	**5,859**	**5,928**	**5,981**	**6,022**	**6,056**	**6,082**	**6,106**
2	18.51	19.00	19.16	19.25	19.30	19.33	19.36	19.37	19.38	19.39	19.40	19.41
	98.49	**99.00**	**99.17**	**99.25**	**99.30**	**99.33**	**99.36**	**99.37**	**99.39**	**99.40**	**99.41**	**99.42**
3	10.13	9.55	9.28	9.12	9.01	8.94	8.88	8.84	8.81	8.78	8.76	8.74
	34.12	**30.82**	**29.46**	**28.71**	**28.24**	**27.91**	**27.67**	**27.49**	**27.34**	**27.23**	**27.13**	**27.05**
4	7.71	6.94	6.59	6.39	6.26	6.16	6.09	6.04	6.00	5.96	5.93	5.91
	21.20	**18.00**	**16.69**	**15.98**	**15.52**	**15.21**	**14.98**	**14.80**	**14.66**	**14.54**	**14.45**	**14.37**
5	6.61	5.79	5.41	5.19	5.05	4.95	4.88	4.82	4.78	4.74	4.70	4.68
	16.26	**13.27**	**12.06**	**11.39**	**10.97**	**10.67**	**10.45**	**10.29**	**10.15**	**10.05**	**9.96**	**9.89**
6	5.99	5.14	4.76	4.53	4.39	4.28	4.21	4.15	4.10	4.06	4.03	4.00
	13.74	**10.92**	**9.78**	**9.15**	**8.75**	**8.47**	**8.26**	**8.10**	**7.98**	**7.87**	**7.79**	**7.72**
7	5.59	4.74	4.35	4.12	3.97	3.87	3.79	3.73	3.68	3.63	3.60	3.57
	12.25	**9.55**	**8.45**	**7.85**	**7.46**	**7.19**	**7.00**	**6.84**	**6.71**	**6.62**	**6.54**	**6.47**
8	5.32	4.46	4.07	3.84	3.69	3.58	3.50	3.44	3.39	3.34	3.31	3.28
	11.26	**8.65**	**7.59**	**7.01**	**6.63**	**6.37**	**6.19**	**6.03**	**5.91**	**5.82**	**5.74**	**5.67**
9	5.12	4.26	3.86	3.63	3.48	3.37	3.29	3.23	3.18	3.13	3.10	3.07
	10.56	**8.02**	**6.99**	**6.42**	**6.06**	**5.80**	**5.62**	**5.47**	**5.35**	**5.26**	**5.18**	**5.11**
10	4.96	4.10	3.71	3.48	3.33	3.22	3.14	3.07	3.02	2.97	2.94	2.91
	10.04	**7.56**	**6.55**	**5.99**	**5.64**	**5.39**	**5.21**	**5.06**	**4.95**	**4.85**	**4.78**	**4.71**
11	4.84	3.98	3.59	3.36	3.20	3.09	3.01	2.95	2.90	2.86	2.82	2.79
	9.65	**7.20**	**6.22**	**5.67**	**5.32**	**5.07**	**4.88**	**4.74**	**4.63**	**4.54**	**4.46**	**4.40**
12	4.75	3.88	3.49	3.26	3.11	3.00	2.92	2.85	2.80	2.76	2.72	2.69
	9.33	**6.93**	**5.95**	**5.41**	**5.06**	**4.82**	**4.65**	**4.50**	**4.39**	**4.30**	**4.22**	**4.16**
13	4.67	3.80	3.41	3.18	3.02	2.92	2.84	2.77	2.72	2.67	2.63	2.60
	9.07	**6.70**	**5.74**	**5.20**	**4.86**	**4.62**	**4.44**	**4.30**	**4.19**	**4.10**	**4.02**	**3.96**
14	4.60	3.74	3.34	3.11	2.96	2.85	2.77	2.70	2.65	2.60	2.56	2.53
	8.86	**6.51**	**5.56**	**5.03**	**4.69**	**4.46**	**4.28**	**4.14**	**4.03**	**3.94**	**3.86**	**3.80**

TABLE I　(*continued*)

Degrees of Freedom in Denominator	Degrees of Freedom in Numerator											
	1	2	3	4	5	6	7	8	9	10	11	12
15	4.54	3.68	3.29	3.06	2.90	2.79	2.70	2.64	2.59	2.55	2.51	2.48
	8.68	6.36	5.42	4.89	4.56	4.32	4.14	4.00	3.89	3.80	3.73	3.67
16	4.49	3.63	3.24	3.01	2.85	2.74	2.66	2.59	2.54	2.49	2.45	2.42
	8.53	6.23	5.29	4.77	4.44	4.20	4.03	3.89	3.78	3.69	3.61	3.55
17	4.45	3.59	3.20	2.96	2.81	2.70	2.62	2.55	2.50	2.45	2.41	2.38
	8.40	6.11	5.18	4.67	4.34	4.10	3.93	3.79	3.68	3.59	3.52	3.45
18	4.41	3.55	3.16	2.93	2.77	2.66	2.58	2.51	2.46	2.41	2.37	2.34
	8.28	6.01	5.09	4.58	4.25	4.01	3.85	3.71	3.60	3.51	3.44	3.37
19	4.38	3.52	3.13	2.90	2.74	2.63	2.55	2.48	2.43	2.38	2.34	2.31
	8.18	5.93	5.01	4.50	4.17	3.94	3.77	3.63	3.52	3.43	3.36	3.30
20	4.35	3.49	3.10	2.87	2.71	2.60	2.52	2.45	2.40	2.35	2.31	2.28
	8.10	5.85	4.94	4.43	4.10	3.87	3.71	3.56	3.45	3.37	3.30	3.23
21	4.32	3.47	3.07	2.84	2.68	2.57	2.49	2.42	2.37	2.32	2.28	2.25
	8.02	5.78	4.87	4.37	4.04	3.81	3.65	3.51	3.40	3.31	3.24	3.17
22	4.30	3.44	3.05	2.82	2.66	2.55	2.47	2.40	2.35	2.30	2.26	2.23
	7.94	5.72	4.82	4.31	3.99	3.76	3.59	3.45	3.35	3.26	3.18	3.12
23	4.28	3.42	3.03	2.80	2.64	2.53	2.45	2.38	2.32	2.28	2.24	2.20
	7.88	5.66	4.76	4.26	3.94	3.71	3.54	3.41	3.30	3.21	3.14	3.07
24	4.26	3.40	3.01	2.78	2.62	2.51	2.43	2.36	2.30	2.26	2.22	2.18
	7.82	5.61	4.72	4.22	3.90	3.67	3.50	3.36	3.25	3.17	3.09	3.03
25	4.24	3.38	2.99	2.76	2.60	2.49	2.41	2.34	2.28	2.24	2.20	2.16
	7.77	5.57	4.68	4.18	3.86	3.63	3.46	3.32	3.21	3.13	3.05	2.99
26	4.22	3.37	2.98	2.74	2.59	2.47	2.39	2.32	2.27	2.22	2.18	2.15
	7.72	5.53	4.64	4.14	3.82	3.59	3.42	3.29	3.17	3.09	3.02	2.96

Reprinted by permission from *Statistical Methods* by George W. Snedecor and William G. Cochran, sixth edition © 1967 by Iowa State University Press, Ames, Iowa.

TABLE J　Exponential Functions

y	e^y	e^{-y}	y	e^y	e^{-y}
0.00	1.0000	1.000000	3.00	20.086	.049787
0.10	1.1052	.904837	3.10	22.198	.045049
0.20	1.2214	.818731	3.20	24.533	.040762
0.30	1.3499	.740818	3.30	27.113	.036883
0.40	1.4918	.670320	3.40	29.964	.033373
0.50	1.6487	.606531	3.50	33.115	.030197
0.60	1.8221	.548812	3.60	36.598	.027324
0.70	2.0138	.496585	3.70	40.447	.024724
0.80	2.2255	.449329	3.80	44.701	.022371
0.90	2.4596	.406570	3.90	49.402	.020242
1.00	2.7183	.367879	4.00	54.598	.018316
1.10	3.0042	.332871	4.10	60.340	.016573
1.20	3.3201	.301194	4.20	66.686	.014996
1.30	3.6693	.272532	4.30	73.700	.013569
1.40	4.0552	.246597	4.40	81.451	.012277
1.50	4.4817	.223130	4.50	90.017	.011109
1.60	4.9530	.201897	4.60	99.484	.010052
1.70	5.4739	.182684	4.70	109.95	.009095
1.80	6.0496	.165299	4.80	121.51	.008230
1.90	6.6859	.149569	4.90	134.29	.007447
2.00	7.3891	.135335	5.00	148.41	.006738
2.10	8.1662	.122456	5.10	164.02	.006097
2.20	9.0250	.110803	5.20	181.27	.005517
2.30	9.9742	.100259	5.30	200.34	.004992
2.40	11.023	.090718	5.40	221.41	.004517
2.50	12.182	.082085	5.50	244.69	.004087
2.60	13.464	.074274	5.60	270.43	.003698
2.70	14.880	.067206	5.70	298.87	.003346
2.80	16.445	.060810	5.80	330.30	.003028
2.90	18.174	.055023	5.90	365.04	.002739
3.00	20.086	.049787	6.00	403.43	.002479

TABLE K   Cumulative Probability Values for the Poisson Distribution

$$P[X \leq x]$$

λt	0.1	0.2	0.3	0.4	0.5	0.6	0.7	0.8	0.9	1.0
x										
0	0.9048	0.8187	0.7408	0.6703	0.6065	0.5488	0.4966	0.4493	0.4066	0.3679
1	0.9953	0.9825	0.9631	0.9384	0.9098	0.8781	0.8442	0.8088	0.7725	0.7358
2	0.9998	0.9989	0.9964	0.9921	0.9856	0.9769	0.9659	0.9526	0.9371	0.9197
3	1.0000	0.9999	0.9997	0.9992	0.9982	0.9966	0.9942	0.9909	0.9865	0.9810
4	1.0000	1.0000	1.0000	0.9999	0.9998	0.9996	0.9992	0.9986	0.9977	0.9963
5	1.0000	1.0000	1.0000	1.0000	1.0000	1.0000	0.9999	0.9998	0.9997	0.9994
6	1.0000	1.0000	1.0000	1.0000	1.0000	1.0000	1.0000	1.0000	1.0000	0.9999
7	1.0000	1.0000	1.0000	1.0000	1.0000	1.0000	1.0000	1.0000	1.0000	1.0000

λt	1.1	1.2	1.3	1.4	1.5	1.6	1.7	1.8	1.9	2.0
x										
0	0.3329	0.3012	0.2725	0.2466	0.2231	0.2019	0.1827	0.1653	0.1496	0.1353
1	0.6990	0.6626	0.6268	0.5918	0.5578	0.5249	0.4932	0.4628	0.4338	0.4060
2	0.9004	0.8795	0.8571	0.8335	0.8088	0.7834	0.7572	0.7306	0.7037	0.6767
3	0.9743	0.9662	0.9569	0.9463	0.9344	0.9212	0.9068	0.8913	0.8747	0.8571
4	0.9946	0.9923	0.9893	0.9857	0.9814	0.9763	0.9704	0.9636	0.9559	0.9473
5	0.9990	0.9985	0.9978	0.9968	0.9955	0.9940	0.9920	0.9896	0.9868	0.9834
6	0.9999	0.9997	0.9996	0.9994	0.9991	0.9987	0.9981	0.9974	0.9966	0.9955
7	1.0000	1.0000	0.9999	0.9999	0.9998	0.9997	0.9996	0.9994	0.9992	0.9989
8	1.0000	1.0000	1.0000	1.0000	1.0000	1.0000	0.9999	0.9999	0.9998	0.9998
9	1.0000	1.0000	1.0000	1.0000	1.0000	1.0000	1.0000	1.0000	1.0000	1.0000

λt	2.1	2.2	2.3	2.4	2.5	2.6	2.7	2.8	2.9	3.0
x										
0	0.1225	0.1108	0.1003	0.0907	0.0821	0.0743	0.0672	0.0608	0.0550	0.0498
1	0.3796	0.3546	0.3309	0.3084	0.2873	0.2674	0.2487	0.2311	0.2146	0.1991
2	0.6496	0.6227	0.5960	0.5697	0.5438	0.5184	0.4936	0.4695	0.4460	0.4232
3	0.8386	0.8194	0.7993	0.7787	0.7576	0.7360	0.7141	0.6919	0.6696	0.6472
4	0.9379	0.9275	0.9162	0.9041	0.8912	0.8774	0.8629	0.8477	0.8318	0.8153
5	0.9796	0.9751	0.9700	0.9643	0.9580	0.9510	0.9433	0.9349	0.9258	0.9161
6	0.9941	0.9925	0.9906	0.9884	0.9858	0.9828	0.9794	0.9756	0.9713	0.9665
7	0.9985	0.9980	0.9974	0.9967	0.9958	0.9947	0.9934	0.9919	0.9901	0.9881
8	0.9997	0.9995	0.9994	0.9991	0.9989	0.9985	0.9981	0.9976	0.9969	0.9962
9	0.9999	0.9999	0.9999	0.9998	0.9997	0.9996	0.9995	0.9993	0.9991	0.9989
10	1.0000	1.0000	1.0000	1.0000	0.9999	0.9999	0.9999	0.9998	0.9998	0.9997
11	1.0000	1.0000	1.0000	1.0000	1.0000	1.0000	1.0000	1.0000	0.9999	0.9999
12	1.0000	1.0000	1.0000	1.0000	1.0000	1.0000	1.0000	1.0000	1.0000	1.0000

λt	3.1	3.2	3.3	3.4	3.5	3.6	3.7	3.8	3.9	4.0
x										
0	0.0450	0.0408	0.0369	0.0334	0.0302	0.0273	0.0247	0.0224	0.0202	0.0183
1	0.1847	0.1712	0.1586	0.1468	0.1359	0.1257	0.1162	0.1074	0.0992	0.0916
2	0.4012	0.3799	0.3594	0.3397	0.3208	0.3027	0.2854	0.2689	0.2531	0.2381
3	0.6248	0.6025	0.5803	0.5584	0.5366	0.5152	0.4942	0.4735	0.4533	0.4335
4	0.7982	0.7806	0.7626	0.7442	0.7254	0.7064	0.6872	0.6578	0.6484	0.6288
5	0.9057	0.8946	0.8829	0.8705	0.8576	0.8441	0.8301	0.8156	0.8006	0.7851
6	0.9612	0.9554	0.9490	0.9421	0.9347	0.9267	0.9182	0.9091	0.8995	0.8893
7	0.9858	0.9832	0.9802	0.9769	0.9733	0.9692	0.9648	0.9599	0.9546	0.9489
8	0.9953	0.9943	0.9931	0.9917	0.9901	0.9883	0.9863	0.9840	0.9815	0.9786
9	0.9986	0.9982	0.9978	0.9973	0.9967	0.9960	0.9952	0.9942	0.9931	0.9919

TABLE K   (*continued*)

λt	3.1	3.2	3.3	3.4	3.5	3.6	3.7	3.8	3.9	4.0
x										
10	0.9996	0.9995	0.9994	0.9992	0.9990	0.9987	0.9984	0.9981	0.9977	0.9972
11	0.9999	0.9999	0.9998	0.9998	0.9997	0.9996	0.9995	0.9994	0.9993	0.9991
12	1.0000	1.0000	1.0000	0.9999	0.9999	0.9999	0.9999	0.9998	0.9998	0.9997
13	1.0000	1.0000	1.0000	1.0000	1.0000	1.0000	1.0000	1.0000	0.9999	0.9999
14	1.0000	1.0000	1.0000	1.0000	1.0000	1.0000	1.0000	1.0000	1.0000	1.0000

λt	4.1	4.2	4.3	4.4	4.5	4.6	4.7	4.8	4.9	5.0
x										
0	0.0166	0.0150	0.0136	0.0123	0.0111	0.0101	0.0091	0.0082	0.0074	0.0067
1	0.0845	0.0780	0.0719	0.0663	0.0611	0.0563	0.0518	0.0477	0.0439	0.0404
2	0.2238	0.2102	0.1974	0.1851	0.1736	0.1626	0.1523	0.1425	0.1333	0.1247
3	0.4142	0.3954	0.3772	0.3595	0.3423	0.3257	0.3097	0.2942	0.2793	0.2650
4	0.6093	0.5898	0.5704	0.5512	0.5321	0.5132	0.4946	0.4763	0.4582	0.4405
5	0.7693	0.7531	0.7367	0.7199	0.7029	0.6858	0.6684	0.6510	0.6335	0.6160
6	0.8735	0.8675	0.8558	0.8436	0.8311	0.8180	0.8046	0.7908	0.7767	0.7622
7	0.9427	0.9361	0.9290	0.9214	0.9134	0.9049	0.8960	0.8867	0.8769	0.8666
8	0.9755	0.9721	0.9683	0.9642	0.9597	0.9549	0.9497	0.9442	0.9382	0.9319
9	0.9905	0.9889	0.9871	0.9851	0.9829	0.9805	0.9778	0.9749	0.9717	0.9682
10	0.9966	0.9959	0.9952	0.9943	0.9933	0.9922	0.9910	0.9896	0.9880	0.9863
11	0.9989	0.9986	0.9983	0.9980	0.9976	0.9971	0.9966	0.9960	0.9953	0.9945
12	0.9997	0.9996	0.9995	0.9993	0.9992	0.9990	0.9988	0.9986	0.9983	0.9980
13	0.9999	0.9999	0.9998	0.9998	0.9997	0.9997	0.9996	0.9995	0.9994	0.9993
14	1.0000	1.0000	1.0000	0.9999	0.9999	0.9999	0.9999	0.9999	0.9998	0.9998
15	1.0000	1.0000	1.0000	1.0000	1.0000	1.0000	1.0000	1.0000	0.9999	0.9999
16	1.0000	1.0000	1.0000	1.0000	1.0000	1.0000	1.0000	1.0000	1.0000	1.0000

λt	5.1	5.2	5.3	5.4	5.5	5.6	5.7	5.8	5.9	6.0
x										
0	0.0061	0.0055	0.0050	0.0045	0.0041	0.0037	0.0033	0.0030	0.0027	0.0025
1	0.0372	0.0342	0.0314	0.0289	0.0266	0.0244	0.0224	0.0206	0.0189	0.0174
2	0.1165	0.1088	0.1016	0.0948	0.0884	0.0824	0.0768	0.0715	0.0666	0.0620
3	0.2513	0.2381	0.2254	0.2133	0.2017	0.1906	0.1801	0.1700	0.1604	0.1512
4	0.4231	0.4061	0.3895	0.3733	0.3575	0.3422	0.3272	0.3127	0.2987	0.2851
5	0.5984	0.5809	0.5635	0.5461	0.5289	0.5119	0.4950	0.4783	0.4619	0.4457
6	0.7474	0.7324	0.7171	0.7017	0.6860	0.6703	0.6544	0.6384	0.6224	0.6063
7	0.8560	0.8449	0.8335	0.8217	0.8095	0.7970	0.7842	0.7710	0.7576	0.7440
8	0.9252	0.9181	0.9106	0.9026	0.8944	0.8857	0.8766	0.8672	0.8574	0.8472
9	0.9644	0.9603	0.9559	0.9512	0.9462	0.9409	0.9352	0.9292	0.9228	0.9161
10	0.9844	0.9823	0.9800	0.9775	0.9747	0.9718	0.9686	0.9651	0.9614	0.9574
11	0.9937	0.9927	0.9916	0.9904	0.9890	0.9875	0.9859	0.9840	0.9821	0.9799
12	0.9976	0.9972	0.9967	0.9962	0.9955	0.9949	0.9941	0.9932	0.9922	0.9912
13	0.9992	0.9990	0.9988	0.9986	0.9983	0.9980	0.9977	0.9973	0.9969	0.9964
14	0.9997	0.9997	0.9996	0.9995	0.9994	0.9993	0.9991	0.9990	0.9988	0.9986
15	0.9999	0.9999	0.9999	0.9998	0.9998	0.9998	0.9997	0.9996	0.9996	0.9995
16	1.0000	1.0000	1.0000	0.9999	0.9999	0.9999	0.9999	0.9999	0.9999	0.9998
17	1.0000	1.0000	1.0000	1.0000	1.0000	1.0000	1.0000	1.0000	1.0000	0.9999
18	1.0000	1.0000	1.0000	1.0000	1.0000	1.0000	1.0000	1.0000	1.0000	1.0000

TABLE K   (*continued*)

λt	6.1	6.2	6.3	6.4	6.5	6.6	6.7	6.8	6.9	7.0
x										
0	0.0022	0.0020	0.0018	0.0017	0.0015	0.0014	0.0012	0.0011	0.0010	0.0009
1	0.0159	0.0146	0.0134	0.0123	0.0113	0.0103	0.0095	0.0087	0.0080	0.0073
2	0.0577	0.0536	0.0498	0.0463	0.0430	0.0400	0.0371	0.0344	0.0320	0.0296
3	0.1425	0.1342	0.1264	0.1189	0.1119	0.1052	0.0988	0.0928	0.0871	0.0818
4	0.2719	0.2592	0.2469	0.2351	0.2237	0.2127	0.2022	0.1920	0.1823	0.1730
5	0.4298	0.4141	0.3988	0.3837	0.3690	0.3547	0.3407	0.3270	0.3137	0.3007
6	0.5902	0.5742	0.5582	0.5423	0.5265	0.5108	0.4953	0.4799	0.4647	0.4497
7	0.7301	0.7160	0.7018	0.6873	0.6728	0.6581	0.6433	0.6285	0.6136	0.5987
8	0.8367	0.8259	0.8148	0.8033	0.7916	0.7796	0.7673	0.7548	0.7420	0.7291
9	0.9090	0.9016	0.8939	0.8858	0.8774	0.8686	0.8596	0.8502	0.8405	0.8305
10	0.9531	0.9486	0.9437	0.9386	0.9332	0.9274	0.9214	0.9151	0.9084	0.9015
11	0.9776	0.9750	0.9723	0.9693	0.9661	0.9627	0.9591	0.9552	0.9510	0.9466
12	0.9900	0.9887	0.9873	0.9857	0.9840	0.9821	0.9801	0.9779	0.9755	0.9730
13	0.9958	0.9952	0.9945	0.9937	0.9929	0.9920	0.9909	0.9898	0.9885	0.9872
14	0.9984	0.9981	0.9978	0.9974	0.9970	0.9966	0.9961	0.9956	0.9950	0.9943
15	0.9994	0.9993	0.9992	0.9990	0.9988	0.9986	0.9984	0.9982	0.9979	0.9976
16	0.9998	0.9997	0.9997	0.9996	0.9996	0.9995	0.9994	0.9993	0.9992	0.9990
17	0.9999	0.9999	0.9999	0.9999	0.9998	0.9998	0.9998	0.9997	0.9997	0.9996
18	1.0000	1.0000	1.0000	1.0000	0.9999	0.9999	0.9999	0.9999	0.9999	0.9999
19	1.0000	1.0000	1.0000	1.0000	1.0000	1.0000	1.0000	1.0000	1.0000	0.9999
20	1.0000	1.0000	1.0000	1.0000	1.0000	1.0000	1.0000	1.0000	1.0000	1.0000

λt	7.1	7.2	7.3	7.4	7.5	7.6	7.7	7.8	7.9	8.0
x										
0	0.0008	0.0007	0.0007	0.0006	0.0006	0.0005	0.0005	0.0004	0.0004	0.0003
1	0.0067	0.0061	0.0056	0.0051	0.0047	0.0043	0.0039	0.0036	0.0033	0.0030
2	0.0275	0.0255	0.0236	0.0219	0.0203	0.0188	0.0174	0.0161	0.0149	0.0138
3	0.0767	0.0719	0.0674	0.0632	0.0591	0.0554	0.0518	0.0485	0.0453	0.0424
4	0.1641	0.1555	0.1473	0.1395	0.1321	0.1249	0.1181	0.1117	0.1055	0.0996
5	0.2881	0.2759	0.2640	0.2526	0.2414	0.2307	0.2203	0.2103	0.2006	0.1912
6	0.4349	0.4204	0.4060	0.3920	0.3782	0.3646	0.3514	0.3384	0.3257	0.3134
7	0.5838	0.5689	0.5541	0.5393	0.5246	0.5100	0.4956	0.4812	0.4670	0.4530
8	0.7160	0.7027	0.6892	0.6757	0.6620	0.6482	0.6343	0.6204	0.6065	0.5926
9	0.8202	0.8096	0.7988	0.7877	0.7764	0.7649	0.7531	0.7411	0.7290	0.7166
10	0.8942	0.8867	0.8788	0.8707	0.8622	0.8535	0.8445	0.8352	0.8257	0.8159
11	0.9420	0.9371	0.9319	0.9265	0.9208	0.9148	0.9085	0.9020	0.8952	0.8881
12	0.9703	0.9673	0.9642	0.9609	0.9573	0.9536	0.9496	0.9453	0.9409	0.9362
13	0.9857	0.9841	0.9824	0.9805	0.9784	0.9762	0.9739	0.9714	0.9687	0.9658
14	0.9935	0.9927	0.9918	0.9908	0.9897	0.9886	0.9873	0.9859	0.9844	0.9827
15	0.9972	0.9968	0.9964	0.9959	0.9954	0.9948	0.9941	0.9934	0.9926	0.9918
16	0.9989	0.9987	0.9985	0.9983	0.9980	0.9978	0.9974	0.9971	0.9967	0.9963
17	0.9996	0.9995	0.9994	0.9993	0.9992	0.9991	0.9989	0.9988	0.9986	0.9984
18	0.9998	0.9998	0.9998	0.9997	0.9997	0.9996	0.9996	0.9995	0.9994	0.9993
19	0.9999	0.9999	0.9999	0.9999	0.9999	0.9999	0.9998	0.9998	0.9998	0.9997
20	1.0000	1.0000	1.0000	1.0000	1.0000	0.9999	0.9999	0.9999	0.9999	0.9999
21	1.0000	1.0000	1.0000	1.0000	1.0000	1.0000	1.0000	1.0000	1.0000	1.0000

TABLE K

λt	8.1	8.2	8.3	8.4	8.5	8.6	8.7	8.8	8.9	9.0
x										
0	0.0003	0.0003	0.0002	0.0002	0.0002	0.0002	0.0002	0.0002	0.0001	0.0001
1	0.0028	0.0025	0.0023	0.0021	0.0019	0.0018	0.0016	0.0015	0.0014	0.0012
2	0.0127	0.0118	0.0109	0.0100	0.0093	0.0086	0.0079	0.0073	0.0068	0.0062
3	0.0396	0.0370	0.0346	0.0323	0.0301	0.0281	0.0262	0.0244	0.0228	0.0212
4	0.0941	0.0887	0.0837	0.0789	0.0744	0.0701	0.0660	0.0621	0.0584	0.0550
5	0.1822	0.1736	0.1653	0.1573	0.1496	0.1422	0.1352	0.1284	0.1219	0.1157
6	0.3013	0.2896	0.2781	0.2670	0.2562	0.2457	0.2355	0.2256	0.2160	0.2068
7	0.4391	0.4254	0.4119	0.3987	0.3856	0.3728	0.3602	0.3478	0.3357	0.3239
8	0.5786	0.5647	0.5508	0.5369	0.5231	0.5094	0.4958	0.4823	0.4689	0.4557
9	0.7041	0.6915	0.6788	0.6659	0.6530	0.6400	0.6269	0.6137	0.6006	0.5874
10	0.8058	0.7955	0.7850	0.7743	0.7634	0.7522	0.7409	0.7294	0.7178	0.7060
11	0.8807	0.8731	0.8652	0.8571	0.8487	0.8400	0.8311	0.8220	0.8126	0.8030
12	0.9313	0.9261	0.9207	0.9150	0.9091	0.9029	0.8965	0.8898	0.8829	0.8758
13	0.9628	0.9595	0.9561	0.9524	0.9486	0.9445	0.9403	0.9358	0.9311	0.9262
14	0.9810	0.9791	0.9771	0.9749	0.9726	0.9701	0.9675	0.9647	0.9617	0.9585
15	0.9903	0.9898	0.9887	0.9875	0.9862	0.9847	0.9832	0.9816	0.9798	0.9780
16	0.9958	0.9953	0.9947	0.9941	0.9934	0.9926	0.9918	0.9909	0.9899	0.9889
17	0.9982	0.9979	0.9976	0.9973	0.9970	0.9966	0.9962	0.9957	0.9952	0.9947
18	0.9992	0.9991	0.9990	0.9989	0.9987	0.9985	0.9983	0.9981	0.9978	0.9976
19	0.9997	0.9996	0.9996	0.9995	0.9995	0.9994	0.9993	0.9992	0.9991	0.9989
20	0.9999	0.9999	0.9998	0.9998	0.9998	0.9997	0.9997	0.9997	0.9996	0.9996
21	1.0000	0.9999	0.9999	0.9999	0.9999	0.9999	0.9999	0.9999	0.9998	0.9998
22	1.0000	1.0000	1.0000	1.0000	1.0000	1.0000	1.0000	1.0000	0.9999	0.9999
23	1.0000	1.0000	1.0000	1.0000	1.0000	1.0000	1.0000	1.0000	1.0000	1.0000

λt	9.1	9.2	9.3	9.4	9.5	9.6	9.7	9.8	9.9	10.0
x										
0	0.0001	0.0001	0.0001	0.0001	0.0001	0.0001	0.0001	0.0001	0.0001	0.0000
1	0.0011	0.0010	0.0009	0.0009	0.0008	0.0007	0.0007	0.0006	0.0005	0.0005
2	0.0058	0.0053	0.0049	0.0045	0.0042	0.0038	0.0035	0.0033	0.0030	0.0028
3	0.0198	0.0184	0.0172	0.0160	0.0149	0.0138	0.0129	0.0120	0.0111	0.0103
4	0.0517	0.0486	0.0456	0.0429	0.0403	0.0378	0.0355	0.0333	0.0312	0.0293
5	0.1098	0.1041	0.0987	0.0935	0.0885	0.0838	0.0793	0.0750	0.0710	0.0671
6	0.1973	0.1892	0.1808	0.1727	0.1650	0.1575	0.1502	0.1433	0.1366	0.1301
7	0.3123	0.3010	0.2900	0.2792	0.2687	0.2584	0.2485	0.2388	0.2294	0.2202
8	0.4426	0.4296	0.4168	0.4042	0.3918	0.3796	0.3676	0.3558	0.3442	0.3328
9	0.5742	0.5611	0.5479	0.5349	0.5218	0.5089	0.4960	0.4832	0.4705	0.4579
10	0.6941	0.6820	0.6699	0.6576	0.6453	0.6330	0.6205	0.6080	0.5955	0.5830
11	0.7932	0.7832	0.7730	0.7626	0.7520	0.7412	0.7303	0.7193	0.7081	0.6968
12	0.8684	0.8607	0.8529	0.8448	0.8364	0.8279	0.8191	0.8101	0.8009	0.7916
13	0.9210	0.9156	0.9100	0.9042	0.8981	0.8919	0.8853	0.8786	0.8716	0.8645
14	0.9552	0.9517	0.9480	0.9441	0.9400	0.9357	0.9312	0.9265	0.9216	0.9165
15	0.9760	0.9738	0.9715	0.9691	0.9665	0.9638	0.9609	0.9579	0.9546	0.9513
16	0.9878	0.9865	0.9852	0.9838	0.9823	0.9806	0.9789	0.9770	0.9751	0.9730
17	0.9941	0.9934	0.9927	0.9919	0.9911	0.9902	0.9892	0.9881	0.9869	0.9857
18	0.9973	0.9969	0.9966	0.9962	0.9957	0.9952	0.9947	0.9941	0.9935	0.9928
19	0.9988	0.9986	0.9985	0.9983	0.9980	0.9976	0.9975	0.9972	0.9969	0.9965
20	0.9995	0.9994	0.9993	0.9992	0.9991	0.9990	0.9989	0.9987	0.9986	0.9984
21	0.9998	0.9998	0.9997	0.9997	0.9996	0.9996	0.9995	0.9995	0.9994	0.9993
22	0.9999	0.9999	0.9999	0.9999	0.9998	0.9998	0.9998	0.9998	0.9997	0.9997
23	1.0000	1.0000	1.0000	0.9999	0.9999	0.9999	0.9999	0.9999	0.9999	0.9999
24	1.0000	1.0000	1.0000	1.0000	1.0000	1.0000	1.0000	1.0000	0.9999	0.9999
25	1.0000	1.0000	1.0000	1.0000	1.0000	1.0000	1.0000	1.0000	1.0000	1.0000

TABLE K (*continued*)—

λt	11.0	12.0	13.0	14.0	15.0	16.0	17.0	18.0	19.0	20.0
x										
0	0.0000	0.0000	0.0000	0.0000	0.0000	0.0000	0.0	0.0	0.0	0.0
1	0.0002	0.0001	0.0000	0.0000	0.0000	0.0000	0.0000	0.0000	0.0000	0.0
2	0.0012	0.0005	0.0002	0.0001	0.0000	0.0000	0.0000	0.0000	0.0000	0.0000
3	0.0049	0.0023	0.0011	0.0005	0.0002	0.0001	0.0000	0.0000	0.0000	0.0000
4	0.0151	0.0076	0.0037	0.0018	0.0009	0.0004	0.0002	0.0001	0.0000	0.0000
5	0.0375	0.0203	0.0107	0.0055	0.0028	0.0014	0.0007	0.0003	0.0002	0.0001
6	0.0786	0.0458	0.0259	0.0142	0.0076	0.0040	0.0021	0.0010	0.0005	0.0003
7	0.1432	0.0895	0.0540	0.0316	0.0180	0.0100	0.0054	0.0029	0.0015	0.0008
8	0.2320	0.1550	0.0998	0.0621	0.0374	0.0220	0.0126	0.0071	0.0039	0.0021
9	0.3405	0.2424	0.1658	0.1094	0.0699	0.0433	0.0261	0.0154	0.0089	0.0050
10	0.4599	0.3472	0.2517	0.1757	0.1185	0.0774	0.0491	0.0304	0.0183	0.0108
11	0.5793	0.4616	0.3532	0.2600	0.1847	0.1270	0.0847	0.0549	0.0347	0.0214
12	0.6887	0.5760	0.4631	0.3585	0.2676	0.1931	0.1350	0.0917	0.0606	0.0390
13	0.7813	0.6815	0.5730	0.4644	0.3632	0.2745	0.2009	0.1426	0.0984	0.0661
14	0.8540	0.7720	0.6751	0.5704	0.4656	0.3675	0.2808	0.2081	0.1497	0.1049
15	0.9074	0.8444	0.7636	0.6694	0.5681	0.4667	0.3714	0.2866	0.2148	0.1565
16	0.9441	0.8987	0.8355	0.7559	0.6641	0.5660	0.4677	0.3750	0.2920	0.2211
17	0.9678	0.9370	0.8905	0.8272	0.7489	0.6593	0.5640	0.4686	0.3784	0.2970
18	0.9823	0.9626	0.9302	0.8826	0.8195	0.7423	0.6549	0.5622	0.4695	0.3814
19	0.9907	0.9787	0.9573	0.9235	0.8752	0.8122	0.7363	0.6509	0.5606	0.4703
20	0.9953	0.9884	0.9750	0.9521	0.9170	0.8682	0.8055	0.7307	0.6472	0.5591
21	0.9977	0.9939	0.9859	0.9711	0.9469	0.9108	0.8615	0.7991	0.7255	0.6437
22	0.9989	0.9969	0.9924	0.9833	0.9672	0.9418	0.9047	0.8551	0.7931	0.7206
23	0.9995	0.9985	0.9960	0.9907	0.9805	0.9633	0.9367	0.8989	0.8490	0.7875
24	0.9998	0.9993	0.9980	0.9950	0.9888	0.9777	0.9593	0.9317	0.8933	0.8432
25	0.9999	0.9997	0.9990	0.9974	0.9938	0.9869	0.9747	0.9554	0.9269	0.8878
26	1.0000	0.9999	0.9995	0.9987	0.9967	0.9925	0.9848	0.9718	0.9514	0.9221
27	1.0000	0.9999	0.9998	0.9994	0.9983	0.9959	0.9912	0.9827	0.9687	0.9475
28	1.0000	1.0000	0.9999	0.9997	0.9991	0.9978	0.9950	0.9897	0.9805	0.9657
29	1.0000	1.0000	1.0000	0.9999	0.9996	0.9989	0.9973	0.9940	0.9881	0.9782
30	1.0000	1.0000	1.0000	0.9999	0.9998	0.9994	0.9985	0.9967	0.9930	0.9865
31	1.0000	1.0000	1.0000	1.0000	0.9999	0.9997	0.9992	0.9982	0.9960	0.9919
32	1.0000	1.0000	1.0000	1.0000	0.9999	0.9999	0.9996	0.9990	0.9978	0.9953
33	1.0000	1.0000	1.0000	1.0000	1.0000	0.9999	0.9998	0.9995	0.9988	0.9973
34	1.0000	1.0000	1.0000	1.0000	1.0000	1.0000	0.9999	0.9997	0.9994	0.9985
35	1.0000	1.0000	1.0000	1.0000	1.0000	1.0000	0.9999	0.9999	0.9997	0.9992
36	1.0000	1.0000	1.0000	1.0000	1.0000	1.0000	1.0000	0.9999	0.9998	0.9996
37	1.0000	1.0000	1.0000	1.0000	1.0000	1.0000	1.0000	1.0000	0.9999	0.9998
38	1.0000	1.0000	1.0000	1.0000	1.0000	1.0000	1.0000	1.0000	1.0000	0.9999
39	1.0000	1.0000	1.0000	1.0000	1.0000	1.0000	1.0000	1.0000	1.0000	0.9999
40	1.0000	1.0000	1.0000	1.0000	1.0000	1.0000	1.0000	1.0000	1.0000	1.0000

TABLE L   Critical Values of D for Kolmogorov-Smirnov
Maximum Deviation Test for Goodness of Fit

The following table provides the critical values D_α corresponding to an upper-tail probability α of the test statistic D. The following relationship holds

$$P[D_\alpha \leq D] = \alpha$$

n	$\alpha = .10$	$\alpha = .05$	$\alpha = .025$	$\alpha = .01$	$\alpha = .005$
1	.90000	.95000	.97500	.99000	.99500
2	.68377	.77639	.84189	.90000	.92929
3	.56481	.63604	.70760	.78456	.82900
4	.49265	.56522	.62394	.68887	.73424
5	.44698	.50945	.56328	.62718	.66853
6	.41037	.46799	.51926	.57741	.61661
7	.38148	.43607	.48342	.53844	.57581
8	.35831	.40962	.45427	.50654	.54179
9	.33910	.38746	.43001	.47960	.51332
10	.32260	.36866	.40925	.45662	.48893
11	.30829	.35242	.39122	.43670	.46770
12	.29577	.33815	.37543	.41918	.44905
13	.28470	.32549	.36143	.40362	.43247
14	.27481	.31417	.34890	.38970	.41762
15	.26588	.30397	.33760	.37713	.40420
16	.25778	.29472	.32733	.36571	.39201
17	.25039	.28627	.31796	.35528	.38086
18	.24360	.27851	.30936	.34569	.37062
19	.23735	.27136	.30143	.33685	.36117
20	.23156	.26473	.29408	.32866	.35241
21	.22617	.25858	.28724	.32104	.34427
22	.22115	.25283	.28087	.31394	.33666
23	.21645	.24746	.27490	.30728	.32954
24	.21205	.24242	.26931	.30104	.32286
25	.20790	.23768	.26404	.29516	.31657
26	.20399	.23320	.25907	.28962	.31064
27	.20030	.22898	.25438	.28438	.30502
28	.19680	.22497	.24993	.27942	.29971
29	.19348	.22117	.24571	.27471	.29466
30	.19032	.21756	.24170	.27023	.28987
31	.18732	.21412	.23788	.26596	.28530
30	.18445	.21085	.23424	.26189	.28094
33	.18171	.20771	.23076	.25801	.27677
34	.17909	.20472	.22743	2.5429	.27279
35	.17659	.20185	.22425	.25073	.26897
36	.17418	.19910	.22119	.24732	.26532
37	.17188	.19646	.21826	.24404	.26180
38	.16966	.19392	.21544	.24089	.25843
39	.16753	.19148	.21273	.23786	.25518
40	.16547	.18913	.21012	.23494	.25205

TABLE L   (*continued*)

n	α = .10	α = .05	α = .025	α = .01	α = .005
41	.16349	.18687	.20760	.23213	.24904
42	.16158	.18468	.20517	.22941	.24613
43	.15974	.18257	.20283	.22679	.24332
44	.15796	.18053	.20056	.22426	.24060
45	.15623	.17856	.19837	.22181	.23798
46	.15457	.17665	.19625	.21944	.23544
47	.15295	.17481	.19420	.21715	.23298
48	.15139	.17302	.19221	.21493	.23059
49	.14987	.17128	.19028	.21277	.22828
50	.14840	.16959	.18841	.21068	.22604
51	.14697	.16796	.18659	.20864	.22386
52	.14558	.16637	.18482	.20667	.22174
53	.14423	.16483	.18311	.20475	.21968
54	.14292	.16332	.18144	.20289	.21768
55	.14164	.16186	.17981	.20107	.21574
56	.14040	.16044	.17823	.19930	.21384
57	.13919	.15906	.17669	.19758	.21199
58	.13801	.15771	.17519	.19590	.21019
59	.13686	.15639	.17373	.19427	.20844
60	.13573	.15511	.17231	.19267	.20673
61	.13464	.15385	.17091	.19112	.20506
62	.13357	.15263	.16956	.18960	.20343
63	.13253	.15144	.16823	.18812	.20184
64	.13151	.15027	.16693	.18667	.20029
65	.13052	.14913	.16567	.18525	.19877
66	.12954	.14802	.16443	.18387	.19729
67	.12859	.14693	.16322	.18252	.19584
68	.12766	.14587	.16204	.18119	.19442
69	.12675	.14483	.16088	.17990	.19303
70	.12586	.14381	.15975	.17863	.19167
71	.12499	.14281	.15864	.17739	.19034
72	.12413	.14183	.15755	.17618	.18903
73	.12329	.14087	.15649	.17498	.18776
74	.12247	.13993	.15544	.17382	.18650
75	.12167	.13901	.15442	.17268	.18528
76	.12088	.13811	.15342	.17155	.18408
77	.12011	.13723	.15244	.17045	.18290
78	.11935	.13636	.15147	.16938	.18174
79	.11860	.13551	.15052	.16832	.18060
80	.11787	.13467	.14960	.16728	.17949
81	.11716	.13385	.14868	.16626	.17840
82	.11645	.13305	.14779	.16526	.17732
83	.11576	.13226	.14691	.16428	.17627
84	.11508	.13148	.14605	.16331	.17523
85	.11442	.13072	.14520	.16236	.17421

TABLE L   *(continued)*

n	α = .10	α = .05	α = .025	α = .01	α = .005
86	.11376	.12997	.14437	.16143	.17321
87	.11311	.12923	.14355	.16051	.17223
88	.11248	.12850	.14274	.15961	.17126
89	.11186	.12779	.14195	.15873	.17031
90	.11125	.12709	.14117	.15786	.16938
91	.11064	.12640	.14040	.15700	.16846
92	.11005	.12572	.13965	.15616	.16755
93	.10947	.12506	.13891	.15533	.16666
94	.10889	.12440	.13818	.15451	.16579
95	.10833	.12375	.13746	.15371	.16493
96	.10777	.12312	.13675	.15291	.16408
97	.10722	.12249	.13606	.15214	.16324
98	.10668	.12187	.13537	.15137	.16242
99	.10615	.12126	.13469	.15061	.16161
100	.10563	.12067	.13403	.14987	.16081

SOURCE : Reprinted by permission from L. H. Miller, " Table of Percentage Points of Kolmogorov Statistics," *Journal of the American Statistical Association*, 51 (1956), pages 111–121.

Answers to Even-Numbered Exercises

2–2 Answers may vary.

2–4 (a)

Class Interval	Frequency
$3,000–under 7,000	10
7,000–under 11,000	26
11,000–under 15,000	8
15,000–under 19,000	3
19,000–under 23,000	1
23,000–under 27,000	2
	50

2–6 (b)

Class Interval	Frequency East	West	Combined Frequency
$2.50–under 3.00	150	0	150
3.00–under 3.50	300	0	300
3.50–under 4.00	150	0	150
4.00–under 4.50	100	0	100
4.50–under 5.00	50	50	100
5.00–under 5.50	50	150	200
5.50–under 6.00	50	150	200
6.00–under 6.50	50	200	250
6.50–under 7.00	50	100	150

(d) Separate graphs are better.

2–8 Intervals of width $.05 would be too small, while $1 and $2 intervals would be too wide.

2–10 (a)–(c) Class intervals must not overlap and must encompass all possible values.

2–12

Consecutive Days Absent	(a) Relative Frequency	(b) Cumulative Relative Frequency
0–less than 5	.620	.620
5–less than 10	.162	.782
10–less than 15	.102	.884
15–less than 20	.064	.948
20–less than 25	.024	.972
25–less than 30	.006	.978
30–less than 60	.022	1.000

2–14

Number of Shares	(a) Relative Frequency	(b) Frequency	(c) Cumulative Frequency
0–under 5,000	.36	360	360
5,000–under 10,000	.27	270	630
10,000–under 15,000	.18	180	810
15,000–under 20,000	.09	90	900
20,000–under 25,000	.07	70	970
25,000–under 30,000	.03	30	1,000

2–16 Answers may vary.

2–18

Class Interval	Relative Frequency	Cumulative Frequency
20–under 25	.18	18
25–under 30	.23	41
30–under 35	.15	56
35–under 40	.13	69
40–under 45	.07	76
45–under 50	.06	82
50–under 55	.05	87
55–under 60	.05	92
60–under 65	.08	100
	1.00	

2–20 (a)

Sex	Frequency
Male	220
Female	130
	350

(b)

Marital Status	Frequency
Married	171
Single	179
	350

(c)

Occupation	Frequency
Blue collar	155
White collar	173
Professional	22
	350

3–2 $\bar{X} = 93.8$ for CompuQuick
$\bar{X} = 192.125$ for Dial-a-Pute

3–4 26.0 feet

3–6 $\bar{X} = 2.75$ $m = 2$ mode $= 2$

3–8 $m = \$2,129$

3–10 Answers may vary.

3–12 $s^2 = 184.3$ $s = 13.6$

3–14 $\bar{X} = 26.15$ $s = 21.11$

3–16 $\bar{X} = 2.75$ $s = .63$

3–18 Firm   A   B   C   D   E
Proportion .0624 .178 .0629 .113 .125

3–20

	(1)	(2)	(3)	(4)
(a) P	.07	.05	.017	.039
(b)	reject	accept	accept	accept

3–22 (a) 4   (b) 2.0   (c) 1.33

3–24 (a) 1,400 to 1,600; 68%
(b) 1,300 to 1,700; 95.5%
(c) 1,200 to 1,800; 99.7%

3–26 $\bar{X} = 126.2$ $s^2 = 385.41$

3–28 (a) $\bar{X} = 77.615$ $s^2 = 208.55$
(b) $\bar{X} = 78.077$ $s^2 = 176.14$
(c) error $= -0.462$

4–2 Answers may vary.

4–4 Answers may vary.

4–6 Answers may vary.

4–8 Answers may vary.

4–10 (a) convenience   (b) judgment
(c) random
(d) judgment or convenience

4–12 Answers may vary.

4–14 A judgment-convenience sample applies.

4–16 Solti, Maag, Abbado, Rozhdestvensky, Bloomfield, Krips, Prêtre, Frühbeck de Burgos, Newman, Schippers

4–18 Beecham, Dragon, Golschmann, Karajan, Krips, Pedrotti, Rignold, Scherchen, Stein, Svetlanov

5–2 (a) $\{(H, H, T), (H, T, H), (T, H, H)\}$
(b) $\{(H, T, H), (T, H, T)\}$
(c) $\{(H, H, H), (H, T, H),$
$(T, H, H), (T, T, H)\}$
(d) $\{(H, H, T), (H, T, H),$
$(T, H, H), (T, T, T)\}$

5–4 (a) (1, 4), (4, 1), (2, 3), (3, 2), (3, 3),
(1, 5), (5, 1), (2, 4), (4, 2), (1, 6),
(6, 1), (2, 5), (5, 2), (3, 4), (4, 3)
15/36

(b) (2, 6), (6, 2), (3, 5), (5, 3), (4, 4),
(3, 6), (6, 3), (4, 5), (5, 4), (5, 5),
(4, 6), (6, 4), (5, 6), (6, 5), (6, 6)
15/36
(c) (1, 1), (1, 2), (2, 1), (4, 6), (6, 4),
(5, 5), (5, 6), (6, 5), (6, 6)
9/36 = 1/4
(d) (1, 1), (2, 2), (3, 3), (4, 4), (5, 5),
(6, 6)
6/36 = 1/6
(e) (2, 1), (3, 1), (4, 1), (5, 1), (6, 1),
(3, 2), (4, 2), (5, 2), (6, 2), (4, 3),
(5, 3), (6, 3), (5, 4), (6, 4), (6, 5)
15/36
(f) (6, 3), (5, 4), (6, 4), (6, 5)
4/36 = 1/9

5–6 Sample space
$= \{0, 1, 2, 3, 4, 5, 6, 7, 8, 9, 10\}$
(a) $\{3, 4, 5, 6, 7\}$ (b) $\{8, 9, 10\}$
(c) $\{0, 1, 2, 3, 4\}$
(d) $\{0, 1, 2, 3, 4, 9, 10\}$
(e) $\{0, 1, 2, 3, 4, 5, 6\}$

5–8 (a) and (b) are not collectively exhaustive, while events in (c) are.

5–10 (a) (1) $\{1, 3\}$ (2) $\{3, 4\}$
(3) $\{2, 3\}$ (4) $\{0, 1, 2, 3\}$
(5) $\{3\}$
(b) (1) $\{0, 2, 4\}$ (2) $\{0, 1, 2\}$
(3) $\{0, 1, 4\}$ (4) $\{4\}$
(5) $\{0, 1, 2, 4\}$

5–12 (a) .7   (b) .5   (c) .7
(d) .3   (e) .6

5–14 Only the Silver Ghost probabilities are correct.

5–16 (a) 1/13   (b) 1/26
(c) 1/2   (d) 3/13

5–18 (a) .7   (b) 0   (c) 0   (d) 1

5–20 (a) 1/2   (b) 1/2
(c) (1) 1/4   (2) 1/4

5–22 (a) 3/8   (b) 5/8

5–24 (a)

Type	Color		Marginal Probability
	Red	Green	
Striped	.20	.10	.30
Solid	.40	..30	.70
Marginal Probability	.60	.40	1.00

(b) .75   (c) not independent

5–26 (a) .729 (b) .001 (c) .243

5–28 (a) 720 (b) 364 (c) 40,320
(d) 138,600 (e) 66,045

5–30 (a) 6 (b) 3 (c) 6 (d) 1,944

5–32 C_{13}^{52}; P_{13}^{52}

5–34 (a) 20! (b) $2(10!)^2$
(c) $10!(2^{10})$

5–36 (a) (1) {K-H, Q-H, J-H, 10-H, 9-H,
8-H, 7-H, 6-H, 5-H, 4-H, 3-H,
2-H, A-H}
(2) {A-S, A-H, A-D, A-C}
(3) {3-S, 3-H, 3-D, 3-C, 2-S, 2-H,
2-D, 2-C, A-S, A-H, A-D,
A-C}
(4) {8-S, 8-H, 8-D, 8-C, 9-S, 9-H,
9-D, 9-C, 10-S, 10-H, 10-D,
10-C}
(b) (1) {A-H}
(2) {8-S, 8-H, 8-D, 8-C, 9-S, 9-H,
9-D, 9-C, 10-S, 10-H, 10-D,
10-C, A-S, A-H, A-D, A-C}
(3) { }
(4) {A-S, A-H, A-D, A-C}
(5) {3-S, 3-H, 3-D, 3-C, 2-S, 2-H,
2-D, 2-C, A-S, A-H, A-D,
A-C}

5–38 1,327,104,000

5–40 (a) neither (b) mutually exclusive
(c) both
(d) collectively exhaustive

5–42 (a) $P[R_1] = .6$ $P[R_2 \mid R_1] = .4$
$P[W_1] = .4$ $P[R_2 \mid W_1] = .7$
$P[W_2 \mid R_1] = .6$
$P[W_2 \mid W_1] = .3$
(b) $P[R_1 \text{ and } R_2] = .24$
$P[W_1 \text{ and } R_2] = .28$
$P[R_1 \text{ and } W_2] = .36$
$P[W_1 \text{ and } W_2] = .12$
(c) (1) .64 (2) .36

5–44 (a) .000005 (b) 5

5–46 (a) (1) 1/15 (2) 1/12 (3) 1/24
(4) 1/4 (5) 4/15 (6) 1/6
(7) 1/8 (8) 17/24
(9) 31/60 (10) 2/3
(b) (1) No (2) No
(3) *A and B*

5–48 .427

5–50 (a) .809 (b) .005

5–52 (a) .8 (b) .2

5–54 (a) .50 (b) 1/3 (c) 1/4

6–2

w	$P[W = w]$
$-\$1$	1/2
$+1$	1/2
	1

6–4 (a)

w	$P[W = w]$
$-\$1$	20/36
$+1$	14/36
$+2$	1/36
$+3$	1/36
	1

(b)

w	$P[W = w]$
$-\$2$	20/36
$+2$	14/36
$+4$	1/36
$+6$	1/36
	1

6–6

w	$P[W = w]$
$-\$1$	20/38
$+1$	18/38
	1

$E(W) = -\$2/38 = -\$0.053$

6–8 $E(X) = 2.1$ $\sigma^2(X) = 1.29$

6–10 (a) \$155.25 for High-Volatility Engineering
\$103.50 for Stability Power

6–12 (a) (1) .1641 (2) .2734
(3) .0078 (4) .2734
(b) They must be the same.

6–14 (a) .1390 (b) .1224 (c) .7822
(d) .0848 (e) .0009 (f) .3105

6–16 $E(P) = .10$

6–18 (a) .0000 (b) .5905 (c) .4095
(d) .0815 (e) .0815

6–20 0.0000 (rounded)

6–22 (a) .1347 (b) .1285 (c) .9672
(d) .3743 (e) .0942 (f) .9096

6–24 (a)

$\bar{x}$	$P[\bar{X} = \bar{x}]$
900	1/25
950	4/25
1,000	4/25
1,050	4/25
1,100	8/25
1,200	4/25
	1

(b) $E(\overline{X}) = 1,060$ $\sigma^2(\overline{X}) = 7,200$
$\sigma(\overline{X}) = 84.90$

6–26

x	$P[X = x]$
5	36/108
10	48/108
20	16/108
50	4/108
100	4/108
	1

6–28 $E(X) = 14.63$ $\sigma^2(X) = 360.90$
$\sigma(X) = 19.0$

6–30 (a) .04   (b) .10   (c) .03

6-32 (a)

$\bar{x}$	$P[\overline{X} = \bar{x}]$
19.5	1/10
20.0	1/10
20.5	1/10
21.0	1/10
21.5	2/10
22.0	2/10
22.5	1/10
23.5	1/10

$\sigma^2(\overline{X}) = 1.29$
$\sigma_{\bar{x}} = 1.14$

(b) $\sigma = 1.85$ $\sigma_{\bar{x}} = 1.31$

7-2 (a) .4332   (b) .1915   (c) .2420
(d) .0062   (e) .0968   (f) .9861
(g) .97585   (h) .0606

7-4 (a) $5'4.175''$ (b) $5'5.9''$
(c) $5'8.7''$ (d) $5'10.625''$
(e) $6'2.1''$ (f) $6'3.825''$

7-6 (a) .0456   (b) .0228   (c) .50003

7-8 (a) .01   (b) .10   (c) .50
(d) 2.00   (e) 10.00

7-10 (a) 4   (b) .4938   (c) .99865
(d) .0401   (e) .0994   (f) .3085

7-12 .9544

7-14 (a) .9876   (b) .7888
(c) Greater variability reduces reliability.
(d) 1 (approximately)
(e) Larger sample sizes increase reliability.

7-16 (a) .3164   (b) 1.3791   (c) .1000
(d) .3000   (e) .4359

7-18 (1) .5000   (2) .9429
(3) 1 (approximately)
Choose rule (3).

7-20 .8904 for $n = 64$; .9544 for $n = 100$; 1 (approximately) for $n = 400$. The probabilities increase with n because of greater reliability.

7-22 (a) .0116 for $N = 500$;
.0150 for $N = 1,000$
(b) .0681 for $N = 500$;
.0708 for $N = 1,000$
(c) No

7-24 (a) .0228   (b) .9544
(c) .99865   (d) .1587

7-26 (a) .6828   (b) .9876

7-28 .00135

7-30 (a) .0207   (b) .0036

7-32 (a) .4525   (b) .0475
(c) 0 (approximately)
(d) 0 (approximately)   (e) .9734

7-34 (a) .0228   (b) .0062

8-2 (a) interval   (b) either
(c) point   (d) interval

8-4 (a) 5   (b) 1.94   (c) No

8-6 (a) 100.53 ± 4.96 (b) $69.2 \pm .15$
(c) $\$12.00 \pm .73$

8-8 105.6 ± 2.88

8-10 (a) $52,346 \pm 1,058$ (c) 77.38%

8-12 (a) 1.812   (b) 2.650   (c) 2.080
(d) 2.358   (e) 2.750

8-14 (a) $\$8.00 \pm 4.12$ (b) $15.03 \pm .40$
(c) 27.30 ± 1.43

8-16 (a) 3 ± 1.43
(b) negligible

8-18 (a) 121.4 ± 6.39 (b) 128.6 ± 6.19
(c) No

8-20 $.59 \pm .03$

8-22 $.42 \pm .097$

8-24 (a) 661   (b) 385
(c) 166; one-fourth as large
(d) 2,642; increases 4 times

8-26 (a) 370 for $N = 10,000$;
357 for $N = 5,000$
(b) 0 (approximately)

8-28 (a) 385   (b) 350; too many by 35

8-30 $1,246 \pm 22.5$

8-32 (a) 8,068   (b) 9,220
(c) 9,604   (d) 3,458

8-34 100 ± 12.7

8-36 (a) 1,537   (b) 385
(c) 97   (d) 16

8-38 (a) 151   (b) 2,401
(c) \$151 for stopwatch; \$120.5 for work sampling.
Work sampling is cheaper.

9-2 (a) (1) correct   (2) Type II error
(3) correct   (4) Type I error
(b) (1) Type II error   (2) correct
(3) Type I error   (4) correct
(c) (1) Type I error   (2) correct
(3) correct   (4) Type II error

9-4 (a) H_0: product will be unsuccessful;
H_1: product will be successful
(b) H_0: product will be successful;
H_1: product will be unsuccessful

9-6 (a) $\alpha = .1190$ $\beta = .1190$
(b) $\alpha = .0228$ $\beta = .0918$
(c) $\alpha = .0170$ $\beta = .0048$

9-8 (a) upper-tailed   (b) 1.28
(c) 103.2

9-10 (a) $z_\alpha = 1.64$; upper-tailed; $z = 2.0$; rejected; .0228
(b) $z_\alpha = 2.33$; lower-tailed; $z = -1.0$; accepted; .1597
(c) $z_\alpha = 1.28$; lower-tailed; $z = -2.0$; rejected; .0228
(d) $z_\alpha = 3.08$; upper-tailed; $z = 2.5$; accepted; .0062

9-12 (a) $z_{.01} = 2.33$; $\bar{X}^* = 512.9$
(b) accepted

9-14 (a) $\bar{X}^* = 83.28$
Accept H_0 if $\bar{X} \leqslant 83.28$
Reject H_0 if $\bar{X} > 83.28$
(b) $\bar{X}^* = 82.62$
(c) $\beta = .1949$ for $n = 64$;
$\beta = .0681$ for $n = 100$
Use $n = 100$.

9-16 (a) $\bar{X}_1^* = -1.96$; $\bar{X}_2^* = 1.96$
Accept H_0 if $-1.96 \leqslant \bar{X} \leqslant 1.96$
Reject H_0 if $\bar{X} < -1.96$ or if
$\bar{X} > 1.96$
(b) .8300   (c) accepted

9-18 *Reject H_0* and conclude that marijuana *lengthens* dream time.

9-20 (a) $t = -3$; lower-tailed;
$t_{.01} = 2.896$; rejected
(b) $t = 1.667$; upper-tailed;
$t_{.05} = 1.711$; accepted
(c) $t = .333$; two-sided; $t_{.05} = 1.753$; accepted
(d) $t = -7.0$; two-sided;
$t_{.005} = 2.797$; rejected

9-22 (a) 2.539   (b) accepted

9-24 Yes

9-26 $\alpha = .0228$ $\beta = .1587$

9-28 (a) upper-tailed   (b) 1.28
(c) .564   (d) accepted

9-30 (a) H_0: $\pi \leqslant .05$, and H_1: $\pi > .05$ upper-tailed
(b) .1814   (c) .086

9-32 (a) $\alpha = .1379$ $\beta = .1539$
(b) α will decrease; $\alpha = .0951$
$\beta = .2061$; β increased

9-34 (a) .0475   (b) .1335
(c) .0668   (d) .0548

9-36 (a) H_0: $\mu = .06$; H_1: $\mu \neq .06$; two-sided
(b) rejecting   (c) accepting
(d) $\bar{X}_1^* = .0594$; $\bar{X}_2^* = .0606$
(e) (1) $\beta = .0918$ (2) $\beta = .83995$

9-38 (a) H_0: $\mu \geqslant 2$; H_1: $\mu < 2$; lower-tailed
(b) Use t (c) *Reject H_0*; terminate

9-40 Kept

10-2 Answers may vary; $a = 20$; $b = .2727$; $\bar{Y}_X = 20 + .2727X$

10-4

	Dependent Variable	Independent Variable
(a)	Time deposits	Employee income
(b)	Income	Stock purchases
(c)	Savings	Wages

10-6 (a) $\bar{Y}_X = 10.0 + 1.0X$
(b) $\bar{Y}_X = 30.0 - 1.0X$
(c) $\bar{Y}_X = -15.0 + .5X$

10-8 (a) $\bar{Y}_X = -3.197 + .3218X$
(c) $s_{Y \cdot X} = .52$; $s_Y = 1.53$; Yes

10-10 $155 \pm .98$ 155 ± 9.8

10-12 (a) $2.5 \pm .01$ (b) $2.5 \pm .196$

10-14 (a) 27 ± 7.25 (b) rejected
(c) rejected

10–16 (a) .987   (b) −.80
(c) .975   (d) −.90

10–18 (a) $\bar{Y}_X = 276.55 + .4121X$
(b) positive   (d) .78

10–20 (a) 99.8%   (b) .999   (c) .999

10–22 (a) $r^2 = .4; r = .6325$
(b) $r^2 = .5; r = -.7071$

10–24 (a) $\bar{Y}_X = -.40 + .1X$

10–26 (a) $12,500 \pm 1,209.3$
(b) $10,000 \pm 1,263.0$
(c) $15,000 \pm 1,263.0$

10–28 (a) $\$80,000 \pm 78.40$
(b) $\$80,000 \pm 1,028$

11–2 (a) 3.189   (b) 3.254
(c) 2.975   (d) 3.708

11–4 (1) (1) 21.847   (2) 26.741
(3) 21.294   (4) 126.612
(b) 4.808
(c) (1) $21.847 \pm .943$
(2) $26.741 \pm .943$
(3) $21.294 \pm .943$
(4) $126.612 \pm .943$
(d) (1) 21.847 ± 9.47
(2) 26.741 ± 9.47
(3) 21.294 ± 9.47
(4) 126.612 ± 9.47

11–6 (a) $b = .6333; a = 1,667;$
$s_{Y \cdot X_1} = 701.2$
(b) $a = -59; b_1 = .6765; b_2 = 323.5$
$S_{Y \cdot 12} = 434.8$
(c) Yes

11–8 (b) $Y_C = -4.443 + 1.1609X_1 + 2.5804X_2$
(d) $\bar{Y}_{X_1} = -.686 - .8477X_1$

11–10 (a) $\bar{X}_{men} = 8.5$ $\bar{X}_{women} = 6.08$
$\bar{Y}_{men} = 5.42$ $\bar{Y}_{women} = 5.2$

11–12 (a) $r^2_{Y1 \cdot 2} = .375$ $r^2_{Y2 \cdot 1} = .5$
(c) The simple coefficients ignore the other independent variable.

12–2
Fall 19X1	$1,000,000.00
Winter 19X2	1,090,000.00
Spring	1,188,100.00
Summer	1,295,029.00
Fall	1,411,581.61

12–4 For Winter, $Y_t = \$540,350$; for Spring, $I_t = 101.42$; for Summer, $S_t = 80.00$; for Fall, $C_t = 104.00$

12–6 (b) $\bar{Y}_X = 200.67 + 9.673X$ ($X = 0$ in 1968)
(c) 374.78

12–8 (a) $\bar{Y}_X = 61.61 + 12.927x + .9207x^2$ ($x = 0$ in 1972)
(b) 282.95

12–10

W	Sp	Su	F
50.6	89.8	150.9	108.7

12–12

	(a)	(b)
Month	Seasonal Index	Cash Required
J	43.0	$430,000
F	99.4	994,000
M	138.2	1,382,000
A	59.9	599,000
M	106.3	1,063,000
J	94.4	944,000
J	87.0	870,000
A	122.3	1,223,000
S	183.3	1,833,000
O	145.4	1,454,000
N	75.0	750,000
D	45.8	458,000

12–14 (a)

1970	W		
	S	97.9	
	S	95.8	
	F	95.5	
1971	W	95.0	
	S	94.3	
	S	94.4	
	F	96.2	
1972	W	99.7	
	S	103.5	
	S	105.0	
	F	103.7	
1973	W	101.7	
	S	99.9	
	S	98.2	
	F	96.7	
1974	W	95.4	
	S	94.3	
	S	93.4	
	F	93.7	
1975	W	95.0	
	S	97.8	
	S	101.2	
	F	102.6	
1976	W	102.7	
	S	102.1	
	S	100.7	
	F		

12–16 (a)

W	Sp	Su	F
73.3	127.6	166.0	33.1

12–18 $\log \bar{Y}_X = 148.465 + .02509X$ ($X = 0$ on Feb. 15, 1973)
153.9 thousand units

13–2 7.4%

13–4 (a) $I = 101.3$, a 1.3 percent increase
(b) $I = 98.7$, a 1.3 percentage increase from 1976 to 1977

13–6

1963	$108.65	1970	$114.99
1964	110.84	1971	117.43
1965	113.79	1972	123.46
1966	115.58	1973	124.76
1967	114.90	1974	119.43
1968	117.57	1975	117.56
1969	117.95		

14-2 43.7 ± 11.7

14-4 $2 \pm .392$

14-6 *Reject H_0 and use ladybugs.*

14-8 accept

14-10 *Reject H_0 and conclude that radial tires are better.*

14-12 $1.5 \pm .86$

14-14 $2,000 \pm 2,184.9$

14-16 No

14-18 commission-only plan

14-20 conclude equal strength in both areas

14-22 (a) Conclude that batting averages are higher for home games.
(b) $.028 \pm .023$

14-24 (a) $\bar{d} = 5.4$; $s_{d\text{-paired}} = 6.096$
(b) rejected

14-26 (a) (1) $H_0: \mu_A = \mu_B$
  (2) $d_1^* = -3.30$; $d_2^* = 3.30$
  (3) $d = 3.60$; rejected
(b) (1) $H_0: \mu_A \geq \mu_B$
  (2) $d^* = -2.76$
  (3) $d = 3.60$; accepted
(c) (1) $H_0: \mu_A \leq \mu_B$
  (2) $d^* = 2.76$
  (3) $d = 3.60$; rejected

14-28 rejected

15-2 (a) accepted   (b) rejected
(c) rejected   (d) accepted

15-4 (a)

	(1) Single	(2) Married	Total
(1) A	12	18	30
(2) B	28	42	70
Total	40	60	100

(b) 12.699
(c) 1; $\chi^2_{.01} = 6.635$
(d) rejected

15-6 (a)

	(1) Male	(2) Female	Total
(1)	27.65	22.35	50
(2)	24.34	19.66	44
(3)	32.08	25.92	58
(4)	18.81	15.19	34
(5)	22.12	17.88	40
Total	125	101	226

(b) 10.683
(c) 4
(d) 13.277; accepted
(e) 9.488; rejected

15-8 Conclude that quality is affected by temperature.

15-10 (a) $13.38 \leq \sigma^2 \leq 35.18$
(b) $56.80 \leq \sigma^2 \leq 244.28$
(c) $.313 \leq \sigma^2 \leq 1.129$
(d) $4.90 \leq \sigma^2 \leq 14.61$

15-12 (a) $2.23 \leq \sigma^2 \leq 5.86$
(b) $1.49 \leq \sigma \leq 2.42$
(c) Yes

15-14 *Accept H_0 and conclude equal regional preference.*

15-16 No

15-18 (a) (1) lower-tailed   (2) 13.848
  (3) $\chi^2 = 13.5$; accepted
(b) (1) upper-tailed   (2) 21.666
  (3) $\chi^2 = 9.45$; accepted
(c) (1) lower-tailed   (2) 10.865
  (3) $\chi^2 = 16.594$; accepted
(d) (1) upper-tailed   (2) 26.296
  (3) $\chi^2 = 26.492$; rejected

15-20 (a) $56.20 \leq \sigma^2 \leq 83.68$
(b) *Accept H_0*

16-2 (a) 6.93; accepted
(b) 3.88; rejected
(c) 3.88; rejected

16-4 (a) $\bar{X}_1 = 87.8$; $\bar{X}_2 = 64.2$;
  $\bar{X}_3 = 76.0$; $\bar{X} = 76.0$
(b) $SST = 1,392.4$; $SSE = 2,001.6$

(c) $MST = 696.2$; $MSE = 166.8$;
 $F = 4.17$
(d) rejected

16-6 (a) No   (b) Answers may vary.

16-8 (a) 87.8 ± 12.59
 (b) 23.6 ± 17.80; yes

16-10 (a) $SSE = 72$; $MST = 21.0$;
 $MSE = 6.0$; $F = 3.5$
 (b) accepted

16-12 (a) $MST = 200,000$;
 $SSE = 1,200,000$;
 $MSE = 80,000$; $F = 2.5$
 No
 (b) $MST = 300,000$;
 $SSE = 1,100,000$;
 $MSE = 68,750$; $F = 4.36$
 Yes
 (c) $MSA = 200,000$;
 $MSB = 300,000$; $SSE = 300,000$;
 $MSE = 25,000$; $F = 8.0$ for A;
 $F = 12.0$ for B
 Reject both.
 (d) Two-factor analysis is more discriminating.

16-14 (a) Yes   (b) No   (c) No
 (d) Yes   (e) Yes

16-16 (a) $SSE = 75$; $MST = 39.25$;
 $MSCOL = 19.25$;
 $MSROW = 35.75$;
 $F = 6.28$ for X; $F = 3.08$ for Y;
 $F = 5.72$ for Z
 (b) The population means are significantly different only for X and Z.

16-18 (a) $\bar{X}_1 = 26$ $\bar{X}_2 = 34$
 $\bar{X}_3 = 50$ $\bar{X}_4 = 58$
 $SST = 3,200$
 $SSE = 1,368$
 Total $SS = 4,568$

Variation	d.f.	Sum of Squares	Mean Square	F
Treatments	3	3,200	1,066.67	12.48
Error	16	1,368	85.5	
Total	19	4,568		

 (b) Yes
 (c) 32 ± 12.4; yes

16-20 (a) $\bar{X}_A = 58$ $\bar{X}_B = 82$ $\bar{X}_C = 103$
 $\bar{X}_{1.} = 78$ $\bar{X}_{2.} = 81$ $\bar{X}_{3.} = 84$
 $\bar{X}_{.1} = 74$ $\bar{X}_{.2} = 82$ $\bar{X}_{.3} = 87$
 $SST = 3,042$ $SSE = 18$
 $SSCOL = 258$ Total $SS = 3,372$
 $SSROW = 54$
 (b)

Variation	d.f.	Sum of Squares	Mean Square	F
Treatments	2	3,042	1,521	169.00
Columns	2	258	129	
Rows	2	54	27	
Error	2	18	9	
Total	8	3,372		

 (c) Reject H_0 and conclude skill affects performance.

16-22 (a)

Variation	d.f.	Sum of Squares	Mean Square	F
Treatments	3	25,271.5	8,423.83	.88
Error	12	114,504.5	9,542.04	
Total	15	139,776		

 No
 (b)

Variation	d.f.	Sum of Squares	Mean Square	F
Treatments	3	25,271.5	8,423.83	4.17
Blocks	3	96,326	32,108.67	
Error	9	18,178.5	2,019.83	
Total	15	139,776		

 Yes
 (c) Their inclusion increases the discrimination of the procedure.

17-2 (a) 5/12   (b) 5/12

17-4 No

17-6 (a) No
(b) .183930 for slump
.084225 for peak
(c) No

17-8 .006738

17-10 (a) .1755   (b) .0067
(c) .0137   (d) .7419

17-12 (a) .606531   (b) .393469

17-14 (a) .20 (b) .40 (c) .39 (d) .30

17-16 .40

17-18 (a) .993 (b) .135 (c) .128

17-20 (a) .0002 school per mile
(b) .632   (c) 11,500 miles

17-22 (a) .2524   (b) .6004   (c) .9671

17-24 (a)

Score	f_e
below 40	7.21
40–50	12.28
50–60	19.87
60–70	23.57
70–80	19.19
80–90	11.45
over 90	6.43

$\chi^2 = 17.47$; rejected
(b) between .01 and .001

17-26 (b) $\chi^2 = 2.8$
(c) *Accept H_0*

17-28 (a) .2880   (b) .3000

17-30 (a) .0596   (b) .8647

17-32 (a) .9763   (b) .9707

17-34 (a) normal   (b) .7698

17-36 Yes

18-2 Yes

18-4 (a) lower-tailed
(b) $W = 25$
(c) accepted

18-6 (a) (1) lower-tailed
(2) 6   (4) rejected
(b) (1) upper-tailed
(2) 62   (4) accepted
(c) (1) lower-tailed
(2) 19   (4) rejected
(d) (1) upper-tailed
(2) 13   (4) accepted

18-8 leaded

18-10 (b) .16; upper-tailed   (c) 2.68
(d) *Reject H_0* and conclude that the
new supplement is more effective.

18-12 (a) (1) upper-tailed
(2) $z_{.05} = 1.64$
(3) $z = -1.98$; accepted
(b) (1) lower-tailed
(2) $z_{.01} = 2.33$
(3) $z = -1.58$; accepted
(c) (1) upper-tailed
(2) $z_{.01} = 2.33$
(3) $z = 2.44$; rejected
(d) (1) lower-tailed
(2) $z_{.05} = 1.64$
(3) $z = -2.05$; rejected

18-14 $V = 5.5$; rejected

18-16 (b) (1) $R_a = 7$; accepted
(2) $R_a = 8$; rejected
(3) $R_a = 2$; rejected
(4) $R_a = 8$; rejected

18-18 (a) 95   (b) .68   (c) .4964

18-20 *Accept H_0* and conclude the appearance
of randomness.

18-22 .61

18-24 $-.50$

18-26 $K = 5.18$; *accept H_0* and conclude that
identical treatment means exist.

18-28 accepted

18-30 rejected

18-32 .88

18-34 (a)

x	$F_a(x)$	$F_e(x)$
0	.08	.1353
1	.27	.4060
2	.55	.6767
3	.79	.8571
4	.93	.9473
5	.95	.9834
6	.98	.9954
7	.99	.9988
8	.99	.9997
9	1.00	.9999

(b) $D = .1360$
(c) .025   (d) 10.56
(e) .10
(f) Kolmogorov–Smirnov test

18-36 *Reject H_0* and conclude non-normality.

19-2 (a) 4; bonds, preferred best; common worst
(b) 3; preferred best; common worst
(c) 5; common best; bonds worst
(d) 7; common best; bonds worst

19-4 A_3 and A_5

19-6 Spring-action movement

19-8 Test market; then market nationally if favorable and abort if unfavorable.

19-12 (a) red
(b) $.98 for red
  $-$.98 for black
(c) $0 for red
  $49 for black

19-14 (b) cauliflower
(c) beets
(d) corn

19-16 (a) Dry underripe loads and preserve ripe loads.

19-18 A_1

19-20 (a) 10,000 tons for A
  33,333 tons for B
(b) 80,000
(c) A
(d) A
(e) Yes

19-22 (a) A_3 (dominated by A_1, A_4, and A_5)
(b) A_4 (c) A_1 (d) A_4 (e) 4

19-24 (b) Market
(c) $250,000
(d) $250,000

19-26 (b) 10   (c) 11

20-4 (a) Yes
(b) Test market; then use concrete if favorable and wood if not.

20-6 (a) 1/2   (d) 2/3

20-8 (c) Buy the information; then if a face card obtained continue and otherwise stop.

20-10 (b)

Number of Children Liking	Proportion $\pi=1/4$	$\pi=1/2$	$\pi=3/4$
$R=0$	.4219	.1250	.0156
$R=1$	.4219	.3750	.1406
$R=2$	.1406	.3750	.4219
$R=3$	.0156	.1250	.4219
	1.0000	1.0000	1.0000

(e)

P	Posterior Probability
1/4	.0278
1/2	.2222
3/4	.7500
	1.0000

20-14 (a) $n=1$ (b) $n=1$

20-18 (b) $C=25$ g   (c) $120.23
(d) $70.23

20-20 (c) reject

20-22 (c) Retain the old box if sales decrease and use the new box otherwise.

20-24 (c) (1) .9633   (2) .4995   (3) .0352

20-26 (b) sponsor   (c) EVPI $= $150

21-2 (a) $.25

21-4 (b) $40,000 for buying
  $25,000 for renting

21-6 The answers will be subjective.

21-8 No

21-10 (a) 1/2   (b) 1/4   (c) 1/2

21-12 (c) Use the test; hire only the applicants who pass it.

21-14 The answers will be subjective.

21-16 The answers will be subjective.

21-18 (a) .105   (b) .15
(c) .38   (d) .73

21-20 The answers will be subjective.

21-22 2.5

21-24 (c) risk seeking

21-26 (a) $\mu=60$ $\sigma=22.4$
(b) (1) .3472   (2) .0594
  (3) .5000   (4) .8732

21-28 (a) 3,440   (b) $472.00   (c) .62790

Index

D E F G H I J
9 0 1 2 3 4 5 6

Symbol	Description
π_A, π_B	Proportions of populations A and B that are compared in two-sample hypothesis tests
q_k	Indifference probability established for winning reference lottery or achieving outcome O_k for certain
q_n, q_0	Quantities of an item in year n and in base period 0; used in constructing index numbers
R	(1) A random variable denoting the number of successes obtained from several trials of a Bernoulli process (2) The test statistic for the matched-pairs sign test for comparing two populations; R is the number of positive sign differences for the paired difference between two sample observations
R_a	Number of runs of type a obtained in a sample; used as the test statistic for the number-of-runs test
$R_{Y \cdot 12}, R_{Y \cdot 123}$	Sample multiple correlation coefficient; the square root of the coefficient of multiple determination
$R_{Y \cdot 12}^2, R_{Y \cdot 123}^2$	Sample coefficient of multiple determination; represents the proportion of variation in the dependent variable Y that can be explained by the multiple regression equation of Y on independent variables X_1, X_2 (and X_3)
r	(1) One of several possible values of the random variable R (2) The sample correlation coefficient; expresses the strength and direction of the relationship between variables X and Y (3) Number of rows in an analysis-of-variance layout
r^2	Sample coefficient of determination; represents the proportion of the variation in the dependent variable Y that can be explained by linear regression on the independent variable X
r_i	The marginal total in the ith row of a contingency table
r_s	Spearman rank correlation coefficient
r_{Y1}^2	Sample coefficient of determination for regression of the dependent variable Y on the independent variable X_1; used in multiple correlation analysis
$r_{Y \cdot 12}^2, r_{Y3 \cdot 12}^2$	Coefficients of partial determination for multiple regression of the dependent variable Y on the independent variables X_1, X_2 (and X_3); measures the proportional reduction in previously unexplained variation in Y by adding X_2 or X_3 to the multiple regression analysis while incorporating the effects of the other independent variables
ρ (rho)	Population correlation coefficient; estimated by r
ρ^2	Population coefficient of determination; estimated by r^2
S	Number of successes in a population; used in conjunction with the hypergeometric distribution
$S_1, S_2, \ldots$	Strategies in a decision structure
S_t	Seasonal component of the classical time series model
$S_{Y \cdot 12}, S_{Y \cdot 123}$	Standard error of the estimate about the multiple regression plane
SSA	Sum of squares between columns for a two-factor analysis of variance; A represents one of the factors about which inferences are to be made
SSB	Sum of squares between rows for a two-factor analysis of variance when: (1) B represents the blocking variable (2) B represents one factors about which inferences are to be made
$SSCOL$	Sum of squares between columns for a Latin-square design in a three-factor analysis of variance
SSE	Error sum of squares: (1) (within columns) for a one-factor analysis of variance (2) (residual) for a two-factor or a three-factor analysis of variance
$SSROW$	Sum of squares between rows for a Latin-square design in a three-factor analysis of variance
SST	Sum of squares: (1) (between columns) for the treatments in a one-factor analysis of variance (2) (between letters) in a three-factor analysis of variance using a Latin-square design
s	Sample standard deviation
s^2	Sample variance
s_A^2, s_B^2	Variances of samples from populations A and B; used in two-sample hypothesis tests
s_X	Sample standard deviation of the independent variable X; used in correlation analysis
s_Y	Sample standard deviation of the dependent variable Y; used in correlation analysis
$s_{Y \cdot X}$	Standard error of the estimate about the regression line; $s_{Y \cdot X}^2$ is an unbiased estimator of $\sigma_{Y \cdot X}^2$
s_d	The estimator of the standard error σ_d for the difference between: (1) two sample means (2) two sample proportions
$s_{d\text{-paired}}$	Sample standard deviation of matched-pairs differences
$s_{d\text{-small}}$	Sample standard deviation of the difference in means of independent samples
Σ	Summation sign
σ (sigma)	Population standard deviation
σ^2	Population variance
$\sigma(X)$	Standard deviation of random variable X
$\sigma^2(X)$	Variance of random variable X
σ_A^2, σ_B^2	Variance of populations A and B compared by two-sample inferences
σ_P	Standard error (also called the standard deviation) of the sample proportion P